HISTORY

OF

TENNESSEE

From the Earliest Time to the Present; Together with an Historical and a Biographical Sketch of Maury, Williamson, Rutherford, Wilson Bedford & Marshall Counties; Besides a Valuable Fund of Notes, Reminescences, Observations, Etc., Etc.

ILLUSTRATED.

Nashville:
THE GOODSPEED PUBLISHING CO.,

This volume was reproduced from
An 1887 edition located in the
Knoxville Public Library,
Knoxville, Tennessee

All rights reserved. No part of this publication
may be reproduced, stored in a retrieval system,
transmitted in any form, posted on to the web
in any form or by any means without the
prior written permission of the publisher.

Please direct all correspondence and orders to:

www.southernhistoricalpress.com
or
**SOUTHERN HISTORICAL PRESS, Inc.
PO BOX 1267
375 West Broad Street
Greenville, SC   29601
southernhistoricalpress@gmail.com**

Originally published: Nashville, 1887
Reprinted with New Material by:
Southern Historical Press, Inc.
Greenville, SC 2017
New Material Copyright 1988 by
Southern Historical Press, Inc.
Easley, SC
ISBN #0-89308-608-8
All rights Reserved.
Printed in the United States of America

CONTENTS.

HISTORY OF TENNESSEE.

CHAPTER I.

	PAGE.
GEOLOGY OF TENNESSEE	13
Area and Boundary of the State	13
Ages, The Geologic	15
Canadian Period, The	17
Coals, The	27
Carboniferous Age, The	22
Crab Orchard Section, The	31
Cretaceous Period, The	22
Cross Mountain Section, The	33
Champlain Period, The	23
Coal of Raccoon District	30
Divisions, The Eight Natural	15
Eastern Iron Region, The	34
Elevations, The Principal	40
Fossils, The Characteristic	36
Glacial Period, The	23
Hamilton Age, The	21
Iron Ore, The	34
Lower Helderberg Period, The	21
Lignitic Period, The	22
Marble Beds, The	39
Metals, The Principal	37
Niagara Period, The	20
Primordial Period, The	16
Recent Period, The	23
Subcarboniferous Period, The	21
Soils, The Various	23
Temperature of the State, The	39
Trenton Period, The	18
Thirteen Tennessee Periods, The	16
Western Iron Region, The	35

CHAPTER II.

THE MOUND-BUILDERS	42
Age of the Mounds	56
Arguments of Judge Haywood	45
Classification of Earthworks	50
Contents of the Mounds, The	53
Carthage Cave, The	54
Evidences of Prehistoric Occupation	42
Fortifications, Etc	51
Location of the Earthworks	49
Mounds of Tennessee, The	51 to 57
Natchez, The	48
Opinion of Bancroft, The	42
Peruvians, The	45
"Stone Fort," The Old	55
Sun Worshipers, The	47
Tribal Resemblances	46
View of Hildreth	44

CHAPTER III.

THE INDIAN TRIBES	57
Avery Treaty, The	77
Battle of Chickasaw Old Field	69
Beloved Town, The	69
Battle of Long Island Flats	73
Battle of Boyd Creek	80
Boundary Established, A New	82
Battle of French Lick	89
Christian's Expediton	76
Chickamaugas, The	79
Chickasaw Treaty of 1786, The	85
Coldwater Expedition, The	90
Cession Treaties, Numerous	95 to 108
Cherokees, The	57
Campaign of Williamson	75
Chickasaws, The	59
Destruction of Indian Towns	65
Expeditions of Sevier	86, 87
Encounter of Untoola and Hubbard	83
Expeditions of Rains	91
English Supremacy and Intrigue	64
Expedition of Col. Grant	68
Earliest Indian Occupation	57
French Trading Stations	62

	PAGE.
"Great Grant" and "Path Deed"	70
Holston Treaty, The	93
Incidents and Anecdotes	74
Killing of the Cavetts, The	94
Massacre of Fort Loudon	63, 66
Massacres upon the Cumberland	89
Nickajack Expedition, The	97
Point Pleasant, Battle of	70
"Pocahontas of the West," The	73
Rutherford's Campaign	75
Shawanees, The	58
Shelby's Campaign against the Lower Towns	80
Sevier's Destructive Campaigns	81
Spanish Influence	90
Traditions of a Former Race	58
Tennessee Soil, First Cession of	61
Treaty of Hopewell, The	84

CHAPTER IV.

SETTLEMENT OF TENNESSEE	108
Brown's Settlement	124
Chisca, The Indian Village	110
Charleville's Trading Station	112
Carter's Valley, Settlement of	124
Daniel Boone	116
Donelson's Journal	129 to 134
Expedition of De Soto	108
French and English Designs	112
Fort Assumption	113
Findley's Excursion	117
French Lick, First Appearance of	123
Fort Loudon, Construction of	114
Henderson's Treaty	124
Hunting Parties, Sundry	116, 117
"Long Hunters," The	121
La Salle and Marquette	111
Results of the Treaty of 1763	118
Regulators and the Scovilites, The	122
Stations on the Cumberland, The	127
Spottswood's Expedition	112
Traders, The French	115
Wood's Tour of Discovery	111
Walker's Expedition	115
Watauga Settlement, The	121
Washington District, Watauga Settlement	125
Washington County, N. C.	126

CHAPTER V.

SETTLEMENT CONCLUDED	135
Affairs on the Cumberland	141
Brown's Disastrous Voyage	144, 145
Continental Land Warrants	139
Clinch-Cumberland Road, The	142, 143
Catalogue of Land Grants	151
Chickasaw Bluffs, The	152
Greene's Reservation	139
Land Companies, The	147 to 150
Military Reservations, The	140
Nashborough	137
Perils on the Cumberland	136
Provisions, How Obtained, Etc	143
Settlers of West Tennessee	154 to 163
Territorial Government, The	146
Transylvania	136
West Tennessee, Settlement of	151
Western Purchase, The	153

CHAPTER VI.

ORGANIZATION	164
Cumberland Compact, The	184 to 188
European Charters, The	164 to 167
Eastern Boundary, The	182
Government of the Notables, The	183
Northern Boundary Question, The	168 to 180
State of Franklin, The	189 to 198
Southern Boundary Question, The	181 to 182
Watauga Association, The	183

vi CONTENTS.

CHAPTER VII.

	PAGE.
ORGANIZATION CONCLUDED	199
Administration of Gov. Blount	205
Acts of the Convention of 1796	213
Acceptance of the Tennessee Cession	202
Census of Tennessee, The First	211
Constitutional Provisions	224 to 228
Constitutional Convention of 1834, The	223
Cession Act of North Carolina, The	199
Constitutional Convention of 1796, The	212
Cession Deed, The	202
Constitutional Convention of 1870, The	227, 228
General Assembly of the State, The First	219
Legislature of the Territory, The	207 to 210
Pioneer Legislation	221
State Governor, The First	220
State Constitution, The First	214 to 218
Tennessee Admitted to the Union	218
Territorial Government Established, The	203
Territorial Officers, The	203

CHAPTER VIII.

GROWTH AND DEVELOPMENT	229
Agricultural Methods, The Early	229
Census Reports, The	252
Corn Crop, The	233
Cotton Gin, The Purchase of	240
Cotton Culture	239
Fruit Crops, The	233, 251
Fertilizers, The Use of	245
Farmers of Middle Tennessee, The	232
Farmers of East Tennessee, The	230
Hay and the Grasses	242
Hemp, Flax, Sorghum, Etc	244
Live Stock	246
Maple Sugar	245
"Money Crops," The	236
Methods of Agriculture Compared	230
Poultry, Butter, Cheese, Honey, Etc	249
Peanuts, The Growth of	241
Potatoes, Sweet and Irish	235
Rye, Barley, Oats, Buckwheat, Etc	235
Tobacco Crop, The	237
Wheat Crop, The	234

CHAPTER IX.

GROWTH AND DEVELOPMENT CONCLUDED	253
Bureau of Agriculture, Etc	279
Coal Productions, The	265 to 267
Copper Ore, The Mining of	270
Cotton Seed Oil	278
Cotton Goods, The Manufacture of	273
Flour-Milling Industry, The	271
Gunpowder	275
Iron Industries, The	260 to 264
Industrial Development	272
Leather, Boots and Shoes, Etc	276
Lumber Productions and Traffic, The	259
Marble Quarries, The	267 to 270
Paper, The Production of	275
Timber of the State, The	253 to 258
Whisky Products, The Enormous	277, 278
Woolen Goods, The Manufacture of	274

CHAPTER X.

STATE INSTITUTIONS	280
Ancient Order of United Workmen	320
Bureau of Agriculture, Mines, Etc	308
East Tennessee Insane Asylum	293
Grand Army of the Republic	322
Institutions for the Blind	289
Insane Hospital at Nashville, The	291
Jackson's Equestrian Statue	284
Knights of Honor, Grand Lodge	315
Knights of Pythias, Grand Lodge	318
Knights and Ladies of Honor	316
Legion of Honor, Grand Council	320
Masonic Grand Lodge, The	309
Odd Fellows Grand Lodge, The	314
Royal Arcanum, Grand Council	321
State Capitol Located, The	280
State Library, The	286
State House, Construction of the	281 to 284
State Penitentiary, The	294
State Historical Society, The	298
State Medical Society, The	302

	PAGE.
State Board of Health, The	305
Tennessee Deaf and Dumb School, The	287
Tennessee Agricultural and Horticultural Society	307
West Tennessee Insane Asylum	294

CHAPTER XI.

STATE INSTITUTIONS CONCLUDED	323
Counties, The Formation of	361, 362
Commercial Highways	335
Funding of the Debt, The	328 to 330
Gubernatorial Election Returns	356
Internal Improvement Systems, The	337
Presidential Election Returns	358, 359
Population of the State, Aggregate	360, 361
Receipts and Expenditures, The Early	323
Railroads, The Sale of	339
Receipts and Expenses, Catalogue of	340
Repudiation, The Question of	329
Railway Enterprises	340 to 348
Railway Commission, The	348
State Indebtedness, The First	326
Steam-boat Navigation	348
State Bonds, Total Issue of	357
State Officers, Catalogue of	350 to 356
State Banks, The	331 to 335
State Debt Proper, The	327 to 329
Treasury of the State, The	324

CHAPTER XII.

BENCH AND BAR OF TENNESSEE	363
Courts of the Watauga Settlement	363
Courts on the Cumberland	367
Circuit Courts, The	376
Courts of the Constitution of 1796	362
Courts of the Constitution of 1834	375
Courts of the Constitution of 1870	378
Impeachment, Cases of	372
Professional Character of Distinguished Members of the Bench and Bar of Tennessee	382 to 412
Territorial Courts, The	368
United States Courts, The	380
Washington and Sullivan County Courts	364

CHAPTER XIII.

EDUCATIONAL HISTORY	413
Colleges Chartered	416
County Academies, The	420
Constitutional Educational Provisions	426
Common School Convention, The	428
Colored Education	434
Common Schools, The	435
Cumberland College	442
Endowment Funds, The	415
Educational Systems Compared	420
East Tennessee College	447
Educational Tax, The First	422
Educational Statistics	441
Graded Schools, The	430
Gigantic Problem of 1865, The	431
Provincial Schools, The	413
Public Schools Established	426
Peabody Fund, The	433
State Colleges Founded	418
School Lands, Disposal of the	423
Superintendents of Public Instruction	428
School Officers, Duties of	438
State Normal School, The	445
Special School Funds	439
State Board of Education	447
School Funds, Creation of the	424
Schools in Tennessee, The First	415
Tennessee Industrial College	451
West Tennessee College	453

CHAPTER XIV.

THE EARLY WARS	454
British, Battles with the	456
Charleston, The Capture of	460
Creeks, The War with the	461
Entochopco, Battle of	464
Jackson's First Battle	462
Jackson, Activity of	470
King's Mountain, Battle of	458
Mexican War, The	473

CONTENTS

	PAGE.
New Orleans, The Movement upon	467
New Orleans, Jackson's Victory at	468
Seminole War, The	469
Tories of East Tennessee, The	454
Talladega, Battle of	463
Tohopeka, Battle of	465
Texas-Mexican War, The	472
Tennessee Troops Sent to Mexico	474 to 476
War of 1812, The	461
Wahoo Swamp, Battle of	472

CHAPTER XV.

FEDERAL MILITARY HISTORY	477
Burnside's Occupation of East Tennessee	490
Bridge Burners Ordered Hanged	488
Campbell's Station, Battle of	491
Confederate Movements	486
Fishing Creek, Battle of	488
Federal Troops Furnished, Total	497
General Movements	489
Greenville Union Convention, The	481
Issue Joined, The	483
Knoxville Union Convention, The	479
Knoxville, Siege of	492
Longstreet vs. Burnside	491
Loyalty of East Tennessee	477
Morgan, The Killing of	495
Regimental Sketches	497 to 512
Skirmishes, The Concluding	496
Union Leaders, The	478
Union Regiments Organized	484

CHAPTER XVI.

CONFEDERATE MILITARY HISTORY	513
Army Bill, The	522
Arms, Condition and Quantity	515
Aid Societies	539
Advance to Columbus, The	543
Army Rolls	595 to 617
Belmont, Battle of	545
Burnside in East Tennessee	558
Call to Arms, The	518
Confederate Government, The	535
Chickamauga, Battle of	556
Confederate Line, Danger to the	547
Confederate Forces, Aggregate	546
Defensive Measures, Extent of	536 to 539
Election Returns of June 8	532 to 534
Evacuation of Middle Tennessee	550
February Convention, The	514
Fishing Creek, Battle of	547
Fort Henry, Fall of	548
Franklin, Battle of	560
Fort Donelson, Fall of	548
Georgia Campaign, The	559
Legislature Convened, The	518
Militia, Reorganization of the	515
Military League, The	528
Militia Transferred to the Confederacy	540
Memphis, Surrender of	553
Military Appointments	530
Murfreesboro, Battle of	555
Missionary Ridge, Battle of	557
Neutrality Question, The	544
Nashville, Federal Occupation of	549
Nashville, Battle of	560
Ordinance of Secession, The	520
Ordnance, The Manufacture of	541
Perryville, Battle of	554
Position of the General Assembly	516
Reserve Corps, The	542
Rock Castle Hills, Battle of	544
Regimental Sketches	561 to 595
State Sovereignty and Secession	513
Shiloh, Battle of	550
Secession Overwhelmingly Favored	517
Tennessee Admitted to the Confederacy	535
Troops, Call for and Refusal to Furnish	517

CHAPTER XVII.

TENNESSEE LITERATURE	617
Brownlow	622
Bright	628
Brunner	625
Baskerville	625
Baldwin	625
Brown	628
Chattanooga Press, The	631

	PAGE.
Crockett	623
Carr	625
Cross	629
Fitzgerald	625
French	627
Geological Authors	623
Guild	624
Graves (Joseph C.)	624
Graves (Adelia C.)	627
Gilchrist	629
Harrison	624
Haywood	618
Journalism	629
Ketchum	627
Knoxville Press, The	629
Law	628
Lindsley (Phillip)	624
Lindsley (J. Berrien)	619
Legal Authors	626
Murfree	626
Memphis Press, The	637
McAdoo	629
McAnally	621
McFerrin	621
Martin	622
McTyeire	622
Medical Authors	622
Maury	623
Nelson	621, 623
Nashville Press, The	632
Putnam	619
Pearson	621
Ramsey	618
Redford	624
Ryan	622
Rivers	622
Summers	625
Tannehill	620

CHAPTER XVIII.

RELIGIOUS HISTORY	638
Arminianism, The Creed of	648
Buildings Erected, The first	646
Baptist Church, The	687
Church and State, Union of	640
Camp-Meeting, The first	650
Creeds, Formation of the	658
Cumberland Presbyterian Church, The	658
Christian Church, The	700
Catholic Church, The	704
Colored Churches, The	708
Episcopal Church, The	694
Irreligion Punished	641
Jerks, The	651 to 655
Jerks, The Cause of the	655 to 657
Jewish Church, The	706
Lutheran Church, The	705
Methodist Church, The	662
Methodist Church South	676
Methodist Statistics	676 to 679
Methodist Book Concern, The	679
Preaching in Tennessee, The first	645
Presbyterian Church, The	680
Revival, The Great	649 to 654
Religious Intolerance	639
Separation of Church and State	644
Slavery Divides the Church	667 to 676
University of the South, The	699

CHAPTER XIX.

BIOGRAPHICAL CHAPTER	708
Blount, Gov. William	716
Bell, Hon. John	733
Brownlow, Gov. William G.	740
Carroll, Gov. William	719
Crockett, Col. David	728
Forrest, Gen. N. B.	742
Grundy, Hon. Felix	729
Haywood, Judge John	714
Houston, Gov. Sam	724
Jackson, President Andrew	720
Johnson, President Andrew	745
Johnson, Hon. Cave	735
Polk, President James K.	738
Robertson, Gen. James	712
Sevier, Gov. John	708
White, Hon. Hugh L.	732
Zollicoffer, Gen. Felix K.	747

CONTENTS.

GILES COUNTY.

	PAGE.
Giles County	749
Buildings	754
County Officers	756, 757
Courts, The	754 to 756
County, Creation of the	753
Churches	769
Geology, Streams, etc.	745
Indian Reserve, Invasion of the	751
Military Record, The	757 to 760
Mills, Cotton-Gins, etc.	751, 752
Productions	749
Powder-Mills	751
Public Highways	754
Settlement	750
Seat of Justice, The	753
Schools	764
Towns, Villages, etc.	760 to 764

LINCOLN COUNTY.

	PAGE.
Lincoln County	767
Act of Creation	770
Boundary, etc.	767
County Officers	771
Courts, The	773, 774
Drainage, Geology, etc.	767
Education	782, 783
Industrial Enterprises	769, 770
Land Grants	767
Newspapers	779
Public Buildings	772
Religion	783, 784
Settlement	768, 769
Statistics	772
Towns, Villages, etc.	778 to 782
War Record	774 to 778

FRANKLIN COUNTY.

	PAGE.
Franklin County	785
County Officers	791
Courts, The	792 to 794
County Created, The	789
Churches	803, 804
Elections	791
Geology and Temperature	785
Industries	788, 789
Land Grants	787
Paupers, The	790
Settlement	786, 787
Seat of Justice	790
Schools	800 to 803
Topography, etc.	785
Towns, etc.	796 to 800
War Matters	794 to 796

MOORE COUNTY.

	PAGE.
Moore County	804
Buildings	809
Courts, The	811, 812
Churches	818, 819
Distilleries	807
Geology, etc.	804, 805
Industries, The Early	806
Military Affairs	812 to 815
Organization of the County	807, 808
Settlers, etc.	805, 806
Schools	817, 818
Seat of Justice	809
Statistics	810
Towns, etc.	815 to 817
Whipping	807

BIOGRAPHICAL APPENDIX.

Franklin County	820
Giles County	846
Lincoln County	876
Moore County	924

PORTRAITS, MAPS AND VIEWS.

Aboriginal Map		Frontispiece
Blind Asylum	Between	124, 125
Bell, John	"	782, 733
Blount, William	"	716, 717
Brownlow, W. G.	"	508, 509
Chapel, University of the South	"	348, 349
Chickamauga	"	556, 557
Crockett, David	"	156, 157
Donelson	"	476, 477
Deaf and Dumb Asylum	"	268, 269
Franklin	"	588, 589
Grundy, Felix	"	380, 381
Hodgson, Rev. Telfair	"	796, 797
Insane Asylum, West Tennessee	"	140, 141
Insane Asylum, East Tennessee	"	92, 93
Jackson's Equestrian Statue	"	284, 285
Jackson, Andrew	"	460, 461
Johnson, Andrew	"	636, 637
Johnson, Cave	"	668, 669
Murfreesboro	"	572, 573
Missionary Ridge	"	492, 493
Nashville	"	604, 605
Normal School	"	428, 429
Polk, James K.	"	396, 397
Robertson, James	"	76, 77
Shiloh	"	540, 541
State Capitol	"	28, 29
Sevier, John	"	220, 221
Thompson's Hall	"	316, 317
Tennessee University	"	444, 445
University of the South	"	700, 701
View on Emery River	"	44, 45
View on Falls Creek	"	188, 189

MAURY COUNTY.

A SUPERFICIAL view of the county would present the picture of a section of a river valley, running almost due east and west, with the dip to the west, and fringed to the north and south by smaller valleys which furrow the sides of irregular ranges of knobs and hills which lie along the northern and southern boundaries. To the west these hills broaden out into the uplands known as the "Barrens," forming a part of the Highland Rim. The bed of this valley is occupied by Duck River, which flows through the whole extent of the county, dividing it almost equally. The river drains the entire county, as all the other streams flow into it. The river is not navigable through the whole extent of the county. The river was much used formerly for flat-boats and barges. It is still much used in floating out rafts during high water. The great value of Duck River is in its excellent water-power, which drives the numerous grist and saw-mills that line its banks. The county is well drained. In several creeks in the western part of the county are some beautiful waterfalls. On the northwest and south the rim which borders the county is slashed by narrow and beautiful valleys of extreme richness; the remaining portion of the county is of a gently rolling surface, stretching out toward the west and south of the river into almost a plain-like smoothness.

Except the small portion around the northern, western and southern edges, invaded by the Highland Rim, the entire county is of limestone formation. It is by no means of one uniform variety, nor is the soil the same over the county. The soil generally is dark and friable, and exceedingly rich. The subsoil is generally a stiff, dark-colored clay, which weathers rapidly into a rich soil. But the characteristic of the county is the cedar timber, which abounds in some places so thickly as to exclude all undergrowth and to shut out every ray of the sun as effectually as the darkest clouds of winter. In "the cedars" the rock comes to the surface. The soil is admirably suited to wheat and grasses, and peach trees do finely in it.

The original settlers in Zion Church neighborhood came from Williamsburg District, S. C. They came in a kind of colony, led by Squire John Dickey, who brought about twenty families with him. A portion of these arrived in 1807, and others in 1808. Five thousand acres of land were purchased of the Gen. Greene Survey, at $3 per acre. Around this as a nucleus clustered the little colony. Among the settlers were Squire Dickey, Moses Frierson, James Blakeley, William Frierson, Eli Frierson, James Armstrong, Thomas Stephenson, Nathaniel Stephenson, "Old Davy" Mathews, Samuel Witherspoon, John Stephenson, James Frierson, P. Fulton, Alexander Dobbins, Moses Freeman, the Flemmings and Mayes. Mr. J. S. Mayes, who is four score and ten, and still vigorous, lives in the Mount Zion neighborhood, and was one of the original settlers, and has a very distinct recollection of the first settlement. Like the Pilgrim Fathers the first thing they did on their arrival was the erection of a church. A place was selected, as near as could be judged, in the center of the purchase for the church site, which proved almost the exact mathematical center. Here was erected a rude log church some time in 1807, which is supposed to have been the first church erected in Maury County. Near the church was laid out a grave-yard in which the body of Robert Frierson was consigned in August, 1808, the first in that vicinity. In this rude church, in the midst of the canebrakes and shades of the forest, the little band of pioneers met regularly every week to hear sermons by the Rev. Samuel Frierson or William Frierson, who poured forth the truths of the gospel with apostolic zeal and simplicity. In a short time the Rev. James N. Stephenson, who had been pastor of the church in South Carolina, became the pastor at Mount Zion. The old log church stood till 1814 or 1815, and was replaced by a brick church of peculiar shape.

It was arranged with the pulpit at the side with the main part of the building arranged for the whites, and a kind of transept at the end for the colored people. The old brick house stood till 1831, when a small body of ground was purchased near the old house and a new building erected. This house still stands, although it has several times been repaired and improved. The people of the Zion neighborhood were largely members of the Mount Zion Church, and being an intelligent class of people have always maintained a talented ministry. After the retirement of Dr. Stephenson, before mentioned, the Rev. James M. Smell was called to the pulpit, who remained till 1850; the next was the Rev. Daniel G. Doak, who remained till 1853, when he was succeeded by Rev. A. A. Doak. Rev. Doak remained but a short time, and was succeeded by Rev. J. T. Hendrick, whose death occurred in 1860. Rev. Hendricks was succeeded in 1860 by Dr. Mack, of Columbia, who served the church till 1863, and then gave place to Rev. C. Foster Williams, who still preaches occasionally. The next pastor was Rev. S. W. Mitchell, who still serves the church.

Inseparably connected with the settlement of Mount Zion neighborhood were the schools of that section. The old church was used for a schoolhouse. Parson Henderson started a Latin school there at an early day. Many of the young men of the neighborhood attended his school. Among them was J. M. S. Mayes, who has distinct recollections of the boyhood days of President James K. Polk, who also was one of his pupils. Among the teachers who have taught at or near Mount Zion are Elias J. Armstrong, Alexander Dobbins Park, White McCollough, T. A. Flemming, Dr. Thomas J. Kennedy, Simeon Smith, James A. Frierson, L. Oatman, J. B. Frierson, Stephenson, J. W. Logan, D. R. Arnell, Prof. J. S. Beecher, A. W. Mayes and James Creighton. Many eminent physicians have also lived in that neighborhood, the most noted of whom are mentioned elsewhere. Among them may be mentioned Drs. Samuel Mayes, D. N. Sansom, J. C. O'Reiley, E. M. Ford, J. W. S. Frierson, J. N. Brown, C. G. R. Nichols, William Armstrong, and Theoodore Frierson, now of Columbia. Moses Frierson built a small water-mill on Lick Creek in the same neighborhood. This was the first mill in the vicinity for some time. Before this each family ground their grain on hand-mills kept by every family.

Not far from Zion is the Polk settlement. The first settler in this place was William Dever, a bachelor, and a maiden sister. They settled in this vicinity in 1807, and were the first settlers between Columbia and Mount Pleasant. They settled on a 5,000-acre tract that was given by North Carolina as a military grant. This fell to Col. William Polk by purchase. The Devers, by parsimonious habits, accumulated considerable means. Col. Polk, who was a Revolutionary soldier, divided this estate among the following four sons: Bishop Leonidas Polk, Lucius J., George N. and Rufus K. Polk. The other two sons received estates elsewhere. This was known as the "Polk neighborhood." The most of this talented family are now gone. Not far from this is what was the former house of Gen. Gideon J. Pillow. Hard by is the old church, St. John's Episcopal, ivy grown with age. This church is a brick building, and was erected in 1841. Here Leonidas Polk did his first preaching, and by his vigor and talent rose to the rank of bishop. He was well known as a minister, lecturer and educator. At the time of his death he held a lieutenant-generalship in the Confederate Army. He was killed by a cannon ball at Kenesaw Mountain, Georgia, during the Atlanta campaign, in the summer of 1864. Ashwood Cemetery is the Polk family burying ground. Here are buried all of the family who have died in that vicinity, the first having been Rufus K. Polk. Rt. Rev. Bishop Otey here has a resting place. Here, too, were consigned the bodies of Gens. Cleburne, Granberry, Ghist and Shahl, who were killed at Franklin November 30, 1864.

The early settlers on Knob Creek were the Sellers, Hanks, McLeans, Williamses, Gwynns, Badgetts and Partees. At a later date came the Goodwins, Vestals, Powells, Neeleys, Coopers and Hudspeths. Perhaps no list of families has been perpetuated more fully than these. The first horse-mill on Knoll Creek was built by John Gwynn, the first water-mill by the Partees. The first ministers were Thomas Hanks, Elijah Hanks and Mr. Dodson. Through the influence of these men Hanks' church was built. This was what was known as an "Old or Hardshell Baptist Church." A schism occurred, and a division headed by Elijah Hanks joined the Missionary Baptists. Elder Hanks was recognized as a leading spirit in building up the missionary cause in the county. Near the mouth of Greene's Lick is Hunter's ford, an old and favorite crossing place for the Indians and early settlers.

In the vicinity of Leiper Creek were the Hamiltons, Crawfords, Oakleys, Neatheringtons, Edgars, Mayes, McCallums, Wrens and Lyons. On the farm formerly owned by Maj. John Brown, is a sulphur spring that was resorted to for a time as a health spring. Near the same place Mr. Goodrich made a boring of 900 feet in depth for oil, but without success. In the vicinity of Bear Creek lived Gen. Isaac Roberts, well known in the county's history and development. Also Daniel Evans, Joseph Hernden, James M. Lewis and Dr. James C. O'Reiley, who is mentioned in the article on physicians. The Gordon family, also the Crawfords, settled in the same vicinity.

Maury County was named in honor of Maj. Shaw Maury, of Williamson County, who represented Williamson County in the lower house of the General Assembly in 1823-24, and again in 1842-43. He also saw military service under Gen. Jackson in 1812 and was connected with one of the best families of the county. The act creating the county passed the General Assembly November 16, 1807, and was entitled "An act to reduce Williamson County to its constitutional limits." Section 2 reads: "Beginning at the above described point, it being the southwest corner of Williamson County; thence south to the Columbia road; thence with said road as it meanders to a point where the Indian boundary line leaves the same; thence with said line to the dividing ridge that divides the waters of Duck River from the Elk; thence with said ridge to a point thirteen miles and fifty-six chains and a half east of the line of the congressional reservation hitherto run and marked; thence north to the Williamson County line; thence with said line, to the place of beginning, to be called Maury County." The survey was made by Henry Rutherford in the fall of 1807, by order of Peter R. Booker, Gideon Pillow, John B. Porter and John Lindsey. These boundaries embraced a much larger area than now belongs to Maury County. It originally embraced parts or all of Lewis, Lawrence, Giles, Marshall and Bedford Counties; as it is now limited it contains 386,309 acres. Section 11, of the act above quoted, declared Maury County to be a part of the Mero District, with as full and ample powers as other parts of said district. Another section of the same act appointed James Gideon to run the line between Maury and Williamson. He was allowed $2 per day for his services and was empowered to employ two chain carriers, the expenses of the above named work to be borne equally by Maury and Williamson Counties.

As is well known, the statutes require the division of the counties into districts according to the number of population, twenty-five being the maximum number. Under the first constitution, this division was not made on the population alone but upon the number belonging to the various militia companies; these of course to some extent represented the number of population. Tax listers were chosen or elected, not for a certain district but for a certain captain's company. The growth of population caused an increase in the number of companies. These were changed every two years. The first available, and possibly the first division made, was in 1809, the following being the heads of companies: Capt. William Polk, Capt. Sellars, Capt. Whitson, Capt. Scott, Capts. James Isom, John Moorehead, Moses Smith, Eli Frierson, James Rutledge, George W. McGahey, William Daniels, Isaac Bills, Thomas Shannon, and Adongah Edwards; fourteen companies or districts. In 1811 the following were the captains of companies: Capts. Scott, Whitson, Booker, Polk, Boyer, Davis, Kirkpatrick, Fitzpatrick, Daniels, Reynolds, Bills, Rutledge, McGahey, Jones, Smith, Gurley, Isom and Moorehead—seventeen in all. In 1813 there were Capts. Looney, Gholson, Farney, Reading, Hurt, May, Osburn, McIntyre, Young, Kirk, Summers, Stockard, Watkins, Kilpatrick, Campbell, Chisholm, McNiell, McLean, Mitchell, Hanks, McCarkin and Dickson. In 1819 the number of divisions had increased to twenty-six, viz: Capts. Cockburn, Gholson, McNutt, Ewing, Dooley, Wilkes, Andreas, Cathel, Allen, Hanna, Crawford, McCarty, Kiley, Short, Torn, Campbell, Bavirey,

Middleton, Powell, Polk, Hamlett, Seargrove, Mills, Cheairs, Gamon and Sherrod Just before the new constitution went into operation there were military districts of Capt. F. S. Alderson of the Columbia Company and Capts. Kerr, Woods, Gill, Edwards, Worthman, Kennedy, Chaffin, King, Martin, Steele, Garrit, Tollman, Dearens, Dyer, Foster, and Mitchell of the Ninety-third Regiment. The Mount Pleasant Company of Capt. J. B. Boyd and Capts. McKee, Cockrill, Oaks, Grimes, Craig, McMakin, Baxter, Graham, Frierson, Stringham and Sites of the Fifty-first; and Capts. Sparkman, Harbison, Cathey. Mitchell, Smith, Black, Oliphant, Kerford, Brown, Ledbetter, Jarrit, Laird and Crawford of the Forty-sixth Regiment. Under the new constitution these divisions came to be known by the ordinal numbers. Various changes have been made in the county boundaries since the organization and much more numerous changes in the civil districts. In February, 1853, Nathan B. Akin, Robert M. Cooper, James Farris, Alfred P. Buckner, C. Y. Hudson, were appointed commissioners to lay off that part of Lewis County which had been attached to Maury into districts. These districts at that time were Nos. 11, 12 and 13. The number of districts as now limited is twenty-five.

Private houses were used as court houses till 1810; the place of meeting was at Col. Joseph Brown's. The session of 1808 was opened December 21, in Columbia. The building used was a small log shanty which stood on the east side of the Square about where East Market Street enters the Square. The act of 1807 required of the commissioners of Columbia that they should contract for the building of a court house, prisons and stocks. They were to use the money arising from the sale of lots not otherwise appropriated. In case there was not sufficient money they were empowered with authority to levy a tax of 12½ cents on each white poll, 25 cents on each black poll, 25 cents on each town lot, $5 on each merchant and peddler or banker, to be collected by the collector of public taxes. The first building was built of brick, within the square, and was completed in 1810.

The above building stood till 1845, after having been repaired and improved many times. At the April term of 1844 a majority of the justices decided to build a new court house, provided the same could be built at a cost not exceeding $15,000, provided said sum should be taken in the claims for taxes then held by Nimrod Porter. A committee consisting of J. B. White, James Brown, Parke Street, Thomas Worthams and E. C. Frierson was appointed for making a contract for the erection of a house. The contract was closed with Nimrod Porter for $15,000, $9,100 were already held by him in tax receipts, and the remainder was to be in money. A bond was executed in the amount of $30,000 by Nimrod Porter, B. W. Porter, Hugh Bradshaw, George Lipscomb, G. W. Gordon, W. H. Pillow and Joseph Brown. By this contract the county was enabled to secure $9,100 of doubtful value. The house now standing was built according to the plans and specifications of this contract. The house was to be 87x49 feet and two stories high. After the house was well under way it was concluded best to build an additional story. This was accordingly ordered at an additional cost of $4,000, making the total cost $19,000. The old house was sold to J. L. Smith for $10, who was allowed one and two years time. Smith failed to meet his obligation, and it was accordingly resold. While the new court house was in course of construction, court met in the old market-house. The court house thus erected is still doing service, but will doubtless soon be replaced by one more in accordance with the wealth and taste of the people of the county. The first jail was erected by the commissioners of Columbia, who were empowered with authority to build a jail. This was erected about 1810, and was of brick, and stood near the second jail site. It was afterward changed to a family residence.

By an act of the General Assembly the citizens of Maury were granted authority to build a new jail. At the February term of court in 1837 James R. Plummer, Joseph Herndon, Tazwell S. Alderson, Patrick McGuire and A. Zillner were made a committee for the erection of a new jail. Lot 46 of the original plan of Columbia was purchased for $1,200 as a jail site. A special levy of taxes was laid for the purpose of raising $3,000 for jail purposes, but the cost greatly exceeded that amount. The work was completed in 1838. The allowances for the jail at the January term of 1839 will indicate the cost. There were allowed to Walter & Benner, $2,385.26; to Thomas W. Ament, $2,832.34; to William Horsley, $1,399.07; to T. W. Ament, a claim for foundation for $929.50. This jail served till 1883, when steps were taken for building a new one. At the October term of court a committee was appointed for the purpose of erecting the proposed building. In January the committee organized by electing W. O. Gordon, chairman, and Robert M. McKay, secretary. The committee purchased the "Thompson property" for $500, and exchanged it for the lot at the head of Embargo, fronting Sixth Street; they also bargained for a lot adjoining with Z. R. Gillespie for $710. The committee were instructed to advertise for plans and specifications, the cost not to exceed $22,500. The committee did its work, and the contract was let to McDonald & Bro., of Louisville, Ky., whose bid was considered the most favorable among six competitors. The fine three-story jail and residence is the result of this contract. Warrants on the county were sold to the amount of $22,500, and cashed by the First National Bank of Columbia for 94 cents on the dollar.

A common mode of punishment in former days was by placing prisoners in the stocks. These were erected by the town commissioners about 1808. They were erected on the Square, and consisted of timbers cut with a groove, so as to clamp around the wrist and ankles. Thus confined the prisoner was so placed that he could move neither hand nor foot. Not unfrequently the prisoner fainted from stagnation of the blood, caused by the pressure of the clamps. Previous to 1830 the poor of the county were farmed out to the lowest responsible bidder. In that year twelve and a half acres of land were purchased for the purpose of establishing a permanent poor farm. In October, 1841, an additional thirty acres were purchased from Dr. Smith for $400, since which time the poor farm has become one of the fixed institutions of the county.

The first turnpike chartered in Maury County was in 1831. It was called the Franklin & Columbia Turnpike; a new charter was granted October 22, 1833. This road, however, was not built till many years after this. The road is now known as the Columbia & Santa Fe Pike, and is an excellent road of eleven miles in length. The Columbia & Hawpasture Turnpike was chartered by William E. Kennedy and others January 23, 1850, and five miles of the road were built in 1856–57. The road was rechartered May 23, 1856, and the road extended to twelve miles in length. The Columbia Central, i. e. the Maury Central, was also chartered in 1856. The charter was granted to Granville A. Pillow, president, and William Gallaway, E. C. Frierson and John M. Francis. The company had the privilege of erecting toll-gates every five miles. The road is now twelve miles long. The Columbia & Mount Pleasant Pike is sixteen miles long, and runs through the finest portion of the county, if not of the State. The Columbia & Little Bigby is a good road, and is ten miles in length. It received its charter in 1880. The Carter's Creek Turnpike was chartered in 1880, and an extension granted in April, 1883. There are also the Columbia & Pulaski Pike of five miles, and the Columbia & Sawell Mill Pike, of five miles in length. The charter to the Columbia & Culleoka Turnpike Company was granted to J. K. Akin, A. F. Brown, W. J. Moore, J. J. Flemming, J. E. Gordon and James T. Akin November 11, 1879. On September 8, 1883, the Culleoka & Mooresville Pike was chartered by R. A. Walker, W. K. Stephens, J. A. Coffey, O. N. Fry and W. A. Bryant. Maury County now has about 100 miles of pike.

The first steps taken to build a railroad through Maury County were some time between 1840 and 1850, when a charter was obtained for what was called the "Columbia & Tennessee River Railroad." The road was surveyed and estimates made and stock taken, but on resurvey it was found that the estimates were far from correct, and the enterprise failed. In 1852 a charter was obtained for the Central Southern Railroad, and soon after for the Tennessee & Alabama Road. In October, 1855, the county voted $200,000 stock in the last named road, and in November of the same year $140,000 was voted in the former road. A charter was also obtained for a road from Nashville to Mount Pleasant. This was afterward changed to Columbia. The road was completed in 1859, and was called the Nashville & Decatur Road. A branch road of eleven miles in length was soon after built to Mount Pleasant through some very fine country. The branch was torn up during the war, and the iron taken for other roads by the Federals. Within the last decade this road has been rebuilt and put in good condition, and a narrow guage road built from Columbia to Fayetteville. In April, 1866, the Tennessee & Alabama Southern Road obtained control of the Nashville & Decatur by lease, and in 1884 the whole system of roads in the county passed into the hands of the Louisville & Nashville Company. Since they have assumed control the road has been greatly improved and its business extended.

The wealth of Maury County and eligible site of Columbia, and the unsettled question of the State capital led the people of this county not only to aspire but to expect the capital to be located at Columbia. While the General Assembly was meeting at Murfreesboro it was thought that if good communication could be had with the Tennessee it would further the claims of Columbia for the State capital. With this as one of the motives in view, a company was formed for the purpose of opening a public highway from Columbia to Clifton, or some other point on the Tennessee, and from that point a steam-boat was to run to New Orleans, thus opening rapid and direct transit to that city. The company was formed about 1820. Among the members were Peter R. Booker, Patrick McGuire, Maj. Samuel Polk, David Gillespie, Dr. McNiel, James Walker, Edward B. Littlefield, John Hodge, John T. Moore, Maj. John Brown, William Bradshaw, Joseph B. Porter, William Frierson and some others. A steam-boat was built at Pittsburgh and purchased by the company for about $40,000. Edward B. Littlefield being a son-in-law of Gen. Nathaniel Greene, of Revolutionary fame, and one of the heaviest stockholders in the company, the boat in deference to him was called the "Gen. Greene." It is remembered that I. P. Minor was captain of the "Gen. Greene;" Lemuel Duncan, clerk, and William J. Dale, a prominent citizen and retired merchant of Columbia, was assistant. The "Gen. Greene" was an unprofitable investment, and it was afterward sold for about one-fourth of its original cost. The "Gen. Greene" brought neither wealth to the company nor the capital to Columbia. This was in the days when to be a steam-boat captain, clerk or even cabin boy was a "consummation devoutly to be wished."

Before the introduction of the steam-boat the produce was conveyed to New Orleans by means of flat-boats. These sluggish vessels were laden with deer saddles, skins, furs, pork, corn and other articles of commerce, and floated to New Orleans, where its owner sold it with its cargo and returned home on foot. He would travel through the canebrakes of Louisiana and Mississippi till striking the "Old Natchez Trace"; thence by this "through the far resounding forest" he reached home after a month or more's absence. Not infrequently, however, he exchanged his cargo for coffee, sugar, rice, salt or other necessaries, and returned by water in a keel-boat, propelled by oars, pushed by poles or drawn by ropes fastened to trees in front. The navigation of Duck River received the attention of the Legislature at a very early day. An act was passed November 2, 1809, forbidding the obstruction of the river for "boats, rafts and flats at least twelve feet wide," and another passed September 30, 1811, forbidding bridges below Shelbyville that would obstruct the river. By an act of November 17, 1813, Alexander Gray, Garret Lane, of Hickman, and Robert Hill, William Cathey and William Stockard, of Maury County, were made "commissioners of Duck River navigation from Gordon's Ferry to the mouth of the river."

Section 4 of the same act gave them power to call upon the commissioners of the town of Columbia for $1,050 of moneys arising from the sale of lands, not otherwise appropriated. Jonathan Webster, Isaac Roberts and Samuel Smith were the commissioners to improve the river from the Bedford line to Gordon's Ferry. On November 9, 1815, Thomas Jones, John Brown and Richard McMahan were the commissioners. These were changed from year to year as necessity required. Among the noted flat-boat men of Duck River were Edwin H. Baird, Moses A. Wiley, Alexander Farris, Andrew T. Gray, John Gordon, Gabe Brown, William Brown, James D. Freeland, Archibald Wray, Powhattan Gordon and Elijah Reeves.

The increased amount of produce in the county brought about the necessity for a better outlet to the outside world. To meet this demand the Duck River Steam Navigation

Company was organized and was incorporated by an act of the Legislature January 27, 1840, with an authorized capital stock of $500,000 divided into shares of $100 each. The following persons were appointed to open books in Columbia for subscriptions of stock: R. B. Mayes, James Walker, Gardner Frierson, H. Langtry, Robert P. Webster, John B. Hamilton and Robert Campbell, Jr. At Centerville there were B. Gordon, Samuel B. Moore, David B. Warren, Edwin M. Baird and John Studdart. Books were to be opened on the first Monday in March in 1840, and when $150,000 were subscribed the commissioners at Columbia were to give notice that an election of directors would be held at such time and place as they deemed proper. An act passed January 20, 1844, by which William J. Rankin, Meredith Helm and Robert Campbell at Columbia; Powhattan Gordon, Abraham Church and Samuel S. Porter at Williamsport, and Samuel B. Moore, Robert Shegoy and Boling Gordon, at Centerville, were appointed commissioners to open books of subscription for a joint stock company with a capital not to exceed $200,000 for the purpose of navigating Duck River with steam-boats. The insufficiency of water in Duck River led to the formation of the Duck River Slack Water Navigation Company. The company was incorporated January 15, 1846, and the capital limited to $650,000 in shares of $50 each. The company was granted the exclusive privilege for fifty years after the passage of the act, to navigate Duck River with steam-boats, barges and keels. The work was to be completed within twenty years else the charter was to become void. The following persons were the members appointed to open books for subscriptions: Robert Campbell, Jr., Christopher Todd, R. B. Mayes, James Smizer, Gideon J. Pillow, George W. Gordon, Robert T. Webster, William F. Rankin, Meredith Helm, Abraham Church, Edwin Baird, M. C. Napier, John Montgomery, D. G. Jones, John B. Gray, Joseph Blackwell and Henry G. Cummings.

A large amount of stock was soon subscribed and a civil engineer was employed who made a survey of Duck River from Columbia to its mouth. According to the engineer's estimate, fourteen or fifteen locks were all that were necessary. It was afterward found that this estimate was only about half the number required. This was not learned, however, until one lock had been completed and that at about double its estimated cost. The lock completed seemed satisfactory but for the immense cost. Under these discouraging circumstances suits of injunction began to be filed against the further prosecution of the work. Before the formation of either of the above companies, the steam-boat, "Madison" came up Duck River. This was in 1839, as is learned from an old file of the *Observer* published at the time.

Before the establishment of the county courts, roads or highways were opened by authority of the State to different settlements or by the General Government for military purposes. Among the last named was the "Old Natchez Trace," called by the older settlers "Notchy Trace." This is supposed to have originally been marked by the Indians in going from one tribe to another or to have been worn by buffalo. The trace, or the military road which followed the trace a portion of the way, was cut out by a detachment of soldiers under command of Capt. Thomas Butler and Lieut. E. P. Gaines, afterward Maj.-Gen. Gaines. This was done by order of President Jefferson in 1801-02. The object was to open easy communication with Indian nations and the Spanish settlements. The terminus at one end was Nashville; the other was at a point about twenty-five miles above Port Hudson. The route is described as leading from "Nashville by Gen. Harding's place, thence through the Perkins settlement, passing about three miles east of Franklin, crossing Duck River at Gordon's Ferry; thence by Debbin's stand on Big Swan Creek; thence to Grinder's old stand on Little Swan; thence by John McClish's; thence across the Tennessee at Colbert's Ferry; thence to Buzzard Roost on Big Bear Creek; thence crossing Brown's Swamp to the Chickasaw agency; thence south a little west of Jackson, Miss.; thence at or near Canton and south to Line Creek." This was the main thoroughfare from Nashville to the lower Mississippi. A branch of this road led into Columbia from the south; it passed through the Athenæum grounds. It was by this route that Gen. Jackson returned with his army from the battle of New Orleans. It was on the old trace that Merriwether Lewis committed suicide. It was along the old route that Aaron Burr traveled in 1806 on his way from Louisiana to meet Jackson at the Hermitage and Blennerhassett in his island home.

The Davis Ford road was the principal thoroughfare from Nashville to Huntsville. This road crossed the river at Davis' Ford below the mouth of Fountain Creek and passed near Hurricane and Culleoka; thence across Elk Ridge near Dodson's Gap where the railroad now crosses. This road took its name from a Mr. Davis who lived on McCutchin's Island near the Indian trail. At the ford Capt. McCutchin overtook and destroyed a marauding band of Indians, and their bodies were buried on the river bank on the north side.

The first bridge across Duck River, at Columbia, was built by Edward B. Littlefield, Peter R. Booker and David Craighead. The consideration for the bridge was $15,000. It was let August 31, 1820, and the contract called for a bridge with stone pillars, the bridge to be covered, weather-boarded, the boarding to be painted white and the roof red. The payments were in installments of $5,000 each, the first due at the time of beginning, the second September 1, 1821, and the third September 1, 1822, the date of completion. The sureties were Robert Mack, James Walker, John Brown, James T. Sandford and Nimrod Porter. The bond was fixed at $30,000. How well the work was done is shown by the fact that the same pillars still stand, but the bridge was burned in the retreat of the Confederates before Buell in 1862. This was improved and temporarily repaired till 1870, when a contract was let to Moore & Vaughn for a new bridge, except the pillars and abutments. The new bridge was completed within the first few days of 1872. Strong efforts are now being made to have a new iron bridge constructed below the old bridge. An effort was made in 1824 to have the bridge a toll-bridge, but was defeated January 26, of that year, by a vote of thirty-three "against" and six "for" a toll-bridge. In 1838 the vote was again taken, and it became a toll-bridge, with rates ranging from 1 cent to 50 cents. J. S. Alderson, John Brown and Joseph Herndon were appointed a committee to employ a bridge-keeper, the first money to be used in repairs on the bridge. As a toll-bridge it was soon discontinued.

The first cemetery was laid off by the commissioners of Columbia in 1807. This lies on the bank of Duck River, north of the city. This is known as "Greenwood," and is a beautiful resting place after "life's fitful fever." It contains the remains of many of the early settlers. "Rose Hill" Cemetery was chartered in 1854 by John B. Hamilton, John Baird, W. J. Dale, Thomas J. Kelly, Nathan Vaught and James Andrews. Many distinguished dead sleep on Rose Hill, among them Judge Dillahunty and Gen. John C. Carter, who fell at Franklin. A large number of Federal soldiers were buried here, but they have been removed to Nashville and Murfreesboro, or other places, and interred in national cemeteries. Over 100 Confederate dead are buried in "Rose Hill" Cemetery. In honor of these heroes is erected a beautiful monument, which is surmounted by a full-sized soldier, who looks with pathos and with downcast eye upon his fallen comrades.

The physicians of 1808[*] were Dr. Samuel Mayes, who was born in Carlisle, Penn., in 1759, graduated from the University of Pennsylvania and settled in South Carolina. He moved to this county in 1808, where he died in 1841. He saw service in the Revolutionary war. Dr. L. B. Estes, well known in the early history of the county, was born in Virginia in 1774, graduated from the University of Virginia, and came to Maury County in 1808, where he died in November, 1814. Dr. James O'Reiley was born in Dublin, Ireland, in 1776, graduated at the university of the same, married in North Carolina in 1805, and came to Maury County in 1809. He was noted for his boldness and originality both in the practice of medicine and surgery. He was well known to the business world. He died in 1850. Dr. G. T. Greenfield was born in Virginia, graduated at the University of Pennsylvania and came to Maury County in 1812. He abandoned the profession and became a cotton planter, and grew rich. He was a noted politician. His death occurred in 1847. Dr. William Fort Brown was a native of North Carolina, where he was born in 1790. He was a student under Dr. O'Reiley; also a partner for a time. He was very much addicted to drink, yet such was the confidence of the people in him that they would send and bring him to their houses and lock him up until sufficiently sober to prescribe. His

---

[*]From an article by Dr. J. M. Towler.

death occurred in 1859. Dr. Thomas Brown was born in Wilkes County, N. C., in 1784, and was a graduate of the University of Pennsylvania. He came to Maury County in 1814; was a popular physician. He died of cholera in 1834. Dr. Isaac J. Thomas was a native of North Carolina, born in 1781, and came to this county in 1814, where he remained till his death in 1844. Dr. John B. Hayes was born in Rockbridge County, Va., in 1796, graduated at the University of New York and settled in Maury County in 1816. He is described as a close student, an acute observer, generous, genial, high-toned, "a fellow of infinite jest that was wont to set the table in a roar." He related a story that well illustrates the superstition of the time: "A member of a family living twelve miles in the country was affected with the shingles; the remedy at the time was the blood from the tail of a black cat. Efforts were made to procure the coveted black cat, but none could be found, the disease became alarming and a runner was started to town with the following instructions from the old lady of the house: 'Johnny, when you get to town try to get a black cat, but if you can't get one, bring Dr. Hayes.'" Dr. Hayes died after a successful practice of fifty-two years. In 1816 Drs. Gale and James G. Smith came to this county; both were from Maryland. Between 1816-20 Drs. J. B. Sanders, Dowell N. Sansom (Horatio Depriest?), McDowell, Silas M. Caldwell, John W. McJimsey, Gillespie and William McNeil; of these Dr. Depriest committed suicide, and all were well known in their profession and in the social circle. Dr. George W. Campbell started out full of promise, but died early in life from septicæmia, originating from a wound. Dr. Grevor abandoned the profession for business, and died at New Orleans of yellow fever. Of the same period were Drs. Cooper, Ford, Turner and Crawford. Dr. J. W. S. Frierson was born in Sumter District, S. C., in 1801, graduated at Greeneville College, and was made a doctor of medicine at Transylvania in 1824, and from that time till his death, in 1872, was in active practice. He was an ornament both to the profession and to society. He was succeeded in the profession by his son, Dr. Samuel W. Frierson. Dr. John Baptiste Alexander Thevenot was born in Paris, France, February 26, 1793, and graduated at the early age of eighteen; was surgeon for a time in the army of Napoleon. He settled at Mount Pleasant in 1824, where he died of cholera in 1834. He was a noted linguist, something of a poet and author, and was regarded as a brilliant and eccentric practitioner. Dr. Jonathan S. Hunt was a native of North Carolina, where he was born in 1790, moved to Williamson County in 1820, graduated at Transylvania in 1822, and moved to Maury County in 1824, and there remained till his death in 1860. Dr. Samuel Porter was born in Chesterville, S. C., February 3, 1793, graduated at Transylvania in 1821, and began practice in this county in 1826. He held an extensive practice about Williamsport till his death in 1873. Dr. Zebina Conkey and A. G. Tracey came to Maury County from New York in 1826. About the same time there came Drs. Hillard Myrick, Mervin Daniel and John Henry Crisp; the two former were graduates of Transylvania, and the latter was a native of North Carolina and a graduate of the University of Pennsylvania. Dr. Amos Gray was born in Prince William County, Va., in March, 1800. He was graduated at Transylvania in 1827, and at once began practice at Santa Fe. He died October 5, 1870. Dr. John S. Law was born in Liberty County, Ga., in 1802, graduated at the University of Pennsylvania in 1827, moved to Maury County in 1833, and died of black tongue in 1844. Between 1828-30 there settled in Maury County Drs. P. P. Barbour, John Littlefield, Eskew, H. S. Roberts, Placebo, Bills and Bracken. Between 1830-40 there were Drs. A. H. Buchanan, S. T. McMurray, of Spring Hill, and Wharton White, who was born in Nashville, January 23, 1819, graduated at Louisville in 1839, and died in 1859. Dr. G. T. Harris was a native of Rutherford County, where he was born in 1806, was a student of Dr. O'Reiley, before mentioned, and graduated at Transylvania in 1826. His death occurred in 1866. Since 1840 there have been the following: Drs. A. M. Kellar, A. M. Hamner, N. W. B. Wortham, James H. Frierson, a native of Maury, born in 1812, graduated at Transylvania and died in 1846; Milton B. Frierson, James Leach, James E. Sealey, Calvin H. Walker, who was born in Columbia in 1823, and graduated at Jefferson College, Philadelphia, in 1847. He was a gallant colonel of a Confederate regiment in the late war, and was killed by a shell near Marietta, Ga. Dr. Wiley T. Perry first saw the light in this county in 1830, graduated at Louisville and died in 1869. Dr. F. S. Woldridge was born in Franklin in 1826, graduated at the University of Pennsylvania in 1850 and died in 1870. A. W. Byers was born in 1815, graduated at Louisville in 1840, and died in 1870. D. J. McCallum was born in Giles County in 1826, graduated at the University of Pennsylvania in 1853, and died in 1864. Dr. Gomar Wing was from Maine, and was a successful practitioner for many years at Spring Hill. In addition there were Drs. A. and J. W. Leftwick, Satterfield and the brothers Kilpatrick, also Dr. McKeithen, who was from North Carolina, and who lived with Gen. Lucius J. Polk at his plantation near Spring Hill. He was regarded as a well-read physician.

The first epidemic in the county was the black tongue in 1813. Gen. Roberts, county surveyor, had a son die of the disease in Nashville. He and another son brought the corpse home for interment. In a short time that son took the disease and died. The disease spread and was more fatal in proportion to its extent than the one in 1844. The epidemic of 1844 occurred early in February, the first case being a young lady who had been visiting Nashville. A great many died of this disease, among them Col. Dew and Dr. Law. The disease manifested itself in different ways: sometimes in acute pains, and in others in nervous and muscular depression without pain. It was very fatal among negroes. It prevailed both in town and country. It was what is now known as cerebro spinal meningitis. An epidemic of scarlet fever of remarkable fatality prevailed in 1837. Cholera has never prevailed in Columbia, although it has visited various parts of the county several times with its wanton violence. Each time imported or sporadic cases occurred in turn, but it invariably died out of itself. In 1834 Col. Whittaker, a planter living seven miles southeast of Columbia, on his return from Nashville, was attacked by the disease at midnight and died the following day. Dr. Brown who attended him died, also seven of his negroes, one of whom died in the office of Drs. Brown & Buchanan, whither he had gone for a physician. It was introduced at Mount Pleasant in the same way, from Nashville, and prevailed with its usual fatality, Dr. Thevenot being one of its victims. At midnight on Saturday, August 14, 1835, it suddenly fell upon the little town of Williamsport, and by the morning of the 15th several were dead or dying and many writhing under its torturing cramps. Twelve citizens of the place died and as many from the country. In every case the individuals had been visiting or doing business in that portion of the town situated in a low, damp flat, nor were any attacked in the country who had not visited that spot of the village on the fatal Saturday. In June, 1849, Dr. Hays was summoned to the bedside of ex-President Polk. He went in the old Polk family carriage driven by Old Joe, the favorite coachman. On Joe's return he was suddenly seized with the cholera and died in a short time, but no other cases followed. In July, 1850, Jim Brown, who kept a wagon-yard in the lower part of town, was suddenly seized with the cholera on his return from Nashville. He recovered after intense suffering, but two colored women caught the disease and died. Those were the last cases of cholera.

Sheriffs: John Spencer was chosen sheriff in 1807 and held the position till 1810, when he was succeeded by Samuel H. Williams, who held the position till 1812. William Bradshaw then held the office from 1812 till 1818, at which time Nimrod Porter was elected and held the office till 1842. Porter was succeeded by J. E. Thomas, who held the office till 1846, and was succeeded by Mumford Smith, who held the office till 1850. Richard B. Moore was elected to succeed Smith and held the position till 1854, when Smith was again elected and held the office till 1856; he was then succeeded by Samuel H. Jones, who held the office till 1860. Thomas J. Cristy held the office from 1860 to 1864, when William M. Sullivan took the office and held it till 1868. Robert D. Rickets held the office from 1868 till the adoption of the new constitution in 1870. Sims Latta held the office from 1870 to 1874, and was succeeded by William A. Alexander, who held the office till 1878. Mr. Alexander was succeeded by Mr. Davis, and he by W. O. Witherspoon, who held it till 1884, and was succeeded by N. Bleheairs. Circuit clerks:

John M. Taylor held the office from 1810 till 1818, and was succeeded by Horatio Depriest, who resigned, and George M. Martin was appointed in his place and held the office till March 11, 1836, when he resigned and was succeeded by J. A. Walker, and he by Pleasant Nelson. Mr. Nelson was succeeded by James O. Potter, who was succeeded by Caleb J. Dickerson; upon his death he was succeeded by Lemuel H. Phillips, and he by Thomas H. Witherspoon, who was succeeded by Samuel P. McGaw. Mr. McGaw was succeeded by the Hon. William B. Wilson, and Mr. Wilson by W. J. Whitthorne. Mr. Whitthorne was succeeded by E. T. Pillow. County court clerks: Joseph B. Porter was chosen clerk in 1807, and was succeeded by his son, T. J. Porter, and he by William E. Erwin. Mr. Erwin was succeeded in 1870 by John M. Hickey, and Mr. Hickey by A. N. Akin in 1874, who still holds the office. Clerks and masters in chancery: On the organization of the chancery court in 1834–35, George M. Martin became master and held the position till 1844, and was succeeded by Hon. William P. Martin, his son. Mr. Martin was succeeded by Rev. John B. Hamilton, and he by A. M. Wingfield. The next master was Joshua I. Williams, followed by D. B. Cooper; after D. B. Cooper came Horace S. Cooper. The present incumbent is Mr. George Childress.

Representatives in the lower house of the General Assembly: Moses Frierson, 1809–11; Amos Johnson, 1811–23; I. J. Thompson, 1823–27; * * * ; A. O. P. Nicholson, 1831–35; James E. Thomas, 1835–39; James E. Thomas and Barclay Martin, 1839–41; Barclay Martin, 1841–42; William H. Polk and Powhattan Gordon, 1843–44; Powhattan Gordon and R. A. L. Wilkes, 1845–46; R. A. L. Wilkes and Barclay Martin, 1847–48; George Gantt and W. Stringham, 1849–50; Barclay Martin and J. L. Miller, 1851–52; Frank Hardeman, 1853–54; A. M. Looney, 1855–56; W. H. Polk, 1857–58; W. C. Whitthorne, 1859–60; J. Gilmer, 1865–67; W. B. Wilson, 1869–73; A. P. Glenn, 1873–77; J. Lee Bullock, 1877–79; John Ballanfant, 1879–81; R. A. Wilkes, 1881–83; Maj. J. T. Williamson and W. T. Porter, 1883–84; George C. Taylor, F. A. Burke and E. W. Carmack, 1884–85. Senators: Thomas H. Benton, 1807–11; Newton Cannon, 1811–15; Thomas Coleman, 1815–19; Benjamin Reynolds, 1819–23; Robert Weakley, 1823–27; Edward B. Littlefield, 1827–31; Lucius J. Polk, 1831–39; A. O. P. Nicholson, 1839–43; James E. Thomas, 1843–47; T. M. Jones, 1847–51; E. R. Osborne, 1851–55; S. B. Moore, 1855–59; Thomas McNeilly, 1865–69; J. B. Frierson, 1869–73; T. J. P. Allison, 1873–77; A. T. Boyd, 1877–81; A. M. Looney, 1883–84. Population by decades: 1810, 7,722; 1820, 15,620; 1830, 18,200; 1840, 17,090 white; 1850, 16,759; 1860, 17,701; 1870, 20,022; 1880, 21,731 whites and 18,178 colored.

The first court in Maury County met at the house of Col. Joseph Brown, about three miles south of Columbia on December 21, 1807. A court of pleas and quarter sessions was organized by the justices, who had previously been appointed by the General Assembly. They were John Dickey, John Miller, William Gilchrist, William Frierson, Isaac Roberts, John Spencer, John Lindsey, Joshua Williams, James Love, Lemuel Pruett, and William Dooley. The commissions of these justices were signed by John Sevier, the governor of the State at that time. It appears that John Dickey, John Miller and William Gilchrist were not present at the opening of the court. The first act of this court was the election of Isaac Roberts, presiding justice. Mr. Roberts afterward became the noted Gen. Roberts. Joseph B. Porter was chosen clerk; John Spencer, sheriff; Edmond Harris, coroner; William W. Thompson, register; Joseph Brown, ranger; Peter R. Booker, solicitor, and Benjamin Thomas, treasurer. Bonds were required of these in sums ranging from $2,000 to $10,000. By order of the General Assembly this court was to meet at Joseph Brown's on the third Mondays in December, March, June and October of each year till the completion of the court house in Columbia. John Spencer returned the following jury: Ephraim McLean, Jr., Alexander Gillespie, Robert Hill, Charles McLean, James Welsh, Griffin Cathey, Thomas Whiteside, William Irvine, Alexander Irvine, Amos Johnson, William Dever, S. Frierson, W. J. Frierson, C. McGee, Bryant Nolin, Martin Hardin Daniel Evans, Josiah Goforth, William Kilcrease, David Love, William Daniel, John Myrick, Thomas Gill, Enos Pipin, John Campbell, Samuel Polk, A. J. Turner, Aaron Cunningham, James Huey, James Craig, David Copeland, A. B. Hudson, George Breckenridge, Isaac Bills, Samuel Smith, James M. Lewis, Andrew Boyd, Silas Alexander and John Davidson. This court seems to have been invested with both appellate and original jurisdiction. Cases being much less numerous than now, this court was sufficient for all cases. Peter R. Booker, the first solicitor seems to have been a practicing attorney at the time of the organization of this court, and to have received his office by appointment. His name is met with but a short time as counselor but frequently as a business man. He became quite wealthy and died in 1839. Joseph Herndon was the first resident lawyer admitted to the bar of this court. He began practice in 1808 and continued before the bar for many years, and died in Columbia in 1862 at a very advanced age. Like Booker he was looked upon as a very high-toned honorable gentleman. This court was mainly occupied in receiving wills for probate, ordering new roads, recording stock marks, and granting ferry license, providing for the erection of mills, and permitting the keeping of ordinaries. The keepers of these ordinaries provided food, lodging and shelter and feed for horses. The "rates" were fixed by the court. The following was the customary price: "Each diet 25 cents; lodging per night, 6¼ cents; horse per feed, 12½ cents; fodder and hay all night, 12½ cents; peach brandy or whisky, 12½ cents per half pint. According to the custom of the time drinks were for sale at these houses of entertainment. A bond was given that the keeper of such house would not suffer or permit gambling, nor on the Sabbath day suffer any person "to tipple or drink more than necessary." The December term of court in 1808 was held in the town of Columbia.

Similar cases as above mentioned were tried; among the punishments inflicted were twenty-five lashes upon the bare back for petit larceny. By an act of November 16, 1809, the circuit court system was established for Maury County. This court took upon itself a great deal of the work formerly done by the county court. The county court continued to have jurisdiction over questions pertaining to the county, such as the erection of public buildings, bridges, dams, ferries, fixing the rate of taxation, changing or making new roads, the appointment of committees on matters of public interest, changing the civil districts, etc.; it also had both original and appellate jurisdiction over petty offenses against the State. The first circuit court was opened in the court house in Columbia on November 25, 1810, with the following officers: Hon. Thomas Stuart, judge of the judicial circuit; John M. Taylor, clerk; Samuel H. Williams, sheriff. The first jurors were J. M. Lewis, James Smith, Benjamin Smith, Thomas Edwards, John Lindsey, John Matthews, Moses G. Frierson, John J. Zollicoffer, James Birmingham, Amos Johnson, John Campbell, Samuel Witherspoon, William M. Berryhill, Lemuel Pruett, William Frierson, James Love, John Miller, James Sanford, Robert Hill, Samuel Polk, Thomas Whiteside, Abner Franklin, Anthony I. Turner, Samuel Lusk, Alexander Cathey and Joseph Brown. Of these J. M. Lewis was chosen foreman, and at the same time William Webb was made constable to attend on the grand jury. The first case taken from this court on appeal was a suit of David Wood against Robert Steele, in which the plaintiff recovered $8 cost with 12 per cent on judgment. The case was taken to the superior court of the "Mero District." On November 28, 1811, Felix Grundy was admitted to practice law before the "inferior and superior courts." The character and standing of this distinguished individual is too well known to require further notice here. At the same time appears the name of Alfred Balch as attorney for the State. Courts and lawyers were as sadly afflicted with "quiddities, quillets, cases, tenures and tricks" formerly as now. James Sellars was refused a new trial in a suit with Andrew Lewis, in which himself was defendant because the exact time for filing his plea had been neglected. Suits for assault and battery were formerly very numerous. Robert Pearce, Andrew Lewis, Joseph Davis and Abner Scott were each given nominal fines by throwing themselves upon the "grace & mercy" of the court. By an act of the General Assembly of November 28, 1809, the judges of the Third and Fourth Circuits were allowed to exchange sittings. Judge Nathaniel Williams, of the Third Circuit, first appears on the records of Maury County on November 27, 1811. Judge Thomas Stuart, the first circuit judge, was a resident of Franklin, Williamson

County. He continued to preside over the courts of Maury County till 1822, when the circuit was changed, yet he continued to sit as judge in the other circuit for a number of years afterward. He is described as a man of profound legal learning and of high moral integrity. He left no issue to perpetuate his name. On November 25, 1812, appears a case on record in which J. B. Hardin was plaintiff and W. L. Hannum was defendant; the case was settled by arbitration. The following is the verdict: "The undersigned, Thomas H. Benton and Alfred Balch, are of the opinion that the said Isaac B. Hardin recover of Washington L. Hannum one hundred dollars. Witness our hands and seals the day and year last written. Thomas H. Benton, Alfred Balch." It is needless to say the former became a distinguished senator from Missouri, and the latter the attorney-general for the Fourth District. This somewhat peculiar entry is made at the September term of the county court in 1810: "Entered one dollar fine against Thomas H. Benton for profane swearing in presence of the court, and the fine was received by the clerk."

The grand jury to inquire "into the body of the county" for 1811 were Amos Johnson, Robert Scott, Joseph Shoat, John Lindsey, William Byers, Isaac Roberts, Daniel Brown, Samuel Smith, Simpson Harris, Ezekiel Polk, John Campbell, A. Franklin, Thomas Hudspeth and James Lewis. James Whiteside became a practicing attorney in 1811, and in the same year the first suit between these two celebrated litigious characters, John Doe and Richard Roe, was begun, without whom it was thought impossible to conduct a case. On the opening of court in November, 1813, appears the name of Archibald Roane as presiding judge. He continued to sit from time to time on the Maury County bench for a number of years. His opinions appear clear and pointed, and without effort at display of self. The following rules were adopted for the government of the court in April, 1814: "All cases, except actions of ejectment, shall be taken up and tried, or continued on the first day of each term, and the parties shall not be compelled to attend suits of ejectment till the second day." The first suits for divorce appear on docket in October, 1815, the parties to the suits were Susannah Adams against William Adams; R. B. Edwards against Margaret Edwards, and Sarah M. Napier against John M. Napier. The recital of their domestic infelicity would be about on a par with a case at present. James Magill was arraigned on the charge of murdering Dr. Simpson April 21, 1816. The case was brought to Columbia on a change of venue. The defendant was in a fair way to suffer the extreme penalty of the law, when the sickness of James Johnson, one of the jurors, caused a delay in the trial and the prisoner escaped by cutting his way out of jail. L. M. Bramlett became an attorney before the court October 24, 1816. At the same court Benjamin Rutledge stood charged with murder by the State, and the following "good and lawful" men decided he was guilty as charged: Joseph Brown, John Zollicoffer, William Daniel, John Mathews, James Love, Alexander Cathey, John Spencer, Robert I. Voorhies, Robert Kelsey, Thomas Stephenson and James Purcell. Before passing sentence he plead the "benefit of the clergy," and received as his punishment a brand of the letter "M upon the brawn of the left hand." The punishment was executed upon him November 26, 1816, at the court house in Columbia; he was further remanded to jail till costs of the suit were paid. On October 25, 1817, Richard Hardin was charged by the State with petit larceny, to which he answered that he could not deny his guilt, but threw himself upon the "grace and mercy" of the court, and for a sentence got three months in the county jail and ten lashes upon his bare back. Jesse Faulkner received the very light sentence of $2 fine for horse-stealing. Horatio Depriest resigned his office as circuit court clerk December 1, 1818, and George M. Martin was appointed in his place. Edmund Kelly, a native of Ireland and a subject of Great Britain, took out naturalization papers on the oath of Daniel Graham. Joseph Brown and Micajah Brooks each received $2 fines for failing to appear as jurors in answer to a legal summons. The name of Parry W. Humphreys first appears as judge over the Maury Court. On December 23, 1821, S. S. Record was put under a bond of $1,000 for offering a challenge to fight a duel. At the June term of 1821, Edmond May and Robertson Rose each applied for pensions under the provisions of the act of Congress passed March 17, 1815. The applications were made before Judge Parry W. Humphreys.

Robert Mack appeared on the bench June 18, 1822, as successor to Judge Thomas Stuart. The vacancy in the judgeship was caused by the formation of a new circuit. Judge Mack remained on the bench till in 1828. He was a native of Pennsylvania, where he was born in 1772; lived in Kentucky for a time, where he taught school and studied law. He became a resident of Columbia about 1809-10, and there began the practice of law. He was a brother-in-law of Gov. Aaron V. Brown, a distinguished lawyer and politician. After retiring from active life Judge Mack devoted himself to literary pursuits. The result of his works were two volumes of poems. The first was called "Kyle Stuart, and Other Poems"; the second, "The Moriad," an epic in twelve cantos, a story founded upon the capture and destruction of Jerusalem by Titus. Judge Mack accumulated abundant means, and lived to enjoy the fruition of his legal and other literary pursuits to the age of ninety-three. He, like Judge Stuart, left no offspring, but what was better a name and fame to be cherished by coming ages. In 1822 the Hon. Joshua Haskell occupied a seat on the bench for one term, and the following attorneys were admitted: A. O. P. Nicholson, J. H. Thomas, W. H. Polk, Bradley Martin and Robert Prince. Another example of old style of justice was a fine of $50, one month's imprisonment and ten lashes upon the bare back of Peter Powell, for a small offense against the State. The latter part of the punishment was inflicted by the sheriff, at the hour of 12 on December 24, 1823. Polly Hicklin was granted a divorce from A. M. Hicklin for five years' "abandonment without cause." Berry White, an old Revolutionary soldier, made application for a pension at the December term of court in 1824. On January 5, 1827, the court adopted the following rule: "All cases of action for debt not really litigated shall be first on trial, the facts to be ascertained from the attorneys on both sides." The first suit for bigamy was brought against W. D. Mitchell December 29, 1827.

About this time was witnessed the close of the much litigated case of Jones Kendrick *et al.* against Dallum. From a condensed statement of the case at hand and from the very long record, it is learned that the suit grew out of a disputed title to land, and it may be here remarked that that arose from the vague terms given to the original description. In 1783 Jones Kendrick made entry in the land office of John Armstrong in the following words: "Jones Kendrick, 5,000 acres of land on the west fork of the second creek above Gen. Greene's land, that empties into Duck River on the south side, beginning near the fork of said creek, and extending up the west fork for complement." A few days later Elijah Robertson made three entries in the same office for 5,000 acres, each lying in the same neighborhood. Grants were issued for these, and one of them was transferred to Dallum in 1790. The portions of the lands of Kendrick and Dallum had passed into the hands of innocent purchasers. The original suit arose as to right of Kendrick or Dallum to make proper title. The main suit was carried to the supreme court twice, once in 1812 and referred, and again in 1813. The principal attorneys in the case were Judge Haywood and Judge Mack for plaintiffs, and Hayes, Dickinson, Whiteside and Cocke for defendants. Numerous suits followed, several of which were taken to the supreme court. The final decisions were favorable to Kendrick's claim.

By the act of the General Assembly of 1809, which established the circuit courts, a "supreme court of errors and appeals" was also established. This was composed of two judges in error and one circuit judge. By an act of the General Assembly passed in 1821, while in session at Murfreesboro, Columbia was designated as one of the places of holding the supreme court. The first session met in Columbia March 4, 1822; the judges present were John Haywood, Thomas Emmerson and Robert Whyte. The second term was held in September, 1822, at which were present John Haywood, Jacob Peck and W. L. Brown. The next term was in September, 1823. The judges present were Robert Whyte, W. L. Brown, John Haywood and John Peck. The next and last session opened September 14, 1824. On June 22, 1826, the grand jury returned "a true bill" for murder against J. R. Bennett. A jury of good and lawful men, Samuel H. Williams, William Allen, John O. Davidson, John Farney, E. E. Davidson, William Kerr, William Pillow, Arthur M. Copeland, William Voorhies, Thomas Gill, F. R. Houston and William Jennings found him guilty as charged in the indictment. Judge Mack ordered that "James R. Bennett be remanded to the county jail of Maury County for safe keeping till Thursday, the 26th day of September, 1826, on which day he shall be conveyed by the sheriff of Maury County to a gallows erected on the common of Columbia, and then hung by the neck until dead, and may the Lord have mercy on his soul." This execution was strictly carried out.

On October 24, 1831, Gideon J. Pillow resigned as solicitor and Edmund Dillahunty was appointed in his place. In the same month A. O. P. Nicholson was admitted as an attorney, and in April preceding Hugh W. Wormley was admitted on motion of Gideon J. Pillow. Whether by chance or otherwise the name of Gideon J. Pillow appears more frequently than any other in assisting young attorneys to a position before the bar. It is needless to say that this was the distinguished Gen. Pillow, whose reputation became national in the Mexican war as well as in the late war. After the close of the struggle he opened a law office in Memphis, where he resided until his death. William E. Kennedy who succeeded Judge Mack, held his first term of court in Columbia in December, 1828. He was judge only till 1833. He was considered a profound lawyer, an able, conscientious and upright judge, and a man of high moral character. Although a married man he left no children to survive him, He died about 1864. These three coincidences seem peculiar to Judges Stuart, Mack and Kennedy; they all lived to be very old, left no children, and were faithful members of the church. Judge William Fleming occupied Judge Kennedy's seat for a time in 1832. Judge L. M. Bramlett, who had previously been admitted to the bar, succeeded Judge Kennedy on the bench of the circuit court October 21, 1833, and remained till October 31, 1835. Judge Bramlett was a resident of Pulaski, Giles County, and under the new constitution, adopted August 30, 1834, he became the first chancellor. Chancery courts had been held as early as 1829, and from that time till 1836, when the new constitution went into full effect, there had been occasional terms of chancery court. Those who held chancery court to this date were William E. Anderson, W. A. Cook, W. B. Reese and Nathan Green. On the adoption of the new constitution Judge Bramlett became chancellor, a position which he held till 1844.

This observation is noticed in regard to a motion to quash indictments: Previous to about 1835 such motions were not offered till after trial or after sufficient progress had been made to develop the weakness of the case. A very efficient weapon had thus been neglected. Numerous cases of "selling liquor to slaves, case, debt, $vi\ et\ armis$, horse stealing, divorce, larceny," were of almost daily occurrence, but a new indictment appears now for the first time, $i.\ e.$, "betting on elections." In 1838 James Hudspeth, John Patten, E. D. Morgan, George W. Kee, W. P. Smith, William Wood, John Thomas and William H. Polk received $5 fines for such offense. At the May term of 1836 Judge Dillahunty, before mentioned, became circuit judge, which position he held till his death in 1852. For several years before his death he was frequently called upon to give place to others on account of ill health. He is described as a "profound, clear-headed, common-law lawyer, an able and pure judge." He was a benevolent, social, public-spirited, Christian gentleman. He was the son-in-law of Abraham Looney, the head of a prominent and respectable family. He lived a happy and congenial married life but left no children.

The first suits of usury began about 1840; be this said, however, they were not numerous. On March 31, 1843, appeared this suit: James K. Polk, governor, to the use of the president and directors of the Bank of Tennessee $vs.$ Henry Turney, J. B. Johnson, Samuel H. Duncan and James R. Plummer. The jury gave judgment for plaintiff in the sum of $22,396, and further against defendants, except as to J. R. Plummer, in the sum of $100,000, and that judgment issued, etc. Numerous suits were brought between the Union Bank of Tennessee and individuals, also between the Planters' Bank of Tennessee and private parties till the war, and some years after the war.

In 1844 the grand jury to inquire into the body of the county found that "William A. Caldwell, late of said county, laborer, not having the fear of God before his eyes, but being moved and seduced by the Devil on the 28th day of October, 1844, with force and arms, did assault Patrick Hornard, in the peace of God and of the State, then and there being feloniously, wilfully, deliberately, maliciously, premeditatedly, with malice aforethought, to kill and commit murder in the first degree with a certain gun of the value of $5, loaded with gun-powder and divers leaden shot, which he, William A. Caldwell, did then and there hold, etc." The prisoner was put under bond, and escaped trial by forfeiture of recognizance. Exacting justice required of Ferdinand Manny, who had stolen eleven knives of the value of $3.30 and had returned but three of them and 60 cents, should get two years at hard labor in the "jail house of the penitentiary" and pay a fine of $2.70. Among the lawyers not specially mentioned who were before the Columbia bar were Doud, Thomas and James B. Craighead, Robert C. Foster, Allen Brown, Francis B. Fogg, Alfred Balch and Robert L. Cobb, all attorney-generals for this district. Francis B. Fogg, J. Egnew, Madison Caruthers and R. H. Almire, gentlemen, were admitted in 1818. Judges: Samuel S. Frierson, Terry H. Cahal, William P. Martin, A. O. P. Nicholson. Others were James K. Polk, W. D. Mitchell, J. H. Thomas, W. H. Polk, Robert Prince, Barclay Martin, Walter Coleman, J. B. White, Russell Houston, John H. Dew, M. S. Frierson, G. W. Gordon, Nathaniel Baxter, J. K. Walker, W. S. Rainey, J. H. Rosborough, W. F. Cooper, W. C. Whitthorne, W. S. Flemming, R. G. Payne, L. D. Myers, George Gantt, W. J. Sykes, Hillary Ward, Amos Hughes, R. F. Looney, A. M. Looney, W. V. Thompson, F. C. Dunnington, N. R. Wilkes, J. L. Bullock, J. H. Fussell, G. P. Frierson, J. T. L. Cochran, J. H. Dew, W. B. Gordon, N. H. Burt, William Voorhies, T. J. Sprinkle, J. M. Sidberry, J. M. Arnold, Nathan Allen, N. R. Wilkes, Nathaniel Armstrong, Mr. Hughes, H. B. Estes, J. W. Allen, Joe E. Johnston, J. S. Bullock, W. B. Gordon, W. L. Pope and H. T. Osborn. Some of these will be mentioned more fully farther on. Terry H. Cahal, who succeeded Judge Bramlett as chancellor in 1844, and served in that capacity till his death in 1851, was a man of strong and vigorous intellect. A committee of the bar of Columbia, of which S. D. Frierson was chairman, resolved May 7, 1851, that "Terry H. Cahal was a man of noble and generous character, and had a heart full of generous impulses. If he was impulsive and ambitious (and we know he was), he was possessed of a generous heart; while he was courageous and fearless, he was ready to forgive and to acknowledge his own faults; a warm-hearted companion, a devoted friend, a liberal lawyer at the bar and a devotee to his profession. He was useful in the Legislative councils, and brave upon the battle fields of Florida. His traits were, however, not sufficient to avert the arrow of death, which truly 'loves a shining mark.'" After the retirement of Chancellor Bramlett the office was filled by special appointment, first by S. D. Frierson, and afterward by A. O. P. Nicholson. Judge J. S. Brine was made chancellor in 1852, which position he held till 1854, and then resigned to resume the practice of the law. As a judge, Chancellor Brine gave eminent satisfaction. On the death of Judge Dillahunty, of the circuit court, the Hon. William P. Martin became circuit judge, and held the position till the courts were closed by the war, which was in September, 1861. Hon. John C. Walker was appointed circuit judge in 1864 in this district, and held the position till 1866, but no courts were held during that time. The last jurors summoned before the war were William Adkinson, E. P. Mays, G. A. Kennedy, Simpson Leggett, A. W. Denham, Henry Hartin, J. L. Renfroe, C. A. Thompson, J. B. Stockard, J. N. Alexander, L. Smith, G. W. C. Maxwell, A. E. Neeley, W. L. Colquit, J. L. Baird, W. B. Wormley, J. H. Joyce, J. H. Frierson, J. H. Coffey, A. Williams, Munford Smith, Richard Blecker, T. J. Smith, D. McClanahan, J. J. Bingham, S. Goodwin, J. Adkinson, Willis Nichols, William Roberts, D. R. Dortch, A. J. Turner, W. H. Davidson, W. D. Bryant, A. S. Dyer and Thomas Hardeman. The first court after the war was opened by Hon. Henry Cooper, in exchange seats with Judge Hillary Ward. The following jurors were summoned: P. C. Church, W. C. Kennedy, J. J. Williams, Robertson Bryant, W. C. Patton, C. A. Tomlinson, W. H. Holt, Samuel W. Scott, J. G. Dobbins, Benjamin Harrison, E. C. Frierson, A. W. Hill, A. J. Lindsley, J. R. Thomason, W. J. Cecil, J. H. Russell, Daniel McKannon, Thomas Baird, H. C. Kirk, J. P. Adkins, J. G. Robinson, J. H. Brown, E. Kirby, M. G. Allen, J. M. Foster, W. F. Moore, C. H. Gray, John Glenn, C. P. Jones, John Nicholson, Sr., and Duncan McKea.

Soon after the assembling of court the bar was called upon to offer suitable memorials of respect to the memory of Chancellor S. D. Frierson, who was the successor of Judge Brine. Judge Frierson died March 11, 1866, while holding a term of court at Pulaski. Judge Frierson was a native of Williamsburg District, S. C., where he was born in 1803, immigrated to Maury County in 1807, graduated at Transylvania University in 1821, was admitted to the bar in 1824, and elected chancellor in 1853. The committee, consisting of Judge W. P. Martin, W. S. Flemming, S. D. Myers, J. H. Thomas and S. S. Merrill, said of him that he was a man of "classic education, extensive reading, thorough and critically learned as a lawyer, and was master of the great principles of equity jurisprudence." On the death of Judge Frierson, Judge David Campbell, of Franklin, was appointed to fill the vacancy, and after acting about one year, was succeeded by Judge H. H. Harrison, who took his seat in April, 1867. He also resigned in a short time, and was succeeded by Judge John C. Walker by appointment. This position he held till the August election in 1870, when Hon. W. S. Flemming was elected. Judge Flemming will have retired from the bench in August, a position which he has held with eminent credit to himself and satisfaction to his constituents for the last sixteen years. In November, 1867, A. M. Hughes became circuit judge and held the position till 1870, when Judge Martin became circuit judge under the new constitution. In 1872 a criminal court was established, composed of the counties of Maury, Williamson, Giles and Marshall. The Hon. William S. McLemore, of Williamson County, was elected judge of this court, a position which he still holds.

James K. Polk, a prominent practicing attorney at the Columbia bar, was elected to Congress in 1825, where he served till 1839. He was speaker of the House from December 5, 1836, to March 4, 1837, and again from December 4, 1837, to July 9, 1838. Other congressmen from Maury County were Barclay Martin, James H. Thomas, William H. Polk (brother of President Polk) and W. C. Whitthorne, recently appointed to the United States Senate to fill out the unexpired term of Senator Howell E. Jackson, who resigned to accept a United States District Circuit Judgeship. A. O. P. Nicholson was a native of Williamson County, where he was born August 31, 1808. He spent his early years near Spring Hill, graduated at Chapel Hill, N. C., in 1827, attended a course of medical lectures in Philadelphia in 1828, and began the practice of law in 1831. He was sent to the Legislature in 1833, and was for a time one of the editors of *The Western Mercury*. He took an active part in organizing the government under the constitution of 1834, and in putting into operation the internal improvements, banking and common school system of 1837. In 1836 he assisted in the compilation of the statutes of the State. In 1835 he was appointed land commissioner for Mississippi by President Jackson, but refused the office. In 1840 he was presidential elector on the Van Buren ticket, and in 1841 was appointed United States senator to fill the vacancy caused by the death of Felix Grundy. In 1844 he canvassed the State for James K. Polk, and in 1845 removed to Nashville and became editor of the *Union*. He returned to Columbia in 1850, and was appointed chancellor by Gov. Trousdale, but resigned at the end of the year. In 1852 he was presidential elector for Franklin Pierce, and in 1853 became editor of the Washington *Union*, and in a short time was elected public printer. He became United States senator again in 1857, and served till the State seceded in 1861. He was a member of the constitutional convention of 1870, and was the same year elected one of the judges of the supreme court, and was chosen by that body as chief justice, a position which he held till his death March 28, 1876.

Hon. W. F. Cooper, of the Supreme Court of Tennessee, was born in Maury County, and graduated at Yale College in 1838, and at once began practice with Hon. S. D. Frierson. In 1861 he was elected one of the supreme judges, but never took his seat on account of the war. He was appointed chancellor of the Nashville District in 1872, and elected to the same position in 1874. In 1878 he was elected one of the supreme judges, a position which he still holds. A fuller sketch of him will be found in this volume.

By an act of the General Assembly in the year 1807 a board of commissioners was created for the purpose of selecting a site for a county seat. The language of Section 3 of said act is "Joshua Williams, William Frierson, Isaac Roberts, John Lindsey and Joseph Brown are hereby appointed commissioners, who or a majority of whom shall, as soon as may be, fix a place most convenient, on or as near Duck River as the nature of the case will admit, for a court house, prisons and stocks for the use of said county of Maury, which place shall not exceed three miles from the center east or west, and after agreeing on a place they shall proceed to purchase or otherwise procure not less than one hundred acres of land, for which they shall cause a deed or deeds to be made to themselves or their successors in office by a general warranty, on which they shall cause a town to be laid off, with necessary streets and alleys, neither of which streets shall be less than one hundred feet wide, reserving two acres as near the center as may be, on which the court house, prison and stocks shall be erected, which town shall be known by the name of Columbia." One half the lots near the square were to be sold to the highest bidder at public auction on twelve months credit. The sale was to be advertised for sixty days in the Nashville *Gazette* and *Impartial Review*. The money arising from the sale was to be used in the erection of the court house, prison and stocks, and, in case there was not sufficient money obtained, the commissioners had power to levy a tax of 12½ cents on each 100 acres of land, the same amount on each white poll and double that amount on each black poll and $5 on each merchant or peddler, to be collected by the collector of public taxes. On May 30, 1808, the commissioners received a deed from John White for 150 acres, more or less, of land, for which White received $500. The land is described as "situate and lying on the south side of Duck River, being a part of 5,000 acres granted to Nicholas Long, bounded on the west by General Greene's Survey." The land was conveyed by Congress to Long, and by Long to Arthur Bledsoe, and by Bledsoe's heirs to John White, and by White to the commissioners aforesaid. The land adjoined the lands of Joseph McDowell and were a part of Grant 216. The sale of lands began August 1, 1808. The following were the original purchasers: Peter Bass, John Caruthers, Lawrence Thompson, William Daniel, Kavanaugh & Berry, John Williams, Lucy White, Joe Brown, William Berry, Peter Cheatham, Hezekiah Almont, James Bruce, Zilman Spenser, B. F. Spenser, Nelson & Cannon, Stump & Johnson, John Spenser, J. B. Porter, Richard Garret, Joseph Lemaster, John Bell, Robert Weakley, William Frierson, Britton Bridges, John Lyon, Nicholas Cobler, Henderson & Rutledge, Samuel Taylor, William and Abner Pillow, McPhail & McGilray, Bird Hurt, Thomas Hardin, J. Neulin, Nicholson & Goodloe, John M. Goodloe, Gabriel Benson, A. C. Yates, James Gullett, Moses Chaffin, George Cockburn, Alfred Balch, Isaac Roberts, John Keenan, McGee & King, Thomas Deaderick, Berryhill King, Edward McGafferty, David Nolen, Samuel Polk, Edwin Mangrum, John Lindsey, E. W. Dale, H. Depriest, Patrick McGuire, William Wallace, William Anderson, L. B. Mangrum, E. B. Littlefield, William Wood, Meredeth Helm, W. T. Lewis, S. P. Maxwell, R. D. Shackleford, James Pearshall, J. W. Egnew, Jethro Brown, John Woodruff, Elisha Uzzell, John Wormley, W. A. Johnson, Isaac Bills, James Huey, Abraham Whitelock, Richard Hanks, Joseph Love and A. R. Alexander. By an act of Section 2, approved November 14, 1809, the commissioners were to appropriate two acres of ground unsold for a church and burying ground. This ground was called "Greenwood," and lies on the left bank and on the south side of the river. This was the chief burying place for the people of Columbia till 1854, when the new cemetery was chartered.

Section 3 of the above act required the commissioner to cause a jail to be built "on some part of a lot not sold, not on the square, other laws to the contrary notwithstanding." Section 5 required the commissioners to build a market-house on the Public Square from the sale of lots. On November 14, 1809, the commissioners of Columbia were authorized to appropriate money from the sale of lots to purchase a bell and clock for the court house. The exact location of the county seat was attended with much difficulty, as conflicting interests divided the opinions of the commissioners. The places taken under serious advisement were the present site of Columbia, and the place owned by Gen. Roberts, a few miles from Columbia, on the north side of the river. It is claimed it received a majority vote of the commissioners, but on reconsideration the vote was given for Columbia.

The place selected was either covered with heavy timber or around the three large ponds; one marked by the site of the Bethell House was covered with heavy canebrakes, where grew very tall cane. Where the Masonic Temple stands was a crossing of timber for footmen over one of these ponds. The timber was soon cleared away, the cane destroyed and the ponds filled or drained, and the infant city started. One of the first business houses erected in Columbia was the indispensable inn. Jeremiah Cherry owned a large inn in Columbia in 1810; how much earlier it was built is not known. Peter Cheatham built an inn a little later near where Black's livery stable now stands, but on the opposite side of the street. Maj. Lewis kept a house of entertainment near where the Guest House now stands, over half a century ago. He was followed in the same house by a Mr. Ransom. The first store in the place, it is thought, was built by John Hodge. This stood where Mr. Taylor Voss now lives, and was a three-cornered brick, the first of the kind in the place, and stood on the south side of the Square. The main building of Hodge was of logs, and the brick was added to it. William W. Berryhill, another store-keeper, had a store also on the south side of the Square. Berryhill's building was of logs, and was two stories in height. Peter Cohea kept what was called the Indian store. Here most of the Indians did their trading. They came in droves, with their pack ponies loaded with peltries and such articles as they had for traffic. They would remain a number of days in town, and would spend what money and trade they might have in whisky and trinkets. They were particularly fond of chinaware. Another store was kept by a widow, Mrs. McCain, as early, it is thought, as 1813. She had two sons, John and Joseph, who assisted her in her work. She was the first female store-keeper in the town or county, and was a woman of taste and culture. Her house was a favorite resort at the time for the ladies for tea parties and social gatherings. Simon Johnson was another pioneer merchant in Columbia, whose place of business was on East Market Street near Black's livery stable. David Martin had a small store near the present site of the Gust House. Patrick McGuire kept a store near the present place of Titcomb & Frierson's drug store. He became quite wealthy, and was the owner of a large quantity of real estate. Other hotel keepers not mentioned above were John Anderson, the father of a very prominent family well known throughout the county, and Mrs. Hocks, whose domineering over her husband is remembered to this day.

The first physicians were Drs. Estes and O'Reilly, who located in or near Columbia about the time the town was laid out. These were both good physicians and high-toned gentlemen. Dr. DePriest settled in Columbia in 1809, and was a man of promise, but committed suicide. Two others were Drs. McNiel and Sansom, each of whom came to Columbia in 1810. In addition to these were Dr. McJimsey, who came about 1813, and Dr. Graves, a man of very fine ability, who came some years later. A paper-mill was run by a Mr. Whiting, but the date is not remembered. There was a coppersmith, by the name of Monroe or McMunn; his shop stood where William Woods' shop now stands. He was considered a very fine workman, and manufactured materials for copper stills.

The first hatter was Elisha Uzzell. As imported hats were not of easy access his work was in great demand. A man named Burns was a leather-dresser and glove-maker. As deer were then plentiful his work was largely confined to the dressing of deer-skins. Burns' Spring was named in honor of Burns. The first saddlers were William and Peter I. Voorhies, John Lowder, and a Mr. Kirkpatrick. The first cabinet workmen were Mathias Warfield and Purcell, the latter was also a carpenter, and did a considerable business. Mr. Vaught, who came to Columbia in 1809, was tutored by Mr. Purcell, and followed his trade till the outbreak of the war, and was rendered unfit for work by age. It is claimed for him that he built more houses in and around Columbia than any other man in the county. At an early period, 1814, there were two rope factories; one of these was owned by a man named McQuidley, and stood where Shepard's grocery store stands. Mebley built a powder-mill at White's Spring, a place well suited by nature for the mill. The saltpeter was obtained at a place about twelve miles southwest of Columbia. The first mill was built by Mr. Henderson, and it stood where the jail now stands. This was a horse-mill, and was afterward changed into a cotton-gin. The first water-mill was built by Mr. Wallace, near where Sewell's mill now stands.

The first silversmith was a man named Cressy, who came to the place about 1814; he was followed by James Wilkins, in 1816, who reached the age of almost four score and ten years. Samuel Northen took up his residence in Columbia in 1820. Soon after him came two of his relatives, James and William R. Hedge. These men prospered in their business and became wealthy. At this period nearly every man was his own shoe-maker, and frequently furnished hides to the numerous tan-yards, with which every neighborhood abounded; there were three of these near Columbia. One of these was owned by Joseph Hart, near what has since been called Noah's Ark, and another, further down, owned by Capt. M. Helm. The latter was run till a comparatively recent date; a third one was owned by John M. Smoot. The last named stood near White's Spring. Alexander Laird has the honor of having been the first brick-mason, and Thomas Norton the first plasterer and painter. The business men, as late as 1820, were Patrick McGuire, William Berryhill, Caleb Longley, John T. Moore, Edward W. Dale, John Hodge, James Leftwick, E. H. Chaffin, David Gillespie, James Walker and R. A. Vail. Between 1820 and 1830 there were, in addition to a portion of the above, Samuel McDowell, Cooper & Hill, Joseph Herndon, Evan Young, James R. Plummer, Henry Langtry, Adlai O. Harris, J. S. Walker, Patrick McGuire, Abram Looney and W. J. Dale. From 1830 to 1840 there were W. J. Dale, Looney & Sons, J. S. Walker, Frierson & Co., Evan Young, Henry Langtry, James R. Plummer and W. J. Dale. These were all general stores, the divisions into special lines not having yet been made. From a paper at hand it is learned that in 1834 Columbia contained 1,500 inhabitants, had 1 college, 1 academy, 4 common schools, 1 printing office, 3 churches, 3 divines, 13 lawyers, 5 doctors, 20 stores, 3 taverns, 2 groceries, 4 blacksmiths, 3 brick-layers, 8 carpenters, 4 cabinet-makers, 3 gunsmiths, 2 hatters, 2 painters, 4 saddlers, 4 shoe-makers, 3 silversmiths, 4 tailors, 2 tanners, 2 tinners, 2 wagon-makers, 1 cotton-gin, 2 carding machines and 1 bank—Union Bank. From 1840 to 1850 the leading business men were W. J. Dale, A. O. Harris, Frierson & Co., Evan Young, James R. Plummer, Henry Langtry, Looney & Bros., J. B. Graves, J. & A. Morgan, Porter & Partee, Hayden & Fisher, J. W. Gamelin and John H. Ewin.

Between 1850 and 1860 there were W. J. Dale, James Akin, James M. Larkin, James R. Plummer, Smith & Davidson, Gardner Frierson, L. H. Duncan. The present principal business men and houses of Columbia are as follows: Dry goods—Mayes & Frierson, McEwen & Dale, O. Cower, A. Gross, George Hedge, Most Hedge. Clothing—Rosenthal & Bro., L. Ottenross and Mayes & Frierson. Groceries—E. W. Gamble (wholesale and retail), Chaffin & Bro., Nichlls & Nichols, Watt Embry, R. Holding, Hinds & Peters. Furnishing goods—George Wilkes. Boots, shoes, hats and caps—R. W. Walkins. Hardware—Elam & Ewing, Street, Embry & Co., Andrews & McGregor. Furniture—W. J. Oakes. Drug stores—Rains & Son, Titcomb & Frierson, Joseph Towler, W. P. Woldridge. Millinery stores—Mrs. Jones, Mrs. Ruttle and J. B. Munter. Book store—S. G. Comstock. Livery stables—Mayes, Dodson & Coperton, Moore & Prewett, J. P. McGaw and W. A. Ruttle & Co. Grain dealers—McLemore & Bro., E. W. Gamble and R. Holding & Cochran. Saw and planing-mill—R. C. Brown. Hotels—Bethell House, Guest House and Nelson House. Jewelers—W. Abe Smith, J. H. James.

The act incorporating Columbia passed the General Assembly November, 17, 1817, by which it became a body corporate and politic under the name and style of mayor and aldermen of the city of Columbia. Various acts pertaining to the city have passed the General Assembly at different times. A somewhat extended charter was passed in 1848 and further changes were made in 1850, 1856 and again in 1870. A destruction of the records render it impossible to follow the city government through all its changes. The record shows that the city has between 5,000 and 6,000 inhabitants, and a taxable property of more than $1,500,000. and a debt of less than $50,000. The city government consists of a mayor, recorder, city attorney, marshal, each elected yearly, and a board of aldermen each of whom is elected for three years. The present executive officers are Joseph Towler, mayor; L. B. Lander, recorder; W. C. Taylor, attorney and John Latta, marshal.

By an act of the Legislature passed April 22, 1807 and approved October 11, 1809, it was enacted by the State of Tennessee, "That Isaac Roberts, John Spencer, William Bradshaw, Joseph Brown, William Berryhill, William W. Thompson, Simon Johnson, Abraham Whitefield and L. B. Estis, and their successors in office be and are hereby constituted a body corporate and politic to be known by the name of the Columbia Water Company, and by that name may sue and be sued, etc." Section 3d provided that they might draw $300 from the commissioners of Columbia, from the sale of lands, the receipt of the company being a sufficient voucher for the money. Additional members were added to the company September 30, 1811, viz.: John Hodge, William McNiel, Samuel Craig, Jeremiah Cherry, Peter Cheatham, Isaac Harden and John M. Taylor. Similar powers were extended to these as to the former members. Water was to be conveyed by some means to the Public Square. It is believed no material steps were taken to effect a supply of water for the city till between 1825 and 1830, when Arnold Zillner, a practical mechanic, constructed a rather rude system of works. Water was conveyed from White's spring by means of a water-wheel to a reservoir placed near the spring. The water being insufficient in quantity a larger wheel was placed at the river. A dam was constructed and by means of the fall of a large quantity of water sufficient force was obtained to elevate all the water necessary for the town. The water was at first conveyed by means of cedar pipes, which were afterward supplanted by leaden ones and these still later by iron pipes. In winter, and when the river was too high for the wheel at the river to work, the one kept at the spring was brought into use. After dong service for a great many years the old water-wheels were supplanted by a steam-engine. A reservoir was constructed so as to hold all the water from White's Spring, which by this means afforded a sufficiency of water.

An ordinance was passed April 30, 1883, and submitted to a vote of the citizens of the town and ratified by them April 12, 1883. The company is known as the Columbia Water Company. For the consideration of $1 the pump house was allowed to be erected on Duck River, the water to be drawn from above the sewerage of the city. For the same consideration the reservoir was allowed to be erected on Mount Parnassus Knob, about 300 feet above the level of Duck River. The contract was made with Travers Daniel, of Clarksville, Tenn., and the mayor and aldermen for the city of Columbia. The company erected an engine of almost 100 horse-power, with a pumping capacity of 1,153,000 gallons per day. The reservoir has a capacity of about 2,000,000 gallons. The company have laid about six miles of mains, and have forty-four double-nozzle fire hydrants, for which the city pays $3,000 per annum. The company have water privilege for fifty years, but at the end of each ten years the city has the privilege of purchasing the works at a price agreed upon by a board selected for that purpose.

June 14, 1883, a steam fire department was organized. It consists of one steam fire-engine, one hose carriage and other apparatus. The company consists of one captain, first and second pipemen, and first and second assistant pipemen, one engine driver, one hose driver and volunteers not to exceed twenty-five men. The Steam Fire Company and the Columbia Water Company afford very ample protection against fire.

The Columbia Gas Company was incorporated in 1883 by Henry Cooper, A. W. Stockell, E. W. Gamble, J. L. Jones, H. D. Fitch and others. The exclusive privilege for furnishing gas light to the city was granted to the company for ten years, with some restrictions. It was known as the Chess-Carley Company. By the contract the company was compelled to begin work within six months and complete the work within twelve months. The company erected a reservoir of 40,000 cubic feet capacity, and make a gas called "fixed oil gas." There were erected at first twenty-five lamps of fourteen candle-power, for which the city was to pay 1 cent per hour while burning, and $3 to the company for each lamp for keeping the same in repair. Some changes have since been made in the contract. The city is kept well lighted. January 13, 1880, an electric light company was organized and chartered. The company was composed of J. B. Rains, Calvin Morgan, Lucius Frierson, J. B. Childress, George L. Thomas and J. M. Mayes. The company, however, did not begin operations.

The difficulty of procuring ice led to the formation of the Columbia Ice Company. The charter was granted February 18, 1880, to M. J. Rushton, E. W. Gamble, R. Holding, L. W. Black, J. M. Mayes and Lucius Frierson. The company at once began work, and since its organization has erected new buildings and procured new machinery, and are now able to supply all demands for ice. The officers of the company are Lucius Frierson, president; E. W. Gamble, secretary and treasurer, and H. L. White, manager.

The Columbia Cotton Mill Company was chartered February 9, 1884, by W. C. Jones, J. M. Mayes, J. P. Street, A. W. Stockell, R. M. McKay, George Childress and G. T. Hughes. The capital stock is $100,000. The buildings are 100x300 feet, one story high, and contain 5,000 spindles and 124 looms, and the machinery is driven by an engine of 200 horse-power. The directors of the company own about twenty acres of land, and on this the 100 operatives live in nice cottages erected for their comfort. The officers of the company are J. M. Mayes, president; W. C. Jones, general manager and treasurer; George Childress, cashier, and C. T. Jones, book-keeper. The product of the mills is about 6,000 yards daily, consisting of sea island cotton, seamless bags, cotton yarns and battings. For this the company find a ready market.

The Maury County Building & Loan Association was organized in August, 1881, and held its first loan meeting in October of that year. The officers were J. P. Street, president; C. W. Witherspoon, secretary and treasurer; Robert M. McKay, attorney; G. T. Hughes, E. W. Gamble, S. G. Comstock, Joseph Towler, A. D. Frierson, W. M. Embry and J. P. Street, board of directors. The Columbia Homestead Building Association was incorporated April 17, 1882, by W. J. Andrews, C. C. Gross, E. W. Carmack, J. H. Andrews, A. Sinclair, R. Holding, S. G. Comstock, W. A. McGregor, Joseph Towler and W. R. Elam. The Columbia Manufacturing Company was chartered on August 20, 1881, by J. M. Hedge, G. D. Hedge, W. C. Taylor, Caleb Taylor and L. Taylor for the manufacture of buckets, churns, dishes, etc. On April 17, 1883, was chartered the Columbia Horseshoe Manufacturing Company by W. J. Embry, T. H. Watkins, A. B. Rains, Lucius Frierson, E. W. Gamble and J. B. Herndon, and on January 4, 1884, a charter was issued to the Columbia Horseshoeing Company on application by A. B. Rains, Lucius Frierson, George L. Thomas, George Childress and J. P. Street. Columbia is also the headquarters of the "Blue Grass Cheese & Butter Association," the "Copolquin Mining Company chartered in 1877, the "Napier Iron Company" chartered in 1879.

The Columbia Jersey Cattle Company was incorporated October 16, 1882, by Campbell Brown, W. J. Webster, J. N. Figures, H. P. Figures, A. T. Brown and W. S. Rainey. Other members have since been added and the company now own some very fine stock. The firm of T. N. Figuers & Co. was organized in 1884 for the purpose of importing and breeding Holstein-Friestan cattle. Their stock are kept on the "Oak Lawn Holstein Farm," about two and one-half miles west of Columbia. The Jersey Stock Company was chartered April 26, 1883, by J. E. R. Carpenter, J. G. Bailey, J. H. Howard, J. W. S. Ridley, J. R. Orr, W. J. Embry and W. V. Wilson. This company embraces some of the best stock men in the county. The Maury Live Stock & Agricultural Association was chartered November 21, 1879, by Campbell Brown, Thomas Gibson, V. Polk, Will Polk and A. N. Akin. The company use the old fair grounds and have fine track for training fast horses. Many of the finest horses in the county are wintered at the company's stables. The Tennessee Trotting Horse & Breeding Association was incorporated in December, 1882, by Will Polk, V. L. Polk, Campbell Brown, G. W. Polk, J. E. R. Carpenter and W. J. Embry.

The Bethell Hotel Company was chartered May 24, 1880, by P. C. Bethell, W. D. Bethell, Lucius Frierson, Eugene Pillow, J. M. Mayes and L. W. Black. The Bethell was open for business in May, 1882. It is considered the third house in size and finish in the State. It has recently passed into the hands of private individuals, Messrs. Mayes & Dodson.

MAURY COUNTY. 771

The Columbia Stock Yards was chartered in 1883, with a capital stock of $30,000. Its officers were J. W. Howard, president; E. W. Gamble, vice-president; T. W. Keesee, general manager; Columbia Banking Company, treasurer, and J. G. Bailey, secretary. The company handle an average of about 8,000 mules per annum. The first four months of the company's existence it handled over 12,000 head of stock.

The charter for the "Exchange" was granted on January 22, 1885, on application by W. J. Andrews, E. W. Gamble, A. B. Rains, W. R. Elam, George W. Wilkes, A. D. Frierson and H. Harpold. The Exchange embraces the most substantial and energetic business men of Columbia, and has for its object and purpose the "collection, preservation and circulation of valuable information relating to the business and progress of the city of Columbia, and its commercial connections and especially the facts relating to the manufacturing and commercial interests."

The Century Club received its charter February 14, 1884. Its officers are G. L. Thomas, president; Horace Frierson, first vice-president; Walter P. Woldridge, second vice-president, and Horace L. Cooper, secretary and treasurer. The Club has magnificent rooms in the Masonic Building and is composed of nearly one hundred of the leading men of the city.

A charter was granted the Cantrell Light Artillery on June 3, 1885, to E. D. Wilson, W. A. Ruttle, R. E. Andrews and A. A. Hodge, and one or two others. The officers are E. D. Wilson, captain; W. A. Ruttle, first lieutenant, and R. E. Andrews, first sergeant. The Witt Rifle Company was chartered on June 13, 1885, on application by Ira C. Witt, W. V. Thompson, C. M. Gamble, T. A. Thompson and R. C. Ewing. The officers are Ira C. Witt, senior captain; W. V. Thompson, captain; C. M. Gamble, first lieutenant; T. A. Thompson, second lieutenant; Alf Horsley, first sergeant.

Under the law governing the Bank of the State of Tennessee, books were opened in Columbia, for the purchase of 800 shares of $50 each, of stock in said bank. Notice was given in the paper for thirty days. Section 27, of the act provided, that when the citizens of Maury County had subscribed $20,000 a branch of the bank should be opened in Columbia, under the same laws as the State bank; it was further provided that the citizens might subscribe "as much as they were able to pay for;" and further, after 120 days, if the directors refuse to establish said branch bank, the citizens of Maury might organize one of their own. The bank to be organized was to be called the "Columbia Tennessee Bank," and to be governed the same as the Gallatin bank. The directors were William Frierson, Samuel Polk, Horatio Depriest, Dorrel N. Sansom, William McNiel, Patrick McGuire, Samuel McDowell, William Bradshaw and Joseph Brown. The time to which they were limited to start this bank was January 1, 1820. This was what was called a loan bank, but soon failed. The bank was organized April 19, 1819, by electing D. N. Sansom, president. The capital stock at that time was $15,000. The results were as above stated. The Union Bank was established in 1832, and the branch for Middle Tennessee was opened in Columbia. This bank had a successful run and its affairs were not entirely wound up till since the war. A branch of this bank was opened in Columbia, in 1834, in the building on the south side of the street opposite the Bethell House. The Planters Bank was chartered in 1833, with a capital stock of $2,000,000. The following were appointed to open books for stock in Columbia on January 1, 1834: James Walker, William McNeill, J. B. Groves, D. P. Frierson, E. W. Dale and James R. Plummer. The bank opened for business in Columbia, in 1838. The building occupied was the one which now stands near the Guest House; this bank was closed by the war.

The Shelby Savings Institution was organized under charter in 1868; by special act of the Legislature, its name was soon changed to the Bank of Columbia. The capital stock of the bank is $100,000, of which $50,000 is paid up capital and $50,000 surplus. The officers of the bank are W. P. Ingram, president; Knox Fleming, teller; Leslie Cullum and J. E. Ingram, book-keepers.

The Columbia Banking Company began business, in 1869, as the First National Bank, and continued as such until July 21, 1885, when it received its charter as the Columbia Banking Company. The capital stock of the company is $100,000, with $20,000 surplus.

The officers are J. M. Mayes, president; J. C. Wooten, vice-president; Lucius Frierson, cashier.

The Second National Bank was chartered in October, 1881. The capital stock and surplus of this bank is about $100,000. The officers of the bank are R. A. Ogilvie, president; Robert M. McKay, vice-president; George Childress, cashier. The board of directors are R. A. Ogilvie, R. J. Banguss, Robert M. McKay, W. R. Webb, A. D. Frierson, W. E. Baird, F. J. Ewing, and O. C. Owen.

Columbia Lodge, No. 31, F. & A. M., was organized by a dispensation from the Grand Lodge of Tennessee, dated November 10, 1819. The officers *pro tempore* were W. G. Dickerson, of the Grand Lodge of Tennessee, W. M.; Harry Hill, S. W.; James G. Craig, J. W.; John Brown, S. and T.; Nathaniel Ives, S. D.; John J. Williamson, J. D., and Alfred Hunt, Tyler. The lodge was opened in the first degree of Masonry when the names of Dowell N. Sanson and Robert L. Cobbs were presented, praying to be initiated. The lodge considering an emergency existing proceeded to ballot and elect the candidates in due form. The lodge was next opened in the Second or Fellow Craft Degree, when the name of Dowell N. Sanson was entered and he was passed to that degree. The Columbia Lodge, No. 31, was incorporated by the Legislature in 1827, with the usual power. On November 12, 1828, the lodge bought of M. D. Cooper the lot where the hall now stands for $600. The same had been purchased of Mrs. R. G. Houston on May 11, 1827, by Mr. Cooper. By an act of the Legislature September 28, 1824, Peter R. Booker, Patrick McGuire, Pleasant Nelson, Henson Grove and E. W. Dale were appointed trustees to manage a lottery for raising a sum not to exceed $8,000, to build a Masonic hall for Columbia Lodge, No. 31. The drawing took place the first Monday in May, 1825. The capital prize was $6,000, and the tickets were $10. The lodge drew the capital prize, but not realizing sufficient means a new scheme was gotten up, in which the drawing took place the first Monday in May, 1826. The capital prize in the second scheme was $3,000, and the tickets $3 each. As in the other case the lodge drew the prize. The cornerstone of the hall was laid with Masonic ceremonies June 16, 1827. The building was of brick, 47x55 feet and two stories high. The building was erected by Levi Ketchum and H. Ward, and was completed in 1828. The new magnificent hall was erected in 1883, and is one of the finest in the State. The lodge now numbers between seventy-five and 100. The following Grand Masters have been furnished by Columbia Lodge, No. 31: Mathew D. Cooper, October, 1826–27; William E. Kennedy, 1828–29; Edmund Dillahunty, 1845–46; Charles A. Fuller, 1851–52, and again in 1865; A. M. Hughes, 1853–54.

De Molay Commandery No. 3, K. T., was organized December 19, 1858. The following are the charter members: Lucius J. Polk, E. C.; A. M. Hughes, G.; J. B. Hamilton, C. G.; J. M. Towler, Prelate; J. H. Devereux, S. W.; L. H. Hankins, J. W.; W. H. Whiton, Recorder; William R. Hodge, Treas.; W. J. G. Hunter, Warden; S. H. Jones, S. B.; C. Foster Williams, S. B., and Jesse Oakes, Sentinel. Later officers were Dr. Robert Pillow, E. C.; Robert M. McKay, G.; S. D. F. McEwen, C. G.; H. L. Hendley, R.; H. B. Cochran, Treas. The following Grand Commanders have been furnished by the Grand Commandery of the State: Sir Charles A. Fuller, in 1859; Sir Lucius J. Polk, in 1860, and Sir J. M. Towler, in 1868–69. Columbia Lodge, No. 3, I. O. O. F., was instituted October 4, 1841. The following were the charter members: Lee Holman, James R. Shelton, George W. McQuiddy, Charles Brandon and James White. Phinteas Lodge, K. of P.: J. H. Fussell, C. C.; J. G. Bailey, V. C.; M. G. Frierson, K. R. and S.; J. J. Elam; M. of E. Uniform Rank: J. W. Fussell, S. K. C.; J. G. Bailey, L. C.; E. E. Erwin, Treas., and William Mayes, Sec. Knights of Honor: M. Ruttle, Dictator; W. D. Cameron, V. D.; A. S. James, Reporter; W. A. Quarterman, F. R.; J. P. Street, Treas.; Dr. J. H. Wilkes, M. E.; T. P. White, Sentinel; M. L. Frierson, Guide. Royal Arcanum: S. D. F. McEwen, P. R.; J. H. Dew, R.; W. J. Dale, Jr., V. R.; H. B. Cochran, Sec.; W. F. Embry, Collector; Lucius Frierson, Orator; Dr. D. B. Harlan, M. E.; Horace Frierson, Treas.; J. P. McGaw, Chaplain; J. J. Elam, Guide. A. O. U. W.: E. W. Gamble, M. W.; S. G. Comstock, Recorder; I. L. Cochran, Overseer; T. J. Fleming, Financier.

The beginning of newspaper enterprises in Columbia was in the year 1811. The man to whom the credit is due was James Walker, a native of Kentucky, but who learned his trade in Nashville. He was entrusted with a printing press by Mr. Estin, his employer, and began work in Columbia at the age of twenty years. Mr. Walker's paper was called the *Western Chronicle;* this was a small weekly paper, and was edited and managed by Mr. Walker for many years. Like all papers at that time, it devoted the major part of its space to foreign news and incidents in remote parts of the United States rather than home news. In 1813 the editor married Miss Jane M. Polk, daughter of Maj. Samuel Polk, who was the father of President James K. Polk. Mr. Walker died in 1864.

Andrew Hayes purchased the press of Mr. Walker and edited the paper for some time, assisted by Mr. Williamson. About 1838 the paper passed into the hands of Hon. A. O. P. Nicholson and Hon. Samuel D. Frierson, both of whom made national reputations on the bench and in other fields of usefulness. The paper at this time was called *The Western Mercury.* Gen. Felix K. Zollicoffer was for a time editor of the *Columbia Observer.* Associated with him for a time was Field, the editor and compiler of the *Scrap Book.* On January 1, 1839, this paper was begun, it is believed by C. P. Bynum. About the beginning of 1837 a paper called the *Southern Cultivator* was started by David Clayton. This was strictly an agricultural paper, and was devoted largely to stock raising and agricultural associations. The *Guardian* was begun in 1841 by the Rev. F. G. Smith, of the Female Institute. Ostensibly the paper was published in the interest of the school, but its matter covered a wide field, and the *Guardian* was filled with the choicest literature and was widely circulated. The paper is still issued by the Smith Bros., but rather as a visitor to old pupils and friends. It was issued at first from the office of Rosborough & Kidd, of the *Observer.* Other editors not already mentioned were C. J. Dickerson, S. W. Mitchell, James O. Griffin, John E. Hatcher, J. J. McDaniel, W. S. Fleming, N. R. Wilkes, James E. Johnson, Hunter Nicholson and W. L. Arnell.

Judge Stanley Mathews, of the United States Supreme Court, was admitted to the bar in Columbia in September, 1843, and resided in Columbia for some time, and while living in Columbia edited the *Tennessee Democrat.* The Columbia *Herald* was established in 1850, and with the exception of one or two short intervals has had a continuous existence. Another paper called the *Mail* was consolidated with the *Herald,* with A. S. Horsley as editor and proprietor. In 1876 the *Columbia Journal,* owned and edited by A. B. Upshaw, and the Maury *Sentinel* were consolidated and became the Columbia *Herald.* In 1881 the Columbia *Herald* was purchased by the Columbia *Herald* Company, composed of A. S. Hendley, A. W. Stockard, A. B. Upshaw, W. J. Embry, Horace Frierson, J. B. Rains, A. N. Akin, H. Williams, H. B. Cochran, J. M. Mayes, E. W. Gamble, W. P. Ingram, L. Marks, R. Holding, Joseph Towler, J. Joseph, J. P. Street, A. Rosenthal, W. P. Woldridge, C. Brown, W. C. Gordon, W. R. Webb, O. C. Owen, J. R. E. Carpenter, J. W. S. Ridley, W. J. Rushton, H. S. Cooper, J. H. Fussell, R. D. Smith and J. L. Jones. The president of the company now is E. C. McDowell, and J. L. Jones is secretary. The managers of the paper are Horace S. Cooper and E. E. Erwin. The *Herald* is on a sound financial basis, is Democratic in politics, but is devoted more to the growth and development of the county than to the discussion of partisan political questions. The Maury *Democrat* was established in the summer of 1882 by J. P. and J. F. Tucker, both natives of Maury County. Mr. J. F. Tucker was for a number of years local editor of the *Herald,* and was for a time connected with the Park City *Times,* of Bowling Green, Ky. Maj. John T. Williamson, a public-spirited citizen, has been connected with the *Democrat* for a number of years, to which he devotes his time and talents. The *Democrat* is a liberal and progressive paper.

The first settlements in and about Spring Hill began about 1808. Abram Hammond, one of the first settlers in this part of the county, moved from Maryland to Kentucky, where he married a Miss Wells; thence he moved and settled within one mile of where Spring Hill now stands. He was the father-in-law of Nimrod Porter, who was sheriff of the county from 1818 to 1842. Col. Russell in an early day cleared the land where Spring

Hill now stands, and built a residence on the eminence just above the big spring. from which the town took its name. The Russell estate was sold to Maj. Winters, who sold it to James Peters, from whom it passed to his son, James P. Peters. Peters' Camp Ground was a gift from the elder Peters, and lay within the present limits of Spring Hill. This was at one time the most popular Methodist camp ground in Middle Tennessee, and was the resort of thousands at their annual gatherings. Another very prominent one of the early settlers in this vicinity was Nathaniel Cheairs, who settled on the old Cheairs homestead in 1810. Mr. Cheairs came with his good wife whom he had married in North Carolina some years before coming to Tennessee. Mr. Cheairs was the father of eleven children, nine of whom lived to manhood and womanhood. Of these Col. Martin T. Cheairs, who still lives, is a venerable and honorable representative of the family. He is now in his eighty-second year, and was born in North Carolina, and came with his parents to the infant State. John W. Cheairs is the father of John W. Cheairs, merchant of Spring Hill and the present sheriff; was for many years a prominent merchant of Spring Hill. Maj. Nat F. Cheairs, the younger brother of the three still living, has been all his life an extensive farmer of the neighborhood. Near the same place settled the families of the Wades, Bonds, Capertons and Pointers. James Black, who lived near Spring Hill, was the grandfather of Henry Waterson, of the *Courier-Journal*, and father-in-law of Judge Stanley Mathews, of the supreme bench, who resided in Columbia in 1843-44. Near Black was the magnificent estate of Gen. Lucius J. Polk. On Carter's Creek lived the Carters, for whom the creek was named. Among them was Daniel F. Carter, a Revolutionary soldier and owner of a 5,000-acre grant. Near these were the Rollands. The Sandfords, Yanceys, Browns, Wellses, Blairs, Chapmans, Crawfords, Stephensons and Dunlaps lived either south or southeast of Spring Hill. A number of very distinguished persons are natives of this place. A. O. P. Nicholson, the distinguished judge and United States senator in 1841-42, was born at Old Sand Spring, where his parents resided. William Parkham, step-father of H. R. W. Hill, who became a merchant prince of New Orleans, lived near here so. Fields, the compiler of the *Scrap Book*, was raised near here. The first store the neighborhood was owned by a man named Brewster, who was afterward the pioneer merchant where Mount Pleasant now stands. His store was on the farm and on the south side of the old Davis Ford road, near the residence of Abram Hammonds. Col. William McKissack was one of the earliest merchants in Spring Hill; in fact he began selling goods there about the time the place came into being—about 1825. Dr. S. McKissack, a brother of the above, was an early settler and a son-in-law of the elder James Peters, and was a man of wealth and influence. William Peters was one of the earliest merchants, and for him Col. Israel McCarroll was clerk. Old Daniel Brown kept a hotel or stand for the traveling public about one mile south of Spring Hill, near the grave-yard in M. T. Cheairs' field. An effort was made to call Spring Hill Petersburg, in honor of James Peters, but his puritanic ideas forbade it, and the name of Spring Hill was given it. Mary Doherty, the widow of George Doherty, together with her son-in-law, George Bond, moved from North Carolina about 1808, and settled on a 5,000-acre grant, made by the State of North Carolina to her husband, George Doherty, for his services as a major in the Revolutionary war. The land lay between Spring Hill and Thompson Station, a little north of Spring Hill. On a creek near where Dr. Sharber now lives was a little mill at a very early time, the only one in the vicinity. About it this tradition prevails: "Maj. Samuel Polk, father of the President, in company with several gentlemen visited this mill and examined it, and when through Maj. Polk remarked to the others: 'A man may fall down and worship that mill and not commit sacrilege, because there is no likeness of it neither in the heavens above, nor in the earth beneath, nor in the waters under the earth.'" The first water-mill of any character was built by Isham Bunch on Rutherford Creek, and it is still in good running order. He also built a distillery at the same place. Maj. Robert Campbell had a distillery in the same neighborhood, as did also Esq. Black.

The first church in this vicinity was built by the Presbyterians about 1814. This was a hewed log house, and stood on the land of Col. Sanford, near where Jackson College stood

MAURY COUNTY. 775

at a later date. Among the leading ones engaged in the erection of this house were Col. Sanford, Col. Hugh Brown, George Blair, Samuel Dunlap, and others. This house has long since been replaced by a substantial brick structure. The leading Presbyterian minister in that early day was the Rev. Duncan Brown, whom many now living have heard with delight, also the Rev. Gideon Blackburn.

The leader and founder of the Cumberland Presbyterian Church in the vicinity of Spring Hill, was the Rev. James B. Porter. The labors of the Rev. Porter were not confined to the one church, but to the establishment of this infant denomination throughout Middle Tennessee. He was active in founding churches and in founding camp grounds so popular in the early history of the church. At a very early period the Methodists established Peter's Ground, before mentioned. Among those who labored for the Methodist cause may be mentioned the Rev. Donaldson Potter, whose labors were untiring and brought their reward.

The first important school taught in this vicinity was kept by William L. Williford before 1820. The school was near Col. M. T. Cheair's place. Here attended the Russells, Cheairs, Winters, Nicholsons, Bonds, Hammonds, and others. Near the same ground, a short time afterward, was built Jackson College, which afterward became Union Seminary. Spring Hall now contains Beachcroft Academy, a female school conducted by Mrs. Estes, and the male college of Prof. Morton. The place now contains a Presbyterian, a Methodist, a Cumberland Presbyterian and an Episcopal Church; and near there is a Christian Church; also two colored churches, one Methodist, the other Baptist. Business: General stores, J. W. Alexander, Campbell & Harman, W. A. Odill; dry goods and clothing, J. W. Cheairs; drug stores, Alonzo McKissack and John Martin; physicians, Drs. J. O. Hardin, J. W. Sharber and E. W. Martin.

A short distance south of Spring Hill, on the railroad, is Ewell's Station, and here is the well known Ewell farm. Here lived the distinguished Confederate general, Richard S. Ewell, who took up his residence at this place after the war and who at the time of his death, was devoting his energies to the breeding and improvement of stock. The somewhat romantic marriage of him and his estimable wife and the coincidence of their deaths are almost fit for a novel. At this place now resides Maj. Campbell Brown, stepson of the former. Maj. Campbell Brown is the well-known breeder of fine stock. In the Twenty-second District, in addition to Spring Hill and Ewell's, there is Woodlawn post-office, a beautiful place on the railroad and Neapolis, the seat of an academy.

Santa Fe is near the center of District No. 22. It is one of the oldest settlements in the county. The Indian title having been extinguished north of the river before they were south of it, settlements began there earlier. The following families are said to have settled in the county in 1806: the Caughrons, Brookes, on Snow Creek, McLeans, Neeley, Cinders, Griffins, Mitchells, Fitzgeralds, Dotys, Aydelottes, Piggs, Ayers, Bakers, Hills, Ladds, Seagraves, Lockharts, Owens and Edmistons. In 1807 came the Reaves, Binghams, Wrens, Hunters and McCrackens. It is said the first white child born on Snow Creek was Samuel H. Willams. The first mill was owned by Andrew Mitchell; this was a horse-mill. The first water-mill was owned by Spencer Griffith. The first blacksmith was Thomas Aydlotte. Carter Linsey was a smith and augur-maker. The first merchant was Jonathan Bullock; the first teacher was Richard Passmore; Mr. Hopkins was also an early teacher. The first physician was Dr. Stribbling, followed in order by Drs. Thomas W. and Samuel Kilpatrick, Dr. Douglas, Dr. Nicholas Scales, Dr. Bateman, Dr. W. W. Dabney, Dr. John Vestal, Dr. Satterfield, Dr. L. B. Forgey, Dr. Samuel Godwin, Dr. James Ragsdale and Dr. Sebastian, all of whom are now gone. The first minister in Santa Fe was the Rev. John Crane, a Methodist, who came there as early as 1807 and died in 1813 and was buried at Goshen Church, the first burial at that place. The Cumberland Church was organized at Santa Fe at a much later date. It is said Santa Fe was called Pinhook at first but was changed later to Benton, but on application for a postoffice, another change became necessary and it was given its present name—Santa Fe.

Mount Pleasant is at the terminus of a branch of the Louisville & Nashville Railroad, which leads from Columbia to Mount Pleasant. The country surrounding Mount Pleasant is claimed to be the finest in the State. To strangers visiting Maury County this question is always put: "Have you been out on the Mount Pleasant Pike?" Mount Pleasant was founded about 1820. Old Father Hunter, a famous bear hunter and Primitive Baptist preacher, was one of the first settlers in that vicinity. Other settlers were the McGees, Griffiths, Craigs, Coopers, Mitchells, Stockards, Pickards and Baileys. Not far from these were the Nixons, Buckners and Grimeses. The first merchant in Mount Pleasant was Lyman D. Brewster, who moved from Spring Hill to that place about 1820. There were formerly some very large landed estates lying in the vicinity of Mount Pleasant, but these have mostly been divided up into smaller farms.

Among the early business men of Mount Pleasant were Hervey Hoge, Lemuel Long, Samuel P. Lea, Messrs. Willson & Jennings. Among the later ones were Henry A. Miller, Ephraim Dickson, Alex Williams and E. O. Cross. Among the noted physicians are noticed Dr. Hamilton, Dr. Thorenot (who died of cholera in 1834), Dr. Sprinkle, Dr. Stockard, Dr. Sansom and Dr. Jordan, who is believed to be the oldest man in the county, and still vigorous. Among the later physicians are Dr. Hunter, Dr. Long and Dr. Williams. Hunter's Church, about one mile south of Mount Pleasant, is contemporary with Zion, and was built about 1810. The first Presbyterian ministers here were Duncan Brown, Hugh Shaw and John S. Frierson. A new church has since been built at Mount Pleasant and the membership of the church transferred there. The early Methodist ministers were John Akin, John Daniel, John Nixon, Kesterson and Tidwell. This denomination has a large and flourishing church at Mount Pleasant. There are also quite a number of Cumberland Presbyterians in this section, and these people have an old camp ground and church at Mount Joy, on the west fork of Bigby, about three miles from Mount Pleasant. Good schools have been maintained at Mount Pleasant for more than a half century. Mathew D. Cooper is said to have taught school there as early as 1809-10. Further notice of the schools of Mount Pleasant and Mount Joy will be made under the head of "Schools." Cross Bridge is the name of a little place about ten miles from Columbia, on the Columbia & Hampshire Pike. At this place is a store, postoffice and an academy. Hampshire is a small village in District No. 15, and is about fifteen miles west of Columbia, and is situated on Cathey's Creek. Lands in this neighborhood were settled in 1807. The first settlers in the neighborhood were the Akins, Loves, Farises, Whitesides, Lusks, Williamses, Erwins, Alexanders, Peytons, Bells, Isoms, Biffles and Burnses. Hampshire is a place of some wealth and business. Game in this vicinity was formerly very abundant. It is said that the wife of William Alexander killed a deer with a smoothing iron in 1808. Near Hampshire on the creek below were settled the Kennedys, Malones and Catheys, the latter giving the name to the stream. The first Presbyterian church in this neighborhood was organized by the Rev. James White Stephenson, who was then pastor of Zion Church. The first church of the Primitive Baptists was organized by the Rev. Mr. McCaleb, who, with the Rev. McConico, was the first minister of that persuasion. The first Methodist preacher was the Rev. John Akin. In the Cathey neighborhood are a Presbyterian and a Christian Church; the latter has quite a large congregation. The first school teachers in the neighborhood were Rev. John Akin, Asoph Enloe and Henry Young. Bigbyville is about nine miles south of Columbia. The origin of the place dates about 1834 or 1835. The village is quite small, and has made little progress, in a commercial sense, for a number of years. It was incorporated a number of years ago, but in April, 1882, it surrendered its charter. Settlements began in the vicinity of Bigbyville about 1807. Among the early settlers were the Hendersons, Reeses, Alexanders, Smiths, Matthews, Hannas, McCains, Perrys, Scotts and Zollicoffers. John J. Zollicoffer, father of Gen. Felix K. Zollicoffer, died on his farm near Bigbyville, and here, too, the General was born. Frederick Zollicoffer, a brother of the General, was one of the first merchants in Bigbyville. The place contains the usual number of business houses of a place of its size; also a Methodist church and a Masonic hall.

Not far from Bigbyville, near the head waters of the Little Bigby, is what is calle

Southport. William McConnell is said to have been the first settler in this vicinity. He built a tannery near where the village stands. Near the place were the McKnights, Galloways, Mathewses and Ralstons. Near here also lived and died Col. William Pillow. The Methodists have a church here and the Christians have one near the place. The first lodge of Good Templars in Maury County was organized at Southport by the Rev. Mr. Hensley in 1868. Near the dividing line between Maury and Giles Counties, at source of Little Bigby, is a cave of considerable size. Here saltpetre was obtained for the powder-mill that first stood in Columbia.

Williamsport is situated in the western part of the county on Duck River. The land where the town now stands was entered by Edward Williams and a ferry was established by him at that place called "Williams' Ferry." The town was laid out in 1817 by Edward Williams, and being on the river was very naturally named Williamsport. The town was incorporated in 1817 by an act of the Legislature, but the charter was allowed to lapse after a time, but was re-incorporated in November, 1845, and the charter amended in 1855. Among the early settlers in and about Williamsport were the Cooks, Williamses, Pools, Edwardses, Comptons, Oliphants, Bullocks and Englishes. Across the river were the Leipers, Greenfields and Colemans. Hugh Leiper gave name to Leiper's Creek. The first physician of Williamsport was Dr. James G. Smith, who came to the county with the Greenfields. Dr. Thomas Greenfield came out from Maryland and settled Greenfield Bend. Williamsport was in an early day an important shipping point, being on the river as it was. The boats used were flat-boats, keel-boats and pirogues. John Muirhead, who lived south of Gordon's Ferry, and Samuel Oliphant are said to have built the first flat-boat that ever floated out of Duck River to New Orleans. Maj. John Bullock, John O. Cook and James Blakely are said to have brought the first salt from the famous "saline works," near Shawneetown, Ill. This was as early as about 1814. The first merchant in Williamsport was George Hicks. Several distinguished business and professional men have lived in Williamsport; among them were Powhattan Gordon, Abraham Church and Dr. Samuel S. Porter. Although in a healthful section of the country, Williamsport was scourged by cholera in 1835. The town is surrounded by good farming country and has its complement of churches, schools, business and professional men. In the same district, No. 14, is a village or settlement called Saw Dust Valley, the center of a prosperous community. In this vicinity is the well-known old Methodist camp ground called Mount Nebo. Near the old camp ground is the modern church of Mount Nebo.

In the First District, in the northwestern part of the county, is a settlement called Kinderhook. The particular place mentioned lies on the line of the old Natchez Trace. The first settler in that region is said to have been a man named Kersey. A county may fail to name some insignificant place Boston or Charleston, but it never fails to have a Kinderhook.

On a branch of the Big Bigby, in the southwestern part of the county, is New York. It is more the name of a settlement than a town. It contains a store, Scott Mill, and one or two shops. Near the place is a Presbyterian Church, and about one mile from the place is a Methodist Church. In the Eleventh District is a neighborhood called Enterprise. There was formerly a store and business shop and a mill there. The place is too far from railroad communication to thrive, although surrounded as it is by fine lands. In the vicinity of Enterprise are a Methodist and a Baptist Church. Rally Hill lies in the eastern part of the county, about fifteen miles from Columbia. The early settlers in this district, the Twenty-fifth, were the Hardisons, Boyds, Peays, Billingtons, Strattons, Hurts, Derryberrys, Smiths, Hueys, Foglemans and others. Other centers in the Twenty-fifth District are Glenn's Store, where there is also a postoffice, Hurt's Cross Roads, Orr's Cross Roads; the latter contains an academy and a church, and Hardison's Mill's. There is a postoffice at the last named place. In former days the settlers about Bear and Flat Creeks were wont to come to Columbia and meet their rivals from the vicinity of Culleoka and engage them in the "manly art" of fisticuff. These contests were often long and sometimes bloody, but were simply tests of muscle.

Among the first settlers in the vicinity where Culleoka now stands was David Love, who built a mill on Fountain Creek. This was long known as Love's mill. Lemuel Prewett settled at Cave Hill, west of Culleoka, in 1807. Col. Joe Brown was another early settler in that locality. John Toombs was an early settler near Culleoka. He once built a distillery near the present site of the county poor-house. Near Culleoka was the old Pleasant Grove Academy; near this is the old Wilkes' Camp Ground and Church. A short distance east of Culleoka is a Baptist Church. At the village of Culleoka is the well-known school of the Wells brothers. This school has long since swallowed up the old Pleasant Grove Academy. In addition to this well-known school Culleoka contains a Methodist and a Presbyterian Church, a Masonic hall, a hotel and numerous business houses.

Hurricane Switch lies six miles beyond Columbia. The village contains two or three stores, a postoffice, several shops and a Methodist Church and camp ground. Pleasant Grove Depot lies on the railroad, ten miles from Columbia. This place contains several stores, a steam flouring-mill, a hotel and other buildings. Campbell's Station lies three miles beyond Culleoka, on the railroad. This was named from the family of Campbells who settled there in an early day. Among the early settlers near there were the Campbells, Gills, Davis Kerr and Amis. Besides a few business houses there is a Christian Church near Campbell's Station. Formerly there was, near this place, Shane's Church and Grave-yard. Mark Jackson, an old Revolutionary soldier, was buried here, as well as many of the old settlers.

By an act passed November 23, 1809, William Berryhill, William W. Thompson, Ludwell B. Estes, Isaac Roberts, William Bradshaw, Joseph Brown, William Dooley and Samuel Witherspoon were constituted a body politic and corporate to be known by the name of the trustees of the Woodward Academy, in the county of Maury. In a few days after Andrew Henderson and Ebenezer Leath were added to the committee to act with above committee. October 22, 1811, the trustees were ordered to draft a scheme for a lottery and publish the same. The tickets were to be of four classes, and the sum to be raised was not to exceed $5,000. The trustees were to enter bond with the chairman of the Maury County Court into a bond of double the amount to be invested in the lottery, and in case the lottery failed the money was to be returned to the purchasers of tickets within six years. It was further ordered that when a sufficient number of tickets had been sold notice should be given for three weeks in the *Western Chronicle*, and the trustees were themselves allowed to purchase tickets subject to the option of the superintendent of the drawing. The act further allowed a small fee to the trustees for their services. Woodward was located a little east of Columbia, near what is known as Burns' Spring. This institution was in a flourishing condition for many years. There were no buildings erected for Woodward till 1815. November 22 of that year Isaac Roberts, Joseph Brown, John C. Wormley, William Dooley, John Mathews, William Bradshaw, Horatio Depriest and David Ogilvie, who were then trustees, purchased two acres of land for $500. The lot is described as "lying on the east of Joseph C. McDowell, six poles and nine links to the chimney of the house built by Horatio Depriest, where Samuel Craig now lives." Woodward was the only institution of the kind for many years in the vicinity of Columbia. Here attended the rising young men of the community, among them A. O. P. Nicholson, Thomas J. Porter, W. P. Martin, George W. Gordon and many others. Among the teachers now remembered are David Weir and Dr. S. P. Jordan, who is still living near Mount Pleasant. Dr. Jordan taught in Woodward about 1821.

It is believed that Spring Hill Academy was in operation before the Manual of Labor Academy or Jackson College; in fact it is claimed the latter succeeded the former. A successful school had been conducted by Dr. Harbin and Prof. Williford at Spring Hill before this time. It is a matter of record that Henry Wade made a deed of two acres of land to Henry Pointer, Henry L. Crutcher, J. W. Cheairs, M. D. Thompson and Henry Wade, as trustees of Spring Hill Female Academy on February 17, 1839.

On the sale of the lands of Jackson College, or the Manual of Labor Academy, the original purchase of eleven and three-fourth acres was retained and a school continued as Union Seminary. September 14, 1840, an additional purchase was made by the trustees of Union Seminary of fifty-three acres of P. H. Junkins, Robert Campbell and J. C. Mitchell. Union Seminary continued as a prosperous school for many years. Dr. Hardin, the president of Union Seminary, resigned in 1840, and was succeeded by R. C. Garrison. The other teachers were J. H. and G. H. Blair.

Jackson College was formerly called the Manual of Labor Academy. On November 11, 1830, James T. Sanders made a deed of eleven and three-fourths acres of land for $297.65 to John Brown, Obediah Jennings, Ephraim W. Foster, James T. Sandford, Phillip Lindsley, Newton Cannon, James W. Brooks, Duncan Brown, William L. Wilford, Robert Hardin, G. M. Martin, Thomas J. Hall, Samuel J. Calvert, Hugh Brown, John Allen, Mathew Rhea, Hugh Barr, D. A. Smith, John White, John Hall, Amzi Bradshaw, Robert M. Ewing, George Newton, Daniel Gilchrist, James M. Linn, John Glass, George W. Ashbridge, James Ellet, Ebenezer McEwin, Alexander Campbell, David Wier, Thomas Lynch, Edward Ward, James Campbell, Benjamin Carter, Benjamin McCullough, W. J. Frierson, Thomas Brown, William Leach and Moses Stephens as trustees of said institution. This was chartered by an act of the General Assembly on November 16, 1829, and October 28, 1833, a purchase of 268 acres of land was made on Rutherford Creek for $3,874. The location not suiting the trustees, they sold 256¼ acres of the land for $5,386 to P. H. and B. W. Junkins. The sale was made on May 8, 1836, and the college moved to Columbia and was afterward known as Jackson College. The new college was opened in 1837, near the railroad, and continued in operation till broken up by the war. The building was destroyed by fire in 1863, and has never been rebuilt, and the grounds have been sold and private residences erected thereon. The presidents of Jackson College in order were Benjamin Larabee, Dr. Sherman, Dr. Mack, B. Ragsdale, Joseph Crawford, Dr. Mack (a second time) and Benjamin F. Mitchell. Among the prominent professors may be mentioned James O. Griffin, David Maxwell, Dr. C. N. Ordway, McClary Blair, S. W. Mitchell and O. H. P. Bennett; the latter occupied the chair of mathematics. In 1848 Jackson College passed into the hands of the Masonic bodies of the county, and was managed by them, i. e., Lafayette Chapter, No. 4; Columbia Lodge, No. 31; Benton Lodge, No. 111; Pleasant Grove Lodge, No. 138; Spring Hill Lodge, No. 124; Mount Pleasant Lodge, No. 57, and St. James Lodge, No. 105. The following was the board of trustees: W. R. Hedge, R. Smith, W. F. Moore, W. Galloway, J. O. Church, Edmund Dillahunty, Nathan Wright, J. S. Campbell, A. M. Hughes, Hugh Forgey, S. C. Newell, J. N. Bills, A. J. Boyd, Nathaniel F. Cheairs, James O. Potter, J. O. Griffith, William J. Hunter, W. W. Coleman and W. W. Jassey.

The Columbia Female Institute was begun in 1835, but did not become a chartered institution till in February, 1836. The building and the early success of this institute is due largely to the Rev. Franklin G. Smith and his estimable wife. Dr. Smith came to Columbia from Lynchburg, Va., and began at once to devote his energies to the up building of the institute. The buildings were erected in 1837-38, and were designed and constructed by Messrs. Drummond & Lutterloh, and are a model of architectural beauty and skill to this day. The institute stands on a four-acre lot, and is 120 feet front with high turrets. The grounds contain fine old forest trees, and are well set in blue grass. Some very fine statuary adorn the front yard of the building. The buildings are owned and controlled by the Episcopal Church of Tennessee. Soon after its erection it took a high position among educational institutions of the country. In 1838 the Rt. Rev. Leonidas Polk, D. D., was its president. Evans Young, S. D. Frierson, James Walker, G. S. Skipwith, Hillary Langtry, Patrick McGuire, Lucius J. Polk, Adlai O. Harrn and P. R. Booker were trustees, and Rt. Rev. James H. Otey, visitor. The institute continued under the immediate control of Rector Smith, who managed both its educational and financial affairs till 1852, when a difficulty arose, which caused the resignation of Rector Smith. He immediately began the Atheneum as a private enterprise. The institute is still in a flourishing condition, and has a large patronage from abroad, particularly from Mississippi and Louisiana.

In the last two decades the Rev. George Beckett has been at the head of this institute. He formerly had control of a female school in Kentucky. There is an excellent corps of teachers in all the departments of the institute. The course embraces all that is usually taught in an institute of its kind.

The Columbia Atheneum was founded by the Rev. Franklin G. Smith immediately after his separation from the institute. The name and fame of Dr. Smith was sufficient guaranty for the success of the Atheneum notwithstanding the embarrassing circumstances surrounding its beginning. The school has had an uninterrupted course since its foundation, even the ravages of war and wantonness of the soldiery were not sufficient to close its doors. Mrs. Smith for a time taught a few pupils alone, and thus prevented the appropriation of the buildings for hospital or other military purposes. The school was conducted by Rector Smith till his death in 1866 and then by his widow till 1871, when at her death the Atheneum fell into the hands of their sons Capt. Robert D. Smith, Dr. William A. Smith and Prof. Frank H. Smith. The former is its business manager. The present management began under very trying circumstances, but by energy and skill the Atheneum is in a very flourishing condition. The principal buildings are the Atheneum proper, the Davis Hall, Orient and Rectory. These buildings are surrounded by a lot of twenty-two acres of beautiful lands covered with forest trees and well set in grasses. The school is divided into these departments: the pestalozzian or primary (one grade), the junior (four grades), and the senior. The senior is divided into twelve schools as follows: 1, The school of ancient languages and literature. 2, The school of modern languages, including the German, Italian, Spanish, and Anglo-Saxon and their literature. 3, The school of modern philosophy. 4, The school of civil history. 5, The school of general literature. 6, The school of elocution. 7, The school of English. 8, The school of mathematics. 9, The school of natural philosophy and chemistry. 10, The school of natural history. 11, The school of music, embracing instrumental, vocal and harmony. 12, The school of art. The discipline and management seem to be of the highest character, and the instructions are by specialists in their respective departments. Aside from the large patronage from home and the States immediately surrounding, a very large number each year attend from Texas. The books of the Smith Bros. show that since the family began teaching in Columbia over 10,000 girls and young ladies have received instructions from them and over 1,000 have graduated. The register for 1884-85 shows an enrollment of 171 pupils. The register for 1885-86 will show an increased number.

The present public school building of Columbia was erected for the "Columbia Female Conference College," under the auspices of the Methodist Church in 1851-52. Rev. J. O. Church was its president, and for a number of years the school was in a prosperous condition. It was largely patronized by the church and by others. As a female school it was closed about the beginning of the war. The building was long known as the Andrews School Building. After the war the Smith Bros. of the Atheneum purchased the building and converted it into a male high school. It was under the management of Dr. W. A. Smith and Prof. John S. Beecher. In 1881 the school board purchased the building from the Smith Bros. and remodeled it for the public schools. The building cost about $14,000, and was called Andrew's Building in honor of one of Columbia's citizens who took great interest in the establishment of the public schools of Columbia. The schools were under the superintendence of Prof. Robert D'Shiel Robertson from September, 1881, until September, 1884. Since that the public schools have been under the management of Prof. S. M. Arnell, who has done much to popularize the public school system. Like the giant oak from the little acorn the schools of Columbia have had a wonderful growth. From a meeting on a dreary winter evening in the chancery court room, lighted by tallow candles, the schools had their origin. Here met James Andrews, E. Kuhn, D. T. B. Rains, Dr. Theodore Frierson, W. J. Andrews, S. N. Arnell and possibly one or two others. At the time there was not only great indifference if not strong prejudice against the common school system. The schools now enroll over 800 pupils, white and black, and are taught by twelve teachers besides the superintendent. The board has under advisement the erection of a fine building for the colored schools, a special appropriation of $3,000 having been set apart for that purpose by the town corporation. The city of Columbia has been quite liberal in its appropriations for its schools. The tax including State, county, and city, amounts to 70 cents on the $100, or something over $8,000 for school purposes, in consequence of which the schools extend over a period of ten months. The course embraces nine grades of one year each, and is intended to fit boys and girls for the various businesses of life.

The Robertson Male High School was established September 7, 1885, by Robert D'Shiel Robertson, to fill a space between the public school and the college or university. The design at first was to limit the number of people to twenty-five, but the pressure being so great a much larger number was admitted and assistants employed. While the school is comparatively a new institution, the varied experience of Mr. Robertson in the University of Nashville, three years in the law department of the Vanderbilt University, three years as superintendent of the Knoxville City schools, besides the work done in Columbia ought to eminently fit him for the work in his male high school.

Ingleside Academy has been under the management of Mrs. S. B. Mack for a great many years. It is a private institution, and is devoted to female education. Mrs. Mack has been engaged in the education of females all her life, a work for which she is eminently fitted.

The present system of public schools of the county was organized in the county in 1872. The county now employs 135 teachers, of whom forty-nine are male white, and thirty-eight are female white; thirty-six are male colored, and twelve female colored teachers. The average length of the school term is about seventy days, although this differs considerably in some of the various districts. The total amount of school money received for the fiscal year ending July 1, 1885, was: From State, $3,568.70; from county, $21,502; from other sources, $6,820.35. The scholastic population for the same time was male white, 4,147; female white, 3,445; male colored, 3,862; female colored, 3,609; total, 15,063. The enrollment was male whites, 2,488; females, 2,317; colored males, 2,067; colored females, 2,165; total, 9,037. The average attendance of whites was 3,603; of colored children, 3,174, making an average attendance of 6,777. The schools are divided into incorporated, consolidated and common school proper, and of the last named there is in the south district one graded school.

Mount Pleasant Academy was built on the lands of Elijah Harbin in 1835. The following trustees were appointed at that time: Willis Ridley, John Dawson and Henry Hays. These were changed from time to time as occasion demanded. Schools of high grade have been maintained there for over a half century. Among the prominent men who have taught here are Hon. William F. Kercheval, R. B. Kercheval, M. Ferguson and Chancellor William S. Fleming. For the last fifteen or sixteen years the Messrs. Webb have been managing a successful school at Culleoka. This is a school for boys, and is known far beyond the confines of the State. Under the "four mile" law the Culleoka Academy was incorporated March 29, 1884. Those in whose names the charter was granted are J. L. Moore, J. M. Stephens, W. H. Wilkes, W. R. Webb, Joseph Love, C. Taylor, J. J. Heulett, N. I. Moore and R. A. Wilkes. This school is in a flourishing condition. Nebo Academy was incorporated December 19, 1877, by W. W. Joice, W. R. McKennon, W. P. Gantt, L. King, George N. McKennon, William F. Kinzer and George Whit Kinzer. Oak Grove was built in 1878 and chartered by Hardin Mayberry, Sampson Liggett, W. C. Liggett, Samuel Clymer, T. M. Savell, W. C. Derryberry, John Craig, H. Green, J. W. Smee, C. S. Richerson, T. H. Richerson and R. W. Tindell. Oak Grove is in the Third District. Cross Bridges Academy was incorporated April 5, 1880, by C. Nicholls, Henry Harlan, A. Bowen, J. C. Webster and J. L. Beard. Spring Hill Male College was chartered December 19, 1881. Those named in the charter are Campbell Brown, J. T. S. Thompson, W. C. Campbell, J. W. Cheairs, J. W. Alexander, A. M. Kissack, J. T. Wade, J. M. Moore, Thomas Gibson, A. M. Bailey and W. A. Bailey. This is now a flourishing school, and is under the control of Prof. Morton.

Beachcroft is the female academy of Spring Hill. This large female school is under the management of Mrs. Estes, and is largely attended outside of the State. A charter for Beachcroft was granted January 11, 1884, to M. C. Campbell, Campbell Brown, H. A. Brown, J. O. Hardin, J. T. Thompson, J. M. Gray, J. W. Cheairs, J. W. Alexander, W. M. Cheairs, H. P. Wade and H. P. Pointer.

Stephenson Academy is a very old one and was chartered in 1848 by Duncan Brown, James M. Arnell, Leonidas Polk, E. W. Dale, J. S. Flemming, J. B. Frierson and J. W. Frierson, Cave Hill. Cave Hill School was incorporated July 9, 1878. The men to whom the charter was given were Jerry C. Notgrass, W. W. Neeley, S. M. Neeley and W. M. Sullivan. Pleasant Mound is located in the Twenty-fifth District and was incorporated about the same time as Cave Hill. Mount Joy School was incorporated in June, 1881, by S. Williams, P. C., Bailey, Thomas Durham, W. H. Bailey, J. H. King, A. C. Sims, B. B. Craig, William T. McCain and T. P. Holmes. Mount Zion Academy was incorporated by charter January 1, 1880, by W. T. Hadley, P. H. Southall, B. L. Mayes, G. H. Fitzgerald, W. S. Alderson, D. Harling, S. E. Witherspoon and W. T. Dodson. In connection with this school is a chartered literary society. Mount Zion is in the Nineteenth District and has maintained a school of some kind for nearly three quarters of a century. Neapolis Academy is in the Twenty-second District and was incorporated in January, 1880. The charter was granted to W. A. Bailey, E. A. Denton, R. C. Allen, W. C. Radley and W. T. Bassham.

In addition to the incorporated schools, schools chartered under the "four mile" law, there are thirteen consolidated schools, schools, however, in which private schools are taught supplementary to the public schools. There is in the Ninth District a graded school of two departments. The remaining schools are the ordinary county schools. The awakening of the people to the importance of an efficient school system indicates that they believe the common schools are the "hope of our country."

The Synod of Kentucky, in October, 1810, ordered that a portion of Transylvania be cut off and a new presbytery formed to be called the Presbytery of West Tennessee, consisting of Rev. Messrs. James W. Stephenson, Samuel Donald, Duncan Brown and Samuel Hedge. This presbytery was duly organized at Bethsaida Church, March 27, 1811. The Rev. Gideon Blackburn and Rev. John Gillespie were received as members at this meeting. Presbyterianism began with the settlement of the State. The following churches had been organized a number of years before the Presbytery of West Tennessee was formed: Bethesda, Bethsaida, Rocky Mount, Ebenezer, Swan Creek, Sugar Creek, Flat Creek, Betherci, Nashville and Franklin. The one at Columbia was formed about 1811. The boundaries of West Tennessee were minutely defined on the north and east, but on the west they extended to Missouri and the Rocky Mountains and southward to the Gulf of Mexico. The old records show that as early as 1813 the presbytery had its missionaries in the Territories of Missouri, Mississippi and West Florida. So rapidly did Presbyterianism grow, and the difficulty of attending so large a territory so great, that the Presbytery of West Tennessee soon became the mother of those of Shiloh, Mississippi, Obion, Nashville and Western District. Mention should be made of Gideon Blackburn, James W. Stephenson and Robert Henderson as active members of the presbytery. The Presbytery of Columbia embraces the counties of Maury, Giles, Marshall and Lincoln. It has under its care twenty-five churches with thirteen ordained ministers and a membership of about 2,000.

The first church organization in Columbia was Presbyterian. The date of the organization is not exactly known as the records have been destroyed, but it was not far from the organization of the county, *i. e.* 1807. The church was organized by the Rev. Gideon Blackburn, well known as an eloquent preacher and a classic teacher of Franklin. The first regular pastor was the Rev. Robert Henderson, well known as a pulpit orator, teacher and scholar. The first brick church erected in Columbia was in 1822-23, on the same lot where the church now stands. Previous to the erection of this church private houses or the court house were used for church services. The church membership embraced many of the leading families in Columbia. Among the early elders were Dr. William McNiell, John Thomas, John Dodge, Benjamin Thomas, Samuel McDowell, George M. Martin, Maj. John Brown, John Frierson, Dr. J. W. S. Frierson and Dr. John S. Law. Dr. Henderson was succeeded by Rev. Robert Hardin about 1830, who was also for a time president of Jackson College while it was located near Spring Hill. The next minister was the Rev. Thomas Scott, who was succeeded by the Rev. Joseph Sherman, who became the second president of Jackson College, after its removal to Columbia. Dr. Sherman, as is well known, lost his life by accident at Nashville in 1849. Rev. Sherman was succeeded by Rev. C. P. Wing, who remained till 1843, when the Rev. William Mack took charge and continued till 1858. Dr. Mack was twice president of Jackson College and was widely known both as a minister and educator. Rev. A. Hartpence succeeded Dr. Mack in 1858, and he gave place to Rev. A. L. Kline about 1860. Rev. A. L. Kline was succeeded in 1868 by Rev. J. M. P. Otts. The Rev. J. C. Mitchell became pastor in 1873, and he still has charge of the church. The present Presbyterian Church was erected in 1843, but was remodeled and repaired in 1874. This church is now well furnished with seats and has an excellent pipe organ. The church membership is 251.

The first Methodist class was formed in Columbia some time between 1815 and 1820, although there were a few members as early as 1815. The first class meeting was held at the house of Thomas White, on Embargo Street. The first church house was built on South Main Street, near E. W. Gamble's large grocery store. This was a frame structure about 35x50. According to Mrs. White the building was erected in 1818, although it is claimed by some not to have been built till 1821. This house was changed to a dwelling and stood till a few years ago. The first regular pastor was the Rev. Thomas Madden, who came to Columbia in 1820. A revival greatly strengthened the church. Dr. Madden was succeeded by Rev. Hartwell H. Brown in 1822. Dr. Madden was recalled in 1823 and remained till 1825, when he was succeeded by Rev. W. B. Beck. The first Sunday-school was organized by Dr. Madden, in 1823 or 1824. The trustees of the first church were John Gordon, Robert Doak, Levi Covey, James Gullett, John T. Moore, Elisha Uzzell and Edward W. Dale. These to a great extent represented the families belonging to the church. The trustees for the new church were E. W. Dale, James R. Plummer, Joseph Herndon, Nathan Vaught, G. I. Voorhies, Rev. William Horsley, John H. Terrill, Samuel A. Hamner and Rev. H. H. Brown. A new brick church was erected in 1836, but this was accidentally destroyed by fire in 1874 and was rebuilt in a few years. The present elegant structure is the fruit of that work. Preaching had been held in Columbia some time before any church was erected. Preaching was had either in the court house or in the grove. One place remembered was the Atheneum grounds, where the celebrated Lorenzo Dow preached. The Methodist is one of the strongest churches in the city, the membership numbering about 350.

The Episcopal Church of Columbia was organized by the Rev. James H. Otey, who afterward became bishop in 1829. The first paster was Dr. Stephens, who was a teacher, as was his son and daughter. The first church edifice was erected just back of the Masonic Hall. The present elegant house of worship was erected in 1860-61. The church has a membership of 149. Rev. George Becket, of the Institute, has been rector of this church for the last nineteen years.

The Cumberland Presbyterians built their church in Columbia in 1848, with the assistance of the Odd Fellows. The symbols of that order are still to be seen over the doors of the church. This house is still standing, and is in a good state of preservation.

The Baptists and Christians each have elegant brick churches on High Street. The former has a new building in course of construction. The date of the organization of these churches is later than any of the former mentioned.

Like most all the counties in Middle Tennessee, Maury was settled largely by Revolutionary soldiers or their descendants. The population of the county in its early history was largely from North Carolina, South Carolina and Virginia. North Carolina gave grants to her soldiers for military services in the Revolutionary war. These grants were located mainly in Middle Tennessee, from which cause large numbers of North Carolina soldiers settled in that part of the State, and not a few in Maury County. These grants varied in size in this county from 200 acres to 25,000 acres, as was the case with Gen. Greene's grant. Among those who served in the Revolutionary war were Maj. James Holland, who died May 19, 1823, at the age of seventy-two; he served in the Legislature of North Carolina, in the Congress of the United States; he was buried about nine miles east of Columbia. William Renfro served through the war, and died in 1830 at the age of ninety-six, leaving a number of descendants in the county. Thomas Wren, the ancestor of a large family, was buried north of the river on the farm where he lived. James White Stephenson was a South Carolinian, and settled near Zion, of which church he was many years pastor. He was a distinguished minister, educator, and a valued citizen. Dr. Samuel Mayes was a soldier at King's Mountain, and other important battles. He was an elder in Zion Church, and was buried at that place. James Armstrong, who was a member of Lee's Legion, came to Maury County in 1807. He, too, was buried at Zion. Another soldier buried at Zion was David Matthews, who served under Gen. Marion. Mark Jackson and Aaron Reynolds, two old Revolutionary soldiers, were buried, one at "Shane's" grave-yard and the other in a private grave-yard near by. Gen. Richard Winn was a soldier and officer from South Carolina. He served in the Legislature of his native State, also in the Congress of the United States. He was buried near Williamsport. His grave was unmarked, and until a few years ago his burial place was in question. Robert Caruthers, an early settler of the county, was also a Revolutionary soldier. The principal Indian fighters were Col. William and Gideon Pillow and Col. Joseph Brown. These men are distinctly mentioned in the settlement of Middle Tennessee by Putnam. Col. Brown had been a prisoner among the Cherokee Indians, and having learned their language he became an effective guide against them afterward. He served as a guide against the Indians in the expedition against Nickajack. In later years he became a distinguished Presbyterian minister. Pillow killed the Indian chief Big Foot in an expedition against the Indians. In the Creek war of 1812-14, Col. Pillow commanded a company, and was severely wounded at Talladega. Both Pillow and Brown died in the county at the age of nearly one hundred years. Cols. Roberts and Gordon were also distinguished leaders in that campaign. Among the last survivors of that campaign were Col. Roberts, M. Cooper, Maj. John D. Fleming and George Donelson.

On the outbreak of the first Seminole war in 1817, Capt. John Gordon raised a spy company which he commanded in that war. It is well known in this war the climate and hardships were far more destructive than the bullet and tomahawk of the Indians. The last survivors of that war were T. S. Pickard and David Hamilton. Soon after the massacre of Maj. Dade and his men in the Wahoo Swamp, and the killing of Gen. Thompson on December 28, 1835, Gov. Cannon called for volunteers. Two companies were raised in Maury County; one commanded by William J. Frierson was raised in the vicinity of Tien and Bigbyville, and the other was commanded by Capt. John B. Hamilton and later by George Lipscomb. This company was recruited mainly in the neighborhood of Cathey Creek. These companies were attached to the First Regiment, of which A. F. Bedford was chosen colonel; T. H. Cahal, lieutenant-colonel; Powhattan Gordon, major First Battalion, and A. C. Goff, major of Second Battalion; W. G. Dickinson, surgeon and A. H. Brown, assistant surgeon. The company commanded by Capt. Frierson consisted of 101 or 102 men and Capt. Hamilton's company contained 105 men. The only loss sustained by these companies was one man who died of measles and a negro belonging to J. M. S. Mayes, who was killed by accident. Mr. Mayes is believed to be the only survivor of that war now in the county. The powder-horn carried by him is now in possession of the Historical Society. A full report of this campaign is given elsewhere.

In the war with Mexico in 1846-47, the call for troops was so quickly filled that but a small portion of those volunteering were accepted. Several companies were tendered the State, but one only, Capt. Albert G. Cooper's company, was accepted. This was a cavalry company and was attached to the regiment of which J. E. Thomas was colonel, Richard

Allison, lieutenant-colonel, and Richard Waterhouse, major. Gen. Gideon J. Pillow, of Maury County, commanded a brigade in that war. He was at Matamoras, Vera Cruz, Cerro Gordo, where he was wounded; also in the battles near the City of Mexico. In that war as given under that head, he made a national reputation for skill and gallantry.

In the war between the States Maury was slow to sever the ties, but when in her whole force was thrown on the side of the South. On May 6, 1861, the county court appropriated $1,000 for the benefit of the families of soldiers who were then in the service. This was to be distributed by the justices in their respective districts. By the report of October 7 it is shown that $1,349.02 had been thus expended. This sum was distributed in the various districts in sums varying from $1 to $539.29. A tax of 10 cents on each $100 was levied for the purpose of keeping up this aid. In the call for 55,000 men, 2,500 of whom were for active service, the county promptly furnished her quota. Home guard companies in each of the twenty-five districts were quickly enrolled and organized by the selection of their officers. Space prevents our giving these officers and men. On May 20, 1861, the court decided that the home guards should serve without pay as it was the duty of "all good citizens to serve in times of peril free of charge."

The first regular troops for the service from this county were Company B, of the Second Confederate. This regiment was organized May 5, 1861, at Nashville, by electing W. B. Bate, colonel; D. L. Goodall, lieutenant-colonel; William Doak, major; William Driver, adjutant; M. W. Clusky, assistant quartermaster; J. A. Moore, assistant commissary-sergeant; Dr. T. J. Kennedy, surgeon and Rev. D. Joseph Cross, chaplain. The regiment was moved to Lynchburg, Va., where it was soon after mustered into the Confederate service by Gen. E. Kirby Smith. Company B was made up at Columbia and joined the regiment at Nashville. The captains of Company B were John G. Anderson, John A. Mackey and Edmund O'Neil. The roll of honor of Company B is J. M. Cathron, died at Fredricksburg, July 16, 1861; John E. Sharber, died at Stafford Court House; John W. Gee, killed at Richmond, Ky., August 30, 1862; William Edwards died at Columbus, Miss. A full sketch of this regiment is given elsewhere.

The Third Tennessee Infantry contained three companies from Maury County, viz.: Companies C, E and F. Company C contained an aggregate of 119 men. The following were its commissioned officers: Captains, D. F. Wade and R. T. Cooper; first lieutenant, J. D. Moss; second lieutenant, Johnson Long; junior second lieutenant, W. S. Jennings. Company E, from both Maury and Williamson, contained 100 men; captains, N. F. Cheairs and H. P. Pointer; first lieutenant, Campbell Brown; second lieutenant, Thomas Tucker; junior second lieutenant, J. T. S. Thompson. Company F contained ninety-eight men. The officers were G. W. Jones, captain; J. B. Murphy, first lieutenant; B. G. Darden, second lieutenant; John T. Williamson, junior second lieutenant. John C. Brown was elected colonel of the regiment; Thomas M. Gordon, lieutenant-colonel; N. F. Cheairs, major, and T. M. Tucker, adjutant. The roll of honor of Company C was thirty-six men; of Company E eight men, and of Company F was sixteen men. This is not a true index of the losses of each, but is given as the only available record. A complete history of this entire regiment is found elsewhere.

The Forty-eighth Tennessee Infantry was made up largely from Maury County, six companies in all. The regiment arrived at Camp Maury, near Nashville, December 12, 1861. It was soon divided into detachments and sent to guard the Cumberland and Tennessee Rivers and railroad bridges in the vicinity of and leading to Forts Henry and Donelson. Upon the approach of the Federals the regiment was concentrated at Fort Henry. In the retreat upon Fort Donelson the regiment lost its clothing and baggage. A detail was sent from each company to collect supplies. In the surrender of Donelson the regiment lost 360 men. The field officers were sent to Fort Warren, Massachusetts; the line officers to Camp Chase, Ohio, but on the 1st of May were sent to Johnson's Island, Lake Erie; the enlisted men were sent to Camp Douglas, Illinois, but in August they were sent to Vicksburg and exchanged. The sick, those on furlough, and those on detached duty were not captured, but were consolidated into a new organization. To these were attached a few new companies, and the whole took the name of Nixon's Forty-eighth, or the little Forty-eighth. This body was attached to Gen. E. Kirby Smith's corps, and took part in the whole of the Kentucky campaign, taking a prominent part in the battle of Richmond, Ky. It was with the Army of Tennessee, at Perryville, on October 8, and at Murfreesboro, Tenn., at the close of the year. Its conduct was such as to receive special mention by its brigade and division commanders.

After the exchange of those captured the regiment was reorganized at Jackson, Miss. An election of officers resulted in the re-election of W. M. Voorhees, colonel; A. S. Godum, lieutenant-colonel; A. J. Campbell, major. Field officers, line officers and non-commissioned officers were sent home to recruit. Capts. Howard and Love's companies had been attached to the Third Tennessee, and were encamped at Holly Springs. These were ordered to Port Hudson in October, and December 27 they were joined by their old comrades, who had been exchanged, and many recruits. They were now reunited. The regiment formed a part of Gen. S. B. Maxey's brigade. The regiment was at the bombardment of Port Hudson on the nights of the 13th and 14th of March, by Farragut's fleet. The regiment left Port Hudson May 3, 1863, to assist in the campaign against Grant around Vicksburg. On the fall of Vicksburg the regiment was sent to the Gulf Department, where it did guard duty from Mobile to Pascagoula. The regiment was sent to Dalton, Ga., in November, and again sent to Mobile, in which department it remained till ordered to join the Army of Tennessee. It united with that army May 27, at New Hope Church, near Marietta, Ga. Before being sent to this department Gen. Maxey had been transferred to the Trans-Mississippi Department, and the brigade placed under Gen. Quarles. In the meantime Maj. A. J. Campbell had died, and Capt. J. D. Howard had been promoted to major. The regiment took part in the battles of New Hope Church, Lost Mountain, Kenesaw, Peach Tree Creek and around Atlanta. The regiment was a part of Loring's division of Polk's corps. After the death of Polk it was in the division of Walthall of Stewart's corps. The regiment met with frightful losses on the 28th, losing more than half its men. The regiment was soon detached to protect the railroad, which was threatened by the Federal cavalry. The regiment was under the command of Lieut.-Col. A. S. Godum. There was some severe fighting around Lovejoy Station and Jonesboro, in which the regiment met with loss, but inflicted severe punishment upon the enemy. The regiment was with Hood's advance into Tennessee, and on its arrival in Maury County the men were allowed a three days' leave of absence, in consequence of which the regiment escaped the battle of Franklin and doubtless many escaped death there. Capts. Love and Tomlinson have furnished the following account of the action of the regiment at Nashville, for Dr. Lindsley's work: "Early in the morning of December 15 Capt. Love was put in command of a force to complete a fort on Hood's left, on the Granny White Pike. About noon he was ordered to report to his regiment near by, and a detail from Quarles' brigade, under Maj. T. E. Jamison, was sent to occupy the work. Scarcely had the brigade moved away before a strong cavalry force attacked the fort, but was driven away with great loss. Shortly they were attacked by infantry. Our men stood heroically; many of them were barefooted in the snow, and when overpowered, fought with clubbed muskets. Sergt. William Trousdale. Charley Jones and Lieut. Maclin cut their way out and joined their commands that night; Maj. Jamison was severely wounded in the thigh and captured and sent as a prisoner to Fort Delaware, where he was kept till August, 1865. Our brigade took position behind a stone wall; soon the enemy captured another fort in our front and turned our guns upon us, and a brigade of the enemy was rapidly moving on our flank. We fell back in good order through a recently plowed field. Here Capt. J. P. Churd had his leg shot off. The next day we occupied an exposed space to the right of Finley's brigade, with no protection. The Federal line was within seventy yards of us and we were compelled to lie down, as the least exposure was sure to result in death. All day long we could see the Federals encircling us. We saw our line give way on the hill above us. Soon the Federals had full possession of the fort; then our whole line gave way." The regiment formed a part of the rear guard, under

Forrest, in Hood's retreat. It took part in the severe skirmish near Pulaski, where a Federal battery was captured. The regiment joined Bragg's forces at Kingston, N. C.; a detachment under Capt. Love took part in an engagement there. The regiment then went to Goldsboro, thence to Bentonville, where it fought its last engagement. It surrendered March 19, 1865.

For the Ninth Battalion Maury County furnished Companies A, B and E. This body was organized in December at a camp near Nashville. The officers of Company A were J. N. Walker, captain; E. N. H. Foster, first lieutenant; Frank J. McLean, second lieutenant; Joe A. Irvine, junior second lieutenant. The officers of Company B were R. N. Moore, captain; T. L. Porter, first lieutenant; J. B. Galloway, second lieutenant; W. H. McFalls, junior second lieutenant. The officers of Company E. were J. H. Akin, captain; A. B. Biffle, first lieutenant; A. A. Kennedy, second lieutenant; A. J. Pugh, junior second lieutenant. The field and staff officers were George Gantt, lieutenant-colonel; B. W. Porter, major; Hunter Nicholson, adjutant. On the reorganization in September, 1862, George Gantt was re-elected lieutenant-colonel; J. H. Akin, major; W. V. Thompson, adjutant. The Ninth lost by sickness and by bullets of the enemy 380 men. For a full account of the Ninth Battalion see elsewhere. Two batteries of artillery and some detached companies make up the men furnished by Maury County, in all twenty-one companies.

WILLIAMSON COUNTY.

THE surface of the county in the Basin is generally undulating, rising in some places into high bluffs or knobs several hundred feet in height. The water-shed is from southeast to northwest. One range of hills or elevated lands rises in Rutherford County, near Stewart's Creek, and extends southwesterly, but gradually sinks into a level a short distance from Franklin. The waters from the northern slope of this range flow into Mill Creek, so named from its early and numerous mills thereon. This drainage extends over the fertile lands of the Sixteenth and Seventeenth Districts. The higher lands afford excellent timber of cedar and other valuable timbers. Separating the Thirteenth and Twenty-first from the Twelfth and Twenty-second Districts is Duck River Ridge, which is the water-shed between the waters of Big Harpeth and the head waters of Rutherford and Flat Creeks. The principal drainage of the county, however, is by the Harpeth and its branches. This embraces a very large portion of the county. The Big Harpeth enters the county at College Grove, near the southeastern part of the county, and leaves it near the northwestern part. Not far from Mount Carmel rises West Harpeth, a stream which flows almost parallel with Big Harpeth, but unites with it a short distance northwest of Franklin. Each of these streams receives small tributaries, the largest and best known being Leiper's Creek, which enters West Harpeth not far from Hillsboro. Within the valley of these small rivers is seen some very fine country. It is even questioned if it can be surpassed anywhere. Formerly it was densely covered with heavy forest trees or a rank growth of cane. A short distance beneath the surface is a bed of limestone, but the soil along the river is a rich, black loam, capable of supporting a luxuriant growth of all the cereals known to the temperate climate, as well as other vegetable products, nor has the cultivation of these been wanting, for the late statistics show Williamson to afford the largest yield of wheat of any county in the State.

Little Harpeth, which flows near the well known Hollow Tree Gap, drains a much smaller amount of land than the other Harpeth, but none the less rich. South Harpeth cuts its way through the Rim or highlands in the extreme western part of the county.

This is bordered by high hills and precipitous rocks, with an ever-changing bed. This feature of these rivers is noticeable within the recollections of men; they are much wider than formerly and not so deep; their rise is much higher and quicker than formerly, and their subsidence is much more rapid. The name Harpeth is said to have originated from two noted outlaws, who had their headquarters on Big Harpeth. Their names were Harp, and from their size were designated Big and Little Harp. After bidding defiance to the law and force for many years they were at last brought to punishment. The country lying along the South Harpeth is quite broken and is sparsely settled. Covering a large portion of districts—first, second, third and sixth—is a heavy growth of timber almost in its primitive luxuriance. In some portions of the county there is a sandy soil, from which there is a heavy growth of cedar, and in other parts there is a fine growth of white oak. Fine springs abound in almost every part of the county; these, with the fine grasses grown, make this an excellent stock-raising county, to which attention has been largely attracted since 1871. Besides the numerous other springs the county abounds in various medical springs. These are known as Smith's Springs, Cayce's Spring, and the best known of these now is the Fernvale Spring, owned by J. B. McEwen. Analyses of the water of the last-named spring have been made by several eminent chemists. These all show the water to possess high medical properties.

A comparison of the amount of cereals grown in Williamson County in 1870 and in 1885 will show the rapid increase in these products, and also the amount of these products grown in the county. The product of corn in bushels in 1870 was 1,010,443; of wheat, 227,294; of rye, 4,662; of oats, 99,933; of barley, 10,536. The corresponding cereals in 1885 were as follows: Indian corn, in bushels, 1,439,445; wheat, 315,966; rye, 2,265; oats, 585,522; barley, 499. The number of domestic animals for the same years were as follows: The number of horses and mules for 1870 were 10,314; cattle, 6,988; sheep, 15,226; hogs, 41,703. The same animals in 1885 were as follows: Horses and mules, 11,442; cattle, 12,906; sheep, 15,809; hogs, 43,132.

In regard to the first settlers of Williamson County, there is an interesting tradition; in fact it must be traditional in part, at least, as Haywood, Ramsey and Putnam do not give it. It is to the effect that in 1797 three men, named, respectively, Graham, Brown and Tindel, accompanied by a negro and a dog, went out on an exploring expedition to the vicinity about Franklin. The men were absent some time, and did not return, neither any tidings of them. A party was sent in search of the men but no trace of them was found until their arrival at Hollow Tree Gap, where the party met the dog in a half starved condition. True to the instincts of his nature the dog led the party to where lay the remains of his masters. It seems the party had found traces of a bear, which they had followed some distance from their course before they came up with the animal. The bear was killed and the party had encamped on the spot. Attracted by the firing upon the bear or by the camp fire, a party of Indians found the lonely party and surrounded the camp and killed the entire number. Fate was generous enough to make these men fight desperately and slay several times their number of Indians. The faithful dog had kept vigil over his dead companions until driven away by hunger.

The Indian titles being extinguished north of Duck River very early settlers began to enter the territory of Williamson before 1800. David McEwen, of Statesville, N. C., with several families, moved to Nashville in 1796, but owing to the disturbances by the Indians, did not proceed on their journey till 1798. In that year Mr. McEwen passed through Hollow Tree Gap and on to Roper's Knob, where he settled. Mr. McEwen was the father of a large and influential family that has been prominent in Williamson County since its inception. William Demumhane, son of Capt. Demumhane, the pioneer settler of Nashville, was born at the mouth of Mill Creek, on the Cumberland. Leaving his parents when quite young he passed through the wilderness of woods and canebrakes and settled near College Grove, where he became a wealthy planter.

Mr. Sledge, who came to the county about the time of De Munbreun, brought only his wife and a few household utensils on a pack-horse, and settled near Peytonsville. Here he lived several years under a temporary shelter. Samuel Crockett, John Wilson and David McEwen, mentioned above, had each settled and built a cotton-gin before 1804, as appears from Dr. Ramsey. In 1798 Andrew Goff, William McEwen, George Neeley and a number of others settled on Spence's Creek. Thomas H. Perkins and Mr. McConnico settled at the fork of the West and Big Harpeth Rivers about 1810. About the same time came Matthew Johnson and William Edmondson. Thomas Spence, Daniel McMahan and Thomas Williamson each settled on the creek bearing the name of the former in 1800. Ewen Cameron is said to have built a house in Franklin in 1797. Abram Maury, upon whose land the city of Franklin was built, and Thomas McKay, at whose house the first court was held, were both residents before 1800. Byrd Hamlet, who settled near Nolensville, has the credit of having raised the first hogshead of tobacco in Middle Tennessee. The following persons had made settlements previous to 1800, the most of whom were connected with the county officially: James Buford, James Scurlock, Nicholas Perkins, Edmond Wall, Chapman White, Solomon Brent, Stephen Childress, William Hulme, William Smith, Sion Hunt, Robert Caruthers, R. P. Currin, Richard Hightower, James Neeley, John Harness and many others. Joel Parish was one of the first to erect a mill on Harpeth; he was also prominently connected with other business interests of the county. The increase of population of the county for the first decade is remarkable, the population in 1810 amuonting to over 13,000, while in 1800 it was numbered by the hundreds. The county in 1810, however, embraced a much larger area than now.

The act establishing Williamson County passed the General Assembly October 26, 1799. The territory was cut off from Davidson County, and embraced the following boundaries: "Beginning at a point forty poles due north of the dwelling house of David McClory on the waters of Little Harpeth, running thence east two miles and one hundred and four poles; thence south seventy degrees, east sixteen miles and two hundred and seventy poles; thence due south to the Indian boundary line; thence with said line westerly to the Robertson County line; thence north with said line to a point due west of the mouth of Little Harpeth; thence in a direct line to the mouth of the Little Harpeth; thence along said river to the place of beginning, to be known as Williamson County." The county was named in honor of Gen. Williamson, of North Carolina. John Johnson, Sr., Daniel Perkins, James Buford, William Edmonson and Capt. James Scurlock were appointed commissioners to select a site for the county seat and to erect a court house, jail and stocks. Henry Rutherford and John Davis were appointed to run the boundary line where not sufficiently designated by nature.

By the same act of the General Assembly establishing Williamson County and appointing the commissioners for the town of Franklin, the commissioners were empowered with authority to reserve two acres of ground for a Square, on which they were to erect a court house. This building was erected some time between the erection of the county and establishing the seat of justice for the same and the year 1801. The order for its erection, the size, dimensions, cost or contractors are not matters of record; however, the county court met in regular session November 3, 1800, in the "new court house." This house was a square brick building, and stood in the center of the Public Square. This building was a very substantial structure and served for a court house until 1857. The first steps taken for the erection of the new building was April 1, 1855, by the appointment of John S. Claybrook, John B. McEwen, Samuel Farmer and C. W. Davis as a committee to investigate the needs of the county. This committee made its report, and a new committee, with full power to contract for and let the new court house, was appointed. This committee consisted of John W. Miller, T. F. Atkinson, John S. Claybrook, Park Street and B. B. Irvin. July 1, the lot on the southeast corner of the Square was purchased of Ferdinand Stitt for $1,000; the court at the same time appropriated $3,000 to commence work on the house. Other appropriations followed from time to time as the work proceeded. The present house is a plain brick structure with stone basement. The portico is supported by long, heavy iron columns. The offices are supplied with substantial fire-proof vaults for the records. The work on the court house not being entirely completed when the war broke out and the neglect during that period required the expenditure of $3,000 in repairs in 1867. This was done through a committee of R. S. Ballow, J. B. McEwen and S. S. House. Prison bounds for insolvent debtors were established in 1803. The bounds were described as "Beginning at the the 'race path,' thence up Main Street and running so as to include John White's Mill; thence to include the court house, jail and down Main Street, and back to the place of beginning."

The first jail was a rude structure, and stood on the Square near the market house. This was a very insecure jail, as prisoners were frequently taken elsewhere for safe keeping. Steps were taken October 8, 1816, for the creation of a new jail, and a committee of Robert P. Currin, Charles McIntyre, H. Petway, Stephen Childress and W. T. Perkins was appointed, whose duty it was to sell the old jail and market house, and to purchase a more desirable lot within the corporate limits. To aid in the erection a jail tax equal to the State tax was levied. A new jail was accordingly erected, which was composed of wood and brick. near where the present one stands. In November, 1828, a committee of H. L. White, E. T. Collins and William Johnston made the following report: "We find that William Clark, jailer, and his family have conducted themselves so ridiculous and have also become a nuisance to their neighbors, and on his family's account we have thought proper to remove the said Clark and substitute Joel Childress in his place." The committee found that the jail was considerably out of repair, that the family part of said jail was open and torn to pieces, and the "whole requires considerable work and considerable improvement, which we believe to be of considerable importance to the county." This jail stood till 1858, when, April 19, a new committee was selected, whose duty it was to report on the propriety of building a new jail. This committee was composed of John B. McEwen, John M. Winstead and Samuel Farmer. The committee recommended that a new jail of stone and brick should be built. The committee visited the Nashville jail and got all the information they could, and flattered themselves that "we will have a first-rate jail." The dimensions of the new jail were to be 40x46 and 24 feet high. There were to be two cells below and two above, and two passages through the building each 10x40 feet. The whole building was to be fire-proof. The contract was let to Robert H. Bradley for the aggregate sum of $8,000, to be completed July 18, 1859, which time was afterward extended to January 1, 1860.

Previous to 1829 the poor of the county were farmed out to the lowest bidder and allowances made for them. On October 5, 1829, a committee of John Thompson, Jabez Owen, William Ditto, Robert McCutchen, G. Marshall and David C. Kinnard reported that they had bought of Andrew L. Andrews, a tract of forty acres of land for $350, a tract of twenty acres from Mark L. Andrews for $90, and contracted with Mark L. Andrews to erect and improve the buildings on the land purchased of Andrew L. Andrews, to the amount of $350. In 1840 W. S. Webb, Mike Kinnard and R. W. Robison, a poor-house committee, bought additional lands to the amount of about 550 acres. At the August term, 1867, a committee consisting of Park Street, W. A. Rodgers and John M. Winstead were appointed a committee to enquire into the propriety of selling a portion of the poor-farm. The report was to the effect that the county owned more land than was profitable. Six small tracts, amounting in the aggregate to 130 acres, were sold. These were purchased by S. S. Short, Thomas Short, J. B. Gray, G. W. Davis, H. S. Reynolds and H. Hanks, respectively. The purchases amounted to the sum of $2,750. The farm yet contains 413 acres of good land, and has good buildings thereon and is managed with little expense to the county.

The date of the building the first market is rather an uncertain quantity, as no order for the erection can be found further than the general order given to the commissioner of Franklin for the erection of a court house, market, jail and stocks. As the others were built during the first year of the present century, it is presumed the market-house was also built then, as frequent orders were given for its government in the first years of the present century. This was not only the place of sale for provisions of all kinds, but also of public sales of various kinds of property, such as slaves, goods, chattels, etc. Within this also was the pillory, a favorite mode of punishment for criminals previous to the passage of the penitentiary law in 1829. This market-house stood till 1831, when, on January 4, "on motion it was ordered by the county court that the mayor and aldermen be permitted to erect a market-house on the Square of the town of Franklin, or any other building they think for the general good of the public, but the sheriff is hereby instructed to see that all rubbish is removed from the Square and streets." This house stood till the Square was cleared of public buildings in 1858, when the old court house and market were removed from the Square.

Members of the State Legislature: Senate—Robert Weakley, 1801-05; Chapman White, 1805-07; N. T. Perkins, 1807-09; Thomas H. Benton, 1809-11; Newton Cannon, 1811-15; Amos Johnson, 1815-17; John Bell, 1817-19; Joel Parrish, 1819-21; Sterling Brown, 1821-25; Newton Cannon, 1827-29; Robert Jetton, 1829-35; Barclay Martin, 1835-41; W. H. Sneed, 1841-45; Abram Maney and J. W. Richardson, 1845-51; W. C. J. Burrus, 1851-53; P. O. N. Perkins, 1853-57; W. L. McComico, 1857-59; J. W. Richardson, 1859-60; A. W. Mess, 1865-66; W. Y. Elliott, 1867-68; D. M. McFall, 1868-70; T. F. P. Allison, 1871-73; A. T. Boyd, 1875-77; W. D. Fullerton, 1877-79; T. F. Perkins, 1879-81.

House— ———, 1801-05; Chapman White, 1803-05; Abram Maney, 1805-07; Moses Frierson, 1807-11; Amos Johnson, 1811-15; William Martin, 1815-21; Abram Maney, Jr., 1821-25; Samuel Perkins, 1825-27; Newton Cannon, 1829-31; R. C. Foster, 1831-35; M. P. Gentry, 1835-39; R. C. Foster, 1839-43; A. P. Maney, 1843-44; S. Venable and R. W. H. Bestick, 1845-46; J. Robison and F. Hardeman, 1847-48; E. Thompson and P. G. S. Perkins, 1849-50; David Campbell, 1851-53; Frank Hardeman, 1853-55; C. W. Beale, 1855-57; W. L. McComico, 1857-58; W. E. Ewing, 1859-60; J. W. Richardson, 1864-65; D. W. McFall, 1865-67; Atha Thomas, 1868-69; Samuel Perkins, 1875-76; F. M. Lavender, 1877-79; T. E. Haynes, 1879-83.

At the February term, 1800, the county court ordered the following roads to be laid off and cut out. Daniel McEwen was to oversee the road from Franklin to Hollow Tree Gap, and the road was ordered to be called the Hollow Tree Gap road. All persons living on the south side of the ridge and north of Big Harpeth were ordered to assist in clearing the road. The first State case in the county grew out of this, but the case was quashed when it was shown that McEwen's help failed to assist him. William Edmunson, William Marshall, John Cummings, Patrick McCutchen, William McGaugh, John Jordan, John Buchanan and William Walker were ordered to lay off the road from the mouth of Arrington's Creek to Franklin. Robert Caruthers, John Ried, John Slocum, Henry Walker, Richard Puckett and Jesse Weathier were ordered to cut out the road from Robert Caruthers' to Franklin, and to the place where the commissioners' trace crosses the Big Harpeth. This road is what was called the Commissioners' Trace road and connected with what was known as the Commissioners road or Natchez trace. The Buford's Ford road was cut out by George Neely. Joseph Porter, John McKinney, Samuel McClary and David Long. This road extended from Franklin to Buford's Ford on the Little Harpeth. The road from Hollow Tree Gap to the Davidson County line by way of Joseph White's was cut out by direction of David White and "all those living on the west side of the road as far down the Little Harpeth as the Plum Orchard and the head waters of Beech Creek" were ordered to assist. The McCutchen Creek road was marked out by Samuel McCutchen, Samuel Edmunson, Ephraim Brown, M. German, John McKay, Thomas Owens and James Scott. This road extended from McCutchen Creek and the Big Harpeth to Franklin.

Natchez trace, the old government road, entered the county from the south near old Harpeth Church, and passed a little east of Beechville postoffice; thence south through Districts Nos. 7 and 6; thence through No. 3 by way of Hillsboro; thence into No. 2 a little west of Boston and out of the county a little east of White Oak postoffice.

The first efforts for a railroad to Franklin were in November, 1831, when books were opened to receive subscriptions for what was then called the Nashville, Franklin & Columbia Railroad, but no success was made till the charter was granted to the Tennessee and Alabama Railroad in 1852. The first road asked for $200,000 to be raised by subscription in shares of $25 each. Books were opened at Franklin and other points on the line. The company reserved the privilege of terminating the road at Mount Pleasant, Columbia, Spring Hill and Franklin. The following persons were made a committee on subscription: Thomas Park, R. G. Foster, John Marshall, J. W. Morton, D. B. Cliffe, J. H. Wilson, S. S. Mayfield, J. H. Bond, R. Ogilvie, S. D. Foster, W. P. Martin, A. Kinnard and E. Thompson. The next call for assistance was made in January, 1853. It was for $100,000 of stock to be taken by the county. The election was held February 12, 1853, under act of 1853 granting the right to continue to take stock in railroads. This also failed when the company again asked assistance to the amount of $2,500 of the county September 11, 1855. The same amount was also asked from the city of Franklin. These amounts were received by the company. The road was not completed to the Alabama line till 1859. On May 1, 1871, it was leased for a period of thirty years by the Louisville & Nashville Company, under whose management it is now controlled.

The Franklin Turnpike was chartered in November, 1830. The first installment of stock was called for November 16, 1831. The call was for $2.50 on each share to be paid to Shadrack Myers and W. S. Childress. The road extended from Nashville to Franklin, and was built by Messrs. Black & Love. The charter was granted for the Franklin & Columbia Pike in 1832. Thomas Peeples had charge of the construction of a part of this road. The Nolensville Pike was built in 1841 of which H. Blackman was president at that time. The county is now well supplied with pikes. The Nolensville Pike is fifteen miles in length; the Nashville & Franklin ten miles; the Franklin & Spring Hill, fifteen miles; the Farmington, ten miles; the Carter's Creek, ten miles; the Wilson & Harpeth, ten miles; the Franklin & Louisburg, ten miles; and the Hillsboro, ten miles. These are in good condition and afford excellent means of transit from one part of the county to another. Instead of the civil districts, as now represented, the county previous to 1834 was separated into militia companies, and over each company was a captain appointed by the county court and for each captain's company was appointed a tax lister. The county was at first divided into three divisions. The listers for these divisions were Daniel Perkins, James Scurlock and Chapman White. In 1801 the divisions had increased to the companies of Capts. Dooley, Nelson, Nolen, Crockett, Maney, Moore and McMay. The divisions for 1802 were Capts. Crockett, McMullen, Hall, Gordon, Hill, Morton, Cannon and Dooley; for 1803 there were Capts. Hill, Cannon, Morton, Crockett, McMullen, Kearney, Gordon, Dooley and Hall. In 1805 the officers were Capts. Nolen, Wilson, McEwen, Dooley, Ogilvie, Williams, Harden, Walker, Miller, Collins, Louis, Stone and Templer. The heads of companies in 1808 were Capts. Hargrave, McEwen, Templer, Mayfield, Stone, Neeley, Sparkman, Buford, Kelly, McKay, Harden, Fitzpatrick, Ogilvie, Wilson, Nolen, M. Johnson and William Johnson. In 1810 there were Capts. Shannon, Stone, Estes, Sparkman, McKay, Wartman, Cooke, Patton, Crawford, Park, Lawrence, Dunn, Robertson, Simmons, Buchanan, Edmuston, Neeley, Ralston and Clifton. The officers in 1815 were Capts. Gantt, Simpson, Auglin, Dalton, Wells, Carson, Hooker, Ridley, Mebaner, McCory, Johnson, Madden and Reeves. These went on increasing as population increased. In 1822 there were Capts. Johnson, Hill, Peper, Dancey, McEwen, Thompson, Bate, Orman, Stacey, Bateman, Garrett, Culbert, Fox, Stanfield, Hall, McLain, Stanford, Munn, Brooks, Timberville, Webb, Price and Boyd. The captains in 1834 were Whitfield, Childress, Foster, Atkison, Porter, Manley, Peach, Williamson, Fleming, McMannis, Fox, Adams, McEwen, Thomas, Matthews, Wallace, Jones, Crockett, Joice, Hampson, Perkins, Shannon, Jackson, Warren, Pickard, Shepard, Hill and Nicholson.

Under the new constitution the divisions were numbered according to the ordinal numbers, viz.: First, Second, Third, and so on to Twenty-fifth. The justices presiding in 1836, when the new constitution went into force, were: No 1, Frederick Ivy; No. 2, Thomas Powell; No. 3, O. D. Moffitt: No. 4, Joseph Burnett; No. 5, I. W. Briggs; No. 6, R. A. Hunt; No. 7, J. S. Breathitt; No. 8, John J. McKay; No. 9, Holland White; No. 10, George Lang; No. 11, Daniel Baughn; No. 12, William Crutcher; No. 13, Mike Kinnard; No. 14, G. W. Hunt; No. 15, Horatio McNish; No. 16, J. A. Holland; No. 17, James Andrews; No. 18, John Bostich; No. 19, R. W. Robinson; No. 20, M. Marable; No. 21, J. W. M. Hill; No. 22, John Hall; No. 23, J. W. Carson; No. 24, John Richardson; No. 25, S. B. Robinson. The work of the division of the districts was not reported to the court till February 4, 1836. The following persons were designated by the General Assembly for laying off the county into districts of convenient size: Richard Hill, James W. Carson, Isaac Ivy, Michael Kinnard and John L. McEwen. The commissioners, before proceeding to make the division, qualified before Gilbert Marshall, a justice of the peace in Williamson County. The committee found that the county contained 3,000 voters, and on that basis divided the county into twenty-five districts. After making the divisions the commissioners designated the following as the places of election in the respective districts: John Graham's, in No. 1; Thompson Davis', in No. 2; John Adams', in Hillsboro, in No. 3; Joseph Yates', at the Sulphur Springs, in No. 4; James Southall's, in No. 5; Robert Hill's, in No, 6; William Leaton's, in No. 7; Mrs. Gracy Goff's, in No. 8; court house, in No. 9; Douglass' Camp Ground, in No. 10; M. M. Andrews', at Pinkney's postoffice, in No. 11; Horton's Camp Ground, in No. 12; Andrew Campbell's, at "Snatchett," in No. 13; Mrs. Holland Davis', in No. 14; Alexander Smith's, in No. 15; John M. Winstead's, in No. 16; Sutherland M. Camp's, in No. 17; H. P. Bostick's, in No. 18; Jason Winsett's, in No. 19; Dr. William S. Webb's, in No. 20; William Munbreun's, in No. 21; Isaac Smith's, in No. 22; Chestly William's, in Manchester, in No. 23; Allen N. McCord's, in No. 24; and Robertson & Ransom's, in Versailles, in No. 25. The number of districts changed from time to time to suit the varying population, the whims, or the conveniences of the people. The boundary lines have been frequently changed. The number of districts was first twenty-five; in 1864 the number was twenty-three, and in 1865 it was raised to twenty-four, at which it remained till 1869, when it was reduced to twenty-two, at which it has since remained.

The court of pleas and quarter sessions was established February 26, 1799, while the General Assembly was in session at Knoxville. The court first met on the first Monday in February, 1800, at the house of Thomas McKay in the town of Franklin. The court continued to meet here till November 3, 1800, when the session was opened in the courthouse. The first justices holding court were John Johnson, Sr., James Buford, James Scurlock, Chapman White and Daniel Perkins. James Scurlock, who had previously qualified before a justice of Davidson County, proceeded to administer the oath to the others. The court organized by electing Scurlock chairman, but after the organization he resigned, and was succeeded by Chapman White. The court then proceeded to elect a clerk, when N. P. Hardeman was chosen and gave bond in the sum of $5,000. Edmund Hall was chosen the first sheriff, and gave bond in the sum of $10,000. Chapman White was made register; Francis Hall, solicitor; Joseph Porter, ranger; Joel Williams and John Harness were chosen constables; Henry Rutherford was made first surveyor; William White, William Ashton and David Logan were made "searchers or patrolers" from Parrish's mill dam; Big Harpeth to the mouth of West Harpeth; thence up to the dividing ridge; Ed Ragsdale and Spencer Buford for the remaining part of the county.

The following constituted the first jury: James Scott, Samuel McCutchen, Samuel Edmunson, Ephraim Brown, James Hopkins, Richard Hightower, Andrew Goff, James Neeley, George Neeley, Joseph Parke, Thomas McKay, George Stringham, William Edmunson, Henry Walker, Isaac Baleman, Reuben Parke, Joseph Stevens, James McComico, Peter Edwards, Samuel McCrary, David McKinney and Henry Childress. The jury for the superior court of the Mero District consisted of Henry Rutherford, David McEwen, Thomas McKay, Abram Maury and Richard Hightower. The tax listers were Daniel Perkins, who had that territory "north of the dividing line between Big and Little Harpeth, thence up Little Harpeth to Richard Hightower's and the Davidson County line," James Scurlock all "east of the commissioner's trace" and Chapman White "all west of the commissioner's trace." Patrick McCutchen appeared the first day and recorded his stock mark as a "crop and slit in the right ear and a half under crop in the left." William Marshall had an "underbit in each ear." The first State case was the State *vs.* David McEwen, for which the grand jury returned a "true bill," but on May 6, 1800, the case was marked "presentment quashed." In May, 1800, Seth Lewis, Jessee Wharten, Joseph Herndon and John Dickinson were admitted as attorneys, and John McNutt was made solicitor *pro tem*. On November 3, 1800, Frances Hall offered his resignation as solicitor, and Joseph Herndon was appointed in his place. Edmund Hall also resigned his office as sheriff, and Henry Childress was appointed in his place. The court allowed Hall $30 for *ex officio* services as sheriff. Bennet Searcy, who became circuit judge a short time after, was admitted before the Williamson bar in February, 1801, and William Smith at a little later date. Henry Rutherford was allowed $24 for running the line between Williamson and Davidson Counties. In 1803 Parry W. Humphreys and G. W. L. Manns became attorneys, and Thomas Stewart, who became the first circuit judge, resigned as solicitor, and was succeeded by Peter R. Booker. Mr. Booker soon after moved to Columbia, and finally quit practice for business. In 1807 there was a trial before the county court of Nelly, a slave of Mr. K. Holcomb, for the murder of her child. The jury was composed of James Hicks, Sion Hunt, Thomas W. Stockett (a justice and owner of slaves), John Johnston, Robert Caruthers, John Soppington and David Justice, owner of slaves. The jury found her guilty as charged in the indictment, and ordered that she should be remanded to jail till Friday, March 20, 1807, when she should be taken to some convenient place near the town of Franklin, "with a good and sufficient rope hung by the neck until dead, dead, dead, and may the Lord have mercy on her." A motion for an appeal was overruled. Felix Grundy and Thomas H. Benton first appear on the records here as attorneys. From 1808 to 1811 or 1812, the name of Benton is connected with more cases than any other lawyer. In 1808 Henry Martin was indicted for stealing, but found not guilty as to the charge, but was fined the cost of the prosecution. At the April term, 1810, L. P. Montgomery, I. Johnston and J. W. Eaton were admitted as attorneys, and Jacob Garrett was fined $10 for improper conduct and "treating the court contemptibly."

The circuit court was authorized by an act of the General Assembly November 16, 1809, entitled an act establishing a circuit court and a supreme court of errors and appeals. By order of the General Assembly of November 14, 1811, Thomas Stuart became judge of the Fourth Judicial Circuit of "law and equity." By the same act the judge was compelled to be a resident within his circuit. Judge Stuart received the oath of office before Justice Robertson in the court house in Nashville. Judge Stuart, the well-known judge and accomplished scholar, was a resident of Williamson County near Franklin. He served from the organization of the court till 1836. The officers of the court were William Hulme, sheriff; William Smith, clerk, with Felix Grundy, R. B. Sappington, Thomas Smith and Henry Childress, as bondsmen. Alfred Balch was the first solicitor before this court. The following attorneys appeared and took the oath on March 24, 1810: Felix Grundy, T. H. Benton, Peter R. Booker, John Reed and Nicholas Perkins. The court announced this rule, "that on the first day the trial of issues should be proceeded with as they appear on the docket and are called, and on the second day suitors shall be compelled to try or continue all issues at law except cases of ejectment." The sheriff returned the following as the regular jury panel: Jacob Garrett, John Witherspoon, Henry Cook, Daniel Perkins, Thomas McEwen, Sion Hunt, George Hulme, Sherwood Greer, Nicholas Scales, John H. Eaton, James Bruff, Archibald Lytle, Newton Cannon, John Bostick, James Allison, Guilford Dudley, Burwell Temple, John Crawford, William Neeley, David Dickson, Stephen Childress, Samuel Perkins, William Bond, Richard Hightower, Berry Nolen, Charles Boyles, Hendley Stone, Thomas Alexander, John Wilson, Samuel Morton, Thomas Simmons, William Anthony, R. P. Currin, Thomas Wilson, Collin McDaniel, Thomas Gooch, Thomas Garrett and N. T. Perkins. The following was the first grand jury: Stephen Childress, William Boyd, N. T. Perkins, Hendley Stone, James McEwen, Samuel Morton, Sr., Guilford Dudley, Sherwood Greer, William Anthony, Thomas Gooch, John Bostick, Sion Hunt, Archibald Lytle and David Perkins.

The first case tried on appeal was a suit of Thomas Talbott against John, Thomas and James Wilson and Robert and James Patton in a suit for debt for $3,200. The suit was begun in the county court on July 18, 1807. The plaintiff got judgment for $800. In November, 1810, Walter L. Fountain and John Hardeman were admitted as attorneys. The trial of David Magness, Perry Magness and Jonathan Magness for the murder of Patten Anderson was begun November 14, 1810. The jury was composed of Henry Cook, James Gideon, James Hicks, Samuel McCutchen, R. Parks, Andrew Goff, Robert McLellan, Thomas Ridley, James Hartgrove, R. Puckett, Tom Berry and Thomas Walker. The jury found David Magness not guilty of "wilful murder," but guilty of "malicious slaying," and for sentence ordered that he should be branded in the left hand with the letter "M," and to lay in jail till costs of suit were paid. At the first term of 1811, Nathaniel W. Williams appeared as judge by "mutual agreement" with Judge Stuart. W. W. Cook and J. Haskell became attorneys before the bar on May 2, 1811. Joseph Venable was charged with "feloniously stealing, taking and carrying away" from Samuel Rodgers twelve Spanish milled dollars of the value of twelve dollars current cash of the United States, and one-fourth of a milled dollar of the value of 25 cents. He was found "not guilty" of the above amount, but was found guilty of taking one-half dime of the value of 5 cents, and for punishment received ten lashes on the bare back immediately. The first term of court in 1812 was opened by Judge Roane, and in 1813 by Judge John F. Jack. Thomas Moore brought suit against Thomas Miles for slander, and by a jury was awarded $75. Alfred Balch brought suit for the State against Samuel Roll for stealing a woolen great coat, who received for sentence twenty lashes upon the bare back.

At the November term Judge Bennett Searcy presided, and John Burkley and James Gordon made oath that they desired to become citizens of the United States. At the May term the court adopted the following rules: First. On the first day of each term trials shall be proceeded with as they stand on the docket, and are called, but no suitor shall be compelled to try or continue any suit of trespass or ejectment. Second. On the second day suitors shall be compelled to try or continue cases as they stand on the docket.

In 1816 Binkley Donaldson was arraigned for the murder of James Skelly, but was found guilty only of "feloniously slaying." He prayed the benefit of the clergy and was ordered to be brought before the bar of the court and branded with the letter "M" in the left hand. Martin Gurley and James Bramblet were convicted of horse stealing and received thirty-nine lashes upon the bare back, were branded "H. T.", and were compelled to stand in the pillory two hours each day for three days, were rendered infamous and sentenced to jail for six months. During the years 1817–19, Judges Nathaniel W. Welhams, Joseph McMinn and Jacob C. Isacks were upon the bench. John Hardeman was tried for horse stealing, but when brought before the court would not say anything, pretended that he could not talk. The court found that he acted in a "rude, vulgar and profane manner," and that his manner was not caused by the "visitation of God." He was ordered to be set in the pillory. The punishment did not seem very effective, as he still refused to talk. The first divorce suit was filed in 1821 by Sally Merrett against James Merritt; however the prayer of the plaintiff was not granted. April 14, 1823, John A. Murrell was fined $50 for "riot." John A. Murrell, James Murrell and William Murrell were bound in the sum of $200 to keep the peace, on the oath of Thomas Merritt. The former was also under indictment for horse stealing, which case was taken to Davidson County on a change of venue in 1827. This was the celebrated John A. Murrell, so well known as a thief, robber and murderer, but who turned an evangelist in his latter days. Indictments for "gaming" were first returned in February, 1825. At that time there were eighteen returned against Joel Childress, Archibald Smith, William Clark, Felix Staggs and others. Each were fined $5 and costs. The following is a list of attorneys practicing before the Williamson bar in 1825: N. P. Perkins, James H. Maney, R. C. Foster, N. P. Smith, C. S. Olmsted, Thomas Washington, Samuel Houston, Jesse Greer, James P. Clark, John Bell, Andrew Hays, Felix Grundy, P. H. Dailey, David Craighead, M. W. Campbell, A. P. Maney, William Thompson, William McGee, John Thompson, W. G.

Hunt, William Hadley, G. W. Campbell and G. S. Yerger. Previous to the passage of the "penitentiary law" in 1829, criminals were punished by branding or whipping rather than by fines and imprisonment. Joel Watkins was found guilty of feloniously slaying Aaron Curtis, and was branded with the letter "M." in the presence of the court. John Hart for horse stealing was given twenty lashes on the bare back "well laid on," branded in the hand with "H. T." ordered to stand in the pillory two hours for three days, given six months in jail, and be rendered infamous and pay costs of his prosecution. George Sandford was fined $250 for forgery, at the same time Daniel Crenshaw for stealing a "gray mare" from N. Woldridge received a similar punishment to Hart as above. John Walker was whipped and fined for counterfeiting. Warner Metcalf got the full penalty for horse stealing, including branding, pillory, jail, fine, whipping and rendering infamous. September 11, 1831, Francis Smith was sentenced to the penitentiary for two years for stealing a "dark colored surtout cloth coat, one fur hat and a branded handkerchief" of W. M. Wright. This was the first sentence to the penitentiary.

On October 12, 1830, the following agreement for deed to land was made between R. P. Currin, W. B. Lewis, Levi Colbert, James Colbert, George Colbert, James Brown, W. McGilvey, Isaac Alberson, "*To Keel Ka Ishto Ke yo Katubler, Ishtokecha Imme houl le tubbe Ishto ya tubbe Ah te Ko wa, In he yo, Chitubbe. Immo mo la Tubbe, Hush ta ta be, In no wa Ka che, Oh hd cubb, kin hi chi tubbe, Im mo la Subbe,*"* and J. M. McClish, representative of the Chickasaw nation of Indians. McClish lived at one of the fords of Duck River, and was a half-breed. McKilvey was also a half-breed. It is believed this record has never been disputed. The following attorneys were admitted at the dates mentioned: Thomas Hoge, February 18, 1831; John Mason, August, 1830; Alexander Hardin, August, 1831; Preston Hayes, February, 1832; John Marshall, 1832; Robert Weldon, August, 1831, and George Collinsworth, February, 22, 1833. J. W. Perkins was admitted February 10, 1834; Nicholas Perkins March 16, 1836; Charles Scott and Richard Hay, March 13, 1837.

The Legislature in the winter of 1835–36 made some changes in judicial circuits, in consequence of which Williamson became a part of the Sixth rather than the Fourth Circuit, and January 25, 1836, Judge William V. Brown appeared on the bench in place of Judge Stuart. Judge Brown remained on the bench till he was succeeded by Judge Thomas Maney in 1842. As a mark of an epoch in financial circles in 1838, there were twenty-five suits against individuals brought by the Union Bank of Tennessee, eighteen by the Planters' Bank and thirteen by the Union Bank. The attorneys between 1840 and 1850 were J. L. McEwen, P. G. S. Perkins, T. S. Foster, J. B. McEwen, William McAllister, Humphrey Marshall, R. C. Foster, David Campbell, Haynes, Hay, Murfree, Figures, Venable, Ewing, Nicholson, Alexander, Allen Reed and Fauntleroy.

In the earlier period of the bar the most distinguished men were Thomas H. Benton and John Bell. The latter was born February 18, 1797, and came to Franklin in 1816, and was sent to the State Senate in 1817, and was a presidential candidate in 1860. His popularity is shown by the fact that he carried the State by a handsome majority. Judge Thomas Stuart occupied the bench the remarkable period of twenty-seven years—1809 to 1836. For clearness of insight, liberality of construction and uprightness of decision he had few superiors. At a later date were such men as N. P. Smith, Nicholas Perkins, Peter N. Smith, Richard L. Andrews, Richard Alexander, R. W. H. Bostick, R. C. Foster ("Black Bob"), M. P. Gentry and Humphrey Marshall. In 1842 Thomas Many became circuit judge in place of Judge Brown, which position he held till 1854, when he was succeeded by Nathaniel Baxter. Among the lawyers immediately before the war were C. A. Harris, J. P. Campbell, E. Baxter, R. M. Ewing, M. L. McComico, E. T. Andrews, R. F. Hill, W. S. McLemore, E. C. Cook, J. B. McEwen, S. Venable, A. Ewing, David Campbell, J. Marshall, R. C. Foster and W. B. Bate; the latter, as attorney-general, resigned July 26, 1857, and was succeeded by W. S. McLemore. The last court before the war met March 10, 1862, with Judge Baxter in the chair, H. Hill, sheriff, and M. L. Andrews, clerk. The last jury called consisted of Zachariah Green, W. A. Rodgers, Matthew Meacham,

---

*These Chickasaw names are quoted *verbatim et literatim* from the records.

John Fitzgerald, L. J. Johnson, J. B. Gray, H. B. Temple, Thomas Brown, G. W. Armstrong, W. B. Hulme, Alexander Moss, W. A. McKay, John W. Miller, F. G. Ratcliff, M. H. Page, M. M. Andrews, William Jones, J. E. Tulloss, T. H. Oder, J. C. Owen, H. B. Fly, E. J. Green, C. S. Bostick, W. D. Patton, J. B. Lane and J. W. Neely. On April 4, 1863, Mark L. Andrews made this entry: "The Federal army being in possession of the court house, I was not able to open court." The first court after suspension by the war was opened by Judge M. M. Brien, who presented his certificate from Gov. Andrew Johnson on July 12, 1864. On July 31, 1871, very touching resolutions were offered on the death of Hon. S. S. House. The committee consisted of David Campbell, Jesse Wallace, J. B. McEwen, W. S. McLemore, H. H. Cook and T. S. Perkins. It is questionable if any bar and bench in the State has furnished more able or accomplished representation than that of Williamson County. Of the latter, the full measure has been filled by Judge W. S. McLemore and Chancellor W. S. Flemming.

A large number of the old settlers of the county took up military claims of grants made by North Carolina to her Revolutionary soldiers. It was of this element that the country was largely peopled. As late as 1832 the following Revolutionary pensioners were living in Williamson County: James Turner, William Watkins, Moses Lindsey, R. Graham, D. McMahon, Patrick Campbell, George Neeley, Robert Guthrie, Isaac Ferguson, John Andrews, Thomas Razius, Alex Lister, Charles Allen, Thomas Cook, Benjamin Ragsdale, David Jocy, George Hulme, Joseph Witherington, Roger Mallory, Robert Parrish, John Beavert, Jacob Grimmer, John Pearce, Henry Cook and William Kennedy.

In the Creek war of 1812-14 a call was made for troops to assemble at Nashville December 10, in addition to those that had been sent by way of Fayetteville. These men were to be transported down the river in boats. Owing to delay in procuring supplies and transportation the men did not embark till January 7. The entire force consisted of over 2,000 men. Col. John Coffee commanded a cavalry force of 670 men. Col. William Hall, of Sumner County, commanded one of the regiments, and Col. Thomas H. Benton, of Williamson, the other. The force amounted to 1,400 men. The cavalry went overland to Natchez. The detachments by water met the cavalry force at Natchez February 15, and both were held there by Gen. Wilkinson, awaiting orders, till March 4, when they were ordered home, as their services were not deemed necessary.

The Seminole war broke out in 1817; it was almost a continuance of the Creek war of a few years earlier. After some pretty severe fighting a treaty was made with the Indians at Moultrie Creek September 18, 1823, by the stipulations of which the Indians were to be restricted to a reservation. This treaty was never satisfactory to the Indians and difficulties occurred in 1828-29, and finally another treaty was made by Col. Gadsden at Payne's Landing, May 9, 1832, by which the Seminoles were to be set on a reservation with the Creeks. A difficulty occurred between Gen. Thompson and Osceola, a Seminole chief, for which Osceola was imprisoned in Fort King for six days. Burning with revenge Osceola waylaid Gen. Thompson near Fort King and killed him December 28, 1835. On the same day Maj. Dade, with over 100 men, was waylaid in the Wahoo Swamp and the entire party massacred. Pursuant to a call of the governor two regiments of troops were called for to serve against the Seminoles. One company was recruited from Williamson County, of which Joel A. Battle was chosen captain; the lieutenants were Gabriel Matlock and Hollingsworth. These men were enlisted for six months, and were attached to the Second Regiment. They were ordered to rendezvous at Fayetteville. The regiment was organized by the election of William Trousdale, colonel; J. C. Guild, lieutenant-colonel; Joseph Meadow, major of First Battalion, and William L. Washington, major of Second Battalion. Dr. D. Smith was made regimental surgeon, and J. P. Grundy became adjutant of the regiment. The Second Regiment was composed of the companies from Sumner, Smith, Wilson, Davidson, Robertson, Dickson and Williamson Counties. This regiment was brigaded with the First Regiment, under Col. J. B. Bedford. The brigade was commanded by Gen. Robert Armstrong. The command left Fayetteville July 4 for the seat of war. For a history of the campaign see another part of this volume.

The success of the Texans in gaining their independence, their sufferings and indignities at the hands of the Mexicans were such as to excite the deepest sympathy of the Americans. On the call for troops to fight the Mexicans the enthusiasm was unbounded. It became a question as to who should be permitted to go. Nearly every county had its political club at the opening of the war, and these largely volunteered their services. So many offered their services that only a portion could be accepted. The Bethesda Clay Guards not only offered their services, but also to furnish their own horses. But few of these were accepted. Those who were received were mustered into service at Franklin by Gen. Bradley. Only about a half dozen men went; of these Moses Carter, now living in Franklin, was one. Only one or two more are still living.

On the issues of 1860 the people were almost a unit for the maintenance of the integrity of the Union. The presidential vote in 1860 was 797 for Breckenridge; 1,587 for Bell, and 32 for Douglass. The vote clearly indicates the feeling of the people at that time. A meeting was called for December 28, 1860, to be held January 11, 1861, to take into consideration the state of the Union. This was called for by W. L. McComico, S. H. Barley and J. A. McNutt. The committee on resolutions consisted of A. W. Moss, J. J. Fogg, S. S. House, W. L. Huff, N. J. Haynes, J. W. Neely and S. H. Barley. The meeting expressed great love for the Union, thought the South had great cause for complaint, but did not believe in secession, and resolved that on the following day the stars and stripes should be unfurled from the summit of the court house. Flags were brought forth at different parts of the county. The Franklin *Review and Journal* in speaking of the action of the people of South Carolina in passing ordinances of secession, said: "They have been taught to hate the Union. If every demand was granted they would not willingly return to the Union. * * * They ask us to follow them like sheep follow their leader, but we must not suffer them to drag us out of the Union."

The country was rapidly drifting into war, and the county, true to its teachings, was soon prepared to follow the fortunes of the State. By an act of the special session of the Legislature in April, 1861, the county court met May 20, and made a levy of 4¼ cents on each $100 for a relief fund for the families of volunteer soldiers. The justices, by unanimous voice, agreed to give their own *per diem* till January following for the same cause. The county judge was ordered to issue script to be sold to the Planters' Bank of Franklin for cash to be used for the immediate relief of families. The home guards were organized in the various districts, John M. Winstead being chosen general commanding.

The first regularly organized body of troops from Williamson County was the Williamson Greys. This body constituted Company D, of the First Tennessee. This regiment was composed of Companies A, B, C, E and F, of Nashville; Companies G and H, of Maury; I, of Rutherford, and K, of Giles. The regiment was organized at Nashville, Tenn., May 2, 1861, by electing George Maney, colonel; T. F. Sevier, lieutenant-colonel; A. M. Looney, major; R. B. Snowden, adjutant; W. L. Nichol, surgeon; J. B. Buist, assistant surgeon; S. H. Ransom, assistant quartermaster, and George W. Menees, assistant commissary surgeon. After organizing the regiment was ordered into Camp Harris at Allisona; here it remained a short time and was then sent to Camp Cheatham, in Robertson County. The regiment spent some time in drill and was then ordered to West Virginia. It served under Gens. Lee and Loring till December, 1861, when it was sent to Winchester to report to Stonewall Jackson. The regiment was ordered to Knoxville February 2, 1862, and soon after was ordered to Corinth, where it arrived in time to take part in the battle of Shiloh. The regiment was in the campaign through Kentucky and in fact in all the important engagements in Tennessee and the Atlanta campaign. Company D was commanded by Capt. James P. Hanna. In April, after the battle of Shiloh, Lieut. John L. House became major, and Lieut. Oscar Adkison became captain. The roll of honor of Company D, as far as is known, consists of William R. Hughes, McNairy J. Thompson, William B. Campbell and Thomas A. Anthony; all killed October 8, 1862, at Perryville, Ky. A complete history of the First Tennessee is given elsewhere in this volume.

Company E, of the Third Regiment was partially made up in Williamson County. The officers of this company consisted of N. F. Cheairs, captain; H. P. Pointer, first lieutenant; Campbell Brown, second lieutenant; Thomas Tucker, third lieutenant. The regiment was organized at Lynnville, Giles County, May 16, 1861. The roll of honor of Company E consists of W. T. Chatman, killed at Fort Donelson February 13, 1862; T. M. Golden, died in prison April, 1862; W. J. L. Johnson, died at Bowling Green; M. V. Sharp, died at Camp Trousdale; J. T. Thompson and W. W. White died at Camp Douglass; J. T. Lamb, died at Nashville in October, 1861, and W. A. Polk, killed at Shiloh. (See State History for sketch of the Third Regiment.)

Battle's regiment, the Twentieth, was organized at Camp Trousdale in the early part of June, 1861. The regimental officers from Williamson County were Moses B. Carter, lieutenant-colonel; Dr. D. B. Cliff, surgeon; John Marshall, quartermaster; Alex Winn, adjutant; John Edmonson, chaplain, and E. L. Jordan, wagon-master. Company B of the Twentieth was recruited at Nolensville and vicinity. The first officers were Joel A. Battle, captain; W. M. Clark, first lieutenant; T. B. Smith, second lieutenant; W. H. Mathews, third lieutenant. On the election of Battle to the colonelcy Lieut. Clark was chosen captain. In 1862 Capt. Clark was made regimental surgeon on the capture of Dr. D. B. Cliff. At the appointment of Capt. Clark, T. B. Smith became captain. He afterward rose to the rank of brigadier-general, and was wounded in the head by a sabre stroke after he had surrendered at the battle of Nashville. From the effects of this wound he became insane. In May, 1862, Orderly Sergt. J. F. Guthrie was elected captain, who was soon after made major, and was killed at Jonesboro, Ga., August 31, 1864. The roll of honor of Company B was Eugene Street, N. M. Johnson, D. G. King and J. G. Nevins killed at Chickamauga; Robert Peel and William Kellom, at Murfreesboro; W. S. Battle, at Shiloh; George Keith, at Fishing Creek; W. A. Hay, at Baton Rouge, and N. C. Peay, at Dalton, Ga. Those who died of disease were G. A. Jenkins, William McClarion, B. Poke, J. H. Potts, J. N. Potts and Robert Walden. It should have been stated that on the reorganization C. S. Johnson was elected first lieutenant; W. J. Murray, second lieutenant, and T. C. Williams, third lieutenant. On the promotion of Capt. Guthrie, Johnson became captain; McMurray, first lieutenant, and Williams, second lieutenant; also George Pea became lieutenant near the close of the war. The company roll showed 153 men enrolled from first to last, and only seven men at the surrender at Greensboro, N. C. Company D. was made up in the vicinity of Triune and College Grove. The officers of this company were William P. Rucker, captain; Fred Claybrook, first lieutenant; —— Pinkston, second lieutenant, and A. Hatcher, third lieutenant. Capt. Rucker resigned, but went out again and was killed in Forrest's attack on Fort Donelson in 1863. Lieut. Claybrook was elected captain, and soon after became major, but was killed at Horses Gap. P. G. Smithson was next made captain. The dead of this company were A. B. Gee, J. G. Crutcher, J. W. P. Kent, G. H. Murray, J. M. Smith, B. W. Yeargin, J. B. Buckman, E. A. Austin, T. P. Couch, W. J. Collett, W. R. Hall, W. H. Merritt, C. R. Moxly, E. T. Pinkston, H. H. Russell, D. T. J. Woods and J. H. Tucker. Company H was recruited in Franklin and vincinity. M. B. Carter was elected captain, but was promoted to lieutenant-colonel. F. De Graffenried then became captain. He was succeeded by N. W. Shy, who passed the grades of major, lieutenant-colonel to colonel, and was killed at Nashville. Thomas Caruthers was next chosen captain, and served till the close of the war. Company H lost J. L. Andrews, Benjamin Armstrong, Daniel Butt, J. S. McAllister, J. G. Boyd, W. E. Boyd, J. H. Alexander, F. M. Andrews, N. J. Davis, E. T. Edney, K. S. Edney, B. M. Givens, H. P. Harrison, F. D. Ham, H. King, W. C. Prichard, Thomas Puett, J. D. Prichard, T. J. Sellers, Thomas Talley, F. A. Truett, W. E. King, A. W. Ivy, C. N. Shelton, H. Sawyers, T. W. Stephens, N. Newcomb, J. T. White, F. Wray and T. J. York. A complete history of the Twentieth Regiment is given elsewhere.

The Thirty-second Regiment, of which Capt. Ed C. Cook's company was a part, was organized in 1861. The company left Franklin October 14, 1861, for Nashville. The officers of the company were Ed C. Cook, captain; Jake Morton, first lieutenant; R. F.

McCaul, second lieutenant, and Thomas Banks, third lieutenant. The regimental officers of this regiment were E. C. Cook, colonel; William P. Moore, lieutenant-colonel; W. J. Brownlow, major; Calvin Jones, adjutant; John T. Shepard, quartermaster; James F. Grant, surgeon; James F. Finley, chaplain. A sketch of this regiment is given in another part of this work.

A company was raised in Williamson County for Holman's battalion by Capt. Jacob T. Martin in August, 1862. The company consisted of 140 men. The commissioned officers were J. T. Martin, captain; Thomas Banks, first lieutenant; David S. Chaney, second lieutenant; A. S. Chapman, third lieutenant. The battalion consisted of four companies and was organized at Columbia October 15, 1862, by Maj. D. W. Holman. The battalion after drilling for a time was attached to Gen. Wheeler's command.

Capt. Thomas F. Perkins, a youth of eighteen, entered the service in June, 1861. He became first lieutenant of a battery, and did good service at Fort Donelson, where the command was captured. Capt. Perkins made his escape and returned to Williamson County, where, in July, 1862, he raised a company of cavalry consisting of sixty-five men. This became Company I of Douglass' battalion. The commissioned officers of this company were Thomas F. Perkins, captain; John C. Bostick, first lieutenant; Richard Clouston, second lieutenant; Malachi Kirby, third lieutenant. February 20, 1863, Holman's and Douglass' battalions were consolidated, and became the Eleventh Tennessee Cavalry. The history of these two bodies is given under that regiment.

Company G of the Third Cavalry was organized May 25, 1862, and mustered into the Confederate service May 26. The officers of this company at the organization consisted of James W. Starnes, captain; W. S. McLemore, first lieutenant; Thomas Allison, second lieutenant; G. Harris, third lieutenant. This regiment was a part of Dibrell's brigade of Wheeler's cavalry corps. Company G left for the front October 10. Other companies, as organized, were the following: Light Dragoons, William Ewing, captain; Burke Bond, first lieutenant; T. S. House, second lieutenant. Capt. J. W. Hill's company, of which J. T. Wilson was first lieutenant; Samuel Lea, second lieutenant, and W. T. Wade, third lieutenant. Capt. John A. Wilson's company, of which N. H. Lamb was first lieutenant; John A. Cathey, second lieutenant, and W. J. White, third lieutenant.

For generations to come Franklin will be pointed out as the place of a terrible conflict on November 30, 1864, between the Confederate forces under Gen. John C. Hood, and the Federals under Gen. Schofield. The Federals were composed of the Fourth and a part of the Twenty-third corps, the former commanded by Gen. Stanley and the latter by Schofield. Schofield, being the senior officer, gave directions to the whole command. The object of the Federals was to fall back as slowly as possible so as to give Thomas time to concentrate his forces at Nashville. The object of Hood in forcing the Federals to a stand was to defeat them in detail—Schofield first and Thomas last. Hood's army was composed of the corps of Lieut.-Gens. Lee and Stewart and the corps of Maj.-Gen. Cheatham. The Federal Army had arrived on the night of the 29th and on the 30th, and being so hard pressed were compelled to give battle to save their trains. The Big Harpeth makes a bend around Franklin in the shape of a horseshoe, and from point to point of this the Federals had thrown up hastily constructed but very strong works and well covered by artillery.

Hood's lines were arranged with Stewart's Corps on the right, Cheatham's on the left and the cavalry under Forrest on the flanks, the main body, however, being under Forrest in person on the right. Only a portion of Lee's corps became engaged; that of Johnson's division on the left.

According to Hood's own words his orders were "to drive the enemy at the point of the bayonet into and across the Big Harpeth River, while, if successful, Gen. Forrest was to cross the river and attack and destroy his trains and broken columns." At 4 P. M. the lines advanced to the attack. Hardly in the annals of military pageantry was a sight more grand than the steady march of these hostile columns. The Federal outposts quickly fell back to their main line. Here with them it was a question of life or death. The advancing columns were soon met by a storm of shot and shell—grape and cannister and musketry, the roar of which seemed to make the earth itself tremble. The conflict was of the most desperate character and became hand to hand; columns driven back reeling and staggering only went to return, if possible, with more desperation. From 4 P. M. till late at night the battle raged. When the morning sun arose, it found the Confederates masters of the gory field. In evidence of the terrible conflict it may be said that Hood's report shows his loss to have been about 4,500. Among the killed or mortally wounded, were Maj.-Gen. P. R. Cleburne, Brig.-Gens. Strahl, Carter, Granbury and John Adams; while Maj.-Gen. Brown, Brig.-Gens. Manigault, Quarles, Cockrell and Scott were wounded and Brig.-Gen. Gordon was captured. Although nearly a quarter of a century has passed since the conflict, many marks are still visible. Between 2,600 and 2,700 Confederates are sleeping in the Confederate cemetery near the scene of this conflict.

On the organization of Williamson County, in 1799, the Legislature appointed a board of town commissioners consisting of Samuel Crockett, Charles McAllister, David Figures, John Sappington and E. Cameron, whose duty it was to select a site for a county seat to be called Franklin; to procure a tract of land for that purpose either by purchase or donation. It was their duty to erect a court house, jail and stocks. The Public Square, consisting of two acres, was donated to the commissioners by Peter Perkins, on condition that the county seat should be located at Franklin. The name was given to the place in honor of Dr. Benjamin Franklin. The town was surveyed and laid out in 1800 by Henry Rutherford, who was chosen county surveyor in February of that year. The plat consisted of between 100 and 200 lots. The most of the lands on which the city of Franklin now stands were entered by Abram Maury, who gave name to the sister county. Among the purchasers of lots in 1801 and 1803 were William Campbell, J. B. Porter, S. Moore, Thomas Harmon, Samuel McClary, Ephraim Brown, Robert Harmon, Ewen Cameron, William Smith, Samuel Chapman, Peter Edwards, James Hicks, Samuel Mitchell, Alexander Myers and John McKay.

The first house is said to have been built in Franklin in 1797 by Ewen Cameron. The court house, as stated elsewhere, was built in the spring and summer of 1800. Thomas McKay, at whose house the first court met, was a resident at that time. Other settlers followed in rapid succession. Benjamin White built an ordinary on the lot adjoining, where Mr. Gault now lives, in 1803. This old building still stands though in a very dilapidated condition. He with his sons became the owners of a tavern, wagon yard, wagon shop, blacksmith shop, butcher shop and gunsmith shop. Alexander Myers and Phillip Many obtained tavern license in 1803. Ordinaries or taverns were supposed to afford food, feed and drinks. The following were the rates established by the county courts: breakfast, dinner and supper, each 25 cents; one-half pint of whisky, 12½ cents; one-half pint of peach or apple brandy, 12½ cents; one-half pint of rum or gin, 37½ cents; one horse feed, 12½ cents. Other tavern keepers during the first decade were Henry Lyon and Stephen Barfield. The bridge across the Harpeth was sold by N. Scales, Thomas Edmundson, S. Green, R. Puckett, D. McEwen, James Boyd, S. Buford and George Hulme to W. Witherspoon, Jacob Gantt, John Witherspoon, Benjamin Nolen, Thomas McKinney and John Blackman on April 8, 1805. In 1820 the contract for paving the Public Square was let to Stephen Childress, John Watson and Hinchey Petway for $1,600. The money was raised by a levy on the county for $1,200, and on the town for $400 additional.

The act of incorporation passed the General Assembly October 9, 1815. The act reads as follows: "That the town of Franklin, in the county of Williamson, and the inhabitants thereof are hereby constituted a body politic and corporate by the name of the mayor and aldermen of the town of Franklin, and shall have perpetual succession, and by their corporate name may sue and be sued, * * * and may use a town seal." It was given power to employ night watches, establish streets, restrain gambling, regulate amusements, establish and regulate markets, fire companies, and other measures for the benefit of the town. The act provided for the election of mayor and aldermen and other town officers. The following are given as the limits as included in the charter: "Beginning in the center of the old Natchez road where a small branch crosses the same, about 150 yards from the margin of said town; thence in a direct line to Big Harpeth River, so as to include the house where Nicholas Perkins, Jr., now lives; thence down the middle of said river with its meanders to the mouth of Sharp's branch; thence up said branch until it receives another small stream on the east side; thence up that small branch to the beginning; provided that no land or lots of ground included within the above described bounds shall be subject to pay a greater tax to said corporation, etc., etc." Amendments were made to the charter in 1833, in 1836, in 1837 and in 1852. The by-laws of Franklin were passed in 1828 while Nicholas Perkins was mayor and Thomas B. White was recorder. Many of these have since become inoperative, and many have been repealed. Among the many laws passed was one requiring every owner of a private house, storeroom or office to procure a leather bucket sufficient to hold two gallons of water; the same was to have the owner's name placed thereon, and to be hung in a convenient place for use in case of fire. All free male inhabitants in the city under the age of fifty-five were organized into a fire company, under the command of a captain and four masters.

From a copy of the *Western Weekly Review*, published in 1831, the following business cards are found. G. W. Neeley had a cabinet shop at the north end of Main cross street near Perkin's tan-yard. James C. Karr also had a cabinet shop two doors above the Franklin Inn. This inn was what is now the Elliott House; this was kept by T. L. Robinson. A boot and shoe store was kept by A. C. C. Carter, father of Moscow Carter. Hugh Duff was a painter and glazier; he was noted for his wit, and "was a fellow of infinite jest." William Cayce kept a jewelry store on Main Street. John E. Gadsey and Phillip A. Yancey each were carpenters and joiners. The female school was taught by Mrs. Moore. The corporation school and Harpeth Academy were managed by Rev. J. H. Otey and J. A. M. E. Stuart. Tailor shops were managed by William Anderson and Peter W. Crouch, Porter & Haffey, Samuel L. Graham and John S. Allen. A book store was kept by J. H. McMahan and J. Hogan, Jr. The Franklin Hotel was kept by Mrs. Smith, and the "Old Bell Tavern" by Thomas Miller & Co. General stores were kept by H. P. Bostick, McComico & Hamner, Joseph W. Baughn & Co., B. S. & E. S. Tappan and C. G. Olmsted. A music store was kept by John D. McAllister, a tin and coppersmith shop by S. N. Sharp, and a grocery store by M. C. Cayce. Perkin & White kept hardware and cutlery. The leading blacksmiths were S. Vaughn and G. W. Lane. The fire company was under command of Thomas Park. An ordinance was passed excusing firemen from militia duty. The Independent Blues was a militia company of Franklin for many years of which company E. S. Tappan was captain and James Park orderly sergeant. This company took part in the reception given to Gen. Lafayette on his visit to Nashville. Before this time there had been a blue dye factory owned by Alexander McCowen. The name of this has been perpetuated in Indigo Street. There had also been a nail factory, but this closed operations about 1820, and a brewery kept by the Daws Bros. The following attorneys were living in Franklin at this time: G. W. & R. C. Foster, John Marshall, P. N. & N. E. Smith, G. W. Campbell, John Bell, J. S. Jones, N. P. Perkins, J. Swanson, C. A. Harney and W. H. Wharton. It is shown by record that in 1835 Franklin contained a population of 1,500; academies, 2 female and 3 male; 4 churches; 3 clergymen; 8 physicians; 7 lawyers; 4 taverns; 5 blacksmith shops; 6 bricklayers; 10 carpenters; 1 cabinet workman; 1 gunsmith; 2 hatters; 3 saddlers; 4 shoe-makers; 3 silversmiths; 3 tailors; 2 tanners; 1 tinner; 2 wagoners and 13 merchants. On January 1, 1815, a contract was entered into between John Sample, Robert P. Currin and Hinchey Petway, by which they purchased of Henry Cook twelve acres of land on the east side of Big Harpeth, upon which they erected a factory for the manufacture of cotton-bagging, etc.

By an act of Legislature, October 21, 1831, a lottery was chartered at Franklin for the purpose of buying a town block. There were 2,024 tickets, which were to be sold at $5, making a total sum of $10,120. The capital prize was $2,000. The committee on management was composed of R. P. Currin, Thomas Hardeman, C. G. Olmsted and E. Breathitt. The tickets were put on sale at Hogan & McMahon's book store. The fond hopes of the citizens were never realized, as the lottery did not prove a success. Races at the Fairview Course, owned by John Sweeny, in 1831, drew out the following horses on the first day: Mr. Meek's Dart, Mr. Pankey's Division, Mr. Rice's filley Conqueror; the second day there were Pankey's Nelly-hoe; Peeple's Graytail, Sneed's Rappahannock and Thweatt's gelding. The sweepstakes premium was $200. There was also a sweepstakes premium for two-year-olds of twenty barrels of corn. On July 4, 1831, there was a celebration at Reader's Spring. The committee of arrangements was composed of J. Park, W. H. Crouch, B. R. White, P. Perkins J. Moore and A. McGan. Among the prominent men living in Franklin at that time were Newton Cannon, W. G. Childress, Thomas Hardeman, Nicholas Perkins, Abram Maury, William Martin, Christopher McEwen and John L. McEwen.

The principal business men between 1840-50 were: Dry goods stores—J. W. Baughn, J. H. Otey, George Seabright and A. & W. Park. Drugs—McPhailt & English. Boot and shoe store—Brown & Littleton. Carriages—H. Eelbeck and R. G. Richardson. Blacksmiths—Brock & Cody. Physicians—Drs. S. S. and A. J. Mayfield, R. Glass, Reid & Perkins and Dr. Crockett. Business men from 1850 to 1860: Dry goods—Horten & Carl, J. R. Hunter, L. F. Beech, House & Bro., Snyder & Frizzell, Shanner, Broham & Co. Drug store—F. S. Wooldridge. Merchant tailors—Cummings & Byers, A. W. Moss, Hyeronemus & Craig. Livery stables—J. K. & C. R. Richardson, Neely & Haynes. Grocery stores—S. H. Bailey, J. M. Casey. Carriage shop—W. G. D. Boehms. Furniture—R. H. Teal & Toon. Iron works—John Pugh, T. P. Pugh & C. B. Beech. Produce dealers—Beale & Toon, Spencer, McCoy & Co. and M. S. Royce. Book store—Thomas Parkes. Cabinet shop—Courtney & Karr. Business men immediately following the war: Dry goods—Joe Frankland & Co., M. Kaufman, J. M. Graverly, J. G. Bliss, T. L. Owen and J. & M. House. Drug Stores—W. G. Clouster, Crutcher & Handy. Groceries, harness, etc., etc.—A. C. Vaughn, J. L. Parkes, Bostick, Moreley & Rozell. Groceries—J. J. Puryear & R. R. Hightower, Cook & Westerfiel. Tinware—James Merrill. Furniture—J. C. Karr.

The present business is as follows: Dry goods and general stores—Smithson, Kennedy Haynes & Co., Theo. Owen, Neely & Campbell, Joseph Frankland, Frank Adle, A. Thorner and Julius Dietrich. Groceries—Reynolds & Wilson, J. W. Bennett, Will Cody, F. Eelbeck, Newton Cannon, John Atwood, Hearn & Haynes, Ed Haynes and Mrs. John Morton. Drug Stores—Beech & Son, Thomas Burus and — White. Agricultural implements—C. V. Holdeman & Co. and W. A. Johnson & Co. Harness, Saddlery, etc.—A. J. Dennis & Co. and James Russell. Book store—Emma Eddy. Livery stables—Vaughn & Son, John Blackburn and Charles Moss. Hotels—Parrish House and Elliott House. Flouring-mills—The mill owned by J. B. Lillie, built in 1870 at the head of Main Street, was built at a cost of about $50,000, and has a capacity of about 300 barrels per day; the Atlas Mills were built in 1882 by Hamilton, Vaugh & Turley; the mill of Y. M. Rezer was built the same year.

A branch of the Union Bank of Tennessee was established in Franklin in 1832. The stock allowed for the bank was $200,000. To give an estimate of the amount of business done by this bank in its early history it is shown that March 4, 1835, there were discounted $26,000, and more that $80,000 were offered. This bank continued in operation till it was closed by the operations of the war. The First National Bank of Franklin, the only banking concern in the place, is on a good financial basis and is well managed.

Hiram Lodge, No. 7, F. & A. M., was originally Lodge No. 55, and was instituted under the Grand Lodge of North Carolina. Authority was granted by Robert Williams, Grand Master of the Grand Lodge of North Carolina and Tennessee of Ancient York Masons. The delegates to the Grand Lodge, which met at Knoxville December 2, 1811, were Archibald Potter, Stephen Booker and John A. Rodgers. At this meeting a Grand Lodge for the State of Tennessee was organized, and Hiram Lodge, No. 55, now became Hiram Lodge, No. 7, of the Grand Lodge of Tennessee. The present lodge building was erected some time between 1818 and 1825. The commandery at Franklin is called DePayen, No. 11, and consists of thirteen members. Its officers are J. L. Parkes, E. C.; Altha Thomas,

G.; T. F. Perkins, C. G.; J. P. Hannes, P.; Burke Bond, S. W.; J. P. Hamilton, J. W.; D. B. Cliffe, Treas.; T. A. Pope, R.; J. H. Rolffs, S. B.; W. Jones, Sword B.; A. Truett, Warden; E. T. Wells, Sentinel; Altha Thomas, J. P. Hanner and J. L. Parkes, Past Commanders.

The date of the foundation of a paper in Franklin is a matter of some uncertainty. It was some time near 1820, but neither the exact date nor its founder is known. In 1831 the paper was called the *Western Weekly Review* and was owned by J. H. McMahan and J. Hogan, Jr. and was edited by Thomas Hoge, of East Tennessee. Soon after the now venerable Don Cameron became editor. In 1852 the name of the paper became *The Review and Journal*. Don Cameron sold the paper and N. J. Haynes and D. L. Balch with S. P. Hildreth, editor. In 1858 Edwin Paschall became editor for a very short time and was succeeded by Hildreth again. Judge W. S. McLemore was editor a short time in 1860 and to June 13, 1861, when Mr. Haynes became editor and proprietor. In 1865 it was owned by N. J. Haynes & Son and in 1870 by Haynes & Bro., with Burk Bond as editor. In a short time T. E. Haynes alone became editor and proprietor. In 1873 Haynes, Andrew & Co. became owners, with T. Dick Bullock as editor. Mr. Bullock was out for a time but returned again in 1876 when Haynes & Andrews became editors and proprietors. On accepting the postmastership under the present administration, Mr. T. E. Haynes retired from the paper and Mr. M. L. Andrews became sole manager. *The Review and Journal* is one of the oldest, if not the oldest paper in the State with an unbroken management. It has always been a clean, high-toned, consistent paper. It is well edited and is good authority on Democratic doctrines.

Thompson Station is located about seven miles south of Franklin, in District No. 4. It is the principal shipping point for that section of the county over the Louisville & Nashville Railroad. The place contains from 100 to 200 inhabitants. The station contains several stores, a cotton-gin and other business houses; also a Methodist and a Christian Church. Historically this place is known by several very severe engagements fought near it in the late war. Brentwood is a station on the Louisville & Nashville Railroad near the line between Williamson and Davidson Counties. It is beautifully situated and contains several business houses, a postoffice, shops and a Methodist Church. A severe skirmish was fought here in Hood's retreat from Nashville. Nolensville is situated on the head waters of Mill Creek in District No. 17. It was named in honor of one of the oldest families in the county. It is surrounded by an excellent farming country. Nolensville dates back in the thirties. The pike leading to Nashville from Nolensville was built in the latter part of the thirties and the beginning of the forties. Nolensville has a large number of business houses for a place of its size. It also has a graded school of three departments and a postoffice. There is an I. O. O. F. Lodge also a Masonic Lodge—a Blue Lodge and Chapter. Triune is the name of a neighboring postoffice in District No. 18. It is on the pike leading from Nolensville to College Grove. This is the seat of a church and has a consolidated school and a cotton gin near by. This place is situated near the head waters of Wilson's Creek, a tributary of the Big Harpeth. Near the corners of Districts Nos. 14, 18 and 20, is a postoffice called Arrington. On Big Harpeth, near the county line is situated College Grove. This has long been a pleasant neighborhood and the seat of an excellent school. It now contains a school of three departments, a Presbyterian and a Methodist Church. On Grove Creek in the same district is Jordan Store postoffice. In the southeast corner of the county, in District No. 22, is Reed's Store postoffice. Bethesda postoffice is situated near the center of District No. 12 in a thickly settled neighborhood. There has been a church at the place since 1839. There is also an academy and one or two business houses.

It is a matter of record that in 1836 Peytonsville was called Snatchett, or as the public now have it—Snatch. Its name originated in the fact, it is said, that one individual owed another $10, and the creditor being unable to collect the debt seized the opportune moment and snatched the money from the unsuspecting debtor. One of the first settlers at this place was Andrew Campbell. Peytonsville now contains one store, a postoffice and a blacksmith shop. It also contains a Methodist Church built in 1857, and a Christian Church of recent construction. There is also a Masonic hall, Lodge No. 337, F. & A. M.; other neighborhoods, points and postoffices are Williamsburg in the Fourth District; Boston postoffice, White Oak postoffice in the Second, and Leiper's Fork or Hillsboro postoffice in the Third. Hillsboro, or Hillsborough as formerly spelled, is an old settlement; James Adams was an early resident at that place. In the First are Christiana postoffice, Basin Springs postoffice and Smith's Springs; in the Fourth is West Harpeth and in the Seventh is Beechville.

Harpeth Academy was authorized by the General Assembly in 1807, under the laws passed for encouraging popular education. The trustees appointed for Harpeth were Abram Maury, Daniel Perkins, Nicholas T. Perkins, G. McComico, Albert Russell, Stephen Childress, William Neeley, Charles Bayles, Robert P. Currin and John Hardeman. The first steps toward building were taken in February, 1810, when the above trustees purchased eighty square poles from William McRay. This land lay between one and two miles from Franklin near the Ball estate. From its vicinity to Harpeth River it was called the Harpeth Academy. On November 4, 1817, an act was passed making not less than five trustees a quorum, and added to the number of trustees William Smith, Andrew Campbell, John Watson, John Bell and John White. The growth of Franklin brought about the necessity of greater facilities for schools and a desire to have the school nearer town. Accordingly Harpeth Academy was sold to Randel McGavack in 1823, and a new site purchased on Main Street consisting of ten acres of ground.

This building stood till it was destroyed by the soldiers during the war. Perhaps the most noted teacher in the early history of Harpeth was the Rev. Gideon Blackburn. Many distinguished educators taught in Harpeth; also many very distinguished sons of Williamson County were educated there.

Harpeth Union Female Academy was established in 1828. In that year a deed to the grounds was made by Newton Cannon to Samuel Perkins, W. S. Webb, T. D. Porter, John Bostick and Newton Cannon as trustees for the academy. This school was managed with success many years. In February, 1837, Lot No. 134 in Franklin was purchased and the foundation laid for the Franklin Female Academy.

The Franklin Female Institute was founded in ——, and was successfully managed till broken up by the war. This institution was founded as a stock concern and was managed by a board of trustees. It was mainly under the control of the Presbyterians. On the organization of the public schools under the present system the institute building became to be used as the public school building. These schools are under the management of Superintendent Wallace, who has brought them to a high state of proficiency. The average length of terms is ten months. A regular course is maintained and the graduates are well qualified for the various duties of life.

In 1848 Moses Cates sold a quantity of land to John Matheral, Joseph Daus, J. W. Allen and James Hardgrave for a house for a school and religious worship. This was on the Big Harpeth near William Armstrong's. A church and school was built on Murfree's Fork of Anderson's Big Spring at about the same time. This was built on the lands of John Pope and Samuel Akin. John Moore and James Patten were made trustees.

The first trustees of Owen Hill Female Academy were appointed November 22, 1850. They were William Burner, W. M. M. Huley, J. P. Allison, E. L. Jordan, J. B. Wilson, J. Jordan and G. C. Kinman. A public school was built on the lands of Thomas Buchanan, in 1848. The trustees were S. S. Bradley, F. W. Jordan and Robert Carothers. A schoolhouse was built on Nelson Creek in 1837. The first trustees appointed were Nelson Fields, G. Vernon, David Hampton, William Fields, Henry Jenkins and A. Carmichael.

College Grove was founded in 1861. It is still a very flourishing school. Its first trustees were W. Jordan, W. W. Healey, A. G. Scales, J. L. Casey and J. P. Allison.

The public school system as organized under the new constitution was put into operation in 1872. It was several years before their efficiency became very marked owing to a lack of schoolhouses and funds for paying teachers. Aside from private schools or schools disconnected with the public school system the schools of Williamson are divided into graded schools, consolidated schools and ungraded common schools. The graded school as here used means schools in which the teacher has succeeded in arranging pupils in classes with regard to their advancement and kinds of text-books without reference to the number of rooms in the building in which schools are taught. The ungraded schools are those in which the teacher has not succeeded in eliminating text-books of different kinds from the school, in consequence of which pupils pursue the same studies of the same advancement, but having different text-books require different classes. The consolidated schools are those in which the expenses of management are met by the public funds and by private subscription. The benefit derived from consolidated schools is that the school terms are made much longer. The most of the consolidated schools are incorporated under the "four mile law;" the result of which is that whisky is driven from the county except in incorporated towns. In the following schools three teachers are employed: Trinity, Nolensville, Owen's Station and College Grove. The following schools are consolidated schools: Trinity, Nolensville, College Grove, Owen's Station, Triune, Forest Hill, Hillsboro, Douglas Church, Mount Carmel, Perkins' School and Boyd's Mill School. From the superintendent's report for both 1884 and 1885 it is learned that the scholastic population in 1885 was male, white, 2,880; colored, 2,154; female, white, 2,764; colored, 2,076. Total scholastic population for 1884, 9,874. The same for 1885 shows males, white, 2,997; female, 2,790; colored, male, 2,245, female, 2,168. Total of both, 10,200. As a comparison the scholastic population for 1839, which of course did not include colored, was only 4,456. Out of the above enumeration the total enrollment of whites and colored for 1884 was 5,529, and the daily attendance was 3,376. The same item for 1885 shows an enrollment of 5,204, and a daily attendance of 3,444. The total number of white schools for 1884 were 51; colored, 20. The number for 1885 was 54 and 28, respectively. The total length of schools in days in 1884 was 108, and in 1885, as per report, 104. The total amount of funds expended for 1884 was $17,764.90; for 1885 it was $20,683.21. Of these amounts there was expended for teachers' salaries for 1884 $11,610.75, and in 1885 $13,557.35. The schools of Williamson County are growing in efficiency and favor.

The Tennessee Female College of Franklin was founded in 1856. One of the principal men engaged in establishing this school was John Marshall. A magnificent building was erected and able instructors were employed. The school soon took a high rank among the educational institutions of the land. The school has had a continuous and prosperous course except for a brief period. The school finally fell into the hands of Bishop Hargrove, of the Methodist Church. The buildings were recently purchased by Prof. Edgerton, who has been conducting a successful school in all the departments for the last year. In March, 1886, the beautiful buildings were consumed by fire, to the great misfortune of Prof. Edgerton and the community. The school was transferred to a large private house, where the school year was finished. The school for 1886 closed with the "Thirty-sixth Annual Commencement," at which nine young ladies were graduated. It is a pleasing fact to know that the arrangements have been consummated for the rebuilding of this institute, and it will again open for work in September, 1886.

The Baptist Church is believed to have been the first church organized in the county, as a record of Harpeth Baptist Church is found in 1803. It is claimed it was built in 1800. It is known to the public as Old Harpeth Church. Among the first members of this church were Andrew Goff and wife. This old church stood about four miles from Franklin. Liberty is the name of another Baptist Church in the county. This also was standing as early as 1803, and how much earlier is unknown. Owing to a division this very popular branch has been greatly weakened in this county. The division on the question of missions led to the two branches known as Old or Primitive Baptists and the Missionary Baptists. There was formerly a Baptist Church in the Perkins' neighborhood, but it no longer stands. The Baptist Church in Franklin was organized in 1839, and an excellent brick church erected in 1849. From lack of numbers preaching is not maintained regularly by this denomination.

The Presbyterian Church at Franklin was organized January 8, 1811, by Rev. Gideon Blackburn. The elders chosen at this time were Alexander White, Samuel Moore, E. Hamilton and Robert Harris. There were at that time forty-six lay members and an addition of seventeen was made the same year and thirty-seven in 1812. Dr. Blackburn remained in charge of the church except the interval of 1817 till 1824. In 1817 Rev. David Wise was called to the charge. The first report to Presbytery in 1813 showed a membership of ninety-three. Dr. Blackburn only gave from one-fourth to one-half his time to the church at Franklin. In 1818 Dr. Blackburn and Rev. J. T. Hamilton both worked on the charge. On the resignation of Dr. Blackburn his son, Rev. J. N. Blackburn, had charge of the church a number of years. In 1826 Rev. Rob Henderson was employed, who gave three-fourths of his time to the church at Franklin. In 1832 Rev. R. H. Lilly was employed; about this time there were twenty-six additions to the church. Rev. M. M. Marshall took charge in 1834 and remained till 1837, when he was succeeded by Rev. A. H. Desheil, who remained till 1840. In 1840 R. A. Garrison became pastor and served till 1843. The church at that time numbered 132 communicants. The following were the elders who for their long service are mentioned: A. Park, T. F. Adkison, William O'N. Perkins and Don Cameron. In 1843 Rev. A. N. Cunningham became pastor and served till 1858, when he was succeeded by Rev. Ira Morey, who resigned and died in 1864. Among the pastors Rev. Gideon Blackburn is, perhaps, best known. Many distinguished men as lay members here belonged to this church. Gilbert Marshall served as clerk of the session from 1824 to 1852. This church suffered the misfortunes of the war, and after the battle of Franklin this house was taken as a hospital by the Federals, during which time it was greatly damaged. The first pastor after the war was the Rev. W. L. Rosser. The first church built in the place was built by the Presbyterians, around which many historic events cluster. The present church edifice at "Five Points" was erected in 1842.

In addition to the church at Franklin, the Presbyterians have an old established organization at Little Harpeth; also one at the ridge called Ridge Church.

The Cumberland Presbyterian Church in Franklin was organized, in 1871, with seventeen or eighteen members, by the Rev. Gill, of Kentucky. The members worshiped at other churches till 1876, when they erected a very elegant church on Main Street at an outlay of nearly $8,000, but of value of nearly $10,000. The corner-stone was laid with Masonic ceremonies and the dedicatory sermon preached June 3, 1876. This is one of the finest churches in the city. This denomination is not strong numerically, yet the regular church services are kept up.

The first Cumberland Church built in the county was erected at Mount Carmel on the Lewisburg Pike about ten or twelve miles from Franklin. October 27, 1827, Allen Bugg made a deed to three and one-half acres of land to T. E. Kirkpatrick, C. Walker, Newton Wall and W. W. Bond, as trustees of the Cumberland Church. The old house has long since been replaced by a new one. There is still a good organization maintained at Mount Carmel.

At a very early period in the history of Cumberland Presbyterianism a church was built near where Pleasant Hill now stands. This was a Union Church built by the Methodists and Cumberlands, but it soon after fell into the hands of the Methodists. The ground was deeded by Moses Cator to Stephen Stockett and G. W. Armstrong, N. Mitchell and Joseph Manley. There is still a good congregation at Pleasant Hill.

Hills Camp Ground was an old Cumberland camp ground. The families of David and Robert Hill and William Byres were members of the congregation at this place. The camp grounds were established about 1832. Huts were built and an open court or an arbor was arranged for the worshipers. There were at one time 115 professors of religion at this place and sixty at another. A house of worship was afterward built at Hills.

The church at McKay was built mainly through the efforts of William and John McKay. It was built about 1855 and has a beautiful location and is in a prosperous condition. West Harpeth Church was built on lands deeded, in April, 1857, to J. Adams, G. W. Mayberry and J. B. Carl, as trustees of West Harpeth. The leading families belonging to West Harpeth were the Binghams and Grays.

Moore's Chapel was built through the instrumentality of Mrs. Moore. This building was erected about 1850. There is a Cumberland Presbyterian parsonage and a strong church at Bellview about nine miles from Franklin on the Murfreesboro Pike. This is one of the strongest congregations in the county. The pastor of Bellview usually preaches to the congregation at College Grove, where there is an organization but no house of worship belonging to the Cumberland Presbyterians. The Cumberland Presbyterians also have organizations at Pleasant Dale, Boiling Springs and Nolensville.

The beginning of Methodism in Williamson County dates back to near the beginning of the present century. The first conference held in Franklin was on October 20, 1816, the presiding bishops being Robert R. Roberts and Enoch George. This was held in a schoolhouse near where the old Methodist Church afterward stood. Among the early members were Thomas Olds, wife and daughter; William Johnson and wife, Sarah; William Davis, Mrs. Foster, Henry Eelbeck, Caleb Maury and wife, William Manning and sons, Mrs. Abram Maury and Mrs. James Park. The first church built in Franklin was built on a lot deeded by James Russell to J. W. McConan, E. T. Collins, James Park, Robert Davis, H. R. W. Hill, Hugh McCabe, William Johnson, Richard Swanson and T. L. Douglas on September 18, 1827, as trustees. This was a brick house, and stood on what was formerly called Water Street, near Mill Street. The Methodists of Franklin now have an elegant house of worship, and maintain a pastor and own a parsonage. Their report shows a membership of 367, and they have a Sunday-school of 155 pupils. This church has given to foreign missions within the last year $253.55, and pays its pastor, Rev. J. E. Harrison, a salary of $1,000.

Douglas Circuit consists of four churches: Thompson Station, Bethel, Colis Chapel and Douglas. Douglas Church, near the old Douglas Camp Ground, was built in 1853. The trustees at that time were L. Henderson, J. Hughes, J. Cove, J. W. Williams, Joseph Barnett, P. M. Hughes and Frank Hardeman. The old camp ground was established about 1827, and in 1836 was made a voting precinct. The total strength of the circuit in membership is 386, and Sunday-school pupils 175. This circuit has contributed $152.35 to foreign missions, and pays its pastor, Rev. W. B. Lowry, a salary of $650, and owns its parsonage.

College Grove Circuit contains two churches. The pastor is Rev. J. A. McFerrin. The total membership of the two churches is 230. The pastor is furnished a parsonage and receives a salary of $600. The circuit has furnished $80 to missionary funds, and has 120 Sunday-school pupils.

Brentwood Circuit has two churches: Brentwood and Johnson Station, with a membership of 258, and of Sunday-school pupils 110. It owns a parsonage and pays its pastor a salary of $400, and contributed last year $128 to the missionary fund. The first church at Brentwood was built in 1857. The trustees were Robert Reams, T. H. Oden, S. B. Frost, D. L. Drake and Stephen Tucker.

The Bethesda Circuit has four churches and a membership of 384, and 130 Sunday-school scholars. The churches have given $128.95 to foreign missions within the last year. They own their own parsonage and pay their pastor, Rev. H. O. Moore, $380. Bethesda is one of the old churches of the county. The first church was built in 1839. The trustees were W. Lavender, John McCurdy, Mark L. Andrews, H. H. Horton, J. Fisher, H. G. Padgett, J. L Morris, H. C. Horton and Blythe Spratt.

Harpeth Station Circuit has two churches. It has a membership of 244, has 139 Sunday-school pupils, contributes $116.25 to foreign missions and pays its pastor, R. P. Ransom, $400. Harpeth was built in 1847. Its trustees were Gideon Ratcliff, Richard Swanson, Richard Reed, Sandford Allen, Phillip Burgh, Isham Lamb and H. B. North.

Pope and Mount Zion Circuit, of which Rev. John Burnett has charge, has a membership of 175, has thirty Sunday-school pupils, pays its pastor a salary of $250, and has given $45 the last year for the missionary cause. The church at Pope's is an old organization. Its first trustees were Samuel Akin, John Moore and James Patton.

The Nolensville charge contains three churches, under charge of Rev. W. T. Rowland,

WILLIAMSON COUNTY.   809

who receives a salary of $450. The membership of this charge number 364, and Sunday-school pupils 180, who have contributed to the missionary fund, $136.55.

The Bethlehem and White Circuit consist of two churches under R. E. Travis, with a membership of 203 and forty-two Sunday-school pupils. These churches have contributed $30.75 to missions, and pay their pastor a salary of $400.

Fernvale Circuit contains four churches under Rev. J. W. Kitchen, whose salary is $125. The mission fund of this charge is $5. The number of membership is 310; Sunday-school pupils, 130. There are in the county 10 pastors, 25 churches, 6 parsonages, and a membership of 2,921. The following is a list of the elders given in order: M. Lindsey, B. McHenry, T. L. Douglas, William McMahan, Rob Paine, James McFerrin, Louis Garrett, James McFerrin, G. D. Taylor, T. L. Douglas, H. E. Pitt, A. L. P. Green, A. F. Driskill, A. S. Riggs, A. L. P. Green, W. Burr, R. P. Ranson, R. K. Hargrave, J. W. Hill and T. A. Kesley. Early pastors were A. Monroe, William Adams, R. W. Morris, Thomas Madden, H. H. Brown, Rob Paine, R. Ledbetter, F. P. Scruggs and J. B. McFerrin.

The first preaching by the Christians in Williamson County was in September, 1833, by Revs. A. Craig and Joel Anderson. Soon after this the county was visited by the celebrated Alexander Campbell. A meeting of several days duration was held by Revs. Absalom Adams and Tolbert Fanning, at which there were fifteen professions and an organization of seventeen members effected. There was not much change in numbers till 1837, when Rev. Tolbert Fanning settled in Franklin and remained till 1841. In that year James C. Anderson became pastor of the church in Franklin, and soon after there was an addition of about thirty members. In 1843 Rev. Adolphus Morse, of the Western Reserve, Ohio, was called to take charge of the church, and remained about one year. Several meetings were held in 1844 by Revs. Wharton and Jones, of Nashville, and seven additions were made to the church; also on April 15 of that year Rev. W. J. Barbee became pastor. In the year 1844 the church was visited by Revs. Ferguson, Smith and Jones. Notwithstanding the difficulties in presenting and establishing the new doctrine it soon took a deep hold upon the minds of the people. Unfortunately, some domestic difficulties embarrassed the church for a time, yet in 1845 the membership at Franklin numbered 100 members, 48 males and 52 females. Worship was generally held in private houses till 1851, when an elegant church was erected. At a church meeting held April 18, 1849, it was resolved to erect a house of worship, and voluntary subscriptions were offered at once for about $1,500. The house is a brick structure about 40x60 feet, and is elegantly furnished. A baptistry has recently been added to the building. The names of the Campbells, the Craigs, the Kirkpatricks, Cayces, Bennetts, are closely connected with the interest of the Christian Church. The membership of this popular denomination is now about 340.

The church at Leiper For k, or Hillsboro, was organized about 1840. Among the early ministers there was Rev. A. Morse, who preached there in 1843. Owing to a difficulty between him and some of the members he did not long remain. This is now a very strong and flourishing congregation. The Christians have a good church at Thompson Station, the organization dating back to about 1845. The Thompsons and Hamiltons were leading members of this church. Boston also is one of the oldest organizations in the county. There is also a large church at Owen's Chapel, a church at Berea, built in 1880, and a new house of worship at Peytonsville, erected in 1885-86. They also have a church building and an organization at Riggs, Cross Roads, and a church organization at South Harpeth and Hill's Chapel. This influential denomination has a membership of from 1,200 to 1,500 in the county.

The St. Paul's Episcopal Church, of Franklin, was organized August 25, 1827, at the Masonic Hall. The following were elected wardens or vestrymen: Thomas Maney, senior warden; Thomas Hardeman, junior warden; William Anderson, B. S. Tappan and Peter N. Smith, vestrymen. Rev. J. H. Otey was chosen first rector, which position he held till November 23, 1835, at which time he resigned. Steps were taken in 1831 for the erection of a church edifice, for which purpose B. S. Tappan and Thomas Hardeman were chosen a committee on building. The committee was instructed to proceed to the erection of a building if the same could be done at a cost not to exceed $2,000. The matter was dropped until 1834, when a new committee, consisting of Messrs. Dickson, Hardeman and Baldwin, were ordered to proceed with the building, the church in the meantime having received $550 from New York and Philadelphia. The corner-stone of the church had been laid on Tuesday, June 28, 1831, by Rev. Bishop Meade, of Virginia.

On the resignation of Rector Otey, Rev. N. Watson Monroe was called, followed by H. T. Leacock, and he by W. P. Sanders, and he by L. S. Sherwell. J. W. Rogers was called in 1845, and Rev. A. S. Royce in 1854. Rev. E. Bradley became rector in 1869, and remained till August, 1873, when Rev. G. N. James became rector. On the death of Rector James, August 16, 1881, Rev. Charles M. Gray was called and took charge January 8, 1882. In 1870 a neat rectory was built adjoining the church edifice. The number of communicants of the church is not large.

RUTHERFORD COUNTY.

GEOGRAPHICALLY speaking Rutherford County occupies the exact center of the State, and almost the exact center of Middle Tennessee. Few if any vertical sections of any great depth have been made, and it is believed no record has been kept. The county embraces an area of over 500 square miles, the outcrop being blue limestone and shales. It is what geologists term lower Silurian. It is probable that the depth of this formation extends from 500 to 1,000 feet with occasional thin strata of other formations.

The soil of this county is exceedingly fertile, being either of a black or brownish red color; the latter color is doubtless due to the iron oxides contained in it. Although there are many places where the ground is apparently covered with stone, yet by careful husbandry there are few places that cannot be made to yield a rich harvest to the careful and industrious husbandman. Fields that have been cultivated for nearly a century, and are apparently worn out by the cultivation of corn and cotton, are soon reclaimed by a few years' growth of red clover, or by seeding in the blue-grass make excellent grazing lands.

The native growth of timber embraces almost every kind grown in the temperate climate. The native trees that are valuable in the markets are oak, hickory, walnut, poplar and cedar, vast quantities of the latter being shipped to all parts of the county, and until within the last few decades was almost the exclusive article of produce for the market, and it is still more largely cultivated than any other one thing, yet large quantities of wheat and corn are raised. The production of these three articles is almost marvelous in some instances with a suitable season. The intelligent farmer has learned the necessity of a rotation in crops for the improvement of the land and to guard against over production in some articles and the necessary consequence—dull prices for that article. His crops are now more varied, more wheat and corn and pasture lands. This brings about a necessity for more stock, and such is now seen. The county is now largely engaged in breeding fine horses, cattle and sheep. These are bringing rich rewards to those so engaged. Large quantities of rye, oats, barley, tobacco, potatoes, hay, peas, beans, wool, butter and cheese are also produced. The product of the orchard and garden embraces everything from the smallest and sweetest berry to the finest apple. The quantity is only limited by the effort of the producer.

The east fork of Stone River enters this county near Reddyville in the eastern part of the county and flows almost in a northwest direction through its entire course. It forms a part of the boundary line between Districts Nos. 17 and 19; from 19 it receives Andrew and McKnight Creeks as tributaries. At the corners of Districts Nos. 17, 19 and 22, it receives Cripple Creek (named from an accident befalling a man while crossing it) as a tributary; this with its branches rises mainly in District No. 22. Stone River passes through the central part of District No. 22, and near the western part receives Cave Creek from the south and Bradley Creek from the north. The last named with Stone River forms the boundary line between Districts Nos. 22 and 15. Near the central part of District No. 21 it receives Bushman Creek. Stone River then forms the boundary line between Districts Nos. 15 and 5 on the north, and Districts Nos. 22, 21, 9 and 6 on the south, where it unites with the west fork of Stone River.

The west fork enters this county near the southeastern part of the county, and forms a part of the boundary between Districts Nos. 21 and 25; at the northern extremity of District No. 25 it receives the waters of Long Creek, which is the boundary line between District No. 25 on the east and Districts Nos. 20 and 11 on the west. The main stream forms the boundary between Districts Nos. 18 and 11; near the center of District No. 11 it receives the waters of Lytle Creek, and near the center of District No. 11 it receives a tributary of its own name. The head waters of the last named is called Dry Fork. West fork passes through Districts Nos. 13 and 9; near Florence Station it receives the waters of Armstrong Creek, the two branches, east and west fork, unite, and form one stream near Jefferson. The river passes out of the county in a northwest direction; from the south on the boundary of Districts Nos. 6 and 2 it receives Stewart Creek. Stone River was discovered and explored as far as Jefferson by Gen. Uriah Stone and four men in 1794. It was for Stone that the river was named. Other streams in the county were named in honor of prominent families.

Previous to 1780 the Indians held undisputed sway in this county. The old trace leading from Nashville to Chattanooga is yet to be seen. Along this route the Choctaws, Chickasaws, and particularly the Cherokees, held undisputed sway from time immemorial. Soldiers sent out by Gen. Robertson went as far as Black Fox Camp Spring in 1793. In 1794 Orr's expedition, sent out by Gen. Robertson, followed the trace by way of Murfreesboro, and September 7, 1794, camped near Black Fox's Spring. This expedition extended as far as Nickajack, where the Indians were defeated. Few Indian troubles occurred after that time. The first settlers in the county were mainly from Virginia and North Carolina. Those coming from Virginia came mainly by water by way of the Ohio and Cumberland Rivers; those coming from North Carolina over the mountains on pack-horses. The parent State, North Carolina, as an inducement to have the lands on the "Cumberland" settled up, offered 640 acres to each head of a family who would live upon the land; hence the large number of 640-acre grants.

Samuel Wilson, grandfather of Col. Jetton, is said to have visited the vicinity of Jefferson as early as 1788–89, and marked out lands. He soon after returned with his family and settled at Wilson Shoals on Stone River. He has the honor of having planted the first corn within the forks of Stone River; also of having killed the last elk in the county, near Murfree Spring. He left a large and respectable family and died in 1827, and was buried with the honors of war near where the United States Cemetery now is. Thomas Nelson, Thomas Howell and William Adkinson settled near Stewart Creek. Col. Robert Weakley and Robert Bedford each owned grants at the confluence of the east and west forks of Stone River. These lands were taken up previous to 1800. It was largely through the influence of these two men that the first seat of justice was located at Jefferson. William Nash, who, with Col. Weakley, surveyed the line separating Rutherford from Davidson, is said to have owned the first store in the county. It was he who administered the oath of office to the justices of the first county court. Nimrod Menifee settled the land now marked by the United States Cemetery. The place is marked by two historic events, one the opening of the second year of the county courts, and the other, fifty-seven years later, within a few days, the opening of the second year of the war and with it one of the bloodiest battles of modern times. Robert Overall settled near Overall Creek, to which his name was given. His family has been prominent in the history of the county since its inception.

Another early settler in that vicinity was Capt. Richard Ransom, who came from North Carolina in 1810 and settled near the head of Overall Creek. Rev. James Bowman was another settler in that vicinity, and was one of the early ministers of the Presbyterian Church. Each of the last was the head of a large family. Charles Ready settled near Readyville, to which his name was given. He settled in the county about 1800, and was one of the seven justices that constituted the first court in Rutherford County; also he was one of the seven commissioners to select a new county seat, appointed by the General Assembly in October, 1811. Of all these he was last to die. Thomas Rucker, another one of the seven justices, lived between Murfreesboro and Jefferson; his place came in one vote of being made the county seat, instead of Murfreesboro. Richard Sanders and family came from North Carolina about 1806, and settled on Stone River, in the neighborhood called "Raleigh." In the same vicinity were the Floyds, Brashears, Wights and Goodloes. Murfreesboro marks the settlement of Capt. William Lytle.

The great natural feature of this county caused more good mills to be erected at an early day than was the case in other places. A few tread-mills were established in the county, but the vast majority of the mills were propelled by water-power. Thomas Rucker built a mill on his place called the "Cave" Mill in 1799. Louis Anthony's mill was built on Stone River, adjoining Henry Gilham's place, in 1804. Cumming's and Smith mills each existed at the beginning of 1804. John M. Tilford built a grist and saw-mill on the west fork of Stone River, near the Salem Pike, in 1814–15; a distillery was added to this later. Samuel Tilford built a mill on the east fork in 1815. David Dickman built a mill on the west fork in 1809, and in the same year James Rucker built a cotton-gin, the first in the county. Rates then were fixed by law as follows: Dinner, 25 cents; supper and breakfast, 20 cents each; lodging, 8⅓ cents; horse, with corn or oats and fodder, 33⅓ cents; oats, per gallon, 8⅓ cents; whisky, one-half pint, 12½ cents; peach brandy, one-half pint, 12½ cents; French brandy, rum or wine, one-half pint, 50 cents. The following kept ordinaries previous to 1820: William Mitchell, William Nash, Harvey Pope, Charles O'Flynn, Hugh Good, James Hill, William Hansbrough, W. R. Hearn, Thomas Mayfield, Peter Williams, William Rather and T. Goodrich.

It is claimed that William Nash started the first trade-store in the county. This was near Jefferson about 1803. The usual stock in trade consisted of a few articles of dry goods, some groceries, a little powder and lead and the inevitable barrel of whisky. Money being scarce a system of exchange was instituted. Large ox hides were rated at about $4; inferior ones proportionately less: wolf scalps, at $2.50 each, receivable for taxes; deer skins, 50 cents; deer "saddles," 50 cents per pair; 'coon skins, 25 cents each. These, with other produce, were sent to New Orleans by flat-boat, a journey requiring a month or more to complete. Dollars were frequently cut into halves or quarters and given for change, hence two "bits," four "bits," etc. Food consisted solely of the product of the farm and forest. A little corn was raised, and either eaten as hominy or made into an indifferent meal, and then into bread. Turkey, deer and elk abounded; hogs were allowed to run at large, and when wanted were hunted down and shot; clothing was made of the coarsest homespun. A maid dressed after the fashion of the day looked as lovely to her rustic lover, though dressed in a homely garb, with cheeks aglow with health, as does now the belle of fashion, in her silks and jewels, to her gay suitor.

Articles of household furniture were simple and plain. Gourds and cows' horns were dressed, and, with a handle adjusted, were used for drinking vessels. Stills were as numerous as the mills, and the whisky barrel as common as the meal tub. Instead of the social "glass" of the more refined society, they were simply asked to take a "horn," *i. e.* a drink; hence the origin of the expression "take a horn." Dr. Thomas Norman was born on the night following the completion of the survey of the county, which had been assigned to William Nash and Col. Robert Weakley, consequently he was the first child born in Rutherford County.

Black Fox Camp Spring was a marked place during the Indian troubles. There is a beautiful tradition of the celebrated Black Fox, who, when he was overpowered by his enemies, rather than fall into their hands, leaped into the spring with his arms and sank from sight. The story would have been incomplete had he not come to light again, and the tradition that buried him brought him out alive at Murfree Spring. About three miles from Murfreesboro is the old Bradley race track, which was a famous resort for sportsmen since 1820. Col. Robert Smith was a prominent figure in those races. Betting, card playing, and the usual accompaniment were common at those races. Near this old race track is the old Indian dance ground, which is a circular track dug out of the earth and rock. Neither history nor tradition tells of its origin.

As the law now is, counties having a population of between 7,000 and 10,000 must be divided into 7 civil districts; those between 10,000 and 15,000 into 12 districts; those between 15,000 and 20,000 into 15 districts; those having from 20,000 to 25,000 into 17 districts; those having from 25,000 to 30,000 into 20 districts, and those above 30,000 have 25 districts. These are numbered by the ordinal numbers. Previous to the constitutional convention in 1834 the districts were named from prominent families, as Sanders, Ready, May and Murphy Districts. The first divisions were made in 1804. The county was then divided into three divisions. Thomas Rucker, John Howell and Thomas Mitchell were ordered to make the divisions. The first was made by a line along the west fork of Stone River to the most westerly branch to the Indian "trace;" thence along the "trace" to the Wilson County line; thence along the county line to Smith's mill; thence on a line to Cummings' mill; thence to the place of beginning. The second contained all west of the river to the western boundary. The third all north of the road leading from Smith's and Cummings' mill and east of Stone River. James Rucker, James Howell and William Lytle were appointed cotton inspectors, each for his own warehouse or district. Tobacco inspectors were appointed after the manner of cotton inspectors. Polls were listed and taxes assessed in the various parts of the county by the justices of the respective districts. The heads of families, when not over age, were enrolled into militia companies, and they were listed by companies. The first of this kind was in 1805, when Justice John Hill listed Capt. John Smith's company; William Nash listed Capt. Samuel McBride's company; W. M. Searsey, W. W. Searsey's company; William Lytle, Capt. John John's company; William Smith, Capt. O. M. Benge's company, and Charles Ready, Capt. Alexander McKnight's company. These companies varied with the population. In 1806 the captains of companies were as follows: Capts. Alex McKnight, Peter Noe, R. Ready, Henry McCoy, Nimrod Junkins, William Robinson, Thomas Yardley, W. M. Searsey, W. A. Sublett, Samuel McBride and John Smith. The districts mentioned above have been subject to many changes since 1834, as well as before that time, this depending upon the whims and conveniences of the people. The county court every few years makes a slight change in these, so many having been made that it would be too tedious to follow all. The usual price paid for listing up to 1834 was $20 to each lister. In 1818 the captains of companies were Webb, Miller, Doaks, Ganaway, Sublett, Morris, Cook, Fox, Thomas, Robertson, Gilfins, Todd, Welton, Moore, Haley, Hubbel, Carson, Patton, McKnight, Thomas Harris, Elliott and A. Harris. In 1821 the number had increased to twenty-three companies, and in 1824 to twenty-six. The number increased yearly till 1833, when the number had reached thirty-six companies. They were as follows: Capts. McGregor, Stevens, Saunders, Clement, Finney, Ridley, Ferguson, Blair, Traylor, Murphy, Harris, Barlow, McLean, Norman, Parrish, Blanton, Hicks, Lillard, Edwards, Osborn, Thomas, Mather, Smith, Bird, Ivy, Hale, Newman, Rowland, Hoover, Robertson, Fowler, Knox, Prewitt, Yourie, Barnett and Brown. From this time on the respect and enforcement of the militia laws gradually grew into neglect.

This county was organized by an act of the General Assembly then in session at Knoxville, October 25, 1803, but the courts for the county were not organized till January 3, 1804. The county was named in honor of Gen. Rutherford, of North Carolina, who was known in the Revolutionary war, and also in contests with the Indians within the confines of this county. It will not seem strange that the county should have been named in honor of a North Carolinian, when it is remembered that previous to 1796, Tennessee was a part of that territory. Rutherford County was formerly included in Davidson and

Williamson Counties. The dividing line was "on the extreme height of the ridge between Mill Creek and Stone River; thence southwardly to the eastern boundary of Williamson; thence with the line of Williamson to the southern boundary of the State; thence with the State line east to the corner of Wilson County; thence with the Wilson County line north to the corner of Wilson; thence with the line of Wilson 6½° west to the southwest corner of Wilson; thence a direct course to the mouth of Sugg Creek; thence a direct line to the place of beginning; that the county so laid off on the east and southeast of the waters of Stone River, etc., be known and distinguished by the name of Rutherford."

The same act that created the county also ordered the county board (justices) to meet in March, June, September and December annually. Rutherford County was declared a part of Mero District. By an act, November 7, 1803, Samuel Weakley and William Nash were appointed to fix the boundary line between Davidson and Rutherford Counties. By an act, August 3, 1804, John Hill, Frederick Barfield, Mark Mitchell, Alexander McBright and Peter Legrand were appointed to select a central site for a seat of justice for the new county. They were to receive by purchase or donation forty acres of land upon which they were to erect or cause to be erected a "court house, prison and stocks;" to lay out a town to be named by the commissioners; lots were to be sold at auction to the highest bidder; lots were to be advertised in the *Tennessee Gazette*, and the proceeds of the sale to be used in the building of the court house, jail and stocks. On December 3, 1807, Bedford County was cut off from Rutherford, thus reducing the latter to the constitutional limits. Minor changes were made in 1815, 1837, 1843, 1844, 1848, 1851, 1852, 1854, 1856, 1860, 1867, 1868, 1870, 1871, 1877, 1879 and 1883.

The above named board selected a site within the forks of Stone River for a county seat. The town was regularly laid out having about 150 town lots and a Public Square on which was erected a good brick court house which stood till 1835. The town was named Jefferson. The following prison bounds were established: "Beginning at the junction of the east and west fork of Stone River running up the west fork of said river at low water mark to the first cross street; thence south to the south boundary of Main Street; thence east with said boundary so as to include the Public Square to a post ten poles below Mitchell's ordinary on the south boundary of said street; thence north to the low water mark of the east fork of Stone River; thence down the same to the place of beginning." Norton Green was appointed overseer of the streets and Public Square. The following were among the first purchasers of lots in Jefferson: Peter Cook, Theophilus Cannon, Joseph Bennett, William Carlisle, Harrison Gilliam, John Bell, Samuel Bell, Daniel Ferguson, J. A. Lewis, George Douglas, Robert Weakley, William Howell, Thomas Stone, H. H. Harris, Norton Green and Mark Mitchell, who kept the first ordinary in the place. The rich farming lands surrounding Jefferson and river transportation gave it a prospect of becoming an important commercial emporium at no distant day. Some very distinguished men attended court at Jefferson, among whom were Felix Grundy and Thomas H. Benton. Dissatisfaction arose as to the location of Jefferson as a seat of justice; a more central location was desired.

October 17, 1811, the Legislature appointed Charles Ready, Hugh Robinson, Hans Hamilton, James Armstrong, Owen Edwards, Jesse Brashears and John Thompson commissioners to select a permanent seat of justice for the county. They were directed to have due regard to good water and a central location. Sixty acres of land were to be procured by purchase or donation. A struggle was made to secure the seat. Readyville Rucker's place, Black Fox Spring and Capt. William Lytles' place were offered. The commissioners visited the various places mentioned. Charles Ready prepared a sumptuous dinner, the Rev. Henderson delivered an address, toasts were drank and strong efforts were made to have Rucker's place chosen. The commissioners were also entertained by Lytle, where the vote was taken on his proposition to donate sixty acres of land south of "Murfree Spring Branch" to the commissioners. The vote stood Robinson, Hamilton, Edwards and Thompson—four in favor of Lytle's offer. The opposition led by Ready had Armstrong, Brashears and Ready—three votes in favor of Rucker's place. Such was their chagrin at their defeat that they refused to sign the deeds to the lots sold.

RUTHERFORD COUNTY.   815

All of the original deeds simply bear the names of Hugh Robinson, Hans Hamilton, John Thompson and Owen Edwards. The only reserve made in the deed was a mutual understanding that Lytle should have one lot redeeded to him. This was accordingly done and the commissioners gave the lot on the southeast corner of the Square. The land now in the hands of the commissioners was a part of the lands originally entered by William Lytle and Archibald Lytle. The sale of lots was advertised in the Knoxville and Nashville *Gazette* to begin on June 12, 1812. The lots sold at auction and were disposed of rapidly. George Smith received Lots 12 and 15 for $116.25. Other purchasers were Daniel Dickinson, William Lytle, Samuel Wilson, Henry Tratt, Robert Jetton, John M. Tilford, Wilson Kerr, Bennett Smith, James Henderson, Blackman Coleman, Fred Barfield, Hezekiah Cartwright, William Bowen, Hugh Montgomery and Abe Thompson. The commissioners as soon as a site was fixed were to effect the removal of records to the new site. Two acres of ground near the center of the seat were to be reserved, on which were to be built a court house and stocks, and another lot near was for a jail. The proceeds of the sale of lots were for the erection of the buildings above mentioned. The act of January, 1812, ordered the commissioners to report to the county court; also allowed the commissioners pay for services rendered, and ordered the records removed. By an act of November 15, amending an act of October 17, 1811, the name of the new county seat was changed from Cannonsburg to "Murfreesborough." An act of October 15, 1813, made Joel Childress, Joel Dyer, J. M. Telford, Abram Thompson, Alex Carmichael, B. Ganaway and Blackman Coleman commissioners of Murfreesboro. This act was repealed in September, 1813, and seven others were elected by the people. An act of November 5, 1813, ordered elections to be held at Murfreesboro instead of Black Fox Camp; they were also to be held at Readyville and at James Johnson's house.

The first court house built in the county was at Jefferson. This house was built in 1804-05. It was of brick and was built at a cost of between $2,000 and $3,000, and stood till 1835 or 1836, when it was sold. It was erected by the commissioners of Jefferson—Peter Legrand, Mark Mitchell, John Hill, Alex M. Wright, Fred Barfield and James Sharp. In 1812 a new court house was erected on the present site of the court house on the Public Square in Murfreesboro. This seems to have been a very indifferent house, as in March, 1818, the court appointed Bennett Small, John Hoover and John Edwards commissioners to repair the same. For this purpose a tax of $12\frac{1}{4}$ cents on each 100 acres of land, 25 cents on each house and lot, 25 cents on each stud horse, 25 cents on each black poll, $12\frac{1}{2}$ cents on each white poll, and $10 on each billiard table was levied. This house was burned in 1822, and a call session in August of 1822 granted premiums for a new levy of taxes for the purpose of building a new house.

On September 11, 1822, the trustees, Robert McCombs, J. S. Jetton, Henry Goodloe, Jacob Wright, David Abbott, Sol Beasley, John Smith, John Dickson, Alex McEwen, O. N. Crocket, Benjamin Johnston, John Edwards, Jacob Wright, John Alexander and J. Williams levied a tax of $37\frac{1}{4}$ cents on each 100 acres of land, 75 cents on each town lot, 25 cents on each free poll, 50 cents on each black poll, twice the season for each stallion, $10 on each four-wheel pleasure carriage, $5 for each two-wheel carriage and $10 for each ordinary where liquors were sold. They were ordered to pledge the taxes thus levied for the years 1823, 1824 and 1825, after deducting costs of collection, to the Nashville Branch Bank of Murfreesboro for the purpose of raising $6,000 for the erection of a new court house. In case the money was not furnished by the bank the commissioners had power to procure it on the most advantageous terms elsewhere. The money was accordingly raised and a brick building erected in due course of time. This house stood until the present substantial structure was erected, in 1859. The present building was erected at a cost of about $50,000. The committee which was appointed to inquire into the propriety of building a new court house was appointed January 3, 1859, and was composed of V. D. Cowan, F. Henry, W. T. Lytle, George Smith and E. A. Keeble. The committee reported that a new court house was necessary, and the court made the old committee a building committee with enlarged powers. The present fence around the court house was erected in 1867, at a cost of nearly $4,000, and the court house was furnished with gas in 1874.

The first prison bonds have already been described. There were four persons imprisoned for debt. Stocks were also built at Jefferson, where persons were bound hand and foot for lighter offenses.

A whipping post was also erected on the corner of the Square for the punishment of graver offenses. Samuel McBride, the sheriff, demanded of the court a suitable jail for prisoners in his possession. A temporary jail was erected at the organization of the court, but he was now accommodated with a better one. On moving the county seat to Murfreesboro a new jail was built by the commissioners of Murfreesboro on College Street, a little north of the present jail. This building was of brick, two stories high and was erected by Mr. Dickson. This building was used as a jail till 1852, when it was sold to William Spence for $700. On October 4, 1850, Mr. J. Lidsey, W. H. Helms, B. Clayton, J. E. Dromgoole, N. W. Carter and John Burke were appointed a committee to investigate the needs of the county in regard to the jail. The committee reported the old jail unfitted for repairs and that a new one was necessary. The contract for the new jail, on the present site, was let to Thomas J. Bulgett September 11, 1852. The total cost of the building was $7,984, with some unfinished work on the outside.

Previous to the passage of the acts of 1826–27 by the General Assembly, the poor, whom we always have with us, were kept at private houses and allowances were made by the court for their care under the head of a "poor woman" or a "pauper." On November 17, 1828, the board of justices appointed John Fetcher, Rob Miller, James C. Mitchell, Thomas Powell and H. D. Jameson, as commissioners "to select and locate an institution" for the poor. The sheriff, U. S. Cummins, was ordered to give notice of such action. February, 1829, they reported that they had decided to purchase 100 acres of land within eight miles of Murfreesboro. It had been decided to purchase a farm of 100 acres of land and to build a brick house, and the commissioners accordingly levied a tax on land and on white and black polls for that purpose. On August 17, 1829, the commissioners purchased 100 acres of land where "John Alexander (deceased) lived" for $400, and in their report stated that it would not be necessary to rebuild as $100 worth of repairs would give ample accommodations. The report of the commissioners was received and met the approval of a majority of the justices. The farm lay on Cripple Creek, within seven miles of Murfreesboro.

The Nashville, Chattanooga & St. Louis Railway was completed from Nashville to Murfreesboro in 1851. A large subsidy in the form of stock was voted by the State, and large sums were given by private citizens. Among those most influential in building the road, outside of the county, were Gov. James C. Jones, Col. V. K. Stevenson and the distinguished Robert Y. Hayne, of South Carolina. So eager were the people for the road that they seemed to vie with each other as to who should donate most liberally toward the road. The first passenger coach over the road from Nashville arrived on the 4th of July, 1851. Flowers and festoons decorated the little city, and a dinner and speeches commemorated the great event. A new world of business was opened up—a communication between the manufacturing cities of the North and the rich fields and seaboard cities of the South. The road extends through the county a distance of nearly thirty miles, entering near the northwest corner of the county at Lavergne and passing out near the southeast part of the county at Fosterville. This road is one of the best and most profitable thoroughfares of the country.

The first turnpike in the county was the Nashville, Murfreesboro & Shelbyville Pike. The charter was granted in 1831, and the work was immediately begun. The State gave aid to the amount of one-half, and the remainder was soon furnished by individuals. Commissioners were appointed and the road was surveyed and ready for work in a short time. John and James Holmes, two energetic and somewhat eccentric Irishmen, obtained the contract for ten miles of the road toward Nashville. Ground was broken July 4, 1832. Feasting, toasting and speech making were indulged in on account of the great event. They were "wined and dined" and lauded over their enterprise. Subsequently these contractors completed five miles more of the road toward Shelbyville. The road was completed and gates erected and ready for business in 1842. The report of the pike superintendent for 1885 shows an old balance, gate receipts, etc., to the amount of $10,315.50, disbursed on repairs and dividend $8,208.60, leaving a balance on hand of $2,106.90, and the road in good condition. The Cumberland & Stone's River Pike was chartered by the Legislature in 1836, and work soon after begun. Thomas Buckley contracted for the first three and one-half miles from Murfreesboro for $1,800, one-half payable in bonds. After many difficulties this road was completed and is now one of the best in the county. The Murfreesboro & Manchester Pike was chartered about the same time as the latter, the State giving aid in each case; the receipts for this road for the last year were $2,408.50, no report of expenditures of the road are at hand. The Woodbury Pike was chartered in 1851. The receipts for this road for the year ending January, 1886, were $3,087.70; expenditure, $3,511.21, being an excess of $423.51.

The Wilkerson Cross Roads Pike show receipts of $936.90; disbursements of $1,054.63, being an excess of $117.73. This road was chartered in 1858 and built by the Wilkerson Turnpike Company. The road is reported in good condition. The Murfreesboro & Salem Road is reported in good condition with receipts at $1,767, and expenditures the same. The superintendent's report shows the Eaglesville & Salem Road to be in good condition, the receipts for the year being $1,233.34; disbursements $1,019.50, leaving a balance of $213.84. The receipts for the Eagleville, Unionville & Shelbyville Pike were $1,086.75; expenditures for repairs, $649.82 with a balance of $436.93. The Murfreesboro, Liberty via Lascassas Road receipts were $1,633.10; the expenditures $1,809.74, being an excess of $165.64. The Murfreesboro & Bradyville gave receipts of $1,793.18, and called for $1,560.78 expenditures, with a surplus of $232.50. The receipts for the Jefferson & Lascassas Road were $1,208.71; expenditure not given. The Murfreesboro & Liberty Road via Hall's Hill, received at its gates $1,088.40 and disbursed $900, the remaining surplus still to be used in repairs. From the above it will be seen that the county is well supplied with pikes. It is doubtful if any county in the State can boast of as many and as good pikes or more efficient and accommodating officials.

The Rutherford County Medical Society was organized in Murfreesboro, June 1, 1852, with the following membership: Drs. B. W. Avent, S. B. Robison, J. W. Richardson, M. Ransom, B. H. Bilbro, B. S. Wendel, J. J. Abernathy, W. T. Baskette, L. W. Knight, T. C. Black, W. C. Martin, R. J. Powell, G. W. Burk, and H. H. Clayton. The following were chosen for officers for the first year: J. W. Richardson, president; J. E. Wendel, vice-president; E. D. Wheeler, recording secretary; S. B. Robison, corresponding secretary, and B. W. Avent, treasurer. The object of the society was the discussion of the theory and practice of medicine and the collateral sciences. The code of ethics of the American Medical Association was adopted for the government of the society. The regular meetings are on the first Thursdays of May and November of each year. The following essays and reports have been read before the Society and nearly all published in the *Nashville Journal of Medicine and Surgery*. In 1852, Cholera Infantum, by W. T. Baskette; Statistics of Fifty Cases of Typhoid Fever, by S. H. Wood; A Case of Amaurosis, by H. H. Clayton. In 1853, Paratitis followed by Meningitis, by L. W. Knight; Sanitation, by S. B. Robison; Reports of Cases of Dysentery, by B. H. Bilbro; Congestion of the Brain, by R. S. Wendel. In 1857, Croup, by L. M. Mason. In 1858, "Intersusception" of the Bowels, by R. S. Wendel; Veratrum Viride by T. S. Smith; Acute Mania Treated by Chloroform, by B. W. Avent; Case of Puerperal Fever, by M. Ransom. In 1859, A Case of Spinal Abcess, by J. B. Murfree. In 1859, Syphilis, by L. M Wasson; Abortion among Negroes, by J. H. Morgan; Blood-letting, by J. B. Murfree. In 1867, Indications for Stimulants, by J. W. Richardson. In 1868, Cholera Infantum, by S. B. Robison. In 1872, Syphilis, by J. B. Murfree. In 1874, Quinia Sulphatis, by H. H. Clayton. In 1877, Dysentery, by W. E. Yourie; Cholera Infantum, by P. C. Coleman; Embolism, and Thrombosis, by G. D. Crosthwait; Diphtheria, by T. D. Miller; Cholera Infantum, by John H. White; Diphtheria, by R. N. Knox; Stricture of the Urethra, by H. J. Warmuth; Erysipelas, by William Freeman; Ostitis, by M. B. Murfree; Malaria, by J. H. Dickson; Bright's Disease, by G.

W. Overall, and Tuberculosis, by R. N. Knox; the two latter in 1878. Dysentery, by M. H. Bonner; Cholera Infantum, by A. W. Manire in 1884. Puerperal Fever, by W. E. Yourie. The following are the officers for 1886: William Whitsen, president; J. J. Rucker, vice-president; M. H. Bonner, corresponding secretary; J. B. Murfree, secretary and treasurer. Other members: M. Ransom, H. H. Clayton, R. S. Wendel, J. F. Rucker, R. B. Haines, J. E. Manson, T. J. Elam, B. M. White, T. J. Bennet. J. H. White, J. F. Byrn, M. E. Neeley, J. M. Dill, W. E. Yourie, R. N. Knox, L. D. Miller, R. W. Reed. A. W. Mainre, A. P. McCullough, William Freeman, W. C. Martin, J. W. Davis, H. J. Warmuth, J. N. Bridges, ——— Dyke, S. N. Crosthwait; H. Yeargan; S. D. Crosthwait; W. Hoover, W. H. Lytle, W. D. Robison, J. H. Dickson.

The Tennessee Central Agricultural and Mechanical Association purchased excellent grounds in 1868, and erected suitable buildings for the association and held several semi-annual fairs, at which there were fine displays of live-stock, products of the field, orchard and garden; also exhibits of the mechanical and fine arts. From some unknown cause the enterprise was not a financial success, and for a number of years the county was without a fair. In 1884 the Rutherford Fair Association purchased the grounds and buildings of the Tennessee Central Fair Association for $5,000. The grounds lie on the Nashville. Chattanooga & St. Louis Railroad and the Shelbyville Turnpike Road, one mile south of Murfreesboro, and embrace thirty acres of land. The track is one-half mile in length and sixty feet wide, and within is the show ring which is encircled by the amphitheater. The first fair under the present management began September 24, 1884, and continued in session four days. The officers at that time were Col. N. C. Collier, president; James A. Moore, first vice-president, and Frank Avent, recording secretary. So successful was the management that a dividend of 10 per cent was declared the first year. Still greater was the success in 1885, as a dividend of 15 per cent was declared, leaving a reserve dividend of 6 per cent still on hand. The association point with just pride to its almost marvelous success since its organization. All the departments usually represented at fairs were well represented at the last, besides one in equestrianism for ladies. The officers for 1885 were Col. N. C. Collier, president; Col. John S. Gooch, Col. W. D. Robison and A. W. Blackman, vice-presidents; Frank Avent, permanent secretary; John E. Richardson, recording secretary, and A. M. Overall, treasurer. The Tennessee State Trotting Horse Breeders' Association held its first meeting on the grounds of the Rutherford County Fair Association. Several of the leading members of the County Association are also members of the State Association.

The market house building, though distinctly a part of the town, is mentioned here as it was used for public purposes. The building stood on the north side of the Square, near the public well. It was built by the first town commissioners in 1815. It was simply a shed 20x40 feet, standing on brick pillars and divided into stalls. January 1, 1830, Jonathan Huggins secured the contract for enlarging and improving the building. This was the common place of auction sales by constables, sheriffs, etc., of negroes and other property. The building was destroyed during the war.

The following are the county officers: Sheriffs—Samuel McBride, 1804-06; O. H. Benze, 1806-13; U. S. Cummins, 1813-34; G. S. Crockett, 1834-36; William P. Watkins, 1836-42; William B. Lillard, 1842-48; J. M. Tompkins, 1848-52; A. M. McKnight, 1852-56; W. N. Mason, 1856-60; * * A. Jones, 1865-67; G. S. Webb, 1867-70; Ed Anold, 1870-76; Richard Ransom, 1876-82; Benjamin Baley, 1882-86. County court clerks—Joseph Herndon, 1804-13; Blackman Coleman, 1813-24; John R. McLaughlin, 1824-34; R. S. Morris, 1834-44; John Woods, 1844-56; John Jones, 1856-60; J. D. Wilson, 1865-70; J. O. Oslin, 1870-78; W. D. Robison, 1878-86. Registers—William Mitchell, 1804; * * John Spence, 1819-23; M. G. Reeves, 1824-36; John Woods, 1836-44; A. T. Reeves, 1844-54; G. W. Holden, 1854-58; B. F. Wharton, 1858-70; Hardy Murphy, 1870-78; J. B. Jetton, 1878-86. Circuit court clerks—Wilham Ledbetter, 1819-34; Richard Ledbetter, 1834-36; Samuel H. Hodge, 1836-46; D. D. Wendel, 1846-61 (on the organization in 1846 D. D. Wendel was made both circuit and criminal court clerk, which he held till the war); M. L. Fletcher,

1864–70; J. B. Fowler, 1870–78; Peyton Randolph, 1878–86. Chancellors—L. M. Bramblett. 1836–42; B. L. Ridley, 1842–62; J. P. Steele, 1864–72; A. S. Marks, 1872–78; J. W. Burton, 1878–83, Ed Hancock, 1883–86. Chancery clerks—White Jetton, 1836–40; G. S. Crocket, 1841–42; G. D. Crosthwait, 1842–48; D. D. Wendel, 1848–62; Peyton Randolph, 1864–86. Chairmen—William Vincent; Silas Reed; John Fletcher, 1848; Joseph Lindsey, 1848–68; John Woods, 1868–86. Postmasters at Murfreesboro—Joel Childress, 1812–17; David Wendel, 1817–39; D. B. Mallory, 1839–52; E. B. McLean, 1852–56; J. M. Leatherman, 1856–60; W. R. Butler, 1860–62; William Burt, 1864; George Booker, ——; J. W. Wilson, 1871–85; Frank White, 1886.

First District—A. H. Smith, T. H. Carter; Second—N. W. Mason, J. S. Gooch; Third—H. H. T. Carter, H. Gregory; Fourth—J. W. Hall, L. A. Rogers; Fifth—W. A. Rushing, A. M. Jones; Sixth—J. L. Barber, H. H. Macon; Seventh—G. W. Smith, J. L. Anderson; Eighth—R. S. Brown, J. T. Wilson; Ninth—Z. T. Dismukes, J. E. Stockard; Tenth—G. W. Burns, W. W. Lamb; Eleventh—J. S. Webb, W. M. Rucker; Twelfth—C. A. Hill, W. L. Leathers; Thirteenth—J. T. McKinley, M. M. Henry, A. G. Tompkins; Fourteenth—W. C. Westbrook, A. W. Leathers; Fifteenth—J. S. Allen, William Hunt; Sixteenth—W. S. Rhodes, Samuel Vaught; Seventeenth—D. M. McKnight, W. G. Malthis; Eighteenth—John Woods, W. J. Knox; Nineteenth—P. M. Puryear, B. R. Bivens; Twentieth—M. S. Lynch, J. D. Gilmore; Twenty-first—E. B. Fathera, B. T. Johnson; Twenty-second—W. A. Jones, J. T. Brown; Twenty-third—F. A. McKnight, C. A. McKnob; Twenty-fourth—John Gum, A. F. Summers; Twenty-fifth—G. C. Dromgoole, J. H. White.

From official information it is learned that the railroad business alone at Murfreesboro amounts to $30,000 in passenger traffic and $50,000 annually in freight, with about $5,000 additional at Lavergne, Florence, Christiana and Fosterville. Of 10,000 or 12,000 bales of cotton raised in the county 6,000 or 7,000 are shipped by rail, and in addition there are shipped 1,000 car loads of cedar lumber, 200 of hogs, 100 of horses and mules, 50 of cattle, 100 of wheat, 200 car loads of other grains and 500 car loads of miscellaneous freight.

The first court in Rutherford County met at the house of Thomas Rucker January 3, 1804, this being the first Monday. The "commissioners of the peace" were Col. John Thompson, Peter Legrand, Thomas Rucker, John Howell, Charles Ready and John Hill, to whom the oath of office was administered by William Nash, till this time a resident of Davidson County. The first act of the court was the appointment of Samuel McBride, sheriff, who gave bond in the sum of $12,000, and Joseph Herndon was made clerk. William Mitchell was appointed register; John Howell, ranger, and Joseph Boyer, John Anthony, W. Ramsey and William Martin, constables. Thomas Overton and John H. Bowen were admitted as attorneys. The sheriff returned the first grand jury as follows: Alex McCulloch, foreman; Henry Davis, George Ransom, J. M. Wright, Sr., Joe Nichols, Samuel Campbell, Daniel Williams, William Felton, Samuel Wilson, Thomas Nelson, James Whitsett, J. Clark, James Lindsey, William Gammel, John Smith, John Kimbro, Simon Miller, Mark Mitchell, John Sullivan, Robert Smith, C. Harmon, Thomas Mitchell, James McGahah, James Hill and James Oliphant. At the close of the first quarter session the court adjourned to meet in April at the "forks of Stone River." At this court Bennett H. Henderson was admitted as an attorney, and Parry W. Humphreys was made solicitor for the county. The court continued to meet at the forks of Stone River (Jefferson) till January, 1805, when the first session of that year was held at the house of Simon Miller, situated about five miles north of Murfreesboro. At this court there were present the "Worshipful" Thomas Rucker, John Howell, John Hill and Thomas Thompson. This court appointed Robert T. N. Smith, revenue collector, who reported forty-six bodies of land subject to double taxation from failure to report the same for taxation; these bodies of land varied in size from 100 to 3,000 acres. The July term of court again met at the forks of Stone River in 1805. The court fined C. Dement $1 for "contemptuous behavior of court," also the first *ad quad damnum* suit was tried. This suit was brought by Henry Gilliam against Lewis Anthony, who had erected a mill-dam on Stone River, but twelve "good and lawful men" said that Gilliam was entitled to no damage. Pending the erection of the court house at Jefferson, which had been selected as a county seat, the court met from this time till April, 1806, at Nimrod Menifee's, near the National Cemetery; while at Menifee's Rucker, Thompson and Ready held court. This court allowed Samuel McBride $40 for services as sheriff, Herndon $50 as clerk, and Bowen $30 as solicitor for 1804. In April, 1806, court again met at Jefferson in the court house. John M. Taylor and Eli Talbot were admitted as counsellors at law at this term, and Parry W. Humphreys was made solicitor for the county at a salary of $30 per annum.

On his resignation, in 1805, Peter Brooker was appointed to fill the same office. The court allowed Joseph Henson the privilege of building a grist-mill on the east fork of Stone River. James Hamilton was fined by this court for beating E. Grady. John H. Bowen was made a solicitor for the year 1808. Abel Russel was fined $50 for slandering William Hamilton, and Peter Legrand got $10 for an assault upon Peter Anderson. Thomas Rucker received a $600-judgment against Col. Edward Bradford for false imprisonment. The case grew out of some supposed misdemeanor on the part of Rucker at a militia drill, in which he incurred the displeasure of Bradford, who ordered Rucker's neck placed between two rails of a fence and he was kept there to await the pleasure of the Colonel. On his release he brought suit against Bradford for false imprisonment with the above judgment. Soon after both became members of the Baptist Church, and as brothers the debt was forgiven. William Bowen was fined $5 for an assault upon Bird Hurst, and Samuel Rogers $92 for a like offense against William Collier, and in a counter suit Collier received a judgment of $375 against Rogers for slander. David Ferguson was assessed 25 cents for slandering J. P. H. Lemon, and the court, that it might not be too severe on Ferguson, divided costs between plaintiff and defendant. Henry Davis was fined 6¼ cents for beating John Thompson "contrary to the form and statutes made and provided." William Edwards was assessed $7 for a like assault upon John Barker. In the court at Jefferson William B. Robinson, Henry Minor and Thomas H. Benton were admitted to the bar. The latter is said to have pleaded his first case at Jefferson. He was at this time a resident of Franklin, Williamson County. He represented Rutherford and Williamson in the State Senate in 1809. His record as a statesman and senator from Missouri for thirty years is well known.

In 1807 Felix Grundy was admitted as an attorney. He was a noted criminal lawyer, and was well known in political circles. He was a member of the Legislature while at this place, and was for many years a United States senator from this State. Bennet Smith was made cotton inspector in 1807, and in 1808 he became solicitor for the county, which position he held for a number of years. He is said to have been a man somewhat eccentric in his ways, a man of strong likes and bitter dislikes. He was a lawyer, farmer and financier.

The development of the county demanded a higher court. By an act of the Legislature Rutherford was made a part of the Fourth Judicial District, and the Hon. Thomas Stuart, nicknamed "old sorrel," was qualified for the position as judge January 2, 1810; John Coffee was made clerk, and Alfred Balch, solicitor-general. Each held his commission from Gov. Willie Blount. Each of the above became well known in the county. The first grand jury impaneled by the circuit court consisted of J. L. Armstrong, foreman; John Hill, John Smith, Joe Morton, James McKnight, L. Davis, John Wallace, A. McCulloch, John N. Reed, E. B. McCoy, Joseph Barton, Charles Ready and Peter Legrand. The first regular jury was composed of Hans Hamilton, John Sharp, Allen Hill, Joseph Dickson, Thomas Hubbard, J. L. Jetton, James Whitsett, J. Rucker, Rob McComb, George Brandon, William Nash and Daniel Marshall. It was in this court that case wherein —— was plaintiff and —— defendant, the point in dispute being a hide taken to the tan-yard, the amount involved at the time being about $2.50. It was continued in court till cost amounted in all to about $3,000. At the first quarter sessions in 1813, Ezekiel McCoy, Daniel Bowman, J. S. Jetton, Fred Barfield and S. Jetton, "Worshipful Justices Esquires" were present.

A negro named "Jess" was found guilty of "house breaking" on the property of E.

Ward, and was sentenced to execution September 3, 1813. He was sent to Nashville to await the day of execution. This was duly carried out at the appointed time. According to the superstition of the time bits of the hangman's rope were in great demand as a talisman against many ills that human flesh was heir to. The October term of court allowed Mathew McClanahan $29 for his services on the above occasion, and William Neugent, James Miller and William Knight were each allowed $2 as guards for the prisoner; and Samuel Williams, A. Miller and James Lowell were each allowed 50 cents as witness fees.

As a reminder of old times Samuel Richardson was allowed $8 for wolf scalps, and Joseph Welton $3 for one scalp. At the October term of 1813 to facilitate business the justices were divided into four divisions as follows: The first year was composed of William Nash, Moses Bellah, Solomon Beesley, George Weton, J. S. Jetton, Thomas Berry, David Allen, John Tutton, James Whiteside, John Edwards, J. D. Irwin, James Gillespie and William Lock; the second, Fred Barfield, Robert Bedford, Hugh Robinson, William Mankin, A. M. Erwin, J. Millford, Thomas Hoover, J. Smith, J. L. Ambrose, W. H. Davis, Owen Edwards, T. A. Cannon; the third, John Hill, John Henderson, Thomas Nash, John Miller, Sam Campbell, Henry Goodloe, John Dickson, Rob Wannick, E. B. McCoy, George Simpson, Rob McCombs and James McKnight; the fourth, W. W. Searsey, Abe Johns, H. M. Henderson, Jacob Knight, John Barter, L. Davis, Dan Bowman, G. W. Banton, H. Hamilton, W. Edwards, J. S. Jetton and James Sharp. In a suit of the State against Samuel Wilson for an offense against its dignity, Wilson was fined the sum of 1 cent. Thomas Wilson was arraigned for petit larceny, "whereupon Thomas threw himself upon the country and the attorney prosecuting did the like;" then came a jury of "good and lawful men" as follows: Mathew Hirst, William Stokes, John Johns, Larken Johnston, Samuel Kilbro, James Devore, James Cantheron, John Williams, John Hill, Thomas Harris and Samuel Mallery, who, being tried on their oaths, said the defendant was guilty, and affixed his punishment at ten days in the common jail, and that he should be taken to the Public Square and there receive one lash upon the bare back. The "gaol" not being considered safe he was taken to Nashville for imprisonment. Blackman Coleman was allowed $40 for taking the tax list and Bennet Smith $50 as solicitor for 1813. In 1814 Daniel Sullivan was fined $5 for failing to obey a *scire facias*, also $5 for gaming, and Joseph Young received $5 for contempt of court. John Lowery and J. W. Peak received $1 each for forfeiture of recognizance. James Caruthers was allowed $29.75 for taking Thomas Wilson to the Nashville "gaol." A. Sharp was fined $245 for seduction, and William Blair $250 for a like offense. October 15, 1815, Alexander Patterson was fined $10 for petit larceny, and in addition received ten lashes upon the bare back at the whipping post on the Public Square, and was sent to jail till the fine was paid. John Foss, V. Robertson, Thomas Noelard, Elizabeth Balle and M. Martin, by throwing themselves upon the "grace and mercy" of the court were each fined 1 cent. In 1818 M. Battin was placed in the scales of justice and was found wanting to the extent of 6¼ cents for neglect of duty as overseer of the road. P. Wilson and N. T. Perkins were each given nominal fines for tilts at *vi et armis*. James Maxwell was indicted for the murder of Caleb Hewett, and was fined, but was released on taking the "insolvent debtor's oath."

At the June term of court in 1818 it was ordered, first, that witnesses shall be questioned by one lawyer on a side only; second, that questions for continuance shall be argued by one attorney alone on a side; third, sheriffs shall have jurymen ready for those accused; fourth, no motion on appeals should be heard unless made. In 1813 the court ordered B. Coleman to have a county seal made, which was executed by Benjamin Liddon, for which the court allowed $10.

In 1819 a man named Thurman was tried for horse stealing and found guilty, and according to the law and custom of the time was condemned to be executed. The day was set and the time arrived. The prisoner was seated on his own coffin and driven in a cart to the place of execution, near where Soule's College now stands. People thronged the place, the Rev. Dr. Henderson delivered the funeral sermon, and pointed out the evils of a sinful life; the hands were pinioned, and the sheriff, U. S. Cummins, was about adjusting the noose when Daniel Graham, secretary of state, appeared and stayed the proceedings by reading to the Sheriff a reprieve for the prisoner who was remanded to jail.

In 1821 began a series of suits between the Nashville Branch Bank and Benjamin Tratt, *et al.*, which continued in court several years. In 1824 John Bishop was arraigned for petit larceny, and the jury, Simpson Harris, Hugh Porter, James Covington, George Moore, William North, D. M. Jarnett, William Bynum, W. Anderson, W. Maury, A. Blackman and E. Wood, found him guilty, and fixed his punishment at ten days in jail and five lashes upon the bare back. This observation may not be out of place here: At this time there was no penitentiary in the State. Punishment was inflicted by standing in stocks, by the whipping-post, the branding-iron, imprisonment in jail and sometimes by clipping the ear. Persons were made infamous by branding the mark indicating the crime of the guilty one, as "T" for thief, "M" for murder. These punishments were not inflicted as marks of brutality by the court, but were looked upon as marks of justice inflicted, and while the lash was being applied to the quivering muscles and the scathing branding-iron to the quivering flesh, the court could cooly proceed with business.

In 1823 R. E. Green was fined $5 for assault and battery; David Thompson, 1 cent, official negligence as road overseer; Henry Bedford and William Leech each got 1 cent for riot. In 1831 Spencer Hazlett was fined $5 for assault and battery; W. Featherston, $5, and P. Featherston 1 cent, for similar offenses. R. Ramsey was fined $2 and three months in jail for "malicious mischief." S. R. McLaughlin turned into the treasury $800 as back taxes for 1823–24. In 1833 H. D. Thompson, William McKey, Samuel Patterson and Joseph Cheatham were each fined $5 for "presentments for gaming," Besides those already mentioned the following attorneys had been admitted to the bar: Thomas Overton, F. H. Johns, Jesse Wheaton, B. H. Henderson, R. S. Caruthers, Rob Hawkins, R. M. Bute, H. C. Whiteside, D. W. Dickman, E. A. Keeble and Alfred Johns. The most of these men became well-known attorneys. "Malicious mischief," affrays, extortion were common offenses at this time. Twelve "good and lawful men" ordered the sheriff to inflict a punishment of twenty lashes upon the bare back of Isaiah Lester for petit larceny. On January 15, 1827, the death of Judge John Haywood was ordered spread upon record, and each member of the bar was requested to wear crape upon the left arm for a period of thirty days.

John W. Childress was appointed attorney-general, *pro tem.*, for the year 1827. Indictments for riot were found against Samuel Green, Samuel Wilson, Moses Baum and Thomas Baum, and a fine of $10 was assessed against each, while William Hicks and Thomas Alexander were each fined nominal sums for keeping "tippling houses." Again in 1827–28, punishments by whipping were inflicted—one of thirty lashes upon Henry Adams, and one of five lashes and three days' imprisonment upon Willis Cooper. In 1829 a case was tried in the Rutherford Circuit Court, known as the "Harding Case," brought from Maury County on a change of venue. This was something of a family quarrel, in which two parties were killed, and a father and son were tried as accessories to the crime alleged to have been committed by two sons who had fled the country. The prominence of the families made the case an exciting one. After an exciting trial of some time the defendants were acquitted.

A further division of the labors of the county court was made in 1836 by the establishment of the chancery court. Judge L. M. Bramblet was elected first chancellor. He served with credit to himself and the county from 1836 to 1842. Bramblet was succeeded on the bench as chancellor, in 1842, by Judge B. L. Ridley, who served with credit and marked ability till the court was suspended by the war. Judge Ridley was a man of moral as well as personal courage, and when the war came up he entered the service. After the close of the war he resumed the practice of law, which he continued till his death. In 1838 a negro named "Charles" was arrested for rape. The evidence was wholly circumstantial but seemed pretty clear, and on the strength he was tried, convicted and executed. There was a strong suspicion at the time that he was not the guilty party. Later a negro was executed in Mississippi for a similar crime, and while under sentence of death owned to have committed the crime in Rutherford for which Charles was hanged.

Another subdivision in matters of litigation was made by the establishment of a criminal court. This was done in 1846. The district of this court included Davidson and Rutherford Counties—being the same as now. The Hon. William K. Turner, of Nashville, was made judge of this court. He held the office from the formation of the court until the court was discontinued on account of the war. Judge Turner is described as a man firm, earnest, clear, prompt and sound in his decisions, but plain and easy in manner.

In 1848 Sarah, a slave, was executed by order of the court. This was done by the sheriff, J. M. Thompson, for which the court allowed him the sum of $12.50; other allowances, for grave, coffin and gallows, amounted to a total of $26.25. A destruction of all the circuit and criminal court records during the war renders a detailed account of the transactions of these courts impossible.

The county court was partially reorganized in June, 1864, while under control of the military authorities. But little work was done by this court. The criminal court was reorganized at the July term, 1864; the Hon. T. N. Frazier was made judge and M. L. Fletcher, clerk. Owing to the occupation of the court house for other purposes, the court first met in the Odd Fellows' hall, but afterward moved to the Masonic hall. The results of the war brought a new feature into the courts, *i. e.*: "State *vs.* —— —— col., Hog Stealing, etc." The chancery court was reorganized at this time; Judge J. P. Steele presiding, with J. M. Tompkins, clerk and master. On the death of the Hon. Charles Ready, who had been prominent before the public for fifty-three years, the entire bar attended his funeral in a body. J. M. Avent and W. H. Washington were appointed a committee to report the memorial of his death to the criminal court; Gen. J. B. Palmer, E. H. Ewing and —— Burton, to the supreme court; H. P. Keeble and B. L. Rielley, to the county court; J. L. Cannon and G. S. Ridley, to the circuit court; J. D. Richardson and J. M. Childress, to the chancery court.

A personal mention of each member of the bar or judge on the bench will not be made; but be this said, the Rutherford County Courts, in all their branches, have been characterized, from the beginning to the present, by men of culture, ability and refinement. The highest judicial seat nor the presidential chair have not been too high to be reached either by her native or adopted sons. Neither the halls of Congress nor the judicial ermine have ever been disgraced by one of her children.

Many of the old Revolutionary soldiers settled in Rutherford County after the admission of Tennessee into the Union, on grants from the State of North Carolina. Among them may be mentioned the Gilbraiths, Grants, Halls, Hills, Murfrees, Hubbards, Joneses, Rutledges and others. Many of them became pensioners after the passage of the act of Congress, of 1832, for their relief. In the Creek war of 1812-14, related elsewhere, a large number of troops went from Rutherford County, although it is believed no regularly organized company was sent. Col. Henderson, who is accredited to this county, was killed in a skirmish near the city of New Orleans. In the second Seminole war, which broke out in 1836, Rutherford County furnished two companies, Capt. Yoakum's and Robert Jetton's. These men enlisted under the call for 2,500 men to serve six months. These men were attached to the Second Regiment, which was organized at Fayetteville, about June 16, 1836, by electing William Trousdale, colonel; J. C. Guild, lieutenant-colonel; Joseph Meadows, first major; William Washington, second major. These two regiments were formed into a brigade, of which Robert Armstrong was elected brigadier-general. The troops left Fayetteville, the place of rendezvous, on July 4, and proceeded direct to Columbus, Ga. The history of this expedition is given under the second Seminole war. In 1846, on the outbreak of the Mexican war, great numbers offered their services to the State and Government. Two political companies from Rutherford tendered their services at once, the one commanded by Capt. Mitchell, called the Spring Blues, and the other by Capt. Childress. The latter only was accepted. These men were not accepted till the second call, and consequently did not see very active service.

The sentiment of Rutherford was strongly opposed to secession or separation till the climax of the political issues was reached, when the people slowly yielded, and in time became earnest supporters of the Confederate Government. The first regiment raised in this county for the Confederate service was the Second Tenneesee Infantry. The regiment was composed of ten companies, averaging 120 men each; two of these companies, A and F, were from Rutherford County. The captains of Company A were S. N. White, John A. Butler, Thomas G. Butler and James T. C. McKnight. The captains of company F were Thomas D. White, W. D. Robinson and William H. Newman. At its first organization William B. Bate was chosen colonel; David L. Goodall, lieutenant-colonel; William R. Doak, major. The regiment was organized at Nashville, May 5, and was ordered to Virginia. It was mustered into the Confederate service May 12, at Lynchburg, by Gen. E. Kirby Smith. The field and staff officers were W. B. Bate and W. D. Robinson, colonels; D. L. Goodall and John A. Butler, lieutenant-colonels; William R. Doak, major; T. J. Kennedy and Alexander Erskine, surgeons; J. H. Erskine and T. L. B. Brown, assistant surgeons; Joseph Cross and G. T. Henderson, chaplains: M. W. Cluskey and W. H. Rhea, quartermasters; W. T. Driver and W. J. Hale, adjutants. The complete account of this regiment is given in the State history.

The credit of raising the Eighteenth Regiment is due largely to Gen. J. B. Palmer, of Murfreesboro. At the outbreak of hostilities Maj. Palmer, as he was then called, was engaged in the practice of law at Murfreesboro, and was a man very much opposed to secession, a doctrine which he opposed with all his force and logic. He said, however, if the worst came to the worst he was with his native State. The determination of Maj. Palmer to volunteer led vast numbers of his neighbors and companions to enlist with him. The following companies were raised, principally in Rutherford County: Maj. Palmer's own company, B. G. Woods' company and B. F. Webb's company. The history of this regiment is best told in the language of Gen. Palmer himself. The regiment was organized on the 11th of June, 1861, at Camp Trousdale, Tennessee, by the election of J. B. Palmer colonel, A. G. Carden, lieutenant-colonel, S. W. Davis, major. It contained ten companies, commanded respectively by Capts. M. R. Rushing, J. W. Roscoe, William R. Butler, H. J. St. John, G. H. Lowe, B. F. Webb, J. B. Matthews, B. G. Woods, A. G. Carden and W. J. Grayson. Col. Palmer's staff consisted of R. P. Crockett, quartermaster, with rank of captain; Thomas Wood, commissary, with same rank; Dr. John Patterson, surgeon; J. W. Gowan, assistant surgeon; James W. Roscoe, adjutant, with the rank of first lieutenant; James S. Baxter, sergeant-major. The first battle in which the regiment participated was at Fort Donelson, where after much suffering, hard and gallant fighting, it, with the garrison and army under command of Gen. Floyd, was captured on February 16, 1862. Col. Palmer and other field officers were imprisoned at Fort Warren, Boston Harbor. The staff and company officers were confined at Johnson's Island, Lake Erie, and the privates at Camp Douglas, Illinois. All the men and officers were exchanged in September, 1862, when the regiment was reorganized by an act of the Confederate Congress. J. B. Palmer was again elected colonel; W. B. Butler, lieutenant-colonel; W. H. Joyner, major; John W. Douglas, adjutant. This reorganization took place September 26, 1862, at Jackson, Miss. This regiment from the beginning to the close of the war belonged to the famous command known at part of the time as Brown's, and subsequently as Palmer's brigade; by its latter name it was surrendered at Goldsboro, N. C., May 2, 1865, on the terms agreed upon by Gens. Joe E. Johnston and William T. Sherman. As a regiment, it was commanded by its first colonel, Palmer, till his promotion to the rank of brigadier-general in 1864. The Eighteenth participated in the great battles of Fort Donelson, Murfreesboro (Stone's River), Chickamauga, Lookout Mountain and Missionary Ridge. It participated in all the engagements in the Atlanta campaign. It made the campaign into Tennessee after the fall of Atlanta, doing active service at all points. After the defeat of Gen. John B. Hood before Nashville, this was one of the regiments of Palmer's brigade which, with other choice troops, covered Hood's retreat from Middle Tennessee across the Tennessee River. This rear guard was under

Maj.-Gen. Walthall, the ranking officer, and consisted of his own division and the brigades of Gens. Palmer and Featherston and some cavalry forces. After this Palmer's brigade was ordered to North Carolina under Gen. Johnston, under whose direction the battle of Bentonville, in that State, was fought. In this fight Palmer's brigade was made the directing column, and it distinguished itself so highly as to be handsomely complimented by Gen. Stevenson, the division commander, in a "general order." This was the last fight of the Eighteenth. The regiment was discharged in May, 1865, which closed its arduous and brilliant career of patriotic duty and service for a period of a little more than four memorable years. At the battle of Murfreesboro Gen. Palmer, then colonel, was wounded three times; in the celebrated Breckinridge fight on January 2, 1863. He received a Minie-ball through the calf of the leg, one through the shoulder, and a shell wound on the right knee, though he did not leave the field till the close of the engagement, and then brought off his regiment in good order. He was next severely wounded at Chickamauga, from which he has never recovered. He was also slightly wounded at Jonesboro and at Bentonville.

The Twentieth Tennessee Regiment was known as Battle's regiment, and was organized at Camp Trousdale near the Kentucky line. Joel A. Battle was elected colonel; M. B. Carter, lieutenant-colonel; Patrick Duffle, major; Dr. D. B. Cliff, surgeon; J. H. Morton, assistant surgeon; John Marshall, quartermaster; M. M. Hinkle, commissary; Alex Winn, adjutant; John Edmonson, chaplain. The only company from Rutherford in the regiment was Company E. John S. Gooch was elected captain of the company at the age of nineteen, and was severely wounded at Fishing Creek. At the reorganization of the army in May, Capt. Gooch was elected lieutenant-colonel at the age of twenty. Col. T. B. Smith, of the regiment was only twenty-two. Col. Gooch was compelled to resign in a short time, and was succeeded by F. M. Lavender. On the promotion of Col. Gooch. William Ridley was chosen captain of Company E, and remained with the company during its term of service. Capt. Ridley received a severe scalp wound at Missionary Ridge; Lieut. Crosswaite was killed at Murfreesboro, and Lieut. Peyton at Chickamauga. A full history of the regiment is given elsewhere. Many other companies and parts of companies were recruited in Rutherford County, but their history is closely interwoven with other regiments.

The battle of Murfreesboro began December 31, 1862, and ended January 2, 1863. The Confederate forces numbering about 35,000 men were under the command of Gen. Bragg, whose right was under Gen. Breckinridge, center under Gen. Polk, and left under Gen. Hardee. The Federals according to Rosecrans, then commander, numbered 37,977 infantry, 3,200 cavalry and 2,223 artillery. Rosecrans' right confronting Hardee, was commanded by Gen. McCook, the center by Gen. George H. Thomas, opposite Polk, and the left, opposite Breckinridge, was commanded by Gen. T. L. Crittenden. Bragg anticipating Rosecrans' intention of attacking his own right, hurled Hardee with irresistible force upon McCook, Rosecrans' right, and crushed it. By night Rosecrans had lost, including stragglers, one-fourth his army and a large portion of his artillery. His right wing was almost at right angles to its position in the morning, but it had been so strengthened as to be impossible to drive it further. The battle so far had been largely in favor of the Confederates. January 1 was a day of comparative quiet save on occasional artillery duel and some skirmishing. On January 2 shirmishing opened about 8 o'clock and grew warmer as the day advanced; the tide rolled toward the right. At about 3 P. M. the picket firing began, which was the signal for the celebrated charge made by Breckinridge on the right. Perhaps no more gallant charge is recorded in history than this one led by Breckinridge and his gallant subordinates, They swept everything before them, crossed the river and seemed ready to crush Rosecrans' left, as had been done by his right, but he had skilfully massed fifty-eight pieces of artillery heavily supported by infantry. Upon this unseen enemy the troops rushed, but were compelled to fall back with much loss. The night was passed with anxious watching, and the following day Bragg slowly began to fall back, leaving the field in the hands of the Federals. Bragg's loss was reported by him at

10,000; Rosecrans' loss was 1,533 killed, 7,245 wounded, besides 6,273 prisoners. On the ground where the battle was fought is now a National cemetery, where were gathered the dead bodies from the various points and buried there. The number thus buried amount to about 6,000. Near Murfreesboro is a Confederate cemetery, where now sleep 2,000 Confederate soldiers.

The city of Murfreesboro was founded by an act of the General Assembly passed October 17, 1811, although no lots were purchased nor houses erected until in June, 1812. The town was originally called Cannonsburg, in honor of Gov. Cannon, but by an act of November 19, 1811, amendatory to the act of October 17, 1811, the name was changed to "Murfreesboro." This name was given in honor of Col. Hardy Murfree, who was a Revolutionary soldier and held lands in the vicinity under military grant from North Carolina. His claim as well as many others, were signed by "Richard Dobbs Spaight, Esq., our governor, captain-general, and commander-in-chief;" such an array it would seem would make the title perfect. As is elsewhere mentioned, Joel Childress, Joel Dyer, John M. Tilford, Abraham Thompson, Carmichael, B. Sanaway and Blackman Coleman, were appointed commissioners (aldermen) of Murfreesboro. These constituted the first town board or council, the former commissioners having nothing to do with the government. The above act was repealed September 28, 1815, and seven commissioners were chosen by the people. Previous to this, November 5, 1813, the election precinct at Black Fox Camp was ordered moved to Murfreesboro. On November 19, 1813, all money in the hands of the commissioners from the sale of lots, after paying these expenses, was ordered turned over to the town board for the benefit of the town.

The act incorporating the town of Murfreesboro passed the General Assembly October 17, 1817. It was declared that the citizens of the town of Murfreesboro, of the county of Rutherford and State of Tennessee were a body corporate and politic with authority to sue and be sued, etc. The town was organized with a mayor and aldermen. Annual elections were ordered to be called by the sheriff on the first Monday in January. On October 13, 1818, Isaac Hilliard and Mary Moore, his wife, of Halifax County, N. C., legatees of Col. Hardy Murfree, deeded Lots 46 to 70 inclusive, except Lots 53 and 65, to the "Citizens, owners and Occupiers of certain Lotts or parcels of land" in the town of Murfreesboro. This was done for a love of the people of the place, a desire to make their titles perfect and for the remembrance of Col. Murfree in the name. On December 26, 1837, Isaac Hilliard's enlargement was incorporated, containing Lots 1 to 24 inclusive. A further addition was made to the city January 10, 1851. On December 6, 1860, Bennett Smith deeded a lot near the Presbyterian Church to the city. On December 12, 1865, the city limits were extended three-quarters of a mile from the Public Square. Town officers: The first town officers elected were Joshua Haskell, mayor, but he resigned and David Wendel was chosen in his place; Burrell Gannaway, Nicholas Tilford, T. C. Watkins, William Barfield, Charles Niles and G. A. Sublett, aldermen; William Ledbetter, recorder; Benjamin Blankenship, town constable. Other mayors, David Wendel, 1819: Robert Purdy, 1820; Henry Holmes, 1821; William R. Rucker, 1822–23; John Jones, 1824; William Ledbetter, 1825; S. R. Rucker, 1826; William Ledbetter, 1827; John Smith, 1828; Edward Fisher, 1829; John Smith, 1830; John C. Moore, 1831; Charles Ready, 1832; Charles Niles, 1833; Marman Spence, 1834–35; Edward Fisher, 1836; L. H. Carney, 1837; E. A. Keeble, 1838; Edward Fisher, 1839; G. A. Sublett, 1840; B. W. Farmer, 1841–42; H. Yoakum, 1843; Wilson Thomas, 1844; B. W. Farmer, 1845–46; John Leiper, 1847–48; Charles Ready, 1849–53; F. Henry, 1854; E. A. Keeble, 1855; Joseph B. Palmer, 1856–59; John W. Burton, 1860–61; J. E. Dromgoole, 1862;   *   *   *   R. D. Reed, 1865–66; Charles Ready, 1867; E. L. Jordan, 1868–69; T. B. Darrach, 1870; J. A. January, 1871; J. B. Collier, 1872–73; Dr. J. B. Murfree, 1874–75; H. H. Kerr, 1876; H. H. Clayton, 1877; N. C. Collier, 1878–79; J. C. Clayton, 1880–84; E. F. Burton, 1882–83; J. M. Overall, 1884–85; H. E. Palmer, 1886. Police officers: A. G. Miller, city marshal; G. W. Myers, R. E. Beard and R. M. Nelson.

The town as originally surveyed by Hugh Robinson, contained seventy lots each 150 feet square, being numbered from the northwest corner to the northeast from one to twelve inclusive. The Legislature passed eighteen rules and regulations to govern the town while under the first town board. In 1815 the General Assembly passed an act for the relief of the seven commissioners of Murfreesboro against any claims that might arise against them while they were discharging their official duties. Capt. William Lytle built a mill, blacksmith shop and afterward a cotton-gin near Murfreesboro in 1808. The first house was built within the corporate limits of the town in 1811. A. Carmichael built the first tavern in Murfreesboro near the "Pump Spring." Col. Joel Dyer moved his tavern from Jefferson to Murfreesboro in 1812; this building stood till burned in 1854. Col. Robert Jetton built a tavern on South Main Street of cedar logs, that stood till burned in 1853. J. Renshaw also built a tavern near the southeast corner of the Public Square. Porter & Spence moved their dry goods store from Jefferson to Murfreesboro in 1813. The town was now growing rapidly. A public warehouse was built near the creek on Main Street in 1813. All cotton and tobacco had to be placed in some one of the three houses in the county for inspection before sale. W. A. Sublett and L. Mathews were made inspectors in 1813. The fees for opening and recooperage was about $1.50 per hogshead for tobacco and cotton in a similar ratio. On November 15, 1817, J. Haskell deeded Lots 71 and 72 to Bradley Academy. In 1818 the market house was built, which, with some improvement stood till destroyed by the soldiers. Hugh Cabell was made sealer of weights and measures for the town and county. The rates fixed were for a bushel measure 50 cents; pecks, 25 cents; half peck, 12½ cents; gallon, half gallon and two quarts, 25 cents. In 1818 the town well was ordered begun, but was not finished till 1824; owing to a destructive fire all wooden chimneys were ordered pulled down, and brick or stone substituted instead. Also a fire-watch of twelve men were put on duty. The Subletts were allowed $98 for printing the town ordinances in 1818. Stumps were ordered removed from the streets. Few buildings at this time were adorned with paint. The first brick house erected in town was built this year by John M. Telford, west of where the present National Bank now stands.

Drs. W. R. Rucker, James Maney, Henry Holmes, J. King and L. P. Yandell were distinguished early practitioners. Lawyers—S. H. Laughlin, Samuel Anderson, S. R. Rucker, W. Brady, Andrew Childress, J. R. Martin, Charles Ready, John Bruce, John Haskell, P. W. Humphreys and I. H. Bute. Visiting attorneys—Rob Butler, John Bell, J. H. Eaton, Andrew Jackson and Felix Grundy. Merchants—David Wendel, Joe Spence, Hill, Snell & Co., M. Spence, Silas Loik, C. O'Flynn, C. R. Abbott, Falls & Christy, David Lineau, John Smith, J. C. Moore & Co., J. Currin, Benjamin Elder and Charles Gugger. Saddlers—Charles Niles, W. Gardner, A. S. & J. Davidson. Tailors—Reuben Bolles, Peter Campbell, Samuel Parrish, Samuel Jones. Hatters—Alfred Miller, A. Staller, Christopher Hist. Cabinet workmen—James Crichlow, Ed Fisher, Samuel Patton. Chair-makers—E. A. Cochran, Isaac C. Brown. Carpenters—Capt. J. Jones, George Anderson, J. McDermott. Blacksmiths—William Gilliam, John Kennedy, William Blanton, P. Parker. Boot and shoe-makers—Willis Barker, B. Kennedy, J. Jones. Tanners—V. Cowan, Rob Jetton, J. Bone. Wagon-makers—William R. Icemeyer, J. D. Scrape. Tinner—Lewis Sperry. Tavern-keepers—James Vaughn, R. Smith, Gen. Robert Purdy, W. C. Emmett. Gunsmiths—Ed Elam, George Baltes. Brick and Plasterers—J. Fletcher, T. Montague. Jewelers—A. Liddon, who made the county seal, and W. Manchester. Milliners—Mrs. A. Staller, Miss S. Warren. Wool-carder—Isaac C. Brown.

The first General Assembly met in Knoxville May 28, 1797, and continued to meet there till 1813, when it changed to Nashville and remained till September 15, 1815, at which time it again assembled at Knoxville, but was changed to Murfreesboro September 19, 1819. It continued to meet at Murfreesboro till early in January, 1826, since which time its sessions have been in Nashville. The bill for fixing a permanent seat of government was called up October 4, 1843. The vote at the third reading in the House stood: Yeas, 40; nays, 34. In the Senate, on motion of Senator W. H. Sneed, for Rutherford and Williamson Counties, the vote on the question of locating the state capital at Murfreesboro stood eleven for and fourteen against. On reconsideration October 10, 1843, the bill was carried in favor of Nashville. During the session while in Murfreesboro the Assembly met in the court house, the representatives using the lower floor and the senators the upper floor. A call session was held August, 1822, but the court house having been burned, the session was held in the Presbyterian Church; the lower house met on the first floor and the Senate in the gallery. On the assembly of the Legislature at this place, Gov. McMinn took his seat as governor, and James McDowell was elected doorkeeper. During the session of 1823 Gen. William Brady was chosen speaker of the House.

The acts were printed on a press owned by the State. This was brought from Nashville, and the work was done in a house on College Street. The year 1823 marked the first appearance of a "Dutchman"—Hoffman by name—into the town. He was a baker by trade, and the novelty of the man was as great as the ginger cakes he sold. Another historic character of this period was Peter Jennings, a free negro, who had served during the Revolutionary war, and for such service was awarded a pension. At this period Murfreesboro afforded two military companies, one of seventy-five men, the Murfreesboro Volunteers, commanded by Capt. G. S. Crockett; the other, the Murfreesboro Sentinels, commanded by Capt. Russel Dance, afterward by J. C. Abbot, and still later by Capt. John Childress. The former company took part in the reception given to Gen. Lafayette at Nashville in 1825. A great semi-centennial celebration was held July 4, 1826, at Murfree's Spring under the auspices of the Sentinels. There was a parade by the company, and speeches made by M. Rooker and others. A committee visited the Hermitage, and invited the hero of New Orleans to visit Murfreesboro January 15, 1828, the thirteenth anniversary of the battle of New Orleans. The invitation was accepted. Dr. William R. Rucker was president on this occasion, and G. A. Sublett, vice-president. Great preparations were made, and a large and enthusiastic assembly greeted him. A magnificent banquet was spread, and the beauty and chivalry of the place did honor to the occasion. Thirteen regular toasts were drank, and responded to with grace; twenty-four additional were offered. A poem was prepared and read for the occasion. "There was a sound of revelry by night," and the reception closed with a magnificent ball. At this time the population of Murfreesboro was 955, and the revenues for the town but $355.81.

In 1831 the Washington Cotton Factory was started by Mr. Lowery; this had a horse head-wheel for motive power. From the success of this a new company was formed, consisting of Messrs. Masterson, Christy, Lowery & Johnson. A large second-hand engine and machinery was placed in position, the whole at a cost of about $25,000. It was an unfortunate financial investment. It soon passed into the hands of Dr. James Maney, then to —— & Watson, next to Moore & Cox, and then to Field for $4,000. William Somerhall finally purchased the entire business for $1,500.

In 1833 a report was made to the city council on the feasibility of establishing a system of water-works. A favorable report was made and the estimated cost was $1,000. It was proposed to raise the water from the Sand Spring in large tubs, to be conveyed to the top of Capitol Hill upon a wooden railway; the same to be elevated by horse-power. The water was to be led from Capitol Hill, by cedar tubes, into an air-tight tank in the court-yard square; thence, by hydrants, to the places of business. The work was completed and the Rose Water-Works were set in operation. After a short time they were found to be a failure. The first drug store was started by H. H. Treadaway, on the east side of the square, in 1837; another was soon after started by Avent & Carney, which was afterward sold to J. H. Nelson. The first grocery store was started by Jacob Decker in 1837; a large carriage factory was started the same year by H. Osborn & Co. Other jewelers than those mentioned were F. Garland, James Reed, A. O. H. P. Sehorn, R. D. Reed, William Roulet and J. Lukins. In 1850 a new drug store was started by John McDermott; a hardware and grocery store, by John C. Spence; a book store, by R. D. Reed; a second book store was owned by Craig & Fletcher, which was sold to Fowler & Davis. The livery stables at this time were owned by Todd & Carnahan, Todd & Barkley. A carriage shop was run by R. & S. Smith. The Cedar Bucket Factory was started by J. C. Spence in 1854.

The Rio Mills were erected in 1855 by W. S. Huggins & Co. The building was a large four-story brick, and was run by two twenty-five horse-power engines, and had a capacity of about 200 barrels of flour per day. The whole cost about $25,000. These mills were sold to William Spence, who, in 1860, added a distillery, and at this place fed many hogs. These mills were used by the armies during the war and were greatly damaged. 1855 was noted for the great fire in this city, in which the City Hotel, as well as many other buildings, was burned. The first gas-works were built in this city in 1857. Mains were laid and the business was started by making gas from resin oil and cotton seed, but, the war interfering, the matter was not fully tested. The opening of the war made Murfreesboro a great military camp. The troops enlisted were usually sent to Camp Trousdale for instruction. The first appearance of Federals in the place was March 7, 1862, and on the 10th Gen. Mitchell took formal possession of the place. July 13, 1862, he made his celebrated raid upon the town, capturing a large number of prisoners. This strange coincident occurred during the engagement: In the attack upon Maney Springs 21 Federals were killed and no Confederates; in the attack upon the court house 23 Confederates were killed and no Federals; in the fight at the river 2 on each side were killed. After the battle of Stone River the city was again in the hands of the Federals, they having taken possession January 4, 1863. All the churches and the colleges were used as hospitals for the sick and wounded, first by the Confederate, afterward by the Federal Army. In 1866 the Cedar Bucket Factory passed into the hands of the Stone River Utility Works. It was started in the old cotton factory, but has since moved to its present building. April 15, 1869, marks the era of the "great fire," in which a large number of business houses were destroyed.

Business of 1870: Attorneys—Charles Ready, H. P. Keeble, J. B. Palmer, J. C. Cannon, B. L. Ridley, G. S. Ridley, E. H. Ewing, E. D. Hancock, B. F. Lillard, R. Beard, F. R. Burrus, J. E. Dromgoole, J. M. Avent, J. W. Burton, T. B. Darrach, J. D. Richardson, J. W. Childress and J. A. Leiper. Physicians—G. D. Cisthwait, J. B. Murfree, W. C. Cook, J. E. Wendel, M. Ransom, L. M. Knight, W. D. Robinson, R. S. Wendel, H. H. Clayton, W. Whitson and N. H. Lytle. Dentists—A. Hartman and S. H. Bears. Hotels—City Hotel, J. A. Crocket; and Planters, W. A. Rapp. Dry goods—Rosenthal & Bro., T. C. Goodrich, E. Rosenfeld, W. Smith, J. Allen, Miles & McKinley, Rich & Wright, Eagleton & Byrn, Tobias & Bro. and A. G. Rosenfeld. Drug stores—J. McDermott, J. W. Nelson and William Wendel. Bakers and confectioners—H. Raymond, G. S. McFadden and H. Osborn. Saddlers and harness-makers—John Kelley, Mosby & Co. and J. H. Boehms. Grocers—L. Burgsdorf, Lane & Crichlow, J. S. McFadden, J. I. C. Haynes, Henry Elliott, James Tompkins, Collier & Eagleton, James & Collier, R. N. Ransom, Smith & Hodge, Jetton & Clayton, Pearce & Abbott, John Barber, H. H. Kerr, Carney & Ransom and W. A. Ransom. Stoves and tinware—Daniel Kelley. Hardware—Street, Andrews & Co., T. B. Ewbanks. Milliners and dress-makers—Mrs. McDougal and Mrs. R. W. January. Jeweler—William Roulet. Commission merchants—Reed & Tally, Leiper & Menifee. Lumber dealer—William A. Ransom. Coal dealer—Rob Martin. Marble and stone—David Neugent. Blacksmiths—W. J. McKnight, N. C. Blanton. Carriage factories W. G. Garrett, Thomas Spain, Bock & Walter.

Present business: Dry goods—B. F. Paty & Co., T. Tobias, J. Frank & Co., M. Hirsh & Co., Moses Henlein, I. Rosenfeld, M. Nathan & Co., —— Fleishman. Grocers—Spain & Co. (also grain and seeds), Henderson & Co., H. Arnold, B. B. Kerr, Butler & Dumwright, J. M. Overall, M. Rosenfeld, Bell & Huggins, Haynes, Hollenell & Co., McFadden & Son, Todd & Morgan, John Johnson, J. B. White, J. Osborn. Groceries, grain, cotton and produce—William Mitchell, Hodge & Smith, Clayton & Overall & Co. Grain dealer—W. F. Leiper. Grain and machines—D. H. Tally. Drug stores—William Wendel, J. Nelson, J. T. Merchant, H. H. Kerr, J. Kerr. Hardware—Street, Burns & Co., Nelson & Ivy. Harness and saddlery—Street, Burns & Co., J. Mosby. Buggies and carriages—Adam Bock, George Walter, W. B. Garrett. Wagons—Rob Blanton, V. Dill. Stoves and tinware—Cantherin & North, Beard & Co. Jewelers—W. R. Bell, W. B. Paty.

Book stores—O. P. Hill, W. B. Smith. Grist-mills—J. A. Ransom, Belmont Mill Co., Murfreesboro Mill. Cotton-gins—Ransom & Co., J. T. B. Wilson, D. H. Talley, White & ——. Cedar Bucket Factory—Stone River Utility Works. Lumber dealers—W. B. Earthman & Co., Kirkpatrick & Ranson. Liverymen—J. H. Allen, Roberts & Oslin, W. R. Fox, James McKnight. Hotels—Miles House, New Ready House. Gas-works— —— Collins. Butchers—W. B. Jones, Mathew Nelson. Milliners—Mrs. L. Gifford, Mrs. Bettie Shelton. Dress-makers—Miss Nannie Prim, Mrs. P. Hooper. Opera house—Jordon & Elliott. Tannery—— Smith. Professional attorneys—Palmer & Palmer, Avent, Avent & Smith, Ed Hancock, Ridley & Richardson, H. P. Keeble, Burrus & Woods, Cannon & Son, P. P. Mason, Sheafe & Smithson, E. L. Jordan, Jr., B. L. Ridley, B. F. Lilliard, Ervin Burton and R. Beard. Physicians—Wendel & Wendel, C. C. Clayton, J. B. Murfree and Dr. Burns. Dentists—Alexander Hartman and J. Bryan.

A new industry is the Stone River Creamery, started in 1884. This establishment is now in successful operation, using about 4,000 pounds of milk per day. Financially, the town has always been solvent; morally, the grade is high; intellectually, it has few superiors. It educated one President and gave him a wife, and has been socially intimate with several. It has recently furnished a prominent character in the field of letters, Charles Egbert Craddock—Miss Mary Murfree.

The charter granting the Murfreesboro Tennessee Bank was issued November 15, 1817. The capital stock was $400,000, divided into shares of $50 each. The limit of the bank was to run till January 1, 1841, with the option of closing sooner, if thought best by the directors. The directors were John Fisher, Joshua Haskell, Samuel P. Black, John Clopper, E. B. Clark, Benjamin McCulloch, Joel Childress, Nicholas Tilford, William Barfield, John Smith and Edmond Jones. The officers elected were Benjamin McCulloch, president; Samuel P. Black, cashier. The bank began business on the north side, but afterward built a house of their own on the northeast corner of the Square. Business with the bank was continued about five years when the directors began closing the business. On the closing of the bank loan-agencies were established in its stead. The agents of these often enriched themselves at the expense of their creditors. In 1838 the Bank of Tennessee was established. Branches of the bank were opened in the leading cities. The capital stock of this bank was $5,000,000. These branch banks took notes at a discount, which were made payable on the installment plan. Notes or tickets on the bank were also issued for a time. The stringency of the money market at that time made these banks a great relief to the business world. A branch of the Planters' Bank was established in Murfreesboro in 1859, with J. W. Childress, president, and William Ledbetter, cashier. The bank continued in successful operation till the war, when the capital was moved to Nashville. After the close of the war the business of the bank was closed out.

The Exchange Bank was established in the summer of 1852, under the free banking system by William and Joseph Spence. The bank was started with a capital stock of $50,000, but was afterward increased to $100,000. The bank did a prosperous business till 1857, when by some improper management the bank became embarrassed and suspended for a time, but resumed business again in 1858, but was permanently suspended in a short time. Much loss and dissatisfaction grew out of the management of this institution.

The First National Bank was established in March, 1869, with a capital stock of $100,000. The first board of directors were J. B. Kimbro, W. N. Doughty, J. W. Richardson, J. R. Collier, J. R. Dillon, J. E. Dromgoole, J. B. Palmer, W. A. Ransom, M. L. Fletcher, W. B. Lillard and A. M. Alexander. The officers were J. B. Kimbro, president; W. N. Doughty, vice-president; J. B. Collier, cashier. In July, 1871, the capital stock was increased to $160,000, and in March, 1872, J. B. Kimbro died and was succeded by J. W. Childress as president. In 1879 Collier, the cashier, died and was succeeded by H. H. Williams, the present cashier. J. W. Childress resigned in January, 1880, and was succeeded by E. L. Jourdan. In 1877 the capital stock was reduced from $160,000 to $100,000, at which it now stands, with $50,000 surplus. The present board of directors are E. L. Jordan, J. B. Palmer, J. M. Avent, J. M. Haynes, Joseph Ransom, R. C. Blackman, N. C. Collier, J. W. Sparks, J. T. Byrn, J. A. Moore and George Beasley.

The Stone River National Bank was organized May 1, 1872. The directors were W. N. Doughty, J. P. Rice, W. R. Butler, W. C. Eagleton, T. C. Goodrich, Theodore Smith, J. I. C. Haynes, D. D. Wendel and C. B. Huggins. The officers were William Mitchell, president; D. D. Wendel, cashier, and C. B. Huggins, teller. The capital stock was $50,000. The present officers are William Mitchell, president; A. M. Overall, vice-president, and J. B. Fowler, cashier. The board of directors are William Mitchell, A. M. Overall, Alex Hartman, J. I. C. Haynes, W. N. Doughty, C. H. Byrn, J. H. Reed, Horace E. Palmer, W. C. Harrison, Jr., W. Barton and C. M. Holden. The Stone River National Banking Company was organized May 1, 1872, with a capital stock of $50,000. The officers were W. N. Doughty, president; D. D. Wendel, cashier, and C. B. Huggins, teller; directors: J. P. Rice, W. R. Butler, W. C. Eagleton, T. C. Goodrich, J. I. C. Haynes and Theodore Smith. The present officers are William Mitchell, president; A. M. Overall, vice-president; J. B. Fowler, cashier. Directors: William Mitchell, A. M. Overall, Alex Hartman, J. I. C. Haynes, W. N. Doughty, C. H. Byrn, J. H. Reed, H. E. Palmer, W. C. Harrison, Jr., W. Barton and C. M. Holden.

The first newspaper ever published in Murfreesboro was *The Courier*. The initial number of this little sheet made its appearance June 16, 1814. It was issued from the office on the corner of Vine and Lebanon Streets, by G. A. and A. C. Sublett. *The Courier* was like other papers; at times it gave the news rather than the expression of opinions. The press was one of the Franklin style, not unlike that on which was printed the Declaration of Independence. Mail service was furnished once a week at this time, but to facilitate exchanges private carriers carried papers to Nashville. The *Weekly Times* was established in Murfreesboro in 1837, and was the organ of the Democratic party. It was edited by Thomas Hegan. The Tennessee *Telegraph* said: "The union of the Whigs for the sake of the Union." Its motto signified its politics. It was edited by E. J. King. This editor, like the modern editor, saw the salvation of the country depended upon the support of his paper and his party. The *National Vidette* was established by G. A. Sublett in Murfreesboro in 1828. It favored the election of Andrew Jackson for President in opposition to John Quincy Adams. It was an "anti-administration" paper. *The Murfreesboro News* was established in 1859 by A. Watkins, and was edited by G. T. Henderson, as a neutral political paper, but in 1852 it was changed to a Democratic paper. The paper was ably conducted by Mr. Henderson till it was suspended on account of the war, the type and press having been destroyed by the Federal Army. *The Telegraph* was the Whig organ of the county and was edited first by T. Taylor and afterward by R. S. Northcott. This paper continued till the war. *The Murfreesboro News* was again started by Mr. Henderson in January, 1866, and was continued till 1878, when it was sold to other parties. *The News* is now owned and edited by W. C. Frost, a young and vigorous writer, who is conducting the paper in a very successful manner. *The Free Press* was started in 1878 by G. T. and R. K. Henderson. It, as well as the *News*, is Democratic in politics yet conservative on all matters in regard to opinion. The pages of *The Free Press* show that the Messrs. Henderson knew how to edit a paper. The *Gold Eagle* is the organ of the colored people. It was begun in January, 1886, but suspended publication until the middle of February on account of machinery. The paper is a seven column edition and is edited by Dr. B. Andrew Franklin. It is issued from the office of Russell & Ransom.

The scourge of cholera first threatened the place in 1832, but fortunately did nothing more than to frighten the inhabitants. A general clearing up and fumigating of the foul place was begun. The cholera went away only to gather strength for its return in 1835, when it came like a terror in all its horrors. Men and women frightened fled from their homes as though they were pursued by a devastating army; business was suspended; relief committees were formed; G. J. Cain, a prominent merchant, died; Gen. William Brady, a prominent lawyer and candidate for Congress, succumbed to the disease; Dr. A. Hartwell, who did yeoman service for the sick, was himself attacked and died. A committee of young men, James and John Holmes, D. D. Wendel, William Spence, W. T.

Leiper, John Leiper, Robert Loik, Samuel Eagleton and James W. Hamilton were formed to act as nurses and attend the needs of the sick, and right nobly was the work done. The women, too, did their share. Providing coffins, digging graves and nursing the sick took all their atteniton. The town seemed depopulated by the disease and fright. Soon the destroying angel raised its wings and fled, but sadness was left in nearly every household.

Mount Moriah Lodge, No. 18, was chartered in the year 1817, on petition of F. N. W. Burton, M. B. Murfree, B. F. McCulloch, John Lytle, A. C. Sublett and John L. Jetton. The lodge met on the north side of the Public Square in their room till about the year 1832, when the discredit attached to the order, by the community, caused it to suspend after a prosperous existence for more than a dozen years. After the excitement above mentioned had died away the lodge again reorganized in 1840. They met for a time in a room on the northwest corner of the Square, then on the west side in a room on the third floor of a building; this room and contents were burned in 1859. The lodge next procured new regalias and filled a room on the east side of the Square. This lodge was compelled to suspend during the war, but was soon after reorganized, and now has a membership of about forty members. The present officers are William Mitchell, W. M.; T. H. Woods, S. W.; George Walter, J. W.; J. H. Allen, Treasurer; J. T. McKinley, Secretary; J. R. Thompson, Chaplain; J. J. McKnight, S. D.; J. C. Dunn, J. D.; W. F. Leiper, S.; J. W. Wigg, T.

Murfreesboro Commandery, No. 10, was chartered May 12, 1870, and was organized by V. E. Sir David Cook assisted by Sir Knights A. B. Martin and Alex W. Wick, of Baldwin Commandery, No. 7. The first officers were Sir J. B. Palmer, E. C.; Sir J. D. Richardson, G., and Sir J. B. Murfree, C. G. The officers for 1886 are W. F. Leiper, E. C.; John Bell, Jr., G.; William Mitchell, C. G.; W. D. Robinson, P.; H. C. Jackson, S. W.; Richard Beard, J. W.; H. W. Kerr, Treasurer; William Ledbetter, R.; Charles King, S. B.; H. Weakley, S. B.; T. M. King, W. Past Commanders: J. B. Palmer, J. D. Richardson, J. B. Murfree, T. H. Woods and H. H. Kerr.

Stranger Rest Lodge, No. 14, I. O. O. F., was instituted December 25, 1845, with the following charter members: J. N. Champion, Andrew Donaldson, J. A. Harrison, S. A. Bivens and R. G. Buchanan. On December 27 W. W. Earthman became a member, the oldest now living. Funds paid to Grand Lodge since its inception, $16,570.51; relief funds, $3,389.65. Two fires within the last decade have made a report on the orphans' educational fund impossible, yet there has been expended under this head $980.35. The lodge now owns a $3,000 building on the South Side. Present officers are R. M. Ransom, N. G.; J. P. Cosbey, V. G.; M. Hoehnlein and W. B. Drumright, treasurers. Orphan fund trustees: N. C. Collier, E. C. Cox and Adam Bock. This body has expended for orphans now under their care, $1,289.55. The Refuge Lodge has furnished the following Grand Masters: Benjamin Johnson, A. O. H. P. Sehorn, E. G. Budd and J. H. Crichlow, the only one now living, and these three grand representatives to the Sovereign Grand Lodge: A. O. H. P. Sehorn, E. G. Budd and J. H. Crichlow, now lieutenant-colonel upon the staff of John C. Underwood, the lieutenant-general and commander-in-chief of the army of Patriarchs Militant. Notwithstanding the misfortune of fires, etc., the order has had a successful career, and now numbers sixty-five active members.

The G. U. O. O. F. Lodge, No. 1822 (colored), was instituted in October, 1878. The lodge now numbers about 200 members.

The origin of temperance societies in Rutherford County dates as far back as 1827, as mentioned in the history of the Presbyterian Church. In this church was organized the first formal society having rules and by-laws. A society was soon after formed called the "Washingtonians," or Washington Temperance Society. After a time the interest in the matter somewhat died away, but was renewed again in 1847 under the name of "Sons of Temperance." This society prospered, and higher degrees were formed in 1851. In that year the degree of Knight Templar was opened in the court house, and in 1857 the K. of H. was organized. These societies continued to prosper till broken up by the war. In 1867 the order of G. T. was organized in the court house, and in 1868 the order of S. of T. was revived. To the efforts of these good people the State owes no little to her excellent temperance legislation.

Lodge No. 161, K. of H., was organized in Murfreesboro, September 25, 1875, with the following charter members: H. H. Clayton, F. H. Crass, W. B. Garrett, S. B. Bowers, J. O. Oslin, T. N. Crichlow, John McDermott, E. Rosenfeld, J. W. Childress, G. H. Baskett, Dr. J. B. Murfree, J. B. Clayton, E. C. Cox, J. R. Osborn, J. T. Rather, R. L. Martin, S. N. Lawing, S. G. McFadden, Ed Ohrenne, H. Hirsch and W. C. Osborn. The present officers are J. M. Wigg, P. D.; H. C. Finch, D.; H. Hirsch, V. D.; E. C. Cox, A. D.; S. W. Lawing, R.; J. J. McKinley, F. R.; J. W. Ewing, C.; Dr. R. S. Wendel, Treas.; G. W. Ransom, G.; H. Eickhoff, I. W. and D. W. Donaldson, Sentinel. Present membership ninety-five. The A. O. U. W., was organized May 2, 1877, with the following members: C. O. Thomas, Dr. J. B. Murfree, J. R. Osborn, J. N. Crichlow, R. F. Osborn, W. Roulet, F. H. Crass, W. B. Earthman, H. Hirsch, W. E. ——— and S. N. Lawing. This popular fraternity now numbers thirty-nine members.

Jefferson is located at the forks of Stone River. The place was selected, as stated elsewhere, as a seat of justice for the county and remained the same from 1804 till 1811. Col. Robert Weakley and Robert Bedford entered the land about Jefferson and had a town platted. A court house, brick, about 40x40 feet was begun in 1804, and ready for use in the summer of 1806. A jail and stocks were also built. Rude houses were rapidly built. The town proper embraced forty acres of land. William Nash opened a store near the place in 1803, said to have been the first in the county. An ordinary was kept in the place by Mitchell in 1805. As communication and travel at this time was mainly by river, Jefferson was an important trading post. Numerous keel and flat-boats were seen at her wharves, many were also built there. Goods were bought largely at Pittsburgh and brought to Jefferson by river; produce, grain, meat, etc., were shipped to New Orleans and sold. These voyages required months to complete. After the removal of the seat of justice to Murfreesboro the town began to decline. In 1815 the old court house was transformed into a seminary of learning under the name of "Jefferson Seminary of Learning." The Legislature made John Coffee, Peter Legrand, S. Crosthwait, George Simpson and Walter Keeble trustees of said institution and to govern the same. The school was of short duration; the old building stood till about 1835.

In 1824 Constant Hardeman built the first and only steam-boat at Jefferson and floated the same down to Nashville to receive her machinery and finishing touches. The boat was of about 100 tons burthen. The broad-ax by which most of the timber was hewed is now in the hands of David Neugent. The town now contains a shop, one or two stores, a postoffice and an Odd Fellow Lodge.

The little village of Milton is situated fourteen miles southeast from Murfreesboro. The first settlers came from North Carolina and Virginia about the year 1790. Among the first were James Doran and ——— Roach; the former entered land and built a house about one mile from where the village now stands; a stone spring-house bears "J. D., 1807," and is still standing. The latter, it is thought, entered the land where the village now stands. The first house was built about 1810. Little further is known of the place until 1830, when Howard and Benjamin Morgan purchased the land and laid out a town, to which was given the somewhat classic name "Milton." The town was incorporated and "constituted a body corporate and politic under the name and style of the mayor and aldermen of the town of Milton." The town soon assumed metropolitan airs, but after an existence of about a half-century the charter was revoked. The place now contains only about 200 inhabitants. The village contains an I. O. O. F. Lodge, Presbyterian Church, a drug store and two general stores. The amount of business in the place amounts to about $40,000 annually. The pride of the village is its seminary, which was erected and incorporated under the "four mile law." This school is in a flourishing condition under the management of Prof. N. D. Overall, assisted by Miss Mattie Hill; in the music and art departments are other competent teachers. The high moral standing, the people, their social culture, the fine lands surrounding and good mail facilities, make Milton a desirable place in which to live. Historically Milton marks the place of a hotly contested engagement between Gens. Morgan and Blackman in the late war, in which the former was defeated. Some of the Confederate dead lie buried in a beautiful grove near the village.

The village of Eagleville, consisting of about thirty families, is situated in the southwest part of the county. The first settlements made in that neighborhood were made about 1790. Pioneer settlers were William and Thomas Jordan, Henry Ridley, James Shepard, Robert Donaldson, James Neal, Daniel Scales, Ab Scales, John Guy, Robert Wilson, James Gillespie, Joe Carson, —— Burgess, George and Robert White.

The Missionary Baptist Church was organized one and one-half miles north of Eagleville November 7, 1839, by Rushing James Keal and John Landrum. The first members were Thomas and Sophia Jordan, Elizabeth Williams, Josiah Johnson, Drury Bennett, William Cullom, Robert and Nancy Palmer, John and Rhoda Hazelwood. It was then called Harpeth Baptist Church, but on removal to Eagleville, in about 1866, it was called Eagleville Baptist Church. Eagleville Lodge, No. 17, I. O. O. F., was organized May 20, 1846. The charter members were John Nunn, William Nunn, Samuel Rankin, Thomas W. Maxfield, S. S. Morgan, Thomas Cheatham, Thomas Moore and William Taylor. Business: Charles Williams sold the first goods in the place in 1832. His old stand is now occupied by his sons, J. C. & R. E. Williams. R. S. Brown has also sold goods for a number of years. Other branches of business are a drug store, cabinet shop, machine shop, tobacco factory, flouring-mill, two blachsmith shops, livery stable and a boot and shoe shop. The school, now under Prof. G. M. Savage, was chartered several years ago. It employs seven teachers, and the curriculum embraces the entire course of mathematics, natural sciences, English, Latin, Greek, Hebrew, French, German and Anglo-Saxon languages, metaphysics, logic, music and art. This school is furnished with a commodious boarding-house for girls, and a row of ten rooms for boys, beside the family buildings. The school building has eight rooms besides the chapel.

Readyville is situated on the Woodbury Pike in District No. 19, in the eastern part of the county. It was named in honor of Charles Ready, who was one of the seven justices that organized the first court in the county, in 1804. He settled in that county not far from the beginning of the present century. In 1833 this was on District No. 6, and George Brandon, A. Tenneson and Joe Macey were made inspectors of elections at that place. Readyville is situated in an excellent farming community, and maintains a flourishing school.

La Vergne was founded after the building of the railroad, and lies in District No. 3, near the Davidson County line. It was incorporated by an act of the General Assembly passed February 28, 1861. It contains several hundred inhabitants, two churches, stores, shops and other business houses. It was at this place that skirmishing began between the armies of Gens. Bragg and Rosecrans previous to the great battle of Stone River. The town fared badly during the war.

Salem is situated five miles southwest of Murfreesboro, on the Salem & Eaglevile Pike. Salem is near the western part of District No. 11. Versailles is the name of a postoffice near the center of District No. 10. It contains a store and other places of business. Middleton is situated near the southern boundary of the county fourteen miles south of Murfreesboro. It contains a Baptist Church, postoffice, store and shops. Christiana lies on the east side of the railroad ten miles from Murfreesboro. It is in the northern part of District No. 20. It contains a postoffice, a school, one or two stores and is a good shipping point on the railroad. Fosterville is a thriving little village situated thirteen miles southeast of Murfreesboro on the railroad. It contains a church, store, postoffice and shops. Carlocksville is situated near the southeastern part of the county fourteen miles from Murfreesboro and in the most thickly settled portion of District No. 24. It contains business houses, a Baptist and a Methodist Episcopal Church and a postoffice,

Stewartsboro, near the Nashville Pike on Stewart Creek, was formerly a place of some little business, but since the completing of the railroad the business has been transferred to Smyrna. In point of population and wealth this is now the second town in the county. It contains a school of excellent merit, a Presbyterian Church, a Masonic Lodge, stores and other business houses. Florence, on the railroad midway between Smyrna and Murfreesboro, has a fine location and is surrounded by excellent farming country. It supports an excellent school.

Rutherford County is divided into forty-three school districts, and has 150 houses for the education of children in the public schools. The schools were organized under the present system in 1869, and put into effective operation in 1873. Besides the 150 schoolhouses above mentioned the county supports seven graded schools, *i. e.* one at Murfreesboro, Smyrna, Milton, Eagleville, Fosterville, Lavergne and one at Florence. The school population for the year ending July, 1885, was white males, 4,069; females, 3,824; colored males, 3,398; females, 3,281. This makes a total school population of 14,572. There was expended for the year as above the sum of $39,556.82. In these schools there were employed 43 male white teachers and 44 females, and 31 colored male teachers and 44 females, making a total of 139 teachers. The total number engaged in both public and private schools amounts to about 200. The average salary for teachers in the public schools for 1885 was $25 per month, the minimum being $18 and the maximum being $60 per month. The average length of term for the year is four months. Excellent private schools of high grade are maintained the greater part of the year at Milton, Readyville, Eagleville, Florence and Smyrna.

The public schools were put in operation soon after the war, but for want of proper accommodations were not efficient until within the last year. An elegant brick building was erected on the site of the old Female Academy, and an efficient corps of teachers employed. The present corps of teachers are Prof. W. W. Millam, principal; Miss Sallie Ralston, assistant; other teachers, Misses Mary Jones, Nannie Wade, Allie Wade, Ida Clark and Janie Murfree. The colored schools are under the charge of Prof. Carney and three assistants.

Soule's Female College was organized in 1825, and was known as the "Female Academy." The first trustees of this school were F. N. W. Burton, Dr. W. R. Rucker, M. B. Murfree and Dr. James Maney. This school was for girls exclusively, those heretofore being mixed schools. Besides the ordinary branches taught there were in addition rhetoric, philosophy, *belles-lettres*, painting, needle-work and music. The teaching was done by the Misses Mary and Nancy Banks.

The Female County Academy was founded in 1829. One acre of ground was purchased in the north part of town for $100, and a two-story brick building of four rooms was erected thereon. A suitable course of study was prepared, and the services of Miss Keyser was obtained. The school was soon in successful operation. The Rev. Mr. Baker, who became the husband of Miss Keyser, was also employed as one of the teachers. After Mr. and Mrs. Baker retired from the institution Mr. and Mrs. G. T. Henderson conducted the school successfully, after whom Mr. and Mrs. Blackington took charge of the school. In 1850 the school had grown to such proportions that an enlargement was found necessary, and one acre of land was purchased of William Lytle and added to the grounds, on which additional buildings were erected. The first teachers in the academy after the enlargement were Mr. and Mrs. Fellows.

In 1852 steps were taken to have a female school of more extended limits. The Rev. Thomas Madden is said to have taken the initiative in this matter. The charter was obtained in 1854, and the following trustees appointed: L. H. Carney, B. W. Avent, D. D. Wendel, Levi Wade, W. R. McFadden, Joseph Watkins, William Spence, W. S. Huggins and W. F. Lytle. The school was founded on a very liberal basis, four of the above being Presbyterians, four Methodist, and one belonging to neither. The school was named in honor of Bishop Soule, of the Methodist Episcopal Church. The following faculty were employed: J. R. Finley, president; Mr. J. Hoffman, Misses Jane and Phœbe Raymond, Julia Knapp and Jane DeWolf. The school was opened in the Female Academy, but owing to disagreement with the trustees of that institution it was decided to erect a new building. About three and a half acres of ground was purchased where the old Methodist

Church stood, and a large brick building, three stories high, about 100x110 feet, was erected at a cost of $25,000. Dr. Finley resigned before the college was completed, and was succeeded by Dr. S. P. Baldwin, who conducted the school successfully two years, and was succeeded by C. W. Callender, who remained two years, and was succeeded by Rev. John Naff. Rev. Naff conducted the school till his death in 1862. Owing to the war the school was suspended, the building having been taken first by the Confederates as a hospital, afterward by the Federals. The building was greatly damaged by the war. The school was reorganized by the Rev. J. R. Plummer after the war, who conducted a school successfully for two years. Owing to a debt overhanging the building it was sold, the Rev. D. D. Moore, D. D., being the purchaser, for $15,000. Dr. Moore managed the school six or seven years, when it passed into the hands of J. D. West, D. D., and later into the hands of Prof. J. R. Thompson, its present owner. The institution has a faculty of nine instructors, the Rev. J. R. Thompson being the president. The school has a preparatory and a collegiate department. In the collegiate department is a freshman, a sophomore, a junior and a senior class, embracing the usual course of a school of its kind. Since 1877 there have been forty-seven graduates from the college. Under the management of Prof. Thompson the school has been eminently successful. The location, the surroundings, the high professional training, the social refinement, and the Christian influence that is brought to bear upon pupils at this institution make it a desirable place for the training of young ladies for the higher duties of life.

Union University was organized by charter dated February 5, 1842, under the title "Union University in Tennessee." The trustees named in the charter were William Martin, Robert Boyd, Crawford Howell, C. C. Trabue, J. H. Marshall, J. H. Shepard, D. W. Dickson, B. Gannaway, H. Maney, J. J. Whittaker, W. W. Searcy, P. F. Norflest, L. Reneau, Charles Watkins, B. Kimbro and L. E. Abernathy. The trustees had power to select a location. It was intended for a Missionary college. That denomination being numerous in East Tennessee Somerville was selected as the site, and G. W. Wilt began teaching a primary grade of work intended as a branch of the college. Owing to the failure to raise the necessary funds for West Tennessee the school was never properly begun at Somerville. A more liberal basis was made, and it was proposed to erect the college at Murfreesboro, still to be under the control of the Baptists, but it was to be in the main non-sectarian. The new name given the college was Union University. The following new board of trustees was appointed: Charles Trabue, Rev. Hiram Young, Rev. B. Kimbro, Hon. W. L. Martin, P. F. Norflest, C. K. Winston, James Avent, E. H. James, T. Vaughn, Rev. W. L. Perry, Thomas Ashford, Rev. T. B. Ripley and Rev. Samuel Baker. The Rev. M. Hillsman was elected treasurer, and J. F. Fletcher secretary of the board. The required subscription ($25,000) being obtained the work of building the university was begun. The corner-stone was laid in June, 1849, with imposing ceremonies by the civic societies of Murfreesboro. The address was delivered by Dr. Eaton, its first president. The building is a fine brick structure, 80x110 feet, and three stories high. The first faculty were Rev. Dr. Eaton, president; Revs. William Shelton, G. W. Jarman, David Bridenthall and P. W. Dobson, professors in the various departments. The Rev. J. H. Eaton, who was chosen the first president, was at the time managing the Bradley Academy, and by an act of the Legislature the Bradley was placed under the same management as the university. The school under President Eaton had a prosperous career. On his death his remains were deposited in a tomb in the college campus, near the scene of his labors. The Rev. Pendelton was chosen the successor of Dr. Eaton, and managed the school successfully till 1861, when it was closed on account of the war. During the period of the war the university building was used as a hospital by the army. In 1853 Eaton College or the Baptist Institute was founded and managed by the same board of trustees as the Union University. For the institute two acres of land was purchased of Dr. James Maney, in the north part of town, on which was erected a brick building, 50x80 feet, and two stories high. The building furnished accommodations for about 100 pupils. This institution passed into the hands of the Christian denomination a short time before the war. School at this place, as elsewhere, suspended during the war, during which period the building was used as a hospital or for other purposes, and was greatly damaged. After the war the Cumberland Presbyterians managed a school there for a time, and then it again passed into the hands of the Christians. The university and its branches has ceased as a university, but instead of the university proper there is in its stead the "Eclectic Normal School," which is now being successfully carried on by Dr. James Waters. The school has a good corps of teachers, a full course of study and a good attendance.

The work of the Cumberland Presbyterian Church began in this county in the early history of the organization. Preaching was at first held in private houses. Norman's camp ground was a favorite place of meeting for a long time. The denomination has churches at Mount Vernon, Jackson's Ridge, Rockvale, Lebanon, Rockspring, Fosterville, Lytle's Creek, Mount Tabor, Lascassas and Jerusalem. The Cumberland Presbyterian Church was organized in Murfreesboro on May 30, 1858, by delegates from Nashville and elsewhere. The first pastor chosen was J. C. Provine; the deacons were C. N. Brooks, J. H. Green, H. Osborn, R. N. Ransom and W. A. Reed. The members were J. N. Clark and wife, C. N. Brooks and wife, J. Reed and wife, H. Osborn and wife, J. Hooker and wife, R. N. Ransom, W. A. Reed, R. D. Reed and some others. Preaching had been held in town as early as 1840–45, by Rev. George Donnell and others from Lytle Creek congregation. The church was begun under the pastorate of Rev. J. P. Campbell, and a lot was purchased in 1859. A Sabbath-school was organized September 25, 1859, with the pastor as superintendent, and H. Osborn and R. N. Ransom, assistants. The school had nineteen scholars and six teachers. The church was only partially completed at the outbreak of the war, but being less damaged than others, services were held in that church by the Methodist Episcopals and Presbyterians for a time. In 1865 preaching was resumed in the church and soon after steps were taken to repair and complete the building, which was done in 1868–69. The class now has a house of worship worth about $9,000, a strong membership and maintains a good Sabbath-school.

Soon after Alexander Campbell began his wonderful career as a minister and theologian, converts began to be made to his doctrines in Rutherford County. The first church was organized in Murfreesboro January 1, 1833, and consisted of twelve members. Steps were immediately taken to build a church. Lot No. 59 of the original plan of Murfreesboro was purchased of F. E. Bicton for $50, and deeded to Peyton Smith, George Morris, William Smith, Thomas Rucker, Sr., Joseph Ramsey, Thomas Rucker, Jr., and G. W. Banton. The church was completed in due time, and the members began worship at their new home and continued till 1859–60, when the church built a new house of worship on Main Street. Services were interrupted here for a short time during the war, but were resumed again in 1865. This denomination has churches at Antioch, Miles Hill, Rock Hill, Science Hill and elsewhere. It is a strong and influential body.

One of the earliest church organizations in the county was the Primitive or Regular Baptist Church. Its first members were from North Carolina or Virginia. The early ministers labored with an apostolic zeal, and were known for their simplicity of habits. The first church organized in the county by the Baptists was McCoy's, in the Norman settlement. This was before 1800. Elder William Keel is believed to have been the first minister. He remained with these people some time and then went away, but returned in his old days. This church grew rapidly, and soon became one of the leading churches in the county. In consideration of $1, love and affection, on May 8, 1813, Thomas Rucker deeded two acres of land to John Warren and Drury Vaugh, deacons, or their successors in office, of that branch of the Baptist Church who believe in the "final preservation of the Saints in Christ, and Baptism by emersion." This church house was erected near Cumming's mill on the east fork of Stone River. This was called Providence. Other early members were the Lillards, Claytons and Clarks, also Dr. Yandell, father of the distinguished Dr. Yandall, of Louisville, Ky. Dr. Watson, one of its early ministers, was distinguished as a physician and a minister, and respected as a citizen.

Beasley's church was built four miles west of Murfreesboro about 1820, on the Beasley farm. There is still a house of worship near the same place. Among the early members of this church were Chrisnhall and wife; Posey, wife and family. Elder Whitesett was one of its first ministers. The denomination is quite strong at this place. Enon Church was built at a later date. The building is a frame structure, and stands about six miles north of Murfreesboro. The membership here is small. Early members were the Reeds, Barksdales and Searceys. Peyton Smith was one of its early ministers. He afterward joined the Methodists, and later the Christians. Lett Bond was a later minister of the church in Murfreesboro. The first church of this denomination was built near the southeast corner of the Public Square, and stood for some years. On the failure of the Bradly Academy early in the decade of 1830, that building was used by these people till the creation of the church which now stands in Murfreesboro. This was built in 1850–51. Prominent among the early families belonging to this church were the Brooks, Powells, Morgans, Lethermans, Ruckers and Claytons. Dr. Watson was a leading spirit in the erection and maintenance of this church. The membership of this denomination has greatly decreased within the last few decades.

Owing to a difference of opinion in regard to missionary work, Sabbath-school work, and other minor matters, there was a division in this branch of the church, the one branch being known by the public as Primitive, Regular or 'Hard Shell" Baptists, and the other as Missionary Baptists; the latter are characterized by Sabbath-schools, educated ministry and foreign missionary work. This denomination is now the strongest in the county, and has from fifteen to twenty churches and a large membership. This denomination was first organized in Murfreesboro, January 7, 1843. Church organizations already existed at Enon, Bethel and Overall Creek. Delegates were sent from these as well as from Nashville to assist the organization in town. The sermon was preached by R. B. Howell, and the deacons assisting in the organizations were J. H. Marshall, J. Thomas, C. C. Trabue and James Avent. The membership enrolled were S. D. Crosthwait and wife, Thomas H. Maney, Fanny Maney, Thomas and Priscilla Dickson, Mary L. Bell, R. Smith, Lorinda Smith, J. H. Eaton, W. H. January and J. F. Fletcher. The first deacons were B. Gannaway, John Malley and Frank Fletcher. At the first meeting J. H. Eaton was ordained to preach, T. H. Maney was elected clerk, and R. B. Howell was chosen first pastor. Steps were soon taken for the erection of a church, which was completed in 1848. This was duly dedicated, and was occupied till April, 1862, when services were interrupted by the war. The church was greatly damaged by the armies, and was afterward sold to the colored people. Services were resumed after the war at the Cumberland Presbyterian Church, the Rev. A. Vanhoose officiating as pastor. In 1868 the church began the erection of a new house of worship on Main Street; this was completed at a cost of about $10,000. The membership of this church is now about 135. A large church is maintained at Braley's Creek, Antioch, Concord, Eaglesville, and in fact in nearly every district in the county.

The origin of the Presbyterian Church is due to the labors of Rev. Robert Henderson, who began his work in June, 1811. The church was organized near Murfrees Spring, in April, 1812, with the following members: Robert Wasson, John Smith and William D. Baird, elders; others were Joseph, Margaret and Mary Dixon, John, Susana, Henry and Frances Henderson, May Stewart, Abigal Baird, Margaret Jetton, Margaret Wilson, Grace Williams, Elizabeth Kelton, Margaret Wasson, Jane and Elizabeth Smith. In 1813 Rev. Henderson gave the church half his time; in 1814 he was succeeded by Rev. Thomas J. Hall, and he, in 1815, by Revs. James Beuman and George Newton, each of whom gave the church one-quarter of his time. In 1816 Revs. George Newton and Jessee Alexander rendered like service, and in 1817 Jesse Alexander gave one-third his time. In 1818 Rev. Henderson again took charge of the church. The sacrament of the Lord's Supper was first administered to this church in October, 1818. The first public collection, amounting to $22.08¾, was taken up to defray the expenses of the church for the last six years. In December, 1823, the Rev. J. W. Hall became pastor. The number of church communicants at this time was ninety-one; the number in 1828 was 138. In 1819–20 the church erected a fine brick church in Murfreesboro; this was 40x60 feet, with gallery and cupola; in the latter was hung a 560-pound bell in the year 1831. This bell cost $220.31. This building stood till destroyed by the ravages of war. It was used as a hospital for sick and wounded soldiers. In 1822 this building was used for the meeting of the General Assembly. Aside from the Rev. Robert Henderson, who was a teacher as well as a pastor, the Rev. William Eagleton was the most noted. The Rev. Eagleton began his labors, December 29, 1829, on the resignation of J. W. Hall, and continued with the church till 1866, the time of his death.

No church history of the place would be complete without mention of this godly man. Many others deserve mention. D. D. Wendel was clerk of the sessions from 1846 till his death in 1873. The church was reorganized after the war by Rev. J. H. Neil, and a new building erected in 1870. This building at that time cost between $17,000 and $18,000. The church is new and out of debt, and has contracted for a $600 pipe organ. The membership at present is about 300 communicants. The Presbyterian Church deserves credit for being the first temperance society in Middle Tennessee. At a meeting of the synod, October 5, 1827, after reciting the evils of intemperance, it was "*Resolved*, that they will abstain from the use of distilled liquors; that they will not permit them to be used by their families or servants except as medicine; that they will not provide them as articles of entertainment for their friends, and they will discountenance the use of them in the community." Another very old church is Cripple Creek, which has a membership of 37; Stone River has 63; Hopewell, 78; Hall, 38, and Smyrna, 69. In the days of camp-meetings the Presbyterians had a camp ground at the Sulphur Springs and one in the McKnight settlement, near Milton.

The progress of the church was slow till December, 1828, when the first conference met in Murfreesboro, at which a great revival was begun, and the church was greatly strengthened. John Lytle, Mrs. Wasson and the Rev. John Lane deserve mention for their zeal and piety; also Capt. Jones, who conducted the first public prayer-meeting at the old Bradly Academy, in 1818. The Rev. Baker was the first stationed preacher in Murfreesboro; he began his work in 1829. Other prominent ministers of that day were the Revs. F. E. Pitt and Alexander. The old church becoming insufficient for the demand, a new church was begun in 1843, on a lot bought of Daniel Lernean, and deeded to F. Yoakum, William Rucker, R. B. Jetton, L. H. Carney, James W. Hamilton, S. B. Christe, John Leiper, W. J. Lytle and John Jones, trustees. The new building was erected at a cost of about $5,000. Preaching was begun in the basement in June, 1843, the Rev. T. W. Randle then being pastor. The dedicatory sermon was preached by Rev. M. L. Andrews, on June 23, of the same year. In 1862 services were discontinued on account of the war, the church having been used at first by the Confederates as a hospital for the sick and wounded, afterward by the Federals. During the period of the war the church was greatly damaged, but in 1873 the house was completely remodeled and rededicated. This church now has the largest membership of any in the city. Special mention should be made of the Rev. Sterling Brown, who held one of the most remarkable religious revivals ever held in the State, at the old Windrow Camp Ground, about the year 1824 or 1825. At this there were over 300 conversions. Meetings were held at that place regularly from about 1812 till 1873, except during the interval of the war. It was long the "Mecca" of the Methodists. The churches of this denomination now dot the enntire county.

The organization of this very popular branch of the church in this county dates back to about 1812. At that time there was held a camp meeting at the Windrow Camp Ground, at which there were many professions of religion. Other camp meetings were held at which itinerant ministers of the Methodist faith were present and worked with that zeal that was peculiar to the pioneer ministers of that faith. Rev. Robert Paine, who became bishop in the Methodist Episcopal Church, was a circuit rider over a district embracing Rutherford County. During the session of the General Assembly, he preached in the court house, and many members were present and took a part in the exercises, among them Felix Grundy, the distinguished lawyer and statesman. A class was organized at a house on College Street in 1821. The following are the charter members: Benjamin Blankenship and wife, Edward Fisher and wife, Thomas Montague and wife, John Lytle and wife, Martin Clark, Willis Reeves, John Jones, William Ledbetter, G. A. Sublett, D. Henry Holmes, Dr. W. R. Rucker, Levi Reeves, J. D. Neugent and David Hannis. Preaching was furnished by traveling preachers at first, and services were held either in the court house or in private dwellings till the year 1823. In 1823 John Lytle deeded a lot, near where Soule's College now stands, for the purpose of having a church erected thereon. The lot was deeded to John R. McLaughlin, Samuel McLaughlin, Simpson Simons, Benjamin Rucker, S. Ogden, A. Childress and Edmond Jones as trustees. A brick house, one story high, with gallery for negroes, and bell, was completed at a cost of about $1,800.

WILSON COUNTY.

WILSON is one of a group of counties which form the bottom of the great Silurian basin of Middle Tennessee. The surface of the land is rolling and varied with plateaus, hills and valleys, and is often picturesque. The surface is on an average elevation of between 500 and 600 feet above the level of the sea, while Jenning's Knob, six miles southeast of Lebanon is the highest elevation in the county, rising to a height of 1,221 feet above the sea level. The lands are based generally on limestones which occur in successive layers nearly horizontal in position, and have a vertical thickness, from the lowest exposed to the highest in the hills, inclusive of about 900 feet. A number of high hills and ridges in the eastern and southeastern part of the county are capped with a stratum of flinty material beneath which is a layer of slate. The limestones belong to the group of formations known to geologists as lower Silurian, the upper part embracing some 500 feet of layers pertaining to the Nashville formation (Cincinnati) and the lower part to the Lebanon (Trenton); as the town of Lebanon rests upon some of its layers. The rocks of the former division are seen on the slopes of the hills and ridges, while those of the latter outcrop on lower grounds and in the valleys. There is an abundance of rocks in the county consisting of varieties of blue limestone and sandstone, much of which is suitable for building purposes.

The supply of timber in the county is abundant, all species of trees growing in the forests, such as oak, hickory, ash, gum, cedar, elm, maple, poplar, cherry, chestnut, mulberry, beech, sycamore, dogwood, walnut, cotton-wood, box elder, sassafras, iron-wood, persimmon and willow. The soils may be divided into four classes: First, the river and creek bottoms, which are alluvial and of great fertility, and upon which may be grown all kinds of crops. Second, the dark soil peculiar to the cedar flats and glades, which is very poor and unproductive, and is the least desirable. Third, that found on the hills, ridges and plateaus of the northwestern and middle portion of the county, and on the slopes of the hills in the eastern and southeastern portion, which is a sandy-mulatto color, loose soil. Fourth, that found in the valleys and lower parts of the county, which is also of a mulatto color, but is more compact and clayey. All the different cereals, such as corn, wheat, oats, potatoes, and all fruits and cotton grow well in the county. The Cumberland River washes the northern boundary of the county for a distance of twenty-five miles, and besides the numerous springs all over the county there are the following important creeks: Cedar Lick, Spring, Cedar, Barton, Spencer, empty into the Cumberland; Sugg, Stoner, Hurricane and Fall empty into Stone River; Smith Fork, Round Lick, Spring and Fall Creeks have their source near each other in a group of hills in the southeastern part of the county, while the other creeks head in the numerous valleys.

Beyond an occasional migratory and venturesome hunter, trapper or scout, who passed through the vast forests and canebrakes in quest of the abundant game or in pursuit of marauding bands of Indians, the presence of white men was unknown in Wilson County previous to 1790. At the close of the Continental war the State of North Carolina made grants of large bodies of land to her soldiers in pay for gallant service in time of battle. The land so granted was situated in Tennessee, then a portion of North Carolina, and it was by the owners of the land that Wilson (then Sumner) County was settled. The following are the names of the parties to whom land was granted in Wilson County during the years between 1780 and 1790: William Ray, 1,000 acres; Isadore Skerett, 640 acres; James Kennedy, 640 acres; Cornelius Dabney, 640 acres; John Burton, 1,168 acres; John Williams, 640 acres; John Conroe, 640 acres; Hardy Murfree, 1,000 acres; Nicholas Conroe, 640 acres; Thomas Evans, 640 acres; John Davidson, 274 acres; Stephen Merritt, 640 acres; James C. Montflorence, 1,000 acres; John Kain, 571 acres; Walter Allen, 912 acres; Redmond T. Barry, 640 acres; William Hogan, 500 acres, and Andrew Bostane, 220 acres. Between 1790 and 1800: Robert Stewart, Jonathan Green, John Boyd, Philip Shackler, John Haywood, William Lytle, Alexander Mebane, Jeremiah Hendricks, James Rogers, John Brown, William Fleming, Bennett Searcy, Ambrose Jones, Edward Harris, Henry Barnes, George Kennedy, Jacob Patton, Reeves Porter, James Menees, Thomas Evans, Gideon Pillow, Delilah Roberts, David Douglas, Johnson Hadley, Joseph Cloud, Daniel Wilbourn, James Barron, Vachel Clark, Jesse Cobb, Samuel Churchhill, Boyd Castlemen, Ephraim Peyton and Alexander Denny, 640 acres each; William Hogan, 500 acres; Willie Cherry, 228 acres; Archibald Lytle, 1,000 acres; Lazarus James, 337 acres; John Wright, 2,000 acres; Henry Ross, 274 acres; John Dabney, 228 acres; William Martin, 1,280 acres; David Gibson, 1,000 acres; Thedford and George Brewer, 1,000 acres; John Boyd, Jr., 228 acres; Samuel Barton, 1,000 acres, and Absolom Tatum, 300 acres.

Many of the above never became settlers of the county, and numbers of the pioneers of Wilson County purchased of them the lands on which they settled. The first settlement of Wilson County was made in the year 1797 at Drake's Lick, near the mouth of Spencer Lick Creek on Cumberland River, which was afterward the northeast corner of Davidson County, by William McClain and John Foster. Two years later John Foster, William Donnell and Alexander Barkley made a settlement on Spring Creek, seven miles southeast of the present town of Lebanon. During the same year settlements were made on Hickory Ridge, five miles west of Lebanon, by John K. Wynn and Charles Kavanaugh, both of whom came from North Carolina, and on the waters of Round Lick Creek, by William Harris and William McSpadden, of North Carolina, and James Wrather and Samuel King, of Virginia, and also on the waters of Spring Creek, about eight miles south of Lebanon, by John Doak, John Foster, David Magathey, Alexander Braden, the Donnells, and probably others. At the time of these settlements the land was covered with vast forests and thick canebrakes, and game of every specie from the bear, panther and deer down to the squirrel and rabbit existed in abundance. Several years before, however, the Indians as a tribe had been driven back, and only friendly ones as a class were met with by the settlers.

From 1799 the settlement of the county was rapid. The lands lying on the waters of the various creeks being the richer and easier of cultivation were naturally the first settled, and hence in giving the following list of names of the early settlers, they have been grouped into creek neighborhoods. On Barton Creek: Charles Blaylock, Elijah Trewitt, Levi Holloway, Henry Shannon, Snowdon Hickman, William Eddings, Thomas Mass, Eleazer Provine, John Lane, Byrd Wall, William Thomas, Samuel Wilson, George Swingler, John Goldston, Benjamin Esken, Jeremiah Still, Thomas Sypert, George Wynn, Benjamin Wineford, William Peace, James Mayes, John Cage, Alexander Chance, Josiah Martin, Henry Reed, William Elkins, James Menees, John Allcorn, Thomas Congers and probably others.

On Spring Creek: James Cannon, Soloman Marshall, James Chappell, Walter Carrouth, Martin Talley, George Alexander, Joseph Moxley, Hugh Morris, Bartlett Graves, Spencer Talley, John Forbes, William Bartlett, William Sherrill, John Steinbridge, Josiah Smith, Alligood Wallard, Thomas Williams, Purnell Hearn, John Jones, John Walsh,

Samuel Elliott, Benjamin Mottley, Richard Hawkins, Gregory Johnson, William Steele, Henry Chandler, Arthur Dew, Daniel Cherry, Adam Harpole, and others.

On Cedar Creek: Hugh Roane, John Provine, Alex Aston, Samuel Calhoun, Perry Taylor, John L. Davis, Mathew Figures, David Billings, Irwin Tomlinson, Joseph Trout, Hooker Reeves, Nathan Cartwright, Lewis Chambers, Andrew Swan, William Harris, William Wilson and Joseph Weir.

On Spencer Creek: John Walker, William White, Brittain Drake, Lewis Kirby, William Gray, Joel Echols, Robert Mitchell, Philip Koonce, James McFarland, Moore Stevenson, Jere Hendricks and Richard Drake.

On Cedar Lick Creek: Theophilus Bass, Clement Jennings, John Everett, John Gleaves, Reuben Searcy, Joshua Kelley, James Everett, James H. Davis, Thomas Davis, Howell Wren, William Ross, Edmund Vaughn, George Smith, Harmon Hays and Daniel Spicer.

On Cumberland River: Edward Mitchell, Elijah Moore, William Sanders, Caleb Taylor, Bartholomew Brett, William Johnson, Josiah Woods, W. T. Cole, Joseph Kirkpatrick, Henry Davis, James Tipton, Thomas Ray, Reuben Slaughter, Daniel Glenn, James Hunter, Ransom King, Henry Locke, Ephraim Beasley, Sterling Tarpley and William Putway.

On Stoner Lick Creek: Blake Rutland, Zebulon Baird, John Graves, Benjamin Graves, Thomas Watson, John Wilson, John Williamson, Henry Thompson, Thomas Gleaves, Ezekial Cloyd, Anderson Tate, Jacob Woodrum, Ezekial Clampet, Andrew Wilson, James Cathom and James Kendall.

On Suggs Creek Benjamin Hooker, Acquilla Suggs, William Warnick, William Rice, Benjamin Dobson, Hugh Gwynn, Jenkin Sullivan, John Roach, James Hannah, Hugh Telford, Green Barr, Peter Devault, John Curry, Thomas Drennon, Joseph Hamilton and Joseph Castlemen.

On Pond Lick Creek: Robin Shannon, John Ozment, Lee Harralson, John Spinks and John Rice.

On Sinking Creek: Thompson Clemmons, William Bacchus, David Fields, Lewis Merritt, Frank Ricketts, Fletcher Sullivan, James Richmond, Robert Jarmon, John Winsett, Jesse Sullivan, William Paisley, John Billingsley, Seldon Baird, Dawson Hancock and Jonathan Ozment.

On Hurricane Creek: William Teague, John Gibson, William Hudson, Nicholas Quesenbury, Charles Warren, Jacob Bennett, Elisha Bond, Robert Edwards, John Edwards, Bradford Howard, George Cummings, John Merritt, Joseph Stacey, Frank Young, Henry Mosier, Charles Cummings, John Woolen, Absalom Knight, Thomas Miles, Peter Leath and Gideon Harrison.

On Fall Creek: William Warren, Samuel Copeland, Joseph Williams, Jacob Jennings, William Allison, Hardy Penuel, Joseph Sharp, Sampson Smith, Frank Puckett, James Quarles, Roger Quarles, Mathew Sims, Shadrack Smith, James Smith, Charles Smith, Aaron Edwards, Hugh Cummings, Isaac Winston, William Wortham, Burrell Patterson, Absalom Losater, John Alsup, Lard Sellars, Joseph Carson, Charles Gillem, Arthur Harris, Walter Clapton, William Smith, John Donnell, Adney Donnell and William Lester.

On Smith Fork: Dennis Kelley, David Ireland, John Adams, David Wasson, John Armstrong, Isaac Witherspoon, John Allen, Richard Braddock, Edward Pickett, Elisha Hodge, Thomas Flood, James McAdoo, Samuel McAdoo, Abner Bone, Thomas Bone, William Richards, George L. Smith, Samuel Stewart, William Beagle, James Johnson, John Knox, William Knox, John Ward, Solomon George, Reason Byrne, James Godfrey, Henry Payne, James Thompson, James Thomas, Thomas Word, James Ayers, William Jennings, Charles Rich, Abner Alexander, William Oakley and James Williams.

On Round Lick Creek, including Jennings Fork: John W. Peyton, Arthur Hankins, James Wrather, Samuel King, William Haines, John Bradley, William McSpaddin, William Coe, Abner Spring, William Harris, John Phillips, Benjamin Phillips, Edward G.

WILSON COUNTY. 843

Jacobs, John Green, Samuel Barton, Alexander Beard, Jordan Bass, Soloman Bass, John Lawrence, Evans Tracy, Joseph Barbee, Shelah Waters, George Clarke, James Shelton, William Neal, Joshua Taylor, Isaac Grandstaff, Daniel Smith, Jacob Vantrase, Duncan Johnson, Joseph Foust, James Hill, Joseph Carlin, George Hearn, John Patton, John Bradley, William New, Robert Branch, James Edwards, William Howard, Edmund Jennings, John White, John Swan, Thomas Byles, William Palmer, Park Goodall, Jerre Brown, Thomas B. Reece, James Scaby, James Hobbs, James Newbry and John Caplinger. The first corn-mill erected in the county was built by Samuel Caplinger some time in 1798. It was a small horse-power affair, the horse being hitched to a pole or shaft and driven around in a circle. The building was a small, unhewn-log house, and stood on the farm now owned by Roland Newby, in the Eighth Civil District. Very good corn meal is said to have been ground by this mill, and the patronage was drawn from a large scope of country. Subsequently the mill was removed to a site on Jennings Fork, and converted into a water-power. The first water-mill is supposed to have been built by Thomas Conger, some time in the same year, on Barton's Creek, about three miles northwest of Lebanon. A horse-power mill was also erected about that time by one of the Donnells, near Doak's Cross Roads, eight miles south of Lebanon.

Before these mills were erected the settlers went to Davidson County for their grinding, or converted the corn into meal by means of the old-fashioned mortar and pestle. In 1799 Mathew Figures built a water-power grist-mill on Cedar Creek, to which he afterward added a saw. In 1800 William Trigg and Joseph Hendricks built a water-power grist-mill on Spencer Creek. Other mills of the early days were those or Isham and Larkin Davis, on Cedar Creek; William Wilson's, on Spring Creek; Jesse Holt's, on Barton Creek; John Scott's on Spring Creek, and John T. Hays', on Smith Fork. Later on William Wharton built a water-mill on Spring Creek, in the Tenth District; Williams & Kirkpatrick built one on Spencer Creek, in the Fourth District; Alex Simmons built one on Fall Creek, in the Seventeenth District; James C. Winford built one on Spring Creek, in the Ninth District, and about the same time a paper-mill was built on the Cumberland River, twelve miles from Lebanon, at which a good article of paper, both news and commercial, was manufactured. The machinery was inadequate, however, and the enterprised was short lived.

With the increase in population there was an increase in the number and facilities of the mills in this county, and at the present W. P. M. Smith, C. H. Cook, J. N. Adams and J. W. Williamson & Bros. have steam saw and grist-mills; Jacob Earhart has a water-power grist-mill on Stone Creek, and W. C. Gillian has a water-power grist-mill on Cedar Creek, in the First Civil District; John Brown and William McFarland have steam saw and grist-mills, and Washington Moore has a water-power grist-mill on Spring Creek, in the Fifth District; B. D. Hager has a steam saw and grist-mill, and William Colquit and William Tomlinson have steam grist-mills, in the Seventh District; J. C. Logue has a steam grist-mill, and J. L. Hubbard a steam saw and grist-mill, in the Twenty-fourth District; Coon Lannon has a steam saw and grist-mill, and William Rice a water grist-mill on Sinking Creek, in the Twenty-third District; John D. Gains has a steam saw-mill, James Johnson a water-power grist, and W. D. S. Smith a steam and water-power saw and grist-mill on Cedar Creek, in the Sixth District; J. N. Cowen has a steam corn-mill and wool factory in the Twenty-second District; Mrs. Pendleton has a steam saw, grist and carding-mill in the Second District; Gains Leach and Hugh & David have water-power grist-mills on Sanders and Smith Forks, respectively, in the Fourteenth District; Dr. James McFarland has a steam saw and grist-mill in the Third District; J. B. Baird has a steam saw and grist-mill in the Twenty-first District; G. W. Wright has a steam saw and grist-mill in the Twenty-fifth District; —— Etherly has a steam saw and grist-mill, and Bailey Hall and William Barrow water-power grist-mills on Barton Creek, in the Fourth District; John Patterson and Patton & Harvey have water-power grist-mills on Smith Fork, in the Fifteenth District; Thomas Mitchell has a carding machine in the Ninth District; John Bryant has a steam saw-mill in the Nineteenth District; John W.

Bennett and John Wynn have steam saw and grist-mills, and S. T. Alsup has a water-power saw and grist-mill on Falling Creek, in the Twentieth District; P. W. & T. R. Hearn have a water-power grist-mill on Falling Creek, in the Seventeenth District; John S. Belcher has a steam grist-mill in the Eighth District; Vick & Miller have a water-power grist-mill on Town Branch, and Bailey Peyton one on Spring Creek, in the Tenth District, and W. L. Waters has a steam-power flour, grist and saw-mill in the Sixteenth District.

Although still-houses were more numerous than schoolhouses in the early days of the county, yet the owner and location of the first one can not be learned. Isham Webb had a still in the Eleventh District at an early day, and later James Carrouth, John Forbs, Jerry Johnson, Bolin Wynn, Robert Thomas, Jack Cook and perhaps others, whose names could not be secured, operated stills in various parts of the county, all of which had capacities ranging from one-half to two barrels per day of mash. The old-fashioned worm was used, and the houses were small, unhewn-log buildings, and in some instances the still was located out of doors. These stills all disappeared several years before the late civil war.

Considerable cotton was grown in the county, and it is claimed that the first crop of this article grown west of the Cumberland Mountains was on the farm of John Donnelson, afterward the father-in-law of Andrew Johnson, in Clover Bottom, this county, some time about the organization of the county. As early as 1802 there were numerous cotton-gins in operation in the county: One by George Alexander, near Center Hill; one by John B. Walker, on Hickory Ridge; one by Moses Echols, on the waters of Spencer Creek; one by Daniel Trigg, and others by Alaman Trigg, Henry Betts, John Watson, Robert Goodloe, Seth P. Pool, Joseph Sharp, Joshua Kelley, Edward Bondward, Thomas Wilson and Thomas Green in various parts of the country, the exact location of which is unknown to the citizens of the present. These have all disappeared, as they ceased to be of use many years ago.

The first store in the county was kept by John Herrod in 1800, but the location of his store can not be learned. It was a small mercantile establishment indeed, the stock consisting of a few standard articles of staple groceries, ammunition, nails, tobacco and whisky, all of which were brought from the older States on pack mules or horses. Salt sold from $8 to $10 per bushel; nails at 25 cents per pound, and everything else in proportion. Herrod also kept tavern at his store, they both being at his dwelling-house. A short time afterward George C. Hodge and Solomon George opened similar stores, or ordinaries as they were then called, in the neighborhood of Smith Fork. Other early store-keepers were John Gibson, Samuel Tillman, Huldah Sherrill, Richard Bryan, William C. Mitchell, George Cummings, John Lumpkins, John Brown, Isham Davis, George Jarrett, Carter White, William Stewart, Elisha Dismukes, Higdon Harrington and David Martin, all of whose stores were located in various portions of the county outside of the county seat.

So far as known, the oldest house now standing in the county was built by Samuel Sherrill, on Barton Creek, about two miles southwest of Lebanon. It was built some time in 1800, of hewn cedar logs, the doors and shutters being made of split boards, smoothed with the drawing-knife, and fastened together with nails made by hand. The house is strong and still serviceable.

Josiah S. McClaim, who was county clerk for a period of over forty years, now dead, is said to have been the first male white child born in the county, he having been born in January, 1797.

Wilson County was established by an act of the Third General Assembly of Tennessee, passed October 26, 1799, three years after the organization of the State. The act establishing the county is in substance as follows: "An act reducing the limits of Sumner County and establishing two new counties," etc., that part referring to Wilson County being in the following language: "Sec. 4, *And be it enacted*, that another new county be established by the name of Wilson, to be contained within the following described bounds: Beginning upon the south bank of the river Cumberland, at low water mark, at the mouth of Drake Lick Branch, the northeast corner of Davidson County; thence with the line of Davidson County to the Cherokee boundary, as run and marked agreeably to the treaty of Holston, and with the said boundary to the Caney Fork, and down the Caney Fork, according to its meanders, to the mouth thereof; thence down the meanders of the Cumberland River, by the south bank to the beginning."

Sections 15 and 16 provide for the holding of the courts of said county on the fourth Monday of December, March, June and September, and designate the house of John Harpole, as the place of holding the first sessions of the courts.

By an act passed by the General Assembly November 6, 1801, a portion of Wilson County was annexed to Smith County, and the present bounds of this were established by an act passed November 13, 1801, as follows: "Beginning on the south bank of Cumberland River at the mouth of the Drake Lick Creek, it being the upper corner of Davidson County, running from thence up said river with the middle of the channel of the same to the Smith County line; thence south twenty-three degrees east along the said Smith County line to the Indian boundary line; thence westwardly with said Indian boundary line to the Davidson County line; thence northwardly along said Davidson County line to the beginning." This act also provides for the appointment of Christopher Cooper, Alanson Trigg, Mathew Figures, John Harpole and John Doak, as a commission to organize the new county, run the boundary lines and locate the county seat, purchasing forty acres for the latter purpose; the said land to be selected with due regard for good wood and water; to lay off the county seat into town lots, sell the same at public auction, reserving sufficient ground for a public square, and with the proceeds of such sales defray the expenses of erecting a court house and jail, and other necessary building for the use of the county.

In the latter part of 1799 the boundary lines were run in accordance with the provisions of the above act, and the county was duly organized. But it was not until in 1802 that the county seat was located, when the present site of Lebanon was selected on account of its almost central location, and of the existence on the land of a large, never-failing spring of pure water, and which spring at the present time is as pure, fresh and strong as at that early day. The land selected was owned by one James Menees, who donated the necessary land.

Wilson County is bounded on the north by Sumner County, on the northeast and east by the counties of Trousdale, Smith and DeKalb, southeast by Cannon County, south by Rutherford County, and west by Davidson County, and has an area of 578 square miles. The county was named in honor of Maj. David Wilson, a native of Pennsylvania, who settled in Sumner County when Tennessee was a part of North Carolina.

Wilson County has a population of 28,747, of which number about 7,200 are voters, a large majority of whom vote the Democratic ticket. Previous to the late elections the county enjoyed the distinction of being the banner Democratic county of the State. Wilson ranks among the best counties in the State. Out of a total of 356,396 acres of land almost 200,000 are improved. In 1885 the cereal products of the county were 1,226 bushels of barley, 1,806,262 bushels of corn, 132,506 bushels of oats, 4,869 bushels of rye and 188,540 bushels of wheat. At the same time there were in the county 15,502 horses and mules, 16,285 cattle, 18,795 sheep and 49,583 hogs. The total valuation of the land in the county in 1885 was $3,500,679; of personal property, less $1,000, $295,836; of all other property, $158,220; total valuation, $4,440,370. There are 173,100 miles of railroad in the county, which has a total value of $204,360, and 620 town lots, total value of which is $485,635. In 1885 the tax assessment was as follows: Poll tax, 3,979; State, 13,821.11; county $15,079.89; school, $17,069.46; railroad, $19,750.98; court house, $2,220.18; highway, $3,503.96; total $72,943.12. The tax levy for 1886 is as follows: On each $100, county 25 cents; poll $1; school 25 cents; poll $1.50; railroad 50 cents; poll 50 cents; highway 11 cents; State 30 cents; total, $4.41.

The county court of Wilson County was organized at the house of John Harpole on Monday, December 23, 1799, the following commissioned magistrates being present: Charles Kavanaugh, Elmore Douglas, John Harpole, John Allcorn, John Lancaster, John Doak, Mathew Figures, William Gray, Andrew Donelson, Henry Ross and William

McClain. The exact place of holding this first session of the court, *i. e.*, the location of Harpole's house, is a matter of much dispute at the present time; yet after diligent search and numerous inquiries from reliable persons the writer is of the opinion that the house stood on the north side of Spring Creek about five miles north of the present county seat. The court was organized by the election of Charles Kavanaugh as chairman; Robert Foster, clerk; Samuel Rosborough, sheriff; John Allcorn, register; John W. Payton, trustee; William Gray, ranger; William Quesenbury, surveyor; and Benjamin Seawell, solicitor. Among the first acts of the court were to admit John C. Hamilton to practice as an attorney, prove a deed of conveyance of 640 acres of land from Michael Coonrad to his brother Henry, and order a road laid off from the forks of Round Lick Creek to the "25-mile tree," nearly opposite the house of Edward Mitchell. The March term, 1800, was also held at Harpole's, as were the June, September and December terms, during which sessions John Hogg and George K. Wynn exhibited their ear marks; John Herrod was granted license to keep an ordinary, permissions were given to William Trigg, Joseph Hendrick and Mathew Figures to erect water grist-mills; Lemuel Herrod, John Dickason, John B. Johnson, Jesse Wharton and Nicholas Perkins were admitted to the bar; $2 was ordered paid for the scalp of each wolf killed in the county; and a tax was levied for county purposes of $6\frac{1}{4}$ cents on each 100 acres of land—$6\frac{1}{4}$ cents on each white and $12\frac{1}{2}$ cents on each black poll.

The court continued to meet at Harpole's throughout the year 1801, during which time John Herrod took out tavern license, Charles Smith was admitted to the bar, and rates for ferrying were fixed as follows: Man and horse, $6\frac{1}{4}$ cents; man or horse, $3\frac{1}{8}$ cents; cattle and other stock, $3\frac{1}{8}$ cents per head; loaded wagon and team, $1; empty wagon and team, 75 cents; four-wheel carriages, $1; two-wheel, 50 cents.

From March until December, 1802, the court met at the house of Henry Turner on Barton Creek, three miles southwest from Lebanon, and from there adjourned to meet at the house of Edward Mitchell, in Lebanon, the new county seat having been laid out and the lots sold on August 16 of that year. Mitchell was allowed by the court 25 cents for each meal and lodging furnished the magistrates during the session of court. During 1803 the court fined Obediah Spradim $1.50 for profanity; James Anderson was granted ordinary license, and the rate of charges for ordinaries was regulated as follows: rum, wine, gin and French brandy, $8 per gallon; whisky or brandy $12\frac{1}{2}$ cents per half pint; lodging $6\frac{1}{4}$ cents; corn or oats 4 cents per gallon; horse with hay or fodder, 25 cents; pasturage for twenty-four hours, $12\frac{1}{2}$ cents.

In 1804 the March term of court was held at James Anderson's in Lebanon, the June term, at Edward Mitchell's and the September and December terms at Anderson's. Throughout 1805 and until June 1806 the court met at Mitchell's house, at which time the court adjourned to meet at the new and first court house, that building having been completed and placed in readiness for the court during the year. The first court house was a small cedar-log building, with a clapboard roof, and stood on the west side of the Public Square. It was large enough only for the holding of the court, the county officers having their quarters in various houses around the Square. Beyond this meager description nothing more can now be learned, as the memory of the present oldest inhabitant runneth not back that far. The jail was completed a short time previous to the court house. It was also a small cedar-log house, having two apartments, and entrance to the cells was through a trap door in the upper floor, the cells resting on the ground.

The court appointed Jeremiah Brown, John Allcorn and John Wynn a committee in 1806 to award the contract for and superintend the building of a bridge across the creek, which flows through the town (now known as Town Branch), and John Doak, John Harpole and Mathew Figures were appointed a committee to have a stray pen erected. Benjamin Tower was granted ordinary license and Robert Goodloe, Seth P. Pool and Joseph Sharp were appointed cotton inspectors.

In 1807 the court licensed Daniel Tillman to keep an ordinary, appointed Peter Mosley and Edward Bondward cotton inspectors, fined William Talbott 1 cent for inciting a riot, allowed Seth P. Pool $200 for building an office for the accommodation of the county officials, and allowed David Marshall $12 for building a stray pen.

In 1808 the court granted ordinary license to William Mann, and John Cartwright was granted permission to erect and operate a cotton gin. In 1809 the court ordered the removal of the stray pen. James Richmond was appointed cotton inspector, and Isham and Larkin Davis were granted permission to erect a water-power grist-mill. In 1810 Thomas Swain was admitted to the bar. Joel Mann was granted ordinary license, and William Wilson granted permission to erect a grist-mill. In 1811 the old jail was torn down, and a new one erected on the same site. The new building was of brick and cost $1,396. William Seawell was the contractor. In 1812 Charles Swain, James Johnson, Ezekial Bass and Reuben Bullard were each fined by the court for committing assault and battery, and Thomas Bradly, the sheriff, was fined $10 for absenting himself during the sitting of the court. In 1817 the court appropriated $500 for the building of a new court house. The building was completed in 1818. It was of brick and stood in the center of the Public Square. The house was square in shape, one story in height, and had a peaked roof, on the center of which was a square belfry and bell. In 1829 the court levied a poor-house tax of 6¼ cents on each 100 acres of land, 6¼ cents on each white and black poll, and 6¼ cents on each town lot. The court also appointed Etheldred P. Harris, William McSwain and Thomas B. Reise a commission to select suitable ground upon which to locate said poor-house, and erect the necessary buildings. The following year a small tract of land, three miles southwest of Lebanon, was purchased, and a cedar-log house, containing three rooms, was erected as an asylum. A few years afterward a new asylum was erected on a tract of land about six miles southwest of Lebanon, which served as a poor-farm until 1866, when 219 acres of good farm land was purchased of James Davis for $30 per acre, upon which stood a substantial weather-boarded log house. Four log cabins were erected, and such is the poor asylum of the present. A new jail was erected in 1832, which was also of brick, which stood until 18—, when the present substantial brick jail, which stands about two squares from the Public Square on West Main Street, was erected. In 1833 a new floor was laid in the court house. In 1846 the court passed an order for the building of a new court house, which building was not to cost in excess of $8,000. In 1848 the court house was completed, when the old building was torn down. The new court house was of brick, two-stories in height, and stood on Lot No. 8 on the south side of the Public Square, one entrance being on South Cumberland Street. The upstairs was devoted to a circuit court room, while on the lower floor were the quarters of the county officers and the county court room. The building stood until 1881, when it was destroyed by fire, and in January, 1882, the court passed an order for the erection of a new court house, appointing H. G. Johns, G. W. Lewis, J. F. Orgain, L. Drifoos and J. A. Brent a building committee. Subsequently W. A. Lewis, W. H. Brown and John D. Owen were added to the committee. The plans and specifications of the building were prepared by Bruce & Morgan, of Atlanta, Ga., and the contract was awarded to J. F. Bowers & Bros., of Nashville. When complete the building cost $18,306.80. It is a handsome brick structure, two stories in height above the ground, has stone cappings, tin mansard roof, and is supplied with fire-proof vaults and all modern conveniences. The front of the building is highly ornamented, and is set off with an imposing brick portico, with a flight of stone steps leading thereto. On the second floor are two large court rooms, one each for the circuit and county courts, while on the first floor are large, light and well ventilated offices. A handsome stairway leads from the main hall to the court rooms. There are three entrances to the building, which stands on the site of the old court house, one on the Cumberland Street side, one on the Public Square and one on the west side. During the building of the court house the courts were held in the Masonic Hall.

The clerks of the county court and their terms of office have been as follows: Robert Foster, 1799 to 1800; John C. Henderson, 1800 to 1802; John Allcorn, 1802 to 1827; John Stone, 1827 to 1831; Josiah McClain, 1831 to 1871; R. P. McClain, 1871 to 1875; Jesse F. Coe, 1875 to 1880; Abraham Britton, 1880 to 1882; W. M. Harkreader, 1882 to 1886.

Sheriffs—Samuel Rosborough, 1799 to 1802; William Wilson, 1802 to 1802 (three months); Nathaniel Perry, 1802 to 1804; George Hallum, 1804 to 1805; John V. Tullock, 1805 to 1806; Thomas Bradley, 1806 to 1819; James Williams, 1819 to 1821; Thomas Bradley, 1821 to 1825; John Hearn, 1825 to 1831; Paulden Anderson, 1831 to 1836; Benjamin G. Mabry, 1836 to 1839; Wilburn R. Winter, 1839 to 1840; Henry D. Lester, 1840 to 1844; John C. Lash, 1844 to 1847; Robert Hallum, 1847 to 1848; John J. Crittenden, 1848 to 1854; Jonathan Etherly, 1854 to 1859; Nathan W. McCullough, 1859 to 1866; William E. Foust, 1866 to 1870; Andrew McGregor, 1870 to 1874; David W. Grandstaff, 1874 to 1876; William P. Bandy, 1876 to 1882; James G. Hamilton, 1882 to 1884; William P. Bandy, 1884 to 1886. Registers—John Allcorn, 1799 to 1801; Henry Ross, 1801 to 1827; James Foster, 1827 to 1836; Thomas Edwards, 1836 to 1837; A. W. Foster, 1837 to 1839; Giles H. Glenn, 1839 to 1844; Robert M. Holeman, 1844 to 1846; Allen W. Vick, 1846 to 1876; John F. Tarply, 1876 to 1886. Trustees—John W. Payton, 1799 to 1800; James Stewart, 1800 to 1814; Edward Crutcher, 1814 to 1821; John W. Payton, 1821 to 1833; David C. Hibbitts, 1833 to 1844; John Shorter, 1844 to 1848; Benjamin Tower, 1848 to 1856; David B. Moore, 1856 to 1860; Jarrett W. Edwards, 1860 to 1872; J. F. Lane, 1872 to 1874; Nathan Oakley, 1874 to 1876; J. N. Cook, 1876 to 1884; D. J. Barton, 1884 to 1886.

The Circuit Court of Wilson County convened for the first time in the court house at Lebanon, September 24, 1810, Hon. Thomas Stuart, presiding. The first case of consequence on the docket was that of the State against Joel Alpin, on a charge of assault and battery. Alpin was found guilty as charged in the indictment, and fined $5. In 1811 Peggy and Solomon Ray were divorced; in 1812 Thomas Martin and Joseph Davis were each fined $10 for assault and battery; in 1813 James Rather, for assault and battery, was fined $5; Isaac and Betsy Cook were divorced in 1814, and in 1815 Betsy and David Hunt were also divorced; in 1820 Jedediah Willie was publicly whipped for larceny, and Robert Easom for assault and battery was fined $10 and sent to jail for twenty days; Hiram McKinley, for larceny, in 1821, was given twenty-five lashes on the bare back and jailed; in 1826 Lewis Yarnell was convicted of murder, and was branded on the left hand with the letter M, and given four months in jail; James Nilms, for horse stealing, in 1828, was sentenced to be hung, and upon the day of execution, after having been placed on the scaffold, was reprieved at the last minute and his sentence commuted; during the same year Joe, a slave, for murder, was branded with the letter M and given thirty-nine lashes, and for horse stealing Pins Simpson was sentenced to receive twenty-six lashes, six months in jail and to stand in the pillory two hours on the mornings of Saturday, Monday and Tuesday, and was branded on the hand with the letters H and T; in 1829 Willis, a slave, was given thirty-nine lashes and branded with M for committing murder; David B. Cole was publicly whipped and jailed for larceny in 1830; John Afflack, for killing his wife in 1830, was branded with M and sent to jail for eleven months, and for murder in the second degree Joseph C. Wilson was sent to the penitentiary for fifteen years; in 1834 Frank McCullough, on two counts for store stealing, was sent to prison for five years on each; Clayton, a slave, was convicted of the murder of a white man and daughter named Hunt , and was hung at Lebanon November 26, 1836; in 1837 Aaron F. Jones and James Lively were each sent to the penitentiary for horse stealing; McDaniel Smith was sent to the penitentiary for four years on a charge of bigamy in 1839, and John Lawrence, for larceny, was given eight years; Isaac Mahaffy was sent to the penitentiary ten years for murder, and Stephen L. Pearson was sent for four years on a charge of forgery in 1841; Leslie Clark, for perjury, and Edward Wyatt, larceny, were sent to prison in 1842; in 1845 Garland Brown and John Jones, on charge of larceny, were sent to prison for two and six years, respectively; for murder in 1848, Britton Collins was imprisoned for ten years; in 1850 Squire Collins and James Young were each sent to the penitentiary for ten years for murder; in 1857 Rufus L. Watson was imprisoned for ten years for murder, and on the same charge Parmelia Smith received a similar sentence in 1858.

In 1867 Russell Sanders, Polk Evans, John Bratton, Mary North, Thomas Clymer, Frank Baird, Isham Jackson and Wash Hardy, on charges of larceny, were each imprisoned one year. In 1868, on charges of larceny, Foster Newby was sent to prison for three years, Fayette Sneed three years, Thomas Waters one year and James Radford one year, and Nancy Elliott, for murder, ten years, and James Tarlton, for horse-stealing, three years. In 1869 Henry Palmer and Henry Sewell, for house-breaking, were each sent to the penitentiary for ten years; Henry Curtis, horse-stealing, ten years, and Frank Smith, for larceny, one year. In 1870 William Porter was sent to the penitentiary seventeen years for bigamy, and for larceny Sam Thompson, Ben Camper, Edward Knight, Marcus Hawkins and John Burch were given terms of imprisonment. In 1872 Hugh Bradley (colored), was sent up for four years for larceny, and Seth Williams, for house-breaking, got two years. In 1875 Jerry Belcher got ten years in prison on the charge of arson, and for larceny William Gooch, Albert McGregor, Burdine Preston and Moses Howell were sent to the penitentiary. In 1876 Porter Williamson and Burr Spinks (colored), were convicted of murder and sentenced to be hung. Williamson was granted a new trial, pending which he was hung by a mob, while Spinks was hung by law. In 1877 sentences were passed as follows: King Walsh, house-breaking, three years in the penitentiary; Jasper Williams, horse-stealing, ten years, and William Claxton, horse-stealing, three years. In 1878 Albert Gibson, for larceny, was sent to prison for three years; Davis Bass, house-breaking, was given three years, and James Scott, for larceny, received one year. In 1879 Scott Bass, for larceny, received three years imprisonment; Jere Evans, for malicious stabbing, one year; Pomp Grizzle, horse-stealing, three years and Bob Williamson, murder, three years. In 1880 John Bond, for rape, was imprisoned for ten years; William Tackett, horse-stealing, and Lee Hardy, larceny, were each sent up for three years. In 1881 Samuel Baird, Wash Hearn, Martin Graves and Pike Ward were sentenced to the penitentiary for larceny; J. W. Conner, for murder, was sent for twenty years; Bob Nipps, horse-stealing, three years, and Joe Harrison, for arson, was sent for five years. In 1882 Joe Campbell was sentenced to the penitentiary for twenty years for murder; Marcus Seay, horse-stealing, went up for five years, and, for larceny, terms of imprisonment were given Jake Neal, Jack Price, Alf Jennier, William Hamler, Bill Oxendine and George Dibrell. In 1883 James Payne, for house-breaking, received three years imprisonment, and in 1884 Frank Jennings and Tom Robertson, for murder, were each given ten and three years, respectively, and Frank Johnson and Bill Davis were given one and five years, respectively, for larceny. In 1885 Berr Officer, for larceny, was sent up for one year; Bernice Richardson, murder, got a life sentence; Hardy Baker, horse-stealing, three years; James Baxter, murder, convicted and sentenced to be hung. Baxter's case was appealed to the supreme court, where the decision of the lower court was sustained. His execution was set for November 3, 1885, but he was granted a reprieve, and on June 4, 1886, was hung at Lebanon; Andrew Church, an accomplice of Baxter in the crime, was sent to the penitentiary for life; both were negroes, and their crime was the murder of Mrs. Lane, an aged widow, for the purpose of robbery. In 1886 George Burns, for bigamy, was sent to the penitentiary for five years; Kate Rhodes, infanticide, sent for ten years; Asbury Johnson, Jesse Hill, George Thompson and Robert Keith, for larceny, were sent to the penitentiary for one year each, and W. H. Smith, marshal of Lebanon, was indicted for murder, he having killed a negro who resisted an arrest.

The judges who have presided over the courts of Wilson County since the organization of the circuit court have been as follows: Thomas Stewart, 1810-30; James C. Mitchell, 1830-35; Samuel Anderson, 1835-52; Hugh L. Davidson, 1852-64; Henry Cooper, 1864-68; John W. Phillips, 1868-70; William H. Williamson, 1870-78; Robert Cantrell, 1878-86.

The attorney-generals were Thomas Washington, 1810-18; Alfred Balch, 1818-24; William R. Hess, 1824-26; Samuel H. Laughlin, 1826-28; Robert L. Caruthers, 1828-32; Samuel Yerger, 1832-36; Thomas C. Whiteside, 1836-42; Hugh L. Davidson, 1842-48; William L. Martin, 1848-52; James L. Scudder, 1852-60; Barclay M. Tillman, 1860-66; Horace Rice, 1866-68; James M. Brien, 1868-69; James F. Stokes, 1869-70; Moses McKnight, 1870-78; Lillard Thompson, 1878-86.

The circuit court clerks have been as follows: Harry L. Douglas, 1810-15; Samuel C. Roane, 1815-17; Henry Shelby, 1817-18; Harry L. Douglas, 1818-21; John S. Tapp, 1821-27; Samuel Yerger, 1827-32; William L. Martin, 1832-42; John W. White, 1842-44; James H. Britton, 1844-48; Harris H. Simmons, 1848-49; Calvin W. Jackson, 1849-54; Plummer W. Harris, 1854-58; Joseph T. Manson, 1858-70; William McCorkle, 1870-73; Samuel G. Stratton, 1873-82; W. W. Donnell, 1882-86.

The Chancery Court of Wilson County convened for the first time July 25, 1836, at the court house in Lebanon, the Chancery Court of the State having been created during that year, having been provided for by the Constitutional Convention of 1834. Hon. Lunsford M. Bramlett was the presiding chancellor, and John H. Dew was appointed clerk and master.

The chancellors have been as follows: Lunsford M. Bramlett, 1836-40; Bromfield L. Ridley, 1840-61; John P. Steele, 1865-70;* Charles G. Smith, 1870-75; Horace Lurton, 1875-77; B. J. Tarver, 1877-78; George E. Seay, 1878-86.

The clerk and masters were John H. Dew, 1836-38; James B. Rutland, 1838-50; John K. Howard, 1850-61;* Orville Greene, 1865-70; Haywood Y. Riddle, 1870-76; R. P. McClain, 1876-83; R. C. Sanders, 1883-86.

Wilson County has furnished more than her quota of public men to the State and county. Among the more prominent was Hon. James C. Jones, who served as governor of the State from 1841 to 1845, and as United States senator from 1852 to 1858. The county has furnished six congressmen, as follows: Samuel Hogg, Robert L. Caruthers, Robert Hatton, W. B. Campbell, Edward I. Golladay and H. Y. Riddle. All of the above, including Sam Houston, Alexander Campbell, Abraham Caruthers and others, have practiced at the Lebanon bar. The present members of the bar are Robert Cantrell, E. R. Thompson, W. H. Williamson, B. J. Tarver, P. K. Williamson, R. C. Sanders, R. P. McClain, E. E. Beard, Lillard Thompson, J. S. Gribble, W. R. Chambers, J. T. Lane, J. P. Eastman, J. C. Sanders, Samuel Gallaway and Robinson McMillin.

Wilson County has a war record extending back to the Continental war of 1776, for among the pioneers of the county were quite a number of the patriots of that war, among whom were John Wynn, Edward Mitchell, John Dabney, John Harpole, Philip Shackler, Anthony Gain, Jeremiah McWhirter and James Scott, the first four of whom were commissioned officers. As early as 1800 the county had an organized militia of seven companies, the captains of which were Capts. Bishop, Moore, Echols, Dillard, Warick, Blalock and Hood. By 1807 the militia had increased to fifteen companies, under command of Capts. McNight, Pitman, Mann, Wilson, Caplinger, Bumpass, Leech, Branch, Alexander, Hunter, Martin, Coonce, Bandy, Joiner and Priestly. The companies had been increased four by 1810, and were commanded by Capts. Hill, Provine, Thompson, Cage, Hallum, Jones, Martin, Swingley, Quarles, Williams, Stiles, Estes, Henderson, Barnes, Smith, Bass, Spink, Davidson and Williamson. Robert Desha was the first brigadier-general of the Wilson County militia.

Wilson County furnished two full companies to the war of 1812, they being under command of Capts. Charles Wade and John Hayes. Out of the two companies only the following names can now be learned: Charles Wade, John Hayes, William and Lawrence Sypert, William Hartsfield, Zachariah Tolliver, Kit Seaburn, William Meyers, James Carson, Grief Randolph, William Martin, Thomas K. Ramsey, William Harrison, John Shackleford, Joseph Settles, William Norman, George Dillage, Fred Askins, —— Williams, —— Goldstone, —— Kirby, —— Aigan and —— Goodall.

Two companies were also sent by this county to the Florida war in 1836. The first company left Lebanon in June, 1836, under command of Capt. J. J. Finley, and the second went out in December, 1837, under command of Capt. W. L. S. Dearing. The following is an incomplete list of the soldiers of the county in the above war: J. J. Finley, W. L. S. Derring, T. J. Stratton, John D. Mottley, Dawson Hancock, John Willburry, P. Hearn, J. N. Kennedy, W. W. Talley, E. S. Smith, Nathan Oakley, Lewis Pendleton, J.

---

*No court during the civil war—from 1861 to 1865.

H. Kennedy, William Woodkins, Samuel T. Mottley, Bern Winford, W. T. Cartwright, George Lewis, Claibourn R. Jarrett, William Powers and John W. Alexander.

Again two companies were sent out from Wilson County in the war with Mexico in 1846. The companies were commanded by Capts. Smith and Hayes, and the following is a list of the names of the soldiers as far as could be gathered after dilligent search: Benjamin Rice, Henry Tyree, Dr. Herbert, David K. Donnell, Gideon Alsup, John Bostick, Nathan Oakley. Coon Dillon, Pleasant Tarpley, William Reeves, W. W. Talley, Moses Reeves, Newton Thomas, William Putnam, Linsey Chapman, Thomas Jones, Calvin Jones, Ross Webb, Thomas Helms, Alexander Neal, J. M. Alsup, M. A. Byers, William J. Coleman, Jesse Alexander, William T. Hobson, William Simms, James Bryant, J. W. Ewing, W. H. George, Thomas Stroud, Farrer Carson, W. A. Willy, Monroe Shelton, William Lewis, Foster Tucker and E. S. Oakley.

When the crisis came at the breaking out of the civil war in 1861, Wilson County promptly espoused the cause of the South, and responding with alacrity to the call for volunteers made by Gov. Harris, began at once the organization of companies to assist in repelling the threatened invasion of the State of Tennessee by the Federal Army. Early in the spring of 1861 the organization of troops was inaugurated, and was continued throughout the whole year and during the year following. Portions of the Seventeenth, Eighteenth, Twenty-fourth, Twenty-eighth, Thirty-eighth and Forty-fifth Regiments of Tennessee Infantry, of the Fourth and Fifth Regiments of Tennessee Cavalry, and of Company C, First Tennessee Heavy Artillery were furnished by Wilson County.

The first company organized was the "Blues," of which Robert Hatton was the captain. Then followed in rapid succession five companies, as follows: The "Grays," Capt. John K. Howard; the "Statesville Tigers," Capt. Nathan Oakley; the "Hurricane Rifles," Capt. Daniel G. Shepard; the "Silver Spring Guards," Capt. J. A. Anthony, and the "Harris Rifles," Capt. Monroe Anderson. The above companies left Lebanon May 20, 1861, going to Nashville, from which city they were ordered to Camp Trousdale, in Sumner County, for instructions. Upon the organization of the Seventh Regiment of Tennessee Infantry, all six of the Wilson County Companies were placed in the regiment, and Capt. Robert Hatton was elected colonel of the same. Thomas H. Bostick succeeded to Col. Hatton's place as captain of the "Blues," and W. H. Williamson succeeded Capt. Howard in the captaincy of the "Grays." The companies were then numbered as follows: Harrison Rifles, Capt. Monroe Anderson, Company D; Statesville Rifles, Capt. Oakly, Company F; Hurricane Rifles, Capt. Daniel G. Shepard, Company G; Grays, Capt. W. H. Williamson, Company H; Silver Spring Guards, Capt. Anthony, Company I; Blues, Capt. Bostic, Company K. Remaining at Camp Trousdale until in the latter part of August of the same year, the Seventh Regiment proceeded to West Virginia, and were in their first engagement at the battle of Cheat Mountain. The next engagement was the battle of Seven Pines in Virginia, in which battle Col. Hatton, who had previously been promoted to a generalship, was killed. The Wilson County companies continued with the regiment throughout the war, and were engaged with the regiment in all its battles and campaigns, and were present at the final surrender of the army of Virginia at Appomattox Court House.

Early in the fall of 1861 four more companies were raised in Wilson County. Leaving Lebanon these companies reported also to Camp Trousdale, where they went under instructions. When the Forty-fifth Regiment of Tennessee Infantry was organized, the Wilson County companies were assigned places therein, as follows: Company B, Capt. Curtis; Company F, Capt. Oldham; Company G, Capt. S. S. Preston, and Company H, Capt. Andrew Beard. With the Forty-fifth Regiment the four Wilson County companies participated in the battles of Shiloh, Vicksburg Landing, Baton Rouge, Murfreesboro, Chickamauga, and all the different engagements of the regiment, and were present at the final surrender at Bentonville, N. C., by which time the regiment had dwindled down from death, sickness, disappearance, etc., to less than 100 men.

During the same fall, 1861, three companies of cavalry were raised in Wilson County, and reported to Camp Cheatham and were placed in the Fourth Regiment of Tennessee Cavalry. They were Company B, Capt. John R. Davis; Company C, Capt. Phillips, and Company G, Capt. Sam Thompson. These companies were engaged with this regiment in the various campaigns, and sustained heavy losses.

During 1861 another company of infantry was raised in the county, and reported to Camp Trousdale. This company was given a place in the Eighteenth Regiment of Tennessee Infantry, upon its organization, as Company K. When Company K left Lebanon W. J. Grayson was captain, but he dying in a few months' time, William P. Bandy, at present sheriff of Wilson County, was elected to the vacancy. The regiment went first to Bowling Green, Ky., and then to Fort Donelson, where they were captured at the fall of that fort, in 1862. After the exchange of the regiment at Vicksburg Company K was reorganized, with 126 men, only one of whom was present at the surrender at the close of the war. In the latter part of 1861 another company was raised in Wilson and DeKalb Counties, and left Alexandria under command of Capt. T. C. Goodner. The company was placed in the Twenty-fourth Regiment of Tennessee Infantry as Company K. At about the same time as above another company was raised in Lebanon, and under command of Capt. E. I. Golladay, reported at Camp Arrington, near Memphis, and was mustered into the Thirty-eighth Regiment of Tennessee Infantry as Company H. A portion of Company D, Capt. John Wiseman, was also raised in Wilson County, and joined the Fifth Regiment of Tennessee Calvary, Gen. John Morgan's command.

In December, 1861, A. F. Orr, E. C. Fite, R. W. Miller, T. H. Norman, T. J. Hankins, W. P. Skeen, D. B. Anderson, Fines Underwood, E. M. Hearn and H. M. Cartwell left Lebanon for Columbus, Ky., where they joined Company C, Capt. Sterling, of the First Tennessee Heavy Artillery. From Columbus they went to Island No. 10, then to Vicksburg, where they were captured. After being exchanged the company was reorganized and was ordered to Battery Tracy, in Mobile Bay, and from Battery Tracy they were ordered to Fort Morgan, where they were captured and sent to Governor's Island, N. Y. All of the Wilson County portion, with one exception—Underwood, who died in prison—survived the war and returned to Wilson County. In the spring of 1862 Capt. Jonathan Etherly took out from Wilson County Company F, of the Twenty-eighth Regiment of Tennessee Infantry. Capt. Etherly was afterward promoted to a colonelcy.

The above is a list of the companies, their letters and captains, and the regiments to which they belonged; and for a detailed account of the campaigns of the several regiments the reader is referred to the war chapter of this volume, to be found elsewhere.

While Wilson County's soldiers were at the front the county, and particularly Lebanon, was the scene of several stirring events. In the spring of 1862 a regiment of Federal troops, under command of Col. Monday, pitched their tents in Lebanon and held full possession of the town for about three months. The *campus* of the university was selected as their quarters, and the college building was converted into barracks. In the latter part of the same year, upon the evacuation of Lebanon by the Federals, Gen. John Morgan, with about 300 of his cavalry, was quartered in Lebanon for a short while. The Federals were at Murfreesboro, and, learning of Gen. Morgan's presence in Lebanon, sent a detachment of cavalry, under Gen. Dumont, to effect his capture. The Federal cavalry arrived at Lebanon at daylight and at once opened on the Confederates. Their pickets were driven in, and, though they had large odds to contend against, the plucky Confederates prepared for action. Gen. Morgan had quarters at the Lee House, and when the skirmishing began had not yet awakened. His men retreated from the college building into the town, and, being pressed, took shelter in the Odd Fellow's Hall, on West Main Street, near the court house, from which place they were dislodged only after a sharp fight. Gen. Morgan and the majority of his command made their escape, though it was a close call. Several on both sides were killed and wounded.

In 1863 Gen. Reynolds, who was stationed at Nashville, made frequent raids into Wilson County, and gathered up all the horses and cattle to be found.

Unlike many of the Tennessee counties, Wilson was not injured to any great extent by guerrillas and jayhawkers, though what were termed "home-made Yankees" committed a few depredations. At Shop Springs, some time in 1864, William Williams was arrested while in bed by supposed "home-made Yankees," and was led out from his house a short distance and shot; but beyond this nothing of a similar nature was done.

Lebanon, the county seat of Wilson, was founded in 1802, at which time the commission appointed by the General Assembly for that purpose, selected the land of James Menees upon which to locate the county seat. The town lots were sold at public auction on the 16th of August of the same year, among the purchasers being William Bloodworth, James Peacock, John Wright, Edward Mitchell, M. Stewart, William Crabtree, William Trigg, S. Harpole, William Gray, John Irwin, J. Providence, Peter Rule, John Impson, William Allen and others. Lebanon is situated on the east branch of Barton Creek (Town Branch), six miles south of Cumberland River, and about six miles north of the geographical center of the county, and on the Tennessee & Pacific Railway, thirty miles east from Nashville, and has a population of 3,000. The first settler on what is now the site of Lebanon, was Neddie Jacobs, who built a small log hut in 1800, and maintained himself and wife by fishing and hunting. He was an odd character, and is remembered chiefly for his fiddling propensities, as he would sit and fiddle by the hour, putting aside his beloved instrument only to replenish his larder with game. The first house after the town was laid out was built by John Impson, which stood near the spring in the Public Square. Thomas Impson, Edward Mitchell, Edmund Crutcher and James Anderson also erected houses at about the same time. The first brick house was erected in 1812 by Dr. Henry Shelby, and soon afterward another brick house was erected by Joseph Johnson. William Allen, an Irishman, was the first man to open a store in Lebanon, and the first hotel proprietor was Edward Mitchell, these two gentlemen engaging in business in 1803. The first physicians were Drs. John Tulloch and Samuel Hogg. The first postmaster was John Allcorn, and the first school-teacher was an Irishman named John Trotter, in about 1805. The first church was the Methodist Church, which was erected in about 1812, of which Rev. German Baker was the first preacher. Previous to this services were held at private residences and in the court house.

In November, 1807, the General Assembly passed an act for the regulation of the town of Lebanon, by which Samuel Hogg, Edmund Crutcher, David Marshall, Joseph Johnson and John Allcorn were appointed commissioners. The act provided further that a majority of the commissioners should constitute a quorum, and that one of their number should be chosen as president to preside over their meetings. The commissioners were given power to levy a tax on all town lots, call out the able-bodied men to work on the roads, and appropriate money for the improvement of the town.

Edmund Crutcher was chosen as the first president of the commission, and consequently was the first mayor of Lebanon. The first newspaper established was the *Lebanon Gazette*, which was established in 1818 by Messrs. Ford & Womack. It was published but a short time. In 1842 the *Banner of Peace*, edited by Dr. F. R. Cassitt, was established in Lebanon and published in the interest of the university until 1851, when it was removed to Nashville. Other papers published in Lebanon have been the *Chronicle*, the *Pocket*, the *Free Press*, and the *Cumberland University Magazine*. The papers of the present time are the *Herald* and *Register*. The *Herald* was established in October, 1853, by W. Z. Neal and R. T. Spillers. It was a seven-column folio, and in politics was Whig. The paper was published until the civil war, when it was suspended for three years. In 1865 the paper was revived by Neal & Ward, the latter having purchased the interest of Mr. Spillard. In December, 1869, R. L. C. White purchased Mr. Neal's interest, and in 1871 Mr. White became the sole proprietor and has continued as such to the present time. The *Herald* is a five-column quarto, has a good circulation, and is independent in politics. The *Register* was established in 1883 by D. C. Williams, who sold out the paper to J. D. Kirkpatrick in 1884. Mr. Kirkpatrick conducted the *Register* until June, 1886, when he sold the property to A. C. Durdin. The *Register* is a seven-column folio, Democratic in politics, and enjoys a good circulation and advertising patronage.

From 1800 to 1820, the business men of Lebanon were John Herrod James Anderson, Edward Mitchell, William Mann, Benjamin Tarver, George Hallum, Joel Mann, David Marshal, Reddick Eason, Leonard Sims, Allan Avery, Patrick Anderson, Yerger & Golladay, Cage & Crutcher, Winchester & Cage, Jaspar R. Ashworth, and Nathaniel Dew. During the same period, Edward Mitchell, David Marshal and John Herrod were the tavern keepers.

The business men of the twenties were James Johnson, Mathew Dew, Yerger & Golladay, Foster Crutcher, Hicks & Johnson, Pauldin Anderson, John Muirhead, David Marshal, Allcorn & Johnson, Harry L. Douglas, Frank Anderson, Thomas J. Thompson, Jasper R. Ashworth, T. J. Stratton and Henry Chambers. The hotels during the same period were conducted by David Marshal, George Helms, William Hartsfield and Harry L. Douglas. During the thirties the business men were Jasper R. Ashworth, Joseph Phillips. Lawrence Sypert, T. J. Stratton, William Hall, Edward and John W. White, John Hearn, John M. Hill, Dr. James Frazier, M. T. Cartwright, P. & T. Anderson, Stiff Harrison, E. A. & J. W. White, White & Price, Henry Smith, Peyton Ewing & Co., Fisher Bros., Dawson Hancock, Allcorn & Johnson, Ewing and Richmond, George H. Bullard, Mathew Cartwright, Gillespie & Mabry, Hearn & Hill, E. A. & J. W. White, and W. H. Wortham. Albert Wynn and a company composed of Obediah Gordon. George F. McWhirter and James G. Robertson, were the innkeepers, and a company composed of Gears, Wilkerson, Pyle, Porter & Co., conducted an extensive carriage factory during that period. At the same time a large cotton factory, owned and operated by a stock company under the firm name of the Tennessee Manufacturing Company, was in full operation, and upward of 500 hands were employed in the manufacture of cotton goods of all descriptions. The property was afterward destroyed by fire and never rebuilt.

The business men of the thirties with but few exceptions, and the following additions, were the same during the forties: L. Drifoos and John W. Price.

During the fifties the business men were George Harsh, Jacob Howard, T. J. Stratton, M. A. Price, W. T. Coles, Daniel R. Fakes, Burr Harris, A. R. Davis, L. Drifoos, J. H. Armstrong, Cook & Owen, P. G. Duffer, N. Cantrell, John A. Haynes, James McCasland, Ed R. Penebaker, Robert L. Williams, R, P. Allison, T. E. Davis & Co., Burgess & Mattley, G. W. Lewis, H. D. Lester & Son, A. M. Springer, J. F. Coe, Lester & Smith, and D. Cook, Jr. In 1854 the Lebanon Flour-mill was established on the site of the old cotton factory by W. W. Carter, for that time it was considered the best mill in the State. In 1859 John A. Lester, purchased a half interest in the mill, and since then several changes have occurred in its proprietorship, and at the present the property is owned by Mr. Lester and his son-in-law, Selden R. Williams. The mill is supplied with the most improved machinery, and has a capacity of 100 barrels of flour per day. The capital invested is $15,000.

The business men of the sixties were Dabney Carr, T. J. Stratton, J. Emanuel, W. H. Armstrong, W. H. Brown, Cash M. Park, D. Cook, Jr., Clark & Cook, Burgess & Co., J. L. White, L. Drifoos & Co., Charles Stone, A. R. Fonville, Kennedy & Aust, J. M. Woolard, J. T. Manson, Brittain & Neal, Coe & Morris, and T. Harrington. In August, 1866, the People's National Bank was established by Mattley & Campbell, and has continued in business up to the present. The officers at this time are Judge Nathan Green, president; Samuel T. Mattley, cashier. The capital stock is $50,000 with $10,000 surplus.

The business men of the seventies were as follows: General Merchants—Robinson & Perry, J. C. Crawford, J. P. Tolliver, W. W. Donnell, J. H. Ozment & Co., J. O. Dillard, W. T. Cartwright, Hughlitt & Harris, Rosenthel & Bros., J. T. McClain & Co., J. B. Halley, C. T. Cox, D. D. Smithwick, Joseph Wharton, Goodbar & Means, G. W. Lewis, John W. Comer, M. J. Watkins, Leggon & Bros., Hatcher & Johnson, Donnell & Young, J. Harding, Thomas Jenkins, Lampton Bros., J. A. Lester & Co., Dillard & Wilson, Fish & Reese, L. A. & J. B. Wynn, C. L. Johns, G. W. Collier and G. W. Martin. Boots and shoes—Samuel H. Matherly and J. A. Haynes & Co. Tin shop and stoves—N. S. Williams. Drugs—A. P. Thompson, and Gwynn & Peyton. Livery stables—Swindle & Shorter, Murphey & Buchanan, and Orgain & Watkins.

In 1870 the Bank of Wilson was established with Dr. John Owen as president and T. J. Stratton as cashier. In 1872 the name of the bank was changed to that of the Second National, with James Hamilton, as president, and Mr. Stratton, cashier. The present officers are S. R. Williams, president; John Palmer, vice-president; W. H. Brown, cashier. The cash capital of this bank is $70,000. In 1875 Waters & Co., erected a large flouring-mill and stocked it with the best of machinery, and the mill is in operation at the present under the same proprietors. The capital invested in the property is $15,000.

The business interests of the present are represented as follows: S. Martin, J. E. Stratton, R. P. Oldham, McClain Bros. and Wilson & Waters, dry goods; J. L. Drifoos, Shannon & Co., Freeman & Whitescower, Monroe Fish, W. D. Chandler, Edward Wheeler, R. S. Haley & Sons, Huggins & Seagraves and Ligan & Bros., groceries; S. M. Anderson & Co., Gwynn & Hinds and McDonald, McKinzie & Co., druggists; H. M. Drifoos and J. F. Odum & Co., merchant tailors; D. L. Brown, clothing; John A. Haynes, Fakes & Co. and Samuel Matherly, boots and shoes; N. J. G. Allen, tinware and stoves; J. P. Cox, undertaker; R. M. Cartwell and Freeman & Whitescarver, saddlers; J. A. Woolard & Bro., J. T. Lee, Billings & Ragland and Ligan Bros., saloons; J. R. Shorter, Neal & Ligan, A. J. Rutherford, Hinse & Hannah, Murphey & Buchanan and Johnson & Vance, livery stables; Trebbling & Smith, butchers; J. M. Watkins, John W. Conner and Mrs. Cal. Woodard, hotels. In 1884 the Bank of Lebanon was established with a cash capital of $25,000. The officers are James Hamilton, president; D. W. Dinges, vice-president, and S. G. Stratton, cashier. The manufactories of the present are the Lebanon Planing-mill and Barrel Factory, Williams & Covington, proprietors; John W. Reede and Pyle & Hartsfield, carriage manufactories, and John Shelton, marble-yard. In June, 1885, the Lebanon Creamery was established by a stock company with J. Moldenhower, a native of Denmark, as manager. Upward of 4,000 pounds of milk are received at the creamery each day, which is manufactured into butter and cheese. The machinery used in the creamery is of the most modern make, embracing a Danish milk separator, which separates the cream from the milk at the rate of 2,000 pounds per hour. The milk for the establishment is supplied by the many herds of fine blooded milk cows for which Wilson County is noted.

Among the early prominent physicians of Lebanon were Thomas Hogg, James Frazier, John Ray, L. W. White, Drs. Allison, Crutchfield, Miles and McCorkle. The present physicians of Lebanon are J. M. Anderson, J. W. Holbert, O. C. Kidder, F. A. Fleming, J. L. Fite, William Hannah and G. L. Robertson. Dentists: W. H. Bennett and A. F. Claywell. Lebanon has eight churches, as follows: Methodist Episcopal, Cumberland Presbyterian, Baptist and Christian (white), and Methodist Episcopal, Baptist, Cumberland Presbyterian and African Methodist Episcopal (colored), all of which are treated of more fully in the chapter on churches.

The secret societies of the town are as follows: Lebanon Lodge, F. & A. M., No. 97, established during the thirties; Magnolia Lodge, No. 69, I. O. O. F., established in 1847; Lotus Lodge, No. 20, organized in 1875; Lebanon Lodge, No 69, A. O. U. W., established in 1883; Lebanon Lodge, K. of H., No. 222, established in January, 1876, and Cedar City Lodge, No. 23, G. T., organized in 1884.

Lebanon was first incorporated in November, 1807, and has continued as a corporation in some shape or other up to the present time, the form of government in force to-day being a taxing district, which went in force in 1881. The present officers are J. Matt Woolen, mayor; E. E. Beard, treasurer; J. P. Eastman, secretary and financial agent; W. H. Smith, marshal.

The Wilson County Agricultural and Mechanical Association was organized in Lebanon in 1852, and with the exception of a suspension during the late war has held annual exhibitions at the fair grounds near Lebanon ever since. The fair grounds enclose twenty acres of splendid land, upon which have been erected substantial and tasty buildings. The amphitheatre is in the shape of a circle, furnishing seating accommodations for about 4,000 people and affording a delightful promenade.

Statesville, a village of about 200 inhabitants, is situated on Smith Fork, in the Fifteenth District, eighteen miles southeast from Lebanon, and has nineteen town lots. The town was established on the lands of William Bumpass in 1812, and was first named Maryville, in honor of Mrs. Bumpass, but was subsequently changed to the present name in honor of Statesville, N. C. The town reached its zenith in about 1835, there being at that time about seven stores and sundry mechanic establishments in the place. From that time until recent years the business of Statesville retrogaded. At present there are three general stores, the proprietors of which are J. R. Hale, J. M. Jennings & Bro. and A. L. Jennings, all of whom do a good business. The blacksmiths are S. T. Moody, J. W. Armstrong and Brittain Barby. A good steam saw and grist-mill is operated by A. T. Young. The public schools consist of one each of white and colored, which are well attended and successfully conducted. The Cumberland Presbyterian and Methodist Episcopal congregations have substantial churches, and both the Masonic and Odd Fellows' fraternities have lodges. The town is situated in a rich and productive farming district, and the people are moral, industrious, and as a rule very well to do.

Cainsville, in the Seventeenth District, is about eighteen miles south of Lebanon, on the Statesville and Murfreesboro Pike, has about 100 inhabitants and nineteen town lots. The village is situated in a healthy and fertile country, and was established in 1829 on the lands of George I. Cain, from whom it derived its name. The present business interests are represented by T. L. Huddleston, R. J. Harris and Florida Bros., general merchants; R. B. Pearcy, undertaker, and Peyton Woods, blacksmith. Both white and colored schools are located in the village, the former being a chartered academy under the "four mile" law. The churches of Cainsville are two in number, Presbyterian and Methodist.

Gladesville is a village of about 100 inhabitants, situated about twelve miles southwest from Lebanon, in the Twenty-fourth District. The village is located on a rocky glade, from whence came its name, and was established in 1852 upon the land of Benjamin Hooker, Jr. The business of Gladesville consists of three general stores owned by I. B. Castleman, Baker & Meyers and F. Y. Begley & Son, two blacksmith shops by Ned Martin (colored) and Richard Murry (colored), wood shop by Robert McPeak, and saddlery shop by Wood Woodrum. The Missionary Baptists and Methodists have good churches. An excellent high school is conducted in the town, which was chartered in 1878 under the "four mile" law.

Mount Juliet is a station on the Tennessee & Pacific Railway, fourteen miles west from Lebanon, in the First District, and was established in 1870 upon the land of Newton Cloyd. Originally the town stood on the Lebanon & Nashville Road, on the land of John J. Crudoup, and was first established in 1835. The merchants of Mount Juliet are Grigg & Smith, general store, and Elly Fuqua is the blacksmith. The Cumberland Presbyterian Church is the only one in the town, and Lodge No. 379, F. & A. M., the only secret society. Mount Juliet Academy, a chartered school, ranks among the best in the county.

Green Hill is situated on the Lebanon & Nashville Pike, fifteen miles from the former place, in the First District, and has a population of about fifty people. The town was established in 1836 on the land of Hugh Robinson, and before the construction of the Tennessee & Pacific Railway was a place of considerable importance, it being the halfway point between Lebanon and Nashville. The present merchants are Cook & Cook, Gillaim & Purdue and J. N. Adams, general stores. Green Hill Academy, a chartered school, furnishes the educational facilities of the town, and one church building serves for the several denominations.

Lagardo is one of the thriving towns of the county, and has a population of about 250. The village lies twelve miles northwest from Lebanon in the Fourth District, and in the valley of the Cumberland, two miles from that river. It was established in 1835 upon the land of Turner Vaughan. The business of the town is at present represented by Wright & Vaughan, Davis Bros. and James A. Woods, general merchants; Greer & Shepard, blacksmiths, and Davis Bros., steam saw, flour and grist-millers. Lagardo has three secret societies as follows: Masonic Lodge, No. 237; Good Templar's Lodge, No. 78, and Y. M.

A. Lodge (a colored organization). A splendid high school is conducted in the town, in which from two to three teachers are employed. Five churches are located in Lagardo as follows: Baptist, Cumberland Presbyterian and Christian, and Colored Missionary Baptist and African Methodist Episcopal.

Leeville is a small station on the Tennessee & Pacific Railway, six miles west from Lebanon, in the Twenty-second District, and was established on the land of Rev. D. C. Kelley, in 1871, and named in honor of Gen. Robert E. Lee. The present merchants are A. E. Beard and A. G. Rogers & Son. The town has an excellent high school and Methodist Episcopal and Baptist Churches.

Taylorsville is a small town lying on Cedar Creek, seven miles northeast from the county seat in the Sixth District. The town was established in 1840 on the lands of John N. Taylor and Philander Davis, and named for the former. J. R. Ware, a general merchant, has the only store in the town, and James Brewington has the only blacksmith and wood shop. A chartered academy is located in Taylorsville, which ranks with the best schools in the county.

Commerce, a village thirteen miles east from Lebanon, in the Twelfth District, was established in 1822 upon the land of Joshua Taylor, and has a Cumberland Presbyterian Church, and an excellent chartered school known as the Commerce Academy. Messrs. Bell & Phillip and Smith & Lanham are the merchants, both of whom keep general stores.

Cherry Valley is a small town on the Sparta Pike, ten miles southeast from the county seat in the Sixteenth District, and was established in 1848 upon the land of Wilson T. Cartwright. The merchants are Phillips & Clemmons, Phillips & Henderson, and Grandstaff & Waters. The town has a chartered school, Methodist Church and Masonic Hall.

Green Vale is a village of seventy-five inhabitants, situated in the Seventeenth District, and was established in 1871, upon the land of W. D. Quarles, and William M. Johns. The merchants are A. J. Quarles and Cox & Gwinnett, general stores; J. Busey, undertaker, and Patton & Reeves and Jennings & Attwood, blacksmiths. Green Vale Academy is located in the town and also Wetumpka Lodge, No. 142, I. O. O. F.

Other villages, or postoffices, are Silver Spring, in the Second District, Tucker's Cross Roads and Bellwood in the Eighth District, Cottage Home in the Thirteenth District, Shop's Springs in the Nineteenth District, Saulsbury, Baird's Mill, Round Top, Fall Creek, Mount View, Oak Grove, Tucker's Gap, Austin, Beckwith and Rural Hill.

From the establishment of the first school in the neighborhood of Spring Creek, in 1800, by Benjamin Alexander, the schools of Wilson County have increased in number and facilities until at the present the county is dotted over with high schools and academies, and can boast of one of the leading universities in the South. As above stated the first school in Wilson County was established some time in 1800, by Benjamin Alexander, on the waters of Spring Creek. The school was taught in a log dwelling-house, from three to four months in the year, and, though humble and unpretentious, furnished the foundation for the present magnificent school system. Another school was taught by Rev. Samuel Donnell in the same neighborhood, in 1802, which was called a classical school, and was conducted in connection with the church of which Mr. Donnell was pastor. Following these schools several others were taught in the various creek neighborhoods, of which no record can be obtained, and in 1810 George McWhirter, a man of finished education, established what afterward became the celebrated Campbell Academy. This school was located on Hickory Ridge, about five miles west of Lebanon. Mr. McWhirter was assisted in the conduct of the school by his two daughters, and all the higher branches were taught. In the course of five or six years the school was removed to Lebanon and a good building erected on a piece of ground donated by Gov. Campbell, for whom the school was named. In 1840 a new building was erected for the academy, and it was continued as such until the late civil war, after which it was turned over to the Cumberland University, to be used as a preparatory department of that institution, and is in use at the present. Among the prominent teachers of this school were Rev. Thomas Anderson, Profs. S. C. Anderson, Myron Kilborn, W. R. Dougal, Lucien Marshall, Poindexter and Kennedy.

Some time in 1815 a very good school was taught at the schoolhouse known as the Washington Schoolhouse, of which Prof. Patterson was the teacher, and about that time another school was taught by Mary Morris, at a point a few miles west of Lebanon. In the spring of 1824 Brevard College, one of the leading schools of that day, was established by Capt. Thomas Brevard, a native of Ireland. The building was an ordinary log house, and stood four miles due east from Lebanon. The higher branches were taught by Capt. Brevard, and not a few of the citizens of the present obtained their education at that institution of learning. After conducting the school successfully for about nine years Capt. Brevard was succeeded by Prof. William Pemberton, who in turn was succeeded by Prof. Robert Simpson, and he in turn by Prof. John Vesa, a Frenchman. The school was abandoned after one year's management of Prof. Vesa.

The next high school established was the Abby Female Institute, in Lebanon, during the thirties, the proprietors and teachers of which were Miss Harriet Abby and her sister, Mrs. Kilborn, both of whom came from the New England States and founded the school. The institute was afterward conducted as a high school by Rev. Mr. Roach, Prof. Edgar and Gen. A. P. Stewart, and was abandoned during the seventies.

Carroll Academy was next established by Prof. Stephen Owen, a Northern man, some time in 1842. This school was situated on the Lebanon & Rome Pike, seven miles northeast from the former place, and was one of the leading schools of that day. The school was afterward moved to Big Spring, and was continued until during the seventies. Among the teachers were Prof. Stephen Owen, Prof. Carroll, Capt. Norris and Prof. J. B. Hancock, the latter being now at the head of Maple Hill Female Seminary.

In about 1842 Princeton College of Kentucky, under the direction of the Cumberland Presbyterian Church, was moved to Lebanon, and Cumberland University established, of which Rev. F. R. Cassitt, D. D., was the first president. The university was first located in the old Cumberland Presbyterian Church, but subsequently a large college building was erected on College Street, which was surrounded by a large *campus*. The building was afterward enlarged, and during the civil war was destroyed by a Confederate soldier, who having attended the college, became incensed at it being occupied by negroes, filled one room with cedar rails one night and applied the match, destroying the entire property. After the war the university was re-established. The private residence of Judge Abraham Caruthers, which stood on the south side of West Main Street, about one mile from the Public Square, was purchased in 1867 and converted into a college building, and is at present the theological department of the university. About the same time the private residence of Andrew Anderson, on the same side of the above street, on the second block west of the Public Square, was purchased and converted into an academic hall. In 1878 Caruthers' Hall was built at a cost of about $22,000, in which is situated the law department of the university. The combined valuation of the property of the university is about $60,000. Caruthers' Hall is a handsome brick building, and is an ornament to the city. The law department of the university was established January 9, 1847, and Judge Abraham Caruthers was the first professor, he resigning a seat upon the bench of the State to accept the position. In 1852 Judge N. Green, father of the present chancellor, resigned a seat on the State bench, and responded to a call to assist Judge Caruthers. Shortly thereafter Judge Nathan Green, Jr., the present chancellor, was elected to a professorship in the school, and these three gentlemen continued as the faculty of the law department until the breaking out of the war in 1861. In 1866 Judge Green, Sr., died, and Hon. Henry Cooper succeeded to his position. Judge Cooper resigned in 1868, when Judge Robert L. Caruthers was called to that position, and he, too, resigned a seat on the supreme bench. Judge Caruthers resigned in 1881, and died the following year. Dr. T. C. Anderson then became the president, and he was succeeded by Dr. B. W. McDonnell, and then Judge Nathan Green was elected chancellor, and occupies that responsible position at the present. In 1878 Andrew B. Martin, one of the present faculty, was elected to a professorship. The theological department was established in 1853, and for twelve years Dr. Beard, father of E. E. Beard, a prominent member of the present bar of Lebanon, was the principal. In

1877 the department was reorganized, and its faculty increased to two regular professors and two lecturers. Dr. Beard died in 1881, and Dr. S. G. Burney, D. D., was called to his position, that of systematic theology, and Prof. J. D. Kirkpatrick, D. D., was given the chair of historical theology. The faculty at present is as follows: Nathan Green, LL. D., chancellor: S. G. Burney, D. D., systematic theology; J. D. Kirkpatrick, D. D., historical theology; R. V. Foster, D. D., exegetical theology; C. H. Bell, D. D., homiletics and missions. Lecturers: W. J. Darby, D. D., and J. M. Hubbert, D. D. More than 10,000 young men have been educated in Cumberland University, and the attendance is large each year. In 1848 or 1849 Dr. N. Lawrence Lindsey, LL. D., at one time a member of the faculty of the university, established a school for young ladies, six miles east from Lebanon, on the Sparta Pike, which was called Greenwood. The school was deservedly popular, and was conducted by Dr. Lindsey until his death in 1868, and afterward by his widow until 1883, when it was discontinued.

The Baptist Church established a high school for young ladies in Lebanon in 1859. A substantial brick building was erected on East Main Street, and Rev. Mr. Powell was placed in charge. Dr. Powell conducted the school until some time in 1861, when he was succeeded by Dr. Griffin, of Nashville, and then followed Rev. J. M. Phillips and Rev. A. Hart as principals. In 1870 the school was discontinued and the property sold to the town of Lebanon, and has since been conducted as a public school, being at present in the charge of Prof. B. M. Mace, a popular educator.

Maple Hill Seminary was founded by Prof. J. B. Hancock in September, 1880, and is located on the Lebanon & Nashville Pike, three miles west from Lebanon, with delightful surroundings of forest and farm lands. The school property embraces twenty acres of land, to which is attached a farm of 250 acres, upon which are produced many of the supplies for the school. The school buildings are of frame, and conveniently arranged and situated. Maple Hill has been a success in every respect since its establishment, and under the judicious and efficient management of Prof. Hancock promises to continue so.

An addition of importance to the educational advantages of Lebanon and Wilson County, will be the Lebanon College for young ladies, which will be opened next fall by Profs. Foster and Weir, of which Prof. Foster will be the principal. The finishing touches are being applied to a handsome and commodious building for this school, which is an ornament to the town in which it is located.

The following is a list of the many excellent high schools and chartered academies in the various districts: Mount Juliet and Green Hill Academies, in the First District; Lagardo High School, in the Fourth District; Cedar Grove High School, in the Fifth District; Austin Academy, in the Seventh District; Bellwood High School, in the Eighth District; Tucker's Cross Roads Academy, in the Ninth District; Linwood High School, and Shop Spring Academy, in the Eleventh District; Commerce Academy, in the Twelfth District; Round Top Academy, in the Thirteenth District; Prosperity Academy, in the Fourteenth District; Statesville Academy, in the Fifteenth District; Cherry Valley Academy, in the Sixteenth District; Cainsville Academy, in the Seventeenth District; Fall Creek Academy, in the Eighteenth District; Mace Institute, in the Twenty-first District; Mount View Acadamy, in the Twenty-second District; Oak Grove Academy, in the Twenty-third District; Gladeville High School, in the Twenty-fourth District; Hamilton Academy, in the Twenty-fifth District, and Leerville Academy, in a school district separate from the civil districts. The academies are all chartered schools, working under the four mile temperance law.

The last report of the school superintendent of the county shows the public schools of Wilson County to be in the following condition: Number of pupils: white male, 3,608; white female, 3,444; total white, 7,052; colored male 1,484; colored females, 1,464; total colored, 2,948; grand total, 10,030; average attendance, 5,000. Number of teachers: white male, 61; white female, 29; white total, 90; colored male, 17; colored female, 14; colored total, 31; grand total, 121. Number of schools: white, 73; colored, 30; total, 103. The county superintendents since 1873 have been as follows: Profs. A. D. Morris, S. G. Shepard, B. M. Mace, J. B. Powell and R. McMillin, the present incumbent.

The first sermon preached in Wilson County was by Rev. William McGee, a Presbyterian minister, in the fall of 1798, at the house of William McClain, in the Drake Lick settlement, near the mouth of Spencer Lick Creek, and the first church organized was Spring Creek Church, which stood on the creek by that name, which was established by Rev. Dr. Hall, a North Carolina Presbyterian minister and missionary in 1800. The church was a small log house, puncheon floor, and Rev. Samuel Donnell was the first pastor. These pioneer Christians were very devout, but had been brought up, as a rule, upon the farm and had not enjoyed the best of educational advantages, and when the split came in their church in 1810 they went with the Cumberland wing, and this first church was also the pioneer Cumberland Presbyterian Church. In the latter part of 1800, or first of 1801, the Methodists organized and erected a church in the Hickory Ridge settlement, which church was christened Bethel Church. Afterward the church was removed to a point on the Lebanon & Nashville Pike, about four miles west from Lebanon, where a new building was erected and which is in use at the present time. Some time in 1803 or 1804 a Presbyterian Church was erected on Suggs Creek, and another of the same denomination at Shop Springs, both of which bore the names of the waters upon which they were located. The Methodists also erected Ebenezer Church at about that time on what afterward became the Cold's Ferry Pike, five miles from Lebanon.

Koonce's Meeting-house was probably the first church erected by the Baptists in this county. The old church stood near the present village of Leeville, and was built some time in 1806. Cedar Grove, four miles north of Lebanon, was the next church erected by the Baptists, and then followed Spring and Cedar Creek Churches. The above were the pioneer churches of Wilson County, and among their pastors were Revs. Samuel Donnell, S. M. Aston, William Smith, Samuel King, S. J. Thomas, Robert Donnell and George Donnell, of the Cumberland Presbyterian Churches; Revs. McKindry, Asbury, Jarrett, Morris, Page and Brown, of the Methodist Churches; Revs. James, Willis, Borum, Wiseman, Maddox and Tompkins, of the Baptist Churches.

Other early churches were Good Hope Cumberland Presbyterian Church, which was erected in the Eighth District some time about 1810 or 1812; Wesley Chapel, Methodist Episcopal, in the Twenty-third District, and Big Spring and Moriah Cumberland Presbyterian Churches.

The first church erected in Lebanon was in 1827 by the Methodists. The church is a brick building, and is in use at the present by the colored Methodists. In 1830 the Cumberland Presbyterians erected a church in Lebanon. This building was a two-story brick, and was built by the church and Masonic Lodge, the Masons occupying the second floor. The old building remains standing at the present time, but has fallen into disuse and dilapidation, as it was abandoned in 1850, at which time the present Cumberland Presbyterian Church was erected. In about 1840 the Baptists erected a church in Lebanon at a cost of about $7,000. Previous to the erection of these churches the different denominations held their meetings in the court house. In 1856 the present Baptist Church in Lebanon was erected, when the old building was sold to the South African Methodists. The present Methodist Episcopal Church was erected in 1855, and the old building sold to the colored Methodists. The Christian (Campbellite) Church in Lebanon was erected in 1874. All of the Lebanon churches are handsome brick buildings, and were erected at about the following costs: Cumberland Presbyterian, $10,000; Methodist Episcopal, $8,000; Baptist, $7,000; Christian, $6,000. The colored churches of Lebanon, of which mention has already been made, are two brick and two frame, the latter costing between $2,000 and $2,500 each.

The churches of Wilson County of the present are as follows: Stoner's Creek, Cumberland Presbyterian; Locust Grove, Cumberland Presbyterian; Prosperity, Methodist Episcopal; Scaby's Chapel, Christian; Hickory Ridge, African Methodist Episcopal; Williamson's Chapel, African Methodist Episcopal, and Cedar Grove, Baptist, (colored) in the First District. Mount Olivet, Baptist, and Cook's Methodist Episcopal in the Second District. Bethlehem, Methodist Episcopal; Salem, Methodist Episcopal; Spencer's Creek,

Baptist; Seay's Chapel, African Methodist Episcopal, and Powell's Grove, African Methodist Episcopal in the Third District. New Hope, Cumberland Presbyterian; Melrose, Cumberland Presbyterian and Sander's Chapel, Methodist Episcopal, in the Fourth District. Horn, Methodist Episcopal; Mount Pleasant, Cumberland Presbyterian; Bareah and Philadelphia, Christian, and African Methodist Episcopal and Baptist (colored) in the Fifth District. Athens, Missionary Baptist; Cedar Creek, Primitive Baptist; Bethel, Methodist Episcopal; Christian and Dickerson's Chapel, Colored Baptists, in the Sixth District. One Cumberland Presbyterian Church and one (colored) Missionary Baptist Church in the Seventh District. Good Hope, Methodist Episcopal; Bethlehem, Christian; Tucker's Cross Roads, Methodist Episcopal, and Bellwood, Christian, in the Eighth District. Zion, Methodist Episcopal; Poplar Hill, Baptist, and Black Zion, African Methodist Episcopal, in the Eleventh District. One Baptist Church in the Twelfth District. Round Top, Methodist Episcopal and one Baptist Church in the Thirteenth District. Prosperity, Baptist, and Prosperity (colored) Baptist, in the Fourteenth District. Smith Fork, Missionary Baptist; Mount Vernal, Old School Presbyterian; Methodist North and Colored Baptist, in the Fifteenth District. Round Lick, Baptist; Cherry Valley, Methodist Episcopal and one Christian Church in the Sixteenth District. Salem, Missionary Baptist, and Salem (colored) Missionary Baptist and Bradley's Creek (colored) Missionary Baptist, in the Seventeenth District. Falling Creek, Missionary Baptist; Mount Pisgah, Methodist Episcopal; Union, Cumberland Presbyterian, and Ramah, Missionary Baptist, in the Eighteenth District. Shapp's Spring, Missionary Baptist; Center Hill, Cumberland Presbyterian; Bethesda, Cumberland Presbyterian, and Bethel, Christian, in the Nineteenth District. Union, Missionary Baptist; Friendship, Primitive Baptist; New Liberty, Missionary Baptist; Cason's Chapel, Methodist Episcopal, and Hebron, Christian, in the Twentieth District. Rocky Valley, Missionary Baptist; Jacob's Hill, Methodist Episcopal, and Beard's Grove, Colored Baptist, and Jacob's Hill, African Methodist Episcopal, in the Twenty-first District. Mount Zion, Cumberland Presbyterian; Hebron, Methodist Episcopal; Liberty Hill, Methodist Protestant; and Ephesis, Christian, in the Twenty-second District. Oak Grove, Methodist Episcopal, and one Christian Church, and Brown's Corners, African Methodist Episcopal, in the Twenty-third District. Rutlins, Missionary Baptist; Suggs Creek, Cumberland Presbyterian; Gain's Church, Baptist; Hall's Church, Methodist Episcopal; and Corinth, Christian, in the Twenty-fourth District. Pleasant Grove, Methodist Episcopal, in the Twenty-fifth District.

BEDFORD COUNTY.

BEDFORD COUNTY lies in the great Central Basin of Tennessee. The prevailing rocks are limestone, generally thinly bedded and flaggy, but with some fine building stone. The limestones belong to the Nashville and Lebanon formations, limestones low in the geological series. West of Shelbyville excellent building stone abounds. Two other varieties of limestone are found in the county, called white rock and sandstone or fire rock. The white rock, found in the northwest corner of the county, bears a good polish and makes a good appearance in buildings, standing the weather well. The sandstone or fire rock occurs in thick beds eight miles west of Shelbyville, and is coarse, soft and easily worked, but in thin slabs is flexible. The sandstones which cover the knobs are of little value.

The surface of the county is undulating and is interspersed with hills and valleys. West of the road that leads from Shelbyville to Murfreesboro, and north of Duck River, the country is comparatively flat, and east of this road it is undulating, with lines of rounded hills. These hills rise in some instances to an elevation of 200 or 300 feet, and are usually capped with sandstones, and together with the slopes and crests, are heavily wooded. The soil is comminuted limestone and sandstone, with an intermingling of rich black humus, and is exceedingly fertile, durable and generous. South of Duck River, and running west as far as Sinking Creek, the surface continues much the same, while west of Sinking Creek the hills rise much higher than anywhere else in the county. Gentry Hill is about 350 feet above the valley lands below. Another hill, and probably the most noted elevation in this part of the country, is Horse Mountain, three miles east of Shelbyville and in plain view from the town. One side of Horse Mountain is heavily timbered, while on the other flourishes an excellent vineyard. At the base of the mountain is a fine spring, and which years ago was the location of a camp ground. During the late war Horse Mountain was used as a signal station by both the Northern and Southern armies. Zinc or copper was supposed to exist in the mountain, and during the war a party of Federal soldiers leased the property for a term of years, and had an Indiana geologist make a visit to the mountain for inspection. Nothing ever came of the venture. There are several varieties of soils, different in color and productiveness. They may for convenience be called the mulatto, the red and the black. The mulatto predominates and is the characteristic soil of the county, and the best of clover, wheat, oats, sweet potatoes and cotton grow well on it. The red soil is confined chiefly to the cedar belt, on the north side of Duck River. The black soil is found upon all streams and on the hill sides. Corn, wheat, oats, cotton, clover, potatoes and all the grasses grow well in the county, and all kinds of fruit, such as apples, peaches, pears, plums, cherries and all the smaller fruits and berries, grow in abundance. The timber of the county is made up of ash, poplar, walnut, butternut, elm, buckeye, sugar, maple, oaks, red bud, sumac, dogwood, hickory, beech, box elder, gum, cedar and mulberry.

The streams of the county are Duck River (which runs nearly centrally through the county from east to west. Its tributaries from the south are Norman, Shipman, Thompson, Little Flat, Big Flat, Sugar, Powell and Sinking Creeks; from the north, Noah Fork, Garrison Fork, Wartrace Fork, Butler Creek, Fall Creek, North Fork and Clem Creek. All of these streams furnish good water-power, particularly Duck River. In the east and southeast part of the county numerous springs of excellent water are to be found, while in the level part they are not so frequent.

Upon the formation of Bedford County, in 1807, the territory embraced in her boundaries was made up of dense canebrakes and vast forests, both almost impenetrable, and was but sparsely settled. From information gleaned from such men as Nimrod Burrow and Thomas S. Word, Esqs., of Flat Creek, and J. E. Scruggs, Esq., of Fairfield, who are among, if not the oldest citizens now living, the writer is of the opinion that the first settlement of the county was made about 1805 and 1806, as follows: Clement Cannon settled near the present site of Shelbyville, in the Seventh District; Philip Burrow, William, Wilbourn and Freeman Burrow settled on Thompson Creek, in the Twenty-fifth District; John Blackwell settled near Three Forks of Duck River; Capt. Mat Martin and brother, Barkley, and William McMahan settled on Garrison Fork of Duck River, in the First District. The above settlements were all made at about the same time, and if any were made prior to them, no information of the same can now be found.

Among the other early settlers were Cuthbert Word, Samuel Card, Thomas Knott, Robert Snoddy, James Eddy, William Hix, Robert Hastings, Henry Hastings, Nathan Hubbard, Stephen Hastings, William Haslett, William Burrow, Banks Burrow, Joseph Hickenbotham, Thomas Gibson, Hazen Blair, John Casteel, Michael Holt, Joseph Walker, Joseph Erwin, William Crutcher, William Hickman, Henry Davis, Isaac Muse, Richard Muse, Anderson Davidson, Andrew Erwin, William Finch, Mrs. Mary Scruggs, William P. Finch, John Tillman, Christopher Shaw, "Salley" Sailors, Robert Furguson, Thomas Dean, Thomas Hudson, James Reagor, David Floyd, Michael Womack, William Pearson, and the Davises, Deerys, Eakins, Armstrongs, Stones, Caldwells, Burdetts,

Galbraiths, Wades, Whitneys, McKissacks, Ruths, Hollands, Marshalls, Nelsons, Moores, Arnolds, Shrivers, Bomars, Mullines, Norvilles, Shaffners; Kings, Youngs, Kimbroes, Hooziers, Ewells, Halls, Hords, Ewings, Davidsons, Smiths, Vances, Stokes, Osborns, Finches, Scotts, Crouchs, Mosleys, Neils, Thomases, Peacocks, Woods, Fugetts, Hoovers, Suttons, Murfrees, Steeles, Harrises, Wilsons, Coopers, Tunes, Mortons, McCuistians, Clordeys, Greens, Browns, Fishers, Thompsons, Parsonses, Turrentines, Tilfords, Allisons, Lents, Blantons, Warners, Worthams, Atkinsons, Andersons, Sharons, Stallings, Sims, Brames, O'Neals, Coffeys, Gaunts, Stephensons, Drydens, Harrisons, Greers, Barretts, Whites, Gambills, Deans, Campbells, Williamses, Floyds, Pearsons, Bobos, Reids, Reeveses, Morgans, Parkers, McGills, Rays, Hastings, Dunaways, Dicksons, Allans, Landers, Landises, Anthonys, Enlisses and Maupins.

The following persons were granted land lying in Bedford County by the State of North Carolina for military services during the Continental war, between the years 1785 and 1790: Amos Balch, 1,000 acres; George and Richard Martin, 3,000 acres; Thomas Talbott, 2,000 acres; George Cathey, 2,500 acres; James Brandon, 1,000 acres; Robert Smith, 5,000 acres. Between 1790 and 1800: John Sloan, 1,000 acres; Ruth Greer, 2,000 acres; James Grant, 5,000 acres; Stokely Donaldson, 1,000 acres; Samuel Patterson, 2,400 acres; Ezekial Alexander, 1,000 acres. Between 1800 and 1810: Norton Pryor, 1,360 acres; David Justice, 2,000 acres.

Below is a list of those who received grants of land from the State of Tennessee between the years 1800 and 1810: George Doherty, 2,500 acres; Andrew Jackson, 320 acres; Thomas Overton and John Brahan, 640 acres; Malcom Gilchrist, 260 acres; John Bright, 122½ acres; James Greenlee, 300 acres; Tilman Dixon, 274 acres; James Bright, 45 acres, James Lewis, 2,000 acres; James Patton, 274 acres; Daniel Ship, 532 acres; John Baird, 2,500 acres; George W. Campbell, 730 acres; Thomas McCrery, 1,000 acres; William Martin, 50 acres; John Smith, 1,000 acres; Ephraim Drake, 275 acres; John Coffee, 100 acres; Edward Harris, 800 acres; Oliver Williams, 60 acres; Joseph Greer, 150 acres; Jesse Maxwell, 320 acres; Robert White, 1,000 acres; Aaron Cunningham, 640 acres.

Probably the first mill erected in the county was the water-power corn-mill built by Mr. Goge, on the creek by that name, in about 1809 or 1810. Previous to the erection of this mill the pioneers carried their corn to Phillips' horse-power mill in Rutherford County, or reduced it to meal by means of the mortar. In about 1812 Joseph Walker erected a water-mill on Garrison Fork of Duck River, near where the town of Fairfield was afterward located, and David Shipman erected a water-mill at the head of the creek by that name. The Wilhoit and Germany mills on Duck River, both water-power, were built about 1814 or 1815. Other early mills were the Cannon Mill, at Shelbyville, on Duck River; Ledford's mill, on same river; James Sharp's mill, on Thompson Creek; John Sim's mill, on Duck River, two miles above Shelbyville; Henry Wiggins' mill, on Flat Creek, and Conway's and Pruitt's mills, on same creek; Horseley's mill and Crowell's mill, all of which were water-power, and Joshua Holt's water-power near Flat Creek. The mills of the present, outside of those located in the different towns heretofore mentioned, are as follows by districts: Third District, James Mullen's and N. C. Germany's corn-mills, water-power; Seventh District, Tune & Co.'s flour and corn-mill, water-power, on Duck River, and Wilhoit Mill, owned by Strick Parsons, on Duck River, water-power; Eighth District, G. W. Gregory's saw and grist-mill, water-power, on Falling Creek; Ninth District, William Taylor's steam grist-mill; Tenth District, N. R. Taylor's horse-power grist-mill; Eleventh District, John Hall's water-power saw, corn and flour-mill, on Duck River, Fletcher Ray's water-power grist-mill on North Fork Creek, and Adams' & Simmons' steam saw-mill; Eighteenth District, J. N. Neeley's water-power corn-mill on Sinking Creek, R. M. Sikes' water-power corn-mill on Rock Creek, and Whitehead's steam corn-mill; Twenty-first District, F. M. Johnson's water-power corn-mill on Flat Creek, and Eugene Blakemore's water-power corn-mill on Duck River; Twenty-third District, Hix Bros. water-power grist-mill on Flat Creek; Twenty-fifth District, Mrs. Smith's steam corn-mill, Joseph Wilhoit's water-power corn-mill on Duck River, and Jacob Anthony's water-power corn-mill on Thompson's Creek.

One of the first cotton-gins in Bedford County was the Cannon Gin, near Shelbyville, built by Clement Cannon about 1812. Other early gins were those of John Tillman and Tom Mosley, in the Fairfield neighborhood, and later L. P. Fields had a gin in the same neighborhood. There were, no doubt, other early cotton-gins, but a faithful effort to learn whose they may have been and their location was unrewarded. The cotton-gins of the present are Taylor & Hester's, in the Tenth District, with which is also a carding machine; William Taylor's in the Ninth District; W. J. Loyd's cotton-gin and carding machine, in the Eighth District; George Vernatti's, in the Fifth District, and Mrs. Smith's gin and carding machine in the Twenty-fifth District. While there were no doubt a large number of still-houses in the early days, yet they all disappeared years ago, and with few exceptions have passed from the memory of the present citizens. One of the first, if not the first still was owned by Philip Burrow, father of Nimrod Burrow, Esq., and was situated near the present town of Flat Creek; John Holt also had a still at about the same time and in the same neighborhood. Other early stills were those of Nathan Evans, in the Twentieth District, on Sugar Creek, and of Simpson Neice and Leslie Bobo in the Twenty-second District, on Flat Creek. Later on distilleries were established. The distilleries of the present are four in number, and are as follows: The Zach Thompson Distillery is the most extensive one in the county, is situated near the town of Wartrace, and full particulars of the same may be found in the history of that town; Marcus L. Rabey's distillery in the Twenty-second District, and Blakemore & Co.'s distillery, in the same district, each have a capacity of sixty gallons per day; T. F. Wooton's distillery, in the Twenty-fifth District, has a capacity of forty gallons per day. So it will be seen that whisky forms quite an item in the products and exports of Bedford County.

In the early days the militia laws were in force in Bedford, as in all other counties in Tennessee. The early officers of the militia were Brig.-Gen. Robert Cannon; Cols. Samuel Mitchell, John A. Moore and S. B. Blackwell. The militia consisted of two battalions, which formed one regiment. Musters were held semi-annually. The battalion muster was held each spring on Sinking Creek, and the general (or regimental) muster was held in the fall at Shelbyville. The officers would bedeck themselves on muster day in close-fitting, homespun coat, half-moon hat, and presented a great sight as they would drill the rank and file, armed with shot-guns and cornstalks, accompanied by music from the piercing fife and drum. After the drill would begin the "fist and skull" fights, which would continue throughout the day.

Bedford County was erected by an act of the General Assembly December 3, 1807, which act is as follows:

"Be it enacted by the General Assembly of the State of Tennessee, that a new county be, and the same is, hereby established south and southwest of, and adjoining the county of Rutherford, by the name of Bedford, in memory of Thomas Bedford, deceased, which said county shall begin at the southwest corner of Rutherford and southeast corner of Williamson County, on the Duck River Ridge, and run thence with said Williamson County line to the line of the county of Maury; thence along the same southwardly to the south boundary of the State; thence eastwardly to the east boundary of Rutherford County; thence along the same to the ridge that divides the waters of Duck River from those of Cumberland; thence along the same westwardly to the east corner of Williamson County, leaving Rutherford County its constitutional limits, and all that tract of country included in the above described lines shall be included within the said county of Bedford."

Section 2 of the act provides for the holding of the courts of the new county at the house of Mrs. Payne, near the head of Mulberry Creek, until the next General Assembly. The county was surveyed and organized in the early part of 1808, the courts being held at the place designated by the act creating the county. Of the courts, court house, etc., but little is now remembered, and as the county was reduced in limits the following year, thereby placing Mrs. Payne's residence and farm in a new county (Lincoln), the county seat was soon removed. On the 14th of November, 1809, the General Assembly passed the following act, which reduced, materially, the limits of Bedford County, the territory being taken in the formation of Lincoln County:

BEDFORD COUNTY. 865

"Be it enacted by the General Assembly of the State of Tennessee, that the lines and boundaries of Bedford County shall be as follows, to wit: Beginning on the northeast corner of Maury County and running south with the eastern boundary line thereof to the extreme height of the ridge dividing the waters of Duck River from the waters of Elk River; thence eastwardly to the extreme height of said ridge to the present eastern boundary line of the said county of Bedford; thence north to the south boundary line of Rutherford County; thence westwardly with the said line to the southern boundary line of Williamson County, and thence with the said line of Williamson County to the beginning."

Section 2 of the act provides for the appointment of John Atkinson, William Woods, Bartlett Martin, Howell Dandy and Daniel McKissack as commissioners to locate a county site for the new county on Duck River, within two miles of the center of the county. Benjamin Bradford and John Lane were subsequently added to the above commission by the Legislature. The county was resurveyed by Malcom Gilchrist, and the county site was located temporarily at the house of Amos Balch, on the Lewisburg road, two and one-half miles southwest of the present county seat. In May, 1810, however, the county site was permanently located at Shelbyville, 100 acres of land being donated for that purpose by Clement Cannon. Amos Balch and William Galbreath each offered to donate to the commissioners fifty acres on which to locate the county seat, but as the site selected was more central and the donation more liberal their offers were rejected.

Bedford County was materially reduced in territory by the formation in 1836 of Coffee County on the east, and again in 1837 by Marshall County on the west. At present Bedford County is bounded on the north by Rutherford County, northeast by Cannon County, east by the counties of Cannon and Coffee, south by the counties of Moore and Lincoln, west by Marshall County, and has an area of about 475 square miles. Originally the the county was divided into twenty-five civil districts, but upon the formation of Marshall County in 1837 a number of these districts were placed in that county, and other districts have since been merged into each other, and at present there are only nineteen districts, they being designated numerically as First, Second, Third, Fourth, Fifth, Sixth, Seventh, Eighth, Ninth, Tenth, Eleventh, Eighteenth, Nineteenth, Twentieth, Twenty-first, Twenty-second, Twenty-third, Twenty-fourth and Twenty-fifth.

In 1810 the population of Bedford County was 8,242, and in 1830 had increased to 30,396. At that time it was the most populous county in the State. The formation of the new counties referred to before and various other causes, reduced the population materially, and in 1870 it amounted to only 24,333, and at present the population is about 26,100. The voting population is about 4,500, and at the presidential election of 1884 Mr. Cleveland received in the county a majority of 171 votes over Mr. Blaine, though the usual Democratic majority far exceeds that given to Mr. Cleveland. Bedford County has a total area of 332,800 acres, of which 203,511 were improved in 1885. During the above year the total value of property assessed for taxes was $5,183,560. There are in the county 741 town lots, at a total value of $522,515. The taxes of 1885 amounted as follows: Poll tax $7,508; State tax $13,787.41; county tax $11,489.51; school tax $21,295.41; road tax $4,399.84. The tax levy for 1886 was 20 cents on the $100 worth of property for county purposes; 20 cents on the $100 and $1 poll for school purposes; 11 cents on $100 for roads and highways.

The cereal products of the county for 1885 were of corn 1,682,358 bushels; wheat 257,425 bushels; oats 87,408 bushels; rye 6,145 bushels, and of barley, 108 bushels. During the same year there was owned in the county live-stock as follows: 11,426 head of horses and mules, 14,188 head of cattle, 16,020 head of sheep and 46,251 head of hogs.

The first court house was erected in 1810 or 1811. The building was of frame, very small, and stood on the northwest corner of the Public Square. A second building, this time of brick, was erected in a few years, and stood in the center of the Square. This building was destroyed by a tornado in 1830. In its stead was soon afterward erected a large brick court house on the site of the one destroyed, which stood until 1863, when it was destroyed by fire, together with a large portion of the county records. A party of Confederate soldiers had taken quarters in the court house, and through their carelessness the building was set fire to and entirely destroyed. Upon the reopening of the courts after the war they were held in various buildings, principally in a hotel which stood on the south side of the Square, and in 1869 the erection of the present court house was begun, but was not completed until 1873. The building is one of the largest and handsomest court houses in the State, and was erected at a cost of about $120,000. It is of brick, with rock foundation. The principal court room is 40x90 feet in size; county court room, 20x40 feet, and chancery court room, 20x40 feet. The circuit and chancery court rooms are on the second floor, while the county court room and county officials' quarters, six in number, are on the first floor. Besides these there are four jury rooms, and in the basement are eight good rooms. Including the porches the building is 120 feet long and 91 feet wide. The pillars for the lower porches are of blue limestone, square, and in Ashler masonry, while those above are of cast iron, Corinthian in style. The building is surmounted by an elegant cupola, containing a clock and bell that cost $1,500. The building stands in the center of the Square, and is surrounded with a grassy plat, inclosed with a neat and substantial iron fence, erected on a stone base. Altogether it is a handsome edifice, and presents a striking appearance, and of which the citizens may well be proud.

Several jails were erected by the county at different times, all of which were of small consequence, until the building of the present jail in 1866 at a cost of $35,000. The jail is a solid stone building, two stories in height, and is one of the most secure jails in the State. It is conveniently arranged into cells and corridors, and light and air are admitted through several long, narrow windows, through which the smallest person could not escape. It is one of the handsomest and most conspicuous buildings in Shelbyville.

In 1832 the first poor asylum was established by the county. At that time 160 acres of land were purchased, lying in the Third District, three miles northeast from Shelbyville, adjoining Horse Mountain, on which were standing several log houses, which were fitted up for the accommodation of the county's poor. In 1883 two substantial frame houses of two rooms each, 16x18 feet, were erected at the asylum at a cost of $2,500. These buildings were burned in May, 1886, and new ones in their place are in course of construction, the county court having appropriated $2,500 for that purpose at its July meeting.

Bedford County is traversed by numerous turnpikes or macadamized roads, a majority of which lead to and from the county seat. The average cost of these turnpikes was $1,500 per mile, and toll-gates are established every five miles, by means of which the expense of construction and maintenance of the pikes is derived. The turnpikes of this county, their establishment and the number of miles of each are as follows: Shelbyville, Murfreesboro & Nashville Pike, built in 1832, 12 miles; Shelbyville & Fayetteville Pike, built in 1852, 9 miles; Shelbyville & Lewisburg Pike, built in 1856, 11 miles; Shelbyville & Unionville and Shelbyville, Richmond & Petersburg Pikes, built in 1858, 18 miles of the former and 9 of the latter; Shelbyville & Fairfield Pike, built, part in 1859 and completed in 1865, 8 miles; Shelbyville, Flat Creek & Lynchburg Pike, built in 1875, 9 miles; Shelbyville & Fishing Ford Pike, built in 1875, 5 miles; Shelbyville & Tullahoma Pike, built in 1874, 10 miles; Shelbyville & Wetumpka Pike, built in 1881, 5 miles; Shelbyville & Versailles Pike, built in 1885, 8 miles; Wartrace & Beach Grove Pike, built in 1874, 6 miles; Bellbuckle & Flatwood Pike, built in 1882, 5 miles; Bellbuckle & Beach Grove Pike, built in 1882, 6 miles, and Bellbuckle & Liberty Gap Pike, built in 1882, 5 miles.

The bridges of importance of Bedford County, together with their cost and earliest time at which bridges were built, are as follows: Shelbyville bridge, across Duck River, built in 1832, present cost $2,000; Fairfield bridge, in the First District, across Garrison's Fork, built in 1856, present cost $1,000; Scull Camp Ford bridge, in the Seventh District, across Duck River, built in 1856, present cost $3,000; Warner's bridge, in the Seventh District, across Duck River, on the Shelbyville & Fishing Ford Pike, built in 1856, present cost $2,000; Hall's bridge, across Duck River, in the Eleventh District, built in 1875; present cost $2,000. Columbia Ford bridge, in the Eleventh District, across North Fork, built in 1881, present cost $400; Unionville Turnpike bridge, across North Fork, built in 1860, present cost $500; Sugar bridge, in the Twenty-first District, across Sugar Creek, built in 1850, present cost $400; Fall Creek bridge, across Fall Creek, in the Eighth District, built in 1860, present cost $500; Flat Creek bridge, in the Seventh District, across Flat Creek, built in 1855, present cost $1,000; Flat Creek bridge, in the Seventh District, on Lewisburg Pike, built in 1850, present cost $800; Lynchburg Pike bridge, across Duck River, in the Seventh District, built in 1876, present cost $3,000, Fall Creek bridge, on the Columbia Pike, in the Eighth District, built in 1885, cost $400. There are numerous small bridges across small streams throughout the county, but are not of sufficient importance to be given special notice.

The Nashville & Chattanooga Railroad has a branch leading from Wartrace to Shelbyville, eight miles in length, while the main line passes through the eastern portion of the county. This railroad, together with the various turnpikes, furnishes means for ample transportation for Bedford County, while, in addition, Duck River can be used for transporting lumber to a great extent. In point of agriculture, manufactures, stock and wealth Bedford County ranks with the best counties in the State, while in health, climate and educational facilities the county has few equals in any portion of the South.

The records of the County Court of Bedford County do not extend farther back than 1848, those previous to that date having been destroyed with the court house in 1863 by fire. Beyond that date but little if anything of the transactions of the court can be ascertained at the present day. The first sessions of the court were held in 1808, at the house of Mrs. Payne, near the head of Mulberry Creek (now in Lincoln County), and the only record extant of those sessions is a marriage license issued by the county clerk to John Tillman and Rachael Martin. During portions of 1809 and 1810 the courts were held, as before mentioned, at Amos Balch's residence, from where they were removed to Shelbyville in the latter part of 1810. The first session of the court of which there remains any record was held in the court house at Shelbyville, beginning October 1, 1848, when the following justices were present: William Galbraith, chairman; John W. Norville, James Hoover, Newton C. Harris, Jacob Serley, Garrett Phillips, James Wortham, John W. Hamlin, Price C. Sterle, Dudley P. T. House, Joseph P. Thompson, John L. Cooper, James Foster, Joseph Anderson, Meredith Blanton, John O'Neil, Green T. Neeley, William Thompson, John A. Brown, Joshua Hall, B. F. Green, Isaac B. Holt, Herrod F. Holt, Lemuel Broadway, Joseph Hastings, James H. Miles, Kindred Pearson and William Taylor.

The transactions of the court during 1848, or at least so much thereof of interest, were as follows: A commission of lunacy was appointed to inquire into the mental condition of Eliza Jane Gambell; Sarah Terry emancipated Bob and John, two of her slaves. The commissioners before appointed to let out the contract for building a bridge across Duck River, at or near Skull Camp Ford, made a report to the effect that the contract for said bridge had been awarded James Wortham, at the price of $1,700. The report was signed by E. J. Frierson, John T. Neil and William Galbraith, commissioners, which report was accepted by the court. The following election judges were appointed for the November, 1848, election: First District—William D. Clark, Anthony Thomas and Samuel McMahan; Second District—G. G. Osborn, John L. Davidson and Francis H. Keller; Third District—Henry Holt, John Shaffner and John A. Moore; Fourth District—John Norville, Robert Clarke and Nathan Chaffin; Fifth District—Andrew S. Lawrence, George W. Bell and William Weaver; Sixth District—James P. Couch, John Knott and Henry Brown; Seventh District—E. J. Frierson, George Davidson and Thomas Holland; Eighth District—Thomas Wheeler, Jacob Fisher and Robert Terry; Ninth District—Ziza Moore, Jason Winsett and Absalom Landers; Tenth District—Alfred Ranson, Fredrick Balt and James Mankins; Eleventh District—William B. Phillips, Robert Rayson and Charles L. Byren; Eighteenth District—Fielding Bell, James Statling and James B. Jones; Nineteenth District—William Wood, John Larne and James H. Curtis; Twentieth District—Miles Phillips, Jackson Wallace and Randolph Newson; Twenty-first District—Samuel Thompson, Richard Phillips and Herbert Smith; Twenty-second District—John C. Hix, Henry Dean and Arthur Campbell; Twenty-third District—James H. Miles, John Hastings and John Reed; Twenty-fourth District—Elisha Bobo, Watson Floyd and Thomas Anderson; Twenty-fifth District—John Koonce, Levi Turner and Gabriel Maupin. The commissioners appointed for that purpose reported that they had let the contract for repairing the bridge across Wartrace Fork of Duck River to Henry Stephens for $79. The report was signed by Samuel Phillips, Philip Cable and Robert Chambers, commissioners, and was received by the court. The tax levy for 1849 was 8½ cents on each $100 worth of property for county purposes, 25 cents on each free poll, and licensed privileges one-fourth of the State tax. During that year William Presgrove and Nathaniel M. Wheeler were allowed $75 for building a bridge across North Fork of Duck River, on the Lower Nashville Road, near Presgrove's mill. The court ordered the census taken in 1851 by districts, which census was as follows: First District, 93; Second District, 163; Third District, 187; Fourth District, 145; Fifth District, 164; Sixth District, 119; Seventh District, 232; Eighth District, 99; Ninth District, 160; Tenth District, 156; Eleventh District, 239; Eighteenth District, 177; Nineteenth District, 151; Twentieth District, 189; Twenty-first District, 109; Twenty-Second District, 209; Twenty-third District, 195; Twenty-fourth District, 205; Twenty-fifth District, 206.

In 1853 John R. Eakin, A. Ervin and John Meyers, bridge commissioners, made a report that the bridge across Garrison Fork of Duck River, heretofore ordered built by the court, was complete, which report was received, the town of Wartrace Depot was incorporated; a bridge was ordered erected across Garrison Fork of Duck River at Wartrace.

In May, 1866, the court passed an order for the erection of a new jail, and appropriated $15,000 for that purpose, and levied a tax of 10 cents on the $100 and 50 cents on each poll to raise the money. The following jail commissioners were appointed to prepare plans and award the contract for building the jail: Thomas C. Whiteside, W. H. Wisdom, Joseph H. Thompson, William Galbraith, W. G. Cowan, Henry Cooper, W. B. M. Brown, William Houston, Jr. and W. T. Tune. In July of the same year the court appropriated $6,000 more to be used in construction of the jail, and several additional appropriations for the same purpose were subsequently made.

In October, 1869, the court ordered a new court house erected, and appointed Thomas H. Caldwell, H. P. Clearland, L. B. Knott, William Gosling and William P. Cowan a building committee to prepare plans, estimates and specifications, and award the contract for building the court house and superintend the same. The building was completed in 1872. In June, 1872, the court issued articles of incorporation to the town of Flat Creek. In 1873 the court appointed John R. Dean superintendent of the county schools.

In 1874 the court ordered a new bridge built across Duck River, at Hall's mill, and for that purpose appropriated $500. In 1883 an order for the erection of two buildings at the Poor Asylum, was passed by the court, said buildings to be of frame, two rooms each, 16x18 feet, and appropriated for the erection thereof $2,500. These buildings having been destroyed in 1886, the court at its last session appropriated $2,500 with which to replace them. Owing to the absence of the records it is impossible to give the term of years the different county officers served, but the following is a correct and complete list of the names of the officers in the manner in which they held office.

Chairmen of County Court: John Atkinson, J. W. Hamlin, H. F. Holt, P. C. Steele, William Galbraith, R. L. Landers, John P. Hutton, Thomas J. Ogilvie, Richard H. Stem, B. F. Foster and John W. Thompson, the present incumbent. County Clerks: Thomas Moore, James McKissack, William D. Orr, Robert Hurst, A. Vannoy, J. H. O'Neal, Joseph H. Thompson, R. C. Couch, Robert L. Singleton and Will J. Muse, the present incumbent.

The first sessions of the Circuit Court of Bedford County were held in 1808 at Mrs.

Payne's house on Mulberry Creek, and were presided over by Hon. Thomas Stuart, circuit judge. Judge Stuart afterward held the courts at Amos Balch's, and was still on the bench when the county seat was located at Shelbyville. However, there remains no record of those early courts, the existing records beginning with December, 1853, at which time Hon. Westly W. Pepper was judge, John H. O'Neal was clerk and James W. Johnson was sheriff. The first grand jury was drawn in the following manner: the names of the venire were written on slips of paper and the papers placed in a hat, from whence thirteen names were drawn out by a child under ten years of age, and of the men whose names were thus selected was the grand jury composed.

During the sessions of the court in 1853, Gilbert E. Holder was fined $200 and sent to jail for three months for carrying a bowie knife. John Record was fined $5 for gambling, and William Neil was sentenced to one year's imprisonment in penitentiary for larceny. In 1854 Martha Dobbins was granted a divorce from William Dobbins. John W. Nelson was fined $5 for malicious shooting. Isaac Williams for larceny, was sent to prison for one year, and Mary Low was fined $5 for permitting one of her slaves to live as a free person of color. In 1855 Isaac Parker pleaded guilty to a charge of libel, and was fined $5. William Ballard was sent to prison for three years on a charge of altering bank bills. James B. Phillips served a judgment of $2,500 against Robert Cannon, for slander and for committing murder. John Wilson was sent to prison for seven years. In 1855 W. H. _____ was sent to the penitentiary for one year on a charge of larceny, and James Wagster, for disturbing public worship, was fined $10 and costs.

In 1857 William P. Puckett was fined $25 for malicious stabbing, and Joel Criscoe was sent to the penitentiary for five years for larceny. In 1858 James Ripley, on a charge of murder, was sent to the penitentiary for twenty-one years; Frank Bagley, for arson, was given a sentence of six years, and Jesse Phillips, for incest, was sentenced to five years imprisonment. In 1859 Bob, a slave, upon conviction of manslaughter, received the following sentence: "That he receive 100 lashes upon the bare back, then be imprisoned for ten days, and then receive another 100 lashes upon the bare back, to be well laid on by the sheriff of Bedford County."

There were no sessions of the court held during the late civil war. In 1864 Alexander Brown, for larceny, was sent to the penitentiary for one year; and on a similar charge, John Morton was sent up for three years. In 1865 Samuel Evans, Charles Ellison, Riley Kizer and Harriet Phillips, all colored, were convicted of larceny, and the first was sent to the penitentiary for one year; the second for three years; the third for one year, and the last one was let off with one month's confinement in the county jail.

In 1866 James Cheatham and Bush Varmory, were each sent to the penitentiary for fifteen years upon a charge of larceny and house-breaking. During that year James Brewer, Pinkney McDonald, Van McFarland, John Bomer, Jesse Barksdale and Mary Ann Stenston, all confined in the county jail on various charges, made their escape. In 1867 James Eakin, colored, was sent to the county jail for thirty days on a charge of larceny, and on a similar charge George Morgan was sent to the penitentiary for one year. In 1868 George Wood, Alexander Aldridge, Ann Jackson and Alexander Elkin, were given terms of imprisonment on charges of larceny. In 1869 Ann Jackson was again imprisoned on a charge of larceny, and on similar charges Arch Cook was sent to the penitentiary for twelve years; Abe Featherstone for two years and six months; Alfred Davis for ten years; John Moore, ten years; Sarah Cannon, three years, and, for stealing a horse, John Brown was sent for ten years.

In 1870, on charges of larceny, William King was sent to the penitentiary for ten years; James Simmons three years, and Caroline Houston three months in jail. In 1871 William Hamilton was convicted of murder and imprisoned for eleven years; Elizabeth Kiser, for larceny, was sentenced to imprisonment in State prison for one year, but her sentence was commuted to ten days in jail on account of her *encientic* condition; Edward Hilton, on a charge of involuntary manslaughter, was sentenced to three years' imprisonment; and on charges of larceny James Jones was given four years in the penitentiary;

James Gregor, two years; Hal Germiny, three years; Charles Dyer, four years; Fal. Hamer, one year; Green Smith, two years, and Ida Kains one year. In 1872 James S. Robinson, Lewis Cannon and Henry Gambell were sentenced, respectively, to terms of seven, three and four years' imprisonment on charges of larceny.

In 1873 John Daniel was sent to prison three years for larceny; Richard Wells, for murder, was sent for five years; and Mitch Pearson was convicted of murder in the first degree and sentenced to be hung February 13, 1874. Pearson took an appeal to the supreme court, where the verdict of the lower court was reversed. He was again tried and convicted of murder in the second degree and sentenced to ten years imprisonment at hard labor. In 1874 John Fogelman, Henry Tillman, Jerry Meadows and David Nealey were convicted of larceny and all sent to the penitentiary for one year each. In 1875 William Campbell and Marion Shaffner were sent to the penitentiary for three and one years, respectively, for larceny, and Dr. Shannon, for horse-stealing, was sent to the penitentiary for twelve years.

In 1876 Joseph Williams was sent to prison for two years, and William Barksdale was sent to jail six months on charges of larceny. Thomas Rippy, for murder, was given ten years; William Holder, for house-breaking, was given ten years; and Abraham McMahan and wife recovered $120 damages from Thomas McEwen for slander. In 1877 John Bourke, for house-breaking, and L. Jones, John T. Dean, John Holt, Henry Cannon, Emmet Thompson, Willis Dallis and Harrison Brown were imprisoned for larceny, and John Jones was sentenced to be hung October 4, 1877, for murder. Jones appealed his cause to the supreme court and the decision was reversed, and upon standing trial a second time was sentenced to imprisonment for life. In 1878 Robert Dixon, Philip Shuman, John Miller and Bill Morton were sent to the penitentiary for one year each, and Lafayette Revis, for house-breaking, was sentenced to five years' imprisonment, and for arson Revis was sentenced to ten years' imprisonment, the second sentence to go into effect upon expiration of the first. In 1879 Willis Frazier, for murder, was imprisoned for twelve years; and for larceny James Eakin, Henry Brown, James Waston and Jerry Ball, were sent to prison for one year each. In 1880 John Gaston, James Woodard and Lewis Thomas were given terms of imprisonment for larceny. In 1881 Mary Brown, Lula Thomas and Bob Chambers were given one year imprisonment in the penitentiary on charges of larceny.

In 1882 Frank Atkinson, for horse-stealing, was sent to prison for three years; James Stewart, murder, five years; and Ambrose Tillman, one year; Louis Kiser, two and a half years; Anderson Sims, one year; Henry Beedy, three years; Henry Lovelace, four years; William Allison, one year; Harrison Williams, one year; Bob Webb, one year, and Lewis Castleman two years on charges of larceny. In 1883 Charles Elkins, for murder, was sent to the penitentiary for twenty years; Jim Gamble, arson, two years; James Warren, murder, three years; Nan Roberson, arson, two years; and for larceny Wylie Chambers, Henry Amos, James Flack, R. C. Wyland, Tom Stamps and Tom Ganaway were each given one year imprisonment in the penitentiary. In 1884 Eliza Pepper, for murder, was sent to prison for life, and George Cross, John Cooper and Nelson Johns were given six and three years each, respectively, for horse-stealing; and Henry Mosley and George Stewart, for larceny, was sent up for one year each. In 1885 Carrie Cleveland, for murder, was sent to the penitentiary for three years, and William McGrew and Henry Carwell, for larceny, were each given one year. In 1886 Willis Rankin and Henry Lamb were sent to the penitentiary for one year each on charges of larceny, and Lamb was sentenced to three years' imprisonment on a charge of horse-stealing, his second sentence to commence upon expiration of the first.

The judges who have served on the Bedford bench were Thomas Stuart, James C. Mitchell, Samuel Anderson, Hugh L. Davidson, Henry Cooper, J. W. Phillips, W. H. Williamson and Robert Cantrell, present incumbent. Attorney-generals: Alfred Balch, William B. Martin, Thomas Fletcher, James Fulton, Abraham Martin, E. J. Frierson, Thomas C. Whiteside, H. L. Davidson, William L. Martin, James L. Scudder, B. M. Tillman, James W. Brien, William H. Wisener, Jr., James F. Stokes, M. W. McKnight and Lillard Thompson, present incumbent. Circuit clerks: Daniel McKissack, John T. Neil, Lewis Tillman, James H. Neil, J. M. Phillip, W. B. McBrame and John T. Cannon, present incumbent.

The Chancery Court of Bedford County convened for the first time in 1836, with Hon. B. L. Ridley presiding as chancellor and Robert P. Harrison as clerk and master. The following is a list of the chancellors and clerks and masters: Chancellors—B. L. Ridley, Thomas H. Caldwell, John P. Steele, A. S. Marks, John Burton and E. D. Hancock, the present incumbent. Clerks and masters—Robert P. Harrison, Robert B. Davidson, W. J. Whilthorn, Lewis Tillman, Sr., Lewis Tillman, Jr., T. S. Steele, William H. Morgan and J. S. Butler, the present incumbent. Other county officers have been as follows, in the order given as to terms: Sheriffs—Benjamin Bradford, John Warner, John Wortham, John Warner, William Norville, K. L. Anderson, D. D. Arnold, James Mulins, J. M. Johnson, James Wortham, Garrett Phillips, R. B. Blackwell, Joseph Thompson, J. M. Dunaway, F. F. Fouville, J. J. Phillips, George P. Muse and D. W. Shriver, the present incumbent. Trustees—John W. Cobbs, William Ward, Peter E. Clardy, Daniel Hooser, S. B. Gordon, J. L. Goodrum, William McGill and J. L. Goodrum, the present incumbent. Registers— John Ake, Thomas Davis, A. Vannoy. D. B. Shriver, M. E. W. Dunaway, John W. Thompson, H. H. Holt and C. N. Allen, the present incumbent. School superintendents —John R. Dean, J. L. Hutson, William H. Whiteside and J. H. Allen, the present incumbent.

Among the early distinguished members of the Bedford County bar were Abraham Martin, who was district attorney at one time, and who afterward removed to Montgomery, Ala., where he was elected to the bench; Archibald Yell, who afterward removed to Little Rock, Ark., and of which State he was elected governor and also representative in Congress, William B. Sutton; William Gilchrist; I. J. Frierson, a member of the Legislature at one time; William H. Wisener, at one time a member of the Legislature and speaker of the Lower House; Henry Cooper, who was judge of the circuit court for a number of years, and who was also a member of the Legislature and for several years president of the Lebanon Law School and United States senator for one term; Hugh L. Davidson, who for ten years was judge of the circuit court and attorney-general for one term, and Thomas C. Whitesides, who was district attorney for a while. The bar at present is composed of Edmund Cooper, who was a member of the Legislature one term, served one term as congressman, was first assistant secretary of the United States Treasury under President Johnson, and was also chosen by President Johnson as his private secretary; Thomas H. Caldwell, who was at one time chancellor of this division, attorney-general for the State, was a Grant and Colfax and Blaine and Logan presidential elector, and was Tennessee's State commissioner to the Philadelphia Centennial in 1876; James A. Warder, who was United States district attorney, and is at present one of the nominees of the Republican party for supreme judge; R. B. Davidson; F. B. Ivey; Walter Bearden; Charles S. Ivey; Gen. Ernest Caldwell, who is the present member of the Legislature and who was commissioned a brigadier-general by Gov. Hawkins, and W. B. Bate.

Not a few patriots of the Revolution were among the first settlers of Bedford County, among whom were Capt. Matt and Col. Barclay Martin, who, with five of their brothers, fought for seven years under Gen. Washington; Capt. Christopher Shaw, William Campbell and James Hurst. There were no doubt others, but their names have long since been forgotten, and of them there is no record.

A full company was furnished by Bedford County to the war of 1812, which company was present at the battle of New Orleans. Among the members of the company whose names have been preserved were William Hazlett, John Farrer, Michael Womack, James Gowan, John L. Neil, Philip, James and William Burrow (brothers), John Casteel, William Woods, "Sallie" Sailors, William P. Finch, Robert Furguson, Andrew Mathus, Townsend Fugett, Wesley Rainwater, Benjamin Webb, Martin Hancock, J. L. W. Dillard, John Murphey, Moses Pruitt, John Pool and James Scott. The company was commanded by Capt. Barrett.

When the Seminole or Florida war began in 1836, Bedford County promptly organized a full company, which, under the command of Capt. Hunter, participated in many of the engagements of that war. Among the volunteers of that war were Albert Smell, John Hudlow, John Stone, Standards Thomas, Abraham McMahan, Lewis Tillman and William Woods.

Bedford County furnished one full company to the war of the United States and Mexico in 1846. The company was commanded by Capt. E. W. Frierson, and was mustered into the First Tennessee Volunteer Infantry, at Nashville. The following are the survivors of the Mexican war who are living at present in Bedford County: James H. Neil, Samuel J. Warner, E. M. Lacy, Stanford Sutton, John B. Fuller, J. W. Buckaloo, C. W. Arnold and John D. Martin. Among those who volunteered from the county and who have since died, were C. C. Word, James Scudder, Berry Logan, Zachariah Lacy, Joel H. Burdette, Thomas G. Holland, Alexander Turrentine, Joshua B. Scott, William McNabb, Appleton Tucker, Chesley Arnold, Sullenger Holt, Stephen Jolly, John A. Moore and James L. Armstrong.

Bedford County was divided on the great questions which led to the late civil war, and when the election was held June 8, 1861, to vote for or against separation from the Union and representation in a Confederate Congress, the county voted in the negative by a majority of nearly 200. When the time came for action the county furnished almost as many soldiers to the Northern as to the Southern army. Indeed, so loyal was Shelbyville to the Union as to earn for the town the name of "Little Boston," and being on the line of march of both armies, witnessed many movements and counter-movements of large bodies of troops, and though much damage was sustained to property and not a few lives lost, yet through the influence of prominent citizens on both sides the consequences were no more serious than could have been expected in time of war.

In September, 1861, the "Shelbyville Rebels," the first Confederate company raised in the county, was organized by the election of A. S. Boon as captain. Immediately following this company, Confederate companies were organized as follows, all of which were mustered into the Forty-first Regiment of Tennessee Infantry: Scudder Rifles, Capt. W. C. Blanton, organized in the vicinity of Unionville; Erwin Guards, Capt. M. Payne, organized at Wartrace; Richmond Guards, Capt. Brown, organized in the vicinity of Richmond; a Flat Creek company, under Capt. Keith, and Capt. J. F. Neil's Bell Buckle company, also about half of Capt. Thomas Miller's company, which went from Marshall County, was made up from Bedford County by those living near the county line.

During the same year a company was organized at Bell Buckle, and James Dennison elected captain, which joined the Second Regiment of Tennessee Infantry. During the summer of 1861 three companies were organized in the county, and joined the Seventeenth Regiment of Tennessee Infantry. They were as follows: a Flat Creek company, Capt. J. D. Hoyl; a Fairfield company, Capt. James L. Armstrong, and Capt. W. A. Landis' company, made up part in Bedford and part in Lincoln County. In 1862 a company of artillery was organized in Shelbyville, of which J. L. Burt was elected captain, and Capt. R. B. Blackwell also took out a company in that year.

In 1862 Capt. Montgomery Little was deputized by Gen. Forrest to raise a company of 100 men to act as an escort to the daring cavalry commander, which company was to be mounted and known as "Forrest's Escorts." Capt. Little proceeded to Shelbyville, where, October 6, 1862, he completed the organization of the Escorts. The company was composed of the picked men from Bedford, Rutherford, Lincoln, Marshall and Moore Counties, and were provided with choice arms and the best horses the county afforded. On the above date the escort fell into line in front of the court house, on the south side, in Shelbyville, from which place they took up their line of march to Nashville, and from that time until the close of the war was with Gen. Forrest through all his campaigns.

The Federal troops furnished by Bedford County were as follows: Those who were attached to the Fifth Regiment of Tennessee Mounted Infantry: Capt. R. C. Couch's company, Capt. J. L. Hix's company, Capt. Robert C. Wortham's company and Capt. Rickman's company. Those of the Fourth Tennessee Regiment of Mounted Infantry: Capt. James Wortham's company and Capt. John W. Phillips'; and Capt. C. B. Word's company, of the Tenth Tennessee Mounted Infantry, known as Johnson's Guards.

Throughout the war Shelbyville was infested with troops at short intervals, first the Confederates and then the Federals having possession. The same troops also visited Wartrace, and at that place entrenchments were thrown up by the Confederates, while the latter also dug a line of rifle pits around Shelbyville, extending from Horse Mountain to Duck River, and on the mountain both armies established signal stations at different times. The first troops to visit Shelbyville was a detachment of Confederates under command of Col. Gordon, during the summer of 1861. During 1862 troops visited the town as follows: Fourth Ohio Cavalry, Gen. Forrest's cavalry, Gen. Mitchell's division, Gen. Lytle's brigade, Seventy-eighth Pennsylvania Regiment of Infantry, Gen. Wood's division, the First Kentucky Cavalry and Gen. Albert Sidney Johnston's entire army corps, who came here on their retreat from Bowling Green, Ky. While here Gen. Johnston replenished his commissary department with about 30,000 head of hogs and a large quantity of beef. In April, 1863, Gen. Bragg's army was encamped in Shelbyville for a month or more. After the battle of Murfreesboro in December, Gen. Bragg retreated to Shelbyville, and going into camp remained until January, 1864. During 1864 Gen. Milroy's division, a Missouri regiment of infantry, under command of Col. Fox, and the One Hundred and Seventh New York Regiment of Infantry encamped in Shelbyville.

At Wartrace, in April, 1862, the Forty-second Regiment Indiana Infantry, was attacked by Col. Starn's Regiment, when a sharp skirmish took place. In 1863 a lively skirmish occurred between the Fifth Tennessee Cavalry and the Confederate Cavalry under Gen. Wheeler at Wartrace, and in October following, Gen. Wheeler again had a brush with the Federal Cavalry, between 3,000 and 4,000 men being in the fight, two miles west of Shelbyville, in which quite a number were killed and wounded. On the 27th of June, 1863, four companies of the Fifth Tennessee made an attack on the Confederates who were holding Shelbyville. The Federals, commanded by Col. Bob Galbraith, advanced from Guy's Gap, and by the time Shelbyville was reached the Confederates were on the retreat. A running fight occurred on Martin Street, during which several were killed on the Confederate side. The Confederates retreated from the town and crossed Duck River at the Scull Camp bridge, at which point, being so closely pursued, they threw a large brass field-piece from the bridge into the river, and the cannon remains to this day in the mud at the bottom of the river. No lives were lost on the Federal side during the hot engagement.

In May, 1864, twelve soldiers belonging to the Fourth Tennessee Mounted Infantry (Federal), were captured while guarding the Shelbyville depot, which was stored with hay, by Robert B. Blackwell, who was at the head of a company of bushwhackers. The depot and contents were burned, and the twelve soldiers escorted a short distance from town and shot.

Shelbyville, the capital of Bedford County, is a beautiful town of about 3,500 inhabitants, situated on the east bank of Duck River, and almost surrounded by that winding stream, and at the terminus of the Shelbyville & Wartrace branch of the Nashville & Chattanooga Railroad, sixty-three miles southeast from Nashville by rail, and fifty-five miles as the "crow flies." The immediate surrounding country is most beautiful and picturesque, the town being enclosed between ranges of hills on the east, south and north. Shelbyville was established in 1810 by the commissioners appointed by the General Assembly to locate the county seat of Bedford County. The land upon which the town was located (100 acres) was donated to the commissioners by Clement Cannon, by deed dated May 2, 1810, and registered June 22, 1811. The town was at once laid off into lots and sold at auction to the highest bidder, and the county seat was then named Shelbyville, in honor of Col. Isaac Shelby, who commanded a regiment of 240 men in the storming of King's Mountain and capture of Col. Ferguson and the British Army under him October 7, 1780.) Among those who purchased town lots of the commissioners were Archibald

Alexander, Ben Brayford, Samuel Bell, Clement Cannon, George Cunningham, Daudy Howell, James Edde, Michael Fisher, Ben Gambell, Thomas Lordmore, William Lack, Lewis Marshall, Robert Murry, Joseph Mengee, William Newson, Abraham Thompson, Jonathan Webster, Joseph Woods, Joseph Walker, Henry Winro and many others. The streets of Shelbyville, all of which are macadamized, are ten in number, those running north and south being Martin, Brittain, Depot, High, Thompson, Cannon and Spring, and those running east and west are Daudy, Main and Bridge.

The town was incorporated October 7, 1819, and has continued as an incorporated town up to the present. At the first municipal election, held on the first Monday in November, 1819, Thomas Davis, David McKissack, James A. McClure, Giles Burdett, William O. Whitney, John H. Anderson and Jacob Morton were elected aldermen, and by them Thomas Davis was chosen mayor and James Brittain recorder. The present municipal officers are as follows: Mayor, John W. Ruth; recorder, John W. Thompson; aldermen: First Ward, J. P. Ingle; Second Ward, W. A. Frost; Third Ward, S. J. McDowell; Fourth Ward, J. R. Burdett; Fifth Ward, J. T. Allison; Sixth Ward, Thomas L. Thompson; police: John Searcy, John Bartlett and Logan Harrison.

The Shelbyville fire department was organized December 2, 1885. In 1883 a good steam fire-engine and a hook and ladder wagon was purchased by the town at a cost of $22,000. A steam force pump was also purchased at a cost of $800, which was placed at the mill of Lipscomb & Co.

The Eakin Library, containing over 1,000 volumes of choice literature, was founded in 1881 by the widow of the late William S. Eakin, and from whom it takes its name.

The first merchant of Shelbyville was James Deery, who opened a general merchandise store on the town site in 1809, one year before the location of the county seat. The first mill was a water-power corn-mill, and was built in about 1815 by Clement Cannon on Duck River, and a mill, known as the "Cannon Mill," is in operation on the same site at the present. The first blacksmith was Henry Tudale, and he was followed by Jeremiah Cunningham, Moses Marshall and Jacob Morton. The merchants of Shelbyville from 1810 up to 1840 were Benjamin Strickler, John Eakin, John and Spencer Eakin, Peter Donnelly, Hugh Wardlow, Robert Stephenson, J. C. and T. M. Caldwell, John A. Marrs Brittain & Escue, Thomas Doris, George Davidson, Alexander Eakin, Thomas Reed, W. B. Brame, Robert Mathews, Robert Moffitt, Wardlow & Thompson, John N. Porter, William Deery, John Cannon & Co., Davidson & Caldwell, and Davidson & Jett. Richard White and R. P. Harrison were the hotel proprietors of that period. The merchants of the forties were John Eakin, Eakin Bros., George Davidson, William G., J. C. & T. M. Caldwell, Robert Mathews, W. W. Wilhoit, Seahorn & McKinney, William S. Jett, Eakin & Moffitt, James H. Deery and T. M. Caldwell & Co. Merchants of the fifties: John C. Caldwell, Jr., C. P. Huston, Baskette & Stamps, Wilhoit Bros., Armstrong Bros., Baskette, Jett & Co., Cowan & Strickler, Caldwell, Cowan & Co., John Wilts, John Nering, Mitchell & Shepard, J. W. Wallace & Bro., Roan & Cable, and Mitchell & Sperry. Merchants of the sixties: Thomas W. Buchanan, O. Cowan, John F. Brown & Co., Mason, Vaudy & Co., Corney & Neiley, H. Frankle & Co., R. C. White, Thomas J. Roan, C. A. Warren, Evans & Shepard, Horner & Co., Buchanan & Woods, Graves & Gillis, George B. Woods, John H. Wells, and Trollinger & Tune. With but few exceptions the merchants of the seventies were the same as during the sixties.

The merchants of the present are as follows: Buchanan & Woods, J. S. Gillis, A. C. John & Co. and A. Frankle & Co., dry goods and notions; J. P. Brown and Rice & Sandusky, clothing; Allison & Hall and Leftwich & Co., dry goods and clothing; Mrs. E. Dalby, Mrs. Martha Rainbow and Mrs. E. Cleveland, milliners; C. A. Warren, B. F. Dwiggins, Green & McGill, John Dayton & Co., E. W. Carney, G. N. Eakin, Morton & Wilhoit, Rutledge & Thompson, T. J. Warner, Hix Bros., Arnold Bros. and R. H. Whitman, groceries; W. R. Haynes & Co., furniture; C. W. Cunningham, books and stationery; F. H. Otte, merchant tailor; Evans & Shepard, Roan & McGrew and S. F. Knott, drugs; John W. Ruth & Son, jewelers; M. A. Rainbow, silversmith; A. J. Jarrell, tinware and stoves; O. Cowan & Co. and J. E. Deery, hardware; Foman & Son, tinware and groceries; Hope & Co., Eagle & Shaffner and W. M. Bryant & Co., grain dealers; H. C. Ryall, lumber dealer; Mathus & Low, commission merchants; N. J. Calhoon & Bro., marble works; M. L. Morton and E. W. Fuller, harness and saddles; J. H. Hix, C. D. Gunter, T. J. Jones, S. P. Freeman, W. V. Allen, Arnold Bros. and T. J. Warner, saloons; W. H. Caul, gunsmith; Benjamin C. Gregory, photographer; G. A. Cleveland, house and sign painter; John Ledbetter and Reidenbery & Turner, butchers; Jack Henderson, T. C. Ryall & Co., T. C. Allison, Hite & Taylor and Collins & Rankin, livery stables; R. M. Bowen, G. F. Davis and J. R. Hunter, shoe-makers. The only hotel of Shelbyville is the Evans House, J. C. Eakin, proprietor, which is a first-class hotel in every respect. James Brown and Simpson & Burkeen are the barbers. J. T. Landis will open a steam laundry, which is now in course of erection, during the fall.

The manufactories of Shelbyville are as follows: The Victor Flouring-mill, built in 1880, present proprietors Lipscomb & Co., is situated on Duck River, and has water and steam-power; capacity 250 barrels of flour per day. The building is a large two-story brick, and the machinery is of the most improved pattern; the Cannon Mill (water-power), which stands directly across the river, is also owned by this company; the Shelbyville Flouring-mill, also situated on Duck River, was built some time during the sixties by Robert Dwiggins. The mill has changed hands frequently, and is at present operated by E. Shepard, trustee; the building is a three-story brick, and the capacity of the mill is 225 barrels per day; Mullins Mill, water-power, situated on Duck River, one mile east of Shelbyville, is owned by J. C. Tune; Shelbyville Carding Machine, established in 1884, owned by Burdett & Co.; Shelbyville Manufacturing Company (stock company), was established in 1883, manufacture hubs, spokes, rims, double and single trees, etc., twenty-five men employed regularly; L. H. Russ & Co., manufacturers of carriages, and the celebrated New South wagon; McDowell Bros., manufacturers of wagons and buggies and general blacksmith; Southern Machine Shops (owned by stock company), established in 1884; A. J. Trolinger, cooper shop; E. H. Kohl, repair shop; H. C. Ryall, planing-mill; W. F. Holman, tannery; J. C. Eakin, fruit evaporator and canning factory. Probably the most important manufactory in the county, and the only one of the kind in the county, is the Sylvan Cotton Mills, situated two miles southwest of Shelbyville. These mills were established in 1852 by Gillen, Webb & Co., but are now owned and operated by a stock company. The mills were destroyed by fire in 1881, but were rebuilt on a larger scale immediately thereafter. The present buildings are of brick, the main building being 50x186 feet, picker-room 40x56 feet and engine and boiler-room 40x60 feet; the machinery is all new and of modern make; the mills are provided with 3,680 spindles and 108 looms, and the daily capacity is 6,000 yards of drilling and sheeting. From 12,000 to 15,000 bails of cotton are consumed annually, and between eighty and ninety operatives are given employment. All of the operatives reside in neat cottages in the vicinity of the mills, forming quite a village. A general store is kept by the company, from which the villagers draw their supplies.

The Shelbyville Savings Bank was established in 1867 by A. W. Brockaway. From its establishment until 1873 William Gaslin was president and A. W. Brockaway was cashier. Brockaway was succeeded as cashier at that time by Dr. R. N. Wallace, and that gentleman was succeeded by his son, John R. Wallace. The bank suspended in September, 1885, with a capital stock of $40,000 and $120,000 on deposits, of which not over 20 per cent will be realized. The failure of the bank caused the failure of several business men. The National Bank of Shelbyville was established in November, 1874, by Edmund Cooper, who became president, with Albert Frierson, cashier, and B. B. Whitthorne, teller. Mr. Cooper is still president and Mr. Whitthorne is cashier and Edmund Cooper, Jr., is teller at present; capital stock $50,000. The Peoples' National Bank, with a capital of $60,000, has been recently organized, with N. P. Evans as president and S. J. Walden, Jr., as cashier. A building for this bank is in course of erection, and the bank will be ready for business during the present fall.

Shelbyville's secret societies are as follows: Shelbyville Benevolent Lodge, No. 122, F. & A. M., organized in 1819, suspended in 1833, and reorganized in 1847; Chosen Friends Lodge, No. 11, I. O. O. F., organized in 1845, suspended in 1885, and will be reorganized in the near future; Sons of Temperance Lodge, organized in 1846, suspended in 1860, and reorganized in 1867, as Shelbyville Lodge, No. 131, I. O. G. T.; Olive Branch Lodge, No. 4, A. O. U. W., organized in May, 1877; Duck River Lodge, No. 10, K. of H., organized in 1875; Corono Council, No. 426, Royal Arcanum, organized in December, 1879; Local Branch, No. 60, Iron Hall, organized in December, 1881; Y. M. C. A., organized in 1884. Colored secret societies. Duck River Lodge, No. 1947, I. O. O. F., organized in May, 1879; Charity Lodge, No. 25, F. & A. M.

The physicians of Shelbyville who have practiced in the town and vicinity since 1830: Drs. James G. Barksdale, James Kincade, George W. Fogleman, Grant Whitney, —— Brazee, John Blakemore and Frank Blakemore; the present practicing physicians are Drs. J. H. McGrew, Thomas Lipscomb, R. F. Evans, C. A. Crunk, Swanson Nowling, S. M. Thompson, G. W. Moody, J. H. Christopher, N. B. Cable and Samuel J. McGrew. The practicing dentists are Drs. G. C. Sandusky, Edward Blakmore and J. P. McDonald. The schools of Shelbyville consist of a graded public school, Dixon Academy, Female Academy and the colored free schools.

Shelbyville has seven white and four colored churches, as follows: Presbyterian, organized in 1815, and brick church erected in 1817. In 1856 the building was sold to the Catholic congregation and the present brick building erected at a cost of $10,000. In donating to the county the land upon which to locate a county seat Clement Cannon set apart a tract of ground upon which any denomination could have the privilege of erecting a house of worship. The Methodists took advantage of the free ground, and in 1820 erected a frame church. The building was destroyed by a severe storm in 1830. The congregation then abandoned the Cannon ground and erected a brick church in 1833, at a cost of $3,000. This building they sold, in 1881, to the Christian congregation and began at once the erection of the handsome brick edifice which is as yet incomplete, but in which services have been held for many years. This building has already cost about $12,000. The Baptist Church was organized in 1845, when a brick building was erected on the Cannon ground, the site of the old Methodist Church, at a cost of about $3,000. This church was destroyed by a wind-storm in 1870, and was rebuilt, at a cost of about $5,000. The Catholic Church was organized in 1855, and in 1856 the congregation purchased the old Presbyterian Church building, and the same is in use at present; the Cumberland Presbyterian Church was organized and a church erected in 1856. The building was destroyed in 1880. The congregation then purchased their present brick building from the Northern Methodists, which church was organized after the civil war, but disbanded The Episcopal Church was organized in 1853, and until 1861 held services in the Odd Fellows' hall. In 1860 the erection of the present brick church was begun. The ground was donated by William Gasling and the church was built by Hon. Edmund Cooper, as a memorial church to his first wife. The building cost $2,500. The Christian Church was organized in 1881, at which time the congregation purchased their present church from the Methodist Episcopal congregation. The colored churches are the First and Second Missionary Baptists, the African Methodist Episcopal South and the Union African Methodist Episcopal.

The first newspaper published in Bedford County was the Shelbyville *Herald*, Theo F. Bradford, editor and proprietor. In 1821 the *Herald* was sold to —— Iredell, and with that gentleman was afterward associated J. Newton, and together they conducted the paper until about 1830. The *Western Freeman* was next established in 1832, with H. M. Watterson as editor, and John H. Laird, publisher. In 1836 the *Peoples' Advocate* was established by William H. Wisener, who was both editor and proprietor. About the same time the *Western Star* was published by Granville Cook. In 1840 the *Peoples' Advocate* was succeeded by the *Western Advocate*, with John W. White as editor and publisher. In 1844 the *Free Press* was published by I. C. Brassfield, and contemporaneous with the *Free*

BEDFORD COUNTY. 877

Press was the *Whig Advocate*, published by John H. Laird. In 1848 the *Star* was published by R. C. Russ. From 1848 to 1862 the *Expositor* was published by James Russ, Jr., and Ralph S. Saunders. R. C. Russ published the *Bedford Yeoman* from 1850 to 1855, and during 1857 and 1858 the *Constitutionalist* was published by J. H. Baskette. About the same time the *Herald of Truth*, a Baptist paper, was published by Dr. R. W. Fain. From 1862 to 1863 J. H. Thompson and T. B. Laird published the *Tri-weekly News*, and from 1863 to 1866 T. B. Laird published the *American Union*. In 1865 the *Republican* was published by James Russ, with Lewis Tillman as editor. In 1871 the *Bulletin* was established by J. L. and J. B. Russ, and previously these gentlemen established the *Commercial*, which paper was published in 1870 by T. S. Steele and S. A. Cunningham. Two years thereafter the *Rescue*, which paper had been started a short time before, was merged into the *Commercial*, and R. C. Russ became editor and proprietor, and occupies that position at the present time.

Besides the *Commercial*, the other papers of Shelbyville are the *Gazette* and *Times*. The *Gazette* was established in 1874 by J. B. and J. L. Russ. In 1880 A. L. Landis purchased the paper and conducted it for two years, and sold it to William A. Frost and William Russell. In 1884 Mr. Frost became sole editor and proprietor, and continues as such at the present. The *Gazette* is one of the most successful newspaper plants in the State. The office is supplied with an abundance of good material, and is equipped with a Campbell power news press and Gordon jobber. The *Times* was established by William Russell and D. M. Alford in the latter part of February, 1886, making its first issue on the 26th of that month, with Mr. Russell as editor and Mr. Alford as publisher. Although young in years, the *Times* is on a sound footing, and has evidently come with the determination of staying. All three of the papers are Democratic.

The first agricultural society of Bedford County was organized in 1857, and the fair grounds were located near Shelbyville. The first officers were as follows: President, Hugh L. Davidson; vice-presidents, R. H. Sims, G. G. Osborn, Thomas Lipscomb, W. W. Gill and Henry Dean; treasurer, Lewis Tillman; recording secretary, J. F. Cummings; corresponding secretary, John R. Eakin. At the close of the civil war the society was reorganized as a stock company, and handsome and commodious buildings were erected on grounds just outside the incorporated limits of Shelbyville. Annual exhibitions are held, and the society has been deservedly successful. The present officers are as follows: President, J. J. Gill; vice-presidents, Oliver Cowan, Martin Euliss and T. C. Ryall; corresponding secretary, Ernst Caldwell; secretary and treasurer, John D. Hutton; general superintendent, C. N. Rice.

In May, 1830, Shelbyville was swept by a terrible tornado, which destroyed the court house, the Methodist Church, and quite a number of other brick buildings, and killed and wounded a number of people. Those who were killed were James Newton, David Whitson, —— Arnold, ——Reideout and ——Caldwell. The town has also been visited at three different times with Asiatic cholera, which caused a large number of deaths each time. The first visit was in June and July, 1833, the second in September, 1866, and the third in July, 1873.

Wartrace, the second town of the county, is situated at the junction of the main line of the Nashville & Chattanooga Railroad and the Shelbyville branch of that road, eight miles east from the latter place and fifty-five southwest from Nashville, and has a population of 800. The town dates its establishment from the time of the completion of the Nashville & Chattanooga Railroad in 1852. The land on which the town stands was originally owned by Rice Coffee, and Henry B. Coffee was the first citizen of the village. Among other early citizens were Robert Buchanan, John Stephens, N. C. Harris, W. H. Clark, W. B. Norville, G. W. Martin, R. P. Ganaway, John R. Coffee, W. T. Grim, Willis Pruitt, S. A. Prince, S. C. Mills, J. D. Payne, Robert Ervin, M. Payne, A. G. Garrett, A. M. Keller and J. W. Tillford. The town was incorporated in October, 1853, under the name of Wartrace Depot, and Daniel Stephens was the first mayor elected. With the exception of the years of the late war the corporation has remained in full force and effect, and the officers at the present are as follows: Mayor, Sidd Houston; board of aldermen, R. P. Maupin, B. I. Hall, J. W. Haynes, R. V. Davidson and T. B. Davis; recorder, W. G. Wood; marshal, W. F. Hailey. Daniel Stephens and William Norville were the first merchants, they opening general stores in 1852. During the next eight years W. P. Green, Thomas Hart, W. K. Raibourn & Co. and Murphey & Stephens were the business men. From 1860 to 1870 the business men were Thomas Hart, L. P. Fields, Fields, Mackey & Co., D. Morris & Co., M. N. McKinney & Co., O. P. Arnold, J. A. Cortner & Co., Arnold Bros., B. W. Blanton, B. F. Davis & Co. and A. Murphey & Co.

From 1870 to 1886 the merchants have been and are as follows: J. D. Houston, drugs; B. I. Hall, Davis & Co., Arnold Bros., B. W. Blanton and Cunningham, Davidson & Co., dry goods; Smith Bros., family groceries; C. B. Murphey, books and stationery; J. W. Haines, furniture and undertaker; W. E. Russell, tinware and stoves; A. Ogle, saddles and harness; Mrs. M. E. Clayton, milliner. The hotels are the Healan House, Mrs. S. D. Healan & Son, proprietors, and the Chockley House, J. C. Chockley, proprietor. The town has two good livery stables, owned by J. W. Tillford and W. G. Petty. The banking house of B. F. Cleveland was established in 1882, of which B. F. Cleveland is president, and R. M. Cleveland is cashier. This establishment does a general banking business, and is of much benefit to Wartrace. The manufacturers of Wartrace are as follows: J. A. Cunningham & Co., flouring-mill, erected in 1880 at a cost of $12,000, and the Wartrace Mill Company, established in 1882, the building of which cost $18,000; these mills are supplied with modern machinery, and do a large custom and shipping business; Ellington Bros., saw and planing-mill, erected in 1885, with $3,000 capital invested; John Butner, wagon-maker and blacksmith, and Harry Erwin, John Price and W. A. Schwarts, general blacksmiths. Near Wartrace is situated the distillery of Zach Thompson, which has been in active operation since 1883, though it has been in existence for about fifty years. This distillery has a capacity of between seventy-five and eighty gallons of whisky per day. The physicians who have practiced their profession in Wartrace from its establishment to the present have been as follows, in the order given: Drs. Walter H. Sims, W. T. Griswold, John M. Murry, T. H. Manier, A. S. Brown, R. F. Fletcher, H. K. Whitson and D. W. Duke.

The secret societies are as follows: I. O. O. F., established in 1850, and reorganized in 1885; K. of H., established in 1878; K. of L., established in 1878; R. A., established in 1861. A Masonic lodge was organized in 1874, but was abandoned after a period of about six years. Wartrace has splendid educational advantages. The Wartrace Academy was established in 1860, and has been continued every year since. In 1885 the present school building was erected. It is a large brick, two stories in height, and cost $5,000. There are five grades in the school, and the school term amounts to an average of ten months each year. The houses of worship of Wartrace are the Missionary Baptist, the congregation of which was organized in 1860, and the building was erected in 1870. It is a substantial frame, and cost about $1,500. The Methodist Episcopal Church was organized and house erected in 1876, at a cost of $1,500. The colored denominations are Baptists and African Methodist Episcopals, both of which have meeting-houses.

The business houses of Wartrace are all of brick, and present a handsome and substantial appearance. The railroad has a large brick depot, for both passengers and freight.

Bellbuckle, the third town of the county, was founded in 1852 by A. D. Fugitt, the original owner of the land on which the town now stands. Bellbuckle takes its name from a small creek by that name, which runs near the town, and the creek derived its name from the fact of a representation of a bell and buckle, which are carved on a large beech tree, which stands near the head of the stream. The carving was discovered on the beech by the earliest settlers, and as to the carver; when the work was done, or the reason thereof, is one of the mysteries, though many traditions concerning the same have been handed down. Bellbuckle is situated on the Nashville & Chattanooga Railway, fifty-one miles southwest from Nashville, and ten miles northeast from Shelbyville, and has a population of about 800. The town was laid off into lots in 1854 and incorporated in

1856. During the war the corporation lapsed, but immediately thereafter a new charter was obtained, since when it has been in force and effect. The present town board is as follows: Mayor, S. P. Jones; aldermen: G. H. Miller, W. R. Muse, T. J. Oglevie, B. E. Thomas, Z. T. Beachboard and J. M. Freeman; George Moon, recorder; A. Melton, marshal.

A. D. Fugitt opened a general store in Bellbuckle in 1852, being the first merchant. Clark & Miller, W. B. Norville, R. D. Rankin, W. R. Pearson and R. D. Blair, all of whom kept general stores, were the other business men of the fifties. The merchants of the sixties were Lamb & Weirback, W. C. Cooper, Norville & Beachboard, R. D. Blair & Son, Thomas & Claxton and R. D. Rankin, all general stores, while R. D. Wallace ran a flouring-mill. Between 1870 and 1880 the merchants were McFarrin Bros., Jamison & Miller, Haggard Bros., W. L. Garner, R. A. Hoover, T. J. Peacock, W. C. Cooper, J. F. Johnson, Johnson & Hite, W. P. Crawford, Oglevie & Crawford and B. E. Thomas, all of whom kept general stores, with the single exception of Thomas, who kept a stock of drugs in connection with the postoffice. The business men from 1880 and of the present are W. P. Crawford, T. J. Peacock, A. H. Newman, R. A. Hoover. J. W. Pattey and E. F. Gomer, general stores; D. W. Shiver & Co., A. L. Haggard and Howland Bros. family groceries; R. L. Justice, drugs and family groceries; B. E. Thomas, drugs and postoffice; and H. Hall, undertaker and cabinet-maker. The manufactories are represented as follows: R. F. Wallace & Co., plows and wheelwrights; George Bailey and Meldon Bros., blacksmiths and wagon-makers; W. S. Putnam, blacksmith and carriage-maker; R. F. Wallace, steam saw-mill and manufacturer of Wallace's patent double shovel. Bellbuckle has a large creamery, which was established in 1885 by a stock company with $5,000 capital. The creamery is supplied with milk from the numerous herds of fine milch cows in the neighborhood. It is fitted up with the latest improved machinery, and has a capacity of handling 6,000 pounds of milk per day.

The one hotel of the town is conducted by Mrs. Winnett. The railroad company erected a good brick depot in 1862, which is in use at the present time.

The streets run north and south and east and west, being continuations of the following pikes: Bellbuckle & Beach Grove Pike, leading east; Bellbuckle & Liberty Pike, leading north; Bellbuckle & Flatwood Pike, leading west, and a short pike leading into the Shelbyville & Fairfield Pike.

The practicing physicians of the town have been in the order named: Drs. Smith Bowlin, T. C. McCrory, W. F. Long, T. C. Henson, W. F. Clairy, J. W. Acuff, W. R. Freeman, T. F. Frazill, and H. E. Finney, dentist.

The secret societies of the town consist of Good Templar, Masonic and Odd Fellow, lodges of those fraternities being organized in 1860.

The first school established in Bellbuckle, and one of the first in the county, was Salem Academy, which was founded in about 1820. Numerous changes were made in the old school, and in 1880, when a handsome brick building was erected and the name of the school was changed to that of Bedford College (see chapter on schools of county). Besides this school the public common schools are conducted for a term of five months each year. An addition of importance to the schools of Bellbuckle, and also of the county, is the Webb School, which was recently removed to that place from Maury County, where it was known as the Kuleoka Institute (see school chapter). The colored school, which is taught five months in the year, is held in the colored church building.

Bellbuckle is supplied with a number of good churches. The Methodist Episcopal Church, a handsome brick, was erected in 1878, at a cost of about $4,000; the Missionary Baptist Church (frame) was erected in 1873, at a cost of $1,500; the Cumberland Presbyterian Church was erected in 1883, is of brick, and cost $4,000; the Christian Church was erected in 1883, is of frame, and cost $2,000. The colored churches are the Baptists and African Methodist Episcopal, both of which are frame buildings which cost each about $400.

Flat Creek is situated seven miles southeast from Shelbyville in the Twenty-fourth District, and has a population of about 150 people. The town was founded in about 1840 upon a tract of school land known as the Sixteenth Section. The first merchant was Thomas Newson, who kept a general store as early as 1841 or 1842. Other early business men were Blanton & Co., Hall & Warnock, Crunk & Friend, Keith & Baker, Long & Morgan, Long & Watson, Evans & Keith, Dean & Keith, Brennon & Dean and Hudson & Co., and during the time of the above business men a Grange store was in operation for several years. The business men of the present are as follows: John E. Wood, Hudson & Co. and Hale Bros., general stores; J. H. Farran, groceries; and John Bryant, saddles and harness. The Flat Creek Saw and Planing-mill was established in 1870, by John D. Floyd, and is now owned by Phineas Hix. The blacksmiths are John Bryant, Nance Green and Matt Thomas. The early physicians of Flat Creek were Drs. J. Blakemore, Russ, Gordon, James Crunk, Shepard, Samuel Rager and Grizard and those of the present are Drs. Frost, Anderson Rager and Williams. Flat Creek has a chartered academy and also good common white and colored schools. The churches are as follows: Cumberland Presbyterian, built during the fifties at a cost of $1,000, frame; Methodist Episcopal South, built in 1885, and cost $1,000, frame; and Christian, built in 1870, and cost $1,500, frame. In 1850 the Primitive Baptists erected a large frame church, which was the first church in the town. This church passed into the hands of the Missionary Baptists, and afterward to the Separate Baptists, and that organization disbanding the church was abandoned, and while still standing and in a comparative state of preservation, is unused The Missionary Baptist (colored) congregation meets in the colored schoolhouse. Both the Masons and Odd Fellows have organizations in Flat Creek, both of which were established in 1850.

Fairfield, fourteen miles northeast from Shelbyville, in the First and Second Districts, is one of the oldest towns in Bedford County. The town lies on both sides of Garrison Fork of Duck River, which stream is spanned by a large bridge at the town, and is distant from Wartrace four and a half miles and from Bellbuckle five miles. The land upon which the town was founded was owned by Dr. J. L. Armstrong and Henry Davis; that on the west side of the creek belonged to Dr. Armstrong and was called Petersburg; that on the east side by Mr. Davis and was called Fairfield. The two towns were laid off into lots, and the lots were sold some time in 1830. From 1835 to about 1850 Fairfield (the name of Petersburg was soon dropped) was one of the most flourishing towns in the county, and a large amount of business was annually transacted. The building of the Nashville & Chattanooga Railway destroyed the business to a great extent, and since that time the town has gradually but steadily declined, and at present there are not over fifty inhabitants. The early business men of Fairfield were Josephus Erwin, William Crutcher, William Hickman, Henry Davis, Isaac Miller, William Clark, Henry Davis, Jr., James Word, John West, ——— Marshall, David Brown, James Martin, ——— Miller and James Simms. Osborn & Bro. are the business men of the present. The blacksmiths are Osborn Bros. & Justice, James Martin and Buck Butner. H. A. Justice & Son have the one corn mill, which is on Garrison's Fork and is of water-power. The physicians of Fairfield and vicinity have been as follows: Drs. James L. Armstrong, Thomas B. Mosley, Needham King, Robert Singleton, George B. Sumner, David King, Allen Hall, J. B. Muse, Jack Morgan and Robert Morgan. Those of the present are Drs. Joshua Ganaway, Smith Bowlin, R. W. Kirch and S. K. Whitson. Fairfield has four churches—two white and two colored. The former are Missionary and "Hard Shell" Baptists, and the latter are Missionary Baptists and African Methodist Episcopal. The schools of the town are the Fairfield Academy (chartered), which enjoys an excellent reputation, and the colored free school.

Unionville, situated in the Eleventh District, twelve miles northwest from Shelbyville, has a population of about 200, and is one of the most prosperous towns in Bedford County. Unionville was founded in about 1827 upon the lands of Meredith Blanton and James Roy, and derived its name from the uniting of two postoffices and establishing the same at that point. In 1828 Meredith Blanton erected a blacksmith shop, which shop has been operated continually from that time to the present by the Blanton family, and is now owned by two grandsons of M. Blanton. The first business in the town was transacted by the firm of McGaffin, Rushing & Covington, who had a general store. Other early business men, who were in the merchandise trade from that time until 1860, were William Collins, Blanton & Keller, Duggan, Moon & Barnes, Little, Brown & Deason and F. S. Smith. From 1860 to 1870 the merchants were Ganaway, Clary & Co., McCord & Ogilvie, Atkinson & McCord, Peter Barnes, Williams & Landis, Williams & Moon, Landis & Bro., Ganaway & Henden, Duggan & Henden, B. F. Duggan, J. M. Moon, McLane & Bro, Winsett & McLane, Winsett & Elkton and Winsett & Covington. From 1870 to 1880: Duggan & Clark, Duggan & Sons, T. N. McCord, J. A. Ganaway, Landis & Winsett, Covington & Landis, W. A. Ott, J. Covington, J. M. Moon, B. F. Duggan and H. R. Frierson. From 1880, including the present merchants: T. N. McCord, Blanton & Blanton, J. Covington, Covington & Blanton, H. R. Frierson and H. R. Freeman. The churches of Unionville are as follows: Methodist Protestant Church, erected in 1840 of logs, and rebuilt of frame on the same site in 1868, at a cost of about $1,500; Methodist Episcopal Church South, frame building, erected in 1856, and cost about $900; Cumberland Presbyterian Church, frame, erected in 1876, and cost $1,600; Christian Church, erected in 1878 at a cost of $1,000. The schools of the town consist of a chartered academy, at which school is taught ten months in the year, and the colored free school. The secret societies are the Masonic and Good Templars lodges, the former of which was organized in 1867, and the latter in 1885. The practicing physicians of the town are Drs. B. F. Duggan, S. S. Duggan and G. L. Landis.

Normandy, at the mouth of Norman Creek, twelve miles east from Shelbyville, in the Twenty-fifth District; Richmond, in the Nineteenth District, ten miles southwest from Shelbyville; Palmetto, in the Eighteenth District, twelve miles west of Shelbyville; Rover, in the Tenth District, sixteen miles northwest from Shelbyville; Haley's Station, three miles south of Wartrace, on the Nashville & Chattanooga Railway, and Cortner's Station, six miles south of Wartrace, on the Nashville & Chattanooga Railway, are all flourishing villages of from twenty-five to fifty inhabitants each.

Bedford County justly prides herself upon her splendid educational advantages, which, indeed, are surpassed by those of but few counties in Tennessee. Of the schools during the first ten years of the county's existence as such, there remains no record whatever, and from this fact one is led to believe that, while it is more than probable that schools were taught in the county as early as 1805 or 1806, they were of an inferior order, and contributed but little to the education of the county. The first school taught in the county, or at least the first one of any consequence and of which there is a record, was Mount Reserve Academy, which was established in about 1815 or 1816 by the Rev. George Newton, who came from North Carolina a few years previous to that time. The school was located three miles east of the present site of Wartrace in a log house at the place now known as Bethsalem Presbyterian Church. Rev. Newton was a classic scholar, and taught with great success the English as well as the higher branches of a liberal education. This school continued at different periods until the civil war, when it was abandoned.

The next school was Dixon Academy, which was established in Shelbyville in 1820, and which in its day, and even at the present, was a noted school. A thorough classical course was taught at the school by such teachers as Rev. Alexander Newton, Prof. James Jett, Prof. Blake and Prof. Gonigal, and many of the afterward prominent men of the county and State were educated there. The building was of log, and stood in the center of an eight-acre plot of ground, which ground was donated to the school by Clement Cannon, Esq., one of the wealthy citizens of that day. The log building was subsequently weatherboarded, and in that shape the building rendered service until 1855, when the present commodious brick building was erected. The school has been in continuous operation (excepting vacations) from its establishment to the present, having been conducted all along as a subscription school. The present principal is Prof. T. P. Brennon, who, in 1885, added a military department to the school, and the pupils are required to wear a neat uniform similar to those in use in the United States Regular Army.

Contemporaneous with Dixon Academy was Salem Academy, which was established by Rev. Dr. Thurston near where now stands Bellbuckle in 1825. This school was taught in a double log house which was erected by the patrons of the school. Dr. Thurston was succeeded as teacher by Prof. Blake. In 1850 the school was removed to town and was known as the Bellbuckle Academy, of which Thomas B. Ivey was the first teacher. In 1870 the school was succeeded by Science Hill School, which was established by Prof. A. T. Crawford; and Science Hill was in turn succeeded by the present Bedford College in 1880, when a handsome brick school building, costing $5,000, was erected. These schools were all a continuation of the old Salem Academy. In about 1828 or 1830 Mrs. James Jett, wife of Prof. Jett, of Dixon Academy, established an excellent female acad my a short distance east from Shelbyville, which was continued for about twelve years, until the death of Mrs. Jett.

The next school of consequence was the Martin School in Fairfield, which was established by Abraham Martin in 1828. Mr. Martin was a very successful teacher, and for eight years conducted a celebrated school. At about the same time Rural Academy was established one mile east of Fairfield on the east side of Duck River, of which Rev. Baxter H. Ragsdale was the first teacher. The school continued until 1846. In 1837 Clark M. Comstack founded a classical school at Big Springs on Sugar Creek, which he taught until 1846, when the school was abandoned.

In 1840 the citizens of Shelbyville erected a building by subscription and founded a female academy, which was first taught by Prof. Alford Dashiall. The school was run for about eighteen years, and the school building stands at the present, being occupied as a residence. The school was succeeded by the present female college, which was established in 1858, when the large brick building now in use was erected at a cost of $15,000. The school is now under the management of Prof. J. P. Hamilton, and is very successful. In 1846 the Baptists established a school about one mile south of Fairfield, of which Abraham Tillman was the first principal. This school continued until the breaking out of the civil war, and after the war the building was remodeled and has since been run as a public high school, of which Prof. Joseph Estill is the present principal instructor.

The Shelbyville University was established in 1852, and continued about four years, Prof. Hamilton being the president. After the war the building, which was considerably damaged, was rebuilt, and the university was continued by Prof. C. W. Jerome. The building, which stands and is in use at the present, is of brick, and cost about $1,200, exclusive of the ground, which was donated by Judge Davidson and Moses Marshall, Esq. In about 1870 the building and grounds were purchased by the school directors of the Seventh Civil District and converted into a public high school. For the ensuing term seven teachers are employed for this school, and a most successful term is anticipated. The school is one of three white public schools in the Seventh District, one of which is at Sylvia Mills, and the other at Fairview.

During the fifties Richmond, Fairfield and Unionville Academies (chartered), and a splendid school near Schaffner's Lutheran Church, known as the Jenkins School, were established, all of which are in use at the present. Wartrace Academy was chartered in 1860, Flat Creek Academy in 1875, Tumtine Academy in the Eleventh District, in 1873, Center Grove Academy in the Ninth District, in 1878, and Liggett's Academy in the Eighteenth District, in 1880. The above is a list of the chartered academies of the county.

The Webb School at Bellbuckle, was removed from Culleoka in the spring of 1886, and buildings are almost completed for the school. They are of frame, the main building being one story in height, with two wing additions, affording a capacity for 150 to 200 students. The chapel has a floor area of forty-two square feet. W. R. Webb, A. M., and J. M. Webb, A. M., are the principals, while the school is owned by a stock company. A classical course is to be taught, and the school will no doubt prove very successful.

Under a general law of the General Assembly, passed March 6, 1873, the present public school system was inaugurated. The number of pupils enrolled the first year in Bedford County was 5,432, and in 1876 the number enrolled was 6,062. On June 30, 1885, the scholastic population of the county was white male, 3,612; white female, 3,354; total 6,966; colored male, 1,484; colored female, 1,417; total 2,901; total white and colored male and female between the ages of six and twenty-one years, 9,867. For the same year there were teachers employed in the county as follows: white male, 50; white female, 39; colored male, 21; colored female, 16; total 126. Number of schools in the county: white, 63; colored, 31; total 94. Number of school districts in the county, 21.

The different religious denominations were organized in Bedford County probably as early as 1806, and the Methodists and Presbyterians had camp grounds at different points in the county, where they would meet during the months of July, August and September. The Methodists had camp grounds at Salem, Steele's, Horse Mountain, Knight's and Holt's; the Presbyterians at Bethsalem, and later on, the Cumberland Presbyterians at Three Forks, Beech Grove and Hastings'. Probably the first meeting-house erected was Salem Church, which was built in about 1807 at Salem Camp Ground, one-half mile from the present town of Bellbuckle. The church was a log house, built of yellow poplar, unhewn logs, and the cane was cut, logs cut and carried on the shoulders of men, and the house built by the individual members of the church. The old building stood until about 1820, when it was replaced with a better log one, and in 1845 a substantial frame building was substituted for the log, and it is in use at the present time. In 1816 the Tennessee Annual Methodist Episcopal Conference was held at Salem Church. Other early Methodist Churches were Pleasant Garden, on Flat Creek, in the Twenty-fourth District, built in 1814; Holt's Camp Ground, near the Fayetteville Pike, in the Twenty-fourth District, built in 1823, and Mount Moriah, near Wartrace, built in 1823. In 1821 the Methodist Circuit extended from below Fayetteville to Hooker's Gap, and from four to five weeks were required to ride the circuit. Rev. John Brooks, one of the ablest of the Methodist Episcopal ministers, was the circuit rider.

The Presbyterians erected their first church at Shelbyville in 1815, and their second and only other one at Bethsalem, near Wartrace, in 1816.

New Hope, at Fairfield, was probably the first Baptist Church in the county, it having been erected in 1809, and though having been rebuilt several times is still in use. Keele's church, named for "Billy Keele," on Garrison's Fork, near Fairfield, was probably the first church erected by the Separate Baptists, some time in 1812 or 1813.

The Cumberland Presbyterians erected their first churches at Three Forks about 1820, and at Hastings' Camp Ground about 1821. The Lutherans came into the county at an early day, and erected a church on Thompson Creek about 1826, though they were organized several years before that time. Their next church was Cedar Hill Church, in the Shaffner neighborhood.

In 1846 the Christian Church was organized in the county, and in 1855 the Catholic Church was organized in Shelbyville. The Episcopal Church was organized in 1853 (see Shelbyville Churches). The Northern Methodists came into the county since the war, yet are very strong at the present, having eleven churches in the county and at Caldwell's Camp Ground, three miles from Shelbyville on the Unionville Pike, which was named in honor of Hon. Thomas H. Caldwell, of Shelbyville.

The Duck River Bible Society, a very important adjunct of the churches, was organized at Shelbyville on the 16th of May, 1718, and has been in continuous operation up to the present. The society is an auxiliary to the American Bible Society, which was organized in 1816, and the Duck River branch was one of the first organized. Its leading object is to distribute Holy Bibles to the needy and destitute.

The churches of the present, outside of those in the towns already mentioned, are as follows by civil districts: Center, Cumberland Presbyterian; Shiloh, Methodist Episcopal South; Bethlehem, Primitive Baptist; Haley's Station, Methodist Episcopal South, and Union Ridge, African Methodist Episcopal, in the Second District. Mount Mariah, Methodist Episcopal South; Bethell, Methodist Episcopal South; Mount Olivett,

Methodist Episcopal North; Phillipi, Methodist Episcal North, in the Third District. Cross Roads, Christian, and Guy's Gap, Baptist, in the Fifth District. Whitesides Chapel, Methodist Episcopal South; Nance's, Missionary Baptist; Hart's Chapel, Methodist Episcopal; Bellview and Browntown, Colored Missionary Baptists, in the Sixth District. Mount Pisgah, Primitive Baptist; North Fork, Missionary Baptist; Hickory Hill, Methodist Episcopal South, and Green Hill, Cumberland Presbyterian in the Eighth District. Blankenship, Methodist Episcopal South; Tarpley, Methodist Episcopal South, and Bethlehem, African Methodist Episcopal, in the Ninth District. Enon, Primitive Baptist; Rover (town), Missionary Baptist; Rover (town), Methodist Episcopal North; Cedar Grove, Methodist Episcopal; Mount Zion, Protestant Methodist Episcopal; Kingdom, Cumberland Presbyterian, and Poplar Grove, African Methodist Episcopal, in the Tenth District. Ray's Chapel, Protestant Methodist Episcopal; Crowell's Chapel, Lutheran; Pleasant Valley, Methodist Episcopal South; Zion's Hill, Methodist Episcopal North, and Corner Meeting-house and Thompson's Ford, both African Methodist Episcopal and Cumberland Presbyterian combined in the Eleventh District. United Presbyterian (at Palmetto); Zion, Primitive Baptist; Shiloh, Methodist Episcopal South; Dryden's Chapel, Methodist Episcopal South; Liggett Chapel, Methodist Episcopal North; Libourn, Methodist Episcopal North, and African Methodist Episcopal and Baptist, in the Eighteenth District. Richmond (town), Christian, and Branchville, Methodist Episcopal South, in the Nineteenth District. Marvin's Chapel, Methodist Episcopal South; Big Springs, Missionary Baptist; Cottage Grove, Cumberland Presbyterian, and Knight's Chapel, Methodist Episcopal South, and one colored church each of Missionary Baptist and African Methodist Episcopal, in the Twentieth District. Center, Methodist Episcopal South, in the Twenty-first District. Mount Harmon, Methodist Episcopal and Separate Baptist combined, in the Twenty-second District. New Hope, Cumberland Presbyterian; Mount Pisgah, Methodist Episcopal South; Hickory Grove, Separate Baptist; Caldwell's Chapel, Methodist Episcopal North; St. Mark, Christian, and St. Mark, African Methodist Episcopal, in the Twenty-third District. Normandy (town), Methodist Episcopal South; Jenkins Chapel, Christian, and Mount Bethel, African Methodist Episcopal, in the Twenty-fifth District. Sylvan Mills, Methodist Episcopal North; Mission, Cumberland Presbyterian; Reed's Hill, Missionary Baptist; Fairview schoolhouse used by Methodist Episcopal, Baptist and Christian congregations; Robison's Hill, colored Missionary Baptist, and Elbethel, Colored Missionary Baptist.

MARSHALL COUNTY.

THE basis of all wealth is the soil of the land. Prosperous cities, towns and huge manufactories seem to spring up and flourish as if by magic and without reference to the agricultural advantages of the country; but such growth will be but temporary unless sustained by a country possessing agricultural wealth. It may almost be reduced to a mathematical problem in which it may be said the soil and climate equal the wealth of the country.

The surface of the county is comparatively level, yet there is sufficient undulation to give ample slope for drainage. The backbone known as Elk Ridge extends from east to west and rises to the height of 300 feet. This is the water-shed south of Duck River and separates the county into two distinct parts in that part of the county. Duck River flowing through the northern part is the main outlet for drainage in that part north of the ridge. The two principal tributaries of Duck River from the north are Caney Spring and

Flat Creek. The two principal streams from the south are East Rock Creek and West Rock Creek. Both these streams take their rise in Elk Ridge but unite before entering Duck River, south of the ridge are Cane Creek, Richland Creek, Bradshaw Creek, Swan and Robinson Forks. Duck River and Richland Creek are the finest streams in the county, affording ample facilities for milling purposes, and their valleys and in fact all in the county, are made up of rich loamy soil. The beds of these streams are usually covered with pebbly limestone. The banks show an outcrop peculiar to the Central Basin. This is what is known as the Trenton formation which is composed of the Carter Creek limestone, this being a light blue or dove-colored limestone, the upper part sometimes gray. This is the upper layer. The next below in the natural order is the glade limestone. This light blue color, is thin-bedded, shaly and is the formation peculiar to the cedar glades. The next stratum in order is the Ridley limestone, below this is the Pierce limestone and lastly is the central limestone. Each of these strata affords a rich fossil plant which is inviting to the paleontologist. The streams above mentioned have sufficient flow to prevent stagnation and the waters are usually clear. The drainage of the county and other physical features are such as to render it comparatively free from malarial or miasmatic diseases. The section of the county north of Elk Ridge is more level than that south of it. The soil here yields a rich harvest in all the cereals, grasses, vegetables and fruits. The iron oxides give the soil a reddish hue yet it is very rich. The spurs and ridges furnish a fine growth of timber, the cedar and poplar being the most valuable. Many of the farms are fenced with rails of the former, and the latter has become a very valuable article of export since the completion of the Duck River Valley Railroad.

The section of the county lying in the vicinity of Chapel Hill is particularly well adapted to the growth of cotton. The section along Richland Creek, south of Elk Ridge, is regarded as the best part of the county and is equal to any in the State. The finest and best improved farms in the county are to be found in this section. All the lands are arable and highly productive except near the tops of the knobs, serrated ridges and glady spots. The ridges are usually fertile to their summits and are covered with a soil of flinty, siliceous, cherty gravel and weathered rocks, that is friable and easily worked. What is known as the Cornersville District is generally considered the finest agricultural section of the county, and will compare favorably with any in the State.

The timbered lands of the county cover from seventy to eighty square miles of territory, and some of this is unsurpassed in the United States. The best of these lands are between East and West Rock Creeks, west of Farmington, between Duck River and the railroad, extending to the neighborhood of Berlin, and in the northwest part. The growth of timber includes oak, poplar, ash, elm, linden, beech, locust, cherry, walnut, sugar tree, hackberry, buckeye, cedar, hickory and chestnut. The growth of oak, walnut and poplar is of immense size.

In addition to the excellent timber the county affords good limestone rock, not only for fencing but also good building material. The sandstone in some places affords good grit for whetstones and grindstones. Excellent lime is made from the limestone rock, which exists in almost unlimited quantities. Within the last two decades there has been a perceptible falling off in the amount of cotton raised, and a great increase in the amount of grain, particularly in wheat, oats and corn. The greatest increase, however, has been in the amount of fine stock, including horses, cattle, hogs and sheep. This change has greatly increased the wealth of the county, is less exhaustive on the soil and is obtained at a less expense of labor.

A landscape view of the territory now included in Marshall County, as it was 100 years ago, would reveal to us an unbroken wilderness visited only by the roaming Indian in pursuit of the game which so abundantly inhabited this section. No settlements were made within the present limits of Marshall County prior to 1807. The first settlers found a growth of cane so rank that they preferred traveling along the beds of small streams to the arduous labor of cutting out roads. Most of the first settlers came here to live on land which had been granted to Revolutionary soldiers by North Carolina, for service rendered in the war. The many indications of a fertile soil and the equable climate caused many others to follow soon, and in 1810 the curling smoke ascended from many of the primitive "clearings," and the hardy pioneers began to call this new land their home.

It is not known where or by whom the first settlement was made. For convenience in treating of the first settlements, the county may be divided into three sections: First, that portion north of Duck River; Second, that lying between Duck River and the Elk Ridge, and Third, that lying south of Elk Ridge.

On Caney Spring Creek, near the village of Caney Spring, Asa Fonville raised a crop in 1807, and a little farther up the creek James Patterson began clearing up a farm early in the same year. Four miles northwest of Caney Spring, Squire Atkisson was a very prominent early settler, and a leader in his community for many years. James Haynes and a man named Kellams settled near together, and between Atkisson and Patterson. Samuel Ramsey settled on the creek two miles from the village, in 1808, and afterward in 1809 removed south of Duck River. He had a water-mill, which was the first one north of the river. It was visited by people from ten or twelve miles distant. Others who lived in that vicinity prior to 1810 were the Allens, Wallaces and Becks. Gen. N. B. Forrest, who was born at Chapel Hill in 1818, was a descendant of this family of Becks.

In the vicinity of Chapel Hill a settlement was made in 1808 by Andrew Patterson, who was a captain, commanding a company in the battle of New Orleans in 1815. Robert Patterson, a brother of Andrew, also settled near in the same year. Northwest of Chapel Hill four miles in 1809, Joseph Brittain settled on his tract of 5,000 acres. He reared a large family of children, and gave them all farms. Several descendents of this man are now living in that section. He built a horse-mill. The Boyds and Riggs lived in the same community as early as 1810, and were probably there as early as 1808. The father of Gen. Forrest emigrated from North Carrlina, and after a temporary stay at other places made his home at Chapel Hill in 1815.

Near Duck River on the north side, a large family of the Billingtons were the first to make permanent settlements. Near there was a Rev. Mr. Warner, a minister in the Baptist Church. Others among the first pioneers were James Patton, Hugh McClelland, Richard Walker and two families of McClures.

Early in the year 1807 James Neil came from North Carolina to where Farmington is now located. He built a cabin just northwest of the turnpike in the village. He was soon followed by two of his brothers, Alexander and Andrew Neil, who both lived within a quarter of a mile of where the village stands.

About the same time John Reed opened up a small farm one mile south of these. Near Reed was John Dysarts about the same time. About three miles from Farmington, on West Rock Creek, Allen Leiper was the first cane cutter. He had a valuable water-mill for those days, which in the years 1808–09 supplied the demand of the central section of the county. In 1808 John Shaw brought his family from North Carolina, and made his home one mile north of the village. Shaw was a hero at the battle of New Orleans.

At Fishing Ford a man named Hazelett was the first to clear away the cane and build a cabin. Southwest of him a short distance was a man named Cleek. Cleek raised several sons, who made good citizens of that section. Who first drove the ax through the wilderness where Lewisburg now stands is not known. At the time of the organization of the county Abner Houston lived just west of Col. J. H. Lewis' house, and across the creek from him lived John H. Bills. Two miles northwest William McClure, the first chairman of the county court, settled in 1808 or 1809. Jonathan Moore came in 1808 from Carolina, and made the first opening in the forest on Globe Creek, and was soon followed by John Wilkes, who has many descendants in the county at present. On the head waters of Rock Creek a settlement was made by James Leiper, a brother of Allen Leiper, in 1808. About this time Benjamin Simmons came from North Carolina to the same neighborhood, bringing with him a slave then eight years old, who is now reverently addressed, by white and black, as "Uncle George McBride." This negro was widely known throughout this section of the State on account of his skill in the use of the violin. Just east of Simmons were Josiah and John Blackwell's farms. Not far from where the railroad begins to ascend Elk Ridge from the north, John and Robin Orr were among the first settlers in the county. In 1808 William Williams settled where Round Hill Church now stands, and soon afterward removed to near Belfast. Then he opened a store. He bought his first stock of goods at Nashville, and hauled it home in a one-horse cart. From a ledger which he kept in 1823 the following prices are quoted: Coffee, per pound, 56¼ cents; sugar, 25 cents; indigo, 31¼ cents; salt, 4 cents; copperas, 12½ cents; nails, 25 cents; madder, 15 cents; cambric, per yard, $1; flannel, 75 cents; calico, 50 cents; muslin, $1; bombazette, 75 cents; whisky, per pint, 18¾ cents; wine, 50 cents; "Bateman's drops," per bottle, 25 cents, etc. A remarkable fact is that calico was bought in quantity from three-fourths to three yards, rarely ever more than one yard being purchased at one time by one party. The book indicates that Mr. Williams did a large business and that his debtors paid their accounts promptly. Early in 1807 Nathaniel Dryden emigrated from North Carolina to his grant of land where Belfast now stands. Thompson Cannon was his first neighbor, and in the same year Francis H. Woods and James Coffey settled near. Further down the creek was Samuel Ramsey, who moved from north of Duck River in 1809. He was the father of John Ramsey, who was born in North Carolina in 1797; was fifteen years old when coming to the county, and is now living at Farmington, at the age of eighty-nine years. Thomas J. Hall, who was a prominent Presbyterian minister, settled near Farmington in 1814, and taught school there for many years.

South of Elk Ridge is some of the finest land in the county, and it was not long in being developed into a well settled community. At Connersville the first to disturb the stillness of the wilderness was John Haynes, who, in 1807, lived near where the flouring-mill stands. William Henderson, in 1808, built the first house on the ground now covered by the town. In a very short time Pearsley Cox became his neighbor on the northwest. Billy Marr came from North Carolina to Robinson Fork in 1808, and in a short time he sold out to Ephraim Massey, who kept a store for several years. Ephraim Patrick, John Dabney, John Cockrell, Billy Alexander and John and Thomas Walker came to this section about the same time. John Parks lived four miles south of Connersville, on Richland Creek, in 1807. On Cane Creek, about ten miles south of Lewisburg, Elisha and Joab Bagley located between 1807 and 1810; James Brown lived very near them. Above Brown, on the same creek, were Josiah McAdams and his two sons, Irvin and James; still further up the creek Jesse McLean and Henry Bagley were the first pioneers. Elisha Bagley had a horse-mill. After these first settlers had opened the first farms settlements rapidly followed, and the names of those coming in after those above mentioned would occupy too much space to be given.

In all parts of the county traces of the Mound-Builders are found. Mounds built of earth and small stones, ranging in height from four or five feet to about fifteen feet, are more numerous in this county than in any other part of the State. North of Lewisburg about a mile is a mound ten feet high, built of larger stones than are commonly found in these structures. It was evidently a burial place, for parts of a skeleton have been taken from it. A thigh bone of a person was recently found in this mound, which, if the other parts were developed proportionately, belonged to a person over seven feet tall. The jaw bone, also found, is much larger than that of any person of whom we now have any knowledge. This body was evidently buried in a sitting posture. Three miles west of Lewisburg is a large clay mound, covering over a quarter of an acre. In the Seventeenth District there is one of small stones and clay seventeen feet high. There is also a very large one in the Fifth District. In these mounds are found fragments of pottery and rude missiles of various kinds, supposed to be weapons of warfare. In various parts of the county are found numerous arrow-heads, battle-axes, pipes, etc., probably relics of the Indian tribes that lived here.

Marshall County was established by an act of the Legislature passed February 26, 1836. It included fractions of Lincoln, Bedford and Maury Counties, when first organized, and in 1870 a part of Giles County, known as the Cornersville District, was given to Marshall. In establishing the first boundaries the line between Marshall and Maury was placed nearer the county seat of the latter than the law allowed, and it was so changed as to conform to the law. In 1871 the line on the west was again slightly changed to include the farms of John B. Wilkes and John Coffey, in Marshall.

October 3, 1836, at the house of Abner Houston, the first county court was organized by the following justices of the peace: William McClure, Thomas Ross, William Wilkes, Peter Williams, Thomas Wilson, David McGahey, James Adams, George Cunningham, James L. Ewing, John Field, Adam Miller, Joseph Cleek, Ephraim Hunter, Asa Holland, James Patterson, Jason B. Sheffield, Sherwood Dunnigan and Andrew Laird. William McClure was elected chairman, and David McGahey was appointed secretary *pro tem*. The court then "adjourned to meet at the camp ground immediately," and upon being again convened the following men were chosen to fill their respective offices: John R. Hill, sheriff; Martin W. Oakley, clerk county court; John W. Record, trustee; John Elliott, register; Joseph McCord, coroner; Isaac H. Williams, ranger, and Hugh McClelland, surveyor. The court then appointed commissioners to lay off the civil districts, and proceeded to the general routine of business, namely, appointing road overseers, etc.

The first money for county purposes was derived from the sale of lots in Lewisburg November 30, and December 1 and 2, 1836. These sales amounted to $22,861, which was appropriated for public improvements. The lots were usually sold on time, and January 4, 1837, the treasurer reported "no money in the treasury." In 1841 the following levy of tax was made: On each $100 worth of property (for county) 6 cents; on each $100 worth of property (for poor) 1¼ cents; on each poll, 25 cents; on each merchant peddler or hawker, $5; on shows, $50.

The tax for 1842 was the same as for the year previous, except that a bridge tax of 6¼ cents on each poll and 4⅜ cents on each $100 worth of property was assessed.

For 1886 the tax levy was at the following rate: County tax, 40 cents on $100; State tax, 30 cents on $100; school tax, 15 cents on $100; railroad tax, 35 cents on $100; highway, 11 cents on $100; total $1.31 on $100. In 1886 there was reported 224,829 acres of land valued at $2,205,117. The total taxable property was valued at $2,578,170. The population in 1880 was 19,260.

Indicative of the rich agricultural resources, the following official report of 1885 is given: Number of acres of improved land, 132,513; number of horses and mules, 9,344; number of cattle, 9,808; number of sheep, 10,118; number of hogs, 37,815; Indian corn, 1,176,536 bushels; oats, 59,567 bushels; rye, 2,050 bushels; wheat, 172,584 bushels.

November 7, 1836, James Osborn, William Williams, Joel Yowell, Aaron Boyd and James C. Record were appointed commissioners to lay off and sell town lots in Lewisburg and to superintend the erection of public buildings; and December 5, 1836, the same body of men, with the exception of James Osborn, was appointed a committee to draft plans and specifications for a court house and a jail. On January 2, 1837, they reported that after due consideration and deliberation they would suggest the said buildings to be similar to those of Bedford County, with some alterations. The first court house, modeled after the one then in Shelbyville, was built at a cost of $8,750, and was completed, received and occupied by October 1, 1838. This building burned in 1873, and the next year the present court house was erected. The contract for its erection was $21,900, and carpeting, desks, chairs, tables, shelves, etc., amounted to about $1,000 more. This is a splendid two-story brick building, and with its yard full of shade trees presents a handsome appearance.

Thomas D. Moore, Samuel Davis, J. B. Ezell, James Hendricks and James W. Nance composed the committee to draft the plans and specifications. A notable fact is that W. H. Wisener made the first and last speech in the old court house, and the first speech in the new one.

MARSHALL COUNTY.   889

The first jail was a brick building 26x50 feet. It was lined with a double wall of hewn oak logs, having a space of eight inches between, which was filled with stones. The floor and ceiling were of two-inch oak plank. It was completed March 1, 1838, at a cost of $3,850. This jail was a secure one, as no prisoners ever escaped from it. It was burned about the close of the war and in 1867 the present one was built of stone, at a cost of $9,108.06.

On January 1, 1838, court appropriated $1,000 for building a poor-house. The poor-farm was located two and a half miles southwest of Lewisburg, and comprised seventy-two acres. In 1858 it was sold, and the present one of 160 acres, was bought. It is ten miles south of the county seat. There are now ten white and seven colored inmates of the asylum.

In 1871 the people of Marshall voted an appropriation of $315,000, to the proposed building of the Cumberland & Ohio Railroad through the county. In 1873 the amount was divided, $200,000 being still appropriated to the above road, and $115,000 to the Duck River Valley Railroad. The panic of 1873 destroyed the hopes of the Cumberland & Ohio Road; but the Duck River Valley Road was completed to Lewisburg from Columbia, in April, 1877, and in October, 1879, it was completed to the Lincoln County line. Besides the $115,000 a large individual subscription was raised. Dr. R. G. McClure and Col. J. H. Lewis were instrumental in securing the road. Dr. McClure was president of the company for three years and was succeeded by Col. Lewis, who was president two years previous to its lease to the Nashville, Chattanooga & St. Louis Road. Marshall County issued bonds for the $115,000. The railroad tax pays the interest on these bonds and also creates a sinking fund, by which the debt has been reduced to $87,600. This road supplies the much needed outlet for grain which has so long been felt, and it has been the means of placing Marshall high in the rank of agricultural counties of the State.

The Shelbyville & Lewisburg, Lewisburg & Franklin, Nashville, Nolensville & Chapel Hill, Cornersville & Lewisburg, and Lewisburg & Mooresville Pikes were built before the war. Since the war the Cornersville & Lewisburg Pike has been extended to Pulaski, and the Lewisburg & Mooresville Pike Road runs to Culleoka. The Nashville, Nolensville & Chapel Hill Pike has also been extended from Chapel Hill to Farmington. Others which have been constructed recently are the Cornersville & Lynnville, Comersville & Spring Place and Lewisburg & Columbia Pikes.

The first bridge was built across Duck River within this county in 1838, at a cost of $6,892. It was a covered wooden bridge supported on stone piers. There are now two splendid iron bridges across the river and one of wood.

The Marshall County Agricultural and Mechanical Society was organized July 7, 1856. Its first officers were as follows: E. A. Wilson, president; W. L. McClelland, vice-president; A. B. Ewing, secretary; James V. Ewing, treasurer. The board of managers were Maj. G. L. Allman, John W. Hutton, Esq., Col. John R. Hill, Gen. Levi Cochran, D. V. Chrisman and Thomas McKnight. Before the war fairs were held every year, the first one being October 30 and 31, 1856. Fairs were also held from 1868 to 1873, and after this the colored people held three annual meetings under this charter. The society owned seven and a quarter acres of land and had constructed the necessary buildings, such as an amphitheatre, halls, stables, etc., which were all destroyed by the war.

The Marshall County Medical Society held its first meeting in August, 1877. The first members were Drs. J. S. Nowlin, J. S. Howlett, T. E. Reed, S. T. Hardison, B. F. Smith, R. A. Orr, T. B. Leonard, Z. W. Neil, J. O. Nowlin, J. C. Crunk, J. W. Huddleston, T. J. Kennedy, W. S. McLean, J. D. Johnson, J. M. Patterson, L. L. Murray, C. A. Abernathy, F. Ferguson, J. W. Percy, J. B. Neil, W. M. Allison, C. C. Neil, A. Jones, J. C. Hill, R. C. McCordy and W. C. Ransom. J. S. Nowlin, S. T. Hardison, J. M. Patterson, A. Jones and F. Ferguson have been presidents of the society. There are now eighteen members.

The county officers have been as follows: Sheriffs—John R. Hill, 1836; Solomon Meadows, 1842; John Laws, 1844; W. B. Holden, 1848; Thomas F. Brooks, 1854; John B. Wilkes, 1856; W. F. Collins, 1860; A. Duncan, 1862; Levi Cochran, 1863; James R. Nei

1864; Stephen Tally, 1868; John W. Champ, 1870; Scott D. Davis, 1874; W. T. Jones, 1878; R. S. Walker, 1882; W. T. Jones, 1886.

Trustees: John W. Record, 1836; James V. Ewing, 1838; James Brown, 1846; James Ross, 1847; Wesley A. Giles, 1850; James B. Chadwell, 1854; Samuel Davis, 1865; Alfred Hobson, 1870; W. G. Massey, 1872; James V. Ewing, 1874; Samuel Orr, 1876; A. V. Stillwell, 1880; N. J. Smiley, 1884.

Chairman: William McClure, 1836; John Hatchett, 1838; Benjamin Williams, 1839; Burgess Hardin, 1842; W. P. Davis, 1846; James V. Ewing, 1846; Burgess Hardin, 1848; James V. Ewing, 1849; J. A. Yowell, 1855; David McGahey (county judge), 1855-58; David McGahey, 1858; Samuel Davis, 1860; W. A. Houston, 1864; W. H. McConnell, 1866; Moses C. West, 1869; J. J. S. Gill, 1871; J. W. Calahan, 1873; J. McBride, 1876; John T. Street, 1877; James D. Cook, 1879; A. M. Davis, 1880; J. F. Brittain, 1883; W. C. McGregor, 1885; W. C. McGregor (county judge, April, 1885); W. J. Leonard (county judge, 1886).

Clerks County Court: Martin W. Oakley, 1836; John Elliott, 1846; Stephen Tally, 1854; R. L. Adams, 1862; W. P. Bullock, 1874;. J. McBride, 1882.

Clerks Circuit Court: David McGahey, 1836; Thomas McKnight, 1846; William D. Fisher, 1865; Thomas McKnight, 1868; L. B. Collins, 1870; W. G. Loyd, 1878; E. M. Miller, 1886.

Clerks Chancery Court: Gideon B. Black, 1836; R. K. Kercheval, 1846; R. G. McClure, 1865; Stephen Tally, 1870; H. N. Cowden, 1872; R. L. Adams, 1876.

Registers: John Elliott, 1836; J. J. Elliott, 1846; W. N. Cowden. 1856; J. N. Waters, 1862; J. A. Yarbrough, 1874.

Coroners: Joseph McCord, 1836; Joseph Cloud, 1846; P. G. W. Goodwin, 1849; F. K. Rambo, 1855; W. C. Stephenson, 1858; Levi Cochran, 1859; John Ramsey, 1864; William Calton, 1865; Alfred Hobson, 1869; John A. Bills, 1870; H. K. Moss, 1870; L. Cochran, 1872; H. K. Moss, 1875; R. H. McCrary, 1876; John Leonard, 1878; E. F. Williams, 1885.

Surveyors: Hugh McClelland, 1836; Samuel Elliott, 1838; W. H. McConnell, 1843; Stephen Tally, 1845; E. I. Hunter, 1852; Ephraim Hunter, 1857; H. B. Allen, 1858; S. Tally, 1863; H. B. Allen, 1864; J. P. Dysart, 1866; James Hendricks, 1870; Joel A. Morris, 1878; James Hendricks, 1886.

Rangers: Isaac H. Williams, 1837; G. W. Moore, 1840; J. M. Yowell, 1845; J. P. Smith, 1857; J. L. Reed, 1864; M. C. West, 1865; Jonathan Bills, 1865; W. D. Hawkins, 1875; L. Cunningham, 1875; H. K. Moss, 1878; J. M. McKee, 1885; H. K. Moss, 1886.

State Senators: Wilson P. Davis, 1843; Richard Warner, 1845; Thomas Dean, 1847; Wilson P. Davis, 1849; J. J. Jones, 1853; Wilson P. Davis, 1857; J. M. Johnson, 1859; W. H. Wisener, 1865; J. M. Patterson, 1871; J. D. Tillman, 1873; E. A. Wilson, 1875; Jesse Aldridge, 1877; W. P. Tolley, 1879; D. S. McCullough, 1881; D. J. McCullough, 1883; C. R. Berry, 1885.

Representatives: T. C. H. Miller, 1843; Benjamin Williams, 1847; W. F. McGregor, 1849; Thomas H. Hardin, 1851; E. A. Wilson, 1855; H. N. Cowden, 1859; A. A. Steele, 1865; A. F. Lillard, 1867; A. H. Steele, 1869; A. Jones, 1871; J. L. Orr, 1873; W. N. Cowden, 1877; Richard Warner, 1879; Ernest Pillow, 1881; W. P. Bullock, 1885. Floaters or joint representatives are not given.

The caption of the first entry of records of the circuit court is as follows:

"At a circuit court held for the county of Marshall, within the Eighth Judicial Circuit in the State of Tennessee, at the house of Abner Houston, being the place appointed by law for holding courts in said county on the fourth Monday in November, in the year of our Lord one thousand eight hundred and thirty-six, being the twenty-eighth day of the month, before the Honorable Edmund Dillahunty, Esquire, one of the judges of. the Eighth Judicial Circuit, and for the State of Tennessee, the following proceedings were had, etc." David McGahey was appointed clerk *pro tempore*, and entered into bond for the faithful performance of his duties. James H. Thomas appeared and took the oath of attorney-general. The sheriff presented the names of twenty-five men upon whom he had served a *venire facias*, whereupon the said names were written on scrolls of paper and drawn from a hat by a child under the age of ten years, when the following body of good and lawful men, citizens of Marshall County, was elected, empaneled sworn and charged to enquire for the body of the county of Marshall, to wit: Henry Bishop, James Brown, John Hatchett, Jesse Morton, James Kennedy, William Rosson, Thomas Ross, Samuel Radford, William Wilkes, James V. Ewing, William M. Orr, James Osborn and James B. Lowry, of whom James Osborn was elected foreman."

This day the attorney-general presented to court an indictment against James Orr for "mare stealing" and for stealing money, notes and other valuable papers. Orr was found guilty as charged and given three years at hard labor in the penitentiary. A judgment was rendered against him to recover $12.25, the amount of unreturned stolen property. This was the first case before the court. To this term were presented five indictments for "affray," three for "unlawful gaming," and one for "assault and battery." A fine of $10 was assessed in each of these cases with one exception, in which the accused was acquitted. In a slander suit for $1,000 damages, William Wilkes recovered from John Wilkes $150. George Purdan was fined $5 for entering court in a state of intoxication. The wounded dignity of the State was healed by two fines of $2.50 each for "contempt shown to this court" by Samuel Bickett and William Perry. The failure of John R. Hill, the sheriff, to preserve order before his Honor, cost him a fine of $10. At the March term, 1837, Robert Liggett, Bryant Crow, Wyatt Hill, William Roane, John Coggins and Wade McCrery were fined $5 each for unlawful gaming, to which they pleaded guilty. For malicious mischief Allen Gates paid a fine of $10 and was "held in jail until sunset." Henry Morris and Charles Thompson pleaded guilty to presentments for affrays, and paid fines of $5 each, and pleading guilty to "assault and battery" by William Wadkins cost him $2.50. In the July term against John A. W. Jackson was instituted the first case of forgery which resulted in Jackson "making good the damages," and paying the cost of prosecution. Indictments for assault and battery and for affrays were the most frequent subjects for the court's consideration this year, and up to the close of the half century the most numerous cases of indictments were "keeping tippling houses," "retailing spirituous liquors," "open and notorious drunkenness," "assault and battery," "affray," "unlawful gaming," and "betting on elections," with the other crimes common to the age.

In 1838 Joseph Winston was found guilty of usury and fined $19.33¾ (the amount of overcharged interest) and costs. In the same year Daniel Doxie was sent to the penitentiary for two years for malicious stabbing, and was the next year followed by James Joyce, who had a sentence for the same length of time for malicious shooting. In 1838, for the first time, the court "absolutely and forever" burst asunder a matrimonial bond liberating James Gates from his sacred vows to Elizabeth Gates. In 1839 Mathew Thomas, Lucy Sorrell, Betsy Turner, Patsy Hicks and Betsy Sorrell pleaded guilty to a presentment for an unlawful assembly, thereby contributing $1 each to the State fund. In the same year Andrew Duncan began a four years' term in the State prison for counterfeiting. Haywood Keith went for three years for horse stealing, and Guilford Paine four years for larceny.

In 1842 the grand jury presented that "Robert Bogle, of said county, yeoman, * * * * * not having the fear of God before his eyes, but being instigated by the devil, with force and arms in the county upon one Caleb Pyle in the peace of God and of the State, * * * * * with a certain piece of timber of no value, did assault feloniously, unlawfully, wilfully, deliberately maliciously, premeditatedly and with malice aforethought," etc., inflicting "mortal wounds of which said Pyle instantly died." Bogle was convicted of manslaughter and given six years' confinement in the State prison. In the same year, after a long and tedious trial, John J. Elzey was found guilty of murder in the second degree, and sent to the penitentiary for ten years. In 1848 Hardy Bloodworth and Mary Ford were indicted for duplicity in murder of the first degree. Bloodworth was found not guilty. After a protracted effort to get a decision, Mary Ford was granted a change of venue. Leth-

Walker, after being on trial for a number of years for the same offense, was also granted a change of venue. These were aggravated cases, both parties having been accused of murdering "infants of young and tender years." Josiah B. and Claiborn W. Black were acquitted of a charge of murder in 1850. In 1855 Martin, a slave, murdered his master, —— Lawrence, and in 1856 was hung. Never has any other capital execution taken place in the county.

In 1866 Marshall Hopewood was cleared of the charge of murdering Robert Ross. Hiram C. Harris, for murdering Willis Frank, was sentenced to ninety-nine years in the penitentiary, the decision of the inferior court having been sustained by the supreme court. About the same time Isaac Daws was found not guilty as charged" of the murder of C. C. Gulley. In 1867 John B. Short was proceeding to the matrimonial altar (to a justice of the peace) with his intended bride on the same horse behind him. He was followed by Sambo and W. J. Cook, brothers of the bride, and shot, from the wounds of which he died in a few days. The Cooks were indicted for murder in the first degree, but broke jail. Isaac B. Collins was accused of instigating the murder, and for five years this case was before the court, costing the State about $2,000, and resulting in his acquittal.

Judge Edmund Dillahunty, of Columbia, sat upon the bench from 1836 to 1852. He was a man of fine personal appearance, benevolent in demeanor and of high moral character. His court was a "temple of moral training," and dignified decorum was required at his bar. He was a fine lawyer and an excellent judge. "His charges to the juries were always sermons," and aside from his official duties he often gave the people of Lewisburg lectures on morality and religion. Judge Dillahunty was succeeded by William P. Martin, also of Columbia, who served until 1860, and was re-elected to another term in 1870, serving until 1877, when age compelled him to give his seat to John V. Wright, who held courts until the expiration of Martin's term in 1878. Judge Martin was a man of great ability, both as a judge and a lawyer. From 1860 to 1865 court was held by special judges. John C. Walker came to the bench in 1865, and was succeeded by Hillary Ward, who served from 1866 until 1868, and he by A. M. Hughes from 1868 to 1870. In 1871 the increased business of the court demanded a special criminal court, of which T. M. Jones was the first judge. In 1872 W. S. McLemore was elected criminal judge, and held until that court was abolished in 1878. He was then elected to fill the judicial term now closing. The attorney-generals have been as follows: James H. Thomas, 1836; Nathaniel Baxter, 1842; Lunsford M. Bramblett, 1847; A. M. Hughes, 1848; Nathan Adams, 1854; James L. Scudder, J. J. Noah and A. C. Hickey, from 1865 to 1868; Noble Smithson, 1868; J. H. Fussell, 1870 to 1886.

The chancery court was established in 1836 with Lunsford M. Bramblitt as chancellor. He was succeeded in 1844 by Terry H. Cahall, who served until 1851, when L. D. Frierson came to the bench, continuing until 1866, and was succeeded by David Campbell. Then John P. Steele was chancellor until 1868, and after his term John C. Walker sat upon the bench for two years. In 1870 W. S. Flemming was elected, and was re-elected in 1878 to serve the term closing in 1886.

At the first circuit court were present Samuel D. Frierson, Erwin J. Frierson, William P. Martin, William T. Ross and W. H. Wisener, all of whom were licensed to practice as attorneys and counsellors at law. Before the war these courts were regularly visited by almost all the prominent lawyers of this part of the State. James K. Polk was a familiar figure at this bar, and it is claimed that he was in Lewisburg attending a lawsuit when the news of his nomination as a candidate for the presidency reached him.

Robert G. Paine, W. P. Davis & Son, Gideon B. Black and —— Powell were able resident attorneys before the war. Since the war R. K. Kercheval, John F. Moore and Thomas F. Lewis were successful members of this bar. At present the following are attorneys at law in Lewisburg: Richard Warner, who was a member of the constitutional convention of 1870, a member of the Legislature in 1878 and a member of Congress in 1880–84; Col. J. H. Lewis;* W. N. Cowden, who served a part of one term in the Legis-

*For sketches see Biographical department.

lature, and was then made clerk of the supreme court; James J. Murray; A. N. Miller, assistant United States district attorney; E. M. Miller; C. T. Swanson;* J. L. Marshall;* P. C. Smithson;* C. A. Armstrong;* H. K. Moss; L. A. Thompson and W. W. Walker.

In the Creek war of 1812-14 a few persons, from what is now within the limits of Marshall County, attached themselves to Gen. Jackson's forces at Fayetteville. These men followed the fortunes of their indomitable leader in that campaign. Among those who were with Jackson were James Orr, of the vicinity of Verona, and Mr. Lawrence near Mooresville. John Hatchett, James Shaw, Capt. Andrew Patterson and Samuel Hillis, of Lewisburg and vicinity, were veterans of the battle of New Orleans, and lived in the county after its organization. John Hay, Christian Harbor, and Richard Warner, father of Hon. Richard Warner, of Lewisburg, were also at the battle of New Orleans, the latter of whom was wounded there in a skirmish in December, 1814. These men were honored with a special mark of distinction on all stated occasions during their lives. In the Seminole war two regiments of troops rendezvoused at Fayetteville in June, 1836; these were the first and second regiments. Over these Gen. Armstrong was elected brigadier-general. They left for the seat of war July 4. No regularly organized company went from Marshall, but a number joined a company while organizing at Crooked Springs near Fayetteville, in Lincoln County.

On the outbreak of the war with Mexico two companies from Marshall were enlisted, one of infantry and one of cavalry. The infantry company was attached to the First Regiment, and was commanded by Capt. Harris Maulden. The lieutenants were W. P. Davis and Wade McCrary; L. Cooper, A. G. Cooper, J. E. Fowler and R. H. McCrary, were sergeants, and H. Hardin, T. F. Winston, Willis Collins and Elisha Luna, were corporals. The muster roll included William Acuff, John Alexander, N. W. Burks, T. A. Bostwick, Alex Bingham, I. B. Cook, Samuel Davis, J. F. Davidson, B. C. Dobson, E. R. Dabney, W. W. Emmerson, J. C. Emmerson, Q. C. Fleming, W. T. Fossett, William Griffin, Joseph Hall, J. B. Kiecham, R. S. Luna, B. F. Luna, A. M. Meadows, Hampton Myers, J. H. Nichols, W. H. Peacock, Moxey Rone, R. R. Maney, T. J. Stokes, Mirach Shehane, G. H. Shehane, J. F. Shehane, R. C. Williams, J. R. Owensby, John Arnold, W. S. Bowers, Isaac Bearden, J. L. Bryant, M. B. Carter, O. Clark, A. S. Duvall, C. Dickson, William Dodd, William Ewing, M. Fowler, T. C. Fluty, G. W. Fluty, R. L. B. Gray, E. H. Gray, James Hagan, Alex Jackson, J. B. Luna, J. A. Moore, R. W. Moore, J. A. Morton, John M. Parks, W. C. Porch, I. Stone, A. P. Short, Elias Snell, F. E. Smith, J. H. Walls, J. Thompson, J. B. Wyatt and James Freeman. The company marched from Lewisburg to Nashville by way of Stegall's Mills, Mr. McEwen's and Beech's farms. The company left Lewisburg May 31, and reached Nashville June 3, boarded the "Commune" on the 6th of June, and was transferred to the "Tennessee" at Smithland on the 8th, and arrived at New Orleans on the 13th. On the 17th the regiment embarked on the "E. N. Chapman," and on the 20th anchored off the Brazos. The regiment was carried up the Rio Grande by vessel and landed at Camargo, thence marched to Monterey, where it took part in that severe engagement, which resulted in the capture of that town. The regiment suffered not only in the battle but terribly from fevers and other diseases. On December 19 the two Tennessee infantry regiments were formed into a brigade under Col. W. B. Campbell. After considerable marching and some desultory fighting, the regiment was put on board the "Jubilee" February 26, and moved to Vera Cruz, where it arrived March 11, and landed March 12. The regiments continued in the siege of Vera Cruz till its capitulation on the 27th. The men were severely engaged at the battle and capture of Cerro Gordo on April 18. The twelve months' men went as far as Jalapa, when they were ordered to Vera Cruz to be discharged. The men arrived at Vera Cruz on May 10, and on the 11th they took ship for New Orleans, where they arrived on the 21st. They were mustered out and paid off May 26. The company arrived at Nashville June 2, and returned home June 5. Of the seventy-three men enlisted in the company forty-three were killed, discharged or died of disease.

---

*For sketches see biographical department.

The cavalry company was commanded by Capt. Milton A. Haynes. The other commissioned and non-commissioned officers were W. B. Richardson, William Chambliss, William Brownlow, Jr., Robert G. McClure, Joseph A. Clayton, J. R. Haynes, R. M. Patterson, Joseph Gresham, John G. Taylor and A. J. Nance. The company was organized at Cornersville, and mustered into the service at Nashville June 8, 1846. The place of rendezvous for the cavalry was near Memphis. These troops proceeded to Mexico by way of Little Rock and Washington, Ark., and through Titus County, Tex. The company consisted of ten officers, eighty privates. two buglers and one blacksmith.

There was great unanimity of sentiment for the South in the late war after the firing on Fort Sumter. The first volunteers from this county were in Turney's First Tennessee, but no whole company was sent out till in April, 1861, when the Seventeenth was raised. This regiment assembled in Franklin County in May, and on the 27th of that month it started for Camp Trousdale, Sumner County. It was organized June 11 by the election of T. W. Newman, colonel; T. C. H. Miller, lieutenant-colonel, and A. L. Landis, major. The companies in the Seventeenth from this county were C, F and H. The commissioned officers of Company C at the organization were R. C. Williams, captain; J. C. Davis and F. M. Orr, lieutenants. The officers of Company F were R. P. Hunter, captain; John Begger, William Wallace and J. B. Hunter, lieutenants. The officers of Company H were R. H. McCrary, captain; W. H. Holder, G. W. Collis and David Sanders, lieutenants. May 8, 1862, the regiment re-enlisted for two years and was reorganized. In Company C J. C. Davis became captain; F. M. Orr, J. W. McCrary and R. H. Armstrong, lieutenants. J. C. Cooper became captain of Company F; R. H. McCullough, William Byers and Lee Carthey, lieutenants. The captain of Company H was G. H. Owen; the lieutenants were J. P. Tally, A. L. Elzy and Z. W. Ewing. On reorganization T. C. H. Miller was elected colonel; W. W. Floyd, lieutenant-colonel, and A. S. Marks, major.

The Seventeenth Regiment left Camp Trousdale July 23, armed with flint-lock guns, and arrived at Bristol, Va., July 26, where it remained till August 3, when it was sent to Russellville, E. Tenn., thence to Cumberland Gap, where it arrived August 8. September 14 the regiment left Cumberland Gap and was with the advance of Zollicoffer into Kentucky. The regiment was engaged at the battle of Mill Spring, or Fishing Creek, January 19, 1862. The regiment arrived at Livingston January 24, and at Murfreesboro February 19. February 28 the regiment left for Iuka and Corinth, where it was armed with English rifles. May 28 the regiment left Corinth and arrived at Tupelo June 8. July 28 the regiment left for Chattanooga, where it arrived August 4. At Chattanooga the army was reorganized, and the Seventeenth became a part of Johnson's brigade, of Buckner's division, of Hardee's corps. It was in the Kentucky campaign, and September 16 assisted in the capture of Munfordsville with its garrison. The regiment was in the severe engagement at Perryville, October 8; thence the regiment went with the army to Middle Tennessee. The regiment arrived at Murfreesboro December 28, and was assigned to the right under Gen. Breckinridge. In the three days of terrible battle the Seventeenth lost heavily, but sustained itself gallantly. It then fell back with the army to Tullahoma, where it remained until active operations began again. After some minor movements the Seventeenth took part in the two days' battle at Chickamauga on the 19th and 20th of September, losing 145 men. It advanced with the army to Chattanooga, where it lay till November 23, when Johnson's brigade, to which it belonged, was sent with Longstreet against Knoxville. November 29 the Seventeenth served as a supporting column to McLaw in an assault upon Fort Loudon. After the defeat at Knoxville the army fell back to Rogersville December 4. The regiment remained in East Tennessee till May, 1864, suffering greatly for want of food and clothing. In March the regiment was asked to re-enlist, and to a man they obeyed. May 2 the regiment took train at Abington, Va., for Petersburg. It was engaged in the defense of Petersburg and Richmond till the close of the war. The regiment was severely engaged at Drury's Bluff May 15 and 16, 1864. Col. Floyd was killed and about sixty men were lost in this engagement. The Seventeenth was again engaged February 5, 1865, at Hatcher's Run. Its last battle was fought April 2, 1865, in the defense of Petersburg, where it lost half its numbers. The remnant of the regiment was surrendered at Appomattox April 9, 1865.

The New Hope Company (Eighth Tennessee) from Marshall County was commanded by Capt. J. L. Bryant. The lieutenants were J. P. Holland, B. B. Bowers, T. F. Brooks, with T. E. Russell orderly sergeant. A sketch of the Eighth Regiment may be found in the State history.

The Thirty-second Regiment was commanded by Ed Cook as colonel, W. P. Moore, lieutenant-colonel, and W. J. Brownlow, major. On the re-organization Ed Cook was re-elected colonel; William P. O'Neal, lieutenant-colonel, and J. P. McGuire, major. The Thirty-second was represented from this county by one company, of which William P. O'Neal was captain, and Jasper Smiley, Calvin Coffey and Frank Hall were lieutenants. On the re-organization Frank Hall became captain, Jasper Smiley, Calvin Coffey and J. Sanford lieutenants. See elsewhere for a history of the Thirty-second Regiment.

One company from Marshall composed of 101 men was sent to the Forty-first Regiment. This company was known as the Lewisburg and Cornersville Company. The company officers of this company were R. G. McClure, captain; J. C. Osborn, J. M. Vancleave and R. P. Robins, lieutenants. The regimental officers at first were Robert Farquaharson, colonel; R. G. McClure, lieutenant-colonel, and T. G. Miller, major. On re-organization Farquaharson was re-elected colonel, J. D. Tillman, lieutenant-colonel, and T. G. Miller, major. From Camp Trousdale the Forty-first was sent to Bowling Green; thence on December 23d to Fort Donelson, where it was captured February 15, 1862. The men were exchanged at Vicksburg in September and the regiment reorganized at Clinton. The regiment marched and counter-marched through Tennessee and northern Mississippi till January, 1863, when it was ordered to Port Hudson. On May 2 it was ordered to Jackson to avert the doom overhanging Pemberton and Vicksburg. After the fall of Vicksburg it was ordered, September 7, to Mobile. It did guard duty on the coast for a time, but was ordered up to Chickamauga and again joined Johnston's army at Dalton in May, 1864. It took part in the Atlanta campaign till the fall of Atlanta; thence was ordered into Tennessee; was at Franklin and Nashville and was then sent to North Carolina, where it surrendered at the close of the war. Its brigade commanders were Bushrod, Johnson, Maney, Gregg and Strahl.

There were three companies for the Fifty-third Tennessee Regiment raised in this county—Companies B, E and D. Company B was raised in Lewisburg and vicinity. W. B. Holden was chosen first captain, but was succeeded by W. F. Collins as captain in 1862. The lieutenants of this company were J. J. Murray, J. M. Hawkins and W. M. Patterson. This company at first numbered about eighty-five men. Company E was raised in the vicinity of Mooresville and Wilson Hill. I. H. Hills was chosen the first captain, but he was succeeded by S. C. Orr. The lieutenants of this company were Andrew Bryant, Joseph Anderson and George W. Moore. Company D was raised at Cornersville by T. F. Winston. On the organization of the regiment Capt. Winston was chosen lieutenant-colonel, and W. H. Wilkes was chosen captain; W. P. Lewis, N. L. Cauless and John A. Perry, lieutenants. On reorganization W. P. Lewis was made captain; N. L. McCauless, John A. Perry and E. A. McCollum, lieutenants. W. H. Wilkes was elected colonel on reorganization, and W. B. Holden, major, who afterward became colonel. The regiment was mustered into the service December 17, 1861. It was engaged at Fort Donelson, Port Hudson, the Vicksburg and the Atlanta campaigns. It took an active part at New Hope Church and at the poor house near Atlanta; at the last engagement it suffered terribly. The regiment was in Hood's advance, participating at Franklin and Nashville. After this disastrous campaign it was sent to North Carolina, where it surrendered with the remnant of its numbers.

Company A, Baxter Smith's Fourth Cavalry, was organized at Nolensville, November 1, 1862, and was sworn into service soon after. The company officers were D. W. Alexander, captain; W. H. McLean, W. C. Green and R. O. McLean, lieutenants. This company originally consisted of 107 men; but a remnant was left at the close of the war.

Company A, Starnes' Fourth Tennessee Regiment, was raised by Capt. P. C. Haynes. The lieutenants were Aaron Thompson, J. C. Cundiff and B. F. Boyd. On reorganization Capt. Haynes became lieutenant-colonel, and Aaron Thompson was promoted to the captaincy. The officers of Company D of this regiment were D. S. McCullough, captain; Alfred Dysart, Monroe Fisher and Dr. McCullough, lieutenants. Alfred Dysart, who had become captain, was killed at Thompson Station, and was succeeded by W. M. Robinson. These men were sworn into the service in October, 1861, and were assigned duty at Camp Cheatham. A full account of this regiment is to be found in the State history.

There were three companies for Marshall, in the Eleventh Cavalry. One company was commanded by Capt. T. C. H. Miller, with E. H. Hamilton,—Rainey, as lieutenants. This company was raised north of Duck River and was composed of about 100 men. The second company was M. M. Swim's company. The commissioned officers were M. M. Swim, captain; James Ferguson and James Swim, lieutenants. These men were also enlisted in the northern part of the county. A third company of this regiment was raised at Cornersville, by Capt. Gordon, of Giles County. The last named company was made up from both Marshall and Giles Counties.

The last company raised in the county was the one recruited by Capt. E. J. Neil. This company was raised in the nothern part of the county in 1864, and was attached to Col. N. W. Carter' regiment. The Eleventh, above mentioned, was surrendered at Washington, Va., and Col. Carter's regiment at Selma, Ala.

It is a noticeable fact that the cavalry and infantry forces raised in this county were nearly equal in number, and that nearly all the cavalry was from the northern part of the country, while the infantry was from the southern part.

On April 19, 1861, Capt. T. C. H. Miller was presented with an elegant flag, by the ladies of Chapel Hill. This was presented by the hands of Miss Narcissa Wilhorte, now the wife of William McLean, of Nashville. Lieut. J. B. Hunter, made an appropriate and impressive response, accepting the flag on behalf of the company. Capt. Alexander's company also received an elegant silk flag, which was presented by Miss Anna Patterson, while the men were *en route* for Nashville. J. L. Orr made a speech accepting the flag, tendering the thanks of the company, and pledging their lives in its defense, saying it should never be "trailed in the dust of dishonor."

By the act of the Legislature, creating the county, Richard Warner, William Smith, Holman R. Fowler, George W. McBride and William D. Orr were appointed commissioners to select and procure by purchase or otherwise not less than fifty acres of land for the county seat, the name of which was to be known as Lewisburg. Abner Houston donated fifty acres where the town now stands, and thus secured its location. This land was estimated to be worth $400. On the last day of November and the first two days of December, 1836, were sold 149 lots for a sum total of $22,861, over five and one-half times the estimated value of the whole fifty acres. Lot 1, Block 7, was purchased by Dale & Phillips for $785, being the highest price paid for any one lot. Willis M. Hopwood paid $700 for Lot 6, Block 5. The lowest price paid was $31.

The town was incorporated by an act of the Legislature December 16, 1737.

The first business establishment of any kind was a small grocery opposite where Col. J. H. Lewis now lives. Abner Houston was the first merchant to sell a general line of goods. Hopwood, Dabney & Co. opened up a store on the south end of the east side of the Square in the spring of 1837. In about two years R. C. Dabney, one of the firm, retired, and the business was continued by Willis M. Hopwood and W. F. McGregor. Eli Dysart, Alexander McClure, Jack Appleby, Lorenzo Anderson and Branson Caple were also merchants before 1840. John Hatchett was the first postmaster. For several years saloons or groceries were the most numerous and most popular business establishments, and it is said that at one time there were not less than a dozen "liquor shops" in the town.

MARSHALL COUNTY.   897

In the forties business was conducted by Abner Houston, Hopwood & McGregor, Fisher & Ewing, Hatchett & Calahan, John Major, James Webb and Samuel Ewing.

In the fifties: Fisher & Ewing, Hatchett & Calahan, John Major, James Webb, Thomas Murray, Laws & Son and Porter & Davis, among others, were the principal merchants. A considerable amount of business was transacted in those days, although there were but a few business houses.

During the war business was almost at a standstill. In the seventh decade the firms which did a general mercantile trade were Ewing & Calahan, Ewing & Bro., James Webb, John Major, Thomas Murray, R. A. Fraley and Ewing & Boren.

In the seventies Thomas Murray, Ewing & Boren, J. M. Hawkins, W. D. Fisher & Co., Neil & Dark, J. K. Davis & Co., M. C. West & Co., Autry & Braley and Montgomery Bros. were general merchants. Druggists were S. D. & J. C. C. Brents, Hardison, Brents & Murray, Elliott & Cunningham, J. A. Braley and P. L. Atkisson. Furniture dealers and undertakers were J. M. & J. H. Haynes and W. H. Wood. Nearly all the general merchants kept groceries.

Since the building of the railroad to Lewisburg, business has rapidly and firmly increased; elegant brick blocks have been built, and it favorably compares with other towns of a larger population. Present business, general merchandising, etc.—V. O. Hays, Ewing & Adams, J. M. Hawkins and J. M. Brown; groceries—J. E. McRady, Woods & McCord, J. H. Wells, J. M. Brown, J. T. Kercheval, C. C. McKinney & Son, W. W. Miller, W. P. Irvine, G. R. Braley and T. C. Beard; drugs—J. A. Braley and T. C. Black; hardware—Hardison & Tate; hardware and grain—Woods & McCord, and Coffee, Woods & Co.; stoves and tinware—T. P. Garrett; saddlery—Willis Menifee & Co.; jewelry—John T. Murray; photographer—J. M. Patterson; livery—George W. Davis and Davis & London; blacksmith and wood shop—London & Knudson; blacksmiths—John W. Hooten, W. J. Looney & Co. and W. C. Buchanan; tan-yard—W. A. Braley; planing-mill—G. A. McClane; flouring-mill—Coffee, Woods & Co.; general produce—A. C. Brents; buggies, etc., Irvine & Black; marble works—W. H. Merritt; hotels—A. B. Stetwell (Stetwell House), and Coffey Bros. & Hardison (Coffey House); saloons—G. W. Davis, J. T. Edwards, J. M. Collins and Hendricks & Edwards; physicians—Drs. S. T. Hardison, J. B. Neil and T. E. Reed; dentist—P. D. Houston; newspapers—in 1847 the Marshall *Democrat* was commenced by Charles A. French, which was of short duration. The publication of the Lewisburg *Gazette*, by R. C. Russ, was begun in 1848, and continued about two years. Another paper, known as the Marshall *Messenger*, was published for a short time by Sewell & Bills. In 1859 the first number of the *Southern Messenger* was published. It existed until the war, and its various editors and publishers were J. H. Sewell & Co., R. Warner, Jr., and J. W. Knight, and Jo. G. Carrigan & Co. In the campaign of 1860 this paper was "an out-and-out Breckinridge sheet." In the absence of Mr. Carrigan, the editor, for a few weeks, it was left under the editorial care of W. N. Cowden, who changed its cast and began supporting Douglas, to the deep regret of Mr. Carrigan, but with an increased patronage.

The Marshall *Gazette* was established in 1871 by Figures, Binford & Brandon. In 1873 it was purchased by Ewing, Armstrong & Kercheval, and in a short time Ewing & Kercheval became sole proprietors. They continue to manage it successfully. From March, 1881, to July, 1883, the Lewisburg *News* was published by Cowden & Reed the first month, and afterward by Cowden & Moss.

The Bank of Lewisburg was organized November 7, 1882, with a capital stock of $30,000. J. N. Sullivan was the first president, and T. W. Brents the first cashier. R. S. Montgomery was the second president, and in a short time was succeeded by R. L. Adams in September, 1885. Brents was succeeded by J. T. Dean, who has been cashier since September, 1885, at which time the capital was reduced to $20,000. The bank has a stated surplus of $4,000.

The secret societies of Lewisburg are as follows: Lewisburg Lodge, No. 7, I. O. O. F., was chartered August 18, 1845, by the following members: Wilson P. Davis, W. F.

McGregor, Brandon W. Cowden, Charles C. Shehan, Levi Cochran, S. B. Ewing, James Beckett and James Smith. It now has a membership of forty-four. Dillahunty Lodge, No. 112, F. & A. M., was instituted October 8, 1845. John W. Laws was Master; George W. Record, Senior Warden, and F. W. King, Junior Warden. Lewisburg Lodge, No. 270, K. of H., was authorized to organize by a charter dated September 5, 1876. The charter members were C. A. Armstrong, W. P. Bullock, A. N. Coffey, J. J. Murray, J. S. Nolen, R. C. Rives, H. H. Smith, R. Warner, Jr., and J. A. Yarbrough. Magnolia Lodge, No. 152, K.& L. of H., began with thirty-four members in 1880. The I. O. G. T. also have a lodge.

Lewisburg has four churches, owned respectively by the Presbyterians, Cumberland Presbyterians, Methodists and Christians. The Christian Church is a fine brick building. The Cumberland Presbyterian Church, built in connection with the Odd Fellows Hall, is also brick. The other two are good frame edifices.

Cornersville received its name from the fact that it was located near the corners of Bedford, Lincoln, Giles and Maury Counties. The first merchandising was done by Thompson & Wardlaw as early as 1815 or 1818. After them an Irishman named Covantry did business one year on the "credit basis" and failed. James Haynes was among the very first to sell goods. Ephraim Massey, Bayne & Simmons and Crutcher & Marsh were merchants before 1835. In 1839 Zenas Baird began merchandising, and in 1848 was succeeded by his son, W. E. Baird, who still continues the trade. McClelland & Harris, James Moffett and John N. Patrick were prominent merchants after 1839.

Present business: W. E. Baird, James F. Kennedy and L. J. Nance are general merchants; John R. Jones, A. C. Clayton & Co. and John R. Fowler keep family groceries; Dr. E. A. Norton is the druggist; the physicians are Drs. L. C. Pillow, A. Jones, E. A. Norton and M. D. Kelley; the town contains but one saloon, owned by W. P. Cochran. The Cornersville Flouring-Mill, owned by Clayton, Davis & Co., was built in 1883, and is now receiving roller process improvements. The Presbyterians, Cumberland Presbyterians and Methodists each have church edifices. The Mount Vernon Lodge, No. 25, I. O. O. F., was chartered April 1, 1847. It now has not more than ten members in good standing. Cornersville Lodge, No. 126, F. & A. M., has about thirty members. The K. of H. also have a lodge.

Chapel Hill is located in the northern part of the county. W. S. Mayfield sold goods there about 1838 or 1840. After him J. B. Fulton did a large business for many years. Other merchants have been E. T. Williams and Williams & Glenn. At present the merchants are William Branson and W. B. Glenn. John Williams has a drug store. Chapel Hill Lodge, No. 160, F. & A. M., was chartered in 1848 or 1849, and is now in a good financial condition. The Odd Fellows once had a lodge. The village contains three church buildings, owned, respectively, by the Christians, Methodists and Cumberland Presbyterian orders.

The physicians are Drs. Womack, A. B. Robinson and J. W. Morton. Earlier physicians have been J. H. Robinson and J. S. Gentry.

Farmington is said to be the oldest town in the State south of Duck River. It was not incorporated, however, until 1830, but as early as 1809 several settlements were made so near together as to present the appearance of a village. It has many years since given up its charter. Its name was derived from its being a "town of farmers," or being in a splendid farming region. From 1823 to 1830 Eakin & Co. did a good business, and in 1830 William J. Whitthorne began merchandising. John Ramsey managed the business for these firms from 1828 to about 1835. Lile A. Ewing and William and Abram Robinson were successful merchants before the war. Since then Hoyle & Carpenter, Boren & Erwin, Carpenter & Montgomery and Neil & Shearin have done busines. At present John Ramsey & Son and Robinson & Liggett are general merchants. W. C. Ransom is the practicing physician. John Ramsey has lived at Farmington since 1823, and is now ninety years old.

Verona, first known as Tyrone, began its village life in 1859. However, J. L. Ewing had a store and mill there forty years ago. Since a short time after the war it has been known as Verona. Merchants have been Houston & Stilwell, Fisher & Robinson, H. C. McQuiddy and Borean & Bro., the last two of whom are now there. A flouring-mill is owned by Regen & Bro. The village contains a saddlery, a blacksmith and wood shop and two churches.

Belfast is the first station on the railroad southeast of Lewisburg. Muse Bros. were the first merchants in 1838. Others were Robert Williams and Smiley & Armstrong. J. L. Orr and James Sims are the business men at present. At "Old Belfast," Robert Williams had a store for many years but it was moved to the station when the railroad was built.

Caney Spring has two stores, one blacksmith shop and a carding factory. A Methodist Church is located near. Caney Spring Lodge, No. 94 was in existence in 1858. The trustees were William McLean, J. W. Carson, J. M. Taylor, J. King, and W. S. Allen.

Holt's Corner, a small village in the extreme northern part of the county, has two stores, a blacksmith shop, two cotton gins, a Methodist Church and an academy.

Spring Place has been a village for many years. Since about 1875 the postoffice has been known by the name of Archer. It is located on the head waters of Richmond Creek. Archer Beasley has a store and McBride & Compton have a saw and grist-mill.

South Berlin dates its beginning with the building of the railroad. It began with one store owned by W. A. Jackson and a blacksmith shop, and has succeeded in "holding its own." Old Berlin, which was near where South Berlin now is, was a good business village and was once incorporated before the war. It does not now exist.

Mooresville was a good business village before the war. S. B. Howlett was a very successful merchant for about forty years. William Bryant, now there, has been a merchant for many years. The place took its name from Ashley Moore who lived there in early days.

Silver Greek, a railroad station at the Maury County line, has a store kept by R. C. Harris, and a blacksmith shop by W. N. Hammonds.

Rich Creek, located between Chapel Hill and Farmington, has two merchants—J. W. Boren and D. A. Reavis. There are several country stores in the county known by the following names: Robinson Fork, New Hope, Lunn's Store, Beasley, Delina, Lillard's Mills and Cochran's Mill. The mill at the last mentioned place was built by Levi Cochran. It is a saw and grist-mill. Lillard's is a flouring-mill.

The Lewisburg Male Academy was incorporated by an act of the Legislature January 18, 1838, by James C. Record, G. W. Haywood, William McClure, B. G. Blackwell, William Williams, H. B. Kelsey, Stephen C. Chitwood and David McGaughey. The house was a two-story brick building and stood on the lot now owned by Richard Warner. The lot on which the academy stood was donated by the town commissioners. This was the principal school for boys until the opening of the war. The Female Academy originated in about the same manner as the Male Academy. The first building was a one-story frame structure, of two rooms. This school supplied the wants of the county till it was closed by the war. Marshall Academy was established February 5, 1842, under the law providing for county seminaries. The trustees of Marshall Academy were J. C. Record, George W. Haywood, James Osborn, Levi Cochran, Thomas Ross, Benjamin Williams and John Paxton. The trustees were made perpetual by law, as in the above institutions. Marshall Academy never fulfilled the expectations of its friends.

The two academies at Lewisburg were sold and the Lewisburg Institute erected in their stead in 1875. The building erected was a three-story brick, but the walls threatening to give way, the upper story was taken down and a two-story building made of it. The first trustees were W. G. Loyd, R. A. Ogilvie, Joe McBride, James A. Woods and W. R. Kercheval. The school was managed as a Masonic institution. The building was purchased by Rev. C. R. Darnell, who conducted a school in the building until his death. The school next became a joint-stock concern, and a school was conducted in it till 1882, when the building was burned. In 1888 a new two-story frame building was erected.

This is also a stock concern and is managed by Prof. J. B. Haynes, county superintendent. This is managed as a consolidated school so long as the public funds hold out. The school is divided into three departments: literary, music and art. The faculty embraces J. B. Haynes, A. B., principal; W. W. McLean, B. S., Miss Emma Kercheval and Miss May F. Whitsitt, assistants in the literary department; Mrs. Fannie Brown, music; Miss Sallie Cayce, art. The curriculum embraces a course of ten years and includes the sciences and the ancient and modern languages.

The report of the scholastic population for that year shows the whites to amount to 3,874, the colored to 1,623; total 5,497. The number enrolled 3,000, the number in attendance 2,250. The total number of white teachers employed 46, the colored 11; total of both 57. The State fund for the same year was $2,564, county, $8,006.73; total, $10,570.73. The report for 1883 gives a male white population of 2,597; female, 2,597; total, 4,943. Colored male, 887; female, 1,615; grand total, 6,558. The last report shows a white male population of 2,861; female, 2,646; total, 5,507. Colored male, 979; female, 905; total, 1,884; grand total, 7,341. The same report shows an enrollment of 5,849, or over 787. The number of days of school is 97; the average compensation for teachers per month, $36.38. The total number of schoolhouses in the county is 38. The number of schools in the county is 85. In these are employed 84 white and 20 colored teachers. The estimated value of school property is $14,053. The expense for running the schools for 1885–86, including repairs on buildings, teachers salaries, etc., was $12,503.18. Superintendent Haynes has prepared a manual of rules and regulations and a course of study for the public schools, which is a well studied work and is destined to materially aid the county teachers in their work. The sentiment and the schools of Marshall have a tendency onward and upward.

Consolidated schools are found in most all the towns and villages of the county; in addition to these schools being consolidated schools, the most of them are incorporated under the "four mile law." Enough have been incorporated to drive saloons from the county except in Lewisburg and Cornersville, which are operating under charters. The Farmington school is both a consolidated and an incorporated school. It is divided into a literary and music department. The school is under the management of Prof. M. M. Gattis. A consolidated school at Cornersville consists of a literary and music course. The Cornersville schools are under the management of Prof. Bridges. The schools of Mooresville are also consolidated schools. The schools are divided into two departments, a literary and a music department. The literary department employs two teachers and the music one. The principal of the Mooresville schools is W. W. McLean. At both Verona and Belfast are consolidated schools, having the two usual courses and each requiring three teachers. The principal of the former is Prof. Luttelow and of the latter Prof. John Green. The public school system was first put into operation in 1874.

The church known as Wilson Hill or Globe Creek Church, was organized in 1811. They were formerly known as the "Schismatics." Here was held the first and only camp-meeting by the Christians in the county. In 1844 the membership of Wilson Hill was 136, including 35 heads of families and 12 servants. The ministers at that time were Revs. Barrett and McCord; the elders A. Lavender and H. Phillips; the deacons, John Wilson and J. Robbins. This church has had a prosperous existence, but was greatly injured for the time being by the J. R. Collinsworth defection. The Year Book for 1885 gives P. Q. Houston as one of the elders, the church membership at 100, the number of Sabbath-school pupils at 50, the number of teachers and officers 6, and the value of church property at $1,000. The Cedar Creek Church was organized in June, 1841. In a few years the membership was 101, and in 1844 it numbered 19 males, 16 heads of families and 3 servants. The house was erected in 1844, with Brother McCord as pastor, Joshua and Joel Hardison and John Fox, elders; J. Beard and S. L. Hardison were the deacons. A new church has since been built within the limits of Maury County, called Antioch, which has taken the place of Cedar Creek.

According to an authority at hand, what is now Cane Creek was separated from the association of United Baptists in 1823; another authority has it much later. The membership in 1844 was 126. Monthly meetings were held till 1839, when semi-monthly meetings were held. On the expulsion of Rev. Willis Hepwood all the heads of families, except John England and John Blackwell, left the church, the whole numbering nearly 500. The members followed Hepwood and built a new church, called Liberty, about one-half mile from the old church. A great revival was held at Liberty in 1851, by Rev. C. R. Collinsworth, at which there were 156 members added to the church. The present membership is reported at 80, Sunday-school scholars 30, and church property worth $1,000.

A division of Liberty Church was made in 1841, and Cane Creek organized with 45 members and a new church erected. The membership of Cane Creek is 200, Sunday-school pupils 60, and church property is worth $2,500. In 1840 there were between 30 and 40 members on Tory Creek with no house of worship, but these have united at Beech Grove or elsewhere since and a new house erected at Beech Grove. In 1828 a church was organized at Berea, near Chapel Hill, by Rev. J. K. Speer. The church soon became quite strong, numbering at one time 120 members. Among the leading members and officers were J. Biddington, J. Patton, H. Wilson, J. M. Barnes and J. A. Manire. The two last named managed a church school for a time at Berea. Owing to the overflow of the river the membership was changed to Old Lasea and Cedar Creek. The church at Lewisburg was organized in 1836, and in eight years the membership numbered 136. The first elders were J. McCord, John Harden and D. B. Bills; the deacons were J. Bills and E. R. Hoover. The first house of worship was erected in 1845, a new brick house is now building in Lewisburg at a cost of about $4,000. The present membership is 200.

The pioneer denomination of Marshall County was the Presbyterian, and its first church was Bethberei. This was organized June 1, 1810, by Rev. Samuel Findley, of Kentucky, with the following members: John, Martha and Margaret Dysart; William and Elizabeth Anderson; David McCurdy; John, Eleanor and Elizabeth Cummings; Robert and Nancy Elliott; Edward Bryant; John and Mary Holmes; John, Phidellas, James, Allen, Rebecca and Mary Leiper; James and Mary Coffey; William and Ann Say; Hugh Cathey, and Francis H. Woods. Two of these, Mrs. Mary Holmes and Mrs. Mary Coffey, were living in 1860. The organization sermon was preached by the minister while standing upon a rock, near where the present church now stands, from the text "Upon this rock I will build my church," etc. The first minister was Rev. John Gillespie, who served the church in 1811; Andrew Morrison served 1812–13; Thomas J. Hall, 1814–49; George H. Blair, 1849–53. Revs. Robert Hardin, Thomas Stone, W. J. Frierson and M. S. Kennedy have completed the service of the church till the present time, except intervals of from four months to three years. The ruling elders at first were John Dysart, F. H. Woods and Allen Leiper. The first church was made up from members who were compelled to travel from four to eight miles for a place of worship. The total number of ministers to the present time is 15; the number of ruling elders, 34; the number of deacons, 9; clerks, 7; number of members, 900; sacramental meetings, 150. Allen Leiper served as clerk of the session from 1810 to 1826; John Ramsey, now of Farmington, from 1826 to 1848; Lile A. Ewing, from 1848 to 1853, since which time James S. Ewing has been clerk. The church membership started with 28; in 1815, it was 144; in 1818, it numbered 183. A great revival occurred in 1832, which resulted in about eighty accessions to the church. Notwithstanding the number that had been separated and united into other churches, this congregation still numbers about 125 members. The Presbyterians started the pioneer Sunday-school in this portion of the county, the Rock Creek Sunday-school, or Bethberei, having been organized in 1827. Other Sunday-schools followed at Farmington, Cedar Creek, Hopewell and Piedmont. An auxiliary Bible society was formed by this church in 1815, which is still in existence. This church was the founder of the first temperance society in 1832, within the limits of this county. Bethberei has paid to its pastors an aggregate of $17,000; to missions, Bible cause, educational purposes, etc., a total of $23,000, making a sum of $40,000 for all purposes. In June, 1860, the church celebrated its fiftieth anniversary by a sermon from Rev. F. A. Ross, and in June, 1885, its seventy-fifth anniversary, the anniversary sermon having been preached by Rev. F. A. Thompson. In 1828 there were churches at Piedmont, or Round Hill, Hopewell, or Bethel, also flourishing Sunday-schools at each of these places, as well as at Farmington and Cedar Creek. The first members at Round Hill, or Piedmont, were Frank Woods, James Coffey, —— Ramsey, Albert Anderson, David McCleary, Bedford Woods, John Miller and others. The elders at Bethel were Robert Orr, L. D. Stockton, Alex Adams, Allen Coffey and Amzi Bradshaw. The two churches above mentioned were known as the Old and the New School, but about 1866 or 1867 the two were again united and formed what is now "Union Church." The Rev. P. A. Atkisson is pastor. This church, like all of the Presbyterian Churches, maintain a weekly Sunday-school and prayer meeting. Its membership now is about 125.

The church at Lewisburg was organized in June, 1847, by Rev. Edward McLean with seven members, viz.: Dr. S. W. Penn and wife, G. B. Black, E. E. Ewing and wife, Jane Ewing, Hugh A. Hall and wife. Dr. Penn and Messrs. Hall and Black were ordained elders. The ministers have been E. T. Brantley, 1848-49; George H. Blair, 1850-52; W. C. Dunlap, 1852-53; Robert Hardin, 1854-59; W. H. Verner, 1859-70; W. T. Roser, 1870-72; J. M. Alexander 1872-75; J. T. Rothrock, 1877-80; M. S. Kennedy, 1880 to present. There have been ten elders; those now living are J. L. Reed, J. S. Ewing, A. L. Ewing, J. L. Marshall, J. A. Woods and T. C. Black. The church now has four deacons and a membership of about 100. The church at Cornersville is under the charge of Rev. M. S. Kennedy, who also preaches for the church at Lewisburg.

The pioneer Cumberland Presbyterian Church in Marshall County is Bear Creek Church, near Mooresville. This church was organized in 1814 by Rev. Samuel King. This was soon after the separation of the Cumberland Presbyterian Church from the Primitive Church. The first house erected was a log building. The present brick building was erected about 1860. This is one of the strongest congregations in the county. It now numbers about 240 members. The church at Farmington was organized in 1818 by some elders and lay-members, who were seceders from the Presbyterian Church at Bethberei. This organization soon erected a house of worship. They now have a good house and a membership of about 100. A Sunday-school has been maintained since 1828. The present pastor is Rev. J. D. Bräley. Beech Hill is one of the old churches. It was organized about 1840. The church is served by Rev. J. N. Holt from Eagleville. The membership is about seventy. The Richland Church was organized about 1836 by Rev. Andrew Smith. Among the first members were Richard McCrea, Henry Bishop, Moses Park and others. The membership now is about 150, with A. F. Rankin as pastor. The Cornersville Church was organized about 1830. Among the first members were Capt. W. Harris, Esq., James Hayes and —— Park. One of the first pastors was Rev. H. B. Warner. This church now has a good house of worship and a membership of about sixty. Rev. W. A. Bridges is the present pastor. The Bethlehem Church near Berlin was organized between 1850 and 1860 by R. P. Atkisson. The church now numbers about fifty members and owns a good house, with Rev. A. F. Rankin as pastor. The Chapel Hill Church was organized in 1856. It owns a good brick house and has a membership of about eighty.

The Cumberland Presbyterian Church at Lewisburg was organized May 29, 1841, by Rev. Willis Burgess, who continued to labor with the church till 1849. The first elders were Elisha Hurt, William D. Fisher and James M. Bowden. Rev. N. P. Modrall, became pastor and served from 1849 to 1855; L. P. Atkisson, 1855-58 W. W. Hendricks, 1858-60; P. L. Atkisson, 1860-66; S. E. Wilson, 1866-69; S. O. Woods, 1869-72; J. M. Brown, 1878 to the present.

The church had seventeen elders since its organization, the present ones being Jo McBride, M. C. West, R. A. McCord and J. B. Haynes. A brick house of worship was erected some time after organization. This building is still in a good state of preservation and is still in use by the church. This congregation has had a quiet but steady growth since its organization.

Since its reorganization, in 1866, the register shows an enrollment of 194 members. The Cumberland Presbyterians were among the pioneer churches to hold camp-meetings. Two noted camp grounds of this church were Rich Creek and at Col. Levi Cochran's.

The date of the organization of the Methodist Episcopal Church South is not exactly known, but it was in the early part of the century. The class was first organized at Carmel, where a house was erected and worship held for many years, when the class was moved to Lewisburg. The class has been at Lewisburg for half a century. The class at Lewisburg belongs to the same circuit as Cornersville, and has a membership of about seventy-five. The present church at Cornersville was built in 1877, the trustees at that time were N. L. McLelland, A. W. Johnson, A. Jones, George T. Allman and J. A. Jarrett. The parsonage for this church and the one at Lewisburg is located at Cornersville.

The church at Chapel Hill was founded by Andrew Patterson between 1840-50. The church was erected in 1847. Lebanon is another one of the old churches of Marshall County. The church at that place was erected in 1844. There are also churches at Berlin, Farmington, Verona, New Hope, Macedonia, Allen's Chapel, McCrary, Mooresville, Mount Zion and Gill's Chapel. The Methodist Church was long celebrated for holding camp-meetings and camp-meeting revivals. One of the old camp grounds was near Lewisburg.

The Primitive Baptists have three churches in Marshall County. This respectable body of the militant was among the pioneer organizations in the county. There are now churches at Rich Creek, Stephen's Grove and Chapel Hill. The church at Rich Creek was organized about 1835-36; the present building was erected in 1871. The membership numbers about 100. Good houses of worship have been erected at each of the other churches.

The Missionary Baptists are represented in the county by churches at Smyrna, Pisgah and one on the Mooresville Pike near Col. John Hill's. These are old churches and have a large membership.

MAURY COUNTY.

JAMES F. AGNEW was born in Maury County, Tenn., February 16, 1839, and is the son of John Agnew, a native of Virginia, born October, 1804. The father began working for himself at the age of twenty, and was a shoe-maker by trade. He followed this for fifteen years, after which he engaged in farming. In 1827 he took for his second wife Catherine Mitchell, who bore him eight children, our subject being one of them. His first wife bore him two children: William and Sarah, but died shortly after the birth of Sarah. The second wife died July 30, 1883. She was a good wife and mother, and her death was universally regretted, as also was the death of her husband, John Agnew, who followed her May 28, 1884. They were both worthy members of the Cumberland Presbyterian Church. The father of John Agnew was also of the same name. He was born in Ireland, was a shoe-maker by trade, and was a soldier in the war of 1812. Our subject remained on the farm until he was twenty-four years of age, when he began farming for himself. In 1861 he enlisted in Company E, Third Tennessee Regiment Infantry, and was in the battle of Fort Donelson. He was captured at the latter place, but was afterward released. He was again captured at Jackson, Miss., where he remained a prisoner for some time, but at last was exchanged and paroled, and came home. September 18, 1862, he married Manda P. Turner, a native of Tennessee, born December 20, 1843, and the daughter of William and M. C. (Candle) Turner. To Mr. and Mrs. Agnew were born three children: Effie D., born December 5, 1864; Rufus F., born February 2, 1867, and Addie C., born February 23, 1870. Our subject is a successful farmer, and he and family are members of the Cumberland Presbyterian Church. He is a Democrat in politics.

ALFRED N. AKIN, clerk of the Maury County Courts, was born in this county February 25, 1841, son of Samuel W. and Eliza C. (Alexander) Akin, natives, respectively, of Williamson and Maury Counties, Tenn. The father was a farmer, and resided in the Twenty-second District until his death October 27, 1856. He was magistrate of his district a number of years and gained some celebrity as a skilled mechanic and inventor, having invented a corn and cotton cultivator, which was acknowledged as a very superior and useful patent. Alfred N. Akin was reared and educated in the county, and began mercantile life as a clerk at fifteen years of age. He was connected with the quartermaster's department under Gen. Marcus J. Wright during the war, and from 1866 to 1871 was engaged in mercantile pursuits in Columbia. He held the position of teller in the Bank of Columbia for a time, when ill health compelled him to abandon business entirely. In August, 1874, he was elected to the office of clerk of the county courts, which he has filled faithfully and efficiently by re-election to the present time. Mr. Akin has two sons by Sarah Jones, whom he married August 29, 1867. He is a Democrat and Mason (Knight Templar's degree) and a member of the K. of P. and K. of H. fraternities.

JOHN C. ALEXANDER, a prominent and time-honored farmer, was born in this county January 8, 1824, and is a son of Abdon J. and Eliza E. (Campbell) Alexander, both natives of North Carolina. The father Abdon was born July 4, 1798, and followed the vocation of a farmer and stock raiser. He died October 1, 1868. The mother died in 1855. Eleazer Alexander, our subject's paternal grandfather, was born November 23, 1763, and was one of the early settlers of this county coming here as early as 1808 and settling on a tract of land given his wife's brother, Benjamin Carter, for services rendered in the Revolutionary war. He was also a neighbor and fast friend of Ezekiel Polk, grandfather of of James K. Polk. The subject of this sketch was reared on the farm and remained with his parents until he was twenty-two years of age, securing a common school education. He then began farming and during the war was engaged in making boots and shoes. December 15, 1845, he married Mary W. Sparkman, a native of Williamson County, Tenn. They have six children by this union, all of whom are living; Sarah R., Ross, Laura L., Enola E., Caroline H. and Mary C. In 1868 he engaged in the steam saw-mill business and remained in this business for nine years. He then returned to his present farm where he has been actively engaged ever since. Mr. Alexander and family are leading members of the Christian Church and have the respect and esteem of all their acquaintances.

JOSEPH W. ALEXANDER, merchant and citizen of Spring Hill, Maury Co., Tenn., is a native of this State, born March 20, 1844, son of Randolph and Elizabeth (Sharber) Alexander, natives, respectively, of South Carolina and Tennessee. The father was one of the early settlers of Rutherford County and was a tiller of the soil in the above named county. In 1830 he removed to Henry County, West Tenn., where he resided until his death which occurred in 1854. The mother followed in 1863. Our subject, Joseph W., was reared on the farm and remained with his parents until he was fifteen years of age, at which time he came to this place and residing with his uncle attended school. In 1861 he enlisted in Company E, Third Tennessee Regiment Infantry, serving as a high private until he was wounded in the right lung at Jackson, Miss., July 14, 1863. He was afterward put on post duty at Selma. Ala., and was captured there by Wilson's troops. He was paroled at Selma and in 1865 returned to Spring Hill, where he attended school for some time and received a good education. In 1868 he began in the mercantile business, clerking about six months. After moving about for some time in 1872 he established his present business. December 12, 1873, he was united in marriage to Miss Mattie D. Crump, a native of this State. They have six children, Charley R., Annie L., Bessie W., Joseph B., Blanch and Marcus O., all of whom are living. Mr. Alexander has been postmaster at Spring Hill since 1878. He is a member of the Masonic lodge, a Democrat, and himself and family are members of the Methodist Episcopal Church.

MRS. REBECCA T. AMIS, a native of Maury County, Tenn,, was born in 1839, and is a daughter of Col. Jonas and Martha (Adkisson) Thomas, who were born in the "Old Dominion." The father came to Tennessee at an early day, and became an eminent lawyer and politician. He represented Maury County in both branches of the State Legislature, and was speaker of the State Senate one term, and as a parliamentarian had no superior. He was once nominated for Congress, but owing to ill health was compelled to withdraw from the race. His demise occurred August 3, 1856. The mother died January 14, 1870. Mrs. Amis, our subject, was married October 13, 1857, to John E. Amis, and two children blessed their union; Bruce E. and Jonas T. Mr. Amis took an active part in the late war, and was a member of the gallant Forty-eighth Tennessee Infantry. He was captured at the fall of Fort Donelson, and died in prison in St. Louis, Mo., in 1863. Mrs. Amis is a finely educated woman, and has won quite a reputation as an instructress, having taught in the Atheneum, at Columbia, and in the Tennessee College at Franklin, and also in the public schools at that place. She is a member of the Presbyterian Church.

PROF. WILLIAM ANDERSON, a prominent minister and teacher of Maury County, Tenn., was born in Williamson County, of this State, October 19, 1848, son of James C. and Lucinda (Newsom) Anderson, who were married January 29, 1843, and the parents of four children. The father was a native of Alabama, and came to Williamson County in 1834. He was ordained a minister of the Christian Church in 1828, and followed th vocation of farming in connection with his ministerial duties. He died September 12, 1857. The mother is still living, and a resident of the old homestead in Williamson County. Our subject remained on the farm until he was nineteen years of age, overseeing the business transactions and caring for his widowed mother. He then began attending school at the Franklin College, remaining there until 1872, teaching and attending school, and has continued that occupation ever since. He is at present teaching school at Carter Creek, and has been the local minister of the Christian Church in that neighborhood. In 1875 he wedded Laura Alexander, a native of this county, and became the father of three children: Effie, Ora and Clark C., all living. Prof. Anderson is an eloquent preacher and a learned teacher, and is classed among the leading citizens of Maury County.

E. F. ANDREWS, M. D., a successful physician of Maury County, Tenn., was born in Williamson County, in 1856, son of Ephraim and Sarah (Bizzell) Andrews. Both parents were born in Tennessee, and the father was a skillful shoe-maker and agriculturist, and is, at the present time, a resident of Hickman County. Dr. Andrews is a graduate of the famous Vanderbilt University of Nashville, Tenn., being one of the class of 1883. He began practicing his chosen profession in Hickman County, and in September, 1884, he removed to Williamsport, Maury County, where he is meeting with merited success. For four years previous to his practice he taught school. He is a stanch member of the Democratic party and belongs to the Masonic fraternity. He is a worthy member of the Methodist Episcopal Church South and is a young man of ability and energy.

ROBERT J. BAUGUSS, another old and prominent citizen of Maury County, and a native of this county, was born one mile from where he now resides, November 16, 1821. He is the eldest child of John and Louisa (Allen) Bauguss, both natives of North Carolina. The father came to this county about 1814, and was a farmer by occupation. He died in 1847 and the mother followed about ten years later. Our subject assisted his parents on the farm and took charge of his father's business at the time of the latter's demise. In 1861 he enlisted in Company A, Forty-eighth Tennessee, and served part of the time as orderly sergeant. At the time of the surrender at Fort Donelson he was captured and taken to Camp Douglas, where he remained for three months. He was afterward discharged from service at Port Hudson and returned to the old homestead where he has been engaged in farming and stock raising ever since. In 1852 he married Miss D. L. Partee, a native of this county, and to them were born five children, only one of whom is living— John T. Mr. Bauguss is a Democrat in politics and has been magistrate of the Twenty-first District for three terms. He is an attendant and Mrs. Bauguss a member of the Methodist Church. He has also been a member of the Masonic lodge for upward of thirty years.

A. A. BARKER is a successful merchant of Maury County, Tenn., and was born in Wayne County, Ky., August 27, 1849, son of Hugh and Kate (Randall) Barker, natives, respectively, of Kentucky and Alabama. The father was an enterprising farmer, and became the possessor of considerable worldly goods. He departed this life in 1875. The mother is still living, and resides in the "Lone Star State." Our subject spent his early days on his father's farm, and was united in marriage to Miss Rhodes, in August, 1872, and four children were born to their union: Carrie H., Alice B., Myrtle J. and Hugh B. Mr. Barker belongs to the Democratic party, and has been postmaster of Cross Bridges for two years. Mr. and Mrs. Barker are members of the Christian Church, and among the prominent families of Maury County.

WILLIAM A. BARKER, a native of Maury County, born December 3, 1850, son of George Barker, who started out on life's rough track for himself at the age of twenty-one. The father had a limited education, but enough for practical purposes. He was a farmer, a Democrat and a member of the Masonic fraternity. He was also a member of the Baptist Church. In 1846 he married Maria L. Byers, and by her became the father of three children: Nancy, William A. and George D. He died in 1861. The mother of these children was born in Virginia, August 15, 1820, and is the daughter of Anderson and Sarah (Dortch) Byers, natives of North Carolina. They were married there, but afterward moved to Virginia, where they remained for some years. They then moved to Tennessee, locating in Maury County. The mother died in 1861. The paternal grandparents of our subject were Alexander and Margaret (Dodson) Barker, who were born in North Carolina and Tennessee, respectively, the former in 1791 and the latter in 1801. They both lived to be old people, the grandfather dying in 1878 and the grandmother in 1885. Our subject was reared on the farm, and at the age of twenty-eight engaged in the mercantile business at Rock Spring, and is at present engaged in that occupation. He is also a mechanic and a blacksmith. In 1879 he married Mollie Usery, a native of Giles County, Tenn., born July 22, 1861, and the daughter of William L. and Matilda (Wright) Usery. To our subject and wife were born three children: Alfred H., born 1880; Florence, born 1881 and died 1882, and Willie T., born 1883. Our subject has a good sound education, and was a school teacher for some time. He is a Democrat, and he and his brother, George, are in the merchandise business together, the firm being known as the Barker Bros.

REV. GEORGE BECKETT, rector and principal of the Columbia Female Institute and rector of St. Peter's Episcopal Church, was born in Wakefield, Yorkshire, England, June 8, 1818, and is a son of William P. and Mary (Harrison) Beckett. Our subject was educated in England, attending Queen Elizabeth Grammar School, at Wakefield, and graduated in 1838. In 1840 he immigrated to the United States and located first at Cincinnati, Ohio, where he prepared himself for the Episcopal ministry. He was ordained, in 1843, by Bishop B. B. Smith, D. D., at Louisville, Ky. His first charge was in Hopkinsville, Ky., where he had management of a school. In 1852 he took charge of St. Matthew's Church and Institute, in Jefferson County, Ky., and in the fall of 1866 removed to Columbia, and began conducting the Columbia Female Institute, and has met with good success. He entered on his pastoral duties in St. Peter's Episcopal Church in 1868. In 1844 he married Miss Ann E. Temple, a native of Logan County, Ky., a great-niece of Gen. George Rogers Clark. They have one son—John Temple.

CAPT. JOHN W. BECKETT was born in Marshall County, September 2, 1836, and is the son of Samuel and Rebecca (Swan) Beckett. The father of our subject was born March, 1809, in North Carolina. He came to Tennessee and settled near Lewisburg, and engaged in farming, in which he was very successful. He was elected justice of the peace, which office he held for several years. He was also postmaster for some time. He was a member of the I. O. O. F. and a Democrat in politics. He belonged to the Methodist Episcopal Church South. Our subject received a good practical education in the country schools, and at the age of twenty-one began business for himself. In 1871 he wedded Mrs. Jane W. Bryant, whose former name was Gresham. Mrs. Bryant had by her first husband four children: Sebastian C., born in 1855 and died in 1862; Ralph G., born 1857; Sallie A., born in 1860 and died in 1865, and Arch S., born in 1862. In 1861 Mr. Beckett enlisted in Company C, Ninth Tennessee Regiment, and was elected orderly sergeant at the organization, and at the reorganization was elected first lieutenant and afterward promoted to captain.

CAPT. ALEXANDER W. BECKWITH, an energetic farmer of Maury County, Tenn., was born October 4, 1830, son of Jonathan and Dolly C. (Madison) Beckwith, both natives of Virginia. The father was a physician of Fredericksburg, Va. In 1823 he moved to Lauderdale County, Ala., and engaged in the practice of medicine. His death occurred in 1856. The mother died in 1847. Our subject grew to manhood on the farm, and received a good education at the St. Joseph College, Nelson County, Ky. At his father's death he took charge of the plantation, and continued to do so up to the time of the late war. In 1861 he enlisted in Company C, Twenty-seventh Alabama Regiment, as first lieutenant, and remained as such until after the battle of Shiloh. He was then made captain of the company, but at the end of eight months was discharged on account of ill health. He then returned home for a short time, but soon joined Johnston's cavalry company, Rogers' command, remaining with them about six months, and then on account of his bad health returned home, where he remained until the close of the war. He then began farming on his plantation, but in 1866 he moved to Mississippi and remained there until 1874, when he removed to his present place, where he has remained ever since, steadily engaged in farming and stock raising. November 14, 1866, he wedded Mary Mason, a native of Alabama, and to them were born five children, only two of whom are living, viz.: Alexander W. and Jonathan. Mr. Beckwith is a Democrat in politics, and himself and family are leading members of the Methodist Church.

WILLIAM M. BIDDLE, of Columbia, Tenn., and native of the city, was born November 1, 1847, son of Daniel M. and Mary (Pride) Biddle, who were born in Sumner and

Robertson Counties, Tenn., respectively. Our subject was reared in Sumner County, where he secured a good education in the common branches, and at the age of twenty years became a disciple of Æsculapius, with the view of making medicine a profession, and graduated from the medical department of the University of Nashville in 1870. He removed to Arkansas, where he practiced about four years and then returned to Nashville and studied the homœopathic system of medicine under Dr. J. P. Dake. In 1877 Dr. Biddle came to Columbia, where he has since practiced homœopathy with extraordinary success. June 15, 1871, his marriage with Miss Julia Rogers was consummated. She was born in Sumner County, and has borne her husband one son and three daughters. The family are members of the Episcopal Church. The Doctor is a Democrat and a member of the State Medical Society of Homœopathy.

RUFUS K. BLACKMAN (deceased) was born in Tennessee October 9, 1826, son of Bennett and Ann (Chinton) Blackman, both of whom were natives of North Carolina. The father moved from North Carolina to Tennessee about 1790. He was an extensive farmer and died in 1833. The mother died in 1849. Our subject was reared on the farm and received his education in the district schools. At the age of eighteen he began operating the farm of his widowed mother, and followed farming and stock raising on the old homestead place up to the time of his demise, which occurred August 10, 1883. He was a leading member of the Christian Church, and was classed among the enterprising and successful business men of the county. He was extensively engaged in raising and breeding fine stock. He also operated a saw and grist-mill in this county for many years. He was always strictly exact in his business transactions, and was a moral, upright citizen. In 1851 he wedded Eliza Eichbaum, a native of Davidson County, Tenn., and daughter of William and Catherine (Stevens) Eichbaum, natives, respectively, of Ireland and Massachusetts. The father immigrated to this country about 1824, and married soon after. His wife was one of the first educators of Nashville, and was for many years a teacher in the Nashville Female Academy. Her death occurred about 1860. The father died in 1871. By her union with our subject Mrs. Eliza W. Blackman became the mother of nine children, all of whom are living: Bennett, Ada L., Mary, Willie, Anna, Edwin, Louisa, Charlie and Albert. Mrs. Blackman and family are leading members of the Christian Church, and are classed among the leading families of the county.

JOHN H. BLAIR, merchant, of Kedron, Maury County, was born January 13, 1844, within one mile of where he now resides, and is one of seven children born to Thomas W. and Catherine C. (Neely) Blair, both natives of Tennessee. The father was from the family of George D. Blair, who was one of the early settlers of this county. Thomas W. died in 1854. The mother is still living at the advanced age of seventy-four. Our subject passed his youth in assisting on the farm and in acquiring a fair education in the common schools. At the age of seventeen he enlisted in Company B, Eleventh Tennessee Cavalry, and served as a high private with the above company until the close of the war. He then returned home and began clerking in the mercantile business with different parties until 1882, when he established his present business at Kedron, and controls the leading trade in that town and vicinity. October 23, 1872, he wedded Miss Ella Blanton, a native of this county, and to this union were born six children, only four of whom are living, viz.: Leonidas O., Julia M., Sue Ella and Ada V. Mr. Blair is a Democrat in politics, and himself an attendant, and family members of the Methodist Church.

REV. JOHN G. BOLTON, a minister of the Methodist Episcopal Church South, was born in Humphreys County, Tenn., February 22, 1841, and February 7, 1868, was united in marriage to Hattie J. Williams and became the father of four children: Samuel I., Cordelia M., Ida S. and Pattie R. Rev. Bolton enlisted as a private in the late war in May, 1861, in Company A, Eleventh Tennessee Infantry, and served in this capacity through the war, also acting as chaplain of the Fiftieth Tennessee Regiment. He was captured the 27th of November, 1864, and remained in prison two months at Johnson's Island. He is a strong supporter of Democratic principles and is a Knight Templar and belongs to the K. of H. He has been an active member of the Tennessee Conference for twenty-seven years. His parents, William T. and Theresa (Warren) Bolton, were both born in the State of Tennessee. The father was a moral, honest man, and departed this life June 3, 1885. The mother's death occurred on the 17th of October, 1863. Both were earnest members of the Methodist Episcopal Church at the time of their deaths.

ANDREW T. BOYD is a son of James Boyd, whose father was a soldier under Gens. George Washington and Nathaniel Greene during the Revolutionary war, and was in the battles of Monmouth and King's Mountain and served through the war. James Boyd was born in Davidson County, Tenn., and there married Elizabeth Henderson, a native of North Carolina. The father was a tiller of the soil and departed this life in 1825. The mother was a member of the Presbyterian Church, and died in 1860. Andrew T. Boyd began studying medicine and took a course of lectures at Lexington, Ky. He afterward attended the University of Philadelphia, Penn. He practiced his profession successfully for about twenty years, and then retired from active duties. In 1878 he married Miss L. Curthirell. In the late war he was surgeon in the Forty-eighth Tennessee Regiment for one year. He is now a Democrat, though formerly a Whig, and belongs to the Masonic fraternity, Royal Arch Degree.

WILLIAM BRANCH'S birth occurred in Bedford County, Va., May 6, 1812, son of James and Martha (Minor) Branch, who were born in Bedford County and Botetourt County, Va., in 1766 and 1770, respectively. They were married in 1792, and became the parents of ten children, our subject being the youngest of the family. They came to Tennessee about 1814, and accumulated considerable means. The father died in 1844, and the mother in 1839. At the age of twenty-one William M. began farming for himself, and, January 28, 1841, married Mary Ann Uzzell, who was born in Maury County July 13, 1823, and daughter of Elisha and Ann (Cohee) Uzzell. Mr. and Mrs. Branch are the parents of the following children: Frances T., born in 1841; John T., born in 1843; Martha E., born in 1845; Nancy A., born in 1848; Mary S., born in 1850; Laura S., born in 1852; Sarah E., born in 1854; Willie T., born in 1857; Joseph H., born in 1859, and Ruth A., born in 1862. Mr. Branch is a Democrat and Mason, and is considered a wide-awake and prosperous citizen of the county. He and wife are members of the Methodist Episcopal Church South.

JOHN B. BROOKS, merchant, was born in Arkansas, November 1, 1854, and is a son of William and Mary (Dodson) Brooks, who were native Tennesseeans. William Brooks was an enterprising agriculturist and is now residing in Maury County. The mother was a member of the Methodist Church and died in that faith in April, 1862. John B. received a somewhat limited education in the common schools, but step by step has climbed the ladder of success until he has accumulated considerable property. December 9, 1879, he was united in marriage to Miss Roxanna Akin, daughter of Anderson Akin, a prominent citizen of Maury County. To them were born two children, both of whom are dead. Mr. Brooks supports the principles of Republicanism, and he and wife are members of the Methodist Episcopal Church and are good citizens and neighbors.

WILLIAM R. BROWN, an old and prominent citizen of Neapolis, Maury Co., Tenn., was b orn in this county, October 15, 1832, and is a son of Solomon and Elizabeth (Sanders) Brown, both of whom were natives of South Carolina. The father was one of the early settlers of this county and followed the vocation of farming. He died about two years after immigrating here from South Carolina. The mother's death occurred in 1864, at the unusual age of eighty-one years. Our subject passed his youthful days on the farm and secured a fair practical education at the common schools. At the age of sixteen he serve d an apprenticeship at wagon-making and followed that business for twelve or fifteen years. In 1852 he began merchandising at Neapolis and was engaged in this business until the beginning of the war. In 1861 he enlisted in Company A, Forty-eighth Tennessee, and served as a sergeant about one year. Being a mechanic he was detailed boss of brigade shops and was afterward made boss of the division shop, and remained as such until the close of the war. He then returned to Neapolis and resumed his former business. In 1881 he removed to his farm, on which he lived one year, then built his present house and shop, where he has been engaged in wagon-making and general repairing. In 1869 he wedded Elizabeth Truelove, a native of this county, who died in 1882. They have four children born to this union, only two of whom are living: Willie E. and Lillie. Mr. Brown is a Democrat and an attendant of the Methodist Church.

W. HUGH BROWN, farmer, was born in Maury County, Tenn., December 11, 1843, and is the eldest son of James W. and Jenette M. (Dobbin) Brown, natives, respectively, of North Carolina and Tennessee. The father came to Maury County about 1816 with his father, Hon. Col. Hugh Brown, of North Carolina, and his brother, Rev. Duncan Brown, who was a well-known preacher of this county. James W. Brown followed the occupation of a farmer to a considerable extent and was very successful. He died June 1, 1885. The mother still survives him, and is living with her son, John S. Brown, on the old homestead. Our subject was reared on the farm and received a good practical education. In 1861, at the age of seventeen, he enlisted in the Spring Hill Company, Third Tennessee Regiment, under the command of Capt. Pointer. He remained with the above company about six months and then joined the cavalry command and remained with this company until the close of the war. He then returned to this county and began farming on his father's tract. In 1870 he removed to his present farm, where he has been steadily engaged in farming and stock raising ever since. In 1870 he wedded Laura B. Cheairs, a native of this county, and to this union was born one child, Nora. Mrs. Laura Brown is the daughter of Col. Martin T. and Martha (Bond) Cheairs. The father was born in North Carolina, May 19, 1804, and is the son of Nathaniel and Sarah (Rush) Cheairs, natives, respectively of North Carolina and Maryland, Nathaniel died in 1846 and his wife followed in 1858. Martin T. Cheairs was reared on the farm and secured but a limited education. At the age of thirty-four he went into the mercantile business with his brother, John Cheairs, at Spring Hill. Eleven years from that time he gave up the mercantile business and engaged in farming and stock raising. In 1837 he was married and became the father of nine children, only three of whom are living, viz.: Mary F., Nannie R. and Laura B., the wife of our subject. Mr. Brown is a Democrat, and himself and family are members of the Old School Presbyterian Church.

ANDREW D. BRYANT, one of Maury County's most enterprising citizens, was born in Franklin County, North Carolina, March 14, 1825, and is the son of John F. and Sarah W. (Amis) Bryant, who were born in 1790 and 1794, respectively. The father, John F., was the son of Roland and Mary (Hunt) Bryant, and Roland was the son of William Bryant, who was born in Ireland. John F. was a successful farmer, was married in 1814, and was the father of ten children. He died December 6, 1857, and his wife followed him to the grave in 1870. Our subject was reared on a farm and obtained a limited education in the country schools, and followed farming for eight years, in Dallas County, Ark. He then moved to Maury County, Tenn., where he now resides, engaged in farming and stock raising, in which he has been quite successful. He was married, January 4, 1852, to Sarah Hill, a native of Tennessee, born in June, 1828, and the daughter of Isaac and Margaret (Steele) Hill. Isaac Hill was born in North Carolina, in 1800, and died in Marshall County, Tenn., in 1840. To our subject and wife were born eight children: James R., born 1854; Isaac H., born 1856; John F., born 1857; William T., born 1859; Ida R., born 1861; Andrew D., born 1863; Patrick H., born 1866, and Lizzie H., born 1869. Mr. Bryant has given his children a good education and has reason to be proud of them. In 1874 he was engaged in building two miles of railroad, and also built switch and station houses. In 1877 he engaged in the saw and grist-mill business. He took an active part in the Confederate service during the late war, enlisting in Company H, Fifty-third Regiment, and served two years. He was first lieutenant, and his captain being wounded at Fort Donelson, Mr. Bryant took his place as captain. Our subject was captured and taken to Indianapolis, Johnson's Island, Camp Chase and at Vicksburg, where he was exchanged. He is an enterprising and successful farmer and stock raiser, and is highly spoken of by his many friends.

THOMAS H. BRYANT is a native of Maury County, Tenn., and was born Au gust 15, 1839, and was reared on a farm. In 1861 he enlisted in Company F, Third Tennessee Regiment, under Col. J. C. Brown. He was captured at the fall of Fort Donelson and taken to Camp Douglas, where he was imprisoned seven months. He was then exchanged at Vicksburg and immediately rejoined the army. He participated in many battles and was wounded and captured at Raymond, Miss. After his release he again joined his command, stationed at Meridian, Miss. He was disabled there and came home on furlough, and was captured and paroled near the first of 1864. June 4, 1866, he wedded Emma J. Howard, born February 20, 1847, in Maury County. They have four children: James H., Hattie W., Frank L. and Bessie M. Mr. and Mrs. Bryant are members of the Methodist Episcopal Church South and he belongs to the Democratic party. His parents, Edward and Elizabeth (Amis) Bryant, were both born in Granville County, N. C., in 1778 and 1797, respectively. The father was a farmer and miller. He was a soldier in the war of 1812 and was a Whig in politics. He died in 1867 or 1868, and the mother about 1835.

JOHN S. CALDWELL, farmer, was born in Maury County, Tenn., February, 1811, and is the son of William H., and Elizabeth (Stanfield) Caldwell, both natives of Virginia. The father came from Virginia to this county in 1806. He was a farmer and secured a very comfortable competency. His death occurred in October, 1854. The mother died in April, 1852. Our subject was reared on the farm and was one of the many old settlers who received their education in the rude log schoolhouses of a former day. At the age of twenty-seven he began farming for himself on Carter Creek, where he remained for five years. He subsequently purchased a farm on Bear Creek and after living there sixteen years removed to his present place, where he has been actively engaged in farming and stock raising ever since. November, 1839, he married Sarah A. Jameson, a native of this county. To them were born eight children, seven of whom are living: Mary E., Robina C., Ellen J. (deceased), Thomas J., John E., Emily O., Robert C. and Dora M. Mr. Caldwell is a Democrat in politics, and himself and family are leading members of the Christian Church. He is a Mason of good standing and is one of Maury County's oldest and most respected citizens.

WILLIE G. CECIL, a progressive young farmer of Maury County, Tenn., was born June 18, 1861, and is one of six children born to the marriage of James H. Cecil and Julia Ingram. James Cecil was born in Hanover County, Va., in July, 1812, and came to Tennessee in 1841 locating on a farm in the Thirteenth District of Maury County, where he lived at the time of his death in 1883. He was strictly honest in his business transactions and was a warm advocate of the cause of temperance. His wife was born in Lebanon, Ky., in 1833. She was a member of the Roman Catholic Church, and her husband belonged to the Methodist Episcopal Church South. Willie G. Cecil attended the Maury County common schools, and entered St. Mary's Agricultural College at Lebanon, Ky., in September, 1876, where he completed his course and graduated with honor in June, 1878. He then returned home and has since been engaged in farming. In his political views he is a stanch Democrat and gives his support to that party on all occasions.

NATHANIEL B. CHEAIRS, the popular sheriff of Maury County, Tenn , was born in the county at Spring Hill, September 8, 1848. He secured a good education in the Washington Lee University at Lexington, Va., and at the age of nineteen became salesman in a wholesale merchandise establishment in Nashville, continuing one and a half years. He then began farming and stock trading at Spring Hill, but in August, 1884, was elected to the office of sheriff of the county, which he has filled faithfully and well to the present time. He is a Democrat of a progressive type and is a member of the K. of H. One son, John M., is the result of his marriage to Miss Annie Alexander, which occurred in October, 1875. His parents, John W. and Susan T. (Pointer) Cheairs, were born in North Carolina and Virginia, respectively. The father was a merchant and farmer by occupation and followed the former occupation in New Orleans and later engaged in both enterprises at Spring Hill, Tenn. He died there in January, 1873, followed by his widow in April, 1874.

BIOGRAPHICAL APPENDIX.

OWEN P. CHEEK, one of Maury County's most enterprising citizens, was born May 7, 1831, son of John L. and Elizabeth Cheek. The father was born in North Carolina, October, 1801, and came to Tennessee with his parents when quite young. He began business for himself at the age of twenty-one as a farmer, and by this occupation he accumulated considerable means. He was married and became the father of a large family. His death occurred in 1873. The mother was born in Maury County March, 1815, and is an exemplary Christian, she is still living at the old homestead. Our subject received a limited education, although enough for all practical purposes. August 17, 1854, he wedded Susan Huey, a native of Maury County, Tenn., born February 17, 1838, and the daughter of William G. and Susan (Bradley) Huey. By this marriage our subject became the father of ten children; Eliza J., Susan E., William L., Calvin B., James M., Ida L., John T., Joseph E. J., Lises E. and one who died unnamed. The mother of these children is a worthy member of the Missionary Baptist Church, and has many warm friends. In 1861 our subject enlisted in Company H, Forty-eighth Regiment Tennessee Infantry, and was sworn in at Nashville. He was captured at Fort Henry and taken to Chicago where he was imprisoned for seven months. He was then exchanged and sent to his command at Vicksburg. He was all through the war and was a brave and gallant soldier. He is a Democrat and is justly recognized as an upright, honest citizen.

NIMROD P. CHEEK, a prominent farmer of Maury County, was born April 22, 1857, and is the son of John L. and Elizabeth Cheek. For further particulars of parents see sketch of Owen P. Cheek. Our subject began business for himself in 1874 as a farmer, and has made that his principal occupation ever since. In 1876 he was united in marriage to Cornelia C. Gilliam, a native of Maury County, born June 19, 1861, and the daughter of Harrison O. and Mary A. (Pinkston) Gilliam, both natives of Tennessee. The father was born in Tennessee, and was one of Maury County's most successful farmers. He was a member of the Christian Church, as also was his wife. To our subject and wife were born an interesting family of four children: John W. H., born April 28, 1877; Huston N., born August 6, 1880; Arthur B., born August 11, 1882, and C. L., born September 7, 1884. Mr. Cheek is in good circumstances, is a Democrat and he and wife are members of the Christian Church.

GEORGE CHILDRESS, the subject of this sketch, a son of Adrian D. and Nancy B. (McGuire) Childress, was born at Spring Hill, Maury County, May 5, 1849. The parents, who also were natives of Maury County, removed to Lawrence County in 1850, where the father now resides, the mother having died in January, 1884. George was reared and received an old field school education in Lawrence County. At the age of eighteen he secured a clerkship in his native town with Mr. J. B. Stephenson, where he remained ten months, coming to Columbia in October, 1868, and secured a clerkship in the well-known house of Harris, Frierson & Co. Upon the organization of the First National Bank of Columbia he was chosen as book-keeper, which position was retained till 1872, when he engaged in general insurance. In 1874 he was elected secretary and treasurer of the Duck River Valley Railroad Company, and was later appointed superintendent, which positions he held for about eight years. In 1882 he was principal in the movement which resulted in the organization of the Second National Bank of Columbia, of which he has ever since been the cashier. In 1883 he was appointed clerk and master of chancery court, which office he manages through his efficient deputy, I. S. Orman. In 1876 he married Annette Estelle Kuhn, daughter of Edward Kuhn, who was several times mayor of Columbia, and one of the most enterprising men of the county. They have two daughters. He is a Democrat in politics. He and wife are strong believers in the doctrines of the Methodist Episcopal Church South.

ALLEN B. CHURCH, senior member of the firm of Church & Jack, dealers in dry goods, groceries, hardware and general merchandise, was born in this county October 16, 1846, and is a son of Robert C. and Lucy (Fitzgerald) Church, natives, respectively, of North Carolina and Tennessee. The father was a tiller of the soil and was very successful in that occupation. He died about 1871. The mother is still living and is a resident of the old homestead. Our subject received a good common education and remained with his parents on the farm until he was twenty-one years of age. Previous to this, at the age of eighteen, he enlisted in Company E, Ninth Tennessee Regiment, and served as a high private with the above company for five months. Then on account of sickness he returned home, and remained there until the close of the war. He then began farming, and soon removed to a farm on Snow Creek, where he remained one year. He then moved to Leiper Creek, and continued farming. In 1879 he began the mercantile business at Theta as a partner of Mr. Jack, and remained there about three years. In 1880 they established their business at Carter Creek, where they are at present. In 1866 he married Emily Oakley, a native of this county, and seven children were born to this union: Stephen R., Oatey, Arthur, Jennette, Tolitha, Bessie, and an infant not named. Mr. Church is a Democrat in politics, and his family are members of the Presbyterian Church.

WILLIAM J. COCHRAN, one of Maury County's most highly respected citizens, was born in this county June 7, 1811, son of James and Jane (Miligan) Cochran. The father was born in North Carolina May 2, 1781, and immigrated to Georgia when a young man, afterward living in Tennessee for a few years. He went back to Georgia, where he was married, after which he came back to Tennessee, and located in Maury County. He died June 30, 1859. He was in the war of 1812 and was a brave soldier. The mother died May 15, 1864. Our subject grew to manhood on the farm, and at the age of twenty-one began business for himself as a farmer. August 14, 1834, he wedded Maria R. Dodson, and to them were born these children: David J., born 1836; James Brooks, born 1838; Ascenith J., born 1844; William H., and an infant not named. Our subject received a rather limited education, but enough for all practical purposes. He is a Democrat, and he and wife are members of the Presbyterian Church.

WILLIAM O. COFFEE, M. D., of Columbia, was born in Ballard County, Ky., in 1859, and after the usual common school training he obtained his literary and medical education in St. Louis, Mo., and graduated from the Missouri Medical College of that city in 1880. He first began practicing in the blue-grass State, and later in Illinois, Missouri, Indiana, Kansas, New York, Pennsylvania, and in May, 1885, came to Tennessee, locating first in Lebanon, and three months later came to Columbia, where his father, William Coffee, was known, and his grandfather, Nathan Coffee, had been a well-known and prosperous business man. William O. has acquired a good practice in the short time he has been in Columbia. He is a member of the Kentucky, Illinois, Missouri, and King's County (N. Y.), Medical Societies, and was one time a member of the American Medical Association. He is a Democrat in politics and a member of the K. of H. fraternity.

JOSEPH M. COFFEY is considered one of the prosperous citizens of Maury County, Tenn. He was born March 23, 1844, son of Hugh W. and Jennie (Gragg) Coffey, and was reared on a farm. At the breaking-out of the war he enlisted in Company F, Forty-eighth Tennessee Infantry, Quarles brigade, and was an active participant in many of the bloodiest battles of the war. He was captured in Nashville and taken to Camp Douglas, where he was imprisoned about four months, and from that time until the close of the war he was a prisoner at Point Lookout, Md. He returned home June 30, 1865, and immediately began tilling the soil. November 30, 1876, he married Maggie J. Coker, who was born in Missouri November 2, 1858, daughter of John M. and Sallie A. (Wilkes) Coker. Hugh M., born in 1877; Roy B., born in 1880; Ollie F., born in 1881; Sallie E., born in 1883, and Shirley E., born in 1886, are the children born to Mr. and Mrs. Coffey's union. They are members of the Cumberland Presbyterian Church, and Mr. Coffey is a Democrat, and an energetic and successful farmer.

WILLIAM R. CONNER, a successful agriculturist of Maury County, Tenn., was born in Davidson County, Tenn., May 28, 1827. He obtained a practical education, and started in life with no capital save his hands and unbounded energy. He has been quite prosperous in his business undertakings, and is now a well-to-do "tiller of the soil." June 4, 1852, he led to the hymeneal altar Miss Martha Blocker, daughter of Elijah Blocker, of

Maury County. Three children blessed their union, these two now living: India B. (wife of Thomas S. Whiteside), and Addie B. (wife of E. A. Pogue). Mr. Conner was opposed to the late war, and accordingly refrained from participating in it. He is a stanch supporter of Republican principles, and belongs to the Masonic fraternity. He is a member of the Christian Church, and is a son of Alfred and Sidney (Kennedy) Conner, who were born in North Carolina. The father was a farmer by occupation, and died in 1843. The mother died in 1873.

HORACE S. COOPER, one of the managers of the Columbia *Herald*, was born in Bedford County, Tenn., in April, 1846, and is a son of Edwin and Mary (Stephens) Cooper, who are natives, respectively, of Williamson County, Tenn., and Virginia. Matthew D. Cooper, our subject's grandfather, moved to Maury County as early as, or prior to, 1830, and was a successful cotton dealer and merchant and a prominent Mason. His death occurred in Columbia in 1878, at the advanced age of eighty-eight years. Horace S. Cooper was raised in his native county, and made his home with his parents until eighteen years of age. He then entered Yale College, from which he graduated, with the degree of A. B., in 1868. He began preparing himself for the profession of law, and began practicing at Shelbyville, Tenn., in 1872, continuing until 1879, when he accepted the position as deputy clerk and master of the chancery court, and was afterward appointed clerk and master, and filled the position faithfullly and efficiently until 1883, when he resigned to resume the practice of law and manage his large farm. He makes a specialty of raising and selling fine stock, and is a successful financier. May 1, 1885, he accepted his position with the *Herald*, and has contributed largely to the success of this well-known paper.

JAMES C. COOPER is a son of Robert and Catharine Cooper, and was born in Maury County, Tenn., November 17, 1826, being the fifth of their fifteen children. He was a soldier in the Mexican war, serving in Company C, First Tennessee Cavalry, and participated in the battle of Vera Cruz and several minor engagements. In 1861 he enlisted in Company C, Forty-eighth Tennessee Volunteer Infantry, and was in the following engagements: Perryville, Chickamauga, Richmond, and numerous skirmishes. He was twice wounded. September 12, 1856, he was married to Miss Emarinthy C. Kinzer, and to them were born the following eight children; John T. (deceased), Albert C., James H., William D., George Lee, Robert Burns, Anna B. and Callie D. Mr. Cooper is a member of the Methodist Episcopal Church South, and an earnest worker in that church. Politically he has been a life-long Democrat, and was constable of the Eleventh District for a period of seven years, and discharged the duties of that office in an efficient manner. He belongs to the Presbyterian Church. His father and mother were natives of the "Palmetto State" and Tennessee, born in 1790 and 1799, respectively. The father was a prosperous farmer, and lived a long and useful life. Our subject's maternal grandmother was a member of the Methodist Episcopal Church for eighty years, and lived to be about one hundred years old.

HENRY S. COX, physician of Columbia, Tenn., is a son of John and Martha C. (Evans) Cox, the father being a successful stock raiser and farmer of the county. He reared his family in Maury County, and in 1863 was shot by a Federal soldier at his home. The mother died prior to the war. Henry S. attended the Jackson College at Columbia, and when twenty years old became a disciple of Æsculapius, studying under the direction of Dr. W. G. J. Hunter. He then attended the University of Pennsylvania in Philadelphia, and graduated as an M. D. in 1860. He enlisted as first surgeon of the First Arkansas Sharpshooters, and later served with Gen. A. M. Stovall as surgeon of the brigade. Since the war he has resided in Columbia, where he has built up a fine practice. In 1866 he was married to Rebecca Martin, by whom he is the father of three children: John, Ella and Martin S. The Doctor was an old-line Whig until that party ceased to exist, and since that time has been a Democrat, but has never aspired to political prominence, and has devoted his energies and talents strictly to his profession.

STEPHEN S. CRAIG was born in the Fourth District of Maury County December 14, 1833, was reared on the farm and owing to circumstances his education was rather limited. January 13, 1859, he wedded Mary A. Sharber, a native of Rutherford County, Tenn., born January 13, 1837, and the daughter of John and Nancy Sharber. To our subject and wife were born nine children: Robert J., born 1859; John W. S., born in 1861, and died in 1882; James C. born in 1865; Nancy E., born in 1868; Lanella R., born in 1869; Mary L. B., born in 1872; Wallace J., born in 1873; L. J., born in 1876; Virgie M., born in 1878, and Joseph A. T., born in 1881. Mr. Craig is a successful farmer and also a wheelwright. During the late war he enlisted in Company C, Forty-eighth Tennessee Regiment of Infantry. He was captured and taken to Nashvile, where he was paroled in 1865. He was elected magistrate in the Fourth District of Maury County March, 1882, and holds that office at the present time in an able and efficient manner. Himself and family are members of the Cumberland Presbyterian Church. His parents, Robert R. and Rachel (Miles) Craig, were both natives of South Carolina, the former born December 15, 1786, and the latter December 8, 1795. The father was married in South Carolina and came to Tennessee soon after, locating in Franklin County, where he engaged in farming for three years. He then moved to Maury County and continued farming, in which he was quite successful. He was in the war of 1812 and was a gallant soldier. He died November 18, 1854. The mother was a member of the Cumberland Presbyterian Church for nearly forty years and was an earnest worker in the cause of Christianity.

JAMES F. CRAIG, a native of Tennessee and well-to-do farmer, was born in Maury County May 1, 1836. His father, Robert Craig, was a native of North Carolina, where he married Mary Sellers, also of that State, and came to Tennessee. He now resides in Maury County and is a widower, his wife having died October 4, 1864. Our subject is a graduate of Erskine College, South Carolina. He took an active part in the late war, serving in Company B, Thirty-second Mississippi Infantry, from March, 1862, to March, 1864. At that time he was transferred to the Third Tennessee and served in this capacity until the close of the war. He is a member of the Old School Presbyterian Church, and is a strong Democrat in politics.

THOMPSON S. CRAIG, was born in the Sixth District of Maury County May 9, 1849, son of Nathaniel H. and Hattie (Scott) Craig. The father was born in North Carolina December 25, 1807. He was reared on the farm and was married in 1828 and became the father of seven children. His death occurred in January, 1886. He was the son of John and Lucinda Craig. The mother of our subject was born in Tennessee December 14, 1807, and died about 1872. She was the daughter of Samuel and Sarah Scott, natives of Ireland. Our subject passed his early life on the farm, and began business for himself at the age of twenty-three as a farmer. February 22, 1877, he wedded Ella Cline, a native of Canada, born January 2, 1858, and the daughter of John L. and Augusta (Simons) Cline. To our subject and wife were born four children: Emmit P., born in 1878; John L., born in 1882; Ruby, born in 1883, and Samuel S., born in 1885. Mrs. Craig is a member of the Methodist Episcopal Church, and is a warm advocate of Christianity. Mr. Craig is a Democrat, and a member of the Masonic fraternity. He is justly recognized by all as an honest, upright young man.

MANN DAWSON, a well known and well-to-do farmer of Maury County, Tenn., was born October 11, 1838, and is the youngest of a family of six sons and five daughters born to John and Martha G. (Hunter) Dawson, who were natives of North Carolina, born in 1786 and 1798 and died in 1843 and 1878, respectively. John Dawson came to Tennessee at an early day and became one of the pioneer settlers of Maury County, and there passed the remainder of his days. Mann Dawson attended the common schools of Maury County and assisted his parents on the farm. Later he attended the college at Lebanon, Tenn., where he finished his education. At the breaking out of the late civil war, in May, 1861, he joined Col. Wade's company, Third Tennessee Volunteer Infantry, and took an active part in the battles of Lookout Mountain, Missionary Ridge, Fort Donelson, Chickamauga, Atlanta and numerous others. He was captured at Fort Donelson, and kept a prisoner at Camp Douglas, Chicago, seven months. He was exchanged at Vicksburg, Miss., in September, 1862, and returned to his home in May, 1865. He was formerly a Whig in politics, but is now a Democrat. He is a Freemason.

GEORGE W. DAVIDSON, farmer, of Maury County, Tenn., is a son of George W. and Elizabeth J. (Wasson) Davidson, and his birth occurred in Lawrence County, Tenn., June 22, 1847. His father was born in the "Old Dominion" in May, 1812, and came with his parents to Tennessee at an early day, locating on a farm in Lawrence County. Our subject spent his early days on a farm and obtained a good common school education. He enlisted in the Confederate Army in the latter part of 1862 in Company D, Ninth Tennessee Cavalry and participated in the battles of Franklin, Thompson Station and several minor engagements. He was paroled May 12, 1865, and returned to Lawrence Co. and engaged in farming. He was married, October 16, 1868, to Chirena I. Alford, and the birth of two sons and one daughter is the result of their union: George M., James W. and Elizabeth J. Mrs. Davidson was born in 1845. She is a member of the Cumberland Presbyterian Church and a faithful wife and mother. Mr. Davidson is a Democrat, and was elected magistrate of the Thirteenth District November 4, 1884, and is giving entire satisfaction. He resides on a farm near Mount Pleasant, and is doing well financially.

WILLIAM H. DAVIS, a native of Maury County, Tenn., was born January 6, 1823, son of Ephraim and Eliza T. (Allen) Davis, whose marriage occurred 1829. The father was a Democrat and was justice of the peace one term. He was a man of sound judgment and good sense. His death occurred January, 1882. The mother was born in Virginia in 1804 and was the daughter of Hamblin and Silvina (Maneer) Allen. They were natives of Virginia and came to Tennessee about 1812 or 1813, locating in Maury County, where they tilled the soil. Eliza, our subject's mother, was a member of the Baptist Church, and died in 1878. Our subject spent his boyhood on the farm, and owing to circumstances received a rather limited education. March 26, 1857, he married Martha E. Cannon, a native of Lincoln County, Tenn., born December 20, 1837, and the daughter of George M. and Nancy M. (Holeman) Cannon, both natives of Tennessee, born 1820 and 1822, respectively. Our subject enlisted in Company G, Ninth Tennessee Cavalry and served until the close of the war. He was in many battles and had some narrow escapes. He is the father of nine children: Jennie M., born in 1858; Benjamin, born in 1859; Felix Z., born in 1862; William E., born in 1866; Eliza M., born in 1869; Mary A., born in 1871; Hay, born in 1873; Leah, born in 1875, and Omega H., born in 1878. Mr. Davis has been constable for four years in the Twenty-first District of Maury County, and was constable from 1876 to 1880. He has been school commissioner for eighteen months, and is a member of the Masonic fraternity. He is also a member of the K. of H., a Democrat in politics and is recognized as an honest, upright citizen.

RALEIGH P. DODSON, a well-known liveryman and one of the proprietors of the Bethel House of Columbia, Tenn., is a native of Maury County, born September 6, 1845, son of Raleigh and Lucinda (Witherspoon) Dodson, who were born in North Carolina and Tennessee, respectively. The father was a prominent farmer and stock raiser, and died a day or so after our subject's birth. Raleigh resided with his widowed mother in the county and secured an ordinary common school education. He served in the late war in Company G, First Tennessee Infantry, and at the battle of Perryville was captured by the Federals and afterward paroled. After his return he engaged in the livery business in Columbia, which he has continued to the present time, being a partner of M. C. Mays. In 1871 he married Loretta Gill, a native of the county. Mr. Dodson is a Mason, Knight Templar degree and a Democrat, and is a prosperous and influential resident of the town.

THOMAS J. DORSETT'S birth occurred in Maryland April 22, 1831. He is a son of Thomas and Harriett (Clagett) Dorsett, of Maryland. The father was a tiller of the soil. He died in the Episcopal faith April 7, 1847. The mother still survives and is a resident of Maryland. The subject of our sketch was married on the 2d of March, 1852, to Miss Mary Robinson, daughter of Stewart Robinson, a resident of Maryland. To Mr. Dorsett and wife were born thirteen children, only six of whom are living: Laura R. (wife of Otey Walker, a successful merchant at Williamsport), Lillie G. (wife of Samuel Gray, of Nashville), Thomas J., Mary E., Harriett and Pauline. Mr. Dorsett did not participate in the late war. He is a warm Democrat and belongs to the Masonic fraternity, Royal Arch degree. Both he and wife are members of the Episcopal Church and are esteemed citizens of Maury County.

WALTER C. DORSET, M. D., was born in Anne Arundel County, Md., July 19, 1841, being a son of Thomas J. and Harriett (Clagett) Dorset, of Maryland, where the father died and the mother still resides. Walter C. was reared to manhood on a farm, and completed his education at the Virginia Military Institute at Lexington, Va. In 1867 he came to Maury County and resided with a relative, Mrs. Jane H. Y. Greenfield. He began studying medicine with the late Dr. Samuel Frierson. Later he attended Belleview Hospital Medical College, of New York City, and graduated there as a physician in 1870. Since that time he has practiced in Columbia, and has met with more than ordinary success. He is strictly a self-made man, and by his own efforts and devotion to his calling has gained an enviable reputation. In January, 1886, he was elected health officer of Maury County by the county court, for a term of four years. Marion and Hallie B. are the children born to his marriage with Miss Janie M. Arnell, which occurred in 1871. Dr. Dorset's political views are Democratic. He is a Mason, and he and family are members of the Episcopal Church.

SHADRACH S. DUGGER is the fifth of eight children born to David and Catherine (Bailey) Dugger. David was born in Virginia, and Mrs. Dugger near Bowling Green, Ky. The father was a Democrat and died about 1829, after living a useful and prosperous life. The mother died about 1860, in Henry County, Tenn. Our subject was born in Maury County February 20. 1830, and has passed the life of an agriculturist. July 20, 1850. he was married to Martha J. Laneare, who was born in Virginia March 12, 1835, and is the daughter of Howell and Elizabeth (Epperson) Laneare. They were born in Virginia and came to Tennessee when our subject's wife was a small child and located in Giles County. The father died in 1845 or 1846, and the mother in 1881. To our subject and his wife were born four sons and four daughters: Samuel G., born in 1851; Thomas J., born in 1852; Corinna, born in 1856; Elizabeth L., born in 1860; Daniel B., born in 1866; Leroy S., born in 1869; Lorinda, born in 1872, and Isolana, born in 1876. Mrs. Dugger is a member of the Christian Church, and her husband is a Democrat. He has resided on his present farm for thirteen years, and success has attended his efforts.

JOHN H. ELLETT, a well-known citizen of Maury County, Tenn., was born on the 29th of October. 1836, the only child of Thomas P. and Susan (Griffith) Ellett. Thomas P. Ellett was born near Richmond, Va., in 1802, and came to Maury County with his parents at an early age. He was a participant in the Seminole war, and was a strong temperance man. He died in Maury County. His wife was born in that county about 1806 and died in 1836, an earnest member of the Methodist Episcopal Church South. Our subject obtained the rudiments of his education in Maury County, and later attended Cumberland University at Lebanon, Tenn. He was married August 15, 1861, to Miss Ophelia Kindel, and to their union five sons and three daughters were born: John C. (deceased), James K. (deceased), William M., Wadkins B., Felix M., Anna L. (deceased), Martha W. (deceased) and Katharine. In 1862 Mr. Ellett enlisted in the Confederate Army, Company D, Third Tennessee Volunteer Infantry, and was a participant in the following bloody battles: Vicksburg, Raymond, Jackson, Miss., Port Hudson, Chickamauga and others. He served as first lieutenant of his company until May, 1865, when he returned home. Previous to the war Mr. Ellett was a Whig, but since that time he has been a Democrat. He belongs to the Methodist Episcopal Church.

THOMAS Y. ENGLISH, farmer, was born in Giles County, Tenn., March 19, 1835, and is one of a large family of children born to John and Clara (Willeford) English. The father was born in North Carolina in 1800, and was by occupation a farmer. He came to Tennessee with his mother in 1810, and settled on a farm in Giles County, where he lived a long and prosperous life. He was a member of the Baptist Church, and died July 26, 1879. The mother was a native of South Carolina, born in 1810. She was a member of the Primitive Baptist Church, and was a faithful, conscientious Christian.

Her death occurred September 26, 1885. Our subject was reared on a farm, and educated in Giles County. He came to Maury County in 1875, and settled on a farm in the Eleventh District, where he has since resided. He enlisted as a private in the Confederate Army May 12, 1861, Company I, Third Tennessee Volunteer Regiment, commanded by Col. John C. Brown, of Tennessee. He participated in the battles of Fort Donelson, Chickamauga, Bayou, Raymond and several minor ones. He was taken prisoner at Fort Donelson, and taken to Camp Morton, Indianapolis, Ind., where he remained until his release May 11, 1865. He was married November 8, 1881, to Lissie Spain, a native of Maury County, and the result of this union is the birth of three sons: Thomas Y., born August 8, 1882; John W., born February 25, 1884, and Robert J., born February 23, 1886. Mr. English is a member of the Methodist Episcopal Church, a Democrat in politics, and one of Maury County's best citizens.

EPHRAIM E. ERWIN, local editor and business manager of the Columbia *Herald*, is a native of Maury County, Tenn., born September 18, 1848, son of William H. and Jemina A. (Voss) Erwin. The father was a native of Maury County, and was a prosperous farmer and stock dealer. He served as constable a few years, and died in 1858 or 1859. Ephraim E. resided under the paternal roof until his father's death, and secured a somewhat limited education in his youthful days. This he overcame in later years by his own efforts. After attaining his majority he served as deputy postmaster of Columbia four years, and was made register, and later served as clerk of the county court. In 1876 he accepted the position of accountant in the chancery court, filling the position with credit to himself and the satisfaction of the people, until 1883. By much desultory study he had become well versed in legal lore, and in 1884 was admitted to the Maury County bar, but never entered into the practice regularly. In March, 1885, he accepted a position on the *Herald*, and it may be truthfully said that the success of the paper is in a large measure due to his untiring energy and ability. In 1872 he married Bessie R. Porter, of Maury County, who died in March, 1874, leaving one son. Mr. Erwin is a Democrat, and belongs to the Masonic, K. of P. and A. O. U. W. fraternities. He is also a member of the Cumberland Presbyterian Church.

ERVIN T. ESTES' birth occurred in Maury County, Tenn., March 16, 1855. He is a successful merchant, and was united in marriage August 5, 1877, to Miss Virginia T. Grant, daughter of Thomas U. Grant. Mr. Estes is a Democrat, and he and wife are members of the Methodist Episcopal Church South, and are considered among the reliable and prominent citizens of the county. Our subject's parents were Orvin T. and Hester J. (McBride) Estes, who were born in the State of Tennessee, and spent their lives as farmers. The father was an honest and upright man, and died in 1855, a member of the Methodist Episcopal Church South. The mother still survives him, and is a resident of Maury County, Tenn.

FLAVIUS J. EWING, a well-known business man of Columbia, Tenn., and partner in the firm of Elam & Ewing, was born in Marshall County, Tenn., August 19, 1831, son of James V. and Elizabeth Ewing, who were born in Virginia and Georgia, respectively. The father was one of the pioneer farmers of Tennessee, and suffered all the privations incident to early life in Tennessee. He died in Marshall County in 1881. Our subject was reared and educated in his native county and finished his education in Jackson College of Columbia, and several of the best Colleges of Virginia. In 1860 he came to Maury County and located on a farm in the Twenty-first District, where he followed farming and stock raising until 1882, when he removed to near Columbia, and in 1883 engaged in his present business in the city, and has by his many good business qualities contributed largely to the success of the firm. Mary L. Akin became his wife in 1859, and their union resulted in the birth of two sons and four daughters. Robert L., the eldest son, is in business with his father. Mr. Ewing was originally a Whig in politics, but since the war has voted the Democratic ticket. He served two years in the quartermaster's department of the Confederate Army, Gen. Hardee's corps. Mr. and Mrs. Ewing are members of the Presbyterian Church.

H. F. FARISS, postmaster of Columbia, Tenn., son of Hugh W. and grandson of James Fariss, who came to Maury County, Tenn., from the Carolinas in 1806. H. F. was born November 19, 1839, and at the age of thirteen removed with his parents to West Tennessee, and secured a common school education. At the age of twenty-two he returned to Maury County and tilled the soil until 1865, when he engaged in the mercantile business in Hampshire, in which he still retains an interest. In 1866 he was appointed postmaster of Hampshire, and served almost continuously until 1882, when he was elected county trustee, serving until 1884, then resigned and was appointed to the postmastership at Columbia, by President Arthur. As evidence of Mr. Fariss' popularity it need only be stated that he has successfully held various public offices notwithstanding the fact that he is a Republican in politics. He is the father of seven children by Mary E. Brooks, whom he married April 15, 1866. Mr. Fariss and wife are members of the Methodist Episcopal Church and he is a Mason and a member of the K. of H.

FRANK L. FITZGERALD, merchant, was born September 23, 1861, and is a son of Francis M. and Caroline (Chandler) Fitzgerald, both natives of this county. The father was born October 8, 1833, and received his education in the common schools. He came to this county at an early date and followed the occupations of farming and stock raising, in which he has been moderately successful. He was married in 1857 and is the father of five children: Margaret L., Frank L., Willie L., George V. and one who died in infancy. Mr. Fitzgerald is a Democrat in politics and he and wife are members of the Cumberland Presbyterian Church. In 1861 he enlisted in the Confederate Army, Company A, Forty-eighth Tennessee Regiment, and served as first lieutenant in that company for three years. He was the son of Maston and Margaret (Harder) Fitzgerald, both born in Virginia. Maston was one of the early settlers of this county and a soldier in the war of 1812. He died in 1879, and his wife in 1868. Our subject's father and mother are still living and are residing on the old Chandler homestead. Our subject was reared on the farm and received a good education in the district schools. At the age of twenty-two he engaged in his present business, in which he has been very successful. He is a Democrat in politics and an enterprising and successful business man.

WILLIAM STUART FLEMING, chancellor of the Eighth Chancery Division of Tennessee, was born in Maury County, April 23, 1816, eldest son of Thomas F. and Margaret E. (Armstrong) Fleming, who were members of a colony that came from South Carolina to Tennessee in 1805. They were of Scotch-Irish descent, and strict Presbyterians. William S. Fleming was taught the English branches by his father, and his preparatory Greek and Latin was expounded to him by John Barland, a teacher of New York City who visited him two years. He entered the Sophomore class of Yale College, and graduated in 1838. He taught school in Maury County a short time, and then began his legal studies, being admitted to practice in 1842. He immediately opened a law office in Columbia and soon commanded a large practice, which he retained as long as he remained in the practice of his profession. In 1860 he removed to his elegant country seat, which was destroyed by fire, during Hood's raid in Tennessee, by the Federal commander as a military necessity, entailing a loss of $22,000. He also had fifty slaves emancipated, and thirty head of horses and mules impressed. In 1870 he was elected chancellor, and has held the position by re-election to the present time. He is quite an eloquent orator, and for a period was editor of a literary paper, and later of a political paper, but at the same time continued his practice. He was a Whig, and although a Southern sympathizer, was not a participant in the war. He is now a Democrat, and had been a ruling elder in the Presbyterian Church for twenty-three years. He has been thrice married, having lost two wives by death. September 5, 1839, he wedded Frances M. Stephenson, who died in 1849, having borne six children, three of whom died in infancy, and only two now living: Thomas F. Fleming and Mrs. A. N. Dobbins. January 12, 1854, he married Mary Witherspoon Frierson, who died in 1858, having borne three children, all of whom died in infancy. February 8, 1860, he took for his third and present wife Ruth A. (Johnson) Booker. To them were born three children, one now living, William Stuart, also a member of the legal profession.

L. G. FLEMING was born on the 14th of February, 1847, in Maury County, Tenn. His parents, William O. and Winnie (Richardson) Fleming, were natives of Maury County, the father born in 1808. He was a farmer, and succeeded well in his business undertakings, and became the father of eight sons and six daughters. He was a member of the I. O. O. F., and a Democrat in politics. He was a man of strict integrity of character, and a successful farmer. His wife died in 1879 and he in 1860. Our subject is a well-to-do farmer and stock raiser, and was married December 1, 1874, to Manda Dodson, a daughter of W. W. Dodson. To them was born one son, George W., August 29, 1875. Mrs. Fleming died October 30, 1875. December 30, 1879, Mr. Fleming married Sammie E. (Evans) Fleming, born in 1855, a daughter of John Evans. She was first married to Nathaniel Fleming, brother of our subject, and by him became the mother of two daughters: Winnie, born in 1873, and Mattie, born in 1875. To her last marriage has been born one son and one daughter: Ella E., born in 1881, and John O., born in 1883. Mrs. Fleming belongs to the Cumberland Presbyterian Church, and her husband to the Christian Church. He is a Democrat and a member of the I. O. O. F.

ARCHIBALD C. FLOYD was born in Granville County, N. C., November 16, 1857, son of John W. and Margaret J. (Campbell) Floyd, of North Carolina, where the father lived and died and the mother now resides. Our subject resided with his parents and was educated at the University of North Carolina at Chapel Hill, graduating in 1882. During this time he had taught school at intervals to secure means to enable him to complete his collegiate course. The year following his graduation he became a disciple of Blackstone, and entered the law department of his old *alma mater*, and graduated October 1, 1883. He then taught school a short time, and obtained a license to practice from the supreme court of that State. In February, 1884, he came to Columbia, and has since practiced his profession with good results. He is a partner of George W. Hayes. Since February, 1886, Mr. Floyd has been principal of the Andrews Public School of Columbia, and is giving good satisfaction. He is a Democrat, and a member of the Methodist Episcopal Church South.

LUNSFORD B. FORGEY, M. D., a successful practitioner and farmer of Maury County, Tenn., was born September 18, 1825, and is a son of Hugh and Salina (Shorter) Forgey, natives, respectively, of Tennessee and Georgia. The father was a wealthy farmer and died about 1879. His widow is still living and is a resident of the "Lone Star State" Dr. Forgey, our subject, began reading medicine under Dr. W. W. Dabner, and graduated at the university of Louisville, Ky., one of the class of 1851. He began the practice of his profession in Maury, his native county, and has met with the success his knowledge of medicine and his skill deserves. In October, 1856, he led to Hymen's altar, Miss Sarah D. Adkin, who has borne him eight children, seven of whom are living: William S.; Charles A., James H., Addison H. and Anna Lee (twins), Walter E. and Thomas B. Dr. Forgey is a Democrat and Mason and his wife is a member of the Cumberland Presbyterian Church.

JAMES M. FRIERSON, an influential farmer of Maury County, Tenn., was born in that county October 18, 1818, son of Thomas J. and M. A. E. (Blakely) Frierson. The father was a native of Williamsburg District, S. C., born October 17, 1784, and was a tiller of the soil. He was a member of the Presbyterian Church and noted for his many acts of charity. He died in Maury County, November 16, 1846. The mother was also a native of South Carolina, born in 1797, and was for many years a faithful servant to the cause of Christianity. She died in December, 1865. Our subject's early life was passed in merchandising in Columbia. After five years of successful business transactions, he retired to the farm where he has since remained. In 1849 he wedded Martha G. H. Dawson, a native of North Carolina, and to this union were born nine children: John D., Anna E. Martha G. (who died in 1880), Ella T., Sallie R., Lillie A., Narcissa A., who died in 1883, Irene H. and Nettie. Mr. Frierson is a well-to-do farmer, having a fine farm of 250 acres, all well cultivated except fifteen acres of good lumber. He is a Democrat, a member of the I. O. O. F. and also a member of the Presbyterian Church.

WILLIS R. FRIERSON, a widely known and prominent citizen of Maury County, Tenn., was born in that county April 24, 1827, son of Thomas J. and M. A. E. (Blakely) Frierson. (For further particulars of parents see sketch of James M. Frierson.) Our subject received a good English education in the schools of Maury County, and September 29, 1851, he was united in marriage to Mary A Goodloe, a native of Maury County, Tenn. The result of this union was the birth of five children: Goodloe M., Willie T., Hinton S., Eustatia (who died May 14, 1858) and Ada V. Mr. Frierson is considered one of the successful farmers of Maury County. He has a good farm of 700 acres on the Columbia & Hampshire Pike, about nine and a half miles west of Columbia. This farm he manages in an admirable manner. Besides farming, he is engaged in merchandising and has a new business room on the pike near his elegant residence. He is a Democrat in politics and a member of the Presbyterian Church.

THEODORE FRIERSON, M. D., a well-known medical practitioner of Columbia, Tenn., and native of the county, was born April 6, 1827, son of John Witherspoon Frierson, who died at the age of twenty-one, while preparing for the Presbyterian ministry, and while our subject was an infant. He was a brother of the eminent Dr. J. W. S. Frierson, and was married to Grace Stephenson. Theodore Frierson was reared to manhood in Maury County, and graduated from Center College at Danville, Ky. He then began studying medicine with the uncle mentioned above, and later attended the medical department of the University of New York City, and graduated in 1850. He practiced in Shelbyville, Tenn., a few months, then moved to Arkansas, but owing to ill-health returned to Tennessee. He served as private parts of two years in the Confederate Army, and resided in Mississippi until the close of the conflict. He returned to Tennessee in January, 1868, and after residing on a farm in Maury County until 1880, he returned to Columbia, where he has since practiced. In 1860 the Doctor wedded Harriett A. Frierson, a distant relative of his. Their children are Grace, Walter B. and Ida. The Doctor is independent in his political views, but was formerly a Whig. He is an able practitioner. He and family are members of the Presbyterian Church.

REV. JOHN STEPHENSON FRIERSON was born in Maury County, Tenn., December 27, 1829, and is one of eleven children born to the marriage of Robert L. Frierson and Jane Eliza Stephenson, born in 1803 and 1807, respectively. The father died March 13, 1857; both he and wife were members of the Presbyterian Church. Our subject was reared on a farm and attended the Stephenson Academy, where he received a good education. In 1848 he entered Center College at Danville, Ky., and graduated in 1851. He then entered the Princeton, N. J., Theological Seminary, where he remained two years. January 11, 1855, he was married to Martha M. Jordan, daughter of S. P. Jordan, and three children were born to their union: Luther L., Mary J. (wife of J. W. Howard) and Ida J. September 10, 1866, Mrs. Frierson died, and February 8, 1870, our subject married Martha L. (Granberry) Duncan. Her parents, Mr. and Mrs. James M. Granberry, were born in North Carolina in 1798 and 1804, respectively. Two children were born to Mr. and Mrs. Frierson: John and Donna Maria. Our subject is a member of the F. & A. M., and has attained the degree of Royal Arch Mason He is a member of the "Beta-Theta Pi," a well-known literary society of the East. Rev. Frierson was formerly a Whig, but is now a stanch Democrat, and for many years has been president of the board of trustees of the Mount Pleasant Female Academy, and for several years has been a member of the board of trustees of the Columbia "Atheneum." He has been pastor of the Presbyterian Church at Mount Pleasant for the last thirty years.

JOE H. FUSSELL, of Columbia, Tenn., and attorney-general of the Ninth Judicial Circuit, was born in Maury County on the 12th of January, 1836, and is a son of Henry B. and Eliza C. (Kincaid) Fussell, who were born in North Carolina and Tennessee, respectively. Both of our subject's grandfathers, John Fussell and Joseph Kincaid were among the very early and prominent pioneers of Maury County. Henry B. was reared in Maury County and removed to Columbia when our subject was six years of age, and died here December 16, 1876. He was a carpenter by trade and was an old-line Whig in politics as long as that party existed. He was one of the founders of the Cumberland Presbyterian Church at Columbia. Joe H. was educated in Columbia and graduated from Jackson College in 1855. He taught school in the preparatory department one year and then took the chair of mathematics and languages in his old *alma mater*. He afterward had charge of the mathematical department of the old Ravenscroft School, but had been a reader of Blackstone in the meantime, and also worked at the carpenter's trade, which he had learned of his father, and taught school alternately, in order to secure means to enable him to complete his law studies. He read under Col. A. N. Looney, and Judges William Martin and A. O. P. Nicholson, and in August, 1860, was admitted to the Maury County bar, and practiced his profession until the breaking out of the war, when he enlisted as a private in Company E, First Battalion Tennessee Cavalry, afterward First Tennessee Regiment, and was made first lieutenant of his company, and the last two years of the war commanded a squadron of the regiment, ranking as captain. He served four years and was with his company in 318 engagements. After the surrender of the South he was not allowed to remain in Columbia by the Federals, owing to his refusal to take the oath of allegiance and was compelled to repair to the Barrens, where he remained a year. In 1866 he resumed his law practice in Columbia, continuing until 1870, when he was elected attorney-general, and has served by re-election up to the present time. In 1882 he was nominated by what was known as the State Credit Democratic Convention for governor of Tennessee, but was defeated by the low tax element. In 1885 he was elected president of the Tennessee State Temperance Alliance. He is now the champion of the prohibition element in the State in the fight against the whisky ring. He is making the race for judge of the Ninth Judicial Circuit, subject to the August, 1886, election. Margaret Roberts became his wife in January, 1873. Mr. Fussell is a Mason, Knight Templar degree, and is Post and Past Commander of DeMolay Commandery, No. 3, of Columbia, and is Grand Commander of the State. He and wife are members of the Cumberland Presbyterian Church, of which he has been ruling elder since 1856.

JAMES A. GALLAWAY, a native of Maury County, Tenn., was born in the Third District of that county September 1, 1832, son of James E. and Marion Gallaway, who were married December 14, 1824. The father was born August 27, 1798, and came to Tennessee soon after his marriage, locating in Maury County, where he engaged in merchandising and farming. He was a graduate of the Chapel Hill College in North Carolina and was widely known in that State and in Tennessee. His parents were James and Elizabeth Gallaway. Our subject's mother was born July 18, 1804, in North Carolina, and was the daughter of Robert and Mary Gallaway. Robert Gallaway was a member of the Old School Presbyterian Church and filled the office of county clerk for a period of forty years. James Gallaway, our subject's paternal grandfather, was born in Scotland, and was also a member of the Old School Presbyterian Church. His wife was a "Hardshell" Baptist. Our subject received a good education at Gourd Vine Chapel and Salem Academy, and began business for himself at the age of eighteen as a farmer and stock raiser. November 20, 1856, he married Prucilla J. Baird, a native of Rutherford County, born May 27, 1837, and the daughter of James W. and Sarah J. (McLane) Baird. By this union our subject became the father of five children: Sarah C., born in 1857; James L., born in 1861; William R., born in 1866; Charles R., born in 1870 and Marion V., born in August, 1874. During the late war Mr. Gallaway enlisted in Company G, Ninth Tennessee Cavalry, and was stationed at different points until 1863, when he joined Joseph Johnson's company. He then left that command and was detailed to Gen. Cherry, taking an active part in the fight from Dalton to Atlanta. He was known as one of the immortal thirteen in Forrest's old brigade. He was paroled at Greenboro, N. C., with Johnson's command, and came home August, 1865. He is a Democrat in politics.

MATTHEW J. GALLOWAY an old and influential farmer of Maury County, Tenn., and a native of this county, was born May 6, 1813. He grew to manhood on the farm, secured a limited education in the rude and primitive log schoolhouse of his boyhood days, and began tilling the soil on the farm where he is now residing. In 1837 he was united in matrimony to Susan Williamson, a native of Giles County; they had six children, only four of whom are living: Enoch W., Samuel W., Irvin T. and Julia. George B., was killed at Franklin, November 30, 1864, and Pattison J., died in 1876. In 1852 our subject purchased a farm in Perry County on which he moved. He remained there fifteen years, and then returned to this county and has ever since remained here. His parents were Enoch and Anna (Beal) Galloway, both natives of North Carolina. The father immigrated to this county about 1809, and followed agricultural pursuits. He died in 1867. The mother preceded him in 1835. Our subject is a Democrat, and himself and family are worthy members of the Christian Church.

CAPT. JOHN B. GALLOWAY may be mentioned as a native and successful farmer of Maury County, Tenn. He was born October 4, 1832, and obtained a fair education. In 1855 he took for his helpmate through life Miss Margaret Hanna, daughter of Samuel Hanna. Anna G. (wife of Rev. S. W. Haddon), Ola and John C., are the three living of the six children born to their marriage. Mr. Galloway served in the late war in Company B, Ninth Tennessee Battalion Cavalry as its first lieutenant, remaining such about two years. He was captured at the fall of Fort Donelson, and remained a prisoner eight months at Johnson's Island. After being released he was made captain of his company, and served as such until the close of the war. He was a brave and gallant soldier and officer. He and wife are Presbyterians and he is a Democrat. His parents, James and Jane (Sellers) Galloway, were natives, respectively of South Carolina and Tennessee. The father was a farmer and died in 1869, and the mother about 1864.

JAMES M. GEDDENS was born in Williamson County, March 23, 1816. His father, James Geddens, was a native of Virginia, born in 1756, and was by occupation, principally, a farmer. He came to Williamson County with his parents in 1801 and was a participant in the war of 1812. He married Priscilla Buford, a native of Virginia, who bore him seven children. Our subject grew to manhood on the farm and September 21, 1837, he led to the hymeneal altar Caroline A. Thomason, an estimable lady and a native of Alabama. To this union were born these children: James, William B., John W., Tully, Josephus T., Matthew D., Eliza H. A., and Carrie. Josephus T. died November 9, 1861, and Eliza H. A. March 6, 1874. Mrs. Geddens died May 6, 1880. She was a member of the Methodist Church and was always faithful to the cause of Christianity. Mr. Geddens was formerly a Whig in politics but is now a stanch Democrat. He has a good farm of 330 acres all under a good state of cutivation except sixty acres of woodland. He has been a member of the Methodist Episcopal Church since his seventeenth year.

JOHN H. GILLIAM, one of Maury County's oldest and most respected citizens, was born in Charlotte, Va., Nov. 24, 1800, and is the son of Thomas and Sarah (Pettnes) Gilliam. They were both born in Charlotte County, Va. The father in April 12, 1778, and the mother in 1782. The father came to Tennessee in 1806 and located in Rutherford County where he engaged in farming very successfully for two years. He then moved to Maury County and locating at Rock Springs resumed his occupation of farming. In 1812 he built the first saw-mill that was ever built on Duck River, known as the Wallace Mill. He lived there seven years and then purchased a tract of land north of Rock Spring and engaged in farming. He was a "Hardshell" Baptist and a Democrat. His death occurred October 1, 1844. The mother died September 6, 1835. Our subject began business for himself at the age of twenty-one as a farmer. January 6, 1822, he married Martha Gilliam, a native of Charlotte County, Va., born October 30, 1799, and the daughter of Robert and Estella (Marsby) Gilliam, both natives of Charlotte County, Va. By this marriage our subject became the father of four children: Sarah P., born in 1824; Edward H., born in 1825; Stephen M. born in 1828, and Charles W., born in 1833. The mother of these children died September 27, 1863, and January 6, 1867, our subject married Julia C. Jones, her former name being Martin. She was born in Maury County March 24, 1824, and is a member of the Christian Church. Our subject enjoys very good health, although in his eighty-sixth year, and has voted the Democratic ticket for many years.

ROLAND GOOCH, farmer, was born in Maury County, Tenn., August 30, 1836, son of William S. and Alacy (Jones) Gooch, both natives of Granville County, N. C. The father was of Scotch-Irish parentage, and emigrated from North Carolina in about 1820. He was a farmer and a minister of the Baptist Church. After teaching that doctrine for a number of years he became a minister in the Christian Church, in which faith he remained until his death, which occurred June 24, 1852. The mother is still living, at the advanced age of eighty-two. Our subject remained with his parents on the farm until he was twenty-two years of age, securing a good classical education. He then removed to St. Francis County, Mo., where he engaged in the mercantile business as a partner with his brother, P. H. Gooch. They had, at that time, charge of the mail route from Farmington, Mo., to Iron Mountain, at St. Genevieve. At the end of eight years he removed to western Canada, and continued the mercantile business. In 1865 he returned to his present neighborhood, where he has been engaged in farming and stock-raising ever since. In 1857 he married Nancy E. Jones, a native of Bedford County, and to them were born eight children, two of whom are dead. Those living are Mary C., Rolena, Benjamin E., Thomas R. and Ada and Bertha, who are twins. Mr. Gooch is a Democrat in politics, and himself and family are leading members of the Christian Church. Mr. Gooch has been a Master Mason since 1859.

HON. WILLIAM B. GORDON, attorney, of Columbia, Tenn., was born in Maury County, July 23, 1839. He is the second son of George W. and Elizabeth (Bradshaw) Gordon, and was reared on a farm. He secured a good education at Jackson College, graduating in 1858. He then began studying law during his leisure hours, and in 1860 was licensed to practice. In the spring of 1861 he enlisted in Capt. Hamilton's company, Second Battalion of Confederate Cavalry, which, after the first year of the war, was consolidated with the First Tennessee Regiment of Cavalry, and sometimes known as Wheeler's brigade. He was wounded and captured, June 4, 1863, near Franklin, and was paroled three months later, but was so badly disabled that he was compelled to abandon further service. He practiced his profession six months at Lewisburg, Tenn., and then returned to Columbia and became a partner of Joe H. Fussell, remaining in partnership with him until the latter's election to the attorney-generalship. Since that time he has conducted a fairly large and remunerative practice for himself. March 13, 1878, he married Miss Mary L. Franklin, of Mississippi. Mr. Gordon is a Democrat, and was city attorney of Columbia three years. In 1870 he was elected without opposition to the Tennessee State Legislature, representing Maury, Williamson and Lewis Counties. He is at present candidate for chancellor of the Seventh District. He is a Mason, Knight Templar, a Knight of Honor, and he and wife are members of the Presbyterian Church.

JAMES T. S. GREENFIELD, M. D., a successful practitioner of his native county of Maury, Tenn., was born September 17, 1831, son of Jerard Greenfield, who was born in Maryland, and came to Tennessee when a young man and married Miss Catharine Sandford. He practiced medicine, and was considered one of the most skillful physicians of the county. In early days he would frequently get lost in the canebrake, and for that reason put a bell on his horse so that he could be found when wanted. In connection with his practice he carried on farming. His death occurred in 1847, and the mother's in 1831. James T. S. Greenfield graduated from the Pennsylvania University of Philadelphia, and was one of the class of 1852. He began practicing in Maury County, and has met with well deserved success. In 1884 Miss Frances O. Lavender became his wife, and to their union three children—James T. S., Jane H. Y. and Zilpha—were born. The Doctor was opposed to secession, but being a Southern man his sympathies were with his people. He is a Methodist and a Democrat.

JOHN A. GRIMES is one of the five children of Henry A., and Elizabeth (Evans) Grimes, and was born in Maury County, Tenn., February 19, 1840. Henry A. Grimes was one of the oldest native inhabitants of Maury County, and died May 9, 1881. The mother was born in Warren County, and was a devoted member of the Cumberland Presbyterian Church. John A., our subject, received a good education in the common schools of Maury County, and was married May 9, 1866, to Miss Alice M. Moss. They are the parents of these five children: Samuel H., John B., Robert L., Archie and Minnie. At the breaking out of the war Mr. Grimes enlisted, July 4, 1861, in Company F, First Tennessee Cavalry, commanded by Capt. A. J. Polk, of Tennessee, and participated in the battles of Shiloh, Corinth, Iuka, Lookout Mountain, Missionary Ridge, Chickamauga and many others. He was taken prisoner in 1862, near Coffee, Miss., and was kept a prisoner at Alton, Ill. After being exchanged he rejoined his command at Spring Hill, Tenn., in the early part of 1863 and was paroled at Charlotte, N. C. in May 1865. He then returned to Maury County where he has since resided. He has always been a Democrat in politics, and is a member of the Methodist Episcopal Church South.

C. DAVIS HAM, a successful dealer in fine stallions and jacks, was born in Lawrence County, Tenn., November 20, 1848, and is the son of Henry and Lucinda (Burns) Ham, born, respectively, in North and South Carolina. Henry Ham was an adept at the blacksmith's trade, a nd followed that occupation in Lawrence County, Tenn., where he resided after coming to this State. The mother's death occurred on the 19th of October, 1879. She was an earnest worker in the cause of Christianity, and was a consistent member of the Methodist Episcopal Church. The subject of this sketch is the owner of the famous stallions, Cleveland, Hendricks and Black Prince, and the noted jack, Starlight. He has long made fine stock breeding his occupation and has met with well deserved success. He is a strong supporter of Democracy and is a substantial citizen of the county. He is a member of the Baptist Church.

THOMAS C. HARDISON was born in Maury County December 30, 1829, and is the son of Joel and Jane (Long) Hardison. The father, a highly respected and successful physician, was born in North Carolina October, 1800, and came with his parents to Tennessee when quite young. He married and located in Maury County, where he lived a long and prosperous life. He had a good education and was a Democrat in politics. He died December 17, 1873. The mother was also born in North Carolina in 1800, and died May 1884. She was the daughter of David and Mary Long, who died in 1846 and 1852, respectively. Our subject received a good common school education, and, May 20, 1847, was married to Frances Fox, a native of Maury County, Tenn., born March 19, 1828, and the daughter of John and Martha (Harris) Fox, who were natives of North Carolina, the former born in 1784, and the latter in 1786. To our subject and wife were born three sons and one daughter named Hampton J., born 1848; Mary J., born 1849; John J., born 1852, and James H., born in 1859. Hampton J., the eldest son, secured a fair education and began business for himself at the age of eighteen. In 1864 he enlisted in Vaughn's company Forty-eighth Tennessee Regiment of Cavalry, and was faithful to his duties. August 10, 1865, he wedded Martha E. Cheek, a native of Maury County, Tenn., born February 20, 1848, and daughter of John L. and Betsey (Rine) Cheek. To Hampton and wife were born these children: John T., born 1866; Texannah, born 1867; William W., forn 1870; Tallie, born 1872; Mary F., born 1874; Jesse P., born 1876; Melvin A., born 1878, and Hampton E., born 1884. The father of these children is a Democrat in politics and a successful farmer. In 1863 Thomas C. Hardison, our subject, was elected magistrate in Maury County and has held that office ever since. He is highly spoken of by all his acquaintances as an upright, honest citizen.

ANDREW J. HARDISON was born November 1, 1856, son of Marshall E. and Eliza A. (Olds) Hardison. The father was born in Maury County July 12, 1827, and was reared on the farm. He was constable of Maury County for several years and filled the office in a creditable manner. He was married November 2, 1853, and four children were born to him. In 1861 he enlisted in the war, but was not in the service very long before he was taken with the measles and returned home, where he remained for a short time. He was afterward captured and imprisoned at St. Louis, Mo., where he died February 28, 1862. The parents of Marshall E. Hardison were Humphrey and Harriet (Woolard) Hardison. Humphrey Hardison was a farmer, a Democrat and a member of the Christian Church. The mother of our subject was born in Marshall County, Tenn., in 1832. She was the daughter of James and Martha Olds. Her father being a soldier in the war of 1812, was a Whig and a member of the Masonic fraternity. Our subject had poor educational advantages, but made the most of what he could get. December 25, 1884, his marriage with Millie A. Hardison was solemnized. She was born in Maury County December 20, 1863, and is the daughter of Ira and Mary Hardison. Our subject is a young man but has been very successful in his undertakings, and is widely known as a good farmer and stock raiser. He is a Democrat, and his wife is a member of the Christian Church.

THOMAS A. HARRIS, a widely known citizen of Mount Pleasant, Maury Co., Tenn., was born in Halifax County, of the "Old Dominion, June 20, 1820. He is the second son of a family of three sons and three daughters born to Thomas F. and Ann L. (Cobb) Harris, natives, respectively, of Powhattan County, Va., and Granville County, N. C., born in 1770 and 1786. The father was a practicing physician, and died in his native county in 1861. The mother and father were Presbyterians in faith, and died in their native State in 1861 and 1870. Our subject resided with his parents on the farm until 1846. In 1839 he was one of the escorts of Gen. Samuel Houston from West Tennessee to the republic of Texas, which trip was made on horseback. In June of 1846 he enlisted in the Mexican war in Company C, Tennessee Cavalry. The regiment was formed at Memphis and commanded by Col. Jonas E. Thomas, of Maury County, and at Matamoras joined Gens. Taylor and Pillow's forces. They then went to Tampico, where the command was assumed by Gen. Winfield Scott. Mr. Harris was discharged at New Orleans in May, 1847. Since that time he has been farming in the Thirteenth District of Maury County. At that date he was married to Miss Sarah H. Cooper, of Maury County, and to them were born one son and one daughter: Millard F. (deceased) and Anna L. In October, 1856, Mrs. Harris died, and December 23, 1859, Mr. Harris wedded Elizabeth J. Stockard. They have one child —Virginia Lee. Mrs. Harris died October 8, 1868. For three months of the civil war Mr. Harris was second lieutenant of the State militia. The company was transferred, or forced in the rebel army, resigned and returned home. He was a Whig previous to the war, and since that time has been a strong advocate of Republican principles and gives his support to that party. He was in Washington when the news came of Robert Lee's surrender, and was in Ford's Theater at the time of the assassination of President Lincoln. Mr. Harris is an ancient Odd Fellow, and is a member of the Episcopal Church. His juvenile career was somewhat checkered and romantic, with many incidents of pleasure and hardships in thirty States and four Governments. His life since the Mexican war has been devoted exclusively to his family duties in Maury County, Tenn.

DUNCAN HASTINGS, an old and much respected citizen and farmer of Maury County, Tenn., was born October 15, 1817, in Orange County, N. C., son of John and Mary Hastings. The father was a native of North Carolina, and died in that State about 1824, when our subject was quite young. In 1825 the mother and family immigrated to this county and were among the early settlers. The mother died February 16, 1861, at the unusual age of one hundred years. Our subject remained on the farm with his mother until he was twenty-one years of age, and as the educational advantages of those early days were not what they are now, his education was rather limited. He then began farming for himself in his present neighborhood, where he remained until 1854, when he removed to his present place and has since resided there. June 7, 1858, he wedded E. N. Thomas, a native of this county, who died July 30, 1863. They had one child by this union, who died in 1862. April, 1868, he wedded his present wife, Elvira Curl, a native of Hickman County. Mr. Hastings is a Democrat in politics and a member of the Baptist Church. Mrs. Hastings is a member of the Christian Church.

SAMUEL D. HAYES, one of Maury County's enterprising citizens, was born in Granville County, N. C., September 20, 1816, son of William and Marinie Hayes, born in Kentucky and North Carolina, respectively. They were the parents of seven children: James, Eliza, Benjamin, Charles, Samuel, Whitman L. and William, all of whom are dead with the exception of our subject. William Hayes farmed very successfully in North Carolina for several years and then came to Tennessee, locating in Maury County. At the time of his death he was residing near Troy. He died in 1874. He held the office of sheriff and constable of his county in North Carolina. He was a Democrat and served in the war of 1812. At the age of eighteen years Samuel D. Hayes became overseer for John Moore in Alabama, but at the end of two years returned to Tennessee and farmed near Duck River for fifteen years. He was married, in 1844, to Fannie Smith, who was born in Virginia in 1828, and was a daughter of John and Nancy (Hayes) Smith, natives of Virginia. The father was a soldier in the late war and died in 1885. Our subject and wife have four sons and six daughters: William S., born in 1848; Nancy E., born in 1852; Eliza B., born in 1855; John D., born in 1857; Marica L., born in 1859; Martha P., who died in 1885; Fannie R., born in 1861; Mary L., born in 1863; Sarah W., born in 1866, and Samuel D., born in 1869. Mrs. Hayes belongs to the Christian Church. Mr. Hayes is a Democrat in political views.

GEORGE W. HAYES, attorney, of Columbia, Tenn., is a son of George W. and Margaret E. (Steuart) Hayes, and was born in North Carolina November 27, 1851. The parents were born in Georgia and North Carolina, respectively. The father died in the latter State and there the mother still resides. Our subject was reared and received a common school education in his native State. He followed agricultural pursuits there until April, 1881, when he began his legal studies and took a two years' course in the law department of the University of North Carolina, and was licensed to practice by the supreme court of that State. He came to Columbia in November, 1883, and began practicing in January of the next year. He is a Democrat, but has never aspired to office. His father, however, was a prominent politician in his native State, being a member of the State Legislature, and was also a soldier in the late war with the rank of colonel. Our subject is a member of the Methodist Episcopal Church South, and is unmarried. He and Archibald C. Floyd are partners in the law practice and are recognized as successful members of the Maury County bar.

HIRAM L. HENDLEY, register of Maury County, Tenn., and native of the county, was born November 26, 1838, son of George S. H. and Elvira E. (Foster) Hendley, who were born in the "Palmetto State." The father came to Tennessee in 1832, where he married and became a successful tiller of the soil. He died when our subject was five or six years of age. Hiram L. resided on the farm in Maury County until 1850, when they removed to Wayne County; thence to Texas in 1854. Five years later he returned to Maury County. He received an ordinary common school education, and in 1860 was united in marriage to Addie E., daughter of Maj. James L. Guest. At the breaking out of the war he enlisted as a private in Company A, Ninth Battalion, Tennessee Cavalry, serving until the fall of Fort Donelson, when he was captured and held a prisoner at Camp Morton seven months. He was exchanged and made first lieutenant of his old company, serving thus until the close of the war. He was in the Dalton and Atlanta campaigns, and was severely wounded in the thigh at Funnel Hill, but returned to his command in time to participate in the battle of Atlanta. After his return home Mr. Hendley clerked until 1878, with the exception of four years spent in the mercantile business for himself. At the latter date he was elected register of Maury County, and has filled that position by re-election to the present time. He is one of the board of aldermen of Columbia, and is an active Democrat. His wife died in December, 1880, leaving three sons and two daughters. Mr. Hendley is a Mason, Knight Templar degree, and is also a member of the K. of H. and the Methodist Episcopal Church South.

JAMES B. HILL, one of Maury County's most highly respected citizens, was born in Georgia May 18, 1807, and is the son of James and Jane (Robertson) Hill. The father was born in Georgia, married in that State and came to Tennessee in 1806, where he followed agricultural pursuits. He was a Democrat, a member of the Cumberland Presbyterian Church and died in 1830. The mother was born in North Carolina, and the results of her union with James Hill were eight children: Alexander, Olive, Midleton, Matilda, Thomas, William H., Jane and James B. The mother was a member of the Presbyterian Church, and died in 1840. Our subject was reared on a farm and began business for himself at the age of twenty-two, as a farmer. In 1830 he married Peggie Denham, a native of the State of Tennessee, and the daughter of Robert and Nancy J. (Turner) Denham. To our subject and wife were born three children: James E., born February 7, 1831; Nancy J., born November 12, 1832, and died August 28, 1860, and Robert H., born June 6, 1834, and died January 8, 1854. Mrs. Peggie Hill died in 1836, and in 1837 Mr. Hill married Nancy Smith, who was born in Tennessee in 1809. By her he became the father of two daughters: Sarah E., born June 2, 1839, and died June 15, 1854, and Margaret F., born March 20, 1844. Our subject's second wife died in 1846, and in 1848 he married Elmira Lancaster, who was born in Tennessee in 1811. He is a Democrat in politics, and he and wife are members of the Cumberland Presbyterian Church.

DR. J. SPENCER HILL, a young and prominent physician of Carter Creek, Maury County, and a native of this county, was born January 19, 1854, and is the son of Ashley and Mary (McKay) Hill, natives, respectively, of North Carolina and Tennessee. The father immigrated to this county when but a small boy, and served an apprenticeship at stone cutting and afterward followed that business as a profession for a number of years, cutting and engraving stone monuments. He afterward followed the vocation of farming, at which he was quite successful. His death occurred about 1869. The mother still survives him at the advanced age of sixty-six years and is a resident of the old homestead. Our subject remained with his parents on the farm until he was twenty years of age, securing a good education in the Stephenson Academy in this county, and also the Concord Academy. He then began the study of medicine with Dr. A. H. Brown and remained with him over a year. He then attended one course of lectures at the medical department of the Washington University, at Baltimore, Md., after which he returned to Columbia and resumed the study or medicine under Dr. Brown. In 1876 he attended one course of lectures at the Missouri Medical College of St. Louis, and graduated from that institution in the sessions of 1876 and 1877. He then returned to Carter Creek and began the practice of medicine at that place. April 19, 1882 he wedded Nona C. Russell, a native of Hickman County, Tenn., and the daughter of Hon. W. B. Russell. She died December 17, 1885, and left one child, Nona. Dr. Hill is a Democrat in politics and a leading member of the Methodist Episcopal Church of which he is a steward. He is a successful practitioner and his practice extends over a wide space of country.

THOMAS J. HOBBS is a son of Jordan and Martha (Nicholson) Hobbs, and was born in Maury County, Tenn., November 13, 1830. The father was born in Georgia in 1802 and the mother in Tennessee in 1803. They were the parents of twelve children, our subject being the fifth. The father was a farmer and a stone and brick-mason and belonged to the Masonic fraternity. He died in 1861 and his wife in 1884. Thomas J., our subject, began farming for himself when twenty-one years of age. November 3, 1852, he married Jane C. Coffee, who was born in Maury County March 13, 1836. To them were born the following children: John C., born in 1853; Jane A., in 1854; Martha O., in 1858; Clarence J., in 1859; Mary A., in 1862; Lizzie A., in 1864; Thomas M., in 1866; Maggie L., in 1868; Emma E., in 1871; Ernest W., in 1874; Cornelia B., in 1877, and Bertha J., in 1880 and one infant son who died. Mr. and Mrs. Hobbs are members of the Christian Church.

GEORGE S. HOGE, native of Maury County., Tenn., was born October 1, 1841, and is the eldest of six children of Moses and Eliza A. (Napier) Hoge. The father was born in West Virginia in 1799, and came to Maury County, Tenn., in 1819, locating on a farm in the Twelfth District, where he spent a long and useful life and died October 7, 1858. His wife was born in 1816. George S. Hoge received a good English education at the Mount Pleasant Academy, and in November, 1862, he enlisted in Company D, Third Tennessee Volunteer Infantry, and was in the battles of Vicksburg, Raymond, Resaca, Murfreesboro, and was with Hood on his campaign through Tennessee. He was captured at Murfreesboro in 1864, and was a prisoner at Columbus, Ohio, until exchanged at Richmond, Va., March 4, 1865. He returned home in 1865 and has followed agricultural pursuits up to the present time. March 8, 1871, he was united in marriage to Miss Leora Long, and to them one son, Willie Long, was born. Mr. Hoge has been a life-long Democrat and is a well-to do farmer.

MAURY COUNTY.

REV. JEREMIAH F. HOLT was born in Maury County October 8, 1821, and is a son of William and Mary (Powell) Holt. The father was born in Burke County, N. C., in 1778, and was by occupation a farmer. He came to Tennessee at an early day and settled on a farm in Maury County, where he lived a long and useful life. He was a member of the Primitive Baptist Church and died in 1833. The mother was also a native of North Carolina, born in 1783. She was a member of the Christian Church and passed from this life in 1862. Our subject passed his youthful days on the farm and received a good English education in the schools of the county. October, 1845, he married Margaret Ball, a native of North Carolina, and a member of the Primitive Baptist Church. She died in 1866. In 1868 Mr. Holt wedded Mary E. (Laird) Harwood, a native of Giles County, and the results of this union were these children: Albert A., Jeremiah, James M. and Robert B., all of whom are living. Mr. Holt has been a life-long Democrat and was magistrate of the Eleventh District for six years. He is a member of the Primitive Baptist Church and has been a minister for thirty-three years. He is a successful farmer, having 255 acres of good land.

JERRY HOLT is a son of William L. Holt, and was born in Maury County, Tenn., October 8, 1856. The father was born in North Carolina, May 12, 1802, and was a son of William Holt, who came to Tennessee when William L. was very young. He was first married to Harriett Snell, who died in 1842, leaving three sons. The father remained single about six years and then wedded Lucy A. Taylor, and by her became the father of four sons and three daughters. William L. was a Democrat, and departed this life March 20, 1878. Jerry, our subject, was the fourth of his family, and began doing for himself at the age of twenty-two. March 1, 1883, he took for his life companion Mollie L. Davis, who was born in Williamson County, Tenn., July 5, 1864, and is a daughter of Owen and Mary (Shaw) Davis. Mr. Holt belongs to the Democratic party and is a young man of energy and good habits.

JOHN A. J. HOWARD was born in Williamson County, Tenn., April 29, 1819, and is the son of John and Fannie (Pinkston) Howard. The father was born in North Carolina December 12, 1784, and came to Williamson County, Tenn., when a young man. In 1806 he was married and became the father of four children. The mother was born in North Carolina June 5, 1786, and died September 4, 1869. The father died October 20, 1847. Our subject began business for himself at the age of twenty-one as a farmer. November 24, 1853, he married Mary M. Denham, a native of Maury County, and the daughter of Robert F. and Eleanor (Watts) Denham. Mary M. Howard, our subject's wife, died April 15, 1869. She was a member of the Methodist Episcopal Church South, and was faithful to her Christian duties. During the late unpleasantness between the North and South our subject enlisted in Company A, Forty-eighth Tennessee Regiment—after the consolidation it was Company C, Forty-eighth Tennessee Regiment. He was in the battle at Richmond, Ky., and served fifteen months, after which he received an honorable discharge and returned home December, 1862, and engaged in farming. Our subject has held the office of constable for one term and the office of magistrate for a number of years.

JOHN W. HOWARD is a son of Thomas and Margaret (Hunter) Howard, and was born in Maury County, Tenn., April 27, 1847, and his early days were spent in laboring on his father's farm and in attending the Mount Pleasant Academy. In September, 1864, he joined the Confederate Army, enlisting in the Ninth Tennessee Battalion, and participated in the following hard-fought battles: Nashville, Franklin, with Hood's campaign through Tennessee. After the close of the war he returned to Maury County, and has since been engaged in farming and mule raising, and is doing well financially. April 24, 1877, he was married to Mary J. Frierson, who died July 1, 1880, leaving one son, William Jordan. In politics Mr. Howard is a Democrat, and belongs to the Masonic fraternity and the Cumberland Presbyterian Church. His father and mother were born in Tennessee in 1812 and 1816, respectively. The father was an agriculturist. The mother was a faithful and conscientious Christian, being a member of the Cumberland Presbyterian Church, and died July 9, 1861.

CAPT. ISAAC J. HOWLETT, merchant, of Culleoka, was born in Davidson County, April 4, 1839, son of Addison B. and Elizabeth (Clemons) Howlett. Addison Howlett is of Scotch parentage, and a prominent farmer of Davidson County, where he yet lives. The mother died in 1872. Isaac J. secured a fair education, and in 1855 began earning his own living by clerking for an uncle, S. B. Howlett, in Mooresville, with whom he remained until 1861. He then enlisted in the Confederate Army, and was captain of Company F, Forty-eighth Tennessee Infantry. He was captured at the fall of Fort Donelson, and was imprisoned at Columbus and Sandusky, Ohio. After his return home he farmed for about a year and a half, and in 1868 went to Gadsden, Tenn., and engaged in merchandising in partnership with William Linder. In March, 1871, he sold his interest and returned to Maury County, and collected for his uncle until December, 1879. He then came into possession of the store by his uncle's will, and has since carried on the business very successfully. He owns fifty acres of land and his business house and residence property. March 28, 1861, he married Mary R. Howard, and they have six children: Kirby S. (a physician of the county), Mary I., Jennie L. and Lizzie D. (twins), Minnie M. and Adah B. Mr. Howlett is a Democrat, and the family are Presbyterians.

HUNTER & CO., who creditably represent the milling interests of Maury County, is composed of James M. and Eugene D., sons of James M. and Mary (McConnico) Hunter, both natives of Maury County Tenn. The father, James M., Sr., followed the milling business all his life up to the last two years, at which time he was stricken with paralysis, which disabled him from business, and from the effects of which he has not yet recovered. He was one of the first millers of the county, and at one time owned the only water-wheel in Maury County. He was very successful in this business, and since he has retired from active life his sons have carried on the business, having erected a large four-story mill at Carter Creek, which is equipped with the latest improved machinery. Their capacity is seventy-five barrels per day, and their chief markets are Georgia, Alabama and Florida. James M. Hunter, Jr., is a native of this county, and was born December 3, 1852. He received a good common school education, and was put in the mill to work at the age of fourteen, being steadily employed in that business ever since. December 19, 1877, he wedded Georgia Jameson, a native of this county, and a daughter of William A. Jameson. To this union were born three children: Aris M., Evan W. and Fred, all of whom are living. Mr. Hunter is a Democrat in politics, and is classed among the leading business men of the county. Eugene D. Hunter was born in this county May 12, 1857. After reaching the years of manhood he began the mercantile business at Carter Creek, and operated this in connection with the milling business. November 20, 1880, he wedded Mary A. Jameson, a native of this county, and a daughter of W. A. Jameson, and to them were born three children: Bessie E., Ethel and an infant not named. Mr. Hunter is a Democrat in politics, and is an enterprising and successful business man.

J. W. IRWIN, farmer, was born in Maury County April 30, 1854, son of William M. and Fannie Irwin. The father was a native of Hickman County, Tenn., born in 1825, and was a tiller of the soil. He was a member of the Methodist Episcopal Church, and died near Macon, Miss., in 1876. The mother was born in Tennessee in 1828, and was a member of the Methodist Episcopal Church. She died July 26, 1885. Our subject's early life was passed in assisting on the farm and in attending school at the Mount Pleasant Academy. May 2, 1876, he wedded Mollie Hunter, daughter of Dr. W. G. J. Hunter, and a native of Maury County. The birth of four children followed this union: Bertram M., Knox H., Horace O. and Lelia I., all of whom are living. Mr. Irwin has been a life-long Democrat, and is a member of the Methodist Episcopal Church. He is justly considered one of Maury County's most enterprising and moral citizens.

SAMUEL E. G. JACK, a member of the firm of Church & Jack, and a prominent citizen of Carter Creek, Maury Co., Tenn., was born in Washington County, Ill., July 14, 1837, son of William and Lecey J. (Fitzgerald) Jack, both natives of this State. The father was a successful farmer, and his death occurred about 1841. The mother is still living and enjoying fair health on the old homestead. Our subject lived on the farm with his Grandfather Fitzgerald until he was about eighteen years of age, securing an education in the common schools. He then began farming on Snow Creek and was steadily engaged in that business until he was thirty-three years of age. In 1861 he enlisted in Maury Light Artillery, and remained with this company until the fall of Fort Donelson, when he was taken prisoner and and retained at Camp Douglas, Chicago, for six or seven months; was then exchanged at Vicksburg, and joined the Heavy Artillery, stationed at Port Hudson, and remained there ten months; he was then paroled and returned home. In 1869 he began the saw-mill business on Knob Creek, where he remained two years. He was then elected constable of the Tenth District, and acted as such for four years; was afterward elected as deputy sheriff for two years. He then engaged in the mercantile business at Theta, as the firm of Church & Jack, and in 1880 established his present business. In 1855 he wedded Miss Louisa Tennessee, a native of this county, and to them were born four children, two of whom are living: William E., Rosena S. G. Mr. Jack is a Democrat, and himself and family are members of the Baptist Church.

WILLIAM J. JACOBS, farmer, was born in Maury County, Tenn, January 14, 1831, and is a son of Joseph R. and Louisa (McKee) Jacobs, both natives of North Carolina. Joseph Jacobs became fatherless when but nine years of age. He was then bound out to Williamson Akins, and learned the blacksmith trade, which occupation he followed the principal part of his life. He also followed agricultural pursuits for some time. His death occurred in 1870. He started in life but a poor boy, with nothing but two strong arms with which to battle, and when the late war broke out, was one of the wealthiest men in the county. This he accomplished by hard work and close attention to business; he was the son of William Jacobs. The mother died in 1875. Our subject remained with his parents on the farm until he was twenty-one years of age, serving an apprenticeship in the blacksmith's trade, which business he followed for seven years. He was one of the many old settlers who received the rudiment of their education in the rude log schoolhouses of those early days. October 14. 1860, he wedded Ann E. Parham, a native of this county, and the daughter of Thomas J. Parham. Mr. Jacobs is a Democrat, and one of Maury County's most successful farmers. He is at present residing in the house built by Ezekial Polk, grandfather of James K. Polk.

ROBERT C. JAMESON, farmer, was born in Maury County, Tenn., September 5, 1832, and is one of ten children born to John and Elizabeth (Rauntree) Jameson. The father was born in North Carolina, and came to this county about 1816. He was a successful farmer, and secured a very comfortable competency. His death occurred in October, 1861. The mother was a native of Tennessee, and died August, 1868. Our subject lived with his parents on the farm until he was twenty-one years of age, securing a good practical education. He then began teaching school, which profession he followed until the breaking out of the war. In 1861 he enlisted in Company I, Forty-eighth Tennessee Regiment, serving as a second sergeant until the reorganization, remaining with that company until the close of the war as high private under his brother Maj. Thomas E. Jameson. After the war he returned home and began farming and stock raising on his present farm, and this he has followed ever since. December 20, 1866, he wedded Margaret R. McMeen, a native of this county, and to them were born three children: Clarence H., John W. T. and Robert C., all living. Mr. Jameson is a Democrat in politics, and himself and family are leading members of the Christian Church.

JOHN C. JOHNSON is a native Tennesseean, born in Hickman County October 14, 1844, and is a son of Andrew and Meddy (Cook) Johnson, who were also born in Tennessee. The father was a tanner and stock trader, and was considered an upright and useful citizen. His death occurred in November, 1865. The mother died in 1872 an earnest member of the Methodist Church. Our subject received a limited education in the common schools, and started in life for himself with only the means to earn his livelihood which nature gave him, and by energy, perseverance under difficulties, and economy he has accumulated a considerable property, and is the owner of 259 acres of very productive land. He was married, January 28, 1869, to Virginia Mayberry, who has borne to him eight children, seven of whom are living: William K., Horace E., Lillian A., Marvin, Ella. Tennie P. and Cordie G. Mr. Johnson served in the late war in Company A, First Tennessee Cavalry, and served until the close of the war. He was captured May 8, 1865, but was released immediately after the surrender. Mr. Johnson and wife are members of the Methodist Church, and he is a Democrat in politics.

WILLIAM J. JONES, a time-honored farmer of Maury County, and a native of that county, was born November 4, 1823, son of Willis and Elizabeth (Gee) Jones, both natives of North Carolina. The father was one of the early settlers of Maury County, and was one of the wealthiest and most successful farmers of his day. He died in 1834; the mother died one month later in the same year, at the age of forty years. Our subject on account of his parents' dying when he was quite young, was reared by his older brothers and sisters. He secured a limited education, and at the age of fifteen began farming near Santa Fe, this county. In 1861 he purchased his present farm of 1,050 acres of good land, which was part of the land granted to Ezekial and Thomas Polk for services rendered in the Revolutionary war. Our subject has been quite successful in farming and stock raising, and has one of the finest farms in Maury County. In 1841 he wedded Emily Hanks, a native of this county and the daughter of Rev. Elijah Hanks, of this county. Her death occurred in 1843. In 1845 he wedded Harriet Miller, who died about 1860. To this union was born one child—John L. In 1862 he married Lucinda McConnico, a native of this county, who died in 1877. They had six children, Walter, Minnie, Eulae E., Hallie, Alverta and Ernest. In 1879 Mr. Jones married his present wife, Nancy Evans, a native of Williamson County. Our subject is a Democrat in politics, and himself an attendant and his wife a leading member of the Methodist Episcopal Church.

JOHN F. T. JONES is a prosperous farmer of Maury County, Tenn. He was born in Bedford County, of the same State, January 15, 1843, and is a son of Lawrence and Nancy (Briante) Jones, natives of Tennessee. The father was an enterprising agriculturist of Bedford County, and is justly recognized as a worthy and honest man. December 29, 1866, John Jones, our subject, was united in the bonds of marriage to Miss Telitha Delk, and one child blessed their union, named Mary Nancy Ann. Mrs. Jones is a daughter of Jacob B. Delk, a well-known citizen of Maury County. Mr. Jones is a Democrat, politically, and was an ardent advocate for the union of the States. Although he favors Democracy he, as a general rule, supports the man and principle rather than the party. He is an Odd Fellow of the third degree; and he and Mrs. Jones are members of the Methodist Episcopal Church South.

JOHN L. JONES, attorney at law, of Columbia, Tenn., was born September 1, 1848, and after receiving a common school training entered Bethel College, Ky., and afterward the literary department of the State University of Lexington, Ky., from which he graduated. He then entered the Lebanon (Tenn.) Law School, graduating in January, 1871, and immediately removed to Missouri where he practiced law until 1878. Since that year he has been a successful practitioner of Columbia. He is an uncompromising Democrat in politics, and although he has never aspired to office heretofore he is at present candidate for attorney-general of the Ninth Judicial Circuit, subject to election in August, 1886. February 28, 1871, Mr. Jones wedded Emma J. Hamilton, of Wilson County, by whom he is the father of three sons and two daughters. Mr. Jones is a stockholder and director of the Columbia Gas Company, and is secretary of the board of directors of the *Herald* Publishing Company, of Columbia. In the winter of 1863–64 he served as private in Company A, First Tennessee Cavalry, being one of the youngest soldiers in the Southern Army, and the youngest in his regiment. He is a son of William J. and Harriett (Miller) Jones, natives of this State and county. The father, who is one of the most prosperous of the county, is a strictly self-made man, and is a resident of the Nineteenth District of Maury County.

SIMON P. JORDAN, M. D., an old and well-known citizen of Maury County, Tenn., was born in Stokes County, N. C., October 1, 1794, and is a son of John and Mary (Sapp) Jordan. The father was born in Pennsylvania about 1756, and his father was of English birth, and came to the United States when quite young. Our subject's mother was born in the same State and county as himself. At the age of sixteen Simon P. Jordan entered the university at Chapel Hill, N. C., from which institution he graduated with honors in 1818, and was a tutor in the same three years. While in the freshman class James K. Polk became a student in this college. In May, 1821, Dr. Jordan became principal of the male academy at Columbia, Tenn., and filled that position four years. While tutor in the University of North Carolina and principal of the academy at Columbia he studied medicine, and in 1825 entered the State University of Lexington, Ky., and graduated with honors in 1827. Since that time he has resided in Mt. Pleasant. In the fall of 1828 he was married to Jane T. Lawrence, born in 1809 in North Carolina, and three children were born to them: Emily, Martha and Mary, all of whom are dead. Dr. Jordan became a Mason at Chapel Hill, N. C., in 1820, and has taken the degree of Master Mason. In politics he is a Democrat.

E. T. JOURNEY was born in Maury County, Tenn., May 7, 1835, and is the son of Nathaniel T. and Mahala C. (Wantland) Journey. The father was born in Virginia March 7, 1811, was a farmer, a Democrat, and he and wife were members of the Baptist Church. He died in 1874 a highly respected citizen. His parents were William and Mary (North) Journey, who were natives of England. They were married there and came to the United States soon after, locating in Virginia. Here William engaged in the tobacco business, which he followed successfully for some years. After this he engaged in the hotel business at Petersburg, Va., but gave that up and spent the latter part of his days in farming. He died at the advanced age of ninety-five. Our subject spent his boyhood days at work on the farm and in attending the country schools. December 7, 1867, he married Virginia F. Evin, by whom he became the father of three children: Frederic A., born August, 1868, and died December, 1868; Cora L., born 1871, and William M., born 1876. The mother of these children died September 22, 1880. She was a consistent member of the Baptist Church. December 12, 1881, Mr. Journey married Esther Denham, and by her had two sons: John W., born in 1882, and Frederic V., born in 1884. Our subject was all through the war; was in most of the noted battles; was wounded at Pine Mountain, and afterward during a skirmish was captured and taken to Camp Douglas. He suffered all the hardships and privations incident to the life of a soldier, but bore up under all with great fortitude. In 1870 Mr. Journey was elected constable, which office he held until 1872. He was then appointed deputy sheriff, and held this position two years.

MARSHALL N. KERR was born in the Sixth District of Maury County, and is the son of A. M. and C. (Moreen) Kerr. The father was born in Orange County, N. C., in 1786, and came to Tennessee in 1810, locating where Spring Hill now stands. He was engaged in farming and wagon-making. In 1811 he was married, and became the father of fourteen children. He had a good education, was a Democrat, and died August 5, 1864. The mother was born in Virginia in 1796, and died March, 1854. Our subject grew to manhood on the farm, and at the age of twenty engaged in the saw-mill business. In 1862 he enlisted in Company B, Fourth Regiment Cavalry. His first battle was near Nashville, and the second at Thompson's Station. He was in the battle at Chickamauga, was captured there and taken to Camp Douglas, Chicago, Ill., where he remained nineteen months. In 1865 he was discharged, returned home and continued the saw-mill business. He married Eliza McGahey, who was born March 8, 1856, and who was the daughter of David and Sarah Orr, and became the father of one son and one daughter: Kint K., born in 1856, and Mary E., born in 1859, and died in 1859. Mrs. Kerr died in August, 1875, and in December, 1875, our subject married Mary L. Park, and had by her four sons: Andrew R., born in 1881, and Marshall B., born in 1884; two children died in infancy unnamed. Mr. Kerr is a Democrat, and is justly recognized as an honest and upright citizen.

JOSEPH B. KERR, of Maury County, Tenn., was born October 19, 1838, son of William and Mary (Crafton) Kerr, born in Orange County, N. C., in 1781, and Tennessee, May, 1800. The father was twice married, the first time to Kate Ross, by whom he reared eleven children. Mrs. Kerr died in 1826, and in 1827 he married our subject's mother, who bore him seven children. The father was a farmer and mechanic by trade, and a Democrat and a member of the Presbyterian Church. He died December 8, 1853, and his widow in 1875. Our subject began working for himself at agricultural pursuits when very young. In December, 1861, he enlisted in Company F, Forty-eighth Tennessee Infantry and served until July, 1864, being a brave and faithful soldier. May 17, 1870, he married Sarah E. Barker, who died a few years after her marriage. October 21, 1875, he led to the hymeneal altar Harriet E. Davidson, who was born in Lawrence County, Tenn., March 28, 1854, daughter of George and Mary E. (Wason) Davidson, natives of Tennessee. To Mr. and Mrs. Kerr were born the following children: William A., born 1876; Daisy E., born 1877; Pearl W. born 1879; George D., born 1881; Louisa A., born 1883, and Rose M., born 1885. Mrs. Kerr is a member of the Cumberland Presbyterian Church and Mr. Kerr of the Christian Church.

FELIX M. KINDLE, farmer, was born in Maury County September 1, 1854, son of William R. and Sarah (Cecil) Kindle. The father was a native of Mississippi, born in 1821, and was by occupation a farmer. He came to Tennessee with his parents in 1826 and settled on the farm where he is now residing. He is a member of the Baptist Church and is one of the best citizens of Maury County. The mother is a native of Ohio, born in 1818, and is a worthy member of the Methodist Episcopal Church. Our subject's early life was passed in farming, saw-milling and in attending school at Hampshire and Mount Pleasant Academy, where he received a good English and Latin education. December 2, 1875, he wedded Mollie Irwin, who was born in Maury County, and the following children were born to this union: Boyd W., William R., Cecil and Sadie. Our subject has been a life-long Democrat in politics. He has a good farm of 165 acres, and is a member of the Methodist Episcopal Church.

ABRAHAM M. KINZER'S birth occurred in Maury County, Tenn., January 25, 1822. He was educated in the common schools, and began doing for himself with little or no capital. He chose farming as his calling through life, and by his own exertions has become the possessor of 299 acres of very productive land. In November, 1844, he was united in the bonds of matrimony to Miss Elizabeth Lurk, daughter of Elias Lurk, and seven children were born to them, five of whom are living: Mary (wife of Joseph Dodson), James H., John W., Bamly (wife of Robert Ladd) and Jefferson D. Mr. Kinzer belongs to the Democratic party, and he and Mrs. Kinzer are members of the Methodist Episcopal Church South. George and Elizabeth (Mayberry) Kinzer were born in the "Keystone State." The father was an agriculturist and departed this life about 1833. The mother died in 1846.

JAMES H. KINZER was born in the county where he now resides in 1849, son of Abraham and Elizabeth (Lurk) Kinzer. Abraham Kinzer was a Tennesseean by birth and was an enterprising farmer and citizen of Maury County. James H. Kinzer was reared and educated in his native county, attending the common schools for some time. He is at the present time the owner of 200 acres of fertile and well-cultivated land, all of which he acquired by his own exertions. In 1874 Miss Julia Johnson became his wife, this lady being a member of the Methodist Episcopal Church South, and the daughter of Marvel Johnson. Mr. and Mrs. Kinzer have three children, named May F., Anna and Lillie. Mr. Kinzer is a member of the Methodist Episcopal Church South, and as a Democrat in politics has done much to assist his party.

GEORGE WHITFIELD KINZER is a son of Henry and Jane (Stockard) Kinzer and was born on the 29th of October, 1826. He resided with his parents until his marriage to Miss Mary J. Lurk, which took place November 4, 1847. She is the daughter of Elias Lurk, a well-known citizen of the county. To Mr. and Mrs. Kinzer were born eight children. The following six are now living: Emma E. (wife of Dr. W. W. Joyce), Addie J. (wife of William Flygs), John W., Marshall W., Mattie and Walter W. Mr. Kinzer was a soldier in the late war, serving in Company A, First Tennessee Cavalry, until the close of the war. He is a Democrat in politics and is a Prohibitionist in the broadest meaning of the term He and his wife are members of the Methodist Episcopal Church South, and he is a member of the Masonic fraternity. Mr. Kinzer's father and mother were born in Virginia and Tennessee, respectively. The father was a skillful wagon-maker and farmer and died in 1871. The mother died in 1867. Both were members of the Methodist Episcopal Church South.

SETH R. KITTRELL was born in Granville County, N. C., December 31, 1800, being the youngest of four sons and two daughters of Joshua and Ruth (Kittrell) Kittrell, both natives of North Carolina. The mother came to Tennessee with our subject in the fall of 1820. Our subject received a good education in Granville County, N. C. He was married, June 1, 1826, to Eliza J. Hunter, and three sons and two daughters have blessed their union: Jacob H., William A., Hinton G., Zulika R, and Larissa K. The two elder sons are deceased. Mr. Kittrell was a strong supporter of Whig principles until the death of that party and since that time has supported and advocated Democratic principles. He is an earnest worker in the Methodist Episcopal Church South, and resides on his farm near Mount Pleasant, and is considered one of Maury County's worthy citizens.

GEORGE W. KITTRELL, an old farmer and merchant of Loco, Maury Co., Tenn., was born in Sumner County that State, January 26, 1825, son of George and Elizabeth H. (Rutherford) Kittrell, natives of North Carolina and Kentucky, respectively. The father came to this State about 1800 and located in Maury County. He was a farmer and a soldier in the war of 1812. He died in 1867. The mother died in 1865. Our subject, after assisting on the farm and attending the district school where he received a limited education, farmed for one year and then enlisted in Capt. A. G. Cooper's company, of J. E. Thomas' regiment and served as a sergeant in the Mexican war until 1847, when he was honorably discharged from service. He then returned to this county and engaged in farming and stock raising. In 1850 he wedded Mary J. Walker, who was born in Davidson County and became the father of five children, three of whom are living: James B., Phelix H. and Cicily A. In 1855 he removed to Perry County and engaged in merchandising and farming. In 1879 he returned to Maury County and located in his present place. In 1879 Mr. Kittrell established his present business, merchandising, which he operates in connection with farming. He is a Democrat and has been postmaster at this present place for five years; was also postmaster and magistrate in Perry County for many years. Himself and family are members of the Christian Church and he has been a Mason since 1858.

CHARLES D. KNIGHT, a native of Giles County, Tenn., was born February 19, 1857, son of Andrew J. and Leathy L. Knight. The father was born in Georgia, and at the age of eighteen began farming for himself. His first wife was Drucilla Hardy, who died a few years after marriage. He then married our subject's mother, who bore him these children: Dewitt C., Martha J., Nancy M., Mary, Charles D., W. M., Luby, Minnie, Ellen and Andrew J. The mother was a native of Giles County, Tenn. Our subject remained on the farm with his parents until he was twenty-two years of age, after which he engaged in agricultural pursuits for himself. He was married February 19, 1880, to Sallie B. Craig; her former name was Foster. She was born December 23, 1853, in Maury County, and is the daughter of Richard S. and Sallie A. (Flemming) Foster. To our subject and wife were born three children: Minnie L., born 1881; Various L., born 1883 and Lillie, born 1885. Mr. Knight is a Democrat in politics and is much respected by all who know him.

WILLIAM H. LANCASTER was born November 29, 1818, and grew to manhood on the farm. At the age of twenty-four he began business for himself as a mechanic, in which he was quite successful. He accumulated considerable means, purchased some good land and engaged in farming. He married, January 6, 1848, Mary A. Hill, who was born December 28, 1829, and is the daughter of Middleton and Elizabeth (Cunningham) Hill. To our subject and wife were born eight children: Samuel L., William L. (deceased), Orison E., Naomi, Ella R., Mary L., William R. and Martha C. Our subject's wife was faithful in her Christian duty and died November 25, 1867. In 1868 Mr. Lancaster was married to Margaret M. Caskey, a native of Maury County, born September

22, 1827, who bore him two children: William R. and Martha C. Our subject is a member of the Primitive Baptist Church, in which he has been a deacon for twenty-five years. In 1861 he enlisted in Company A, Forty-eighth Tennessee Regiment, and served nine months. He became disabled, received an honorable discharge and came home. Michael and Susan (Anderson) Lancaster, our subject's parents, were born 1780 and 1781, respectively. Michael Lancaster was the son of Nathaniel and Hope Lancaster, and was a mechanic by trade. He was married in Buckingham County, Va., and came to Tennessee in 1808, locating in Maury County. He was in the war of 1812 and was a brave soldier. He died in 1862. The mother lived to see her children all grown. She died November 5, 1876.

FRANK D. LANDER, recorder of the city of Columbia, is a native of Hopkinsville, Ky., born February 25, 1855, but removed to Columbia, Tenn., with his mother at the breaking out of the war, his father being in the Confederate service. He completed the common branches at Clarksville, Tenn., and in 1875 accepted a clerkship in the Bank of Columbia, which position he held two years. In the meantime he began versing himself in legal lore and in 1877 was admitted to practice in the Maury County Courts. In 1883 he was elected city recorder for a term of two years and has served by re-election up to the present time. He votes the Democratic ticket but belongs to the younger and more progressive school of Democracy. He is one of the successful practitioners of the county and bids fair to succeed in his profession. His parents, Russell B. and Bettie (Dunnington) Lander, were natives of the Blue-grass State.

ADDISON LEFTWICH, M. D., is a successful physician of Hampshire, Tenn., and was born in Maury County on the 8th of August, 1835, and is a graduate of the Nashville University of Medicine, being one of the class of 1857. He began practicing his profession in his native town, and has met with the success his skill merited. March 4, 1861, the nuptials of his marriage with Miss Mary Jones were celebrated. She is a daughter of Edwin Jones, a prominent citizen of Maury County, and became the mother of eight children, five of whom are living: Francis T., Albert, Arthur, Sue M. and Anna V. Our subject advocated the union of the States in the late war, and now supports the Republican party. His wife belongs to the Methodist Episcopal Church. Our subject's parents were Dr. Joel and Mary (Thorp) Leftwich, were born in the Old Dominion, where he was a prominent physician. He died November 12, 1865, and the mother April 7, 1857. Both were members of the Methodist Episcopal Church.

GEORGE LIPSCOMB, farmer, of Maury County, Tenn., was born in North Carolina in 1813, and is a son of Archibald and Dorothea (Pembelton) Lipscomb, who were born in the "Old Dominion." The father was a well-to-do farmer of that State. His death occurred in March, 1837, and the mother's in March, 1862. Both parents were members of the Baptist Church. The father was a Revolutionary soldier, and drew a pension in compensation for his services in that war; this his wife drew up to the time of her death. In June, 1837, our subject was married to Miss Mary C. Erwin, daughter of Alexander S. Erwin, a prominent citizen of North Carolina, and one of Maury County's early settlers. To Mr. and Mrs. Lipscomb were born eight children, six of whom are living: Archibald A., Emma (wife of William H. McFall), William H., Theodocia E., Benjamin B. and Ida (wife of William J. Erwin), of Arkansas. Mr. Lipscomb served in the Florida campaign in 1836, serving as first lieutenant, and a part of the time as captain. He is a Democrat in politics, but was a Whig previous to the war. He was an advocate for the union of the States, but being a Southern man his sympathies were naturally with the South. He is a Good Templar and a Methodist. His wife is a Presbyterian.

HENRY LONG, M. D., of Mount Pleasant, Maury Co., Tenn., was born on the 28th of September, 1835, and is the second son of six children born to Lemuel and Mary (Craig) Long, natives of North Carolina and Tennessee, respectively. The father was a farmer, and came to Maury County, Tenn., in 1826, and there died October 14, 1864. Our subject received the rudiments of his education in Mount Pleasant, and afterward studied medicine under Dr. S. P. Jordan for a period of three years. In 1855 he entered the medical department of the State University of Nashville, where he pursued his studies for two years, and graduated from the Medical University in Philadelphia, Penn., with honors, March 20, 1858. He practiced his profession in Mount Pleasant until the breaking out of the war, when he was appointed by the State board of Nashville as assistant surgeon of the First Tennessee Regiment. In 1862 he was appointed surgeon of the Ninth Tennessee, and served in that capacity until the close of the war. He resided at Mount Pleasant for a brief period, and then took a course of lectures at New Orleans, La., and has since practiced in Maury County, Tenn. September 9, 1872, he was married to Fannie B. Scurlock, and an interesting family of six children have blessed this union: Henry H., Joseph S. (deceased), Clarence B., Frank, Leon M. and Katie W. (deceased). The Doctor and his wife are members of the Episcopal Church, and he is a Democrat and is a warm advocate of the principles of his party. He is a skillful physician, and has a lucrative practice.

RUFUS LONG was born in Maury County, Tenn., September 16, 1841, and is the youngest of six children of Lemuel and Mary P. (Craig) Long. Lemuel Long was a prosperous farmer, and was born in Northampton County, N. C., in 1799. He came to Tennessee in 1820, locating in Maury County. He was a strong advocate for the cause of temperance, and was noted for his many deeds of charity. His death occurred November 14, 1865. Rufus Long's boyhood days were spent on a farm. He received a good English education in the common schools of Maury County, and in the fall of 1861 enlisted in Company C, Ninth Tennessee Cavalry, commanded by Col. Jacob Biffel. He was at Lexington, Chickamauga, Spring Creek, Day's Gap, and was with Forrest in his movements through Georgia and Alabama. He was captured at Paper Mills in 1862, and was taken to East Tennessee, where he was paroled after being a prisoner only one week. He then returned to Maury County, where he has since resided and farmed. December 28, 1874, he was married to Jennie Gillespie, and four children have been born to them, namely: Archie, Washington, Eula and Katie W. Mr. Long had been a life-long Democrat, and is a member of the Presbyterian Church.

WILLIAM H. LONG, a prosperous young farmer of Maury County, Tenn., was born in Jackson County, Fla., December 15, 1860. He is the youngest of three children of Felix H. G. and Emily B. (Dickson) Long. Felix Long was born in North Carolina June 25, 1819, and when a young man went to Florida and settled on a farm, where he lived a long and useful life. The mother was born in North Carolina December 1, 1822, and died March 3, 1864, in Jackson County, Fla. She was a member of the Methodist Episcopal Church and a true Christian. Our subject received a good education in Franklin County, Tenn., and was married October 3, 1882, to Miss Elizabeth B. Long, born June 12, 1862, and to them was born one daughter, named Emily Maria Murphy Hay. Mr. Long votes the Democratic ticket, and resides on his farm three miles from the enterprising village of Mount Pleasant.

WILLIAM MACK, D. D. (deceased), late of Columbia, Tenn., was born in Flushing, N. Y., July 29, 1807. He obtained a fine classical education in Union College, Schenectady, N. Y., graduating in 1831, and pursued his theological studies at Princeton, N. J., where he remained three years. After entering upon his ministerial labors he became pastor of the Third Presbyterian Church in Rochester, N. Y., and remained such five years. In January, 1840, he came to Tennessee and took charge of the Second Presbyterian Church at Knoxville, where he continued his labors until December, 1843. He then removed to Columbia, Tenn., where he served as pastor of the Second Presbyterian Church a number of years, and was also president of Jackson College. He resigned the latter position in 1849, but continued pastor of the church till 1857. About the last twenty-two years of his life was spent in Evangelical work in Middle Tennessee, where he was beloved for his many virtues and truly Christian spirit. Dr. Mack was a diligent and painstaking student, frequently, during his college presidency, spending whole nights in study. He was an independent thinker, and a man gifted with more than ordinary culture and ability. His sermons, which were usually extemporaneous, were characterized by method, solidity and reasoning power, and were effectual in producing a most salutary and holy influence. He was instrumental in leading many young men to embrace Christianity, and his affectionate and fatherly personal appeals to them led many from the haunts of vice. Owing to age and failing health he went to Columbia, S. C., thinking that a more southern climate would prove beneficial, but his shattered health continued to fail, and January 9, 1879, his eyes were closed in their last sleep. He died at the residence of his son, Rev. J. B. Mack, of Columbia, S. C., leaving a wife and several children to mourn his loss. His daughter Mollie, who accompanied him South, was also with him at the time of his demise. He has a son, E. G. Mack, residing on a farm near Columbia, Tenn., who is an honorable citizen. Rev. Mack was an honorary member of the Y. M. C. A., and his assistance and talks did much good. His memory will remain green in the hearts of many, and his good deeds and influence will prove a lasting monument to his memory.

HENRY W. MANN was born in Marshall County January 19, 1845, and is the son of William and Mary P. (Wilson) Mann. The father of our subject received a good education and was at one time a prominent merchant in Shelbyville and Lewisburg, Tenn., but the latter part of his life was spent in farming, in which he was quite successful. He died January 9, 1853. His wife, Mary Mann, was born in Marshall County, Tenn., June 15, 1822, and was the daughter of Thomas and Martha (Goodwin) Wilson. Mrs. Mann is a worthy member of the old Baptist Church. Our subject began business for himself at the age of twenty, as a farmer. In 1861 he enlisted in Company H, Seventeenth Tennessee Regiment, and was in many battles and skirmishes. He was captured, exchanged, and acted as scout for two months. He then joined the Eleventh Tennessee Cavalry, Company E, and was in the 100 days' fight from Dalton to Atlanta, and was again captured near Pulaski as a bushwhacker, and had his choice, death or an oath. He took the oath. He then went back to Company E, Eleventh Tennessee Regiment, and remained with this until the surrender in 1865. January 28, 1869, he wedded Nancy W. Dillahay, a native of Maury County, Tenn., born February 27, 1853, and the daughter of John W. and Louisa (Murphey) Dillahay. To our subject and wife were born four children: Josie I., William T., Lee, and Edgar (deceased). Our subject is a Democrat and finished a good education at New Hope Academy.

WILLIAM G. MARTIN is a native of Sumner County, Tenn., born September 22, 1825, and reared on a farm. July 27, 1852, he wedded Mary J. Barrett, born January 10, 1841, and daughter of Wade and Amelia (Jones) Barrett, of North Carolina, and early settlers of Tennessee. The father died in 1870 and the mother in 1886. The children born to Mr. and Mrs. Martin are Ann C., Mary E., Henry B., James T., Jessie L., John H. D. and William M., and three infants deceased. She was a member of the Christian Church, and died March 28, 1876. October 24 of that year Mr. Martin married Callie Barrett, born in 1840. They have three children: June F., George E. and Amelia W. In the fall of 1862 our subject enlisted in Company E, Eleventh Tennessee Regiment, Cavalry, and served until January, 1865. He was a faithful and brave soldier. He is a Democrat and a son of Henry and Sarah Martin. The father was born in Caldwell County, N. C., in 1797, and was a son of Richard Martin, a Baptist minister and a North Carolinian. Henry Martin came to Tennessee when a young man and married a Miss Carrol, who died, leaving two daughters. He then married our subject's mother and became the father of ten children. He died in 1843 and his wife in 1870.

THOMAS T. MARTIN was born in the Sixth District of Maury County, Tenn., October 14, 1841, son of Henry and Sarah (Burnley) Martin, born in North Carolina and Virginia, respectively. Henry Martin was born in 1793, and was a son of George W. Martin. At the breaking out of hostilities between the North and South our subject (in 1862) enlisted in the Eleventh Tennessee Battalion, and participated in the battles of Thompson's Station, Chickamauga, Knoxville and Franklin, and in 1864 was detailed as special scout, and served in this capacity until the surrender in 1865. After his return home he attended school at Hartsville, Tenn., for some time, and then engaged in farming, and was married, March 3, 1869, to Mattie H. Perry, who was born in Maury County September 8, 1850, daughter of Burkley Perry. The following children were born to Mr. and Mrs. Martin: James M., born in 1871; Lizzie M., born in 1873; Sarah T., born in 1876; Lillie G., born in 1878; Burkley V., born in 1881; Ivy B., born in 1883, and Willie T., born in 1886. Our subject is a successful farmer and a Democrat, and he and wife are members of the Cumberland Presbyterian Church.

THOMAS G. MARTIN was born in Giles County, Tenn., September 27, 1831, and is one of ten children of George W. and Narcissa (Pillow) Martin. The father was born in the Old Dominion, and came to Tennessee with his parents at the age of six years, and located with them in Nashville, and was engaged in that city for many years as a wholesale dry goods merchant. He died August 19, 1854, from an accidental gun-shot wound. He was prominently connected with political affairs, and was once nominated as candidate for governor of Tennessee, which he declined. Thomas G.'s mother was born in Maury County, Tenn., in 1811. His paternal great-grandmother in the early settlement of Virginia, killed a huge black bear in a hand-to-hand conflict. She was going to one of her neighbors, and had to pass through a dense canebrake, in which she saw the huge monster reared in the attitude of battle. Realizing that to run was certain death she advanced and dealt him a blow with a hickory wagon standard, which happened to be lying near, and crushed in his skull. His maternal grandfather, Gideon Pillow, was an aid-de-camp of Gen. George Washington during the Revolution. December 21, 1854, our subject was married to Mary M. Wingfield, who died in June, 1858, having borne two children: George W. and Ellen W. November 22, 1860, Mr. Martin wedded Larissa Kittrell, and one son, Seth Kittrell, blessed this union. In September, 1862, Mr. Martin enlisted in the Ninth Battalion of Tennessee Cavalry, but was transferred to the Ninth Regiment Tennessee Cavalry, and served in the Georgia campaign. He was paroled in 1865, and returned to Maury County, where he has since resided. He is a member of the Episcopal Church.

WILLIAM R. H. MATTHEWS is a successful tiller of the soil and a native of Maury County, Tenn., and was born in 1838. Newton Matthews was born in this State, and was married to Miss Eliza Mack. He was fairly well to do in worldly goods. His death occurred March 23, 1886. His widow is yet living, and is a resident of this county. William Matthews' early education was indifferent, but by energy and economy he has advanced in the world and has accumulated some property, being the owner of a stock of merchandise and sixty acres of land. William, Fannie D. (wife of Philip Evans), Bedford L., Elenora, Juba F., Jerome, Robby and Sallie E. are the children born to his union with Fannie Garrett, which was solemnized February 16, 1858. Mr. Matthews served in the late war in Company B, Ninth Battalion of Cavalry, commanded by Maj. James Akin, serving with his company two years. Owing to impaired health he then returned home, but afterward joined the Ninth Regiment Cavalry, and served about six months, when he was again compelled to return home, and refrained from further participation in the war. He is a Democrat, and the present magistrate of his district, having served in that capacity twelve years. He and wife are members of the Methodist Episcopal Church South, and he is a Mason.

HENRY MAYBERRY is one of Maury County's successful agriculturists. He is a son of Michael and Margaret (Williams) Mayberry, and was born in the county where he now resides May 31, 1808. He resided with his father on the farm, and after attaining a suitable age began following the same occupation for himself. December 25, 1827, he was united in marriage to Miss Ella Kinzer, and twelve children were born to their union, ten of whom are now living: George W., Alice E. (wife of F. O. Howser), Martha A. (wife of James Nance), Mary J. (wife of James Hill), Robert N., Henry N., Columbus P., Margaret G. (wife of Scott Lurk), Virginia and William G. Mr. Mayberry is a Democrat and belongs to the Masonic fraternity, and he and Mrs. Mayberry are members of the Methodist Episcopal Church South. Our subject's parents were natives of Virginia, and the father was an enterprising farmer. He was a Methodist, and died about 1851. The mother was a Baptist, and died in 1876.

JAMES M. MAYES, president of the Columbia Banking Company and a prominent business man of the town, is a native of Maury County, born March 3, 1827, son of John M. S. and Rebecca S. (Witherspoon) Mayes, both South Carolinians by birth. John M. S. came to Tennessee with his father, Dr. Samuel Mayes, in 1806, locating in Williamson County, and the following year removed to Maury County. He has been a farmer all his life, and is one of the old and respected citizens of the county. His early life was much devoted to hunting, fishing and field sports, and although his fortunes suffered severely during the late war he still retains a comfortable competency, and attained his ninetieth year May 29, 1886. He served six months in the Seminole war in 1836, and was an old-line Whig as long as that party existed. At the breaking out of the war he was a firm supporter of the Union, but after the State seceded his sympathies were with the Southern cause. Two of his sons were in the Confederate Army. Our immediate subject resided on his father's farm and secured a good education at Centre College, Danville, Ky., graduating in 1848. He then began the study of law, which he abandoned six months later and entered mercantile life as a clerk. From 1851 to 1861 he was engaged in mercantile pursuits, and after the close of that conflict, up to 1875, he kept a hardware store, and then retired from active business life and took a tour through Europe. In 1878 he became connected with the First National Bank of Columbia, and has acted as its president up to the present time. In September, 1884, he became connected with the large dry goods firm of Frierson, Mayes & Co., of which his son Walter M. is active manager. In 1857 Willie B., daughter of John W. Cheairs, of Spring Hill, became his wife, and two sons and three daughters were born to their union. Mr. Mayes is strictly independent in politics, but has generally supported the Democratic party since the war.

MILES C. MAYS, one of the proprietors of the Bethel House, of Columbia, Tenn., was born in Maury County January 11, 1846, son of Miles H. and Elizabeth P. Mays, who were born in Virginia and Tennessee, respectively. The father was a successful farmer before the war, but was financially ruined during that conflict. During the close of the war he followed merchandising until the latter part of 1865, when he removed to Nashville, and from there to Dickson, Tenn., where he owned and operated a hotel until his death September 10, 1885. Miles C. Mays acquired a good education in Jackson College, being a student at the breaking out of the war. He (in 1864) enlisted as a private in Company E, First Tennessee Cavalry, serving until the conflict closed. Shortly after he engaged in the livery business, with which he has been connected ever since, R. P. Dodson being his partner. From 1872 to 1880 Mr. Mays conducted the Nelson Hotel of this city. In 1883 he managed the Bethel House, and two years later he and Mr. Dodson purchased the hotel which they have operated very successfully since April, 1886. January 20, 1885, he married Maggie Lee Shaffer, of Terre Bonne, La. Mr. Mays is a Democrat, and is an enterprising citizen of Maury County.

ROBERT N. McBRIDE, farmer and stock dealer, is a son of John and Hannah (Kinzer) McBride. John McBride was born in Maryland, and came to Tennessee at an early period, where he followed farming until his death in 1859. His wife is yet living, and is a resident of Maury County, Tenn. Robert N. McBride was born August 31, 1841, and spent his early days in attending school and laboring on his father's farm. May 12, 1871, he led to the hymeneal altar Miss Helena Williams, daughter of W. D. Williams, a prominent man of the county. They became the parents of six children, four yet living: Dora B., William D., Mattie P. and Robert L. Mr. McBride took an active part in the late war, enlisting in Company A, Forty-eighth Tennessee Infantry, and served throughout the struggle. He was captured at New Hope, Ga., in 1863, but made his escape in a few hours. Our subject is a warm Democrat, and is a Mason of the Blue Lodge degree. He and Mrs. McBride are members of the Methodist Episcopal Church South.

WILLIAM T. McCLAIN is a son of John and Elizabeth (McMillan) McClain, and was born in Bedford County, Tenn., August 29, 1820. He spent his early days in farming, and was united in marriage, July 30, 1839, to Miss Mary Coleman, a native of Virginia, and to them were born four children: Robert C., Luther, Catharine and Livonia, all of whom are dead. January 29, 1845, Mrs. McClain's death occurred. Mr. McClain wedded Mrs. Martha (Williams) Dixon August 24, 1847, and to them were born three sons: Newton, John (deceased) and Jasper. Our subject is an advocate of Democratic principles, and was constable in Maury and Lewis Counties for a perion of sixteen years. He belongs to the Cumberland Presbyterian Church and the Masonic fraternity, and resides on a farm about five miles from Mount Pleasant. His father, John McClain, was born in North Carolina March 16, 1777, and was a soldier in the war of 1812, participating in the battle of New Orleans. He died in Maury County April 5, 1881. The mother was born in the Blue-grass State, and was a Cumberland Presbyterian in faith.

CAPT. ROBERT B. McCORMICK, farmer, was born in this county May 4, 1832, son of William C. and Dorcas (Irwin) McCormick, both natives of North Carolina. The father immigrated to this county from North Carolina in 1829, and settled where Carter Creek Station now stands. He farmed for a livelihood and was quite successful. His death occurred September, 1834, at Spring Hill. He was a man of strong religious feeling, and was a leading member of the Presbyterian Church. The mother died in 1870. Our subject remained and assisted his parents on the farm until he was twenty one years of age, securing a good, practical education in the district school, and subsequently attended the Franklin University, graduating from that institution at the sessions of 1858 and 1859. He then came to his present neighborhood and established the Union University, of which he was principal until May, 1861. He enlisted in Capt. Pointer's company of the Third Tennessee Regiment, serving as a high private for about six months. He was a non-commissoned officer until the capture of Fort Donelson, when he was captured and remained in prison at Springfield, Ill., for seven months. He was then exchanged, and after the reorganization of the Confederate forces was elected captain of Company E, Third Tennessee Regiment, and remained as such until the close of the war. In 1866 he wedded Anna Adkinson, a native of this county, who died June 19, 1879. They had four children by this union; Maury M., Lizzie D., Robert B. and Dot, all living. Mr. McCormick taught school until 1868, when he engaged in the grist and saw-milling business. In 1879 he returned to school teaching, and in connection farmed to some extent. In 1883, on account of ill health, he quit school teaching and began farming, and this he has followed ever since. January 11, 1885, he wedded his present wife, Amanda Eason. Capt. McCormick is a Democrat in politics and an attendant of the Methodist Episcopal Church.

MALCOLM McDONALD, son of John and Mary (McAuley) McDonald, was born in North Carolina February 28, 1808. The parents were natives of Scotland and North Carolina, respectively. The mother died in Marshall County, Miss., in 1845. Angus McDonald, our subject's grandfather, owned a boat and followed coasting as an occupation. John McDonald came to Tennessee in 1820 and followed the following occupations: merchandising, tobacco inspection, teaching, book-keeping and farming. He was a Mason and died in Marshall County in 1853. At the age of twenty-three our subject began farming for himself. October 18, 1836, he married Caroline K. Essleman, born in North Carolina in 1810, daughter of James and Ann (Campbell) Essleman, natives of Scotland. Malcolm and Mrs. McDonald are the parents of one son, James E., who was born April 3, 1839, and died August 3, 1839. Both husband and wife are members of the Presbyterian Church, and he has been an elder for ten years.

ALEXANDER W. McDONALD was born in Maury County, Tenn., September 2, 1837, and is a son of Allen and Temperance (Henderson) McDonald, born in Maury County October 16, 1800, and March 23, 1805, respectively. After attaining his twenty-first birthday the father followed farming and attained a comfortable competency. The mother died October 30, 1848, and September 27, 1849, he took for his second wife Olivia C. Caskey. His death occurred June 26, 1862. Alexander W. has always followed the life of a farmer. In 1861 he enlisted in Company F, First Tennessee Cavalry, but at the end of three years was detailed to superintend a saddle factory, serving in this capacity until the close of the war. During his war campaign he was orderly sergeant. After his return home he engaged in the saddlery business at Culleoka, which he followed very successfully several years. He then resumed farming and the lumber and saw-millin business. At the end of a few years he sold out and began keeping a confectionery store in Columbia and was also engaged in the book and stationery business, and later sold pianos and organs. August 21, 1865, he married Sarah D. Gracy, born October 26, 1843, in Giles County, daughter of Joseph B. and Elizabeth (Bradshaw) Gracy. They have nine children: Barnet A., born in 1866; William E., in 1868; Lizzie E., in 1869; Donald G., in 1871; Alexander N., in 1873; James B., in 1875; Luther B., in 1878; John O., in 1881; and Lura, in 1883. Mr. McDonald and his family are members of the Cumberland Presbyterian Church. He is a well educated man and is recognized as an upright and honest citizen.

COL. EDWARD C. McDOWELL is a native of Fayette County, Ky., born November 5, 1840, son of Capt. John L. McDowell, who was also a native of Kentucky, and was married to Nancy Vance. Edward C. was reared and educated in Kentucky, attending both the collegiate and law departments of the Transylvania University at Lexington, Ky., and graduated in law from the same institution in 1859. In 1861 he began practicing in Memphis, Tenn., and the same year was made colonel of the State troops at that place. After Tennessee's secession he resigned this position and joined the Tennessee Artillery Corps as lieutenant, and served until July 9, 1863, when he surrendered with the army at Port Hudson, La., and was held as prisoner of war at Johnson's Island and Fort Delaware until June 16, 1865. He then resumed his practice at Memphis, where he remained until October, 1874, and since that time has resided and practiced his profession in Columbia. September 16, 1873, he wedded Bettie, daughter of Leonard D. Myers. whose sketch appears in this work. Three sons and three daughters were born to their union. Col. McDowell is a Democrat and a Scottish Rite Mason of the thirty-second degree.

SAMUEL D. F. McEWEN, a well-known merchant of Columbia, Tenn., is a native of Maury County, where he was born July 10, 1850, son of John A. McEwen (deceased), attorney at law, of Nashville. Our subject's early education was obtained in his native county. He attended Yale College two years and in 1870 started in business in Columbia as clerk in the bank of that city. He afterward became book-keeper, and for two and a half years was teller. Up to 1879 he was in the grocery business in the city. Since that time he has been a dry goods merchant, and has shared in the success of the well-known firm of McEwen & Dale. He married Margaret A. Phillips, May 15, 1873, of Monroe, La. They have two daughters. Mr. McEwen is a Democrat in his political views, and is a Mason—Knight Templar degree. He is treasurer of the Columbia Jersey Cattle Company, and secretary and treasurer of the Maury County Trotting-Horse and Breeding Association. He and wife are members of the Presbyterian Church.

ROBERT MARTIN McKAY, son of Richard A. and Eliza J. (Jennings) McKay, was born in Maury County, Tenn., June 5, 1852. His father was a well-to-do farmer of the county, and still resides in the Nineteenth Civil District of Maury County, where he is magistrate. At the age of nineteen years Robert M. began the study of law, and when twenty-one years of age was admitted to the bar and soon established a fairly remunerative practice. He is considered a safe counsellor and earnest advocate, and has won decided distinction and eminence among the leading lawyers of the State. He may properly be said to be a self-made man, and is endowed with qualities which have enabled him to surmount obstacles which would have discouraged many men. Since 1875 he has been a partner of Hardin P. Figuers, the style of the firm being McKay & Figuers. Mr. McKay is a Democrat, and is secretary of the Democratic State Executive Committee and member of the same from his congressional district. He is chairman of the Democratic Executive Committee in his Seventh Congressional District. In 1884 he was one of the committee appointed by the County Court of Maury County for the erection of the new jail. He is vice-president of the Second National Bank of Columbia and one of its directors, and an active member of the Merchants & Manufacturers Exchange of the city. He also belongs to the Columbia Board of Education, and is a Mason (Knight Templar), and was one of the committee who superintended the erection of the handsome Masonic temple of

Columbia, Tenn. In 1883 he was candidate for mayor of Columbia and was defeated by twenty-four votes, the whole number of votes being 840. Mr. McKay was united in marriage to Miss Alice F. Rankin, to whom he had been engaged twelve years.

HARDIN PERKINS FIGUERS, of the firm of McKay & Figuers, was born at Franklin, Tenn., April 15, 1849, and was educated in the Carnton High School, from which institution he graduated in December, 1866. He then began teaching the "young idea" at Gum Springs, Williamson County, continuing until 1867. The following year he entered business life as clerk in the dry goods establishment of J. L. Parks, and there acquired a thorough knowledge of business life. In the early part of 1869 Mr. Figuers engaged in the newspaper business, becoming one of the editors and proprietors of the Franklin *Review*, the oldest weekly newspaper in the State. In January, 1872, he removed to Columbia and became one of the editors and proprietors of the Columbia *Herald*. Four years later he began editing the Columbia *Journal*. In 1875 he formed a law partnership with Mr. McKay, and is one of the most trusted and successful practitioners of the Maury County bar. He is an eloquent speaker and writer, and the author of the volume "Tennessee Manual of Chancery Pleadings and Practice," consisting of 700 pages, which has won high praise from all parts of the State. Mr. Figuers is a Mason (Knight Templar) and Worshipful Master of F. & A. M. December 4, 1873, he wedded Lily Dale, who has borne him one daughter. His parents, Thomas N. and Bethenia H. (Perkins) Figuers were natives of Williamson County, Tenn.

RICHARD A. McKAY, Esq., an old and prominent citizen of Carter Creek. Maury Co., Tenn., was born in this county February 28, 1819, son of Alexander and Rebecca (Claymaster) McKay. The father was a native of North Carolina and one of the early settlers of Maury County. He was a farmer and in very comfortable circumstances. He died July 21, 1870. The mother was a native of Tennessee, and died February 19, 1850. Our subject passed his boyhood on the farm in assisting his father and in the schoolroom in securing an education. He remained at home until the death of his father, and then purchased his father's estate and was steadily engaged in farming and stock raising until 1876, when he removed to his present place. In 1870 he established a store at Carter Creek and engaged in merchandising in connection with his farming interests until about 1883. In 1882 he was appointed agent of the Louisville & Nashville Railroad at Carter Creek, which position he now fills. January 31, 1843, he wedded Eliza Jennings, a native of this county. They had eleven children, three of whom are dead. Those living are Alexander W., Robert M., Cameron H., Anna E., Sallie R., Ashley J., Thomas J. and Phineas E. Mr. McKay is a Democrat in politics and has been magistrate of the Nineteenth District for ten years; was postmaster at Carter Creek about twelve years up to the present administration, and he and family are leading members of the Cumberland Presbyterian Church, of which he is an elder. He is also a member of the K. T. Lodge.

ALONZO McKISSACK, a prominent citizen of Spring Hill, Maury Co., Tenn., was born in North Carolina January 14, 1835, son of Orville W. and Ellina (McKissack) McKissack, natives, respectively, of Tennessee and North Carolina. The father was from the family of Archibald M. McKissack, who was one of the pioneer settlers of this State, and still survives at the advanced age of seventy-seven. The mother also survives at the age of seventy. Our subject remained with his parents until he was twenty-one years of age, securing a good school education at Cumberland University, and graduated from the law department of that institution in 1861. May, 1861, he enlisted in Company F, Third Tennessee Regiment, serving as an orderly sergeant and remaining as such until the close of the war. He was a prisoner six months at Fort Donelson, eleven months at Fort Delaware, seven months at Fort Lookout and four months at Fort Elmira. At the close of the war he returned to Maury County and began farming, which occupation he followed for two years, after which he engaged in the dry goods business at Spring Hill. In 1873 he established his present business, carrying a full and complete line of drugs and medicines and has been quite successful. September 1, 1880 he wedded Miss Almira Hardeman, a native of Williamson County, Tenn. He is a Democrat and he and wife are members of the Methodist Church.

SAMUEL H. McKNIGHT, M. D., was born in Maury County, Tenn., December 25, 1846, son of Augustine and Keziah (Roper) McKnight, who were born in North Carolina and Tennessee, respectively. The father was a much respected and well-to-do farmer and departed this life in 1888. The mother died in 1869. Samuel H. McKnight received the rearing and early education of the average farmer's boy, and later attended the medical department of the Vanderbilt University, at Nashville, Tenn., and graduated from that institution in 1881. He immediately began practicing his profession in his native county and is doing well. In 1868 he took for his life companion, Miss Mary McKnight. Luther, Lelian, Cora, Kate, Samuel, Mattie Lee and two deceased are the children born to this union. Dr. McKnight served in Company B, Ninth Tennessee Battalion, Cavalry, from the time of his enlistment until the close of the war. He has been a licensed Methodist minister for fifteen years, and belongs to the Republican party.

JOHN D. McLEMORE, farmer of Maury County, and a native of Williamson County, was born April 12, 1832, and is one of nine children born to A. J. and M. S. (Debrey) McLemore, natives, respectively, of North Carolina and Tennessee. The father was a farmer by occupation and came to Williamson County at an early day His death occurred in 1849, and his wife followed soon after. He was the son of Robert McLemore, who was of Scotch-Irish parentage. Our subject remained with his parents until he was twenty-one years of age, securing a common school education. He then began farming on his father's tract and remained with his mother until her death. He then went into the grocery business at Thompson's Station, at which he remained for three years. He then removed to this county and located close to Columbia, where he engaged in farming and stock raising. In 1862 he enlisted in McLemore's company, Starn's regiment, as a high private, but was discharged in 1863 on account of bad health. He then returned home and was assigned a position in the commissary department at Columbia. In 1866 he moved back to Williamsom County, where he engaged in farming and stock raising until 1884, when he removed to his present place, and he has been steadily engaged ever since in farming and stock raising. December 8, 1858, he married Lesey Pope, a native of Williamson County, and to them were born seven children, only four of whom are now living: Atkins P., Sidney G., Jamie and Robina. Mr. McLemore is a Democrat in politics, and himself and family are leading members of the Presbyterian Church, and he has been a member of the Masonic Lodge for twenty-four years, and is also a member of A. O. U. W. He is one of Maury County's best citizens.

LEMUEL P. McLEMORE, an energetic farmer, was born in Maury County, Tenn., April 23, 1841, and is a son of A. J. and M. S. (Debrey) McLemore. [For further particulars of parents see sketch of John D. McLemore]. Our subject secured a good practical education in the common schools, and remained with his parents until he was sixteen years of age. He then resided with his brother until the close of the war. In 1872 he purchased his present farm on which he has resided ever since, engaged in farming and stock raising. November 14, 1872, he wedded Lesey M. Frierson, a native of this county, and by this union is the father of two children: Wickliffe F. and Mary M. Mr. McLemore is a Democrat in politics, and himself and family are members of the Methodist Church. He is one of the most enterprising farmers of the county, and is justly recognized as a moral, upright citizen.

JOHN A. McMEEN, a successful farmer of Maury County, Tenn., and a native of this county, was born January 21, 1838, and is a son of Thomas F. and Elizabeth (McKay) McMeen, both of whom were natives of this State. The father was a tiller of the soil, and in connection with this carried on a blacksmith shop His death occurred May 12, 1854. The mother died March 10, 1849. Our subject grew to manhood on the farm, and secured but a limited education. At the age of nineteen he began merchandising, and followed this business three years, after which he began farming. In 1861 he was engaged in the commissary department of the Confederate Army, and February 9, 1863, he enlisted in Company G, First Tennessee Heavy Artillery, serving with them until captured at Port Hudson. He was then kept prisoner at St. Louis a short time, and was afterward stationed at Camp Morton, Indianapolis, Ind., where he remained until the close of the war. He then returned to Tennessee, and engaged in farming until 1880, when he removed to his present place, and he has been steadily engaged in farming and stock raising ever since. November 14, 1859, he wedded Harriet D. Cook, a native of Kentucky, and to this union were born five children, only three of whom are now living: Thomas S., John W. and Charles W. Charley died in 1870, and Ashley in 1868. Mr. McMeen is a Democrat, and himself and family are members of the Cumberland Presbyterian Church.

WASHINGTON W. MILLER, an old and prominent farmer of Maury County, Tenn., and a native of that county, was born March 21, 1811, and is the youngest son of John and Catharine (Hall) Miller, both natives of Virginia. The father immigrated to this country in 1806, and was an extensive farmer. His death occurred in 1848. The mother died when Washington W., our subject, was but a small boy. He passed his early life on the farm, and had no such school advantages, in the rude log schoolhouses of his boyhood days, as exist at present. Nothwithstanding all these drawbacks he secured a good practical education. In 1851 he removed to his present place, on which he has been steadily farming ever since. In 1837 he was married to Susan Hadley, a native of this State, and to this union were born four children, only two of whom are living: John A., and Jemima S. Melville J. died in 1878, and William C. was killed in the army in 1863. Mrs. Miller died August, 1884, at the advanced age of seventy-one years. Our subject is a Democrat in politics, and is classed among Maury County's oldest and most honorable citizens.

WILLIAM F. MOORE, an old and influential citizen, was born in Maury County, Tenn., January 22, 1817, son of Matthew and Sarah (Smith) Moore, natives, respectively, of North Carolina and Virginia. The father moved to this county from North Carolina in 1807 or 1808 and was a farmer of considerable note. He held the position of magistrate of the Third District for thirty-five years. He died in 1839, was a Democrat in politics and the son of Reuben Moore, of North Carolina, who was a soldier in the Revolutionary war. The mother of our subject died about 1865. William F. was reared on the farm with his parents until he was sixteen years of age, securing a good common school education. At that age he began clerking in the mercantile business at Columbia, where he remained for seven or eight years. He then went in business for himself, at which he was very successful. In 1848 he moved back to the farm but at the same time carried on his dry goods business at Columbia. In the same year he wedded Nannie Boyd, a native of this county, and to them were born twelve children, ten of whom are now living: Mary J., Dora M., William L., Imogene, Lillie B., Laird B., Julia R.. Robert S., Walter and Lucy. Matthew B. died in 1850 and John in 1860. In 1853 Mr. Moore sold out here and removed to Texas, where he was engaged in the cotton business and also in stock raising. In 1860 he returned to the old homestead where he now resides. He is a Democrat in politics and has been a member of the Masonic lodge for upward of forty years.

LEONARD D. MYERS (deceased) was a native of Alabama, born May 1, 1821. He was reared in his native State and educated in the East Tennessee University at Knoxville. He removed to Columbia in 1845 and read law under Judge Edmund Dillahunty, and was admitted to practice at the Maury County bar in 1847 and remained in the practice of his profession here until his death May 14, 1876. He married Sara H. Caruthers, of this county, a member of the distinguished family of that name, who, with four daughters, still survives him. He was an active Democrat but never aspired to political honors. He served as a private in the Confederate Army, in the Ninth Tennessee Battalion. Although not a member of any religious denomination he was a firm supporter of Christianity and contributed generously to all religious and charitable enterprises. He was an enterprising, liberal-minded citizen and was remarkable for a retentive memory. His mind was stored with legal lore, ready at his bidding, and he was acknowledged as the leading practitioner of the Maury County bar for a number of years and had a State reputation for legal ability. He was a man of strong convictions and manly resolutions, and was noted for his devotion to his friends. His nature revolted at anything that tended to lower the standard of higher manhood, and yet the gentler elements of his nature, guided by charity for all, softened the rude asperities of life.

T. P. NOWLIN, M. D., is a well-known and prominent physician of Maury County, Tenn., was born in what is now Alcorn County, Miss., January 30, 1853, son of Janway W. and Sarah H. (Williams) Nowlin. The father was a native of Marshall County, Tenn., and was a dry goods merchant in Nashville for a number of years. The mother was a native of Nashville and a member of the Methodist Episcopal Church. In 1861 our subject and his father came to Lawrence, Tenn., located on a farm and engaged in a tannery. In 1870 he entered the Farmington Academy where he received a good education. In 1871 he began the study of medicine under Dr. J. S. Swanson, with whom he remained two years and in November, 1873, entered the medical department of the Vanderbilt University of Nashville, Tenn., from which he graduated with honors in February, 1880, and since that time, has followed his profession in Maury County. November 29, 1876, he was married to Callie M. Payne and one daughter was born to them, named Mattie Lee (deceased). November 15, 1878, Mrs. Nowlin died. She was a member of the Methodist Episcopal Church South and was a devoted Christian. November 7, 1883, Dr. Nowlin wedded Fannie S. Payne. The Doctor belongs to the Democratic party and is a well-known and successful physician of Maury County.

DR. HILLARY L. OLIVER, a successful practitioner, was born in Maury County, Tenn., December 8, 1828, and is the son of Hezekiah and Mahala (Lewis) Oliver. The father was born in Virginia in 1787, was married in 1822 and came to Tennessee in 1825. He located in the Fourth District in Maury County, and engaged in farming and school teaching. He was a member of the Methodist Episcopal Chuch South for over sixty-years. He was a Democrat and was in the war of 1812. The mother was also born in Virginia in 1800 and was a member of the Methodist Episcopal Church South. By her union with Hezekiah Oliver she became the mother of six sons and two daughters. The mother died in 1840 and the father in 1867. Our subject grew to manhood on the farm and obtained a good English education. At the age of twenty-one he began farming for himself and in 1855 began the study of medicine. He graduated in his medical studies at New Orleans School of Medicine in 1860. December 19, 1867, he wedded Valderia A. Dillehay, a native of Maury County, Tenn., born in 1850, and the daughter of Marcus G. and Mary (Lancaster) Dillehay. Our subject became the father of nine children—six sons and three daughters—named G. Meldon, Emma L., Dalton A., Edith, Milton L., Ethel (deceased), Hillary G., Carl L. (deceased), Hubert L. In 1861 our subject was elected captain of a volunteer company, and at the organization of the regiment was elected lieutenant-colonel of the Fifty-second Tennessee Regiment. After remaining in the service for four months he received an honorable discharge and returned home. He is a Democrat in politics and is highly spoken of by all.

WILLIAM L. ORMAN, an old and prominent citizen of Spring Hill, Maury Co., Tenn., was born in that State December 25, 1817, and is the eldest child of Adam and Martha (Reams) Orman, natives, respectively, of North Carolina and Virginia. The father came to Williamson County about 1814, and followed agricultural pursuits as a livelihood. His death occurred about 1850. The mother followed in 1874. Our subject received a good common school education, and after attaining the years of manhood served an apprenticeship at the carpenter and cabinet trade, making that business a profession until a few years ago, and at which he was quite successful. In 1840 he led to the hymeneal altar Mary North, a native of Tennessee, who died about 1850. They had five children by this union, three of whom are living, viz.: William E., Robert and Rhoda. In 1853 Mr. Orman married Sarah Childress, a native of this county, who died in 1873: They had seven children by this union, viz.: James S., Maggie, Anna L., Henry, Sallie B., Jannie C. and Julia, all of whom are living. Mr. Orman was an old-line Whig in politics, but at the present time does not bother much about politics. Himself and family are consistent members of the Cumberland Presbyterian Church. Mr. Orman is classed among the leading men of the county.

GEORGE W. PARK, a prominent farmer and a leading citizen of Maury County, was born October 1, 1840. He is the son of J. J. A. and Althere E (Oliver) Park, was reared on a farm and was attending school at the commencement of the war. In 1861 he enlisted in Company F, First Tennessee Regiment, served throughout the war in that company and was in many battles. After the war he engaged in farming for one year. He then engaged in the milling and general merchandise business. He has been ticket, express and freight agent, and also postmaster at Park Station, where he is now living. He obtained a fair country school education and was married, August 28, 1866, to Adelia C. Lancaster, who was born August 28, 1846. To this union was born, December 17, 1867, one child, Erastus J. Mrs. Park was a devoted wife and mother, and was a member of the Cumberland Presbyterian Church. She died March 17, 1870, and December 15, 1870, our subject was married to Emma C. Wright, her former name being Emma C. Denton. She was born in Maury County, Tenn., September 3, 1849, and by her union with Mr. Park became the mother of these children: Thomas H., Martha E., George W., Cordie D. and Katie L. Our subject has built up a very thriving business, and has accumulated sufficient means to enable him to enjoy the comforts of life. In politics he is a Democrat.

JAMES S. PERRY, farmer, was born June 2, 1826, and remained with his parents on the farm until he was twenty-one years of age, securing a good common school education. He then began farming for himself in the southern portion of the county, near Bigbyville, where he remained but a few years. He then leased a farm near Columbia, on which he remained until the breaking out of the war. In 1863 he enlisted in Company G, Ninth Tennessee Cavalry, serving as a high private for a short time. He was afterward engaged in the commissary department, and remained in this capacity until he was captured and paroled in 1864. He then returned to Hickman County, remaining there a few days. Previous to this, in 1853, he had wedded Susan Hamilton, a native of Davidson County, and to this union was born one child—Susan D. Mrs. Perry died November 21, 1855, and January, 1859, he wedded Ann Smoot, a native of this county and a daughter of Dr. Smoot. To this union were born two children, Annette and Maggie A., who died January 20, 1885. The second Mrs. Perry died in May, 1871, and, December 21, 1876, Mr. Perry married his present wife, E. J. Elvira Sellers, a native of this county and a daughter of Hardy Sellers. They have one child by this union—Alma A. T. After the death of his first wife, Mr. Perry taught school for six years, and, in 1877, he purchased his present farm, on which he has since lived. He is a Democrat in politics and has the confidence and esteem of all who know him. He is the son of Simpson and Elizabeth (Thompson) Perry, natives, respectively, of North Carolina and Tennessee. The father was a farmer and died September 6, 1859. He was the son of William Perry, who emigrated to this State about 1803. The mother of our subject died in 1880, at the advanced age of eighty-two.

NATHAN PERRY, M. D., is a son of William Perry, who was a native and farmer of North Carolina, and there wedded our subject's mother, Elizabeth Shaw. William died in 1822 and his wife, who was a consistent member of the Methodist Episcopal Church, died in 1846. Nathan Perry, when a young man, began reading medicine with Dr. John H. Crisp, of Salem, Miss., and afterward attended the famous University of Pennsylvania, at Philadelphia, from which institution he graduated. He then returned to his native county, where he has since successfully practiced his profession. In October, 1849, his marriage with Miss Mary J. Amis was solemnized, and to their union eight children—Nancy E. (wife of Leroy Scott), Charles A., Josiah A., Willie A., Lena, John S., Lulu J. and Katie C.—were born. In 1884 Dr. Perry was called upon to mourn the death of his wife. He is a member of the Methodist Episcopal Church South, and is a Mason of the Royal Arch degree. In politics he is a Democrat.

LEWIS C. PICKARD may be mentioned as one of Maury County's worthy tillers of the soil. He is a native of the county, born July 22, 1848, and is the eldest of six children of Alex S. and Rachel (King) Pickard. The father was born in North Carolina and came to Tennessee, locating on a farm in the Twelfth District of Maury County, where he died in 1869. His mother was always a resident of Maury County and was an earnest worker in the Cumberland Presbyterian Church. The nuptials of our subject's marriage to Miss Sally Craig were celebrated February 15, 1872, and they have rejoiced in the birth of eight children—four sons and four daughters: William A. (deceased), Herbert B., Hardy O., Joseph L., Josie C. (deceased), Mary D., Katie G. and Sallie F. Mr. Pickard supports the principles of the Democratic party. He resides on his farm near Mount Pleasant, and is a good farmer and honest citizen.

ANTHONY L. PILLOW, M. D., of Columbia, Tenn., was born in Maury County, October 7, 1819, son of Abner and Mary S. (Thomas) Pillow, of North Carolina and Virginia, respectively. They were early settlers of Tennessee, the grandfather, John Pillow, having settled near Nashville when it was a small place. Abner Pillow's brothers were Col. Way Pillow, Gideon and Mordica, Gideon being the father of Gen. Gideon J. Pillow. Abner Pillow, who was a farmer and practical surveyor, was engaged in locating lands. He was a magistrate, and at one time was deputy sheriff of the county. He was an old line Whig in politics, and died in the fall of 1860. Anthony L. Pillow was reared and secured a good literary and classical education in Maury County. In 1841 he began studying medicine, and graduated from the Jefferson Medical College of Philadelphia, Penn., in 1845, and began practicing in Columbia the same year. The Doctor has also given some attention to farming, and was a Whig before the war, but is now a Democrat. In 1847 he wedded Mary F. Young, of Maury County, who died in 1873, leaving three children: Evan Y., Eugene and James C. (deceased).

EVAN Y. PILLOW, clerk of the Maury County Circuit Court, was born in the old residence of James K. Polk at Columbia, Tenn., October 12, 1848, son of Dr. Antony L. and Mary F. (Young) Pillow. Evan Y. was reared in Columbia, and received a collegiate education in Lee College, of Lexington, Va., then under the control of Gen. Robert E. Lee. In 1870 he began storing his mind with legal lore, studying under the direction of Hon. James H. Thomas. He was admitted to practice in the Maury County courts in 1872, and did so until 1877, when he was elected to the office of city recorder, which office he held by re-election until the latter part of 1878. He then resigned and made the race for circuit court clerk, and was elected the same year. He served a term of four years so faithfully and efficiently that he was re-elected in 1882, and is now discharging the duties of that office. Mr. Pillow is a Democrat of the younger and more progressive class, and has taken an active and leading part in the political campaigns during the last ten years. He is a Mason of the Royal Arch degree, and is a member of the Episcopal Church, and is prominently connected with the public and private enterprises in city and county.

ROBERT PILLOW, M. D., Columbia, Tenn., is a native of this city, born April 4, 1852, son of William H. and Elizabeth T. (Porter) Pillow, who were Tennesseeans by birth. The father was a well-known and prosperous money speculator of Columbia, and died December 5, 1864. He was at one time constable and deputy sheriff, and was an old-line Whig and a firm supporter of the Union during the late war. Robert Pillow was reared in Columbia, and finished his education in the Davidson (N. C.) College. In 1870 he became a medical student under Dr. A. L. Pillow, and later attended lectures in the medical department of the University of Pennsylvania, graduating March 12, 1874, as an M. D. He then began practicing with his uncle and former preceptor, and in 1879, in connection with W. P. Woldridge, engaged in the drug business, continuing two years. Dr. Pillow has been a successful practitioner, and is a "Sky Blue" Democrat in politics. He is a Mason of the Knight Templar degree, and is Eminent Commander of De Molay Commandery, No. 3, of Columbia. October 7, 1885, he was married to Miss Sara R. Parrott, of Cartersville, Ga.

JAMES M. PHILIPS, citizen of Maury County, Tenn., was born in Williamson County June 3, 1846, and is the son of Jesse H. and Margaret J. (May) Philips, natives of Davidson County, Tenn., born in 1812 and 1816, respectively. Jesse Philips followed farming throughout life, and was married in 1836, becoming the father of two sons and four daughters: Mary W., Mattie H., Hugh L., Annie B., James M. and Eliza M. The father was a Whig in politics, and was one of the most successful farmers of Williamson County. He died in October, 1852, mourned by many friends. Our subject was engaged in the merchandise business in Nashville in 1871. In 1872 he married and engaged in farming in Williamson County for several years, and moved to Maury County in 1882, where he has since been engaged in tilling the soil. He was married to Madora Owen, who was born July 19, 1852, daughter of John C. and Judy A. (Davis) Owen. To Mr. and Mrs. Philips were born three sons: Robert L., born in 1873; Jesse H., born in 1876, and John O., born in 1883. The father and mother are devoted members of the Christian Church. Mr. Philips is a Democrat, and is much respected and esteemed by all his friends.

GEN. LUCIUS E. POLK, a well-known and respected farmer and citizen of Maury County, Tenn., was born in North Carolina July 10, 1833, son of William J. and Mary R. (Long) Polk. The father was a native of North Carolina, born in 1794, and was by occupation a farmer. He came to Tennessee in 1836, and settled in the Twenty-second District of Maury County, where he remained one year, after which he moved to Columbia and lived there until his death, which occurred in 1860. The mother was a native of North Carolina, born in 1797, and was a consistent member of the Episcopal Church. She died at Columbia in 1885. Our subject's early life was passed on the farm. In 1849 he entered the University of Virginia at Charlottesville, and remained there until 1852, securing a good classical education. In April, 1861, he enlisted as a private in the Confederate Army, First Company of Yell's Rifles of Arkansas. In July following the company was transferred to Company B, Fifteenth Arkansas Volunteer Infantry. Our subject was in the battles of Shiloh, Richmond and Perryville, Ky., and Murfreesboro, Chickamauga, Missionary Ridge and Ringgold Gap, Ga., where he displayed the greatest efforts of his military career. April 11, 1862, for gallant services rendered at the battle of Shiloh, he was promoted to the rank of colonel of his regiment. In the following December he was promoted to the rank of brigadier-general, in which capacity he served until the close of the war. He was paroled at Courtland, Ala., in June, 1865, and immediately went to his home in Arkansas, where he engaged in agricultural pursuits. August 19, 1863, he wedded Sallie M. Polk, a native of Lauderdale County, Ala., and the birth of four sons and one daughter followed their union: Rufus K., Mary R., Lucius E., William J. and James K., all of whom are living. Mrs. Polk was born September 2, 1843, and is a consistent member of the Episcopal Church. In 1866 our subject came to Tennessee and settled on a farm in the Eleventh District of Maury County, where he has since resided. He was president of the Columbia Central Turnpike for three years, and for a like number of years was its efficient secretary and treasurer. He has a farm of 900 acres, all under a good state of cultivation. Politically he has been a life-long Democrat, and was magistrate of the Eleventh District for one year.

WILLIAM T. PORTER is a merchant and farmer of Maury County, Tenn., and was born in Williamsport in 1836, son of Dr. Samuel and Catherine (Todd) Porter, born in South Carolina and Virginia, respectively. The father was a successful practitioner of Williamsport for forty years. He was a soldier in the war of 1812, and died in 1873. His widow draws a pension from the Government in compensation for his services. William T. was a school teacher for thirteen years, and was married, September 11, 1866, to Mary Jane Russell, daughter of M. M. Russell, a prominent citizen of the county. Eight sons were born to them: Otey J., Madison R., Samuel S., Walter J., Hugh V., Joseph F., Henry A. and one deceased. In 1862 Mr. Porter enlisted in Company C, Ninth Battalion Tennessee Cavalry. He served as hospital steward for four months previous to his enlistment, and soon after that time was made quartermaster-sergeant, and served in this capacity throughout the war. Mr. Porter is a warm Democrat, and has represented his county two years in the State Legislature, and while there introduced a bill to repeal the corporation charter of Williamsport. His motive was to banish whisky from the town. The bill was hotly contested by both sides, but was passed. Mr. Porter is a Mason of the third degree, and he and wife are worthy members of the Methodist Church.

AUSTIN W. POTTER, an old and influential farmer of Maury County, Tenn., was born September 29, 1811, in Williamson County, Tenn., and is one of six children born to

Donaldson and Jane (Wright) Potter, natives, respectively, of Ireland and Virginia. The father, a man of strong mind and undoubted piety, settled in this county and was a minister of the Protestant Methodist Episcopal Church. He was for many years the only resident preacher in the neighborhood, and almost every Sunday he had an appointment to preach either at some private house or under the wide-spreading branches of the tall trees of the forest. In 1806 he removed to this State, and in 1865 his second wife, the mother of our subject, died. Donaldson Potter died in 1849. Our subject was a farmer boy and secured a good classical education in Jackson College, of this county. After attaining the years of manhood he began teaching school in this county. He afterward taught school in Williamson County for six months and then began the mercantile business at Spring Hill, beginning as clerk for his brother, but afterward entered the firm as a partner. In 1849 he was united in marriage to Amanda Ellen Haddox, a native of Kentucky, who died June 7, 1881. She was a noble woman, and her death is deeply regretted. She was the mother of four children: Ellen F., Andre J. (deceased), Mary A. and Austin W., Jr. In 1850 our subject began trading in mules, and this he continued until the breaking out of the war. After the war he began farming and stock raising on the farm where he is now residing, which consists of 796 acres. Mr. Potter is a Democrat in politics and was appointed postmaster at Spring Hill in 1845 by James K. Polk, and remained as such until he resigned in 1850. He and family are leading members of the Christian Church, and he has been a Mason for many years.

THOMAS J. REA is a son of John and Mary (Ussery) Rea, who were both Tennesseeans by birth. The father was a prosperous farmer and was considered a substantial citizen of Maury County. His demise occurred in 1862. The mother still survives and makes her home in Giles County, where our subject was born, in 1845. He attended the common schools near his home and started in life for himself with a small capital. By all the virtues necessary to success in worldly affairs he has become the owner of 339 acres of very productive land and two houses and lots in Columbia. John C. and Nannie B. are the children born to his marriage with Miss Luira Locke, which was solemnized in 1869. Mrs. Rea is a daughter of W. A. Locke, a prominent citizen of Giles County. Mr. Rea was a participant in the late war, serving in the Ninth Tennessee Cavalry about three months, when his company was disbanded and he returned home. He and Mrs. Rea are members of the Cumberland Presbyterian Church, and he is a Democrat, politically.

R. H. REESE may be mentioned as a skillful wheelwright and carpenter of Maury County, Tenn. He is a son of M. J. and Elizabeth (Cook) Reese, who were born in Alabama and Tennessee, respectively. J. M. Reese was also a wheelwright by trade and followed that occupation in Tennessee until his death April 21, 1866. He belonged to the Presbyterian Church. The nuptuals of our subject's marriage to Jane Roach, daughter of John M. Roach, a prominent citizen of Maury County, was celebrated on the 21st of November, 1882. Two children were born to them, only one of whom is now living, Addie E. Mr. Reese is a Democrat and gives his support to that party on all occasions. He and wife are among the respected and esteemed citizens of Maury County. His birth occurred November 25, 1852.

JAMES S. RENFROE'S birth occurred in Maury County, Tenn., February 14, 1818, son of William and Eliza A. (Craftin) Renfroe, the former born in South Carolina in 1798, and the latter in Virginia in 1800. The grandparents of our subject were early pioneers of this county and State, and the father was married at the age of nineteen, and became the father of eleven children, James S. being the eldest. He was constable of this county several terms and died in 1846. His wife died in 1856. Our subject was reared on a farm. In 1848 he was married to Delia R. Calvert, who was born in Maury County, in 1824, daughter of Joseph W., and Catharine (Lawrence) Calvert. William C., born in 1849; Narcissa E., born in 1851; Eliza C., born in 1855; Joseph S. and Mary D., born in 1858, and Alice D., born in 1864, were the children born to this union. Mrs. Renfroe died October 28, 1872, and her husband remained single until 1883 when he married Sarah M. (Collier) Davis. She was born in 1829 and is a daughter of Archie and Mary (Hight) Collier, and a member of the Methodist Episcopal Church South. Mr. Renfroe has been an elder in the Baptist Church for twenty-five years. He has been magistrate of his district for twenty-six successive years, and is a Democrat, and belongs to the I. O. O. F.

WEBB RIDLEY, JR., is a well-to-do young farmer of Maury County, Tenn., and was born on the 15th of January, 1859. He is the eldest of four children born to J. W. S., and Annie (Pillow) Ridley. Both parents were born in Maury County; the father, December 31, 1824. He was a tiller of the soil in the Ninth District. The subject of our sketch was a student in the Mount Pleasant Academy until 1875, when he entered the Central University of Richmond Ky., where he received a good English, Latin and German education. He then returned to his father's farm, and on the 26th of September, 1883, was united in matrimony to Miss Madge Whitney, a resident of Montgomery County, Ky. She is a member of the Christian Church and is an earnest worker in that faith. Mr. Ridley has a good and well cultivated farm near the village of Mount Pleasant, and has been fairly prosperous in his business ventures.

JOHN J. ROUNTREE, farmer, was born in Williamson County August 18, 1815, and is a son of Andrew and Mary (Robison) Rountree, both natives of North Carolina. The father immigrated from North Carolina to Williamson County about 1800 and in 1817 removed to this county. He was a tiller of the soil and died in 1841. The mother followed in 1864 at the age of eighty-two. Our subject remained on the farm until he had reached man's estate and secured a good common school education for the advantages that were to be had at that early day. In 1838 he wedded Margaret McTee, who was born in this county. This union was blessed by the birth of eight children, six of whom are living: Charles W., William A., Emily J. (deceased), Mary A., Margaret J. (deceased), John M., Thomas F. and Kansas L. In 1867 our subject removed to his present location, where he has been engaged in farming and stock raising ever since. In 1872 he wedded his present wife, Susan H. Borders, who was born in Mississippi. They have two children: Ida R. and Johnnie E. Mr. Rountree is a Democrat and he and family belong to the Christian Church.

DANIEL RUDY, a well-known and prominent citizen of Maury County, Tenn., was born in Pickaway County, Ohio, November 23, 1841, son of Henry and Elizabeth (Ludwick) Rudy. The father was a native of Switzerland, born in 1797, and immigrated to America in 1810. He went to Ohio in 1822 and was engaged in milling in Pickaway County. In 1832 he retired to a farm where he lived until his death in 1852. He was for many years a magistrate and filled the office in a capable and satisfactory manner. The mother was a native of Pickaway County, Ohio, born in 1808; she died in her native county in 1860. Our subject's early life was passed principally in farming. He received a good English education in the common schools of Pickaway County and in October, 1868, he married Mary Zeiger, a native of Pickaway County. To this union were born seven children: Philip Z., Jacob L., Daniel, Charles, Herman, Mary A. and Catherine, all of whom are living. In 1880 Mr. Rudy came to Davidson County and settled on a farm near Nashville, where he remained until 1886, when he moved to Maury County and settled on a farm in the Thirteenth District where he has since resided. Politically he has been a life-long Democrat.

WILLIAM J. SCOTT'S birth occurred in Maury County, Tenn., April 19, 1821; he is a son of Andrew Scott, who was born in South Carolina, and was brought to Tennessee when very young. He was a son of Samuel Scott, and was married to Mary D. Matthews, of North Carolina, who bore him fourteen children, our subject being the third of the family. Andrew Scott was a member of the Presbyterian Church; and was a magistrate in Maury County for a number of years. He was a farmer of considerable means and died about 1874. His wife's death occurred about a year previous. William J. spent his early days on his father's farm, and when twenty-one years of age began farming for himself. May 1, 1856, he wedded Mahala T. Martin, born near Hartsville, May 8, 1832, daughter of Henry Martin. They have five sons and two daughters: Henry C., born in 1857; Miles E., born in 1868; Andrew D., born in 1860; James F., born in 1863; Leah, born in 1866; Mary A., born in 1868, and William A., born in 1870. Mr. Martin and wife are members of the Presbyterian Church.

GEORGE W. SCRIBNER was born in the Eighth District of Maury County, September 16, 1822, and is the son of John and Nancy (Noles) Scribner, The father was born in North Carolina in 1798, and was the son of Lewis S. Scribner, who was born in North Carolina and moved to Tennessee when John Scribner was but eight years old. He died in 1836. John Scribner was reared on a farm, was married October 27, 1817 and became the father of six children: James N., George W., Butler N., Sarah B., John A. T. and Susan R. Nancy Scribner was born May 3, 1798, was a member of the Primitive Baptist Church, and died in 1851. John Scribner was then married to Rebecca A. Aoidlett, and by her has six children. He was an elder in the Cumberland Presbyterian Church, and was a truly good man. He died in 1878. Our subject was reared on the farm and began business for himself at the age of nineteen. In 1841, Matilda J. Hiland became his wife. She was born in Dickson County, Tenn., in 1825, and is the daughter of Joseph D. and Eliza (Baxter) Hiland. To our subject and wife were born eight children—Sarah C., Mary E., Marsus M. (deceased), John H., Nancy T., Thomas C. and James M. The fourth daughter died in infancy. In 1875 our subject was married to Sarah M. Perry, who was born in Marshall County, Tenn., April 9, 1859. She is the daughter of Jerry and Mary M. (Jones) Perry. To Mr. and Mrs. Scribner were born two sons: Jeremiah B. and George B. Our subject has been engaged in the milling business for fourteen years. He was a brave soldier and was all through the war.

JOHN A. T. SCRIBNER was born in Maury County, Tenn., December 18, 1832, and is the son of John and Nancy (Noles) Scribner. For further particulars of parents see sketch of George W. Scribner. Our subject remained on the farm until he was twenty years of age; he then began working for himself. He received a limited education, though by diligence he managed to secure enough for the business of life. In 1852 he married Huldah G. Garrett, who was born in Maury County, Tenn., and who is the daughter of William and Dolly (Ham) Garrett. To Mr. Scribner and wife were born an interesting family of six children: Mary J., born in 1851; Willie J., born in 1853; George W., born in 1855; Nancy A., born in 1859; James W., born in 1865, and Laura A., born in 1868. September, 1868, Mrs. Scribner died, and in 1869 Mr. Scribner wedded Mollie E. Benton, who was born October 8, 1844. By her he became the father of four children: Alice O., born in 1870; Butler M., born in 1872; Malcia, born in 1873, and Sue A., born in 1875. Mr. Scribner's second wife died August 1, 1876, and he took for his third wife Mrs. Margaret F. Turner. Our subject is a Democrat and a worthy member of the Cumberland Presbyterian Church.

HIAL PAUL SEAVY, manager of the Grand Opera House, of Columbia, Tenn., was born near Woodstock, of the "Green Mountain State," May 21, 1842, son of Isaac and Rebecca (Paul) Seavy, of New Hampshire. Hial's early days were spent in Vermont, where he secured an academical education. At the age of twenty he left the farm and learned photography in New York City, where he remained three years as apprentice and journeyman. In 1868 he came to Columbia, Tenn., and purchased a gallery in the city, and has successfully carried on the business ever since, but has done this in connection with other callings. He is an accomplished musician, and served in the Federal Army as leader of the Second Vermont Brigade Band. He organized the celebrated Columbia Helicon Band, of which he was leader for eight years until it disbanded. He has also been connected with journalism for the last ten years, and has been regular correspondent at Columbus for Nashville dailies during this time. Since the erection of the new opera house he has been its efficient manager. In 1869 he married Louise G. Strachauer, a native of Nashville, and they are the parents of two sons and one daughter. He belongs to what is popularly known in Tennessee as the "sky-blue Democracy." He is a Mason, Royal Arch degree, and is Post Chancellor of the K. of P. lodge, but is not a member of the present lodge.

DR. JOSEPH W. SHARBER, a prominent citizen and physician of Maury County, Tenn., was born in this State November 4, 1818, and is one of the children born to John E. and Parthenia (Jones) Sharber. The father was born in North Carolina, and was one of the early settlers of Williamson County, Tenn. He was a farmer by occupation and was quite successful in that pursuit. His death occurred in 1859. The mother was a native of Tennessee and died in 1833. Our subject was a farmer boy and remained with his parents until he was eighteen years of age. He then attended school at Murfreesboro for three sessions, after which he taught two sessions of school at Mount Vernon and half a session at Dogwood Grove, Bedford County. While teaching at Mount Vernon he began the study of medicine with a view of making it a profession, and about 1841 began studying medicine with Dr. Boskett, and in 1843 began practicing with the above named physician. At the end of a year he located at Eagleville and practiced medicine for three years. He then attended one course of lectures at the University of Pennsylvania, and graduated from that institution in 1845. He then returned to Eagleville and resumed the practice of medicine. In 1847 he moved to his present place and practiced medicine, and also farmed to some extent. His reputation as a learned and skillful physician spreads far and wide, and his practice covers a large scope of country. In 1846 he wedded Mary J. Porter, a native of this county, and a daughter of James B. Porter. To them were born nine children, only one of whom is living. Her name is Fannie P. James P. died in 1848; John P. died in 1855; Joseph W. died in 1855; Lura died in 1865; Mary E. died in 1865; Dr. Willam B. died in 1879; Walter S. died in 1879, and E. Burk, died in 1888. Dr. Sharber has been a Mason for eighteen years and an Ancient Odd Fellow for nearly forty years. He is a Democrat, and himself and family are leading members of the Cumberland Presbyterian Church, he being an elder in that church for about forty-four years.

WILLIAM F. A. SHAW is a native of Orange County, N. C., born April 1, 1809, son of Joseph B. and Martha (Gooch) Shaw, born in Maryland and Virginia. The father was born in 1774 and is a son of Joseph Shaw, a native of Maryland and a Revolutionary soldier. The Shaw family came to Tennessee when our subject was about eighteen years of age. The father died in 1863 and the mother in 1854. William was one of ten children and was reared on a farm and educated in the common schools. He has always followed the life of a farmer and is very successful. In 1835 he married Jane Rountree, daughter of Andrew Rountree, of North Carolina, and to them were born Mary O., Thomas B., Martha I., James P., Emily E., Margaret E., William F. A., Joseph J. and Andrew J. Mrs. Shaw died July 22, 1864, and November 15, 1865, Mr. Shaw wedded Mary A. E. Renfroe, who was born in Maury County in 1827. To them was born one son, Barclay R., born in 1868. Mr. Shaw is a member of the Baptist Church, and was a magistrate of Williamson County a number of years. He has been a citizen of Tennessee for about sixty years and is recognized as an honest, upright citizen.

THOMAS D. SIMMONS, farmer, was born October 6, 1842, and received a good common school education. At the age of eighteen he enlisted in Company H, Thirty-second Tennessee Regiment, and served as a high private in that company until the close of the war. He then returned home and began farming. In 1866 he removed to his mother's farm in this county, where he remained until 1871. He then purchased his present farm and has been successfully engaged in farming and stock raising. In 1870 he wedded Sarah A. McKee, a native of this county, and to them were born nine children: Robert H., Thomas G., Mary A., William C., McKee, Quinton, Eva, Charlie and Edward, all of whom are living. Mr. Simmons is a Democrat in politics, and himself and family are consistent members of the Christian Church. He is classed among the enterprising and successful farmers of the county and is a respected citizen. His parents were Thomas A. and Eliza A. (German) Simmons, both natives of Tennessee. The father was a farmer and was moderately successful in this occupation. His death occurred in 1862. The mother still lives at the advanced age of seventy-seven and is a resident of Maury County.

REV. FRANKLIN G. SMITH (deceased) was born in Bennington, Vt., December 14, 1797, and was educated at Princeton (N. J.) Theological Seminary and graduated at the remarkably early age of fifteen. He began preparing himself for the Presbyterian ministry, but changed his views while in college and espoused the Episcopal faith. He conducted a private school in Milledgeville, Ga., some years, and then went to Lynchburg, Va., and started a school for young ladies, and also organized the St. Paul's Episcopal Church of that city in 1822, of which he was rector during his residence there. He was married to Sarah A. Davis, in 1835, and a year later removed to Columbia, Tenn., and took charge of the Female Institute of that city. In 1852 he established the Atheneum, which he has conducted during his lifetime. During the war he was a refugee, owing to his outspoken sentiments in favor of the Confederate cause. His wife conducted the school, and at the close of the war he returned, but died August 4 of the following year. He bequeathed his property to his wife and she managed the Atheneum until her death, January 11, 1871. Of their eight children three sons and two daughters are now living: Fannie P. (wife of Maj. L. M. Hasea, of Cincinnati, Ohio,), Capt. Robert D., present principal of the Atheneum; Dr. W. A., Prof. Frank H. and Carrie E., all of whom are teachers in the various departments of the school. Rector Smith was a man of extraordinary literary ability. He was editor and founder of *The Guardian*, a monthly journal of high order, started in 1841, and is yet published by the family. He may be called the founder of the educational interests in this part of the State, and was never known to turn away a pupil, no matter how poor, who was desirous of obtaining an education. He was one of the finest educators in the country and his views and teachings were acknowledged as undoubted authority by many of the best educators of the land.

CAPT. ROBERT D. SMITH, principal of the Columbia Atheneum, was born October 9, 1842, son of the late Rev. Franklin G. Smith. He was educated by his father, and completed a scientific and literary course with him. He served in the late war in Company B, Second Tennessee Infantry, enlisting in April, 1861. He was promoted at the battle of Shiloh to first lieutenant on Gen. Claiborne's staff, and served with Gens. Claiborne, Polk and Walthall until the surrender, being promoted to the rank of captain during the Dalton-Atlanta campaign. He participated in every battle of the war that the Army of Tennessee was engaged in except Chickamauga, when he was sick in the hospital. At the close of the war he returned home and completed his education, having, however, made great progress in mathematics while in the service by much desultory study with members of the engineer corps of the army. He assumed management of the Atheneum after the war, which he has ever since retained, and upon the death of his mother became the principal and prime manager of the school. In 1867 he married Margaret I., daughter of Hon. James H. Thomas, of Maury County. Two sons and one daughter have blessed this union. Mr. Smith is a Mason, Knight Templar degree, and he and family are members of the Episcopal Church.

MUNFORD SMITH is a well-known and worthy citizen of Maury County, and was born August 18, 1842, and is one of nine children of Munford and Elizabeth (Byrum) Smith. Munford Smith, Sr., was a native of East Tennessee, born in 1805, and his wife of Maury County, Tenn. Our subject's early days were spent on a farm, and he was educated at Mount Pleasant, Columbia, and Florence, Ala. May 17, 1861, he joined Company C, Third Tennessee Volunteer Infantry, and was in the battles of Fort Donelson, Chickamauga, Port Hudson, Raymond, Miss., and many engagements of lesser note. He was paroled at Greensboro, N. C., in May, 1865, and immediately returned to Maury County and settled on a farm. He was married, November 21, 1871, to Miss Anna M. Cecil, and they became the parents of six children: William C., Julia I., Flora K., Anna M., Julia E. and Virginia L., the latter two being deceased. Politically Mr. Smith is a Democrat. He is a member of the F. & A. M., and of the Methodist Episcopal Church South, and is considered one of Maury County's moral and energetic citizens.

PATRICK H. SOUTHALL, JR., was born in Maury County, Tenn., September 9, 1853, son of Patrick H. Southall, a farmer and stock raiser of Maury County. Our subject was reared in the county, and in 1872 entered the Cumberland University of Lebanon, Tenn., graduating from the literary department in 1875, and a year later graduated from the law department of the same institution. In the fall of the same year he came to Columbia, where he has became a successful practitioner, and was for a time a partner of L. P. Padgett. He is now practicing alone, and is doing well. He is a Democrat, and favors a protective tariff, and is a member of the Masonic fraternity and Methodist Episcopal Church South. He is vice-president of the city board of education, and takes quite an active interest in the local campaigns, and has won quite a reputation as an orator.

THOMAS W. SOWELL, one of Maury County's most enterprising citizens, was born December 28, 1856, son of William J. and Emily J. (Hardison) Sowell, both of whom were born in Maury County in 1824 and 1833, respectively. The father was a successful farmer and became the owner of several hundred acres of land. He enlisted as colonel (in the late war) of the Forty-eighth Tennessee Cavalry, and was a brave and faithful officer. He was married in 1850 and became the father of the following family: William I., Alice J., Thomas W., Fannie P., Felix, Emily E., Wallace T., Carrie E., James D. and Albert B. The father was a teacher in early life. He died on the 13th of August, 1884. The mother is yet living. Our subject was reared on a farm and began working for himself at the age of eighteen as clerk in the mercantile business for about eighteen months. He then worked in his father's mill one year, and then engaged in the mercantile business for himself two years, being fairly successful. October 25, 1883, he wedded Jennie R. Chisholm, born in Alabama January 15, 1860, daughter of Dr. Lewis C. and Jane Chisholm. The father was born in Alabama in 1821 and the mother in 1827. Dr. Chisholm graduated from a dental college in Nashville and was professor in the same one year. The mother died in 1862, and the Doctor afterward married Isabel Dickson, of Alabama. Our subject and wife have two children: Barkley, born August 30, 1884 (deceased), and Nina, born September 15, 1885. Mr. and Mrs. Sowell belong to the Christian Church and he is a supporter of Democratic principles.

GEORGE W. STACKARD, a well-known agriculturist of Maury County, Tenn., was born in Rutherford County November 6, 1823, son of Nathan and Mary (Kinzer) Stockard, natives, respectively, of North Carolina and Virginia. The father was an enterprising farmer and was regarded by all as a moral, upright man. His death occurred in 1879 and the mother's in 1853. They were Methodists in belief. The subject of our memoir was united in matrimony in 1862 to Miss Sallie Walker. Mr. Stackard is a Democrat in his political views and gives his support to that party on all occasions. He is at the present time magistrate of his district and has served in this capacity for the last fifteen years. In 1865 Mr. Stackard engaged in the mercantile business, but abandoned that in 1877. By his energy, enterprise and economy he has accumulated considerable property.

WILLIAM W. STANLEY, a young and enterprising farmer of Maury County, and a native of that county, was born February 27, 1846, and is a son of Austin C. and Rhoda C. (McConnico) Stanley, both of whom were natives of Tennessee. The father was a farmer and the son of Wright Stanley, and during the late war enlisted in the Fourth Tennessee Regiment and served as a high private until he was killed at the battle of Wartrace, Tenn., in 1862. The mother died in 1856. Our subject remained with his parents until he was seventeen years old, receiving his education in the district schools. He then enlisted in Company H, Forty-eighth Tennessee, serving as high private until December, 1864, when he joined the Sixteenth Confederate Cavalry Regiment and remained there until the close of the war. He then returned to this county and began farming. About 1868 he purchased his present property, and has since been engaged in farming and stock raising. In 1866 he was married to Ellen Rountree, a native of this county. They have five children, only three of whom are living: Thomas A., Carrie I. and William W., Jr. Mr. Stanley and family are leading members of the Christian Church.

WILLIAM K. STEPHENS, a successful merchant of Culleoka, Maury Co., Tenn., was born in Marshal County, January 7, 1852, son of Thomas M. and Mary (Goodrich) Stephens, born, respectively, in Virginia and Tennessee. The father came to Culleoka, Tenn., in 1858, and followed the mechanic's trade several years, but lately has gived his attention to farming. Our subject received his education under Prof. Webb, of Culleoka;

at the age of seventeen he began doing for himself, and became a partner in the firm of C. B. Abernathy & Co., and after Mr. Abernathy's death he purchased his interest, and since 1883, has been sole proprietor with the exception of one month. Mr. Stephens has succeeded well in his business enterprises and has a fine stock of goods. He has a farm consisting of seventy acres, and May 8, 1873, was married to Miss Ida O. Wilkes, daughter of B. L. Wilkes; they have five children: Thomas N., William K., Leroy W., Walter S. and Mary C. Mr. Stephens is a Democrat, and was appointed postmaster of Culleoka, March 3, 1874. He and wife are members of the Methodist Episcopal Church South.

SAMUEL R. STONE, farmer, was born in Fayette County, Ky., July 21, 1827, and and is a son of John and Mary (Berry) Stone, both natives of Kentucky. The father was an extensive farmer, owning at his death 1,200 acres of as good land as Kentucky affords, to be divided among his children. His death occurred in 1872, and the mother followed in the same year. Our subject assisted on the farm until he was twenty-one years of age, securing a good education in the common schools. He then began farming for himself in Kentucky until 1884, when he removed to this county, renting his Kentucky land. He purchased the Cooper farm of 587 acres, on which he has been steadily engaged ever since. In 1854 he wedded Mary Marshall, native of Kentucky, and they have five children by this union: Walker J., William, Birdie, Samuel and Jessie. Mr. Stone is a Democrat in politics, and himself and family are members of the Christian Church.

REV. JOSEPH HART STRAYHONE, a well-known farmer and influential citizen of Maury County, Tenn., and a native of Orange County, N. C., was born October 12, 1821, son of Daniel and Penelope (Berry) Strayhone. The father of our subject was also born in Orange County, N. C., and came to Tennessee in 1822. He located on a farm in Maury County and lived there until his death, which occurred in 1824. He was a worthy member of the Presbyterian Church. The mother was born in North Carolina, and was also for many years a member of the Presbyterian Church. In later years she became a member of the Methodist Episcopal Church. Her death occurred in 1848. Our subject passed his youthful days in aiding his father on the farm. January 6, 1843, he wedded Mary C. Aikins, a native of Maury County and the daughter of John Aikins. The fruits of this union were the following children: Nellie C., John Alison, Jennet E. and William Bascom. In March, 1859, Mrs. Strayhone died; she was an excellent woman and a devout member of the Methodist Episcopal Church. In September, 1859, our subject took for his second wife Olevia A. Mullins, a native of Bedford County and the daughter of Rev. William Mullins. This second union resulted in the birth of two children: H. Elizabeth B. and William D., both living. In 1852 Mr. Strayhone became proprietor of a tannery in Lawrence County, which business he successfully managed for twenty years. In 1861 he enlisted as a private in the Confederate Army, in the Forty-eighth Tennessee Regiment Volunteer Infantry, to serve as chaplain. He participated in the battles of Richmond and Perryville, Ky., and was honorably discharged at Shelbyville, Bedford County, in 1862. He immediately returned to Lawrence County and resumed the tannery business. He received a good education in the schools of Maury County, and has been, politically, a life-long Democrat. He is a member of the Methodist Episcopal Church South, and has been a minister of the gospel since 1849. He is also a member of the Tennessee Conference, joined that body in 1868, and had traveled as itinerant preacher three years previous to joining the conference. He has a farm of 157 acres, and is a member of the Masonic fraternity.

PATRICK SULLIVAN, farmer, was born in Ireland in September, 1823. He is one of eight children born to Flourence and Honora (Reyney) Sullivan. The father was a native of Ireland, born about 1800, and was by occupation a well-to-do farmer. He was an ardent advocate of the cause of temperance, and was a member of the Roman Catholic Church. He died in 1882. The mother was also a native of Ireland, born about 1803; she was a member of the Roman Catholic Church and a devout Christian. She died in 1884. Our subject's early life was employed in the shoe-making business. He came to America in 1849, and in 1851 settled in Maury County, where he was employed as a laborer. In

1853 he wedded Mary J. Hand, a native of Maury County, and to this union were born these children named: Flourence, Patrick S., John, James, Timothy, Honora, Julia, Kate and Margaret, all living except Mary A., who died in 1856. Mr. Sullivan is a Democrat, and has a good farm of eighty-five acres. He is a prominent member of the Roman Catholic Church, and is a well respected citizen.

C. TAYLOR was born in Giles County, Tenn., July 6, 1818. At the age of twenty he began business for himself. He has given his attention to farming. December 24, 1839, he married Elizabeth B. Foster, born in 1819, daughter of Richard and Elizabeth Foster. To Mr. and Mrs. Taylor were born the following children: James R., William, Sarah P., Frances M., George C., Jasper, Callie D., Martha, Cornelia, and an infant deceased. At the latter's birth the mother died, and May 10, 1866, Mr. Taylor married Mary E. (Thompson) Fowler, and by her is the father of four children: Calabie M., Burt F., Floyd A. and Earl F. (deceased). Mr. Fowler is a Democrat and a wealthy farmer. His wife is an earnest worker in the Methodist Episcopal Church South, and is the mother of two sons by her former marriage: Walter W. and Joseph C. Both are in Texas, the former a physician, and the latter a salesman in a drug store. Our subject's parents were James and Martha (Washam) Taylor, both born in Virginia. They were married in 1815, and came to Tennessee soon after the birth of their first child and located in Giles County. They died in 1821 and 1836, respectively.

HON. GEORGE C. TAYLOR, attorney at law, of Columbia, Tenn., and member of the Forty-fourth General Assembly of Tennessee, is a native of Maury County, born December 9, 1848, son of Claybourne Taylor, a well known and worthy farmer of the county. George C. Taylor was reared and educated in his native county. In 1862 being only fourteen years of age, he ran away from home, and entered the Confederate Army, enlisting in Company F, Forty-eighth Regiment Tennessee Infantry, and serving until the close of the war, being one of the youngest soldiers of the Tennessee army. He was seriously wounded in the hip at Atlanta, from which he still suffers. After his return home he attended school and clerked in a store until 1866, when he went to Arkansas, where he farmed and taught school. In 1869 he returned to Columbia, and began studying law with Hon. James H. Thomas, and was admitted to the bar in 1871. He is an uncompromising Democrat, and as such was elected to the State Legislature in the fall of 1884, and served with credit. In 1872 he wedded Laura Burte, who died less than a year after. June 8, 1874, he married Mrs. Susie D. Stone. They have two daughters: Laura C. and Georgie C. Mr. Taylor is one of the successful members of the Maury County bar, and is an able and popular representative of the people.

WILLIAM C. TAYLOR was born October 18, 1852, in Marion County, Ky., and is a son of Clark and Frances M. (Tucker) Taylor, both of whom were Kentuckians by birth, and are now deceased. The father was a resident of Sumner County, Tenn., at the time of his death. William C. was reared and educated in Kentucky and Tennessee, attending the Lebanon Kentucky Seminary, and also St. Mary's College, near that city. At the age of twenty-one he began his legal studies at Danville, Ky., continuing there until 1875, when he came to Columbia and engaged in the practice of his profession, which he has continued up to the present time, and has met with very flattering success. He is a strong supporter of Democratic principles, and has held the office of city attorney for five years, giving the best of satisfaction in the performance of his duties. He is a Mason of the Knight Templar degree.

DR. HEZEKIAH TERRELL, a prominent physician and farmer of Maury County; was born February 15, 1815, in Williamson County, Tenn. He was reared in the country and secured a good common school education. At the age of twenty-two he began the study of medicine at Franklin, Tenn., where he remained over two years. He then attended a course of lectures at the Medical University, of Louisville. In 1843 he began the practice of medicine, which he has been engaged in ever since. He has an extensive practice and has been very successful. December 20, 1838, he wedded Margaret S. Dabney, a native of Williamson County, and to them were born eight children, only five of whom are living: Mary E., William J., Alexander C., Joel and Anna. Dr. Terrell was an old line Whig before the war, but since that time has voted with the Democratic party. Himself and family are members of the Christian Church. The Doctor has been a member of the Masonic lodge since 1852. He is the son of James and Mary (House) Terrell, both natives of North Carolina. The father was a pioneer settler of Williamson County, emigrating from North Carolina to that county in 1806. He was a farmer and blacksmith. His reputation as a skilled mechanic spread far and wide. He died April 25, 1826. The mother followed August 13, 1842.

JOHN M. TERRY, a well-known citizen of Maury County, Tenn., was born in Warren County, N. C., February 21, 1821. He is the sixth of eleven children—six sons and five daughters—born to the marriage of David Terry and Nancy B. (Jordan) Terry. The parents were born in Warren County, N. C., and came to Maury County, Tenn., about 1831, and settled on a farm in the First District, where they resided until their respective deaths in 1834 and 1856. John M. Terry's early life was spent on his father's farm. He attended school at the Mount Pleasant Academy, where he secured a good English education. May 16, 1867, he was united in marriage to Miss Sarah A. Caldwell, of Maury County, and five children—two sons and three daughters—blessed their union: John O., Madison, Nannie Seymoura, Carena G. and Zula. Mrs. Terry was born May 12, 1841. She was a member of the Methodist Episcopal Church South, and was a faithful helpmate to her husband. She died February 11, 1882. Mr. Terry has been a life-long Democrat and is a strong advocate of the principles of his party. He is a member of the Methodist Episcopal Church South.

JAMES M. TINDEL was born in Bedford County, Tenn., February 10, 1838, and is the son of Anderson Tindel, who was born June 2, 1809, and who came to Tennessee when young, locating in Bedford County. He engaged in farming, which he followed very successfully for several years. He then moved to Maury County and located in the Fourth District, where he still continued farming, but in connection worked at the shoemaker's trade. By his marriage to Lety Caffe, who was born in 1808, he became the father of eleven children, of whom our subject is one. The mother of these children was a member of the Christian Church and was faithful to her Christian duties. She died January 1, 1873. The father was also a member of the Christian Church and died June 14, 1879. Our subject reached his majority on the farm, and in 1863 enlisted in the Forty-eighth Tennessee Regiment of Infantry. He was at Fort Henry guarding stock about the time of the battle at Fort Donelson. He escaped from Fort Henry and came home, where he remained but a short time. He then went through Mississippi to Jackson, and afterward came home. January 2, 1868, he wedded Adeline Jones, a native of Maury County, Tenn., born May 7, 1850, and the daughter of Jesse and Sarah (Moore) Jones. To our subject and wife was born one child, a daughter, Lettie A., born August 29, 1868. Mr. Tindel and wife are worthy members of the Primitive Baptist Church and have the respect of all who know them.

THOMAS J. TINDEL was born in Bedford County, Tenn., May 2, 1845, and is the son of Anderson and Lety (Caffe) Tindel. (For further particulars of parents see sketch of James M. Tindel.) Our subject was reared on the farm, and owing to circumstances his education was rather limited, but by his own exertions he has gained sufficient education for the business of life. November 7, 1867, he led to the hymeneal altar Van D. Cheek, and by this union he became the father of an interesting family of five children—four sons and one daughter: George W., born May 4, 1869; Lillie L., born November 16, 1871; Jackson P., born September 3, 1874, and died September 15, 1876; Wilburn, born April 17, 1878, and Henry M., born October 24, 1881. Mr. Tindel is justly recognized as an honest, upright citizen, and has many warm friends.

DR. JAMES T. S. THOMPSON was born in this county February 6, 1836, and is one of six children born to the union of Capt. Absalom and Mary B. (Sanford) Thompson, natives, respectively, of Virginia and Tennessee. The father was from the family of John Thompson, one of the pioneer settlers of Williamson County, who was born in 1800.

Capt. Thompson has filled a large space in the history of the community for the last half century. He has taken a lively interest in developing the resources of the country and in promoting the cause of education. He was one of the projectors and liberal supporters of Jackson College, and after its removal to Columbia he was an active participant in the establishment of both the Female and Male Academies of Spring Hill, and was a trustee of both schools for many years. He has been a member of the Presbyterian Church since 1833, and was ordained one of its ruling elders in May, 1844. His death occurred February 17, 1881. The subject of this sketch passed his youth on the farm with his parents. At the age of twenty-two he began reading medicine with Dr. S. T. McMurray with a view of making it a profession. He attended two courses of lectures at the Nashville Medical College, and graduated from that institution at the sessions of 1857–58. He then returned to Maury County and began the practice of medicine. At the breaking out of the war he enlisted in Company E, Third Tennessee Regiment Infantry, serving as lieutenant until the fall of Fort Donelson, after which he served as assistant surgeon of Robertson's battery, and at the exchange of his regiment was made surgeon of the Third Tennessee Regiment, and remained as such for three years, after which time the regiments consolidated, and he then joined Gen. Joseph E. Johnston's staff, and remained with him until Gen. Hood took charge of the army, and served in the same capacity under the latter General until the close of the war. He then returned home and resumed the practice of medicine. At the end of a year he removed to Corinth, Mississippi, and engaged in farming and milling. He remained in this State until 1876, when he returned to this county, locating on the old homestead, where he has been engaged in farming and stock raising ever since. November 30, 1870, he was united in marriage to Mary L. Cheairs, a native of this county and the daughter of John W. Cheairs, whose sketch appears elsewhere in these pages. To Mr. and Mrs. Thompson were born nine children, eight of whom are living, viz.: Mary P., John C. (deceased), James M., Thomas St. C., Leo Duloney, Hattie C., Myra R., Susie P. and an infant not named. The Doctor is a Democrat in politics, and a member of the Presbyterian Church. Mrs. Thompson is a member of the Methodist Church.

HARVEY S. THOMPSON'S birth occurred in Giles County, Tenn., June 20, 1843. He is of Scotch-Irish descent, and was raised and educated in his native county. His education consists of good common schooling, which he greatly improved by much desultory reading and study. After the breaking out of the late war he enlisted as private in the Third Tennessee Infantry in 1863, and served about one year in the Confederate Army. He followed farming and school teaching in Marshall and Maury Counties, Tenn., also in Mississippi two years, and in the meantime stored his mind with the legal lore of Blackstone. In 1876 he had so mastered the profession that he gave up pedagoging and came to Maury County, Tenn., and was admitted to the Columbia bar, and there he has since practiced his profession with success. Mr. Thompson was raised a Whig, but is now Independent in his political views. In 1883 he was appointed United States commissioner for the Middle District of Tennessee, and has since filled the position in a highly satisfactory manner. Mr. Thompson is unmarried, and is a son of David N. and Eliza (Shields) Thompson, who were born in Giles County, Tenn., where they have both long been tenants of the grave-yard at old Elkridge, which contains one of the most ancient and honored Presbyterian Churches in that county. The subject of this sketch is strictly a self-made man; the war left him entirely penniless.

WILLIAM E. TOMLINSON, a successful farmer of Maury County, Tenn., was born in Giles County, this State, in 1833, being a son of John and Anna (Murphy) Tomlinson, who were born in North Carolina, where the father followed the life of an agriculturist and became quite well to do in worldly goods. He died about 1838. The mother is still living and is a resident of Giles County, Tenn. William E., our subject, assisted his father on the farm and was married in March, 1874, to Martha English, and one child blessed this union: Mary S. Mr. Tomlinson took an active part in the late war, enlisting in Company E, Forty-eighth Tennessee Infantry, and served for three years, at the expir ation of which time he was transferred to Gen. Forrest's division and served until the surrender of Lee. Mr. Tomlinson is a Democrat politically, and belongs to the Masonic fraternity. He and wife are members of the Methodist Episcopal Church South.

JOHN H. TOOMBS was born near Culleoka, Tenn., January 6, 1819, son of John and Catherine (Wems) Toombs. The father was born in Virginia in 1793, and came to Tennessee with his parents, Edmund and Sabra Toombs, when a small lad. He became a prosperous farmer of Davidson County, and died in 1830, and his wife about 1852. John H. was their third child. He spent his boyhood days on his father's farm, and after attaining his majority began earning his own livelihood at farming. In 1844 he was united in marriage to Elizabeth P. Hill, who was born in Maury County May 20, 1822, daughter of William C. and Maria (Dickson) Hill, born in North Carolina and Georgia in 1795 and 1797, respectively. They were early pioneers of Tennessee and were farmers of Maury County. The father died in 1835 and the mother in 1870. Mr. Toombs is a Democrat and his wife is a member of the Baptist Church.

JOSEPH M. TOWLER, M. D., was born in Lexington, Ky., July 17, 1822, and is of English-Scotch descent. His father died when he was eleven years of age, and he removed to Maury County, Tenn., in 1833, and was educated in La Grange College, Alabama, and afterward served as one of the faculty in the same eight years. After attaining his majority he began studying medicine under Dr. B. W. Dudley, and graduated from the medical department of the University of Pennsylvania in 1847. He then returned to Columbia, where he has since continued the practice of his profession and is considered a highly eminent physician. He is a member of the American Medical Association, and ex-president of the Tennessee State Medical Society. Joseph is his son, born to his marriage with Catharine Chapman Voorhies, of Maury County, which occurred March 16, 1847. He is a prominent Mason, being Past Grand Commander of the State. He and family are members of the Presbyterian Church, and he is an elder in the same. He was originally an old-line Whig, but since the war has affiliated with the Democratic party. He served as first surgeon of Col. Biffle's regiment in the civil war, and later as brigade surgeon of Gen. John Adams until he was captured and paroled. He has been resident physician of the noted summer resort at Waukesha, Wis., for the last ten years, where he annually spends his summers.

JOSEPH F. TUCKER, editor and manager of the *Maury County Democrat* at Columbia, Tenn., is a son of Joseph F. and Mary J. (Faris) Tucker, who were Tenneesseans by birth. Joseph F. was born December 14, 1853, and attended the schools of his native county and finished his education at Louisville, Ky., taking an academical course. He was salesman in a mercantile establishment a number of years, and afterward accepted the position as traveling salesman for a Louisville firm. For several years he was local editor of the Columbia *Herald* and conducted a campaign paper at Bowling Green, Ky., during the campaign of 1884. In February, 1885, he returned to Columbia and has since edited the *Democrat* of that city, in which he is ably assisted by his brother, Jesse P. Nannie May is a daughter born to his marriage with Miss Ada B. Webster, which occurred in October, 1884. Mrs. Tucker is a native of Williamson County, and our subject belongs to the K. of H. fraternity.

OTEY WALKER, merchant and agriculturist, is a son of Asberry and Sarah (Jossey) Walker and is a native of Maury County, Tenn., born July 31, 1849, and May 30, 1878, united his fortune with Miss Laura Dorsett, daughter of T. J. Dorsett, a well-known citizen of Maury County. To their union was born one child, Sarah E. Mr. Walker is a strong supporter of Democratic principles and is a believer in Episcopalianism, and his wife is a worthy member of that church. Asberry Walker was an enterprising merchant and was regarded as one of Maury County's most substantial citizens. His death occured in 1860. The mother is still living, and is a resident of Maury County.

MRS. SARAH J. WEBSTER, is a daughter of Samuel and Sallie (Vaughn) Weakley, and was born in 1818. Her parents were both born in the "Old Dominion," the father being a skillful surveyor and enterprising farmer of that State, where his death occurred about 1830. The mother died ten years later and she and her husband were worthy members of the Methodist Church. Our subject was married, on the 17th of March, 1836, to James H. Webster, an industrious farmer of Maury County, and their union was blessed with eleven children, the following seven of whom are living: Fannie P. (wife of Thomas S. Porter), Roenia C., James J., Mattie J. (wife of Shade Murray), Lizzie D., Kate W. and Frank W. Mr. Webster died in 1873. His widow is an accomplished lady and is a member of the Methodist Episcopal Church South. She owns considerable land, and is much esteemed by her neighbors and friends.

WILLIAM J. WEBSTER, attorney at law, of Columbia, son of William J. and Mary A. (Porter) Webster, and grandson of Jonathan Webster and Nimrod Porter, who were early pioneers and farmers of Maury County. The former was for many years sheriff of the county. William J. Webster, Sr., was a farmer, a Democrat and a member of the Presbyterian Church. He died in 1859, followed by his widow in 1868. Our subject was born October 17, 1847, and in addition to the common school education he attended the Washington-Lee University, of Lexington, Va., and then entered the Lebanon (Tenn.) Law School, from which he graduated in 1869. During the year 1869 he was admitted to practice at the bar of Maury County, and has followed his profession in Columbia with well-deserved success. October 23, 1872, Mary C. Allison became his wife and the mother of his three children: William J., Hyleman A. and Virginia M. Mrs. Webster is a member of the Episcopal Church. Mr. Webster is a member of the Presbyterian Church and a Democrat in politics. He has given much attention to raising and breeding fine stock, and is a one-half owner and president of the Columbia Jersey Cattle Company.

PROF. HENRY Y. WEISSINGER, an enterprising farmer of Maury County, Tenn., was born in Wilson, Ala., February 9, 1842, and is the youngest son of Leonard Weissinger by his second wife, Eliza M. (Bond) Weissinger. His first wife was a Miss Cobb, who died in 1839. The father of our subject was a native of Georgia, and was a farmer by occupation. At one time he edited a paper in Perry County, Ala., but moved to this county in 1872. His death occurred in 1876. The mother of our subject was born in North Carolina, but resided the principal part of her life in Marion, Ala. She was gifted with rare moral and intellectual endowments, which were carefully cultivated under the judicious supervision of Miss Mary Burk, her mother's sister, one of the best educators, as well as one of the best women of her day. Our subject received a collegiate education at the Howard College of Alabama, and graduated from that institution in 1862 with the degree of A. M. He then enlisted in Company A, Twenty-eighth Alabama, serving as a high private, but afterward sergeant of the company. He then joined Company I, of the Twenty-fifth Alabama Regiment, and served as lieutenant of the company. In 1864 he joined his brother's staff and served as captain until the close of the war. He then returned home and began teaching school, and followed that profession in that State until 1868, when he returned to Mount Pleasant, Maury County, and continued teaching school, remaining there until 1873. He then moved to West Tennessee and taught in a high school for three years. In 1875 he removed to Spring Hill, Maury County, and taught there until 1881. In 1884 he began farming on his present place, where he has been steadily engaged ever since. In 1870 he wedded Emily E. Miller, a native of this county, and to them were born seven children: Henry Y., Mary L., Charles M., George J., Leonard A., William M. and Anna M., all of whom are living. Prof. Weissinger is a Democrat in politics, and he and all his family, with the exception of one, are members of the Old School Presbyterian Church.

JAMES L. WHITE was born in Maury County, Tenn., December 31, 1842; was reared on the farm and received his education in the common schools. At the age of twenty-one he began farming for himself, and, September 6, 1866, he was married to Ophelia T. Davidson, a native of Maury County, Tenn., born September 5, 1847, and the daughter of John and Martha (Davis) Davidson. To our subject and wife were born these children: John W., George M., Willie E., E. M., Margaret E., James E., Pattie, Grover C.

In 1862 Mr. White enlisted in Company F, Forty-eighth Tennessee Infantry, and left for Jackson, Miss., where he remained a short time and then came home. He then joined Company F, First Tennessee Regiment Cavalry and went to Mississippi, Alabama, Georgia, South Carolinia and North Carolina, after which he was paroled and returned home. In 1878 he was elected constable and served four years. In 1882 he was elected magistrate, and holds that position at the present time. He is a Democrat in politics. Our subject's parents, William and Margaret White, were born in North Carolina and Tennessee, respectively. The father was born in 1811, and was the son of Lewis and Nancy White. He was a farmer, an upright citizen and had many friends. He died in 1855. The mother was a member of the Christian Church and was always ready and willing to aid in the cause of Christianity.

WASHINGTON CURRAN WHITTHORNE was born in that part of Lincoln County subsequently made a part of Marshall County, Tenn.; was raised in Bedford, attended school at Arrington Academy in Williamson, Campbell Academy in Wilson, and graduated at East Tennessee University. He was a student of law under James K. Polk at the time of his election to the presidency, and entered into the politics of the State at an early age; was a member of the State Senate in 1855-56 and 1857-58, and was speaker of the House of Representatives in 1859-60, having been elected to the House over W. L. McConnico, the Whig candidate, and one of the foremost orators in the State. In 1860 he was selected by his party as a candidate for elector for the State at large. He canvassed the State from one end to the other, meeting more competitors of the ablest of his opponents than was ever done in any former political canvass in the State. Upon the breaking out of the war he became assistant adjutant-general, serving with Gen. Anderson in West Virginia in 1861. At the close of the war he returned to the practice of his profession at Columbia, in which he achieved great success until the year 1871, when he was elected to the Forty-second congress where he continued to serve without intermission until the close of the Forty-seventh Congress. During his service in Congress, his most marked work was as a member of the Committee on Naval Affairs, of which he was chairman for six years. Of Gen. Whitthorne's services to his party and country since the war, it is unnecessary to speak at length. He has served both with untiring zeal, energy and ability. While earnest, bold and energetic by nature, he combines with those qualities a prudence, conservatism and sagacity which gives them extraordinary weight and influence. He was appointed to the Senate by Gov. Bate to fill the unexpired term of Senator Howell E. Jackson, appointed United States Circuit Court Judge.

REV. WILLIAM H. WILKES, a native of Maury County, Tenn., was born May 7, 1821. He is the son of Richard A. L. and Judith (Harris) Wilkes, who were natives of the "Old Dominion," immigrating to Tennessee in 1806, which remained their home until their respective deaths in 1867 and 1880. The subject of this sketch was educated principally at the Triune and Pleasant Grove Academies. At eighteen years of age he entered the ministry of the Methodist Episcopal Church. His appointments have included the towns of Springfield, Wartrace, Mount Pleasant, Spring Hill, Pulaski, Franklin, Nashville and Columbia. Mr. Wilkes was married January, 1848, to Miss Mary K. Amis, who died in 1856, leaving three children: Izora (Mrs. C. S. Williamson), Richard (who served in the State Legislature in 1881 and 1882), and Alice (Mrs. Rev. W. R. Peebles). His second marriage was to Miss Zurelda Amis, who died soon after her marriage leaving one daughter, Mary K., wife of Thomas E. Andrews. His present wife was Mrs. Elizabeth (Martin) Johnson. Mr. Wilkes has been for many years connected with the movements to advance the interest of education by the establishment of schools of high grade.

COL. NATHANIEL ROBARDS WILKES was born in Oxford, Granville Co., N. C., July 26, 1833, son of James H. and Eliza (Robards) Wilkes, who were born in Virginia and North Carolina, respectively. The father removed with his wife and family to this State in 1837, and located in Maury County. Here he farmed and taught school. He served about six years in all as magistrate, and was also superintendent of the county schools two years. He died in 1879. Nathaniel R. Wilkes was reared in Maury County, and graduated from Jackson College in July, 1854. A year later he began the study of law with a view to making it a profession and remained with Frierson & Fleming until 1857. He advanced rapidly in his profession as a lawyer of ability and promise, and for two years was a partner of William H. Polk. At a later period he was associated with N. H. Burt, an eminent member of the Chattanooga bar. From 1865 to 1867 he practiced with H. T. Osborne, and from 1870 to 1872 with J. L. Bullock. Mr. Wilkes is a partner of Mr. Padgett, and his well-established reputation as a lawyer has contributed largely to the success of this firm. Col. Wilkes is a Democrat, but was a Whig previous to the war. He twice enlisted in the Confederate Army, but after a service of ten months he was discharged on account of physical disability contracted during service. In October, 1858, he and Miss Jennie Thompson were united in marriage. Mrs. Wilkes died in 1859, leaving no issue. June 23, 1875, he married Miss Anna Y. Baird, who was born in Nashville. Col. Wilkes is a Mason, Knight Templar degree. He is a member of the I. O. O. F., K. of P. and K. of H. Mrs. Wilkes is an Episcopalian in faith.

MRS. LENNIE M. WILKES, widow of James H. Wilkes, was born in Maury County, Tenn., November 21, 1835. She is a daughter of W. R. and Cynthia (Davidson) Caldwell, who were born in North Carolina and Tennessee, respectively. The father followed the occupation of tilling the soil, and accumulated considerable property, and is now a resident of Mississippi. The mother was an earnest worker in the Cumberland Presbyterian Church, and died in 1862. Mrs. Wilkes, our subject, was twice married; the first time to G. W. Kinzer in 1857, and six children were born to them, four of whom are living: William J., E. C., Ella M., W. O., Charles H. G. and Ethel G. Mr. Kinzer was a good business man, and was much respected by his fellow-men. He departed this life in 1873. His widow was married, in 1874, to James H. Wilkes, and to them was born one child, a son, Joseph T. In 1879 Mr. Wilkes died. Since that time Mrs. Wilkes has managed her farm, and is doing well financially. She is a member of the Presbyterian Church.

JAMES H. WILKES, M. D., of Columbia, Tenn., was born in Maury County July 26, 1839, and is a brother of N. R. Wilkes, whose sketch precedes this. James H. attended the Jackson College, of Columbia, and in 1858 became a disciple of Æsculapius under Drs. A. H. & W. H. Brown. Later he attended lectures in the medical department of the Nashville University (now Vanderbilt), graduating in 1862. He was assigned hospital duty for the Confederate Army as assistant surgeon, continuing one year, when he was promoted to first surgeon. At the time of the surrender he was acting surgeon for Gen. Thomas Harrison's Texas brigade of cavalry. He remained at home during 1866, but in 1867 removed to Arkansas, where he remained two years, and then returned to Maury County, Tenn., but shortly after began practicing in Edgefield, a suburb of Nashville. In the latter part of 1869 he returned to Maury County, and in 1880 removed to Columbia, where he has since resided and practiced. He is a member of the State Medical Society and the Masonic fraternity, Knight Templar degree, and a Democrat. In 1868 he was married to Dora I. Davis, of Franklin, Tenn., and two sons and two daughters have blessed their union.

GEORGE C. WILLIAMSON was born near the waters of the Little Harpeth River January 19, 1815, son of Samuel and Judith (Woodfin) Williamson, born in the Old Dominion in 1786 and 1796, respectively. The father was a son of Cutbert Williamson (who was a farmer and an 1812 soldier) and followed the mechanical trade until his death. He was the father of eight children, and he and wife were worthy and consistent Christians. He was in the war of 1812 and was a Whig in politics. He died in 1860 and the mother in 1873. Our subject began farming for himself at the age of twenty and March 31, 1836, he married Mildred A. Brown, born in Maury County in 1818, daughter of Charles E. and Elizabeth (Acres) Brown. The children born to Mr. and Mrs. Williamson are Charles S., born in 1837; John T., born in 1839; James G., born in 1842. Mr. and Mrs. Williamson are members of the Presbyterian Church and he belongs to the Masonic fraternity and is a Democrat.

JOSHUA L. WILLIAMS' birth occurred in Maury County, Tenn., October 13, 1829.

He attended the common schools and later in life began farming and merchandising, in which he was very successful, and now owns 600 acres of very productive land. He was married in 1874 to Miss Martha Peller, daughter of David W. Peller, and four children have blessed their union: Samuel W., Lottie G., Sarah G. and Archibald D. Mr. Williams is a Democrat in politics, but was formerly a Whig, and has served his county in the capacity of clerk and master of the chancery court six years. He and Mrs. Williams are members of the Presbyterian Church and he is a Freemason and a son of Gen. William D. and Sarah G. (Earley) Williams, who were born in North Carolina and Tennessee, respectively. The father was a farmer and was one of the first settlers of Maury County, Tenn., coming to this State in 1806. His death occurred in 1859. The mother was a member of the Cumberland Presbyterian Church and died in 1884.

MAJ. JOHN T. WILLIAMSON, attorney at law, of Columbia, Tenn., was born in Maury County August 11, 1839, son of George C. and Mildred A. (Brown) Williamson, the former born in Giles County and the latter in Maury County. John T. was brought up on a farm in the county and finished his literary education in the Cumberland University at Lebanon, Tenn. He became a student of Blackstone shortly before the war, but in 1861 entered the Confederate Army as brevet second lieutenant, Capt. Jones' company, Third Regiment Tennessee Infantry. In 1863 he was promoted to major of the Fifty-first Tennessee Infantry, and served until the close of the war. He then returned and resumed his legal studies, and was admitted to practice in 1868. Since that time he has been a successful practitioner of Columbia and has met with the success his knowledge of legal lore and his industry merited. In 1869 he married Miss Albina G. Bugg, of Charlotte County, Va. They have four children—one son and three daughters. Mr. Williams is a Democrat, and was mayor of the city of Columbia in 1877-78. In 1882 he was elected to the State Senate from Maury and Lewis Counties. He is a Mason, Knight Templar degree, and is a member of the Royal Arcanum. He and wife belong to the Cumberland Presbyterian Church.

WALTER P. WOOLDRIDGE is a son of Dr. Ferdinand S. and Louise T. (Parrish) Wooldridge, both natives of Williamson County and members of prominent families of that county. The father was a prosperous physician and druggist of Franklin, and died there in 1869. Our subject was born in Franklin, Tenn., May 31, 1856, and after securing an ordinary high school education, came, in 1870, to Maury County and engaged as clerk in the drug business with Titcomb & Williams, and afterward with R. M. Frierson and T. B. Rains, of Columbia. In 1878 he engaged in selling drugs on his own responsibility, in which he has remained to the present time. He has met with more than ordinary success, which fact is due to his energetic and industrious business habits and strict integrity. He is identified with many private and public enterprises of Columbia. April 27, 1882, he married Miss Eliza Keesee, of Clarksville, Tenn. They have one daughter, named Louise D. Mr. Wooldridge is a Mason and a Knight of Pythias, and he and Mrs. Wooldridge are members of the Episcopal Church.

JAMES C. WOOTEN, vice-president of the Columbia Banking Company, was born in Fayetteville, N. C., June 18, 1832, and is a son of Shedrick O. and Elizabeth (Blake) Wooten. The father came from North Carolina to Maury County, Tenn., in 1833. He was originally a hatter by trade, but followed milling and farming in this county. He died in 1851. James C.'s rudimentary education was limited, but he afterward attended the Jackson College during 1852-53. He then began clerking for S. F. Mayes, and soon became a partner in the firm of Mayes, Wooten & Co., but at the breaking out of the war he abandoned the business and enlisted as a private in Capt. Gordon's company, of the Forty-eighth Tennessee Infantry. He was afterward appointed to the quartermaster's department in the Confederate Army, ranking as captain. After his return home he was made agent for the Nashville & Decatur Railroad and held the position three years, after which he engaged in the wholesale grocery and cotton business, with T. W. Keesee & Co., remaining one year. He was married in 1869 and then removed to Leighton, Ala., and was engaged there for fifteen years in buying and selling cotton to Memphis and to

Eastern spinners, but returned in 1885, and has since been identified with the Columbia Banking Company in the capacity of vice-president, and is one of the leading stockholders. He still retains a large interest in Leighton, Ala, owning and managing several large cotton plantations there, as well as other property. He married Hattie A. Abernathy, of Alabama, in 1869, and by her is the father of three children: John T., William B. and Emma. Mr. Wooten is a Democrat, a Mason and a member of the K. of P. He is essentially a self-made man and has a handsome competency, which he has acquired by his own exertions. He spent one year traveling in Europe, visiting most of the large cities in England and on the Continent, and has of late years traveled over all the Western Territories, having visited, at various times, all the States of the Union. He owns a handsome residence in Columbia, which he now occupies.

WILLIAMSON COUNTY.

WILLIAM E. ALEXANDER, a prominent citizen of Williamson County, was born in this State July 8, 1831, and is the son of Jesse W. and Phœbe (Williams) Alexander, both natives of Tennessee. The father was born July 8, 1800, and moved to this county in 1807. He was a Mason in good standing and was noted for his hospitality. The mother was born in 1799, and is still living at the advanced age of eighty-seven years. The father died October 19, 1870. Our subject followed agricultural pursuits from early boyhood. In 1852 he wedded Miss Antoinette Lavender, a native of Tennessee, born in 1834, and the daughter of Nelson and Purmelia (White) Lavender. To our subject and wife were born eight children: William C., Laura A., Ebenezer C., Lucy F. (deceased), Antoinette V. (deceased), Volona L., Viola V. and Nora L. In 1865 Mr. Alexander moved to his farm, which lies in the southeastern portion of the county, and contains 107 acres of finely cultivated land. He is a Democrat in politics, and he and wife are worthy members of the Cumberland Presbyterian Church.

S. ANDERSON, an influential citizen of this district, was born in Williamson County in the year 1825, and is one of eight children born to Joseph and Sallie (Hartley) Anderson. Mr. Anderson has followed farming from early boyhood. In 1847 he married Miss Ella Hartley, a native of this county, born in 1827, and the daughter of Laburn and Nancy (Carson) Hartley. To our subject and wife were born nine children : Sarah C., born August 14, 1849; Thomas W., August 14, 1851; John W., August 27, 1853; William P., March 27, 1854; Sophia E., April 11, 1856; Robert B., deceased, born April 27, 1858; Berry G., born January 27, 1861; Eliza J., August 27, 1864, and Tennessee, March 29, 1868. In 1857 our subject moved to the farm upon which he is now living, which is known as "Cross Keys." It contains 190 acres of land in a fine state of cultivation. He is a member of the Masonic fraternity and a Democrat in politics. He and wife are worthy members of the Cumberland Presbyterian Church.

REV. MARK LYELL ANDREWS was born on the 2d day of December, 1796, between Lexington and Richmond, Ky. His parents were born and reared in the State of Virginia, married and moved to Kentucky in the latter part of the year 1795. In 1810 the father of our subject, George Andrews, moved to Williamson County, Tenn. May 16, 1816, our subject married Eliza Dean, and in the fall of 1819 he became impressed religiously and sought for and found pardon, after which he joined the Methodist Episcopal Church, November, 1819, and was licensed as a local preacher in September, 1822. In 1826 he was ordained deacon by Bishop Soule, and in 1836 was ordained an elder, at Columbia, by Bishop Roberts. In the economy of the church, there being no provision made to support her local ministers, he was forced to look to other sources for employment to support a large and growing family. In March, 1840, he was elected clerk of the Circut Court of Williamson County, and re-elected thereafter from time to time until the year 1874, having held the offfice continuously for a period of 34 years. This is a long time to hold an office, especially in a country notoriously fond of rotation in public life. In 1874, his health declining at that time, he withdrew from any further wish to serve the public, and retired to private life. He died at his residence two miles west of Franklin, November 16, 1878, at the age of eighty-one. He was a blessing to the dying, and stood by the bedside of more dying men and women than most any one else in our State history. He was an example to the living and a benefactor to his race. The world is vastly better off from his having lived in it, and is indeed poorer in Christian charity now that he has gone to his reward.

JOHN ANDREWS, an influential citizen of Williamson County, was born in this State December 18, 1813. His father, James Andrews, was born in North Carolina, in 1785, and in 1805 was married to Jane McGuire, also a native of North Carolina, who was born in 1787. To this union were born seven children—six sons and one daughter—all dead but our subject. The father fought in the Creek Indian war and died in 1850. The mother died in 1845. Our subject took to the hymeneal altar, September 20, 1840, Minerva Matthews, who was born in this State February 28, 1818, and who is the daughter of Isham and Mary B. (Simms) Matthews, the former born in 1782 and died in 1862, and the latter born 1788 and died in 1865. Our subject and wife are the parents of three children: Nannie R., born July 18, 1841; Mary E., born January 20, 1845, and Lucy J., born August 23, 1846. Mr. Andrews followed farming until 1838, after which he clerked in a drug store at Franklin. In 1847 he began merchandising at Peytonsville this district and was very successful in that business. He was also postmaster there for two years. In 1853 he moved to his present farm which consists of 223 acres of good land. He has besides this farm 144 acres of land in this district. He and family are members of the Methodist Episcopal Church South, and Mr. Andrews is a stanch Democrat.

WILLIAM ARMSTRONG, deceased, was born in Virginia in the year 1809, and like the average country boy received his education in the primitive schools. In 1813 he came to Tennessee and located in Williamson County. He entered on life's journey with Miss Elizabeth Leigh as his companion November 2, 1836. Mrs. Armstrong was a daughter of Benjamin Leigh, a native of North Carolina, who immigrated to Tennessee in 1812, and married Martha Whitby. Only two children blessed the union of Mr. and Mrs. Armstrong: William W. and Benjamin F., both of whom are dead; William W. died November 18, 1860, and Benjamin F. died while in the service of his country during the late civil war between the North and the South. Our subject moved to the Seventh District, Williamson County, in 1838, to the place known as "Rocky Hill," where he died February 20, 1879. He was a man who had the respect and esteem of all who knew him, and was a worthy member of the Cumberland Presbyterian Church. Mrs. Armstrong is still living at "Rocky Hill," six miles north of Franklin, and is a consistent member of the Methodist Episcopal Church South.

JOHN ATWOOD was born in what is now Stokes County, N. C., October 22, 1846, son of William F. and Mary (Steele) Atwood, and of English descent. The father was born in Virginia in 1803, and the mother in North Carolina in 1808; they both died in North Carolina. Our subject came to Tennessee in 1868 and settled at Nashville, where he engaged in the broom-making business. This he continued in that city until 1873, after which he clerked in a grocery store until 1876. He then engaged in the grocery business for himself and has since continued that occupation. He is one of the leading business men of the county, and handled last year over 400,000 pounds of broom corn. May 28, 1878, he wedded Maggie A. Sinclair, of this county, and this union resulted in the birth of three children: John B., Bessie May and Jeneva V. Mr. Atwood is a Democrat, a member of the K. of H., and also a member of the Methodist Episcopal Church South. Mrs. Atwood is a member of the Christian Church.

ROBERT A. BAILEY, son of Albert H. and Louise A. (Figuers) Bailey, was born in the town of Franklin, Tenn., September 11, 1849. The father was born in Virginia, and at an early day immigrated to Tennessee and settled in Franklin. He was both a farmer and merchant, and in early life was married to Miss Louisa A. Figuers, and four children were born to them: John H., William T., Patrick R. and Robert R. The father died in 1852, and his son John H. died August 4, 1845. William T. was killed at the battle of Missionary Ridge. Our subject resided on his father's farm until the year 1868, when he engaged as salesman in the dry goods house of J. W. Harrison, where he remained six years. He then engaged in the same business for himself, but in 1875 sold his stock of goods in Franklin and purchased a farm in the adjoining county. In 1872 he was united in marriage to Miss Leonora Mayberry, and three children have blessed their union: Henry M., William T. and Robert A. Mrs. Bailey is a member of the Methodist Episcopal Church.

THOMAS R. BARRICK, station agent and general manager for the Louisville & Nashville Railway at this place, was born in Glasgow, Ky., November 7, 1862, and is the son of J. R. and Lou M. (Moss) Barrick. His parents were both natives of Barren County, Ky. The father was born in 1824, and for a number of years was editor of the Atlanta *Constitution*, and gained some prominence as a writer and contributor to some of the leading papers and magazines of the country. He died at Atlanta in 1869. The mother was born in 1820 and died in 1885. The subject was educated at the schools of his native county, and the early years of his business life were spent in the drug and dry goods business as clerk. At sixteen years of age he began the study of telegraphy. In 1880 he was telegraph operator at Columbia, Tenn. In 1882 he came to Franklin, where he has ever since been station agent. He attends to all the railway business at this place, and enjoys a lucrative and responsible position with the Louisville & Nashville Company. He is thoroughly posted in railway affairs, and is one of the most popular railroad men on the Louisville & Nashville line. January 20, 1886, he wedded Miss Mattie A. Brown, a daughter of Benjamin and Virgia Brown, of this county. He is a Democrat and a member of the Presbyterian Church. Mrs. Barrick is a member of the Christian Church. They are leading young people of the county.

JOHN J. BEECH, druggist, was born in Williamson County November 12, 1826, son of Robert A. and Martha C. (Beech) Beech, and is of English extraction. His father was born in Nottaway County, Va., in 1798, and his mother in Charlotte, Va., in 1800. His paternal grandfather, John Beech, was also a Virginian, and was a faithful soldier in the Revolutionary war. The Beech family came to Williamson County from Virginia at a very early day, and here, in 1843, the mother of our subject died, and his father followed in 1855. Our subject, John J. Beech, passed his youthful days on the farm and secured a good education in the Franklin schools. In 1844 he went to Nashville and began learning the drug business, and in 1851 commenced the same business for himself in Nashville in partnership with Dr. Samuel Flemming. This he continued until 1860, when he removed to Austin, Tex., and for four years was very successfully engaged in the drug business in that city. In 1865 he removed to Franklin, and in 1866 began the drug business in this place, where he has since continued. He is the oldest druggist in Franklin and one of the oldest in the State. In 1851 he wedded Sarah J. Johnson, of Williamson County, and became the father of one son, Eugene L. Mr. Beech is a Democrat, and he and wife are members of the Christian Church.

THOMAS O. BETTS is a son of Thomas and Clarissa (Whittington) Betts, and was born in Davidson County, Tenn., November 21, 1834. The Betts family are natives of Pennsylvania, the grandfather of our subject moving to Nashville at an early day, and erecting the first hotel in the place. He afterward moved to Belleview and operated a grist-mill and distillery for a number of years. Our subject's father was a tanner by trade, and owned a farm on Harpeth River. He became the father of ten children, and died in 1845. Our subject is one of five surviving children, and from early youth has shown aptitude for merchandising and has always followed that occupation. In 1875 he was married to Miss Margaret M. Burk, who is a native of Washington City. Mr. Betts began merchandising in Thompson's Station in 1877, under the firm name of T. O. Betts & Co. They carry a stock of $8,000, and do an annual business of $13,000.

WILLIAM F. BINGHAM was born in the county where he now resides, September 25, 1838, son of James J. and Amelia (Haley) Bingham, and is of Irish lineage. The parents born in Guilford County, N. C., and Halifax County, Va., in 1800 and 1807, and died in Williamson County, Tenn., in 1876 and 1872, respectively. Their family consisted of nine children, our subject being the sixth. He received a common school education, and learned the tanner's trade, which he followed three years. He enlisted in the First Regiment Tennessee Infantry, and served four years. He was slightly wounded at the battle of Murfreesboro, Tenn., and was a participant in some of the hardest fought battles of the war. Since the close of that conflict he has followed farming, with the exception of six years, when he served as sheriff of Williamson County. He was married, March 1, 1867, to Miss Susan Davis, of the same county as himself. Mr. Bingham is a Democrat, and belongs to the Masonic and Odd Fellows fraternities. He and wife are members of the Christian Church.

JAMES J. BINGHAM, farmer and merchant, was born November 22, 1840, in Williamson County, Tenn., son of J. J. and Amelia (Haley) Bingham, and is of Irish descent. The family came from North Carolina to Tennessee at a very early day. Our subject received a common school education, and has made farming his chief occupation through life. He was in the Eleventh Tennessee Cavalry, Confederate States Army, and served one year. He was married to Miss Luversa E. Dodd, September 27, 1864. They have had five children, four now living: Thomas R., born in 1865; Laura Lee, born in 1868; Jennie D., born in 1870, and Sallie M., born in 1872. Mr. Bingham and wife belong to the Christian Church. Mr. Bingham, by his untiring application to business, has secured reasonable results, and is now spending a happy life with his family.

THOMAS H. BOND was born July 26, 1826, and is a son of William Bond, who was an early settler of Tennessee and a native of Virginia. He located in Williamson County in 1804 and a year later was married to Miss Nancy Dabney, of North Carolina, and thirteen children were born to them : Sidney S., Margaret, Lucy, Elizabeth, Bethenia, John D., Morris L., Charles A., William J., Thomas H., Robert W., Benjamin F. and Nancy D William and Nancy Bond died in 1850 and 1868, respectively. They were members of the Christian Church. The place of our subject's nativity was Williamson County, Tenn., where he was educated in the common schools. September 12, 1850, he wedded Miss Mary M. Banks, who bore him twelve children—Henry M., Laura E., Bethenia D., Annie M., James D., Benjamin F., Thomas H., Florence L., William W., John D., Morris L. and Nannie D. Bethenia died in 1861, Morris L, in 1867, and John D. in 1884. In 1845 our subject began merchandising in Nashville, continuing six years, and then returned to Williamson County and resumed farming. He owns a very fine tract of land and is a member of the Christian Church. In politics he is a Democrat and was a Whig before the dissolution of that party.

JAMES C. BOSTICK was born in 1835, in Williamson County, Tenn. He is a son of James A. and Nancy Bostick, and grandson of John and Mary G. Bostick, who were born in North Carolina, and settled in Tennessee in 1809. Our subject's mother was the daughter of William and Sarah King, born in North Carolina, and settled in Tennessee at an early date. The parents of our subject were married in this State in 1827. To them were born eight children : Thomas K., Mary J., James C., Manoah H., Sarah P., Martha E., John and William. James C. attended the Hardeman Academy, near Triune, in 1854–55, and the Western Military Academy, in Sumner County, Tenn., where he fitted himself for civil engineering, and in 1856 served in that capacity for the Louisville & Nashville Railroad. Three years later he abandoned this and engaged in the lumber business in Nashville, Tenn., the firm being known as Bostick & Abston. At the breaking out of the war in 1861 he enlisted in the Thirteenth Tennessee Cavalry under Gen. Morgan, and participated in all the principal battles. At the close of the war he returned to Sumner County, where he remained until 1869, when he moved to Williamson County where he now resides. In 1859 he wedded Fannie L. Abston, daughter of Merry and Mary Abston. To Mr. and Mrs. Bostick five children were born : James A., Merry C., Mary A., Sallie P. and Fannie M. Mr. Bostick was elected county surveyor in 1873, and justice of the peace in 1871, which office he still holds. Mrs. Bostick died in 1885. She was a member of the Methodist Episcopal Church as is her husband. He is a Democrat in politics and is of English descent.

JOSEPH H. BOWMAN was born July 5, 1847, in Madison County, Miss., where he remained until the death of his father. He then came to Tennessee and located near Franklin, where he received his education. March, 1863, Mr. Bowman shouldered his musket and enlisted in Company D, Thirty-second Tennessee Regiment of Infantry. He was in Bragg's retreat from Tennessee, and also with Johnston in Georgia. He received a wound June 22, 1864, from which he feels the effects to this day. He was paroled May, 1865. After the war he clerked in a store in Franklin, and afterward went to Nashville and clerked there for some time. Leaving Nashville he wedded Miss Jennie E., second daughter of Thomas and Margaret S. Brown. Mr. Brown died January 13, 1870. Mrs. Brown is still living, and is a member of the Christian Church. Our subject moved to Williamson County and engaged in farming, and by his union with Jennie E. Brown became the father of ten children: Thomas B., William H., Joseph H., Maggie B., Elizabeth M., George B., Jennie B., Inez B., Dunklin C. and James G. Mr. Bowman has a fine farm of about 148 acres, and it is known as the "Owl Nest Farm." Mrs. Bowman is a worthy member of the Christian Church. Our subject's father, William Bowman, was born January 8, 1809, and received his education in the University of Nashville. September 20, 1843, he wedded Miss Elizabeth M. Maney, daughter of William Maney, of Franklin. William Bowman was a Master Mason, and died at his residence in Mississippi, June 27, 1853. The mother is still living, and is a consistent member of the Presbyterian Church. She was for many years a teacher in Ward's Seminary at Nashville.

PHILIP BOXLEY, son of Harrison and Nancy (Claude) Boxley, was born July 16, 1841, in Williams County, Tenn. Harrison Boxley was born in Virginia, and immigrated to Tennessee about 1828, and settled in Williamson County, where he afterward became a well-to-do farmer. His wife was born in Tennessee, and to them were born two children: Philip and James. Mrs. Boxley died in 1844, and Mr. Boxley wedded Mrs. Maury (a widow), who bore him one child, a daughter named Mary. Our subject was educated in the country schools, and in 1871 was united in marriage to Miss Hattie Boxley. He enlisted in the Southern Army in 1861, in the Twentieth Tennessee Regiment, under Col. Battle, and was a participant in the following battles: Shiloh, Missionary Ridge, Chattanooga, Franklin, Atlanta and Vicksburg. In 1869 he removed to Arkansas, where he remained two years, when he returned to Tennessee and located on the West Harpeth River, in Williamson County, where he owns a fine farm and is a good citizen.

WILLIAM W. BROOKS was born in Franklin County, N. C.. in 1817, and is the son of Christopher and Martha Brooks, who were married in North Carolina, December 22, 1808, and came to Tennessee in 1824. They became the parents of six children: Martha A., Susan, Christopher B., William W., Mary F. and Alexander N. B. Our subject received good educational advantages, and has spent his days in farming and blacksmithing. He located on his present farm in 1852. It consists of 198 acres of valuable land, well-improved, near Owen's Station. Mr. Brooks started in life with but little capital, except his hands and willing heart, and by his energy and good management is in very comfortable circumstances, financially. July 11, 1847, he wedded Martha Alley, who was born in August, 1828, in Williamson County. She is a daughter of Walter and Perna C. Alley, of North Carolina. Mr. and Mrs. Brooks have these four children: William, Mary E., Martha J. and Eliza L. Mrs. Brooks died May 29, 1872, and Mr. Brooks took for his second wife Mary C. Brown (widow of Dr. H. T. Brown), daughter of David and Mary C. Beech. She was born August 14, 1833, and became the mother of one child, Kate B. Mr. Brooks belongs to the Democratic party and is of English extraction.

JOHN A. BUCHANAN was born in Rutherford County, Tenn., December 16, 1835, son of Moses and Sarah Buchanan, and grandson of Maj. John Buchanan, who emigrated from Scotland to America about 1750 and was a participant in the Revolutionary war and the war of 1812. The father of our subject was born in Tennessee April 4, 1806, and the mother July 16, 1810. She was a daughter of James and Ann Ridley who were born in Tennessee. Moses Buchanan and his wife were married about 1826 and became the parents of these children: Sarah A., Mary J., James A., Elizabeth C., John A., Katherine L., Tennessee L., George R., Samuel J.. Moses R., Hance H., Henry S., Nannie A. and Virginia L. John A., our subject, received a liberal education and in early life was engaged in the milling business with his father. At the breaking out of the war in 1861 he enlisted in Douglas' regiment and was third lieutenant of Carter's company. At the end of two years he was captured and taken to Murfreesboro but after a short time was paroled and returned home to Rutherford County. March 21, 1860, he wedded Miss Ridley who was born in Giles County, September 23, 1842, daughter of William and Minerva T. Ridley. Our subject located on his present farm of 160 acres in 1879. He is the father of these children: Moses R., born July 14, 1861, and died January 8, 1885; Sallie M., born November 7, 1863; John B., born December 29, 1866, and died September 24, 1872; Henry L., born October 16, 1869; Nannie, born October 6, 1871, and died October 12, 1872; Mattie L., born August 18, 1873; Willie M., born October 21, 1875, and died October 1, 1876; Scrap H., born December 31, 1877, and Jimmie, born May 8, 1880. Mr. Buchanan is a Democrat in politics and in 1880 was elected justice of the peace. Mr. and Mrs. Buchanan have two adopted daughters: Nannie P., born December 11, 1866, and Beulah C., born November 8, 1871, daughters of William and Isabella Ridley.

E. B. BUCHANAN, farmer, was born in Williamson County, Tenn., August 9, 1840, son of Robert S. Buchanan, who was born in this county February 3, 1818. He received a common school education and was married in 1838 to Miss Harriet Bateman and our subject is the second of their twelve children. The father died in June, 1883, and the mother in March, 1862. The family first came to Tennessee from Pennsylvania in 1778, and were among the first settlers of Nashville. Our subject received an academic education at Franklin, Tenn., and assisted his father on the farm until twenty years of age, when he began working for the Memphis & Charleston Railroad Company, and resided in Collierville until the breaking out of the war. He then enlisted in Company C, Fourth Tennessee, and was in the battles of Perryville, Corinth, Murfreesboro, and the Atlanta campaign. He was captured June 21, 1864, but made his escape at Murfreesboro and returned home but soon re-enlisted and was in the battles of Franklin and Nashville. After his return home he began clerking on a steam-boat, continuing one year and then engaged in the mercantile business in Nashville one year. He then taught school the following year and later engaged in farming. He was deputy sheriff from September, 1870, to September 1874, and has been justice of the peace from 1874 to the present time, his term expiring in 1888; has also been deputy county clerk. He was married, Febuary 2, 1868, to Miss Mattie McKay, daughter of John P. and Margaret McKay. They are the parents of these children: John M., Hattie, R. D., and Willie E. Mr. Buchanan is a Democrat and belongs to the Masonic fraternity, I. O. O. F., K. of H. and A. O. U. W. He and wife belong to the Cumberland Presbyterian Church.

REV. CLAUDIUS BUCHANAN, a native of Williamson County, was born December 17, 1842. His father, Joseph Buchanan, was born in this State about 1809, and in 1836 he wedded Martha Edmiston, a native of Tennessee, born about 1809. To this union were born seven children, two of whom are yet living, our subject being one of them. The father died in 1876. Our subject's grandfather, John Buchanan, was born in Washington County, Va., in 1772, and married Margaret Edmondson in 1798; she was also a native of Virginia, born about 1774. They came to Tennessee about 1800 and purchased 200 acres of land in this district on what is known as the "Old High Tower Road." He died in 1820 and the grandmother in 1858. Our subject has followed agricultural pursuits the principal part of his life. In 1861 he enlisted in Company D, Twentieth Tennessee Regiment, was taken prisoner at Missionary Ridge, imprisoned at Rock Island, Ill., and retained there fifteen months. At the close of the war he returned home and in 1866 was married to Miss Dolly J. Smithson, a native of this State, born October 12, 1844, and the daughter of Sylvanus and Louisa Smithson, natives, respectively, of Virginia and Tennessee. The father was born about 1791 and served as a private in the late war; was wounded in the Cheat Mountain campaign. He died in 1872 and the mother in 1850. To our subject and wife were born six children: Josephine E., born September 11, 1867; M. Blanche, born December 29, 1869; William C., born August 10, 1871; John B., born July 24, 1874; Lillian M. born September 10, 1877, and Gerald M., born March 28, 1870. In January, 1867, Mr. Buchanan moved to the farm upon which he is now living and in 1870 purchased it from his father. It contains 300 acres of medium land in a fair state of cultivation. In 1871 he obtained license to preach, and has since been a local preacher. He is a member of the Masonic fraternity and is a Democrat in politics. He and wife are devout members of the Methodist Episcopal Church South.

JOSIAH BUTT was born in Bedford County, Tenn., February 6, 1832, son of Nathaniel and Rebecca Butt, who were born in this State. Nathaniel Butt was the son of James Butt, who came to this State from the "Old Dominion" and settled in Davidson County about 1814. The mother, Rebecca Butt, was a daughter of Joseph E. Cook, who came from North Carolina to this State in the early part of the present century. The parents of our subject were married about 1828, and to their union were born five children—three sons and two daughters: Arthur, Josiah, Mary, Rebecca and Nathaniel. Our subject was educated in the common schools, and in 1866 located on his present farm, where he has followed tilling the soil, wagon-making and blacksmithing, and is the owner of 175 acres of valuable farming land. By the sweat of his brow he has acquired his present property, and deserves much credit therefor. January 19, 1854, he wedded Martha Jackson, daughter of John J. Jackson, a native of North Carolina. Both Mr. and Mrs. Butt are members of the Missionary Baptist Church at Concord. To them were born nine children: Porterfield, Theodore, Clara, Joanna, Willie, Georgiana, Ada, Olive and Nettie. Mr. Butt is a member of the Democratic party, and the family are of German-Irish descent.

ANDREW CAMPBELL is a son of William and Margaret (Stewart) Campbell, and was born in the year 1818 in Donegal County, Ireland. His father was a native of the same country, and died there about 1839. He was the father of five sons: John, William S., Andrew, James and Patrick. John, William and James are dead. Our subject's mother was of English descent, belonging to the Stewart family of that country, who settled in the northern part of Ireland in 1690, and in 1790 came to the United States and located in East Tennessee. Our subject came to Tennessee in 1839, and located near Franklin. He received an excellent education at Bethany College, Va., and after graduating returned to Tennessee, where he followed school teaching in Williamson and Davidson Counties thirty-five years. Since 1883 he has followed farming on a large scale, and in politics was a Whig until the death of that party, when he became identified with the Democratic party. The family have always been prominent citizens of the county.

NEWTON CANNON, dealer in hardware and groceries, was born near Franklin June 14, 1846, son of William P. and Susan A. (Perkins) Cannon, and of French and English descent. The family is traced back to three brothers who came to America. One settled in Maryland, one in South Carolina, and the other in North Carolina. Our subject is traceable to the North Carolina branch of the family. The paternal grandfather of our subject was Newton Cannon, who was born in North Carolina, and came to Williamson County in early life. He was a saddler by trade, a colonel in the Seminole war, under Jackson, and was twice governor of Tennessee, and a member of Congress. He was one of the early prominent men of this State, a leader of the Whig party, and died at Nashville in 1842. The father of our subject was born in this county in 1816, and was a farmer by occupation, and was wounded in the Florida war. He now lives in southern Kentucky. The mother was born in this county in 1821 and died in 1849. Our subject was reared on the farm, attended Franklin schools, and in 1862 enlisted in Company I, Eleventh Tennessee Cavalry, Confederate States Army, and was paroled in May, 1865, at

Gainesville, Ala. At the close of the war he returned home, and in 1873 was appointed deputy county court clerk, which position he occupied for one year. For thirteen years he has been engaged in merchandising, five years of which time were spent in the wholesale hardware business in Nashville. He is now engaged in retail merchandising in Franklin, but in connection with this carries on farming on 250 acres of valuable land near Franklin. February, 1873, he wedded Miss Jennie B. McEwen, daughter of John B. McEwen, and by this union became the father of five children: John B., Leah A., Cynthia G., Newton and Samuel P. Mr. Cannon is a Democrat, and his wife is a member of the Presbyterian Church.

JOSEPH CARL is a native of Williamson County, Tenn., and was born April 5, 1828, son of Jacob B. and Jane B. (Stewart) Carl, born in 1802 and 1806, in Dutchess County, N. Y., and Todd County, Ky. Jacob B. Carl was brought to Williamson County, Tenn., when a child by his parents, and died January 1, 1854. The mother is yet living. Our subject was reared on a farm and received a common school education, and always followed agricultural pursuits. He enlisted in the Confederate Army and belonged to the Twelfth Tennessee Cavalry. He served three years and surrendered with his regiment in Georgia by order of Gen. Johnston. Since the cessation of hostilities he has made agriculture his chief pursuit and at the present time owns 250 acres of well-tilled land. On the 20th day of February, 1851, he was united in matrimony to Miss Mary J. Alston, of Williamson County, Tenn. To them were born twelve children—ten sons and two daughters; one son and one daughter are deceased. Mr. Carl is a Democrat and Mason and he and wife belong to the Christian Church.

COL. MOSCOW B. CARTER, one of the leading men of the county, was born in Franklin December 5, 1825, son of Fountain and Mary A. (Adkinson) Carter, and of French-Scotch origin. The father was born in Halifax County, Va., in 1797, and the mother in the same county in 1806. The Carter family immigrated to Williamson County, Tenn., in 1809, and here our subject's father died in 1872 and the mother, in 1852. Our subject received a good education in the Franklin schools, and in 1846 enlisted in the Mexican war, and served one year. He is one of five living Mexican soldiers of this county. He then came home and engaged in farming and surveying, carrying on these occupations until the breaking out of the late war. In 1861 he raised a company for the Confederate States Army, of which he was elected captain, and in May of the same year, was commissioned lieutenant-colonel. January, 1862, he was captured at the battle of Mill Springs and held as a prisoner of war for nine months. He remained in the service until the latter part of 1863, when he came home. Since the war he has been engaged in farming and now has 120 acres. On this farm the battle of Franklin was fought. Prior to the war, in 1851, Mr. Carter wedded Callie Dobbins, and three children blessed this union: Lena, Walter and Hugh. Mrs. Carter died in 1860, and in 1866 Col. Carter wedded America Cattles, and this union resulted in the birth of two children: Alma and Moscow. The second Mrs. Carter died in 1876, and our subject married his present wife, Mrs. Pamelia Miot, a native of South Carolina, and to this union were born two children: Emma L. and Frank F. Col. Carter is a Democrat, a Mason, and he and wife are members of the Presbyterian Church.

JOSEPH T. CHADWELL was born on the 7th of November, 1824, in Williamson County, Tenn. His parents, John and Mary (Thompson) Chadwell, were the father and mother of nine children, our subject being the third. The father's native State was North Carolina, and he came to Tennessee at a very early day, settling near Nolensville, Tenn., where he was a tiller of the soil and owned a fine tract of land. His children were Robert, Thomas, Joseph T., John, Everett, George, Martha H. and Sarah; only five are now living. The father died in 1854, and in 1863 his widow followed him. Our subject's early days were spent on his father's farm and in attending the county schools near his home. In 1859 he was united in marriage to Mrs. Mary Parks, a widow lady. Mr. Chadwell owns an excellent farm of 220 acres, and is one of the enterprising and leading men of Williamson County, Tenn.

WILLIAMSON COUNTY. 973

JOEL CHAMPION may be mentioned as a prominent farmer and stock raiser of Williamson County, Tenn. He was born in Hancock County, Ga., son of Alexander and Mary (Benson) Champion, who were also born in Georgia, and were married about 1810, and to them were born these three children: Joel, Nancy and Rebecca. The family came to Tennessee in 1822. The father died in Putnam County, Ga., in 1817, and the mother in Maury County, Tenn., in 1859. Joel Champion's early education was limited. His early days were spent on a farm, and agriculture has been his chosen calling through life, at which he has been fairly prosperous, as he started in life with little or no money. He owns 140 acres of land on which he settled in 1840, and which is in a good state of cultivation. December 2, 1851, he married Elizabeth C. McMahon, who was born December 9, 1827, and became the mother of these children: Ann E., Louisa J., Susan I., John R., Mary F. and Minnie J. Both husband and wife are members of the Methodist Episcopal Church, and in political views our subject is a Democrat.

JOHN GILLEM CLAY, M. D., is a son of the late Judge Thomas J. and Sarah A. (Green) Clay, and was born at Madison, Ala., May 3, 1859. Thomas Jefferson Clay was a Virginian by birth, born in Petersburg, January 12, 1819. His father was Thomas Clay, a native of Virginia, whose ancestry were prominent among the most wealthy families of that period. He was married to Miss Nancy Webb and resided many years in Petersburg, and subseqently lived in Nottaway County five years. At that time Thomas Jefferson moved to Madison County, Ala., and while a youth came to Williamson County, Tenn., and entered Arrington Academy. He was there a classmate of Gen. W. C. Whitthorne and others who have become eminent in the history of Tennessee. His education was completed at Huntsville, Ala. Being educated as a teacher, he taught school at Nolensville, Tenn., after which he returned to north Alabama, where on January 29, 1850, he wedded Miss Sarah Armistead Green, daughter of Dr. William B. Green, of Madison County, Ala., who was from Newbern, N. C., where he was born and married to Sarah Bass. After Mr. Clay's marriage he engaged in the mercantile business and in 1856 moved to the town of Madison on the Memphis & Clarksville Railroad, being one of the first settlers of the place and one of its most successful business men. He served as mayor of the town for a number of years and also as district judge. In 1883 he moved to the city of Montgomery, remaining there two years, when he moved to his home at Madison, and there died April 25, 1886. He was a member of the Missionary Baptist Church and was noted for his Christian virtue. John G. Clay, M. D., our subject, was reared in Madison, Ala., and there received his academic education. He spent two years at Salado College, in Texas, and graduated in the commercial department of that institution. He returned to Alabama in 1879 and in the autumn of the same year entered the medical department of Vanderbilt University at Nashville, Tenn., from which institution he graduated in the spring of 1882, and in 1883 also graduated at the University of Nashville. At the former date he began practicing medicine at Thompson's Station, Tenn., and at a later date he also engaged in the drug business at the same place. He carries a stock of $1,500 and does a business from $2,000 to $3,000 per year. He is a member of the Missionary Baptist Church and is an honest dealer with his fellow-man.

JOHN S. CLAYBROOKE is a son of John and Sarah Claybrooke, who were born in the "Old Dominion," and a grandson of William and Sarah (Overton) Claybrooke, who were of the F. F. V.'s. The Claybrooke family was of English descent, and came to America and settled on the James River, in Virginia, about 1600. Our subject's father, John Claybrook, was born about 1767, and was a farmer and merchant by occupation. He married our subject's mother in 1796. She was born in 1773 and died in 1850. They were the parents of these children: Elizabeth P., James O., Mary A., Sarah W., John S., Thomas W., Jane R. and Lucretia. Our subject was born in Louisa County, Va., March 28, 1808. He received his education in Virginia, and came to this State in 1828, and made his home with his uncle, Judge John Overton. He taught school in Hardeman Academy, near Triune, for twelve sessions. In 1836 he settled where he now lives and owns 550 acres of valuable and well improved land. He also owns 1,800 acres of land in

Haywood County, Tenn., and several other tracts in West Tennessee. Mr. Claybrooke was married to Mary A. Perkins, April 24, 1834, daughter of Samuel and Sallie Perkins, who were born in Virginia and Tennessee, respectively. Mr. and Mrs. Claybrooke became the parents of ten children: Frederick, John P., Sarah, Annie W., Samuel P., Mary E., Elvira L., Susan F., Eliza M. and Virginia O. In politics our subject is a Democrat, and his ancestors were among the early pioneer settlers of Tennessee, and several of them participated in the Revolutionary war and the war of 1812. Our subject has a fine education and is one of the esteemed men of the county, and was the first president of the Nashville & Decatur Railroad, holding the position from 1852 to 1868. His wife's death occurred November 10, 1868.

WILLIAM COLLINS, son of John and Mary (Cole) Collins, was born December 7, 1838. The father was born in Virginia, and came to Tennessee when quite young. He was a farmer, and became the father of eight children: William, Sallie J., John, James, Zibbie, Lewis, Fannie and Franklin. The father died August 22, 1872. He was twice married, his second wife being a Miss M. Johnson. William Collins was the only child born to John and Mary Collins. He was reared on a farm and educated in the country schools, and in 1861 enlisted in the Twenty-fourth Tennessee Regiment, under Col. Wilson, participating in the battles of Shiloh, Chickamauga, Atlanta and others of lesser note. In 1866 he was united in marriage to Miss Mary Rease, a native of Williamson County, and daughter of Joe T. Rease. Both Mr. and Mrs. Collins are members of the Cumberland Presbyterian Church, and are esteemed citizens.

HENRY HOWE COOK was born in Williamson County, Tenn., November 23, 1843, son of Lewis and Margaret Jane Cook. Lewis Cook was born in South Carolina in 1801, and moved to Maury County, Tenn., when a boy with one of the members of Gen. Nathaniel Green's family. From thence he went to Nashville and learned the carpenter's trade, which occupation he followed for years, but spent the latter part of his life as a farmer. He died in 1873. His father's name was William, and his mother's maiden name was Howe. Margaret Jane Cook was the daughter of Nathan Owen, who came from Petersburg, Va., and settled on Mill Creek, in Davidson County at an early day. He married Jennie Hightower, mother of Margaret Jane. Our subject spent his boyhood on the farm, and at fifteen years of age entered Franklin College, near Nashville, where he remained until April, 1861, when he enlisted in Company D, First Tennessee Regiment, Confederate States Army, and went to Virginia. He was discharged on account of ill health in the winter of 1861. Soon after his return from Virginia he went to Fort Donelson, from which place he made his escape about 8 o'clock on the morning of the surrender. He then joined the Fifty-fifth Tennessee Regiment at the battle of Shiloh. After the consolidation of the Forty-fourth and Fifty-fifth Tennessee he was elected lieutenant in the Reed and McEwen consolidated companies, and was with the regiment at the battles of Perryville and Murfreesboro. At the last named place he was wounded twice. After Capt. Samuel Jackson was mortally wounded, at the battle of Chickamauga, our subject commanded the company, and was in the assault on Fort Sanders at Knoxville, at the battle of Bean's Station, Port Walthall Junction and Drury's Bluff, where he was captured and taken to Fortress Monroe, Point Lookout and Fort Delaware. He was one of the 600 officers who were selected at Fort Delaware and put under fire of the Confederate batteries at Morris Island, off Charleston, and from thence he was taken to Fort Pulaski for purposes of further retaliation; thence he was taken back to Fort Delaware. He suffered greatly in prison from hunger and cold, and his health was much impaired. In June, 1865, he reached home and began the study of law, and was licensed to practice in 1867. In 1870 he was elected county judge of Williamson County for a term of eight years, and was re-elected in 1878. He is a Democrat in politics, a Mason and a member of the Christian Church. In 1882 he married Miss Fanny Crockett Marshall, a daughter of the late John Marshall, one of Tennessee's best lawyers. To this marriage was born one daughter—Genevieve. Judge Cook is a citizen of Franklin, Tenn., where he is engaged in the practice of the law.

MRS. SARAH E. COOKE was born in Maury County, Tenn., June 4, 1837. Her father, Lemuel Jones, was born in North Carolina in 1811, and her mother in South Carolina in 1815. The father came to Tennessee at an early day, and resided in Maury County until his death, which took place September 6, 1845. The mother died July 26, 1885. The father's family consisted of four children, our subject being the eldest. Mrs. Cooke was educated in the common schools and at Springhill College, Tennessee. She was married December 1, 1857, to Mr. P. H. Cooke, of Maury County, Tenn., who was born September 3, 1830, in Maryland. He was educated at Jackson College, Tennessee, and was of Scotch descent. He was a Confederate soldier and belonged to the Maury Artillery, being captured at Fort Donelson and died July 11, 1862, while a prisoner in Camp Douglas, Chicago. Mrs. Cooke has one son, John L., who was born January 23, 1860, and educated at Culleoka College, Tennessee. He manages their farm of 200 acres in a very satisfactory manner, and he and mother are members of the Presbyterian Church.

DR. J. D. CORE, a successful practitioner, was born in Tennessee November 3, 1839, and was the son of John D. and Deborah (Carroll) Core. The father was born in North Carolina February 1, 1787, and was a strict member of the Methodist Episcopal Church for over sixty years, and died November 6, 1877, with the full assurance of a blessed hereafter. The mother was born in Moore County, N. C., December 25, 1801, and was also a worthy member of the Methodist Episcopal Church for many years. As a wife and mother she was kind and affectionate; as a neighbor she had the respect and esteem of all who knew her, and her death, which occurred June 24, 1875, was universally regretted. Our subject was reared on a farm and educated in the best county schools. At the age of sixteen he began reading medicine with his brother, Dr. Jesse G. Core, and remained with him until 1857, when he entered the University of Nashville, took the courses of 1857-58, also 1859, and graduated from that institution in 1860. In 1861 he enlisted as a private in the army, but at the expiration of two years he was promoted to second lieutenant and held that office until the close of the war. He then returned home and located at Bethesda, and has since been engaged in the practice of his profession. January 22, 1867, he was wedded to Miss Bettie J. Blythe, and by her he became the father of one child, named John B. Mrs. Core died November 11, 1872. Dr. Core then married Mary R. Blythe, May 7, 1874. She was the daughter of Andrew T. Blythe, and was born in this State in 1825. To our subject and wife were born two children: Willie T. and Richard E. The Doctor is a member of the Masonic fraternity, a Methodist in belief and a Democrat in politics. Mrs. Core is a member of the Old School Presbyterian Church.

DAVID R. CORLETT was born in this county November 19, 1830. His father, John C. Corlett, was born in North Carolina May 28, 1798, and came to Tennessee when a young man. He was married, February 25, 1830, to our subject's mother Mary A. Chriesman, a native of this county, born July 7, 1807. The father died in 1862 and the mother in 1885. Our subject was reared on a farm, and is now living near the farm of his birth. In 1854 he wedded Miss Lucy J. Roberts, a native of this State, born April 4, 1833, and the daughter of John R. and Annie (Giles) Roberts. April 18, 1857, Mrs. Corlett died, and in 1858 Miss Martha H. Warren became his second wife. She was a native of Tennessee, born May 31, 1831, and died February 6, 1862. Our subject then married his present wife, Sarah C. Thompson, December 28, 1865. She was born in this State May 21, 1837, and is the daughter of Hugh and Mary A. (Blackwell) Thompson, natives, respectively, of South Carolina and Alabama. To Mr. Corlett and wife were born four children: Mary T., born 1870; David H., born 1874; Annie P., born 1876, and Marvin, born 1878. In 1862 he enlisted in Company C, Eleventh Tennessee Cavalry, and was captured and taken to Camp Chase, where he was retained until the close of the war. In 1867 he moved to his present farm, which contains 319 acres, in the Twelfth District. In Marshall County he has another farm of about 111 acres. In 1876 he was elected justice of the peace, and re-elected in 1882 and holds the office at the present time. He and wife are members of the Methodist Episcopal Church South, and Mr. Corlett is an unswerving Democrat.

R. F. COTTON was born in Davidson County, Tenn., July 24, 1838, and was the sixteenth of seventeen children born to Allen and Mary (Barham) Cotton. The father was born in North Carolina and died in 1867, and his wife in 1863. Our subject received a good English education, and taught school a number of years. He enlisted in Company F, Fourth Tennessee Cavalry, in 1861. At Richmond, Ky., he captured a Federal captain and fifteen men by making them believe he had a large force. He was promoted on the field to a first lieutenant, and was in the secret service, under Gen. Bragg, until captured September 19, 1863. He was discharged in May, 1865, and after his return home engaged in farming. At the end of one year he came to Williamson County and purchased a farm near Franklin, which he has increased to where he now owns 325 acres of good land. In September, 1865, he wedded Lucinda J. Smith, daughter of Turner Smith. She died in May, 1868, leaving one daughter, Amanda. He then married Mary E. Owen, daughter of Richard and Mary Y. (Temple) Owen, October 22, 1871. Their children are Alcenia G., Mary E., Owen T., Robert A., Lucila, Maggie and Park. Mr. Cotton is a Democrat and a member of the K. of P.

ROBERT S. COWLES is a son of John and Mary (King) Cowles, born in Virginia in 1801 and 1811, respectively. John Cowles came to Tennessee in 1825 and located near Cowles Chapel. His occupation was school teaching and farming, and he was a member of the Methodist Episcopal Church South. He and Mary King were married in 1830, and to them were born ten children: William H., Mary F., James B., Sallie E., John W., Lucy, Alice, Robert S., Susie, Samuel and Ann J. John Cowles died May 14, 1882, and his wife February 22, 1886. Robert S. Cowles was born in Williamson County, Tenn., January 31, 1844, and was educated in the county schools. At the breaking out of the war he enlisted in the Forty-fourth Tennessee Regiment, under Col. Mitchell. He was in the following battles: Shiloh (where he was wounded), Murfreesboro, Chickamauga, all the battles in the Georgia campaign, second battle of Murfreesboro, Nashville and surrendered at Greensboro, N. C. Since that time he has farmed. In 1872 he was married to Maggie North, daughter of H. B. North. They have two children: James B. and Maggie R. Mr. Cowles owns a fine tract of land and is one of the leading farmers of Williamson County Both he and wife are members of the Methodist Episcopal Church South.

COL. N. N. COX was born in Bedford County January 6, 1837. C. and N. Cox, his father and mother, moved from North Carolina about 1811 and settled in Bedford. When our subject was about nine months old his father died, leaving thirteen children, our subject being the youngest. The mother, with some of the younger children, moved to Arkansas, and from there to southwestern Texas, in 1847. She located in Seguin, near San Antonio. Her son, N. N., spent his early years on the frontiers of Texas and was in several scouts and fights, protecting the settlers from the Indians. He left Texas, in 1857, to enter the law school at Lebanon, Tenn., and graduated from the law department in June, 1858. He located in Linden, Perry County, and commenced the practice of law. In 1860, being quite young, he was placed on the electoral ticket representing Breckenridge and Lane. He enlisted in the army in 1861 as captain in the cavalry service. At the organization of the battalion to which his company was attached he was elected major, and when the battalion was organized into a regiment, just after the battle of Shiloh, he was ordered to organize another command, which he did. This command was placed under Gen. Forrest. At the battle of Parker's Cross Roads, in West Tennessee, Maj. Cox was captured, with a number of his men. He was confined in Camp Chase for some time. During his imprisonment his troops were organized into the Tenth Tennessee Cavalry, and Maj. Cox, while in prison, upon the recommendation of Gen. Forrest, was appointed colonel of the regiment, by the War Department at Richmond. He continued to command the regiment until the close of the war. He then located in Franklin, Tenn., and resumed the practice of law. In 1872 he was one of the electors of the Democratic party again for his district. In one of the hottest contests ever known in Tennessee for congressional honors he was one of the contestants. He was twice rewarded for gallantry by Gen. Forrest, and was made a full colonel without his knowledge. He has never held a civil office, and at this writing is still engaged in his profession.

WILLIAM H. CROUCH is of Scotch-Irish descent, and is a son of William H. and Eliza (Stone) Crouch. The father was born in Virginia in 1804, and came to Tennessee when a boy. He learned the shoe-maker's trade, and in 1832 or 1833 was married to our subject's mother, and to them were born seven children: Mary, William, John (deceased), Peter, Barton (deceased), Charles (deceased) and Eliza. The father was twice married, his second wife being Lucy Carter. He died in 1874, and the mother some time in the forties. Our subject was reared in Franklin, Tenn., and he was educated at the Harpeth Male Academy. He was first employed in his father's merchandise store in Franklin, and remained with him until 1859, when he engaged in the ready-made clothing business under the firm name of Cummins & Crouch. In 1860 he sold out his interest and began clerking for Mr. Cummins, continuing until 1861, when he went to work for C. A. Bailey & Co. In 1862 he enlisted in the Fourth Regiment of Tennessee Cavalry, under J. W. Starn. He was wounded in the thigh in a skirmish at Sugar Hill, Tenn., and was compelled to go on crutches four years. In 1857 he was married to Miss Mollie Hodge, of Franklin, who died in 1862, leaving one son, John H. Mr. Crouch is now in business in Harpeth Station for R. H. North, and is agent for the Louisville & Nashville and Great Southern Railroads, and is postmaster and a member of the Methodist Episcopal Church South.

JAMES P. CRUTCHER, a prominent citizen of this district, was born in this county May 22, 1825, and is the son of Robert and Nancy (Children) Crutcher, both natives of Virginia. The father was born September 22, 1788, and was married about 1815. In 1824 he came to Tennessee and died in that State January 3, 1866. The mother was born April 26, 1803, and died April 18, 1861. Our subject's grandfather was James Children, who was born March 25, 1771, and his great-grandfather was Samuel Matthews who was born in 1742. Our subject was a country boy and received a fair education in the county schools. He was a dentist by occupation, and practiced his profession for twenty-seven years. In 1851 he wedded Miss Susan V. Bond, a native of this State born March 5, 1830, and the daughter of John and Mary L. Bond. To Mr. Crutcher and wife were born seven children: Robert S., William H. (deceased), Mary T. (deceased), Sina V., Jane E., James M. and an infant daughter, deceased. In 1866 Mrs. Crutcher died, and our subject wedded Tennessee McConnico in 1867, and by her became the father of three children: Magnes V., David P. and Susan C. In 1864 our subject volunteered in the service when Hood made his advance into Tennessee, and remained but a short time. In 1876 he removed to his farm which contains 110 acres in a fine state of cultivation. He and children are members of the Cumberland Presbyterian Church, and his wife is a member of the Methodist Episcopal Church South. In politics he is a Democrat.

CHARLES H. DAVIS is a son of F. H. and Mary A. (Gray) Davis, and is of Scotch-Irish descent. Both parents were born in Williamson County, Tenn., in 1822. The Davis family came to the State at an early date, and the mother died in 1869. Our subject was reared in Franklin, Tenn., and received his education in the male Academy of that place. He was a soldier in the Confederate Army, and belonged to the Thirty-second Regiment Tennessee Infantry. He was at the fall of Fort Donelson where he was captured and was held at Camp Norton, Indianapolis, Ind. He afterward participated in the battles of Chickamauga, Mission Ridge, and all the various battles of the Georgia campaign. Since the war he has followed farming and merchandising. He was married, November 27, 1867, to Miss Alabama V. Reaves, of Maury County, Tenn. Mr. Davis is a Democrat, and he and wife belong to the Christian Church.

JOHN D. DE GRAFFENRIED, county clerk of Williamson County, was born near Franklin, November 17, 1854, son of M. F. and M. M. (McLemore) de Graffenried, and of Swiss-French origin. The family came to America from Berne, Switzerland, and settled in North Carolina, and from thence, in an early day, the family immigrated to this county. The father of our subject was a general under Gen. Jackson. By occupation he was first a lawyer, but later in life turned his attention to farming, and at one time was one of the wealthiest men in this part of Tennessee. He died in 1869. The mother of our subject died in 1861. Our subject is the eighth child by his father's second marriage. He was educated at the Military Institute at Nashville, at which school he was adjutant for some time. Later he was a clerk in the county clerk's office, and subsequently engaged in the dry goods and lumber business. Politically he is a thorough Democrat. In 1882 he was elected county court clerk, defeating some of the county's strongest men. He has made one of the best officers the county has ever had. In 1883 he wedded May Sneed, of Rutherford County, and this union resulted in the birth of one daughter, Patti Russ. He and wife are members of the Methodist Episcopal Church South. He is one of the prominent young men of Williamson County, and the family one of the best known in this section.

JOHN F. DEMUMBRAN was born in this State in 1841, and is the son of William and Mary A. (Patton) Demumbran. The father was born near Nashville in 1793, and was a farmer by occupation. The mother was also born in this State, in 1865, and by her union with William Demumbran became the mother of eleven children, five of whom are yet living. The father died January 11, 1870, and the mother in 1854. Our subject was united in marriage, in 1761, to Miss Sallie Merritt, a native of this State, born in 1840, and the daughter of John and Susan (Burden) Merritt. To Mr. and Mrs. Demumbran were born seven children: Minnie M. (deceased), William, Francis E., Hattie, John W. B., Wallace and Carrie D. In the fall of 1861 our subject enlisted in Company D, Twentieth Tennessee Regiment, and remained with that company for about six months, when he joined the artillery, and remained in that until the close of the war. In 1868 he was elected justice of the peace in this district, and re-elected in 1874, and again in 1880. He is holding the office at the present time, and is giving evident satisfaction. He is a stanch Democrat.

JOSEPH T. DEMUMBRAN, an influential citizen of this district, was born in this State January 19, 1826, and is the son of William and Mary A. (Patton) Demumbran. Our subject was reared on a farm, and has followed agricultural pursuits all his life. He has been quite successful, and has a splendid farm of over 400 acres, with an elegant residence erected on it in a good location. February 14, 1855, he wedded Miss Elizabeth Redman, daughter of Thomas J. and Julia A. (Bayne) Redman, and a native of Virginia, born in 1834. By this union our subject became the father of one child, Mary E., who was born in 1855. His first wife having died, he married Ann T. Redman, a sister of his first wife. She was born in Virginia May 11, 1836. Our subject directs his attention principally to raising corn, small grain and stock. He was formerly a considerable cotton grower. In 1861 he enlisted in Company D, Forty-fifth Tennessee Regiment, and at the death of Second Lieut. Helm he was elected to fill his place, and held that position until wounded at the battle of Shiloh in 1862. He was taken care of by relatives until sufficiently recovered to travel, when he returned home. In politics he is an unswerving Democrat.

ALEXANDER DODD, farmer, was born in Williamson County, Tenn., September 7, 1824, son of Samuel and Xernia (Johnson) Dodd. His father was born in 1795 and was a native of the Carolinas, and came to Tennessee at an early day. He was a soldier in the war of 1812, and participated in the battle of New Orleans and aided in erecting the famous cotton breastworks. In early life he was married to Miss Johnson, who was born in 1796, and they became the parents of eleven children, our subject being the sixth. He was reared on a farm and secured a common school education and has followed agricultural pursuits through life. He was united in marriage to Miss Jane Davis, of Williamson County, September 17, 1846, and by her became the father of seven children—five sons and two daughters; one son is dead. Mrs. Dodd died May 5, 1885. Our subject belongs to the Democratic party and is a member of the Masonic fraternity. He owns 200 acres of good land, on which he has lived over thirty years. He and family belong to the Christian Church.

TALBOT F. DODD, dealer in general merchandise at Thompson's Station, Tenn., is a son of A. and Jane (Davis) Dodd, and first saw the light of day December 28, 1863, in

Williamson County. The father is a native Tennesseean, and he and wife became the parents of seven children. He has always been a tiller of the soil and owns a tract of land in the Second District of Williamson County. The mother died April 5, 1885. Talbot F. Dodd was reared on his father's farm and was educated in Franklin, Tenn. In 1882 he began business with Dodd, Dudley & Lipscomb, but remained in this connection only a short time, when he went to Shaw, Tenn., and engaged in the same business under the firm name of Dodd Bros., but remained only a short time when he went to Birmingham, Ala., and from there to the town of Thompson's Station, where he has since resided. He carries a stock of goods valued at $2,000, and does a business of $8,000 per annum.

ROBERT M. DOSS was born on the 3d of June, 1856, and was reared on a farm and received a good education in the schools of Mobile, Ala., and in 1881 came to Tennessee with his father and settled in Williamson County. In 1882 he led to the hymeneal altar, Miss Mattie Reams, daughter of Robert Reams, and one child has blessed their union, named Robert R. Mr. Doss is a farmer and stock raiser and owns a good tract of land in Williamson County. He and wife are members of the Methodist Episcopal Church south and are prominent citizens of the county. His parents are William and Elizabeth (Moore) Doss. The father was born in Alabama, where he lived a number of years and then became a resident of Mississippi. William Doss was twice married and by his first wife became the father of these children: John B., Alice I. and Robert M., and by his second wife (Bettie Jones), became the father of three children: William W., Edward L., Maggie and Sawrie.

EDWIN H. DOUGLAS is a son of Byrd Douglas, who was a native of Lynchburgh, Va., and came to Tennessee in 1830 settling in Fayetteville. He was always a merchant and followed that calling in Nashville. In 1839 he wedded Martha R. Bright, sister of Hon. J. M. Bright, and to them were born these five children: Edwin H., Hugh B., Lee (deceased), Byrd and Mary M. Mrs. Douglas died and Mr. Douglas married a Mrs. Cook (widow), who bore him two children: Ellen and Bruce. After his second wife's death he married Sarah Cragnall, of Davidson County. They have one son, Dr. Richard Douglas. The father died in December, 1882, leaving a large sum of money to his children. Edwin H. Douglas was born May 11, 1840, and was educated at the Western Military School of Nashville and graduated in 1860. He was a soldier in the late war and was first lieutenant of Freeman's battery when the war closed. He participated in many of the principal battles and was a true soldier and commander. After the war he engaged with his father in the grain and cotton business for several years. He was married in 1869 to Miss Bettie McGavock, who died shortly after her marriage. In June, 1883, he wedded a Mrs. Woodfin (widow), of St. Louis, Mo., and to them was born one child, Margaret Richards. In 1871, Mr. Douglas moved to Williamson County, and purchased the J. R. McGavock farm, where he has since been engaged in rearing stock, and has owned some speedy runners, trotters and pacers, and also breeds Short-horn cattle.

HENRY C. EDMONDSON was born June 15, 1828, in Williamson County, Tenn., son of John and Mary (Cummins) Edmondson, and grandson of John and Barbara Edmondson, of Virginia, who came to Tennessee in the latter part of the eighteenth century. Our subject's parents were born in 1805 and 1811, respectively, and were married September 18, 1827, and became the parents of seven daughters and four sons. The father died December 11, 1880. Our subject was their eldest child and received a liberal education, and from early boyhood has tilled the soil. He owns 180 acres of valuable and well improved farming land, on which he located in 1856. December 27, 1853, he wedded Bethenia H., daughter of Constant P. C. and Susan Sneed, natives of Virginia and Tennessee, and to them were born six children—one daughter and five sons: John, Constant P. C., William H., Thomas, Charles and Sarah. Mr. and Mrs. Edmondson are members of the Methodist Episcopal Church South, and he belongs to the F. & A. M. fraternity, and is of Scotch-Irish origin.

David C. Edmondson, farmer of Williamson County, Tenn., was born October 7,

1881, and is a son of John and Mary Edmondson, who were natives of the State. To them were born these children: Henry C., David C., Barbara H., John A., Mira L., Elizabeth B., Jane W., William A., Mary, Martha and Caroline. Our subject's boyhood days were spent in farming and attending the common schools, where he received a good education. He has always followed the occupation of farming and has succeeded well financially, and owns at the present time a comfortable home and 205 acres of as good land as Williamson County produces, on which he located in 1882. December 22, 1858, he was married to Priscilla O'Neal, who was born June 16, 1840, daughter of John F. and Matilda O'Neal, of Davidson County, Tenn. Mr. and Mrs. Edmondson became the parents of three interesting children—one daughter and two sons: Jennie P., Starnes W. J. and John F. Mrs. Edmondson died May 20, 1879; she was a member of the Presbyterian Church. Our subject is a member of the Methodist Episcopal Church South, and in politics is a Democrat. The family are early settlers of Tennessee, and of Scotch-Irish descent.

EDMOND W. EGGLESTON, a native of Virginia, was born January 14, 1825, and came to Tennessee in 1850. His father, Josiah C. Eggleston, was born in Virginia December 21, 1802, and February 7, 1822, was married to Sarah M. Smith, our subject's mother, who was also a native of Virginia, born March 14, 1800. The father died December 26, 1827, and the mother then married James L. Harris, by whom she had five children. She died July 27, 1842. Our subject's grandfather, Edmond Eggleston, was born in Virginia January 24, 1773, and married the Widow Epperson, formerly Susan Smith, who was also a native of Virginia, born November 22, 1772. Our subject was reared on a farm and followed agricultural pursuits until 1847, when he clerked in a store for about four years; later he resumed farming and has continued that up to the present time. In 1854 our subject was united in marriage to Miss Elizabeth H. Flemming, a native of this county, born November 16, 1833, and the daughter of Josiah and Jane B. (Sharp) Flemming, natives, respectively, of Kentucky and Virginia. The father was born January 24, 1798, and died November 18, 1853. The mother was born January 5, 1800, and died January 5, 1856. To our subject and wife were born five children: Josiah, Junius V. (deceased), Edward E., Sarah J. (deceased), and Thomas B. (deceased). April 25, 1866, Mrs. Eggleston died, and December 23, 1869, he married Miss Hilu A. Flemming, a sister of his first wife. Mrs. Eggleston was born January 12, 1844, and by her union with Mr. Eggleston became the mother of four children: James F., Susan C., Robert W. and William C. In 1852 he moved to this district, and in 1870 purchased his present farm for the second time. He and wife are members of the Methodist Episcopal Church South. He is a member of the Masonic lodge and a Democrat in politics.

JOSIAH E. ELLIOTT, son of Exom and Jeannette (Mebane) Elliott, was born November 2, 1817, in North Carolina. The father came to Tennessee in 1820 and became a successful farmer of Williamson County. He and wife became the parents of seven children: Mebane, Seth, Robert, Josiah, George, Alexander and Allen, all of whom are deceased with the exception of our subject and Seth. Exom Elliott died in 1827 and his widow in 1870. Our subject's early days were spent on his father's farm and in attending the country schools. In 1848 he wedded Miss Mary D. Tucker, and to them were born twelve children: Mary J., Exom A., James L., Josiah H., William, Seth M., John M., Charles E., Minerva B., Lillian H., Addie L. and Claude E. Mary J. Elliott died in 1885. She was the wife of E. W. Napier and was married in 1874. Our subject owns a tract of land in the Tenth District and is a thrifty farmer. He is a member of the Presbyterian Church and the family are of Scotch-Irish descent.

WILLIAM H. EVANS, an old and prominent citizen, was born October 16, 1812, and is the son of William G. and Mary S. (Saddler) Evans. The father was a native of North Carolina, assisted his father on the farm and received a limited education in the common schools. He was one of the first settlers of Davidson County and his death occurred in 1844. The mother died in July of the same year. They were both members of the Methodist Episcopal Church South. Our subject spent his boyhood on a farm and received his education in the common schools. February 19, 1835; he married Miss Margaret A.

Charlton, daughter of G. W. Charlton, and by this union he became the father of these children: G. W., Sallie A., E. C., Nancy H., Margaret E., Cleo, Emma S., S. W. and Jackson Z. In 1878 Mr. Evans moved to the Seventh District of Williamson County, Tenn., where he now resides on his place known as Rough Rock. Mr. Evans is a Democrat in politics, and he and wife are worthy and consistent members of the Methodist Episcopal Church.

JOHN T. FLEMING is a son of William and Mixey (Thompson) Fleming and was born in Williamson County, Tenn., May 14, 1823. The family are of Irish and Welsh descent, and William Fleming was a native of Campbell County, Va., and emigrated to Tennessee in 1814. He was married in 1815, and five children were born to them: Elizabeth, Samuel, Elmira, John T. and William. The father died in 1875. John T. was reared on a farm and educated in Franklin. He has followed farming from boyhood, and in 1852 was united in marriage to Miss Bettie Mann, and nine children have blessed their union; namely: Blanche, Della, Mary, William, Charles, John, Robert, Sallie, and Myra. Mr. Fleming is a well-to-do farmer, and owns a fine tract of well cultivated land, and is one of the leading citizens of Williamson County.

JOHN T. FLEMING, son of Samuel Fleming, was born November 27, 1827. Samuel Fleming was born in the "Old Dominion," and came to Tennessee in 1812, locating on a farm in Williamson County. In 1814 he married Miss Jane Thompson, of Virginia, and to them were born ten children: Elizabeth, Keziah, Malissa J., Virginia, David R., William T., Watson, John T., E. L., and Samuel. The father died in 1876 and the mother in 1839. They were members of the Presbyterian Church. Our subject was reared on a farm and was educated in the country schools. In 1854 he was united in marriage to Miss Elizabeth Mallory, and their union was blessed with eleven children: Philip M., Adelbert W., Mattie, James, Albert, William, John, Lizzie, Joe, Nathaniel and one who died in infancy. Those who are dead are Nathaniel, Albert, William and Lizzie. Mr. Fleming ownes 223 acres of land, and is a prosperous farmer of the county. His family are of Scotch-Irish descent.

WILLIAM C. FLEMING was born October 4, 1859, in Williamson County, Tenn., and is a son of Dr. Sam and Lizzie (Brooks) Fleming. The Doctor was born and reared in Williamson County. He acquired his medical education in Philadelphia, Penn., graduating from the medical school of that city. He was a druggist of Nashville, Tenn., for some time, but soon returned to Williamson County, where he died in January, 1875. He was the father of these seven children: Fillmore, Malvina, William C., Samuel, Lee, Thomas and Mickey. Dr. Fleming was a man of some means, and was a leading citizen of the county in which he resided. William C. Fleming, our subject, was educated in the country schools, and took a course at Jackson, Tenn. In 1883 he was united in matrimony to Miss Addie Reams, daughter of Henry Reams, of Williamson County. To them was born one child, Reams. Mr. Fleming is a prosperous farmer and owns 400 acres of land.

A. BRICE FLEMING is a native of Williamson County, Tenn., born April 18, 1849, son of David R. and Emily M. (Andrews) Fleming. The father was of Scotch-Irish descent, a native of Kentucky, and came to Tennessee with his father when an infant. He became the father of two sons, David B. and A. Brice, and was a farmer and a member of the Methodist Episcopal Church. He died December 15, 1858, and the mother in January, 1876. Our subject spent his juvenile days on a farm, and finished his education in the Presbyterian University, at Clarksville, where he remained three years. In 1876 he was married to Miss Sarah Haddox, of Maury County, who died in 1878, leaving one child, Mary. He was in the commission business at Nashville two years, and then returned to Williamson County and married Lelia Steele. One child has blessed their union, named Pauline. Mr. Fleming owns 900 acres of fine land, and is a stock dealer and farmer of note. He belongs to the Presbyterian Church.

CHARLES FULTON was born August 5, 1862, and passed his early life in assisting his father on the farm and in getting a fair education at the common schools. He is now engaged in running his father's farm, which consists of 1,050 acres. Mr. Fulton is a member of the Presbyterian Church, and a Democrat in politics. He is the son of W. D. and Sarah M. J. (Henderson) Fulton. The father was a native of Georgia, born November 17, 1820, and received a common school education. At fifteen years of age he was clerk in the postoffice at Athens; shortly afterward he was made clerk in the bank of Athens, and at the early age of seventeen was made teller in the same bank. Here he remained until he was about twenty years of age, when he began the study of law in the office of Mitchell, a prominent lawyer of the Athens bar. Soon after he was admitted to the bar, and practiced at Summerville and Trenton. In 1844 he married Sarah M. J. Henderson, daughter of James Henderson, of Georgia, and to this union were born ten children. W. D. Fulton continued to practice law until 1847, when he enlisted in the Mexican war, August 30. He was captain in the Mounted Battalion of Georgia Volunteers. At the close of the war he returned home and, moving to Atlanta, superintended the Georgia State Railroad. Here he remained until 1852, when he went to Chattanooga, Tenn., and was cashier of the Bank of Chattanooga until the late war. He then moved to Nashville and superintended the completion of the Maxwell House. In 1869 he moved to Williamson County and located in the Seventh District, north of Nashville. Here he died November 15, 1882. He was a member of the Presbyterian Church and a Democrat in politics.

WATSON MEREDITH GENTRY, M. D., was born near Stockett's Church, Williamson County, Tenn., January 31, 1831, the second son of Theophilus L. and Rebecca B. Gentry, and is of Welsh and English descent. Theophilus Gentry was born in North Carolina in 1802, but came with his father to Williamson County when a boy and settled at College Grove. He died at his home in Marshall County in 1883. He was a man noted for his great piety, vigorous mind, exceeding pleasantness and sobriety, and was considered, by those who knew him best, equally smart as his distinguished brother, Col. Meredith P. Gentry, who for sixteen years was one of Tennessee's most popular and eloquent statesmen. He had a wonderful memory and was a very gifted conversationalist. Dr. Gentry, on his maternal side, was also of distinguished ancestry; his mother's father, Dr. Thomas Sappington, of Tennessee, was the inventor of "Sappington's Pills," noted for their wonderful curative properties; he made a large fortune out of them; they are considered a very fine medicine in this progressive nineteenth century. Dr. Gentry's mother was born in this country in 1810, and died in 1837. The Doctor was named for his paternal grandfather, Watson Gentry, a North Carolinian, received an academic education at Owen's Hill and Triune Academies, after which he was a professor of mathematics and the languages for two terms. At this time he was only seventeen years of age. In 1852 he began the study of medicine under Dr. E. Edmonson, of Bethel, Giles Co., Tenn. The latter part of 1852 he went to New York to attend lectures at the University of New York City, where he graduated with honors in March, 1855. Immediately after his graduation he went to Europe, and visited and studied at the most noted colleges of that continent. On his return to this country he accepted a position as surgeon of Bellevue Hospital, N. Y., which he held for two years. In 1857 he located at Shelbyville, Tenn., where he practiced until May, 1861; in June of that year he was commissioned a surgeon of the Seventeenth Tennessee Regiment, Confederate States Army. In 1862 he was promoted to chief surgeon of Gen. Crittenden's division, which position he held until 1863, when he was sent to Montgomery, Ala., to take charge of the hospitals there. He had nine hospitals under his charge, with 2,300 beds. In 1866 he located near College Grove, on the place formerly owned by Dr. Reuben Gentry, his cousin, where he farmed for four years. In 1870 he moved to Franklin and resumed the practice of medicine, where he still lives. In 1858 he married Miss Martha A. Jones, of Nashville, who was a great belle in her day, being a woman of remarkable beauty and sprightliness; daughter of Dr. John R. Jones, a retired cotton planter of Marshall County, Tenn., who died in 1866. Dr. Gentry has but one child, a daughter, who is said to be quite accomplished in art and music. He is a a nch Democrat and a Mason of high order, being a member of the Commandery. Himself, wife and daughter are members of the Old School Presbyterian Church.

DANIEL GERMAN, M. D., was born near Franklin, March 19, 1831; son of Daniel and Elizabeth (Rounsaville) German, and is of French-Dutch extraction. The father was born in North Carolina in 1787, and when quite young came with his parents to Tennessee and settled near Nashville, but subsequently the family removed to Williamson County, and here the father of Dr. German died in 1858. The mother of our subject was a Tennesseean, born in this county in 1805 and died here in 1882. The early life of Dr. German was spent on the farm and in getting an education in the Franklin schools. He began studying medicine in 1850, and graduated from the University of Pennsylvania in 1854. He then located in Franklin and practiced his profession until the beginning of the war. During that conflict he was a surgeon in the Confederate Army, and as such was one of the very best. In 1863 he was transferred from the Eleventh Tennessee Infantry, Cheatham's division to Roddy's division of cavalry, of north Alabama, as chief surgeon. He surrendered May 20, 1865, at Decatur, Ala. Since the war he has been actively engaged in his profession in this town, and has won for himself an extensive and lucrative practice. He was married, in January, 1869, to Miss Adalitia McEwen, daughter of John B. and Cynthia (Graham) McEwen. They have five children, the two eldest being daughters, Misses Graham and Alice, the other three boys, Daniel, Richard McEwen and Horace Bright German. He is a man with many friends, and stands high in the estimation of the best people of this and adjoining counties; he is a Democrat, a Mason and a member of the Methodist Episcopal Church.

MOSES G. GOSEY, an old and a prominent citizen of this district, was born in Tennessee December 2, 1815. His father, James Gosey, was born in Virginia about 1770, and was married in 1798 to Rebecca Bowers, a native of Virginia, born about 1785. In 1801 they came to Tennessee, where the father followed the occupation of a farmer. He was a good, pious citizen, having joined the Methodist Episcopal Church at an early day. He died in 1856, and his widow followed in 1859. Our subject was united in marriage to Miss Mary A. Nevils in 1846. She was a native of this State, born August 12, 1824, and the daughter of Josiah and Sallie (Beech) Nevils. Our subject and wife became the parents of five children: James G., Sarah E., Mary T., Mattie L. and an infant not named. All have crossed the dark river into the valley of the shadow of death, and only two lived to be grown. In 1849 our subject began merchandising at Peytonsville, and carried on a thriving business there until 1860. During the war he was very unfortunate, losing about $17,000 of hard-earned money. He lives on a farm of seventy-two acres on the edge of Peytonsville, and since the war has directed his attention to farming. He is a member of the Masonic fraternity, and he and wife are members of the Methodist Episcopal Church South.

WILLIS K. GREEN, of the firm of Green & Fitzhugh, of Nolensville, Tenn., dealers in groceries and general merchandise, first saw the light of day September 18, 1824, son of John and Elizabeth Green, who were born in North Carolina, and were married January 29, 1807. To them were born ten children: Green B., Pollie, Thomas, Henry, Robert, Willis K., Susan Patsie, Jane and one infant daughter. Our subject was educated in the common schools, and in early life was engaged in the grocery and liquor business at Nolensville, Tenn. In 1860 he sold out his business and worked as clerk for J. Pick & Co., of Nashville, dealers in groceries and general merchandise. Here he remained until 1865, when he moved back to Nolensville and formed a partnership with John A. Fitzhugh in the grocery and general merchandise business. January 11, 1848, Mr. Green wedded Sarah A. Holiway, who was born October 13, 1827. They have three children: Mary J., Maggie and Madison G. Mrs. Green died February 22, 1856, and Mr. Green took for his second wife Martha J. Fields, August 13, 1856. She was born January 26, 1830, and died October 17, 1879, after becoming the mother of four children named Ella M., Charley B., Sarah M. and Katie E. Mr. Green is a Democrat, and he and family are members of the Methodist Episcopal Church South. He is a member of the F. & A. M. and I. O. O. F. He owns 100 acres of land, and is of Irish descent.

MADISON G. GREEN, M. D., was born on the 1st of September, 1854, in this county.

He is one of three children born to Willis K. and Sarah A. (Holiway) Green (see sketch of Willis K. Green), and in his boyhood days received a common school education and spent the free and happy life of a farmer's boy. In 1874 he began the study of medicine with Dr. T. G. Shannon, of Nolensville, and a year later entered the Vanderbilt University at Nashville, Tenn., and after receiving two courses of lectures graduated from that institution as an M. D. He then located in Arkansas and practiced his profession until 1877, when he returned to Nolensville, Tenn., where he has since remained actively engaged in the practice of his profession, and is regarded, and deservedly, as a skillful physician. May 29, 1879, he was united in matrimony to Cora E. Hailey, who was born November 11, 1859, and is the daughter of William N. and Mary A. Hailey. Mr. and Mrs. Green have two children, Mary A. and Clifton H. Both husband and wife are members of the Methodist Episcopal Church South, and Mr. Green is a member of the K. of H., and favors Democratic principles.

DeWITT C. GRIGGS is of English descent, and was born in Williamson County, Tenn., June 28, 1833, son of John and Jane Griggs, who were married in North Carolina about 1810, and came to Tennessee in 1811. They were the parents of these nine children: William, Mary, Lucy A., Thomas J., James B., John A., Madison, Virginia T. and DeWitt C., who received a liberal education in the common schools. He has been engaged in farming and carpentering all his life, and located on the farm of fifty-five acres where he now lives in 1865. His farm is well tilled and fertile, and the principal products are corn and wheat. He was married to Mary A. Hawkins August 16, 1857. She was born October 15, 1839, and was the daughter of Lucas P. and Eleanor Hawkins, natives of Virginia. To Mr. and Mrs. Griggs were born the following family of children: Adelaide, William M., Effie J., Mary E., John L., Edgar C., Henry C. and Owen J. Mrs. Griggs died July 14, 1873, and December 11, 1873, Mr. Griggs wedded Elizabeth H. Hawkins, born August 1, 1844, widow of William Hawkins and daughter of Moses and Jane N. Watkins, of Tennessee. To Mrs. Griggs' first marriage were born two daughters: Mariah J. and Millie H. To her marriage with Mr. Griggs this family: Lena, Daisy D., Lucy M., St. Elmo, Maude E. and Ruby B. were born. Mr. Griggs is a Democrat and a member of the I. O. O. F., and he and family are highly respected citizens of the county.

RICHARD T. HAILEY, a prominent wagon and carriage manufacturer at Nolensville, Tenn., was born May 11,1832, in Rutherford County, Tenn., and is the son of Henry and Joanna Hailey, who came to this State about 1822 and were married in 1828. Henry Hailey settled near Nolensville in 1834, and worked at carpentering until his death in 1854. He was a soldier in the Revolutionary war and the war of 1812. Our subject was the second of five children, and received his education in the public schools. From boyhood he has followed wagon and carriage-making, and has been very successful. In 1850 he went to Louisiana, and was overseer of a large cotton plantation, but after remaining a short time returned to Tennessee, and is yet a resident of Nolensville. He was married to Elizabeth Hamlet in 1854, and to them were born four children: Laura, Mary, Kittie and Henry. In 1861 Mr. Hailey enlisted in the First Tennessee Cavalry under James T. Wheeler, and participated in many battles. In 1882 Mr. Hailey was elected justice of the peace, and has faithfully performed the duties of his office. He is a Democrat and a member of the K. of H., and he and wife belong to the Methodist Episcopal Church South.

JOHN C. HALEY, an influential citizen of Williamson County, was born in this State in 1839, and is the son of John and Tolitha (Garrett) Haley. The subject is of English descent and received his education in the best schools of the county. He was reared on a farm and followed agricultural pursuits for seventeen years, when he began trading in stock, and has made that a specialty ever since. In 1860 the subject was united in marriage to Miss Mary Powell, a native of Mississippi, born about 1840, and the daughter of Thomas and Sallie Powell. To our subject and wife were born two children—Beulah E., born in 1865, and Clarence B., born in 1877. Mrs. Haley died in 1877, and Mr. Haley took for his second wife Mrs. Mary (Pierson) Berry, widow of Thomas Berry. She was born in Tennesee in 1841 and was the daughter of William and Mrs. (Williams) Pierson. The subject has about 240 acres of good land, well watered and in a fine state of cultivation. It lies on the pike, near College Grove. On this he has erected a neat residence, which is beautifully located. He is an extensive stock trader and well known in Nashville, this and adjoining counties. He and wife are members of the Methodist Episcopal Church South. Politically Mr. Haley is a Democrat.

WILLIAM C. HALEY, a prominent citizen and stock trader of this county, was born in Tennessee October 12, 1844, and is the son of John and Tolitha (Garrett) Haley. The subject was reared on a farm and educated at Triune Academy, this county. He has lived on a farm from boyhood, with the exception of three years from 1882, when he lived in Nashville and a portion of the time in Winchester, educating his children. In 1884 he returned to his farm near College Grove, and has since been engaged in farming and trading in stock. He has a splendid farm containing ninety acres with a neat residence on it. It is situated near the pike leading through College Grove. In 1864 our subject was married to Miss Anna E. Withoite, a native of this State, and the daughter of Young and Eliza (Dunaway) Wilhoite. To Mr. and Mrs. Haley were born ten children: Mattie E., born December 13, 1865; Kate M., born January 4, 1867; Nannie T., born April 29, 1868; John A., born December 31, 1869; Samuella, born December 13, 1871; Young W., born September 25, 1873; Lula H., born July 14, 1875; Annie B., born September 11, 1879; Willie D., born November 6, 1880, and died March 27, 1883, and Linus P., born April 12, 1885. In 1862 he enlisted in Company F, Eleventh Tennessee Cavalry, was taken prisoner near Murfreesboro in 1863, he then took a non-combatant oath and came home. He is a Democrat and member of the Masonic lodge, No. 172. He, wife and six of his children are members of the Methodist Episcopal Church South.

WILLIAM E. HAMILTON was born in Tennessee December 26, 1827, and was educated in the county schools. In 1845 he was married to Miss Maggie Shy, and three children were born to them, named William E., Lizzie M. and William N. William E., Jr., died in 1860, and Lizzie in 1862. Our subject died in 1872 and was a member of the Cumberland Presbyterian Church, and in 1849 moved to Missouri and purchased a tract of land, where he lived until his death. His widow then took charge of the farm, managing it until 1882, when she was stricken with paralysis. Since that time her youthful son William N., has operated the farm and cared for his mother. They own forty-six acres of land in the Fifth Civil District of Williamson County, and also a tract of land in Missouri. The Hamilton family is one of the best in the county. Our subject's parents were James and Eliza (Swisher) Hamilton.

DANIEL A. HAMPTON, a resident of Williamson County, Tenn., was born March 4, 1814, in Brunswick County, Va., and is the fifth of nine children born to David and Elizabeth Hampton, who came to Tennessee in 1832 and located in Williamson County. Their children were named as follows: Richard C., Louisa, Emily, Hammeditha, Daniel A., Rufus S., Joseph H., Ann and Mary E. Our subject received a common school education, and has been engaged in farming from boyhood. He has been fairly prosperous in his business enterprises and has a good home, and is the owner of 153 acres of fertile and well improved farming land. He located upon this farm about 1831. In 1849 he was married to Mary Mitchell, daughter of David A. and Eliza Mitchell of Tennessee. Mr. and Mrs. Hampton became the parents of twelve children: David, Richard, Eva G., John H., James C., Harris B., Lulu B., Nancy E., Louella, Thomas P., Aubra A. and Emily C. Mr. Hampton is a member of the Methodist Episcopal Church South, and in politics is a Democrat. The Hamptons are of English descent, and are highly respected citizens, being residents of this State for almost a century.

JAMES P. HANNER, M. D., was born in Nashville, Tenn., July 4, 1835; son of Rev. John W. Hanner, who was born in North Carolina in 1810, and who has for many years been a leading Methodist clergyman and is now a resident of Clarksville. The mother of Dr. Hanner, Rachael E. Park, was born in Maryland, January 31, 1814, and died in Nashville February 18, 1841. Dr. Hanner was educated at the Western Military Institute, and was instructed in mathematics by James G. Blaine. He began the study of medicine in 1855 at Franklin, and attended one course of lectures at the University of Nashville, and later he attended the University of Pennsylvania from which institution he graduated in March, 1857. In 1861 he was mustered into the Confederate service as captain of Company E, of the First Tennessee Regiment, and at the end of one year resigned his commission and was appointed surgeon of Morton's battery, Forest's command, and thus continued until the close of the war. Came home in 1865 and has since been engaged in the practice of his profession. He has been for many years a leading practitioner of this part of Tennessee. November 30, 1865, he wedded Miss Mary Walker, a Mississippian by birth—resident of Franklin since early childhood—and by this union is the father of four children : Loulia A., James P., Jr., John W. and Lizzie McR. Mr. Hanner is a Democrat, a Mason (Knight Templar), and he and wife are members of the Methodist Episcopal Church. He has the respect and esteem of all who know him, and is one of the best men of Franklin.

TURNER L. HARRISON was born in Tennessee June 5, 1838. His father. Nathaniel L. Harrison, was born in Warren County, N. C., December 2, 1808, and came to Tennessee with his parents when quite young. He remained in this county many years and held the office of constable and deputy sheriff. He was a good neighbor, a kind father, and reared and educated his children to become useful men and women. His home was in the Tenth District until 1843 when he moved to the Thirteenth. His death occurred November 21, 1885. Our subject's mother, Christiana Knight, was born in Tennessee in 1812, and in the year 1832 was wedded to Nathaniel L. Harrison, by whom she became the mother of eleven children. Her death occurred in 1863. Our subject was united in marriage, in 1863, to Ella A. Martin, a native of this State, born in 1843, and the daughter of Benjamin F. and Jane D. (Alston) Martin. To her union with Mr. Harrison she became the mother of four children: Covoda, born in 1863, Modera, born 1865; Odo, born 1870, and Goldie, born 1877. Our subject followed agricultural pursuits until 1858, when he began merchandising in Nashville. In 1861 he enlisted in the Confederate service, was promoted to third lieutenant, and stood at his post of duty during the entire war. In 1865 he returned home and began. blacksmithing in the village of Peytonsville, his present location. In 1881 he was elected justice of the peace. He and wife are members of the Christian Church, and he is a Democrat in politics.

JAMES W. HARRISON was born near Franklin, Tenn., August 21, 1847, and is of English extraction. His father, William Harrison, was born in this county in 1820, was a tiller of the soil and died in this county January 8, 1878. The paternal grandfather of our subject was William Harrison, a Virginian, born in 1799. He came to Williamson County in early life and was sheriff of that county for the years 1836–42. He died in the year 1865. The mother of our subject, Martha (Terrell) Harrison was born in this county in 1820 and died in 1854. James W. Harrison, our subject, is fourth in a family of eleven children. Like the average country boy he spent his early life in assisting on the farm and in acquiring an education in the common schools. In 1865 he went to Spring Hill and began clerking in a store where he remained until 1867, when he came to Franklin, and in April of that year engaged in the dry goods business which he successfully continued until 1885. October 10, 1869, he married Miss Anna Briggs, of Franklin, daughter of Isaac W. and Dorithy M. Briggs. Mr. and Mrs. Harrison have an adopted child—Annie James. He is a thorough Democrat, and he and wife are members of the Presbyterian Church.

ABRAM W. HATCHER was born in this county in the year 1835. His father, William Hatcher, was born in Virginia in 1796, and in 1814 was united in marriage to Lucy Rucker, a native of Virginia, born in 1797. The father died in 1867 and the mother in 1884. Our subject was married to Mary S. Dodson, a native of this State, born June 23, 1841, and a daughter of Eli and Elizabeth (Fitzgerald) Dodson. To Mr. Hatcher and wife were born three children, Ernest L., born July 11, 1859; William D., born May 14, 1861; Robert A., born August 26, 1865, and died October 7, 1865. Our subject had the misfortune to lose his wife September 2, 1865, and married for his second wife Martha E.

Chriesman, a native of this State, born December 27, 1844. Her father, George W., was born in this State in 1801, and died in 1868. Her mother, Jane Sprott, was born August 25, 1817, also in this State, and died December 27, 1881. Our subject became the father of eight children by his last marriage: Mary S., born 1870; James C., born 1871; Charles W., born 1873; Lucy J., born July, 1875; Sallie A.; Elizabeth R., born 1880; Madeline, born 1881; and George A., born 1885. In 1861 our subject enlisted in Company A, Forty-fifth Tennessee, as a private, but was promoted to the rank of second lieutenant, and fought through the entire war. He was hit by spent balls six different times, but was never disabled. Since the war he has been engaged in tilling the soil. He is a member of the K. of H., and he and wife are members of the Methodist Episcopal Church South. He is a Democrat in politics.

HON. THOMAS ELLIOT HAYNES was born near Franklin, Tenn., October 17, 1842, son of N. J. and Elizabeth H. Haynes, and is of English extraction. The father was born in Williamson County in 1820, and died in this town in 1876. The mother was born in the same county in 1822, and at the present is residing in Franklin. She is a daughter of the late Rev. M. L. Andrews, and the mother of ten children, four of whom are living. Our subject's grandfather came to Williamson County at an early day, and was a soldier in the war of 1812. Our subject received the rudiments of his education in the county schools, and subsequently attended Franklin Male Academy. He learned the printing business in Franklin, and in 1865 he with his father resumed the publication of the *Review*, which had suspended during the war, and Mr. Haynes continued with the paper until March, 1886, when he sold out to the present owners. Mr. Haynes was formerly a Whig, but since the war has been a persistent Democrat. In 1879 he was elected to the lower house of the General Assembly to represent Williamson County, and was re-elected in 1881. He was a delegate to the National Democratic Convention in 1884, and in June of the same year was elected chairman of the Williamson County Democratic Executive Committee. For twenty years he has been one of the leading politicians of this part of Tennessee. November 2, 1865, he wedded Bettie Hill, who was born near Franklin in 1846. To this union were born five children: Minnie, Metta, Natus, Narcissa, and Lizzie, who died in 1884. Mr. Haynes joined the Masonic fraternity in 1866, and he and wife are worthy members of the Methodist Episcopal Church South. February 24, 1886, he was appointed postmaster.

E. MARCELLUS HEARN, attorney at law, was born in Sumner County, Tenn., May 7, 1842; son of Whitson P. and Anna E. (Dickason) Hearn, and is of English descent. The father was born in Wilson County, Tenn., April 12, 1820, and was a tiller of the soil. He died September 14, 1881. The mother was a native of Sumner County, Tenn., born August 17, 1824, and died May 30, 1884. Our subject was reared on a farm near Lebanon in Wilson County, to which place he removed with his parents when but four years of age. He was educated at Linwood Academy in Wilson County, and in 1861 he enlisted in the Confederate Army in Capt. Sterling's company, First Regiment of Heavy Artillery, commanded by Andrew Jackson Donaldson. He was at the battle of Columbus, Ky., Island No. 10, Fort Pillow, siege of Vicksburg (where he was captured, paroled and exchanged), and the siege of Fort Morgan, where he was again captured. He was taken to New Orleans, thence by water to Governor's Island, N. Y., and later to Elmira, N. Y., where he remained a prisoner of war six months. Just before the surrender he was exchanged, and came home in the spring of 1865. In the fall of the same year he entered the law department of Cumberland University at Lebanon, and graduated from that institution in 1867. He then went to Memphis and began the practice of law, which he continued in that city until 1878, when he came to Franklin, and here has since continued the practice of law. In 1868 he wedded Miss Louisa D. James, by whom he had two children. Mrs. Hearn was born October 25, 1847, and died March 3, 1874. November 8, 1877, Mr. Hearn married Mary Alice McEwen, daughter of John B. McEwen, of Franklin. To this union was born one child, named John B. Our subject is a true Democrat, a Mason, and a member of the I. O. O. F. and K. of H. He and wife are members of the Methodist Episcopal

Church South. Mr. Hearn was a true and brave soldier, and is a prominent lawyer and a good man.

JOHN H. HILL, was born January, 25, 1814, spent his early life on a farm and in getting an education. In 1839 he wedded Miss Susan A. Cox, daughter of Samuel Cox, of Franklin, Tenn. To this union was born one child, James R., who died in infancy. In 1842 Mr. Hill married his second wife, Susan E. Hughes, daughter of James and Susan Hughes, and to his last union Mr. Hill became the father of eight children: James N., Talitia C., John R., Ophelia H., Susan J., Emma P., Mary W., and Thomas R., two of whom are dead. In 1850 Mr. Hill moved to the farm now known as "Harpeth Home," in the Sixth District of Williamson County, and engaged in farming and stock raising. He is a Democrat in politics and he and wife are members of the Cumberland Presbyterian Church. Our subject's father, Robert Hill, was born in North Carolina about 1775, spending his early life on a farm and receiving his education in the common schools. He married Miss Jane Fisher, and by this union was the father of these children: Joseph F., James B., Hugh, John H., Margaret C., Easter J. In 1807 Mr. Hill immigrated to Tennessee and located in the Sixth District. He died here in 1850.

CHARLES H. HILL, a prominent young farmer, was born in Williamson County, Tenn., November 5, 1856, son of John H. and Sallie A. Hill, natives of Tennessee. Charles H. received a liberal education, and early in life was engaged in farming, but owing to bad health was obliged to abandon this work and in 1878 commenced teaching school and followed this occupation until 1883, when his health was much improved. In 1879 he began reading law with Thomas & Turley of Franklin, Tenn., but soon abandoned this and since 1883 has been a tiller of the soil. He owns 100 acres of valuable and well improved land, and his principal products are corn and wheat. In politics he is a Democrat and a member of the Methodist Episcopal Church South. The Hill family are of Scotch-Irish descent and were among the settlers and esteemed citizens of the county.

JAMES H. HOGE may be mentioned as a well-to-do farmer of Williamson County, Tenn. He was born in Maury County March 28, 1833, and was reared in Mount Pleasant, where he remained until twenty-five years of age, when he moved near Columbia and there resided twenty-three years. He then sold out and came to Williamson County, where he purchased 142 acres of land in 1881. He was in the late war, enlisting in the Ninth Tennessee Regiment under George Gant. He was taken prisoner at the fall of Fort Donelson and was retained two months at Terre Haute, Ind., and was then taken to Indianapalis, where he remained five months when he was exchanged at Vicksburg, Miss. James H. Hoge is a son of Harvey and Lucy A. (Lester) Hoge. The father was born in Virginia, and came to Tennessee at an early day, being one of Maury County's pioneer settlers. He followed merchandising and became the father of eight children; all of whom are dead save our subject. The father died in 1856 and the mother in 1868.

C. H. HOSKINS, son of Robert T. and Tennessee (Abernathy) Hoskins, was born in Davidson County, November 22, 1838, and received a common school education. From 1857 to 1862 he taught school and then enlisted in Company F, Fourth Tennessee Cavalry, and was in many of the principal battles of the war. He returned home in April, 1865, and commenced farming and has followed that occupation up to the present time. He was married, October 26, 1862, to Fannie E. Mays, of Cheatham County, Tenn. To them were born these children: Charles H., Robert J., John W., Nannie E., James T., Sterling F., Josie T., Lulu T., Fannie E., and William B. Mr. Hoskins is a supporter of Democratic principles and his wife is a member of the Christian Church. Our subject's father was born in Wilson County, Tenn., in 1809, and went to Davidson County when a young man and worked for D. Young. He then engaged in the grocery business in Nashville in 1868, and after following this several years his health failed and he retired from the business. He died March 22, 1882, and his wife in 1880.

WILLIAM HOUSE, a member of the Williamson County bar, was born in Franklin, December 6, 1849, son of Hon. Samuel S. and Sarah J. (Parks) House, and is of Scotch-Irish descent. The father of Mr. House was born in Williamson County in 1822, and in his early life was a Franklin merchant. Later he began the study of law and was admitted to the bar in 1856. For many years he was one of the leading lawyers of this section, and a member of the law firm of Ewing & House. In 1861 he was a member of the Tennessee General Assembly and of the Constitutional Convention in 1870. After the war he was one of the first to shape and advocate a new policy for the people of this county. Previous to the war he was one of the projectors of the Tennessee Female College at this place and with others who were then prominent citizens he contributed both money and effort for the building and success of the college, etc., and was secretary and treasurer for many years. He was a prominent member of the Methodist Episcopal Church South and did much for the church all through life. He wedded Miss Sarah J. Parks, a native of this county, and left a large family, nearly all of whom still reside in Williamson County. He died July 31, 1876. No man stood higher in the estimation of the people; his life was useful and "his end was peace." Our subject received his education at the private schools in Franklin and the University of Virginia. He began the study of law in the office of Judge Turley and was admitted to the bar in 1872 and has since been engaged in the active practice of his profession. He is now a law partner of Atha Thomas, whose sketch appears elsewhere in this volume. In 1873 he married Miss O. C. Wood, of Bolivar, Tenn. They have five children. He is a Democrat, a Mason, and he and wife are leading members of the Methodist Episcopal Church South. The family is particularly traced to Mansfield House who came here from North Carolina in the very early settlement of the county.

S. J. HOUSE, M. D., was born in the town of Franklin, Tenn., June 8, 1855, son of Samuel S. and Sallie J. (Parks) House, and is of English descent. He was educated in the Franklin schools, reared on a farm near the town, began the study of medicine in Franklin in 1874, under the direction of Dr. James P. Hanner, attended lectures at Vanderbilt University at Nashville, and graduated from that institution in March, 1876. He then located in Franklin and has since been engaged in the active practice of his profession. For nearly six years he held the office of jail physician, and in January, 1885, he was elected county health officer of Williamson County and re-elected to the same office in January, 1886. He is one of the leading physicians of this section and has made his own way in life. December 18, 1884, he was united in marriage to Sallie E. Gooch, of Rutherford County, Tenn., daughter of N. and E. Gooch, of Nashville. To our subject and wife were born one child, Evie. Dr. House is a Democrat, and is a representative of one of most prominent and widely known families of Tennessee. He and wife are leading members of the Methodist Episcopal Church South.

B. R. HUGHES, a native of Virginia, was born August 10, 1819, and was the son of Richard and Elizabeth (Reynolds) Hughes, natives of Virginia. The father immigrated to Tennessee in 1827. B. R. Hughes, the subject of this sketch, was reared on a farm and received his education in the common schools. August, 1841, he wedded Mrs. E. Cox, and by her he is the father of six children, only two of whom are now living: George R. and Narcissie. Mrs. Hughes' death occurred during the late civil war, she was a consistent member of the Primitive Baptist Church, and had the love and esteem of all who knew her. In 1865 our subject wedded Miss Nannie Simmons, daughter of Thomas Simmons, and by this union is the father of six children, three of whom are living: James T., William S. and Fannie. In 1874 Mrs. Hughes died and in 1875 our subject wedded his present wife, Permelia A. Hulme (Hungarford), who is a member of the Methodist Episcopal Church South. Mr. Hughes is an extensive farmer and stock raiser, owning at the present about 324 acres of good land. He has been magistrate in his district for about eight years and filled the office in an able and satisfactory manner.

G. R. HUGHES, son of B. R. and E. P. (Reynolds) Hughes, was born June 1, 1848, and spent his early life on his father's farm in the Sixth District of Williamson County. He received his education in the common schools of the county, and later appeared on life's grand stage as a blacksmith and wagon-maker. In December, 1864, he enlisted in Company F, Fourth Tennessee Cavalry, at the youthful age of seventeen, and participated in the battle of Nashville and numerous skirmishes. At the close of the war he returned home and engaged in farming. September 20, 1868, Mr. Hughes was united in marriage to Miss Narcissie Johnson, daughter of Louis Johnson, of Williamson County. To this union were born four children, two of whom are now living: L. B., Ennis, Willie and Leonard. Mrs. Hughes is a worthy and consistent member of the Primitive Baptist Church. He was elected magistrate of his district in August, 1882, which office he now fills.

LEE HUGHES, SR., a prominent citizen of Williamson County, was born in this State September 6, 1828. His father, Arch Hughes, was born in North Carolina November 28, 1787, and was a farmer by occupation. In April, 1811, he wedded our subject's mother, Martha Rogers, a native of North Carolina, born February 10, 1791. To this union were born ten children, three of whom are yet living. The mother died in 1850, and the father followed in 1854. Our subject has followed agricultural pursuits from early youth, and is at present living on the farm of his birth, which he inherited from his father. It consists of 225 acres of good land with a large brick residence on it in a suitable location, and is known as "Locust Hill." In 1854 our subject wedded Miss Lucy Pope, a native of Tennessee, born November 4, 1837, and the daughter of John and Dolly (Etta) Pope, natives of this State. To Mr. and Mrs. Hughes were born five children: Martha A., born May 29, 1855; Alexander R., born April 18, 1857; Nancy P., born February 17, 1859; Leander, born April 9, 1861, and an infant not named. Martha A. died May 14, 1881. On the 22d of June, 1863, our subject had the misfortune to lose his wife. He is a Democrat in politics.

JOHN H. HUNTER, farmer, was born in Williamson County, Tenn., August 15, 1828, within two miles of where he now resides. He is a son of Henry and Jane W. (Bennett) Hunter, and is of Irish descent. His father was born in Chatham County, N. C., in 1786, and his mother in the same county in 1801. They were married in 1821, and died in Williamson County, Tenn., in 1762 and 1871, respectively. The Hunter family were among the very early settlers of Tennessee. Our subject received his rudimentary education in the common schools of the county, after which he took an academic course in Marshall County, Tenn., and finally completed his education by a collegiate course in the Cumberland University at Nashville. At the breaking out of the war he joined the Confederate Army, enlisting in the Forty-fourth Tennessee, Johnson's brigade and Hardee's corps, and finally surrendered at Appomattox Court House, Va. Since the war he has farmed, with the exception of two years (1867 and 1868) spent in Texas. He was married, January 26, 1859, to Miss Martha M. Bennett, of Columbus, Miss., who also received a collegiate education at Nashville. They have three children: Henry, born in 1868; Hendly B., born in 1873, and Roberta G., a daughter. Mr. Hunter is a Democrat, and is the owner of 1,200 acres of fine land and a model farmer. His wife is a member of the Christian Church.

DR. GEORGE B. HUNTER was born on the 17th of June, 1831, in District No. 3, of Williamson County, Tenn. His parents were Henry and Jane (Bennett) Hunter (see sketch of John H. Hunter). Our subject is the youngest of their five children and spent his boyhood days on a farm and in attending the common schools. He afterward attended Jackson College at Columbia, Tenn., and read medicine with Dr. John W. Morton, of Franklin, Tenn., and afterward graduated with high honors from the Medical University of Philadelphia, Penn. He practiced his chosen profession before the war, when he received an injury by being thrown from a horse, which prevented his joining the army, but left him with a greater burden, that of medical attendant of over sixty families of widows and orphans. Since the war he has given his entire attention to his large farm of 1,300 acres of fine land. August 31, 1871, he was married to Miss Lou M. Bennett, daughter of Judge H. S. Bennett, of Granada, Miss. They have one daughter, Anna M. Dr. Hunter was a Whig, but is now neutral in politics. Mrs. Hunter belongs to the Christian Church.

JAMES P. JOHNSON, farmer and stock raiser, of Williamson County, Tenn., is a son of Thomas B. and Harriet C. (Patterson) Johnson, and was born in Fayette County, Ky. The father was born in the same county in 1808, and in 1832 came to Tennessee and settled twelve miles south of Nashville. His occupation was farming and stock raising.

About 1840 he moved to Mississippi, but soon returned and purchased the Laurel Hill Stock farm, which he cultivated very successfully. He was, for a number of years, president of the State Agricultural Association, and was contractor on the Nashville & Chattanooga Railroad while it was building. In 1828 he was married to Miss Harriet C. Patterson, of Virginia, and seven sons were born to them. James P. and Andrew H. are the only living descendants of this union. Thomas B. Johnson was a member of the Methodist Episcopal Church, and died in 1874. Our subject was educated in the Nashville University and graduated in 1847. In 1852 he began farming, but four years later he sold his farm to the State for the benefit of the Insane Asylum. He then purchased the Laurel Hill stock farm, and in 1853 became a member of the firm of Johnson, Brown & Gibson, stock dealers, but retired at the end of four years. In 1853 he wedded Sarah J. Sykes, daughter of Jesse Sykes. Ten children were born to them; James W., Harriet L. (deceased), Thomas B., Jesse S., Jennie S., William A., Addie L., James P., Andrew V. and Richard E. Mr. Johnson and his children are members of the Methodist Episcopal Church South. His wife is a Missionary Baptist.

S. A. JOYCE was born in Alabama November 10, 1839. His father, Jackson Joyce, was born in Tennessee about 1810, and went to Alabama when a young man. His mother, Lutitia Dunnagee, was born about 1819, and died in 1851; the father followed in 1866. To their union were born six children, one sister and the subject are the only ones living. Our subject followed farming until 1865, when he began trading in stock, and has made that a specialty ever since. In 1861 he enlisted in Company F, Seventeenth Tennessee Infantry, under Gen. Crittenden, and was captured near Cleveland, East Tenn. He was then taken to Rock Island, where he was held about eighteen months. At the close of the war he returned home, and in 1868 was married to Mrs. Mary E. (Sheppard) Holt, widow of John H. Holt, and daughter of Clinton and Polly (Riggs) Sheppard. By his union with Mrs. Holt our subject became the step-father of three Holt children, named: Eva, born April 30, 1857; Willie, born January 10, 1860, and Josie, born September 13, 1863, and the father of five children: Joseph, born November 7, 1868; Maggie, born February 19, 1870; Mary E., born June 30, 1872; Eula, born October 28, 1874, and Samuel M., born May 27, 1878. Mrs. Joyce died June 25, 1884. In 1870 he moved to his farm, which contains 100 acres of medium land, and is situated in the southeastern part of the county. The principal products of this farm are corn and small grain. He has a neat residence, situated near the pike and two miles from Alisona. He is a member of the Cumberland Presbyterian Church and a stanch Democrat in politics.

DAVID J. KENNEDAY, dry goods merchant, was born in Oxford, Lafayette Co., Miss., August 21, 1850, son of D. J. and Eliza (Harris) Kenneday, and is of Irish lineage. The father was born in North Carolina in 1816. In early life he emigrated from North Carolina to Mississippi. He was married twice, and is the father of eleven children. He now resides in Mississippi. The mother was born near La Grange, Miss., and died in that State in 1852. Our subject was the fifth child by his father's first union. He received his education at Oxford (Miss.) University, and in 1867 he came to Franklin and began clerking in a store. In 1869 he accepted a position in the dry goods house of J. W. Harrison, and with him remained as salesman until March, 1885, when he became a member of the firm of Smithson, Kenneday, Hodge & Co., the leading dry goods firm of Franklin, and is doing a successful business. January, 1876, he wedded Miss Florence Scruggs, of this county, daughter of Joseph and Angeline Scruggs. To Mr. and Mrs. Kenneday were born five children: Joseph S., Annie D., David J. (twins), James W. and Theodore. Mrs. Kenneday is a member of the Christian Church and Mr. Kenneday of the Methodist Episcopal Church South. He is a Democrat, a prominent young business man and a true gentleman.

DR. T. H. KENNEDY is the son of Richard and Martha R. (Early) Kennedy, niece of Bishop Early. Richard Kennedy became the father of eight children and in his religious views was a Baptist. Our subject first saw the light of day in Virginia. He was born October 25, 1827, and was educated in the Old Dominion. In 1848 he entered the Philadelphia College of Medicine, and, after graduating in 1850, immigrated to Tennessee and began practicing his profession. The same year he led to the hymeneal altar Miss Sallie H. Waldron, of Virginia, who died in 1851. He afterward married Miss Fannie H. Humphries, who is a woman of intelligence and is in every sense of the word a helpmeet. Dr. Kennedy owns a fine farm, comprising 265 acres of fertile and well cultivated land in the Fourth District of Williamson County, and he may truly be said to be a leading citizen. He is a member of the Methodist Episcopal Church.

JOHN W. KING was born in Rockingham County, N. C., April 27, 1808. His parents, William and Mary King, were married about 1807, and came to Tennessee three years later. The father was a farmer, and he and wife became the parents of the following children: John W., George P., Elizabeth, Leana P., Mary, Alias, William. Thomas, James, Robert and Nancy. William King the father, died in 1863, and the mother in 1834. Our subject received a limited education. January 2, 1834, he wedded Lucy A. Alston, who was born March 26, 1810, daughter of John and Jane H. Alston, of North Carolina. Our subject owns 350 acres of land on which he settled in 1835. He has succeeded quite well in his financial undertaking and is very comfortably situated. Mr. and Mrs. King became the parents of this family: John A., James C., Thomas S., William, Mary E., Eliza, Laura J., Sarah J. and one infant son. Mr. King is a Democrat, and he and family are members of the Methodist Episcopal Church South.

WILLIAM KING, undertaker and funeral director at Nolensville, Tenn., was born October 7, 1841, in Williamson County, Tenn, and secured a fair education in the country schools. He farmed until 1869, when he engaged in the grocery and general merchandise business in Nolensville, but in 1872 sold out this store and has since been engaged in his present business, in which he has been quite successful. His marriage to Annie Massey was celebrated in 1869. She was born in 1852, and is the daughter of Thomas J. and Frances C. Massey, who were born in Tennessee. Mr. and Mrs. King were the parents of two children—a son and daughter: William E. and Fannie G. Mrs. King died in 1873, and a year later Mr. King wedded Addie King, born in 1852, her parents being Benjamin and Susan J. King, natives of Tennessee. Our subject and wife became the parents of the following children: Susie M., Lucy E., Walter H., Bessie L. and John M. Husband and wife are members of the Methodist Episcopal Church South, and he belongs to the K. of H. and in politics is a Democrat. Mr. King was a soldier in the Twentieth Tennessee Regiment of Volunteers under Col. Battle, and was in many of the principle engagements of the war.

B. F. KING was born June 2, 1856, and was the son of John B. and Sarah V. Philips. The father was a native of Portugal and spent his boyhood at home, receiving a common school education. At the age of fourteen he left home and took passage as cabin boy in a ship engaged in the slave trade running from Africa to South America; while on the voyage the ship was captured by an English cruiser and the prisoners taken to the nearest English port. Here the boy was released, owing to his youth. He afterward came to America and located at Nashville, Tenn., where he engaged in the block and tackle business used in erecting the State Capitol. Here he remained about seven years and while in Nashville was married to Miss Mary Philips and by her had one child, viz.: John A. Mr. King lost his wife in 1847 and the following year he married Miss Sarah Virginia Philips, sister of his former wife and the mother of our subject. Mrs. King died February, 1867. She was a member of the Methodist Episcopal Church South. Mr. King is still living on his farm in the Twelth District of Davidson County. He is a Democrat, a member of the I. O. O. F., and also a member of the Methodist Episcopal Church South. Our subject spent his life on a farm and received his education in the common school. At the age of seventeen he left the home of his youth, went to Nashville and served an apprenticeship at the carpenter's trade. He remained here five years after which he went to Clarksville where he worked at his trade. In 1883 he came to Forest Home, in the Sixth District of Williamson County, Tenn., and engaged in the mercantile business with B. F. Tatum. The following year he bought out his partner. November 26, 1884, he wedded Miss Ella

Hows, daughter of Jack Hows, of Davidson County. To this union was born one child, Albert Edward. Mr. King is a member of the K. of P., also a member of the Cumberland Presbyterian Church. He is a Democrat in politics.

CLAIBOURNE H. KINNARD, Sr., was born in Williamson County, Tenn., October 1, 1857. Here he was reared and educated, attending the Southwestern Presbyterian University at Clarksville. In 1877-78 he attended the Vanderbilt University and took a course of lectures in the medical department. October 17, 1882, he was married to Miss Rebecca Campbell, of Williamson County, and daughter of John and Rebecca Campbell. To Mr. and Mrs. Kinnard were born two children: Rebecca M. and Claibourne H. Mr. Kinnard owns 540 acres of fine land, and he and wife are members of the Presbyterian Church. His parents were Claibourne H. and Elizabeth (Fleming) Kinnard. The father was born and raised in Williamson County, and by occupation was a farmer. In 1834 he married our subject's mother, who was a daughter of William Fleming, and the following seven children were born to them: Ann F., Susan E., Adella B., George, Orlena C., Kate C. and Claibourne H. The father died in 1863, and the mother August 29, 1884.

GEORGE M. KITTRELL, son of M. J. and Annie A. (Hunter) Kittrell, was born December, 20, 1829, near Mount Pleasant, Maury County. The parents were born in North Carolina, and about 1814 the father came to Tennessee and followed the occupation of farming. To him and wife were born seven children: Riddic, Loretta, Martha, Jacob, George M., Armesa and Eudora. George M., Reddic and Loretta are the only ones living. The father died in 1874 and the mother in 1854 or 1855. George M. attended the Mount Pleasant school, and in 1855 was united in marriage to Miss Anna W. Fleming, daughter of Thomas F. Fleming. They have five children: Whitney F., Laura R., William H., Thomas F. and Annie A. At the breaking out of the war Mr. Kittrell was living in Arkansas and enlisted in McNeal's regiment (Infantry), and was in many engagements. After the war he lived in Mount Pleasant, Tenn., nine years, and in 1875 located on a farm in Williamson County, where he has since resided. He is a member of the Methodist Episcopal Church South, and is a good citizen.

ROBERT H. KITTRELL is a son of George and Bettie (Rutherford) Kittrell, and was born in Maury County, Tenn., November 30, 1839. The father was a North Carolinian by birth, and in 1805 immigrated to Tennessee and settled in Maury County, near Hampshire. He was a tiller of the soil and owned considerable land in that county. He and our subject's mother were married in 1818 and thirteen children were born to them, four being dead. Those living are Elizabeth, James, William, George, John, Benjamin, Adaline, Robert H. and Rufus. George Kittrell, the father, died in 1868, and the mother in 1861. Both were members of the Christian Church. Our subject attended the common schools in boyhood, and in 1861 enlisted in the First Tennessee (Cavalry) Regiment, under Col. Wheeler, and was a participant in most of the principal battles of the late war, and surrendered at Durham, N. C., in April, 1865. In 1857 he was married to Miss Josephine McDonald, and their three children died in infancy. Mr. Kittrell was engaged in the mercantile business in Isom's Store, Tenn., for about nine or ten years, when he sold his interest and moved to Williamson County. For his second wife he took Miss Sue Underwood, in 1883. They have had two children born to them, Blanche C. and Anna L., who died October 4, 1885. Our subject owns a fine stock farm and is a prosperous agriculturist.

GILBERT H. LAMB, resident and farmer of Williamson County, Tenn., was born April 11, 1829, and is the son of Davis and Mary (Evans) Lamb, natives of North Carolina who settled in Tennessee in 1810. They were the parents of ten children—seven daughters and three sons, namely: Charity, Penina, William, Luticia, Hannah T., Abraham, Celia, Gilbert H., Mary and Elizabeth. The subject of our sketch received a very limited education in the common schools, and has been engaged in agricultural pursuits from boyhood. He settled on his farm of 109 acres in 1859, where he has been quite successful in his calling, and has a comfortable home. April 7, 1853, he was married to Matilda A. Vernon, who was born January 28, 1829, daughter of Obadiah and Ellen Vernon, who were born in North Carolina. To our subject and wife were born eight children: William H., George D., Abraham, Martha, Louis M., Mary F., Cora A. and Gilbert T. Mr. and Mrs. Lamb are members of the Methodist Episcopal Church South.

DR. HIRAM A. LAWS is a son of Col. John and Mary M. (Cathey) Laws. The father was born in Orange County, N. C., and came to Tennessee in 1828 and settled at Chapel Hill, Marshall County. He was a farmer and represented Marshall County three times in the lower house of the State Legislature and one time the upper house. He was also sheriff of the county, and filled every office from justice of the peace to State senator. He died in 1874. Hiram A. Laws was born November 10, 1850, in Marshall County, and attended the common schools. He also studied medicine in the University of Nashvile and graduated from the same in 1873. He practiced some time at Thompson's Station and in 1884 was licensed to preach the gospel. In 1877 he married Miss Mary E. Thompson. daughter of Dr. Elijah Thompson, and to them these children were born : Daisy C., E. H. and Mary F. Dr. Laws is in good circumstances, and he and wife are members of the Methodist Episcopal Church South and are one of the leading families in the county.

JOSHUA B. LILLIE, proprietor of the Franklin Flouring mills, was born near Watertown, N. Y., September 6, 1828, son of James and Caroline (Akins) Lillie, and is of French-Dutch descent. The father of Mr. Lillie was born in New York and the mother in Connecticut. They both died in Canada. When our subject was six years of age he was taken by his parents to Canada, where he received a common school education, and served an apprenticeship as house carpenter and joiner. Continued this business until 1861. He came to Tennessee in 1855, and in 1864 engaged in the saw-mill business, which he continued until 1869. He then bought the Franklin Mill, which was then very imperfect, and began at once to improve it and adopted the "roller process" in 1884. The capacity now is 200 barrels of flour per each twenty-four hours and 500 bushels of meal. In 1860 he was married to Miss Sallie M. Smith, of this county, and is the father of an interesting family of three children : Emma, James and Pryor. During the late war he was a Union man, and is now a Republican in principle. His first wife died in 1875 and the next year he married Lucy A. Smith, a sister of his first wife. He and wife are worthy members of the Christian Church. He is one of the leading millers of the South, and is a fair business man.

THOMAS MAHON, SR., was born January 6, 1779, in County Cork, Ireland. He was of wealthy parentage and a descendant of one of the noblest families of the Emerald Isle. He was educated for the priesthood, but as that life was not congenial to him he never assumed the duties of a priest. At the age of sixeeen he left his home in Dublin, Ireland, and came to New York to transact some important business for his father, who was a merchant, and being charmed with this country, determined to make the "land of the free" his future home. After residing five years longer in Ireland he returned to America and spent some time in Philadelphia, where he married Miss Abigail Shute, a young lady of French descent, and a resident of North Carolina, who only lived a few years, and died in 1808 when their only child was two years old. Five years later Mr. Mahon wedded Miss Emily T. Brooks and came to Maury County, Tenn., where he spent the remainder of his life. He was a teacher for many years, and for a long time was surveyor of Maury County. He and his son by his first wife, Thomas E., were for many years engaged in erecting mills, but the venture proved disastrous. They lost, by floods and other misfortunes, seven mills and a factory. Mr. Mahon died in 1856 and his widow in 1872. Thomas E. Mahon, Jr., was born February 1, 1806, in North Carolina, and came to Tennessee with his father. He married Nannie B. Brooks, April 7, 1841. She was born July 17, 1818, daughter of Thomas and Nancy (Jones) Brooks, who came to Tennessee from North Carolina on horseback. The father was a good farmer and operated one of the finest mills in Tennessee. At his death he left a handsome legacy to each of his thirteen children. Thomas E. Mahon, like his father, was for many years a school teacher and county surveyor. He and his wife became the parents of the following family : Thomas E., Martha M., James, William S., George W., Brooks, John and Julia. His life was characterized by his strong religious principles and conscientious integrity. He was educated in Jackson College. He died July 14, 1883, leaving his widow and seven surviving children.

JOHN W. MALLORY is a native of Northampton County, Va., born in 1780, and came to Williamson County, Tenn., in 1812, locating on a farm near Franklin in 1814. The same year he was married to Miss Sarah E. Crockett, daughter of Andrew Crockett, of this county. To them were born these six children: Lucinda, Andrew C., James H., John, Newton and Sarah E. Lucinda is the only one now living. The son, James H. Mallory, was born March 14, 1818, a graduate of the University of Nashville, and was afterward a teacher in Franklin and Gallatin. He established a nursery on the farm owned by his father, and carried on this business very successfully until his death January 19, 1857. He wedded Miss Susan S. Jones, of Logan County, Ky., in 1855, who bore him one child, J. W. Mallory, who was born June 29, 1856, and received a common school education, and May 23, 1878, wedded Miss Mamie, daughter of Thomas S. Buford, of Williamson County. They have two children: Clarence B. and Mamie L. J. W. Mallory owns 200 acres of land, where his grandfather, John W. Mallory, settled. Mr. Mallory is a Democrat, and he and his wife are members of the Presbyterian Church.

CLEMENT W. MALLORY is a son of Philip and Martha (Nance) Mallory, and was born March 25, 1833. Philip Mallory was born in Virginia and came to Tennessee at an early day, locating in White County. He afterward became a brick contractor in Nashville and was a soldier in the war of 1812. Of a large family born to him these are living: Elizabeth, Clement W., William M., Mary A., Harriet S. and Josiah. The father died of cholera in 1854. His wife died in 1849. Clement W. Mallory was educated in Nashville, and his first work for himself was done for a dry goods firm of that city. At the breaking out of the war he enlisted in Col. Ewing's company, and participated in many battles of note. On account of physical disability he was discharged, and since that time has resided in Williamson County, Tenn., and is a thrifty farmer. He was married, in 1865, to Malissa Fleming, and they are the parents of three children: Lemuel P., Martha J. (deceased in 1874) and John R. Mr. Mallory is a member of the Presbyterian Church and his wife is a Baptist.

FULTON A. MAYBERRY, son of Americus C. and Elizabeth M. (Dotson) Mayberry, was born October 17, 1851, in Williamson County, Tenn. His father was born in Tennessee and his grandfather in Virginia, and came to Tennessee at an early day. He was a mechanic and started in life very poor, financially, but at the time of his death, in 1840, was worth $150,000. Americus Mayberry was a farmer and owned a large tract of land in Williamson County. He was a successful farmer and business man, and at one time sold family groceries in Columbia, but at the breaking out of the war sold his stock of goods and turned his attention to farming. He was the father of six children: Fulton (deceased), John H. (deceased), Fulton A., John H., Presley (deceased) and Nannie. Americus Mayberry died in November, 1868, a believer in the Methodist faith. His widow married H. G. Mayberry, a brother of her first husband, and is living in Williamson County. Our subject was reared on a farm and was educated at Franklin, and in 1879 was married to Miss Nannie Seal, daughter of W. H. Seal. They have one child: Bessie. Mr. Mayberry owns 626 acres of land in Williamson County, and is a member of the Methodist Episcopal Church South. The family are of English descent.

W. L. McCALL, a prominent citizen of this county, was born in Tennessee, March 15, 1842, and is the son of Lycurgus and Emeline M. (Hartley) McCall. The father was born in Tennessee December 19, 1814, and married our subject's mother January 26, 1837. The mother was also a native of Tennessee, born October 15, 1817. She died October 4, 1866, and the father followed September 23, 1877. Our subject's grandfather, Laburn Hartley, and grandmother, Nancy Carson, natives of North Carolina, emigrated to Tennesee about 1800. Our subject has followed farming from early childhood, with the exception of two years when he was elected as constable. In 1866 he wedded Miss Marilda Irvin, a native of this State, born September, 1842, and the daughter of Andrew and Elizabeth (Evans) Irvin. The father was born in North Carolina December 17, 1804, and ried March 27, 1868. The mother was also born in North Carolina. To our subject and wife were born six children: Dora M., born 1866; Anna L., born 1867; Lizzie E., born 1870; Wallace E., born 1872; Andrew L., born 1875, and Louisa J., born 1879. Mr. McCall has 109 acres of medium land, situated in the southeast portion of the county. He is a member of the masonic fraternity, and is a stanch Republican.

AARON C. McCORD is a native of Williamson County., Tenn., born October 3, 1823, son of James and Rebecca (Curtis) McCord, natives of Georgia and North Carolina, respectively. In 1300 the father came to Tennessee. He was a cabinet-maker by trade, but also followed farming on a small scale. He and wife became the parents of twelve children: Mary, Martha J., Russell, Myra, Aaron C., Benjamin S., Calvin, Marshall P., James A., Harriet, Fountain and Sarah J. Mary and Martha are dead. Benjamin S., and Marshall P. left Tennessee before the war, and have never been heard of since. Husband and wife died in 1849 and 1841, respectively. Our subject was educated in the common schools, and in 1843 was married to Miss Elmina Caskey, of Maury County, and to them were born the following children: James C. (deceased), Russell F., William F., Milton A., Rebecca J. and John Wesley (deceased). In 1875 Mr. John McCord was elected justice of the peace for the Eleventh District, Williamson County., and still holds that office. He is a member of the Cumberland Presbyterian Church, and a representative man of the county.

JAMES McEWEN is a son of Maj. J. L. and Tabitha H. (Barfield) McEwen, and was born in Williamson County, Tenn., on the farm where he now lives. The father was born in Madison County, Ky., in 1794, and came to Tennessee with his parents, in 1798. He was major of the State militia in Williamson County, and was a soldier in the war of 1812. He was a farmer and was married in 1821. The father died April 15, 1879, and the mother December 28, 1853. Our subject's grandfather, David McEwen, was born in Pennsylvania in 1756, and came to Indiana in 1798, where he died in 1821. James McEwen received an academic education, and resided with his parents until the breaking out of the war, when he enlisted in Company D, First Tennessee Infantry, in April, 1861. After his return home in May, 1865, he took charge of his father's plantation, and now owns 550 acres of as good land as there is in the county. Mr. McEwen makes a specialty of raising fine stock, and was the breeder and owner of the celebrated trotting mare, Annie W. Mr. McEwen's house, one of the best and oldest brick houses in the county, was destroyed by fire April 6, 1877. He belongs to the Democratic party.

JOHN McGAVOCK was born in Williamson County, Tenn., April 2, 1815, son of Randal and Sarah (Rogers) McGavock. The family are of Scotch-Irish descent, and Randal was born in Virginia and came to Tennessee in 1786, locating in Nashville, where he was clerk of the superior court and clerk of the land office. In 1825 he moved to Williamson County, and located near Franklin. He was married in 1810 and became the father of these four children: John, Mary, Elizabeth and James R., all being dead except our subject. Randal McGavock died in 1843 and his wife in 1850. They were pioneer settlers of Tennessee, and leave a name behind them that will remain green in the hearts of those who knew them. John, our subject, was educated at the University of Nashville and graduated from that institution in 1837. He has always been a farmer. In 1848 he wedded Miss Carrie Winder, of Louisana, and two children were born to them: Winder and Hattie. In 1845 he was appointed colonel in the Army of the Tennessee by James K. Polk, and was made director of the Bank of Tennessee by Andrew Johnson, which office he held eight years. Mr. McGavock has always been a Democrat and cast his first presidential vote for Martin Van Buren.

WILLIAM S. McLEMORE, circuit judge, was born ten miles south of Franklin, in Williamson County, February 1, 1830, son of A. J. and Bethenia S. (Dabney) McLemore, and is of Scotch-Irish extraction. The father of our subject was born in this county in 1801, and died here in 1849. The mother was born in 1803 and died in 1857. Of thirteen children born, our subject was the fifth child and second son. He was reared on the farm and received his education in the common schools of the neighborhood in which he lived.

At seventeen years of age he entered the Transylvania University at Lexington, Ky., and in 1849 he entered Lebanon Law School, where he graduated in 1851. In the same year he began to practice in Franklin, and in 1856 he was elected county court clerk, and held this office until 1860, when he declined re-election and resumed the practice of law. In 1861 he enlisted in Company F, Fourth Tennessee Cavalry, Confederate States Army, and was promoted to first lieutenant, then captain, major, and in 1863 was commissioned colonel. The last six months he was colonel, commanding a brigade of cavalry, and was a brave and gallant soldier. In 1865 he returned home and immediately began the practice of law, which he continued until 1872 when he was elected criminal judge, the circuit then being composed of Williamson, Maury, Marshall and Giles Counties. He held this office six years and in 1878 was elected circuit judge of the Ninth Judicial Circuit; his present term expires in August, 1886. He has made a splendid record as judge, and as a lawyer has been quite successful. May 15, 1856, he wedded Miss Anna S. Wharton, daughter of Dr. W. H. Wharton, of Nashville. To Judge McLemore and wife were born five children: Annie L., Bethenia, Albert S., William W. and Lizzie M. He was formerly a Whig but since the war has been a thorough Democrat. He is a Mason and a member of the Methodist Episcopal Church South. Mrs. McLemore is a member of the Christian Church.

JOHN A. MILLER, a native of Maury County, was born November 25, 1838, and is the son of W. W. and Susan J. (Hadley) Miller. The father is a native of Tennessee, and spent his early life in assisting his father on the farm and in attending the common schools. He is a member of the Baptist Church. The mother died at her residence in Maury County in 1883. Our subject, in 1855, entered the Jackson College, at Columbia, Tenn., where he finished his education. May 1, 1861, Mr. Miller enlisted in Company G, First Tennessee Infantry, and participated in the battles of Shiloh, Chickamauga and other engagements. In 1864 Mr. Miller was captured and carried to Fort Delaware, where he was paroled February 6, 1865. After the war he engaged in farming, and in December, 1866, he was married to Miss B. A. Brown, daughter of Thomas Brown, of Williamson County, Tenn., who was born in Virginia, near the old battle-field of Manassas. In early life he immigrated to Tennessee, locating near Nashville, and at the age of twenty-nine he married Miss Nancy Allison, of Davidson County, and after her death was wedded to Mrs. Hunter. Mr. Brown died in February, 1870, and was a worthy member of the Christian Church. To our subject and wife were born six children: John, Maggie B., Thomas B., William W., Joe A. B. and Mary M., deceased. January 1, 1874, he moved to the Sixth District of Williamson County, to the farm known as "Old Town," where he now resides. Mr. Miller is a member of the Presbyterian Church and of the Masonic fraternity, and is a Democrat in politics.

J. G. MOODY, an enterprising farmer of the Fourteenth District of Williamson County, Tenn., was born December 27, 1838, in Davidson County, Tenn., and is one of two children of William and Eliza B. (Roy) Moody. The father was born in Tennessee and was of Scotch descent. He was a farmer and married in 1836, and died August 14, 1841. The mother was born October 12, 1818, and survives her husband. Our subject was reared in his native county and was educated in the country schools. When only fourteen years of age he left home and learned the carpenter's trade, at which he worked fourteen years. At the breaking out of hostilities, in 1861, he enlisted in Company D, First Tennessee Volunteers, and was in the battles of Chickamauga, Franklin, Nashville and Stone River. December 30, 1867, he wedded Mary Lou (Page) Moody, born December 17, 1847, in Williamson County, Tenn., daughter of J. T. and Mary (Harrison)Moody. Our subject and wife have seven children: William P., James A., John T., Charley E., Mary O., Walter B. and Ida. Mr. Moody supports Democratic principles and is a member of the Masonic fraternity, and he and wife are members of the Methodist Episcopal Church.

ALEXANDER MOORE, an old and retired farmer, was born in Lincoln County, N. C., March 2, 1798, son of James and Eleanor (Irvin) Moore. The father of Mr. Moore was born in North Carolina in 1764, and died in Tennessee in 1838. The mother was also born in North Carolina in 1771, and died in Williamson County, Tenn., in 1809. Our subject's grandfather, Gen. Robert Irvin, was a delegate to the Independent Convention at Charlotte, N. C., in May, 1775. Our subject is the fourth of seven children. His eldest brother, Robert I. Moore, was born in 1791, and was a leading merchant in Nashville for many years; he died in that city in 1848. Our subject grew to manhood on the farm. In 1818 he began teaching school, and continued that occupation until 1825, when he began farming, and this he continued successfully until 1874, when he removed to Franklin, and here he now resides. He still owns 380 acres of fine land and the place is known as Moore's Lane. In 1824 he married Miss Nancy Merritt, a native of North Carolina, who was born in 1800. Mr. and Mrs. Moore have now lived together for sixty-two years, perhaps the oldest couple in the county. They have one child, James P., now a prosperous farmer. Our subject is a Democrat and cast his first vote for Gen. Jackson in 1824. He has been successful in life and one of the first men of this county. He and wife are members of the Cumberland Presbyterian Church.

JOHN B. MURREY was born in Williamson County, Tenn., July 6, 1822, and spent his boyhood on his father's farm, receiving his education in the common school. At the age of twenty-two he wedded Miss Adaline Wilson, a daughter of Thomas Wilson, a native of North Carolina, but a resident of Williamson County, Tenn. To Mr. and Mrs. Murrey were born two children; Sallie E. and Maggie J. In 1846 our subject moved to the Eleventh District in Davidson County, and was elected collector and served his county in that capacity as well as deputy sheriff until 1861. In the spring of 1872 he moved to the Sixth District in Williamson County, on the farm known as "Mount Pier," where he now resides. His farm contains 1,173 acres. He is a member of the Old School Presbyterian Church and his wife is a member of the Methodist Episcopal Church South, and has been since quite young. Our subject is the son of Ennis and Anna (Buchanan) Murrey, natives, respectively, of Tennessee and Virginia. The father was born in 1795, and received a common school education by his own exertions. In 1818 he was married to Miss Anna Buchanan, daughter of John Buchanan, a native of Virginia. In 1822 our subject's father was elected collecting officer of his district. In 1833 he went to Nashville and located on a farm where North Nashville now is, and afterward moved to Franklin, Williamson Co., Tenn. He was a Democrat in politics, and a member of the Methodist Episcopal Church South. He died March, 1824.

ISAAC L. NEELY'S birth occurred February 5, 1821, in Williamson County, Tenn. He is a son of John C. and Elizabeth Neely, who were born in Virginia and North Carolina, and grandson of Isaac and Fannie Neely. The father, John Neely, came to Tennessee about 1800. He was in the war of 1812 and died in 1867. The mother died in 1872. They were married about 1814, and our subject is the third of their eleven children. He has always been a farmer, and in 1878 purchased 131 acres of land near Nolensville on which he is doing well. In 1841 he was married to Sarah E. C. Burk, who was born about 1818, in North Carolina, daughter of John and Lucy Burk, and who died May 1, 1861, leaving one child, Miles E. Mr. Neely then married Eliza Pyner, October 18, 1861. She was the widow of Mason Pyner, and daughter of Samuel and Peggy Burke. The Neely family are highly respected citizens and were among the first families who settled in this State. Mr. Neely and wife are members of the Methodist Episcopal Church, and he is a member of the Masonic fraternity and I. O. O. F., and in politics is a Democrat.

J. W. L. NEVILS, a leading citizen of Williamson County, was born in this State July 14, 1834. His father, Josiah Nevils, was born in Virginia in 1794, and the mother, Sallie Beech, was also born in Virginia, about 1809. They both came to Tennessee in the year 1821 and in 1823 were united in marriage. The father left his farm to fight in the war of 1812, and was in the memorable battle of New Orleans. He died in the year 1854 and his wife in 1852. Our subject wedded Miss Ella G. Low in 1871. She was born in Tennessee September 13, 1851, and was the daughter of Gabriel and Vina H. (Pinkston) Yarbrough Low. To our subject and wife were born six children: John L., deceased, born in 1872; Augie V., born in 1874; Josiah W., deceased, born in 1876; William W., born in 1877; Sallie M., born in 1880, and an infant not named. Our subject engaged in the mercantile business in Maury County, Tenn., in 1856, and in 1861 closed out and enlisted in the Confederate Army, serving his country until the close of the war. One year after returning from the war he engaged again in the mercantile business at Peytonsville for about ten years, after which he sold out his stock of goods and gave his undivided attention to farming. He has 104 acres of good land near Peytonsville. He is a member of the Masonic lodge, also of the I. O. O. F., and he and wife are worthy members of the Methodist Episcopal Church South. Mr. Nevils is a Democrat and in 1874 he was elected magistrate in this district.

JOHN M. NEVILS, sheriff of Williamson County, was born in Maury County, Tenn., October 3, 1835, son of Josiah and Sarah (Beech) Nevils, and of Dutch-English descent. Our subject was reared on the farm and secured a good practical education in the common schools. He followed the occupation of a farmer until the beginning of the late war, when he enlisted in the Confederate Army, Company B, Eleventh Tennessee Regiment, and served four years. In 1865 he engaged in merchandising in Nashville, but soon removed to Peytonsville, this county, and continued farming and merchandising. In 1868 he wedded Lydia A. Lowe, who died in 1878. In 1879 he wedded Alice Merritt, and to them were born three children: Emmett, Annie C. and an infant unnamed. To his first marriage were born two children: Robert H. and Edward M. Mr. Nevils is a member of the Masonic fraternity and of the I. O. O. F. He has made one of the best sheriffs the county has ever had. He is a member of the Methodist Episcopal Church and is one of the prominent men of this county. Mrs. Nevils is a member of the Christian Church.

JAMES A. NORTH, M. D., is the son of H. B. and Martha J. North, who were natives of Virginia. The North family came to Tennessee at a very early day and settled in Williamson County. H. B. North was a Methodist minister and belonged to the Tennessee Conference and was preaching the gospel in Montgomery County when he married our subject's mother, and nine children were born to their union: R. H., James A., Ann W., Margaret S., Thomas B., Alice, Ida, Elizabeth and Lucy. The father died about 1878 and the mother March 4, 1882. James A. North was born in Williamson County, January 4, 1838, and was educated in Thompson Academy, and in 1859 entered the medical University at Nashville and graduated in 1861. At the breaking out of the war he enlisted in First Regiment Tennessee Cavalry, and participated in the battle of Fishing Creek, after which his command went to Mississippi under Col. Bartow and later were united with Gen. Forrest's force and was in all its exploits. In 1879 he was married to Miss Eliza Baker, and five children have blessed their union: Jesse W., Henry B., Carrick H., Eloise and Robert J. Dr. North began practicing his profession at Harpeth Station in 1865. He owns 150 acres of fine land and is one of the prosperous farmers of the county.

JEROME J. O'CONNER, farmer, formerly a merchant, was born in Manchester, England, July 3, 1827, and came to America in the year 1838. His parents, William and Anne (Synnott) O'Conner, were born in County Wexford, Ireland, in 1790 and 1789, respectively. The former died in St. Louis, Mo., in 1852, and the latter in the same place in 1858. Our subject was educated in the common schools, after which he learned the shoe-maker's trade. He commenced merchandising in 1865, but at the breaking out of the war enlisted in the Confederate Army in the Sixth Regiment Tennessee Infantry, and served fifteen months. He was married, in 1873, to Miss Henrietta Blackman, who has borne him five children: Miles, Albert, Annie, Laura and one deceased. Mr. O'Conner is a Democrat in his political views, and belongs to the Masonic fraternity; is a temperance man in every respect. He started in life in straightened circumstances, but by his energy and perseverance has surrounded his family with the comforts and conveniences of life. His wife belongs to the Christian Church.

DR. URBANE G. OWEN, a successful practitioner, was born in this State June 2, 1833. His father, Richard C. Owen, was born in this State December 12, 1809, and was a farmer by occupation and manufactured tobacco for several years before his death. The subject's mother, Henrietta (Rivers) Owen, was born in this State May 22, 1810, and married to Richard C. Owen in 1832. The father died April 17, 1860, and his widow followed him in death September 8, 1868. The subject is of Welsh descent and was educated in the best country schools. In 1855 and spring of 1856 he attended the old University of Pennsylvania and in the fall of 1856 he went to New York and then graduated in the spring of 1857. He practiced in the Brooklyn hospital twelve months, when he resigned and went to the city of New York and practiced until January, 1859. He then returned to Tennessee and located at Owen Hill, where he practiced until 1861. In September, 1859, Miss Laura Dobson became his wife; she was born in this State June 29, 1843, and was the daughter of Matthew and Letitia (Hughes) Dobson. To the subject and wife were born five children: Annie L., Richard G., William T., Letitia and Polly P. In 1861 he enlisted as private in Rucker's company, Battle's regiment and remained with it until the fall of 1861, when he was ordered to report to the Fourth Confederate (Churchwell's) Regiment at Knoxville, which he did and was made medical surgeon of that regiment. Here he remained until the close of the war, after which he returned home and located at College Grove, where he resumed the practice of his profession. Since locating there eight of his consulting physicians have died. The subject has not taken a dose of medicine in nineteen years. He has a good practice and is conceded to be very successful. He is a member of the Masonic lodge, No. 172, and he and wife are members of the Christian Church. In politics Mr. Owen is a Democrat.

PETER D. OWEN, a prominent farmer and stock raiser of Williamson County, was born February 3, 1833, in Davidson County, Tenn., near Nashville, and is the son of Peter and Charity Owen, natives of Virginia, who were married about 1816, and had born to them these children: John T., Floyd H., Elizabeth, Sarah G., Ambrose R., Herbert H., Peter D., Obadiah F., Carrie L., Hiram and Betsy. The subject of this sketch received a liberal education in the common schools and has been engaged in farming from boyhood. In 1882 he settled on his present farm of 200 acres, which is very valuable, all well improved, and a part of the same in a high state of cultivation. December 3, 1873, he was married to Sallie F. Waller. She was born September 10, 1851, and is the daughter of Pierce and Elizabeth Waller, natives of Tennessee. Mr. Owen and wife are the parents of these children: Mary, John F. and Willie. The early members of the Owen family were among the first families that settled in Tennessee and were highly respected citizens. They are of Scotch-Irish origin. Our subject started in life very poor, financially, but by industry and good management has made himself a very comfortable home and is well-to-do in this world's goods.

D. C. PADGETT was born in this State May 15, 1843, and is the son of Henry G. and Mary W. (Anderson) Padgett, both natives of Virginia. The father was born in 1796 and came to Tennessee about 1817 after his return from the war of 1812. He taught school for several years after he became of age, and was a life-long member of the Methodist Episcopal Church South. His death occurred in 1853. The mother was born in 1797, and died August 2, 1885. By her union with Henry G. Padgett she became the mother of eleven children—seven males and four females—seven of whom are yet living. Mrs. Padgett was a kind neighbor and was esteemed by all who knew her. Our subject is at present living on the farm formerly owned by his father; it lies in the southeastern portion of the county and contains eighty-seven acres of very good land, the products from it being corn, tobacco and small grain. Mr. Padgett is a Democrat in politics.

JACOB T. PAGE is of Scotch-Irish descent and a son of David D. and Charity Page, who were born in North Carolina, and settled in Tennessee about 1800. The early members participated in the war of 1812. Jacob T. was born October 30, 1819, in Williamson County, Tenn., and in early days received a liberal education. He has been a farmer from boyhood and located on his present farm of 125 acres in 1855. His land is well improved and under good cultivation. January 26, 1843, he was united in marriage to Mary J. Harrison, the daughter of William P. and Edith Harrison, of this State and county. Mr. and Mrs. Page have had born to them six children—two daughters and four sons: William F., Mary L., John D., Thomas H., Jacob S. and Olivia E. Mrs. Page died in 1878.

She was a member of the Methodist Episcopal Church South, her husband being a member of the same. Mr. Page belongs to the Democratic party and is a member of the F. & A. M.

JOHN PAGE (deceased), was born in 1798, in Wayne County, N. C., and was the son of John and Lovey (Davis) Page, who came to Tennessee from North Carolina and located in Williamson County about 1801. To their union were born nine children—five sons and four daughters: David D., John, Jacob, Harvey, Frederick, Nancy, Sarah, Betty and Martha. Our subject came to this State with his parents when three years of age, and was educated in the common schools. His early days were spent in farming, and about 1826 he engaged in the grocery and general merchandise business in Triune, in which he was fairly successful. In 1830 he was married to Margaret A. Wilson, who was born in 1814 in Williamson County, daughter of Samuel and Martha (Davis) Wilson, natives of Ireland and North Carolina, respectively. The father came to America about 1770, and was married to Martha Davis in 1802 in Tennessee. Our subject, Mr. Page, sold out his business at Triune in 1827 and moved to Nolensville, where he carried on the same business until 1833, when he sold out and removed to Louisiana, where he managed a cotton plantation until his death, in 1873. He and wife became the parents of ten children: Eudora M., John J., Walter, Katie, Robert W., Almira, Jason W., Harry H., Maggie and Webb M. Mr. Page was a Democrat in politics, and he and wife were members of the Methodist Episcopal Church South.

JOHN W. PARHAM, carpenter, was born April 10, 1851, in Williamson County, Tenn., son of George W. and Eliza (Bingham) Parham, and is of Irish descent. The parents were born in the same county as our subject, in 1824 and 1830, respectively. The mother died January 9, 1885. John W. was the second of their ten children, and was reared on a farm and attended the common schools. He afterward learned the carpenter's trade, at which he has since worked. He was married, April 22, 1877, in Williamson County, Tenn., to Miss Nancy V. Thweatt, of the same county. She was born February 12, 1857, and has borne her husband two children: Oscar, born February 12, 1878, and Florence, born August 23, 1881. Mrs. Parham was a daughter of W. H. Thweatt, who was born in 1808 and died in 1876. Her mother was born in 1820 and died in 1882. Their family consisted of sixteen children—eight sons and eight daughters. Of the number five are dead. Mr. Parham belongs to the Democratic party.

JAMES PATTON, a prominent citizen of Williamson County, was born July 17, 1812. His father, Jason Patton, was born in North Carolina in 1787, and came to Tennessee about 1802, where he was engaged in tilling the soil. His mother, Bithunia Bostick, was born in North Carolina about 1789, and came to Tennessee with her father in 1809. In 1811 she was married to Jason Patton and became the mother of nine children, three of whom are yet living. Mr. Patton died August 7, 1841, and his widow followed him in death May 10, 1870. Our subject's grandfather, James Patton, was born in Tennessee in 1760. The grandmother, Margaret (Wilson) Patton, emigrated from Scotland to Ireland and from there to North Carolina, where she was married. Our subject was reared on a farm, and with the exception of a few years that he spent trading in slaves, might be called a life-long farmer. In 1839 he married Miss Susan Thompson, a native of this State, born June 2, 1820, and the daughter of Jason and Susan (Cobb) Thompson. To Mr. and Mrs. Patton were born four children: Mary B., born December 7, 1841; Jason H., born August 5, 1849; Agnes J., born November 19, 1851, and Joseph J., deceased, born November 6, 1854. Mrs. Patton died December 18, 1881. Shortly after marriage he moved to Mississippi and ran a cotton plantation for ten years, after which he moved back to Tennessee. In 1850 he purchased the farm on which he now resides, it consists of 500 acres of first-class land in a fine state of cultivation. In 1854 he was elected justice of the peace and served the people in that capacity for about eighteen years. He was a conscript officer with the rank of major in the Confederathe service. In politics he is a Democrat.

THOMAS F. PERKINS, Sr., first saw the light of day March 12, 1809, in Williamson County, Tenn. He was reared on a farm until seventeen years of age, and then engaged in mercantile business in Triune, Tenn., where he remained twelve months, when he removed to Harpeth Lick, where he resided five years. In 1833 he wedded Miss Leah A. Cannon, who bore him seven children: Louisa, Letitia, Laura, Samuel F., Newton C., Thomas F., Jr., and William C. All the sons were soldiers in the Confederate Army. Only two of the children are living: Thomas F., Jr., and Newton C. Our subject was a merchant for twelve years and then engaged in farming, and at the breaking out of the war was the owner of 127 slaves. He now owns a farm near Memphis, Tenn., and also one in Williamson County. He is a member of the Cumberland Presbyterian Church, and is a leading man in the county. His parents, Samuel and Sarah P. Perkins, were natives of Virginia and Tennessee, respectively. About 1804 the father came to Tennessee, where he tilled the soil. He held several offices in Virginia, and in 1807 was married and became the father of seven children: Louisa, Eliza M., Mary, Sarah P., Elvira, Susan and Thomas F., all being dead except our subject. Mrs. Perkins died in 1824, and Mr. Perkins then married Nancy Richardson, who bore him one child, Samuel. Mr. Perkins represented Williamson County, Tenn., in the State Legislature, and was a very influential man of his day. He died in March, 1843.

SAMUEL F. PERKINS (deceased), son of Thomas F. Perkins and grandson, on his mother's side, of G. Cannon, of Tennessee, was born July 1, 1833. He spent his early boyhood on a farm, attending the common schools of the county. Quite early in life he entered the Jackson College at Columbia, Tenn., and after finishing his education he returned home and engaged in farming, and also the mercantile business in Franklin. At the age of twenty-five he wedded Miss Theresa G. (Ewin) Perkins, daughter of Henry C. Ewin, of Todd County, Ky. Mrs. Perkins was a granddaughter of D. H. Hill, one of the first settlers of Nashville, and grandniece of Col. Ewin Hickman, who was killed by the Indians near the place where Centerville now stands, in Hickman County, and after whom Hickman County received its name. Mr. Perkins is the father of nine children: Leah L. (wife of Leland Jordan, of Murfreesboro), Lizzie E. (wife of John H. Henderson), Thomas F., Samuel F., Theresa (wife of Frank Y. McGavock), Henry C., Newton C., Leah M. and William Ewin. In 1861 Mr. Perkins obeyed his country's call and volunteered to fight her battles. He enlisted in Company C, Fifty-fifth Tennessee Infantry, and was promoted to a lieutenancy in his company. He participated in the battle of Corinth, Miss. He was also in numerous skirmishes. In 1862 Mr. Perkins returned to his rural pursuits, and also engaged in the mercantile business in Franklin, Tenn. In 1879 he moved to his farm on the Hillsboro & Nashville Pike. He died June 9, 1885, at Franklin. Mr. Perkins was one of the most successful farmers in the county, his farm consisting of about 700 acres. Mrs. Perkins is still living at "Hill Side," the home place, and is a member of the Christian Church.

N. EDWIN PERKINS was born in Williamson County in 1821, and received the rudiments of his education in Franklin and subsequently attended college in Danville, Ky. Being fond of the country, he passed his life in rural pursuits. He wedded Miss Martha T. Maury, and to this union were born three children: Edwin M., Leighla O. and Maud C. (wife of J. W. Reid, grandson of Maj. John Reid, aid-de-camp to Gen. Jackson at the battle of New Orleans). Our subject was a member of the Protestant Episcopal Church, and a member of high rank in the I. O. O. F. He was a man of unblemished honor and was universally respected. His death occurred in 1871 at his place, "The Meeting of the Waters." He was of Welsh descent, and the grandson of Hardin Perkins, who was a native of Virginia, a captain in the Revolutionary war, and one of the first settlers in Williamson County. He was one of the most successful farmers in the State, and amassed a large fortune. Nicholas Perkins, our subject's father, was born in Davidson County. After reaching manhood he went to Fort Stephens, then on the confines of the territory of the United States, where he entered into partnership with George S. Gaines in the practice of law. While there he was instrumental in the capture of Aaron Burr, who was attempting to make his escape to the Spanish possessions. He carried Mr. Burr to Richmond and delivered him up to the authorities. Nicholas Perkins wedded his cousin, Miss Mary Perkins, practiced law in Franklin and served several terms in the State Legislature, and died one of the largest property holders in the State. He was a man of fine practical ability. Our subject's wife, Martha T. (Maury) Perkins, was the granddaughter of Mr. Abram Maury, who was a descendant of the Maury and Fountaine families, of Virginia. They were a Huguenot family, who were forced to leave France on account of the revocation of the Edict of Nantes by Louis XIV. Mr. Abram Maury was born in Virginia, and was the first settler in Williamson County. He was the founder of the town of Franklin, and Maury County was named in honor of him. He held many offices of honor and trust in his State, and was a man of erudition and nobility of character. His son, the Hon. A. P. Maury, father of Mrs. M. T. Perkins, was a worthy man of a noble sire. He served his country both in the State Legislature and in the Congress of the United States. His greatest eulogium was that he was an incorruptible politician. His wife, Mary Claiborne, belonged to the Lewis and Claiborne families of Davidson County. They have three children now living: Mrs. M. T. Perkins, Mrs. W. S. Reid and Mr. F. C. Maury, of Nashville, Tenn.

CAPT. HENRY P. POINTER is a son of Henry and Wilmoth (Boyd) Pointer. The father was born in the "Old Dominion" and emigrated to Tennessee in 1827, settling near Spring Hill, Maury County. He was a farmer, and eventually became the possessor of a fine farm in Williamson County. In the earlier part of his life he wedded a Miss Ragland, and three children were born to their union: Martha, Mary (deceased), and Elizabeth. Mrs. (Ragland) Pointer died and Mr. Pointer then married Wilmoth Boyd, of Virginia, who bore him eight children: William, Susan, Henry P., Thomas G., Sammie, Ellen, Harriet and one who died in infancy. Henry Pointer, Sr., died in the year 1863. His wife died several years previously. Our subject, Henry P. Pointer, was born May 5, 1822, in Halifax County, Va., and came to Tennessee with his parents when a small lad. He was educated in Jackson College, Maury County, and was reared on a farm, and in 1853 was united in marriage to Miss Martha J. Caldwell, who died shortly afterward; and he then wedded Miss Virginia Brown, and one child was born to their union, named Henry Strange. At the breaking out of the war Mr. Pointer enlisted in the Third Regiment Tennessee Infantry under John C. Brown, and was taken prisoner at the battle of Fort Donelson and carried to Camp Chase, where he was kept two or three months, when he was taken to Johnson's Island, and at the end of two or three years was exchanged at Vicksburg, Miss., and went on Gen. Forrest's staff and remained with him until the close of the war. In 1861 he was made captain of Company E (Infantry), and was wounded near Memphis. After the close of the war he came home and has since been engaged in farming on his 200-acre farm, and is one of the principal stock raisers in the county.

GEORGE W. POLLARD, farmer and stock raiser, was born in Williamson County, Tenn., February 7, 1815, son of Joseph and Martha (Nicholson) Pollard, natives of Virginia and North Carolina, respectively, and married in 1814 and became the parents of eleven children: George W., Isaac N., Malachi W., Joseph J., William C., Robert L., Newton N., Nancy D., Martha E., Mary J. and Virginia A. The father died in 1839, and the mother in 1852, in Williamson County, Tenn. Our subject, George W. Pollard, received a liberal education, and the greater part of his life has been spent in farming. In 1831 he began clerking in the dry goods store of Charles R. Abbott, of Murfreesboro, Tenn., remaining two years, when he went to Columbia, Tenn., and became clerk for James S. Walker. In 1835 he began clerking for a house in Nashville, and in the spring of 1836 commenced business for himself in Mississippi under the firm name of Pollard & Shattuck, of Carrolton. In 1837 he wedded Mary J. Tindall, born August 20, 1819, daughter of Noah B. Tindall, of Maury County, Tenn. Mrs. Pollard died July 9, 1839, leaving one child, Isaac C. In 1842 Mr. Pollard returned to his native county and married Martha E. Mebane, who was born February 9, 1824, daughter of William and Mickie Mebane. In 1844 Mr. Pollard purchased 500 acres of land, but in 1868 again engaged in the general merchandise business on his farm. Since 1878 he has given his time and attention to farming and stock raising. He and wife have four children : William M., Julia, Laura (who died December 14, 1854), and Martha G. Mr. Pollard is a Democrat in politics, formerly a Whig. He was elected justice of the peace in 1848 and served until 1854. After his father's death he was the only support of his mother and younger brothers and sisters, but by hard work managed to give them a good education He and his wife are members of the Methodist Episcopal Church South, and they are highly respected and esteemed citizens of the county.

JAMES H. PORTER, son of Stephen S. and Mary (Henry) Porter, was born September 11, 1850, in Blount County, East Tenn. Stephen S. Porter came to Tennessee from Virginia about 1840. In early life he married, and to him and wife were born three children : Isabella, Lou and James H. Mrs. Porter died in the fall of 1807, and Mr. Porter then married Miss Catharine Peck, and four children were born to them: Amelia, Mary, Saunders and Robert. Saunders died in 1866. In 1865 Stephen S. Porter moved to Maury County, where he has since lived, engaged in farming. He is a member of the Methodist Episcopal Church South. James H. Porter was educated at Spring Hill, Maury County, and in 1876 was united in marriage to Miss Alice A. Potter. They have three children : Walter S., Ellen A. and Florence E. In 1877 Mr. Porter came to Williamson County and purchased his present farm of 131 acres of fine land. He is one of the leading farmers of the county, and is a member of the Methodist Episcopal Church South.

PETER H. REED, farmer and fruit grower of Williamson County, Tenn., was born in this county in 1824 and is one of four children—one daughter and three sons—born to the marriage of Andrew and Nancy Reed, natives of North Carolina and Virginia, respectively, who came to this State and county at an early day. Our subject was the eldest of the family and following him were Andrew J., Mary F. and William F. Peter H. received a very limited education and from early boyhood has been engaged in agricultural pursuits on the farm where he now resides. Of late years he has given a great deal of attention to raising fruit, and is known throughout the county as a successful fruit raiser. He has been fairly prosperous in all his undertakings and is regarded as a very industrious farmer. He served two years in the late war in the Twentieth Tennessee Regiment, under Col. Battle. He is a Democrat in politics, and his father, Andrew Reed, was a captain in the war of 1812 and participated in the battle of New Orleans. Our subject is a bachelor and of Irish descent.

GIDEON W. RIGGS, deceased, was born in this county November 17, 1845, and is the son of Gideon and Catharine (Holden) Riggs, natives, respectively, of North Carolina and Ireland. The father was born March 8, 1790, and came to Tennessee when but a lad. He died November 17, 1879. The mother was born September 1, 1815, and at an early age immigrated to Alabama, and from there to Tennessee, where she married Mr. Riggs, she being his third wife. She died August 10, 1864. Our subject followed farming the principal part of his life and in 1862 entered the Confederate service, where he remained two years, being discharged on account of ill health. In 1866 our subject married Miss Nannie Jordan, a native of this county, born December 28, 1842, and the daughter of Newton and Mary Jordan, both natives of this State. The father was born in 1803 and the mother in 1805; they were married in the year 1827 and had thirteen children born to their union, five of whom are yet living. The mother died February 10, 1885. Our subject and wife became the parents of seven children: Gideon, born in 1867; Kate, born in 1868; Lillie M., born in 1870; Emmet, born in 1871; Jordan, born in 1873; Oliver, born in 1876, and Earl, born in 1877. May 17, 1879, our subject passed from life, and since that time the widow assumed control of the farm, cultivates a portion and rents the remainder out. This farm contains 250 acres of land in a fair state of cultivation. Mrs. Riggs and eldest daughter are members of the Methodist Episcopal Church South.

HIRAM E. RING, deceased, was the son of George Ring, and spent his early life in the city of Lancaster, Ohio. At the age of nineteen he entered the college at Granville, Ohio, from which he afterward graduated and then began teaching, which he continued until 1845. About this time Mr. Ring volunteered in Company I, Second Regiment of Ohio Volunteers, commanded by Col. George W. Morgan, and participated in some of the battles of the Mexican war. In 1847 he was discharged at New Orleans and returned home. He then came to Nashville and engaged in teaching, where he remained until 1848, after which he moved to Williamson County and located in the Sixth District. June 12, 1849, he wedded Miss Emma T. Motheral, daughter of Joseph Motheral, of Williamson County, whose father was one of the first settlers of this county. To the union of Mr. and Mrs. Ring were born two children: Henry H. and Leonidas R., both living. After his marriage Mr. Ring lived two years in Sumner County, after which he moved to Dover in Stewart County, and took charge of the Male Academy at that place. He continued teaching until his death, which occurred October, 1858. He was a member of the Presbyterian Church and of the I. O. O. F. After her husband's death, Mrs. Ring returned to her home where she lived with her father until 1872, when his death occurred. Mrs. Ring is a member of the Presbyterian Church, and is still living at her residence in the Sixth District.

W. T. ROBERTS, a successful farmer, was born in this State October 11, 1850, and is the son of William R. Roberts, a native of this State, born April 17, 1817, and who married our subject's mother, Charity E. Demumbrane, in 1840. She was a native of Tennessee, born about 1820. Mrs. Roberts died October 27, 1855, and William Roberts married Rebecca J. Merrett, June 24, 1858. The second Mrs. Roberts died October 5, 1859, and in 1873 Mr. Roberts took for his third wife Miss Ella Bradley, a native of this State, born July 27, 1840. Our subject's grandfather, Benjamin Roberts, was born in Virginia May 20, 1776, and was a farmer by occupation. His wife, Juda Fuqua, was also born in Virginia. Our subject was reared on a farm, and is at present living with his father at the old homestead; this farm lies in the eastern portion of the county and contains 110 acres of average land. He directs his attention principally to raising corn and small grain. He has a large, commodious residence, well located on the farm. His father is a member of the Cumberland Presbyterian Church. In 1876 our subject was united in marriage to Elizabeth T. Bradley, a native of this State, born June 29, 1853. To this union were born two children; one died in infancy; the other, William R., born August 31, 1879, is still living. Mrs. Roberts is a member of the Methodist Episcopal Church South. Politically Mr. Roberts and father are Democrats.

CAPT. WILLIAM J. ROBINSON was born September 28, 1832, and his early life was passed in assisting on the farm and in attending the district school. In 1861 he enlisted in Company A, Twentieth Tennessee Infantry, and participated in the battles of Fort Donelson, Fishing Creek, Parker's Cross Roads, and was also in many skirmishes, where he was wounded. In 1863 he was promoted to captain of Company D, of Napier's battalion, and afterward of Cox's Tenth Tennessee Regiment. Capt. Robinson was captured September, 1863, and carried to Johnson's Island, Ohio, where he remained eighteen months. He was paroled just before Lee's surrender. At the close of the war he returned home, and in 1866 was married to Miss Sallie N. Newsom, daughter of James E. Newsom, of Davidson County, and by her he is the father of five children: Walter, Catharine L., Bellefield N., Baley P. and Sallie N., four of whom are now living. Capt. Robinson was married a second time to Miss Ella V. Newsom, June 28, 1877, and five children blessed this union: William J., James T., Susie N., Sallie M. and Ella V., all of whom are now living. Our subject is the son of James C. and Susan (Litton) Robinson. The father was born in Virginia, October 5, 1795, and in quite early life he served an apprenticeship with a cabinet-maker. After finishing his apprenticeship he went to Kentucky and there followed his trade. He afterward moved to Nashville, where he was married, February 6, 1828. In 1840 he moved to Williamson County and located in the Sixth District, on the place known as Blue Springs. He was a member of the Legislature during the years 1847-48. He was a member of the Presbyterian Church, and died October 13, 1852. His widow died July 23, 1863. She was a worthy member of the Methodist Episcopal Church South.

JOHN HENRY ROLFFS was born in Hanover, Germany, May 25, 1843, son of John and Kate (Von Bastel) Rolffs, and of German lineage. The parents of Mr. Rolffs were both born in Germany. Our subject's father was a soldier in the battle of Waterloo under Wellington. The Rolffs family came to America about 1850, landing at New Orleans, and came by river to Nashville, where the parents of our subject died. He is the eighth of nine children, was reared in the city of Nashville and attended the schools there. In 1859 he began working as an apprentice at the tinner's trade and worked at this for some time. In 1866 he came to Franklin and engaged in the house-furnishing business, which he has followed nearly ever since. In 1871 he led to the hymeneal altar Miss Mary Jane Pugh, of Franklin, though a native of New York City, and to this union was born one child, Anna Pugh. Mr. Rolffs is a Democrat and a Mason (Knight Templar). He is one of the oldest merchants of Franklin and also one of the most successful.

ASHLEY B. ROZELL may be mentioned as a prominent farmer and stock grower of Williamson County, Tenn., was born in the Palmeto State June 11, 1802, and is a son of Solomon and Mary Rozell, who were born in Maryland and North Carolina, respectively. They were married in North Carolina in 1800, and immigrated to this State about 1804 and located in Williamson County, but soon moved to West Tennessee where they remained several years, afterward moving to Shelby County, locating near Memphis, where both father and mother died. To them were born six children—five sons and one daughter—named Ashley B., Yerbie P., Rufard A., Martha D., Blackman L. and Claybion W. Our subject received a common school education and always followed the occupation of farming. In 1821 he became a minister of the gospel in the Methodist Episcopal Church, and was a member of the Methodist Episcopal Tennessee Conference until 1833. Since that time he has been a local minister and is widely known in the State. In 1828 he was married to Margaret M. Rolston, who was born in 1809, and the daughter of Maj. Alexander Rolston. She died in 1830, and in 1832 he wedded Henrietta S. Burnett, born in 1810, daughter of Brooken Burnett, of Rutherford County. They have five children: Mary T., Logan D., Ruford B., Martha C. and Ashley B. Mrs. Rozell died in 1846, and for his third wife Mr. Rozell took Martha A. Chambers. She is a daughter of Thomas and Nancy Chambers, of Virginia, and was born in 1823. To them were born four children: William R., Henrietta, Lockie B. and Lizzie B. The family are all members of the Methodist Episcopal Church South, and their early ancestors were among the first families that settled in the State. They are of French descent. Mr. Rozell has been quite prosperous, and in 1865 located on his farm of 420 acres of valuable land, known as the Mount View stock farm.

A. G. SCALES, an old and prominent citizen of this county, was born in Tennessee October 14, 1821. His father, Joseph G. Scales, was born in North Carolina about 1795, and came to Tennessee with his father when seventeen years old. He was of English extraction and a farmer by occupation. Our subject's mother, Frances Webb, was born in Virginia about 1801, and came to Tennessee, where she married Joseph G. Scales in 1815, and became the mother of sixteen children, five of whom are yet living. Mr. Scales died in 1870, and his widow followed him in 1875. October 16, 1845, our subject wedded Miss Martha E. Lavender, a native of Tennessee, born December 5, 1821, and the daughter of Nelson and Nancy (Bugg) Lavender. To our subject and wife were born eight children. William N., Fletcher A., Laura M., James A., Allie A., Joseph D., Charles E. and Samuel W. Mrs. Scales died April 22, 1863, and he took for his second wife Eliza L. Westervelt, a native of Pennsylvania, born November 20, 1839, and the daughter of Dr. Peter A. and Ann W. (Gribble) Westervelt. By this last union Mr. Scales became the father of five children: Frank B., born in 1867; Peter S., born in 1869; Risdon G., born in 1871; Willis C., born in 1875, and Frances H., born in 1882. Our subject was reared on a farm and lives in sight of his birth-place. He started out to make a living for himself when quite young, and by close application and hard work accumulated considerable wealth, which he retained until the close of the war. He was chairman of the Vigilance Committee organized during the war. His farm was often made the camping grounds of both armies at different times, who destroyed his fences and carried off his stock and also his slaves, who numbered about thirty, leaving him nothing to cultivate his farm. About the close of the war he was elected justice of the peace in this district. He was substantiated before the United States Court as a loyal man and succeeded in getting a claim of $1,260 some time after peace was declared. He has donated money for the erection of churches in all directions. He has a fine farm of 300 acres lying on both sides of the Farmington & Fayetteville Pike. He takes great pride in rearing fine stock and has some fine blooded animals at his place. He has been trustee of the Male and Female College at College Grove from its beginning. He is a Democrat, and he and wife are devout members of the Methodist Episcopal Church South.

JOHN SCALES first saw the light of day on the 24th of January, 1829, in this county. His parents, John and Sallie Scales, came to Tennessee from North Carolina about 1820. They were the parents of six sons, our subject being the third. From early boyhood he has been a farmer and now deals also in stock and owns seventy-nine acres of valuable and well improved farming land, a part of the same in a high state of cultivation. He located on his farm in 1885. September 4, 1884, he was united in marriage to Bettie E. Sayers, who was born August 28, 1856, and is a daughter of Abner and Jane Sayers, who are natives of Virginia and Tennessee. Mr. and Mrs. Scales have one child, a son named John. Mr. Scales is a strong supporter of Democratic principles. The family were early settlers of Tennessee and have always been considered valuable citizens. They are of Scotch-Irish descent and some of their early ancestors were participants in the Revolutionary war and the war of 1812.

PLEASANT D. SCALES, son of Samuel and Melissa A. A. (Wilson) Scales, was born in Tennessee, October 1, 1839. His father died in 1841, and his mother then married Matthew Wilson, by whom she had three children. Our subject lived on a farm in Rutherford County until eleven years of age, when he came to this county and farmed until 1857. He then clerked in a store two years, after which he attended school at College Grove, where he remained until 1861. He then enlisted in Company D, Twenty-fourth Tennessee Regiment, and remained in service until the close of the war. In 1865 he came home and began merchandising at Bethesda, which he has continued ever since. He is also postmaster at the same place. May 24, 1876, our subject led to the hymeneal altar Miss Mary O. Ratcliffe, a native of this State, born March 11, 1852, and the daughter of Francis G. and Martha (Reams) Ratcliffe. To Mr. and Mrs. Scales were born four children: Ella, born June 23, 1877; Eva M., born February 14, 1879; Annie C. (deceased), born May 16, 1881, and Frank E., born April 23, 1884. In 1883 Mr. Scales was elected magistrate in this district and holds the office at the present time. He is a member of the Masonic fraternity and a Democrat in politics. He is a member of the Cumberland Presbyterian Church, and his wife a member of the Methodist Episcopal Church South.

YOUNG SCRUGGS, son of Edward and Althea (Hassel) Scruggs, was born in Williamson County, Tenn., February 17, 1840. His father was a native of Virginia, and at an early day came to Tennessee and settled in Williamson County. He was a soldier in the war of 1812 under Gen. Jackson, and when about thirty years of age was married to Miss Althea Hassel, and nine children were born to them: Thomas (deceased), William, Joseph, Edward, John, Drury (deceased), Theo, Young and Nancy. Edward Scruggs, Sr., died in 1847. Our subject was reared on a farm and educated in the town of Franklin. He has always followed the occupation of farming, and owns 360 acres of fine and well cultivated land. In 1874 he was married to Miss Ida Bennett, and four children have been born to them, named Allen M., Edward H., Mattie T. and Louie, who died in 1880. Mr. Scruggs was a Confederate soldier and enlisted in the First Tennessee Regiment under Col. George Manny, and was a faithful and brave soldier. Since that time he has been a resident of Williamson County, Tenn., and is much respected and esteemed by all who know him.

THEO SCRUGGS is a son of Edward and Althea (Hassel) Scruggs, and was born December 4, 1834, in Williamson County, Tenn. (For parents' life see sketch of Young

Scruggs.) His boyhood days were spent on his father's farm, and his education was obtained in Franklin, Tenn., under Andrew Campbell. He has always been a tiller of the soil and has met with good success. He owns 400 acres of fertile and well cultivated land and is doing well financially. In 1878 he took for his companion and helpmate through life Miss Lizzie Bond, who died shortly after her marriage, and he then wedded Miss Isabella White. They have no children. Mr. Scruggs is a leading member of the Christian Church and is one of the first citizens in the county.

COL. SAMUEL E. SHANNON is a son of Samuel R. and Elizabeth Shannon, and was born March 12, 1838, in Williamson County, Tenn. The parents were married in 1828, and to them were born eight children: Tennessee E., Robert W., Mary F., Sarah A., Thomas G., Samuel E., Cornelia P. and Martha V. The subject of this sketch received a good education in the common schools, and was a teacher of the county until 1861, when he enlisted in the Twenty-fourth Tennessee Regiment with the rank of second lieutenant, and was promoted to captain, then major, and lastly to lieutenant-colonel. He participated in the battles of Shiloh, Corinth, Miss.; Perryville, Ky.; Murfrees' boro, Chickamauga, Missionary Ridge, Jonesboro, Atlanta and Franklin. Since the war Mr. Shannon has been engaged in farming, and owns 280 acres of well improved land. He has been quite prosperous in his undertakings, and by his industry and good management has made himself a good home. He was married to Elizabeth H. Roberts March 7, 1866. She was born November 4, 1837, and is the daughter of Benjamin F. and Margaret Roberts, who was born in Tennessee. Mr. Shannon is a Democrat, and in August, 1876, was elected justice of the peace, and has been a faithful and efficient performer of his duties.

J. A. SHORT, a prosperous farmer and stock raiser, was born April 25, 1839, and received his education in the common schools. In 1861 he obeyed his country's call and volunteered to fight her battles. He enlisted in Company H, Twentieth Tennessee Infantry, and was a participant in several battles of note, viz.: Shiloh, Murfreesboro, Chickamauga and Atlanta, Ga., and also numerous minor engagements. He was wounded three times during the war, and at its close returned home, and is now engaged in farming and stock raising. He and B. F. Short, his brother, own about 700 acres of land. Our subject's parents were William H. and Juda (Atkinson) Short. The father was a native of Halifax County, Va., and in 1808 he left his native State and immigrated to Williamson County, Tenn., where he engaged in farming and stock raising until his death, which occurred July 28, 1881. The mother was a daughter of the late Elder John Atkinson, of Virginia, who was a noted preacher of his day, and a descendant of one of the first families of Virginia.

WILLIAM H. SMITH was born in Powhattan County, Va., February 6, 1829, son of Francis S. and Elizabeth C. (Lockett) Smith, who were of English and French descent, and born in 1801 and 1808, respectively, in Virginia. The family removed to Missouri in 1839, and then to Alabama in 1846, after which our subject came to Nashville, Tenn., in 1852. He received his preparatory education in the country schools, and afterward graduated from Howard College, Ala. He then took a Latin and Greek course in Franklin College, Nashville, Tenn., and at the breaking out of the war enlisted in the Forty-fourth Tennessee, afterward transferred to the Thirty-fifth Tennessee, Polk's brigade, and was clerk in the quartermaster's department. He was married, January 18, 1854, to Miss Mary E. Moore, of Davidson County, Tenn. Mrs. Smith was born near the Hermitage November 17, 1830. To them were born seven children, two of whom are dead. Mr. Smith is a Democrat, and he and wife are members of the Christian Church. He is a farmer and nurseryman, and for about twelve years before the war taught school. Mrs. Smith's parents were John and Mary (Stewart) Moore, born in North Carolina and Tennessee in 1795 and 1800, and of Irish-Scotch descent, respectively. The father died in 1878, and the mother in 1862. Their family consisted of seven children. Mrs. Smith's grandfather, William Stewart, came from Scotland to America when eighteen years of age, and was elder of the Presbyterian Church at the Hermitage, and died about 1848. He was a soldier in the war of 1812 under Gen. Jackson.

SAMUEL A. SMITH was born in this county June 4, 1844, and is the son of William M. and Margaret M. Smith, natives of Tennessee. The father was born in 1809, and died about 1872. The mother was born September 26, 1814, and died November 20, 1857. Our subject's grandfather, John Smith, was born in the last century, and came to Tennessee in 1809 and located on the farm on which our subject is now living. Samuel A. Smith passed his youthful days on the farm, and is now living on the farm of his birth, which lies in the southeastern portion of the county, and contains eighty-five acres of land in a good state of cultivation. In 1863 he enlisted in Company C, Eleventh Tennessee Cavalry, and remained with that company until captured at Middleton, Tenn. After remaining a prisoner about six weeks he was exchanged. In 1864 he, with several others, left the company and went to Mississippi and joined Gen. N. B. Forrest's command, where they remained until the close of the war. He was in the memorable battle of Franklin, and had many narrow escapes, but never received a wound. November 8, 1866, he wedded Miss Mary F. Smith, a native of Tennessee, born July 8, 1849, and the daughter of William N. and Martha A. (Giles) Smith. To our subject and wife were born four children: William N. M. (deceased), born in 1867; Margaret A., born in 1870; Annie, born in 1873, and Jennie P. (deceased), born in 1875. Mrs. Smith died January 9, 1878, and our subject then married Miss Louella Chriesman, in January, 1879. She was born in this State September 11, 1860, and is the daughter of David V. and Lydia A. (Dunlap) Chriesman. By this last union our subject became the father of two children: Samuel D., born in 1880, and Effie M., born in 1882. In 1876 Mr. Smith was elected constable, and held the office for six years. He is at present deputy sheriff. He and wife are worthy members of the Methodist Episcopal Church South, as is also his two eldest children. In politics he is a Democrat.

NATHANIEL N. SMITHSON, a respected citizen of Williamson County, was born in this State April 2, 1826. He received his education as the average country boy in the district schools. November 30, 1851, he was married to Miss Margaret K. Johnson, a native of Tennessee, born March 8, 1833, and the daughter of Jesse and Dolly (Smithson) Johnson. Our subject and wife were blessed by an interesting family of ten children: James M., born in 1852; Joseph P., born in 1855; Tandy (deceased), born in 1857; Elijah K., born in 1860; Dolly A., born in 1863; Martha P., born in 1865, Permelia (deceased), born in 1867; Mary E., born in 1879; Lydia O., born in 1874, and Jesse W. (deceased), born in 1877. In 1870 our subject moved to his present location in the edge of Peytonsville, where he has a fine farm of 190 acres; besides this he has another farm of 400 acres in another part of the county. He is a Mason, a stanch Democrat and a member of the Methodist Episcopal Church South. His wife is a member of the Baptist Church. Mr. Smithson is the son of Tandy S. and Ann (Cheatham) Smithson. Her father, a native of Virginia, was born in 1802, and died in 1873, and the mother was born in 1804.

GEORGE W. SMITHSON, of the firm of Smithson, Kenneday, Hodge & Co., is a native of Lunenburg County, Va., his birthday being December 30, 1838, son of William G. and Mary Smithson, whose maiden name was Crenshaw. The parents were born in Virginia, the father in 1819 and the mother in 1820. The family is of English extraction and came to Tennessee about 1840. There the mother of our subject died in 1846 and the father in 1852. Our subject lived on a farm until he reached the age of thirteen, when he began clerking in the store of Charles W. Smithson at Peytonsville, this county. He continued as clerk until 1859, when he engaged in business for himself at Peytonsville in partnership with John C. Helms, and remained in this business until 1861. He then enlisted in Capt. Ewing's company, First Battalion, Tennessee Cavalry. He was twice wounded, once at Paducah, Ky., and again at the battle of Franklin, Tenn. In 1865 he came to Franklin and engaged in the dry goods business and the same he now continues. From October, 1883, to March, 1885, he was cashier of the Farmers' National Bank, of Franklin. In the spring of 1885 he became a partner of the firm, Smithson, Kenneday, Hodge & Co. This is the most extensive dry goods store in Franklin, and is doing a large trade. In 1871 he wedded Miss Sallie M. Henderson, daughter of Dr. Samuel Henderson of this county. To

Mr. and Mrs. Smithson were born four children: Janey, George H., Mary and Sallie. Mr. Smithson is a first-class citizen, a Democrat, a Royal Arch Mason, and his wife is a member of the Methodist Episcopal Church South.

DR. SETH C. SPARKMAN was born in Williamson County, Tenn., November 27, 1830, son of Seth and Rebecca (Latta) Sparkman, who were of Scotch-Irish descent, and were born in Tennessee and North Carolina, respectively, in 1797. After his fourth year the father was a resident of Williamson County, where he died October 18, 1884, and the mother April 20, 1883. Our subject is the fourth of seven children, and received his education in the best schools of the county, after which he chose the profession of medicine and read with Dr. J. T. Cox. He attended lectures at Macon, Ga., and obtained a diploma. He was married September 27, 1866, to Lucy M. Cummins, daughter of William Cummins. They have two children: Ernest, born March 9, 1868, and Lena, born December 23, 1870. The Doctor has practiced his profession successfully for twenty years. He owns 576 acres of land, and is neutral in politics. He is a Mason and his family belong to the Church of Christ. John Latta, father of Mrs. Sparkman, was born about 1764, and came to Tennessee from North Carolina in 1813, and died September 15, 1827. Our subject's father, Seth Sparkman, was reared on a farm in the cane in Williamson County, Tenn. His early education was limited, but with advancing years he acquired a fair education. July 9, 1822, he was married, and followed blacksmithing and farming through life, and also practiced medicine to some extent. His father was William Sparkman, born in 1764, in North Carolina. He came to Nashville, Tenn., in 1796. He moved to Williamson County, Tenn., in 1801. He died March 15, 1832.

JAMES T. SPARKMAN, farmer and stock breeder, was born in Williamson County, Tenn., August 16, 1836, son of Seth and Rebecca (Latta) Sparkman, and is of Scotch-Irish descent (for history of ancestors see sketch of Dr. S. C. Sparkman). Our subject was educated in the common schools, and spent the free and happy life of a farmer's boy. He has been twice married. The first time to Miss M. J. Dabney, who bore him four children: Dabney, born December 30, 1860; Latta, born July 4, 1864; Tabitha C., born September 15, 1862, and died June 1, 1863; and Mary P., born September 23, 1867, and died December 16, 1869. Mrs. Sparkman was born March 21, 1842, and died June 4, 1873. October 10, 1876, he wedded Miss Laura King, of Williamson County, Tenn., born June 23, 1849. The entire family belong to the Christian Church. Mr. Sparkman owns a farm of 280 acres, which is under good cultivation and which yields fair profits.

THOMAS W. SPARKMAN was born on the same farm where he now resides June 14, 1812. He is a son of William and Rosanna (Williams) Sparkman (see note of father in Dr. S. C. Sparkman's sketch). William Sparkman's family consisted of nine children—four daughters and five sons. Our subject was the youngest, was reared on a farm, and received a common school education, and has made farming his chief business through life. September 23, 1840, he was married to Miss D. Fitzgerald, and for his second wife married Miss Nellie Ann White, March 16, 1843. His first wife died August 11, 1841. His second wife was born November 2, 1822, and died August 21, 1879. She became the mother of twelve children—eight sons and four daughters. Four sons are dead. Mr. Sparkman was in the Home Guard service during the war, being too old for the army, but was represented by both sons and sons-in-law. He and family belong to the Christian Church.

JOHN B. SPROTT was born in this State May 19, 1826, and is the son of Blythe and Rachael Sprott, the father born in North Carolina December 29, 1792, and died June 15, 1868. He was a soldier in the war of 1812, and took an active part in the Creek and Indian war. The mother was a native of North Carolina, born in the year 1794, and died April 1, 1840. Our subject was joined in marriage to Miss Sarah A. Crutcher, a native of this county, born June 4, 1831, and the daughter of A. P. and Jane P. (Children) Crutcher. To Mr. and Mrs. Sprott were born ten children: Ophelia Z., born 1851; Absalom B., born 1853; Rachael, born 1855; Mary V., born 1857; Sarah M., born 1861; Emma C., born 1863; John A., born 1865; Thomas P., born 1868; Nora P., born 1871, and James F. P., born

1877. Our subject lived on a farm till 1845, after which he taught school for several years. He traded considerably in stock in early life, and during the late war was the errand man for the neighborhood. In 1866 he was elected magistrate in this district, which office he held for several years. In 1853 he moved to his farm, which lies in the southeastern portion of the county, and contains 250 acres of good land. He formerly raised considerable stock, but of late years directs his attention chiefly to raising corn, tobacco, and small grain. He has a farm of 193 acres in the Eleventh District, and another of seventy acres. He had the misfortune to lose his wife in November, 1878. He is a Democrat, and he and family are members of the Methodist Episcopal Church.

WILLIAM H. SPROTT was born March 23, 1835, and is the son of Blythe and Rachael Sprott, natives of North Carolina. Our subject led to the altar, in 1860, Mary S. Foster, a native of Maury County, Tenn., born August 7, 1846, and the daughter of Henry and Susan (Stevenson) Foster, natives, respectively, of South Carolina and Tennessee. To our subjct and wife were born three children: Rachael J., born March 10, 1866; William H., born July 20, 1869, and Minnie M., born December 16, 1875. Mr. Sprott was reared on a farm and is living in the house of his birth. He has followed farming from early boyhood and has been quite successful. In 1861 he enlisted in the Forty-fifth Tennessee Regiment and remained with his company until captured in Georgia April 17, 1864, when he was taken to Indianapolis, Ind., and retained eleven months. He returned unscathed from the war with the exception of a slight wound. His farm lies in the southeastern portion of the county and contains ninety-one acres of land in a good state of cultivation. Politically Mr. Sprott is a Democrat. He and wife are members of the Methodist Episcopal Church South.

JAMES P. SPROTT was born in Williamson County, June 19, 1832, and is the son of Joseph and Elizabeth (Podgett) Sprott, natives, respectively, of North Carolina and Virginia. The father was born January 26, 1791, and came to Tennessee with his father when but a child. He died April 1, 1876. The mother was born about 1802 and died about 1830. Our subject passed his early life on the farm, and when a young man learned the saddler's trade and also the tailor's trade which he followed for about two years. In 1857 he married Miss Caroline Pratt, a native of Tennessee, born in the year 1842, and to this union was born one child, Caroline G. He had the misfortune to lose his wife September 19, 1860, and took for his second wife M. M. Herron, a native of Tennessee, born March 2, 1833, and a daughter of James H., and Maria (Bond) Herron, natives, respectively, of Tennessee and Virginia. To this last union one child, Jimmie, was born. Mr. Sprott is at present living in the southeastern part of the county on a farm of 225 acres. In 1861 he enlisted in the army and after remaining there about eighteen months he returned home and resumed his life-long occupation of farming. Mrs. Sprott is a worthy member of the Cumberland Presbyterian Church. Politically Mr. Sprott is a Democrat.

JAMES W. STEVENS first saw the light of day May 12, 1828, in Williamson County, Tenn., son of Edward and Nancy Stevens, who had born to their union ten children—eight sons and two daughters. Our subject was the ninth child and was educated in the common schools. He began life very poor financially, but by industry and good management made himself a very good home, and is comfortably situated. In 1870 he purchased 114 acres of land, upon which he has since resided. February 9, 1848, he took for his life companion Nancy Westbrook, who was born June 10, 1832, a daughter of Thornton and Betsy Westbrook, of Tennessee. To Mr. and Mrs. Stevens were born these children: Mary E., Adaline, Robert L., Nancy J., Henry, Effie, Ernest, Walter D., James A., Josephine, Beulah, Thomas and Sarah. The family are members of the Cumberland Presbyterian Church, and in politics Mr. Stevens was formerly a Whig, but now declines to side with either party. His ancestors were English.

PARK STREET, farmer, of Williamson County, Tenn., was born August 3, 1807, in Lunenburg, County, Va., son of Anthony and Mary Street, born in the "Old Dominion" and came to Tennessee in 1811. They were married in 1803 and became the parents of four sons: Alexander, James, Park and Anthony G. The father served very conspicuously in the Revolutionary war, and was a farmer. He died in 1809 in Virginia. His wife died in Marshall County, Tenn., in 1849. Our subject received a common school education in the Marshall County schools, and in 1828 engaged in the grocery and general merchandise business, at Fishing Ford, until 1830. He then purchased a farm near Columbia, in Maury County, where he tilled the soil until 1851, and then purchased his present farm. He owns 155 acres of valuable land and is well-to-do financially. July 28, 1829, he married Mary J. Smith, born September 10, 1813, daughter of James and Martha Smith, of Virginia. To Mr. and Mrs. Street were born eight children: William M., John M., Ann P., James P., Eugene, Mary J., James A. and Grief. Mrs. Street died November 23, 1848, and May 8, 1850, Mr. Street married Christiana Rainey, who was born February 2, 1807, widow of Maj. Jesse G. Rainey and daughter of John and Frances Raines, natives of West Virginia. The second wife died December 19, 1860, and for his third wife Mr. Street took Tennie E. J. Barns, February 5, 1862, born January 27, 1830, daughter of Thomas and Mourning Barns. To them were born one son, Claud P. Both husband and wife are members of the Methodist Episcopal Church South. Mr. Street is a Democrat and a member of the I. O. O. F. He was justice of the peace in Maury County, and was elected to the same office in this county in 1852, holding the office until 1882, when he declined re-election. The Street family are highly respected citizens and were among the first to settle in Tennessee.

JAMES J. SAYERS, deceased, was a prosperous farmer of Williamson County, Tenn.; he was born March 14, 1801. His parents, Robert and Nancy Sayers, were born in Virginia and were the parents of six children—four sons and two daughters. The parents came to Tennessee the latter part of the eighteenth century. Here our subject was educated in the best schools of the State and spent several years of his early life as a pedagogue, and instructed and ruled his pupils with more than ordinary ability. He wedded Ann M. Taliaferro January 29, 1835. She was a daughter of Baldwin and Nancy (Spotswood) Taliaferro, and was born March 6, 1806. Her parents were born in Virginia, and the Spotswood family were among the F. F. V's. To the above mentioned union were born four children: Robert B., Mary E., Jimmie A. and Sarah J. Our subject settled on the farm where he died, in 1844. He owned 700 acres of good land, and his death, which occurred April 16, 1863, was felt as a universal loss. His wife, Ann M., died April 18, 1886. She was a woman endowed with more than ordinary intellect and was for many years a successful teacher in the county. Both parents were members of the Methodist Episcopal Church South, and the father was a Democrat and a member of the F. & A. M., and the early members of his family figured very conspicuously in the Revolutionary war.

JOHN M. STREET, deceased, was a prominent farmer of Williamson County, Tenn., and was born February 26, 1834, son of Park and Mary J. Street, who were born in Virginia. Our subject's early life was spent in working at the carpenter's trade. February 7, 1858, he wedded Mary J. Vernon, who was born October 16, 1844, and is the daughter of Ashlem and Nancy Vernon, who were natives of North Carolina. To Mr. and Mrs. Street were born ten children: Nancy E., Mary A., Lazinka U., Jennie, James P., William D., Eugene, John A., Moffitt and David A. At the time of his death, October 4, 1879, our subject owned 212 acres of good land. Mr. Street was a man of noble impulses and his death was mourned by all who knew him. His widow, Mary Street, married Capt. William T. Ridley December 29, 1882, and to them was born a son named Bunk. The Street family are highly respected citizens, have been known in Tennessee for almost a century and are of English descent. Mr. Street was a Democrat in his political views and favored the principles of that party.

JOSEPHUS L. SWEENY, blacksmith, was born on the 21st of February, 1842, in Williamson County, Tenn. He is one of seventeen children—eleven sons and six daughters—born to the marriage of Charles P. Sweeny and Sallie Huggins, who are of Irish descent, born in Virginia and Tennessee in 1816 and 1818, respectively. Both are yet living. Our subject was educated in the common schools and was reared on a farm, after which he learned the blacksmith's and wagon-maker's trade. He was a soldier in the late war and served in Baxter's artillery for over two years. Since the close of the war he has worked at his trades and has been quite successful. April 19, 1866, he was married to Miss Minerva Jane Gathire, born in Edgefield, Tenn., December 25, 1849. To them, were born six children: Lemuel F., born June 10, 1867; Edward L., born August 29, 1869; John L., born July 17, 1875; Bonie L., born August 26, 1878; Charles D., born February 15, 1885, and Annie L., born September 18, 1872. Mr. Sweeny is a Democrat and he and wife belong to the Christian Church.

REV. STEPHEN ALLEN TAYLOR is a son of William Taylor, who was born in North Carolina and was a farmer in Georgia for about eighteen years. In early life, was united in marriage to Miss Malinda Nunp, of North Carolina, and of their twelve children eleven grew to manhood and womanhood: George, Hiram, Sallie, Mary, John, Nancy, Solomon, Stephen, Martha, James and Margaret. William Taylor died about 1835, and was buried in Georgia. He was a member of the Baptist Church. His wife died in 1853. Our subject was born in the State of Georgia February 15, 1829. He received his rudimentary education in the country schools, and in 1850 entered the University of Lebanon and graduated in June, 1854. He first followed school-teaching and was licensed to preach the gospel in 1849. In 1854 he was united in marriage to Miss Rachel D. Miller, a native of Tennessee, and five children have been born to them: John M., William A., Christina B., Carrie Bell and Elbridge G. Mr. Taylor's ancestors were of English birth and came to the United States, locating in Virginia or North Carolina. Mr. Taylor has been a minister of the Cumberland Presbyterian Church nearly forty years. He owns the Independence farm of 459 acres of land, and is highly respected by all who know him.

HERBERT R. TEMPLE (deceased) was born May 1, 1815, and passed his early life in assisting his father on the farm and in attending the common schools. Later he went to Texas and engaged in farming, but at the age of thirty-four he left Texas and returned to Tennessee, locating in Williamson County. August 26, 1852, he was married to Miss Susan Brown, and to this union were born four children: William E., Mary F., Roberta L. and Herbert R. Mr. Temple was a member of the Masonic fraternity and at the time of his death, which occurred August 28, 1880, was living at his farm known as "Oakland." Mrs. Herbert Temple is still living at her residence in the Sixth District of Williamson County, and is a worthy member of the Christian Church. Mr. Brown, father of Mrs. Temple, is a native of Virginia and immigrated to Tennessee where he engaged in farming in which he was quite successful. August, 1832, he wedded Miss Fannie Claud, and by her he is the father of these children: Susannah, Catharine, Virginia, Nannie E., Mary F., Coleman and Enoch. Mr. Brown is a member of the Christian Church.

HON. ATHA THOMAS, attorney at law and ex-treasurer of State, was born in Williamson County, October 5, 1829, and is the son of William and Eliza Thomas, both natives of Virginia. In a family of twelve children the subject is the tenth and is of Welsh-English extraction. The father of Mr. Thomas immigrated to Tennessee in 1796 and settled in Davidson County, but in 1801 he removed to Williamson County and here he and his wife died. Our subject was reared on the farm and received a liberal education at private schools and at Wirt Academy in Sumner County. In 1851 he began teaching school and about the same time he began reading law. He continued teaching for two years and then entered the Lebanon Law School and graduated from that institution in 1853. In 1854 he took charge of Thompson's Academy in this county where he conducted a most successful school until the beginning of the war. From 1861 to 1864, he had charge of Harpeth Academy in Franklin and was one of the most successful teachers the county has ever had. In 1865 he began the practice of law in this and adjoining counties and was, for a number of years, associated in the practice with G. W. Hicks, and was a member of the House of Representatives in 1869-70. In 1883 Mr. Thomas was elected State treasurer of Tennessee, and accepted that office at an inauspicious time, which was during the greatest financial crisis the State has ever experienced. He held the office one term and then resumed the law practice, which he now continues in partnernership with William House, and together they constitute one of the best law firms in the county. In 1856 our subject wedded Miss Sarah E. North, daughter of Rev. Henry B. North. Mrs. Thomas died in 1858, and in 1882 Mr. Thomas was married to Mrs. Bettie Sikes, of Rutherford County. To the last union were born two children: Atha and Woodlief. Mr. Thomas has always been a true Democrat. He is a Mason (Knight Templar) and a member of the Methodist Episcopal Church South. In addition to his extensive law practice, he has held many positions of trust and is one of the first men of the State. Mrs. Thomas is a worthy member of the Baptist Church.

PROF. HUGH BLAIR TODD, one of the best known men in the State, was born in Spottsylvania County, Va., June 2, 1815, and is a descendant on both sides of distinguished English and Scotch families. Some of his ancestors were noblemen and were among the early adventurers to America. His maternal grandfather, Col. Winslow, of the British Army, finally settled in America, where he died. His paternal grandfather, Richard Todd, settled in Virginia, and there his father, William Todd, who was an Episcopal clergyman, was born. His father died in that State in 1854. Our subject was educated in the private schools of Virginia, and at the age of seventeen began teaching. In 1835 he moved to Fayette County, Ky., and there established his first boarding school, and after four years of success purchased "Green Hill," near the home of Henry Clay, and there established a school which became famous throughout the State. He conducted schools at Lexington, Ky.; Carlisle, Ky.; Mount Sterling, Ky.; Camden Point College, Mo., and Platt City, Mo., where he remained until the beginning of the late war. He then cast his fortunes with the South, but on account of failing health was compelled to resign, after which he returned home, and in 1862 took charge of the Rogersville Academy, in East Tennessee. Our subject has been married three times—the first was in 1836; he wedded Eliza Dickenson, of Virginia, and by this union has three living children. In 1862 he wedded Mrs. Kate Carr, of Tennessee, and has one child by her. In 1868 he took for his third wife Mattie T. Gorth, a native of Todd County, Ky., and by her has one son, Hugh Blair, Jr. Prof. Todd is one of the most successful and distinguished teachers the South has ever known. He is an able and fluent speaker, and carries with him the feelings of the people. For years he was the friend of Henry Clay, whom he resembled somewhat. He is an active worker and member of the Christain Church. During the year 1883 he was chief of the department of agriculture, horticulture, floriculture and decorator of the grounds at the Louisville Exposition. In 1884 Prof. Todd moved to Franklin, where he expects to pass the remainder of his days. He is a Democrat in politics.

HON. B. B. TOON, an old and influential citizen of Williamson County, Tenn., was born in this State August 20, 1816. His father, James Toon, was a native of Virginia, born in 1779, and in 1815 was wedded to Dorcus Dodson, a native of Virginia, born October, 1788. The father came to Tennessee in 1811 and located in West Harpeth, in this county. He fought in the war of 1812 and also in the Creek Indian war. He died in 1839, and the mother died in 1863. Our subject was united in marriage to Miss Sarah Nolan, a native of this county, born May 13, 1832, and the daughter of Stephen Nolan, a native of Virginia. To our subject and wife were born seven children: Michael M., born in 1850; Fannie D., born in 1852; James M., born in 1855; Florence M., born in 1857; William B., born in 1860; Rufus C., born in 1866, and Vera P., born in 1874. Our subject was reared on a farm, and in early life taught school in this county. In 1849 he moved to his present farm, which lies on Harpeth River, about seven miles from the county seat, and which contains 330 acres of good land in a fine state of cultivation. In 1842 he was elected justice of the peace in this district, and re-elected in 1850, which office he held until 1876, with the exception of four years during the war. In 1874 he was elected to the State Legislature, representing Williamson and Maury Counties. He and wife are members of the Methodist Episcopal Church South, and he is a member of the Masonic fraternity and a Democrat in politics.

ALPHEUS TRUETT, son of Henry M. and Sarah (Clampett) Truett, was born May 17, 1823, in Hickman County, Tenn. His father was a native of North Carolina and at an early day immigrated to Hickman County, Tenn, where he followed agricultural pursuits and was also engaged in the nursery business. He had the first fruit nursery in the State. His mother was a native of Delaware and by her union with Henry M. Truett became the mother of twelve children, only two, our subject and James M., now living. The father died in 1833 and the mother followed in 1840. Our subject was reared and educated in the country. In the year 1849 he wedded Miss Roena A. Beard, a native of this State. By this union they became the parents of one child, Edwin C. Mrs. Roena Truett died in 1850, and in 1852 our subject wedded Miss Susan E. Meritt, who bore him five children: Sallie A., Jennie, Alice R., John H. and Susan J. Sallie A. died in 1873. Our subject's second wife died in 1863, and in 1865 Mr. Truett married Miss Sarah J. Taylor. Three children blessed this union: Lanie E., Richard E. and William A. Richard E. died in 1872. Mr. Truett is at present engaged in the nursery business at Franklin, Tenn. He has a good stock of all kinds of fruit trees, and in connection with this runs a flower garden which is very fine. He also owns a tract of land adjoining the town of Franklin. He is a member of the Methodist Episcopal Church South, and is one of Franklin's best citizens.

C. R. TURNER was born in Williamson County July 10, 1831, and is the third of nine children born to John and Sallie (Richerson) Turner. Our subject was reared on a farm and had reached the age of seventeen when his father died, leaving him control of the farm and care of the large family. In 1867 he wedded Miss Martha J. McCord, a native of this State, born March 1, 1846, and the second of eight children born to Newton and Sallie A. (Knott) McCord. To Mr. and Mrs. Turner were born six children: William H. C. (deceased), born January 16, 1877; James R. (deceased), born March 1, 1882; John N., born February 3, 1868; Sarah E., born March 24, 1875; Anna T., born September 30, 1874, and Maggie L., born October 15, 1879. Mrs. Turner died October 25, 1882, and our subject then married, November 15, 1883, Martha J. Wood, a native of this State, born June 14, 1843, and the daughter of William T. and Louisa E. (Crocket) Wood. In 1862 our subject enlisted in Company D, Holeman's regiment, and remained in the 'army until the fall of 1864, when he returned home. In 1867 he moved to his present farm, which contains 145 acres of good land. Mr. Turner is a Democrat in politics.

WILLIAM M. TURNER, M. D., was born in Williamson County September 26, 1831, son of Joseph R. and Elizabeth H. (Marshall) Turner, and is of English and Scotch-Irish descent. The father was born in Maryland in 1801 and his mother, who was a sister of Hon. John Marshall, was born in Williamson County, Tenn., in 1808. The maternal grandfather of our subject came to Tennessee in the pioneer days of the State, and the Marshall family was one of the most distinguished of Tennessee families. The Turner family came to Tennessee and settled in Williamson County about 1828, but subsequently removed to Marshall County, and there the father of Dr. Turner died in 1879, the mother having died in 1856 in Marshall County. Our subject is the eldest of eleven children, ten of whom lived to be grown. He was educated at Chapel Hill Academy in Marshall County, Tenn., and in 1854 began the study of medicine. In 1857 he graduated from the old medical college in Nashville and subsequently located at Chapel Hill, where he began the practice of medicine and dentistry until 1872. He then moved to Franklin and here makes a specialty of dentistry, having almost entirely abandoned the practice of medicine. He is considered one of the best dentists in this section. In 1863 he wedded Ann L. Bain, *nee* Bullock, of Franklin, who for many years was one of the leading teachers of the Tennessee Female College of Franklin. To Dr. Turner and wife were born one son, Dr. Dick B. Our subject is a Democrat and he and wife are leading members of the Methodist Episcopal Church South.

ANDREW C. VAUGHAN was born in Hardeman County, Tenn., April 16, 1837, son of William and Mary M. (Craig) Vaughan, and is of Irish-English lineage. The parents of our subject were both born in Tennessee, the father about 1804 and the mother about 1806. His paternal grandfather, William Vaughan, was a native of Virginia and emigrated to Tennessee at a very early date. Our subject's father died in Perry County,

Tenn., in 1864 and his mother died in the same county. Our subject grew to manhood on the farm and at the age of eighteen went to Franklin and learned the harness-maker's trade. He engaged in that business for about eight years. In 1860 he was married to Lutitia A. McAlpin, a native of this county. The fruits of this union were seven children: William T., Lulu E., Dan E., Jessie E., Myrtle, Lutitia and Ada. In 1862 Mr. Vaughan enlisted and served three years in the Confederate service. He was taken prisoner in 1863 and conveyed to Camp Butler, Ill., but was exchanged at the end of six weeks. He then came home and resumed the harness business, which he continued for quite a number of years. He has also been engaged in the manufacture of brick, and was in the livery business. He is a Democrat, a Royal Arch Mason and he and wife belong to the Christian Church. He is a leading citizen of the county.

JOHN H. WAGGONER is a son of John and Sarah Waggoner, who were born in Tennessee. Their ancestors were North Carolinians by birth, and the father of our subject was in the war of 1812, and his father was a Revolutionary soldier. Our subject was born on the 30th of April, 1824, and received a liberal education. He has followed farming from boyhood, and was first married to Jane Burnett, who was the daughter of Henry and Sarah Burnett, of Davidson County. Mr. and Mrs. Waggoner became the parents of seven children: James L., William S., Robert S., Benjamin S., Neal S., Joel S. and Mary F. Mr. Waggoner's wife died in 1862, and in 1863 he wedded Sulula A. Beech, daughter of William and Jane Beech. To Mr. and Mrs. Waggoner were born eleven children: Merry E., L. M., Ophelia B., Laurence, Emily K., Vida P., Flurida A., Thomas J., John H., Lee and Andrew. Our subject settled on his present farm of 165 acres in 1865. He and his wife are members of the Methodist Episcopal Church South.

OBADIAH WALLER, M. D., was born in Davidson County, Tenn., February 3, 1827, and is the son of Joel Waller, who was born in Virginia. The family were early pioneers of Tennessee, and are of Scotch descent. In early life Joel Waller married a Miss Scales, by whom he had eleven children, our subject being the youngest. He was educated in the Franklin Male University and finished his literary course at Nashville, after which he studied medicine under Dr. S. S. Mayfield and Dr. John W. Morton, and in 1849 he attended the Louisville (Ky.) Medical College, and was a member of the *Societas Louisvillensis Medica*, and completed his medical studies in the Medical University of Pennsylvania, at Philadelphia, and received his diploma in 1851. He served as surgeon in the late war in the Forty-fourth Tennessee Regiment, and since the close of that conflict has followed his profession in Williamson County and also superintends his farm. He was married, March 3, 1854, to Miss Nannie Marion Carl, whose mother, Mrs. Jane B. Carl, is now residing with the Doctor, and was born in 1806, but is yet hale and vigorous. Dr. Waller is a Democrat and a Master Mason, and he and wife are members of the Methodist Episcopal Church.

J. E. WALTERS is a son of Eli A. and Mary (Carsey) Walters, and was born in Williamson County, Tenn., June 23, 1849, and received a common school education. In 1869 he was united in marriage to Miss Alice Bond, daughter of Page Bond, of Maury County, and their union was blessed with five children; those living are James, Nannie, Morris and Tommy. Mrs. Walters' death occurred in 1884. Mr. Walters is a Democrat in his political views and is a member of the Cumberland Presbyterian Church. His father, Eli A. Walters, was born in the Old Dominion in 1807, and came to Williamson County, Tenn., with his parents, when twelve years of age. After attaining his majority he began farming for himself, and in 1836 was married to Mary Carsey, daughter of Thomas B. Carsey, of this county. They have four children: J. E., W. C., Dora P. (Mrs. James Mahon, of Maury County,) and Thomas. The father died January 19, 1861. Thomas P. Carsey was born in Maryland, in 1797, and came to Tennessee about 1812. The Walters family are also old settlers of the county, having come to this State in 1819.

JOHN C. WELLS, carriage manufacturer and undertaker, was born in Nottoway County, Va., September 12, 1812, and is the son of Coleman and Elizabeth (Phillips) Wells. The father and mother were born in Virginia, the former in 1781 and the latter in 1786. The father was a soldier in the war of 1812 and died in 1833. The mother died in Virginia in 1882. Our subject's grandfather, Giles Wells, was a Virginian and a soldier in the Revolutionary war. He died in Virginia, at a good old age. At the age of fifteen our subject began serving a four years' apprenticeship at the wagon-maker's trade and worked at that trade in his native State until 1839, when he immigrated to Williamson County, Tenn., and settled in Franklin, where he carried on the wagon business for nineteen years and then began the carriage business, which, in connection with the undertaking business, he has carried on since the war. June 3, 1834, he married Catherine Robinson, a native of Virginia, born November 27, 1810, and by this union became the father of an interesting family of seven children: James C., Posthenia E., Sarah F., John W., Edward T., Richard P. and Virginia H. Mr. and Mrs. Wells are the grandparents of twenty-seven children. Mr. Wells is a Democrat and a Mason, and this aged couple have been members of the Baptist Church for half a century. He is one of the prominent men of the county and a leading citizen.

WILLIAM WHITE, M. D., was born in the town of Franklin, Williamson Co., Tenn., son of William and Mary (Bennett) White, and of English extraction. The father was born in this county in 1810, as was also the mother in 1814. The former died in 1850 and the latter in 1874. Our subject's early life was passed on the farm. He received the rudiments of his education in the country schools, and subsequently attended the Franklin schools. In 1867 he began the study of medicine under Dr. J. D. Bennett, of Maury County, Tenn. In the fall of 1868 he went to New Orleans and entered the Medical University of Louisiana. In 1871 he was elected resident student of Charity Hospital in the Crescent City, and in March, 1873, graduated from the University of Louisiana. He then returned to Williamson County and engaged in the practice of his profession, which he continued until 1877, when he engaged in the drug business in Franklin, and in this has since continued. He is one of the most reliable druggists in that town, and is doing a successful business. In 1881 he wedded Sallie Watson, of Franklin, a daughter of Thomas J. and Kate Watson. Our subject is a Democrat, and he and wife are members of the Methodist Episcopal Church. December, 1885, he was elected director of the National Bank of Franklin. He is an honorable man and is in every sense a gentleman.

DR. THOMAS W. WHITFIELD, deceased, was born in February, 1827, and spent his early life in assisting his father on the farm and in attending the country schools. In 1853 and 1854 Mr. Whitfield attended lectures in the Nashville Medical College and graduated from the same the next year. Dr. Whitfield located in Davidson County and began practicing his profession. Miss Sarah M. Berry became his wife March 4, 1855, and to them were born eight children: John H., Mattie H., Anna E., Julia W., Jimmie D., Thomas W., William B. and Clifton B., all of whom are living. In 1860 Dr. Whitfield left Davidson County and located in Henry County, West Tenn. Here he remained about fifteen years, when he removed to Williamson County, and there died July 13, 1879, on his farm known as "Hill Side Home." He was a member of the Masonic fraternity and was also a member of the Christian Church. John Berry, father of Mrs. Whitfield, died October 7, 1856. Her mother died September, 1876, and was a member of the Christian Church. Our subject's widow is still living and is also a member of the Christian Church.

JAMES T. WILHOITE was born January 19, 1846. His father, Young Wilhoite, was born in Tennessee January 5, 1817, and was reared on a farm but left it in early boyhood and began merchandizing, which might be termed his life-long occupation. The subject's mother, Eliza (Dunaway) Wilhoite, was born in Tennessee July 14, 1817, and by her union with Young Wilhoite became the mother of nine children, three of whom are dead. The mother died in 1852. December 25, 1866, the subject wedded Anna M. Hume, who was born in this State October 24, 1848. She was the daughter of Alfred and Mary Hume. To the subject and wife was born one child, Annie E., who was born November 7, 1867. His wife died December 21, 1867. He then married for his second wife Miss Bettie E. Johnson January 31, 1871. She was born in this State April 6, 1850, and was the daughter of Joshua and Minnie T. Johnson. By the subject's last union he became the father of five children: Jimmie Y., born November 7, 1871; Minnie P., born May 17, 1875; Willie, born December 28, 1882, and two boys, twins, not named, born February 20, 1886. The subject was born in Shelbyville, Tenn., and was educated in the best schools of that town. When sixteen years of age he lived four years on his father's farm near Shelbyville. In 1865 he came to Allisona and engaged in the mercantile business, where he remained about ten years. He then returned to Shelbyville and engaged in the grocery business, where he remained two years, after which he again returned to Allisona and engaged in agricultural pursuits. In 1879 he engaged in the mercantile business, and continued to do so until 1883. Since that time he has directed his attention to farming. He has 200 acres of good, level land. He has been a considerable stock raiser and trader, and his fine farm is situated in the southwest corner of the county and has a good pike road running by it. He is a Mason, a member of the Cumberland Presbyterian Church and a stanch Democrat in politics.

CLEM W. WILLIAMS was born July 11, 1814, in Davidson County, Tenn. His parents, Freeman and Martha Williams, were born in Virginia, and were married about 1795, and became the parents of twelve children: Jourdan, Herbert, Joseph, Susan, Nancy, Joshua, Clem W., Luke, Rachel, William, Levi and Berry. Our subject was educated in the common schools, and in early life was engaged in farming. In 1838 he began the shoe-maker's trade, and also worked at stone-masonry, following this until 1871, when he again commenced farming. He owns 470 acres of valuable land, on which he located. He was married to Adaline Barns in 1839. She was the daughter of George and Nancy Barns, and died in 1841. In 1847 Mr. Williams wedded Tabitha Barns, daughter of Peter and Pollie Barns. To them were born these sons: John W., Thomas L. and Samuel L. This wife died in 1853, and Elizabeth Osborn became his third wife in 1857, and bore seven children: Mary H., Fannie P., Ada, Robert, Noble, Martha C. and Charley. The present Mrs. Williams was the daughter of Noble and Hannah Osborn, natives of North Carolina. Mr. Williams is a Democrat, and he and wife are members of the Methodist Episcopal Church South.

JOHN WILSON (deceased) was born in the year 1806, in Georgia. When about six years of age he went with his father to Mississippi, and after finishing his education entered on life's rough track as a planter in Mississippi. October 9, 1836, he was united in marriage to Mahala H. McPherson, daughter of Joseph McPherson, and by this union became the father of an interesting family of children. Mr. Wilson located on Harpeth River, in the Seventh District, where he remained nine years engaged in farming. In 1849 he removed to Richland, where he died August 8, 1852. He was a member of the Methodist Episcopal Church South. Mrs. Wilson's father, Joseph McPherson, was a native of North Carolina. He wedded in early life Miss Mary Taylor, and by her became the father of thirteen children, three of whom are now living. Mrs. McPherson was a member of the Methodist Episcopal Church South, as also is her daughter, Mrs. Wilson.

WILLIAM E. WINSTEAD, clerk and master of chancery court, was born near Franklin, in this county, January 18, 1838, son of John M. and Nancy A. (Whitfield) Winstead, and is of Scotch ancestry. The father of our subject was born in this county in 1807, and for twenty-five years was a magistrate of the county. He is still living. The mother was born in Davidson County in 1811, and died in February, 1885. Of twelve children our subject was the fifth son; he was reared on the farm, and received the rudiments of his education at the country schools, and subsequently attended Shelbyville University, from which he graduated in 1859. In 1860 he taught school ten months, and in 1861 he was appointed deputy clerk and master of this county. In the fall of 1861 he enlisted in Capt. John L. McEwen's company, and in 1863 was discharged on account of physical disability. In 1865 he was appointed clerk and master, and has held the office ever since, and has been one of the leading officials of this county for twenty years. He was one of five brothers who was in the Confederate Army. He was formerly a Whig but is now a Democrat. November 1, 1870, he wedded Miss Anne E. Bradley, daughter of R. H. Bradley, of Franklin. To Mr. and Mrs. Winstead were born two daughters: Maggie A. and Katie Niel. Mr. Winstead is a Mason, a member of the I. O. O. F., and he and he and wife are members of the Methodist Episcopal Church. He is a representative of one of the earliest families of Tennessee, and is one of the leading citizens of Franklin.

JOHN M. WINSTEAD was born March 9, 1807, in Williamson County, Tenn., son of John and Mary Winstead, natives of Virginia and North Carolina, and grandson of William and Elizabeth Winstead, of Virginia, who settled in Tennessee in 1795. The mother's maiden name was Chapman and her parents came to Tennessee about 1800. Our subject's father was a farmer and was married about 1795, becoming the father of seven children, our subject being the sixth. The father died July 28, 1822, and the mother in 1837. Our subject is the only living member of his father's family, and has always been engaged in farming. He was educated in the common schools, and March 8, 1827, was married to Nancy A. Whitfield (daughter of Harrison and Mary Whitfield), born August 5, 1811, in Williamson County. They became the parents of twelve children: James M., Harrison W., John M., Walker W., William E., Robert O., Meredith P. G., Thomas E., Mary E., Winfield S., Lucy T. and Ida. Our subject owns 500 acres of very valuable land. His wife died February 7, 1885. In politics he is a Democrat and a member of the I. O. O. F. In 1854 he was chosen justice of the peace, continuing until 1882. Our subject comes of a prominent family and some of his ancestors were soldiers in the Revolutionary war and the war of 1812, and were prominent men in this State.

RUTHERFORD COUNTY.

COL. JOHN H. ADKERSON, an enterprising farmer, was born in this county and State October 15, 1831, and is the son of James A. and Percilla (Jones) Adkerson, both natives of Virginia. The father was one of the early settlers of this county, coming here in 1820. He was one of the leading farmers of the county, and his death, which occurred December 3, 1853, was a sad shock to all who knew him. The mother died September 12, 1877. The subject of our sketch, John H., was reared on the farm and received his education in the county schools. At the age of twenty-one he took charge of his father's fram, and in the year 1861 enlisted in Company I, Forty-fifth Tennessee Regiment, as first lieutenant, and served in that capacity for eight months, when, on account of his health failing, he was honorably discharged September, 1861. He then returned to his farm, and has since been engaged in farming and stock raising. On January 20, 1854, Mr. Adkerson was united in marriage to Miss Sallie Sneed, a native of this county, and to them were born the following children: Sallie M. (deceased), Ida, Ella, Katie N., George M., James A., John N., Mabel and Clinton. Mr. Adkerson is a Democrat in politics, and served as deputy sheriff for four years in this county. He is also a member of the Missionary Baptist Church, and the balance of the family are members of the Cumberland Presbyterian Church. Mr. Adkerson is justly recognized as one of the leading citizens of the county.

ANDREW M. ALEXANDER, born May 19, 1815, is a son of Andrew M., Sr., and Nancy (Doran) Alexander, who were born in Maryland and Virginia respectively. The father was one of the pioneer settlers of the county, and was killed at New Orleans during the war of 1812, in which he served until his death in 1814. The mother's death occurred in 1865. Andrew M.'s boyhood days were spent on the farm with his mother and in securing a limited education. At the age of eighteen he engaged in the mercantile business with Gilman & Moore, with whom he remained two years. He afterward clerked for J. L. Moore & Co., remaining three years. In the spring of 1838 he began farming close to his present place, and in 1850 purchased the farm where he now resides and where he has since been steadily engaged. In 1855 he erected a grist-mill on his place which has a capacity of thirty barrels per day. He controls the leading business in that line in his part of the county, and is doing well financially. December 3, 1837, he wedded Miss Rebecca Wright, a native of North Carolina. Her death occurred November 1, 1882. This marriage was without issue. Mr. Alexander is a Democrat and a leading member of the Presbyterian Church.

MRS. ANNIE E. ALEXANDER, widow of Albert G. Alexander, a prominent farmer of Rutherford County, Tenn., was born March 31, 1814, in Virginia. Mr. Albert G. Alexander, a native of this State, was born August 8, 1810, and is the son of Daniel and Sarah (Alexander) Alexander. He was one of the early settlers of this county, coming here with his parents about 1827. He was an extensive and very successful farmer, and himself and family were leading members of the Methodist Episcopal Church. His death occurred February 26, 1862. His wife, Mrs. Annie E., still lives on the old homestead. To Mr. and Mrs. Alexander were born five children: Eliza J. Madison (who died in March, 1862, in the prison of Camp Butler, Ill., during the war), Robert L., Elizabeth and Ophelia. Mrs. Annie E. Alexander and family are members of the Methodist Episcopal Church and are justly recognized as one of the leading families of the county.

HON. B. F. ALEXANDER, a native of Rutherford County, Tenn., was born January 20, 1849, and is the son of Madison H. and Catharine (Suttle) Alexander, natives, respectively, of Tennessee and Virginia. The father, who is a well-known and prosperous farmer, still resides in this county. The mother, who died in this county November 23, 1877, was reared in the immediate neighborhood of Thomas Jefferson, and often spoke of that illustrious statesman in warmest terms of praise. Our subject graduated at Union University, Murfreesboro, Tenn., in 1870, and a year later took the degree at the law school of Cumberland University. He then practiced his profession for several years at Murfreesboro, editing the Murfreesboro *Monitor* in the meantime. In 1878 he was chosen over four competitors to represent Rutherford and Bedford Counties in the House of Representatives, where he served in a faithful and highly efficient manner. In 1880 he was nominated by acclamation by the Democrats of Rutherford County to represent his senatorial district in the Forty-second General Assembly, and although his party was divided he was elected by a handsome majority. In 1881 he was elected temporary speaker of the Senate. He was made chairman of three different committees and was appointed a member of a committee sent to New York to compromise with holders of Tennessee bonds, but declined on the ground that a sovereign State ought to settle her local concerns without dictation from her creditors. Mr. Alexander always advocated the rights and worked in the interest of the laborer and producer of the country, and the people of his district manifested their approval by electing him without opposition to a seat in the Forty-third General Assembly, and although he had declared himself not a candidate for the position he was elected speaker after a few hours' balloting. Mr. Alexander is a Democrat of the old Jefferson type, a man of affable and generous nature, and was reared in the Methodist faith, to which he still inclines. He is unmarried and is engaged in agriculture, which is his favorite pursuit.

JAMES H. ALLEN, proprietor of the livery, feed and sale stable at Murfreesboro, Tenn., was born in Warren County N. J., August 26, 1831, son of Obadiah A. and Elizabeth (Harris) Allen, both natives of New Jersey, where the father died and the mother still resides. James H. spent his early days on a farm in his native State where he acquired but a limited education such as was common to farmers' children at that day. At the age of seventeen he left home and began learning the harness-maker's trade which he mastered and at which he worked in Pennsylvania, North Carolina, Alabama and his native State, and on the 27th of March, 1857, he came to Murfreesboro, Tenn., and followed his trade until the breaking out of the war when he was employed by the Confederate Government in the quartermaster's department, continuing until the battle of Stone River, when he was employed in the quartermaster's department of the Federal Government and continued until the close of the war. In 1866 he engaged in his present business and has met with good and merited success. He controls a large share of the trade in town and county and is also engaged extensively in the sale of horses and mules. February 2, 1860, he was married to Sarah E. Lane, a native of the county. To them were born four children, two of whom are living: Harris L. and Emmet C. Mr. Allen was a Whig as long as that party existed. Since the war he has been independent in his political views. He is a Mason and he and wife are members of the Presbyterian Church.

MAJ. CHARLES W. ANDERSON, a prominent and successful farmer of Rutherford County, Tenn., was born in Franklin, Ky., November 28, 1825, and is a son of Harry I. and Adaline (Hickman) Anderson, both natives of Kentucky. The father came to this State in 1835, and took charge of the Tennessee State prison at Nashville, where he remained for thirteen years, after which he commenced farming. He died in the year 1882. The mother died when our subject was an infant. The subject of this sketch received a good education and then went into the mercantile business in Nashville, where he remained for six years. In 1848 he became interested in steam-boats, owning an interest in the following steamers: "Milwaukee," "Colorado," and commanded the "North Carolina," "Colorado" and the "Embassa." He was the first man to take out a contract for the semi-weekly mail packet between Nashville and Memphis for the government. In the winter of 1851, he sold out the mail line and took a position as general freight agent, where he remained for some years. At the breaking out of the war he received notice from Quartermaster Meyers, appointing him transportation quartermaster of all the troops passing through Chattanooga, with headquarters at the above place. After the battle of Shiloh he returned to his present farm and found his home burnt out by the Federals. He then joined Gen. Forrest's staff with the rank of lieutenant, was aid-de-camp of Gen. Forrest till the close of the war. Mr. Anderson was in many of the principal battles, and never received a wound of any kind during this time. He returned to his home, repairing and mending up his broken fortune as best he could. Mr. Anderson is a Democrat and his family are leading members of the Baptist Church. In 1852 Mr. Anderson was united in marriage to Miss Mattie Love, and to this union were born six children, three of whom are living, namely: Harry J., Lillie L. and Mattie C. Maj. Anderson is one of the leading farmers of this county and is respected by all.

JAMES L. ANDERSON, a well-known farmer, was born in Rutherford County, Tenn., June 16, 1826, and is the son of George W. and Martha M. Anderson, natives of Virginia. The father, a successful carpenter and farmer, came to this county in 1818, located on a farm where he lived until his death, which occurred in 1847. The subject was reared on the farm and obtained a fair education at the common schools, and at a proper age began farming on property inherited from his father. Afterward he sold out and moved to the place where he now resides. In 1845 he was married to Miss Emily M. Beesley, and to them were born three children, namely: Martha H., George D. and Sallie T., wife of Arthur M. Edward. Mr. Anderson is an unswerving Democrat, and in 1862 enlisted as a private in Company I, of the First Tennessee. He took an active part in most of the battles in which his company was engaged, received a wound at Missionary Ridge, and was unfit for active service for about two months; after recovering he joined the command at the battle of Atlanta. He then joined a cavalry company and served until the close of the war. Mr. Anderson is an influential citizen, and has held the office of justice of the peace for some time.

HORACE N. ARNOLD, merchant, of Murfreesboro, Tenn., was born in Rutherford County, Tenn., March 29, 1860. He is a son of Capt. Ed and Harriett (McLanahan) Arnold, natives, respectively, of Virginia and Tennessee. The father came to Tennessee when a young man and followed farming, contracting and building and brick-masonry. He built probably two-thirds of the brick buildings in Murfreesboro, which were erected before the war. He was captain of a company in Gen. Forrest's regiment, and led that body in the capture of Murfreesboro from the Federals. He died suddenly of supposed heart disease in the streets of Murfreesboro November 11, 1884. He was a Democrat and was sheriff of the county about sixteen years. He was a member of Methodist Episcopal Church. Horace N. Arnold obtained a collegiate education and served four years as deputy sheriff under his father. In 1880 he engaged in the book and stationery business, but from 1882 to 1883 followed farming, and then engaged in the grocery and dry goods business in Murfeesboro. In January, 1886, he moved to his present commodious business rooms on the Square where he carries a full and select line of staple and fancy groceries, dry goods, boots, shoes and general merchandise. December 17, 1885, he was married to Fannie B. Butler, a native of the town. Mr. Arnold is a Democrat and a member of the board of aldermen in the city. He and wife are members of the Methodist Episcopal Church South.

JAMES MONROE AVENT, a prominent and wealthy attorney of Murfreesboro, Tenn., was born December 10, 1816, in Greenville County, Va. His parents, James and Mary Avent, were natives, respectively, of Virginia and North Carolina, and removed from the father's native State to Alabama, from whence they came to this State and county in 1830. They resided here until 1856, when they removed to Hardeman County, Tenn., where the elder Avent died in 1868. James M. Avent's boyhood's days were spent on the farm and in the schools, differing from the experience of many lads of his day, insomuch that his education was superior to that of the ordinary youth. He secured a good literary education at the Clinton College, in Smith County, Tenn. At the age of twenty-one he had decided to make the law his profession for life, and entered the office of Charles Ready, of this city, with whom he read law until he was admitted to the Rutherford County bar in 1840. He then engaged in the practice here, rapidly growing in reputation and character as a lawyer, and was for many years a partner of the late ex-Chancellor B. L. Ridley. Mr. Avent is now the senior member of the well-known law firm of Avent, Smith & Avent, and it may be justly said that he has contributed largely to the success and high standing of this firm at the Rutherford County bar. February 27, 1857, Mr. Avent married Mary W., the daughter of the late Maj. John W. Childress, of this county. The result of this union has been five children, the following four now living: Frank, James M., Bettie B. and Sarah W. Mr. Avent is a Democrat of the old "Jacksonian school," and has always been an active and zealous worker for his party, but never aspired to office. He has frequently been appointed judge *pro tem* of our courts, and discharged the duties of this highly responsible position in a manner that indicated his superior qualities as a jurist. He is a prominent member of the Masonic fraternity, and has been identified with all public and private enterprises that were calculated to promote the prosperity of the city or county. He was one of the organizers of the Stone's River Creamery Company, of which he is now the president. Himself and wife have been lifelong members of the Methodist Episcopal Church South, and he is justly and universally recognized as one among the leading and successful citizens of our county, a lawyer of fine judgment and ability and a consistent Christian gentleman.

FRANK AVENT, junior member of the firm of Avent, Smith & Avent, attorneys at law of Murfreesboro, Tenn., was born March 7, 1858, in Rutherford County, Tenn., and is a son of James M. Avent, senior member of the firm. Frank received the rudiments of his education in the public schools of Murfreesboro, and afterward entered the Vanderbilt University at Nashville, from which college he graduated in 1878. In the fall of 1879 he entered the law department of the Cumberland University at Lebanon, Tenn., graduating in 1880. He spent several months in the West, and in 1881 was a law partner of his uncle, Capt. John W. Childress. He then joined his father in this city, and they control a large share of the legal business done in the county. Mr. Avent is a Democrat, and was a candidate for nomination to the State Legislature, but was defeated. He is a member of the K. of P., post chancellor of the local lodge, and is secretary of the County Fair Association. He is a member of the Methodist Episcopal Church South, and is a rising young barrister of Rutherford County.

BAIRD & MARTIN, stove and tinware merchants of Murfreesboro, Tenn., began their business in February, 1886. They keep a fine and extensive stock of goods, and do a large business. They also deal extensively in harvesting machinery. James S. Baird, of the firm of Baird & Martin, was born in Rutherford County, April 15, 1861, son of Josiah M. and Sarah (McKnight) Baird, both natives of the county (see father's sketch). James S. was reared on a farm, and received a common school education. At the age of twenty he came to Murfreesboro and engaged in the coal business, in which he has retained an interest to the present time, being a member of the coal firm of W. N. Perry & Co. In April, 1883, he purchased the Murfreesboro *News*, which he conducted creditably one year, and in February, 1886, engaged in his present business as above stated. He is a Democrat, unmarried, and a member of the Presbyterian Church, and is one of the reliable young business men of the county.

STERLING B. BARING, a prominent farmer of Rutherford County, was born April 17, 1823, in this county, and is the son of Amos and Nancy (Ethel) Baring, natives respectively of Green County, Tenn., and Petersburg, Va. The father, a mechanic and farmer, came to this county in 1820 and lived here until his death, which occurred in 1839. The son was reared on the farm and received a fair education in the country schools, and at the age of sixteen began learning the house carpenter trade. After finishing this, he started to contracting for himself, following this with success for twenty-five years. He then purchased the farm where he now resides, which contains 270 acres of good land. In 1854 he married Elizabeth Edward and became the father of eight children : Mamie L., the wife of D. N. Fain, Tennie V., Ella, Lizzie C., Julia P., Mary E., Josie J. and Lydia. Mr. Boring is a Democrat, and has held the office of justice of the peace in four districts for twelve years. He is a Master Mason, and his wife is a member of the Methodist Episcopal Church South.

BENJAMIN BATEY, sheriff and native of Rutherford County, Tenn., was born on the 4th of July, 1846. His parents, Benjamin and Tabitha (Searcy) Batey, were natives respectively of Virginia and Tennessee. The father was born in 1801 and came to Tennessee in 1807 or 1808, being among the first settlers of Davidson County. About a year later he came to Rutherford County where he was reared, married and raised a large family of children. He was a successful farmer and served as magistrate several years. He died in 1873. Our subject was educated in the Cumberland University at Lebanon, Tenn., and graduated from the Law Department of that institution. In 1863 he enlisted as a private in Company D, Twenty-first Tennessee Cavalry, and served in the Southern Army until its surrender. He then returned home and completed his education as above stated. He followed farming until August, 1882, when he was elected by the Democratic party to the office of sheriff of Rutherford County, and re-elected in 1884. He has proved an excellent man for the position, and has given good satisfaction. He is a Mason, Knight Templar, and is also a K. of P.

FRANK BATTLE, an influential farmer of Robertson County, was born April 5, 1841, in Davidson County, Tenn., and is the son of Joel and Adaline (Morely) Battle, natives of Davidson County. The father served as captain in the Florida war, after which he was elected general of the Tennessee Militia. In 1861 he enlisted as colonel in the Twentieth Tennessee Regiment Infantry, and was captured at Shiloh; during that fierce and bloody battle his horse was killed, and, falling on him, disabled him from active service. After his return he was appointed treasurer of the State of Tennessee, serving in that capacity until the close of the war. He was then appointed by Gov. Brown superintendent of the State prison, and held this office until his death, which occurred in September, 1872. Our subject was reared on the farm and received an academic education at White Creek Academy of Davidson County. He has been quite successful in farming, having at present 200 acres of well improved land. January 1, 1866, he was married to Miss Bettie House, and to them were born eight children : Joel A., Alfred B., George S., Addie M., Frank P., Paul, Julia H. and James M. Mr. Battle is an unswerving Democrat. In 1861 he enlisted as private in Company B, of the Twentieth Tennessee Regiment, and after the battle of Murfreesboro was promoted to captain of a company of Wheeler, scouts. In July, 1862, he was captured by the Federal Army and taken to Johnson's Island and held as hostage for Capt. Harris, and later was removed to Fort Warren, where he was held for eight months, and then sent through as especial exchange. After the war he was appointed sheriff of the Supreme Court in Nashville, served three years and then moved to Rutherford County, where he now resides. He is a Mason, and he and wife are members of the Cumberland Presbyterian Church.

GRANVILLE C. BATY, a native of Rutherford County, Tenn., was born September 4, 1848, being a son of William G. W. and America (Crockett) Baty, both natives of this State and county. The father, who was a well-known and successful farmer of the county, died in 1872. Granville was reared on a farm with his parents, and secured an ordinary common school education in his boyhood days. When he was ten years of age his mother died, and at the age of fourteen he began life for himself; working about on a farm until he was eighteen years of age, and then engaged as clerk in the mercantile business in this city, continuing until 1869. He soon after erected a store-house about six miles from Murfreesboro on Franklin road, to engage in the business. Being disappointed in this went to West Tennessee and engaged first in railroading and later in the mercantile business in Dyer County, continuing there until his father's death, when he returned to this county and settled up his father's estate, and then followed farming in this county until 1883, when he engaged in his present business as wholesale and retail merchant. In 1876 he married Lucy L., daughter of Ivy J. C. Haynes. They have five children: Lizzie G., Martha J., Fannie B., Hal C., and Rufus H. Mr. Baty is a Democrat in politics, and he and wife are members of the Methodist Episcopal Church.

CAPT. RICHARD BEARD, attorney at law, notary public, and general insurance agent at Murfreesboro, Tenn., was born near Canton, Miss., February 28, 1842, son of Rev. Richard Beard and Cynthia (Castleman) Beard, natives, respectively, of Virginia and Tennessee. The father was born in 1799, and was educated for the ministry in the Cumberland College at Princeton, Ky. He began his professional career as president of his *alma mater*, and filled the theological chair of Cumberland University from 1854 until his death in 1881 or 1882. The immediate subject of this sketch was reared in Princeton, Ky., and Lebanon, Tenn., securing a good education in the latter place, and graduating from its college in 1858. He then spent another year studying English literature, and during 1860 entered the legal department with the view to making the practice of law his profession. In the spring of 1861 he enlisted in Company H, Seventh Regiment Tennessee Infantry, and served until after the battle of Seven Pines in 1862, when he was severely wounded, and was afterward appointed second lieutenant in the Fifth Confederate Regiment, and after the battle of Perryville, Ky., was promoted to first lieutenant. At the battle of Murfreesboro he was appointed adjutant, and after Chickamauga was raised to the rank of captain, being also wounded in this engagement. He was an eye witness to the death of Maj.-Gen. McPherson, commander of the Federal Army of the Tennessee, and refutes the charges made by the Federals that McPherson was murdered, and since the war wrote an article on the same, which has been published throughout the country, North and South. In 1864 Capt. Beard was captured and kept a prisoner at Johnson's Island, Lake Erie, until the close of the war. He then returned home, and in the spring of 1866 graduated in law and came immediately to Murfreesboro, where he has built up a good practice. During the fall of 1869 and years of 1870-71 he owned and edited the Murfreesboro *Monitor*, a weekly paper devoted to the interests of Democracy. He finally disposed of his paper advantageously. He is a Democrat, a Mason and Knight Templar. February 15, 1870, he wedded Marie L. Dromgoole, who has borne him four children: Sallie, William E., Richard, and Marie L. He and wife are members of the Cumberland Presbyterian Church.

WILLIAM BEESLEY, farmer, was born December 28, 1838, and is the eldest child born to Christopher and Susan (Ridoubt) Beesley, natives of Rutherford County, Tenn. Our subject was reared on the farm and secured a good common school education. At the age of twenty-one he began trying to make a livelihood by farming for Arthur Miller and others, and so continued up to the time of the war. In 1866 he rented a farm in the Seventh District, where he lived for twelve years, at the end of which time he was able to buy land. In 1878 he purchased the property where he now resides. Mr. Beesley has met with evident success in his occupation of farming and at present owns 112 acres of land. In 1866 he married Miss Alice G. Elliott, a native of Rutherford County, Tenn., and to this union were born eight children: Adelaide S., Christopher E., Mattie T., Carrie E., Susan W., Ethel L., William A. and John R. Mr. Beesley is a Democrat, and enlisted in 1861 in Company I of the First Tennessee Regiment as a private. He was engaged in some of the noted battles, such as the battles of Shiloh, Chickamauga, Perryville, Franklin, Murfreesboro and Bentonville. He was wounded in the leg during the battle of Chickamauga, which disabled him from active service for about six weeks. In 1863 he was wounded for the second time in the leg, and at the battle of Franklin he received a flesh wound which disabled him for three months. After the war he returned home and resumed his business of farming. He is an influential citizen and a good neighbor.

JOHN BEESLEY, brother of William and Christopher Beesley, whose biographies are found elsewhere in this work, was born September 3, 1840, in Rutherford County. He was reared on the farm and received a good English education at Salem Academy. At the age of twenty-two he engaged in farming on rented property, and four years later purchased land in the Fourth District, where he remained three years. He then sold out and bought the farm where he now resides. Mr. Beesley has an excellent farm of 100 acres. In 1865 he married Miss Martha A. Job, and by her became the father of two children, viz.: Minnie P. and Mary S. In January, 1883, he married for his second wife Miss Mary E. Mathews, a native of Weakley County, Tenn. Mr. Beesley is a Democrat, and April 2, 1861, enlisted as private in Company I, First Tennessee Regiment of Infantry, where he remained until the close of the war. Mr. Beesley and family are members of the Methodist Episcopal Church South, and he is justly recognized as one of the leading farmers of the county, and a moral, upright citizen.

CHRISTOPHER BEESLEY, a prominent farmer of the Seventh District, was born March 20, 1853, in Rutherford County, Tenn., and is the son of Christopher and Susan J. (Ridoubt) Beesley. The father, a well-known pioneer farmer, died at his old homestead in this county March 9, 1879. The mother is still living. The subject was reared on a farm, receiving but a limited education in the common schools of the county. After reaching his majority he began farming for himself, and rented land for the first five years, after which he purchased the farm on which he is at the present living. It consists of 261 acres of well improved land. In November, 1876, he married Miss Bettie O. Pope, a native of Williamson County, Tenn., and to this union were born three children: Mary O., Huston D. and Sarah G. Mr. Beesley is an unswerving Democrat, and he and wife are members of the Primitive Baptist Church.

WILLIAM R. BELL, watch-maker, jeweler and musical instrument dealer, of Murfreesboro, Tenn., is a son of Robert F. Bell, of this city, and was born in Rutherford County, September 14, 1857. William R. obtained a fair education and at the age of seventeen began learning the watch-maker's trade, which he mastered and at which he worked until 1879, when he engaged in his present business on his own responsibility, and has met with the success his honesty and industry has merited. He has one of the best stores in the city, well stocked with jewelry of all kinds, silver and plated-ware, watches and clocks, and controls the majority of the trade in this city and county. Besides this he keeps a fine stock of pianos, organs, and other musical instruments, in which he does a thriving business. October 25, 1881, he was united in marriage to Nellie Frost, a native of Rutherford County. They are the parents of three children: Lizzie M., William R. and Lyda. Mr. Bell is a Democrat in his political views and is a member of the I. O. O. F

SAMUEL P. BLACK, M. D., an enterprising citizen of Rutherford County, Tenn., and proprietor of the Smyrna grist-mill, was born in Tennessee April 10, 1837, and is a son of Dr. Thomas C. and Catharine W. (Morton) Black, both of whom are natives of this State. The father was born in Sumner County March 15, 1809, and is the son of Samuel P. Black, a native of North Carolina, who received a liberal education in that State, and was noted for his learning and morality. Dr. Thomas C. Black received his literary and classical education entirely from his father; he afterward attended Bradley's

Academy, where he commenced the study of medicine. He graduated at the Transylvania University, of Kentucky, and was one of the founders of the Rutherford County Medical Society. His death occurred May 28, 1878. The mother still survives and resides on the old homestead. Our subject, Samuel P., was reared on the farm and secured a good classical education, attending school at the Stone's River Academy and Washington Institute. At an early age he began the study of medicine with his father, and later attended lectures in the medical department of the College of Nashville, graduating at that institution with the degree of M. D. He then returned home and practiced medicine with his father until 1859, when he engaged in the milling business. In 1862 he was appointed assistant surgeon of the hospital at Nashville, where he remained for some time, but returned home on account of sickness, shortly afterward he enlisted in the Fourth Tennessee Cavalry Company, and was transferred to the medical department of East Tennessee, where he filled the position of assistant surgeon. At the close of the war he returned home and resumed his milling business, which he has since continued and in which he has been quite successful. Mr. Black is a single gentleman, a Democrat in politics and has been a Mason since he was twenty-one years of age.

ADAM BOCK, carriage and buggy manufacturer, of Murfreesboro, Tenn., was born in Hessen-Darmstadt, Germany, February 8, 1833, being a son of John and Margaretta (Flath) Bock, both natives of Germany, where they lived and died. Adam received a fair collegiate education in his native language and learned the carriage-maker's trade of his father. In 1851 he came to the United States, landing at New York City and soon after came to Louisville, Ky., where he followed his trade about eight years. In the spring of 1860 he came to Murfreesboro, and at the breaking out of the war enlisted in Company I, First Tennessee Infantry, and served in the Confederate Army until the close of the war. In November, 1865, he engaged in his present businesss, in company with others, under the firm name of Osborn, Bock & Co., but since 1879 Mr. Bock has conducted the business alone. He manufactures superior carriages and buggies and is doing well from a financial standpoint. In 1869 he wedded Virginia C. Jordan, of Tennessee. They have four children: Margaret J., George I., John A. and Estelle. Although independent in politics Mr. Bock rather favors Democratic principles. He is a member of I. O. O. F. and he and Mrs. Bock are members of the Presbyterian Church.

COLUMBUS T. BRITTAIN, a prominent farmer and fruit grower of Third District, was born July 13, 1834, in Rutherford County, Tenn., and was the son of John and Martha M. (Smith) Brittain, natives of North Carolina and Tennessee, respectively. The father, a cabinet-maker by trade, came to this county in 1818, and afterward farming with such evident success, that at the time of his death, which occurred in 1859, he left 300 acres of land. The son was reared and educated as the average farmer boy, and at the age of twenty-five commenced farming for himself on his father's place. Mr. Brittain has met with well-deserved success, having one of the largest and best improved farms in the county. In 1862 he enlisted in Company F, Fourth Tennessee Cavalry, as a private and and took an active part in most of the battles in which his command engaged. He was mustered out in 1865, returned home and resumed his farm duties. In 1869 he married Miss L. Brothers, who died October 31, 1871, leaving one child, Margaret M. In 1873 he was again married to Miss Frances M. Batey, and by this union had two children: John W. and Frankie D. Mr. Brittain is a Democrat, a Master Mason and he and wife are members of the Christian Church.

ROBERT S. BROWN, a widely-known and energetic merchant of Eagleville, was born in Bedford County, October 27, 1844, and is the son of Solomon and Evaline (Kimmons) Brown, both natives of North Carolina. The father was a prominent farmer and a soldier in the Mexican war; his death occurred in 1850. The mother still survives him and is the wife of Thomas Chambers. The subject of this sketch was married, February 11, 1864, to Miss Alice Booker, and this union was blessed by eight children: Thomas E., James W., Ada, Robert, Nina, Mary, Irene and Horace. Mr. Brown took an active part in the late war, being captain of a company of Federal scouts, operating in this State for one year, at the expiration of which time he resigned his commission and refrained from further participation in the war. He returned home to engage in business and is now the leading merchant in Eagleville. Mr. Brown is a Republican in the broadest meaning of the term and is the present magistrate of a strongly Democratic district.' Mr. and Mrs. Brown are members of the Christian Church and have the respect of all who know them.

BUTLER & DRUMRIGHT, merchants. The business was estalished in 1878, by I. H. Butler and J. C. Mosbey, who conducted it two years and then divided the stock, and Mr. Butler and John W. Childress were partners for two years longer. Mr. Butler then purchased his partner's interest, and Thomas Kerr became a partner, continuing so one year. He then dropped out and Horace Arnold became associated in this business, and remained a partner until 1885. Mr. Butler continued alone until February, 1886, when it came into the hands of the present firm, who keep a general merchandise store, and do an extensive business. Isaac H. Butler was born in Murfreesboro, July 26, 1844, son of Thomas O, and Permelia (Ware) Butler who were born in North Carolina and Louisiana respectively. They were married about 1838, and the father followed farming until his death in 1865. Isaac H. was prevented from receiving an extended education by the breaking out of the war. In 1861 he enlisted as first lieutenant of Capt. Lytle's company, Eleventh Tennessee Cavalry, and after serving one and a half years, was discharged on account of his youth, but re-enlisted in Carter's regiment of cavalry, and was made captain of Company C, of that regiment. He was captured near Murfreesboro in 1864, and was imprisoned on Johnson's Island in Lake Erie until the close of the war. He then returned home and farmed until 1873, with the exception of one year (1867) spent in Texas. He came to this city and operated the City (now Miles') Hotel one year, and then engaged in the liquor business for the same length of time. He was elected to the police force and served during 1876-77. In 1878 he engaged in his present business, but has since been compelled to close out on account of ill health. In 1865 he wedded Mary E. Murphey, who bore him six children. Mr. Butler is a Democrat, and in 1878 was elected city recorder, an office he held continuously until 1886. He and wife are members of the Methodist Episcopal Church South.

JOHN A. CAMPBELL, a successful and well-to-do agriculturist, was born in Rutherford County, Tenn., in the year 1853, and is a son of Samuel and Elvira (Eagleton) Campbell, who were native Tennesseeans. The father was also a farmer of thrifty habits and had established a wide reputation as a successful tiller of the soil. He died in 1875, the mother's death occurring three years later. They were both earnest members of the Presbyterian Church. Our subject, John A. Campbell, took for his life companion Miss Nettie Sumpter, in 1877. Two children were born to their union, one of whom is living: Sumpter. Mr. Campbell favors Democratic principles and gives his aid and support to that party. Both he and wife are members of the Presbyterian Church and he is one of the wide-awake and enterprising farmers of the county.

JOSEPH L. CANNON, attorney at law, was born in Rutherford County, Tenn., April 29, 1835, son of Alanson and Elizabeth (Sharp) Cannon, natives of Rutherford and Sumner Counties, Tenn. The father, who was an active and successful farmer, is now living a retired life with our subject, who received a good literary education and graduated from the literary department of the Cumberland University at Lebanon, Tenn., in 1858. In 1859-60 he took a course in law at the same institution and then located at Shelbyville, where he opened a law office. Owing to the war he was compelled to abandon this, and in 1862 enlisted in Company C, Eighteenth Regiment Tennessee Infantry, and served until the close. He began practicing law in Murfreesboro in 1865, and has met with good success. During 1872-73 he was a partner with J. W. Burton. October 9, 1860, he married Margaret, daughter of Richard Beard, D.D., and to them were born eight children, seven now living: Alanson B., Elizabeth E., Annie W., Minnie, Nellie L., Franklin B. and Sarah L. Mr. Cannon has always been a Democrat and has been temporary judge of the court, also chancellor by appointment numerous times. He and wife are members of the Cumberland Presbyterian Church.

THOMAS F. CARLTON, a widely-known and successful merchant, was born in Rutherford County, Tenn., March 7, 1853, and is the son of Blake and Mary (Walker) Carlton. The subject of this sketch, Mr. Thomas F. Carlton, is an uncompromising Democrat, and is known by all his acquaintainces as a moral, upright citizen.

ALFRED M. CAWTHORN, a well-known business man of Murfreesboro, Tenn., was born in Wilson County, Tenn., November 28, 1840, being a son of James and Nancy (McDowell) Cawthorn, natives of Virginia and North Carolina. The father came to Rutherford County, Tenn., in 1840, and spent the remainder of his life in Murfreesboro, where he followed the carpenter's trade and later gunsmithing and the locksmith's trade. His death occurred in the spring of 1882. Alfred M. Cawthorn was reared in Murfreesboro and learned the tinner's trade at which he worked until the breaking out of the war, when he enlisted in Capt. White's company, Second Tennessee Infantry, and served one year as private, when he was honorably discharged on account of ill health. At the close of the war he engaged in the stove and tinware business in Murfreesboro, and has continued to the present time, with the exception of eight or nine years which he spent in McMinnville, Tenn., engaged in the same business. Mr. Cawthorn controls the leading trade in his line in the city and county. In 1865 he wedded Vienna Manor, a native of Rutherford County. They have two children: Anna M. and Mary A. Mr. Cawthorn is a Democrat and was alderman of the city one term before removing to McMinnville. He also served as constable one term, and is a member of the I. O. O. F., Strangers' Refuge Lodge, No. 14, and is also an ex-member of the K. of H., and he and wife belong to the Cumberland Presbyterian Church.

HENRY H. CLAYTON, M. D., is a son of Benjamin and Lockey (Quarles) Clayton, and was born in Rutherford County, December 27, 1826. His parents were born in Virginia. The father came to Tennessee from Kentucky as early as 1815. He died in 1864. Henry H. resided on the home farm with his parents and secured a good academic education. At the age of eighteen he began studying medicine in the office of J. M. Watson & J. E. Wendel, where he remained a student three years. He then took a course of lectures in the medical department of the University of Kentucky and graduated from the University of Tennessee in 1849. He then returned home and practiced two years in the county and then removed to Murfreesboro, where he has met with excellent success in the practice of his profession. In June, 1849, he married Maria Helen, a native of Kentucky, who died in 1873, leaving five children: John B., Jennie M., Mary, Henry H. and William L. In 1874 Dr. Clayton married Mrs. Hattie A. Keeble. In 1861 he raised Company I, Forty-fifth Tennessee Infantry, and served as captain two years, when he was elected first surgeon and served as such on the battle field one year, and the rest of the time was hospital surgeon. He is a member of the K. of H., and A. O. U. W., and was mayor of Murfreesboro in 1877. He is a member of the Methodist Episcopal Church South, and is one of the ablest practitioners of the county,

JAMES CLAYTON, senior member of the firm of Clayton, Overall & Co., are dealers in general merchandise at Murfreesboro, Tenn. The business was established in 1865 by James Clayton and Rufus Jetton, who kept a grocery store until 1870, and then added a line of dry goods and other merchandise. At this time Mr. Jetton retired and T. B. Ivie took his place. Two years later Mr. Ivie died and in 1875 Mr. Asbury Overall and his brother, John H., became connected with the business, but the latter retired in 1881 and James H. Crichlow purchased an interest in the business and since that time the firm has been as above—doing a successful business, and they are now one of the most firmly established firms in the city. James Clayton, senior member of the firm, was born March 7, 1833, and is a son of Benjamin Clayton, Sr. (see sketch of Dr. H. H. Clayton). James received an ordinary education, and at the age of nineteen came to this city and became salesman in the mercantile business. In 1857 he engaged in a similar business in Nashville, but a year later came to Murfreesboro and kept a hat, cap, boot and shoe store with Rufus Jetton. In 1861 he enlisted in the Twenty-third Regiment Tennessee Infantry, and oon after became quartermaster, with the rank of captain. In 1864 he was commissioned major. At the close of the war he and other comrades started home on horseback, but were robbed by bushwackers in the Cumberland Mountains, being compelled to come the rest of the way on foot, and, as above stated, engaged in his present business. October 29, 1868, he wedded Haddeassa Cowan, who bore him seven children. Mr. Clayton has always been a Democrat in politics, and was mayor of the city for the years 1881-82, during which time the corporation debt was very considerably reduced and its affairs placed upon a firm and solid basis. He is a member of the I. O. O. F. and K. of H. and he and wife are members of the Presbyterian Church. Asbury Overall, general merchant, and member of the above firm, was born on the 20th of April, 1844, and is a son of James and Rachel W. (Davis) Overall. The father was a farmer and died in Rutherford County in 1874. Our subject secured a fair education and resided on the farm with his parents. In 1875 he removed to Murfreesboro, where he became a member of the present firm. In 1881 Mr. Crichlow became a partner and they are now doing a thriving business. In 1878 Mr. Overall married Hudie Lowe. They have two children, Gertrude and Floyd. In November, 1862, he enlisted in Company C, Eighteenth Regiment Tennessee Infantry. He was captured at Atlanta and held at Camp Chase, Ohio, until April, 1865. He is a Democrat and he and wife are members of the Methodist Episcopal Church South.

ROBERT A. COLEMAN, a merchant of Rutherford County, Tenn., was born February 6, 1859, in this county, and is the son of Edwin and Mary E. (Wrather) Coleman, natives, respectively, of Virginia and Tennessee. The son was reared on a farm and received a moderate education, attending the common country schools. At the age of twenty-one he started in business for himself, clerking in the store that he has since purchased in partnership with his brother, W. B. Coleman. He has met with evident success, and has the postoffice in connection with one of the best general supply stores in the county. In September, 1882, Mr. Coleman was married to Miss Ida Fly. Mr. Coleman is a Democrat and he and wife are members, respectively, of the Methodist Episcopal and Christian Churches South. He is justly considered as one of the leading merchants of the county, a conscientious Christian and one of the influential men of the county.

CARROL COLLINS, superintendent of the Murfreesboro Gaslight Company, was born in the State of New York, September 3, 1851, son of Edward H. and Rosanna (Bennett) Collins, also natives of New York. When a small lad our subject removed with his parents to Peoria, Ill., where he learned the gas-fitters trade. At the age of twenty years he accepted the position as superintendent of the gas-works at Pekin, Ill. He was then assistant superintendent of the gas-works in Detroit, Mich., and afterward went to Chicago and there had charge of the Hyde Park gas-works some months. At a later period he engaged in the manufacture of retorts and fire-brick, and in 1880 accepted the position as superintendent of the gas-works at Cairo, Ill., where he remained until May, 1883, when he came to Murfreesboro and has taken almost complete control of the gas works of that city. Mr. Collins owns a controlling interest in the works and the citizens have profited greatly by his experienced management. He has greatly improved the quality of the gas and added many new and needed improvements. In November, 1884, Mr. Collins married Lizzie Garrett, of Rutherford County, and daughter of an old and highly respected citizen of the county. Mr. Collins is a worthy citizen and reliable business man of the county.

THOMAS W. COX was born October 7, 1845, in Alabama, and is the son of Middleton and Louisa (Oden) Cox, both natives of Georgia. The subject of this sketch, who is an energetic and successful farmer, was married February 1, 1870, to Miss Emma Overall, and to this union were born five children, four of whom are living: Minos L., Jessie L., Thomas W. and William M. Mr. Cox took an active part in the late war, enlisting in Company A, Thirtieth Alabama Infantry. He was courier for Gen. Pettus during the Georgia campaign, was captured May 16, 1863, and remained a prisoner until July 7, when he was exchanged and returned to his original command, where he served with distinction until the close of the war. Mr. Cox is a Democrat of the most pronounced type, and a member of the Baptist Church. Mrs. Cox is a worthy and consistent member of the Methodist Episcopal Church, and they are justly recognized as influential citizens of Rutherford County.

JAMES H. CRICHLOW, a well-known business man of Murfreesboro, Tenn., was born in this city February 11, 1850. His father, Thomas H. Crichlow, who was a native of the State and for many years a successful merchant of Murfreesboro, removed in 1853 to Florida, where he died two years later. James H. then returned to this county with his mother and family, and here our subject was reared, securing a fair education in his youthful days. At the age of thirteen he accepted a clerkship in a hotel and restaurant here, and later in a mercantile business, continuing at the latter until 1869, when he acted as assistant postmaster for two years. He then engaged in the grocery business with J. B. Lane two years, when he again returned to clerking, in which he continued until 1881, when he entered into his present partnership with the firm of Clayton, Overall & Co., in which he has contributed to and shared equally in the success of this well-known business firm. October 25, 1874, Mr. Crichlow was united in matrimony to Miss Emma Lane, of Rutherford County. By this union they have three children: Laila J., Newton C. and Helen M. Mr. Crichlow is a Democrat in his political views, and a member of the I. O. O. F., K. of P. and K. of H. fraternities, also of the R. A. He has held high positions in both the local and State lodge of Odd Fellowship, being Past Grand Master of the State lodge; was also Grand Representative to the Sovereign Grand Lodge. Himself and wife are leading and active members of the Methodist Episcopal Church. Mr. Crichlow is very popular as superintendent of the Methodist Episcopal Sunday-school, and possessing unusual musical ability as a vocalist, together with other commendable faculties, he is rendered singularly fit for this position; besides, he is invariably called upon by the public to preside over all public and social entertainments given in the city, and he fulfills the part of master of ceremonies on all such occasions in a highly satisfactory and efficient manner.

DR. GEORGE D. CROSTHWAIT, one of the oldest and most prominent physicians of Rutherford County, Tenn., and a native of Virginia, was born May 4, 1808, and is the son of Shelton and Elizabeth (Thompson) Crosthwait, both of whom were natives of Virginia. The father was one of the early settlers of this county, coming here in the year 1804, and engaged in farming and milling. His death occurred in 1825 and the mother's in 1864. Our subject received a good classical education at the common schools, and at the age of eighteen attended the University of Virginia at Charlotte, Va., taking one course in the medical department with a view to making it a profession. He afterward attended the medical college at Lexington, Ky., where he graduated with honor in 1832. He then returned to Murfreesboro, where he practiced medicine in that town and vicinity. He then moved to Iowa City, Iowa, and practiced medicine there for some time. In 1862 he returned to this county, but did not take an active part in the war, being over fifty years of age at that time, but he warmly sympathized with the Southern cause, having lost three sons in the war. He was a Whig in politics before the war, and in 1852 represented Johnson County in the State Senate of Iowa. At the close of the war he went to California, where he remained three years. In 1849 and 1850 he was a representative of Rutherford County in the State Legislature, and was clerk of the chancery court of Rutherford County from 1844 to 1849. In 1836 Mr. Crosthwait was united in marriage to Miss Eliza Burton, a native of North Carolina, and to them were born eight children, only three of whom are living: Lavina C., Dr. George W. and Eliza F. Mrs. Crosthwait died December 22, 1860, and in 1862 Mr. Crosthwait was united in marriage to Caroline Harding, a native of this State. On account of his advanced age Dr. George D. Crosthwait retired from practice in 1883, and has since lived a quiet life. He is a Mason, and himself and family are members of the Missionary Baptist Church.

DR. JAMES W. DAVIS, a prominent and well-known physician of Rutherford County, Tenn., and a native of this State, was born September 22, 1821. His parents were William H. and Mary (Broughton) Davis, natives respectively of North and South Carolina. The father was one of the early settlers of the county, came here in 1804 and engaged in farming. He was a Democrat, holding the office of magistrate in his district for twelve years. His death occurred in June, 1852. The mother died in 1830. Our subject was a country boy, and received a good classical education. He taught school in this county for two years and then began the study of medicine, and afterward attended lectures at the medical department of the Louisville College, graduating at this institution at the sessions of 1850 and 1851. He then returned to this county and began the practice of medicine at which he has ever since been engaged. His reputation as a learned and skilled physician is well known. Mr. Davis did not take an active part in the late war but his sympathies were with the South. In 1860 he was united in marriage to Mrs. Mary J. Weakly, a native of this State, and to this union were born four children (only one of whom is living): James W., Mary E. (deceased), Samuel L. (deceased), and Sue H. (deceased). Mr. Davis is a Democrat, and himself and family are leading members of the Presbyterian Church, of which he has been an elder for upward of eighteen years. He is a prominent citizen and a good man.

WILLIAM L. DAVIS is a native of Tennessee, born April 17, 1833, son of Charles L. and Elizabeth (Sanders) Davis, both of whom were born in Virginia. The father came to Tennessee in 1825, where he became a well-to-do farmer. His death occurred in 1874. The mother died in 1841. Our subject, William L., secured a common education, and at the age of twenty-one purchased a farm in Bedford County, on which he lived two years. In 1860 he returned to Rutherford County, and took a half interest in his father's mill, of which he is now proprietor. The mill was established at an early date, and is now classed among the best custom mills of the county, outside of Murfreesboro, having a capacity of thirty barrels per day. Mr. Davis is always strictly accurate in his business transactions and accordingly controls the leading trade in his section of the country. In 1856 he was united in marriage to Sallie Searsey, a native of this county. They have this family: Robert O., John; Mollie E., wife of Robert Bell; Ella, wife of Joseph Blake; and Samuel B. Mr. Davis is a Democrat in politics, and he and family are members of the Presbyterian Church.

JASPER F. DICKENS (deceased) was a prominent and energetic farmer of Rutherford County, Tenn., and was born in Cannon County, Tenn., November 18, 1828, son of Baxter B. and Nancy (Holt) Dickens, who were also natives of the State. His death, which was a great loss to his family and friends, occurred March 21, 1885. In 1858 he was united in marriage to Miss Mary J. Prater, who was born in Tennessee, and still survives him. They became the parents of eleven children, only eight of whom are now living: Nancy C. (wife of J. A. Todd), died May 7, 1880; William T., Martha E. (died August 15, 1884), Baxter M., Thomas P., Quitnian, Rufus G., Edna F., John T., Charley G. and James, who died February 16, 1886. Mrs. Dickens is a member of the Missionary Baptist Church, and since her husband's death has resided on and managed the farm, being quite successful in her business transactions. She belongs to one of the leading families of the county.

DR. JAMES M. DILL, a widely known practitioner, was born in Rutherford County in 1831, and is a son of Isaac and Gilley (Cooper) Dill, who were natives of South Carolina, the father being an active agriculturist. He departed this life in 1847; the mother died in 1851. They were earnest and faithful members of the Christian Church, and died earnest believers in that faith. The subject of this sketch was united in matrimony to Miss Jestina Kelton August 11, 1857, and to this union seven children were born, only two of whom are living, Joseph W. and Nettie F. Mrs. Dill died February 9, 188–. She was an excellent and charitable lady, and was held in high esteem by a large circle of acquaintances. The Doctor took for his second wife Miss Mary Hill, September 19, 1883. He is a Democrat of the Jacksonian order, and he and his wife are worthy and consistent members of the Christian Church, and are recognized as worthy and influential citizens of the county.

WILLIAM B. DRUMRIGHT, of the firm of Butler & Drumright, merchants of Murfreesboro, Tenn., was born in Williamson County, Tenn., July 8, 1841, son of Richard and Elizabeth (Rainey) Drumright, both of the Old Dominion. The father located on a farm in Williamson County in 1825, and spent the remainder of his days a tiller of the soil. He died in 1844. Our subject resided on the farm with his mother until her death, in 1858, and secured a common school education. He came to Murfreesboro at the latter date and learned the brickmason's trade, which he followed until the beginning of the war, when he enlisted in Company I, First Regiment Tennessee Infantry, and served as private and non-commissioned officer until the surrender of the Southern Confederacy. He then worked at his trade in Jackson and Madison Counties, Tenn., two years and then returned to Murfreesboro, and has since been engaged in contracting and building, and has erected some of the finest buildings in the city. In February, 1886, he engaged in the general merchandise business, and has been quite prosperous. November 15, 1868, he married Martha F. Rather. They have six children—one son and five daughters. Mr. Drumright is a Democrat, and has been a member of the board of aldermen of the city one term. He is a member of the I. O. O. F., and he and family are members of the Methodist Episcopal Church South.

DR. JOHN N. DYKES, a successful practitioner, was born near Rogersville, Tenn., November 14, 1833, and is the son of Henry and Rebecca (Curry) Dykes. The father departed this life in 1857, and his widow followed him in 1885. The subject of this sketch was married April 19, 1857, to Miss Sallie Long, and their wedded life was blessed by four children, three of whom are living, viz.: Henry E.. James M. and Sidney B. Mrs. Dykes departed this life in 1876; she was a worthy member of the Missionary Baptist Church, dying with a full possession of all Christian hopes. Dr. Dyke married the second time in 1880 to Mrs. Maggie Smotherman, having by this union two children, one of whom is living, namely, Horace G. The Doctor is a stanch Democrat and took an active part in the late war, enlisting in Company G, Thirty-first Tennessee, remaining with his company until after the fall of Vicksburg, when his company was changed from infantry to cavalry, and the Doctor changed from surgeon to lieutenant. He was with John H. Morgan at Greenville and saw Miss Williams when she rode out of town to direct the Union troops through the Confederate lines. The Doctor and wife are leading members of the Baptist Church and are regarded as prominent and influential citizens of the community in which they live.

W. B. EARTHMAN & CO., manufacturers of red cedar lumber, of Murfreesboro, Tenn. For the past eight years Murfreesboro has grown to be a cedar market of greater importance and reputation than any other city in the country, considerably overshadowing many other cities of a much larger population. This result has been attained on account of the superior advantage Murfreesboro has in locality, being surrounded by immense cedar groves, and because the above named firm has had the necessary capital, capability and push. The business of this firm reaches out over a large extent of territory; their chief markets are St. Louis, Cincinnati, Louisville and Indianapolis. The business was first established by W. B. Earthman & Co. in 1878, and they have been very successful in the business. They started in with no capital but that which nature had endowed them with, and the fact of their owning the building and yards in which they do business gives them superior advantage now. William W. Earthman was born December 3, 1818, and is a son of James and Margaret (Webber) Earthman, natives, respectively, of Tennessee and Mississippi. The father was a farmer and afterward a merchant of Winchester, Miss. He came to this State in 1829 and died in the spring of 1830. The mother died in 1858. The subject of our sketch was reared on the farm and secured a fair education at the common schools. At the age of fifteen he went into business for himself. In 1847 he was united in marriage to Miss Elizabeth Bumpas, a native of this State, and to them were born five children: William B., Ira O., Ella M., V. K. Stephenson and Fannie, who died in 1884. Mr. Earthman is an old-line Whig in politics. Himself and wife are members of the Cumberland Presbyterian Church. Mr. William W. Earthman is one of the oldest and most reliable business men of the county, and is justly recognized as a moral, upright citizen. William B. Earthman, a native of this State, was born December

3, 1848, and is the son of William W., senior member of the firm, and Elizabeth Earthman, both natives of Tennessee. The father engaged in farming in the county for many years, and also engaged in the lumber business in this place in 1847. William B. was reared on the farm and secured a good common school education. At the age of eighteen he engaged in the mercantile business and afterward, in 1878, engaged in his present business. In 1877 he was united in marriage to Miss Mattie T. Frost, a native of this State, and to them were born four children: Hewett F., Weber B., John B., Christine R., all of whom are still living. Mr. Earthman is a Democrat in politics, and himself and family are members of the Methodist Episcopal Church. He is classed among the enterprising and successful business men of the county. Ira Overton Earthman, junior member of the firm, is a native of this county, and was born January 3, 1852. He is a son of William W. and Elizabeth Earthman. Ira Earthman was reared on the farm and secured a good common school education, afterward attending the Union University, at Murfreesboro, and Franklin University, near Nashville. At the age of nineteen he began the mercantile business, which he continued for three years; he was then employed by Hodge & Smith, and remained with them for five years. In 1878 he engaged in his present business. December 1, 1885, he was united in marriage to Miss Anna Rivens, a native of this State. Mr. Ira Earthman is a Democrat in politics, and he and wife are members of the Methodist Episcopal Church.

DAVID F. ELAM may be mentioned as an energetic and prosperous farmer of Rutherford County, Tenn., born in Murfreesboro, July 27, 1829, son of Edward and Rebecca (Wade) Elam, who were born in Virginia and Maryland, respectively. Edward Elam was a descendant of Daniel Elam, one of the pioneer settlers of the county, and a school teacher in his day, being one of the early educators of Murfreesboro. Edward Elam was a mechanic and farmer, and at the time of his death was a merchant of Jacksonville, Ala. He was one of the first men that ginned cotton at Murfreesboro, and made quite a fortune at that business. He was a Jacksonian Democrat. His death occurred in 1839, and the mother's in 1858. The subject of this sketch made his parents' house his home until twenty-one years of age. He then began for himself, and in 1858 purchased a farm in West Tennessee, but in 1865 returned to Rutherford County and purchased his present farm, consisting of 600 acres of excellent land. In 1856 his marriage to Miss Ellen P. Crawford was celebrated. They have these children: Franke E. (wife of Samuel P. Black), Edward E., Mamie (wife of Dave Miller), Annie, Wade H. and Washington E. Mr. Elam is a Democrat, and he and wife are members of the Presbyterian Church.

DR. THOMAS J. ELAM, a prominent physician of Rutherford County, Tenn., born November 25, 1832, and is a son of Edward and Rebecca (Wade) Elam, who were born in Virginia and Maryland, respectively. The father was a Robertson County pioneer and farmer, and died in the fall of 1839. He was a participant of the war of 1812, and was in the battle of New Orleans under Gen. Jackson. Our subject spent his boyhood days on a farm, and received a collegiate education, attending Irving College in Warren County in 1856. He began studying medicine under Drs. J. E. & R. S. Wendel, of Murfreesboro, and attended the medical college of Nashville, and received his diploma in 1858. He has since practiced in Rutherford County, and has met with good success, owning 400 acres of land on the Stone River. February 6, 1861, he married Elizabeth Snell, and to them were born eight children—three of whom are dead. Those living are Samuel B., Franklin, Francis C., Thomas J. and Elizabeth. Mr. Elam was a Whig previous to the war, but since that time has been a Democrat. He was a surgeon in the late war, serving the Forty-fifth Tennessee Regiment. In 1864 he was discharged on account of ill-health and returned home. He is a Master Mason, and his wife is a member of the Cumberland Presbyterian Church.

HON. EDWIN H. EWING, LL. D., of Murfreesboro, Tenn., was born in Nashville December 2, 1809, being a son of Nathan and grandson of Andrew Ewing, who was one of the first settlers of Nashville. The names of Nathan and Andrew Ewing appear in the county court records as clerks successively from 1783 to 1830. Our subject secured a good literary education and graduated with the degree of A. B., from the University of Nashville in 1827, and later had the honorary degree of LL. D., conferred upon him. He began studying law without a preceptor, using the books of an elder brother and occasionally appealing to that able lawyer, Francis B. Fogg, who generously assisted him in his struggles to rise. In 1830 he was licensed to practice and was admitted to the bar a year later. He was a partner of James P. Grundy until 1837, and grew rapidly in character and standing as a lawyer. He and his brother Andrew formed a partnership, and in 1840 he worked with so much vigor for the election of the Whig ticket that he was honored by an election to the State Legislature in 1842, where he became reputed for his able speeches. In 1844 he favored Henry Clay for the presidency, and in 1845 he was elected to fill a vacancy in Congress for the Nashville District. He served two sessions in that body, when he declined to fill a seat in the House longer. While there he delivered several able speeches, one on the Oregon question; one on the Tariff of 1846, which was favorably commented on by his room mate, Alexander H. Stephens; one on the River and Harbor Bill of 1846, and one on the Mexican war. Meanwhile his reputation as a lawyer increased and he was frequently chosen special judge on the supreme bench, and his opinion delivered on the great Winchester case won him a wide-spread reputation. In 1850 he made a fortunate speculation in real estate, which rendered him financially independent. He then decided to make a tour of the globe, and in 1851 left for the Old World, taking copious and interesting notes of the many countries he visited. Mr. Ewing practiced his profession in Nashville until 1856, when he came to Rutherford County and resided with his daughter until 1860, when she removed to Nashville and he continued to make his home with her until 1861. At the breaking out of the war he spoke and voted for the Union in the election of February, 1861, but after Lincoln's proclamation he took a position against coercion. In the latter part of 1863 he advised the people of the State to submit to the Federal Government. His letter to this effect was published and subjected him to much criticism and aided probably in his defeat for judgeship of the supreme court afterward. After the war he practiced his profession in Murfreesboro, but of late years has retired from active duties and is spending his declining years at his residence in this city. Mr. Ewing has always been an energetic student in literature and has contributed largely to newspapers and has been much sought after throughout the State as a public lecturer.

JOSIAH W. EWING is a well-known citizen of Murfreesboro, Tenn., and is the eldest of two children and only son of Hon. E. H. Ewing, whose sketch precedes this. He was born in Nashville August 11, 1834, and attended the Nashville University, his father's old *alma mater*, being in the sophomore class at the classing of that institution. He then completed his education at Bethany College, Virginia, graduating with the degree of A. B. in 1881. He then removed to this county and followed agricultural pursuits until 1861, when he enlisted in Capt. Ledbetter's company, First Regiment Tennessee Infantry, and served in this capacity until after the battle of Stone River, when he was made provost-marshal of the court of Hardee's military corps, continuing thus about fifteen months, when he was made assistant inspector of field transportation for the Confederate forces of Tennessee, which position he retained until the surrender. He then returned to Rutherford County and resumed the management of his farms, but in 1873 came to Murfreesboro, where he has since resided. November 21, 1855, he wedded Miss Ada B. Hord, of this county. They have three sons and one daughter. Mr. Ewing, like his father, was an old time Whig until that party ceased to exist. Since that time he has affiliated with the Democratic party. He and wife are members of the Presbyterian Church.

JOHN W. FARIS, a successful farmer, was born in this county September 30, 1846, and is the son of Rev. C. B. and Mary (Ransom) Faris, natives of this State. The subject of this sketch was united in wedlock, April 18, 1866, to Miss Lizzie Hopkins, and to them were born the following children: Mary A., Sue E., Charley B., James R., Ada, Sallie and Lena M. Mr. Faris took an active part in the late war, enlisting in Company

A, Twenty-fourth Tennessee, serving as second lieutenant, but was afterward promoted to lieutenant of Company F, Alabama State troops. Later he joined Company D, Eleventh Tennessee Cavalry, where he remained until the close of the war. He was a gallant soldier and a brave man. Mr. and Mrs. Faris are members in good standing in the Methodist Episcopal Church, and are regarded with esteem and affection in the community in which they reside.

R. W. FARIS, a prominent merchant, saw-mill owner, proprietor of a well-boring machine and manager of a blacksmith shop, is financially embarrassed, and was never otherwise. Mr. Faris is an uncompromising Democrat from away back. In youth he was noted for mule riding and coon hunting. He enlisted in the army at the age of sixteen, in Company A, Twenty-fourth Tennessee, and was as timid a soldier as ever shouldered a musket. He served one year, was discharged for youthfulness, and was sworn in the next day for three years, and served until 1865. He joined the Kuklux, Good Templars, Free Masons, and is a consistent member of all the above named societies. Mr. Faris has been twice married; the first time to Miss Elizabeth Z. Jackson, having three children: Walter R., Mary J. and Charles R. The second time he was married to Miss Mattie Mathews, and one child was born to this union, Angre. Mr. Faris is now superintendent of the Methodist Episcopal Sunday-school, and is in many respects the equal of Sam Jones.

MINOS L. FLETCHER, farmer, was born in this county in 1822, and is the son of John and Martha (Howlet) Fletcher, both natives of North Carolina, who immigrated to this State in 1818, and fully participated in all the hardships and inconveniences of those times. The father died in 1849, and the mother in 1828. They were prominent members of the Primitive Baptist Church, and died in full faith of a blessed hereafter. The subject of this sketch was married, June 7, 1841, to Miss Lucretia H. Overall, and to this union were born two children, both of whom died in infancy. Mr. Fletcher was an ardent advocate of the union of States, but being a resident of the South he refrained from participating in the late war. Mr. Fletcher supports the man and the principle rather than the party. Our subject was elected magistrate by the Democratic party, and served his county in that capacity for sixteen years. He was also elected circuit court clerk by the Republican party, and served in that capacity for six years. Mr. Fletcher is independent in politics, and has the confidence and friendship of both parties. Mr. and Mrs. Fletcher are worthy members of the Methodist Episcopal Church.

THOMAS B. FOWLER, cashier of Stone River National Bank of Murfreesboro, Tenn., was born in Cannon County Tenn., July 7, 1838, son of R. and H. (Craft) Fowler, who were natives of the same place. The father was a farmer and was clerk of the county courts twelve years. He represented his county in the lower house of the State Legislature, the sessions of 1851-52. His death occurred in 1863. At the age of twelve years our subject left home and came to Murfreesboro, where he became clerk in a book store and later acted as book-keeper in the dry goods business until the war, when he enlisted as a private in Capt. S. N. White's Company, and served until after the battle of Franklin, where he lost a leg in a skirmish near Overall Creek. He was raised to the rank of lieutenant and adjutant. He was revenue collector for Rutherford County for the years 1866-67. After he had recovered from his wound he accepted a position as book-keeper at the Savings Bank and later became teller of the First National Bank. In 1870 he became clerk of the circuit court and filled the position until 1882. He then accepted his present position. February 8, 1868, he wedded Mrs. Sallie (Major) Richardson. They have an adopted daughter named Katie B. Mr. Fowler is a Democrat and is a Mason, Knight Templar and Scottish Rite degrees. He is a member of the K. of P. and K. of H. and he and Mrs Fowler are members of the Presbyterian Church.

WILLIAM R. FOX, proprietor of the livery, feed and sale stables of Murfreesboro, Tenn., which were established by Fox & Smith, in 1884, was born in this county July 31, 1860, and is the son of William and Tennie Fox, natives, respectively, of Ireland and this State. The father is known in this county as the leading trader in stock since the war, making a specialty of cattle. He is a Democrat, politically, and his family are members of the Methodist Episcopal Church. The subject of our sketch, William R., was reared with his parents and secured a good education, attending the University of Tennessee, at Knoxville, and at the age of twenty engaged in business with his father, dealing and trading in all kinds of live-stock. In 1884 William R. Fox purchased his partner's share in the livery business and has since conducted it. He has from twenty to twenty-five head of good livery horses on hand at all times and carriages and vehicles of all styles. On October 27, 1885, he was united in marriage to Miss Lizzie E. Robertson, a native of this State. Mr. Fox is classed among the energetic business men of the county and has the respect of all.

CAPT. THOMAS FRAME, a well-known citizen of Rutherford County and superintendent of the Stone River National Military Cemetery, is a native of Ireland, and was born in Londonderry in 1829. He is the son of John and Bessie (Black) Frame, both natives of Ireland. The father followed the occupation of farming and his son Thomas was reared on the farm, securing a good common school education in the country schools. At the age of sixteen he was engaged by the surveyors of Ireland, and here he remained for ten years. He then studied architecture for one year at the city of Londonderry and in the summer of 1850 he immigrated to this country and engaged in surveying in the State of Louisiana. In 1854 he enlisted in the regular army at New Orleans, and served three years. When the slavery question came up in Kansas, in 1857, he was stationed at that point to keep peace, and in 1858 was sent to quell the Mormon trouble, and afterward was engaged in fighting the Indians. In 1863 he started south with Company F, United States Cavalry, and their first engagement was at Chickamauga, and afterward in all the principal battles until the close of the war. He was then appointed first sergeant of the metropolitan police, which position he held until 1870 when he was appointed to his present position. In 1869 Mr. Frame was united in marriage to Mrs. Sarah (Graham) Hawthorn, widow of Adam Hawthorn. To Mr. and Mrs. Frame were born two children: Irene H. and Lula T. Mr. Frame is a member of the Odd Fellows and the Grand Army of the Republic and he and wife are members of the Presbyterian Church.

W. C. FROST, editor and proprietor of the Murfreesboro *News*, was born in Yazoo County, Miss., November 9, 1859, and is the son of William D. and Mattie L. (Brown) Frost, natives of Tennessee. The father is a practicing physician of good standing in Bedford County to-day. Walter C., our subject, was reared to agricultural pursuits in his boyhood days, securing a fair literary education, preparing himself for teaching, which profession he followed for about one year; then, at the age of twenty, he began the study of law at Fayetteville, Tenn., reading in the office of Holman & Holman, and at the age of twenty-one was admitted to the Lincoln County bar and entered into the practice of law. There, in partnership with S. W. Carmack, and later at Columbia, Tenn., with John V. Wright and Lee Bullock. In the spring of 1884 he removed to Nashville with a view to establishing practice there, but in September, 1885, he came to Murfreesboro and bought out the *News* of that city, and has since conducted the paper in a faithful and highly efficient manner. Mr. Frost is an unswerving Democrat in politics, and his paper, which is devoted to the interests of this party, is free and fearless in proclaiming the principles and sentiments of the Democracy in Rutherford County. Although comparatively a new comer in Rutherford County, Mr. Frost bears the respect and esteem of the entire community, and is justly recognized as one among the enterprising and successful young citizens of Murfreesboro and an efficient newspaper man.

JOHN A. GILLEY, a prominent and enterprising farmer and a native of the county, was born February 4, 1843, and is a son of Peterson and Elizabeth (Cornehan) Gilley, both natives of Tennessee. The father was a farmer and a distinguished minister of the Separate Baptist Church. He departed this life July 13, 1884. The mother is still living and is a resident of this county. Our subject was married to Miss Nancy McCrary May 8, 1866. To them were born four children: Ephraim D., John F., Jessie P. and Arthur T. Mr. Gilley was a soldier in the late war, and served in Company G, Fourth Tennessee

Cavalry, until his capture shortly after the evacuation of Savannah. He remained a prisoner about two months, and then returned home and refrained from further participation in the war. Mr. Gilley is a believer in Democratic principles, and gives his aid and support to that party.

JOHN BUCHANAN GOODWIN was born in Davidson County, Tenn., October 6, 1827, son of George and Jane T. (Buchanan) Goodwin, natives, respectively, of North Carolina and Tennessee. The father was a mechanic of Nashville, and was an extensive lumber manufacturer, in which business he secured a very comfortable competence. His death occurred in 1837. The mother was a daughter of Maj. John Buchanan, one of the prominent settlers of the State and a noted surveyor. She died in 1838. Our subject, John B., was reared on a farm with his eldest sister until he was twelve years of age. He then attended school until seventeen years of age when he purchased a farm in this county; since 1869 he has resided on his present farm, and March 29, 1845, he united in marriage to Miss Ledocia Thompson, a native of Alabama. They have eight children: Mary J. (deceased), Sarah E. (Buchanan), Margaret L. (Burnett), George M., Tennessee L. (Sanders), Ledocia (Sanders) Mrs. Goodwin died in 1859 and he took for his second wife Mrs. Sarah (Buchanan) Mobry, who bore him five children, only three now living: Henry M., William H. and Joseph D.; she was the mother of one child, Sarah A. (Goodwin) by her first marriage. Mr. Goodwin is a Democrat in politics and held the office of magistrate for seventeen years; he and family are leading members of the Baptist Church, and he is among the successful farmers and upright citizens of the county.

JOSEPH P. HALE, trustee of Rutherford County, Tenn., was born in Franklin County of the same State, December 14, 1828, son of Ellis H. and Mary E. (Miller) Hale. The father was born in North Carolina in 1801, and came to Tennessee in 1826 or 1827. He was married December 20, 1827, and about 1830 came to this county and followed farming with fair success until his death October 21, 1877. His wife died March 25, 1885. Our subject resided on the farm with his parents. His early education was limited but in later years he prepared himself for teaching, which profession he followed for a number of years. He is a natural mechanic, so abandoned school teaching and began following the carpenter's trade. In August, 1882, he was elected county trustee and served one term of two years in so faithful and efficient a manner that he was re-elected to the office in 1884, and is now discharging the duties of that office. December 14, 1853, he wedded Elizabeth C. Vaughn. They have these children: Thomas J., William S., Edgar P., Laura P. (Barber), Charles V. Branch P., James D., and Rufus O. Mr. Hale is a Democrat and was a warm advocate for the Confederate cause during the late war. In November, 1861, he enlisted in Company D, Forty-fifth Regiment Tennessee Infantry, and served until he was wounded at Shiloh, when he was raised to the rank of first lieutenant. He was discharged in 1862 but re-enlisted and served until December 7, 1864, at which time he was severely wounded in an engagement in front of Murfreesboro, having his right arm broken and his left hand badly mangled. Mr. Hale is a member of the Primitive Baptist Church and is an able official and excellent citizen.

JOHN W. HALL, Esq., a prominent farmer and fruit grower of Rutherford County, was born June 25, 1834, in this county, and is the son of John and Charlotte (Gambill) Hall, natives, respectively, of Virginia and Tennessee. The father came to this county in 1812 and employed his time in teaching school and farming. He died in the fall of 1846. The son was reared on a farm and received a fair education in the common schools of the county. At the age of eighteen he started to farm for himself on a rented farm, attending school and farming. He purchased a farm in the Fourth District, but seven years later sold it and still later bought the farm on which he is now living. On February 8, 1859, he was married to Mary J. Shelton, and to this union were born the following children: William A., Larraphine, Charlotta, Sarah E., Jimmie S., Mary L., and John W. Mr. Hall is a Democrat, and in 1862 enlisted in Lytler Eleventh Tennessee Cavalry as a private. He participated in most of the battles that the command was engaged in; was taken sick soon after the Franklin battle and was left in Davidson County until he was able to get home. In 1876 he was elected justice of the peace of the Fourth District and has held the office up to the present time. He and wife are members of the Christian Church and are respected and esteemed by all.

MRS. JULIA A. HALL, a widely known and eminently successful land-owner, was born in Bedford County, this State, and is the daughter of Isaiah and Mary (Rainy) Gault. The father was a gentleman highly respected as a kind neighbor and a warm friend. His death occurred in the year 1852 and the mother, who was loved and esteemed by all who knew her, followed her husband to his last resting place in the year 1876. They were devout Baptists and died in full fruition of all Christian hope. The subject of this sketch was united in marriage in the year 1858, to John L. Hall. To this brief but happy union were born six children, five of whom are living: Rainy I., John B., Albert S., Delphia C. (wife of James E. Floyd) and Thomas J. Mr. Hall's death, which occurred in 1873, was a sad blow to his bereaved family and friends. He was justly considered a moral, upright man. Mrs. Hall is a worthy and consistent member of the Baptist Church and occupies a prominent position in the community in which she resides.

JOHN C. HARRIS, a prominent and well-known farmer of Rutherfotd County and a native of this State, was born June 1, 1842. He is the son of John C. and Jane P. (Ragsdale) Harris, natives of Tennessee. The father was born February 17, 1800, and was one of the wealthiest and most prominent farmers of the county, and one of its pioneer settlers, coming here as early as 1823, and securing, when land was cheap, one of the finest farms in the county. In 1853, having lost his companion in life, he conceived the idea that he would be his own administrator, hence about twenty years ago he divided his landed estate among his children, giving to each one an excellent farm. Many are they who can testify to the kind hospitality and broad benevolence of this noble man. He was an elder in the Presbyterian Church for a period of sixty years, and on his death, which sad event occurred February 10, 1885, he lacked just seven days of being eighty-five years old. The subject of this sketch was reared on the farm, and secured a fair education at the common schools. At the age of eighteen he enlisted in Company E, Forty-fifth Tennessee Regiment, serving as a private for two years, and was afterward made first lieutenant of his company until the close of the war; was imprisoned at Camp Chase, Ohio, in December, 1863, where he remained until March, 1865. He then returned home and attended school at College Grove, Williamson County, for three years, and at the age of twenty-five commenced farming for himself on his father's tract. His first wife, Miss Annie M. Green, died in April, 1883; they had one child—Janie R. In May, 1884, Mr. Harris was united in marriage to his second wife, Miss Maggie Green, a native of this county.

ROBERT B. HARRIS, M. D., a prominent man of Rutherford County and a native of this State, was born September 6, 1837, and is the son of John C. and Jane P. (Ragsdale) Harris, natives of Tennessee. The subject of our sketch was reared on the farm, and secured a good common school education. In 1856–57 he attended the Cumberland University, of Lebanon, Tenn., and returning home in 1858, commenced the study of medicine, and in 1858 attended two courses of lectures at the University of Pennsylvania, at Philadelphia, medical department, with a view to making it a profession. In March, 1860, he graduated at this institution with the degree of M. D., after which he returned to Rutherford County, and followed the practice of medicine as a business. He is known all over the county as a learned and skillful physician. On account of his health failing Dr. Harris was compelled to withdraw from practice in 1876, and has since been engaged in farming. In 1861 he enlisted in Company A, Twenty-third Tennessee Regiment, serving as a private until the organization of the regiment, when he was made assistant surgeon, and after the battle of Shiloh was promoted to surgeon of the regiment, and continued with this regiment until after the fall of Petersburg, when he was detailed to hospital service at Montgomery, Ala., remaining there until the close of the war. In 1883 he was married to Mrs. Kittie V. Byers, a native of this county, and Mr. Harris' second wife, his first wife, Miss Susie R. Hill, having died in 1879. To the last union two children have been born: James P. and Robert G. Mr. Harris is a Democrat, in politics and he and family are leading members of the Cumberland Presbyterian Church, of which Mr. Harris has been an elder for some time.

HAYNES, HOLLOWELL & CO. are merchants of Murfreesboro, Tenn. In 1882 the business was established by Thomas R. Hollowell (see sketch) and his brother George S., under the firm name of G. S. Hollowell & Co. The following year Thomas R. assumed complete control of the business, and conducted it alone until the latter part of 1883, when Mr. G. C. Batey took an interest, continuing until January, 1885, when William R. Haynes purchased an interest. They carry a large and select stock of general merchandise, and are doing a lucrative business. William R. Haynes was born in Cannon County, Tenn., February 11, 1840, being a son of Ivy J. C. and Elvira (Fletcher) Haynes, natives, respectively, of North Carolina and Tennessee. The father came to Tennessee about 1823, and located in Rutherford County, where he learned the cabinet-maker's trade, which he followed until 1853. He then engaged in the general merchandise business, but in 1881 retired to a farm near the city, where he now resides. Our subject, William R., worked in his father's store, and in 1877 became a partner in the business. In 1881 he retired from business, and two years later removed to the country, but in 1885 returned to the city and engaged in his present business. In 1878 he married Miss Sophia M. Reeves, of Bedford County, Tenn. Mr. Haynes is a Democrat. In 1861 he enlisted in Company C, Forty-fifth Regiment Tennessee Infantry, and served in the commissary department of the Confederate Army until its surrender. He and wife are members of the Methodist Episcopal Church.

JAMES F. HENDERSON, a pioneer farmer of Rutherford County, was born May 4, 1811, in Lincoln County, N. C., and was the son of Logan and Margaret E. (Johnson) Henderson, natives of North Carolina. The father immigrated to this county in 1818, settling on a farm in the vicinity of Murfreesboro, and was a successful farmer, and was elected justice of the peace, which office he held for a number of years. He died in this county in the fall of 1846, leaving a large estate. The son was reared on a farm, and received a good education at Nashville University. After reaching his majority he took charge of his father's farm for eight years, and then moved to the place where he now lives. He has been a successful farmer, giving each of his three sons a farm of over 100 acres of land. On December 20, 1832, he married Miss Amanda Veoores, a native of Tennessee, and to this union were born eleven children, seven of whom are living, namely: Medra, Octavine, Vansinderan, Hortense, Frank, Clifford C. and Estella. Mr. Henderson is a Democrat, a Royal Arch Mason, and he and wife are members of the Presbyterian Church. He is a leading farmer of the county and an excellent citizen.

JAMES W. HILL, a farmer of Rutherford County, was born October 1, 1841, and is the son of William G. and Eliza M. (Westall) Hill, natives of Texas. William Hill was a wealthy farmer of Texas and one of the leading citizens; he died in 1859. The subject was reared on a farm, receiving a moderate education at the University of North Carolina. In 1871 he moved to Rutherford County, where he engaged in farming, and met with evident success, having 165 acres of well improved land. He was married in 1863 to Sarah M. McLean, a native of Rutherford County, and to this union were born eight children, six of whom are living: Charley B., Annie B., John W., Herbert N., Florence S. and Sadie C. Mr. Hill is a Democrat. In 1861 he enlisted in the Confederate Army with Terry's Texas Rangers, as a private, serving until the close of the war. He and wife are members of the Methodist Church. Mr. Hill is justly recognized as one of the leading farmers and a moral and upright man.

SAMUEL H. HODGE, a prominent business man of Murfreesboro, Tenn., a native of this city, was born November 6, 1838. His parents, Samuel H. and Sarah C. (Mitchell) Hodge were both born in North Carolina, in 1800, and immigrated to this county with their respective parents, about 1814 or 1815. Our subject's father was raised, married and raised his family in this county, following farming the greater part of his life, in which he was very successful. He was an old-time Whig politically, and took an active part in the local campaigns in his day. He was elected by his party to the office of clerk of the circuit court, which he filled continuously and in a faithful and efficient manner for several terms. His death occurred in 1846, but his widow survived him twenty years. The immediate subject of this sketch secured a good education in his youthful days at the Cumberland University at Lebanon, Tenn. In May, 1861, he enlisted as a private in Company I, First Regiment Tennessee Infantry, and served in this capacity in the late war until 1863, when he was detached from his regiment to serve as a secret scout for Gen. Bragg, and was captured in the latter part of the same year, while engaged in discharging the duties of this most perilous and difficult task, and held as a prisoner of war at Fort Delaware until March, 1865. He was then exchanged and at the close of the war returned home. Here he began business life as a clerk, and in 1868 he established a mercantile establishment for himself, and has remained in the same to the present time, meeting with more than ordinary and well-deserved success. In January, 1885, Mr. Smith became his partner in business, Mr. William Mitchell, his former partner, having withdrawn to engage in business for himself. Alexander Smith was also a partner previous to Mr. Mitchell's connection with the business, this partnership being severed by Mr. Smith's death. Under the firm name of Hodge & Smith the present firm carry a large and well-selected stock of general merchandise of nearly every conceivable description and command the leading trade in their line in the city and county. They also buy and sell, probably, more cotton, grain and seeds than any other firm in Rutherford County. In December, 1868, Mr. Hodge married Emma Smith, of this county, by whom he is the father of five children: George W., Samuel H., Florence, Lillian and Emma Sue. Politically he is an unswerving Democrat. He has attained the Knight Templar and Scottish Rite degrees in Masonry and himself and wife are zealous members of the Presbyterian Church of this city.

THOMAS R. HOLLOWELL, a native of Rutherford County, Tenn., was born September 16, 1839. His parents, Edwin C. and Ann M. (Crockett) Hollowell, were born, respectively, in North Carolina and Rutherford County, Tenn. At an early period the father came to Tennessee and followed farming and carpentering for a living. The latter part of his life was spent in Murfreesboro, where he died in 1868. Thomas R. secured a common school education and followed the carpenter's trade until the breaking out of the war, when he enlisted in Company H, Twelfth Regiment Tennessee Infantry and served as private in the Southern Army until the battle of Shiloh, where he was wounded and left on the field for dead. He was captured by the Federals and held until the September following, when he was exchanged and re-enlisted, serving in the commissary department. In 1864 he was made captain of Company I, Twenty-first Tennessee Cavalry, serving until the close of the war. From that time until 1878 he farmed, and at the latter date he was elected county trustee and served faithfully and well four years. He is at present engaged in the general merchandise business and is doing well financially. In 1867 he married Nannie P. Jobe, of Murfreesboro, and four children have blessed their union: Mary Ann, Thomas, Bessie and Lena. Mr. Hollowell has always been an unswerving Democrat. He is a Mason, Knight Templar degree, and he and wife are members of the Methodist Episcopal Church South.

M. HIRSCH & CO. are dry goods and notion merchants, of Murfreesboro, Tenn. The firm is composed of Moses Hirsch, resident partner, and Joseph Franklin, of Nashville, and the business was established in January, 1884, Mr. Hirsch having active management and control. They carry a fine line of goods pertaining to their business and have a dress-making department in connection. Mr. Hirsch is a well-known business man and a native of the city. He was born March 9, 1859, and is a son of Henry Hirsch, of Murfreesboro (see sketch). Moses was reared with his parents and secured an ordinary business education. At the age of fourteen he began his career as clerk in the mercantile establishment of his uncle, E. Rosenfeld, continuing with him and A. Tobias & Bro. until January, 1884, when he engaged in his present business as above stated. He is unmarried, a Democrat in politics, and is a wide-awake young business man of the city.

CAMILLUS B. HUGGINS, a citizen and native of Murfreesboro, Tenn., was born June 5, 1822. His parents, Jonathan and Elizabeth W. (Smith) Huggins, were born, respectively in North Carolina and Davidson County, Tenn. The father came to Rutherford County, Tenn., in 1818, and spent the greater portion of his life in mercantile pursuits, in which he met with good success. In politics he was a Whig before the late war, and was a participant in the war of 1812. His death occurred at Manchester, Tenn., September 30, 1870. Our subject's boyhood days were spent in his native county, where he received limited educational advantages. He began his business career as clerk in a mercantile establishment, and afterward engaged in the grocery business two years with J. W. Nelson, in Lebanon, Tenn., and then returned to Murfreesboro, and after clerking a number of years, engaged in the dry goods business with Isaac Lohman, and afterward with his father and brother in the grocery business, continuing until 1857. Mr. Huggins was in the commissary department of the Confederate Army after the battle of Stone River until the surrender. Since that time he has followed different occupations. He was connected with the First National and Stone River Bank as teller, but of late years has devoted his time and means to general trading and speculation. In January, 1855, he wedded Miss Sarah E. Ridley, of Rutherford County. To them were born eight children, the two eldest, a son and daughter, dying young. Those living are four sons and two daughters. Mr. Huggins is now a Democrat in politics, although a Whig before the war. He is a member of the Methodist Episcopal Church and his wife of the Cumberland Presbyterian Church.

THOMAS G. IVIE was a successful merchant at Murfreesboro, born in this county September 17, 1837, and was the son of Charles D. and Judith (Wood) Ivie, natives, respectively, of Virginia and Tennessee. The subject of this sketch was wedded December 18, 1870, to Sallie Sawing, and to this brief but happy period of wedded bliss were born two children, one of whom is living, namely: Thomas G. Mr. Ivie was a consistent Methodist and one of Rutherford County's best citizens, and by his unswerving integrity was highly esteemed by all. His death which occurred March 13, 1872, was a sad blow to his bereaved family and acquaintances. Mrs. Ivie still survives him and is an accomplished lady and a devout Christian, being a leading member of the Methodist Episcopal Church South and is held in high esteem by all who know her.

NATHAN R. JACKSON, a well-known and successful agriculturist, was born in this county December 27, 1845, and is the son of Nathan and Indiana Jackson, natives, respectively, of Virginia and Tennessee. The subject of this sketch was married January 29, 1873, to Miss Emma L. Dawson, and to this union were born five children: William F., Clara, Cora and Flora (twins) and Ruth. Mr. Jackson took quite an active part in the late war, enlisting in Capt. Miller's company of cavalry, was captured at Columbia, Tenn., and remained a prisoner for a short time. At the close of the war he took the oath and returned home. Mr. Jackson is a Democrat with prohibition tendencies, and a Methodist by inclination. His wife is a member of the Cumberland Presbyterian Church and they are justly recognized as prominent and influential citizens of the community in which they live.

PROF. ROBERT D. JAMISON, a prominent farmer and stock raiser, was born April 13, 1838, in Rutherford County, and is the son of Henry D. and Sarah W. (Thomas) Jamison. The father, a well-known saddler and farmer, came here at an early date and settled at Murfreesboro, where he remained for fifteen years. He then moved on a farm near a place where he has since resided. He was secretary and treasurer of the Murfreesboro & Nashville Turnpike Company, was a follower of the old Whig party and a successful farmer, having a large estate at the time of his death, which occurred in March, 1858. Our subject was reared on a farm and received a good education at Thomson Academy, in Williamson County. At the age of eighteen he taught school in Williamson County for a year and a half. After his father's death he took charge of the farm, which he conducted until 1861. In 1865 he purchased a farm in the vicinity of Murfreesboro, erected a schoolhouse and taught school and attended the farm until 1878, when he took charge of Union University, conducting it in an able manner for five years. He then retired from a professional life to a farm that he had purchased near Murfreesboro, and where he now resides. December 26, 1860, he was married to Miss Camilla T. Patterson, of this county, and to them were born seven children, one dying in infancy; those living are Atha T., Evis C., Samuel P., Henry D., Ella and Maddie. Mr. Jamison is an unswerving Democrat. He enlisted in 1861 as private in Company D, Forty-fifth Tennessee Regiment of Infantry, and was promoted to surgeon of ambulance train. Mr. Jamison is a member of the K. of H., and he and wife are members of the Baptist Church.

JAMES F. JENKINS, a native of Rutherford County, Tenn., was born July 5, 1840, by the marriage of Hiram and Nancy (Puckett) Jenkins, natives, respectively, of Pettis County, Mo., and Rutherford County, Tenn. Hiram H. Jenkins came to Rutherford County in 1832, and settled on a farm, which he improved and enlarged to a great extent. Here he remained and farmed until his death, which occurred in December, 1870. The subject was reared on the farm and received a fair education at Union University, after which he commenced farming on his father's place until the breaking out of the war, when he enlisted in Company I, of the First Tennessee Infantry, as a private, serving three and a half years. In 1865 he went to farming again on the old place. He left there, and after moving around for some time and after his father's death, which occurred in 1868, he came back on the old place. He has since followed farming and has purchased a part of his grandfather's estate, where he has since resided. He has been quite successful and owns about 250 acres of good land. The subject was married in 1864, to Lizzie Wilson, who died in 1868. He then married Beulah Clement, a native of Gainesville, Ala. One child, Anna M., was born to him by his first wife; and by his second wife seven children have been born, namely: Clement B., Mary A., James F., Minnie S., Kate B., Ruby M. and Beulah. Mr. Jenkins is an unswerving Democrat and a member of the Methodist Episcopal Church. His wife is a member of the Baptist Church. Mr. Jenkins is one of the leading farmers and an excellent citizen.

COL. ROBERT B. JETTON, register, and native of Rutherford County, Tenn., was born February 15, 1818, and is one of eight children born to the marriage of Robert Jetton and Nancy Wilson, both natives of North Carolina. The father came to this State about the beginning of the present century. He was a farmer and a Democrat of the Jacksonian school, being a major under Jackson in the Seminole war. He was a member of the Legislature a number of terms, and was recognized as one of the leading spirits of Democracy in the county during his time. He was prominently identified with all private and public enterprises and was a member of the Old School Presbyterian Church, in which faith he died December 26, 1840. Our subject resided with his parents on the home farm and received a good collegiate education, attending the Nashville University. At the age of twenty-two he began farming for himself, continuing the same until the ravages of war almost ruined him financially. After the war he made an attempt to regain his former financial standing, and succeeded in part. Later, owing to financial embarrassments, he was compelled to abandon farming and seek other employment as a means of livelihood, and for a time was deputy under Hardy Murfree, register of the county, and served two years. Mr. Murfree died about this time and Mr. Jetton was elected to fill the unexpired term, and in 1882 was elected to the office by the people. He has been unfortunate in matrimonial affairs, having lost two wives by death. His present wife was Miss Esther L. Murfree, whom he married in 1857. They have five children living. He had one daughter by his first wife, now Mrs. G. W. Fall, of Nashville, who was reared by ex-President Polk's wife. Mr. Jetton is a Democrat and he and family are members of the Presbyterian Church.

ELIHU C. JOB, one of the enterprising farmers of Rutherford County, was born August 7, 1809, in Murry County, Tenn. He is the son of James and Catharine (Pitt) Job, natives, respectively, of Virginia and North Carolina. The father came to Maury County at an early date and settled on a farm. He is one of the constructors of the first cotton-gins in that county. His death occurred in 1833. The son was a farmer boy, and received a good common school education. At an early age he served an apprenticeship in a cabinet shop. After finishing his trade he started in business for himself in Rutherford

RUTHERFORD COUNTY. 1043

County. He purchased the farm on which he now resides, and has met with evident success. In 1833 he married Miss Mary W. Smith, and to this union were born eight children, of whom six are now living, namely: Luke E., Elizabeth C., Benjamin A., Nancy P. (wife of T. H. Hollowell), Martha A. (wife of J. T. Beesley) and Lavina S. (wife of W. T. Edwards). Mr. Job is a Master Mason and a Democrat. He is considered a good citizen and a kind neighbor.

COLUMBUS N. JOHNSON, a successful farmer, was born in Rutherford County, Tenn., in 1831, and is the son of John and Jane (Miller) Johnson, both natives of this county. The father died in the year 1866, and the mother in 1838. They were consistent members of the Baptist Church, and died happy in the faith of a blessed Redeemer. The subject of this sketch was married, in 1854, to Miss Mary Davis, and to them were born eight children, six of whom are living: Tilman D., Robert B., Raymond R., Sillie G., Charles C. and Tabitha J. When the late war broke out Mr. Johnson shouldered his musket, and with many a gallant companion enlisted in Company D, Forty-fifth Tennessee Infantry, serving in this capacity for three years. At the expiration of that time, owing to ill health, Mr. Johnson left the army and refrained from further participation in the war. Mr. Johnson is a stanch Democrat, and he and wife are members of the Baptist Church, and are kind neighbors and good citizens.

WILLIAM S. JONES & BROS., dealers in dry goods and groceries, boots and shoes, queensware and general merchandise at Jefferson, Rutherford Co., Tenn. The junior member of the firm succeeded his uncle, W. E. Jones, in 1878, in the business, and in 1886 his brother, A. M. Jones, purchased a partnership in it. The subject of our sketch, William S., was born September 9, 1840, in this State, and is the son of Albert and Nancy J. (Jones) Jones, natives, respectively, of Tennessee and Virginia. The father was one of the leading farmers of the county, a Democrat in politics, and was elected sheriff of this county for one term, and was magistrate of the Fifth District for twelve or thirteen years. Himself and family were leading members of the Presbyterian Church. Our subject was reared on the farm, and received an education like the average country boy. At the breaking out of the war he enlisted in Company E, Forty-fifth Tennessee, serving as a high private until the close of the war, when he returned home and engaged in the mercantile business with his uncle until he started in his present business in 1878. Mr. Jones is a single gentleman, a Democrat in politics and a member of the Cumberland Presbyterian Church. He is spoken of as one of the enterprising and successful business men of the county.

MRS. LIZZIE H. JONES, widow of Amzi Jones, who died November 18, 1878, is a native of this State, born at Murfreesboro September 23, 1846, being a daughter of Alfred and Narcissa (Bradford) Miller, natives, respectively, of Alabama and North Carolina. The father was a money broker of considerable note in this county. Amzi Jones was a prominent and energetic farmer of this county, born near Smyrna October 7, 1841. He lost both of his parents when an infant, and was adopted by his half-brother, Dr. George Jones, and lived the greater part of his younger days with him in Memphis, Tenn. He received his education at Georgetown, D. C., and enlisted in the army of the Confederate States at the breaking out of the war. He was wounded in the battle of Stone River, but continued in the army until the war closed. He contributed largely to the literary department of the county papers, and was a gentleman of much intelligence and possessed an untiring energy, which was depicted in a business transaction only a few hours before his death. He was always strictly exact in his business transactions, meeting his obligations faithfully and promptly. At the close of the war he was engaged in the cotton business, being a very successful trader. In 1870 he came to this county, purchasing a farm close to the one his widow now resides on, and in January, 1878, removed to her present farm, at which place he died one month later. Mr. Jones was a successful farmer, was universally esteemed, and had many friends. The subject of our sketch, Mrs. Lizzie Jones, has lived on and controlled the farm since his death, and in 1882 finished building a grist-mill which her husband had commenced shortly before his death. She has conducted this business in connection with her farming interests up until the present time. Their marriage occurred in 1869. They have one child by this union—Amzi. Mrs. Jones is a pleasant and very intelligent lady; is a member of the Methodist Church, and is justly recognized among the leading families of the county.

EDWARD L. JORDAN, president of the First National Bank of Murfreesboro, and one of Rutherford County's wealthiest and most prominent citizens. Our subject first saw the light of day in Williamson County, Tenn., July 23, 1817. Archer Jordan, our subject's father. was born in Lunenberg County, Va., about 1770, where he was reared to manhood and married our subject's mother, Elizabeth Walker, also a native of that county. In 1795 Archer Jordan emigrated West, locating first in Kentucky, but the following year came to Tennessee, and crossing the Cumberland River on the ice with his wife, and his father and family, and all their earthly possessions, which was limited to a few essential household articles, he located in Davidson County, but soon afterward removed to Williamson County, where he was elected magistrate of the district, in which he resided until his death in 1835. Edward's mother dying when he was but fourteen years of age, and his father three years later, he was left upon his own resources at the age of seventeen, and consequently his education was somewhat limited. At the age of eighteen years he entered a mercantile house at Hardeman Cross Roads, now Triune, Williamson County, as clerk, continuing three years in this capacity, when, in company with William P., son of the late Gov. Cannon, he bought out his employers, Thomas F. Perkins & Co. The new firm conducted the business successfully together until Mr. Cannon's withdrawal, in 1841, after which Mr. Jordan owned and conducted the business alone three years. He then repaired to a farm in that county, where he resided until 1851. He then removed to this city and conducted a mercantile business successfully until the breaking out of the late war, when he was compelled to close out the business, as well as many others, at a great sacrifice. Mr. Jordan was a non-participant in that bloody strife, but strongly maintained his position in favor of the preservation of the Union, although he extended a sympathizing and helping hand to his suffering and sometimes helpless brethren of the South. Mr. Jordan has always taken an active lead in all public and private enterprises in this city, and has contributed largely to the prosperity of the county. He was one of the directors of the Planters' Bank prior to the war, which was never reopened after that time, but in company with others Mr. Jordan established the savings bank, of which he was president until it united with the First National, when he became one of the directors of the latter, and finally its president, which position he fills in a faithful and highly efficient manner. He has also, since the war, devoted a great amount of time and attention to the collection of war claims from the United States Government, in which he has been very successful. Mr. Jordan has been very unfortunate in matrimonial affairs, having lost two wives by death. In 1840 he married Martha, daughter of the late Montford Fletcher, of this county. She died in 1852, leaving four children—three of whom are now living: Montford F., Mary (the widow of the late Dr. G. S. Nuckolls, of Alabama) and Leland. His union with Mrs. Jane Cook, daughter of the late James Carothers, of Williamson County, was without issue. In 1858 he was united in matrimony to Mrs. Mildred Williams, his present wife, and daughter of the late Dr. George Hopson, of Montgomery County, Tenn. The following named children are the result of this union: Maggie (the wife of the Rev. E. A. Taylor, of Knoxville, Tenn.) and Edward L. Mrs. Jordan has three children by her former marriage. They are Mrs. E. R. Thomas and Mr. H. H. Williams, of this city, and John P. Williams, vice-president of the First National Bank of Nashville. Mr. Jordan was formerly an old-line Whig before the war, but has, since that party ceased to exist, been strictly independent in his political views. Himself and wife are leading members of the Missionary Baptist Church of this city, and he is justly recognized as one of the most enterprising and successful business men of Rutherford County, and is a reliable and consistent Christian gentleman. His aged brother, Dr. Clement Jordan, is living a retired life at our subject's home, at the advanced age of eighty-five years. He also has a sister,

Mrs. Ralston, eighty-six past, living in West Tennessee. Mr. Jordan is one of six sons and six daughters who lived to maturity, who all raised large families with exception of two—three sons and one sister now living.

MINOR C. JORDAN (deceased) was a very successful agriculturist, and was a native of Rutherford County, Tenn., where he was born September 29, 1820, and is a son of Johnson and Rachel (Hill) Jordan, who were born in the "Old Dominion." Our subject was married July 20, 1842, to Miss Elizabeth W. Jordan, and to their union fourteen children were born, seven of whom are living: Martha J. (wife of D. S. McCullough), Mary W. (wife of W. T. Allison), Clement J. (married to Martha Lytle), John A., Minor C. E. James S. and Lulu B. Mr. Jordan, who was a member of the Missionary Baptist Church, died February 14, 1879. Mrs. Jordan still survives and is a member of the same church as her husband. She is very charitable to the poor and is a woman worthy of all respect.

DR. ROBERT F. KEYES, a well-known and eminently successful practitioner, was born in Ontario, in 1844, and is the son of Henry and Martha (Taylor) Keyes. The father was one of the few men who were born on the Atlantic Ocean. The mother was a native of Ireland. The subject of this sketch is a graduate of the Queen's Medical College at Weymouth, is a licentiate of Great Britain, a member of the United States Board of Health, and also a member of the State Medical Association of Tennessee. He was one of the representatives of this association at the World's Fair. The Doctor was married March 27, 1867, to Miss Josephine Hood, and this union was blessed by the birth of two children: George L. and John W. Our subject is a radical Democrat of the most pronounced type, and is a consistent member of the Baptist Church. His wife is a devout and worthy member of the Methodist Episcopal Church. The Doctor and wife are prominent and respected citizens of the community in which they reside.

CAPT. WILLIAM D. KILLOUGH, a prominent farmer of Rutherford County, Tenn., who was born in said county March 15, 1838, and is son of James and Matilda (Martin) Killough. The father was a prosperous agriculturist and engaged in commercial brokerage to a considerable extent. He was a Presbyterian and died in 1863. The mother is still living and is a resident of this county. Our subject was united in matrimony to Miss Alice Cunningham in 1872, and two children blessed their union: Martin C. and William D. Mr. Killough took an active part in the late civil war and enlisted in Company I, Forty-fifth Tennessee Infantry, and was soon made fourth corporal. He achieved distinction in this position and was raised to the rank of orderly sergeant, and was soon after promoted to first lieutenant, and later was made captain of his company and served in this capacity two years. He was wounded at Stone River and was brought home. He was paroled to report when his health would permit his rejoining his regiment, but, as there was no exchange of officers, he never reported but remained at home, not participating further in the war. The Captain is a very firm Democrat, and he and his wife are members of the Presbyterian Church and are worthy citizens of the county.

MRS. AMANDA (FRAZIER) KIMBRO, a widely known and eminently successful land-owner, was born in north Alabama, October 11, 1832. The subject of this sketch came to this country in 1852, and was wedded to John Bell Kimbro October 12, 1852. Mr. Kimbro was a gentleman possessing large business ability and wealth. He was the first president of the First National Bank at Murfreesboro, and a Union man; did not take an active part in the late war, being religiously opposed to it. In 1872 Mr. Kimbro died, leaving his wife and eight children, six of whom are now living: Clarence S., John B., Frazier, Azariah, Fitzie and La Salle. Mrs. Kimbro is a devout and consistent member of the Baptist Church; is an enterprising and estimable lady, and is justly recognized as a prominent and influential member of the community in which she lives.

COL. JAMES MOORE KING (deceased), who was one of Rutherford County's most highly respected pioneer citizens, was born near Clinton, Sampson Co., N. C., November 18, 1792. He came to this county with his mother in 1809; was a soldier in the war of 1812. He participated with his regiment and company in the battle of New Orleans, and was also a volunteer in Jackson's expedition against the Seminole Indians, taking an active part in all the battles of that campaign. He was not a regular enlisted soldier in the late war, but was engaged in seven battles and cavalry skirmishes, spending the greater part of his time during this period in the camps and on the battle field. In 1863 he went south and did not return until after the close of the war. November 29, 1821, he married Miss Martha Batey, an excellent woman, and to them were born nine children: Julia, wife of C. W. Moore; Helen J., widow of Capt. Lythe; James M.; Charles H.; Bettie K., wife of Col. Thomas G. Morley; Thomas M.; Morrison D.; John H. and William H. Charles H. King, a prominent farmer of Rutherford County, was born October 8, 1835, and is a son of Col. James Moore King. He was reared on a farm and received a fair education at Salem Academy, and at the age of eighteen took charge of his father's farm, and two years later engaged in farming on the place where he now resides, inheriting the land, which now consists of 262 acres, from his father's estate. July 18, 1856, he was married to Miss Ann Wood, and to them were born seven children: Nettie M., Mary F., George W., Pattie B., Charles H. and Anna M. Our subject is a Democrat, and in 1861 enlisted as private in Company I of First Tennessee Regiment; was promoted to lieutenant, and served one year in that capacity. He then volunteered as private in the same company, remaining until 1863, when he was paroled, and went on detached duty as a scout afterward. During the battle of Perryville he received a wound in the left arm, which disabled him from active service for three months. He is a Knight Templar, a Mason, and he and wife are members of the Methodist Episcopal and Primitive Baptist Churches respectively. John H. King, a brother of Charles H. King and a son of Col. James Moore King, was born October 10, 1845, in Rutherford County; was reared on a farm, and received a limited education. In 1867 he took charge of his father's farm and remained there one year. He then commenced for himself, farming on a portion of his father's land, where he lived until his father's death, which occurred in 1879; he then purchased the old homestead, where he now resides, and supports his aged mother. May 18, 1882, he was married to Miss Ophelia (Alexander) Rucker, and to this union was born one child—Robert P. Mr. King is a Democrat, and at the age of fourteen, in 1862, he enlisted in the war. He was a participant in all of the battles in which the command was engaged, and in 1865 returned home. He is a Master Mason, a member of the Methodist Episcopal Church, and a moral and upright citizen. William H. King, another son of Col. James Moore King, was born December 7, 1847, in Rutherford County, and received a collegiate education at Union University, in Murfreesboro. At the age of twenty-one he began farming for himself on a portion of his father's property, it afterward being deeded to him. He has succeeded remarkably well in his farming interests, and at the present he has over 200 acres of excellent land. November 29, 1871, he was married to Miss Olivia M. Jamison, and this event took place the same night of his father's golden wedding. To Mr. and Mrs. King were born seven children: S. Moulton, Jeannette M., Anna B., Henry J., John C., James R. and Dorsey T. Mr. King is a Democrat, and he and wife are members, respectively, of the Old and Primitive Baptist Churches. He is respected by all who know him, and is an honorable, upright man.

ROBERT N. KNOX, a prominent physician and farmer, was born April 7, 1846, in Rutherford County, and is the son of William F. and Armenia E. (Brown) Knox, natives of Rutherford County. The father, a successful farmer of this county, died about 1850. The son was reared on a farm and received a good literary education at Oak Hill and Science Hill Seminary of Tennessee. After reaching his majority and in order to make a livelihood, he first taught school in this county. and two years later he entered the medical university at Nashville and Vanderbilt of the same place. He graduated and received his diploma from both institutions. In 1874 he began the practice of his profession in Coffee County, and after living there one year moved to this county, where he purchased the farm where he is now living. January 4, 1871, he was married to Miss Lucy Catharine Fox, a native of this county, and to them were born the following children: Sallie E. and William C. Mr. Knox is a stanch Democrat, and enlisted in 1864 in Company E, Fourth Tennessee Cavalry, as a private, serving until the close of the war. He and wife are members of the Missionary Baptist Church.

JOHN J. LEE, farmer, was born May 1, 1845, in Rutherford County, Tenn., son of Asa and Elizabeth (Jacobs) Lee, both born in Tennessee, the former in Coffee County and the latter in Rutherford County. The father was a house carpenter, and was born in 1819 and died in 1868. He was a Democrat and a leading member of the Baptist Church. Our subject received an academic education, attending the Big Spring Academy, and after reaching his majority worked at his trade seven years. He then purchased a farm, which he worked four years. After residing in different parts of the county, he in 1881 purchased the farm where he now resides. He has made his own way in the world, and has met with well deserved success. September 9, 1866, he married Amanda M. Jernigan, who bore him nine children: Sarah E. (wife of Calvin Lowe), Anna E., Mary M., William A., Thomas E., Zoror E., Shelley J., Oder M. and Kate. Mr. Lee is a Democrat, and in July, 1864, enlisted as a private in Company E, Fourth Tennessee Cavalry, and served until the close of the war. He is a member of the I. O. O. F. and is a Master Mason, and he and wife are members of the Baptist Church.

NATHANIEL M. LEWIS, M. D., a prominent physician and merchant of Florence Station, Rutherford Co., Tenn., is a native of this county, born November 24, 1849, son of John W. and Elizabeth (Miller) Lewis. The father was a successful farmer, and is now extensively engaged in stock raising. He is a Democrat, and himself and family are members of the Primitive Baptist Church. Our subject spent his boyhood days on a farm and received but twenty months schooling until he was twenty years of age, at which time he engaged in the mercantile business under W. H. Alexander. At the age of twenty-one he returned home and attended school, and also assisted his father on the farm. He studied medicine at nights. In 1875 he engaged in the dry goods business for himself at Walter Hill, and met with good success. In 1880 he attended the Vanderbilt University at Nashville, Tenn., and graduated with first honors in 1881. He practiced medicine in Nashville during the small-pox epidemic of 1882. He then returned to his father's farm, and in 1883 engaged in merchandising in Florence, where he has continued to the present time, meeting with good success. February 6, 1883, he was married to Miss Estella L. Andrews, daughter of John T. Andrews, deputy clerk of the Williamson County Court for a number of years. Dr. Lewis is a well known and prominent physician, and is one of the leading business men of the county.

L. K. LOWE, an enterprising and successful farmer, was born in Wilson County, this State, January 9, 1837, and is the son of Neri and Elizabeth (Keeling) Lowe, both of whom were natives of this State. The subject of this sketch was married September, 1860, to Miss Mary E. Davis, and to this short but happy wedded life were born three children, two of whom are living, namely: Margaret E. and Rosy B. Mr. Lowe was soon called to mourn the death of his wife which occurred in 1866. In the year 1870 he took for his second wife Miss Sophia P. Williams, and to this happy union nine children were born, seven of whom are living: Elizabeth P., James W., William T., George K., Leonard K., Effie S. and Mary D. Mr. Lowe took an active part in the late war, enlisting in the Third Kentucky Cavalry, serving in this capacity until his capture, which occurred May 10, 1863. He was soon exchanged, and returned to his original command, where he remained until the close of the war. He is a Democrat of the most pronounced type, and he and wife are worthy members of the Missionary Baptist Church, and are respected by all who know them.

JAMES M. LOYD, a prominent teacher and citizen of Smyrna, Tenn., is a native of the State, born in Wilson County, March 9, 1838, son of James and Matilda (Morris) Loyd, born in Alabama and Tennessee, respectively. The father was a farmer, and died February 17, 1852. The mother died in 1869. Our subject secured a limited early education, but finished his education by hard study at home. At the age of twenty years he began teaching school, and has since made that his profession. August 12, 1885, he came to Smyrna, where he has had charge of the schools, and is considered an excellent instructor. He is very original in his methods of instructing, and does not confine himself to the text-books. He has gained the confidence and respect of the patrons, and has made the school a complete success. January 29, 1885, he wedded Miss Sallie Garrett, daughter of George C. Garrett.

MOSES S. LYNCH may be mentioned as a successful farmer and blacksmith of Rutherford County, Tenn., and was born July 27, 1833, son of Ecasmur C. and Sallie (Swan) Lynch. The father was a farmer and brick-mason, and at the present time is a resident of Georgia. The mother was a worthy member of the Presbyterian Church, and died in 1864. May 20, 1858, our subject, Moses S., married Drucilla Numan, and they became the parents of the following children: Robert H., Catharine (wife of Thomas Hayes), James S., Oliver S., Arthur B. and Leonard. Mr. Lynch was an active soldier in the late war, and enlisted in Company F, Forty-fifth Tennessee, and served two months. At the expiration of that time he was detailed to the railroad, owing to his superior mechanical qualifications, and remained in that service until the close of the war. He is a very stanch Democrat, and is at the present time magistrate of his district, serving in this capacity for fourteen years. He is a Presbyterian in belief, and his wife is a member of the same church. They are excellent citizens, and have many friends where they reside.

DR. WILLIAM H. LYTLE, a practicing physician, was born in this county September 30, 1827, and is the son of William and Violet (Henderson) Lytle, natives, respectively, of Tennessee and North Carolina. The father was a man of energy and perseverence, and his death was universally regretted. The Doctor studied medicine under the eminent physicians—Drs. Wendel & Watson. Our subject's marriage to Miss Lavinia J. Dashiell, was solemnized in 1849. To this union were born six children—three of whom are living: Annie R., wife of John B. Johns: Violet H., wife of Leroy B. Wade, and Sophia D., wife of Frank Henderson. The Doctor did not participate in the late civil war between the North and South, but his sympathies were with the South. The Doctor and wife are exemplary members of the Presbyterian Church, and have the confidence and respect of all their acquaintances.

MRS. JULIA LYTLE, an enterprising and eminently successful land owner, was born in this county in 1824 and is the daughter of Col. William and Sarah (Morton) Searcy, natives, respectively, of North Carolina and Virginia. The father died in the year 1846, and the mother in 1832. The subject of this sketch was married June 12, 1844, to Col. Ephraim F. Lytle, and to this union were born eight children—seven of whom are living: Mary E., wife of Henry Murphy, a prominent farmer of this county; Catherine, widow of Robert Lytle; Sallie E., wife of E. C. Cannon, a merchant at Murfreesboro; John; Lizzie S., wife of H. D. Nichol, of Davidson County; E. F. and Thomas B. Mr. Lytle took an active part in the late civil war between the North and South, and was made lieutenant-colonel of the Forty-fifth Tennessee Infantry, and served in this capacity until the beginning of 1863. At that time his health failed and he resigned his commission and refrained from further participation in the war. He was a Methodist in inclination and was justly regarded a moral, upright man. He departed this life February 10, 1868. Mrs. Lytle still survives him and is a consistent member of the Methodist Episcopal Church.

DR. A. W. MANIRE, a prominent and eminently successful practitioner, was born in this county February 8, 1837, and is the son of Lemuel and Susan (Jackson) Manire, both natives of Virginia. The subject of this sketch was married March 11, 1858, to Miss Julia W. White, and to this union were born the following children: Dr. John W., Eliza J., wife of John Lamb; Josephine, wife of J. N. Cothran; Florence E.; Julia A.; Susan O. and Ella M. The Doctor is a stanch Democrat and is now a candidate for, and will probably be elected, clerk of the circuit court. The Doctor took an active part in the late civil war, enlisting in Company A, Twenty-fourth Tennessee, serving in the capacity of hospital steward and detailed assistant surgeon. He resigned his commission in 1862, came home and resumed his practice and has been an active practitioner ever since. The Doctor is a member of the Primitive Baptist and his wife of the Cumberland Presbyterian Church, and they are justly recognized as influential citizens of the community.

WELCOM MANKIN was born October 5, 1835, in Rutherford County, Tenn., son of

John and Elizabeth (Hodge) Mankin, natives of North Carolina and Tennessee, respectively. The father came to Tennessee at an early day and located on a farm in Rutherford County, where he resided until his death, June 8, 1883. The mother departed this life February 14, 1879. Welcom Mankin received a fair English education in the common schools and at the age of twenty years began earning his own living by farming on his father's place, which was subsequently deeded to him. In 1871 he purchased the place where he now resides, and is well fixed financially. February 25, 1860, he was married to Miss Sarah Lyon, who bore him two children: J. E. (wife of W. R. Manley), and John P. Mrs. Mankin died December 3, 1863, and September 17, 1866, he wedded Mrs. Louisa Harrison, and to them were born three children, only one now living: Samuel W. In April, 1861, Mr. Mankin enlisted as a private in Company F, Second Tennessee Regiment, and served in that capacity until the close of the war. July 19, 1864, he was taken prisoner at Peach Tree Creek and was kept at Camp Douglas, Chicago, Ill., nine months, and was then moved to Point Lookout, Md., and there remained until the close of the war. Mr. Mankin and wife are members of the Christian Church.

BENTON P. MANKIN, a successful farmer and stock raiser of Rutherford County, was born November 12, 1843, and is the son of John and Elizabeth (Hodge) Mankin, natives, respectively, of North Carolina and Tennessee. Our subject was reared on a farm and received a limited education as he attended school but a short time before the war broke out. After reaching his majority he began farming and so continued until the death of his father, when he moved to the old homestead. In 1884 he purchased and moved to the place where he now resides. In 1877 he was married to Miss Alice F. Hearn, of Wilson County, and to this union have been born two children: Mardilla H. and Mary L. In 1884 he married Miss S. J. Atkinson, of this county, and one child, Jessie J., has blessed this union. Mr. Mankin is a stanch Democrat and enlisted in Company E, Fourth Tennessee Cavalry, as a private. He took an active part in most of the battles in which his command was engaged, and was wounded at Thompson's Station and a second time near Knoxville, being off duty one month. At the close of the war he returned home and attended school, going at intervals and farming until 1869, when he attended strictly to his farm duties. He and wife are members of the Christian Church and he is justly considered one of the leading farmers of the county.

REV. JOHN J. MARTIN, a retired minister of Milton, Rutherford Co., Tenn., was born in Wilson County, Tenn., March 24, 1811, being a son of Jacob and Mary (Wallace) Martin, both of whom were born in South Carolina. The father was of German parentage and came to this State in 1810, being one of the early settlers of Wilson County, and a farmer by occupation. He was an old-time Whig and was magistrate in his county for upward of twenty years. His death occurred in 1864 and the mother's in 1873. The subject, John J., was reared by his parents on the farm, where he remained until he was twenty-one years of age, securing but a limited education in early days. He subsequently attended the Lascasas Academy with a view to making school-teaching his profession, and afterward taught the young idea in that vicinity for fifteen years, also giving part of his attention to ministerial work. He afterward gave all his attention to the ministry until his health failed in 1885. In February, 1849, he wedded Mrs. Elizabeth Winsepp, his first wife being Miss North Vaughan. She died in 1848. To them were born two children, both of whom are dead. Mr. Martin has a wide-spead reputation as a learned minister of the gospel and is recognized as an excellent citizen.

WILLIAM MASON, an enterprising farmer, was born in Rutherford County, Tenn., July 31, 1827, and is the son of Reynear H. and Elizabeth (Moss) Mason, natives, respectively, of Virginia and this State. The father, an early settler of Williamson County, Tenn., came to this county in 1821 and purchased the farm William Mason now lives on. He was a Whig in politics and was constable of the Second District from 1824 to 1833, also justice of the peace. His death occurred January 2, 1852. The mother died in 1881. The subject of our sketch was a country boy and received his education in the country schools, which at that early time were held in the primitive log schoolhouses. At the age of twenty-one he was elected constable of the Second District, and in 1849 he purchased his present farm, which consists of 1,400 acres of good land. He was re-elected constable in 1852 and deputy sheriff in 1856. In 1858 he was again elected sheriff and was re-elected in 1862. He was elected magistrate of the Second District, and is now holding the office. On October 3, 1864, he was married to his second wife, Miss Frances J. Sanders, a native of this State, and to this union were born eight children : William A., Dora C., Daisy L., M. A., Eulolia P., Sanders, R. H., Moss G. and Parthenia M. His first marriage was with Miss Martha J. Hoover, who died August 22, 1862. To this union were born four children : Isabella H., Robert T., Pleasant P. and Martha J., all of whom are living. Mr. Mason is an attendant at and his family are leading members of the Methodist Episcopal Church. He is classed among the enterprising and successful farmers of the county.

PLEASANT P. MASON, attorney at law, of Murfreesboro, Tenn., was born March 23, 1860, and is the son of William N. and Martha J. (Hoover) Mason, both born in Rutherford County, Tenn. The father is a well-to-do citizen of the county. Pleasant P. secured a good literary education in the public schools and also by desultory study. At the age of twenty he entered the law department of the Cumberland University at Lebanon, Tenn., and graduated in June, 1881. He came to Murfreesboro and in January, 1882, was admitted to the bar and practiced his profession two years with ex-Congressman Sheafe. Since that time he has practiced his profession alone and has met with well-deserved success. November 29, 1882, he was united in marriage to Miss Richie H. Keeble, who was born in the county. They have one son, Richard K. Mr. Mason is a Democrat in politics and has taken quite an interest in the political affairs of the State and county, being appointed State's attorney February 1, 1885, and at the same time was chosen attorney for Rutherford County. He is at present a candidate for attorney-general for Davidson and Rutherford Counties, subject to election August 5, 1886. He was nominated by a convention composed of the justices of the peace of Rutherford County, on the 5th day of April, 1886, as Rutherford County's candidate for this position, defeating his opponent, Edgar P. Smith, a lawyer many years his senior and considered among the most popular men in Rutherford County. He is one of the rising members of the Rutherford County bar, and belongs to the K. of H., and he and wife are members of the Presbyterian Church.

JOHN B. McCLANAHAN, an eccentric old resident of Rutherford County, Tenn., was born February 17, 1820, being a son of Matthew and a grandson of Samuel McClanahan, who came from Culpepper County, Va., to Rutherford County in 1801, Samuel's father having come to that State from his native country (Ireland) with his two brothers presumably 300 years ago. Samuel McClanahan was a major in the Revolutionary war, and after his removal to this county participated in the war of 1812 with Gen. Jackson, as major, Matthew being also a participant in the latter war and a colonel in the Florida war. He (our subject's father) was born in Virginia, and after the Indian trouble had subsided he followed farming in this county, being, as was his father, a Democrat politically. He was the second sheriff of the county and afterward represented the county in the State Legislature. Our subject's maternal grandfather, Mr. Bradley, had a noted race track on his farm two and one-half miles north of Murfreesboro, on what is now the Johnson farm. This course was largely attended yearly by some of the most noted turfmen of Tennnessee, Mississippi, Kentucky, Alabama and Virginia. John B. was a professional rider at these races in his boyhood days and has set astride of many of Gen. Jackson's coursers, as well as others equally noted, often riding sixteen miles in one race before it came to a finish. Our subject's father and grandsire died in this county, both having spent long and useful lives, the latter having attained his one hundredth year and outliving our subject's father, who died about 1835. John B. has emulated the example of his sires only partially. He adheres to their strict examples of honesty and sobriety but has never aspired to any honors or position other than to attend to his farm and command the respect of his neighbors and friends. He has in his possession, as relics, a pair of silver knee-buckles that were made in Ireland over 300 years ago, and a glass bottle that was made there which is nearly as old. He has been twice married, having lost his first wife by death. He has two sons. He was a private in Company I, Forty-fifth Regiment, Tennessee Confederate Infantry, and served until the surrender. He has quite a notoriety in the county as a breeder and raiser of game chickens, having some handsome specimens of the same at his little place near Murfreesboro. He is a Democrat.

MR. LEVI McCLURE, a native of Augusta County, Va., and son of John and Elizabeth (Graham) McClure, who emigrated, or were driven from Georgetown, S. C., by the Tories during the Revolution, was born May 29, 1806. Our subject received a limited education, but being a lover of literature, particularly historical and biographical, read all that came in his way, and by this means his education was considerably enhanced. Leaving Virginia at the age of twenty-one, with his mother and brother and sister, he immigrated to Green County, Ohio, near Xenia, where he worked at the brick-mason's trade until he had accumulated a sufficient amount to purchase a large farm in Shelby County, Ohio. In the year 1841 he married Miss Charlotte Moffet, whose parents were from Lexington, Ky., her father a descendant of the celebrated hunter, Daniel Boone, and her mother a near relative of Jesse Grant, father of U. S. Grant. Mr. and Mrs. McClure's wedded life was blessed by these children: John H. (deceased), Frank W., William G., James F., Curtiss H., Augustus L., Sarah E. (deceased), Mary J. and Margaret A. During the late war our subject took quite an active part, sending four sons to assist the Federals during the civil war. After moving about for some years he concluded to pass the residue of his life in the "Sunny South," and bought a large farm and settled near Murfreesboro, Tenn., on the Franklin road. The family was trained under the influence of the Old School Presbyterian Church.

DR. WILLIAM H. McCORD, a successful practitioner, was born in Marshall County, Tenn., September 1, 1838, and is the son of Allen and Jane (Jordan) McCord, both natives of this State, who with their parents endured all the hardships and privations of those early times. The Doctor is a graduate of the University of Louisiana City of New Orleans. His marriage with Miss Sarah Williams was solemnized November 24, 1868, and by this union the following children were born: William E., John H., Emmet A. and Anna V. The Doctor is a Democrat in politics and took an active part in the late civil war between the North and the South. He enlisted in Gen. Forrest's company and was surgeon in the Eighth Tennessee Cavalry, serving in this capacity throughout the entire war. The Doctor and wife are leading members of the Missionary Baptist Church, and the Doctor is considered one of the best physicians in the county, and has an extensive practice.

McFADDEN & SON, merchants of Murfreesboro, Tenn. The business was begun by James S. McFadden in 1852, but was closed at the beginning of the war and resumed in 1866. For the last two years his son, Edgar S., has been his partner. He sold out his stock in March, 1885, and in September of that year established his present general merchandise store, and is making life a success financially. James S. McFadden is the oldest merchant of Rutherford County, and was born near Murfreesboro December 14, 1823, being a son of Samuel and Hollie (Posey) McFadden, natives of South Carolina. The father came to Tennessee when a boy and was reared on a farm in Davidson County. He came to Rutherford County and located on a farm where he reared his family of fourteen children, and was a successful farmer. He was magistrate of his district a number of years and died in 1852. James S. McFadden secured a fair education in his boyhood days, and at the age of eighteen came to this city and engaged as clerk in the mercantile business and worked one year for W. H. Lytle & W. R. McFadden, and then went to Milton with the latter, with whom he remained one year. He engaged in the business for himself in 1844 in Milton, following that occupation there and in Wilson County for nearly two years, and then went to Mississippi, where he remained about six years. In 1851 he returned to Murfreesboro, and in 1852 engaged in the general merchandise business, which he has continued ever since, with the exception of four years during the war, when he was badly crippled financially. March 13, 1844, he married Miss Elizabeth A. Morgan, who bore him six children, five living: Anna E., James T., Laura C., Walter M. and

Edgar S. Mr. McFadden was an old time Whig, but is now a Democrat. He was not a participant in the war, but sympathized with the Southern cause. He has been alderman of the city for a number of terms, is a Mason, Knight Templar degree, and he and wife are members of the Presbyterian Church.

JAMES L. McKNIGHT, proprietor of a livery stable at Murfreesboro, Tenn., is a successor of J. H. Major in the business, commencing in 1881. In 1885 his buildings caught fire and were consumed together with about $4,500 worth of stock and vehicles. He afterward opened his present stables and now has an excellent lot of horses and carriages. Mr. McKnight is a native of Tennessee, born May 22, 1857, and is a son of A. D. and Mary (Hare) McKnight, also born in Tennessee. The father was a farmer for many years and good luck attended his efforts. He is now residing with the subject of our sketch, who remained on the farm with his parents until seventeen years old, securing a good education. He was then engaged in the mercantile business with E. Rosenfield for five years, and afterward with H. H. Kerr, with whom he remained until 1881, when he engaged in his present business. December 27, 1882, he was married to Miss Susie Pitts, who bore him two children, both now deceased. Mr. McKnight is a Democrat in politics, and his wife is a member of the Methodist Church. He is courteous and accommodating in his business transactions, and has a fair share of the trade in city and county.

GEORGE W. McLAUGHLIN, a prominent farmer of Rutherford County, Tenn., was born August 5, 1827, in Davison County, Tenn., and is the son of William H. and Catharine (Peebles) McLaughlin, natives respectively of Rowan and Warren County, N. C. The father immigrated to Davidson County in 1800, and settled on the farm, operated a tannery and attended the farm duties. In 1810 he was elected colonel of the State militia, between Nashville and Stewart Creek, and was trustee and one of the founders of the Washington Institutions. He resided in Davidson County until his death, which occurred in February, 1854. The son was reared on the farm and received a good literary education at Pleasant Grove Seminary and Washington Institute. After reaching his majority, he taught school in different localities. September 16, 1855, he was married to Miss Tennissee L. Morton, and became the father of five children: Joseph W., James M., Mary N., William H., Ervin M. After his marriage, he purchased the farm where he now resides. Mr. McLaughlin was a Whig before the war, and since has voted the Democratic ticket. He held the office of justice of the peace from 1865 till 1877. He and family are members of the Christian Church, and are good conscientious people.

THOMAS B. MILES. Pattison Miles, the father of Thomas B., was a son of Thomas and Nancy (Pattison) Miles, natives respectively of Virginia and North Carolina. Thomas Miles served seven years in the Revolutionary war in the capacity of lieutenant. He came to Tennessee with his family and negroes in 1792, settling in Williamson County. He died in 1837, and his wife in 1846. Pattison Miles died in 1873; he was an old time Whig, a member of the Methodist Church and a farmer by occupation. His wife, formerly Dicey Moore of Kentucky, died in 1882. Thomas B. Miles, the subject of our sketch, was born near Triune, Williamson Co., Tenn., February 14, 1814, and remained on the farm until seventeen years of age. He received a limited early education, but at the age of eighteen, engaged in the mercantile business in Jefferson, Tenn., remaining until 1840, and for the next five years resided on a farm which he had purchased near Murfreesboro. From that date until 1850, he managed a cotton plantation in Mississippi, meeting with good success. At the latter date he returned to Tennessee, farmed near Overalls Creek for about eight years, and then resided on another farm near Murfreesboro. In 1866 he moved to the town where he was engaged in mercantile pursuits until 1874, and then clerked for different firms until 1882, when he engaged in his present business of keeping the hotel known as the Commercial Men's Home at Murfreesboro. He keeps a first-class house in every respect, and is known to be strictly exact in all his dealings. June 9, 1841, he wedded Miss Catherine E. Johns, born in Tennessee, in 1822. Thomas B. is a Democrat, and he and wife are leading members of the Methodist Church.

I. D. MILLER, an eminently successful agriculturist, was born in Rutherford County,

Tenn., January 6, 1855, and is the son of Alfred and Narciora (Bradford) Miller, natives, respectively, of North Carolina and Alabama. The father was a hatter by trade but spent the latter part of his life in commercial brokerage, and his death, which occurred June 24, 1867, was universally regretted by all his acquaintances. The mother was a good Christian woman and died with full confidence of a blessed hereafter, April 14, 1875. Our subject received a collegiate education attending the noted military college of Frankfort, Ky.; he also took a thorough course at the Commercial College of Evansville, Ind. On September 18, 1883, his marriage to Miss Mamie Elam was solemnized; the fruits of this union was one child, I. M. Mr. Miller is a Democrat and is now a candidate for, and will probably be elected county court clerk. Mrs. Miller is a leading member of the Presbyterian Church, and the family are respected by all who know them.

WILLIAM MITCHELL, president of Stone River Bank, and a prominent business man of Murfreesboro, Tenn., first saw the light of day in Rutherford County, July 8, 1840. Col. Addison Mitchell, our subject's father, was a native of North Carolina and came to this county with his parents, locating on a farm where he was raised. He was married in this county to our subject's mother, Mary A. Hodge, and they raised a family of three children, including William. The father was a colonel in the Confederate Army and met his death in the spring of 1863 at Iuka, Miss. William obtained a good education in his youthful days at the Union University of this city and the Cumberland University of Lebanon, Tenn. Upon the breaking out of the late war, he enlisted as a private in Company I, First Regiment of Tennessee Infantry, serving one year in this capacity, when he was prompted to first lieutenant of the Fourth Confederate Tennessee Regiment, serving in this capacity and later as captain of Company I, of this regiment, until near the close of the war. He then repaired to his farm in this county, which he managed in a successful manner until 1879, when he moved to Murfreesboro and engaged in the general merchandise business with Hodge, Smith & Co., with whom he remained, sharing equally in the success of that well-known firm until January of 1885, when he engaged in a similar business for and by himself and has met with his usual good and well-deserved success in this enterprise. He dealt exclusively in grain, cotton and provisions during 1885, but in 1886 added a large stock of groceries and general merchandise, and now controls a large share of the trade in this combined line in the city and county. In 1871 Mr. Mitchell took unto himself a wife in the person of Mary E. Howse, of Rutherford County. He is one of the firm and unswerving but progressive Democrats of the county, has attained the Knight Templar and Scottish Rite degrees in Masonry, and has been among the foremost in all public and private enterprises that are conducive to the prosperity of his native county. He has been a stock-holder in the Stone River Bank for some years, and January 1, 1885, was made its president, which position he has since filled in a faithful and efficient manner. Himself and wife are members of the Presbyterian Church.

DR. JAMES B. MURFREE, an old and prominent physician of Murfreesboro, Tenn., is a native of this county, born September 16, 1835, and is the son of Matthias B. and Mary A. (Roberts) Murfree, both of whom were natives of North Carolina. The father was one of the first settlers of this county, from whose family the town of Murfreesboro derives its name. His death occurred September 15, 1856. The mother died July, 1857. The subject of our sketch was reared on the farm and received his education at Union University, Murfreesboro, and received the degree of A. M., from that institution. At the age of eighteen he was engaged in the mercantile business for two years. In the summer of 1856 he commenced studying medicine with a view of making it a profession, and October, 1856, entered the medical department of the University of Nashville. In 1857 Mr. Murfree entered the Jefferson Medical College, of Philadelphia, taking two courses of lectures. In March, 1859, he graduated at the above college with the degree of M. D. He then returned home and began the practice of medicine, which he continued until the breaking out of the war, when he enlisted in Company I, First Tennessee Volunteers, and served as a private until June, when he was appointed surgeon and was afterward ordered to Knoxville, Tenn., and assigned to duty as assistant surgeon at that place. In September, 1861, he was commissioned assistant surgeon of the Confederate Army. At the close of the war he returned home and resumed the practice of medicine with good success up to the present date. Dr. Murfree is a Democrat in politics and served two terms as mayor of Murfreesboro during 1874-75. Himself and family are leading members of the Presbyterian Church. In 1862 Mr. Murfree was united in marriage to Miss Ada J. Talley, a native of this county and a daughter of Maj. P. C. Talley. To Mr. and Mrs. Murfree were born nine children: Hordy, Talley, Jane R., Ada J., James B., Fannie D., Libbie M., Mary R. and Matthias B., all of whom are living. Dr. Murfree is classed as one of the leading physicians of Murfreesboro and Rutherford County.

JOHN M. NAYLOR, a retired merchant of Rutherford County, was born October 6, 1848, in Bedford County, Tenn., and is the son of Wade H. and Hannah (McMinn) Naylor, natives, respectively, of South Carolina and Bedford County, Tenn. The father, a prominent farmer of this county, moved to Bedford County in 1827, and came to this county some years later, and settled on a farm where he remained until his death, which occurred November 17, 1857. Our subject was reared on a farm, and received a fair education at the common schools of the county. At the age of fifteen he was left in charge of his mother's farm, where he remained until after the war, attending school until 1872, when he engaged in merchandising in Fosterville. In 1885 he sold out and moved to the place where he now resides. He has met with well deserved success, having a good farm of 120 acres. January 20, 1876, he was married to Miss Jessie Robinson, daughter of Dr. George W. Robinson, an eminent practitioner of this county, and captain of a company of cavalry under Forrest; was killed at Richmond, Ky. To Mr. and Mrs. Naylor were born three children: Eugene B., William E. and Arthur T.; they also have an adopted child, Lavie M. Robinson, who was an orphan of his wife's brother. Mr. Naylor is a Democrat, and he and wife are members of the Missionary Baptist Church.

MOSES A. NELSON was born in Bedford County Tenn., September 22, 1838, son of Benjamin A. and Agnes J. (Nelson) Nelson, natives also of Bedford County, and residents of the same. Our subject's grandfather, Moses Nelson, was one of the first settlers of Middle Tennessee. The subject of this sketch was reared on a farm in his native county, and received an ordinary education. In May, 1861, he enlisted in Company B, Eleventh Regular Tennessee Infantry, and served in the Confederate Army until the close of the war. He was promoted during service, to first lieutenant, and paroled as such at Greensboro, N. C. He then returned home, and in 1868 removed to Murfreesboro and engaged in the liquor and restaurant business, and has continued to the present time. He keeps a strictly first-class house, and controls the leading trade in his line in the city. In July, 1855, Mr. Nelson leased the opera house in Murfreesboro, and has managed it very successfully to the present time. In 1866 he was united in marriage to Miss Kate R. Melchar, a native of Arkansas. They have six children living—three sons and three daughters. In politics Mr. Nelson is a Democrat, though he was raised a Whig and voted that ticket previous to the war.

JOSEPH G. NELSON, druggist, of Murfreesboro, Tenn., and a native of the city, was born September 17, 1843, being a son of the late Joseph W. and Mary (Graves) Nelson, natives, respectively, of Prince Edward's County, Va., and Alabama. The father was born in 1803, and came to Rutherford County, Tenn., in 1815, and was a resident of Murfreesboro for more than half a century. He was energetic, industrious and possessed the attributes that make an excellent man and citizen. His death, which occurred when he was seventy-nine years of age, was much deplored by his many relatives and friends. He was buried in Evergreen Cemetery by the side of his wife, whose death preceded his several years. Joseph G. Nelson received an ordinary education, and in 1861 enlisted as private in Company C, Eighteenth Tennessee Regular Infantry, and served until the close of the war. After his return home he clerked in his father's store until the latter's death, in 1882, when he assumed control and management, and has since carried on his drug store with perfect success. Mr. Nelson is a Democrat and is unmarried. He is wide awake and promises to be one of the first business men of the city.

JAMES O. OSLIN, of Murfreesboro, Tenn., was born in Rutherford County, Tenn., September 22, 1835, a son of Lucas and Mary A. (Arnold) Oslin, who were both born in Virginia, and came to Tennessee in 1825 and settled in Rutherford County. In January, 1850, they removed to Murfreesboro, at which place his father died in 1851, and his mother in 1864. After the death of his father his mother remained a widow the balance of her life. They both died members of the Methodist Episcopal Church South. James spent his early days on a farm and secured a limited education. He learned the brick-mason and plasterer's trade, and followed that occupation until the war between the States, when he, in April, 1861, enlisted as private in Company A, Second Tennessee Infantry, and served until the battle of Chickamauga, where he lost his left leg. He was in the first battle of Manassas, Shiloh, Richmond, Ky.; Perryville, Ky., and Stone River. He never missed a battle or skirmish that his regiment engaged in until after he had lost his leg, as above stated. After he was wounded he remained with kind friends and relatives in Alabama and Georgia until the close of the war. He returned home in July, 1865, and engaged as clerk in a mercantile store, and after a year or more he accepted the position of deputy register of Rutherford County, continuing until January, 1870, when he was elected recorder of the city of Murfreesboro, serving but three months, when he resigned and became a candidate for the office of county court clerk, and was elected in August, 1870, under the new State constitution, and served by re-election until 1878. In March, 1879, he engaged in the sale and livery stable business, and while he remained as one of the proprietors of the "City Stables" he did the leading business of the city, and has been fairly prosperous. Mr. Oslin is an own cousin of the gunner, James Oslin, of Vicksburg, Miss., who threw the grape-shot referred to in the history of the Mexican war at the battle of Buena Vista, where Gen. Taylor told Capt. Bragg to "give 'em a little more grape, Capt. Bragg, a little more grape." Mr. Oslin in a stanch Democrat and a member of the Methodist Episcopal Church South. He belongs to the I. O. O. F., K. of H. and A. O. U. W. fraternities. He is the owner of the Stone River Stock Farm, near the city, and gives nearly his entire time and attention to breeding Holstein, Friesian cattle, some of which are second to none in America.

REV. WILLIAM B. OWEN was born in the "Old Dominion" June 29, 1825, and is a son of Thomas and Sallie (Stewart) Owen, who were born in the same State. They came to Rutherford County, Tenn., in 1840, and followed the lives of farmers. The father was also a minister of the Baptist Church. He died November 20, 1859, and the mother in 1835. William B. Owen was reared on the farm with his father, and secured a good common school education. He attended the Stone River Academy, and at the age of twenty-two began working for himself on his father's farm. In 1850 he purchased the place where he now lives, and March 8, 1860, he wedded Betty M. Nance, a native of the State and daughter of Elder Josiah C. Nance, a well-known farmer and minister of Davidson County. To them were born these children, all of whom are dead: Josiah W., died April 15, 1883, and Eugenia S., died April 14, 1883. Mr. Owen is classed among the successful farmers of the county in which he resides, and is a man strictly honest and fair in his business transactions.

NATHANIEL OWEN, an old and prominent farmer of Rutherford County, Tenn., was born in Virginia October 9, 1820, and is a son of Thomas and Sallie (Stewart) Owen, who were also born in the State of Virginia. Nathaniel Owen, the subject of this memoir, remained and assisted his parents on the farm until he was twenty years of age, securing but a limited education. He then began tilling the soil on his own account, and has since been steadily engaged at that work, and has met with the success that has always attends industry, economy and fair dealing. December 23, 1857, he was united in marriage to Miss Mary E. McNeil, of Rutherford County. They have six children: Mary A. (wife of John Pitts), Thomas E., Martha L., John W., Lillie V. and Sally C., all of whom are living. Mr. Owen is independent in his political views, and he and family are leading members of the Baptist Church.

GEN. JOSEPH B. PALMER, a well-known and prominent member of the Rutherford County bar, was born in this county November 1, 1825. He is a son of William H. and Mildred C. (Johns) Palmer, who were natives, respectively, of Halifax County, Va., and Rutherford County, Tenn. William H. Palmer secured a liberal education in his early days, attending not only literary but medical institutions of learning in his native State. About the year 1820, having attained his majority, he immigrated to this county, where he married soon after, and locating on a farm followed agricultural pursuits until 1830, when his wife died and he removed to Illinois and followed the practice of medicine until his death in that State, when Joseph B. was still quite young. After his mother's death and his father's departure for Illinois, our subject, Joseph B., was taken to raise by his maternal grandparents, Joseph B. and Elizabeth Johns. He received a good collegiate education early in life, attending the old Union University of Murfreesboro. After completing his literary education he followed school teaching in the county one year, in order to secure means enough to enable him to begin the study of law. Later he entered the office of Hardy M. Burton, of this city, with whom he read law until March, 1848, when he had so far mastered his profession as to be admitted to the Rutherford County bar, and opening an office in this city he engaged in the practice, gradually increasing his reputation as a lawyer until the breaking out of the late war, when he renounced a large and lucrative practice, and in May, 1861, organized a company of infantry from here, of which he was elected captain, but immediately proceeded to organize the Eighteenth Regiment of Tennessee Infantry, and was elected colonel of the same. He served with this renowned and gallant regiment in the capacity of colonel, and later in command of a brigade until July, 1864, when he was commissioned a brigadier-general. The history of this well-known regiment will give evidence of the gallant and soldierly bearing of our subject during its many and repeated engagements throughout the entire war. As an instance of the same we might mention the capture of the General with nearly his entire regiment and Floyd's entire command at the battle of Fort Donelson. He was imprisoned by the Federals at Fort Warren eight months, when he was exchanged and soon after returned to his command. In the engagement at Stone River the General was three times wounded while leading his regiment in the famous and fatal Breckinridge charge, but, notwithstanding his wounds were severe, he did not leave the field until the close of the battle, when he lay disabled from his wounds until April, 1863. He then resumed his command at Tullahoma, and was again seriously wounded at Chickamauga while leading a charge, it being thought at the time that his wound was mortal; but he so far recovered as to participate in the Dalton-Atlanta campaign; then returned with Hood's campaign to Tennessee, and in company with other brigades covered Hood's retreat from Nashville to across the Tennessee River. The General was a participant in the closing battle of the war, at Bentonville, N. C., having his horse shot from under him and himself receiving a slight flesh wound. As is well known, shortly before the close of the war Gen. Palmer was placed in charge of all the Confederate Tennessee soldiers, and he surrendered and disbanded them, as brave a body of men and officers as ever raised a weapon in defense of their property, wives and families. At the close of the war the General returned home and resumed his legal practice, in which he has remained continuously to the present time, meeting with more than ordinary and well-deserved success, the law firm of Palmer & Palmer, of which he is the senior member, ranking among the first at the Rutherford County bar. In February, 1854, the General was united in matrimony to Miss Ophelia M. Burrus, who died July 8, 1856, leaving one son, Horace E. June 10, 1869, he married his present wife, who was Mrs. Margaret J. Mason, of Pulaski, Tenn. There are no children of this union. The General was originally an old-line Whig, and was the acknowledged leader of the party in this county a number of years prior to the war. He represented this District in the State Legislature in the session of 1849-50, also 1851-52. Gen. Palmer was a firm supporter of the Union before and up to the firing upon Fort Sumter, being decidedly averse to secession of the Southern States. But when the unfortunate crisis was attained and the Union was virtually broken and out of existence, he took up the cause of his people, solely from a strict sense of duty and his conscientious convictions of honor and right, and so conducted his course through the entire war as to emphasize and verify this fact beyond a doubt. Since the war he has been an uncompromising Democrat in his political views. The General is a Mason of high standing, having attained the Knight Templar and Scottish Rite degrees, and is Past Grand Commander, also Knight Templar of Tennessee. He is a leading member of the Methodist Episcopal Church South, of this city. His entire military, official and legal career has been such as to command the love and esteem of his friends and the respect of his enemies, if any there be of the latter, and he is justly recognized as an enterprising and reliable business man, an able and experienced jurist and practitioner and a consistent Christian citizen, to whom the citizens of "old Rutherford" may refer with pride and esteem.

HORACE E. PALMER, attorney at law, and mayor of the city of Murfreesboro, Tenn., a native of the city, and only son of Gen. Joseph B. Palmer, was born September 26, 1855. Horace was educated in the Union University, his father's old *alma mater*, and would have graduated there, but for the suspension of the institution in September 1873. He then attended the University of Virginia at Charlottsville, taking an eclectic course. In the fall of 1875 he began the study of law in his father's office, and the following year attended the Lebanon (Tenn.) Law School, from which he graduated June 7, 1877. He was admitted to the Rutherford County bar the following month and began the practice alone, continuing successfully until January 1879, when he formed his present partnership with his father, in which he has shared equally the success of this well-known legal firm. May 15, 1879, he married Willie T. Mason, of Giles County, Tenn. They have three children by this union, named William M., Joseph B., and Horace E. Mr. Palmer is a Democrat of the active, progressive and younger class. He was elected November 10, 1885, to the office of mayor, and is now discharging the duties of the office in a zealous and efficient manner. Himself and wife are members of the Methodist Episcopal Church South, and he is known as an active and rising attorney, a reliable citizen and justly popular official of the city and county.

COL. WILLIAM K. PATTERSON, an influential farmer of Rutherford County, Tenn., and a native of this State, was born October 22, 1828. He is the son of Hugh K. and Cynthia (Murray) Patterson, both natives of North Carolina. The father was one of the early settlers of Sumner County, Tenn., coming here in 1800 and engaging in farming and milling, conducting the latter business for sixty-five years. He was a Democrat in politics, of the old Andrew Jackson type; himself and family are members of the Presbyterian church, and in 1872, at the unusual age of ninety-two he passed from this earth. The mother died in 1866. Our subject was reared on the farm and secured a good education, attending the Wirt College of Sumner County; at the early age of seventeen he commenced teaching school and studying law in Sumner County. He studied law for eight years, and in 1853 removed to Arkansas where he purchased a farm and commenced the practice of his profession. He was soon afterward appointed presiding judge of the cavelry court of Arkansas, under Gen. Kirby Smith, with the rank of colonel, remaining as such until the close of the war, when he resumed the practice of law. In 1876 he removed to Tennessee, purchasing the farm on which he now resides; and has since been engaged successfully in farming and stock raising, having 600 acres of excellent land. On November 27, 1849, he was united in marriage to Miss S. J. Ridley, a native of this State and a daughter of Moses Ridley, a prominent farmer of this county, whose sketch appears in this volume. To Mr. and Mrs. Patterson were born four children, only two of whom are living: Thomas R., deceased; Mary J., deceased; William K. and Ella M. Col. Patterson is a Democrat in politics, a member of the Masons (a Knight Templar), and I. O. O. F., and himself and family are leading members of the Presbyterian Church.

BURR F. PATY, the leading and senior member of the firm B. F. Paty & Co., is a native of Smith County, Tenn., born August 28, 1839. His early life was spent upon the farm in that county with his parents, John W. and Frances (Parker) Paty, who were both natives of Middle Tennessee. At about the age of fourteen years our subject left home and began life for himself as a clerk in a mercantile business at Alexandria, and later in

Lebanon, Tenn. At the breaking out of the war, he enlisted from the latter place in 1861 as private in Company A, of Gen. Hadden's regiment, and seven months later was transferred to the commissary department and promoted to the rank of captain, but never received his commission, as he was honorably discharged at the time on account of ill health, caused by exposure during his service. After the war Mr. Paty engaged in a mercantile business for himself at Viola, Warren Co., Tenn., where he continued successfully until his removal to this city in 1878. In 1879, he engaged in his present business as above stated, and it may be truthfully said that he has contributed largely to the success of this enterprising firm, by his energy, industry and practical business tact and experience. In 1872 Mr. Paty married Miss Flora Lillard, of this city, who died five years later. In 1879, he married Mary Lillard, his present wife. They have no children of their own, but have an adopted daughter named Mattie G. Mr. Paty is a Democrat in politics, although he was formerly an old-line Whig, having cast his first vote for John Bell. He has never aspired to any official position, having been too wholly engrossed with his business matters to give any time to such matters even were he so inclined. He has been a life-long member of the Methodist Episcopal Church South, and he is popularly conceded to be one of Rutherford County's most energetic and successful business men, and is held in high esteem by his fellow citizens for his many excellent qualities as a consistent Christian gentleman.

B. F. PATY & CO., of Murfreesboro, Tenn., dealers in dry goods and general merchandise. The firm is composed of the following named persons: Burr F. Paty, M. F. Leatherman and E. C. Cannon. This business was established in 1879 by Messrs. Paty & Leatherman, who conducted it in a successful manner up to August, 1884, when Mr. Cannon, who had been their book-keeper up to this time, was admitted as a partner. These gentlemen carry a large and well selected general stock, consisting of dry goods, gents' clothing and furnishing, hats, boots and shoes, making a specialty of the latter, and control probably the leading trade in this combined line in the city and county.

DANIEL P. PERKINS was born in Hinds County, Miss., June 27, 1839, son of Peter and Sarah P. (Camp) Perkins, who were born in Tennessee and Virginia, respectively. When Daniel P. was but one year old his father died in Mississippi, and he and his mother came to Tennessee and located in his father's native county (Williamson). Here Daniel was reared and secured a fair literary education. At the age of eighteen he began his business career as clerk in a mercantile store, where he continued until the breaking out of the war. In 1861 he enlisted from Nashville, in Company I, Forty-fourth Regiment Tennessee Infantry, and served in the Confederate Army until April 2, 1865, when he was captured at Hatcher's Run, near Petersburg, Va., and held a prisoner at Fort Delaware until after the close of the war. He returned home much impaired in health, and until 1870 was engaged in farming. At that date he began keeping a retail boot and shoe store in Nashville, and continued until 1873, when he came to Rutherford County and located on a farm near the city. In 1883 he engaged in the lumber business with George W. Ransom. Mr. Perkins was married in 1861 to Miss Kate Morgan, who died in 1872, leaving five children, all now living: Mary M. (wife of J. B. Ransom), Morgan, Charles F., Jennie and Kate. In 1873 Mr. Perkins wedded Mrs. Florence (Ewing) Fletcher, daughter of Hon. E. H. Ewing. To them were born three children, two now living: Rebecca W. and Sarah L. Mr. Perkins is a Democrat, and is a member of the Presbyterian Church and K. of H.

HENRY CLAY PIERCE, proprietor of the Pierce Grist and Saw-mills of Rutherford County, Tenn., was born in this county March 3, 1845, and is the son of Granville S. and Elizabeth (Abbott) Pierce, both of whom were natives of this State. The father engaged in milling and farming, and was also one of the leading physicians of the county. He was a Democrat in politics, and his death occurred April 22, 1879. The mother died January 19, 1883. The milling business at Walter Hill postoffice was established by Maj. Abbott, grandfather of Henry C., and he was succeeded by Granville S., father of Henry C. After the death of Granville S., his son, Henry C., took control of the mill and operated it with success one year, after which he rented it to his cousin, Lee Pierce. Our subject was never married. He is a Democrat in politics, and also a member of the Old School Presbyterian Church. He resides on the old homestead with his two sisters, Tennie and Annie Pierce. Mr. Pierce is well known in the county and is respected by all.

WILLIAM P. PRATER, a prominent and well-to-do farmer of Rutherford County, Tenn., was born November 28, 1850. His parents, Monroe and Caroline (Knox) Prater, were natives of Rutherford and Bedford Counties, respectively, and the father was a well-known farmer and Democrat, and he and wife were members of the Missionary Baptist Church. Our subject's early days were spent on a farm, and his educational advantages were limited, only attending the common schools of the county a short time. At the age of twenty years he began working for himself, and farmed two years on the old home place. He then rented land in the Twenty-fourth District, and farmed one year. He then returned to the paternal roof, and there resided until 1875, when he moved on his present property. Mr. Prater has met with good and well deserved success, and now has a well improved farm of 100 acres. In 1871 he was united in marriage to Lethie Pruiett, and their union has been blessed with four children: Sallie C., D. J., Fannie P. and Mary L. Mr. Prater is a stanch Democrat, and he and Mrs. Prater are members of the Missionary Baptist Church.

BEVERLY RANDOLPH, clerk of the circuit and criminal courts of Rutherford County, Tenn., is a descendant of the old and time-honored Randolph family of Virginia, and is a son of Beverly and Lucy (Searcy) Randolph, natives, respectively, of Virginia and Kentucky. The father came to Rutherford County in 1816, and was here married in 1818, and was a successful merchant of Murfreesboro a number of years. Later he operated a large plantation, continuing until his death February 9, 1868. He was an active, old-time Whig, and was a magistrate of more than ordinary ability. He was a member of the Cumberland Presbyterian Church, and was well and widely known as a successful and honorable business man. Our subject was reared in Rutherford County, and secured a fair literary education in the Cumberland University at Lebanon, Tenn. He has always been a farmer, and has met with more than ordinary success in that vocation. In 1882 he was elected to his present office, which he has filled ably and efficiently. Mr. Randolph still resides on his farm, which is situated about eight miles north of the city. December 19, 1865, he was married to Elizabeth C. Wade, a native of the county. They have six children: Sallie L., Annie, John B., Catherine, Henry S. and Walter A. Mr. Randolph was formerly a Whig, but has been a Democrat since the war. He served four years as a private and non-commissioned officer in the Forty-fifth Regiment Tennessee Infantry, but was a prisoner at Camp Morton, Ind., sixteen months. He is a Mason of the Royal Arch degree, and himself and family are members of the Cumberland Presbyterian Church.

RANSOM & PERKINS. This firm, composed of George W. Ransom and Daniel P. Perkins, are dealers in lumber and operate a saw and planing-mill at Murfreesboro, Tenn. The business was established in the fall of 1879 by G. W. Ransom, who conducted it successfully until January, 1883, when Mr. Perkins purchased an interest. They do an extensive and lucrative business, and are one of the leading firms of the city. George W. Ransom was born in Rutherford County, July 29, 1838, and is the youngest son in a family of thirteen children (seven now living) born to the marriage of John Ransom and Elizabeth Bowman, natives of North Carolina and Pennsylvania, respectively. Both father and mother came to Tennessee at an early period with their parents, and in this State our subject's father reared his family. He was a farmer and cotton dealer, a Whig in politics, and was magistrate of his district a number of years. He died September 9, 1849. George W. secured a good education, taking an academic course in his boyhood days. In 1857 he took a prospecting trip through Texas, but in 1858 returned and followed merchandising in this city and Fayetteville, Tenn., until the war. In 1862 he enlisted in Company D, Eleventh Tennessee Cavalry, serving until the close of the war. Since that time he has been engaged in merchandising and the lumber business. In 1859 he married Bettie Bostick, who died in 1863, leaving two sons: John B., of this city, and George T., of Williamson County. In 1869 Mr. Ransom married Margaret Buchanan, of Davidson County. They have seven children—five sons and two daughters. Mr. Ransom is a Democrat, and has served several terms as alderman. He is a member of the K. of H. and A. O. U. W., and he and wife are members of the Methodist Episcopal Church South.

DR. JOHN W. RICHARDSON was born in Charlotte County, Va., November 28, 1809, and died in Rutherford County, Tenn., November 19, 1872. He came to Tennessee with his parents about 1815, and settled at Old Jefferson, Rutherford County. He received a fair education, and studied medicine at Transylvania University. He never removed from the civil district of the county in which his parents first settled. Here he practiced his profession actively until his last illness, and was for a number of years one of the leaders of the Whig party in Rutherford County. He was elected to the lower house of the State Legislature as a Whig for four terms—for the years 1843-44, 1845-46, 1851-52, 1857-58; to the Senate two terms—for the years 1847-48, 1859-60. In the session of 1857-58 he was the choice of his party for speaker of the House, and in 1859-60 for speaker of the Senate. His father, James Richardson, and his mother, Mary Richardson, died in Rutherford County. In 1833 he married Miss Augusta Mary Starnes, who still survives him, as his widow, living in Murfreesboro, Tenn. At his death he left four children, who are still living: Mrs. Sue W. Jolly, of Alabama; James D. Richardson; Mrs. Mary H. Batey and John E. Richardson, of Rutherford County. He was a devoted member of the Christian Church, and on many occasions publicly conducted religious exercises. After the war between the States he acted and voted with the Democratic party.

HON. JAMES D. RICHARDSON, congressman from the Fifth Congressional District of Tennessee, was born in Rutherford County March 10, 1843. He secured a good education in the common branches during his boyhood days, and on the breaking out of the civil war was attending Franklin College, near Nashville. Before graduating, and at eighteen years of age, he entered the Confederate service, serving the first year as private and the succeeding three years as adjutant of the Forty-fifth Tennessee Infantry. At the close of the war he began the study of law, and January 1, 1867, began the practice of his profession at Murfreesboro, where he soon became recognized as one of the foremost lawyers of that locality. As a Democrat he was elected to the lower house of the State Legislature in 1870, and on the organization of that body was made speaker, at that time being only twenty-eight years of age. The year following he was elected to the State Senate, serving in the session of 1873-74. In 1876 he was a delegate to the National Democratic Convention that met at St. Louis, and the same year was elected to the Forty-ninth Congress. He was also chairman of the Democratic Convention of that year that nominated a candidate for governor of Tennessee. Mr. Richardson is a prominent member of the Masonic fraternity, having served as Grand Master and High Priest of the Grand Chapter. He is also the author of "Tennessee Templars," a work containing the biographies of all the Knights Templar of the State. Mr. Richardson is a member of the Christian Church. He wedded Miss Alabama R. Pippin in 1865, and by her is the father of five children, all living but one.

JOHN E. RICHARDSON, junior member of the firm of Ridley & Richardson, attorneys at law, of Murfreesboro, Tenn., is a native of Rutherford County, born January 7, 1857, son of John W. and Augusta M. (Starnes) Richardson, who were born in Virginia and Georgia, respectively (see sketch). John E. was reared in the county of his birth, and entered the Princeton (N. J.) College, from which he graduated in 1877 with the degree of A. B. He then entered the legal department of the Cumberland University at Lebanon, Tenn., graduating in June, 1878. He then returned home and was admitted to the bar, and has since been engaged in the practice of law at Murfreesboro. May 18, 1882, he was united in marriage to Miss Annie Lou McLemore, of Williamson County, Tenn., and daughter of Judge W. S. McLemore. They have had two children: William M., living, and Augusta, deceased. Mr. Richardson, in 1879, entered in partnership with James D. Richardson, continuing until July 1, 1885, when he formed his present partnership. He is a Democrat, and he and wife belong to the Christian Church.

G. S. RIDLEY, of the firm of Ridley & Richardson, attorneys at law, of Murfreesboro, Tenn., was born May 12, 1847, son of James and Almira (Russwurm) Ridley, who were born in Tennessee. The father was a physician, and the greater part of his life was spent near Smyrna Depot, where he successfully followed his calling. He was a Democrat, and was a member of the State Senate during the sessions of 1871-72. He is now practicing his profession in Nashville. Our subject resided with his parents in Rutherford County, and secured a good literary education. At the age of twenty he entered the law department of the Cumberland University at Lebanon, Tenn., and graduated in June, 1868. He was admitted to the bar in this county, and has since continued to practice his profession here. He is a Democrat in politics, but has never aspired to office. He has been connected with B. L. Ridley, Jr., and Judge John W. Burton in the practice of his profession. Subject is a grandson of Henry Ridley, late of Rutherford County, who was a public man in the county in his day, and was a member of the State Constitutional Convention of 1834.

THOMAS RIDOUT, a prominent citizen, was born in Virginia November 25, 1795, and came to this county in February, 1827. He was united in marriage, December 19, 1822, to Elizabeth A. Butts, and to this union were born ten children, three of whom are living, namely: Jessie B., Anna R. Blackborn, wife of Raven C. Blackborn, a successful farmer of this county, and Mrs. Mary Henry, wife of T. B. Henry, a prominent farmer. Mr. Ridout was a man of pronounced type, and was justly recognized as a moral and upright citizen. His death occurred in 1875. Mrs. Ridout is a consistent member of the Methodist Episcopal Church, and is respected and esteemed by all who know her.

LINSFORD M. ROBERTS was born in Tennessee November 12, 1844, and is the son of James M. and Louisa (Conly) Roberts, natives, respectively, of North Carolina and Tennessee. The father came to this State at an early day, and has spent a long and useful life on the farm. He is in very comfortable circumstances, and now resides in Cannon County with his wife, at the age of seventy-two. Our subject was reared on a farm, and secured an ordinary education. In 1862 he enlisted in the Confederate Army, but being under age could not enlist until the following year, when he enlisted in Capt. Nicols' company, Smith's Fourth Tennesee Cavalry, and served as private until the close of the war, when he came home and returned to farming until 1868, when he removed to this city and engaged in the grocery and general merchandise business with evident success until 1879, when he engaged in his present livery business. In 1876 Mr. Roberts married Josephine Arnold, of this county, and to them one child—Erskine P.—was born. Mr. Roberts is a Democrat, and is recognized as one of the leading business men of Murfreesboro.

COL. WILLIAM D. ROBISON, clerk of the Rutherford County Court, a native of this county, was born June 30, 1840. His father, Samuel B. Robison, a native of North Carolina, removed to this county with his parents about the year 1824. Soon afterward his parents emigrated to Illinois where they both died. Samuel B., being of age at the time of his parents' removal to the West, remained in this county and engaged as clerk in the mercantile business at old Jefferson. A few years later he engaged in business for himself at Versailles, continuing two years, when he began the study of medicine with a view to making it his profession for life. He attended lectures in the Jefferson Medical College, of Philadelphia, from which institution he graduated, and soon after located at Salem, this county, where he practiced his profession until 1852, when he removed to Murfreesboro, where he soon acquired a large and lucrative practice. Politically, the Doctor was an old-time Whig before the late war, but after this event he affiliated with the Democratic party. He was a Mason of high standing and a life-long member of the Methodist Episcopal Church South. Soon after his removal to this county he married Mary North, a native of Virginia and mother of our subject. She died January, 1862. The Doctor's death occurred in 1871, while on a visit to his daughter near Rome, Ga. William D., the subject of this sketch, was reared in this, the county of his birth, with his parents, securing a fair literary education. Upon the breaking out of the late war he enlisted in

April, 1861, as a private in Company F, Second Regiment of Tennessee Infantry, under Col. Bate, now governor. He was promoted early in the service to second lieutenant, and after the battle of Shiloh to captain of his company. After the promotion of Col. Bate to brigadier-general, our subject was made colonel of his regiment, in which capacity he served in a faithful and valiant manner until the battle of Jonesboro, Ga., where he received a severe bullet wound in the left hip, which totally disabled him for further service, confining him to his bed eight months. At close of the war, having partially recovered from the effects of his wound, Col. Robison returned home and obtained employment as clerk and book-keeper in mercantile establishments in this city, and being elected to the office of county trustee in 1866, fulfilled the duties of this office also. In 1869 he was elected county tax collector, serving the remainder of the unexpired term of his predecessor, who had died. He also, in the meantime, continued his clerkship in mercantile houses until 1876, when he engaged in the grocery and general merchandise business for himself. He conducted this business with good success until 1878, when he was elected county court clerk, and he has filled this office continuously by re-election in a faithful and highly efficient and satisfactory manner to the present time. September 15, 1869, Col. Robison was united in marriage to Miss Fannie Rice, a most estimable lady, daughter of John P. Rice, who was a highly respected resident of this county from after the war until his death. Our subject's wife departed this life March 6, 1885, leaving no issue, but her memory will ever be cherished by the bereaved husband and a large circle of admiring friends and relatives. Col. Robison has always been a firm supporter of Democracy, and his many terms of public office give evidence of the esteem in which he is held by his constituency in this county. He is a Mason of the Knight Templar and Scottish Rite degrees, being Past Grand Commander of the Tennessee State Commandery of Knights Templar. He is a zealous member of the Methodist Episcopal Church South, and is justly recognized as one among the leading and enterprising business men of old Rutherford, and a highly popular official.

L. A. ROGERS, ESQ., an energetic and prominent farmer of Rutherford County, was born November 14, 1842, in Jefferson County, Tenn., and was the son of Elisha and Mary (Statham) Rogers, natives of Jefferson County. The father was one of Jefferson County's leading farmers, and died in 1879 in that county. The son was reared on the farm, received a moderate education, and at the age of sixteen started out for himself. At the close of the war he purchased the place where he now resides, and has been successful in farming. In 1869 he married Miss Mattie A. Carter, and to them were born three children: Charlie E. (deceased), Sallie M. W. and Maggie M. Mr. Rogers is a Democrat and enlisted in 1861 in Company C, Thirty-seventh Tennessee Regiment, and participated in many of the battles. After the battle of Franklin he was detailed to care for the wounded, and served in that capacity until the close of the war. Mr. Rogers is a Master Mason. He and wife are members of the Methodist Episcopal Church South. He has held the office of justice of the peace and has given evident satisfaction. He is one of the leading men of the district and a moral, upright citizen.

MORRIS G. ROSENFELD, merchant, of Murfreesboro, Tenn., was born in the kingdom of Wurtemburg, Germany, February 3, 1850, and came to the United States in July, 1867. He came to Murfreesboro soon after landing in America, and became a clerk in his uncle's (E. Rosenfeld) store, remaining with him until 1870, when he engaged in his present business. He carries a full and select stock of staple and fancy groceries, dry goods, boots, shoes and general merchandise, and has succeeded well in his business ventures, and controls a large share of the trade in town and county. October 15, 1873, he was united in marriage to Miss Minnie Hirsch, of this city, and the following five children have blessed their union: Gabriel, Ruby, Sylvia, Sigmond and Emanuel. Mr. Rosenfeld votes the Democratic ticket, and is a member of the I. O. O. F. and A. O. U. W. He and Mrs. Rosenfeld belong to the Jewish faith, and are considered worthy citizens.

CAPT. CHARLES A. SHEAFE is a prominent attorney of Murfreesboro, Tenn., and came to Tennessee from his native State in 1865, and located first at Manchester, Coffee

County, where he engaged in the practice of his profession, and continued there until January, 1872. In 1868 he was elected by the Democratic party to Congress for this district, but was prevented from taking his seat by the governor giving the certificate to the Republican candidate. In 1872 he removed to Murfreesboro, where he soon acquired a fairly large and remunerative practice. He is a Democrat. In 1862 he was made captain of Company I, Fifty-ninth Regiment Ohio Volunteer Infantry. The second year he served as provost-marshal on the staff of Gen. H. P. Van Cleve, and during the Georgia campaign was in command of his regiment, and was mustered out in February, 1865, as captain of his company.

JOHN B. SHELTON, constable of the Fourth District, Rutherford County, was born February 10, 1846, in this county, and is the son of John and Sallie A. (Bennett) Shelton, natives, respectively, of Patrick County, Va., and Rutherford County, Tenn. The father, a widely known farmer of this county, died January 6, 1872. The subject was reared and educated like the average country boy, and upon reaching his majority engaged in farming for himself, and purchased the property where he now resides. He has been quite successful, having at present 106 acres of well improved land. In 1868 he was united in marriage to Miss Susan E. House. Mr. Shelton is a solid Democrat, and in 1862 enlisted as a private in Company K, Forty-fifth Tennessee Regiment Infantry; took an active part in most of the battles in which his company was engaged. After the battle of Mission Ridge he was detailed as guard of commissary. Upon returning to the command he was captured and held until the close of the war. He and wife are members of the Methodist Episcopal Church. Mr. Shelton is justly recognized as one of the leading farmers of the county, and an honest, industrious man.

CAPT. WILLIAM H. SIKES, a successful farmer, was born in Rutherford County, Tenn., April 27, 1834, and is the son of Jesse and Martha L. (Howse) Sikes, natives, respectively, of Georgia and Virginia. The father was one of the first settlers of this county, coming here in 1824 and engaging in farming and stock raising, and his death, which occurred in 1869, was a sad blow to the county and community. The mother still survives at the advanced age of seventy-eight. Mr. William Sikes was reared on the farm and received his education at the Union University at Murfreesboro. At the age of twenty-four he purchased a farm, where he remained two years. In 1861 he enlisted in Company E, Forty-fifth Tennessee Regiment, as first lieutenant and retained this rank until after the battle of Shiloh, when he was appointed captain of his company, serving in this capacity from the summer of 1862 until the autumn of 1863 when he was put on the staff of Maj.-Gen. Brown, serving with him but a few months when he was transferred to Maj.-Gen. Stephenson's staff, subject to a requisition issued by the General himself and was with the General in all his commands until the surrender in April, 1865. Mr. Sikes did not receive any wounds whatever during his service in the army; he then returned to Rutherford County, purchased a farm adjoining his father's on which he remained until 1882, when he removed to the old homestead where he now resides. Mr. Sikes is a Democrat in politics and he and family are members of the Baptist Church. In 1866 he was married to his second wife, Miss Bettie Thompson, a native of Alabama. To this union were born four children: Mary L., Mattie N., Bessie T. and William H., Jr. His first wife, Miss Mattie Gooch, a native of this State, died in 1861, and his second wife died in 1884. Capt. Sikes is one of the leading farmers of this county and is an estimable citizen in every respect.

JAMES M. SMITH, a well-known and eminently successful farmer, was born in this county February 6, 1831, and is the son of John P. and Elizabeth (Sims) Smith. The father died in 1862 and the mother followed in 1885. Our subject was united in marriage to Miss Fannie Beckton in the year 1857. To this union was born one child, Jennie The sad event of Mrs. Smith's death occurred in 1858 and Mr. Smith realizing that it is not well for man to live alone took for his second wife Miss Margaret Hutton, in 1860. To them were born seven children: John H., Sallie J., Mary M., James D., Ruth, William S. and Sidney B. At the breaking out of the war Mr. Smith shouldered his musket and enlisted in the Eleventh Tennessee Cavalry, serving nearly three years; at the expiration of that time he returned home and refrained from further participation in the war. Mr. Smith is a strong Democrat and he and his wife are worthy and exemplary members of the Presbyterian Church.

JOSEPH P. SMITH, farmer, of Rutherford County, Tenn., was born July 28, 1840, and is a son of Daniel D. and Lockie (McAdoo) Smith, both of whom were natives of this county. The father is a descendant of Samuel Smith, one of the pioneer settlers of the county and State. The father was a prosperous farmer, a Whig in politics, and he and family were leading members of the Cumberland Presbyterian Church. He died in 1871 and the mother in 1841. Our subject, Joseph P., was reared by his grandmother, Mrs. Mary McAdoo, until he was twelve years of age, when he removed to his father's, living with him until he was twenty years old, and securing a common school education. In 1861 he enlisted in Company C, Eighteenth Tennessee Regiment, and served as a high private during the war. He was captured at Fort Donelson, and was a prisoner at Camp Butler seven months. He was again taken prisoner at Atlanta in July, 1863, and held as such until April, when he returned home and purchased a farm in this county, where he has since been steadily engaged. In November, 1865, he was married to Lockie W. Weatherly, who bore him two children: Ida L., and Joseph W. Mrs. Smith died in October 1883. Mr. Smith is a Democrat and a member of the Presbyterian Church.

EDGAR P. SMITH, of the firm of Avent, Smith & Avent, attorneys at law, of Murfreesboro, was born in Rutherford County, Tenn., February 21, 1850, son of Ephraim and Carolina (Miles) Smith, who were born in Middle Tennessee. The father spent his lifetime on a farm in the county, and his death occurred in October, 1855. Edgar P. resided with his parents and secured a good education, graduating from the Union University of Murfreesboro in 1872. He then entered the law department of the Cumberland University of Lebanon, Tenn., and was graduated from that institution in 1874. He then returned to Murfreesboro and was admitted to the Rutherford County bar in May, 1874, and immediately began the practice of his profession with W. H. Washington, continuing until four years after the latter's election to the office of attorney-general for Davidson and Rutherford Counties, acting as his assistant during that time. In 1885 Mr. Smith entered into his present partnership and has shared equally in the success of this well-known firm. April 29, 1880, Mr. Smith married Miss Eloise Childress; they have two children: Saline and Mary. Mr. Smith belongs to the Democratic party and to the Masonic fraternity, and is a rising member of the Rutherford County bar.

DEWITT H. SMITH, of the firm of Hodge & Smith, merchants of Murfreesboro, Tenn., and a son of George W. Smith, the well-known magistrate of the Seventh District, was born in this county March 31, 1860. He was reared on the farm in his boyhood days, securing a fairly good literary education. In 1880 he graduated from the Southern Business College of Louisville, Ky., and, returning home, he found employment as clerk and bookkeeper with the firm of McKinley & Jackson, remaining with them until they became insolvent, when Mr. Smith was appointed assignee, and he closed out and settled up the business of the firm. In 1882 he entered the store in which he is now a partner, and remained here in the capacity of a clerk until 1885, when he entered into partnership. January 8, 1885, Mr. Smith was united in matrimony to Miss Lulie J. Collier, of this city. By this union they have a daughter, named Jessie. Mr. Smith is a Democrat in politics, and himself and wife are Presbyterians in their religious faith.

FOUNT SMITHSON, attorney of Murfreesboro, Tenn., was born in Williamson County, July 31, 1849. His parents, John G. and Ann V. (Ladd) Smithson, were born in Virginia and Tennessee, respectively, and the father came to the latter State in 1827 or 1828 and followed the life of a farmer. Both parents now reside in Giles County. Our subject attended Giles College two years and paid his expenses while there by teaching school. In 1870 he began reading law in the office of his brother, Noble Smithson, and two years later was admitted to the Giles County bar. In August, 1882, he came to Murfreesboro, where he has practiced his profession successfully to the present time. December 17, 1879, Mr. Smithson married Alma E. Doughty, daughter of Capt. W. W. Doughty, of this city. They have one daughter named Sarah W. Our subject is a Democrat and a member of the K. of P. and K. of H. and is Past Grand Dictator of the State for the K. of H. He and wife are members of the Methodist Episcopal Church South.

JOSEPH P. SMOTHERMAN, a widely known and eminently successful tobacco manufacturer, was born in this county October 21, 1850, and is the son of Eldridge and Sue (May) Smotherman. Our subject's early life was passed as most boys' in attending school, and at the age of manhood he was wedded to Miss Gray. This was in 1873. Their wedded life has been blessed and they have five children: Sue L., Robert T., Alice T. Fred and Joseph. Mr. Smotherman is a Democrat of the most pronounced type. He and wife are zealous members of the Methodist Episcopal Church, and are regarded as prominent citizens of the community in which they live.

JESSE W. SPARKS, clerk and master of the Chancery Court of Rutherford County, Tenn., was born in Nacogdoches County, Tex., January 1, 1837. His father, James Sparks, who was a soldier in the battle of San Jacinto, where he lost four brothers, was born in South Carolina, and died in Texas in 1840 or 1841. The mother, whose maiden name was Massey C. Wadlington, was a native also of South Carolina. Jesse W. spent his boyhood days upon a plantation in his native State with his parents. At the age of seventeen years he, in company with three lads in his neighborhood, were sent to this State to complete their education, their objective place being Nashville, but they entered the Union University of Murfreesboro instead and from this institution our subject graduated in July, 1860. Early in 1861, upon the breaking out of the late war, Mr. Sparks enlisted as a private in the company commanded by Capt. Richard S. Walker (at present one of the judges of the Supreme Court of Texas). Soon after entering the service Mr. Sparks was promoted, through the influence of Judge W. B. Ochiltree, to a second lieutenantcy in the Regular Confederate Army, with orders to report to Gen. Van Dorn, at San Antonio, Tex. Soon after complying with this order he was ordered by Van Dorn to muster in and organize a lot of troops at Houston, Tex., which he proceeded to do, and among them were the afterward famous Texas Rangers, of which regiment Lieut. Sparks was made adjutant, serving as such about one year, when in 1863 he was promoted to major with instructions to report to Gen. Kirby Smith west of the Mississippi River. Complying readily with this injunction, Mr. Sparks served under Smith as major in the adjutant-general's department until he was made lieutenant-colonel of a cavalry regiment and served in this capacity with ardent vigor until the surrender of his regiment at Houston, Tex., June 5. 1865. Returning to his home in Texas, Maj. Sparks soon made preparations for removing to this State and county. In December, 1865, he started for here and after being captured, imprisoned and released various times by the Federals whom he encountered on the way, arrived in the spring of 1866 and locating on a farm, followed agricultural pursuits successfully until 1875, when he was appointed to his present office, which he has filled by appointment until the present time, and it may be truthfully said that Maj. Sparks has discharged the duties of this important office in a faithful and highly efficient manner. The Major is and always has been an uncompromising Democrat in his political views, and this together with his generosity, natural wit and affable manners, has made him justly popular in Rutherford County as an official and citizen. April 18, 1866, he was united in marriage to his presnt wife, who was Miss Josephine Bivens, a native of this county. The result of this union has been six children, all of whom are living: Jesse W., Henry B., Docie, James, Fannie and Ingraham Twohig. Maj. Sparks is a Mason of the Royal Arch and Scottish Rite degrees, and is justly recognized as an enterprising and reliable citizen.

JOHN C. SPENCE. The subject of this sketch is of Irish-American descent, the father, John Spence, having been born in Ireland, and the mother, Mary Chism, in Virginia. John C. Spence was born November 14, 1809, in Rutherford County, Tenn. He had about the usual experience of boys of his day. His school days extended over a period of about seven years. Eighteen months of this time were spent in Hopewell Academy.

Within this period he obtained a fair knowledge of the English language, and learned the rudiments of the natural sciences. At the age of fourteen years he entered the store of his uncle, Marman Spence, with whom he remained eight years, at which time he went to Somerville, West Tenn., and opened a store on his own account. He remained in business at Somerville from 1832 to 1847, when he moved to Memphis, and continued in business there till 1849, at which time he returned to Murfreesboro. He remained in the mercantile business at the latter place until age unfitted him for the active duties of life. He was married to Elizabeth Spence, their family name being the same, September 16, 1834, in Murfreesboro. The result of this marriage was eight children; of these, Ellen, Henry C., John C., William J. and Ellen S. are dead; and Mary S. Roulet, Henry and Florence still survive. The wife, Elizabeth, died January 13, 1884. Our subject became a member of the Methodist Episcopal Church South October 15, 1882, under the ministration of the Rev. J. R. Plummer. Mr. Spence has since lived a consistent member of said church. Politically he was always a Whig so long as that party existed. At the outbreak of the Rebellion he bitterly opposed secession, but when the war began his influence and feelings were with the South. His course was such as to maintain the friendship of his friends and command the respect of his enemies. Since the war Mr. Spence has voted the Democratic ticket. For a number of years Mr. Spence was engaged in writing annals of Rutherford County, which has been valuable as reference to the compilers of this work, and is cited frequently herein. In these he has a large collection of facts, incidents and reminiscences of the past. Mr. Spence has always borne the reputation of an honest, upright, intelligent gentleman.

SQUIRE JAMES E. STOCKIRD, a farmer of Rutherford County, Tenn., was born in the county where he now resides, September 9, 1817, son of William and Jane (Elliott) Stockird, who were natives of North Carolina. The father settled in this county in 1809, and was an energetic and successful farmer, and lived a long and useful life. He was a Whig in politics, and a member of the Presbyterian Church. He served a number of years in the Indian war, and his death occurred in August, 1876. James E. was reared by his grandmother, Deborah Elliott, on a farm, and secured a limited education. At the age of eighteen he served an apprenticeship in mechanics and engaged in making cotton-gins, and followed this business for sixteen years. At the age of thirty-four he purchased the farm of 300 acres where he now resides. On February 17, 1842, he was married to Lucy McGowen, daughter of Rev. E. McGowen, a prominent Methodist Episcopal minister. To Mr. and Mrs. Stockird were born these eight children: Frances J. (Sander). William F. (deceased), Mary C. (Hunt), James E. (deceased), Alice E. (Miles), Nancy F. (deceased), and Thomas A. Mrs. Stockird died April 28, 1866, and in 1869 Mr. Stockird married Mary L. Russwurm, daughter of Gen. John S. Russwurm. They have four children: Samuel R., Rosalind D., John E. and Virginia L. Mr. Stockird did not take an active part in the late war, but sympathized with the Southern cause. He is a Democrat, and has been squire of the Ninth District for twenty years. He and family are members of the Methodist Episcopal Church.

STREET, BYRN & CO. are dealers in general hardware, agricultural implements, saddles, harness, etc., of Murfreesboro, Tenn. The business was established in January, 1869, by W. M. Street and others under the firm name of Street, Andrews & Co. In March, 1875, Mr. Street purchased the entire stock and conducted it until December 15, 1877, when he sold to Binford & Wade; in 1879 the business fell into the hands of the present firm, who carry on a successful business. William M. Street, senior member of the firm, was born in Maury County, Tenn., September 13, 1830, son of Park and Mary J. (Smith) Street, who were born in Virginia and were married in that State in 1828, and came to Tennessee the same year. The father was a successful farmer, and now resides in Williamson County. The mother died in 1848. William M. received a good rudimentary education in the common schools, and attended the Emery & Henry Virginia College two years. At the age of eighteen he engaged in the dry goods business in Columbia, Tenn., first as clerk, and later as partner in the business, but closed out shortly before the war. In 1862 he enlisted in Company G, Ninth Tennessee Cavalry, serving in this and Col. N. W. Carter's Regiment until the close of the war, and was then engaged in the hardware business in Columbia until 1869, when he removed to this city and established his present business. June 14, 1855, he married Elizabeth C. Johnson, of Columbia, Tenn. Mr. Street was a Whig in olden days, but is now identified with the Democratic party. He and wife are members of the Methodist Episcopal Church South. Charley H. Byrn, a junior member of the above named firm, is a native of Rutherford County, born February 8, 1856, son' of William B. and Sarah C. (Hunt) Byrn, who were born in Wilson and Williamson Counties, Tenn. The father spent the greater part of his life on a farm in Rutherford County, where he died August 5, 1883. He was a Whig before the war, but after that time was a Democrat. He was a magistrate a number of years and a life-long member of the Baptist Church. Charley H. was reared on a farm and secured an ordinary education in the country schools. In April, 1875, he engaged as clerk for W. M. Street, and in November, 1879, became a partner in the business. He is a Democrat and a member of the Baptist Church.

ROBERT T. TOMPKINS, a well-known citizen of Murfreesboro, Tenn., a native of Rutherford County, was born January 3, 1835, being a son of James M. and Kitty G. (Ruckel) Tompkins, both natives of Fluvanna County, Va. The father was born in 1807, came to this county in 1831 with his wife and located on a farm in the Seventh District, when he followed farming very successfully until 1855, when he removed to this city and engaged in the mercantile business until the war. He was an old-time Whig in politics and was magistrate of this district a number of years, and served also as county surveyor. Before the war he served three terms of two years each, and in 1855–56 represented this county in the State Legislature. After the war he was appointed clerk and master of chancery court, which office he filled in a highly efficient and satisfactory manner until his death, June 3, 1870. Robert T. was reared with his father on a farm until after he attained his majority. In 1861 he enlisted as a private in Company C, Forty-fifth Regiment, Tennessee Infantry, and served in the Southern Army one year. He was promoted to sergeant and then to first lieutenant of his company, when he was honorably discharged on account of ill health. Before the war he was in the mercantile business, and in 1860 was appointed deputy sheriff, which position he filled until he enlisted in the service. In July, 1865, he was appointed deputy clerk and master of chancery court under his father, and served in this capacity, having almost the entire work and responsibility resting upon him until his father's death, when he was appointed to his father's position, which he held one year during the change of the constitution. Since that time he has acted as deputy in the office, and has also been engaged in the mercantile and general trading business. He was a member of the board of aldermen and treasurer of the city during 1871–72, and has been a member of the city school board twelve years, being clerk and treasurer of the same. June, 1869, he was married to Mary J. Clark, of this city. They have one daughter, named Mary J. In politics Mr. Tompkins is a conservative Democrat, and has taken an active part in the political affairs of the county as his numerous terms of office testify. He is a Mason of Knight Templar and Scottish Rite degrees, and he and family are members of the Presbyterian Church.

ALBERT G. TOMPKINS, of Murfreesboro, Tenn., is a dealer in produce, hides, furs, poultry, eggs, etc., etc. The business was established in 1879 by Tompkins & Riee, and was purchased, a year later, by our subject, who has carried on the business very successfully to the present time. The chief markets for his produce are in Georgia and Alabama, and for furs, in the East. He controls the trade in this line in Murfreesboro and is doing extremely well financially. Mr. Tompkins was born in this State December 31, 1842, and is the son of James M. and Kittie G. (Rucker) Tompkins, both of whom were natives of Virginia. He resided on the farm until fifteen years of age and secured a good common school education. At the age of sixteen he began attending the military school at Murfreesboro. April 16, 1861, he enlisted as a private in Company C, Eighteenth Tennessee Regiment, and served in that company until after the battle of Stone River, when he was transferred to the Forty-fifth Regiment, Company C, and served as a private until the close of the war, and at the battle of Fort Donelson he received a serious wound in the head. August 31, 1864, he was imprisoned at Camp Douglas, Chicago, and was released in April, 1865. He then returned home and engaged in the mercantile business with Tompkins, Singleton & Co. From 1869 to 1870 he was engaged in speculating in cotton and grain and was afterward engaged in the boot, shoe and hat business in this place, with a Mr. Singleton as partner. He afterward engaged at millinery work in the firm of Jamerary & Tompkins. At a later period he, in company with a Mr. Jetton, began keeping a grocery store and continued until 1880, when he engaged in his present employment. February 7, 1867, he was united in marriage to Lizzie Jamerary, a native of this State. They became the parents of nine children, six of whom are still living: Martha H., Margaret M., Wade H., Robert T., Albert S. and Speer T. Mr. Tompkins is a Democrat, being a magistrate for the Thirteenth District for three years. He and family are members of the Methodist Church, and he is classed among the enterprising business men of the county, and is justly recognized as a moral, upright citizen.

THOMAS TOBIAS was born in Poland, December 24, 1851, and came to the United States in 1865, locating immediately in Nashville, Tenn., where he resided until 1869, when he came to Murfreesboro, where he has since resided. April 2, 1878, he married Hannah Abrahams, of Nashville, and three children have blessed their union: Emory Lee, Daisy and Nettie. Mr. Tobias is a Democrat in politics and a member of the A. O. U. W., and is proprietor of the leading dry goods and clothing house of Murfreesboro. The business was established in Nashville, Tenn., by Amos & Abraham Tobias, about the close of the war. At Amos' death, in 1866, Thomas purchased a one-half interest, and in the latter part of 1869 came to Murfreesboro and opened a branch store, called "The Nashville Store." The entire business was removed here in 1870 and was conducted successfully under the firm name of A. Tobias & Bro. until Abraham's death, in 1883. In January, 1884, Solomon Tobias, a younger brother, was taken into the business, but December 28, 1885, our subject became sole proprietor and manager. His store is the largest of the kind in Rutherford County, and is well stocked with dry goods, clothing, carpets, gents' furnishing goods, hats, boots, shoes and millinery. He and Mrs. Tobias belong to the Hebrew faith.

AARON TODD, a farmer of Rutherford County, Tenn., was born August 8, 1840, and his early days were spent on a farm. He received a limited education, and at the age of eighteen began doing for himself, and farmed on rented property until 1872, when he purchased a farm of 185 acres on which he resided until 1882. He then moved to his present farm. He has been quite prosperous in his undertakings, and now owns two well improved farms, consisting of 436 acres in all. In 1867 he was united in marriage to Miss Elizabeth Prater, and to them were born six children, one of whom is deceased; those living are Josephine, Andrew, Mattie K., George and Ida F. July 16, 1861, Mr. Todd enlisted in the Twenty-third Regiment Tennessee Infantry, and served until the close of the war. In 1864 he was taken sick with small-pox, and fell into the hands of the Federals and was taken to Camp Douglas, Chicago, where he was retained until the close of the war. Mr. Todd is a Democrat, and has been constable of the Twenty-fourth District, and in January, 1886, he was elected sheriff of the county, and is one of its leading men and prosperous citizens.

TODD & MORGAN, merchants, of Murfreesboro. The business was established in October, 1883, by Thomas J. Todd and W. W. Sageley, who conducted it until February, 1884, when Mr. Todd purchased his partner's interest and carried on the business part of the time alone and part with a partner until November 1, 1885, when J. A. Morgan purchased a one-half interest. Thomas J. Todd was born in Cannon County, Tenn., October 26, 1855, son of Jefferson and Mary (Simmons) Todd, both natives of Tennessee. The father died when our subject was two years of age, and the mother when he was sixteen. Thomas' early days were spent on a farm, and at the age of nineteen he engaged in mercantile pursuits in his native county, continuing until his removal to this city. December

29, 1882, he wedded Martha B. Creson. They have two children: Herman A. and Palmer D. Mr. Todd is a Democrat and Mason and a member of the Baptist Church. James A. Morgan was born in Cannon County, Tenn., October 26, 1851, being a son of Allen and Sylvia (Barrett) Morgan, natives, respectively, of North and South Carolina. They came to Tennessee at an early day, and located on a farm in Cannon County, where they both died. James A. resided with his parents on a farm, and secured an ordinary education. He worked at farming and shoe-making until 1878, when he engaged in the drug business in Auburn, Tenn., continuing two years. He was salesman in a mercantile store until 1884, and in November, 1885, engaged in his present business. In 1870 he wedded Sarah E. Reed. They have one daughter—Hattie E. Mr. Morgan is a Democrat, a member of the I. O. O. F., and belonged to the Christian Church.

LEONIDAS S. TUCKER, an energetic and prominent farmer, was born in Rutherford County, Tenn., March 21, 1850, and is the son of Silas and Ellen M. Tucker, natives of Tennessee. The father was one of the first settlers of this county, and one of its leading and successful farmers. His death occurred June 27, 1863. The mother died August, 1867. Our subject was reared on the farm and attended the Cumberland University, of Lebanon, where he secured a good education. At the age of twenty-one Mr. Tucker took charge of his father's homestead, which he inherited at his father's death, and which contains 550 acres of good land. October 11, 1871, Mr. Tucker was united in marriage to Miss Lizzie C. Davis, a native of this county, and to this union were born six children: Oscar D., Johnnie M., Lee S. (deceased), Silas, Collier B. and Carrie T. In politics our subject is a Democrat, and he and family are members of the Presbyterian Church. He is a good, conscientious, Christian man, and is esteemed and respected by all.

CAPT. CHARLES F. VANDERFORD, a well-known and prominent farmer of Rutherford County, Tenn., was born in South Carolina August 21, 1833, and is the son of Charles and Eliza (Duatt) Vanderford, natives, respectively, of Massachusetts and South Carolina. The father was a sailor, being the captain of the first steam-boat that went up Cape Fear and the Peedee River, and mate of the privateer "Obellina" in the war of 1812. His death occurred in 1843 and the mother's in 1870. Our subject received a good education and engaged in business as a telegraph operator, being one of the first operators in the country. After being with them about eight months he was employed by Henry Misroon as shipping merchant and steamship agent, and here he remained until he was twenty-one years of age. He then took the position of assistant secretary of an insurance company of St. Louis, then book-keeper, and afterward manager of a firm at St. Louis. At the beginning of the war he returned to Nashville, offering his services to the vigilance committee to put electric torpedoes in the Cumberland and Tennessee Rivers to protect the forts. In 1861 he enlisted in Capt. W. H. Sike's company, Forty-fifth Tennessee Regiment, as a private, but was soon appointed ordnance officer of the troops. Afterward he was transferred to the brigade commanded by Col. Palmer. He soon received the rank of captain, and received orders to report to Gen. P. R. Cleburne, and afterward to Gen. Johnston, then commander of the Confederate forces in Mississippi. He was afterward made acting chief ordnance officer of the army, and discharged the duties of that position to the satisfaction of the generals. At the close of the war Mr. Vanderford returned to his present home and engaged in farming and stock raising. He has been postmaster and agent at Florence Station for twenty years. In politics he is a Democrat, and he and family are members of the Presbyterian Church. December 16, 1858, Mr. Vanderford was united in marriage to Florence Anderson, a native of this State, and to them were born six children: Eugene S., Charles R., Harry A., Mary F., Silas M., Bertha E. Capt. Charles F. Vanderford is one of the energetic and successful farmers of the county, and is a moral, upright citizen.

GEORGE WALTER, manufacturer and dealer in carriages, buggies, phaetons and spring wagons at Murfreesboro, Tenn., was born in Germany, State of Baden, County of Offenburg, town of Zunsweierer, April 23, 1837, and is a son of Kasper and Katherine (Bittmann) Walter, who lived and died in Germany. George left his native home at the age of sixteen, and came to the United States by way of New Orleans, and learned the carriage-maker's trade at Memphis, Tenn. He came to Murfreesboro, Tenn., July 17, 1857, and worked for N. G. Garrett until January 1, 1860, when he engaged in business for himself with William Fox and John Gilbert, under the style of Fox, Gilbert & Co. At the breaking out of the war between the States he enlisted as private in Company I, First Tennessee Regiment. In 1866 he began business again for himself under the style of Osborn, Bock & Co., continuing until January, 1879, when the above firm dissolved by mutual consent, when he engaged in business for himself, and has established a good trade. Mr. Walter married his second and present wife, Miss Emily E. Parrish, a native of London, England, May 3, 1883. Our subject is a Democrat and a Mason, and he and wife are members of the Presbyterian Church.

CHARLES A. WARD, a young and enterprising farmer of Rutherford County, was born in Tennessee June 15, 1852, and is the son of Jackson J. and Mary J. (Leath) Ward, natives of this State. The father was one of the early settlers of this county, and was extensively engaged in farming, owning 1,900 acres of the best land, and was known as one of the wealthiest men of the county. He was a Democrat in politics, and his death, which occurred February 1, 1886, was a sad blow to the community. The mother still survives at the age of sixty-two, and resides on the old homestead. The subject of our sketch, Charles A., was reared on the farm with his parents, and secured a good common school education, and has for the last four years conducted his father's business. Mr. Ward is a single gentleman, and is respected and esteemed by all who know him.

DR. H. JOSEPH WARMUTH, a prominent physician of Rutherford County, was born January 19, 1840, in the City of Mexico, and is the son of Joseph and Maria (Munoz) Warmuth, natives, respectively, of Bavaria and Madrid, Spain. The father, an importer of merchandise in Mexico died in 1859 in that city. Our subject was reared in the City of Mexico until he reached his sixth year; he was then taken to New Orleans, and from there to Paris where he commenced his studies in a preparatory school, then at Lycee Bonaparte; finished a literary course at the gymnasium at Wurzburg and entered the university at the same place as medical student. After his father's death he returned to the United States and graduated from Rush Medical College in 1862. During the late war he entered the army as a private in the Ninth Georgia Battalion, Artillery, and was promoted to first assistant surgeon in the same, after passing the Medical Army Examining Board, at Chattanoogo. March 23, 1863, he was promoted to surgeon in the same command, and passed the examination at Shelbyville, Tenn. After the battle of Chickamauga, he was sent to the rear as hospital surgeon, at Marietta, Rome, and Covington, Ga. In the fall of 1864 he returned to Johnston's army as surgeon of the Seventeenth and Eighteenth Texas Regiments. After the Franklin fight he took charge of the Thirty-seventh Georgia Infantry, and was left by Forrest in charge of all the hospitals between Smyrna and Murfreesboro, Tenn. After the war he began the practice of medicine in Atlanta, Ga., where he remained until January, 1866, when he moved to Tennessee and married Miss Mary Worsham Peebles, born in this county in 1846, and the daughter of Mr. Isham R. Peebles. To Mr. and Mrs. Warmuth were born three children: Sallie A., Laura (deceased), and Mitchell P. W. Dr. Warmuth has practiced his profession ever since in this county. In politics he is a Democrat, and has held the office of president of Rutherford County Medical Society, and vice-president of the medical society of the State of Tennessee. He is a Master Mason, an Odd Fellow and member of Encampment, and he and wife are members of the Christian Church.

FRANCIS WHITING WASHINGTON, a well-known and prosperous farmer and citizen of Rutherford County, is the son of Francis Whiting and Elizabeth Mason (Hall) Washington. Our subject is a descendant of John Washington, who was an uncle of George Washington and a grandson of the original John Washington, who immigrated to the United States from the North of England in 1657. Francis Whiting Washington, the father of our subject, was born in Frederick or Clark County, Va., in 1781, and was educated at Liberty Hall, Lexington, Va., afterward called Washington College. In 1806 or 1808 he immigrated to Tennessee, settling first in Franklin, Williamson County, where, in 1813, he married, and soon after moved to Logan County, Ky. By this union he had five sons: Beverly, James, Allen H., John and Francis Whiting. In 1834 he removed to Nashville, in order to facilitate the education of his children, and afterward to Augusta, Ga., where he died at the residence of his son, Dr. Beverly Washington, in 1871. All the sons have died, with the exception of our subject, who is the sole survivor of the family. He resided at Nashville from 1834 until his marriage, which occurred soon after attaining his majority, to Miss Sarah Catharine Crockett. He then removed to this county, where he has since resided on the Ancient Manor of Springfield, except during the late war, when he served with distinction in the Confederate Army. Springfield is a majestic and antique mansion on the bank of Overalls Creek, and was built in 1814. Our subject's wife was a descendant from the Virginia Crocketts. Her grandfather, Col. Anthony Crockett, was a first cousin of the famous David Crockett. Our subject's married life has been blessed with three children: William Hunter, America Isabella (deceased) and John Henry.

SAMUEL B. WATKINS, an old and prominent farmer of Rutherford County, Tenn., and one of the early settlers of the county, was born in Montgomery County, Md., April 18, 1813, being a son of Thomas S. and Mary (Magruder) Watkins. Samuel B. Watkins was raised with his parents until he was fifteen years of age, securing but a limited education. He then engaged in business with his father, who was a contractor on the Chesapeake & Ohio Canal. He witnessed the first shovel of dirt taken in the construction of that famous canal in 1829, and worked with his father until 1830, at which time his father retired. He then, with his two brothers, succeeded their father in contracting on this work. In 1840 he immigrated to Texas staying in that country six months; he then came to this county in 1841, purchasing his present farm, where he has since lived. Mr. Watkins is a Democrat in politics and did not take any active part in the late war, but sympathized with the Southern cause, as he had one son in the Southern Army. Himself and family are leading members of the Methodist Church. In 1842 Samuel B. Watkins was united in marriage to Miss Mary Anne Wade, a native of this county and daughter of Walter Wade, one of the pioneer settlers of this county. They have five children by this union, of which only two are living, viz.: Samuel S. and Mary S., wife of William Roberts, a well-known farmer of this county. The death of Mrs. Watkins, which was a sad blow to the bereaved family and friends, occurred September 8, 1877. Mr. Watkins is classed among the energetic and successful farmers of the county and is justly recognized as a moral, upright citizen.

ADALINE W. WATKINS, widow of Col. Wilson L. Watkins, was born in Virginia March 6, 1815, and is the daughter of Ambrose and Mary (Hartwell) Howse. Wilson L. Watkins, one of the first settlers of this county, was born in Maryland in 1802, and came to this county when quite young. He was the son of Thomas and Catharine (McGrudy) Watkins, both natives of Maryland. Col. W. Watkins was a Democrat in politics and held the office of sheriff of this county for eight years and for many years was colonel of the militia in this State; his death, which was a sad blow to the bereaved family and friends, occurred in March, 1861. He was a strong Union man up to the time of his death. In January, 1851, Mr. Watkins was united in marriage to Mrs. Adaline W. Howse, the subject of this sketch, and by this union two children were born: Louise S., wife of Jerome Winford, a farmer of this State, and Wilson L. Mrs. Adaline Watkins had three children by her first union, which was with Hubbard P. Wilkinson, in 1832. These children are Mary E., widow of Col. Thomas B. Johnson, William A. and George H. The mother lives on the farm and with the help of her oldest son, William A., carries on farming and stock raising. She and family are leading members of the Methodist Episcopal Church and justly recognized as one of the leading families in the county.

JAMES E. WENDEL, M. D., one of the leading practitioners of Rutherford County, Tenn., was born at Cheek's Cross Roads, Jefferson Co., Tenn., November 29, 1812. He is the eldest son of four surviving members of the family of David and Sarah H. (Neilson)

Wendel. David Wendel was born in Virginia and removed to Tennessee with his father, Christopher Wendel, at or shortly before the beginning of the present century. The family located on a farm near Nashville, where our subject's grandparents spent the remainder of their lives. In 1801 David was apprenticed to his uncle in a mercantile business in East Tennessee, remaining with him in the capacity of a clerk until March, 1806, when he married our subject's mother, who was a native of that section of the State, and succeeded his uncle in business, continuing there until August, 1817. He then removed to Rutherford County and established a store in Murfreesboro, which he conducted successfully until 1839. After that date he retired from active life, having accumulated sufficient means by his frugal and industrious habits in early life to enable him to spend his declining years in peace and comparative luxury and ease. He was one of the most active politicians of the county in his day, and gained considerable local notoriety for his antagonistical views to Gen. Jackson's administration, basing his views upon the grounds that no military man should hold civil office. Notwithstanding this opposition to Jackson he was postmaster of Murfreesboro, under as well as before and after that gentleman's term of office. He was a strict Presbyterian in his religious views, as was also his wife, who died in August, 1838, followed by her husband October 8, 1840. There were few, if any, better or more enterprising and reliable pioneer citizens of Rutherford County than was David Wendel. James E. Wendel, the immediate subject of this sketch, secured a good literary education in his boyhood days. He took a common school and classical course in this county and then after a four years' attendance at the Nashville University, graduated from that institution in 1831. Returning home he entered the office of his uncle, Dr. Patrick D. Neilson, under whom he read medicine until 1834, when he entered the medical department of the University of Pennsylvania at Philadelphia and remained there during the winter and summer months continuously for a period of eighteen months, when his health failed him, and abandoning his studies he traveled rather extensively through the New England States, Canada, and finally returned home, but the following fall returned to the university, where in the winter of 1836 he was elected a resident physician of Blockley Hospital, Philadelphia. He held the position one year, when he resumed his studies at the university, from which he graduated in 1839. Returning home the Doctor entered into the practice of his profession in this city. And the fact alone that after nearly fifty years residence in our midst, during which time he has given his whole time, attention and energy to the success and advancement of his profession, and yet retains a large and lucrative practice, speaks more highly in his favor than words or pen can portray. Dr. Wendel is Democratic in politics, although he was formerly a warm advocate for the principles of the Whig party until it ceased to exist. He is a zealous member of the Presbyterian Church of this city, and is justly recognized as one among the leading and successful members of the medical profession of Middle Tennessee and an enterprising and reliable citizen of our county.

ROBERT S. WENDEL, M. D., brother af Dr. James E. Wendel, and a well-known and successful physician of Murfreesboro, Tenn., was born in Rutherford County July 14, 1821. He secured a good literary education in his early days, and in 1839 began the study of medicine with a view to making it his profession for life. He graduated from the medical department of the University of Louisville, Ky., in March, 1843. He first began the practice of medicine in Mississippi, where he remained six years; then returned home, where he has since been wholly engaged in the practice of his profession, meeting with good and well deserved success. In 1852 the Doctor was united in marriage to Emma C. James, a native of Virginia. They have ten living children by this union—one son and nine daughters. Dr. Wendel is Democratic in his political views, although like his brother, he was formerly an old-line Whig. During the late war the Doctor participated in it in his professional capacity as hospital surgeon for a term of three years, being stationed during the time at Dalton, Marietta and Forsyth, Ga., and Columbus, Miss. Himself and wife are members of the Methodist Episcopal

Church South, and he is one of the acknowledged enterprising and reliable citizens of our county, and a physician of equally high standing.

DR. BARTLEY N. WHITE, a widely known and eminently successful practitioner, was born in this county August 16, 1841, and is a son of Burrell G. and Mary (Donley) White, natives, respectively, of Tennessee and Ireland. The father was an enterprising merchant and farmer, and departed this life October 31, 1884. He was a consistent member of the Christian Church. The mother still survives him and is a resident of this county. Our subject is a graduate of the University of Nashville, and is one of the class of 1867. He was married in May of that year to Sue Ransom, of Bedford County, and five children have blessed their union: Walter M., Sallie W., William R., Burrell G. and Bartley N. The Doctor took an active part in the late war, enlisting in May, 1861, in Company F, Second Tennessee Infantry, serving in the capacity of sergeant for three years. He was captured July 20, 1864, at Peach Tree Creek, Ga., and was a prisoner nine months. At the expiration of that time he was exchanged. He was on parole for sixty days, and during that time the surrender of the Confederate Army was announced. The Doctor is a Democrat of the most pronounced class, and is at present a candidate for and will probably be elected clerk of the circuit court. He and wife are members of the Christian Church, and are recognized as prominent and influential citizens of the community in which they reside.

FRANK WHITE, postmaster at Murfreesboro, Tenn., first saw the light of day August 5, 1843, son of Burrell G. and Mary M. (Donley) White, natives, respectively, of Tennessee and the Emerald Isle. Our subject was brought up to the mercantile business by his father, and secured a good business education. At the breaking out of the Rebellion he was chosen second lieutenant of Company E, Fourth Tennessee Cavalry, and served until the reorganization of the company a year later, when he was made first lieutenant. After the close of the war he returned home and engaged in mercantile pursuits. In 1878 he was appointed deputy clerk of the county court, and removed to Murfreesboro. In December, 1885, he was appointed by President Cleveland postmaster of Murfreesboro, and is now discharging the duties of that office. March 6, 1866, he wedded Miss Joe E. Miller. They have three children living: Mary L., Kate and Frankie. Mr. White is a Democrat and a member of the K. of H. He and wife are members of the Christian Church.

LEVI B. WHITE was born in Tennessee February 18, 1813, son of Henry and Elizabeth (Ward) White, natives, respectively, of this State and North Carolina. The father's family were old settlers of the county, and were prominent people of their day, and he was an old-time Whig. He was strictly exact in all his business transactions, and his death occurred in 1855. The mother died in 1815. Levi B. White, our subject, was reared on a farm by his uncle, Levi White, and secured a common school education in the old log schoolhouse of long ago. When thirty years of age he began farming for himself, and has met with good success in that work. July 7, 1846, he was married to Miss Eliza J. Hall, born in Alabama. She died April 25, 1865, having borne these children: Sallie B. (Alexander), Henry H., Kate (Goodloe), John M. and James L. In August, 1867, Mr. White was married to his second wife, Mrs. Kate Mays, widow of Samuel Mays and sister of his first wife. They have one child, Azile. Mr. White is a Democrat in politics, and he and family are members of the Methodist Church. He is very prosperous, and owns from 1,000 to 1,100 acres of good land.

WILLIAM B. WHITE was born near Gallatin, Sumner Co., Tenn., September 10, 1814, and is a son of Stephen and Jane (Bell) White, natives, respectively, of North Carolina and Tennessee. The father was one of the early educators of Sumner County, and was a school-teacher in that part of the State for many years. He was a farmer of considerable note and his death occurred in 1821. The mother died in 1859. William B. made his home with his uncle, John Bell, of Gallatin, and served an apprenticeship at tailoring, and followed that occupation for ten years. He removed to Milton in 1833 and began merchandising there in 1844. In 1855 he purchased a farm south of Milton on which he remained five years and then purchased his present farm. June 5. 1850, he was married to Miss Martha C. Peebles, a native of the State, and daughter of George Peebles. They have four children: Sarah J. (deceased), wife of George Martin; Martha F. (wife of R. T. Knox); George A. and William Thomas. Mr White was twice married, his first wife being Sarah A. Wilson, who died March 13, 1847. He was the father of four children by this union: Hugh L. (died in 1862), John H. (died in 1870), Elizabeth A. (wife of W. J. Hooper) and Mary A. Mr. White is a Democrat and he and wife are members of the Old School Presbyterian Church. He is good farmer and takes considerable interest in stock raising.

JOHN V. WHITE, merchant, of Murfreesboro, Tenn., is a native of Monroe County, Miss., born September 24, 1850. His parents were Peyton H. and Sarah (Lee) White. The father died in Mississippi and the mother still resides in that State. John V. was reared on a Mississippi plantation and secured a good practical education in his boyhood days. In 1877, he came to Murfreesboro, Tenn., and was salesman in a mercantile store two years. He then engaged in the same business for himself and has continued to the present time, meeting with good and well deserved success. Mr. White started in business with a limited capital and small stock, but by industry, economy and strict business integrity has climbed the ladder of success until he now is one of the first merchants of the city, and controls a large share of the trade in city and county. April 15, 1882, witnessed the celebration of his nuptials with Miss Bettie Jarrett, of this county. They have one son named Thomas V. Mr. White's political views are Democratic, and he and wife are members of Methodist Episcopal Church, and he is justly considered one of the reliable and prosperous business men of Murfreesboro.

DR. WILLIAM WHITSON was born near Nashville, Tenn., August 22, 1821, and is a son of George and Mary (Deth) Whitson, both natives of Virginia, and the father a skilled mechanic and farmer. He was a worthy member of the Christian Church and died about 1840. The mother was a devout Methodist and died in 1833. The subject of this sketch was a member of the first class that graduated from the Nashville University of Medicine. He was married the 22d of February, 1844, to Miss Mernira Newman; to them were born two children, one now living, Lurenza D., a resident of Columbia, N. C. Mrs. Whitson died December 31, 1849, and the Doctor took for his second wife Maria E. Phillips, November 6,1850. To them were born five children, three now living: George D., Hygene and William W. On the 3d of November, 1885, the Doctor's second wife died. She, as well as the first wife, was an earnest member of the Christian Church. Dr. Whitson was an active participant in the late war, being surgeon of the Forty-fifth Tennessee Regiment, and served two years. Owing to ill health he resigned his commission and returned home. He is an enthusiastic Democrat and a worthy and consistent member of the Christian Church. He has a thorough knowledge of his profession and is doing well financially.

CHESLEY WILLIAMS, a retired merchant of Eagleville, was born in Williamson County, July 22, 1809, and is the son of James and Sallie (Allison) Williams, both natives of North Carolina. The subject of this sketch was married December 9, 1830, to Miss Elizabeth Jordan, and to this union were born eight children, namely: Martha J., wife of Whit. Ransom; Mary V., wife of Joseph Ransom; James C.; Macon S., wife of Dr. W. H. McCord; Sophia P., wife of S. K. Lowe; Fannie F., wife of Prof. Savage; Emma, wife of Jesse E. Sullivan, and Robert E. Mr. Williams did not take an active part in the late war, but had a son in the Confederate Army, and for that reason his sympathies were with the South, and yet he was always in favor of the union of States. Mr. Williams is an old-line Whig. He has served his county in the capacity of magistrate for a number of years, and was postmaster at Eagleville for thirty years. He and his wife are devout and consistent members of the Baptist Church, and are respected by all who know them.

JAMES C. WILLIAMS, a prominent and successful merchant, was born in Williamson County, Tenn., September 22, 1842, and is the son of Chesley and Elizabeth (Jordan) Williams, both of whom are natives of Tennessee. The father served as magistrate for a number of years and was postmaster at Eagleville for thirty years. The subject of this sketch was married November 12, 1868, to Miss Mary T. McLean, and their wedded life has been blessed by seven children, namely: Minnie, Samuel, James C., Horace, Granville, Edward L. and Thomas S. Mr. Williams took an active part in the late war, shouldered his musket, and in 1862, enlisted in Company C, Eleventh Tennessee Cavalry, and served in that capacity with Maj. Deering until the close of the war. Mr. Williams is now a Democrat, formerly a Whig. He and wife are worthy and consistent members of the Missionary Baptist Church, and are respected and esteemed as kind neighbors and excellent citizens.

JOHN A. WILLIAMSON, a successful farmer and saw-mill owner, was born in this county May 24, 1845, and is the son of Thomas and Jane (Jordon) Williamson, both natives of this State. Our subject was united in marriage November 28, 1865, to Miss Lizzie Faris, and became the father of eight children: Charles T., Horace S., Eula D., Sue M., Abbie L., Richard W., Maggie E. and Alfred F. Mr. Williamson took an active part in the war, enlisting in Company D, Twenty-fourth Tennessee Infantry, was honorably discharged in 1863, but re-enlisted, after a few months' recreation, in Company D, Twenty-first Tennessee Cavalry, serving with that company until the close of the war. Mr. Williamson is a Democrat with prohibition tendencies. Mr. and Mrs. Williamson are worthy and consistent members of the Methodist Episcopal Church and are justly recognized as influential citizens of the community in which they live.

JOSEPH T. B. WILSON, a cotton dealer, of Murfreesboro, Tenn., established his business in that city in 1874. He controls the leading trade in his line (cotton-ginning) in the county, and is doing well financially. He was born in the "Keystone State" at New Castle, and is a son of John and Martha (Graham) Wilson, who were natives, respectively, of Maryland and Pennsylvania. The father was a merchant for a number of years and afterward became a successful tiller of the soil in Pennsylvania. The subject of this memoir, Joseph T. B. Wilson, spent his boyhood days at work on the home farm and in attending the common schools, where he received a good education. He located in Murfreesboro, Tenn., about 1874 and engaged in his present occupation, at which he has since been steadily engaged. He does an annual business of about $40,000 and is always strictly accurate in his business transactions and prompt in the discharge of his duties. Mr. Wilson is a strong supporter of Republican principles, and is a member of the Presbyterian Church.

MAJ. JOHN WOODS, the well-known and highly respected chairman of the Rutherford County Court, was born to the marriage of Thomas Woods and Susan Baldridge, who were both natives of Orange County, N. C., and came to this county after their marriage, in the spring of 1807. Thomas Woods was one of the sturdy pioneer blacksmiths of Rutherford County and he plied his trade on Overall Creek, also in Murfreesboro, a number of years. In 1827 he removed to near Hickman, Ky., where he died in March, 1838. Our subject was born in Rutherford County, September, 11, 1807, and spent his youthful days on the farm and in his father's shop. Like his father he was a natural mechanic, but was prevented early in life from following his father's trade, by meeting with an accident which permanently disabled his left hand and arm. His early education was such as could be procured by a few months attendance each year at the subscription schools, held in the primitive "log structures," which were common at that early day. In May, 1827, Mr. Woods entered public life by being elected, by the court, to the office of constable of the district on Overall Creek. He served in this position two terms of two years each; then engaged in the grocery business one year at Middleton, this county, and thence until 1833 was engaged as clerk in Murfreesboro. During 1833–34 he was engaged in business for himself again at Salem. In the latter year he repaired to his farm, to which he devoted his entire time and labors until 1840, when he was elected register of the county, serving by re-election until 1848. During his term of office he served also as deputy clerk of the county court. In 1848 he was elected clerk of the county court, filling this office by re-election until 1856. It is a fact worthy of recording that Maj. Woods' popularity as an official, as was evinced by his almost continous term of office, for nearly thirty years before the war, was due entirely to the efficiency of the man, as his party the Democratic, were largely in the minority during that time. In 1859 he was elected to represent this county in the State Legislature. He served in the regular and called sessions during 1859-60-61. The Major was not a participant in the late war, but was a warm advocate for the cause of the people of the South and this, together with the fact that he had been a member of the General Assembly that passed resolutions of secession, probably caused him much annoyance from persecution by the Federal soldiery after they had invaded these parts. They even went so far as to conspire with one of his former slaves and go though with a sham of arresting him, but the matter was dismissed without serious trouble. In March, 1866, Mr. Woods was elected a magistrate of this district, and the following January was elected chairman of the county court, and it may be said to his credit that he has filled these offices, continously, by re-election to the present time, discharging his duties in a highly satisfactory manner, to his constituency and the people of the county at large. October 30, 1383, Maj. Woods married Mary F. Jarratt, of this county, who died August 19, 1884. October 15, 1885, he married Mrs. Nancy (Boring) Jetton. He has no children of his own, but has raised and taken care of a great many friendless children. He has always been prominently identified with all public and private enterprises in the city and county; before the war he was one of the foremost in establishing in the city a branch of the Planters' Bank, and was afterward a director and stockholder in the savings bank and also First National Bank of this city, but has withdrawn from the latter of late years, having by his economical and industrious habits acquired a sufficient competency to support him in a comfortable manner in his declining years. He has never belonged to any secret society or church, but is a firm believer in the Bible, and his life has been spent in comformity with these views. He has been a life-long Democrat and his many and continued terms of office give evidence of the esteem in which he is held by the Democracy of old Rutherford County, and know him only to respect his many superior qualities as an official and a moral, upright citizen.

THOMAS H. WOOD, undertaker, of Murfreesboro, Tenn., was born in Rutherford County, Tenn., April 28, 1838, son of Hughes and Sarah (Kelly) Wood, natives of Virginia. The father came to Rutherford County shortly before our subject was born, and died in Evansville, Ind., while there on a visit about 1840. Thomas H. resided in Murfreesboro with his mother, and secured an ordinary education. At the age of sixteen he began learning the cabinet-maker's trade, which he mastered and at which he worked until 1859. At the breaking out of the war in 1861 he enlisted as a private in Company D, Eleventh Tennessee Cavalry, and served until the close of the war. He then returned to Murfreesboro, and worked as clerk in the merchandise business until 1875, when he began to keep furniture and undertaking goods, continuing until 1882, and since that time has carried on the undertaking business alone. In 1858 Mr. Wood married Lucy McKnight, of Bedford County, Tenn. They have one daughter, Lizzie. Mr. Wood is a Democrat in politics, and was alderman of Murfreesboro during 1874-75. He is a Mason, Knight Templar and Scottish Rite degrees, and is one of the worthy citizens of Murfreesboro.

ROBERT H. YOUNG may be mentioned as a successful farmer and native of Davidson County, Tenn. He is a son of Joseph and Nancy (Alford) Young, who were natives of this State. The father was a skilled ornamental painter, and acquired quite a reputation as a master of his trade in Nashville. He died in 1849. The mother is yet living, and is the widow of George Moxley, of Texas. Our subject was married March 19, 1872, to Miss Sarah Davis, who has borne him one child, named Earnest. Mr. Young took an active part in the late war, enlisting in the Eighteenth Tennessee Infantry, serving in this capacity until the capture of Fort Donelson, when he escaped without being captured, and attached himself to Forrest's independent company of scouts, and remained with them until the close of the war. He is now a Democrat in politics, but was formerly a Whig. His religion is humanity to all. His wife is a consistent member of the Methodist Church, and they are highly esteemed and respected citizens of the county.

WILSON COUNTY.

JAMES N. ADAMS, farmer and merchant, was born in Davidson County, Tenn., August 17, 1851, and is one of three children born to the marriage of Harvey Adams and Mariah Wasson, natives of Bourbon County, Ky., and of Irish and English descent, respectively. The father was born in 1815, and before his marriage (in 1840) was a dealer in fast horses. After residing some time at Nashville he removed to Wilson County. where he owned a farm of 187 acres. In 1876 he sold this farm and again removed to Nashville, where he yet resides. Our subject was reared at home, and received the degree of A. B. from Bethany College, West Virginia, and LL. B. from the law department of Cumberland University of Lebanon, Tenn. He afterward became a teacher in the Oakland Seminary, and continued in that capacity two years. He began practicing law in Nashville, but owing to ill health was compelled to discontinue. May 11, 1881, he wedded Ladie M., daughter of John C. and Mary R. Fowler. She was born August 7, 1862, in Nashville, Tenn. They have two children: Eldon and Charmian. After his marriage Mr. Adams resided on a farm near Nashville until 1885, when he removed to the farm where he now lives, and engaged in his present business. He is a believer in the principles of Democracy, and votes according to the dictates of his conscience. His wife is a member of the Methodist Episcopal Church South.

JOSEPH M. ANDERSON, M. D., was born in the town of Lebanon, Tenn., on the southeast corner of the Public Square, October 17, 1815, being the oldest natural born citizen now living, and is one of the two sons of Patrick and Fannie (Chandler) Anderson. The brother, Thompson Anderson, resides in the city of Nashville and is worthy of its citizenship. The father was born in Virginia in 1779, and the mother in North Carolina, in 1779. The father was a merchant and one of the pioneers of Tennessee and suffered the privations incident to early times. His death occurred in 1817, and his widow married Maj. William Hartsfield and became a resident of Davidson County, where she resided at the time of her death, in 1838. Our subject was reared without a father's guidance and obtained his education in the schools of Lebanon and at a school called Porter's Hill Academy, afterward Clinton College, in Smith County, Tenn. At the age of eighteen he began the study of medicine under Dr. John Ray, and in 1835 he entered the Transylvania Medical College of Philadelphia, Penn., remaining one session. On September 24, 1835, he wedded Mary Dixson Lypert, a daughter of Lawrence and Mary Lypert. Mrs. Anderson was born October 27, 1820, in Wilson County, and she and her husband became the parents of twelve children, only three of whom are living: Joseph B., Samuel and Kate Lee. In the fall of 1836 Dr. Anderson returned to college at Philadelphia, where he graduated as an M. D. in March, 1837. He is now the oldest and one of the most successful physicians and surgeons of Lebanon as well as one of the most enterprising, public-spirited and progressive citizens of the county. He was formerly a member of the old Whig party, but since the death of that party has affiliated with the Democracy. He is a member of the following fraternities: Lebanon Masonic Lodge, No. 98; he became a Master Mason in 1843; Royal Arch Mason, in 1849; Knight Templar, in 1886; Junior and Senior Warden of the Grand Lodge; served as Grand Master for two years, which fact stands unequaled and established a precedent in the Tennessee Grand Lodge for forty years; was Most Excellent Grand High Priest of the Grand Chapter of the State of Tennessee; Thrice Illustrious Grand Master of the Grand Council of the State of Tennessee, Deputy Grand Commander of the Grand Commandery, and served as Grand Commander the same year. He is a member of the Baptist Church, and his wife of the Christian Church. Our subject has lived a long and useful life, and no man occupies a more exalted place in the estimation of his neighbors and fellow-citizens.

JAMES AUST, a young and energetic farmer of District No. 3, was born in 1855, in Wilson County, Tenn., and is the son of Thomas P. and Sarah (Riggin) Aust. The father was of German descent and was born in Virginia in 1811. He was a farmer by occupation. When but a youth he left his native State with his father, who went to West Tennessee and took possession of a large tract of land for services rendered in the war of 1812. Thomas Aust lived in Wilson County at the time of his marriage, which occurred in 1832. Soon afterward he bought 140 acres of land and engaged in farming. In 1848 he sold out and bought 202 acres three and a half miles from Lebanon. Here he died in 1876. The mother was born in 1812, in North Carolina, and is now living with her son James. Our subject received his education in the country schools and in addition he attended the preparatory schools of the University at Lebanon, and also at Transylvania University, at Lexington, Ky. For the past eight years James has had control of the old home place and has managed it in a skillful manner. He is a young man of temperate habits and is courteous and unassuming. His mother is a member of Methodist Episcopal Church South.

DR. R. H. BAKER, a prominent citizen and physician of Watertown, Tenn., was born in Davidson County June 1, 1847, one of a family of eight children of William D. and Mary (Fuqua) Baker. The father was born in Tennessee October 9, 1812, and was married in 1831. He was a farmer by occupation, and held the office of magistrate for twenty-seven years. Since 1883 he and wife have made their home with our subject, Dr. R. H. Baker, who spent his boyhood days on a farm. He attended the common schools and completed his education at the Nashville University, and afterward entered the medical department of that institution and graduated in 1873. He located at Cherry Valley, where he remained two years, but since his marriage has lived in Watertown, with the exception of a short time spent at a Medical College in Cincinnati, Ohio, where he took a course in homœopathy. He has had good success as a physician, and is a member of the Philadelphos Society, of Cincinnati, Ohio, an institution for the mutual advancement of students and professors. He owns 100 acres of land which he manages in connection with his practice. The Doctor is conservative in politics. For some time he was a member of the Masonic fraternity and I. O. O. F., being a Master Mason in the former, but since joining the Christian Church he has ceased to be an active worker in either order.

CAPT. WADE BAKER, a successful farmer and stock raiser, was born in Smith County, Tenn., January 30, 1824, and is one of a family of two children born to John E. and Elizabeth (Benshy) Baker. The father was of German lineage and a native of Virginia, born January 8, 1781. He was a farmer and stock raiser by occupation. He was in the war of 1812 and participated in the battle of New Orleans. January 8, 1822, he was married. At the time of his death, which occurred October 23, 1866, he owned a considerable amount of property, both personal and real. The mother was born February 2, 1804, in Smith County, and died September 9, 1829. Our subject was reared in Wilson County and received his education in the country schools. In 1850 he commenced farming for himself, and in the space of ten years had accumulated a considerable amount of property. During the late war he enlisted in the Confederate service, and in 1861 was made captain of Company F, Twenty-eighth Tennessee. He was in the battles of Fishing Creek and Shiloh. August 19, 1862, he returned home and married Mary E. Hudleston, a native of Tennessee, born March 27, 1843, and the daughter of William W. and Mary Hudleston. Capt. Baker continued to till the soil and in 1870 he engaged in merchandising in connection with farming, which he continued for eight years. He then retired to his farm where he now lives, enjoying good health, with his wife and three children, named Lee, John E. and Wade. The Captain is a Democrat and a member of the Christian Church. He has been postmaster at Rural Hill for ten years. Mrs. Baker is a worthy member of the Methodist Episcopal Church.

CAPT. WILLIAM P. BANDY, sheriff and native of Wilson County, Tenn., was born on the 4th of July, 1828, one of five children of Epperson and Harriet (Pierce) Bandy, of German and French origin, born in 1794 and 1804, in Virginia and Tennessee, respectively. The father was a farmer, and in 1800 came to Tennessee with his parents and became the owner of 300 acres of land. He was twice married, his second wife being Betsy (Denton) Walker. He died in 1863 and the mother in 1831. Our subject attended the county schools, and June 11, 1850, was married to Lucinda Lane, daughter of Bennett Lane. She was born in 1830 and became the mother of these children: Mildred C., wife of George W. Lanius, and Harriet, wife of James Boss. Mr. Bandy moved to Arkansas in 1855, and there his wife died in 1857. He then returned home. In 1861 he enlisted in Company K. Eighteenth Regiment Tennessee Infantry, being first lieutenant, and rose to the rank of captain. He was in many of the principal battles of the war and was wounded at Murfreesboro and Chickamauga, but not seriously. He was captured at the fall of Fort Donelson and sent to Camp Chase, Ohio. He returned home in May, 1865. He served as deputy sheriff from 1865 to 1872, and in 1876 was chosen sheriff, serving as such six years, and the following year was deputy. Since 1884 he has held the office and is a candidate for re-election. In 1871 he wedded Mrs. Virginia (Holmes) Brown, born in New York in 1840. They have three children living: Sallie L., Edward P. and Henry J. Capt. Bandy came to Lebanon in 1880. He owns 183 acres of the old home place. He belongs to the Masonic fraternity and I. O. O. F. and he and wife are members of the Methodist Episcopal Church South.

JONATHAN BANDY, one of the prominent farmers of the Fourth District, Wilson County, was born in Sumner County, Tenn., February 20, 1829, and is one of five children born to Epperson and Harriet Bandy. (See sketch of W. P. Bandy). Our subject remained at home until he was twenty-five years of age, receiving his education in the schools of the county. In 1815 he wedded S. M. Ross, a native of Wilson County, Tenn., born November 12, 1842, and the daughter of Samuel and Susan Ross. To Mr. and Mrs. Bandy were born four children: Corrie E., Pierce J., Sudie S. and Maxie R. In 1854 he bought land in Wilson County and engaged in agricultural pursuits. He has added to his land from time to time till at the present he has 450 acres. He is a Democrat in politics and a member of the Methodist Episcopal Church.

DANIEL J. BARTON, trustee of Wilson County, Tenn., is a native of this county, born February 6, 1842, son of Gabriel and Jane (Johnson) Barton. The father was of Irish birth, born in Nashville, Tenn., April 4, 1794, and followed the occupation of farming. His father, Samuel Barton, was a native Virginian, and came to Nashville when there were but four families residing in the place, and when it was necessary to take every precaution to guard against the Indians. Gabriel Barton was the possessor of 333 acres of land at the time of his death, June 5, 1862. The mother died in 1857. Our subject was educated in the country schools, and in July, 1861, enlisted in Company K, Twenty-fourth Regiment, Tennessee Volunteer Infantry, and was an active participant in the battles of Perryville, Murfreesboro and Chickamauga, where he was severely wounded in the right arm from the explosion of a shell, the limb having to be amputated. He then remained in the commissary department until the close of the war. He then returned home and attended school at Taylorsville two years, and in 1868 began farming. In 1874 Mr. Barton was appointed revenue collector for Wilson County for two years, and after farming until 1883 was elected county trustee, and now holds the office. December 14, 1882, he was united in marriage to Eudora, daughter of Robert C. and Anna B. Scobey. Mrs. Barton was born September 21, 1857, in Wilson County, and she and Mr. Barton are members of the Christian Church.

J. P. BASHAW, an enterprising farmer and stock raiser, was born December 7, 1842, in Wilson County, Tenn., and is one of a family of five children born to J. W. and Charlotte (Cherry) Bashaw. The father was born May 6, 1804, in Davidson County, Tenn., and was of French descent. He was a farmer by occupation, and December 5, 1833, he married and moved to Wilson County, Tenn., where he carried on stock raising in connection with farming. He died November 6, 1884. The mother was born September 24, 1816, and died August 30, 1844. Our subject was reared in Wilson County, Tenn., in the Twenty-fifth District, receiving his education in the country schools and at Washington and Lee Universities. November 10, 1870, Salura Cook became his wife. She was born March 19, 1851, and is a daughter of Dr. L. M. N. Cook. To Mr. and Mrs. Bashaw were born four children: Kate E., Pierce, Eulixis and James B. Mr. Bashaw holds to the principles of Democracy, and he and wife are worthy members of the Missionary Baptist Church.

REV. RICHARD BEARD, D. D. (deceased), was born November 27, 1799, in Sumner County, Tenn., and died December 2, 1880, at Lebanon, this State. On March 10, 1819, he joined the Nashville Presbytery of the Cumberland Presbyterian Church, was licensed to preach October 12, 1820, and July 29, 1822, was ordained. He attended Cumberland College at Princeton, Ky., from which he graduated in September, 1832, and the day following this event was made professor of ancient languages in that institution, a position he retained six years. In the summer of 1838 he was elected to the professorship of languages in Sharon College, Mississippi, entering upon the duties of that position the succeeding fall. In September, 1843, he was made president of Cumberland College, Kentucky, and in the spring of 1853 was made professor of systematic theology in Cumberland University, at Lebanon, Tenn. He moved to Lebanon, and in March, 1854, assumed the position to which he had been elected, and so continued until his demise. Dr. Beard was a man of keen intellect, extended information, an able instructor, an excellent counselor and zealous Christian. He wedded Miss Cynthia E. Castleman, in Davidson County, Tenn., January 21, 1834. Mrs. Beard was born November 22, 1804, in the county where she was married, and died at Lebanon, Tenn., May 27, 1886.

HON. E. E. BEARD, a son of Rev. Richard Beard, D. D., and Cynthia E. Beard was born at Princeton, Caldwell Co., Ky., August 27, 1850. His father removed with his family to Lebanon, Tenn., in 1854, where Mr. Beard has resided since that time. He graduated in the academic department of the Cumberland University in 1870, and in the law department in 1871. He has practiced law at Lebanon since his graduation and is now a member of the firm of Williamson & Beard. In December, 1877, he was elected mayor of Lebanon and re-elected in 1878 and 1879. In the year 1881 Lebanon became a taxing district of the second class and Mr. Beard has held the position of treasurer of the board of commissioners since that date. In January, 1879, Mr. Beard was elected treasurer of the trustees of the Cumberland University and now holds that position. In January, 1885, he was elected to represent Wilson County in the lower house of the Tennessee Legislature, filling a vacancy caused by the resignation of John C. Forr. On the 12th of October, 1876, Mr. Beard married Miss Sarah Livingston, of Davidson County, Tenn.

MAJ. ROBERT BELL, one of the old citizens and farmers of the Twenty-third District, was born in 1805 in Davidson County, Tenn. He is the son of James and Mary (Dean) Bell. The father was born in 1777, in North Carolina, and in 1783 came with his parents to Sumner County, Tenn., but afterward moved to Davidson County. His father, Robert Bell, our subject's grandfather, was the father of nineteen children, eighteen of whom lived to be grown. He was a captain in the Revolutionary war, and died in 1816 at the age of eighty-five years. In 1819 James Bell came to Wilson County and bought 515 acres in the Twenty-third District, settled and remained here until his death, which occurred in 1823. The mother was born in 1777, in Virginia, and died in 1829. They had nine children, three of whom are now living. Our subject received his education mostly outside of the school room. During his boyhood days and youth the schools were few and far between, and educational advantages were very poor. After the death of his father, Robert being the eldest child, the responsibility of the family fell largely upon his shoulders. January 21, 1830, he married Polly Hooker, a native of Wilson County, born in 1811, and the daughter of Benjamin Hooker. To them was born one child, Erastus P., who resides in Rutherford County. Mrs. Bell died June 3, 1841, and the following year he married Sarah A. Furgason, a native of Virginia, born in 1818, and by her became the father of ten children, five of whom are living: Jane M., wife of James A. Neal, who lives in Lebanon; Samuel S., Byron, George F. and Willie S., wife of A. D. Peyton. Maj. Bell is now living on the old homestead and is esteemed as an honest and upright citizen. In politics he was formerly a Whig, casting his first vote for Andrew Jackson. February, 1876, he lost his wife, and since then his son, G. F., has been living with him. Maj. Bell is a member of the Methodist Episcopal Church South, and has led a conscientious Christian life for the past forty-seven years.

W. H. BROWN was born in Lebanon, Tenn., December 18, 1837, and is one of seven children of Samuel and Lucy (Chandler) Brown, born in North Carolina and Virginia in 1800 and 1804, and died in 1852 and 1872, respectively. The father was a saddler by trade and after coming to Tennessee always made Lebanon his home. Our subject was educated in the academies of Lebanon, and at the age of thirteen began clerking for A. R. Davis, for whom he worked ten years. February 2, 1860, he wedded Mattie C. Davis, daughter of Robert and Elizabeth Davis. Mrs. Brown was born September 18, 1834, and to her and husband were born seven children: Dixon Lee, Frank William, Mary, Robert Samuel, Jordan Harry, Charlie Brittin and Fannie. In 1865 Mr. Brown established a dry goods store in Lebanon with a capital of $1,195, $1,000 of which was borrowed. In 1876 he added ready-made clothing to his stock, continuing until January 1, 1885, when he sold his stock to his son, Dixon Lee. In 1874 Mr. Brown succeeded in organizing the Springfield National Bank, and was appointed cashier, but resigned at the end of six months as he did not wish to leave his old native town and county. In 1881 he organized the Peoples Bank, of Lebanon, a private bank, with a capital of $25,000, and was appointed cashier. This bank paid to its stockholders 13 per cent the first year. January 1, 1883, the capital stock of the bank was increased to $40,000. In June, 1884, Mr. Brown and his stockholders bought out the Second National Bank, of Lebanon, a bank organized in 1872, with a capital of $50,000. June 9, 1884, the People's Bank of Lebanon was consolidated with the Second National Bank, and the capital was increased to $70,000. In the reorganization Selden R. Williams was elected president, successor to James Hamilton, and W. H. Brown was appointed cashier, successor to T. J. Stratton. Mr. Brown owns $23,000 stock in the bank, two business houses in Lebanon, seven houses and lots, a small farm, and has a herd of pure bred Short-horn cattle. He belongs to the Democratic party, and is a member of the Masonic fraternity in Lodge No. 98, of Lebanon. He and wife are members of the Christian Church.

T. B. BROWN, farmer and proprietor of a saw-mill, was born in Page County, Va., March 31, 1844. He is one of six chidren born to Isaac and Rachel A. (Wood) Brown. The father was of German-Irish lineage and was born in Virginia in 1819. He was a cooper by trade and this occupation he followed the principal part of his life. He died in 1885. The mother was also of German-Irish lineage and was born in Virginia in 1821, and is at present living in De Kalb County, Tenn. The subject of this sketch assisted at home until he was twenty-two years of age, receiving his education in the schools of the county. In July, 1862, he enlisted in Company B, Fifth Tennessee Cavalry, Volunteers. He took an active part in the battles of Stone River, Missionary Ridge, Nashville and many other minor engagements. He remained in the field until the close of the war, when he returned home. In 1867 he wedded Cauras, daughter of Howard and Pattie Compton. Mrs. Brown was born in Tennessee in 1846. In 1869 Mr. Brown married Annie, daughter of Isaac and Sarah Smith. To our subject and wife were born four children: Candis, Sally, Lulecta and Daisy. In 1871 Mr. Brown bought four town lots in Alexandria, Tenn., and the year previous had purchased the saw-mill which he is at present operating and has operated successfully for the past sixteen years. In 1876 he purchased 155 acres of land in Wilson County and began tilling the soil. He is now the owner of over 300 acres of land and in connection with his farming carries on the saw-milling business. He has been quite successful in life. He is a Republican in politics and a worthy member of the Christian Church.

J. W. BRYAN, an enterprising farmer of Wilson County, Tenn., was born in Halifax County, Va., March 7, 1822, and is one of a family of ten children of Richard and Mary (Brown) Bryan. The father was a native of the "Old Dominion," born in 1792, and was married about 1818, and came to Tennessee in 1826. He was a soldier in the war of 1812 and died June 30, 1855. The mother was born in the same State as her husband in 1800, and died March 27, 1884. Our subject's early educational advantages were limited. July 15, 1849, he wedded Unity, daughter of John H. and Elizabeth Bryant. She was born in May, 1821, and died December 15, 1855, leaving three children, one now living. Samuel H. In 1846 Mr. Bryan became a soldier in the Mexican war, enlisting in Company B, First Tennessee Cavalry, and was under Gen. Scott in the bombardment of Vera Cruz for twenty-six days. He returned home in 1847 and resumed tilling his farm of 120 acres, which he had purchased in 1845. April 29, 1856, he married Margaret C., daughter of Thomas and Elizabeth (Carr) Turner. Mrs. Bryan was born in Sumner County, November 8, 1838. They have eight children: Sarah A., Tennessee, Mary, Alice, Thomas M., Hugh B., Ervin and Zula. To his first purchase of land he has added to until he at one time owned 700 acres, but now owns about 530 acres of valuable farming land. He has been exceptionally prosperous and has given his children good educations, and is himself well posted on all the topics of the day. He is a Democrat and cast his first presidential vote for Henry Clay. He and his wife belong to the Missionary Baptist Church.

PROF. E. S. BRYAN is a resident and native of Wilson County, Tenn., and was born October 13, 1856. He is the second son of six children of Algernon and Elizabeth C. (Phillips) Bryan. The father was a physician, born in 1822. He purchased 177 acres of land in Wilson County, Tenn., and there remained until his career ended. He was educated in the Eclectic Medical Institute, at Cincinnati, Ohio, and at the University of Nashville, graduating from both institutions. He was a successful physician and died in August, 1884. The mother was born in Wilson County, Tenn., in 1830, and like her husband was of Irish descent; she died July 18, 1881. Our subject, after attending the common schools, became a student in the Big Spring Seminary and Cumberland University. In 1880 he became a student in the Commercial College, at Nashville, and graduated in November of the same year. In 1881 he became book-keeper for a Nashville firm, but at the end of six months returned home. He was an instructor of the young about five years, the last two and a half years in Santa Fe, Tenn., and was a good educator and disciplinarian. After serving as book-keeper for J. T. McClain & Co., he went to Louisville, Ky., and attended a business college, devoting the most of his time to penmanship, after which he taught in Santa Fe, as above stated. Prof. Bryan is a Democrat and cast his first presidential vote for Hancock. In 1879 he was deputy postmaster of Lebanon. He is a member of the Masonic fraternity and K. of P., and belongs to the United Brethren Church.

P. B. CALHOUN was born on the 12th of December, 1819, in Wilson County, Tenn., son of Thomas and Mary (Johnson) Calhoun. The father was of Scotch-Irish origin, born in North Carolina in 1782, and came to Wilson County, Tenn., in 1801. He was married in 1809 and died in 1855. The mother was also born in North Carolina in 1784 and died in 1850. Our subject spent about one year and a half in Clinton College, Smith County, and afterward entered as sophomore at Miami College, Oxford, Ohio, graduating in 1841. In 1855 he was united in marriage to Elizabeth, daughter of Dr. and Sarah Jennings, and two children were born to their union, named Mary (wife of John Lamb), and P. J. Mrs. Calhoun lived but three years after her marriage. In 1864 Mr. Calhoun married the widow of Thomas Johnson, who has borne him the following family: Mattie S., Ewing G., Lilla M., Thomas Wayne and Corrie M. Mr. Calhoun was a resident of Columbus, Miss., a number of years and was clerk of the circuit and county courts for three years. In 1850 he went to Texas and there taught school three years, and was engaged in the land business five years. He then returned home and remained until the war, when he was made commissary agent of the Confederate States and remained in Georgia until the close of the war. Mr. Calhoun is a distant relation of John C. Calhoun. While in Texas he owned 8,000 acres of land, but suffered severe losses during the war. He now owns a good home, and is a Democrat and Mason, and he and wife are members of the Cumberland Presbyterian Church.

JOSEPH CAMPER, a farmer and stock raiser, was born October 31, 1812, in Botetourt County, Va., and is a son of John and Sallie (Level) Camper. The father was born in 1782 in Virginia and was a farmer by occupation. He died in Missouri in 1858. The mother was born in 1778 in Pennsylvania and died in Tennessee in 1838. Our subject received his education in the country schools, and at the age of twenty-two began tilling the soil for himself. In 1840 he was licensed to preach by the quarterly conference of the Methodist Episcopal Church and continued to travel and preach for four years. May 30, 1844, he married Elizabeth A. (Brewer) Camper. She was born February 15, 1826, in Tennessee, and is the daughter of M. and S. Brewer. After marriage he settled in the Twenty-second District of Wilson County on 260 acres, where he now lives. He is the father of three children: Mary J., S. E. and Willie Lee. He is a Democrat, a Mason, and he and family are members of the Methodist Episcopal Church. He was elected president of the Tennessee Annual Conference and has the respect and esteem of all his fellow-men.

HON. ROBERT CANTRELL, judge of the Seventh Judicial Circuit, is a native of Warren County, Tenn., and is a son of Isaac and Nancy (Adcock) Cantrell. The parents were of English lineage, born in South Carolina in 1784 and 1790, and died in 1840 and 1872, respectively. He was twice married, his first wife being Bettie Cantrell. He was the father of eleven children, and came to Tennessee in 1816. Robert Cantrell, the seventh son, was educated in the pioneer schoolhouse and in the Fulton Literary Academy at Smithville, Tenn. After his father's death Robert looked after the interests of the farm and cared for his mother. December 23, 1846, he and Martha Magness were married. She is a daughter of Perry and Mary Magness, and was born December 15, 1831. They have eight children living: Mary J., Kate, Harriet P., William M., Robert, Bailey, Minnie and Mattie. He worked on a farm until twenty-one years old, for some time as clerk in a store and afterward became interested in the dry goods business. About 1848 he abandoned this and began studying law. February 9, 1849, he was admitted to the bar, and is now one of the leading lawyers of Wilson County. In 1861 he enlisted in Company F, Twenty-third Regiment Infantry, and was chosen captain of his company, and was afterward elected lieutenant-colonel and in 1862 was tendered the position of colonel, and was assured he would have no opposition in case he became a candidate, but declined on account of ill health. He assisted in collecting stores for the quartermaster and commissary departments. He was captured by a scouting party in 1863, but was soon after paroled. Since the war he has been a resident of Lebanon. In 1858 he was elected to the lower house of the State Legislature and in 1860 was nominated for the Legislature again, but having no desire to enter into politics declined the race. In 1878 he was elected to his present position. He is a prominent and popular judge and to-day stands at the head of his profession. He is a Mason, and he and wife are members of the Methodist Episcopal Church South. He is a zealous temperance worker and has been ever since 1848, and says he will continue the war on whisky as long as it continues to produce crime, causes murders, makes widows and orphans, fills jails and alms houses and causes our helpless women and children to cry for help as against their oppressors—men who ought to aid as husband, parent and friend.

JOHN D. CARSON is one of seven children of James and Lucinda (Dalton) Carson, and was born in Sumner County, Tenn., in 1826. James Carson was of Irish descent and a North Carolinian by birth. He was brought to Tennessee by his parents when an infant and was a resident of Sumner County at the time of his marriage. He came to Wilson County in 1835 and became the possessor of 230 acres near Lebanon. He died in 1875. The mother was born in Virginia and died in 1852. Our subject made his home with his parents until twenty-six years old and February 4, 1852, was united in marriage to Nancy C. Johnson, born in 1835, daughter of John and Elizabeth Johnson. To Mr. and Mrs. Carson were born the following children: Cornelia (wife of R. M. Williams), Alice, Kit, Bell, Laura (wife of William King), Ida, Dora and Walter. Mr. Carson possesses 377 acres of land in Wilson County. In 1844 he had a stroke of paralysis, which has unfitted him for manual labor, and although in good health is obliged to walk with the aid of canes. He takes but little interest in politics and has not voted for a presidential candidate since 1860. Both husband and wife belong to the Christian Church.

MAJ. SAMUEL A. CARTER (deceased) was one of the leading business men of Lebanon, Tenn. He was born February 29, 1832, in Wilson County, being one of eight children of William W. and Isabella (Roane) Carter. Maj. William W. Carter was born in Culpepper County, Va., in 1798, and when quite young moved with his parents to Kentucky, and at a later period moved to Tennessee, where he engaged in various pursuits, dealing extensively in tobacco, built and owned two large flouring-mills: one at Lebanon, Wilson County, and the other in the city of Nashville. He also dealt extensively in real estate, owning some of the largest and best farms in the county; notably the celebrated Big Springs farm, containing 1,000 acres, lying seven miles east of Lebanon, and what is now known as the Grigby farm, containing 1,000 acres, three miles from Lebanon. Mr. Carter was noted for his honesty and fairness in all his dealings, and his word was always considered as good as his bond, and with his great energy and good financiering he accumulated a handsome fortune. He was a member of the Cumberland Presbyterian Church for a number of years, and died at his home near Lebanon in 1877 at the ripe old age of seventy-nine. Isabella (Roane) Carter, mother of our subject, was of a distinguished family of this State. Two of her brothers, Samuel and John Roane, were governors of Arkansas. She was also a niece of Gov. Roane, of Tennessee. She died at the old homestead near Lebanon in 1883. Our subject was educated in the schools of Lebanon, and July 4, 1876, was married to Miss Jennie Jackson, daughter of Thomas R. and Elizabeth Jackson, who were born in 1804 and 1814 in North Carolina and Missouri respectively. Mr. Jackson died May 6, 1883. Mrs. Carter was born March 22, 1853. She and husband became the parents of four children: Estelle, Willie W., Inez and Sammie. Maj. Carter lived all his life in and around Lebanon, and was closely connected with some of the town's principal business interests for years, and by his industry and fine business capacity acquired a considerable estate, and at his death was a large stockholder in the Second National Bank of Lebanon. In 1858 he and J. A. Lester established a family grocery, which they conducted three years. He was also a member of the tobacco firm of Carter & Lester. In 1861 Maj. Carter enlisted a large company of volunteers in Wilson County for the Confederate Army, and was elected their captain, and when the Forty-fifth Tennessee Regiment was organized he was elected major of the regiment. After his father's death he settled on his farm of 220 acres near Lebanon, and there died March 27, 1884. His widow and her mother have since lived on the home farm. Maj. Carter was a member of the Methodist Episcopal Church, as is his wife.

JOHN L. CASTLEMAN, farmer, was born January 15, 1838, near his present home. He is the son of Robert and Artimenta (Reed) Castleman. The father is of Welsh descent, born 1814 in Wilson County, and was a tiller of the soil. His father, Jacob Castleman, was a native of North Carolina, and came to Wilson County, Tenn., about 1800. He was a soldier in the war of 1812. Robert lived in his native county at the time of his marriage, which occurred in 1834. He settled five miles from Lebanon on the Murfreesboro Pike and bought 150 acres, and here he has since resided. He is one of Wilson County's old citizens. He believed that a rolling stone gathers no moss, as he has never lived more than one mile from his birth-place, and never been farther than Nashville from home. The mother was born 1810 in Wilson County, and died September 2, 1885. They had three children, all of whom are living. Our subject received his education in the county schools of his native county, and in addition he attended the Cumberland University of Lebanon for one year. In 1859 he wedded Sarah J. Holloway, daughter of Ezekiel Holloway. Mrs. Castleman was born 1837 in Wilson County, and by her marriage to Mr. Castleman became the mother of three children: Jef L., Edward and Val. Mr. Castleman bought 140 acres near his old home place, where he has since resided. The Castleman family do not possess the disposition to be dissatisfied. They are content to live in Wilson County.

In politics our subject is a Democrat. In 1861 he enlisted in Company A, First Tennessee Regiment, but was soon changed to the Thirty-eighth Tennessee. He took an active part in the battles of Shiloh, Murfreesboro, Corinth, and numerous minor engagements. He is a member of the Masonic fraternity, and he and wife are members of the Christian Church.

J. P. CAWTHON first saw the light of day in Wilson County, Tenn., September 27, 1817, and is one of three children of Thomas F. and Susan (Daniel) Cawthon. The father was born in Prince Edward's County, Va., August 31, 1792, and came to Tennessee in 1808. He was a farmer and stock raiser, and died in June, 1873. The mother was born in 1794, and died in March, 1874. Our subject was reared in the Twenty-fifth District of Wilson County, and obtained his education in the country schools. After attaining his majority he began learning the saddlery business, which he mastered in four years' time. December 3, 1840, he was united in matrimony to Ann (Robbins) Cawthon, who was born March 15, 1827, daughter of Thomas and Ruth Robbins. Mr. Cawthon resided for some time at Mount Juliet, Tenn., and in 1850 purchased 100 acres of land, which he has since increased to 220 acres. Since 1857 he has held the office of squire and has given good satisfaction. Mr. Cawthon has eight children: Lunsford Polk, Allie, William H., Sue W., James Edward, Thomas Preston, Mary A. and Emma Lee. Mr. Cawthon supports Democratic principles, and belongs to the I. O. O. F. His wife is a member of the Cumberland Presbyterian Church.

J. D. CHAMBERS, an enterprising farmer, was born in Wilson County, Tenn., September 17, 1844, and is a son of John and Edna (Johnson) Chambers. The father was of Scotch-Irish descent, and was born in Wilson County, Tenn., in 1806, and followed agricultural pursuits the principal part of his life. He never left his native county, and died there in 1865. The mother was of Scotch-Irish extraction, a native of Tennessee, born in 1812, and died in Wilson County, of that State, in 1878. The subject of our sketch was reared at home, and received his education in the schools of the county. After the death of his father he took charge of the estate which he superintended, with the assistance of his brothers, for about ten years. In 1874 he was married to Woody, daughter of John and Mary Miller. Mrs. Chambers was born in Wilson County, Tenn., December 19, 1849. In 1867 he bought forty-five acres of land in Wilson County, where he commenced farming on his own responsibility, and is now the owner of 243 acres of land, all lying in Wilson County, Tenn., where he is at present living. He is a Democrat and a member of the Christian Church.

H. A. CHAMBERS, farmer, was born in Wilson County, Tenn., December 23, 1841, and is a son of John and Edna (Johnson) Chambers (for sketch of parents see biography of J. D. Chambers). Our subject assisted in agricultural pursuits on the farm and attended the county schools. September 18, 1861, he enlisted in Company E, Twenty-eighth Tennessee Infantry, Confederate States Army, and took an active part in the battles of Shiloh, Chickamauga and many other minor engagements. At the close of the war he returned home, and in 1866 he was united in marriage to Marcia Holman, a native of Wilson County, Tenn., born August 20, 1844, a daughter of William S. and Sophia A. Holman. To our subject and wife were born eight children: Lelia, Eugene, Pearl, Hortense, Daisy, Sophia, Pauline and Bessie. In 1867 he purchased 165 acres of land in Wilson County, where he engaged in agricultural pursuits. He now possesses and controls about 400 acres of land in the Fifth District. He is a Democrat in politics and a member of the Christian Church.

D. D. CLAYTON, an energetic farmer of Wilson County, was born in Macon County, Tenn., in 1827, and is one of five children born to John and Phœebe (Hogg) Clayton. The father was born in North Carolina, and was a tiller of the soil; he died in 1830. The mother was born in Tennessee and died in Wilson County July 8, 1848. Our subject passed his early life on the farm, and received his education in the schools of the county. In 1866 he was married to Ann E., daughter of A. and E. Kirkpatrick. Mrs. Clayton was born in Wilson County, Tenn., in 1831, and the fruit of her union with Mr. Clayton was one child—Alexander A. Mr. Clayton is a man of energy and perseverance, and is quite a successful farmer. He is the present owner of 100 acres of land lying in the Fourth District, where he is at present living. He is a Democrat in politics.

LEMUEL N. M. COOK, M. D., was born in Wilson County, Tenn., August 15, 1815, and is a son of Green and Mary A. (Nicholson) Cook, North Carolinians, born in 1788 and 1787, and died in 1875 and 1853, respectively. The father was a soldier in the war of 1812, and was married in 1814. He was a farmer by occupation. Our subject attended the common schools, and his medical education was obtained in the Medical College of Louisville, Ky., from which institution he graduated in 1838. He was married, April 16, 1845, to Alvira Lassiter, daughter of Enos Lassiter. She was born in Tennessee in 1823 and died February 26, 1883, leaving eight children: E. K. (elsewhere written), Chloe N. (wife of Prof. Kennedy), Seluria (wife of J. P. Bashaw), Joseph L., Ella (wife of Prof. B. M. Mace), Mary, William and Emma (wife of H. L. Pickett). In 1876 Dr. Cook was elected trustee of Wilson County, and served in that capacity four successive terms, returning to his home in 1884. He is an old and highly esteemed citizen, and is a supporter of Democratic principles. He belongs to the Masonic lodge, and also of the K. of P. lodge, No. 20, of Lebanon, and the I. O. O. F. He belongs to the Methodist Episcopal Church South.

CHARLES H. COOK, farmer, was born in Davidson County, Tenn., March 29, 1826, and is one of six children born to James H. and Jane (Hope) Cook. The father was born in North Carolina in 1779, and was of English-German lineage. He was a mechanic by trade, and was elected constable and served in that capacity for several years. He was also magistrate, and held that office up to the time of his death, which occurred in 1844. The mother was born in 1800 and was of English lineage; she died in 1866. Our subject was reared in Davidson County, Tenn., and learned the plasterer's trade, which he followed successfully for twenty years. In 1850 he wedded Rachel A. Carver, who was born in June, 1824, and who is the daughter of Isaac Carver. Our subject has been engaged in the shoe business, the blacksmithing and wheelwrighting and the saw and grist-mill business since 1861. In 1865 he wedded Cleopatra Ozment, who was born August 5, 1834, and is the daughter of James H. and Martha Ozment. This union resulted in the birth of these children: Mary J., Seleta Ann, Zuella S., James E., Martha L., Oliver C. K., Evalena, Green G. and D. Lillian. Mr. Cook is a Democrat, and he and wife are members of the Missionary Baptist Church; he is also a member of the I. O. O. F. In 1875-76 he was elected constable, and filled that office in an able and satisfactory manner.

DAVID COOK was born in Rhode Island in 1795, and died June 17, 1878. He was educated in Newport, R. I., Com. Perry being his schoolmate. He was quite a mechanical genius, and after serving an apprenticeship in a machine shop became a workman of superior ability and was made foreman in large factories in Lowell. In 1841 he came to Lebanon, Tenn., to take charge of a cotton factory, and the following year sent for his wife (formerly Mary Colburn) and family. He worked at several occupations through life, and was a resident of Lebanon for thirty-eight years, being one of the substantial and influential citizens of the town. This tribute to his memory was proclaimed by the mayor of the city at his death: "To the citizens of Lebanon—Death has been among us; he has taken the oldest of our numbers. David Cook is no more. His clear, sound judgment; his moral, upright walk; his active, industrious life; his manly, Christian bearing, all call for our respect and admiration. For more than forty years he has gone in and come out before this community, and we can all bear witness to his many virtues. It is exceeding appropriate that we should show our esteem for such a life. I therefore request that all the business houses of the city be closed from 12 to 4 P. M. as a mark of respect to the deceased. E. E. Beard, mayor." He was a strong adherent of the Masonic fraternity, and was highly honored by that order. Besides having filled all the chairs of the Blue Lodge, Chapter, Council and Commandery, he officiated as Deputy Grand High Priest of the Grand Royal Arch Chapter and Deputy Grand Commander of the Grand Commandery. He was one of Tennessee's brightest Masons, and before the time of his death was said to have been the oldest living Sir Knight in Tennessee. His wife was a sister of Warren Colburn, the author of Colburn's Arithmetic, which is widely known throughout the United States.

CLARK COOK, farmer, of the Third District, was born in Lowell, Mass., November, 1832. He is the son of David and Mary (Colburn) Cook. [For further particulars of parents see sketch of Julia A. Jones, of the Tenth District.] Our subject came to Wilson County with his parents in 1841, and received his education in the Cumberland University. In 1856 he commenced clerking in a dry goods store in Lebanon. In 1858 he went to South Carolina, and from there to Alabama, where he began buying and selling carriages. During the four years of the war he was a traveling druggist dealing out medicine to the soldiers. In 1864 he clerked in a drug store in the city of New York. The following year he came to Nashville and clerked for his brother. The same year he and Mr. McCarty established a dry goods and grocery store in Lebanon, the first goods brought to the town after the war. In 1870 he went to Missouri and kept a first-class restaurant for eighteen months. In 1873 he came to Wilson County, Tenn., bought 125 acres in the Third District and began farming, which he has continued nearly ever since. January 7, 1869, he married Alice Smith, a native of Canal Dover, Tuscarawas Co., Ohio, born March 27, 1854, and the daughter of John and Annie Smith. To our subject and wife were born four children: George, Harry, David and Mary. Mr. Cook is a man of good moral character, and a useful and enterprising citizen.

E. K. COOK, farmer, was born in Wilson County, Tenn., March 3, 1846, and is one of eight children born to the marriage of L. N. M. Cook and Alvira Lassiter. (See sketch of L. N. M. Cook). Our subject was educated in his native county, and resided under the paternal roof until he was twenty-six years of age. In 1863 he enlisted in Company B, Fourth Tennessee, Confederate States Army, Cavalry, and was with Jeff Davis in Georgia when the forces were surrendered. He was in all the principal engagements with Sherman on his march to the sea. June 9, 1880, Mr. Cook wedded Susan, daughter of Samuel and Martha Young. She was born March 11, 1864, and has borne her husband two children: Bashie and Mamie. Mr. Cook is a Democrat in politics, and is a member of the I. O. O. F., and he and family are members of the Methodist Episcopal Church South.

M. W. COWEN, M. D., farmer, was born in Wilson County Tenn., March 7, 1828, and is one of seven children born to James and Nancy (Walker) Cowen. The father was born in Wilson County Tenn., in 1800, and was living in that county at the time of his marriage and followed the occupation of a farmer during his entire existence. He died in his native county August, 1838. The mother was born in Wilson County in 1806, and died in that county in 1847. Our subject passed his early life in assisting on the farm and attending the schools of the county. Later he graduated from the medical department of the University of New York. Having received his first course of lectures from the University of Louisville, Ky. In 1851 he was married to Adeline, daughter of B. and M. F. Hill. Mrs. Cowen was born in Wilson County Tenn., October 12, 1828, and by her union with Dr. Cowen became the mother of an interesting family of six children: Julius E., James B., George W., Matthew W., Albert B. and John W. In 1847 Mr. Cowen came in possession of sixty-six acres of land and in 1851 he bought 150 acres more, in Wilson County and began farming for himself. He has added from time to time and is at present the owner of over 400 acres of land, all lying in the Fourth District, where he is at present living and engaged in agricultural pursuits. He is a Democrat, a member of the Christian Church, and a successful practitioner of this county.

J. P. COX, undertaker, of Lebanon, Tenn., was born August 15, 1834, in Wilson County, son of Andrew and Sarah A. (Palmer) Cox, born in Virginia and Tennessee, in 1800 and 1804, respectively. The father came to Tennessee when ten years old with his parents, and became a prosperous farmer of Wilson County. He died in 1856 and the mother in 1876. After her husband's death she married W. A. Robinson. Our subject was educated in the common schools and in 1856 married Maria Freeman, daughter of Josiah Freeman. She was born November 4, 1837. Mr. Cox was operating a carriage factory at the breaking out of the war, and in November, 1861, enlisted in the Fourth Regiment, Tennessee Cavalry, and participated in many of the principal battles of the war. He was captured at Lebanon in 1864 and was kept a prisoner at Nashville until the fall of Richmond. In 1865 he lost his wife, and April 16, 1871, he married Jackie Maud Wright, daughter of James Wright, who was born in 1815. She was born December 19, 1854, in Arkansas. They have four children: Edgar E., Beulah M., W. Andrew and Fannie O. In 1869 Mr. Cox engaged in photography, traveling in Tennessee, Alabama, Georgia and Kentucky. In March, 1882, he engaged in his present business. He is a Democrat and in 1875 he was elected city marshal, holding the office eight years. He is a Knight of Pythias and his wife belongs to the Christian Church.

W. T. CRAGWALL, farmer, was born in Wilson County, Tenn., August 21, 1847, and is one of nine children born to William J. and Ellen B. (Harris) Cragwall. The father was of English extraction, a native of Virginia, born April 21, 1807. He came to Tennessee in 1835 and bought about 100 acres of land and began tilling the soil. He is at present living in Wilson County, and is still engaged in farming. The mother was born in Hanover County, Va., March 2, 1811, and died in Wilson County, Tenn., July 15, 1861. Our subject passed his youthful days in assisting on the farm and in getting a fair education in the schools of the county and at White Creek Spring in Davidson County, Tenn. In 1875 he married Sally Welkisen, a native of Wilson County, Tenn., born March 4, 1853, and is the daughter of Isaac J. and Elizabeth J. Welkisen. To Mr. and Mrs. Cragwall were born four children: Albert O., Tepuple O., James W. and Willie C. In 1873 our subject bought 231 acres of land in the Fifth District where he is at present living. He is a Democrat in politics and a worthy member of the Christian Church.

JAMES A. CURD is a native of Prince Edward's County, Va., born in September, 1809, and is one of twelve children of John and Elizabeth (Lumpkin) Curd. The father was a Virginian by birth, born in 1761, and came to Wilson County, Tenn., in 1818, where he settled and became the possessor of 800 acres of land. He died in 1821. The mother was born in 1775 in Virginia, and died in Wilson County, Tenn., in 1835. James A. Curd was united in marriage to Susan Everett, November 18, 1833. She was born in Wilson County, July 4, 1809, and is a daughter of John Everett. After his marriage Mr. Curd began to till the soil for himself, and by his energy and industry accumulated about 600 acres of good land, where he and wife now live. To them were born the following children: John, Eliza and Emma. Mr. Curd is a prominent farmer of the county, and favors and supports Democratic principles. He and Mrs. Curd are members of the Missionary Baptist Church.

J. N. CURD, M. D., of Mount Juliet, Tenn., was born in Wilson County, Tenn., in 1834, and is a son of William and Susan (Davis) Curd, natives, respectively, of Virginia and Tennessee. The father came to Tennessee at an early period and during his lifetime he followed the occupation of farming, owning at the time of his death, in 1842, about 420 acres of land. After her husband's death the mother, who was born in 1814, resided on the home place with her children and added 200 acres to their already extensive farm. She died in June, 1870. Our subject received his early education in the schools of his native county and in addition attended the Union University of Murfreesboro, Tenn., for one year. At the age of twenty-five he began studying medicine under A. J. Winter. In 1860 he attended the medical department of the Nashville University, remaining until the breaking out of the war, when he enlisted in Hardy Brett's company of the Forty-fifth Regular Tennessee Infantry, and served in the capacity of hospital steward and assistant surgeon. He was in many of the principal battles of the war and numerous skirmishes. He returned home May 20, 1865, and resumed his practice. In 1866 he returned to the University of Nashville, from which he graduated as an M. D. in March, 1867. He has a thorough knowledge of his profession and has met with good success. Owing to ill health he has farmed principally for the last eleven years and is the possessor of 469 acres of land. In May, 1869, he wedded Ella Winter, daughter of Dr. A. J. Winter. She was born in 1849 and became the mother of five children: Gela, William E., Elmer, Edgar and May. Dr. Curd is a Democrat and was formerly a Whig, casting his first presidential vote for Gen. Scott. He is a member of the Baptist Church and his wife of the Methodist Episcopal Church South. The Doctor is a member of the Masonic fraternity, being a Master Mason.

W. P. DAVIS was born in Wilson County, Tenn., August 19, 1833, and is one of seven children of I. F. and Sarah E. (Curd) Davis. The father was a native of Virginia, born in 1800. He was brought to Tennessee when only four years old, and afterward became a prosperous farmer and stock raiser, owning 1,500 acres of land at his death January 20, 1880. The mother was a native of the same State as her husband, born November 10, 1802, and is yet living in Wilson County with her son, R. T. Davis. Our subject was educated in the common schools and the Union University at Murfreesboro, Tenn. October 25, 1855, he was married to Margaret Elizabeth (Lindsey) Davis, born in 1834, and daughter of Lewis Lindsey. Mr. Davis was a soldier in the late war and served as quartermaster until its close. He returned home and farmed one year, and then went to Columbus, Ga., and was engaged in the livery business for six years. He then returned to Wilson County, where he manages his farm of 425 acres. He and wife have five children: S. E., Mattie A., Ella B., James L. and A. T. Mr. Davis is a Democrat, and he and family are members of the Missionary Baptist Church.

R. T. DAVIS may be mentioned as a prominent farmer and stock raiser of Wilson County, Tenn.; was born April 18, 1843, and is one of five children of I. F. and Sarah (Curd) Davis. (For parent's history see sketch of W. P. Davis.) R. T. Davis was reared to manhood on a farm in the Second District of Wilson County, Tenn., and there received his education. In 1867 he became a tiller of the soil on his own responsibility, and on the 14th day of July, 1870, the nuptials of his marriage with Alice Reynolds was celebrated. She was born in Cumberland County, Va., July 25, 1844, and is a daughter of Obadiah Reynolds. She died October 5, 1875, and Mr. Davis took for his second wife Miss Rachel J. Winter, who was born January 10, 1854, in Wilson County, Tenn., daughter of Dr. Winter. To Mr. and Mrs. Davis were born these children: Ovie W., Alice R. and Nora E. Our subject is the owner of about 650 acres of fertile land, and is doing well financially. He is a Democrat, and is a member of the Missionary Baptist Church. His wife belongs to the Methodist Episcopal Church South.

I. J. DODSON, merchant, of Lebanon, Tenn., was born July 3, 1853, in Wilson County, Tenn., and is one of four children of Isaac J. and Levina (Edwards) Dodson. The father was born in Davidson County, but was a resident of Wilson County at the time of his marriage. He was twice married and the father of eight children. He died in 1853. His widow married S. T. Nix, with whom she lived until her death in 1883. Our subject was left without a father at the age of one month. His education was obtained in Lawrence College, De Kalb County, Tenn., and Cumberland University, Lebanon. November 17, 1874, he married Sallie Cox, daughter of T. J. Cox. She was born September 8, 1857, and is the mother of five children: Tommie, Sallie L., Maggie, Harry and Isaac J. From 1871 to 1873 Mr. Dodson was salesman for Fondill & Bennett, grocers, of Lebanon, and he then engaged in the business on his own responsibility. A year later he sold out, and he and his father-in-law formed a partnership in the hardware business, the firm being known as Dodson & Cox. Later they disposed of their stock, and Mr. Dodson purchased 400 acres of land and began tilling the soil. In 1879 he sold out and returned to Lebanon, and with John W. Price started a hardware store, and later became connected with J. T. McClain in business, and the firm was later known as McClain Bros. & Co. They have about $30,000 stock, and are doing an extensive business. Mr. Dodson is a man of fine business capacity, and in politics is a Democrat. He is a member of the K. of P. and belongs to the Methodist Episcopal Church South. His wife is a Baptist.

G. T. DODSON, an enterprising farmer of the Twenty-fourth District, was born January 29, 1835, in Wilson County, Tenn., and is one of six children born to I. J. and Octavia (Ballard) Dodson. The father was born in 1808 in Tennessee, and was of Scotch-Irish extraction. He was married in 1829, and in 1850 moved to Wilson County and tilled the soil until his death, which occurred August 5, 1853. The mother was born in 1813, in Wilson County, and was the daughter of George Ballard. Her death occurred in 1842. The subject of this sketch was reared in the Twenty-fourth District, and received the rudiments of his education in the country schools and subsequently attended college three terms. He soon purchased 180 acres of land in the Eleventh District, and May 12, 1857, he wedded Sarah J. Edwards, daughter of James Edwards. Mrs. Dodson died October 5, 1871, and April 7, 1881, he was married to Maggie A. Eatherly. Mr. Dodson is the father of two children: Stonewall Jackson, born May 21, 1866 (who has received a thorough English education, and will take a collegiate course, and will then study law), and Kate, who was born September 13, 1883. In 1861 our subject volunteered in the Confederate service, and was elected captain of the Forty-fourth Tennessee (under Col. J. S. Fulton). He was in the battles of Shiloh and Murfreesboro, received a gun-shot wound, and was captured and taken to Fort Delaware, where he remained for six months, when he was exchanged at Petersburg, Va. He came back, enlisted again, was at Richmond, Petersburg and Knoxville, and was with Lee at Appomattox Court House at the time of the surrender. He then returned home and engaged in farming and stock raising. He is a Democrat in politics and a good man.

WILLIAM W. DONNELL, clerk of the Circuit Courts of Wilson County, Tenn., was born October 25, 1850, and is one of twelve children born to Robert P. and Cleopatra (Hearn) Donnell. The father was of Scotch-Irish descent, born in Virginia, and came to Tennessee in his youth. He was a farmer and owned about 200 acres of land. He was one of the early settlers of the county, and died in March, 1862. The mother was born in North Carolina and after the death of her husband made her home with our subject. She died in 1876. When William W. was but twelve years old his father died. His elder brother being in the army the burden of supporting the family fell upon William. He has only attended school about fifteen months, but in spite of this disadvantage he has a good, practical business education, acquired through study and early contact with business life. He early began speculating in stock, and when eighteen years of age hired out as a clerk in the general merchandise store of C. C. Hancock, and remained with him seven years. In 1870 he purchased Mr. Hancock's entire stock, and same year the building in which he did business caught fire, and was consumed with the entire contents. He and Marshall Young opened a similar store, but in 1881 disposed of the stock. A year later Mr. Donnell was elected to his present office by the Democratic party for a term of four years, and is now filling the duties of that office very efficiently.

G. L. DRIFOOS, groceryman, of Lebanon, was born August 14, 1849, in Nashville, and is one of twelve children of L. and Eliza (Harsh) Drifoos. The father was born in Switzerland in 1806 and at the age of seventeen years came to the United States and began his life as a pack peddler. He was economical and persevering and in a few years had accumulated sufficient means to enable him to establish a dry goods store, which he did in Harrisburg, Penn. After his marriage, in 1838, he removed to Cincinnati, Ohio, and in 1843 came to Lebanon, Tenn., where he has been in the mercantile business nearly ever since. Since 1870 he has lived a retired life. The mother was of German descent, born in Harrisburg, Penn., in 1820. Our subject was educated in Cumberland University and Franklin College, Nashville. When about seventeen years of age he engaged in business with his father but in 1870 began farming on 326 acres of land belonging to his father. In 1883 he purchased his brother Harry's grocery store, which he manages in connection with his farming. January 19, 1871, he married Laura Smith, born in 1850. They have seven children: Leopold, Frank, Alice, Harry, Mary N., Carrie and Annie Laura. Mr. Drifoos is a Democratic Prohibitionist and is a Good Templar and a member of the Cumberland Presbyterian Church. His wife belongs to the Methodist Episcopal Church South.

JOHN EATHERLY, farmer and stock raiser, was born February 3, 1821, in Wilson County, Tenn., and is a son of Warren and Peggie (Robertson) Eatherly, both natives of North Carolina. The father was born in 1780, followed agricultural pursuits, and was married in 1805. He was quite well off in this world's goods, owning over 200 acres of land besides a good many slaves. His death occurred in 1854. The mother was born in 1780 and died in 1866. She was the daughter of Hugh Robertson. The subject of this sketch grew to manhood on the farm and attended the country schools, where he received a practical education. December 28, 1843, he wedded Margaret J. Wilson, a native of Wilson County, Tenn., born February 18, 1824, and the daughter of John R. Wilson. To our subject and wife were born eleven children: Nancy C., John W., Margaret, Ann Eliza, T. Hugh, Martha E., Wilson R., Lem R., Charles H., Andrew and Mary F. Mr. Eatherly is the present owner of nearly 300 acres of good land well stocked. He was elected constable of the Second District from 1848 to 1851, which office he filled in a satisfactory manner. He was also elected magistrate and holds that office at the present time. During the late war he was one of the boys in gray and was appointed quartermaster under Gov. Harris.

DR. J. C. ESKEW, physician and surgeon, was born in 1840 in Wilson County, and is the son of Dr. Andrew and Matilda (McFarland) Eskew. The father was born March 16, 1811, in North Carolina, and was a physician and surgeon by profession. His father, Benjamin Eskew, was one of the pioneer settlers of Wilson County, and assisted in forming one of the first settlements in the district. Andrew Eskew was married in 1840, and after studying medicine for some time he took a course of lectures in the Transylvania College at Lexington, Ky. About the time of his marriage he entered upon his practice, which he continued until his death, which occurred May 6, 1854. The mother was born August 16, 1818, and died November 27, 1854. Our subject was reared at home, and received his literary education in the county schools and at Mount Vernon Academy. At the age of sixteen he began teaching and met with good success. At the age of nineteen he commenced the study of medicine under John Logue, where he remained for one year, after which he entered the medical department of the University of Nashville, from which institution he graduated in 1865. In 1861 he enlisted in Company H, Forty-fifth Regiment Tennessee Infantry. He was appointed surgeon in his regiment, and afterward commissioned as hospital steward. He was in the battles of Shiloh, Chickamauga, Missionary Ridge, Jonesboro, Atlanta, Murfreesboro, Franklin and others. He returned home in May, 1865, and began practicing medicine. November, 1865, he bought 112 acres in the Twenty-second District, a part of the old homestead, where he has since lived. November, 1867, he wedded Martha (Rogers) Carver, born in Wilson County in 1845, and to them were born five children: Alice A., James O., Andrew O., Viola G. and Lula B. Mrs. Eskew had one child, Jonas, by her first husband. Dr. Eskew is one of the leading surgeons of Wilson County, and bears an unsullied reputation. He and wife are members of the Christian Church.

J. M. FAKES, senior member of the boot and shoe store of Fakes, Taylor & Co., and senior member of the firm of Fakes & Co., dealers in coal and lumber, was born June 21, 1844, in Wilson County, Tenn., and is a son of W. C. and Elizabeth (Moser) Fakes. The father was of Scotch-Irish descent, born in 1816, a farmer by occupation, and was married in 1834. The mother was of Scotch-German descent, born in 1818 in Wilson County, and she and her husband are yet living. Our subject received a common education, and began doing for himself at the age of twelve. He clerked for some time in Lebanon, and at the breaking out of the war joined the Confederate Army in May, 1861, in Company K, Eighteenth Regiment Tennessee Volunteer Infantry. He was captured at Fort Donelson and taken to Camp Butler, Ill. Three months later he made his escape and joined Morgan's command. He afterward joined his own command, and later was one of Hawkins' scouts. He was again captured and taken to Fort Delaware. June 11, 1867, he wedded Rosa A. Gugenheim, born in Nashville in 1848. They have five children: Sally, Mark, Daisy, Gertrude and Clarence. He has been engaged in business in Lebanon for twenty-one years. He is a member of the Masonic, K. of H. and K of P. fraternities. He and wife are members of the Cumberland Presbyterian Church.

COL. O. G. FINLEY was born in Kentucky in 1787, and came to Tennessee when a young man, locating in Lebanon in 1807. He was a son of Samuel Finley, who was born in the north of Ireland and was of Scotch descent. At what date he came to the United States is not known. He was married to Mary Gains, of Kentucky or Virginia. Col. O. G. Finley wedded Mary Lewis Johnson, of Sumner County, Tenn., in 1811, daughter of Jesse Johnson, of North Carolina, who was a Revolutionary soldier. His wife, Mary Lewis, was also born in North Carolina, and they came to Tennessee, locating in Sumner County at an early period. Col. O. G. Finley's wife died in 1830, leaving the following children: Jesse J., William M., John B. (deceased), Foster G., Sarah A. and Mary (deceased). Col. Finley served in the Creek war, and was a member of the State Senate about 1812 or 1813, when Knoxville was the capital of the State. He was a leather manufacturer, and retired to his farm near Lebanon in 1830. He was a man of strong character, reared in Kentucky when it was a frontier State. He received a limited early education, but owing to his fondness for books and thirst for knowledge he became a finely educated man, and was pronounced by the Rev. Dr. Lindsly, president of the Nashville University, one of the best-read historians in the State. As the epitaph on his tombstone indicates, he was "an honest man." Jesse J., his eldest son, was born in Wilson County, Tenn., November 18, 1812, and received an academic education. He was captain of mounted volunteers in the Seminole war, and afterward studied law and was admitted to the bar in 1838. He located in Arkansas in 1840, and was elected to the State Senate in 1841. He removed to Memphis, Tenn., in 1842, and began practicing law. He was elected mayor of Memphis in 1845, but a year later removed to Florida and was there elected to the State Senate in 1850, and was appointed candidate for presidential elector on the Whig ticket in 1852. He became judge of the Western Judicial Circuit of Florida in 1853, and was elected to the same two terms without opposition. In 1861 he was elected judge of the Confederate States Court, but resigned in 1862 and enlisted as a private in the Confederate Army, and arose to the rank of captain, colonel and brigadier-general. In 1871 he located in Jacksonville, Fla., and in 1874 was elected to the United States Congress, and re-elected in 1876, but declined to be a candidate in 1878. He was again elected in 1880, but is now practicing law in Ocala, Fla. He has four children: Lucius, George, Charles A. and Maggie. William M., second son of O. G. Finley, was born in Lebanon, Tenn., October 11, 1816; received an academic education, and in 1836 volunteered and served as private in the Seminole war. He returned home in 1837 and began studying medicine, and in the following fall entered the Cincinnati College of Medicine, but in 1838 removed to Transylvania University at Lexington, Ky., where the title of M. D. was conferred upon him in 1839. He traveled over the "Lone Star State," but in 1840 located in Arkansas. In 1842 he was elected to the lower house of the State Legislature. In 1843 he removed to Clarksville, Tenn., where he practiced his profession thirty years. In 1871, owing to impaired hearing, he gave up his profession and purchased and located on the old homestead. He was last married to Mrs. V. C. (Corad) Boyd. They have two children: Virgie Lee and Jessie C. John B., third son of O. G. Finley, was born in Lebanon in 1820. He received a practical education, and early evinced a fondness for military tactics. He possessed a splendid *physique,* and at the commencement of the late civil war was made captain of a corps of men from Arkansas, where he then resided. Owing to disease he was compelled to resign his command, and, after several painful operations, died at Searcy, Ark., in 1868. He had taken the degree of doctor of medicine, and ranked high in the community where he practiced. Foster G., fourth son of O. G. Finley, was born in Lebanon in 1822, and received a fair English education. He was reared on his father's farm, and immigrated to Arkansas in 1843. He soon after returned to Wilson County, Tenn., where he now resides, and is noted for his generous hospitality and kindness of heart.

FOSTER G. FINLEY may be mentioned as one of the oldest citizens and farmers of Wilson County, Tenn. He was born March 22, 1822, and is one of eight children of O. G. and Mary L. (Johnson) Finley. (See Dr. Finley's sketch.) Foster was educated in the Campbell Academy at Lebanon, and in 1842 married Mary Buckner, who died the same year. In June, 1845, he wedded Almira Taylor, born October 10, 1826, daughter of Isaac and Margaret Taylor. To Mr. and Mrs. Finley were born this family: Isaac, Mary (wife of Louis Peyton), Maggie (widow of Gus Lampton), William, Charles and Obadiah. Isaac has an orange farm in Florida, and William is in Alabama practicing medicine. Mr. Finley spent five years in Arkansas and some time in Florida, but the greater part of his life has been spent in Tennessee. In 1884 he purchased 50 acres of land in the Ninth District where he yet resides. He has devoted his life to the tilling of the soil, with the exception of three years' residence in Nashville, where he was in the grocery business a short time and then clerked on a steamer on the river. Mrs. Finley is a member of the Methodist Episcopal Church South.

ROBERT V. FOSTER, A. M., D. D., professor of exegetical theology and the Hebrew language in Cumberland University, Lebanon, Tenn., was born in Wilson County, Tenn., August 12, 1845, and is a son of Rufus H. and Sarah (Spain) Foster, who were born in Tennessee in 1814 and 1818, respectively. The grandfather of our subject was John Foster, who came from North Carolina to Tennessee in 1796, and followed the life of an agriculturist. He participated in the war for independence, being a soldier in the army of Washington. Rufus H. Foster was married in 1841 and settled on a portion of the old home place, and eventually became the possessor of 240 acres. His wife died in 1876, and he has lived with his son John and our subject since that time. His children are John S., Benjamin S. (the principal of the Lebanon College for Young Ladies), Mrs. Addie Ellington, Mrs. Charlotte Brantly and Robert V., who was reared on a farm and received his rudimentary education in the neighboring country schools. At the age of twenty-two he entered the sophomore class of Cumberland University at Lebanon, graduating as an A. B. in 1870. The following year he was elected to the chair of mathematics in the Cooper Institute at Daleville, Miss., which position he held four years. In 1875 he returned to Cumberland University and graduated from the theological department with high honors, receiving the degrees of D. D. and A. M. The following year he entered the senior class of the Union Theological Seminary, New York City, and remained one year, receiving the graduating degree, and while there was proffered the professorship of mathematics in the Waynesburg (Penn.) College. He remained one term and received a call to his first *alma mater* to become professor of *belles lettres* and Hebrew, and entered on his duties in the fall of 1877, occupying the chair four years. He was then tendered his present position, which he has since filled with credit to himself and honor to the institution. While teaching at Waynesburg he formed the acquaintance of Miss Belle Braden, to whom he was married November 7, 1882. She is the daughter of D. W. Braden, M. D., and was educated in the Waynesburg College and at Vassar, and has traveled in Europe and visited the leading cities of this country, being a very intelligent and refined lady. Prof. Foster is one of the leading educators of the South, and is a member of the Blue Lodge of the Masonic fraternity. He and wife are members of the Cumberland Presbyterian Church.

JOHN H. FREESE, merchant tailor, of Lebanon, Tenn., was born in Hanover, Germany, September 4, 1850. His parents were Wessel and Angelia (Ahrens) Freese, the father being a forester by occupation employed by the Government. They were born in 1812 and 1822, and died in 1881 and 1853, respectively. Wessel Freese was twice married and was the father of seven children, four by his first wife. John H. Freese was educated in the schools of Hanover, attending until fourteen years of age, when he became an apprentice at the tailor's trade and worked as such two and a half years. In 1867 he came to the United States, locating in Louisville, Ky., where he worked at his trade until 1872, with the exception of one year spent in Chicago. At the latter date he went to Chattanooga, Tenn., remaining two and a half years and has resided in the following places: Huntsville, Ala., fifteen months; Fayettville, fifteen months; Tullahoma, three years; Nashville, two years, and in 1881 came to Lebanon, where he has since reresided. June 8, 1876, he married Alice Crawford, of Tullahoma, Tenn., born in 1858. They have two children: Eva and Katie. Mr. Freese is a skillful tailor and has built up a lucrative trade. He belongs to the following fraternities: Masonic, I. O. O. F., K. of P. and K. of H. He and wife are members of the Cumberland Presbyterian Church.

JESSE H. GLEAVES is a son of Guy T. and Julia A. (Jennings) Gleaves, and was born May 6, 1859, in Wilson County, Tenn. The father was born in 1814 and was a farmer by occupation, and also followed the mercantile business. He was married in 1851 and died in 1867. The mother was born in 1817 and died in 1885. The subject of our sketch was reared and educated in Wilson County. When only sixteen years of age he began tilling the soil for himself and afterward purchased a farm of thirty-five acres and is now a well-to-do citizen. On the 28th of November, 1880, his marriage with Miss Annie T. Hawks was celebrated. She is a daughter of Preston and Cassandra Hawks. Our subject is a highly respected citizen of the county in which he resides, and a strong supporter and believer in the principles of Democracy. His wife is a member of the Christian Church.

EUGENE C. GLEAVES is a native of Nashville, Tenn., born March 24, 1864, and is one of five children of James W. and Emma L. (Stroud) Gleaves, natives of Wilson County, Tenn. They were married in 1861 and six years later moved to Green Hill Tenn., where the father opened a dry goods and grocery store, continuing until 1873, when he began ginning cotton. In 1883 he sold his cotton-gin and removed to Nashville, where he now resides. The subject of our sketch was educated in the common schools of Wilson County, and at the age of eighteen began doing for himself. He was married November 30, 1882, to Rosa B., daughter of Leonard and Elizabeth Lowe. She was born March 7, 1865, and became the mother of two children. Mr. Gleaves has the reputation of being an honest and trustworthy gentleman, and in politics is an old line Democrat and belongs to the I. O. G. T. at Green Hill.

J. B. GRANDSTAFF, a thrifty farmer and native of the Sixteenth District of Wilson County, Tenn., was born February 17, 1831, and is one of eight children of David and Margaret (Phillips) Grandstaff. The father was born in Wilson County about 1805, and was married in 1828 and immediately began farming. He died January 1, 1852. The mother was born in Wilson County two years later than her husband and died about 1865. Our subject was educated in the schools near home and remained on the home farm until twenty-seven years of age. In 1857 he wedded Miss Arsula, daughter of Stacy and Jane (Anderson) Young. Mrs. Grandstaff was born in Wilson County in 1836. She and her husband became the parents of these children: William D., Jane, Frank, Mary and Martha. Mr. Grandstaff is a well-to-do farmer and owns about 230 acres of valuable and well improved land. He has been very industrious and by his own efforts has accumulated a large amount of property. He is conservative in his political views but on national tickets votes usually with the Democratic party. He belongs to the Masonic fraternity and he and wife are members of the Baptist Church.

WILLIAM J. GRANNIS, A. M., principal of the preparatory school of the Cumber land University, was born April 24, 1823, in Morristown, St. Lawrence Co., N. Y. He was educated in the Jefferson County Institute at Watertown, N. Y., and the State Normal School at Albany, N. Y., graduating from the latter in 1847. He began his first work in teaching November 29, 1841, and afterward followed that occupation in Chaumont, N. Y., and the following year was elected principal of the graded school at Cape Vincent, being also superintendent of the town schools, which position he held four years. In 1852 he came to Wilson County, Tenn., having been chosen principal English teacher of the preparatory school of Cumberland University. Owing to the war the school was suspended in 1862, and Prof. Grannis was given a clerkship in the quartermaster's department of the Union Army, stationed at Nashville, holding the position until 1866, when he was appointed as deputy internal revenue collector of the Fifth District of Tennessee. In 1873 he resigned, having previously been elected principal of the preparatory school of Cumberland University, and was at once elected to his former position, thus forcibly illus. trating his ability as an educator and a disciplinarian. Previous to the war the degree of A. M. was conferred upon him by the Cumberland University, which demonstrates how high a position he held in the estimation of the faculty and board of trustees. In October, 1849, he was united in marriage to Lucy A. Gates, born in Oneida, N. Y., in

September, 1829, daughter of Eliphas and Lucy Gates. Prof. and Mrs. Grannis are the parents of the following family: Herbert W., who is assistant teacher in the preparatory school of the university; Hattie, who is music teacher in the girls' department, and Henry. Prof. Grannis and family are members of the Cumberland Presbyterian Church. His parents, John and Marian (Dunlap) Grannis, were natives of Oneida County and Schoharie County, N. Y., born in 1798 and 1802, respectively. The father was a farmer, and always made "York State" his home. He was married three times, and was the father of two children. He died in 1877 and the mother in 1846.

J. S. GRIBBLE, attorney at law, of Lebanon, was born in Warren County, Tenn., in October, 1834. His education was received in Videmour College and Burrett College, of Warren and Van Buren Counties, respectively. J. S. speculated in stock for several years after leaving his parents, and in 1856 commenced merchandising in his native county, and continued until the breaking out of the war. In September, 1861, he enlisted in Company B, Fifth Regiment Tennessee Infantry, and the same month was appointed commissary of his company, holding the rank of captain. He was captured soon after the battle of Missionary Ridge, and taken to McMinnville, where he was paroled with the condition that he was to report every thirty days. After the surrender of the Confederate Army he returned to Lebanon, and entered the law department of the Cumberland University, remaining two sessions. In February, 1856, he went to Woodbury, Tenn., and began practicing with Judge Robert Cantrell, but in 1879 dissolved partnership by mutual consent. In April of the following year Mr. Gribble came to Lebanon. In 1870 he was appointed judge of the Cannon County Court, and held the office one year. In July, 1857, he wedded S. J. Webb, daughter of B. W. Webb. She was born in 1836, and is the mother of these children: Nora (wife of F. B. Martin), Clingman, Gertrude (wife of J. E. Miller), Hilda (wife of Stokely Black), Robert E., Power, Cannon and Vida. Mr. Gribble is an earnest advocate and safe counselor, and has arisen to distinction in his profession.

J. V. GRIGSBY, a prominent farmer and stock raiser of Wilson County, Tenn., was born in Clark County, Ky., in 1826, and is one of five children of Lewis K. and Fanny (Bush) Grigsby, natives of Clark County, Ky., born in 1801 and 1804, and died in 1864 and 1849, respectively. They were married about 1822, and the father was a wealthy farmer, owning at the time of his death 300 acres of land. J. V. Grigsby was educated at Winchester, Ky., and after the death of his mother assumed control of the old homestead, of which he became the owner, and to which he added acres until he owned 600 acres of land. October 16, 1867, he married Mary C. Robinson, daughter of Dr. Thomas H. Robinson. Mrs. Grigsby was born April 5, 1848. They have six children: Fannie, Mary W., Thomas R., Amanda C., John V. and Lewis K. In 1878 Mr. Grigsby sold the old home place and came to Wilson County, Tenn., where he purchased 618 acres of land. For the past twenty years he has been dealing in fine horses, cattle and mules. His average price for cattle is about $1,000, but he has received as high as $3,000 for one animal. He is a Democrat, and he and wife are church members.

WILLIAM HAY HALBERT was born in Lincoln County, Tenn., March 26, 1847, being the son of Pleasant and Nancy (Crawford) Halbert, both of whom were born and raised in the above county. Our subject was brought up on the farm, and attended college at Cain Hill, Ark., for three years under Prof. Buchanan. In about 1867 he began the study of medicine, and in 1872 entered the Eclectic School of Medicine in Cincinnati, and remained until 1873, at which time he returned to his native county and began the practice of his profession. He enlisted in the Ninth Regiment of Tennessee Confederate Cavalry, and before he had reached his eighteenth year was commissioned color-bearer of the same. After six years and a half spent in the practice of medicine in Lincoln County, our subject removed to Lebanon, Wilson County, in order to give his children the benefit of the excellent schools, and also to practice medicine. In September, 1870, he was married to Susan J. Beatie, who was born also in Lincoln County in 1846. To them have been born two children: Thomas Edwin, born in July, 1872, and Mary Beatie (deceased), born September, 1876. Our subject and wife are members of the Cumberland Presbyterian Church. Though practicing in a comparatively new school of medicine (the eclectic), Dr. Halbert has succeeded in building up a large practice, and occupies a prominent position in the medical fraternity of Wilson County. He is a member of the National Eclectic Medical Association, and makes a practice of attending all the meetings of the State Association. He is devoted to his profession, and is one of the very few physicians who practice for love of the profession as well as for gain. Our subject's father was one of the wealthiest land and slave owners in Lincoln County before the war.

W. F. HAMBLEN, an enterprising farmer and stock raiser of the Twenty-fourth District, was born March 30, 1817, in Wilson County, Tenn., and is one of a family of eleven children born to Joseph F. and Martha (Hill) Hamblen. The father was born in Virginia in 1790 and was of Turkish extraction. In 1815 he immigrated to Wilson County, Tenn., purchased land in the Second District and engaged in farming. By energy and perseverance he accumulated considerable means which enabled him to enjoy the comforts of life. He died May, 1861. The mother was also a native of Virginia, and died in Wilson County in June, 1871. Our subject was reared in the Twenty-fourth District of Wilson County, Tenn., and secured a fair education in the country schools. November 3, 1841, he purchased a farm of 112 acres in the Twenty-fourth District, and in the same year he was united in marriage to Sallie Foster (Cloide) Hamblen. Mr. Hamblin has always followed the occupation of a farmer and in this he has been quite successful. He is a Democrat in politics.

HON. JAMES HAMILTON, president of the Bank of Lebanon, and one of Wilson Counties prominent farmers, was born August 14, 1814, in Loudoun County, Va., and is one of six children born to William and Margaret (Hugley) Hamilton. The father was of Irish descent, born in Virginia, and was a farmer by occupation. In 1815 he came to Wilson County, Tenn., and located in the Twenty-fourth District. He was quite successful as a farmer, owning 1,000 acres at one time. His death occurred in 1840 or 1841. The mother was of English descent and was also a native of Virginia. She died about 1870 at the advanced age of eighty years. Our subject was educated in the country schools and later in the Cumberland University at Nashville. At the age of twenty-two he began teaching, which he continued for several years. May 20, 1841, he married Jane McFarland, daughter of James and Dicy McFarland. Mrs. Hamilton was born August, 1824, in Wilson County. They have five children: Nannie, wife of Dr. W. G. Miller; Emma, wife of John L. Jones; James W., a farmer; John M., a druggist, and Robert Hatton, a lawyer. In 1856 he bought 1,200 acres in the Third District, where he now resides. In 1881 he succeeded Dr. Owen as president of the Second National Bank of Lebanon, where he remained until 1884, when the Bank of Lebanon was organized, and he was elected as its president. About 1881 he was elected president of the Humbold Carriage & Wagon Factory. Mr. Hamilton has dealt largely in buying and selling land, and at one time was running 1,800 acres, and is a man of marked business capacity and a successful financier. In politics he is a Democrat, and in 1843 he was elected to the Legislature and in 1847 he was elected to the Senate in the State Legislature, and again in 1872. During the war he was appointed colonel of the State militia in Wilson County, and thus he is known as Col. Hamilton.

J. W. HAMILTON, JR., was born August 10, 1853, in Wilson County, Tenn., and is the eldest son born to Col. James and Jane (McFarland) Hamilton. Our subject was reared on the farm, and received a rudimentary education in the county schools. At the age of fifteen he entered the Central College at Fayette, Mo., which institution he attended for two and a half years, graduating from the mathematical department. After leaving school he secured the position of passenger conductor on the Nashville & Chattanooga Railroad, his line of travel being from Nashville to Lebanon. This position he held for eight years. During the time he was on the railroad he was in partnership with J. R. Shorter in the livery and feed stable business in Lebanon for a period of two years. September 14, 1883, he wedded Ruth Lee Powell, who was born in 1865, and who is the daughter of William and Sarah Powell. To our subject and wife was born one child, James W. In 1884 Mr. Hamilton abandoned the railroad business and turned his attention to agricultural pursuits. He owns 780 acres on the Nashville Pike, five miles west of Lebanon. The first county court ever held in the county assembled on his farm. Mr. Hamilton is a young man of push and energy, which are essential to success. He is a practical business man, and understands the modern idea of cultivating and enriching the soil. He is very conservative in regard to politics, voting for principle rather than for party. His wife is a member of the Methodist Episcopal Church South.

SAMUEL HAMILTON, farmer, was born in Guilford County, N. C., March 7, 1818, and is the son of George and Rebecca (Greer) Hamilton. The father, born in Guilford County, N. C., in 1795, was of Irish extraction. He was a farmer by occupation, and in 1819 left his native State and immigrated to Williamson County, Tenn., where he bought 200 acres of land. His death occurred in 1869. The mother was born about 1793 in North Carolina, and died at the unusual age of eighty-five. Our subject was reared on the farm, and secured his education in the country schools held in the old-fashioned log-houses, with stick and mud chimney, greased paper for window lights, puncheons for seats, and the wide fire-place so prevalent in those early days. October 31, 1844, he married Fredonia Rice, daughter of James Rice. She was born about 1825 in Wilson County. This union resulted in the birth of two children: Andrew J. and Rebecca A. After marriage Mr. Hamilton settled on 180 acres in the Twenty-fifth District, which his Grandfather Hamilton received for services rendered in the Revolutionary war. He is very conservative in politics, voting for principle and not for party. He was formerly a member of the old Whig party, casting his first vote for W. H. Harrison in 1840.

HON. R. A. HANCOCK, farmer, was born in Wilson County, Tenn., January 17, 1827, and is one of twelve children of Lewis and Frances (Adams) Hancock, born in Virginia in 1788 and 1791, and died in Tennessee in 1866 and 1864, respectively. The father was of English origin, and came to Tennessee with his brother, Richard, in 1809. He was married in 1812. The subject of this sketch spent his boyhood days on a farm and acquired the rudimentary portion of his education in the schools near his home, and afterward attended the Liberty school in DeKalb County, Tenn. January 12, 1858, he married Ann J. Sneed, daughter of John and Annie Sneed. Mrs. Hancock was born in Wilson County, January 29, 1835. She and husband became the parents of these children: Delta (deceased), Etna (wife of Jacob Young), Addie (deceased), Walter, Hallie and Myrtle. After attaining his majority, Mr. Hancock began farming for himself, but at the end of three years went to Texas where he remained six years. He then returned and purchased 500 acres of land in Cannon County, where he remained until the fall of 1879. In 1870 he purchased his present farm and now owns 250 acres of valuable land, also 166 acres of fine land in Cannon County, including the old home place of his father. Mr. Hancock has held various civil offices, and in 1884 was chosen to represent Wilson County in the State Legislature. He is a Democrat and a member of the Masonic fraternity, and is always ready to assist laudable enterprises, and has been instrumental in organizing and starting a number of schools. He is a grandson of Benjamin Hancock, who helped prepare the Declaration of Independence. He and wife are members of the Baptist Church.

WESLEY HANCOCK, farmer and stock raiser, was born in 1829 in Wilson County, and is the son of Wesley and Polly (Lee) Hancock. The father was born 1787 in the State of North Carolina, and in his early life was a hatter, but in his latter days engaged in farming. He was married in 1815, and in 1818 emigrated to Wilson County, Tenn,, where he died in 1865. The mother was born in 1796 in North Carolina, and after the death of her husband made her home with her son, James H. She died January 13, 1883, at the advanced age of eighty-six. Our subject received his education in the schools of his native county, and remained at home until twenty-one years of age. June 6, 1856, he married Margaret Drake, daughter of James and Jane Drake. Mrs. Hancock was born in 1834 in Wilson County, and by her marriage to Mr. Hancock became the mother of three children: Samuel L., Hettie L. and Kate. After marriage our subject bought 244 acres in the

Twenty-first District, four miles south of Lebanon, on the Murfreesboro Pike, where he now resides. He has added to his land from time to time, and at the present owns 564 acres. Mr. Hancock is highly esteemed as a good citizen and neighbor. During the late war he was a Union man, but was formerly a member of the old Whig party. His wife is a member of the Methodist Episcopal Church South.

PROF. J. B. HANCOCK, A. B., A. M., principal of Maple Hill Seminary, was born in July, 1848, in Wilson County and is the son of Martin and Martha (Handcock) Hancock. The father was of Scotch lineage and was born in 1827 in Wilson County. He was a farmer by occupation. His parents, our subject's grandfather and grandmother, were natives of Virginia, coming to Tennessee as early as 1796. They remained in the fort at Nashville for a short time and then came to Wilson County. The grandfather settled on Pilot Knob and assisted in farming the first settlement. Martin Hancock located in the Nineteenth District and purchased 300 acres of land. Here he remained uniii his career ended. He died April 16, 1876. The mother was of Scotch lineage, a native of Wilson County, Tenn., and her birth occurred in 1832. Since her husband's death she has been living with her son, Prof. J. B. Hancock. The subject of this sketch was reared at home and received the rudiments of his education in the county schools. At the early age of fourteen he assumed control of his father's farm and managed it successfully for some time, and when nineteen years of age he entered the sophomore Class of the Cumberland University, graduating with honors June, 1870. He then entered the teacher's profession and was elected president of Woodbury College, Cannon County, where he remained for two years. Subsequently he was president of different colleges and at the present is president of Maple Hill Seminary, of which institution he is the founder and proprietor. It was organized September 1, 1880, for the purpose of educating young ladies. It is beautifully situated west of Lebanon on the Nashville & Lebanon Pike. It had a gradual increase from its organization and at the present accommodates 118 pupils. Prof. Hancock owns 268 acres of land and supplies his boarding school from the products of this fertile farm. He also owns the old homestead of 300 acres. As an educator, Prof. Hancock ranks among the leaders of the county and is universally recognized as a very able instructor and disciplinarian. In 1870 his *alma mater* conferred on him the degree of A. B., and in 1873 the degree of A. M.; October 15, 1874, he wedded Julia J. Harris, daughter of Baker W. and Sarah Harris. Mrs. Hancock was born October 29, 1852, in Wilson County. Our subject is a member of the Masonic fraternity (Knights Templar) and K. of P., having taken all the degrees. He is a member of the Methodist Episcopal Church South, and his wife of the Christian Church.

J. E. HANCOCK, an enterprising farmer of District No. 21, was born August 19, 1852, where he is now living. He is the son of William and Sophia (Hines) Hancock. The father was born June 14, 1818, in District No. 21, Wilson County, and was a farmer by occupation. At the time of his marriage, which occurred February 10, 1842, he was living in his native county. In July, 1845, he bought 185 acres in the Twenty-first District, where he located and remained until his death, which occurred August 18, 1872. He was quite successful as a farmer, owning at one time upward of 1,000 acres. The mother was born January 17, 1824, in Lincoln County, Tenn., and died July 30, 1866. There were seven children born to this union, six of whom are living. Our subject received his education in the country schools, and in addition he attended Woodbury College at Woodbury, Tenn. October 10, 1877, he wedded Carrie Alsup, a native of Wilson County, born September 17, 1860, and the daughter of Rev. A. H. Alsup. To Mr. and Mrs. Hancock were born two children: Homer and Howard. After marriage our subject remained on the old home place where he now resides. He is a young man of push and energy, and owns 590 acres in the Twenty-first District, and he and his wife own 295 acres in the Twenty-third District. In politics he is a Democrat, and a member of the Masonic fraternity. His wife is a member of the Cumberland Presbyterian Church.

WILLIAM HANNAH, M. D., is a son of John M. and Amelia (Jones) Hannah, and was born October 12, 1828. The parents were of Welsh and Scotch descent, born in 1802 and 1806, respectively, in Tennessee. The father was a farmer, and died in 1830. His widow then married Dr. Hardin Ragland, and died December 15, 1885. Our subject was educated in the Cumberland University, and when twenty-one years old began studying medicine under Dr. Ragland. In 1851 he graduated from the Louisville (Ky.) Medical College, and in February of that year wedded S. E. Hankins, born in 1835 in Wilson County, and daughter of Matthew C. and Martha P. Hankins. They have one child living—John Matthew. Dr. Hannah was with Dr. Ragland two years, and then moved to Cherry Valley and practiced about the same length of time. In 1860 he bought 160 acres of land, and carried on farming with his practice. In 1885 he sold out and moved to Lebanon, and a year later established a livery and feed stable, with Merrit House as partner, still continuing his practice. The Doctor and wife are members of the Methodist Episcopal Church South, and he belongs to the Good Templars.

DR. J. S. HARALSON, farmer, was born August 2, 1832, in Davidson County, Tenn., and is the son of Jara and Margaret (Hessa) Haralson The father was of English descent, born in 1802 in Halifax County, Va., and was a farmer by occupation. He came to Tennessee, and in 1824 was married. In 1839 he bought 500 acres in the Twenty-second District, Wilson County, where he died in 1879. He was twice married, and was the father of six children, three of whom are living. The mother was of Irish descent, born in 1803 in Virginia. She died in 1836. Our subject was reared without a mother's love or training, she having died when he was but four years old. He was educated in the country schools and in Booth Spring Seminary. At the age of twenty-four he commenced the study of medicine, which he continued for three years. In 1854 he entered the medical department of the University of Nashville, and took a course of lectures. October 18, 1856, he married Sarah Sanders, a native of Tennessee, born in 1840, and the daughter of Thomas Sanders. To Mr. and Mrs. Haralson were born five children: Leonard. James, Samuel, Chorus and Beulah. In 1857 he began practicing, and continued until the war, when he enlisted in the Second Tennessee Cavalry. He was in the battle of Coffeeville, Belmont, and numerous skirmishes. In February, 1863, he was discharged, and returned home, settling near the old home place. After his father's death he moved to the old homestead, where he has since resided. Dr. Haralson lost his wife in 1872, and in 1881 he married M. F. Gleaves, a native of Tennessee, born in 1854, and by this union became the father of three children: Zara, Mary and Etta G. The Doctor now owns 394 acres, and is a Prohibitionist. He is a member of the Masonic fraternity, and he and wife are members of the Baptist Church.

WILLIAM M. HARKREADER, clerk of the Wilson County Court, was born February 9, 1839, the youngest of three children born to John F. and Judith (Oldham) Harkreader. The father was of German origin, born in Virginia in 1805, and a wheelwright and farmer by occupation. He came to Robertson County, Tenn., in his youth, but after residing some time in Kentucky came to Wilson County, Tenn., and there resided until his death in 1878. The mother was born in 1810, and came from Virginia to Tennessee in her youth, and here died in 1878, only a few hours previous to that of her husband. William M. was educated in the schools of Wilson County, and at the breaking out of hostilities between the North and South he enlisted in Company I, Seventh Regiment Tennessee Infantry, and participated in many of the bloodiest engagements of the war. He was so severely wounded at the second battle of Manassas that his left arm was amputated. At the reorganization of the army he was made second lieutenant, and rose to the rank of first lieutenant. After receiving his wound he was given post duty until 1864, when he resigned, but was captured at Rome, Ga., and taken to Johnson's Island, where he remained until the surrender. After his return home he attended school ten months, and in 1870 was elected revenue collector of Wilson County for two years, and in 1873 was appointed to fill an unexpired term in the same office by the county court. In 1877 he was appointed deputy clerk of the county court, and served until 1880. Since 1882 he has held his present office, and has given good satisfaction. December 5, 1878, he married Ella L. Coe, daughter of J. F. Coe. Mrs. Harkreader was born in 1859 in Lebanon. They have one child, Mary L. Mr. Harkreader is a Mason, a member of the I. O. O. F., K. of P. and A. O. U. W.

J. A. HAYNES, proprietor of a boot and shoe store and manufacturing establishment of Lebanon, was born March 2, 1825, in Williamson County, Tenn., son of Anderson and Margaret (Swift) Haynes, born in Virginia, the father in 1784. He was a carpenter, and after his marriage came to Williamson County, Tenn., where he died in 1830. The mother died in 1827, thus leaving our subject without a protector. At the age of eight years he was bound out to John M. Wright, of whom he learned the shoe-maker's trade, continuing four years, at the expiration of which he was bound out to William Denning, of Nashville, remaining with him seven years. In 1844 he came to Lebanon and in 1845 established a boot and shoe establishment. At the latter date he married Elizabeth Harrington, daughter of H. and L. Harrington. Mrs. Haynes died in 1848, having borne two children, both of whom are deceased. September 2, 1849, Mr. Haynes married Martha Smith, born in 1831, daughter of James and Elizabeth Smith. Mr. and Mrs. Haynes have two children: John and Elizabeth. Mr. Haynes is the oldest business man of Lebanon, and his boot and shoe establishment is the next oldest in the United States. By his straightforward course through life he has deservedly prospered. He is a Democrat, and cast his first presidential vote for James K. Polk. He is a Mason and a member of Lodge No. 98, of Lebanon, and he and wife are members of the Missionary Baptist Church.

LEE HAYS, farmer, was born at Cottage Home, Tenn., in September, 1834, and is one of nine children born to James T. and Marlinda (Knight) Hays, natives of North Carolina, born in 1803 and 1807 and died in 1864 and 1875, respectively. They were married in Tennessee in 1825. Our subject was educated in the schools near his home, and on the 24th of April, 1861, wedded Miss M. P., daughter of James M. and Nancy Weatherby. She was born in Rutherford County in 1844, and departed this life April 12, 1877. To them were born five children, four of them now living: Martha L., James P., Hattie M. and Lockie D. In March, 1880, he wedded F., daughter of Thomas and Elizabeth Kiolon. Mrs. Hays was born in 1854, and has borne three children: Stokley B., Mary E. and Fannie. Our subject remained under the paternal roof until he was twenty-six years of age, but began farming for himself some time before. Since his marriage he has lived on the old homestead and now owns 100 acres of valuable land. In 1859 he began merchandising at Cottage Home, continuing until the war. In 1881 he began the business in partnership with J. B. Eastes, and at the end of one year became sole proprietor. Later he disposed of his stock and has since given his attention to farming, and has dealt extensively in mules and hogs for upward of thirty years. He is a Democrat and a member of the I. O. O. F., and he and wife are members of the Baptist Church.

JAMES B. HORN, farmer and an old citizen of District No. 3, was born in 1828, near his present residence, and was reared without a father's care or training, his father having died when our subject was but six years old. His education was received in the pioneer schools of his native county. May 4, 1854, he married Margaret A. Vaughan, who was born November 5, 1833, in Davidson County, Tenn. To this union were born three children: Bettie, Fannie and James A. Mr. Horn is living on the old place and owns 128 acres of the old home tract, but his son James looks after the interest of the tract in a skillful and successful manner. Mrs. Horn died September 12, 1861, and for the past seventeen years Bettie Horn has been keeping house for her brother and father. Mr. Horn was at one time a member of the Masonic fraternity, and is a member of the Methodist Episcopal Church South. In politics he is a Democrat. He is the son of Etheldred P. and Elizabeth N. (Baker) Horn. The father was born in 1796, in the State of North Carolina, and was a tiller of the soil. He came to Tennessee in the early part of the present century, and bought 640 acres in District No. 3, five miles west of Lebanon, where he settled and where his career ended September 1, 1835, while he was yet in the prime of life. The mother was born about 1792, in Baltimore County, Md. After the death of her husband she lived on the old home place with her son James, our subject, until her death, which occurred in 1873.

J. M. HORN, farmer, was born in 1843, in Smith County, Tenn., son of Burrell and Abigail (Traywick) Horn. The father was of English descent, and was a native of Hanson County, N. C. He was married in his native county, and was a farmer by occupation, immigrating to Smith County, Tenn., about 1837. At the time of his death, which occurred in 1866, he was living in Lawrence County, Ark. The mother was of Welsh descent, a native of Hanson County, N. C., and since her husband's death has been living in Arkansas. They were the parents of ten children, five of whom are living. At the age of sixteen our subject left home, and when hostilities broke out between the North and South he enlisted in May, 1861, in Company B, Seventh Tennessee Regiment Infantry, Confederate States Army. He took an active part in the battles of Cheat Mountain, Romney, Seven Pines, Cold Harbor, where he was wounded in the right arm and released from active duty for about two weeks. He afterward fought in the battles of Cedar Run, Second Manassas, Harper's Ferry, Fredricksburg, Chancellorsville and Gettysburg, where he was captured and taken to Fort Delaware, but was kept a very short time. He returned to Smith County after the war, and in a few days came to Wilson County, and has lived there ever since. In connection with farming he began the study of law, and in 1869 was admitted to the bar, and from that date to the present he has been practicing his profession. December 31, 1882, he married Isabell R. Harris, a native of Wilson County, born December 6, 1860, and the daughter of W. D. Harris. Mr. Horn commenced life as a poor boy, but by perseverance and industry is doing finely. He now owns 1,400 acres, and is an honest and respectable citizen. In politics he is a Democrat, casting his first vote for Jefferson Davis. His wife is a member of the Missionary Baptist Church.

J. W. HUDDLESTON, retired physician and surgeon, of Lebanon, was born in Tennessee in 1834, son of W. W. and Mary (Tarver) Huddleston. The father was born in Buckingham County, Va., in 1808, and was a farmer and merchant by occupation. He came to Tennessee in his boyhood and was married in 1827, dying in 1855. The mother was born in Tennessee in 1812, and died in 1854. J. W. Huddleston attended the academies of his native county and the University of Nashville for nearly two years. At the age of twenty he began studying medicine under Dr. Alsup, and the following year entered the medical department of the Nashville University, graduating in March, 1857, as an M. D. He practiced for some time in Nashville, afterward in Wilson County; thence to Marshall County, in 1877. In 1884, he finally located in Lebanon, where he purchased property and has since resided. He has been a leading man in his profession, and in 1862 was surgeon in the Confederate armies. In politics the Doctor is a Democrat, but was a Whig while that party was in existence. In February, 1858, he was married to Alice Robertson, daughter of Dr. Peyton and Ellen (Davis) Robertson, and granddaughter of Gen. James Robertson, one of Tennessee's most noted pioneers. He was a sturdy, brave and influential man, and Robertson County was named in his honor. (See history for further facts concerning him.) Mrs. Huddleston was born in Nashville, in 1838, and she and husband have two children, Nellie (wife of W. R. Chambers) and Josie.

R. M. IRELAND, agent of the Southern Express Company and freight agent of the Nashville, Chattanooga & St. Louis Railroad at Lebanon, was born in Sumner County, Tenn., July 28, 1844, and is one of twelve children born to the marriage of Benjamin W. and Fannie (Stratton) Ireland, who were of Irish descent, born in North Carolina and Tennessee in 1789 and 1817, respectively. The father was a teacher by profession, but later in life followed merchandising and farming. He died in 1853. The mother was a daughter of James and Fannie Stratton and after her husband's death lived on the old home place with her children until 1875, when she broke up housekeeping and afterward resided with her children. She died in Nashville in 1881. Our subject attended the common schools and one session at Chapel Hill Seminary in Marshall County. In 1871 he was appointed deputy sheriff of Sumner County, and held the office four years. In 1861 he enlisted in Company A, Second Tennessee Cavalry, and participated in many of the battles of the war, serving until the close, not being wounded or captured during his service. December 9, 1867, he married Maggie Scroggin, who died in January, 1875. A year later he came to Lebanon and became night watchman for the Lebanon Depot, and eight months later was appointed express messenger and baggage master on the railroad between Lebanon and Nashville, and in 1878 was given his present position. October 2, 1878, he married Addie Kelly, daughter of Hanson and Annie Kelly, of New Orleans. Mrs. Ireland was born October 2, 1857. They have three children: Laura, Hanson and Fannie. Mr. Ireland is very popular as a railroad official, and in politics is a Democrat. He is a member of the K. of P., and he and wife are members of the Methodist Episcopal Church South.

THOMAS JENKINS is one of ten children born to Simon and Nancy (Muse) Jenkins, and was born in Warren County, Ky., September 10, 1822, and there received his education. He made his home with his parents as long as they lived and then he and a brother managed the homestead for several years. In 1869 he came to Lebanon and in 1871 engaged in the grocery business, and after continuing for seven years he added hardware to his stock, but sold out in 1855. In July, 1884, he purchased a beautiful home, consisting of fifty-eight acres in the suburbs of Lebanon. During Mr. Jenkins' career as a merchant in Lebanon he carried a No. 1 stock and was one of the leading business men of Lebanon for fifteen years. During his long lease of life he has proved himself to be "an honest man, the noblest work of God." He is liberal in all benevolent movements, and is an earnest member of the Baptist Church. He is a Democrat. The father and mother were born in Virginia in 1793 and 1800, and died in 1845 and 1847, respectively. They were married in Virginia about 1809 and moved to Warren County, Ky., and there purchased 680 acres of land and became a very successful farmer. He at one time owned 1,826 acres, but gave liberally to his children.

J. M. and J. L. **JENNINGS** constitute the firm of Jennings Bros., merchants of Statesville, Tenn. They are two of five children of J. L. and Martha (Doss) Jennings, who were born in Wilson County, Tenn., and DeKalb County, Tenn., October 20, 1827, and July 7, 1828, respectively. They were married in 1830 and located near Statesville, where they still reside. J. M. Jennings, the older member of the firm, was born in Wilson County September 31, 1836, and in 1880 entered into partnership with his cousin A. L. Jennings in the mercantile business, continuing for about eighteen months when he purchased his cousin's interest, and up to 1885 carried on the business by himself. At that time his brother J. L. became his partner. He was married January 26, 1885, to Miss Lena, daughter of J. P. Hale. She was born August 17, 1867, and has borne one child—Mamie. Mr. Jennings is a Democrat, and his wife is a member of the Methodist Episcopal Church. J. L. Jennings was born December 25, 1858, and remained with his parents until he attained his majority. He purchased a farm near Statesville, on which he lived several years, and in 1885 became a partner with his brother in the mercantile business. He is also proprietor of a hotel in Statesville, and controls a large share of the traveling public. October 13, 1881, he wedded Miss S. A., daughter of Dr. T. H. Knight. He is a Democrat, and he and his brother are recognized as honest and upright business men.

C. L. JOHNS was born in Lebanon, Tenn., in 1850, being one of two sons of Charles L. and Elizabeth (Davis) Johns. The father was a Baptist minister of the State of Tennessee, and after his marriage also worked at the printer's trade. At the time of his death, in 1850, he was a resident of Lebanon. The mother was born in 1823, and since her husband's death has been living with her mother and son in Lebanon. C. L. Johns was educated in private schools and in the Cumberland University. When quite young he began working in a brick-yard, receiving 25 cents per day for his services, and also clerked in W. H. Brown's dry goods store in Franklin, Ky., and in Lebanon for several years. In 1871 he went to Nashville, and after clerking there two years returned to Lebanon and resumed work with Mr. Brown, with whom he remained until 1879, when he established a dry goods store of his own in Lebanon, which he has conducted very successfully to the present time. February 5, 1879, he was married to Kate Cowen, who was born in 1854, daughter of Dr. M. W. and Addie Cowen. Mrs. Johns died June 28, 1880, and since that time Mr. Johns has resided with his mother. Mr. Johns is a good business man and one of the first merchants of Lebanon. He is a Democrat and a member of the I. O. O. F. and K. of P., and is a member of the Methodist Episcopal Church South.

J. C. JOHNSON is one of nine children born to the marriage of James and Cassandy Johnson, natives of the Old Dominion. were born in 1772 and 1774, and died in 1848 and 1846, respectively. They were married about 1800, and came to Tennessee in 1806, where they purchased land and followed the occupation of farming. Our subject, J. C. Johnson, was born in Wilson County, Tenn., December 20, 1816. He was reared on a farm, and his education was obtained in the district schools near his home. December 23, 1841, he led to the hymeneal altar Miss Locky Craddock, daughter of Richard and Nancy Craddock. She was born in February, 1817, and departed this life July 20, 1864. To them were born these children: Richard, Locky (wife of Lewis Tribble), Mary J. (wife of H. C. David), Emily (wife of T. K. David) and Dr. J. H., now a practicing physician of Nashville. After attaining his twenty-first birthday our subject went to West Tennessee, where he remained one year and then returned home and began managing his father's farm. For his second wife he wedded Mrs. Malissa (Bedel) Branch, who was born June 24, 1833. They have three children: Joseph M., Andrew and Ida. Mr. Johnson is a well-to-do farmer, and has always contributed liberally to church and school organizations. He is a Republican, and was strongly opposed to secession. He and wife are members of the Missionary Baptist Church.

CALVIN JONES, an enterprising farmer of Cherry Valley, Tenn., was born in Wilson County, November 23, 1819, being one of eight children of William and Lucy (Wamack) Jones, natives of Virginia, born in 1791 and 1798 respectively. The father came to Tennessee when a boy, and was married September 25, 1816. He was a farmer by occupation, and died December 7, 1848, and the mother in 1885. The subject of our sketch was reared on a farm and received his education in the schools near his home. June 18, 1846, he was married to Miss Susanna, daughter of Ethelrid and Nancy Barby. Mrs. Jones was born November 3, 1824, and has borne her husband two children: Nancy A. (wife of George Donnel), and Mandy (widow of John M. Berry). At an early day Mr. Jones learned the blacksmith's trade, and after his marriage worked at that business for twenty-two years. After his father's death he and his brother Alfred purchased about 170 acres of the home farm and discontinued smithing. He has devoted his time to farming, but spent a few years in operating a saw-mill. He now owns 211 acres of land, on which he erected a fine dwelling house. Mr. Jones is noted for his honesty, and is much esteemed by a large circle of friends and relatives.

J. H. KENNEDY is one of thirteen children of William B. and Drusilla (Hobson) Kennedy, and was born in Wilson County, Tenn., June 23, 1816. The father was born in the "Old Dominion" in 1781, and went to Kentucky with his widowed mother when a youth, and later came to Tennessee and died in September, 1840. The mother was born in Tennessee in 1801, and died in 1853. Our subject was educated near home, and February 28, 1839, married Lucinda C., daughter of James and Nancy Ewing. Mrs. Kennedy was born in 1819, and has borne five children: J. W., N. D. (wife of Horace Knight), Mary E. (wife of Daniel Smith), J. T. and S. A. (wife of C. P. Rich). At the age of eighteen our subject began working for Tally & Bro., merchants, of Statesville, and a year later became a soldier in the Seminole war. and his company acted as advance guard for the regular army. After again serving some time as salesman he purchased 200 acres of land where he now lives, and which he has increased to 300 acres. He suffered large losses from the effects of the civil war, but in the main, fortune has dealt kindly with him. He belongs to the Democratic party and the Masonic fraternity. His wife is a member of the Baptist Church.

JOHN D. KIRKPATRICK, D. D., professor of historic and practical theology in Cumberland University and editor and proprietor of the Lebanon *Register*, was born July 8, 1836, son of Anderson and Eliza (Moss) Kirkpatrick, who were the parents of nine children. The father was of Scotch-Irish lineage, born in Wilson County in 1808, a farmer and stock raiser by occupation. He was married about 1828, and has since resided on the the old homestead, which consists of several hundred acres. The mother was born in 1814 in Christian County, Ky., and died in 1875. Our subject received his rudimentary education in the county schools, and afterward attended the Hartsville High School for three years and the high school at Mount Juliet two years. At the age of nineteen he entered Cumberland University, remaining two years. In 1857 he entered the Theological Seminary of the same institution. He began teaching in 1854, and in 1858 became a minister of the Presbyterian Church, being ordained in 1860. In April, 1861, he enlisted in Maney's company, First Tennessee Regiment. In 1862 he returned to Sumner County and raised Companies C and D, and was elected captain of Company C, Seventh Tennessee Cavalry. He participated in many of the principal battles of the war, and rose to the rank of colonel. He was seriously wounded at Cynthiana, Ky., and was compelled to give up active duty, and was given charge of the enrolling department at Richmond, Va. He was also chaplain of his regiment. After his return he resumed teaching, and November 1, 1866, he married Susan Kirkpatrick, who has borne him four children: Curry B., Donnell B., John D. and Harry B. In 1865 he was given the pastorate of the Goodlettsville Cumberland Presbyterian Church, where he remained four years, and then took charge of the Second Cumberland Church of Nashville. In 1875 he was called to Lebanon to become the financial agent of Cumberland University, and at the same time accepted the chair of historic and practical theology, which he has since filled with credit to himself and honor to the institution. In 1880 he was made managing editor and proprietor of the *Cumberland Presbyterian Review*. This he disposed of, however, and in 1885 took charge of the *Register*. In December of the same year the building caught fire, and was consumed with all its contents. He immediately re-established himself and is at present editing a newsy and valuable paper. In 1884 the degree of D. D. was conferred upon him entirely unsolicited. He is a man of unsullied reputation, a gentleman and a scholar. He is a member of the Masonic fraternity, and K. of H. and K. of P.

N. P. LANOM, farmer and miller, of District No. 23, was born in 1839, in Wilson County, and is the son of William R. and Sallie (Leath) Lanom. The father was born November 25, 1809, in Rutherford County, Tenn., and was a farmer by occupation. Soon after his marriage he moved to Bedford County, and in four or five years moved back to Wilson County, where he bought upward of 400 acres of land in the Twenty-third District. He died in 1874. The mother was born July 22, 1811, and is now living with her daughter, Mrs. W. N. Flowers. Our subject's grandfather, Nathan Lanom, was a native of North Carolina, and came to Wilson County previous to the year 1800, and was one of the first settlers of that county. Our subject was reared at home, and remained with his parents until he was twenty-five years of age. At the breaking out of the war he enlisted in Company G, Seventh Regiment Tennessee Infantry, Confederate States Army, and fought in the battles of Seven Pines, Richmond and Cedar Run. In the last named battle he was wounded in the thigh, the cause of which relieved him from active duty about four months, he being in the hospital at Charlottsville, Va. After recovering from his wounds he received an unlimited furlough and returned home. In the fall of 1863 he enlisted in Company D, Tennessee Cavalry, and remained out until after the surrender. February 2, 1864, he married Caldonia Tennessee Burke, who was born in Wilson County December, 1844, and the fruits of this union were six children: Sallie A., William J., Lucy J., Laura L., Freddie and Nannie A. In 1866 Mr. Lanom bought 160 acres in the Twenty-third District, where he now lives. He has been a hard-working and industrious man, and now owns 600 acres of land. In 1884 he purchased a saw-mill, and the following year added a grist-mill, both of which he runs in connection with his farm. He is a Democrat in politics, casting his first vote for John Bell in 1860. He and wife are worthy members of the Baptist Church.

JOHN A. LESTER, merchant, miller and farmer, of Lebanon, Tenn., was born on the 21st of April, 1827, in Wilson County, and is a son of Henry D. and Malinda (Jones) Lester. The father is a native of Virginia, born in 1800. He came with his parents to

Tennessee when he was about nine years old and located in Wilson County. He became a wealthy farmer and an influential citizen and held several county offices. He died in 1875. The mother was born in Tennessee in 1805, and died in 1874. Our subject was educated in the Campbell Academy of Lebanon, and in 1855 formed a partnership with his father in the grocery business, continuing two years. In 1858 he and Mr. S. A. Carter became partners in the grocery business, continuing until the breaking out of the war. In 1863 he began milling and formed partnerships with the following gentlemen: W. Hallum, William Carter and J. D. Lester. Mr. Lester is the oldest and one of the most successful merchants and millers in the State. He owns a farm of 800 acres and resides in a beautiful and substantial dwelling-house. June 12, 1860, he wedded Martha (Dillon) Williams, daughter of Thomas and Harriet (Roane) Dillon. The mother's uncle, Archibald Roane, was the second governor of Tennessee. Her brother, John Seldon Roane, was governor of Arkansas, and her brother, Samuel C. Roane, was judge of the Supreme Bench of Arkansas. Mrs. Lester was born September 9, 1833, and had two children by her former marriage, Seldon R. and Dixon C. Seldon is president of the Second National Bank of Lebanon, and Dixon is the noted evangelist of Tennessee and is at present in California. Mr. Lester and family are members of the Cumberland Presbyterian Church.

WILLIAM J. LESTER was born in 1825 in Wilson County, Tenn., the eldest son of Henry D. and Malinda (Jones) Lester. (See J. A. Lester for parents' sketch.) William was educated in the Campbell Academy of Lebanon, and after residing with his parents until twenty-one years old he worked at the blacksmith's trade and the following three years tilled his father's farm. December 18, 1851, he was married to Othelda Haney, daughter of Elijah and Clarkey Haney. Mrs. Lester was born in 1833 in Smith County, Tenn., and bore her husband one child, Matilda E., who wedded Anderson Crookshankes and died in 1885. Mr. Lester purchased 237 acres of land near Lebanon, where he now resides. His wife died in 1853 and in 1856 he took for his second wife, Sarah F. (Seay) Belcher, daughter of Daniel and Elizabeth Seay. Mrs. Lester was born in 1835 and died in 1885, having borne one child, Daniel R. who is a farmer in Smith County. Mr. Lester joined Company F, Fourth Tennessee Cavalry, and was in the battles of Murfreesboro, Wartrace, Chickamauga, Missionary Ridge, Marietta, Ga., and many minor engagements. He was so severely wounded in the left leg at the last named engagement that amputation was performed June 22, 1864. He kept a grocery in Georgia for some time but returned home in June, 1865. He has been a prosperous farmer of Wilson County for many years and previous to the war speculated in mules. He is a Democrat in politics, formerly a Whig, and belongs to the order of Good Templars and is a member of the Methodist Episcopal Church South.

J. R. LESTER, M. D., was born November 1, 1836, and is one of nine children of Henry D. and Malinda (Jones) Lester; the family is of English descent. Our subject resided with his parents until he reached man's estate. He received his education in the Cumberland University, and at the age of nineteen began studying medicine and graduated, in 1860, from Jefferson University, Philadelphia, Penn. He then returned to his birth-place, where he has ever since practiced his profession. May 20, 1861, he enlisted in the Seventh Tennessee, Hatton's regiment and was appointed assistant surgeon. After the battle of Seven Pines, Va., he became commander of a company of cavalry in Col. Baxter Smith's regiment and served in this capacity until the close of the war. August 16, 1865, he wedded Miss Sallie, daughter of William Williamson, of Wilson County, and became the father of five children: Nellie, Jennie, Jimmie, Marie and John. Dr. Lester is a stanch Democrat and cast his first presidential vote for Buchanan. The Doctor and his wife are leading members of the Cumberland Presbyterian Church, and he is one of the leading physicians of the county.

J. D. LESTER'S birth occurred near Lebanon, Tenn., in 1839; son of Henry D. and Malinda (Jones) Lester. He received his education in Cumberland University and Jefferson College, and at the breaking out of the war between North and South he enlisted in Company D, Seventh Regiment Tennessee Cavalry, and during his service took an active part in many of the principal battles and skirmishes of the war. He returned home May 20, 1865. June 18, 1862, he was married to Marcella Henderson, daughter of William and Mary Henderson, and by her became the father of nine children: Henry D., Gertrude, Robert E., Albert D., Floyd H., Jessie F., Blanche, Wade H. and Joseph A. In 1867 Mr. Lester began working in the flouring-mill of Carter & Lester, as book-keeper, remaining with them in this capacity eight years. In 1875 Mr. Lester purchased a one-fourth interest in the mill, but in August, 1877, sold his interest and purchased 200 acres of land near Lebanon, which he has since increased to 330 acres. He uses modern methods of cultivating the soil and his land yields him rich returns. In politics he is a Democrat and is a member of the Baptist Church and his wife of the Cumberland Presbyterian Church.

N. LAWRENCE LINDSLEY, LL. D. (deceased), one of Tennessee's most prominent and influential educators, was born September 11, 1816, in Princeton. N. J., and is a son of Philip Lindsley, who was also a leading educator of New Jersey and Tennessee. In 1817 he was elected as vice-president of the college of New Jersey, and in 1822 was acting president of the same. The following year he was chosen president of the University of Tennessee, but declined the honor. In 1824 he was again elected, and January, 12, 1825, he assumed control and was president of that institution until 1850. In May of the latter year he was elected professor of ecclesiastical polity and Biblical archæology in the New Albany (Ind.) Theological Seminary. In 1853 he resigned, and from that date until his career ended, in 1855, his time was spent in study and devotion to his friends. Lawrence Lindsley left his native State in 1825 and came to Nashville, Tenn. with his parents. At the age of sixteen he was nominated to a cadetship at West Point, being appointed by President Jackson, who was a personal friend of his father's, but remained only two years, owing to the severity of the climate. He entered the University of Nashville. graduating with honors in 1836. In 1841 he wedded Julia M., daughter of Moses B., and Sarah (Bedford) Stephens, the father being a prominent educator of his day. Mrs. Lindsley was born July 30, 1823, in the building now known as the Nicholson House, in Nashville. To Dr. and Mrs. Lindsley were born these children: Philip, a lawyer of Dallas, Tex.; Henry S. (deceased); N. Lawrence (deceased); John B., a stock trader of Lebanon; Joseph W., a farmer of Wilson County, and Kate S. (wife of Edgar Waters). The maternal grandfather was a student in Princeton (N. J.) College and was a soldier in the Revolutionary war from North Carolina, receiving for his bravery the "Lawrence Grant" of 2,640 acres of land in Wilson County, Tenn. of which our subject received 500 acres. In 1844 Lawrence Lindsley was elected professor of Latin and Greek in the Cumberland University, and in 1852 established the Greenwood Seminary for young ladies, which became a model of its kind. The degree of LL. D. was conferred upon him by the Cumberland University. He died October, 10, 1868 and it may be truly said of him that he was an accomplished and profound scholar. At the time of his death he was engaged on the production of a work called "An Encyclolexicon of the English Language," which was intended to be a complete dictionary of the English Language. He was the soul of honor and manliness, a philanthropist and Christian. At his desire his wife became principal of the school he had founded, and conducted it successfully until her death July 8, 1883. She was a lady of more than ordinary accomplishments and energy, and her object and aim was to give to young ladies a grand conception of real life, and while her death occurred in the midst of a prosperous work, her life was such that its good influences have not ended, and her name is a house hold word in many Southern families. Both husband and wife were members of the Cumberland Presbyterian Church.

FRANK LINDSLEY, farmer of Twenty-First District, was born in Davidson County, October 13, 1856, son of Hon. Adrian V. S. and Eliza (Trimble) Lindsley. The father was born in Princeton, N. J., September, 14, 1814, and immigrated to Davidson County when but a boy, and soon after entered the University of Nashville where he graduated at the very early age of seventeen. He then commenced the practice of law in which he was quite successful, During the war he was postmaster at Nashville after which he was for some time president and secretary of the Mount Olivet Cemetery, and also had an important railroad position. In 1867 he represented Davidson County in the State Senate, and was for forty-six years president and secretary of the board of trustees of Nashville University. In 1834 he married Miss Eliza Trimble, by whom he became the father of twelve children, nine of whom are living. His father, Philip Lindsley, was president of Princeton College, but resigned that position to accept the presidency of the University of Nashville. Our subject remained at home until he was twenty four years of age, receiving his education at the University of Nashville, and graduated from that institution when but eighteen years of age. He then entered the medical department of the Nashville and and Vanderbilt University, where he remained two years. About seven years subsequent to his leaving school he was engaged in assisting his father in his railroad business. In 1881 he purchased 530 acres of land in District No. 21, Wilson County, a part of a tract which was donated to his great-grandfather, Nathaniel Lindsley, for services rendered during the war of Independence. October, 13, 1880, he wedded Lucy Brutton, of Cincinnati, Ohio, and by her became the father of two children: Eliza V. and Lucy. Mr. Lindsley is one of the most substantial members of the Cumberland Presbyterian Church.

T. G. LOGUE, deceased, was a farmer and the proprietor of a tannery, and was one of six children born to C. and M. (Randels) Logue. His birth occurred March 11, 1820. The father was born June 29, 1778, and was of English descent. He was a tiller of the soil and after reaching a good old age died March, 1863. The mother was born in Robertson County and died in Wilson County, Tenn, in 1843. Our subject received a fair practical education in the country schools and for some time carried on the tannery business for his father. July 11, 1844, his marriage with Nancy Bass, was solemnized. To this union were born eleven children: Margaret E. Mary E. James R., Tapley G., Catharine B., Robert H., Tennessee, Joshua C., Lucy A. Martha and Franklin L. Mr. Logue had accumulated considerable land and at his death, which occurred July 28, 1882, was the owner of about 1,200 acres. He had an unsullied reputation and was much esteemed by all who knew him. He was a supporter of the principles of Democracy, a member of the I. O. G. T. and belonged to the Cumberland Presbyterian Church. Mrs. Logue, is a member of the Methodist Episcopal Church.

ANDREW B. MARTIN LL. D., attorney at law and professor of law in Cumberland University was born in Smith County, Tenn., in 1836, son of Matthew and Matilda (Crow) Martin, both born in Virginia and Ireland, respectively. The father was born about 1800 and was married about 1822. He was a physician and was educated at Clinton College. At the time of his death in 1849 he was a resident of Paris, Texas. The mother was born in 1804 and came to the United States with her mother in 1812. Soon after her husband's death she returned to Tennessee with her family of twelve children. She devoted her life to their welfare and died in 1876. Our subject early cherished the idea of becoming a lawyer, but owing to the untimely death of his parents and other adverse circumstances, he was compelled to abandon the idea for some time. At the age of eleven years he worked in a brick-yard all summer for $13 and at the age of thirteen he left home and began earning his own living. In April, 1852, he reached Lebanon, Tenn., an entire stranger, without money and eighty-five miles from home. He secured a position in the drug store of Allison & Cook with whom he remained five years. His leisure hours were spent in study and in 1857 he began reading Blackstone. He was aided by the faculty of Cumberland University and was made their book-keeper for his tuition. In 1858 he graduated from the same and immediately entered upon the practice of his profession and was regarded as a successful, earnest advocate and safe counselor. He formed a partnership with W. H. Williamson, but at the breaking out of war he enlisted in Company H, Seventh Tennessee Volunteer Infantry and fought in many bloody battles. He served as third lieutenant of his company for some time and was then made adjutant-general upon the staffs of Gen. G. G. Dribrell and Gen. Wheeler. He served about four years and returned home May 20, 1865. He immediately resumed his practice and May 6, 1868, wedded Alice Ready, daughter of Hon. Charles Ready, of Murfreesboro. She was born in 1842 and has borne her husband five children: Mary, Martha, Andrew, Helen and Bennett.

In 1876 he was elected professor of law in his old *alma mater* and has since held the position. In 1871-72 he was a member of the lower house of the State Legislature, being chairman of the Judiciary Committee. In 1880 he was elector of the State at large in the election of Hancock and English and canvassed the State in their behalf. He has been special judge of the circuit and chancery courts numerous times and is in every sense of the word a self-made man, and from his childhood has displayed qualities of head and heart which have enabled him to surmount obstacles which would have discouraged many men.

J. B. MARTIN is one of six children born to George W. and Judith (Bradley) Martin. The father was born in Virginia in 1796 and came to Tennessee with his parents when but two years of age. In 1820 he married and located on a farm in Wilson County, where he lived until his death. The mother was born March 8, 1808. Our subject was born August 23, 1828, and educated in the district schools and remained at home looking after the interests of his father's farm until October 31, 1850, when he married Lucinda R., daughter of J. and Mary Holmes. She was born in Rutherford County, Tenn., in 1833, and died June 19, 1879, leaving two daughters: Mary (wife of A. B. McKnight), and Annie (wife of R. G. Byrn). November 6, 1884, Mr. Martin married Mrs. Thompson of the Fifteenth District, born in Wilson County, in November, 1836. Since his first marriage Mr. Martin has resided on the home place, where he owns 169 acres of land. He and wife are members of the church, and he is a Democrat in politics and belongs to the I. O. O. F.

W. D. MARTIN, one of the old citizens and farmers of the Twenty-first District, was born September 28, 1826, in Wilson County. He is the son of Lindsey C. and Nancy)Stacy) Martin. The father was born about 1794, in Virginia, and was a farmer by occupation; he moved to the Twenty-second District near Gladesville, where he settled and remained until his death, which occurred in December, 1884. He was ninety years of age. The mother was born August, 1791, in North Carolina, and came to Wilson County when quite young. They crossed the mountains by team. She died in 1877 at the advanced age of eighty-six. Our subject received his education in the county schools and October 2, 1851, he wedded Mary J. Shannon, a native of Tennessee, born April, 1836, and the daughter of James and Mary Shannon. To our subject and wife were born two children: Mary D., wife of Dr. Finis Shannon, Jr., and James L., who married Fanny Steed, to this last union were born four children: John A., Elsie M., Marcus W. and Mary O. After marriage our subject bought 150 acres in the Twenty-third District, where he lived sixteen years. He then sold out and bought 273 acres in the Twenty-first District, where he has since resided. He is one of Wilson County's old citizens and is highly spoken of as an honest citizen and good neighbor. In politics he has been a life-long Democrat, and he and wife members of the Baptist Church. In 1876 he was elected magistrate of the Twenty-first District, which office he held in an able manner for six years.

HON. R. P. McCLAIN, attorney at law, of Lebanon, Tenn., is a son of John A. and Minerva (Ross) McClain, and one of their ten children. He was born February, 1838, in Wilson County, and received his rudimentary education in the academies of his native county, and afterward entered the Cumberland University as a junior at the age of twenty, graduating in June, 1860. In 1861 he enlisted in Company H, Seventh Regiment Tennessee Infantry, and in 1862 was given a position in the quartermaster's department. In 1862 he was made paymaster in A. P. Hill's division, and held the position until the close of the war. From 1866 to 1867 he studied law in Cumberland University, graduating at the latter date. February 26 of the same year he married Hettie McKenzie, daughter of Alexander McKenzie. Mrs. McClain was born in Illinois in 1842, and is the mother of four children: Jennie, Minnie, Alexander and Hettie. Mr. McClain first practiced his profession with A. Vick as partner, continuing until 1870, when he was appointed deputy clerk of the county court, succeeding his uncle, J. S. McClain, who had been clerk for forty years in succession. He held the position, by re-election, for eight years. In 1875 he was elected to the lower house of the State Legislature, and from 1876 to 1883 was clerk and master of the Chancery Court of Wilson County. Since then he has practiced

WILSON COUNTY. 1109

law. In 1875 he and his brother, J. T., became proprietors of a dry goods store, and since 1884 the firm has been known as McClain Bros. & Co. They keep a general line of goods and occupy eight rooms 100 feet long. Mr. McClain has been a leading man of Lebanon for the past twenty years, and is a shrewd business manager and successful financier. The father, John McClain, was of Scotch-Irish descent and was born in Tennessee in 1807. He was a farmer and the possessor of 400 acres at the time of his death in 1867. The mother was of Scotch descent, born in Wilson County in 1809.

JOHN B. McCLAIN, farmer, was born in Wilson County, Tenn., April 26, 1842, and is the son of Anson and Minerva (Rocks) McClain. Our subject received his education at Silver Spring High School, of Wilson County, and made his home with his parents until hostilities broke out between the North and South, when he became one of the boys in gray. He enlisted May, 1861, in Company B, Forty-fifth Regiment of Tennessee Infantry. He took an active part in the battle of Shiloh and numerous other engagements. The last two years of the war he was in the quartermaster department, being stationed most of the time at Petersburg. He returned home in the spring of 1865 after an absence of nearly four years. August 9, 1877, he married Sue Brent, daughter of Joe and Amanda Brent. Mrs. McClain was born August 23, 1849, in Davidson County, Tenn., and by her union with Mr. McClain became the mother of two children: Anson Brent and Lollie Bell. After marriage Mr. McClain remained on the old home place and cared for and looked after the interest of his father and mother. In 1881 he bought 125 acres in the Third District, six miles west of Lebanon, where he settled and has since resided. Mr. McClain bears the reputation of being an industrious and conscientious citizen. He is a Democrat in politics, and his wife is a member of the Methodist Episcopal Church South.

ROBINSON McMILLAN, attorney at law, is a son of Frank P. and Jane F. (Robinson) McMillan, and was born March 25, 1857. The parents were both native Tennesseeans, the father having been born in 1829, and the mother in 1832. Of their seven children but three are living: Robinson, Edward E. and Frank P., Jr. Frank P. McMillan was a farmer in Giles County before the war. Having lost all his property he moved to Rutherford County in 1870 to begin life anew. It was then that he took Robinson from school, and put him in the cotton field, where he worked with the negroes till his twenty-first year. At this age young Robinson was a pretty fair scholar, notwithstanding his lack of opportunities. He had improved every spare moment by studying standard works of various kinds, especially works of mathematics, history and poetry. On obtaining his majority he came to Wilson County to try his luck at pedagogy. After teaching a school in the Seventeenth District he went to the Twenty-fifth, to Hamilton Academy, where he began with sixteen pupils. At the end of four years he ended his school at that point with 115 pupils present. He afterward taught at Gladeville with similar success. His precarious state of health continually interfering with his duties as a teacher, he entered Cumberland University to study law. In 1885 he graduated with honor, representing the entire senior class by their unanimous choice. In the year 1885 he was elected superintendent of public schools for the county of Wilson. As county superintendent he has exerted himself to disentangle the county finances, to raise the standard among teachers, and to rouse the people on the subject of education. At the beginning of the year 1886 he associated himself with Rufus P. McClain, of the Lebanon bar, with whom he has since been practicing his profession. In April, 1883, he was married to Josephine Hewgley, daughter of C. W. Hewgley, of Nashville, Tenn. Mrs. McMillan was born January 13, 1861. They have one son—Murray. Mr. McMillan is a Democrat in politics, and a liberal Methodist in religion. He is a Good Templar, a Pythian knight and a Free Mason.

MRS. E. C. McMURRY was born December 25, 1809, in Sumner County, Tenn., and is a daughter of Thomas and Elizabeth (McCorcle) Anderson, born in North Carolina and Kentucky, in 1779 and 1791, and died in 1852 and 1870, respectively. They were married in 1809. He was quite successful as a farmer, owning upward of 400 acres of land. The mother came to Tennessee with her maternal grandparents, and resided in a fort a number of years to protect themselves against the Indians. After her husband's death she lived with her daughter, Mrs. E. C. McMurry. Our subject was educated in the female department of a college at Gallatin, and December 27, 1838, was married to Rev. John M. McMurry, son of David and Anna McMurry. Rev. McMurry was born in Wilson County in 1804, and attended school in Gallatin. He entered the ministry in 1833, being a circuit rider for a short time, and then was given local work. In 1847 he became agent of the endowment fund for the Cumberland University, serving eight years. During that time he was very successful, raising about $60,000. In 1856 he became pastor of the church at McMinnville, Tenn., remaining seventeen years, with the exception of a few years during the war. Owing to ill health he gave up ministerial work in 1869, and retired to his farm, where he died in April, 1875. He was very public spirited, and was a man of talent and influence in the county. His wife and daughter reside in Lebanon, both being earnest workers in the Cumberland Presbyterian Church.

JAMES NELSON is a native of Fayette County, Ky., and is a son of James and Theodica (Bush) Nelson, born in Virginia and Kentucky in 1799 and 1803, and died in 1864 and 1834, respectively. The father was a teacher in early life, and at a later period became a tiller of the soil, and owned 425 acres of land. He became the father of twelve children, nine of whom are living. Our subject was born in 1828, and received his rudimentary education in his native county, and later attended Bacon College, Harrodsburg, Ky., for two years. In September, 1862, he enlisted in Company E, Eighth Kentucky Cavalry, Gen. Morgan's command, and was with him on his raid through Kentucky, Indiana and Ohio. He was captured at Buffington, Ohio, and sent to Chicago, where he was retained until spring. He returned home in March, 1865. Before the war (1859) he purchased 117 acres of land in Wilson County, on which he located and where he has since lived. He is a man of good business capacity, and is at the present time the possessor of 470 acres of fertile and well cultivated land. He has been a life-long Democrat in politics, and cast his first presidential vote for F. Pierce in 1852. In 1876 he was elected magistrate of his district, and has held the office to the present time, to the satisfaction of all concerned.

JOHN D. OWEN, M. D., is a son of John Owen and Mary A. (Goodwin) and was born in Smith County, Tenn., June 21, 1825. The father was of Welsh descent, and his ancestors first located in Maryland and Virginia. He was born in North Carolina in 1787, and was a physician and surgeon by profession. He married and came to Tennessee in 1812, locating in Smith County, where he practiced medicine. He and his wife organized and established the first Sabbath-school ever taught in Smith County. He died September 5, 1826. He was a stockholder and president of a branch of the old Bank of Tennessee at Carthage, and was a member of the town board for several years. The mother was born in 1787 in North Carolina. She was a devout church-member, and a life member of the American Bible Society. She died at our subject's home, in Lebanon, January 2, 1879. John D. was educated in the Cumberland University, of Lebanon, and the Nashville University. At the age of twenty he began the study of medicine under the direction of his brother, Dr. B. R. Owen, and in the fall of 1846 went to Philadelphia, Penn., and entered the same institution from which his father graduated. He graduated in 1848. He has always practiced in Smith County, and has met with well-deserved success. In 1853 he moved to Lebanon, and November 1, of the same year, married Fannie Jamison, daughter of J. and A. (Porter) Jamison. Mrs. Owen was born April 9, 1835. Dr. Owen and another gentleman established a drug store in Lebanon, but was soon compelled to abandon the business owing to ill health. In 1870 he was the prime mover and stock-holder of the Bank of Wilson County, and was made its president, continuing such after it became the Second National Bank. He resigned in 1882, and has since lived a retired life. He has in his possession a copy of the old stamp paper which was issued by the British Government in 1765, compelling the colonies to use stamped paper, it being the only original copy on record; its value is 5 shillings. The Doctor is an enterprising man of Lebanon. His wife died January 6, 1886. He is a member of the Methodist Episcopal Church South, as were all the Owen family of his branch.

J. HARRISON OZMENT, an enterprising farmer, was born September 11, 1853, in Wilson County, Tenn., and is one of three children born to John C. and Amanda (Wright) Ozment. The father was born October 5, 1833, in Wilson County, and is a farmer by occupation. He is the owner of about 100 acres of land, and is now living in the Twenty-fifth District. The mother was born March 4, 1834, and is the daughter of Hollis and Elizabeth Wright. Our subject was reared in Wilson County, and received a practical education in the country schools. In 1877 he began farming for himself, and December 20, 1876, Emma A. Clemmons became his wife. She is the daughter of William L. and Elizabeth (Carver) Clemmons, and was born March 12, 1857. Mr. and Mrs. Ozment are the parents of three children: Clara, Lenna and Horace. Mr. Ozment has a fine farm of 200 acres in the Twenty-fifth District, and is a gentleman in every respect. He is a Democrat in politics, and a consistent member of the Missionary Baptist Church. Mrs. Ozment is a member of the Christian Church.

JOHN PALMER, one of the old settlers of Wilson County, Tenn., was born in that State April 13, 1804, and is the eldest of thirteen children born to William and Sarah (Rankins) Palmer. The father was of English extraction, born in North Carolina in 1777, and immigrated to Tennessee in 1804. At the time of his marriage he was living in Sumner County, Tenn., and followed the occupation of a farmer during his entire life. He died in Wilson County in 1858. The mother was born in North Carolina, in 1782, and died in Wilson County, Tenn., in 1859. The subject of this sketch passed his early life in assisting on the farm and in securing an education. In 1826 he was married to Mary Reese, daughter of Thomas B. and Margaret Reese. Mrs. Palmer was born in Wilson County in 1803, and by her union with Mr. Palmer became the mother of five children: Margaret A. (wife of H. W. Robb), Louisa (wife of J. S. Chambers), Richard H., Henry Clay and Ella. In 1828 he bought 154 acres of land in Wilson County, where he commenced the occupation of farming, and is at present the owner of 1,600 acres of land, the principal part being in Wilson County. Mr. Palmer is one of Wilson County's oldest citizens. By his energy, industry and close application to business he has accumulated gradually from year to year and at present is one of the wealthiest farmers in the county. He is always obliging and kind to the poor, and is highly esteemed as an honest and useful citizen. He is a Democrat in politics and a member of the Christian Church.

THOMAS A. PARTLOW, chairman of the Wilson County Court, was born September 5, 1825. He received his education in the Gladesville school, and remained with his parents until twenty-two years old. May 19, 1847, he wedded Margaret Williamson, a native of Wilson County, born in August, 1825, and the daughter of Thomas Williamson. To our subject and wife was born one child, Cloe. After marriage Mr. Partlow located near the old home and followed agricultural pursuits. January 20, 1859, his wife died, and in 1863 our subject married May Ann Robins, who lived only eighteen months after marriage. In September, 1866, our subject was again married to Martha E. Wray, a native of Wilson County, born April 2, 1836, and the daughter of William Wray. To Mr. and Mrs. Partlow were born four children: William A., James R., Natlie M. and Haywood R. In 1865 Mr. Partlow moved to the Twenty-second District, and previous to this, in 1840, he had learned the tanner and currier's trade, which he carried on for some years. In 1861 he enlisted in Company G, State guards. He took an active part in the battles of Lexington, Oak Hill and Springfield. In 1865 he came home, and in the fall of the same year enlisted again, and was with Gen. Morgan until he made his famous raid through Kentucky, Indiana and Ohio, after which he returned home. Our subject is the son of Thomas and Cloe (Hooker) Partlow. The father was of French descent, born in 1796 in South Carolina, and was a farmer by occupation, owning at one time 513 acres. He was a soldier in the war of 1812, and fought in the battle of "The Horse Shoe Bend." The mother was of German descent, born in 1797 in North Carolina, and died in November, 1876. Mr. Partlow has always taken a very active part in public education. He is a Democrat, and he and wife are members of the Methodist Episcopal Church South.

THOMAS PHILLIPS, a farmer of the Eighteenth District of Wilson County, Tenn., was one of nine children and born June 10, 1826. He was educated in the district schools and reared on a farm. November 15, 1848, he wedded Miss Henrietta Henderson, daughter of Preston and Dorothea (Teague) Henderson. Mrs. Phillips was born January 11, 1832, and became the mother of the following children: H. A., William P., David B., Bettie (wife of John Bass), Mary D. (wife of Samuel Ashworth), Sally E. (wife of Andrew Short), Laura J., Minnie, T. W., John M. (deceased), Ada, Mattie and Eugene. Mr. Phillips resided with his parents until he was twenty-two years of age. He then purchased 105 acres of land which he has since increased to 165 acres, and also owns 112 acres of land in the Seventeenth District. He served as constable two years, and six years as magistrate. He is conservative in politics and was strongly opposed to secession. He and wife are members of the Baptist Church. His parents were David and Mary (Waters) Phillips, who were born in Wilson County in 1794 and 1802, and died in 1846 and 1873, respectively. The father was a farmer and a soldier in the war of 1812.

HARDIN PHILLIPS, merchant, of Cherry Valley, Tenn., was born in Wilson County May 11, 1848, one of nine children of Josiah and Malinda (Bass) Phillips. The father was of English descent, born in Pennsylvania in 1800 and followed farming through life. His death occurred in Wilson County November 15, 1868. The mother was born about 1818 and died December 23, 1882. Our subject was educated in the common schools, and October 15, 1868, he married Miss Lizzie Pendleton, daughter of Lewis and Nancy (Moore) Pendleton. Mrs. Phillips was born April 22, 1851, and to her and her husband were born three children, two now living: Josiah, Hattie and Bessie (deceased.) At the age of eighteen Hardin began working for himself, and in 1869 was elected constable, an office which he held for six successive years, and then became associated with Henderson & Co., merchants, of Cherry Valley, continuing until 1877, when he and Dr. Grantstaff became partners, but in about one year their building and goods was consumed by fire. A short time after Mr. Phillips began business for himself and has met with flattering success. He is a Democrat in politics, and he and wife are members of the Christian Church.

HON. S. S. PRESTON, an old citizen and farmer of the Twentieth District, was born November 22, 1827, in Bedford County, Va., and is the son of John and Martha (Early) Preston. The father was born about 1798, in Bedford County, Va., and was a farmer by occupation. At the time of his marriage he was living in the Old Dominion, but in 1835 he immigrated to Wilson County, Tenn., where he died in 1853. He was a soldier in the war of 1812, and was the father of ten children, six of whom are living. The mother was born in 1799, in Bedford County, Va., and died in 1850 in Wilson County. Our subject was educated in his native county and in Wilson County. At the age of twenty-one he left home and went to Huntsville, Ala., and hired as a clerk in a dry goods store, where he remained for nearly three years. January 12, 1853, he married Ann M. Keyes, a native of Alabama, born June, 1835, and the daughter of James H. Keyes, of Mississippi. To our subject and wife were born seven children: James H., John F., Laura (wife of William T. Watson, of Texas), S. S., Jr., Ella, Alice and Mattie. During the late war our subject enlisted in Company G, Forty-fifth Tennessee Regiment, and was made captain of his company. He took an active part in the battles of Shiloh, but soon after, on account of ill health, was discharged and returned home. Mr. Preston owns 260 acres, and is one of Wilson County's much respected citizens. January, 1872, he was elected as chairman of the county court, and in November of the same year he was elected to the lower house of the State Legislature. In October, 1882, he was again elected chairman of the county court, which position he held for three successive years. During the years 1884-85 he was a resident of Lebanon, where he lived for the purpose of educating his children.

G. A. PURSLEY is a son of William B. and Sophia (Rutherford) Pursley, and was born September 13, 1837, in Sumner County, Tenn. The father was of Irish descent, and was born in Tennessee in 1802, and was a tanner and currier by trade, but later devoted his time to agricultural pursuits. He came to Wilson County in 1839, where he became quite a prosperous farmer, owning 500 acres of land at one time. He died May 16, 1880.

He was twice married, his first wife being Harriet Johnston. The mother was of Scotch-Irish descent, born in 1814 and died in 1885. Our subject came to Wilson County when only two years old. He attended Irving College in Warren County, and the Cumberland University in Lebanon. September 22, 1857, he married Ann Vance, daughter of Ed R. and Mary Vance. Mrs. Pursley was born November 11, 1840, and became the mother of seven children: Hattie (wife of J. R. Gollithan), Minnie (wife of J. M. Hannah), Lizzie A., Alice M., Brice B., Edwin V. and Philip H. Mr. Pursley was first the owner of sixty acres of land, but by industry and economy is now the possessor of 305 acres. He has been a life-long Democrat, and cast his first presidential vote for Stephen A. Douglas. September 10, 1861, he enlisted in Company B, Fourth Regiment Tennessee Cavalry, and after the reorganization of the army was appointed second lieutenant of his company, but returned home in the summer of 1862, owing to ill health. He was arrested and kept a prisoner at Murfreesboro for about three months. He belongs to the Good Templars, and he and wife are church members.

JAMES H. RAGLAND, resident of Lebanon, Tenn., born in 1845, and is a son of Dr. Hardin and Amelia A. (Jones) Ragland. Hardin Ragland was born in Tennessee in 1812, son of Pettis Ragland, of Virginia. Hardin was educated in Campbell Academy and received his medical education in the University of Lexington, Ky. After his marriage he located in Cherry Valley, where he continued to practice until 1878, when he gave up active work and came to Lebanon. He had a thorough knowledge of his profession and for many years was the leading physician in his section of the country, and was a much respected citizen. He died February 6, 1882. The mother was of Scotch descent, born in Wilson County in 1806. She died December 13, 1885. They were the parents of three children, two of whom are living: Mrs. Hattie Page and our subject, who was reared and educated in his native county and White Springs, Davidson County. When sixteen years of age he enlisted in Company C, Fourth Tennessee Regiment, and was in the battles of Chickamauga, Bentonville, Knoxville, Perryville, and numerous lesser engagements. After the surrender of Richmond he returned home, and August 10, 1870, he married Agnes A. Clark, daughter of L. J. Clark. Mrs. Ragland was born in 1852, and is the mother of two children: Hardin and Clark. Soon after returning from the war he, his father and W. S. Phillips kept a general merchandise store at Cherry Valley for three years. He then sold goods at Tucker's Cross Roads for two years, and about 1879 he and W. G. Page established a family grocery and hardware store in Lebanon. Our subject has since sold his interest to P. Y. Hill, and has been speculating in notes and securities. He is a Democrat. His wife died in 1878 and his sister has since been keeping house for him.

JOHN H. RAMSAY, farmer, was born in 1828 in Sumner County, Tenn., and is a son of William and Diana (Austin) Ramsay. The father was a native of the State of Virginia, and in early life worked at the hatter's trade. In late years he followed agricultural pursuits, having purchased upward of 100 acres in Sumner County, where he lived until his death, which occurred in 1850. The mother was born in Sumner County about 1816. After the death of her husband she lived on the old place for some time, but at present she is living with her daughter, Polly Hobson, who is a resident of the Fifth District. Our subject received his education in the county schools, and at the age of fifteen left the parental roof and served as an apprentice to a house carpenter, working thus for two and a half years; after which he worked on his own responsibility. In 1853 he bought 188 acres in the Third District of Wilson County, where he located and where he has since resided. The same year Lucinda Tarver became his wife, but died the following year. In 1855 he married Roxana Tompkins, who died February 5, 1880, and in October, 1881, he married Mary C. Ramsay, a native of Indiana, born January 2, 1858, and a daughter of John and Rebecca Isom. To Mr. and Mrs. Ramsay were born two children: William H. and Ella Myrtle. Mrs. Ramsay has one child, John I., by her first husband. Mr. Ramsay has been a hard working and an industrious man. By his energy and good management he now owns 336 acres of good land. During the late war he was agent, assisting the Commissary Department in supplying food and clothing to the boys in gray. In politics he advocates the principles of Democracy. He is a member of the Masonic fraternity, and he and wife are worthy members of the Baptist Church.

J. M. RICE, an enterprising farmer, was born September 19, 1859, in Rutherford County, Tenn., and is one of a family of eight children, born to J. H. and T. A. (Welsh) Rice. The father was born June, 1837, in Wilson County, Tenn., and was a merchant, which occupation he followed for twenty-five years. About this time he felt a strong desire to preach the gospel, which inclination he followed. At the same time he carried on the merchandising business. The mother was born in April, 1838, in Wilson County, Tenn., and is the daughter of Mitchell Welsh. Our subject was reared in Rutherford County, and received a good practical education in the country schools. February 9, 1882, he led to the altar Jeffella Brett, a native of Wilson County, born May 16, 1862, and the daughter of Alexander Brett. Our subject and wife's married life was happily blessed by the birth of one child, Clide Alexander. Mr. Rice is a member of the Methodist Episcopal Church South, and is a Democrat in politics. Mrs. Rice is a member of the Baptist Church.

G. L. ROBINSON, M. D., of Lebanon, Tenn., was born October 8, 1821, in Smith County, one of eight children of Stephen and Mary (Lancaster) Robinson, who were of English origin. The father was born in Virginia in 1778, and was a farmer by occupation. He came to Tennessee in his youth and his parents were among the very first settlers of Middle Tennessee. He died in January, 1846. He was a soldier in the war of 1812, and was twice married, being the father of nine children. The mother was born June 6, 1798, in Tennessee, and died the same year as her husband. Our subject's early education was acquired in the common schools, and served in the Mexican war in Joseph E. Thomas' Tennessee Cavalry, serving twelve months. After his return he began studying under Dr. G. M. Alsop, of Statesville, and in 1848 entered the medical department of the Louisville (Ky.) University and graduated as an M. D. in 1850. He practiced his profession in Statesville, Alexandria, and in 1854 came to Lebanon, where he has since resided. September 7, 1851, he married Emily D. Anderson, daughter of Frank Anderson; she died June 7, 1875, leaving one child, Churchwell, who died in 1877. In 1878 the Doctor married Valeria Huddleston, daughter of Winston and Mary B. Huddleston. She was born January 21, 1839, and she and the Doctor are members of the Christian Church.

HON. R. C. SANDERS, clerk and master of the Chancery Court of Wilson County, Tenn., was born July 23, 1826, in Sumner County, and is one of three children of James and Letitia (Carey) Sanders. The father was born in North Carolina, in 1779, and in youth came with his parents to Sumner, Tenn., where he followed the occupation of farming. He was married to Letitia Carey in 1825, and died in 1861. He was twice married and was the father of ten children. The mother was born in Sumner County, Tenn., in 1800, and died April 16, 1871. Our subject graduated from Enon College and for one session was a student in the law department of the Cumberland University at Lebanon. In 1847 he began teaching school and continued that and farming until 1849, when he became principal of the Smithfield (Tenn.) High School, continuing until 1853. December 23 of that year he wedded Rhoda A. Reeves, daughter of John and Sarah Reeves. Mrs. Sanders was born February 17, 1836, in Smith County, Tenn., and became the mother of the following children: Nora, John C. and Nat. In 1854 Mr. Sanders was chosen superintendent of the high school at Carthage, Tenn., and in 1857 was elected to represent Smith County in the State Legislature. After his return to Carthage upon the adjournment of the Legislature, he again began the study of law, and in 1859 was admitted to the bar and practiced his profession until the breaking out of the war. In June, 1861, he enlisted in Company F, Twenty-fifth Regiment Tennessee Infantry, and was immediately appointed its adjutant and served until the re-organization of the army at Corinth, when he was elected lieutenant-colonel of the same regiment. He had command of the regiment for several months, the colonel, S. S. Stanton, being absent. He and Col. Stanton, owing to trouble with the brigadier-general in command, resigned, and returned to Middle Tennessee and raised another regiment (infantry), the Eighty-fourth Tennessee; this was consolidated with the Twenty-eighth Tennessee Infantry. Col. Sanders was appointed quartermaster and acted as such until the close of the war, receiving his parole at Washington, Ga., June 9, 1865. Col. Sanders, although quartermaster, went into the ranks as a private, and took part in the capture of Dalton, Ga., in the battle of Spring Hill and Franklin, and in the engagements around Nashville. After the close of the war he resumed the practice of law and formed a partnership with Judge Cantrell, of Lebanon, with whom he remained eight years. In 1874 Col. Sanders moved to Louisville, Ky., but after a two-years residence, returned to Tennessee and resided one year in Gallatin and then came to Lebanon. He and his son, John C., are partners in the practice of law, the latter being a graduate of the law department of the University of Louisville, Ky., and of the same department of the Cumberland University of Lebanon, Tenn. In 1881 Col. Sanders represented Wilson County in the lower house of the State Legislature. He was made chairman of the Committee of Claims and in 1883 was appointed to his present position. He is a member of the Masonic fraternity and he and his son constitute one of the leading law firms of the county.

ERVIN K. SHANNON is a farmer of the Nineteenth District, of Wilson County, Tenn., and son of J. H. and Isabella (Braden) Shannon. He was born March 22, 1841, in the county where he now resides. His father was of Irish descent and was born December 19, 1803. When he was about twenty-five years of age he came to Tennessee. His parents died when he was quite young and he was reared by a man by the name of Shaker, with whom he learned the tanner's trade, and followed this occupation in Tennessee for about ten years. He then moved to a farm belonging to his wife. He was married about 1834, and became the father of seven children, five now living. He was a soldier in the late war and his death occurred in June, 1870. His widow died in 1876. Our subject resided with his parents until their respective deaths. He received his education in the district schools of the neighborhood, and in 1862, in company with his brother, assumed control of the tanning business, continuing about eight years. Since that time our subject has been engaged in farming, and owns the old homestead. He enlisted in the Forty-fourth Tennessee, Company C, and was in the battles of Shiloh and Perryville, Ky., and was wounded in the latter engagement and returned home. In politics he is a Democrat, and his wife is a member of the Cumberland Presbyterian Church.

ALEX SHANNON, proprietor of a grocery and hardware store in Lebanon, Tenn., is a native of Wilson County, born in 1844, and is one of five children of J. H. and Isabella (Braden) Shannon. Alex Shannon was reared on his father's 180-acre farm. He was educated in the country schools, and December 22, 1870, was married to Maggie Holloway, daughter of Richard and Eunice (Shannon) Holloway. She was born in 1847 and is the mother of two living children; James R. and Nebar. In 1872 Mr. Shannon bought 146 acres of land and followed agricultural pursuits until 1882, when he sold out and removed to Lebanon and clerked in the hardware store of McClain Bros. for two years. Since November, 1885, he has been connected with J. K. Buchanan in the grocery and hardware business, and is doing well. Mr. Shannon is conservative in politics, and he and wife are members of the Christian Church.

FINIS E. SHANNON, Sr., one of the oldest citizens of District No. 22, and a prominent farmer, was born November 20, 1814, in Wilson County. He is the youngest child of Henry and Jane (Hayes) Shannon. The father was of Irish descent, born January 10, 1766, in Virginia and was a farmer by occupation. About 1795 he came to Davidson County but afterward removed to Wilson County where he died September 25, 1844. The mother was born March 22, 1772, in Virginia, and died December 10, 1832, in Wilson County. The subject of our sketch received his education mostly outside of the schoolroom. July 31, 1838, he married Nancy Hearn, daughter of Milbry Hearn. Mrs. Shannon was born February 6, 1818, in Wilson County and by her marriage became the mother of two children: Norman P., who is a farmer, and Mary C., wife of James Doughty. After our subject's marriage he located on the old home place. In 1856 his wife died, and in the following year he married Rosanna A. Hunt, a native of Rutherford County, born in 1826, and the daughter of

Samuel Hunt. To Mr. and Mrs. Shannon were born three children: Finis E., Texannah and Frusey. In 1861 he sold the old home place and bought land in District No. 22, where he is now living. He lost his second wife in 1862, and in 1867 he married E. J. O'Neal; she lived but a short time after marriage and December, 1868. he married Elizabeth J. Etherley, a native of Wilson County, born in 1829. Mr. Shannon is one of Wilson County's old citizens and has been quite successful, owning at the present time 500 acres of land. He has been a life-long Democrat casting his first vote for Martin Van Buren. He has also been an active business man, is obliging and courteous and is a good neighbor.

REV. S. G. SHEPARD, an enterprising farmer, was born in 1830 in Wilson County; son of John and Frances G. (Graves) Shepard. The father was of Scotch descent, and was born about 1785 in Prince Edward County, Va. He was a teacher by profession, and in connection with this did farming. At the time of his marriage, which occurred in 1807, he was living in Wilson County. He was not permitted to live the time allotted to man, but was cut down in the prime of life. He died in 1835 with the cholera. The mother was of French origin, and was born in Virginia about 1800; she died in 1860. There were eight children born to them, four of whom are living. Our subject's grandfather, Samuel Shepard, was a soldier in the Revolutionary war, and was present at the surrender of Cornwallis, at Yorktown. About 1800 he immigrated to Wilson County, Tenn., where he settled and lived to an advanced age. He cast his first vote for George Washington, and his last for Henry Clay. Our subject received his education in the county schools, and at the breaking out of the late war he enlisted in Company G, Seventh Tennessee Infantry, Confederate States Army, and was made captain of his company. After the death of Gen. Hatton, May 31, 1862, our subject was appointed lieutenant-colonel of his regiment. He led his men in twenty battles, the leading ones being Seven Pines, seven days around Richmond, second Manassas, Sharpsburg, etc. At the close of the war he returned home, and August 3, 1865, married Mattie Major, a native of Wilson County; born in 1845, and the daughter of Samuel and Fanny (Chambers) Major. To our subject and wife were born four children: Samuel G., Alice, John and Agnes. After marriage our subject began farming, and now owns 300 acres, and is a well-to-do farmer. He is a Democrat in politics and a member of the Masonic fraternity. In 1870 he was elected as one of two representatives from Wilson County to assist in revising the constitution of the State of Tennessee. In 1872 he was elected as member to the State Legislature, and in the same year he was ordained as a Missionary Baptist minister. His ministerial duties have been principally confined to Wilson and Rutherford Counties. At present he has charge of four churches, three in Rutherford and one in Cannon County at Woodbury.

J. R. SHORTER, proprietor of a livery and feed stable, at Lebanon, Tenn., was born in Wilson County in 1845, and is a son of James and Martha P. (Wyoone) Shorter, who were of Irish descent, born in Tennessee in 1815 and 1819, respectively. They were married about 1836, and tilled a farm of 200 acres until 1858, when they purchased a 150-acre farm. Here the father died in 1860, and the mother in August, 1884. Our subject only attended school about three months during his life. September 19, 1867, he lead to Hymen's altar Easter C. Graves, daughter of Lorenzo J. and Mary Graves. Mr. and Mrs. Shorter have three children: Lorenzo J., Susie and Robert. In 1869 Mr. Shorter came to Lebanon and established a retail liquor store, but in 1871 bought a family grocery store, continuing three years. He then farmed three years, and in 1877 returned to Lebanon, and with W. G. Swindell began keeping a livery and feed stable. A year later Samuel Golliday purchased Mr. Swindell's interest, and he in turn was bought out by J. W. Hamilton. Since 1883 Mr. Shorter has carried on the business alone. He keeps ten horses, nine single and six double vehicles, and runs a buss to each train, and has met with merited success. He is a member of the K. of H. and K. of P., and he and wife are members of the Baptist Church.

W. H. SMITH, farmer, was born in Wilson County, Tenn., May 29, 1834, and is one of fifteen children born to James and Martha (Johnson) Smith. The father was a native of Virginia, born in 1796. He followed agricultural pursuits during his lifetime. He died in Wilson County in 1874. The mother was born in Kentucky in 1800, and died in Wilson County in 1853. The subject of this sketch was reared on the farm and educated in the schools of the county. In 1858 he wedded Lucy J. Johnson, daughter of Berry and Miranda Johnson. Mrs. Smith was born in Wilson County, Tenn., in 1836, and by her union with Mr. Smith became the mother of seven children: Martha J., James B., Miranda E., William H., Eddie W., Emma and Bubie. In 1862 our subject bought 141 acres of land, and began tilling the soil; he added to his farm quite often, and is at present the owner of 240 acres of good land. In 1881 Mrs. Smith died, and in 1883 he married Mary F. Williams, daughter of Elijah and Polly Williams. Mrs. Smith was born in Wilson County, Tenn., in 1849, and by her marriage with Mr. Smith she became the mother of two children: Winfield and Lelia. In politics Mr. Smith is a Democrat.

J. E. STRATTON, dry goods merchant of Lebanon, Tenn., was born February 27, 1842, son of Thomas J. and Caroline M. (Golladay) Stratton. J. E. Stratton was reared at home and was educated in the Cumberland University. In May, 1861, he enlisted in Company D, Seventh Regiment Tennessee Infantry Volunteers, and participated in all the battles of the Virginia campaign in 1861-62. He was severely wounded at the battle of Seven Pines. He was cared for in the house of the Misses Forbes, sisters of Col. Forbes, of Clarksville, Tenn. He resided for some time with his uncle, in Granada, Miss. In 1862, while in Kentucky, he was arrested by Federal troops, but after taking the oath of allegiance was released and remained in Kentucky until the fall of Richmond. March 24, 1864, he married Mary Grimes, who was born in 1842, in Kentucky, daughter of James and Fannie Grimes. To Mr. and Mrs. Stratton were born these children: James G., Thomas E. G. and Caroline May. In 1866 Mr. Stratton returned to Lebanon, where he was engaged in the general merchandise business with his father and brothers. He soon after went to Todd County, Ky., where he engaged in the same business three years and farmed six years. From 1873 to 1876 he was a druggist in Allensville, and at the latter date went to Nashville and established a merchant and tailor's establishment. In the fall of 1879 he returned to Lebanon, clerking until 1881, when he engaged in the dry goods business in the same room as that occupied by his father in 1865-66. In 1881 the building burned, and a year later he erected his present fine building. He is one of Lebanon's first merchants and citizens and is a member of the K. of P., and he and family are members of the Methodist Episcopal Church South.

S. G. STRATTON. The Bank of Lebanon, Tenn., was organized in August, 1884, with a capital stock of $25,000, James Hamilton, president, and Thomas J. Stratton as cashier. In January, 1885, Mr. Stratton died, and S. G. Stratton, our subject, was chosen as his successor. He was born January 30, 1844, in Lebanon, and is one of five children of Thomas J. and Caroline M. (Golladay) Stratton. The father was born August 5, 1818, in Sumner County, Tenn., and was a resident of Lebanon at the time of his marriage, in May, 1838. He established a general merchandise store in Lebanon, but a few years later began dealing in dry goods only. He was engaged in the Florida war. His partners at different periods were Benjamin Ireland, Maj. Andrew Allison and lastly, before the war, Samuel Golladay. Mr. Stratton was a leading business man of Lebanon and an influential citizen. In 1870 he was elected cashier of the Bank of Wilson County, and he continued its cashier after it became the Second National Bank, continuing as such until August, 1884, when he was chosen cashier of the Bank of Lebanon, continuing until his death, in January, 1885. He was twice married and became the father of six children, his second wife being Fannie (Watkins) Helm. Our subject's mother died August 15, 1865. S. G. Stratton was educated in the Cumberland University. During the war he first attached himself to the Thirty-eighth Tennessee Infantry, under Col. Looney, of Memphis, and afterward enlisted in Capt. J. W. Britton's company, Fourth Tennessee Cavalry, and was in the service until the fall of 1864. November 9, 1865, he married Alice Fisher, who was born October 10, 1844, who bore him two children: Houston F. and Franceway C. Mr. Stratton was first after the war engaged in the mercantile business with his father, and afterward with R. Green. In 1872 he was appointed clerk of the circuit court, to fill an unexpired term, and was twice afterward elected and held the office until 1882. In 1881 he became engaged in the dry goods business, in the firm of J. E. Stratton & Co., and at present is one of the firm of J. T. Odum & Co. October 22, 1877, Mrs. Stratton died, and December 1, 1881, he married Leila M. Owen, born in 1861, in Talbot County, Ga., daughter of Sidney Owen. By this marriage he has one daughter, Mildred Owen, born February 2, 1883. Our subject succeeded his father as cashier of the Bank of Lebanon. In 1873 he was elected mayor of Lebanon, having served several years, before and after, in the city council. He is a member of the Masonic fraternity, Lebanon Lodge, No. 98, and has filled, among other offices, that of Worshipful Master, Most Excellent High Priest of the Chapter, Eminent Commander of the Commandery, and is a member of the K. of H. and K. of P. He and wife belong to the Methodist Episcopal Church South.

L. D. STROUD born in Wilson County, Tenn., Oct. 7, 1842, is one of eight children of O. B. and Lucie (Lester) Stroud who were born in Halifax County, Va., and Wilson County, Tenn., May 2, 1803 and June 29, 1824, and died April 14, 1863, and March 11, 1875, respectively. They were married November 11, 1841. The mother was a daughter of Joshua Lester, founder of the Baptist Church at Smithfork, Tenn., and its pastor for thirty-seven years. Our subject received his education at what was known as the "Three Forks Institute" and afterward attended the Mount Vernon Institute. When sixteen he entered the teachers' profession continuing until the breaking out of the war when he enlisted in Holton's Seventh Tennessee Infantry and participated in the battles of Seven Pines and Cedar Run; was wounded in the arm at the former battle and yet carries the ball in his shoulder. He was severely wounded at the latter battle and has never entirely recovered from its effects. After his return home he resumed teaching and paid off a debt of $300 which his father had contracted for his schooling. In 1877 he accepted the presidency of the Woodbury College for a period of two years, but ill health obliged him to abandon the profession entirely. March 13, 1865, he wedded Leathy A., daughter of John and Anna Sneed, born December 22, 1841, and has borne six children: Cornelia (Mrs. A. G. Penuel), Minnie (Mrs R. B. Penuel), Angie, Nettie, Bernice and Garland. In February, 1884, Mr. Stroud took a trip to Mexico for a business house at Nashville, and while there acquired a thorough knowledge of the Spanish language. Mr. Stroud is the owner of 250 acres of fine land and his home is pleasantly and picturesquely situated. He is a Democrat in his political views and took an active part in State politics in 1879. He is a member of the I. O. O. F., and his wife belongs to the Baptist Church.

A. SULLIVAN, an enterprising farmer and stock raiser of the Twenty-fourth District, was born March 22, 1815, in Wilson County, Tenn., and is one of a family of nine children born to A. and S. Sullivan. The father was born in Guilford County, N. C., and was a farmer by occupation. He married in his native State and immigrated to Wilson County and settled in the Twenty-fourth District, where he purchased 141 acres of land. He died in March, 1835. The mother was born in Guilford County, N. C., in 1775, and came to this county with her husband, where she remained until her death, which occurred in 1855. Our subject was reared in Wilson County, Tenn., and like the average country boy, received his education in the common schools. June 16, 1839, he wedded Clerky Patterson, daughter of Elijah Patterson. The fruits of this union were three sons, only one of whom is living. One son was killed at Richmond and another at Corinth, Miss. Mr. Sullivan is the owner of 300 acres in the Twenty-fourth District, and by his affable and courteous manner has made many friends. He is a Democrat in politics.

B. J. TARVER, attorney at law of Lebanon, was born in Warren County, N. C., and is one of two sons of Silas and Nancy (Harris) Tarver. The father was a Welshman by descent, and was born in 1794 or 1795 in North Carolina. He was a farmer, and came to Tennessee in 1808 with his father, Benjamin Tarver, one of the pioneers of the county. After his marriage, in 1823, Silas located on a farm where Tucker's Gap is now situated, and there remained until his career ended in 1862. The mother was of English birth, born in North Carolina, and died in 1845. Our subject secured an academical education, and afterward entered the law department of Cumberland University, graduating in 1851.

He has since practiced his profession, and has met with marked success. He commenced at the bottom round of the ladder, but by perseverance and knowledge of his profession he has steadily climbed upward in his profession until he ranks among the first of the Wilson County bar. In 1878 he was appointed judge of the chancery court of Tennessee, and held the office for one year. In 1875 he wedded Susan White, who was born in 1829, and a daughter of James D. White. Mr. and Mrs. Tarver are members of the Methodist Episcopal Church South.

J. B. TARVER, farmer and resident of Tucker's Gap, was born June 14, 1835, in the house where he is now residing. He is the youngest son of a family of seven children, only two of whom are now living: our subject, and Judge B. J. Tarver, of Lebanon. Silas and Nancy (Harris) Tarver were their father and mother. Our subject received his education in the Cumberland University at Lebanon in the literary department. February 28, 1856, he married Lucy Hobson, daughter of Henry and Lucy (Tarver) Hobson. Mrs. Tarver was born August 2, 1837, in Wilson County, and by her union with Mr. Tarver she became the mother of six children: Mattie E., A. Benjamin, John E., Walter A., Nannie and George. In 1858 our subject entered the law department of the Cumberland University, attending two sessions. In 1856 he went to Arkadelphia, Ark., and commenced his law practice, which he continued until the breaking out of the war. In February, 1862, he returned to his birth-place, where he has since lived engaged in agricultural pursuits. Mr. Tarver now owns 440 acres, and is an honest, enterprising and successful farmer. In politics he is a Democrat, but was at one time a Whig. He is a Good Templar, and he and family are members of the Methodist Episcopal Church South.

WILLIAM B. TATUM, one of the prominent farmers of the Twenty-second District, was born in 1821, in Sumner County, Tenn., and is the son of Ira and Martha (Eddins) Tatum. The father was a native of North Carolina and a teacher by profession in his younger days, and later in life he followed farming. He was a soldier in the war of 1812, and died in 1825. The mother was born in North Carolina in about 1800, and died about 1872. Our subject at the age of seventeen commenced working at the tanner's trade, which he continued for four years. At the age of twenty-one he went to Macon, Tenn., and bought 130 acres and commenced farming on his own responsibility. In three years he returned to Wilson County, and in March, 1846, he wedded Sarah A. Goldston, a native of Wilson County, born in 1823, and a daughter of Eli and Elizabeth Goldston. To Mr. and Mrs. Tatum were born eight children: Martha E., A. Frank, Mary E., William A., Emily A., Thomas E., Edward L. and Ira J. About 1851 our subject bought 111 acres in the Twenty-second District, where he located and is now living. In connection with farming he carried on the tannery business for a period of twenty-five years. Mr. Tatum started in life as a poor boy, but by energy, economy and good management he now owns 440 acres. He is a Democrat in politics, and he and wife are members of the Christian Church.

JAMES H. TAYLOR, one of the old settlers of Wilson County, was born in Tennessee, August 24, 1807, and is one of ten children born to Perrygan and Sarah (Wilson) Taylor. The father was of English descent, born in North Carolina in 1761, and came to Sumner County about 1800. He was a farmer by occupation, and at the time of his marriage was living in North Carolina. He died in Wilson County, Tenn., in 1826. The mother was of Irish descent, and was born in Maryland in 1764. She died in Wilson County, Tenn., in 1822. At the age of twenty our subject left home; he had received a fair education at the county schools, and in 1827 Martha Hunter became his wife. She was born in Wilson County, Tenn., in 1810, and was the daughter of Isaac and Selina Hunter. To our subject and wife were born seven children: Caroline, Evaline, Lashophine, Leona (wife of R. C. Morris), Isaac, John and William. In 1832 Mr. Taylor bought 150 acres of land, and from that time to the present has added to his land from time to time, and now owns 262 acres, upon which he is at present living. In politics he is a Democrat, and he and wife are consistent members of the Cumberland Church.

COL. R. E. THOMPSON, a citizen of Wilson County, Tenn., descended from the old Thompson, Cockrell, McNairy and Robertson families of Tennessee. Gen. James Robertson and John Cockrell were the first white men that ever stood on Capitol Hill. Col. Thompson was born at Cockrell's Springs, near Nashville, in 1822. He was partly educated in Nashville, and in 1840 came to Lebanon and finished his education at Cumberland University. He married Miss Mary E. Tolliver, the eldest daughter of Col. Zach Tolliver, of Lebanon, Tenn., by whom he has six living children—two sons and four daughters—all of whom are doing remarkably well. His youngest son, Lillord, is attorney-general of the Seventh Judicial Circuit. Col. Thompson is a lawyer and farmer, and is noted as a criminal lawyer, and defends nearly all the criminals in his section of the county, but refuses to prosecute, never having prosecuted a man, although offered large fees to do so. In politics he is a low-tax Democrat, and is opposed to taxing the people to pay the railroad debt. He has been seven or eight times elected to the State Legislature, three or four times to each branch, and took a very active part in common school education and in the cause of temperance. He is not a very zealous advocate of the four-mile law, and offered a bill, and got it passed, excluding intoxicating liquors from every place in the State, excepting Nashville, Knoxville and Memphis, but the supreme court decided it was unconstitutional. He is a bold and fearless advocate of the rights of the masses of the people, and zealous of encroachments upon their rights by the monied corporations, consequently is often before the people, securing large majorities over very popular men. He still practices his profession, in which, together with other resources, yield him a competency in his old age. He is a Missionary Baptist in faith.

WILLIAM T. THOMPSON, an enterprising farmer, was born August 13, 1846, in Wilson County, and is the son of George and Martha (Baird) Thompson. The father was of Irish descent, born October 17, 1822, in Wilson County, and is a farmer by occupation. His father, Moses Thompson, was born in 1782, in the State of North Carolina, and came to Wilson County at a very early date. He died in 1842. George Thompson lived in his native county at the time of his marriage, which occurred November 11, 1845. He settled in the Nineteenth District, where he has since resided, moving only once since that time. He has lived on the farm where he now resides since 1851, and has been quite successful as a tiller of the soil, owning at the present time upward of 550 acres. The mother was born July 4, 1826, in Wilson County, and died July 12, 1878. Our subject is one of eight children who are living. He received his education in the country schools and February 6, 1868, wedded Fanny Martin, a native of Wilson County, born March 19, 1849, and the daughter of John Martin. To our subject and wife were born four children, three of whom are living: Emma, John B. and Fannie E. In 1869 he bought forty-five acres in the Twenty-first District, where he resided until 1877, when he bought 200 acres where he now resides. Mr. Thompson lost his wife August 5, 1876, and September 12 of the following year he married Lucy Logue, a native of Wilson County, born December 20, 1852. To this union were born four children: Samuel, Mattie, Nannie and Spurgen. Mr. Thompson is an enterprising business man, and now owns 382 acres. His wife has 120 acres in Davidson County. In politics our subject is very conservative, voting for principle and not for party. In connection with farming he has speculated in timber; has been employed several years by the Western Union Telegraph Company to furnish poles to them. He has also furnished Nashville with many telegraph poles.

ED. L. VANCE, JR., junior member of the livery and feed stable of Johnson & Vance, of Lebanon, Tenn., is a son of Edward R. and Drucilla (Hearn) Vance, and was born in Wilson County November 28, 1859. The father is of Irish extraction, born in 1817, in Rutherford County, Tenn., and is a farmer by occupation. In 1837 he came to Wilson County, where he purchased 300 acres of land, and was married in 1839. He has been twice married and is the father of fifteen children. Our subject was educated in the schools near his home and in the Big Spring Seminary. At the age of eighteen years he left home and leased 396 acres of land, which he farmed two years, and the following three years worked on a tract of 400 acres of land in Davidson County. In 1884 he and his brother, Joseph T., purchased the livery and feed stable of Orgain & Ragland, in Lebanon, but at the end of six months M. House became one of the proprietors. In October, 1885, Mr. W. A. Johnson bought Mr. M. House's interest, and since then the firm has been Johnson & Vance. They keep about fifteen horses and twelve single and eight double vehicles, and are doing a good business.

B. J. VANHOOK, superintendent of county poor of Wilson County, was born in 1849 in Wilson County, Tenn. He is the son of Joel N. and Mary T. (Hickman) Vanhook. The father was of German lineage, born in 1822, on the line between North Carolina and Virginia, and was a farmer by occupation. He came to Tennessee with his mother, and at the time of his marriage, which occurred in 1841, was living in Wilson County. He bought land in Barton's Creek, in the Twenty-first District, where he lived for forty years. In 1885 he moved to the Twenty-second District, where he now resides. He is the father of six children, all of whom are living. The mother was born about 1824, in Wilson County, Tenn., and is also living. Our subject received his education in the county schools. December 31, 1869, he wedded Virginia Ligon, a native of Wilson County, born March 31, 1850, and the daughter of Richard L. and Roseline Ligon. To Mr. and Mrs. Vanhook were born six children: Riley C., Orrie, Bettie V., Carrie, Huston and Howard. Our subject settled on Barton Creek, and in 1877 he was elected to the position he now occupies. The county farm contains 220 acres and is located five miles west of Lebanon. The average number of poor is about thirty, and they are properly fed, clothed and cared for by Mr. and Mrs. Vanhook. In politics Mr. Vanhook is a Democrat. In 1882 he was nominated and elected as magistrate of District No. 22, and is at present holding the office. In the same year he bought 130 acres in the Twenty-second District. Mrs. Vanhook is a worthy member of the Methodist Episcopal Church South.

W. C. WALKER, farmer, was born in Wilson County, Tenn., January 8, 1838, and is the son of James D. and Celia L. (Hamilton) Walker. The father was born in North Carolina in 1777, and followed the occupation of a farmer. At the time of his marriage he was living in Wilson County, where he died May 29, 1849. The mother was born in Sumner County, Tenn., in 1795, and died in Wilson County January 18, 1884. Our subject was reared on a farm and received his education in the schools of the county. In 1820 he was married to Katie, daughter of James and Eliza ———. Mrs. Walker was born in Wilson County, Tenn., in 1844, and the fruits of her marriage to Mr. Walker are an interesting family of eight children: Edwin L., Munroe V., Cornelia L., Edna E., Lillia, Addie, William C. and Washington B. H. Mr. Walker is the present owner of 315 acres of good land in the Fourth District, where he is now living. He is a successful farmer and has the respect of all who know him. In politics he is a Democrat.

W. H. WALLACE, a dealer in lumber, was born April 6, 1852, in Wilson County, Tenn., and is a son of J. F. and Catherine Wallace. The father was born in 1836, in Sumner County, and in 1849 he moved to Wilson County and settled in the Second District. He followed agricultural pursuits, and in 1883 moved to Davidson County. The mother was born in 1834, Wilson County, and lived there until her death, which occurred in 1867. Our subject received a fair education in the country schools, and at the age of nineteen began working for himself. September 22, 1870, he married Martha J. Gibson, a native of Wilson County, Tenn., born September, 1852, and the daughter of Thomas W. Gibson. To Mr. and Mrs. Wallace were born six children: James W., Lillie, Lizzie, Daisie, Harvey W. and Alvin. Mr. Wallace, by his industry and energy, has accumulated a considerable amount of this world's goods and is respected by all who know him.

J. S. WAMACK is a native of Wilson County, Tenn., born October 14, 1818, and is one of five children of Richard and Agnes (Smith) Wamack. The father was born in Virginia about 1790, and came to Tennessee, when about twelve years of age. He was a farmer, and married when about twenty years of age, and about thirty years afterward, his wife died, and he then married Mrs. Elizabeth (Pucket) Bailey. J. S. Wamack was educated in the district schools, and August 8, 1839, he married Miss Dorcas Hall, daughter of Samuel Hall. She was born in Wilson County, in 1821, and died August 24, 1857, leaving five children: John K., a theological student at Louisville, Ky.; America (wife of H. C. Patton), Josephine (wife of Eli Vaught), James R. and A. P. Mr. Wamack began doing business for himself after attaining his majority, and became the possessor of 100 acres of land near Cherry Valley, which he has increased to 325 acres of valuable farming land. In November, 1857, Mr. Wamack wedded Mrs. E. E. (Thomas) Boyle, but about a year after her marriage, she died, leaving one child—E. E. (wife of James M. Berry). April 13, 1859, Mr. Wamack lead to Hymen's altar, Mary (Anderson) Vick: she was born in Wilson County October 11, 1832, and bore her husband four children: California, Jourdan (deceased), Agnes (wife of S. Henderson), and an infant (deceased). Our subject and family reside on a farm of 100 acres near Cherry Valley, and in connection with farming, has kept a nursery for about ten years. He has been quite an extensive traveler, and has always contributed liberally to all public and private enterprises. He is a Democrat and cast his first presidential vote for Harrison. He and wife are members of the Baptist Church.

J. M. WATKINS, proprietor of the Watkins Hotel, at Lebanon, Tenn., was born April 3, 1841, and is one of eight children of Moses and Jane (Scoby) Watkins. The father was born in 1812 in Virginia, and was a farmer through life. He came to Tennessee with his parents when about six years of age, and resided on different farms up to 1876, when he moved to Lebanon, where he died in the fall of 1884. The mother was born in Smith County, Tenn., and since the death of her husband has lived with her daughter Mary (Mrs. D. W. King). Our subject attended the schools of his native county, and in 1862 enlisted in Company B, Forty-fourth Regiment Tennessee Infantry, and took an active part in the battle of Shiloh. He returned home in 1864, and after farming two years became clerk in the Sweeney House, in Nashville. December 22, 1868, he married Dora Cartwright, daughter of Wilson T. and Elizabeth Cartwright. Mrs. Watkins was born in 1852 in Nashville. She and her husband have three children: Archie Wilson, Emma Bell (deceased) and Lena May. In 1877 Mr. Watkins came to Lebanon, and he and W. M. Organ purchased a livery and feed stable, which they managed for eighteen months, and for the following year Mr. Watkins conducted the business on his own responsibility. In 1879 he and Mr. D. C. Williams became partners, continuing one year. In 1881–82 Mr. Watkins kept a grocery and restaurant, and in 1883 established himself in the hotel business, and is an obliging and courteous landlord. In politics he is a Democrat, and he and wife are members of the Missionary Baptist Church.

DR. R. L. C. WHITE, editor and proprietor of the Lebanon *Herald*, was born June 11, 1844, in Wilson County, Tenn., and is the only living child of Capt. John W. and Sally C. (Cannon) White, who were of English descent, born in North Carolina and Tennessee in 1804 and 1807, respectively. The father died in 1871. He was a merchant in early life, but later became engaged also in manufacturing interests. He came to Tennessee in 1821, and in 1831 became a resident of Lebanon, and was always an active worker for the old Whig party. He was clerk of the circuit court a number of years, and was married in 1841. The mother resides with our subject, who was educated in the Cumberland University, of Lebanon. In 1862 he enlisted in Company K, Fourth Tennessee Cavalry, and participated in the battles of Perryville, Chickamauga, Murfreesboro, Atlanta, and numerous minor engagements. He remained in the field until the surrender of Johnston's army, when he returned home and entered upon the study of medicine in the Nashville Medical College, remaining one year. In 1867 he attended the Jefferson Medical College, at Philadelphia, and graduated in 1868. In 1869 he purchased a one-half interest in the Lebanon *Herald*, and since 1871 has been sole proprietor and editor. Previous to 1872 the Doctor practiced his profession, but since that time has given his time and attention to his paper, which is very newsy and instructive, and is quoted throughout the State as one of the leading journals. The Doctor is a member of the Masonic fraternity (Lebanon Lodge, No. 98, F. & A. M.), of Baldwin Commandery, No. 7, Knights Templar; Magnolia Lodge, No. 30, I. O. O. F.; Lotus Lodge, No. 20, K. of P.; Lee Lodge, No. 22, K. of H. In 1878 he was elected Grand Chancellor of the State of Tennessee of K. of P., and held the position nearly two years. In 1883 he was elected Grand Keeper of Records and Seal of the State of Tennessee of the same order, and now holds the position. Since 1880 he has been one of the two Supreme Representatives of Tennessee of the Supreme Lodge of the World, K. of P. He has also been Grand Treasurer of K. of H. of Tennessee since 1880. Until 1882 the Doctor was a Democrat, but at that time, owing to a controversy on the State debt, the party was split, the Dr. taking sides with that faction which favored the payment of the debt. He was secretary of the State Executive Committee of the State credit wing of the Democratic party during that canvass. His faction was disastrously defeated, and since that time he has affilliated with no party. Since 1882 he has been magistrate, and has held the position of notary public, and is one of the directors of the Bank of Lebanon. May 23, 1869, Dr. White married Ella M. Wade, daughter of M. B. and Elizabeth Wade, of Rutherford County. She was born in 1851, and is the mother of five children: Ethel, Opal, Coral, Mabel and Kenneth.

J. H. WILLIAMS is a native of Wilson County, Tenn., born March 6, 1841, son of J. H. and Margaret (Coson) Williams, born in North Carolina in 1794 and 1802, respectively. The father came to Tennessee when about twenty years of age, and was married some three years later. He soon purchased a small tract of land, and at the time of his death had acquired 2,000 acres of valuable land. He died April 13, 1862. The mother yet resides in the old home place. Our subject was educated at Cold Spring Academy, and June 10, 1862, was married to Miss S. C. Owen, daughter of Daniel and Mary (Robertson) Owen. Mrs. Williams was born in Wilson County, Tenn., June 29, 1844, and has borne her husband nine children: Bettie, R. B., Mahala C., Mattie M., William H., J. H., Margaret I., Alex and Earnest. In 1862 Mr. Williams purchased 200 acres of his father's estate, and is very comfortably situated. After the war he met with some financial embarrassments, but by his industry and business ability has overcome these difficulties. In 1882 he was elected magistrate, and still holds the office. He is a Democrat and belongs to the Masons and I. O. O. F. He and wife are members of the Baptist Church. In 1861 he enlisted in Company I, Eighteenth Tennessee Infantry, and was in the battles of Fort Donelson (where he was wounded and disabled for six months) and Chickamauga. He was in cavalry service, and was engaged in numerous cavalry fights. He returned home in May, 1865.

W. W. WILSON is one of the firm of Wilson & Waters, proprietors of a dry goods house at Lebanon, Tenn. He was born October 9, 1858, in Mississippi, and is the son of Eaton G. and Margaret L. (Roberts) Wilson. The father was born in Alabama and was a farmer. His death occurred in 1884. The mother was born about 1832 in Alabama, and is now residing with her son, W. W., in Lebanon. The latter was educated in Selma, Ala., but his school days were previous to his fifteenth year. He then began the battle of life for himself, and came to Lebanon and began clerking in the dry goods store of Price & Paty. About a year later he hired out to J. T. McClain & Co., with whom he remained seven years. During these years he was improving his education by study during his leisure moments, and is now a well educated man. In 1881 he owned a one-half interest in a jewelry store, his partner being B. J. Dillard, and for about a year owned a one-half interest in a livery and feed stable, the firm being styled Murphy & Wilson. In January, 1882, Mr. Wilson and Edgar Waters formed a partnership in the dry goods business, and have continued successfully in the same up to the present time. Mr. Wilson is a good business man and a skilled financier, and bears the reputation of being one of the finest salesmen in the city.

R. Q. WORD, a trader and farmer, was born in Wilson County June 6, 1840, and is one of seven children of John and Elizabeth (Quarles) Word. The father was of Irish extraction, and was born in Virginia about 1798. He is a farmer, and came to Tennessee when but six years of age. He was married three times, and is now living in the Fifth District. The mother was of Irish extraction also, and was born in 1798 and died in 1870. Our subject was reared at home, and received his education in the common schools. At the breaking out of the war he enlisted in Company H, of the Seventh Tennessee Infantry, Confederate States Army, and was captured at the second battle of Manassas. He remained a prisoner about thirty days, when he was returned to the Confederate States Army authorities. He was in all the principal battles, and at one time was the only man in his company (officer or private) able to report for duty. After the war he was engaged for some time with the Louisville Oil Company, for which he traveled. February 21, 1867, he wedded Pemelia Freeman, a native of Tennessee, who died March 13, 1871. To this union were born two children, Charles and Elizabeth. He contracted a second marriage May 31, 1872, with Rachel Patton, a native of Kentucky, and the daughter of James H. and Sallie Patton. In 1871 Mr. Word went to Lawson, Ray Co., Mo., and at different times was in a grocery, furniture and hardware store. In 1873 he returned to Tennessee and became one of the proprietors of the Silver Springs Mills. This occupied his attention for five years, since which time he has followed trading in live-stock. He has lately become a candidate for county trustee, subject to the county election August 5, 1886. He holds to the true principles of Democracy. He is a member of the Masonic lodge No. 98, and of the Royal Arch lodge and the K. of P. He is a member of the Methodist Episcopal Church South, and his wife of the Baptist Church.

GEORGE W. WRIGHT, an enterprising farmer and merchant, was born November 21, 1838, in Wilson County, Tenn., and is one of a family of eleven children born to Lewis and Tempie (Eddings) Wright. The father was born in 1794 in the State of Virginia, and when only fifteen years of age immigrated to Wilson County, Tenn., and located in the Twenty-fifth District. He was married in the year 1820, and by industry and perseverance soon purchased about 220 acres. Death called him away March 10, 1872. The mother was born in 1800 in Wilson County. Our subject received a practical education in the county schools, and June 18, 1862, he was united in marriage to Lucy (Guill) Wright. She was born September 26, 1843, and is the daughter of James Guill. To Mr. and Mrs. Wright were born two children: Monroe A. and Tempie E. Mrs. Wright's death occurred January 28, 1868. June 20, 1869, Mr. Wright married Mary Robison, daughter of John Drennan. She was born in Wilson County, and by her union with Mr. Wright became the mother of five children: John, Lee, Cora, Lena and Annie. Mr. Wright is a good man, and one of the most energetic farmers of the Twenty-fourth District.

J. K. WRIGHT, an enterprising merchant and farmer of the Fourth District, was born in Sumner County, Tenn., October 24, 1847, and is one of six children born to William and Margaret J. Wright. The father was born in Sumner County, Tenn., in 1814, and followed the occupation of a merchant and farmer, and at one time was owner and proprietor of the first woolen factory that was operated in the State of Tennessee. He was married in his native county, and died there in 1870. The mother was born in Montgomery County, Tenn., in 1819, and died in Sumner County, Tenn., in 1859. Our subject passed his youthful days at home, and when twenty years of age received the rudiments of his education in the schools of the county, and subsequently attended Boyd's Commercial College at Louisville, Ky. In 1869 he was married to Eliza G., daughter of Dr. Henry B. and Susan Vaughn. Mrs. Wright was born in Wilson County, Tenn., in 1850, and by her union with Mr. Wright became the mother of five children: Maggie S., Alice B., James K., William H. and Graham C. In 1873 he bought eighty-five acres of land in Williamson County, where he commenced farming on his own responsibility, and at the present owns 145 acres of land, all lying in the Fourth District, where he still continues to farm. In 1867 Mr. Wright opened a grocery and dry goods store in La Guardo, and followed this business until 1873, when he sold out his store and continued farming until 1880, when he purchased his present store. He is postmaster at La Guardo, a Democrat and a member of the Cumberland Presbyterian Church.

ROBERT YOUNG (deceased), a successful farmer, was born May 7, 1822, in Wilson County, Tenn., and was one of twelve children born to James and Nancy (Branch) Young. The father was born in Wilson County, Tenn., in 1797, and is of Irish descent. He was a farmer by occupation, and lived to a good old age, his death occurring June 7, 1881. The mother was born in the year 1800 in Wilson County, and died April 17, 1875. Our subject was educated in his native county, and December 1, 1842, was married to Nancy Neal, and by her became the father of eight children: James W., Mary E. (wife of George Sullivan), George, Pallas, David, Nannie (wife of T. Hamilton), William F. and Effie L. In the year 1866 he moved and settled in the Twenty-fourth District, where he purchased 325 acres of land, and carried on farming and stock raising until his death, which occurred June 22, 1885. He was a good man, and had the respect and esteem of all who knew him. He was a member of the Masonic fraternity and held to the principles of Democracy, and was a worthy member of the Missionary Baptist Church. Mrs. Young survives her husband, and manages the farm in a skillful manner. She is a consistent Christian and a member of the Missionary Baptist Church.

G. D. YOUNG, a farmer of the Fifteenth District of Wilson County, Tenn., was born October 23, 1823, and is a son of Joseph D. and Margaret (Stewart) Young, who were born in North Carolina and Tennessee in 1785 and 1796, and died in Tennessee in 1873 and 1875, respectively. They were married in 1812. G. D. Young, our subject, received his education in the schools of his native county. January 8, 1846, he married Miss Miranda, daughter of Andrew and Ritter (Kelly) Thompson, by whom he had six children: A. R., wife of J. D. Pemberton; Joseph D., A. T., Margaret E., J. M. and William B. After attaining his majority Mr. Young began farming on his own responsibility. After his marriage he purchased 135 acres of land which he has since increased to 185 acres. Mr. Young has been quite successful as a farmer and business man, and in addition to his farming has given some attention to the shoe-maker's trade and stone-masonry. He was a Whig as long as that party existed, but is now a Democrat. He belongs to the I. O. O. F. and he and wife are members of the Methodist Episcopal Church.

JOSEPH YOUNG was born near Big Springs, Wilson Co,. Tenn., August 1, 1826, son of D. and Sarah Young, who were of Irish descent, and born in Tennessee and Virginia, respectively. The father was born in 1804, and resided in Wilson County until his death in 1874. He was married about 1825. Our subject was educated in the district schools, and December 20, 1849, was married to Nancy Marks, who was born in Wilson County, Tenn., March 3, 1827, daughter of John and Mary Marks. She died April 19, 1858, having borne three children, one—Laura—is now living. November 23, 1860, he wedded Emily Sneed, born December 30, 1839, daughter of Abraham and Elizabeth Sneed. To Mr. and Mrs. Young were born these children: Sarah E., Mary, James, William, H., Holly and Joseph. Soon after his first marriage Mr. Young purchased a grist-mill and has carried on that and farming to the present time. He owns about 200 acres of land. He was involved to the extent of $3,600 during the war, but by indomitable and persevering will has overcome these difficulties, and has since purchased and paid for 120 acres of excellent land. He is a Democrat politically and has held the office of justice of the peace a number of years. He and Mrs. Young are members of the Missionary Baptist Church.

J. W. YOUNG, a farmer, is a son of Robert and Nancy (Neal) Young, and grandson of James Young, who were of Irish descent. Robert Young was born in 1822, in Wilson County, Tenn., and followed the occupation of farming, owning at the time of his death, in 1885, 325 acres of land. The mother was born in 1824, and is yet residing on the old home place. They were the parents of twelve children, eight of whom are living: Mary, George, Palace, David, Foster, Nannie, Effie and J. W., our subject, who was born in Wilson County, in 1842, was reared at home and educated in his native county. At the breaking out of hostilities between the North and the South in 1861, he enlisted in Company C, Fourth Tennessee Cavalry, and was in many of the principal battles and skirmishes of the war. At the battle of Stone Mountain he was shot in the left hand and was released from duty sixty days. He served until the fall of Richmond, and then returned home after an absence of nearly four years. October 22, 1868, he married Mary L. Luck, born in 1846, and daughter of W. W. and Fannie Luck. Mr. and Mrs. Young have four children: Robert, Elbert W., James and Omar A. From 1866 to 1880 our subject resided with his grandfather, James Young. He now has a good farm and a comfortable home. He is a Democrat and cast his first presidential vote for Horace Greeley. He and wife are members of the Baptist Church.

BEDFORD COUNTY.

JOHN W. ADAMS is a son of Archibald Adams, who was born September 30, 1811, in Tennessee. He was married to Jane Ramsey, who was born July 21, 1810, and our subject, John W., was born to their union December 26, 1836. The father died in 1850 and the mother in 1854. Our subject was their second child, and assisted in tilling his father's farm until twenty-one years of age. For two years he followed photography in Tennessee and Arkansas, and then joined the Confederate Army, Company H, Seventeenth Tennessee Infantry. He was wounded at Murfreesboro, and was disabled from work two months, and was wounded in the foot at Petersburg, Va. After the close of the war he returned home and was engaged by R. L. Adams, of Lewisburg, Marshall County, as assistant county court clerk, and continued about two years. He then (in 1868), engaged in farming, in which he has been fairly prosperous. He was elected magistrate in April, 1884, to fill an unexpired term. December 10, 1866, Mary H. Glenn, of Marshall County, became his wife. She is a daughter of Hugh K. and Lucretia E. Glenn, and has borne her husband three children, all of who are dead. Mr. Adams is a worthy citizen of the county and is a Democrat, and taught school in 1865-66.

J. C. AKIN, proprietor of the Evans Hotel, was born July 2, 1827, in Granville County, N. C. His father, Thomas Akin, moved with his family from North Carolina to Maury County, Tenn., about 1830, and lived there till his death. He was a farmer and raised a large family. The genial subject of this sketch was reared on a farm. He came to Shelbyville in 1854, married and engaged in the mercantile trade for a short time. He then farmed till 1857, having bought a farm near Shelbyville. He then removed to McMinville, Warren Co., Tenn., and engaged in the grocery business there a short time, and then at farming till the war, in the meantime having bought two farms and stocked them. During the war he was in the drug business till early in 1865. He then went to Maury County and raised a crop of cotton; thence he returned to McMinnville, and remained till 1878, when he again moved to Shelbyville, and for six years ran the Barksdale House. Since then he has been running the Evans Hotel, the only first-class hotel in the city. He also runs a fruit evaporator in Shelbyville. He was married, September 18, 1854, to Mrs. America Lane, the widow of Robert Lane, of Marshall County. Her father was Isaac Holman, who was once a member of the Legislature. Mr. Akin and wife have been members of the Missionary Baptist Church for many years, and are among the leading members of the church at Shelbyville. Mr. Akin has been chairman and treasurer of the executive board of the Duck River Baptist Association for many years, and at one time was president of the Baptist Sunday-school Association, and of the Bedford County Sunday-school Association. He is a member of the K. of H. Politically he was formerly an old-line Whig, but is now a conservative Democrat. He is justly regarded as an enterprising and influential citizen of the county, who has always taken special and active interest in all charitable, religious and moral enterprises. The wife was the mother of four children by her former marriage, two of whom are now living.

D. M. ALFORD, publisher of the *Bedford County Times*, was born November 30, 1861, and is the son of A. J. and Margaret (Russell) Alford, both of whom are natives of Lincoln County, Tenn., though now living in Shelbyville, Tenn. Our subject is a practical printer, and as such has filled responsible positions on the Fayetteville *Express*, Shelbyville *Gazette*, Chattanooga *Times* and Murfreesboro *News*. In February, 1886, he engaged with William Russell in the publication of the *Bedford County of Times*, which paper he is publisher, and has succeeded in building up a good newspaper.

JOHN H. ALLEN, superintendent of public instruction of Bedford County, was born November 19, 1848, son of William and Elizabeth (Ray) Allen. The parents were born in 1824 and 1827, respectively. The ancestors of our subject emigrated from Smith County, Tenn., to Illinois, and after remaining there some time moved to Bedford County, where our subject was born. William Allen was a tiller of the soil and the father of five children—four of whom were reared to maturity. These are Isaac S., Sarah, James E. and John H. The father was a pious member of the Methodist Episcopal Church South, and a respected citizen of the county in which he lived. His death, which occurred in 1874, was universally regretted by all who knew him. Since the death of her husband Mrs. Allen has been living with the subject of this sketch. She is also a member of the Methodist Episcopal Church South. Our subject, at the age of nineteen, left the farm and, having had the advantage of a good English education, chose school-teaching as his profession. He has given the best of satisfaction where he has taught, and is considered quite a success as an educator. In 1885 he was elected superintendent of public schools of Bedford County, and by his energy and untiring zeal has done much to further the advancement of the schools of the county. November 10, 1881, he married Miss Susan E. Hobbs, and two children have blessed this union: Lora V. and Ewitt P. Mr. Allen is a member of the Methodist Episcopal Church South, of which he has been a steward for eight or ten years.

A. E. ATKINSON was born in Marshall County, Tenn., January 23, 1817. His father, John Atkinson, was born in Virginia about 1774, and first married a Miss Dunn, who bore him seven children. His second wife was Nancy McClaren, and our subject is the fourth of their eight children. John Atkinson came to Tennessee about 1800, and was one of the first pioneers of the country, and was elected magistrate soon after his arrival. There being no other magistrate in the county, he was obliged to swear himself into office, and held the position until his death in 1829, with the exception of one year, when he was a member of the State Legislature. He also served as chairman of the county court several terms. Our subject has been a school-teacher for thirty-five or thirty-six years, teaching twelve months in the year a portion of the time. He also farmed, and June 5, 1838, he wedded Elizabeth C. Stem, and the following children are the result of their union: F. M., Mary A. (Mrs. A. S. Turrentine), Christina C. (Mrs. W. H. Clark), W. E. and J. R. Mrs. Atkinson died November 2. 1867, a worthy member of the Methodist Episcopal Church. Mr. Atkinson married his second wife, Jane Edwards, April 6, 1870. Mr. Atkinson has a fair education, which he has obtained mainly through his own exertions. Up to the date of the late war he was an old-line Whig. Since that time he has been a Democrat.

JOHN A. BARRETT, farmer and stock raiser, was born July 11, 1843, son of Leroy W. and Lucy B. (Knight) Barrett. The father was born in Bedford County March 29, 1818. and has been a merchant and farmer all his life. March 11, 1841, he was united in marriage, and is the father of three children, all dead with the exception of our subject. The mother was born March 20, 1824, and had been a worthy member of the Christian Church for a period of thirty years. She died March 22, 1875. The father, Leroy W. Barrett, is living at the present time in Rome, Ga., and after the death of his first wife married Mrs. Mary Dolby, a native of Wheeling, Va. He is engaged in the mercantile business. Our subject was born in Bedford County, was given a fair education in the town of Shelbyville, and at the age of eighteen enlisted in the Confederate Army in the Forty-first Tennessee, Infantry, Regiment. He was in the battles of Vicksburg, Port Hudson, Raymond, Jackson, Chickamauga, Lookout Mountain, Missionary Ridge, and numerous other important battles. After the war he came back to this county, and February 21, 1865, was married to Miss Jane B. Holt, of this county. This union resulted in the birth of three children: James L., Eugene A. and Charlie. Mr. Barrett has been quite successful in business, and owns 650 acres of fine land. He is considered one of the leading farmers of the county.

A. P. (DOCK) BAXTER, a native of Tennessee, was born September 1, 1844, son of

James M. and Sarah R. (Grant) Baxter, both natives of Tennessee. Our subject's maternal grandfather was a soldier in the war of 1812, and for services rendered received a pension for a number of years prior to his death. Our subject remained with his parents on the farm until he was twenty-one, and received a limited education on account of the late civil war, which broke into his schooling. He has followed agricultural pursuits in which he has been moderately successful, the principal part of his life. August 26, 1866, he was united in marriage to Lucinda C. Stephenson, of this county, and to this union were born four children: William G., Effie, Mollie and Joseph C. He and family are leading members of the Methodist Episcopal Church. He is a Republican in politics.

WALTER S. BEARDEN, a prominent attorney of Shelbyville, was born in Lincoln County, Tenn., January 10, 1843, being one of two children (twins) born to the marriage of Dr. B. F. Bearden and Susan M. Blake. The father was a native of South Carolina, but lived and died in Lincoln County, Tenn. He was a man of great learning and breadth, and was eminent in the profession of medicine. He died in 1870 and five years afterward the mother died. He received a good early education and at the age of fifteen began teaching as an assistant in an academy. He entered the Emory and Henry College of Virginia and was in that school when the war broke out. He then enlisted in Company E, Forty-first Tennessee as second lieutenant, and remained in the service throughout the war. He was elected second lieutenant of the company upon its second organization, and commanded the company the last year of the war. He received three wounds, one of which was serious. Returning from the service he began the study of law, and in 1866 began the practice of his profession in Shelbyville, where he has made himself a leading member of the bar. He has never aspired to political honor till this year (1886), when he was announced as candidate for chancellor of his district. He was married, February 17, 1874, to Maggie C. Whiteside, daughter of Col. T. C. Whiteside. He has a family of four children by this marriage. Politically, he was reared a Whig, but is now a Democrat. Himself and wife are members of the Presbyterian Church. He is a Knight Templar Mason and at one time was the youngest High Priest in Royal Arch Masonry of the State. As a citizen he is well known and highly respected.

ROBERT B. BIGHAM, farmer and trader, was born in Rutherford County, Tenn., July 4, 1828, son of Elihu H. and Mary (Lisenby) Bigham, and of Irish descent. The father of our subject was born in North Carolina in 1799, and his mother in Anson County, N. C., in 1805. They were married in Rutherford County, Tenn., about 1823, and became the parents of five children, of whom our subject is the third. The Bigham family were among the early settlers of Tennessee, having come to the State when the father of our subject was a small boy and settled in Rutherford County, Tenn. Elihu H. Bigham died on the old homestead in 1873, and the mother, who is eighty-one years old, is still living and enjoying good health and an unusual amount of activity for a person of her age. Our subject received a fair education in the common schools and remained with his parents until he reached his majority. Since then he has followed the business of farming. During the civil war he enlisted in the Confederate Army and was assigned a position in the commissary department under Maj.-Gen. James F. Cummings, where he served throughout the war. Our subject has been married twice, the first time, January 21, 1851, to Miss Mary J. Hoover, who was born October 6, 1833, and who is the daughter of William Hoover. To this union were born five children: William L., Granville H. Samuel B., Robert L. and Sallie A. Mr. Bigham was married the last time, February 15, 1883, to Miss Sue F. Burks, of Bedford County, Tenn., born April 13, 1853. To this union was born one son, Roy B. Mr. Bigham is a Democrat, a Mason, and he and his wife are members of the Christian Church. The grandfather of our subject, Samuel Bigham, was a soldier in the Revolutionary war. He participated in the battle of Camden, under command of Gen. Gates, where the American forces were totally defeated. There is a $2 bill of the old Continental issue still in possession of the family and in a good state of preservation, which he received from the government in payment for services in that war.

WILLIAM BLACKBURN, a well-to-do citizen of this county, was born in Tennessee May 30, 1831. His parents, Robert and Lucy (Ferguson) Blackburn, were born in the Old Dominion February 5, 1796, and June 25, 1799, and died December 28, 1874, and September 6, 1865, respectively. They were married in 1818, and to their union were born five daughters and two sons. Three of the children are yet living. Our subject has spent the greater part of his life on a farm and has followed farming from early boyhood. In 1859 his marriage to Mary M. Sutton was celebrated. She was born in Tennessee December 1, 1840, and is the daughter of John and Jane (Marr) Sutton. Mr. and Mrs. Blackburn have four children born to their union, as follows: Lucy J., born March 4, 1860; Elizabeth, born December 20, 1861; John, born June 13, 1864, died May 5, 1883; and Martha, born November 28, 1866. Our subject's farm consists of 270 acres of good land. He deals quite extensively in tobacco, and although he began life a poor boy, he has accumulated considerable property. He has been a member of the Baptist Church for twenty years and his wife for over thirty years. In politics Mr. Blackburn is neutral.

JOHN N. BLACKWELL is a son of James Blackwell, and both are native Tennesseeans. The former was born October 5, 1828. The mother's maiden name was Delilia Darnall; she was a native of Illinois. John N. has farmed for himself since attaining his twenty-first year. He is a self-made man, and has accumulated a comfortable competency by his unaided efforts. In 1853 he was united in marriage to Miss Martha Wood, a native of Bedford County, and daughter of W. M. and E. Wood. This union resulted in eleven children. The following are those who are living: William N., John A., Thomas J., Samantha A. (Mrs. C. A. Shaw), Samuel J. and Charley D. Mr. Blackwell is an honest and respected citizen. He has never been before a court of justice or was in a law-suit in his life. He was a soldier in the late war, enlisting in Company G, Thirty-second Regiment Tennessee Infantry, in 1862. He was captured at Tullahoma in 1864 and took the oath of allegiance and gave bond for his appearance. He is, politically, a Democrat.

BENJAMIN W. BLANTON, a leading merchant of Wartrace, was born November 22, 1835, in Rutherford County, Tenn. He is the fifth of ten children born to Benjamin and Martha (Farmer) Blanton, natives, respectively, of Virginia and Tennessee, and both of English descent. In 1818 the father of our subject immigrated to Rutherford County, Tenn., and partly on his farm was fought the battle of Murfreesboro. During the battle his dwelling-house and other buildings were used as a hospital for the Federal Army, and the farm was completely devastated. In 1865 he sold this farm and moved to Unionville, Bedford County, where he lived until his death, which occurred in 1885. The mother of our subject died in 1869. Our subject was educated at Asbury Academy, near Murfreesboro, and at the high school in the latter place. He remained with his parents until reaching his majority, and then followed railroad bridge building until 1873, when he went into the mercantile business at Wartrace, where he still remains. He carries a large stock of goods and does a very successful business. In 1871 he married Miss F. E. Bray, of Lincoln County, Tenn., and the fruits of this union were three children: Lula, Annie and Robert Lee. Mr. Blanton is a member of the Masonic and Odd Fellows' fraternities, and, with the exception of three years prior to the present year, he held the office of mayor of Wartrace ever since 1873. He is now president of the Wartrace Male and Female Institute, also of the Wartrace Hollywood Cemetery, and a member of the board of education, of Wartrace. He is secretary of the Democratic Executive Committee, of Bedford County, and he and family are members of the Methodist Episcopal Church South.

EUGENE BLAKEMORE, the genial postmaster of Shelbyville, was born July 28, 1852, at Lewisburg, Tenn., being a son of George F. Blakemore, a native of Lincoln County, Tenn. The father read medicine in his native county, and commenced the practice of his profession at Flat Creek, Bedford County. He afterward practiced in Shelbyville for a time, and then removed to Lewisburg. He then again returned to Shelbyville, where he died in 1874. The mother of Eugene was Cassie E. Winston, a native of Marshall County. The father was married three times; his last wife is now living in Tullahoma, Tenn. Eugene was reared in Shelbyville, and had the advantages of the schools here. He married at the age of twenty, and engaged in farming near Shelbyville for four years. He then removed to Shelbyville, and for two years ran a dray line; he then farmed another year, and then bought and ran a grist-mill at Shelbyville for six months. After this he engaged in the livery and mule-trading business for three years, doing the leading livery business of the place. He sold out that business in 1884, and has since been farming and trading. He was appointed postmaster March 29, 1886, and has filled the office with efficiency. He was married, in 1872, to Miss Ludie P. Newton, a daughter of James S. Newton, deceased, a farmer of this county. Two children have been born to this union, viz.: Frank N. and Eugene W. Mr. Blakemore and wife are members of the Methodist Episcopal Church South. He is a Democrat in politics, and is one of the enterprising and respected citizens of the county.

COL. GEORGE W. BOUNDS was born in Scott County, Va., September 25. 1818. His parents and grandparents were natives of the same State, and his maternal grandfather was a Revolutionary soldier. Our subject learned the saddler's trade, serving an apprenticeship from thirteen to twenty years of age. He then worked at his trade in Estillville a short time, and came to Tennessee in order to vote for Gen. Harrison, as the right of suffrage was extended only to those who were householders or freeholders in their native State. He worked at his trade about six years, and then joined Col. Haskell's regiment, and served in the Mexican war as orderly sergeant and then as second lieutenant, participating in many of its bloodiest battles. He was mustered out of service, but at the call for more troops he again joined, and was elected lieutenant-colonel of the Fifth Tennessee Regiment, which was independent, George B. McClellan being colonel. During a short time while the latter was sick our subject acted as colonel in his place. He was discharged at Memphis in July, 1848. At the breaking out of the civil war he was not in sympathy with the Southern cause, and, although he was forced to join a company of militia, he was honorably discharged at the reorganization of the army. He then held aloof from the army as far as it was in his power to do, it being wholly against his will or desire to take up arms against the Government. Since the war he has voted the Republican ticket exclusively. He was married, November 18, 1853, to Mary A. Pope. Their union has resulted in six children: James C., born September 23, 1854, and died March 23, 1876; Bettie, born April 30, 1856, wife of Thomas Joyce; John, born November 14, 1857; Fannie, born June 21, 1859; Ann, born July 3, 1860, and died April 23, 1878, and June, born July 6, 1863, and died July 13, 1863. Our subject has been a successful man throughout life, and was considered a brave and faithful officer and soldier in the Mexican war. He is a substantial citizen of Bedford County and a man of influence.

F. M. BOWLING, son of Joseph and Elizabeth Bowling, was born eight miles east of Murfreesboro, Rutherford Co., Tenn., September 23, 1847. He resided with his parents near Bradyville, in the same county, till ten years old, then removed with them near Murfreesboro, where they are (1886) living. The first twenty years of our subject's life were spent upon the farm, devoting his leisure time to study, and caring for his disabled father and four brothers and one sister. In January, 1868, he entered Union University at Murfreesboro, Tenn., and remained there until June 12, 1873, receiving the degree of A. M. Previous to this he had chosen teaching as his profession, and in August, 1873, he took charge of a large school at Leeville, Tenn., and after successfully conducting it to its close he accepted a position with Prof. J. E. Nowlin in the Masonic Institute, Hartsville, Tenn., and afterward became a partner with him in the school. While in this school, August 26, 1874, he wedded Miss Susan E. Sanders, daughter of Jesse B. and Mary A. Sanders, who resided near Murfreesboro. To them were born three children: Herbert Manly, born July 9, 1875; Edna Frank, born June 29, 1877, and Mary Myrtle, born May 23, 1882. Mr. Bowling and Prof. Nowlin dissolved partnership by mutual consent, and in January, 1876, he took charge of Unionville High School, where he is now (1886) living. He has been principal of the school ever since, with the exception of the spring term of 1881, when he was associated with Prof. B. F. Hooker, as joint-principal of Milan College, Milan, Tenn. He has devoted himself earnestly and faithfully to the cause of education, and has taken part in many educational enterprises in the hope of elevating his chosen profession, and has been called upon to fill prominent positions in different educational institutions in the county. He follows no text-book in particular, but selects the best methods from different books. He joined the Missionary Baptist Church in the fall of 1865, and takes a deep interest in Sunday-school work, and is now superintendent of the Unionville Sunday-school, which has an average attendance of ninety-five. He is also a strong supporter of temperance.

JOHN A. BRAMBLETT was born August 13, 1813, in Georgia. His father, John Bramblett, was a native of South Carolina, and of Irish descent. He immigrated to Georgia when young, and there married Miss Jennie Couch, a native of Georgia. To this union were born twelve children, our subject being the ninth. About 1832 John Bramblett moved from Georgia to this State, locating in this county, near Wartrace. He was a farmer by occupation, and died in 1861. The mother died in the same year. Our subject was educated in the country schools of Bedford County, and on reaching his majority was married to Miss L. C. Culley, a native of this county. To them were born these children: William E. (deceased), Mary J., Elizabeth F., James M., Newton A., George D. (deceased), Ada B. (deceased), Walter T. and Idella. Mr. Bramblett is a farmer by occupation, and has 255 acres in District No. 2. In 1863 he was conscripted by the Confederate Government and held as a soldier six months against his will. He then left them and returned home inside the Federal lines. He was a strong Union man during the war, and fully believed and still believes that the best friends of the South were those who adhered to the union of the States. He is a Republican in politics, and he and wife are members of the Primitive Baptist Church.

JAMES P. BROWN is one of the family of children who were born to the marriage of William Brown and Jane G. Goodrum. The father was born in North Carolina in 1803, and about 1824 came to Shelbyville where he lived and died. He was a trader in live-stock, lands, etc., and became a well-to-do and prominent citizen of the county. He died in 1880. The mother was born in South Carolina in 1809, and died in 1882. The subject of this sketch was born July 30, 1838, in Bedford County. He was educated in Shelbyville, and remained with his parents until the war. He then enlisted in Company B, Forty-first Tennessee, and was in the service throughout the war. Returning from the war he engaged in the pursuit of farming, in which he continued very successfully till 1875. From 1868 to 1871 he lived in Texas, returning from there to Bedford County. In 1874 he went to Columbus, Miss., and engaged there in the brick-making and contracting business, and he yet continues that business here. In October, 1885, he opened his clothing trade, and carries a stock of about $8,000. He was married, in 1881, to Miss Kate Goodrum, a native of Forsyth, Ga. Two children have been born to this union, viz.: Paul M. and Annie L. Mr. Brown and wife are members of the Methodist Episcopal Church South. He is a member of the I. O. O. F. Politically he is a firm Democrat. He has never aspired to office, but is a worthy and respected citizen of the county.

MRS. MARY A. (CLARY) BROWN was born September 14, 1816, in North Carolina, daughter of William and Nancy (Wright) Clary, both natives of North Carolina. Our subject is the elder of two children born to her parents. May 23, 1834, she married J. R. Brown, a native of East Tennessee, born May 10, 1811. He was a tailor by trade, and worked at this profession about twelve years. He was married in Madison County, Ala., and while in that State was engaged in these different occupations: tailoring, merchandising and farming. In 1850 he immigrated to Tennessee, and engaged in the merchandise business at Unionville, and continued there several years. He then engaged in the saw-mill business, but at the same time continuing his farming interests, and was engaged in the latter business at the time of his death, which occurred January 22, 1875. He was an exemplary member of the Methodist Episcopal Church. To our subject and husband were born thirteen children, seven of whom are dead. Those living are Nancy J., William C., Lucinda C., James P., Thomas D. and Joseph E. Our subject is a woman of considerable influence in this section. Her son, Thomas D., is living with her, superintending the farm. He is a local minister of the Methodist Episcopal Church.

JAMES B. BROWN is a son of Henry Brown, a native of Wake County, N. C. The father received a limited education, and came to Tennessee in 1833, locating in Bedford County where he engaged in farming. He was married in 1830 to Miss Sarah K. Alston, whose ancestors were from North Carolina. To Mr. and Mrs. Brown were born the following family of children: Aley A., Comer N., S. L., L. S., J. J., A. S., J. B., Lucy F. and G. A. and one who died in infancy. Mr. Brown died at his residence near Shelbyville in 1875. He was a member of the order of Sons of Temperance, and he and his wife, who died in 1873, were members of the Missionary Baptist Church. James B., our subject, was born May 1, 1848, and spent his boyhood days on a farm. He entered the United States Military Academy at West Point when but eighteen years of age, and remained there about one year. He finished his education at the Union University at Murfreesboro, Tenn., after which he served an apprenticeship at photography, and followed that occupation three years. He then turned his attention to farming and horticulture, and his farm is known as the "Home Nursery Farm." He was married December 15, 1875, to Sarah J. Hix, daughter of John C. and Emily Hix, and by her is the father of five children: Cora E., Abbie P., Maud M., Alice E. and Lula S., who is deceased. Mr. Brown is a member of the Masonic and K. of H. fraternities, and of the Missionary Baptist Church.

T. G. BUCHANAN, senior member of the firm of Buchanan & Woods, was born March 25, 1852, in Lincoln County, Tenn. His father was T. W. Buchanan, who moved to this county before the war and to Shelbyville about the close of the war. He was an extensive merchant of Shelbyville. In 1878 he was joined by the subject of this sketch, and the firm was then known as T. W. Buchanan & Son. He died November 4, 1884, leaving a family of five children and their mother, Sarah (Davis) Buchanan. T. W. Buchanan was a very prominent citizen of this county. He was a director of the National Bank, a director of the Sylvan Mills, and was prominently connected with the school interests of Bedford County. He was a member of the Cumberland Presbyterian Church, and a liberal supporter of all charitable and benign institutions. The immediate subject of this sketch was reared on a farm, and received a good early education. He clerked in his father's store five years previous to entering the firm (1878). Since then he has been very successfully engaged in merchandising. The firm now do a yearly business of about $50,000 and carry about $25,000 stock of dry goods, clothing, hats, caps, boots and shoes, gents furnishing goods, etc. Mr. Buchanan is a director in the Sylvan Mills, and owns about 1,000 acres of land. He married, in 1878, C. S. White, born in this county. She is a member of the Presbyterian Church. Mr. Buchanan is an enterprising and influential business man of Shelbyville. J. A. Woods, junior member and buyer in the firm of Buchanan & Woods, was born November 8, 1861, near Wartrace, Bedford County, being a son of George B. Woods, who was a merchant of Shelbyville. The father was born in Coffee County, and in his childhood moved to Bedford County, near Wartrace, where he lived till 1863 when he came to Shelbyville. He was president of the Bedford County Temperance Association; he was also identified with the school interests of the county. He married Miss Margaret Clark, who became the mother of three children, J. A. being the eldest. The father died August 12, 1880, and the mother is now living. J. A. was reared in Shelbyville, and clerked in his father's store. After his father's death he engaged with T. W. Buchanan & Son as salesman and buyer, continuing in that capacity till January 1, 1884, when he entered the firm of Buchanan & Woods. He is a member of the Presbyterian Church and of the Royal Arcanum. He is a member of the Y. M. C. A., and takes an active interest in Sunday-school work; he is now assistant superintendent of the Presbyterian Sunday-school here.

JOHN S. BUTLER, clerk and master of the chancery court of Bedford County, was born in Rutherford County, Tenn., March 13, 1832, being one of nine children raised by William S. and Nancy E. (Campbell) Butler. The father was a native of North Carolina and came to Shelbyville in 1816, and till 1830 pursued the carpenter's trade. In 1819 he removed to Rutherford County, where he married the mother, and followed farming after 1830. He died in 1873; the mother is still living. The subject of this sketch engaged at the age of eighteen on the Nashville & Chattanooga Railroad, occupying various positions, among which were, conductor, telegraph operator, ticket and express agent, remaining in that employ for eleven years. He enlisted in Maney's First Tennessee Regiment, Confederate States Army, and was captain on the first and second organization of Company F. He was appointed military superintendent of telegraph lines in 1863, of Bragg's division, and served in that capacity throughout the remainder of the war. After the war he lived one year in Nashville as agent of the Nashville & Northwestern Railroad. In 1866 he came to Shelbyville and engaged at farming and saw-milling and still continues farming. He was elected magistrate of the Twenty-first District about 1876, and September 5, 1883, was appointed to his present office. Politically he is a Democrat. In 1866 he was married to Mary A. Sims, a native of this county. Four children have been born to this union, viz.: Nancy J., Laura, Mary and John S.

CHARLES L. CANNON was born February 14, 1813, in Shelbyville, Bedford Co., Tenn., and is now the oldest living person born in that town. His father, Clement Cannon, was a native of North Carolina, born in the latter part of the last century. He was of English descent and immigrated to Tennessee with his parents, locating in Williamson County, where he was reared and became a surveyor of lands. He afterward purchased a large tract of land in Bedford County, and in 1806 he donated 100 acres of this to the county where Shelbyville now stands for a county seat. He married Miss Susan Lock, a native of Virginia and a resident of Rutherford County. To this union were born six children. The father was a soldier in the war of 1812 and died January 19, 1860. Our subject was educated at Shelbyville and upon reaching his majority began the business of farming, which he has always followed. December, 1842, Miss Mary A. Hooser, a native of this county and a daughter of William and Rebecca (Coots) Hooser, became his wife. To this union the following children were born: Susan R. (deceased), Maria L. (deceased), William H., Thomas C. (deceased), Lettie C. (now Mrs. Phillip Wilhoite), John H. (deceased), Mary R. (now Mrs. William H. Tilferd), Charles L. (deceased), Macon B. and Charles B. Our subject owns a farm of 550 acres about five miles east of Shelbyville, where he now resides. He is a Democrat in politics and he and family are members of the Methodist Episcopal Church South. Mr. Cannon is a nephew of Gov. Cannon and also a nephew of Gen. Robert Cannon.

JOHN T. CANNON, the genial clerk of the Circuit Court of Bedford County, is a grandson of Clement Cannon, Sr., one of five brothers, who came from North Carolina to Williamson County, Tenn., in the first decade of this century. Clement Cannon, Sr., had five sons, the father of our subject, Henry Cannon, being one of them. Henry Cannon was born in 1812. He lived in this county till 1852, when he moved to Shelby County, Tenn., where he died in 1873, having been a farmer all his life. Of those five brothers, who came to Williamson County, four soon afterward came to Bedford County. Their father's name was Minos Cannon and their mother was a Thompson, of Scotch-Irish descent. The mother of John T. was Sallie C. M. Tillman, a descendant of the Martin family, so numerously represented in the county, and a descendant of the Clay family of Kentucky. She died when John T. was but two weeks old, and he was then reared with Col. Lewis Tillman and other relatives. At fourteen he began his own support and attended school on money earned by himself. He clerked in a store three years and then taught school about four years, having married at twenty-two. He then settled down to farming. In 1861 he enlisted in Company K, Twenty-third Tennessee, as first lieutenant, and served eighteen months. He has been farming very successfully since the war, and now owns nearly 400 acres of good land. He was elected to his office in 1878 and has efficiently served to the satisfaction of his constituents. His birth was December 7, 1835. He was married in 1857 to Narcissa Sutton, a native of Bedford County. Mr. Cannon has a family of four children, viz.: Sallie C. M. (the wife of C. J. Moody), Walter S., Lizzie H. and Narcissa W. All the family are members of the Methodist Episcopal Church South. He is a Royal Arch Mason. His ancestors were old-line Whigs and he is a Democrat.

ALEXANDER CORTNER is a native Tennesseean, born December 20, 1827, and of Swedish lineage. He has always resided on a farm and by his energy has accumulated 145 acres of land on which is erected a neat residence, and also has two other tracts of land, containing seventy-five acres. November 16, 1852, he was united in marriage to Mary E. Landers, who was born December 22, 1836, daughter of Robert and Susan (Carter) Landers. To Mr. and Mrs. Cartner were born the following children: Susan M., born March 23, 1854, and died April 4, 1878; Henry, born November 15, 1855, and died August 21. 1857; George R., born March 23, 1858; Letitia C., born January 24, 1860; Alexander F., born June 3, 1863; William L., born March 11, 1866; Victor H., born October 27, 1867; Roy E., born October 21, 1871; Albert E., born July 1, 1876, and Sarah E., born March 24, 1879, and died July 13, 1879. Mrs. Cortner died May 11, 1879. In 1862 Mr. Cortner enlisted in the Confederate service under Gen. Forrest's escort and was in many hotly contested battles. He is a Democrat, and his parents, George and Delilah (Troxler) Cortner, were born in North Carolina November 15, 1801, and October 6, 1807, respectively. They were married in 1823 and became the parents of four sons and seven daughters. The father died October 7, 1884, and the mother in 1871.

JOSEPH H. CATES, son of John S. and Elizabeth (Himes) Cates, was born March 22, 1837. His father was born in 1808, near Knoxville, Tenn., and was given a limited education in the country schools. He chose farming for his occupation. He was also a stone-mason and worked at this trade for a number of years in Bedford County. He was the father of eleven children, viz.: Mary A., John R., Martha J., Daniel E., Joseph H., James P., Giles P., Phenettie F., Sadie R., Jestinie E. and Caldonia C. James and Giles P. are dead. The father, John S. Cates, died June 1, 1880. He was a consistent member of the Cumberland Presbyterian Church and was highly respected by the community, being a man of high integrity. Our subject grew to manhood on the farm, was educated in the country schools and is a farmer and stone-mason. In 1879 he was married to Miss Levina Oakley, and two children blessed the union: John S. and Willam P., both living. Mr. Cates and wife are members of the Cumberland Presbyterian Church. The family are well respected in the county.

JOHN CATNER is a native Tennesseean, born in 1805, son of Lewis and Polly (Smith) Catner, who were born in North Carolina. The father's birth occurred about 1795. He came to Tennessee in 1813 and located in Bedford County, where he lived until his death. Our subject was his second child and assisted his father on the farm until twenty-two years of age. He then worked as a farm laborer seven years and then purchased a small tract of land to which he has since added until he nows owns about 1,200 acres, which he has secured by his own exertions. He is worth about $75,000, and was married, in 1839, to Polly Ray, who bore him one child, Martha (wife of Samuel Wood), and died at her birth. In 1861 Mr. Catner married Mrs. Margaret (Smith) Hall. He is a man of limited education, but is abounding in common sense and wholesome doctrines. In politics he is a member of the Democratic party, and is a strictly honest and upright man.

PETER CATNER, born in 1819, in Bedford County, Tenn., was reared on a farm, and assisted his father until he was about twenty-four years of age. He, at that time, began relying on his own resources for a livelihood, and has prospered beyond his expectations. Through his own energy and economy he is at present worth about $6,000. He has been twice married—the first time to Sarah Ray in 1848. She died in 1850, leaving one child—Mary C., wife of Frank Johnson. In 1854 Mr. Catner wedded Susanna Helton, who bas borne him nine children, three of whom are dead. Those living are John, William, Hannah M., Lewis, James and Thomas. Mr. Catner is one of the honest and worthy citizens of the county. His early advantages were very limited, but he is a strong advocate of the promotion of education. He belongs to the Methodist Episcopal and his wife to the Cumberland Presbyterian Church. Politically he is a Democrat.

J. W. CLARY, M. D., is a North Carolinian by birth, born July 28, 1821. His occupations while in that State were school teaching, deputy county sheriff, deputy county clerk and hotel-keeping. In 1848 he became a disciple of Æsculapius, studying under Dr. Scroggs.

In the spring of 1849 he entered the Medical College, of Castleton, Vt., from which institution he was graduated as an M. D. the same year. In the spring of 1850 he immigrated to Tennessee, and located at Unionville, where he successfully practiced his profession until 1870, and then took up the mill and merchandise business. The Doctor was married December 15, 1852, to Ann McCord, who died May 21, 1859, leaving two children: Allan and Thomas. Dr. Clary took for his second wife Mattie Ogilvie, and their union has resulted in these children: James D., Charley B., George, Emma and Irvin. Dr. Clary is a Democrat. His parents, Benjamin and Alla D. (Barnard) Clary, were born in 1778 and 1802, and died in 1860 and 1884 respectively.

J. C. CLAXTON'S birth occurred April 12, 1830, in Tennessee. He is a son of James and Temperance (Ratler) Claxton, born in 1802 and 1812, and died about 1866 and 1877, respectively. Our subject was the sixth of thirteen children. He assisted his father until twenty-one years of age, and up to the present time has followed farming. Annie E. Jones, who was born in Bedford County, Tenn., September 16, 1836, became his wife August 16, 1854. Their union has resulted in the birth of nine children: Temperance Mahala, Amanda Tennessee, Philander Priestly, Elizabeth Allen (who died in 1863), James Jonas, Minerva Jane, Melvina Jones, Ophelia Adaline and Alice Casander. Mr. Claxton is an enterprising farmer, and a man who wields much influence in the community in which he resides. Although his early education was somewhat limited, he has always taken considerable interest in the education of the rising generation. He has given all his children liberal educations, and his eldest son is completing his education in Europe—Leipzig College, Germany. Mr. Claxton is a Republican in politics, and up to the date of the late war was an old-line Whig.

THOMAS S. CLEVELAND was born April 25, 1840, in Bedford County, Tenn. His father, Jeremiah Cleveland, was a native of Greenville, S. C., born March, 1806, and of English and German descent. About 1833 he immigrated to Bedford County, Tenn., and located on the farm where our subject is now living. He married Miss Sallie E. Stone, a native of Maury County, born about 1815, and of English descent. To this union were born six children. Jeremiah Cleveland was a merchant before his coming to this State, and a farmer afterward. He owned about 1,500 acres of land on Duck River, in this county, besides a large tract of 3,000 acres on the Mississippi River. He had about $50,000 of stock in the Nashville & Chattanooga Railroad, and was one of the first board of directors to locate the road. He died in 1878. The mother of our subject died in 1840. Thomas S. Cleveland was educated at the Cumberland University at Lebanon, and lived with his father until May, 1861, when he enlisted in Company G, Seventeenth Tennessee Infantry, and was elected as third lieutenant of his company, and as such served twelve months. He then joined the artillery of Gen. John H. Morgan's command, and was captured in Ohio in July, 1863, and retained until 1865. He then returned to Wartrace, Bedford County, where he has ever since remained engaged in farming. In 1867 he married Miss Annie E. Wright, a native of Floyd County, Ga., and a daughter of Moses R. Wright, and a niece of Judge Wright, who was a member of the United States Congress. To our subject and wife were born five children: Sallie S., Lizzie H., Hattie D., Annie L. and Carrie C. Mr. Cleveland is a member of the Masonic fraternity, also of the R. A. He and wife are members of the Baptist Church, and live on the old homestead, consisting of 600 acres of land. Mr. Cleveland is a grandson of Capt. Robert Cleveland, and a grandnephew of Col. Benjamin Cleveland, both of whom served with distinction in the Revolutionary war.

B. F. CLEVELAND was born August 11, 1848, in Georgia. His father, Robert M. Cleveland, was a native of North Carolina, and married Miss Fannie L. Wight, a native of Rhode Island. To this union were born the following children: William C., Jeremiah, Vannoy, Caroline, Harriet D., B. F. (our subject), Georgia A. and Robert M., Jr. The father of these children was a manufacturer and capitalist, and moved to this State in 1866, locating at Wartrace, where he died in 1876. The mother is now in Marietta, Ga. Our subject was educated in the high school of Greenville, S. C. In 1864 he enlisted in the Second South Carolina Cavalry, and served with the command until the close of the war. He then returned home to this county and engaged in the business of farming, which he followed until 1882. He then opened a private bank in Wartrace, which he still continues to manage in a very successful way. In 1872 he married Miss Lizzie Pepper, a native of this county. The result of this union is a family of four children: Mattie W., William P., Jesse F. and Eliza P. Mr. Cleveland is a member of the K. of H., a Democrat in politics, and he and wife are members of the Presbyterian Church.

THOMAS H. COLDWELL was born in Shelbyville August 29, 1822. His father, John Campbell Coldwell, was born January 8, 1791, in Hawkins County, Tenn., and removed with his father, Ballard Coldwell, and family to Bedford County, January 1, 1807. John Campbell Coldwell served two campaigns under Gen. Jackson, one against the Creek Indians, in which he participated in the battle at Horse Shoe, and the other against the British, in which he was a participant at New Orleans, January 8, 1815. After this campaign he settled at Shelbyville, and was a merchant from 1818 to 1843, at which time he retired to his farm, where he died July 17, 1867. Thomas H. Coldwell's mother was Jane Northcott, born in Fleming County, Ky., the daughter of Rev. Benjamin Northcott. Thomas was the eldest of two boys and two girls in this family. He was educated at Dixon Academy, Shelbyville, and studied law with Irwin J. Frierson, Esq. He was licensed to practice in January, 1844, and has ever since been in his profession at Shelbyville, and is one of the leading members of that bar. He first married Mary J. Hodge, at Murfreesboro, November 24, 1844. After her death he married Sarah E. Goling, in Cincinnati, May 6, 1851. After her death he married Mrs. Mary H. Bosworth, in Shelbyville, September 20, 1854, and after her death he married Carrie Hopkins, in Cincinnati, November 11, 1875. The last wife died December 4, 1884. For many years Judge Coldwell was an active worker in the Sons of Temperance, and was elected Grand Worthy Patriarch for the State of Tennessee in 1851. He was an unflinching Union man throughout the war. In 1864 he was commissioned by Gov. Andrew Johnson chancellor of the Fourth Chancery Division of Tennessee, but resigned in a short time. In October, 1865, he was commissioned attorney-general of the State and reporter of the supreme court, and in May, 1867, was elected by the people to that office without opposition. While serving in this capacity he reported seven volumes of the decisions of the Supreme Court of Tennessee, and considers this the most pleasant part of his professional career. While attorney-general he entered a *nolle prosequi* in all cases that came to the supreme court, when persons were indicted for treason against the State—a class of indictments which grew out of the late civil war, the disposal of which in this manner won for him the earnest gratitude of his fellow-citizens. In 1868 he was the Grant and Colfax elector for the Fifth Congressional District of Tennessee. From 1865 to 1871 he served as one of the directors of the Nashville & Chattanooga Railroad. He was a lay member of the General Conference of the Methodist Episcopal Church at its session, held at Brooklyn, in 1872, and while there was the author of the resolution sending fraternal delegates from the Methodist Episcopal Church to the Methodist Episcopal Church South. He has always been a zealous worker in the church, giving most liberally to all of its enterprises, and has always been an active Sunday-school worker. During 1871-72 he was president of the Bedford County Agricultural Society. He was instrumental, in 1869, in securing the building of the Bedford County Court House, and was chairman of the building committee. He has been one of the directors of the Shelbyville Savings Bank ever since its organization, and was president of that bank three years. He has been a member of the board of directors of the Central Tennessee College, in Nashville, ever since its organization, and for thirteen years has been president of the board. He is a fearless advocate of the education and Christianizing of the negro. For fifteen years he has been president of the board of school directors of the Seventh District, and at his last election he received every vote cast. In 1871 he was appointed by President Grant, at the recommendation of Gov. DeWitt C. Senter, as commissioner for the State of Tennessee to the Centennial Exposition, at Philadelphia, in 1871. He served till 1877. He was on many of the important committees and was elected first vice-president of the commission, being one of the most active participants in those measures that made the exhibition so great a success. Judge Coldwell has two children: Gen. Ernest Coldwell, the child of the third wife, who is his partner in law, and Carrie ("Sunshine") Coldwell, the child of his last wife. Judge Coldwell is an outspoken Republican. He is a friend to the poor and oppressed, a liberal supporter and patron of education and religion, and a leading and enthusiastic member of his party.

GEN. ERNEST COLDWELL was born at Shelbyville, November 12, 1858. He was educated at Shelbyville and at Carbondale, Ill. After reading law two years in his father's office he was licensed, by Judges Robert Cantrell and Peter Turney, to practice. In September, 1882, he was appointed special revenue collector, under A. M. Hughes, Jr. While a law student he was secretary of the Middle Tennessee and Bedford County Sunday-school Associations. He is a director in the Bedford County Agricultural Society, a director and secretary of the Bedford County Stock Breeders' Society and Register and a director and secretary of the Eakin Library Society. He was appointed, May 21, 1881, on Gov. Alvin Hawkins' staff, with the rank of brigadier-general. In 1884 he was elected Representative from Bedford County to the Forty-fourth General Assembly of Tennessee, overcoming a Democratic majority of 600 by 226 majority, he being a firm and outspoken Republican. His mother, nee Mary Henderson, was a lady of versatile accomplishments and of marked firmness of character. She was born in New York, was raised in Ohio and died in Tennessee in 1874, fifty-three years of age.

WILLIAM COLLIER is a son of Lockey Collier, who was born in Virginia about 1770 and died about 1840. The father came to Tennessee about 1789. Our subject was his only child and resided with his father until twenty-one years of age, and afterward followed the occupation of farming. He is a self-made man and is worth between $8,000 and $10,000, which he has made by his own exertions. He was married, in 1820, to Mary B. Garrett, who bore him twelve children, six of whom are dead. Those living are Martha (Mrs. W. W. Pennington), Nancy J. (Mrs. L. Madison), Don, Eliza F., Mary A. (widow of Morgan Drydaw) and Richard R. Our subject's son, Don, was born August 21, 1832, and was married March 28, 1854, to Martha Billington, who bore him one child that died in infancy. In 1854 he moved to Arkansas, where he lived until 1881, when he returned to the old homestead to provide for his father until his death. Both father and son are influential citizens and Republicans. Don and his wife are members of the Methodist Episcopal Church South.

MRS. IDA J. COLLINS was born October 6, 1837, daughter of David and Sarah (Harris) Williams, who were born in Tennessee in 1814 and 1818, respectively. Mrs Collins' paternal ancestry were originally from the State of Virginia, and her mother's people were North Carolinians. Our subject was united in marriage, April 29, 1858, to W. J. Collins, who was born October 25, 1835. He was a merchant at Unionville up to the date of the late war. He was a member of the Methodist Episcopal Church at the time of his death, which occurred July 21, 1866. His union with our subject resulted in the birth of six children: Spencer D., born March 19, 1859; Edward E. and John B. were twins, born October 25, 1860; Lycurgus F., born January 11, 1863; Emmet C., born December 15, 1864; Ellen J., born December 29, 1866. Mrs. Collins is an earnest member of the Methodist Episcopal Church, and is a woman who has won the respect and esteem of all. She has managed her farm successfully and is a credit to the county in which she lives.

JOHN JACKSON COMER. Samuel Comer was a native of England and came to the United States with his wife (formerly a Miss Randolph), a short time before the Revolutionary war and settled in Virginia. He served in the war against the mother country, and was subsequently killed by the Tories. Reuben D. Comer, son of Samuel Comer, was raised by a man named Abner Lea, of Johnson County, N. C. He married a daughter of Thomas Wright, who came from England to South Carolina. Her parents died when she was an infant, and she was raised by Col. Elliott Lee. After her marriage with Mr. Comer they came to Wilson County, Tenn., and became the parents of five sons and two daughters. John Jackson Comer, the subject of this sketch, was the fourth of their children and was reared on a farm and had charge of his father's mill and cotton-gin. His early education was limited, never having attended school after attaining his fifteenth year. About this time he professed religion. A short time after he began learning the blacksmith business of the Rev. D. B. Moore, with whom he lived three years. His father at this time moved to Warren County, Tenn., and there our subject worked at his trade. He was happily married to Miss Martha P. Parker. In 1845 he was licensed to preach, and in 1853 was received into the Tennessee Annual Conference, and he has followed his calling in Hickory Creek, Bedford, Smith Fork, Mill Creek, Harpeth, Wesley and Carthage. He was appointed presiding elder of the following districts: Carthage, McMinnville, Savannah and Centerville. At the last conference he was appointed to the Unionville Circuit. In 1880 Mrs. Comer died, and after living a lonely life two years, Rev. Comer married Miss Ella Lacre. His first marriage resulted in four children: Sophronia A. (Mrs. J. P. Walton), Nannie J. (Mrs. Prof. S. V. Wall), John B., Moltie P. (died in 1880, wife of J. S. Keton). Rev. Comer is now past sixty years of age, but hopes to continue his good work many years. He is much loved and respected by all who know him and is an influential man where he resides.

J. B. COOPER, ESQ., was born January 25, 1831, in Bedford County, son of George and Sallie (Rutlege) Cooper. The father was born about 1796, and the mother about 1798. They both died when our subject was an infant and he was reared by his aunt, Matilda Rutlege, whom he assisted on the farm until her death, which occurred about 1871. He has been engaged in agricultural pursuits ever since. In 1870 he was elected to the office of magistrate and filled that position in an able and efficient manner. He then began the study of law, and about 1876 the county court granted him license to practice law before the county court and before magistrate courts. He has been quite successful and has made quite a reputation as a lawyer. May 15, 1856, he wedded Rebecca F. Landers, of this county, and this union resulted in the birth of thirteen children: Cicero W., Alice A. (deceased), Lula S., Ella L., Callie T. (deceased), Maggie M., Eddie A. (deceased), Rebecca J., Algie B., America L., Johnnie E., Lattie B. and William E. Mr. Cooper received a common district school education in his early days, but having cultivated a taste for good reading while young, he acquired the major part of his education from the perusal of good books after having grown to maturity. In politics Mr. Cooper is a Democrat.

ALEXANDER A. COOPER was born January 12, 1832, in Rutherford County, Tenn., son of Micajah T. and Sarah (Vincent) Cooper. The father was a native of Rowan County, N. C., born December 28, 1806. When nine years of age he moved with his parents to Cannon County, this State, and in 1829 he was married. To this union were born twelve children, our subject being the second. The father of our subject died February 16, 1874, and the mother in May, 1864. Our subject was educated in the country schools and at Union University at Murfreesboro. After reaching his majority he followed various occupations, such as teacher, merchant and trader up to the late war, when he was appointed by the commissary-general and permanently detailed by the Secretary of War as general purchasing agent of the commissary department for the Confederate Army, which position he held during the war. He then returned home and resumed merchandising at Wartrace, which he continued for two years. He then located on the farm where he now lives. He also served as deputy clerk of the county court of this county for ten years. He has held several minor offices and has been magistrate of his civil district six years. October, 1862, he married Miss Mary E. Singleton, daughter of Dr. Robert L. Singleton, of Fairfield, now deceased. To our subject and wife were born the following children: Robert S., Henry V., Constance, Alexander A. and Sarah A., all living. Mr. Cooper is a member of the Masonic and Odd Fellows' orders, and owns a farm of 100 acres near Fairfield on the Wartrace & Beech Grove Turnpike. He is a member of the board of trustees of the Duck River Academy, and takes an active part in educational matters.

REV. G. W. COOK was born near Shelbyville, Tenn., November 14, 1833, son of

William and Nancy (Lentz) Cook, who were born in 1802 and 1810, in North Carolina and Tennessee, respectively. The father died of cholera in June, 1854. Our subject is the third of eight children. At the age of twenty years he became overseer for Thomas Shearren and then began farming for himself. He joined the Methodist Episcopal Church when a boy, and when about twenty-six years old was licensed to preach. In 1870 he was ordained deacon at Pulaski, Tenn., and in 1874 he was ordained elder. He has had regular work since 1870, and has conscientiously fulfilled the duties of his calling. He was married December 20, 1855 to Mary E. Pickle, daughter of Major and Catharine Pickle. Rev. and Mrs. Cook became the parents of eleven children, four of whom are dead: William T. S., a minister of the gospel; Mary E. (Mrs. C. M. Spruce), Emily M. (Mrs. William Darnell), Rosanna (Mrs. E. Stalling), Henry C., Eliza and Nora A. Our subject acquired the most of his education by dint of hard study after acquiring his growth. He is a Democrat, but up to the date of the late war was an old-line Whig.

J. P. COTHRAN, a successful farmer, was born in Person County, N. C., July 8, 1828, son of Samuel and Polly (Burton) Cothran, who immigrated to Tennessee in 1844, and settled in Williamson County. Our subject was the fourth child born to his parents. His educational advantages were limited, but notwithstanding this fact he has always manifested a willingness and a desire to aid in any enterprise pertaining to the advancement of education. December 18, 1851, he was united in marriage to Mary R. Cothran, of Williamson County. The fruits of this union were eleven children, seven of whom are still living. Mr. Cothran is a self-made man, having accumulated his property by his own exertions. Politically he is a Republican, but up to the late war was a Democrat.

DR. ROBERT W. COUCH was born March 13, 1834, in Bedford County, Tenn., and is the son of Joseph and Catharine Patton Couch. (For further particulars of parents see sketch of R. C. Couch.) Our subject received a practical education in the Duck River Academy at Fairfield, in this county, and his medical education at the University of Nashville, from which institution he graduated in 1855. He then began the practice of his profession, and was surgeon of the Tennessee Iron Works in Wayne County until the beginning of the late war. He then joined the Ninth Tennessee Confederate Cavalry as a lieutenant, and was afterward appointed surgeon of the regiment. He was captured at Fort Donelson and held as a prisoner until May, 1862, when he made his escape from Mound City, Ill., and walked to Corinth, Miss., and from there to his relatives in the county. Since that time he has been engaged in agricultural pursuits. May, 1860, he married Miss Lucy Tucker, a native of Rutherford County, and daughter of Maj. Lewis and Harriet Tucker. To our subject and wife were born the following children: Robert, John R., Kittie, William, Lizzie and Mary, all living but John R. Mr. Couch owns a farm of 315 acres in District No. 2, all well cultivated and in a flourishing condition. He is an Independent Democrat in politics, a Mason, and he and wife are members of the Christian Church.

HON. REUBEN C. COUCH, farmer, was born in Bedford County, Tenn., January 13, 1830, son of Joseph and Catherine (Patton) Couch, and of Scotch Irish descent. The father was born in South Carolina October 9, 1787, and the mother in Buncomb County, N. C., July 10, 1796. They were married in 1813, and to them were born twelve children. The father was a soldier in the war of 1812 under Gen. Jackson. He was a farmer by occupation, and died March 19, 1861. The mother followed March 10, 1886. Our subject's maternal grandmother was a daughter of Rhoda Cunningham, who came from Ireland. She is living in Bedford County, Tenn., and is in her ninety-third year. She has at this time 306 living descendants, children, grandchildren and great-grandchildren, even to the fourth generation. What is most consoling to the declining years of this most venerable matron, is that out of this long line of descendants none have yet done aught to detract from the character of an honest family. Our subject received his education in the common schools, and followed farming up to the time of the war. He enlisted with the boys in blue in the Fifth Tennessee Cavalry. He was commissioned as lieutenant, and afterward promoted to captain, in which capacity he served through the war. He participated in the battle of Stone River, and various skirmishes. After the war he was elected clerk of the county court, and served several years in the revenue department. He was a member of the lower house of the Thirty-eighth General Assembly. November 23, 1865, he wedded Miss Mary J. Dyer, daughter of William H. Dyer, and to them were born three children: Ruben C., Lester and Emily G. James Patton, our subject's maternal grandfather, was one of the pioneers of Tennessee. He reared a family of twelve children—eleven daughters and one son. All lived to be married. Among the daughters there were seven living at one time, all widows, and the youngest over seventy years of age. The mother of our subject, just before her death, had descendants to the number of 266, children, grandchildren, great-grandchildren and great-great-grandchildren. Mr. Couch is a Republican, a Mason, and he and wife and daughters are members of the Baptist Church. He has a fine farm of 275 acres in a fine state of cultivation.

OLIVER COWAN & CO., dealers in hardware and farming implements, is composed of Oliver and Robert Cowan, brothers. Oliver Cowan was born February 13, 1831, in Londonderry, Ireland. The father, Alexander Cowan, died in Ireland, having been a farmer. The mother and six children came to Shelbyville in 1851, and the mother died in 1868. There are five of the family now living. Oliver being the youngest. He was reared on a farm, and received his education in an agricultural college in Ireland. Upon coming to Shelbyville he engaged as clerk in the dry goods trade for three years. He then entered a dry goods business with a brother, and continued successfully till 1874, when he sold out that business and entered the hardware business with his brother, Robert. The firm carries about a $10,000 stock, and transacts about a $20,000 business annually. Mr. Cowan was married, in 1869, to Miss Sarah Bryson, of Lincoln County, daughter of the Rev. Henry Bryson. He has a family of two sons and two daughters, viz.: Henry B., William G., Jennie and Olive. Himself, his wife and two sons are members of the Presbyterian Church. He is a Knight Templar Mason. Politically he adheres to no party rigidly, but supports the man who he thinks is best qualified to fill public office. Robert Cowan was born September 24, 1813, in Londonderry, Ireland. He came from his native land to this county in 1851. He clerked in a store till 1874, at which time he entered the firm of Oliver Cowan & Co. In Ireland he followed farming. He was married, in 1836, to Miss Esther Buchanan, who bore him two sons, viz.: Alexander, who was killed in the Confederate Army in 1863, and William B., who is now a farmer of this county. Mr. Cowan has for many years lived a widower, his wife having died in Ireland in 1841. He is a devout member of the Presbyterian Church, and is one of Shelbyville's oldest and most highly respected citizens.

DR. THOMAS CHAPMAN McCRORY, an eminent physician, was born in Bedford County, November 13, 1834, and is the son of John and Annie (Wilson) McCrory. He is of Scotch-Irish extraction. The father was born in Mechlenburg County, N. C., February 5, 1788, and the mother in Georgia, October 11, 1791. They were married in Marshall County, Tenn., and were the parents of twelve children. The father died October 15, 1874, and the mother January 22, 1864. Our subject had the advantage of a good common school education, and afterward read medicine with Dr. Smith Bowlin. He then attended the Ohio Medical College at Cincinnati and completed his studies, receiving his diploma from the Medical University at Nashville, from which institution he graduated in 1867. He enlisted in Company D, Second Tennessee Regiment, Confederate States Army, and served as lieutenant of the regiment under Col. (now Gov.) Bate. Dr. McCrory was made assistant surgeon, but preferred a more active part and took his place in the regiment. He participated in the battle of the first Manassas, Murfreesboro, Shiloh, Chickamauga and the various battles between Chattanooga and Atlanta. He was captured during Hood's advance in Tennessee, and taken a prisoner to Fort Delaware, where he remained until Lee's surrender. Since the war he has followed his chosen profession, and has at this time a very large and lucrative practice. February 28, 1860, he wedded Miss Sallie J. Knott, daughter of Iverson Knott. This union resulted in the birth of eight children, only three of whom are living: Thomas F., Eugene and Alva. The Doctor is a Democrat and a Mason. Mrs. McCrory is a member of the Methodist Episcopal Church South.

J. M. CROWEL was born November 5, 1847, in Bedford County, Tenn., and is the son of Benjamin and Margaret (Anderson) Crowel. The father was born in the year 1815, in Bedford County, and died in the year 1865. The mother was born in North Carolina about 1817, and died September, 1885. Our subject was the youngest child and only son of his parents. He passed his youthful days on the farm, and after reaching the years of manhood began farming for himself. November 16, 1873, he wedded Susan A. Molder, of this county, who was born in 1857. The fruits of this union were three children: Thomas L., Jennie L., and Edwin Harper. Mr. Crowel is a self-made man, and is now worth about $5,000, which he has made in the last twelve years. He was never sued or had a lawsuit in his life. He is upright, honest and law abiding. His educational advantages were rather limited, but sufficient for all practical purposes. In politics he is a Democrat.

CYRUS W. CUNNINGHAM, dealer in books, stationery, wall paper, jewelry, etc., was born in Bedford County, January 28, 1850, being one of five children of Joseph A. and Elizabeth W. (Williams) Cunningham. The father was a native of Bedford County, his father having come here from North Carolina in the very early settlement of the county. The father was a farmer; his death occurred in 1880. The mother is a descendant of Virginia parentage, is a native of this county, and is now living. The subject of this sketch was reared on a farm to the age of twenty-three, receiving a common school education. He taught school and clerked in a store for two years before leaving home. He then came to Shelbyville, and purchased a one-third interest in a book store, and in 1875 became sole proprietor. In 1876 he failed, but has paid out fully, and now does a thriving business, and owns a desirable and beautiful home in Shelbyville. He now holds the appointment of deputy internal revenue collector of the Fifth Revenue District of Tennessee. He was married, March 9, 1875, to Miss Susan A. Cannon, grandniece of Gov. Newton Cannon. This union has been blessed in the birth of four children, viz: Kate T., Elizabeth, Jennie C. and Mary J. Mr. Cunningham and wife are members of the Presbyterian Church. He is a member of the K. of H. and R. A., being a member of the Grand Lodge of the K. of H. He is a Democrat in politics, and an enterprising citizen of the county.

J. M. CUNNINGHAM, M. D., is a native of Marshall County, Tenn., born June 17, 1849, and is the second of six children of S. D. and Elizabeth (Armstrong) Cunningham, who are now living in Marshall County. Our subject spent his early days in tilling his father's farm, remaining until eighteen years old, at which time he entered the high school at Lewisburg, then under the supervision of Calvin Dornal, and paid his own way for about three years, his father refusing to pay his tuition. He entered the Medical College of Nashville in 1871, and during the vacation in the summer of 1872 he taught school to enable him to take the course of lectures in the fall, which he did, and graduated in the spring of 1873. He began practicing his profession in April of that year at Bedford postoffice, seven miles west of Shelbyville, where he has successfully continued up to the present date. June 14, 1876, he married Lizzie T. Lock, daughter of James Lock. This union has resulted in six children: Vera C., Clare G. (deceased), Ewing B., Hattie S., Lillie R. (deceased) and Horace L. Dr. Cunningham is a Democrat in politics, and he and wife are members of the Methodist Episcopal Church South.

B. M. CURTISS is a native of Bedford County, born July 7, 1859. His father, J. H. Curtiss, was born November 12, 1803, in Connecticut, and died in August, 1866. The mother was Teressa (Moseley) Curtiss, who was born November 22, 1824, in Georgia. She is yet living. Our subject aided his mother until he was twenty-two years of age, and since that time has followed agricultural pursuits for himself, and is a prosperous farmer. In connection with his farming he carried on merchandising about three years. November 17, 1872, he wedded Sallie E. Dysart, who was born July 6, 1859, and is the mother of seven children: Alex, Nola T., R. Dennie, James R., Fannie, Polk and Tint. Mrs. Curtiss died June 3, 1886, an earnest member of the Presbyterian Church. Our subject was elected magistrate of his district in August, 1882, and has served as such up to the present date. He is a well educated man, and one who supports all enterprises for the public welfare. He is a Democrat politically.

I. S. DAVIDSON, M. D., was born near Fairfield, Bedford Co., Tenn., April 25, 1816, son of Andrew D. and Sarah (Muse) Davidson, who were natives of Wales, England. The paternal grandparents of our subject were born in the "Emerald Isle." Andrew D. and his first wife came to America at an early day. During his absence from home at one time the Indians, which were very numerous at that time, seized his wife and two children, and a young man and woman living with them, and made their escape to their camp. After a long and seemingly fruitless search he found his wife, but his children were both dead, and his wife shortly afterward died from fright and exposure. Our subject assisted his father in clearing their farm, and labored under many disadvantages. His education was limited, owing to poor school facilities, at that time, but after he began earning his own living he attended school several sessions, and in this manner acquired a very good education. For over two years he was a medical student of Dr. Barkesdal, of Shelbyville, and attended lectures at Louisville, Ky., in 1841–42. March 27, 1843, he located at Richmond, Tenn., where he successfully practiced his profession up to the present time. May 16, 1844, he wedded Martha R. Smith, daughter of Reason and Sarah Smith. To Dr. and Mrs. Davidson were born eight children, two dying in infancy and one (Barkesdal) was killed in the late war. Those living are John R., George H., Sarah A., Alice, Mary A. and Maud. Dr. Davidson has accumulated all his property since he began his practice, and deserves much credit for the same, as he started in life for himself with nothing. The family are church members. The Doctor is a Democrat, and previous to the war was an old-line Whig.

ELNATHAN G. DAVIS, farmer and trader in live-stock, was born in Bedford County, Tenn., on the farm where he is now living, December 29, 1825. His father, Elnathan Davis, was born in South Carolina in 1795, and in 1817 was married to Rebecca (Sivley) Davis, who was born in Tennessee in 1797. Of this union there were eight children reared to maturity. The father died August 12, 1856, in Bedford County, Tenn., and the mother November 6, 1885. Our subject received a practical education in the common schools, and has followed farming as his chief occupation. He has been married twice, the first time February 20, 1851, to Miss Mary E. Wilson, of Marshall County, Tenn. The fruits of this union were two children: John W. and Cleopatra. January 13, 1870, he took for his second wife Miss Jeffie E. Norton, daughter of H. W. Norton. To this union was born one child, Eugene G. Our subject, from physical disability, was exempt from the army, but the Davis family was represented by other members. Mr. Davis is an old-line Democrat, and a member of the I. O. O. F. He has 300 acres of as fine land as the country affords, all well cultivated, and he and wife are members of the Methodist Episcopal Church South.

WILLIAM G. DAVIS, farmer, was born in Bedford County, Tenn., November 12, 1837, son of Elnathan and Rebecca (Sivley) Davis, and of Irish-German descent. (For further particulars of parents see sketch of Elnathan G. Davis.) Our subject was reared on the farm and received a rudimentary education in the common schools. He subsequently attended Fairfield College, at Fairfield, Tenn., and October 28, 1858, he wedded Miss Mollie J. Norvell, daughter of Dr. A. S. Norvell, of Coffee County, Tenn. The fruits of this union were five children: Charles E., born October 1, 1861; Willie J., born February 13, 1864; Frank P., born July 8, 1867; Emma Smith, born November 18, 1869; and Lena Bell, born October 28, 1871. Mrs. Davis was born in Shelbyville, Bedford Co., Tenn., March 22, 1842. Her father, Dr. A. S. Norvell, was born June 8, 1813, and her mother was born July 13, 1819. The former died in Coffee County, Tenn., February 29, 1876, and the latter died in the same county April 28, 1886. They were married in the year 1839. Mr. Davis has a farm of 140 acres in a fine state of cultivation. He is a Democrat in politics, and he and wife are worthy members of the Methodist Episcopal Church South.

J. B. DICKENS is a son of Daniel and Matilda (Putnam) Dickens, who were born in 1814. The father died October 13, 1874. The mother was drowned June 20, 1870, while crossing Duck River in a canoe. Our subject was the youngest of their eight children.

He was born in Bedford County, Tenn., October 13, 1852. The names of the children are Jasper N., Andrew J., Nellie F., William C., Nancy J., Elizabeth C., Newton and our subject, who was married December 12, 1872, to Jennie Foster, who was born November 21, 1852. To them were born a family of four children: Malcolm A., born in 1873; Clara A., born in 1876; Matilda F., born in 1880, and Sarah G., born in 1884. The mother was the youngest of seven children, their names being Eliza J., Almira M., Malcolm A., Sarah G., Caldonia T., Mary A. and Jennie. Our subject has been a fairly successful financier, and is one of the few men who have made their property through their own exertions. He and wife are members of the Methodist Church, and he is a Republican.

HENRY C. DICKERSON was born June 13, 1854, in Bedford County, Tenn. His father, Capt. James W. Dickerson, a native also of Bedford County, was born October 15, 1815. He married Miss Nancy Young, a native also of Bedford County, born in 1822. To this union were born nine children, of whom our subject is the sixth. Capt. James W. Dickerson, our subject's father, held several county offices, and since the war has followed agricultural pursuits, and now lives near Wartrace. The mother died October 12, 1871. Our subject was educated in the country schools, and lived with and assisted his parents on the farm until he reached his majority, when he was elected to the office of constable of his civil district, and served four years. In 1884 he was the Democratic nominee for sheriff of his county, but was defeated by a very few votes. July 11, 1885, he was appointed deputy internal revenue collector by Col. John T. Hillsman for the Fifth Collection District of Tennessee, which office he now holds. On December 30, 1885, he married Miss Mary E. Shofner, a native of Bedford County, and a daughter of P. W. and Nancy Shofner, born January 1, 1860. He is a member of Shelbyville Lodge of F. & A. M. His wife is a member of the Methodist Episcopal Church. Our subject has two brothers, William J., a prominent business man of Union City, Obion Co., Tenn., and John W. Dickerson, a prominent farmer of this county. This is one of the prominent families of Bedford County.

REV. A. G. DINWIDDIE, D.D., was born July 12, 1840, in Montgomery County, Tenn. His father, William Dinwiddie, was born October 15, 1810, in Kentucky. He was by profession a local minister in the Methodist Episcopal Church South, and was also a farmer. He died April 4, 1872. The mother, nee Mary Cole Alexander, was born in Kentucky, June 15, 1814, and is yet living in Montgomery County, Tenn. The subject of this sketch was reared on a farm and received fair early educational advantages. He was principally educated under Prof. L. E. Duke, of Chapel Hill, N. C., then conducting an academy at Asbury, Montgomery Co., Tenn. At the age of nineteen he engaged in the ministry of the Methodist Episcopal Church South, and has since been so engaged. He joined the Tennessee Annual Conference in October, 1859, and was appointed junior preacher to the Wesley Circuit, where he remained one year. Thence in 1860 he was appointed junior preacher to the Dover Circuit, and at the close of that year he was ordained deacon by Bishop Early. His third year's work was on the Bellefonte Circuit in northern Alabama and on November 19, 1861, he was married to Miss Rachael Odil, of Columbia, Tenn. In 1862 he was appointed to the Trinity Station, Alabama. After the war, in 1865, he was appointed to the Santa Fe Circuit, in Maury County, Tenn. Thence, in 1866, he was appointed to the Duck River Circuit, which pastorate he held two years. In 1868 he organized the Culleoka Institute and was appointed principal of the same, also retaining the appointment of junior preacher on the Duck River Circuit. In 1869 he was relieved of the pastoral charge and appointed to the full principalship of the Culleoka Institute which he held until May, 1870. In October following he was appointed to the Savannah District and remained there four consecutive years. He then took pastoral charge of Pulaski Station for four years. Thence he was appointed to Cedar Hill, Robertson Co., Tenn., for one year. In 1879 he was appointed to the Lebanon Station, which he held until 1882, when he was appointed to the Murfreesboro Station, and June 7, 1885, received the honorary degree of D. D., from the Soule College of Murfreesboro. In October, 1885, he was appointed to the Shelbyville Station, where, as elsewhere, he has enjoyed great success in his work. He has a family of five children: Emma, Willie H., Mary B. Maggie L. and Frank G.

JAMES N. DRYDEN, a native of Tennessee, was born January 6, 1835, son of David and Malinda (Guest) Dryden, natives, respectively, of Tennessee and Georgia. The father was born in 1800 and was by occupation a farmer. The mother was born August 27, 1806, and is still living with our subject at the extreme old age of eighty. Our subject like the average country boy, assisted his father on the farm and attended the district school. At the age of twenty-one he began farming for himself on the farm where he is now living. September 27, 1855, he married Nancy C. Stephenson, of this county, and this union resulted in the birth of four children: William J., Martha M. B., Lucinda E. M. and David O. Mr. Dryden is a very influential man in this section of the country. He is also a man of strong religious sentiments although he is not a member of any church. Mrs. Dryden is a member of the Methodist Episcopal Church. In politics Mr. Dryden is a Republican.

NATHANIEL L. DRYDEN was born January 22, 1839, and is one of three children born to the union of Thomas and Mary H. (Dickson) Dryden. The father was born in Virginia in 1796, and when a youth he, with his father, immigrated to Tennessee and settled in Bedford County. He was married in 1824 and became the father of eleven children. The father and mother of our subject were members of the Cumberland Presbyterian Church. The former died in 1863 and the latter in 1876. Our subject was born in Bedford County, Tenn., and was given an education in the country schools of the day. In 1867 he wedded Miss Sarah J. Llewellyn, a native of Indiana. To this union were born eight children: Hubert E., John W., Mary L., Annie, Maggie H., Daniel D., Thomas F. and Nathaniel L., Jr. Daniel D. died March 31, 1884. Mr. Dryden owns 375 acres of land in the Twentieth District, and deals in cattle, sheep, etc. He is a member of the Cumberland Presbyterian Church, and a leading man in the county. The family is of Scotch-Irish descent.

BENJAMIN F. DUGGAN, M. D., is a son of John and Sarah A. (Burroughs) Duggan, and is of Scotch English descent. The father died a few weeks before our subject was born. Benjamin F. was born January 22, 1820, in Martin County, N. C., and was apprenticed to learn the tailor's trade at the age of ten years. Six years later he began business as a journeyman, and at the age of eighteen he immigrated to Tennessee and began working at his trade at Beech Grove, and while here was ordained as itinerant minister of the Methodist Protestant Church. In 1883 he received the degree of D. D. from the college located at Westminster, Md., and was one of the commissioners that formed the basis of union of the Methodist and Methodist Protestant Church in 1875-77 at Baltimore, Md., and has been a member of the general conferences of his church at Baltimore in 1850; Lynchburg, Va., in 1858, and Montgomery, Ala., in 1867. About 1850 he began the study of medicine, and entered the Nashville University in the fall of 1853 and graduated in 1877, and located in Unionville. He was married, October 23, 1838, to Nancy A. Elliott, who has borne him five children: Benjamin F., Solon S., Algie A., Sarah A. and Salome J. Our subject has been successful in life, but has also met with many adversities. In December, 1861, he became commander of Company A, Fifty-fifth Tennessee Infantry, and was acting colonel from February until the fall of Fort Donelson. When the regiment was organized our subject was made surgeon, and continued in this capacity until the battle of Shiloh.

H. C. DWIGGINS was born October 8, 1844, in Alabama. His father, R. S. Dwiggins was born in this State about 1820 and died about 1880. The mother was Ann (Wadkins) Dwiggins. Our subject was the eldest of two children born to their union. When about fifteen years old he began milling for his father at Shelbyville. His father built the first three steam-mills ever erected in Tennessee. In the fall of 1862 he enlisted in Company D, Fourth Tennessee Cavalry, and served until the close of the war. He was in several noted battles, but was not wounded or captured during service. After his return he followed the milling business for his father until 1871, when he erected a mill at

Branchville, which he has conducted in connection with merchandising ever since. He was the founder of the village of Branchville, and succeeded in getting a postoffice in 1876. He has done much to assist in the prosperity of the county, and is a man of influence and a highly honorable gentleman. October 8, 1873, he wedded Mary Curtiss, of Richmond, Tenn. She is a daughter of James H. and Teresa Curtiss, and was born in 1854. They have six children: Cassie C., Ethel E., Robbie E., Mamie L., Harry C. and one unnamed. Mr. Dwiggins is a Mason, an Odd Fellow and a Democrat. He has been school director for twelve years, and is still holding the same office.

JAMES H. DYER, son of William and Harriet (Brown) Dyer, was born April 8, 1841, in Bedford County. He received a good, practical education in the schools of the county, and followed agricultural pursuits. In 1872 he was married to Miss Belle Arnold, who bore him seven children: Annie H., James H., Thomas, Roy, Grace B., Harry and Ernest G. Harry died April 26, 1873, and Ernest G. died June 4, 1880. Mrs. Dyer is the daughter of Thomas and Nancy A. Arnold. Mr. Dyer owns 600 acres of fine land in the Twentieth District of Bedford County. He is respected as a man of sound judgment and good sense. He is a member of the Missionary Baptist Church, and is one of the leading farmers and stock raisers of the county. His farm is well adapted to the raising of corn, wheat, hay and clover.

HENRY C. DYER was born October 25, 1844, and is the son of William H. and Harriet (Brown) Dyer. The father was born in Bedford County in 1817. He was a farmer and stock raiser and a successful man in business. He was the father of seven children, four of which are living: James H., Mary J., Henry C. and Emily. Mrs. Harriet Dyer died in 1856, and in 1874 Mr. Dyer was married the second time. Mr. Dyer was a member of the Missionary Baptist Church, and died October 1, 1880. Our subject was born in Bedford County, and educated in the common schools. His first employment was farming, and this, in connection with stock raising, he has always followed. In 1871 he was united in marriage to Miss Eliza Evans, daughter of Nathan Evans, of this county, and one child has blessed their union, Mary B. Mr. Dyer owns 705 acres of good land, and is a leading farmer of the county. He and wife are worthy members of the Missionary Baptist Church.

J. F. ELLIOTT, a native of Rutherford County, Tenn., was born April 24, 1824, son of B. and R. (Freeman) Elliott. The father was born about 1784, in Virginia, and immigrated to Tennessee in about 1804. His death occurred in 1869. The mother was also a native of Virginia, and lived to be very old. Our subject worked for his father on the farm till he was twenty years of age. He soon went to West Tennessee and engaged in agricultural pursuits. He remained there about ten years, after which he returned to Middle Tennessee and engaged in the same business. In 1861 he entered the Confederate Army, Forty-fifth Tennessee Infantry, under Capt. Lytle, and was discharged at Shiloh on account of bad health. After returning home he engaged in agricultural pursuits again. In 1867 or 1868 he moved to Kentucky and remained there but one year, after which he moved back to Tennessee and has lived there ever since. In 1846 he wedded Harriet C. Daniel, of Rutherford County. This union resulted in the birth of seven children: Tennessee, Rebecca C., James M., Sarah K., Josie, Albert J. and Harriet L. Our subject is a good, substantial citizen and is so considered by his neighbors. He and wife are members of the Methodist Episcopal Church South. Mr. Elliott is a Democrat in politics.

REV. ASA W. ELKINS was born July 10, 1821, son of Eli and Nancy (Riggins) Elkins. The father was born in North Carolina, and when a young man immigrated to Tennessee and settled in Bedford County in about 1816. He was a farmer by occupation and in early life was married to Miss Nancy Riggins, a native of North Carolina. The fruits of this union were ten children: Deletha, William S., Mary, Asa W., James, Sarah, Nancy K., Evaline, Eli and Richard, who died during the late war. Eli Elkins immigrated to Alabama in 1833 and settled in Jackson County, where he died in 1835. After his death Mrs. Elkins married Lewis Page, and to them were born one child, Nancy W., who died during the war. Mrs. Page died about 1876. The Elkins family is of English descent. The grandfather of our subject was in the Revolutionary war and was a gallant soldier. Our subject was born in the present limits of Coffee County. The educational advantages at that early day were not what they are now, consequently the education that he acquired at school was rather limited. By his own efforts he has gained considerable information, and is considered a man of sound judgment and good sense. In 1846 he married Miss Lucinda Stafford, a native of this State, and one child blessed the union, Mary A. Mrs. Lucinda Elkins died in 1848, and in 1849 Mr. Elkins married Miss Angeline Hufman. The results of this union were eight children: Sarah J., Nancy V., John W., Martha E., Margaret A., Lafayette, Robert E. and George T. Sarah J. died July 26, 1850; Nancy V. died June 12, 1875: Lafayette died March 19, 1885, and one died in infancy without being named. Mr. Elkins was licensed to preach the gospel in 1868 and has since been a local preacher. He was ordained deacon by the annual conference. He and family are members of the Methodist Episcopal Church South.

MARTIN EULES, a worthy citizen of Bedford County, Tenn., is a son of Adam and Dorothea (Shofner) Eules, who were born in North Carolina in 1775 and 1778, respectively. They were married about 1803 and immigrated to Tennessee in 1810. To them were born eleven children, four of whom are living. The father died in 1843, and the mother in 1872. On the 8th of November, 1843, our subject was united in marriage to Miss Casander Bobo, who was born December 10, 1825, and a daughter of Elisha and Lucy (Dean) Bobo, natives of South Carolina, and who died in 1860 and 1830, respectively. To Mr. and Mrs. Eules were born eleven children: Eli S., born in 1845 (deceased); Mary E., born in 1846 (deceased); Elisha A., born in 1848; Allen F., born in 1850; John M., born in 1852 (deceased); Harriet E., born in 1855; Ella J., born in 1857 (deceased); Minnie A., born in 1860; Lula B., born in 1862; Della C., born in 1865, and Lucy T., born in 1867. Martin Eules started in life for himself almost penniless, but by energy and perseverence has accumulated considerable property. His farm, consisting of 500 acres, is about eight miles from Shelbyville, besides this he owns seventy acres in Coffee County and forty acres in this county. He and wife are members of the Lutheran Church and their children belong to the Cumberland Presbyterian Church. In politics Mr. Eules is neutral.

DR. ROBERT F. EVANS, a prominent and leading physician of Shelbyville, was born August 24, 1821, in Caroline County, Va., being the only son of a family of eight children born to the marriage of David S. Evans and Judith Bowlware, both natives of Virginia, of Welsh and English descent, respectively. The father came with his family to Bedford County in 1832; and followed farming until 1840, when he bought the Evans House and began the hotel business, which he continued till the war. He died in 1869, the mother surviving him one year. Dr. Evans was eleven years old when coming to this county, and was reared on a farm. He assisted his father in the hotel business a short time and then studied medicine for several years. He graduated in the University of Pennsylvania in 1847, and then returned to Shelbyville, where he has been successfully engaged in the practice of his profession ever since, except in 1850–51, when he was on a western tour. He was married, December 24, 1867, to Mrs. Mary C. Fite, who was the mother of two children by her former marriage, viz.: Dr. C. C. Fite, assistant physician at the East Tennessee Insane Asylum, Knoxville, Tenn.; and Jennie M. Fite, now the wife of Surg. A. M. Moore, of the United States Naval Service, Washington, D. C. The marriage of Dr. Evans has been blessed in the birth of two children, Stella and Mary F. He, his wife and youngest daughter are members of the Episcopal Church, and his eldest daughter of the Presbyterian Church. He has been senior warden of the church ever since its organization. He is a Knight Templar Mason. He is a member of the Tennessee Medical Society, and was elected president of that body in 1878. Politically he was reared a Whig, but is now a conservative Democrat.

W. L. FARIS, a native of Franklin County, Tenn., was born June 17, 1864, son of G. W. and Eliza (Tucker) Faris. The father was also a native of Franklin County, and died June 5, 1882. The mother was born about 1838 in Bedford County. Our subject assisted his parents on the farm until he was about twenty-two years of age, after which he worked for himself at farming. At the end of three years he began the mechanics trade in connection with farming and still follows that business up to the present date. December 21, 1875, he wedded Amanda R. Kirk, of this county, who was born August 3, 1856. She was the daughter of Edwin Kirk, who was born in 1809, and died November 22, 1883. To our subject and wife were born five children: E. E., Julian L., Lee G., S. I. and Cassie B. Mr. Faris is a self-made man, having made his property by his own unaided efforts, and is consequently a good substantial citizen. He and wife are worthy members of the Methodist Episcopal Church South. He is a Democrat in politics.

J. C. FISHER'S ancestors were from North Carolina. His father, George W. Fisher, was born in August, 1812, and was brought to Tennessee by his parents when only four years old. George W. Fisher married Elizabeth Helm who was born in North Carolina, in 1814, and died in Tennessee in 1846. Our subject was born in Marshall County, Tenn., January 16, 1838, and is the third of seven children and of Irish descent. At the age of twenty years he began clerking for W. S. Hurst, at Hurst's Cross Roads, Murray County, continuing two years. When the war broke out he joined the Confederate Army, Company D, Fourth Tennessee Cavalry, but after serving faithfully for some time was compelled to abandon the service to some extent. For about two years after the war he farmed and stock-traded and then engaged in the merchandise business in Verona and followed that business four years with good results, the style of the firm being Fisher & Robinson. In 1871 he sold his interest and moved to Fayetteville where he was a partner of W. S. Hurst in the merchandise business two years. The firm then divided their stock, and for three years longer Mr. Fisher followed that occupation in that place and in 1877 moved to Shelbyville. Since 1885 he has been exclusively engaged in farming. May 1, 1872, he wedded Mattie Bell (daughter of G. W. and E. Bell), who has borne him six children: Oscar B., Stella (deceased), Elbert H., James D., Hugh C. and George B. Mr. Fisher has accumulated his property by his own exertions and is perhaps the most thoroughly self-made man in this section of the county. The greater part of his education has been acquired through self-exertion. He is a member of the Methodist Episcopal Church South, and his wife of the Christian Church. politically he is a Democrat.

B. F. FOSTER, Esq., was born Janurary 10, 1829, in Rutherford County, and was the son of James and Celia (Gentry) Foster. The father was born April 22, 1800, and was a very successful farmer for his day. The mother was born in 1803, in Georgia. Our subject received a practical education in the district schools, and at the age of nineteen engaged in the saw-mill business. This he continued for about two years and then began teaching school. At the end of fifteen months he gave this up and engaged in farming. In 1870 he was elected magistrate, and served in this capacity for twelve years. January, 1877, he was elected chairman of the county court and held this position for about six years. Prior to this, in 1851, he wedded Nancy A. McBride, of this county, and the fruits of this union were three children: James J., Charles R. and the eldest, Harriet M., who died in infancy. The mother of these children died June 11, 1862. Mr. Foster was married to Frances Hoover, nee Rankin, August 27, 1871. This union resulted in the birth of one child, Lela G. Mrs. Foster was the mother of two children by her former husband; they were named Thomas R. and H. C Hoover. Mr. and Mrs. Foster are members in good standing in the Cumberland Presbyterian Church, he is also a member of the Masonic fraternity and also a Chapter member of the same. He represented his lodge in the Grand Lodge in Nashville five years in succession. He is a Democrat in politics.

H. R. FREEMAN was born in Bedford County, Tenn., December 25, 1835. From twenty-one years of age until 1861 he farmed for himself, and at the latter date enlisted in Company F, Seventeenth Tennessee Infantry, and fought in many of the most noted battles. He was commissary sergeant during the latter part of the war. After his return he farmed until 1874, and then began merchandising in Unionville. He has been very successful. October 13, 1867, he wedded Salome Duggan, who died November 28, 1878. March 9, 1882, he married Emma Barker. They have one child, Enid Freeman. Mr. Freeman is a Democrat and Prohibitionist. His parents, Hartwell and Nancy (Harris)

Freeman, were born in North Carolina in 1797 and 1801, respectively. The father was a well-to-do farmer, and died in 1871. The mother is yet living, and is eighty-five years of age.

JOHN G. FROST is a son of John E. Frost, a minister of the Primitive Baptist Church, who was born April 7, 1825, in Alabama. His mother was Alsie D. Hicks, daughter of D. D. and Malinda Hicks. John G. Frost was born in Bedford County, October 13, 1859, and was the eighth of nine children. He assisted his father on the farm until twenty-one years of age, and then began tilling the soil on his own responsibility. In 1882 he went to Missouri, where he farmed one year, but the same year traveled over the State of Kansas and the Indian Territory. Since that time he has been engaged in the farming interests in Tennessee. November 30, 1882, he was married to Mattie J. Coleman, daughter of N. A. Coleman. She was born January 12, 1861. They became the parents of three children, two of whom died in infancy. Joshua Wright is the child living. Mr. Frost has been a church member since the fall of 1878. He belongs to the Democratic party, and is worth about $2,500.

WILLIAM D. FROST, M. D., was born in Madison County, Ala., August 12, 1830, and is one of six children born to Ebenezer and Nancy (Wright) Frost. The father was born in North Carolina, and in 1827 immigrated to Alabama where he remained until 1835, and then removed to Bedford County, Tenn. He was one of the successful farmers, of the county. In 1837 he was employed by the Government to aid in removing the Indians to the territory to which they were assigned, and during one of these trips he died. He reared a family of which the county is proud. All of them are prominent citizens of the county. The subject of this sketch passed his boyhood on the farm, and received a fair education in the county schools. In 1850 he began the study of medicine, and in the same year entered the Ohio Medical School of Cincinnati, where he remained one term. He then went to Obion County, Tenn., and began the practice of his profession, remaining there eight years, after which he went to Mississippi, where he remained nine years. He then came back to Tennessee, and has since that time been a faithful practitioner of Bedford County. In 1854 he wedded Miss Martha L. Brown, of Obion County, Tenn., a member of the Missionary Baptist Church, who died in 1874. Mr. Frost was a soldier in the late war; was in the Thirtieth Mississippi Regiment, and was severely wounded at the battle of Chickamauga, which rendered him unfit for general service. After this he acted as assistant surgeon of the regiment until the close of the war. Mr. Frost has a family of four children: William A., who is editor of the *Shelbyville Gazette*, Walter C. who is editing a paper at Murfreesboro, Clarinda E. and John W.

WILLIAM A. FROST, editor and proprietor of the Shelbyville *Gazette*, was born September 30, 1855, in Troy, Obion Co., Tenn., being the eldest of five children of William D. and Martha L. (Brown) Frost. The father is a physician and resides at Flat Creek in this county. The mother died September 24, 1874. The subject of this sketch was reared on a farm in Moore County, Tenn., and in Mississippi. He remained with his parents to the age of nineteen, when he entered Mulberry Institute, Lincoln County, Tenn., in which he took a two years' course. He then was appointed deputy clerk of the Circuit Court of Moore County. After one year as deputy he was appointed clerk of the same court and held the office three years. In December, 1878, he bought the Lynchburg *Sentinel*, and published that paper till December 4, 1884, at which time he was burned out. In 1880, June 30, he was appointed clerk and master of the Chancery Court of Moore County, and served four years. January 1, 1884, he took charge of his present enterprise. He has refitted the office with an entirely new outfit and made his the leading paper of the country, and he is regarded as the most successful county newspaper man in the State. He was elected alderman of the Second Ward of Shelbyville in October, 1885, and is chairman of the finance committee. He is justly regarded as a prominent and enterprising citizen. He was married, May, 4, 1880, to Miss Katie Whitaker, of Lincoln County. This union has been blessed in the birth of one son, William W. Politically Mr. Frost is a firm Democrat.

ALFRED D. FUGITT, farmer, was born in Rutherford County, Tenn., November 8, 1813, son of Townsend and Jane (Campbell) Fugitt, and of Irish-French descent. The father of our subject was born in North Carolina in 1780, and the mother was born about 1784. They were married in North Carolina about 1799, and to them were born eight children. The father emigrated from North Carolina to Kentucky in 1804, and owned the land where Danville, Ky., now stands, but concluding the land was too poor for successful farming, moved to Tennessee in 1806. He was a soldier in the war of 1812, and died November, 1878, at the advanced age of ninety-eight, the mother died in 1837. Our subject received a fair education and followed farming and merchandising ever since. He was married, January 10, 1837, to Miss Jane M. Norvell; of this alliance there were born ten children—three sons: Glodolphus C., John N. and Alfred T., and seven daughters: Sallie E., Mattie J., Maggie N., Cassie M., Mollie B., Ada J. and Annie N. Mr. Fugitt was formerly an old-line Whig, and while he entertains no particular love for the name of Democracy he votes that ticket. He has 600 acres of good land, which he devotes almost exclusively to stock raising. Mrs. Fugitt, wife of our subject, was born in Bedford County, Tenn., September 5, 1814. Her father, John Norvell, emigrated from North Carolina about 1806, and was among the pioneers of the State. Our subject had two sons in the late war, Glodolphus C., who was a captain in the Second Tennessee Regiment under Col. Bate, was killed at Shiloh. The second son was a member of the same regiment and was killed in Lincoln County, Tenn., in 1863. While our subject was too old to partake of active service in the army, he displayed his liberality and State pride in contributing the amount of $1,000 a month to Capt. Fugitt's company. The grandfather of our subject, Benjamin Fugitt, was a soldier in the Revolutionary war and served seven years.

JOHN A. GANNAWAY was born in Tennessee May 17, 1824, son of John and Mary W. (Robertson) Gannaway, of Virginia. The father was born in 1788, married in 1811 and came to Tennessee in 1814. He was a farmer and mechanic, and died July 12, 1851. Our subject's ancestors on both sides were from England. He was the fifth of eleven children and resided with his parents on the farm until twenty years of age. He then became overseer of a cotton factory at Murfreesboro, and worked the first year for $50, the second for $100, the third for $200. At the expiration of this time he started to school, attending about five months. He clerked for a short time in Murfreesboro, and then sold goods for A. J. Wood. He then began traveling for a saddle and dry goods firm, continuing five years, and then began the mercantile business at Wartrace, Tenn., with a very small capital. At the end of eight years he had accumulated considerable money and in the fall of 1858 sold out and purchased a farm near Bellbuckle, which he managed about seven years. Since the war he has been postmaster of Unionville, and was a merchant of that place for some time. In 1877 he retired from active business life. September 14, 1853, he married M. R. Tarpley, of Bedford County, and daughter of Edward Tarpley; she was born October 25, 1832, and has borne her husband twelve children: Emma D., Maggie E., John E., James W., Josephus, Nannie R., Mary C., Elijah T., Cora L., Clarence E., Horace B. C. and Cornelius V. Mr. Gannaway was elected magistrate of his district November 8, 1870, and held the office about six years. He and wife are members of the Methodist Episcopal Church South.

BRADLEY GAMBILL was born April 17, 1820, in Tennessee, son of Aaron and Elizabeth (Cannady) Gambill, natives of Tennessee and Maryland, respectively. Our subject was the youngest of twelve children born to his parents, all dead but three. The father was a farmer and a soldier in the Revolutionary war. He received land warrants for services rendered during that war. Our subject worked on the same farm with his brother till he was twenty-two years of age. He is a successful farmer and has followed that occupation the principal part of his life. December 24, 1840, he wedded Sarah C. Anderson, of Tennessee, and this union has been happily blessed by the birth of a large family of children. In 1848 our subject was elected to the office of constable and served the people in that capacity for six years. In 1854 he moved to Mississippi and engaged in the cotton business, but the late Rebellion swept the greater part of his property away. He moved back to Tennessee during the war and was elected to the office of magistrate in 1866, and was elected the two following terms, making a total of sixteen years in all that he served the people in that capacity. He and wife are members of the Methodist Episcopal Church South, and he is also a member of the Masonic order. In politics he is a Democrat. He was a major in the militia before the war.

THOMAS J. GAMBILL, an excellent farmer and the son of Bradley and Sarah C. (Anderson) Gambill, whose sketch appears above in this volume, was born December 14, 1852. He assisted his parents on the farm and secured a fair practical education in the district schools. In 1874 he began to fight life's battles for himself as a farmer. In 1877 he led to the altar Lucy Templeton, daughter of Newton Templeton, and the fruit of this union was an interesting family of four children: Minnie E., Marvin E., Joshua Cleveland and Newton E. Mr. Gambill is one of the enterprising and successful citizens of the Twenty-third District. He has a farm well watered and in a fine state of cultivation in Coffee County, and an interest in a tract in this county. He and wife are exemplary members of the Methodist Episcopal Church South.

N. C. GAMBILL, JR., was born May 28, 1846, in Tennessee, son of N. C. and Minerva (Phillips) Gambill, both natives of this State. The father was born in 1812 and was a tiller of the soil; his death occurred in 1861. The mother was born in 1815, and died in 1866 or 1867. Our subject remained on the farm with his parents until their death. He then began farming for himself in 1867, and has successfully continued that occupation up to the present date. November 29, 1866, he wedded Nancy L. Ladd, of Williamson County. The result of this union was five children: Sallie J., Jesse C., James B., Nannie E., and one who died in infancy. Mr. and Mrs. Gambill are leading members in the Christian Church, and Mr. Gambill is a Master Mason. His education was rather limited, but he has always manifested a willingness to aid in any or all enterprises pertaining to the advancement of education. He is a Democrat in politics and a strong temperance man and an advocate of Christianity in all its phases, sects and denominations.

R. C. GARRETT was born February 11, 1844, in Bedford County, and is the son of Darington and Nancy (Gentry) Garrett, both natives of Tennessee, and both died when our subject was quite small. R. C. Garrett, our subject, enlisted in the Confederate Army in the fall of 1862. He entered as Gen. Forrest's escort, and sustained this relation to the army throughout the entire war. He was wounded in the right arm just above the elbow during the battle of Chickamauga, which disabled him from active duty for about six months. He was again wounded at Plantersville, Ala., was hit by a spent ball on the left jaw, but this disabled him for only a short time. At the close of the war he came home and began tilling the soil on the farm where he is now living. November 30, 1865, he led to the altar Martha L. Jackson, of this county. She was the daughter of John and Rebecca (Lytle) Jackson, natives, respectively, of North Carolina and Virginia, and of Irish and English lineage. To Mr. and Mrs. Garrett were born ten children: Ella N., William T., John J., Robert C., Robecca G., Lizzie L., Fannie C., Darlington J., Fane S. and the tenth, a daughter, died unnamed. Mr. Garrett received rather a limited education, but enough for all practical purposes. He is a Democrat in politics, and Mrs. Garrett is a member of the Baptist Church.

L. T. GAUNT was born March 15, 1852, in this State, son of Lewis and Mary S. (Shearen) Gaunt, both natives of Tennessee. The father was born December 28, 1803, and died February 20, 1860. The mother was born May 2, 1816, and died in 1873. Our subject assisted his mother on the farm and received a rather limited education in the common schools. At the age of seventeen he began farming on his own responsibility and continued this occupation until the fall of 1884. September 29, 1869, he wedded Margaret M. E. Stallings, of this county, and by her became the father of six children: Mollie E., Mattie E., James L., John T., Joe U. and Dan S. In 1882 Mr. Gaunt was elected constable in the Eighteenth District, and served two years. In 1884 he was appointed deputy sheriff under the present sheriff, which position he now holds. In 1885 he en-

BEDFORD COUNTY. 1151

gaged in the merchandise business at this place, and is at present engaged in that occupation. In the fall of 1885 he was appointed United States deputy marshal, which office he now holds. He is a Democrat in politics.

JOHN J. GILL, farmer and stock raiser, was born May 26, 1841, and is one of five children born to the union of Winston W. and Sarah A. (Whitaker) Gill. The father was born in Kentucky March 10, 1809. In 1831 or 1832 he immigrated to Tennessee and settled in Lincoln County. He was for the greater part of his life a merchant, and sold goods at Gill's Store. In 1840 he was married, and became the father of these children: John J., Mary R., Martha C., Sallie J. and Winston W. Martha Gill died in 1851; Sallie J., in 1860, and Winston W., in 1878. In 1846 our subject's father moved to this county and bought a tract of land in the Twenty-second District. Mrs. Gill died in 1855, and Mr. Gill married a Miss Moore, and after her death he married a Miss Wiley, of Alabama. The Gill family were originally from Maryland, and are of English descent. Our subject was born in Lincoln County, and was given an education in the county schools. In 1870 he was married to Miss Susan S. Riggs, a native of Maury County and a daughter of Adam S. Riggs. To this union were born two children: Sallie R. and Winston W. Sallie R. died in 1874, and Winston W. February 11, 1879. Mr. Gill owns one of the finest farms of Bedford County. It contains 650 acres lying five miles south of Shelbyville. He is president of the agricultural society of Bedford County.

J. S. GILLIS, a leading merchant and enterprising citizen of Shelbyville, was born April 12, 1840, in New York State. He was the younger of two children born to the marriage of James Gillis and Isabella Stalker, natives of Scotland. His parents removed to Canada from New York, and he was reared there, receiving a common school education. In 1859 he went to Trenton, Ky., and engaged in the pursuit of farming till 1871. He then removed to Shelbyville and opened his merchandising establishment, which he has continued very successfully. He now carries a stock of about $20,000 and does an annual business of about $35,000 to $40,000. He was married September 25, 1864, to Eliza Bradley, the result of this union is one son—George D. Mr. Gillis is a member of the Missionary Baptist Church, and has been superintendent of the Sunday-schools for about twelve years. His wife is also a member of the Missionary Baptist Church. Mr. Gillis is of old-line Whig ancestry, but he is now a Democrat. He is one of the leading citizens of Shelbyville, and bears the highest esteem of his fellow-citizens.

JAMES B. GREEN, of the firm of Green & McGill, dealers in groceries and provisions, was born in Bedford County, Tenn., January 20, 1856, being a son of Blount G. and Salina F. (Stewart) Green. Blount G. Green was born October 14, 1815. His father, William Green, came to Bedford County in 1808 with his parents. William Green was married in 1811 to Miss Sarah Phillips. Blount G. has always been a farmer and has been very successful, now owning 1,121 acres of land in Bedford County. He was married, in 1841, to Miss Salina F. Stewart, the result of this union being eleven children, viz.: Canzada P., Mary E., Nancy C., Susan C. E., Emily J., Lewis D., Samuel E., James B., Harriet F., Tennessee A. and Thomas B. Three of the family have died, viz.: Canzada P., Thomas B. and Emily J. Mr. Blount Green is one of the prominent farmers of the county, and has been identified with the public offices of the county. James B. was reared on a farm and secured a common school education. At the age of twenty-one he began farming for himself, and continued till 1881, when he engaged at clerking in a grocery store for a short time. He then went back to farming. In December, 1885, he began his present occupation, and has since done a good business in the grocery line. He was married, May 10, 1883, to Mrs. Tennie (McGill) Gallaher, daughter of W. M. McGill, Esq., of this county. The wife is the mother of one child, Mary Gallagher, by her former marriage, and has borne two children to her union with Mr. Green, viz.: Jessie B. and James F. Mr. Green and wife are members of the Christian Church. He takes no very active interest in political affairs, but is an energetic and respected business man.

B. T. GREGORY, the photographer of Shelbyville, was born August 17, 1847, in Shelbyville, being one of a family born to the union of Joseph P. Gregory and Elivira

Jones, natives, respectively, of Virginia and Alabama. Joseph P. was brought to Bedford County when young by his father, Thomas Gregory. He was a dentist by profession. He practiced his profession in Shelbyville, and thence removed to Stevenson, Ala., which place he named in honor of V. K. Stevenson, a prominent railroad man. He (the father) returned to Shelbyville, where he died in 1881. The mother died at Stevenson, Ala., when our subject was young. B. T. received a common school education. At the age of twenty-two he started out in life for himself, having learned and practiced dentistry prior to this time. He then learned the photographer's art, and has ever since been engaged in that art. He permanently located in Shelbyville in 1876, since which time he has done a good business in his line. He was married, December 26, 1881, to Miss Annie Calhoun, daughter of N. J. and Elizabeth Calhoun. Her father was a stone-cutter and marble dealer. One son has been born to this marriage—Benjamin T. Mr. Gregory is a Democrat in politics. He and his wife are members of the Christian Church.

JOHN H. GRIDER was born December 27, 1844, in Jackson County, Ala. His father, Ananias A. Grider, was born in Putnam County, Tenn., in 1812. He married Miss G. Bullington, a native of the same county. To this union seven children were born, our subject being the fifth. Ananias A. Grider died August, 1856, and his wife died in the same month. Our subject was educated in the country schools of his native county. In May, 1861, he enlisted in Company I, Seventeenth Tennessee Regiment, and served with this command up to and including the battle of Chickamauga. During this time he never was absent from his command a single day. The principal battles were Wild Cat Mountain, Fishing Creek, Perryville, Stone River and Chickamauga. At the latter place he was captured and taken to Camp Douglas, at Chicago, Ill., where he remained until March 28, 1865. He was then taken to Point Lookout, Md., where he took the oath of allegiance, was released and returned home. He then worked two years on the Nashville & Chattanooga Railroad, and ever since then has followed farming in Bedford County, where he now resides. On July 1, 1866, he married Mrs. Sarah J. Mooney, and to this union were born five children. Mr. Grider owns a farm of 135 acres in District No. 3, and he and wife are worthy members of the Methodist Episcopal Church South.

SAMUEL B. GORDON, one of Bedford County's old and respected citizens, was born February 14, 1813, in Bedford County. He is one of seven children, the fruits of the marriage of David Gordon and Mary Reynolds, natives of South Carolina. The parents came to this county about 1809 and the father followed farming all his life. He died when Samuel B. was quite small. The mother died in 1836; she was a member of the Presbyterian Church. Mr. Gordon, our subject, was reared on a farm and secured a common school education. At the age of twenty-three he married and settled to farming four miles east of Shelbyville. He afterward moved to Flat Creek, in this county, and lived there eighteen years; thence he moved to where he now lives. He owns about 190 acres of fine land, having been successful as a lifetime farmer. He was married, October 20, 1835, to Amelia Eules, a native of this county, born in 1817. Twelve children have been born to this union, all of whom have lived to be grown, but four of whom have since died, viz.: Mary C. (wife of Thomas Hutton, a farmer of Marshall County); George W. (deceased); Harriet E. (wife of J. R. Burrow, a farmer of this county); Adam E. (deceased); Amzi C. (deceased); William J., a labor superintendent in Alabama; Mitchell S., a merchant in Texas; Martin L. (deceased); John A., a States district attorney in Texas; Samuel B., Jr.; Margaret E. and Amelia E. (wife of G. S. Sanders). Mr. Gordon, his wife and several of the family are members of the Lutheran Church. He is a Master Mason in Blue Lodge Masonry, and a Republican in politics. He was trustee of Bedford County for about three terms about the close of the war.

RICHARD D. GORDON was born February 8, 1834, and is the son of Dr. William J. and Louisa B. (Hix) Gordon. The father of our subject was born in North Carolina February 16, 1813, and when a young man immigrated to Tennessee and settled in Bedford County. He received his medical education at the medical school of Gainesville, Ala., and began the practice of his profession in Bedford County. He was very successful as a physician, and won distinction in the county where he resided. In 1846 he was married to Miss Louisa B. Hix, and to this union were born four children: Dosia, Richard D., and two who died in infancy that were not named. Dr. Gordon died at his home in Bedford County August 20, 1875, beloved by all. Our subject had the advantage of a good practical education in his native county. In 1875 he was married to Miss Callie Burrow, and five children blessed this union: Euphus A., William F., Clawson R., Albert P. and Anna B., all living. Mr. Gordon has made farming a success. He owns 160 acres of land in the Twenty-third District, and is esteemed by all his acquaintances.

N. W. HALEY is a son of E. T. and Susanna (Pratt) Haley, natives of Virginia and North Carolina, respectively. The father was born in 1779, and received a fair education. When about seventeen years of age he went to North Carolina and engaged in farming, and was there married in 1804, and became the father of these nine children: Anderson, James, Mary B., Nancy, Martha, William S., George, E. T. (Jr.), and N. W. Mr. Haley came to Tennessee in 1806, and located in Rutherford County, but in 1829 came to Bedford County, and in 1841 moved to the farm known as "Oak Grove," where he died March 23, 1858. He was an 1812 soldier. Mrs. Haley died March 26, 1844. Our subject was born in Bedford County February 1, 1824, and his early days were passed in laboring on his father's farm. His educational opportunities were limited, owing to his services being required at home, but by contact with business life he has gained a fair business education. He is a farmer and stock raiser, and a Democrat in his political views. He belongs to the Methodist Episcopal Church South.

JOHN V. HALL was born March 31, 1841, in Bedford County, Tenn., and is the elder of two children born to Joshua and Margaret (Swift) Hall, both natives of Bedford County. The father was born about 1804, and died in 1854. The mother was born September 14, 1815, and is still living. Flower Swift, our subject's maternal grandfather, was a native of North Carolina, born June 3, 1787, and died in January, 1851. His wife, Catherine Swift, was also born in North Carolina, October 16, 1791, and died in 1861. The paternal grandparents of our subject were born about 1775 or 1776, in the State of North Carolina, and immigrated to Tennessee at a very early date. Our subject was reared on the farm, and remained on the same until the breaking out of the war. He then entered the Confederate service in Company F, Forty-first Tennessee Infantry, and was captured together with the entire regiment at Fort Donelson. He was taken first to Lafayette, and after remaining there about three weeks was taken to Camp Morton, Indianapolis, Ind., where they remained about seven months. They were then exchanged at Vicksburg, Miss. Mr. Hall was in but two battles in Tennessee: Chickamauga and Missionary Ridge. After these battles his regiment was ordered to Georgia and Mississippi. He was discharged at Dalton, Ga., in 1864, on account of his health. He then came home and bought a half interest in the mill property that he now owns, known as "Hall's Mills." In 1874 he bought the entire interest of the mill, and since that time he has operated the mill on his own responsibility. April 6, 1871, he wedded Ella F. Turrentine, of this county. She was born November 24, 1854. This union resulted in the birth of five children: William J., Emmett E., John T., Joseph E. and Sammy B. Mr. Hall was elected to the office of magistrate in the year 1871, and has served in that capacity for the last fifteen years. He is magistrate at the present time, and fills the office in an able manner. He received a comparatively good education, and is a Democrat in politics.

HIRAM HARRIS, ESQ., was born September 17, 1814, in Roane County, N. C., and is the son of John Harris, a native of Harrisburg, Penn., born about 1775. That city derived its name from our subject's great-great-grandfather, John Harris, who donated the property where Harrisburg now stands to the State of Pennsylvania for the purpose of building that city. Our subject passed his early days on the farm, and after reaching years of discretion began farming for himself. He also partially educated himself, and chose school-teaching as his profession. May 5, 1842, he wedded Lucy A. Tillford, of this county. In 1850 he taught ten months in Texas, and in 1862 taught five months in the State of Mississippi. Since then he has been teaching exclusively in this State. In 1844 he was elected to the office of magistrate in the Sixth District, but resigned the office at the end of two years, and was elected magistrate of the Eighteenth District in 1878 and re-elected the following term. In 1880 Mr. Harris was one of the delegates to the convention in Nashville, to nominate a candidate for governor. He is a Democrat in politics, and he and wife are members in good standing in the Methodist Episcopal Church South.

JOHN HART is a son of James and Sarah (Fossett) Hart, who were born in North Carolina, and became the parents of nine children: Stephen, Thomas, Susan, Rachel, John, Lucretia, Nathaniel B., Mary A. and William G. Mr. Hart came to Rutherford County, Tenn., in 1816, and in 1827 moved to Bedford County, where he died December 10, 1856. Mrs. Hart died August 30, 1860. She was a member of the Methodist Episcopal Church. Our subject was born April 29, 1819, in Rutherford County, and the major part of his life has been spent on a farm. He began doing for himself as a merchant, and clerked in the store of William G. Cowan, of Shelbyville. He was married in December, 1842, to Virginia Holder, daughter of John W. Holder, and by her is the father of four children: James H., Catherine E., John W. and Carrie B., all of whom are dead save one. For his second wife Mr. Hart took Narcissa (Phillips) Jennings, daughter of Garrett Phillips. They have one child, Lillian C. In 1847 he removed to his present place of abode, on the Murfreesboro Pike, five miles from Shelbyville. Mr. Hart served in the United States Army for about one year in the late war. He is a Republican in politics, and is a member of the Masonic fraternity. Both he and Mrs. Hart are members of the Methodist Episcopal Church.

W. R. HAYNES, furniture dealer and undertaker, was born June 29, 1844, in Williamson County, Tenn., being a son of R. R. and Sarah A. (Merritt) Haynes. The father was born in Rutherford County, Tenn., about 1808, was a cabinet-maker by trade and died in Williamson County, Tenn., in 1867. The mother was born about 1810 and is yet living. The subject of this sketch was reared at Triune, Williamson County, and learned his father's trade. He served throughout the war in Company F, Fourth Tennessee Cavalry, and received a wound at Wartrace in a skirmish. He was in all the important battles of the southwest with Forrest's brigade. For a time he then earned his living at manual employment and then for two years he conducted a furniture and undertaking business at Triune. In October, 1872, he came to Shelbyville and opened up his business and has been very successful ever since. He was married May 31, 1876, to Mollie E. Summers, the result of this union being four children: Mary B., Kate S., Sadie and William R., Jr. All the family are members of the Methodist Episcopal Church South, Mr. Haynes being a steward in the church. Politically he is a Democrat, and he is an enterprising citizen of this county.

W. G. HIGHT, proprietor of the National Livery Stable, was born March 27, 1845, in Bedford County, being a son of W. G. and Naomi (Patterson) Hight, both natives of Bedford County. The father was a farmer; he was born in 1818. He was a successful farmer and trader, and was prominently connected with public affairs of the county. He died in 1881 in Arkansas, where he had moved in 1867. The mother died about 1875; now but two of the family are living in the county. Our subject was reared on a farm; at the age of twenty he married and began farming, and continued to farm till 1871. He then engaged in merchandising at Rover, Bedford Co., Tenn., till 1878, and also owned an interest in a mercantile trade at Wartrace from 1876 till 1878. He then ran a mill and stock business at Rover till 1884, when he went to Bellbuckle, and for a short time sold goods there. He then engaged in the livery business in Shelbyville, now doing an extensive trade. He also owns a farm of 140 acres and a saw-mill. He was married in 1865 to Miss Lucy J. Taylor, the result of this union being six children, five of whom are now living, viz.: Eula R., Naomi E., Mary N., William E. J., Alice (the one who died) and Nola P. Mr. Hight and family are members of the Missionary Baptist Church. He is a member of the F. & A. M. Politically he is a Democrat. He is one of the enterprising citizens of Shelbyville, and takes special interest in securing to his children good educational advantages.

WILLIAM S. HIX, farmer, was born May 14, 1825, and is the son of Demarcus D. and Malinda (Stewart) Hix. The father of our subject was born in Halifax County, Va., in 1801, and when only five years of age he, with his father, immigrated to Tennessee and settled in Bedford County. He was a farmer and stock raiser, and was married when quite young. He was the father of twelve children, all of whom were reared to maturity. He died September 19, 1872, a pious member of the Primitive Baptist Church. His wife followed him April 30, 1874, and was a member of the same church. Our subject has always been a farmer, and in 1847 was married to Miss Martha A. Word, a native of Bedford County. The result of this union was twelve children, viz.: John A. (deceased), James H. (deceased), Benjamin F., Asenith M. (deceased), Demarcus D., William W., Martha W. J. (deceased), Ailsey C., Louisa F. (deceased), Mary E., Joseph J. and Lillie A. Mr. Hix owns 474 acres of land in the Twenty-third District of Bedford County, is a member of the Primitive Baptist Church and a leading citizen.

J. H. HIX was born August 15, 1855, in Bedford County, being a son of J. L. Hix, a retired farmer, living in Shelbyville. The father was born and raised in Bedford County, as was the mother, nee Hulda Holt, also. She died in 1883. The subject of this sketch was reared on a farm to the age of fifteen, when he began clerking in the grocery business. In 1880 he opened up the bar and confectionery business, which he has ever since very successfully continued. He was married, January 27, 1881, to Miss Ada Harmon, a native of Warren County, Tenn., then living in Nashville. One son, John, has been born to this union. Mr. Hix is a member of the Republican party. He has never aspired to any public office, but he does a thriving business in his line.

BERRY D. HOLT was born March 4, 1824, in Bedford County, Tenn., on a farm adjoining the one where he now resides. His father, Henry Holt, was a native of Orange County, N. C., and immigrated with his parents to Tennessee when a small boy. He was born in 1792, and married Miss Elizabeth McGuire, a native of Kentucky, who came to this State when a child, and who was of Irish descent. Henry Holt was of German descent, and a farmer by occupation. He died in 1864. The mother still survives. Our subject was educated in the country schools of his native county, and lived with his parents until reaching his majority. For a number of years after this he followed farming and trading in stock. About 1860 he began railroading as a train conductor on the Nashville & Chattanooga Railroad, and on the accommodation train between Nashville and Wartrace for about fifteen years. After that, and up to the year 1885, he ran a through train between Hickman and Chattanooga, and superintended his farm. In 1885 he quit railroading on account of failing health, and now devotes his attention principally to farming. In 1848 he married Miss Lucretia Hart, a native of this county, and to them were born five children: Bettie, William T., John W., Mattie and James B. The mother of these children died May, 1863, and in 1869 their father married Mrs. Mary Roundtree, formerly Mary Kubley, a native of Switzerland. She is the mother of one child—Maggie —by her first husband, Maj. William Roundtree. Our subject was a colonel of the militia during the fifties, and during the late war, while acting as railroad conductor, his railroad was held by the Federal Army. He is one of the trustees of the Wartrace Male and Female Institute, and owns a fine farm of 290 acres. He and wife are members of the Methodist Episcopal Church South.

JOHN W. HOLT was born February 22, 1855, in Bedford County, Tenn.; son of B. D. and Lucretia (Hart) Holt, natives also of this county. The father is one of the prominent farmers of the county. The mother died in 1863. Our subject was educated at the Wartrace High School, and lived with and assisted his father on the farm until he was about seventeen years of age. He then took a course in the telegraphing department of the Cumberland University at Lebanon, Tenn. In 1875 he took charge of the telegraph office at McEwen, Tenn., and remained there seven months. He was then assigned the office at Johnsonville, which he declined, and in 1877 took charge of the office at Christiana and remained there three years. He then took charge of the agency of the railroad and telegraph office at McMinnville, where he remained but a short time. He then went to Nashville and entered the general book-keeping office, where he remained eight months. He then took charge of the Western Union telegraph office at Bowling Green, Ky.; in five months he left, and in 1880 took charge of the ticket, telegraph and Southern Express office at Wartrace, where he now resides. In 1882 he married Miss Blanch Halbach, a native of Virginia, and this union was blessed by two children: Cecil R. and Herbert F. Our subject is a member of the Royal Arcanum, and he and wife are members of the Methodist Episcopal Church South.

JAMES HOOVER was born July 29, 1814, in Rutherford County, Tenn., son of Christopher and Elizabeth (Lotspeech) Hoover. The father was born about 1776, in Germany, as also was the mother of our subject. James Hoover was the eleventh of thirteen children born to his parents. He worked on the farm until he was twenty-three years of age after which he engaged in farming for himself. He has lived in this and the two adjoining counties (Rutherford and Coffee) all his life. December 26, 1837, he was united in marriage to Susan Moore, a native of Virginia, born about 1820. This union resulted in the birth of nine children: Robert W., Clementine F., Calladona J., Martha A., Mary E., Elizabeth E., Susan O., Charles M. and Hugh L. The mother died about 1859 in the full fruition of the Christian's hope. In February, 1862, Mr. Hoover was married to M. J. Winn, of this county. This union resulted in the birth of eleven children: Alice D., Effie M., George C., Edward O., Harvey F., Cleopatra, James F., Benjamin, Nancy E., Albert A. and Anna M. Mr. Hoover was elected to the office of magistrate several years ago, but only served a short time. He is a member of the Cumberland Presbyterian Church and is politically a Democrat.

SYD HOUSTON, mayor of Wartrace, was born January 18, 1850, in Bedford County, Tenn. His father, C. P. Houston, was a native of North Carolina, born in 1809, and immigrated to this State when about twenty years of age. Here he married Miss Jane Worke, who was also a native of North Carolina. To this union nine children were born, of whom our subject is the sixth. The parents of our subject are still living, and his father is one of the leading farmers of the county. Our subject lived with his parents until he was sixteen years old, and then went to Shelbyville and clerked in the store of his brother, C. P. Houston, Jr. He attended school at this place for three years, and then taught school for twenty months. He then read medicine and took a full course of lectures in Louisville, Ky. In April, 1878, he opened a drug store in Wartrace, where he still continues the business, and has a large and successful trade. In 1881 he married Miss Lilian Shealey, a native of Georgia. Our subject is a member of the K. of H., and is serving his first term as mayor of Wartrace. In politics he is a stanch Republican.

JAMES B. HUNTER, farmer and teacher, of Bedford County, Tenn., is a son of E. W. Hunter, who was born in North Carolina, and came to Tennessee with his father when a mere lad. He was married in 1830 to Susanna Wilson, and by her is the father of six children: Sarah M., Robert P., Emily, Margaret M., Thomas H. M. and J. B. Mrs. Hunter's death occurred in 1848, and in 1849 Mr. Hunter wedded Margaret B. Jones, and to them were born three children, only one of whom is living. Mr. Hunter died in 1876 at his residence in Marshall County. James B. Hunter was born April 27, 1838, and was reared on a farm and educated in the common schools. He began teaching when quite young, and then clerked in a dry goods store until the breaking out of the Rebellion, when he enlisted in Company F, Seventeenth Tennessee Infantry. He was lieutenant of his company and acted about half the time as adjutant of the regiment. In 1862, when the army was reorganized; he enlisted in the Twenty-second Tennessee Cavalry and was captured near Montgomery, Ala. He was a participant in the battles of Murfreesboro, Chickamauga, Chattanooga, Knoxville, Franklin and numerous lesser engagements. At the close of the war he returned home and in 1867 was married to Mary C. Cooper, who bore him the following family of children: Ida L., Sarah E., Frank W. and Charles P. Mr. Hunter resides near Bellbuckle, and he and his wife are members of the Methodist Episcopal Church South.

GEORGE C. HUFFMAN, farmer, born April 13, 1830, in Bedford County, Tenn.; son of John and Mary (Cortner) Huffman, natives of North Carolina. The father was born in 1800 and moved to Tennessee in 1819. He was of German descent and one of the best farmers of the county. He died in 1877, and his wife preceded him in 1875. Our subject received the rudiments of his education in the county schools, and subsequently at Fairfield. He began teaching at the age of twenty-one and taught two sessions. He then bought a farm near where he is at present living. In 1858 he married Miss Eliza Phillips, a native of Bedford County, and the fruits of this union were Mary A., Mattie J., Sallie A., Thomas L. and Alice, all living. The eldest, Mary A., is now Mrs. William Bennett, and they reside in California. He owns a large farm of 480 acres of as good land as lies in the county. It is in a most excellent state of cultivation and is known as Adams' Bottom. He has most excellent buildings, well located, and his house, lawn and premises are kept in a neat and tasteful manner. He is of the Cumberland Presbyterian faith and his wife is a member of that church. In politics he is a Democrat.

A. J. JARRELL, one of Shelbyville's best business men, was born March 15, 1845, in Davidson County, Tenn., being a son of Wesley and Martha (Lovell) Jarrell. The father was a native of Kentucky. He died about 1854. The mother was born in 1812, and is now living. The subject of this sketch was reared on a farm. In 1860 he came with his mother to Shelbyville, and farmed a short time, and then worked about in different vocations till 1866. He then learned the tinner's trade, and in 1868 opened up his business, dealing in stoves and tinware. He has been quite successful, and carries on farming also, now owning a fine farm adjoining Shelbyville. He carries about $5,000 stock, and does the leading business of the kind in the county. In 1867 he married Miss Helen Givens, who bore him six children. This wife died in 1881, and in 1882 he married Miss Lina Givens, a sister of the former wife. One child has been born to this union. Mr. Jarrell, his wife and eldest daughter are members of the Missionary Baptist Church. Mr. Jarrell is a Blue Lodge Mason and a member of the I. O. O. F. Politically he is a Republican. He served one year in Company A, Fourth Tennessee Mounted Infantry, United States Army. He is thoroughly a self-made man, and one of the very prominent citizens of the county.

JAMES D. JEFFRESS was born August 18, 1841, in Bedford County. His father, Thomas B. Jeffress, was born in Virginia in 1803 and came to Tennessee in about 1836. While in Virginia he wedded Pollie H. Carter, who was born about 1805. They died in 1876 and 1856, respectively. James was the fifth of their seven children. He entered the Confederate Army in 1861, in Company C, Twenty-third Tennessee Regiment, and was through the entire war, but was not wounded. He was in many of the principal battles, Shiloh, Perryville, Murfreesboro and Knoxville being examples. Since the war he has farmed, and since 1878 has tilled the old homestead, which he purchased, March 7, 1867, he was united in marriage to Frances A. Clay, born in Bedford County, February 16, 1846. Three children were born to this union: Annie Lee, Sallie H. and Thomas Ewing. Mr. Jeffress has a comfortable competency and is a man of intelligence and education. He and wife are members of the Missionary Baptist Church, and he is a Democrat politically.

L. E. JONES is a native of Tennessee, and was born in the year 1816. His parents were North Carolinians by birth, and his maternal grandfather served his country faithfully in the Revolutionary war. The subject of our sketch was reared on a farm by one of his uncles, Isaiah Hammond, and lived with him until after attaining his twenty-first birthday, and then began the battle of life for himself, and has been a tiller of the soil up to the present time. In January, 1840, he united his fortunes with Miss Nancy Bryant, of Bedford County, and their union resulted in the birth of twelve children, seven of whom are now living. Our subject has been quite prosperous in his farming enterprises, and is now living in sight of the first house that was ever built in Bedford County. He received limited educational advantages, but has always manifested a willingness to aid in any and all enterprises pertaining to the advancement of educational interests. His political views are Democratic, and he gives his support to that party. He has always been scrupulously honest in all his business transactions, and is considered one of Bedford County's most substantial citizens.

THOMAS J. JONES was born November 2, 1842, in Lincoln County, Tenn., near Petersburg, being one of the family of children born to the union of Minos C. Jones and Fannie Melson. The father was born and raised in Bedford County. At the age of eighteen he went to Lincoln County, where he married, lived and died, being a farmer by occupation. Thomas J. was reared on a farm with his parents to the age of twenty-one, when he married and moved to Bedford County and farmed a short time. In February, 1867, he came to Shelbyville and opened a bar and confectionery business. He removed to Richmond, Bedford County, in a short time, and in 1870 he returned to Shelbyville, where he has remained ever since in the bar and confectionery business. He was married April 14, 1864, to Mary E. Harrison, a native of this county, who has borne to him eight children, five of whom are now living, viz.: William H., Fannie E., Katie E., Samuel R. and Albert B. Politically Mr. Jones has always been a Democrat. His wife is a member of the Missionary Baptist Church, and his eldest daughter is a member of the Methodist Episcopal Church South. He has been very successful in his business, and is a substantial business man of Shelbyville.

THOMAS J. JOYCE was born August 20, 1847, in Bedford County, and was the eldest of twelve children born to Anderson and Elizabeth Joyce. The father was born December 24, 1820, and died November 17, 1881. He was a successful farmer and at the time of his death was worth about $8,400 that he had accumulated by his own unaided efforts. The mother was born about 1830 and is still living. Our subject grew to manhood on the farm, and at the age of seventeen enlisted in the Confederate Army, Company A, Col. Hill's cavalry regiment. He was in but one battle before the surrender—the battle of Franklin. At the age of twenty-two he and his eldest brother engaged in the stock business, buying and selling horses and cattle, and this they continued very successfully up to 1882. September 24, 1874, he wedded Bettie Bounds, of this county. The results of this union were two children: C. A., born February 7, 1876, and L. P., born December 12, 1879. Mr. Joyce is a good citizen and is scrupulously honest in every particular. He is a law-abiding man; never was sued or had a lawsuit in his life. He and wife are members of the Methodist Episcopal Church South. He is politically a Democrat and a member of the Masonic lodge, which body he joined about 1870.

SAMUEL F. KNOTT, a genial and enterprising citizen of Shelbyville, is a son of Anderson B. and Elizabeth (Tune) Knott. The father is now residing in Chattanooga, where he follows the carpenter's trade. He came to Shelbyville in his childhood and remained here till about 1876, when he removed to Chattanooga. The mother died in 1871. The subject of this sketch was born September 3, 1848, in this county. He secured only a common school education. At the age of fifteen he began clerking in a drug store and continued in that vocation for fourteen years. He then went to Nashville and traveled for William Litterer & Co., wholesale druggists, for nearly five years. He then returned to Shelbyville, and established the drug trade, in which he has met with well deserved success. He carries a stock of about $7,000 and does a large business. He was married in 1870 to Julia B. Steele, a native of this county. Three children have been born to this union, two of whom are living, viz.: Willie and Annie. He is an elder in the Presbyterian Church, and his wife and daughter are also members of that church. For four years he has been an elder of the church, and was a deacon for ten years previous. Politically he is a Republican. He is one of the highly respected, energetic business men of the county.

C. M. KINCAID was born December 24, 1830, in Anderson County Tenn. His father, Clingan Kincaid, was also a native of that county. His paternal grandparents were both natives of Ireland and his maternal grandparents were natives of England, the grandfather serving in the Revolutionary war and when peace was declared took the oath of allegiance to the United States. Our subject was reared on the farm and worked on the same till he was twenty years of age, after which he began working for himself at the same business until the beginning of the late war. He entered the Confederate Army in 1863, enlisting in Company B, Fifth Tennessee Cavalry. At the close of the war he returned home without a wound or without ever having been captured during the time he was in service. Up to the time of the war he had been quite prosperous but that fearful catastrophe swept away nearly all his property. Since that time he has met with many reverses but the scale of fortune finally turned in his favor, and he is now in comparatively good circumstances. Previous to the war, in 1850, he wedded Elizabeth Barnard, of Tennessee. Her father was one of the first settlers of Barnardsville, the town deriving its name from him. To our subject and wife were born eight children: Louisa, Syrene, Sarah G., Clingan, Alta, Erie, Cilena and Albert J. Mr. Kincaid and wife are members of the Primitive Baptist Church, and he is a Democrat in politics.

WILLIAM L. KIMBRO, a merchant of Singleton, Tenn., was born February 8, 1856, and is one of three children born to Riley J. and Martha A. (Span) Kimbro. The father was born and reared in this State, and was by occupation a farmer and mechanic. He was married twice, our subject's mother being his first wife. She was the mother of these children: William L., James and Frederick D., and died in 1861. Mr. Kimbro took for his second wife Mrs. Margaret Raney (nee Robertson), and six children blessed this union: Charles H., Henry, Minnie, Walter, Ira and Zannie. Riley Kimbro was a member of the Lutheran Church, and died October 4, 1885. Our subject had the advantage of a good practical education, and in 1879 was joined in the holy bonds of matrimony to Miss Tennie J. Coleman. The result of this union was four children: Marvin L., Roy E., Argie L. and Hoyt. Roy E. died in 1883. In 1882 Mr. Kimbro engaged in the mercantile business at Singleton, Tenn., and has since that time continued the business at that place. He carries a stock of $1,500, and is doing a business of $3,500, and also runs a blacksmith shop in the same town. He is a member of the Lutheran Church, and is a leading and highly respected citizen.

JACKSON G. KIMERY, a prominent farmer of the Twenty-third District of Bedford County, was born January 30, 1854, son of Edwin and Caroline (Greer) Kimery. The father was a native of North Carolina, and in 1828 he, in company with his father, immigrated to Tennessee, settling on the place where they now reside. Edwin Kimery was the father of nine children, having been twice married. His first wife was Miss Bettie Kiser, and there were four children born to this union. After her death, which occurred some time in 1840, Mr. Kimery married Miss Caroline Greer, our subject's mother, and five children were born to them. Our subject grew to manhood on the farm. At the age of twenty-two he was married to Miss Harriet Parks, daughter of Dr. Parks, and five children blessed their union: Edward L., Alice, Joseph W., Leona and Frederick. Leona and Alice died in 1880 and 1884, respectively. Mr. Kimery has always been a farmer, and has been quite successful in this occupation. He owns 100 acres of good land in a fine state of cultivation.

HENRY H. LANDESS is a native of Tennessee, born July 22, 1818. He resided in Lincoln County, Tenn., until 1851, when he moved to Bedford County. He traveled considerably in Missouri and Arkansas in early life, being absent about six years. Shortly after moving to Bedford County he located on his present farm, consisting of 212 acres of fertile land, furnished with a neat cottage. December 3, 1850, he was married to Lucinda S. Hix, who was born October 6, 1832, and died July 8, 1852, leaving one child—Henry D., born in 1851 and died July 16, 1852. May 24, 1853, Mr. Landess wedded Susan C. Campbell, daughter of Alfred and Sallie (Reeves) Campbell. Mrs. Landess was born May 10, 1835, and has borne her husband the following children: Sarah M., born in 1854; Alfred G., born in 1856; George W., born in 1860; Mary F., born in 1862; Grace C., born in 1865; William G., born in 1867; Mittie M., born in 1872, and Henry H. born in 1875. Mr. Landess is a Democrat in politics, and he and wife are church members. His parents, Henry and Grace (Thompson) Landess, were born in North Carolina and Kentucky in 1777 and 1778, respectively. The father moved to Kentucky in 1789, and there married our subject's mother in 1798, and became the father of thirteen children. They came to Tennessee at an early period, and died in Lincoln County in 1863 and 1801, respectively.

GEORGE L. LANDIS, M. D., was born in Bedford County March, 31, 1847, son of Bryant and Margaret (Ogilvie) Landis. His early days were spent in laboring on his father's farm and in attending the common schools. October 5, 1865, he began the study of medicine with his brother, Dr. J. A. Landis, of Kentucky, and in September, 1869, he entered the Medical University of Nashville, Tenn. He practiced a short time and continued to read under Dr. W. F. Clary, and in the fall of 1870 again entered the University of Nashville, and graduated in March of the following year. Since that time he has practiced in Marshall and Bedford Counties, and since May 7, 1883, has been a resident of Unionville, and is one of the leading physicians of the place. He attended the New York Polyclinic of Medicine and Surgery in the fall of 1885. He was married, November 4, 1875, to Mrs. Carrie Locke, and by her became the father of five children, two of whom are dead. Those living are Alice, Florence and Robbie. Since eleven years of age the Doctor has been a church member, and is now a member of the Methodist Episcopal Church South. In politics he is a Democrat.

CHARLES W. LEFTWICH, although not long a resident of Bedford County, is one of the enterprising dry goods merchants of Shelbyville. He was born in Moore County, Tenn., April 16, 1850. His father, Littleberry Leftwich, was born in this State. He has been a farmer and merchant most of his lifetime, and is now conducting a mercantile trade for Charles W. at Talley, Marshall Co., Tenn. The mother died in 1854. The subject of this sketch was reared on a farm. He received his education mainly in Mulberry Academy of Lincoln County, Tenn. He then taught school about four years. In 1879 he engaged in merchandising in Moore County, Tenn., and continued successfully until the spring of 1885, when he established his business at Talley, which is now conducted by his father. In December, 1885, he began his business here and has continued successfully ever since, with a stock of $10,000 or $12,000 of dry goods and notions, boot and shoes, hats and caps, clothing, etc. He was married, in 1875, to Miss Maggie Morring, of Alabama. This union has been blessed in the birth of five children, four of whom are now living, viz.: Clayton W., Thomas E. Nina P. and Littleberry. Mr. Leftwich and wife are members of the Missionary Baptist Church. Politically he has always been a Democrat.

JAMES M. LENTZ was born in Bedford County February 15, 1828. His father, Benjamin Lentz, was born in 1800 in North Carolina, and immigrated to Tennessee in 1818, settling five and a half miles southwest of Shelbyville, and lived there to the date of his death, which occurred in 1878. Our subject's mother, Penelope (Bussy) Lentz, was born about 1808, and is still living. Our subject grew to manhood on the farm, and received his education in the common district schools. At the age of twenty-one he went to New Orleans, and engaged in the lumber business, remaining there about six or seven years. He then engaged in the carpenter's trade, and continued this business about six or seven years, after which he began farming, and has successfully continued this occupation up to the present time. He was married, February 14, 1861, to Elizabeth Lawell, a native of Tennessee, born April 15, 1837, and to them were born nine children: John H., Samuel J., Robert M., Ethan A., Babe, Mary L. A., Necy, Eddie E., and one died unnamed. Mr. Lentz is politically a Democrat. He is a self-made man, having accumulated his wealth by his own unaided efforts.

DR. THOMAS LIPSCOMB, one of Bedford County's oldest and best citizens, was born in Louisa County, Va., July 22, 1808, to the marriage of William Lipscomb and Ann Day Cook, natives of Spottsylvania and Louisa Counties, Va., respectively. The father was killed by a falling tree in January, 1829, having been a farmer. The mother attained the ripe age of ninety years, and her old age was marked with great vitality. With her own hands she knit over 100 pairs of socks for the Confederate soldiers after she had passed eighty years of age. She lived nearly forty years a widow. The subject of this sketch was reared with his parents on a farm, and received a common school education. At the age of twenty-one he went to Winchester, Tenn., and began the study of medicine. Thence he attended the Medical University of Pennsylvania, at Philadelphia, whither he proceeded and returned the most of the way on horseback. After one course of lectures he returned to Franklin County, Tenn., where his parents had moved in 1826. In 1831 he came to Shelbyville, where he has spent a lifetime in the practice of medicine, surgery and obstetrics, and has attained eminence in his profession. He has been president of the Medical Society of Tennessee, of the Bedford County Medical Society and of the Female Institute at Shelbyville. Since entering into the practice of his profession the honorary title of M. D. has been conferred upon him by the University of Louisville and by the University of Tennessee. He has been successful financially. Since 1855 he has carried on farming. He is the president and largest stockholder of the Victor Mills, of Shelbyville, and was the president of the Branch Bank of Tennessee at Shelbyville at the opening of the war. The advancement of the schools and churches is due greatly to him. For two years he held the Shelbyville postoffice, the emoluments of which he allowed to the widow of a former postmaster. He is not now actively engaged in the practice, but at the age of seventy-three he successfully performed the difficult ovariotomy operation for the first time in his life. He was married, May 22, 1832, to Rebecca Stevenson, who bore him ten children, all of whom were raised. This wife died December 6, 1880, and he then wedded, October 26, 1882, Miss Mary A. Cowan. Dr. Lipscomb and wife are members of the Presbyterian Church, as was his first wife. Politically he is a Democrat, and wields large influence as a worthy citizen of the county.

JACOB LYNN, farmer, was born in Warren County, Tenn., December 23, 1827, son of Andrew J. and Isabella (Hawes) Lynn, and of English extraction. The father of our subject was born in Warren County, Tenn., in 1805, and the mother in Virginia about 1808. They were married about the year 1826, and reared a family of seven children. The father died in Coffee County, Tenn., February 13, 1850, and the mother died in Arkansas in 1865. Jacob Lynn, Sr., the grandfather of our subject, and Benjamin Stinnett, the grandfather of the last Mrs. Lynn, the wife of our subject, were both in the war of 1812, and participated in the battle of New Orleans. Our subject received a practical education in the common schools, and at the age of twenty-one he began business for himself. During the civil war he enlisted in the Twenty-third Tennessee Regiment Infantry, and served eighteen months, participating in the battle of Shiloh, and was discharged at Tupelo, Miss., on account of his age. He has been married four times. The first marriage occurred in 1847 to Miss Sarah Stroud, of Coffee County, Tenn., and resulted in the birth of one son, John A., who was a soldier in the late war. Our subject was married the second time, October 13, 1859, to Mrs. Mary E. L. Giles, daughter of Noble L. Majors. Of this alliance there were two children, one son and one daughter, named, respectively, Joseph T. and Louise Jane. Mrs. Lynn was born July 4, 1820, and died in the same county October 15, 1876. Mr. Lynn was married the third time, September 14, 1877, to Mrs. Mary A. Moses, a native of Tennessee, born March 2, 1832, and died January 26, 1884. His last marriage occurred April 23, 1885, in Bedford County, Tenn., to Miss Rebecca Hill, daughter of Jacob Hill. This lady was born November 24, 1841. Mr. Lynn is a Democrat, and he and wife are members of the Christian Church.

LEVI MADISON'S birth occurred July 1, 1822, in the State of Kentucky. His parents James and Minnie (Loyd) Madison, were also born in Kentucky, and died when our subject was quite young. He made his home with Samuel Thompson until he was fourteen years old and in 1839 went to Texas, where he lived one year and then returned. He worked at the blacksmith's trade in Shelbyville four years and then farmed one year, and then continued his trade seven years. In 1852, he purchased the Ransom Stephens farm, where he lived up to 1883. He then moved to his present place of residence. William D. W. is a son born to his union with Nancy J. Collier, which took place March 22, 1849. She was born in Bedford County, and is a daughter of William and Polly Collier. Our subject has accumulated a comfortable competency by his own unaided efforts, and he and wife are members of the Methodist Episcopal Church South. He is a Republican, and up to the date of the late war was an old-line Whig.

GABRIEL MAUPIN is a native Virginian, born September 7, 1810, and son of Blan and Sallie (Brown) Maupin, who were born in the "Old Dominion" in 1770 and 1772, respectively. They were married about 1790. and became the parents of five sons and five daughters, our subject being the only one living. The family came to Tennessee about 1811, and here the father died in 1829 and the mother in 1852. Our subject has followed farming from boyhood, and in early life was engaged in stock trading. He owns a farm of 500 acres on Duck River, also some valuable property near Shelbyville. His business career has made him well known throughout the county, and he is considered one of its worthy citizens. He was married, September 1, 1844, to Miss Sallie Hickerson, who was born January 2, 1820, daughter of Joseph and Nancy (Russeau) Hickerson. Mrs. Maupin died July 27, 1884, having borne these children: Nancy R., born September 5, 1846; Blan, born November 22, 1847, and died September 7, 1884; Sarah Ann, born March 10, 1849; Joseph H., born August 21, 1851; Gabriel, born September 12, 1853, and died April 15, 1879; Thomas H., born December 18, 1855; Marietta, born Dcember 23, 1858, and Thornton P., born December 23, 1861. Mr. Maupin is a member of the Methodist Church, and is a life-long Democrat.

T. S. MAYES. James Mayes was born about 1788 in Georgia. and came to Tennessee in 1816. He married Polly Sparks, who was a native of Georgia, and our subject was born to them December 16, 1814. He resided on his parents' farm until twenty-one years of age and then began farming on his own responsibility, and has continued very successfully up to the present date. He served the people of his district in the capacity of constable for six years, being first elected in 1840, and in 1852 was elected to the same office for two years. Since that time he has farmed exclusively and has accumulated a good property through his own exertions. Anna Catner became his wife, January 4, 1848, and this union has resulted in ten children, seven of whom are living: Mary E. (Mrs. J. D. Blackwell), Eliza J. (Mrs. W. R. Woodard), William W., John A., Martha A. (Mrs. J. A. Woodard), James L. and Harriett F. Mr. Mayes is a man of great decision of character and is strictly honest and exact in his business transactions. He and Mrs. Mayes are members of the Christian Church and he supports the Democratic party.

WILLIAM McGILL, a prominent farmer and stock raiser of Bedford County, was born May 14, 1820. He is the son of James and Sallie (Parker) McGill. The father of our subject was born in Dublin, Ireland, in 1787, and at an early day immigrated with his father to the United States and settled in Virginia, where he remained several years. He then moved to Rutherford County, Tenn. He was a soldier in the war of 1812, and was in the battle of New Orleans. He was married in 1816, and was the father of seven children: Nancy, William, Lucy, Elizabeth, Sallie, Priscilla and James. The father died in 1860 and the mother in 1884. Our subject was reared on the farm, educated in the country schools, and in 1840 was married to Miss Mary Gardner. Eight children were the result of this union: John A., Sarah J., Robert P., Thomas B., Franklin, Lewis Cass (who died September 28, 1874), Bedford and Tennessee. In 1874 Mr. McGill was elected trustee of Bedford County, which office he held for two terms in a very able manner. He is member of the Christian Church, owns a fine tract of land in the Twenty-third District, and is one of the representative men of the county.

JOHN A. McGILL is the oldest child born to William and Mary (Gardner) McGill- (For particulars of parents see sketch of William McGill). Our subject was born November 1, 1841, and had the advantage of a practical education in the common schools. When the war broke out he enlisted in the Confederate Army in the Seventeenth Tennessee Regiment under Col. Newman, and participated in most of the battles of the war. During the battle at Drury's Bluff he was wounded, and this disabled him for service. He was given a furlough and went to Alabama, where he remained one year. He then came back to Tennessee, and in 1867 was married to Miss Mary E. Terry. To this union one child was born, viz.: Ida I., born January 23, 1870. Mr. McGill and family are consistent members of the Christian Church, and are one of the leading families of the county.

THOMAS B. McGILL, son of W. McGill, whose sketch appears in this work, was born December 15, 1848, in Bedford County. He was reared on a farm and remained with his parents to the age of eighteen. He then engaged as a clerk in a dry goods store in

Shelbyville till 1875. He then went to Nashville and clerked in a wholesale dry goods store for about a year. He then traveled in Kentucky for the Nashville Nursery one year. He then returned to Shelbyville and dealt in live-stock, etc., till 1881, when he established a mercantile trade in the Twenty-third District and secured the establishment of the post-office at Singleton, and held the office in connection with his store three years. In September, 1883, he sold out and farmed for one year. In December, 1885, in connection with James B. Green, he opened the grocery and provision trade in Shelbyville, and the firm does a thriving business. He was married, June 4, 1884, to Miss Kittie Elliott, the result of this union being one son, Robert S. Mr. McGill is a member of the Christian Church, and his wife is a member of Methodist Episcopal Church South. Politically he is a Democrat. He is one of the enterprising and respected citizens of Shelbyville.

E. H. McGOWAN was born and reared in Rutherford County, Tenn. His birth occurred September 26, 1842. At the age of nineteen he entered the Confederate service, enlisting in Company C, Twenty-third Tennessee Regiment, and served out his term of enlistment (twelve months). From that time up to 1869 he farmed, and then engaged in the merchandise business at Poplins' Cross Roads, where he has done well, from a financial standpoint. November 8, 1863, Nancy A. Crowell became his wife and the mother of nine children: Robert F., Henry C., William C., Margaret J., Nancy F., Rebecca W., Florence, Isabella and Eddie. Mrs. McGowan was born in 1844 and died August 30, 1885. Mr. McGowan is a Democrat and is a son of Samuel G. McGowan, who was born in Tennessee, and who married Rebecca Balts. They died, respectively, in 1853 and 1852.

DR. JOSEPH H. McGREW was born February 13, 1826, in Bedford County, Tenn., being the youngest of eleven children of William McGrew. The father was a native of Kentucky, and when young went to South Carolina, where he married Nancy Goodwin. In 1811 they came to Bedford County, where they lived and died, the father being a farmer. The father's death occurred in 1852, and the mother's in 1860. Our subject was reared on a farm. When seventeen years of age he came to Shelbyville, and began the study of medicine in 1844. He attended lectures in Louisville in 1845-46, and in Philadelphia in 1846-47, graduating in March, 1847. He then returned to Shelbyville, and has since been engaged in the practice of medicine successfully. He was married, in 1851, to Letitia Cannon, who bore him two children: James H. and Samuel J. The wife died in 1857, and January 31, 1866, he was married to Mary B. Evans. Himself and wife are members of the Missionary Baptist Church. He is a member of the F. & A. M. and I. O. O. F. fraternities. Politically he is a firm Republican. Dr. McGrew is examining surgeon in the pension service, and ranks among the able practitioners of the county. He is now practicing with his younger son, Samuel J., who was born December 11, 1854. He (S. J.) studied medicine with his father. He attended lectures in the University of Pennsylvania, graduating in 1881, and has proven himself well-informed in his profession. He is a member of the Missionary Baptist Church. Politically he is a Republican.

JAMES W. C. MITCHELL, a merchant of the Twenty-fourth District of this county, was born January 29, 1842, son of T. F. and Margaret (Binkley) Mitchell. The father was a native of North Carolina, and in early life immigrated to Alabama and settled in Huntsville, where he was married. He was the father of eleven children: Sarah A. (deceased), John (deceased), Mary, Martha, James W. C., Joseph (deceased), Robert H., Bates, Nancy, Logan and Elizabeth. Joseph Mitchell was killed in the battle of Franklin and was buried at Columbia. Our subject's father is still living at the advanced age of eighty-six. James W. C. Mitchell was reared on the farm, given an education in the country schools and when in his eighteenth year entered the Confederate Army in the Thirty-seventh Tennessee Infantry; was in the battles of Perryville, Chickamauga, Atlanta, Murfreesboro, Franklin and others, and was wounded twice. After the war he came back to this county and has since that time resided here. In 1873 Miss Catharine Bomar became his wife. The results of this union were four children: Oscar L., James W., Bibbie B. and one not named. In 1875 Mr. Mitchell went into the mercantile business in the Twenty-fourth District, and in 1881 went into the distillery business at the same place, making about sixty-five gallons of whisky per day, and is doing a $3,000 business.

BIOGRAPHICAL APPENDIX.

ROBERT S. MONTGOMERY was born November 30, 1829, in South Carolina, and is a son of Thomas Montgomery, who was born in 1808 and is of Irish parentage. He came to Tennessee in 1844, locating near Palmetto and in 1854 erected a dwelling-house, in which our subject now lives. Robert S. began to reside permanently in the State in 1855, and the same year engaged in merchandise business with Samuel Carpenter, continuing up to the date of the late war. After its close they again resumed business and, in 1874, T. S. Montgomery purchased Mr. Carpenter's interest, the style of the firm being then changed to Montgomery Bros. In 1885 they sold out to J. O. Montgomery, a cousin. March 13, 1855, he married Miss Susan Dysart, daughter of James P. and Leah Dysart. To Mr. and Mrs. Montgomery were born eight children: Alice E. (Mrs. J. F. Tillman), Mary (deceased), Jimmie (deceased), Thomas A., Lillie (wife of Dr. W. C. Ransom), Denny, Gertrude Inez and Robert H. Mrs. Montgomery died April 19, 1881. He is a Republican and a strict member of the Presbyterian Church.

T. S. MONTGOMERY was born March 30, 1843, in the "Palmetto State." At the age of fifteen he left home and engaged in the dry goods business, clerking for his brother Robert S. at Palmetto. He entered Union Academy at the end of eighteen months, where he remained about ten months. He then returned and remained with his brother until the war. At its close he again resumed his clerkship and at the end of two years commenced farming. From 1868 to 1874 he was in the mercantile business at Farmington, but then returned to Palmetto, and in 1885 he and his brother sold out to their cousin. Since 1882 he has served as magistrate of his district. September 27, 1866, he wedded Magie L. Hagle, daughter of Peter and Esther Hagle. They have five children: Flora Esther, T. Clarence, Ethel, Susie and Hoyle. Mr. Montgomery is a Republican and a member of the United Presbyterian Church.

DR. GEORGE W. MOODY, a leading physician of Shelbyville, was born November 5, 1848, being a son of Samuel S. Moody (see sketch of C. J. Moody). He was reared with his parents to the age of twenty-one, and had begun the study of medicine. In 1869 he graduated in the University of Pennsylvania at Philadelphia. He then located in Shelbyville, where he has met with justly-deserved success in the practice of his profession. He was married, March 16, 1861, to Miss Georgie Strong, a native of this county. Her parents were from northern Alabama, and her mother is the daughter of Gen. Moore, of Tullahoma, Tenn. Dr. Moody's married life has been blessed in the birth of two children, viz.: Winston G. and Samuel S. Himself and wife are members of the Methodist Episcopal Church South, and he is steward and trustee of the same. He is a member of the Medical Society of Tennessee, a Democrat in politics, and is a worthy and highly respected citizen of the county.

CLEMENT J. MOODY, one of Bedford County's prominent attorneys is a son of Samuel S. and Letitia (Cannon) Moody. The father was born in Henry County, Tenn. He was a minister in the Methodist Episcopal Church and was a member of the general conference of 1844, when the churches divided and he adhered to the Methodist Episcopal Church South. He was one of the most eminent ministers of the church and for many years was presiding elder of this district conference. He held very prominent positions in various places. His death occurred May 7, 1863. The mother was a niece of Gov. Newton Cannon, and her father was one of the most prominent pioneers of this county, and gave the land whereon the town of Shelbyville was built. She died July 24, 1880. The subject of this sketch received a good early education, graduating at the Centre College, Kentucky, in 1865. He then read law in Shelbyville and in 1867 graduated in the law department of the Cumberland University at Lebanon, Tenn. He was then admitted to the Bedford County bar and has been justly successful in the profession, ranking among the leading criminal lawyers of the State. He was married January 18, 1881, to Miss Sally C. M. Cannon, daughter of John T. Cannon, whose sketch appears in this work. Mr. Moody and wife are members of the Methodist Episcopal Church South. Mr. Moody is a Royal Arch Mason and Past Grand Master of the Shelbyville Lodge. Politically he is a firm Democrat, and is one of the leading spirits in his party.

JOHN R. MOON, M. D., is the eldest of seven children born to the union of Pleasant B. and Mary Ann Moon. His birth occurred November 12, 1853. He received good educational advantages, and attended the Unionville Academy. He began studying medicine when quite young, and in October, 1876, entered a medical college, from which he graduated in March, 1878. He practiced his chosen profession about three years with average success, and in May, 1882, he located in Poplin's Cross Roads, where he has since lived and established a good practice. William U., born November 26, 1877; Bertha Erie, born January 6, 1880; James P., born November 1, 1881; John R., born September 1, 1883, and Mary Myrtle, born May 29, 1885, are the children born to his union with Mattie M. Dryden, which took place May 7, 1876. Dr. Moon and wife are members in good standing of the Methodist Episcopal Church South, and in his political views he is a Republican.

Q. E. MORTON was born September 25, 1835, in Bedford County, Tenn., and is the son of Jacob and Annie (Fisher) Morton. The father was born February 17, 1787, in North Carolina, immigrated to Tennessee about 1814, and engaged in the blacksmith trade. He was the first alderman of Shelbyville. The mother was also a native of North Carolina, and her marriage to Jacob Morton, September 12, 1815, resulted in the birth of fourteen children. Our subject grew to manhood on the farm, and at the age of twenty began farming for himself, and this he continued very successfully up to the time of the late war. In the spring of 1861 he enlisted in the Confederate Army, in the Twenty-third Tennessee Infantry, remaining but thirteen months in the regular service, when he was appointed sutler of his regiment. He was soon captured, and upon being released returned home and engaged in agricultural pursuits, which he has continued up to the present time. Previous to the war, in 1855, he wedded Nancy M. Jackson, of this county. To them were born seven children: John J.; Martha E., wife of E. C. Barnes; Mark J., a practicing physician of Center Grove, who was born September 8, 1864, and graduated from the medical department of the State University, of Nashville. Prior to entering the university he had studied medicine for three years. He has at present quite a good practice, which is constantly increasing. The fourth child of our subject is Q. Emmet; sixth, Rufus H., seventh Nannie R. and eighth James L. Mr. Morton is a Republican, and he and wife are members of the Primitive Baptist Church. He was elected magistrate in 1882, and this office he filled in a highly satisfactory manner.

EDWARD A. MOSELEY, JR., farmer, is a son of Thomas G. and Mary T. (Sikes) Moseley, and was born in Bedford County, Tenn., February 17, 1850, of English and Welsh descent. The father was born in Limestone County, Ala., December 13, 1824, and was married December 16, 1846. To them were born nine children. Thomas G. Moseley served in the commissary department of the Confederate Army under Maj. James F. Cummings. He served one term in the Confederate Legislature of Tennessee as a member of the House of Representatives. He was a member of the Senate in the Thirty-ninth General Assembly representing Bedford and Rutherford Counties. He was a Henry Clay Whig prior to the war but has been fully identified with the Democratic party since that time. Our subject's early days were spent on a farm and in attending the common schools, after which he took a business and commercial course in Bryant & Stratton's Commercial College at Nashville, Tenn. June 30, 1869, he wedded Miss Mattie Thomas, born August 12, 1852, daughter of William Thomas, born in 1807 and died in 1861, and Jane (McCrary) Thomas, born in 1816 and died in 1882. To them were born the following interesting family: Jesse T. L. P., Mary S., Maggie E., Janie T., Carrie Drue, Mattie Louise and Bessie. Mr. Moseley is a Democrat and a member of the Masonic fraternity. He and wife and three eldest daughters belong to the Missionary Baptist Church. Mr. Moseley is the owner of 200 acres of land, and the most of his attention is given to raising Norman and Clydesdale horses, of which he has many fine specimens.

GEORGE P. MUSE, farmer, was born in Bedford County, Tenn., January 29, 1844, and is the son of Orville and Malinda M. (Ross) Muse. His father was born in Virginia November 13, 1806, and his mother was born in South Carolina April 26, 1809. The Muse family are among the early settlers of the State, coming here when Tennessee was but a wilderness. Our subject lives on a farm adjoining the one his grandfather settled on after immigrating to this State. Our subject is the sixth in a family of ten children born to his parents. He was reared on the farm and received a fair practical education. He enlisted in the Second Regiment Tennessee Infantry, Confederate States Army, under Col. (now Gov.) Bate, at the youthful age of sixteen, and served throughout the entire war. He participated in the battles of first Manassas, Shiloh and Richmond, Ky. He was severely wounded in the latter engagement, captured and paroled within the Federal lines. After recovering sufficiently he was taken to Camp Douglas, where he was held three months and then exchanged. He then joined his regiment in Tennessee. After this he was clerk in Cleburne's commissary department, and was again captured while retreating from Dalton. He was held in Rock Island, Ill., until near the close of the war. Since the war our subject has served the public fourteen years; six years in the capacity of constable, four years as sheriff and four years as deputy-sheriff. November 8, 1866, he wedded Miss Mary J. Wright, of Bedford County, Tenn., and the daughter of Whitfield Wright. Their children are seven in number—four sons and three daughters. Mr. Muse has a fine farm of 110 acres, and he is a Democrat, an Odd Fellow, a Knight of Honor and a Royal Arcanum. Mrs. Muse and one son are members of the Methodist Episcopal Church South.

WILL J. MUSE, clerk of the County Court of Bedford County, was born December 5, 1844, near Shelbyville. The Muse family originated in the United States from two brothers, James and George Muse, who came from England to North Carolina. George went to Virginia and James remained in North Carolina. Our subject is a descendant of the latter. The father of Will J. was Jo C. Muse, and the mother was Mary A. Muse, the parents being cousins. The father was a farmer and mechanic, and was identified with the public interests of this county. The maternal grandfather, John T. Muse, was, when quite young, among the first settlers of this State. He was an able minister of the Missionary Baptist Church, and founded the first church of that denomination in this county. He died suddenly while in the preparation of a sermon, having eloquently preached away a lifetime. Will J. was reared on a farm and had limited educational advantages. At the age of seventeen he entered Company B, of Turney's First Tennessee and served throughout the war. He was promoted from a private to the captaincy of his company. He received eleven wounds, three of which were very serious. Returning from the army he attended school three years and taught one year. For three years he then clerked in a store. Subsequently he and a brother engaged in merchandising till 1882. He was elected to his office in August, 1882, and has filled it with general satisfaction to his constituents. He was married in 1872 to Nannie Russell, the results of this union being two children: Henry Kirk White and Georgie Avva. Both Mr. Muse and his wife are members of the Missionary Baptist Church. He is a member of the I. O. O. F. In politics he is a firm Democrat.

THOMAS NANCE is a son of Clements Nance, of Bedford County, Tenn., who was born in 1810 and spent his boyhood on a farm. He received a practical education, and wedded Mary Tune, daughter of William Tune, of Virginia, and to them were born William T., Thomas, Mary, Reuben and Clement. Three of the children are now living. In 1826 Mr. Nance immigrated to Tennessee, locating near Shelbyville, where he engaged in agricultural pursuits. In 1833 Mr. Nance went to Missouri and died in Ray County in 1841. Thomas Nance, our subject, was born October 17, 1837, in Missouri. He came to Tennessee when he was but seven years of age, and his early days were spent in laboring on a farm and in attending the common schools of his neighborhood. He began blacksmithing and followed that occupation for about twenty years. In 1872 he moved to where he now resides. December 14, 1859, he wedded Miss Sarah B. Coates, daughter of P. H. Coates, and six children have been born to their union: Thomas H., James E., Julia E., Carrie E., William G. and Martha E., all of whom are living. In 1883 Mr. Nance was elected magistrate of his district and is filling the duties of that office at the present time. Mr. Nance is a Mason, and he and Mrs. Nance are members of the Missionary Baptist Church.

P. W. NORMAN was born June 20, 1818, and spent his boyhood days on a farm, receiving a common school education. He began life as a farmer, and was married in 1840 to Miss T. E. Webb, daughter of Isaac Webb, of Rutherford County, and six children have blessed their union: Elizabeth A., Catharine J., Sarah G., Amanda R. and James L., and one who died in infancy. Mrs. Norman died in 1874, and Mr. Norman took for his second wife Mrs. Fannie E. (Smith) Webb. Her father, Morgan Smith, died at his home near Shelbyville, October 4, 1875. He was a Democrat. Mr. Norman's last marriage occurred November 2, 1884. His wife is a member of the Methodist Episcopal Church South, and he belongs to the Masonic fraternity. His father, Henry Norman, was born in the ' Palmetto State," and came to Tennessee with his father when he was but nine years of age. He was married when quite young to Elizabeth Aubery, and by her became the father of seven children, only two of whom are now living. Mrs. Norman died in 1850, and her husband took for his second wife Mrs. Sallie White, in 1851. She died in 1854, and he then married, in 1857, Mrs. Becky Caldwell. Mr. Norman died in 1867.

W. C. ORR and family reside in the Eighth Civil District of Bedford County, Tenn., six miles north of Shelbyville, their home being located on the Middletown road. The family consists of the father, above named, born February 14, 1829, and four children: William M., born November 6, 1854; David F., born June 6, 1859; Mary A., born March 18, 1862, and Minnie J., born August 3, 1866. There are two vacancies in the family, caused by the death of the mother, Temperance Orr (*nee* Miller), born in August, 1830, and died May 14, 1876, and John Fain, the eldest child, who died in infancy. W. C. Orr is of Scotch-Irish descent, and is a son of John and Penelope (Morgan) Orr, who were early settlers of Bedford County, being emigrants from the Carolinas. Mr. Orr is a farmer, and served as magistrate of his district from 1870 to 1876. His wife was a daughter of Nathaniel Miller, of Rutherford County, and married our subject in 1854. She was a member of the Primitive Baptist Church. Mr. Orr obtained a fair education in the common branches, and became an adept in penmanship, which he taught a few years. In 1878 he began the study of medicine under Drs. Evans & Fite, of Shelbyville, and the same year attended lectures in the medical department of the Vanderbilt University, of Nashville, Tenn., and read and practiced at home until the fall of 1881, when he attended his second course in the same institution and took his degree at the close of the spring term of 1882. Returning home he located with his father, where he has since practiced his chosen profession. D. F. Orr, son of W. C. Orr, received a common school education, and attended the Shelbyville Normal and High School for three years, and graduated in 1879. He afterward taught in the various public schools of Bedford and Rutherford Counties, and in the fall of 1884 attended his first course of lectures in the Vanderbilt University. He returned home and taught school eight months, and then returned to college and graduated at the close of the session in 1886. Mary A. Orr also received a good education, having attended the Shelbyville Normal and High School, the Soule Female College at Murfreesboro and the Winchester Normal College. For several years she has been teaching in Bedford and Rutherford Counties. Minnie J. Orr attended school two years at the Winchester Normal, and is now teaching her first school.

ISAIAH PARKER, farmer and stock raiser, was born June 5, 1830. He is the son of Joseph and Fana (Howard) Parker. The father was a native of South Carolina, born in 1805. In 1819 he immigrated to Tennessee and settled in Lincoln County, where he remained until 1828. From there he went to Bedford County and bought land in the Twenty-second District. He was a farmer and stock raiser, and at his death, which occurred in 1885, he was worth a large amount of property, owning a large number of slaves before the war. He was a member of the Primitive Baptist Church. The mother was born in Virginia August 12, 1812, and died August 12, 1859. The family is of English-Irish descent. Our subject was born in Lincoln County, received a limited education, and was married to Miss Mary Razier, a native of this county. To them were born eight children: Charles G., B., A. F., Edward, Joseph, Lizzie, Dora and Willie. Mr. Parker is one of the substantial farmers of the county, owning about 1,200 acres of fine land. He is a firm Democrat and a leading citizen. From 1854 to 1859 he was postmaster in Lincoln County. He was also colonel of the militia in 1858, and was justice of the peace about the same time.

GEORGE W. PARSONS was born in 1821 in the State of Tennessee. His father, G. W. Parsons, was born in Virginia in 1788 and came to Tennessee in 1807, and here married our subject's mother, Margaret Fisher, in 1809. They became the parents of thirteen children—four daughters and nine sons. The father was a farmer and millwright by trade, and served in the war of 1812. He died in 1842 and the mother in 1854. Our subject began farming for himself at the age of twenty years, and in 1843 purchased part of his present farm, which he has increased to 247 acres. In 1857 he was elected justice of the peace of his district and held the office until 1870. In 1882 he was again elected, and has held the office up to the present time. He has been a director of the Shelbyville & Unionville Pike for the past twelve years, and is a stockholder in the same. He is well known throughout the county and has been a member of the Lutheran Church since 1849. He belongs to the Masonic lodge, No. 315, and in politics is an old Whig-Democrat. He was married in 1843 to Elizabeth Allison, who was born in Tennessee in 1825 and is the daughter of Robert and Elizabeth (White) Allison. To them were born these children: Mary F., born in 1844; Anna L., born in 1846; Michael F., born in 1850; William J., born in 1848 and died in 1866; Volney S., born in 1852; Sarah E., born in 1854; Cynthia J. born in 1856; John C., born in 1860; Safrone A., born in 1862; George N., born in 1865, and Bunie C., born in 1868.

JOHN W. PARSONS is a son of George W. and Margaret (Fisher) Parsons (see G. W. Parsons for father's sketch), and was born in Bedford County, Tenn., January 3, 1824, and has spent the greater part of his life on a farm. At the age of twenty-two he left home and began the battle of life for himself, and by his energy and perseverance accumulated considerable property. In 1846 he located on his present farm of 343 acres, and erected a neat residence. He lost considerable property in the late war, but did not participate in that struggle. October 6, 1846, he married Ruth C. Allison, daughter of Robert and Elizabeth (White) Allison. She was born August 12, 1818, and bore her husband the following children: George A., born in 1848; Robert, born in 1850; William C., born in 1853; Sarah J., born in 1854; Mary E., born in 1856 and died in 1873; Newton H., born in 1858. June 20, 1881, Mrs. Parsons died, and Mr. Parsons then led to Hymen's altar Catharine Sanders, daughter of Alexander and Jane (Robinson) Sanders, who were born in Kentucky and Tennessee, respectively. Mrs. Parsons was born August 10, 1838, and is a member of the Methodist Episcopal Church South. Mr. Parsons is a stanch supporter of Democracy.

GRANVILLE C. PEARSON, farmer, was born in Rutherford County, Tenn., July 20, 1831, son of Hiram and Matilda B. (Wilson) Pearson, and of English descent. The father was born in Pittsylvania County, Va., April 9, 1797, and in the year 1819 he wedded Matilda Wilson, who was born in Sumner County, Tenn,, May 12, 1802. The father died November 29, 1876, and the mother February 14, 1877. To this worthy couple were born ten children, our subject being the sixth. The Pearson family was among the early settlers of Tennessee, the father of our subject having settled in Rutherford County in 1818. Our subject received a fair education in the common schools, and at the breaking out of the late war he enlisted in the Confederate Army, Fourth Tennessee Cavalry, under Col. Starnes. He took an active part in the battles of Chickamauga, Knoxville, Resaca and other actions. He was with Gen. Forrest when he captured the large Federal forces under command of Gen. Straight, and was a member of Jefferson Davis' escort from Raleigh, N. C., to Washington, Ga. He has now in his possession eighteen Mexican silver dollars of the coinage of 1861, which were paid to him by the order of President Davis for services in the army. These he prizes very highly as relics of that memorable struggle. Our subject has a fine farm of 110 acres, on which he lives, surrounded with the general comforts of life. He devotes the principal part of his time and attention to raising fine stock—horses, cattle and mules. The father of our subject was among the most enterprising stock raisers of his locality, owning at one time 500 acres of land, but lost heavily in the war.

THOMAS B. PHILPOTT, son of Charles T. and Rebecca (Hix) Philpott, was born in Bedford County, December 7, 1847. His father was a native of Virginia, immigrating to this State with his father when quite young, and settled in Bedford County. He was a saddler by occupation, and worked at his trade forty-five years in this county. He is now living at the advanced age of eighty-four years, and is the father of ten children: William, John H., Sarah (deceased) Joshua A. (deceased), Demarcus (deceased), Elisha C. (deceased), Nancy A., Charles N. (deceased), James and Thomas B. Our subject grew to manhood on the farm, and was educated in the common schools. In 1864 he was married to Miss McFarland, and nine children blessed this union: Rebecca E., Charles N., Edward L., Nancy A. James, Jacob, Ernest, Minnie and William, all living. Our subject has all his life followed agricultural pursuits and has been quite successful. He now owns 360 acres of finely improved land in the Twenty-third District, and is a leading man of the county.

M. P. PICKLE was born August 24, 1838, in Farmington, Marshall Co., Tenn. His father, Maj. Pickle, a native of Bedford County, was born in 1813, and was a successful farmer. He died in March, 1862, in this county. Our subject's mother, Catherine Pickle, was born in Williamson County in 1813, and is still living at the advanced age of seventy-three. Our subject remained with his parents on the farm until he was twenty years of age. He then engaged in farming for himself. In 1869 he engaged in the merchandise business in this county, which he continued for about six years. He then moved his business to Rich Creek, Marshall County, where he sold goods for about two years, after which he sold his interest and again returned to agricultural pursuits, together with stock raising. Since 1884 he has been engaged in the lumber business, shipping cedar lumber exclusively. July 29, 1859, he was married to Mary Ann Frances Atkisson, of this county, who was born April 23, 1837. This union resulted in the birth of nine children, two of whom, Andrew and Murry F., are dead. The names of the seven living are, respectively, Major A., James M., George W., Sarah E., Henry J., Annie C. and Minerva P. Our subject's educational advantages were not of the best, consequently he received but a district school education. Owing to this he has always felt a deep interest in all enterprises pertaining to the education of the rising generation. He and wife are members of the Missionary Baptist Church, of which he was ordained deacon about 1868. He has always been a peaceful, quiet man, and has never been summoned before the court for any misdemeanor whatever. He is a Republican in politics.

M. A. PICKLE, a native of Bedford County, Tenn., was born April 11, 1859, son of P. Murry and Mary Ann Frances (Atkisson) Pickle. (For further particulars of parents see sketch of M. P. Pickle.) Our subject worked on the farm with his father and received a rather limited education. At the age of nineteen he entered the high school at Palmetto, Tenn., and continued there two years. He then engaged in farming in connection with school-teaching, working on the farm in the spring and teaching in the fall. This he continued for about four years, after which he engaged in the merchandise business at Bedford with very flattering prospects. January 5, 1881, he wedded Ella Dryden, of this county, and to this union was born one child—William Franklin. Our subject is a good citizen and an honorable man. He is a member of the United Brethren Church, and Mrs. Pickle a member of the Methodist Episcopal Church North. In politics he is a Republican, but strictly speaking he is not a party man.

C. B. RANEY, farmer, of Bedford County, was born June 18, 1838, son of John W. and Catharine (Rolinson) Raney. The father was a native of Virginia, born in 1806, and immigrated to this county at an early day, settling in Bedford County. He was the father of a family of eight children, six of whom lived to be grown. John W. Raney was a farmer, and was accidentally killed in 1841. He was a worthy member of the Free-Will Baptist Church. The mother is still living. Our subject grew to manhood on the farm, and in 1865 began working for himself. Previous to this he had enlisted in the Confederate

Army, in the Forty-first Tennessee Regiment, and in 1861 was elected lieutenant in the company, but gave up his position to make harmony in the ranks, and acted as orderly sergeant. He was again elected lieutenant, and was soon made second lieutenant of the company. He was captured at Fort Donelson and carried to Camp Morton, where he remained eight months. He was then exchanged, and went back into service, and was in the battles of Vicksburg, Jackson, Raymond, Port Hudson, Corinth, Chickamauga and numerous other important battles, as his regiment was never in any important engagement without him. In 1878 he was married to Miss Victoria Campbell, and to this union two children were born: Eunice and William. In politics he is a stanch Democrat.

GEORGE W. READ was born in Dyer County, Tenn., November 29, 1824, and is a son of Robert and Elizabeth (Gentry) Read. The father was born October 28, 1796, in Virginia, and immigrated to Tennessee about 1802. He remained in this State up to the time of his death, which occurred in December, 1883. The mother was born in 1802 and died about 1841. Our subject's educational advantages were rather limited, but, notwithstanding, he is considered a man of sound judgment and good sense. September 30, 1846, he wedded Ann E. Brooks, of Rutherford County, Tenn., and the result of this union was the birth of eleven children: Sarah E., Robert C., Mary J., Martha W., Ann E., James C., John B., William L., Lou H., Aldora and George S. The five eldest died within ten days of each other, of scarlet fever. The tenth died in early childhood. Mr. Read has been very successful in his businesss transactions. He is scrupulously honest and honorable in every particular. He is a member of the Methodist Episcopal Church. He is a Democrat in politics.

J. C. READ was born February 3, 1859, in this State. He is the son of G. W., and Ann Eliza (Brooks) Read. (For further particulars of parents see sketch of G. W. Read.) Our subject was reared on the farm and assisted his father until he was twenty-two years of age. In 1882 and 1883 he was sight seeing, traveling over Texas, Arkansas, Missouri, Mississippi, Alabama and Kentucky. Upon returning home he engaged in agricultural pursuits and this he continued until 1885 at which time he engaged in the merchandising business at Center Grove, in partnership with his brother, W. L. Read. December 18, 1881, our subject wedded Callie J. Bullock, of this county, and to them were born three children: Richard L., Robert A. and George W. Mr. Read is an energetic and active young business man, and has the power and determination to make his mark in the world. Politically he is a Democrat.

ROBERT REAVES, a farmer and stock raiser, of the Twenty-third District of Bedford County, was born November 14, 1833, and is the son of Isom and Rachel (Morgan) Reaves. The father was a native of North Carolina and when a young man immigrated to Bedford County, Tenn., and settled in the Twenty-third District. He was a farmer and stock raiser, and was successful in all his undertakings. He was worth considerable property at the time of his death, which occurred January 1, 1871. He was the father of five children: Benjamin, John, Robert, Frances M. and Jane. Isom Reaves was twice married, his first wife being a Miss Chaney Coggens; three children were born to them, all dead but one, named William. Our subject was reared on the farm and received a limited education in the common schools. In 1855 Miss Martha Morgan became his wife, and this union resulted in the birth of five children: Bettie F., Mary J., Robert A., Dulcenia and Emmet. Mary J. died in 1869 and Robert A. died the same year. When the war broke out our subject acted as escort to Gen. Forrest. He was under Capt. Little and participated in all the battles in which his command was engaged. He owns a fine tract of land and is one of the leading citizens of the county.

WILLIAM RUSSELL, editor of the *Bedford County Times*, was born April 27, 1852, being the son of B. L. and Ermine (Clark) Russell, natives of Kentucky. The father is a retired citizen of Shelbyville, Tenn., and during active life was a merchant tailor by avocation. Mr. Russell is a practical printer, and has held positions on the following papers: The *American Union, American Reserve, Commercial, Gazette*, of Shelbyville, and on the *Rural Sun*, of Nashville, the Clarksville *Tobacco Leaf*, Pulaski *Citizen*, Fayettville *Ex-*

press and Chatanooga *Times*. The Bedford *Times* was established in February, 1886, and is in a flourishing condition.

ROBERT COLUMBUS RUSS, editor and proprietor of the Shelbyville (Tenn.) *Commercial*, was born in Fayetteville, N. C., September 5, 1824, being one of twelve children—six boys and six girls—born to James and Eunice (Steeley) Russ, both natives of North Carolina; the former being born June 29, 1790, and the latter October 17, 1791, and both of whom died in Shelbyville, Tenn. Our subject's paternal grandparents were William and Hannah Russ, the former being a native of Russia, and the latter of Scotland; and his maternal grandparents were William and Lexy Steeley. Only three of the twelve children born to our subject's parents are living, viz.: Our subject, his brother, A. J. Russ, and his sister, Mary Jane Fausett. Our subject set in to learn the "art preservative" in 1840 with his brother James and William L. Berry, in Fayetteville, and began editing and publishing a paper in Shelbyville in 18—, and has continued in that capacity to the present, having published eight papers altogether. Our subject was married to Euphamie M., daughter of John Crawford, at Cedar Springs, Marshall Co., Tenn., December 14, 1848, and to them have been born twelve children—six boys and six girls—all of whom have died except four boys and one girl. The *Commercial* is the oldest newspaper in Shelbyville, is Democratic, and wields considerable influence as a local and party paper.

L. H. RUSS was born in Lewisburg, Tenn., March 3, 1843. His father, James Russ, was a printer and publisher. He came to Bedford County in 1847 and established a newspaper and continued to publish papers until his death in 1869. The mother was Margaret E. Laird. She died in 1857. Our subject was reared in Shelbyville and learned the printer's trade. In 1869 he, with a brother, established the *Shelbyville Commercial* and published that paper one year. He then engaged in the grocery business a short time. From 1870 to 1873, he was not settled in any regular business. In 1873 he established the wagon and buggy manufactory which he yet runs. He manufactures the New South wagons, buggies, carriages, etc. He has a stock of about $6,000, and does about $12,000 annual business. He was married in October, 1869, to Theodosia H. Hobbs, daughter of George W. and Sarah Hobbs, residents of this county. Five children have been born to this union, three of whom are now living: George H., James L. and Lucy E. Those who died were Harry L. and Thomas B. Mr. and Mrs. Russ are members of the Methodist Episcopal Church South, and Mr. Russ is a Royal Arch Mason and a member of the I. O. O. F. He was one of the "boys in gray," serving in Forrest's escort from 1863 till December, 1864, when he was captured and held a prisoner till the close of the war. He was fourth corporal of the escort.

JOHN W. RUTH, the clever and enterprising jeweler of Shelbyville, was born February 27, 1839, in Shelbyville, being a son of George W. Ruth. The father was born in Granville County, N. C., in 1799. A short time before George Washington died, when on his last Southern tour, he passed by the house where George W. Ruth was born only a short time before. He stopped and lifted the infant in his arms, and then and there it was named George Washington Ruth in remembrance of the incident and of the great man. The father came to this county in 1822. He married, lived and died here, being a jeweler by occupation. He was a very prominent citizen of the county, and for many years was a magistrate. He was mayor of Shelbyville two terms, and was identified with the public interests all his life. He was a leading member of the Methodist Episcopal Church, and for many years was a steward. Politically he was a Democrat. His death occurred in August, 1858. His father was a soldier in the Revolutionary war. The mother of John W. was born in Baltimore County, Md., and came to Shelbyville when quite young. She was born in 1804 and died in 1863. The ancestry of John W. were of Scotch-Irish descent, predominating in Scotch blood. The immediate subject of this sketch was reared in Shelbyville and learned his father's trade, which has been his life time business. He is also joined by his son in the business now, the name of the firm being John W. Ruth & Son. He was elected to the office of mayor of Shelbyville in 1873, and served till 1875. In 1885 he was re-elected to the same office, and is now the incumbent. He was married, in 1865, to Miss Fannie E. Newton, who bore him three children, viz.: Albert H., Anne C. and Weakley D. Mr. Ruth and his two oldest children are members of the Methodist Episcopal Church South. He is a Knight Templar Mason and a Knight of Honor. Politically he is a Democrat, but conservative in his views. He is a popular, genial and enterprising citizen of Shelbyville.

JOHN W. RUTLEDGE, SR., one of Bedford County's farmers, was born January 12, 1823, in Bedford County, being a son of John and Sarah Davenport Rutledge, natives of South Carolina. The parents were married in their native State and came to Bedford County in the very early settlement of the county. John W. was reared on a farm and secured but a common school education, the schools then being in an undeveloped condition. He began farming for himself when grown, and at the age of twenty-seven married. He continued to farm and deal in live-stock extensively. He now owns 108 acres of land, with seventy-five acres under cultivation. He was married November 22, 1849, to Eunice M. Warner, daughter of John and Eunice (Dixon) Warner, natives of North Carolina. They came to Sumner County, Tenn., when small, and thence to Bedford County, where they lived and died. The father was born in 1783, and the mother in 1792; they were married November 11, 1810. The father was a sheriff of Bedford County for many years; he was a farmer by occupation. He died May 17, 1834, and the mother died October 2, 1852. Mr. and Mrs. Rutledge are parents of four children, viz.: John G., who died young; Warner G.; Eunice M., the wife of Thomas L. Thompson, and John W. All the family are members of the Missionary Baptist Church, and all are Democrats in politics. Warner G. Rutledge was married December 4, 1874, to Miss Julia L. Phillips, who died January 16, 1876, after becoming the mother of a child, Julia L., who also died July 16, 1876. He is store-keeper and gauger in the revenue service in the Middle and West Divisions of Tennessee.

RUTLEDGE & THOMPSON, dealers in a general line of groceries and provisions in Shelbyville, do a leading business in the town. The firm is composed of John W. Rutledge, Jr., and Thomas L. Thompson. John W. Rutledge, Jr., was born July 20, 1860, being a son of John W. Rutledge, Sr. He was married, December 26, 1884, to Katie Nease, the result of this union being one son, John H. Mr. Rutledge is captain of the Shelbyville Hook and Ladder Company and an enterprising young business man. Thomas L. Thompson was born August 4, 1850, to the marriage of Thomas Thompson and Tranquilla Stephens. Both parents were natives of Bedford County, the mother being of North Carolina ancestry. The father was a farmer and Thomas L. was reared on a farm. He was married, February 25, 1875, to Miss Eunice M. Rutledge, daughter of John W. Rutledge, Sr. Four children have been born to this union, viz.: Thomas L., Mary A., John W. and Hiram S. The firm of Rutledge & Thompson was established October 24, 1878. They were burned out October 22, 1885, and are now preparing to build a commodious brick building. They also deal in mules and fine horses.

ALBERT P. RYALL, M. D., son of Thomas C. and Elizabeth (Scudder) Ryall, was born March 30, 1840. His father was a native of New Jersey, born in April, 1809. Eight children were born to him, viz.: Johnston S., Albert P., Walter S., Thomas, Henry C., Elizabeth R. (deceased), Juliet S. and William (deceased). Mrs. Elizabeth Ryall died in August, 1856. She was a worthy member of the Episcopal Church. Thomas C. Ryall, our subject's father, had the advantage of a good education, and in early life began the study of law. He entered the law school at Trenton, N. J., and graduated from that institution. He then began the practice of law at Freeholm, N. J., but remained there but a short time, as his health was failing. He then traveled extensively in South America, and is now living in Bedford County, and is one of its most highly respected citizens. Our subject had the advantage of a good education in Shelbyville, and in 1860 began the study of medicine. The war coming on broke into his studies, as he enlisted in the Confederate Army in the Twenty-sixth Tennessee Regiment, and was assistant surgeon of that regiment, which position he held thirteen months. He was then assigned surgeon in the hospital at Montgomery. Ala., where he remained ten months. From there he went to Columbus, Ga., in the same capacity. After the war he returned to his county, and in 1865 entered the University of Pennsylvania, at Philadelphia, graduating with honors from that institution in 1867. He then went to Augustine, Fla., and began the practice of medicine. At the end of two years he came to Bedford County, and has been practicing his profession here ever since. He has an extensive practice, and is one of the progressive and leading men of the county. He now owns a finely improved farm of 400 acres, and is quite successful in a financial sense.

THOMAS C. RYALL, SR., a prominent retired citizen of Bedford County, was born April 19, 1809, in Trenton N. J., his parents being natives of New Jersey, and of English descent. He read law and at the age of twenty-one began the practice of that profession, which he continued in New Jersey for five or six years. He then, on account of his health, accepted an offer from Post Capt. David Deacon, United States Navy, who was ordered to command of the United States Frigate "Brandywine," to accompany him on a cruise three years to the Pacific Coast. In this expedition he served as captain's clerk, judge advocate on court martial and officiated *pro tempore* as secretary to Com. Wadsworth, the commander of the squadron. On his return, in reward for his services, he was presented with a written request signed by all the officers of the squadron to the proper authorities, to procure a pursership in the naval service, but in New Jersey he met Miss Elizabeth Scudder, of Nashville, and granddaughter of Dr. John Scudder, the famous East Indian missionary. He soon came to Nashville and married her. He has ever since lived in Tennessee and followed farming until about 1880, when, on account of his age, he retired from active business life. He owns about 800 acres of land and a very fine fruit orchard. Mr. Ryall's married life was blessed in the births of nine children; six of whom are living, viz.: Johnston S., a farmer and merchant in Alabama; Dr. A. P. Ryall, a physician, of this county; Walter, growing oranges in Florida; Thomas C., merchandise broker, of Shelbyville; Henry C., lumberman, of Shelbyville; and Juliet, wife of Brom R. Whitthorne, cashier of the National Bank of Shelbyville. Mrs. Ryall departed this life August 18, 1857. Politically, Mr. Rydall was a Whig, but is now a Democrat. He is now one of the prominent and highly respected citizens of the county.

THOMAS C. RYALL, JR., son of Thomas C. Ryall, Sr., was born October 5, 1843, in Bedford County. He was reared on a farm. At the age of sixteen he enlisted in the Forty-first Tennessee Regiment in the late war. He was in the service about three years, making his escape from Camp Morton prison, Indianapolis, Ind. He then returned home and remained for three or four years. He then lived in Alabama for about three years, engaged in farming and merchandising. He then returned to Shelbyville, where he has been engaged in merchandising and the brokerage business. His main line of brokerage is in tobacco. He was married, January 11, 1881, to Miss Mattie Baldwin, of Canton, Miss., the fruit of this union being one daughter—Ellie. Politically he is a Democrat, and, as are the other members of the family, he is highly respected for his enterprise.

REV. G. C. SANDUSKY was born January 25, 1834, in Wayne County, Ky., being one of a family of ten children born to the union of Jacob Sandusky and Elizabeth Burnett, natives of Kentucky, where they now live. Our subject was reared on a farm. At the age of twenty-four he immigrated to Tennessee and followed farming till the war. He then raised Company H of the Third Tennessee Confederate Cavalry, and was in the service nearly throughout the war. After the battle of Stone River he was promoted to lieutenant-colonel of his regiment. Upon returning from the war he had lost his property and his health. He then began the study of dentistry, and has practiced that profession ever since. In 1870 he located at Shelbyville, and has lived here ever since, and does a thriving business in his profession. He was married, September 7, 1856, to Miss Ellen T. Rogers, a native of Meigs County, Tenn. Eight children have blessed this union, all of whom are living: John A., a dentist in Southern, France; Mary E., wife of W. S. Tipton, editor of the Cleveland *Herald*, Cleveland, Tenn.; Annie, wife of Walter Craigmiles, a hardware merchant of Chattanooga; Dick, a clothing merchant of Shelbyville; Frederick

R., clerk in a dry goods store; Fannie, Cecil and Nellie. Dr. Sandusky and wife are members of the Missionary Baptist Church, and he has pastoral charge of a congregation near Shelbyville. He is a Royal Arch Mason. He is a member of the Democratic party, having been a Whig before the war. As a citizen he is enterprising, and commands the respect of his fellow citizens.

REV. WILLIAM M. SHAW, one of Bedford County's old and prominent citizens, was born July 5, 1806, in Orange County, N. C., and immigrated to Bedford County' Tenn., in the year 1816. He was the son of John and Elizabeth (Scott) Shaw, natives, respectively, of South Carolina and Maryland. The father was born November 8, 1771, and died November 4, 1845. The mother was born in the year 1778 and died February 26, 1842. Our subject was reared on a farm and engaged in the farming interest till the year 1853, at which time he joined the Methodist Conference South, but was licensed to preach as a local preacher previous to this in the year 1845. In 1827 he wedded Mahala Wilson, of this county. She was born January 9, 1809. This marriage resulted in the birth of nine children only six of whom are living: John W., William S., Alexander M., Ambrose D., Ann E. and Mary L. In 1849 Rev. Shaw was ordained deacon at Shelbyville by Bishop Capers and retained this position until October, 1853, at which time he was ordained elder at Franklin, Tenn., by the same bishop. October, 1854, he joined the conference and has been a traveling minister of the Methodist Episcopal Church South up to the present date. Mrs. Shaw died July 31, 1885; she was a consistent member of the Methodist Episcopal Church South. Up to the time of the late war Rev. Shaw was an old-line Whig, but since that time he has been a Democrat.

WILLIAM S. SHAW is a native of Bedford County, Tenn., and a son of William M. and Mahala (Wilson) Shaw, natives of North Carolina. Our subject was born May 26, 1834, and was reared on a farm, and received limited educational advantages. At the age of twenty-two he began farming for himself, continuing until 1862, when he entered the Confederate Army, Company G, Forty-fourth Tennessee Infantry, but served only a short time. He resumed farming, and December 16, 1858, was married to Nancy Clark, who was born September 1, 1839, and who died March 27, 1864, leaving one child—Martha H. September 12, 1867, our subject took for his second wife Julia Haskins. Mrs. Shaw died October 7, 1871, and for his third wife Mr. Shaw took Susan O. Steen, December 1, 1872. She was born March 26, 1852, and became the mother of three children: John Rufus, William Marvin and Edward Driskill. Mr. Shaw is a Democrat, and prides himself on never having been sued or in a lawsuit.

WILLIAM J. SHOFNER was born in Lincoln County, Tenn., May 3, 1819, and is a son of Christopher and Elizabeth (Jenning) Shofner, who died in 1826 and in 1845, respectively. To them were born four daughters and four sons, three of whom are yet living. Our subject resided with his widowed mother on a farm until her death, and about four years later located on his farm of 480 acres. He has been very successful in his business ventures, and has given his five married sons a good farm each. In 1846 he married Rhoda Boone, who was born May 19, 1828. She and husband became the parents of the following family: Jeptha B., born in 1847; James B., born in 1849; Christopher H., born in 1851; George F., born in 1854; William H., born in 1856; Albert, born in 1859, and died in 1861; Elizabeth M., born in 1861; Daniel W., born in 1864, and Newton M., born in 1868, and died in 1871. Mrs. Shofner's parents were William and Sallie (Howard) Boone. The father was born in Kentucky, and is a distant relative of Daniel Boone. Her mother was born in 1803 and died in 1843. Her father then married Margaret Moore. He died in 1854 and the stepmother in 1873.

MONROE SHOFNER was born in Tennessee September 16, 1833, son of Austin and Rebecca (Cook) Shofner, natives of North Carolina, born August 16, 1801, and April 21, 1798, respectively. The father was brought to Tennessee in 1807, and in 1818 married our subject's mother and became the father of eight children: Plummer W., Mitchell D. (killed in the battle of Chickamauga), Henderson, Catherine (deceased), John (deceased), Martin (deceased), Monroe, Purline and Isom (deceased). Our subject's father was reared on a farm and followed farming and stock trading, accumulating considerable wealth. He operated a distillery for about six years, and was well known throughout the county as a dealer in fine horses. He died October 18, 1852, and his wife October 10, 1875. Monroe spent the life of a farmer's boy and is now residing on the farm settled by his grandfather, Martin Shofner, which consists of 200 acres. In 1863 he entered the Confederate service, and remained one year. He followed pedagoging sixteen years, but discontinued that in 1878. Mr. Shofner takes much interest in laudable public enterprises, and gives them his support and patronage. He believes in Republican principles and he is a devout supporter of temperance, and has on divers occasions delivered temperance lectures.

BENJAMIN FORSYTH SMALLING was born in what was Bedford County but now is part of Marshall County, Tenn., November 24, 1825. He is the son of Samuel and Elizabeth (Bostic) Smalling, and is of German lineage. His father was born in Sullivan County, Tenn., about 1800, and his mother was born in Wilkes County, N. C. about the same year. They were married in early life and from this union were born three children. Our subject was reared on the farm and received a practical education in the common schools. Farming has been his chief occupation, although he has spent some time in trading, saw-milling, etc. During the civil war he was commissioned enrolling officer of his district and afterward as an officer of the commissary department in the Confederate Army, where he remained during the war. While he participated in no battles he was often exposed to the dangers incident to war. October 5, 1847, he was married to Miss Ann F. Morton, who was born in Hardeman County, Tenn., January 13, 1830. To this union were born nine children, six of whom are living; these are Forsyth, James M., Constantine W., Benjamin, Mary C. and Elizabeth B. Mr. Smalling has a farm of 100 acres of fine land which he manages in a profitable way. He is a Democrat and he and family are members of the Methodist Episcopal Church South. Our subject's grandfather, Col. Benjamin Forsyth, was a commanding officer in the war of 1812, and was killed in a skirmish near Lake Champlain. He wore a sword at the time of his death which he had captured from a British officer. He made the remark when putting the sword on that he would "fight them with their own weapons." He was killed soon after this occurence. The sword was labeled with its full history by Gen. Scott and sent to the widow of Col. Forsyth and may be seen at this time at the home of James M. Smalling, four miles east of Nashville, Tenn., on the Lebanon Pike.

GEORGE SMITH was born December 12, 1831, in Bedford County, Tenn., son of John E. and Nancy (Mayfield) Smith, natives of North Carolina and Tennessee, respectively. The father was born in 1801 or 1802 and died about 1840. He was a successful farmer. The mother was born about 1806. Our subject was the second of five children born to his parents. He was reared on the farm and remained there until he was eighteen years of age. He then attended school at Chapel Hill, Tenn., and continued there about fifteen months, after which he returned home and engaged in farming as well as in stock and negro trading up to the time of the late war. He enlisted in the Confederate Army in 1861 in Col. Starnes Cavalry Company B. He remained with this company about two years and was then transferred to the Forty-fourth Tennessee Infantry, Company G. He was wounded at the battle of Murfreesboro which disabled him from active service about fifteen months. He again returned to service and remained throughout the entire war. Previous to the war, in 1852, he was married to Martha Rainey, a native of this county, born August 29, 1832. This union has resulted in the birth of eight children: Nancy A., Emmet, Andrew J., John M., Sallie C., Mattie G., Robert E. and Emma. Our subject has been quite successful and has accumulated the greater part of his property since the late war. He and wife are members in good standing in the Missionary Baptist Church.

JOHN A. SMITH, farmer, was born in Bedford County, Tenn., October 27, 1855, son of Jasper N. and Sarah E. (Carrothers) Smith, and of English extraction. The father was born in Bedford County, Tenn., November 7, 1828, and the mother was born in the same county December, 1839. Our subject is first of eleven children born to this worthy couple. He was reared on the farm and received a fair education in the common schools.

October 4, 1882, Miss Mattie Chambers, of Bedford County, Tenn., became his wife. She was born December 25, 1863, and by this union with Mr. Smith became the mother of two children: Jasper E. and Anna M. The Smith family originally came from North Carolina, and were among the very earliest settlers of the State of Tennessee. Our subject is a Democrat in politics and a member of the Baptist Church. Mrs. Smith is a member of the Methodist Episcopal Church South.

W. B. SNELL was born February 2, 1850, in Bedford County, Tenn. He is a son of J. C. Snell, who was born in 1817, and is a native of the county. The mother's name was Sarah H. Snell. Our subject was reared on a farm, and worked on the same with his father until he was twenty-five years of age, at which time he began farming for himself, and has continued successfully up to the present date. He was married, October 29, 1874, to Virginia C. Carlyle, of Bedford County, and daughter of James and Elizabeth Carlyle. They have two children: Jasper B. and Thomas Kelly. In his political views Mr. Snell favors the Democratic party and gives it his support on all occasions. He takes an active interest in all enterprises pertaining to the public good, and is a man who commands the respect of all.

W. T. SOLOMON was born in Lincoln County, Tenn., May 18, 1855. His father, W. C. Solomon, was born in 1818, in North Carolina, and came to Tennessee when quite small. About 1853 he wedded Sallie C. Tarver, born in Columbus, Ga., in 1824. The father died in 1880. At the age of sixteen our subject became a clerk in the merchandise business for J. C. Fisher, of Fayetteville. Two years later he engaged in the grain and produce business at the same place, the style of the firm being Bryson & Solomon. Two years later Mr. Solomon began work for Anderson, Green & Co., of Nashville, as traveling salesmen, and has successfully continued up to the present date. Sue B. Thompson became his wife October 23, 1879. She is a daughter of Newcomb Thompson, and the mother of two children: Alice Cary and William Tarver. Our subject is a man of influence in the community in which he resides, and received a good education in his boyhood days. He and wife are church members, and he is a member of the K. of P. and the Democratic party.

RICHARD HENRY STEM, Esq., was born Feburary, 11, 1822 in North Carolina, Granville County. He immigrated to the State of Missouri in the fall of 1843, where he remained about fifteen months. He then came to Tennessee, and settled a mile and a half east of Unionville. He was the son of Jacob and Mary (Primrose) Stem. The father was born about 1763 and died about 1828. He was a native of Pennsylvania, and moved to North Carolina in his juvenile days, where he lived until the time of his death. The mother was born about 1788 and died about 1865; she was a native of North Carolina. In July, 1839, our subject wedded Sallie Garrett, of North Carolina, who was born February, 1822. On his arrival in Tennessee Mr. Stem engaged in agricultural pursuits and about ten years later engaged in the cattle trading business in connection with farming. He was elected magistrate of the Tenth District in this county a number of years ago, and has served every term since. He was elected as chairman of the county court in 1874 and served in that capacity four years, and was also associate justice two years prior to this election. He is now officiating justice of peace. He is a member of the Methodist Episcopal Church South, professing faith about 1856. Mrs. Stem is also a member of the same church. Our subject is a Master Mason and is also a Chapter member. He is a Democrat in politics and since his childhood days has traveled over these different States: Tennessee, Mississippi, Alabama, Georgia, South Carolina, North Carolina, Virginia, Kentucky, Illinois and Missouri.

FELIX TURRENTINE is a Tennesseean, born May 12, 1811, son of James Turrentine, who was born in Virginia in 1773. The father came to Tennessee in 1807. His wife, Eleanor Neily, was born in North Carolina. Our subject has always been a farmer. May 12, 1842, he married Martha Ann Orr, who was born January 26, 1822. To them were born seven children, all of whom are dead except David A. and Eleanor F. Mrs. Turrentine died February 1, 1882. Mr. Turrentine was an old-line Whig, but since the war has been a

Democrat. His son, David A. Turrentine, was born February 14, 1847. Up to June, 1880, he was a farmer. Since that time he has been engaged in the merchandise business at Hall's Mills. February 24, 1875, he married Mollie F. Shearin, who was born October 21, 1851. To them were born four children: Alice R., Sallie A., Lucy J. and Felix. Mr. Turrentine has been prosperous in his business enterprises. He is a Democrat, and was elected to the office of constable in 1878, and served about ten months. He has also been a delegate to the Democratic Convention from his State several times. William H. Stephens, partner in the merchandise business with David A. Turrentine, was born in Bedford County, Tenn., February 24, 1840. He was reared on a farm, and when twenty-one years of age entered the Confederate Army, enlisting in Company G, Forty-fourth Tennessee Infantry, and participated in the battles of Shiloh, Murfreesboro, Chickamauga, and others. He served throughout the war and was not wounded. After his return he engaged in farming and has followed that occupation to the present time. In connection with this he has been in the merchandise business since 1880. In February, 1886, he was married to Martha Ray, born February 8, 1838. They are the parents of Robert H., Etta, Thomas and Pearlie Lee. Mr. Stephens and Mr. Turrentine are doing a good business in the mercantile line. Mr. Stephens is a very firm Democrat in politics.

HENRY H. STEPHENS was born in the year 1818, in the State of North Carolina and in 1836 immigrated to Tennessee and settled in this county on the farm where he is now living. He was the youngest of nine children born to the union of Hardie and Mary Stephens. He is a mechanic by trade and built the bridge on the Chattanooga Railroad when the road was first laid off. After this he followed the business of a millwright for about five years. He has also carried on farming in connection with his other occupations. May 27, 1839, he was married to Nancy Mullens, of this county, who was born September 21, 1818. This union resulted in the birth of ten children, two of whom are dead. The eight remaining are living in this county. Our subject has been quite successful and has accumulated considerable means. In politics Mr. Stephens is a Democrat and he and wife are leading members of the Methodist Episcopal Church South. His health has been quite poor for a number of years, and he has not been able to see to any out-door business for about six years.

J. M. L. STEPHENS is a son of John and Martha A. (Gulley) Stephens, who were born in North Carolina in 1776 and 1796, and died in 1831 and 1879, respectively. The father was an early pioneer farmer of Tennessee, and was a soldier in the war of 1812, and received land grants for his services. Our subject was born February 28, 1831, in Bedford County, and worked on a farm to support his mother until he attained his majority, when he began farming for himself, and in the winter season taught school for several years. He entered the Confederate service in 1862, in Company F, Forty-first Tennessee Infantry, and was in the battles of Chickamauga, Raymond, Jackson and others, but was not wounded or captured during service. After his return home he resumed farming, and in 1866 was elected constable and served two years. November 22, 1858, he wedded Margaret F. Robinson, of Bedford County, and their union has resulted in the birth of six children: Ransom, Kate, Joseph, John, Lizzie and Hiram. Mr. Stephens is a man well versed in the affairs of the times, and he and family are church members. His eldest son is preparing for the ministry. Mr. Stephens is a Mason, and a Democrat in his political views.

WALTER W. SUMMERS was born January 5, 1819, in Fleming County, Ky. His father, Lewis Summers, was a native of Culpepper County, Va.; about 1796, he immigrated to Kentucky, where he married Miss Mary Armstrong, a native also of Virginia. He was of English descent, and she of Scotch-Irish. To this union were born fourteen children, our subject being the eleventh. The mother died in 1859, and the father died in 1865. Our subject was educated in the common schools of his native county, and remained with his parents on the farm until he reached his majority. He then followed merchandising for about a year and a half, and then devoted his attention to trading in stock, which he followed about thirty years. In 1847 he married Miss Mary Gore, a native of Nelson County, Ky., and to this union three children—Lewis (deceased), Henry and Thomas—were born.

The mother of these children died in 1858, and in 1861 our subject married Miss Hettie Armstrong, a native of Bedford County, Tenn., and to this union two children have been born, both of whom are dead. In 1877 our subject took for his third wife Miss Kincannon, a native of Rutherford County, Tenn., and to them were born two children: Otie P. R. and Wattie R. M., both living. At the breaking out of the late war, Mr. Summers left Louisville and ran a large distillery at Chattanooga until it fell into the hands of the Federal authorities. After the war he returned to Louisville, and in 1867 purchased and moved upon the farm where he now lives, which consists of 320 acres. In 1876, Centennial year, he exhibited the largest steer and largest mule perhaps ever reared, and a three-legged cow. Mr. Summers is a member of the Masonic and Odd Fellows orders, and is independent in politics.

WALTER FINLEY SUTTON, a resident of the Fourth District, Bedford Co., Tenn., born in the district in which he now resides, November 25, 1840, son of John and Elizabeth A. (Harris) Sutton, and is of English-Scotch descent. His father was born in Prince William County, Va., March 5, 1775, and died August 5, 1855. His mother was born in Bedford County, Tenn., in 1813, and died in the same county in 1879. His father was married twice, the second time to the mother of our subject, Miss Elizabeth Harris, a relative of Gov. Harris, of Tennessee. Our subject received a common school education, and has followed farming as his chief occupation. He enlisted in the Confederate service in the Twenty-third Tennessee Infantry and was afterward transferred to the Fourth Tennessee Cavalry, where he served three years. He was in the battle of Stone River, Chickamauga, besides various cavalry skirmishes during the Georgia campaign, and was finally discharged at Atlanta just prior to the general surrender. In the fall of 1865 Mr. Sutton was elected magistrate of his district, which position he has held ever since. December 27, 1858, he was married to Miss Bettie Hicks, of Bedford County, Tenn., born March 13, 1842, and to this union was born one child, William, whose birth occurred October 8, 1868.

WILLIAM B. SUTTON, farmer, was born in Bedford County, Tenn., July 12, 1834, son of John and Elizabeth (Harris) Sutton, and of English-Scotch descent. (For further particulars of parents see sketch of Walter Finley Sutton.) Our subject received his preparatory education at Triune, Williamson Co., Tenn., under Prof. E. B. Crocker, and completed at the Union University, Murfreesboro, Tenn. For several years prior to the war he was engaged in the mercantile business as salesman. When the war broke out he enlisted in the Confederate Army and was assigned duty under Maj. James F. Cummings, commissary for the Confederate Army, with headquarters at Atlanta, Ga. Here he remained until the close of the war. Our subject has been married twice; the first marriage occurred July 10, 1860, to Miss Kate Suttle, daughter of Richard Suttle. To this union were born two sons: John L., born August 1, 1865, and Ernest, born January 29, 1875. The second marriage occurred November 17, 1885, to Miss Elizabeth Alexander. Mr. Sutton is a thorough Democrat, an Odd Fellow, and he and wife are members of the Methodist Episcopal Church South. He has 665 acres of land, 400 of which are in a fine state of cultivation. He gives considerable attention to the raising of live-stock.

C. N. TAYLOR, a native of Bedford County, was born December 1, 1850, and is the son of James P. and Margaret A. (Ransom) Taylor. The father was born about October, 1820, and died January 9, 1880. The mother was born in 1826. Our subject's educational advantages were comparatively good, and at the age of twenty-seven he engaged in farming on his own responsibility. December 19, 1877 he wedded Mary O. Wood, of this county. She was born April 18, 1860, and was the daughter of Johnson W. and Louisa F. (Jordon) Wood; the former born in 1836 and the latter in 1829, and died in 1884. To our subject and wife were born two children; their names are, respectively, Annie R., born December 18, 1879, and John W., born October 8, 1882. Mr. Taylor is a man of good standing in his community, always willing to aid in any enterprise pertaining to the advancement of the educational or moral interests. He is a Democrat in politics.

JOHN W. THOMPSON, chairman of the county court of Bedford County, is a son of Newcom and Amy (Fisher) Thompson, natives of North Carolina. The parents moved to this county in about 1809. The father was a carpenter and he built the first houses of Shelbyville. He afterward engaged in farming two and one-half miles west of Shelbyville and there raised his family and became wealthy, but the war involved him. He died in 1879 at the age of seventy-five. The mother died at eighty-one, in 1886. Our subject was born January 8, 1831, and was reared on a farm. He remained with his parents till April, 1846, when he engaged at clerking in a store. After several years he opened a family grocery trade which he continued until the war. During the war he was engaged in the Adams Express office at Nashville. In 1857 he was elected recorder of Shelbyville and held the office till 1866. In that year he was elected register of Bedford County. In 1868 he was appointed deputy circuit court clerk, which office he held till 1882. He was elected magistrate in 1870, and in 1882 was elected chairman of the court. He was mayor of Shelbyville from 1872 to 1877, having been an alderman for five years previous. He was elected recorder of Shelbyville, in 1885, without his knowledge or consent, and now holds that office. He was united in marriage, in December, 1849, to Miss M. J. Pannell; a native of this county. Five children have been born to this union, four of whom are now living. For thirty years Mr. Thompson was a member of the I. O. O. F. He is now a member of the K. of H. and A. O. U. W. fraternities.

GEORGE W. THOMPSON, one of the old and highly respected citizens of Bedford County, was the oldest son and second child of Newcom and Amy (Fisher) Thompson. He was born February 1, 1823, near Shelbyville, and was reared on a farm, his father being a wealthy farmer and manufacturer. At the age of eighteen he engaged in the tanner's trade, and continued till he was married, when he moved to Shelbyville and served as constable, then a lucrative office, for two years. He then ran a saw-mill for four years and also bought a large tract of timber land. He then returned to Shelbyville and served as constable or collecting officer again for four years. He then engaged in the family grocery business till 1861. During the war he was a Union man and was not engaged in any special avenue of business. In 1866 he was elected to the Legislature and attended the regular and call sessions of 1866 and of 1868. During this time, and ever since, he has been a farmer. He was married, May 18, 1843, to Martha M. Cannon, who bore him five children, three of whom are now living, viz.: Amy F., the widow of C. A. Warren, Sr.; Letitia, the wife of C. A. Warren, Jr., and Mollie G. Mrs. Thompson departed this life July 14, 1874. Mr. Thompson is a member of the Masonic fraternity and I. O. O. F. Politically he is a firm Republican, and he is and always has been an enterprising and energetic citizen of Bedford County.

W. THOMPSON, one of the numerous members of the Thompson family of Bedford County, is a farmer living about four miles west of Shelbyville. He was born August 20, 1842, in Bedford County. His father, John F. Thompson, was born in Bedford County, being a son of one of those Thompsons who came to Bedford County from North Carolina in the very early settlement of this part of the State. He was a farmer all his life, his death occurring August 23, 1883. The mother is now living five miles northwest of Shelbyville. The subject of this sketch was reared on a farm. At the age of twenty-two he married and continued farming, which he has successfully followed ever since, now owning 300 acres of good land well improved. He was one of the boys in gray, serving from July, 1861, till June, 1862, in Blanton's company of the Twenty-third Tennessee. At the battle of Shiloh he lost a leg and in June, 1862, returned home. He was married in 1864, to Hulda B. Wilhoite, the results of this union being ten children, seven of whom are now living, viz.: Eunice, Richard, Lydia, Warner, Charles, Purdey and an infant. Mr. Thompson is a Democrat in politics. He, his wife and eldest daughter are members of the Missionary Baptist Church.

THOMAS C. THOMPSON was born February 8, 1843, in Bedford County, Tenn., son of W. F. and Harriet P. (Hall) Thompson. The father was a native of North Carolina, born September 9, 1816, and of English descent. The mother was of Irish descent, and by her union with W. F. Thompson she became the mother of four children. She died in 1850, and in 1857 the father married Mrs. Mary Muse, a native of this county. To this union were born four children. The father was a tiller of the soil. He died in 1865 and his widow is still living. Our subject was educated in the country schools, and assisted his father on his farm until December, 1861, when he enlisted in the Twenty-third Regiment, Tennessee Confederate Infantry, and served with that command nineteen months. The principal battles in which he was engaged were Shiloh, Perryville and Murfreesboro. In 1866 he married Miss Achsah King, a native of this county, and a daughter of C. B. and Mary C. King. To our subject and wife were born the following children: Mary B., Hattie V., Charles F., James B., Sarah E., Robert E., Thomas E. and George E., all now living with the exception of Sarah E. The mother of these children died May 9, 1882, and in 1885 Mr. Thompson married Miss Maggie A. Rankin, a native of Ohio, and a daughter of Rev. Alexander F. and Mary Rankin. Our subject is a member of the Masonic fraternity, and at present is a magistrate of his civil district. He owns a farm of over 200 acres, all under a good state of cultivation. Himself, wife and four eldest children are members of the Cumberland Presbyterian Church, and he is a Democrat in politics.

ZACH THOMPSON was born July 7, 1844, at Lebanon, Wilson Co., Tenn. His father, Col. Robert E. Thompson, is a native of Bedford County, Tenn., born in 1822 and of Irish descent. He moved to Williamson County with his parents when a small boy and subsequently was educated at Lebanon, Wilson County, and began the practice of law at that place. He has been a member of the Legislature several times and is a prominent lawyer of Lebanon. He married Miss Mary Tolliver, a native of Lebanon, and to this union nine children were born, of whom the subject is the eldest. Zach Thompson was educated at Cumberland University, Lebanon, and upon passing sixteen years of age he enlisted in the Seventh Tennessee Confederate Infantry. He served in that regiment about eighteen months and was then transferred to the Fourth Tennessee Cavalry and with that command served until the close of the war. He then returned home and read law and practiced at Lebanon until 1873. November 21, 1872, Miss Lettie Cannon, a native of Bedford County, became his wife. To this Union were born two children: Robert E. and Mary L., both living. In 1873 they moved upon the place where they now reside, which is about six miles northeast of Shelbyville. The farm consists of 320 acres, all under a good state of cultivation. In connection with farming Mr. Thompson has run a distillery for the last three years. In politics he is a stanch Democrat.

W. E. A. THOMPSON, A. B., a native of Bedford County, Tenn., was born Nov. 28, 1848. His father was a licensed preacher in the Methodist Church, but having an affection of the throat was obliged to give up his ministerial duties and engage in farming. His mother was Ellen C. (Williams) Thompson. Our subject remained with his parents on the farm until he was twenty-one years of age, attending school when he could be conveniently spared from the farm. In the fall of 1869 he taught school at Mount Zion, Bedford County, and in 1870 clerked in a dry goods house at Unionville. The spring of 1871 he spent in school at Chapel Hill and spent the fall at Unionville in the same manner. Early in 1872 he entered the Tennessee University, where he graduated in 1874 with the degree of A. B. He chose teaching as his profession and began work at Unionville, his native village. In the summer of 1875 he left Unionville and taught five months at Middleton, Rutherford County. In the spring of 1876 he accepted the principalship of the Center Grove High School, where he is engaged at the present writing. December 26, 1876, he wedded Nannie Floyd, of this county, and by her became the father of four children: Benjamin H., Mary G., Annie E. and Ellen F. Our subject is a member of the Methodist Episcopal Church South, and is a man of good social standing and influence in this section.

COL. LEWIS TILLMAN (deceased) was born in Bedford County, August 18, 1816, being a son of John and Rachel P. (Martin) Tillman, natives of South Carolina. Both parents immigrated to this county when young. The father was born February 5, 1786, and came to Bedford County about 1810. He was a farmer, and was one of the prominent early citizens of Bedford County. He was a member of the State Legislature of Tennessee in 1820, but would never accept further political honor. His death occurred October 3, 1854. The mother was born May 16, 1789, and attained the age of ninety-two, dying in 1881. Both the grandsires of our subject were soldiers of the Revolutionary war. Col. Lewis Tillman was reared on a farm, and secured but a limited early education because of the rude accommodations of the schools in his boyhood. At the age of twenty-five he married, and settled where he pursued farming till his death. In 1836 he served in the Florida war in the campaign against the Creek and Seminole Indians. He has held the commission of major, lieutenant-colonel and colonel in the Sixty-first regiment of State Militia of Tennessee. From 1852 to 1860 he was clerk of the Circuit Court of Bedford County, and for a few years immediately following the war he was clerk and master of the Chancery Court of Bedford County. Throughout the war he was a firm Union man. In 1868 he was elected to represent the Fifth Congressional District of Tennessee in the Forty-first Congress of the United States of America, without any solicitation on his part. Since then he never would accept any public office. He was married, in 1840, to Mary Catharine Davidson, daughter of James Davidson, one of the early citizens of the county. Mrs. Tillman's mother is still living, aged eighty-two years. Mrs. Tillman was born March 1, 1823. Col. Tillman's married life was blessed in the birth of eleven children, seven of whom are now living, viz.: James D., a prominent attorney at Fayetteville; Lewis, a prominent attorney of Knoxville; Samuel E., professor of chemistry, mineralogy and geology in the West Point Academy, of New York; George N., United States marshal of the Middle District of Tennessee; Hattie A., residing with her mother; Edwin H., in the United States Naval service on the coast of Japan, and Abram M., a law student and clerk in the Internal Revenue Department at Washington, D. C. Col. Lewis Tillman's private and public career was one of unimpeached integrity, undismayed energy and unsurpassed hospitality. The poor, especially, received bountifully from his hand, and no charitable institution went unaided by him.

MICAGER TROXLER is a native Tennesseean, born January 25, 1839, and is residing in the home of his birth, where he owns 110 acres of good land. In 1862 he enlisted in the Confederate Army under Bushrod Johnson and served until December, 1863, when he was taken sick and captured. He was paroled and sent home but never returned to service. November 20, 1860, he married Mary A. Shofner, who was born December 3, 1842. She was a daughter of Frederick and Mary (McKaig) Shofner, and died April 11, 1864. Mr. Troxler then wedded, in 1865, his second wife, Mary A. Dean, a daughter of John and Sarah (Shofner) Troxler, who were born in 1791 and 1796 and died in 1871 and 1869, respectively. Mrs. Troxler was born October 20, 1838. Our subject is a member of the K. of H., and is also a member of Freemason lodge No. 308. He and Mrs. Troxler are members of the Cumberland Presbyterian Church and he is a stanch supporter of Democratic principles. His parents, Isaac and Elizabeth (Payne) Troxler, were born in North Carolina and Tennessee, respectively, in 1803. The father was brought to Tennessee by his parents in 1810, and November 2, 1825, he wedded our subject's mother and became the father of ten children. His death occurred March 15, 1866, and the mother's June 20, 1848.

JOHN C. TROXLER was born January 5, 1840, in Tennessee. His parents, Anthony and Sarah (Cortner) Troxler, were born in North Carolina in 1802 and 1810, respectively. The father came to Tennessee about 1817, and died in 1843. The mother's death occurred in 1886. Our subject has followed farming from early boyhood. In 1861 he enlisted in the Confederate service and remained until 1863, when he was captured while making a visit home, was paroled, and never returned to the service. He was constable of his district two years, and served as deputy sheriff one year. In 1866 Mr. Troxler was married to Mrs. Margaret A., widow of Gilbreth Chambers. She was born in Tennessee in 1848. Nine children were born to Mr. and Mrs. Troxler, named George R., born in 1867; William T., born in 1870; Nancy D., born in 1872; Sarah, born in 1874; John A., born in 1876; Daniel M., born in 1878; Edward, born in 1880; Polly, born in 1882, and Ambrose, born in 1884. In March, 1876, Mr. Troxler was elected justice of the peace in his district, and has held the office up to the present time He owns 126 acres of land, and is a member of the K. of H. He and wife are members of the Cumberland Presbyterian Church, and he is a Democrat politically.

WILLIAM T. TUNE (deceased) was a son of John Tune, one of the first settlers of Bedford County, Tenn. He was born in 1818, in Smith County, and was reared on a farm. He was married, in 1844, to Miss C. E. Morton, and thirteen children were born to them: Mary A., James C., Mattie J., Eliza F., Sallie., Charles W., Emma S., John M., Will R., Thomas C., Louis T., Horace G., and Bettie E. Mr. Tune was a farmer of Bedford County for many years. He died March 5, 1871. Mrs. Tune is still living at her residence, "Cottage Home," and is a member of the Cumberland Presbyterian Church. William R. Tune, fourth son of William T. Tune, was born October 12, 1860, and spent his boyhood days on a farm. He finished his education in the schools of Shelbyville, and then took a traveling tour over the greater part of the United States. At present he is living with his mother, and he is a member of the Cumberland Presbyterian Church.

KESTER L. TUNE, farmer, of Bedford County, Tenn., was born in this State December 6, 1829. His parents, John and Mary (Cooper) Tune, were born in Virginia and Tennessee in 1791 and 1797, respectively. They were married September 12, 1816, and fifteen children were born to their union. The mother died in August, 1853, and the father in 1881. After attaining his majority our subject began the battle of life on his own responsibility, and by industry and economy became the possessor of 465 acres of well cultivated and fertile land. He gives considerable attention to stock trading also. September 1, 1858, he was united in marriage to M. C. Wells, born May 8, 1838, and died January 13, 1862, having borne two children: Joseph E., born April 27, 1860, and died November 1, 1861, and Susan E., born October 13, 1861. For his second wife Mr. Tune married Eliza J. Landers, born October 19, 1835. They have three children: Thomas O., born December 29, 1865; John C., born November 14, 1868; and William S., born March 28, 1872. Mrs. Tune's parents were Thomas and Elizabeth (Thomas) Landers, who were born in North Carolina and Tennessee in 1812 and 1814, respectively. They were married December 20, 1834, and became the parents of twelve children—eight daughters and four sons. The father died May 5, 1879. Mr. Tune's first wife was a member of the Cumberland Presbyterian Church. His present wife is a member of the Methodist Protestant Church. Mr. Tune was a Whig until the death of that party; and since that time has been identified with the Republican party.

JAMES L. TURNER was born July 8, 1823, in Sussex County, Va., son of Littlebury and Mary (Winn) Turner. The father was born April 28, 1788, and died June 18, 1869. The mother was born September 28, 1787, and died February 25, 1879. Our subject's educational advantages were not of the best, but, notwithstanding, he is considered a fine mathematician, and has acquired the major part of his education without a teacher. At the age of twenty-one he engaged in the farming interest with his father, and so continued until about 1851. Previous to this, in 1848, he was elected to the office of constable, which position he held for about eleven years. In 1850 he wedded Margaret N. Murphy, who was born August 12, 1830, and to them were born nine children: Sarah J., James W., William F., Margaret F., Elizabeth A., Nancy F., Tennessee M. (deceased), Joseph H. and Lavinia. Mr. Turner was elected to the office of deputy sheriff in 1858, and held that office one term, and again in 1868 he was deputized to fill the same office. In 1876 he was elected magistrate of the Eleventh District, and has held that office up to the present time. He has also carried on his farming interest, and has been quite successful in that occupation. He is a Republican in politics.

JAMES VANNATTA was born February 9, 1811, in Williamson County, Tenn., and was reared and educated in the country. January 12, 1831, he was united in marriage to Miss Martha Watson, and by her became the father of three children: Samuel, Hibernah K. and John S., only one of whom is living. Mrs. Vannatta died in 1839, and for his second wife Mr. Vannatta took Mrs. Jerusha (Clardy) Nash, and to them were born the following children: Delphia A., Joseph R., George W., Charity A., Eliza F., Christopher C.

and Nannie D. In 1850 Mr. Vannatta moved to Bedford County, where he engaged in farming and stock raising. Both he and wife are members of the Methodist Episcopal Church South. Mr. Vannatta's parents were C. C. and Nancy (Louder) Vannatta, born in North Carolina and Kentucky, respectively. The father came to Tennessee at an early day, locating in Williamson County, near Triune. To him and wife were born the following children: Maria, James and Katie; only one, James, is now living. The father was in the war of 1812, and was with Jackson at New Orleans. He died on his way home from that place. His widow died in 1839. Both were earnest workers in the Methodist Episcopal Church South.

WARREN WAITE, a prominent farmer of District No. 2, was born June 9, 1827, in Bedford County, near Wartrace. His father, George Waite, was a native of Person County, N. C., born November 18, 1790, and was of English lineage. Our subject's paternal grandfather, Robert Waite, emigrated from England to North Carolina during colonial times, and was a surveyor of lands. George Waite, when a boy, moved with his parents to Tennessee, first to Williamson County, and subsequently to Bedford County, where his parents died. He married Miss Nancy B. Warren, a native of North Carolina, born November 30, 1796, and of English-Irish lineage. To this union six children were born. The mother died December 5, 1838, and the father December 21, 1857. The father was a natural mechanic in wood and iron work, and was also a farmer. Our subject received a practical education in the country schools, and remained with his parents until he reached his majority, when he began merchandising, which he continued about twenty years; also carried on farming at the same time. In 1853 he married Miss Rutha S. Yell, a native of Coffee County, Tenn., and to this union were born the following children: George E., Nancy A., Warren S. and James W., all living. Mr. Waite owns a farm of 600 acres, all under a good state of cultivation. He was formerly a Whig, but is now a Democrat in politics, and he and wife are members of the Cumberland Presbyterian Church.

PROF. SIMEON V. WALL was born in Williamson County, Tenn., August 22, 1844, son of John B. and Martha E. (Wilson) Wall, and of Scotch-Irish descent. The parents were born in North Carolina and Tennessee in 1799 and 1803 and died December 31, 1870, and April 15, 1859, respectively. They were married in 1819 and were the parents of thirteen children. The father was a soldier in the Confederate Army notwithstanding the fact that he was over age. He was an old-time Whig, although an intimate friend of James K. Polk. He was a soldier in the Indian war of 1836. His father, Clement Wall, came to Williamson County, Tenn., in 1804. Our immediate subject, Simeon Wall, was a student in Harpeth Academy before the war. He enlisted in the Twentieth Tennessee Regiment and participated in the battles of Shiloh, Chickamauga and Franklin and was in many of the battles of the Georgia campaign. Of his war record the *Review and Journal* of Franklin, Tenn., said: "It is well known that when a mere boy he left this county to serve in the Southern Army and he was recognized all over the army as a brave and gallant soldier." After the war, owing to the financial embarrassment of his father, he completed his education through his own exertions. He has been professor in academies and colleges for nearly twenty years and is one of the successful educators of Tennessee. He is proprietor of the Bedford Academy at Bellbuckle, Tenn., but is soon to sever his connection with this school and take charge of the Culleoka Academy as co-principal. July 28, 1868, our subject married Miss Nannie J. Comer, daughter of Rev. J. J. Comer of the Methodist Episcopal Church South. Mr. and Mrs. Wall are the parents of nine children—seven sons and two daughters. Prof. Wall is a Democrat and a member of the Masonic fraternity and he and wife are members of the Methodist Episcopal Church. South.

CAPT. JAMES A. WARDER, a leading member of the Bedford County bar, was born September 24, 1843, at May's Lick, Ky. His father, Walter Warder, was a native of Kentucky, and was an eminent physician of that State. He died when James A. was but about thirteen years of age. The mother now lives in her native State, Kentucky

Capt. Warder was reared near Maysville, Ky., and received his education at Maysville and at Centre College, Kentucky. When eighteen years of age, in 1861, he enlisted in Company L, Second Kentucky Cavalry, as a private. He was subsequently made first lieutenant of the company and afterward was made captain of Company C, of the same regiment. He held that commission till the close of the war, actively serving in most all the important battles throughout the southwest. Returning from the war he read law, and in October, 1866, was licensed to practice, since which time he has been successfully engaged in that profession, ranking among the ablest lawyers of the State. In 1867 he was commissioned attorney-general of a judicial district, but declined the nomination. He was on the Hayes electoral ticket in 1876, and under the administration of Hayes held the office of United States district attorney. He was nominated by his party for the congressional race in 1884, but the Democratic party being largely in the majority he was not elected, he being a Republican and one of the leading men in his party in this part of the State. He was married, January 2, 1865, to Laura D. Gosling, a daughter of William Gosling, a manufacturer in Shelbyville. Two children have been born to this union, one of whom, Inda Artus, is now living. Mrs. Warder is a member of the Episcopal Church. Capt. Warder's name has frequently been connected with all the important offices of the State. A wide-spread desire existed to nominate him for the Republican candidate for governor, but owing to the time neccessarily required from his profession to make the race against so great a Democratic majority, he discouraged the movement. Just now he is being instructed for, by a number of counties, for one of the supreme judges of the State.

THOMAS W. WARNER, dealer in a general line of groceries and provisions, was born October 26, 1838, in Shelbyville, being a son of William D. and Mary (Swift) Warner, both natives of Bedford County. The father was killed when our subject was but one year old, and the mother is still living, having been married three times. Thomas W. was raised by his grandmother, Swift, on a farm, and secured but a common school education. At the age of fifteen he began his own support. He has been engaged as a clerk and merchant for about twenty-five years. He also owns 143 acres of fine land and carries on farming, his residence being one and three-quarter miles west of Shelbyville, on the Fishing Ford Pike, in an excellent location. He was married May 20, 1866, to Emma R. Trail, a native of Franklin, Ky. Six children have been born to them, viz. : Hugh, Frazer, William F., Thomas W., Henry W. and one who died. Mr. Warner and wife are members of the Missionary Baptist Church. He is a member of the Democratic party. He has in his possession a $1 United States coin, bearing the date of 1798, which his father and grandfather each carried. Mr. Warner is a member of the I. O. O. F. and K. of H.

CHARLES A. WARREN (deceased) was born May 21, 1820, in Blount County, Tenn., His father, Thomas S. Warren, was born and partly raised in Virginia. He immigrated with his parents to East Tennessee when young. He was married in 1809. The mother, Susan Sevier Snyder, was born in Nashville. When she was quite young she was taken to Clarksville, where her parents were murdered by the Indians and she was the only one of the family who escaped. She was then reared by her grandfather, Valentine Sevier, and also lived a great part of her time with Gov. Sevier. The parents of our subject moved to Bedford County in about 1828. The father died in 1856, having been born in 1782. The mother was born in 1791, and died in 1863. There is now but one of the family of ten children raised by them living: Mrs. Jennie Ivie, the widow of C. D. Ivie, of Rutherford County. She was born December 27, 1821. Charles A. Warren was reared on a farm. He served as deputy sheriff of Bedford County for many years in his younger days. He carried on farming all his life and was one of the most extensive business men of the county. He was engaged in stock dealing, merchandising, etc. He was noted for his public spirit and public enterprise and charity to the poor. He was a Democrat in politics. He was married May 2, 1865, to Miss Amy Thompson, daughter of G. W. Thompson. Mrs. Warren died October 29, 1883, leaving a family of three children: George, Josephine and Stanley S. Five children have been born to the union but two, Mattie Lee and William S., have died.

MADISON H. WEBB, farmer, was born in Bedford County, Tenn., February 5, 1836, and is the son of Benjamin and Elizabeth W. (Reeves) Webb. The father was born in Sevier County, Tenn., June 16, 1792, and died in Bedford County, June 18, 1884. The mother was born July 18, 1796, in Orange County, N. C., and was married to Benjamin Webb September 16, 1821. To this union were born six sons, of whom our subject is the youngest. He was reared on the farm, educated in the common schools, and assisted his parents on the farm until twenty-one years of age. He was a lieutenant in the Confederate Army, enlisting in the Eighteenth Tennessee Infantry, but was afterward transferred to the Fourth Tennessee Cavalry, under Col. Starnes. He participated in the battles of Fort Donelson, Murfreesboro, Chickamauga, and some actions in the Georgia campaign. He was captured at Fort Donelson and held a prisoner at Lincoln Barracks, Springfield, Ill., for the space of one month, when he escaped. December 11, 1867, he wedded Miss Elnora Elam, daughter of James A. Elam. The fruits of this union were five children— three sons and two daughters. Our subject has a fine farm of 600 acres. He is a Democrat; a Mason (Knight Templar), and he and wife are members of the Cumberland Presbyterian Church.

JOHN W. WELLS was born May 15, 1843, in Rutherford County, Tenn. His father, Thomas P. Wells, was a native of Virginia, born in September, 1811. When a young man he moved to Williamson County, where he married Miss Susan Smith, a native of this State. To this union six children were born, of whom our subject is the fourth. The mother of these children died when our subject was about nine years old, and the father afterward married Miss Frances Tune, and by her he became the father of two children— a son and daughter. Thomas P. Wells moved to Illinois in 1866, where he now resides; he is a minister of the Cumberland Presbyterian Church and is also a farmer. Mrs. Frances (Tune) Wells is now dead. Our subject came to this county with his parents when but eight years of age, and here he was educated at the Flat Creek Academy. In October, 1861, he enlisted in the Forty-first Tennessee Confederate Infantry and served in that command about two years. He was then left at Jackson, La., on account of illness, and was there captured and paroled by the Federal Army. He had been captured with his regiment at Fort Donelson and held as a prisoner of war until September, 1862, when he was exchanged. In September, 1866, he married Miss Sarah E. Shoffner, a native of this county and a daughter of Col. L. Shoffner. To this union were born two sons, Othniel D. and Willie S., both living. The mother of these children died September 4, 1873, and in 1874 their father married Miss Margaret C. Jenkins, a native of this county and a daughter of Rev. William Jenkins. To this union the following children were born: Susan M., Thomas E., Edgar J., Ethel and Herbert, all living. Our subject owns a farm of 235 acres on Duck River, all rich bottom land. He is a member of the Masonic fraternity and belongs to Shelbyville Benevolent Lodge, No. 122, and he takes an active interest in educational matters. He and wife are members of the Evangelical Lutheran Church.

WILLIAM D. WHEELER is a son of W. W. Wheeler, who was born in Tennessee in 1809, and died in April, 1855. His mother was a Mrs. White; she was born in 1811 and died November 7, 1857. William D. was the eldest of their seven children. He was born in Rutherford County March 12, 1836, and assisted his father on his farm until twenty-one years of age. He followed farming up to the date of the late war. He enlisted in Company G, Forty fourth Tennessee Infantry in 1861, but owing to ill health only remained in the service three months. After his return home he engaged in farming, and has been a fairly prosperous "tiller of the soil." Martha L. Maxwell became his wife January 22, 1861. She was born August 21, 1840, and is the mother of the following family: Mary Ann, Etta Valonie, Malissa Alice and John Watson. Our subject received a common school education and is a supporter of Democratic principles.

ROBERSON A. WHITAKER, farmer, was born in Lincoln County, Tenn., November 9, 1859, son of Dr. Philander and Rebecca M. (Moseley) Whitaker, and supposed to be of English descent. The father was born in Lincoln County, Tenn., October 19, 1826, and

November 12, 1850, he wedded Rebecca Moseley, who was born November 12, 1833. To this union were born six children—four sons and two daughters. The father died July 3, 1869, and the mother July 3, 1885. The Whitaker family were among the early settlers of the State. Our subject was a farmer boy, was educated in the common schools, and at the age of seventeen began working for himself. February 3, 1880, Miss Bettie S. Thomas, daughter of William Thomas, became his wife, and by her he became the father of two children: William T. and Mattie M. Mrs. Whitaker was born in the house where she now resides September 9, 1857. Her father, William Thomas, Sr., was born January 31, 1807, and died March 29, 1861. Her mother, Mrs. Jane (McCrory) Thomas, was born in Bedford County, Tenn., May 28, 1816, and died December 1, 1882. The ancestors of Mrs. Whitaker on her mother's side were formerly from Ireland, and in an ancient Bible, whose leaves are yellow with age, was found the following statement: Hugh McCrory (the great-great-grandfather of Mrs. Whitaker) was born in May, 1759, in the county of Antrim, Ireland. He sailed to America in April, 1775. He joined the regular army, and served as colonel under Gen. Washington, and was killed at Alexandria in October, 1777. Our subject is a Democrat, and he and wife are members of the Missionary Baptist Church.

THOMAS A. WHITE, farmer, was born May 15, 1819, and is one of seven children born to the union of Thomas and Margaret (McGarrah) White. The father was born in Jefferson County, Va., in 1780, immigrated to Tennessee and settled in Maury County. He remained there until 1825 when he moved to Shelbyville and followed the hatter trade. He also kept hotel in Shelbyville several years. In 1801 he was married and became the father of these children: James R., Joseph, Elizabeth, Nancy, John, Susan and Thomas A. Thomas White, Sr., and wife were worthy members of the Methodist Episcopal Church South. The former died in 1846 and the latter in 1850. The subject of this sketch was born in Columbia, Tenn., and is of Scotch-Irish descent. He received a limited education in the Bedford County Schools, and in 1841 was married to Miss Ary A. Williams, a native of this county. Five children blessed this union: Mary, Robert, Isaac H., Margaret and Julia. Three of these have died: Robert, Margaret and Julia. Mrs. White died in 1853, and in the same year Mr. White married Margaret Dryden, of Bedford County, and to this union were born nine children: Ary (deceased), Julia, Lula, Thomas C., William D., James L., Anna, Walter C. and Susan. Mr. White was a tailor for twenty years of his life but in 1853 turned his attention exclusively to farming. He owns 200 acres of land, and is a member of the Methodist Episcopal Church South.

DR. WILLIAM H. WHITTEMORE, of Haley, was born October 6, 1853, in Davidson County, Tenn. His father, William B. Whittemore, was a native of the same county and is of Scotch-Irish descent. He is a prominent farmer of that county, and married Nancy E. Hays, a native of Davidson County and daughter of John Hays. To this union were born ten children, our subject being the eldest. The father and mother are both living. The Doctor was educated at Franklin College, near Nashville, where he graduated in 1869. He received his medical education in the medical department of the University of Tennessee, from which institution he graduated in 1878, and then commenced the practice of his profession at Antioch, Davidson Co., Tenn. Here he remained two years and then moved to Nashville, and was elected as county health officer, and held this position three years. He then moved to Haley, Bedford Co., Tenn., where he continues the practice of medicine and has already established an extensive practice. November 8, 1882, he married Miss Georgia M. Tolmie, a native of the city of Nashville and daughter of Alexander McD. Tolmie, a prominent citizen and machinist of that city, who ran the first engine that was run on the Nashville & Chattanooga Railroad, and was for a long time master mechanic of that road. To Dr. W. H. Whittemore and wife was born one child, Maggie T. The Doctor is a member of the K. of H. and the Iron Hall. He is a Democrat and a member of the Missionary Baptist Church. Mrs. Whittemore is a member of the Presbyterian Church.

JOHN W. WIGGINS, a successful farmer and stock raiser, was born December 26, 1812, in North Carolina. He is the son of Harrel and Sallie (Royster) Wiggins. The father was born in North Carolina in 1788, and when quite young immigrated to Indiana, where he remained but a few months. He then went to Kentucky, and from there to Coffee County, Tenn., where he remained until 1830, when he immigrated to Bedford County, and settled in the Twentieth District. He reared a family of seven children, three of whom are living at the present time: John W., David and Harbert. Harrel Wiggins was a member of the Missionary Baptist Church and died in 1851. Mrs. Wiggins died in 1873. Our subject was given a fair education in the common schools. In 1835 he was married to Miss Mary Greer, a native of North Carolina. To this union seven children were born, only two of whom are living: Mary A. and Hundley. Mrs. Wiggins was a consistent member of the Methodist Episcopal Church South, and died September 15, 1885. Mr. Wiggins has always been a tiller of the soil, has been rather successful and owns 450 acres of good land.

J. GREER WIGGINS, a farmer of Bedford County, was born December 29, 1842. He is the son of Benjamin F. and Jane H. (Greer) Wiggins. The father was born in North Carolina, and in the early part of his life immigrated to Tennessee and settled in Bedford County. He left and went to Mississippi, but in a short time returned to Bedford County. He was a farmer, and reared a family of eight children: J. Greer, John S., Sarah E., Mary J., William J., Benjamin F., Thomas H. and Fannie E. Sarah E. and Mary J. are both dead. Benjamin F. died in 1883. Mrs. Wiggins died about 1880. Our subject was a country boy, and received a good practical education in the common schools. In 1871 he was united in marriage to Miss Emily V. Evans, daughter of Hampton Evans. To this union were born four children: Bessie F., A. F., Edward H. and Hampton Evans. Mr. Wiggins has always been a farmer, and is also a carpenter by trade. He owns 149 acres of land, and is one of the leading farmers of the Twenty-second District. He is a member of the Cumberland Presbyterian Church.

DAVID WILLIAMS is a native of Bedford County, Tenn., born in May, 1815. His father, Joseph Williams, was born in North Carolina, in 1777, and came to Tennessee at a very early period. He was a farmer, and a soldier in the war of 1812, participating in the battle of New Orleans. In 1813 he wedded our subject's mother, Charity Turrentine, who was born in North Carolina in 1791. The father died in 1876, and the mother two years later. David Williams and Sarah T. Harris were united in marriage in 1836. Mrs. Williams was born in 1816, and her parents, James Harris and Nancy (Thompson) Harris, were born in Pennsylvania and South Carolina, respectively. The children born to Mr. and Mrs. Williams are Almeda, born in 1837; Lou, in 1839; Elvira, in 1841; James H., in 1845; Lafayette, in 1854; Mollie J., in 1859, and Samuel K., in 1861. Our subject was reared on a farm and has followed farming from early boyhood. He was postmaster of Hickory Hill for several years, before and after the war, and in 1869 located on his present farm of 230 acres. He has a neat frame residence, and he and wife are members of the Methodist Episcopal Church South. In politics he is a Democrat.

THOMAS W. WOOD, M. D., of Shelbyville, Tenn., is a son of James and Eliza (Oberall) Wood, natives, respectively, of North Carolina and Virginia. The father was born February 10, 1798, and the mother May 13, 1806. They were married September 17, 1829. Ten children blessed their union: John A., William J., Melissa J., Thomas W., Sarah A., Horace O., Nancy P., Martha H., Eliza T. and James G. Mr. Wood came to Tennessee about 1810, and located in what is now Cannon County, where he remained about two years, and then moved to near Woodbury, where he died November 16, 1865. He had been a member of the Methodist Episcopal Church South for nearly forty years. The mother died September 11, 1874. Thomas W. Wood was born in Cannon County, where he received a good common school education, and attended the Lawrence Academy at Woodbury Station. At the breaking out of the war he joined the Eighteenth Tennessee Infantry, and participated in the battle of Shiloh and numerous skirmishes, and was selected as the one to receive the banner for his company, presented by the young ladies of Woodbury. Owing to ill health he was soon compelled to abandon active service, but was given a position in the commissary department and served as commissary sergeant until the close of the war. He was paroled at Macon, Ga., and after his return home engaged in farming and school teaching. He began his medical studies in 1867, and attended his first course of lectures in the medical department of the University of Nashville in 1868, 1869 and 1870, graduating the latter year. He has since practiced in Bedford County, and has built up an extensive practice. Dr. Wood was appointed by the county commissioner as physician for the poor asylum, and has held that position ten years. He was twice appointed deputy county clerk of Cannon County, and at one time lacked only a few votes of being the nominee of the Democratic party for representative of Bedford County. He was at one time salesman in a wholesale hat house in Philadelphia.

J. P. WOOD. William Wood was born in North Carolina in 1802, and was married to Elena Meris, also of that State, and our subject was born to them September 20, 1838, in Orange County, N. C. He has always followed the life of a farmer, and at the breaking out of the late war he entered the Confederate Army, in the fall of 1862, enlisting in Company G, Thirty-second Tennessee Infantry. At the battle of Chickamauga he was wounded in the left thigh and was compelled to abandon service. August 15, 1861, he led to Hymen's altar Miss Martha C. Woodward, who bore him nine children, only five now living: Mary L., Nora W., William W., Joseph O., Winnie L. Mr. Wood is a self-made man, and has been fairly successful in his business undertakings. He is a member of the Methodist Episcopal Church, and his wife of the Christian Church. Mr. Wood is a Democrat.

MOSES WOODFIN, farmer, was born in Bedford County, Tenn., March 7, 1829, and of English-Irish lineage. His father, Samuel Woodfin, was born in Buncomb County, North Carolina, in 1791, and about 1815 married Maria Barnhill, a native of South Carolina, born December 9, 1798, and to them were born fifteen children. The father died April 29, 1863, and the mother in the same county March 8, 1863. Our subject received a good practical education and has followed farming as his chief occupation. He learned the trade of wheelwright which he followed in a regular way for over fifteen years. At the breaking out of the war he enlisted in the Confederate Army, Forty-fifth Tennessee Infantry, and participated in the battles of Murfreesboro, Chickamauga and Missionary Ridge. At Chickamauga he was wounded and at Missionary Ridge he was wounded again, captured, and taken to Rock Island, Ill., where he remained a prisoner until the end of the war. September 11, 1856, he was married to Miss Rachel A. Clark, daughter of William Clark, and the fruits of this union were eight children—three sons and five daughters; the sons are William J., Samuel N. and James M. P.; the daughters: Mollie E., Emma L., Alice, Ida and Maggie L. Mr. Woodfin is a Democrat, a Mason, and he and wife and five children are members of the Cumberland Presbyterian Church. Mrs. Woodfin, our subject's wife, was born in Rutherford County, Tenn., August 9, 1835. Her father was born in North Carolina, in 1807, and her mother in 1817. Her father died October 20, 1881, and was of Irish lineage. Our subject's grandfather, Nicholas Woodfin, was a soldier in the Revolutionary war, and was distinguished for his gallantry and bravery on many occasions. Our subject's father was a soldier in the war of 1812, and participated in the battle of New Orleans.

JAMES C. YELL, a native of Coffee County, Tenn., was born December 31, 1842, son of Francis M. and Judia (Short) Yell, both natives of Tennessee. The father was born near Wartrace, and is of English extraction. He has been a merchant, but at present is engaged in agricultural pursuits on a farm of nearly 200 acres. During the late war he was a guide for the Federal Army between Nashville and Chattanooga, from 1862 to the latter part of 1863, and was a stanch Union man. The mother is also living. Our subject received a practical education in the country schools and at Tullahoma. In August, 1862, he enlisted in the Fifth Tennessee Federal Cavalry, and served in that command until the close of the war. He was in the battle of Murfreesboro. His regiment was mostly engaged in contending with guerrillas and Confederate cavalry. When the war closed he returned home and sold goods at Normandy for about a year. He then moved to the farm where he now resides, and engaged in tilling the soil. He owns a farm adjoining that of his father, consisting of nearly 200 acres, and another a mile distant of 114 acres. December, 1879, he married Miss Ada Waite, a native of Coffee County, and this union was blessed by these children: Gordentia W., Warren S. and Frances M., all living. Mr. Yell is a Republican in politics, and member of the Masonic fraternity and also K. of H. He and wife are worthy members of the Cumberland Presbyterian Church.

BENJAMIN B. YELL, farmer, was born in Bedford County, Tenn., July 25, 1829, son of James and Jerusha (Barton) Yell, and of English descent. The father was born in 1791, and he and his brother Archibald Yell were volunteer soldiers in the war of 1812, and participated in the battle of New Orleans. Archibald Yell was at one time governor of the State of Arkansas, and, on a monument, erected to his memory at Fayetteville, may be seen the following: "Born in North Carolina, August, 1797; A volunteer in the battle of New Orleans; District Judge of Arkansas Territory in 1832; First member of Congress from the State; Governor, 1840; Again elected to Congress in 1844; Resigned and accepted a Colonelcy of Arkansas for the Mexican war, in 1846; Killed at Buena Vista, February 22, 1847; A gallant, soldier, an upright Judge, a fearless champion of popular rights, a sincere friend, and an honest man." The father of our subject died at his residence in Coffee County, Tenn., November 20, 1839. The mother was born in Georgia, in 1797, and was a member of the Methodist Church South. Our subject was reared on the farm and educated in common schools, January 12, 1848, to Miss Ann B. Waite, and the result of this union was four children: George C., Abner W., Bettie A., and Edith N. Mr. Yell is a Democrat, a Mason, and he and wife are members of the Separate Baptist Church. He has a farm of 280 acres of fine land, which he devotes to the cultivation of cereals and the raising of stock.

JOSHUA YELL is a son of James Yell, who was born in North Carolina, and came to Tennessee with his father when young, locating in Rutherford County. He was married to Jerusha Barton, daughter of William Barton, and by her became the father of twelve children, only seven of whom lived to maturity. Archibald Yell, brother of James Yell, was governor of Arkansas two terms previous to the Mexican war, and was killed in that war while commanding the Arkansas troops. The subject of this sketch was born September 15, 1832, and spent his boyhood days on a farm and in attending the common schools. He was married October 2, 1852, to Miss Rebecca A. Waite, and ten children were born to them: Nancy B. (deceased), A. D., James A., Annie, Benjamin, G. E., Bettie, Joshua, Adah and Charley. In 1879 Mr. Yell removed to his present farm of 200 acres. He is a member of the Masonic fraternity, and he and wife are church members.

PROF. JOHN S. YOES is a son of Thomas Yoes, who was born in Tennessee in 1819. He was a farmer, and married Sallie Perryman, who was born in Tennessee about 1825, and by her became the father of fourteen children. Our subject was their sixth child, born October 9, 1849, and began doing for himself at the age of twenty. He chose school-teaching as his profession, and has continued with good success up to the present time. Margaret E. Hopkins became his wife March 14, 1871. She was born May 29, 1847, and has borne him six children: Marzie S., William T., Margaret E., Joseph W., Rebecca A. and John S. Prof. Yoes has been a teacher in Turrentine's Academy since January, 1886. His early educational advantages were limited, but by much desultory study and reading has acquired an excellent education. He has mastered several of the sciences without a tutor, and in every particular has been the architect of his own fortune. He belongs to the Democratic party.

MARSHALL COUNTY.

ROBERT L. ADAMS, clerk and master of the Chancery Court of Marshall County, was born June 15, 1833, in that part of Bedford County now included in Marshall County. He was reared on the farm but on account of physical disability did not engage in hard manual labor. He received a good practical education in the country schools and at the age of nineteen commenced teaching in the schools of this county, where he continued for ten years. In 1862 he was elected county court clerk and held that office for a period of twelve years. In 1876 he was appointed clerk and master of the Chancery Court and is still holding that position. When the Bank of Lewisburg was re-established in 1885, Mr. Adams was elected as its president, besides he is one of the directors of the same institution. Previous to this, in 1860, he wedded Jane E. Bell, and by her became the father of seven children, six of whom are living. Politically Mr. Adams is a firm supporter of Democratic principles. For fifty years he has been a citizen of Marshall County and for twenty-two years of that time he has held positions of trust and honor. This fact alone speaks louder for his ability and popularity than mere words. His parents were Alexander D. and Elizabeth (LaRue) Adams, both natives of Virginia and both members of the Presbyterian Church. The father was a stanch Democrat, although all his brothers were Whigs previous to the war. He died in 1866, and the mother passed away in 1875.

T. RIGGS ADAMS is one of ten children of Joseph and Eveline W. (Garrett) Adams, who were born in Bedford and Lincoln Counties, Tenn., respectively. They were married in Bedford County, and there lived until 1853, when they came to Marshall County, and there the father followed farming and stock raising. He was a Whig in former days, but now supports the Democratic party. The mother died in 1885, and the following year Mr. Adams wedded Mrs. Rachel McLean. T. Riggs' ancestors on his father's side were Irish, and on his mother's German. He was born in Bedford County, on the 11th of January, 1840, and received the rearing and education of the average farmer's boy. In 1862 he volunteered in Company C, Eleventh Tennessee Cavalry, and during nearly three years' service was never wounded and only once taken prisoner, and then held but a few days. He has given his time and attention to farming, and owns 165 acres of land. He is unmarried, and a Democrat in politics.

WILLIAM V. ANDREWS, son of Jones and Lucy (Lanier) Andrews, who were born in Virginia in 1791 and 1803, respectively. They both came to Tennessee when young, and were married in Williamson County. To them were born eleven children, only three of whom are living at the present time. The father was an agriculturist, and one of the most successful of his day. He served in the war of 1812, and was a Whig in politics; he died in 1843. His widow and children lived on the old homestead until 1861, when the mother's death occurred. William V. was born November 1, 1824, and spent his early days on a farm. His father, though wealthy, believed in teaching children to work, and he was sent to the field with the servants and earned his living by the sweat of his brow. At the age of eighteen he took charge of the farm of 500 acres, which he managed until his marriage, in 1849, to Tennessee Tucker. To them were born seven children, four of whom are living. Mr. Andrews was a Whig previous to the war, but now votes the Democratic ticket. He owned 342 acres of land, but gave largely to his children. He has given his children good educational advantages, and contributes largely to the support of laudable enterprises.

CLINTON A. ARMSTRONG, junior member of the firm of Smithson & Armstrong, is a son of George and Margaret (Orr) Armstrong, natives, respectively, of Virginia and Tennessee. After marriage they settled in that part of this county, formerly included in Bedford County. Their family consisted of ten children, nine of whom are living. The father followed the occupation of a tiller of the soil and was also engaged in stock trading. He did not aspire to public places, but rather chose to perform the duties of a quiet citizen. The mother was a member of the Associate Reformed Presbyterian Church, and is still living on the old homestead at the ripe old age of seventy-six. Our subject was born in Marshall County, was reared on the farm and educated in the common schools. He subsequently attended Lewisburg Academy. In 1868 he commenced reading law with Col. W. N. Cowden, and the following year was admitted to the bar. In 1869 he led to the altar Maggie Kercheval, by whom he had two children, one of whom is living. For seven years he was a partner of Col. Cowden, but afterward went into partnership with Smithson, which continues to the present. Mrs. Armstrong was a member of the Presbyterian Church; she died April 20, 1886. Mr. Armstrong is a Democrat, and has been practicing his profession for seventeen years in Lewisburg, and has received his share of the business of the county.

REV. P. L. ATKISSON is a son of Pleasant and Sophronia (Holmes) Atkisson. The father was born in Virginia, and when young came to Tennessee, where he married, and after a short residence in Giles County moved to Alabama, and a few years later went to West Tennessee. He was a shoe-maker by trade, and also farmed. To him and wife were born two sons. In 1835 the mother died, and later he wedded Emily Woods, who bore him one son. He was an 1812 soldier and a Jacksonian Democrat. Our subject was born in Mooresville, Ala., October 7, 1825, and was reared on a farm in West Tennessee. He received an academic education, and after studying medicine for some time took a course of lectures at Memphis and practiced that profession a number of years. At the age of twenty-five he commenced his ministerial work, in which he has been engaged ever since. His marriage with Mary O. Ellison was solemnized in 1850, and to them were born eight children, seven of whom are living. Mrs. Atkisson is a member of the Cumberland Presbyterian Church, in which her husband is a minister. He is a Democrat, and in addition to his ministerial work runs a large farm of 500 acres.

ANDREW J. BARTLETT. Cyrus Bartlett was probably born in the Old Dominion, and when a young man came to Tennessee and married Elizabeth Bedford, probably a native of the State, by whom he had twelve children. He was a house carpenter by trade, and many houses are now standing which bear the evidence of his skillful workmanship. He was a Whig in politics, but always cast his vote for Gen. Jackson, because his father fell while serving under him, and the General took upon himself the education of Cyrus. In 1876 he died, being nearly seventy years of age. The mother is yet living. Andrew J. Bartlett, the immediate subject of this sketch, was born in Marshall County, November 2, 1834, and while young received a fair education in the common schools. Having learned the carpenter's trade, he worked at it until the breaking out of the war, when he volunteered in Company D, Fourth Tennessee Cavalry, and served for three and a half years, being sergeant-major the greater part of the time. In 1865 he wedded Martha E. Turner, by whom he has had one child—Alma. Mr. and Mrs. Bartlett are members of the Methodist Episcopal Church South. He is a Democrat, and since 1869 has followed agricultural pursuits, owning at the present time 150 acres of good land in the garden of Tennessee.

HARTWELL G. BAKER was born September 25, 1804, in Davidson County, Tenn., where he was reared on a farm and educated in the common schools. At the age of twenty-four he left home and began clerking in a store, and at the end of five years bought out his employer's stock, valued at $9,000, on credit, and by close attention to business succeeded in paying his debt. He sold goods for about twelve years and made a snug little fortune, but the war breaking out about this time, swept away about $25,000 worth of property. He has redeemed his fortunes somewhat and owns 225 acres of excellent farming land. In 1837 he was married to Narcissa J. Haynes, born October 9, 1817, in Cornersville, and eight children have been born to them, six of whom are living. Mr. Baker was a Whig, but is now a Democrat. About 1845 he quit the mercantile business and turned his attention to farming. He has been a resident of the county forty-three years and belongs to the Masonic fraternity. His parents, Humphrey and Sallie (Hyde) Baker, were born in Virginia and North Carolina, respectively. The father moved to Kentucky when a boy and finally located in Davidson County, Tenn., where he was married. He was a blacksmith by trade and a Democrat in politics, and became the father of ten children. The mother died in 1834, and the father afterward wedded Mrs. Furr, by whom he had two children. Shortly after their marriage they moved to Kentucky, where the father died during the war.

THOMAS H. BELL, farmer, was born February 27, 1820, in Wilson County, and had a limited advantage for schooling though he has supplied the deficiency by private study. At the age of nineteen he was joined in marriage to Martha A. O'Neal, who was born in 1824. This union resulted in the birth of six children. At the end of ten years the mother died and in 1854 our subject wedded Elizabeth J. Bruce, who was born April 27, 1834. This union was blessed by the birth of twelve children. Mr. Bell is a supporter of Democratic principles, and he and wife are active members of the Cumberland Presbyterian Church. He has held the office of constable, deputy sheriff and magistrate, respectively. He was a strong Union man and is a solid prohibitionist. He has one of the best farms of 130 acres in the county though he has devoted considerable time to house carpentering, running engines and superintending mills. He is a son of Fielding and Elizabeth (Jenkins) Bell. The father was born in Virginia and came to Tennessee in 1802. The mother was a native of Tennesee and was a daughter of Col. Jenkins of Revolutionary fame. After marriage they moved to Wilson and finally to Bedford County in 1826 where they spent the remainder of their days. In 1854 the father died and in 1879 the mother, too, passed away.

DR. G. W. BILLS, a retired physician of Marshall County, was born November 24, 1819, in this county and received a rather limited education. He is the son of Daniel G. and Rachel (Summers) Bills, natives of North Carolina, where they were married and lived until 1816 after which they came to this State and located in what is now Marshall County. The father was a doctor and farmer, and he and wife were members of the Christian Church. He was a Democrat in politics and his death occurred in 1862. The mother followed in 1883 in her ninetieth year. The subject's ancestors on both sides were of English-Irish descent. After reaching manhood he taught school for a short time. In 1843 he wedded A. E. A. Richardson, a native of Marshall County, born April 10, 1823. To this union were born five children. In politics he is conservative, having voted the national ticket but once since the war. He and wife are members of the Christain Church. About 1847 he began the study of medicine and after practicing for nearly six years, took a course of lectures at Macon, Ga. He then returned to this county and practiced his profession until 1867, when he turned his attention more exclusively to farming. He has a farm of 325 acres, and for twenty-two years has practiced his profession in this county. He has lived to see all his children, except the youngest, become members of the Christian Church, and marry companions who belong to the same. His eldest daughter, Rebecca C. (deceased), was the wife of Thomas J. Allen, a wide-awake young farmer; the second child is C. T., who married Elizabeth Blackwell, and is farming successfully; the third, Daniel W., married Josie Cowden, and is accounted a good farmer; Mollie G. is the wife J. T. Wolland, who is also a tiller of the soil.

REUBEN BILLINGTON, son of James and Sarah (Walker) Billington, was born March 23, 1823, in what is now Marshall County, and while receiving a common school education, worked on a farm. Like a dutiful son, he remained on the farm until twenty-one years of age, and a year later began the duties of a farmer, and has followed that calling up to the present time. It 1845 he married Matilda Wallace, who was born February 2, 1825, and four children were the result of their union: Malissa (wife of Charles Jones), William K., Amanda M. (wife of C. J. Farris), and Thomas J. Mr. Billington is a stanch Democrat, and after a year's faithful service in the late war in Col. Haynes' company, he was discharged on account of failing health. He owns a farm of 190 acres, and gives considerable attention to breeding stock. His parents were born in North Carolina; the father in 1792 and the mother in 1793. They came to Marshall County, Tenn., when young, and after their marriage always followed agricultural pursuits. Of their nine children seven lived to be grown, and five are still living. James Billington served for some time in the war of 1812; was magistrate and a Democrat. Mrs. Billington died in 1862, and he two years later. Both our subject's grandfathers were Revolutionary soldiers.

THOMAS C. BLACK, a leading druggist of Lewisburg, and a native of Rutherford County, was reared on the farm and educated in the common schools. He is the son of Thomas C. and Catherine W. (Morton) Black. The parents were natives of Rutherford County, Tenn.; the father born in 1808 and the mother 1816. They were married in their native county and were the parents of twelve children, eleven of whom are still living. The father was a physician and farmer. He died in 1876, and the mother still lives on the old homestead. Grandfather Black, a Scotch-Irishman, came in an early day from Scotland and taught one of the first schools of Murfreesboro. Our subject, after reaching manhood, began the mercantile business as salesman for Miles & McKinley, in Murfreesboro. After conducting business in that county on his own responsibility for a short time he came to Marshall County in 1875 and engaged in the lumber business. Five years later he opened a drug store with Dr. S. D. Ewing, in Lewisburg. After dissolving partnership Mr. Black opened the store where he now does an active business. For twelve months he served as a soldier in Col. W. S. McLemore's company. In politics he is a Democrat and is a member of the Presbyterian Church.

JOHN T. BLAKE, a leading merchant of Marshall County, Tenn., and a son of John W. and Mary A. (Morgan) Blake, was born on the 3d of January, 1834, in Lincoln County, Tenn., and received the education and rearing of the average farmer's boy. After attaining man's estate he attended and taught school a short time and then turned his attention to his trade and farming. He had access to the tools in his father's shop, and in time became proficient as a worker in wood and iron. Five children were the result of his marriage, in 1857, to Martha Phillips. Their son, John M., is a traveling salesman for Grayfall & Co., of Nashville, Tenn. Both Mr. and Mrs. Blake are members of the Cumberland Presbyterian Church, and in politics he votes the Democratic ticket. Since 1857 he has resided on the farm where he now lives. He has a general work-shop and as a business man has been fairly successful. His father and mother were born in North Carolina and Virginia, respectively. After marriage they settled in Lincoln County, Tenn., where they spent the remainder of their days as tillers of the soil. Their family consisted of fourteen children, only five of whom are living. The father was an old-line Whig, and after a long and active life died in 1862. The mother, who was a member of the Cumberland Presbyterian Church, outlived him several years.

THOMAS A. BOYD, farmer, was born July 25, 1844, in Williamson County, Tenn. He had the advantages of a common school education, but the war cut short all thoughts of continuing his studies. In 1861 he volunteered in Company C, Eleventh Tennessee Cavalry, Confederate Army. While scouting in East Tennessee he was captured, and after a short imprisonment at Camp Chase he was taken to Fort Delaware, where he remained until the close of the war. He then returned home and went to work on the farm. In 1866 he wedded Mattie S. Wilson, who was born December 2, 1849, in Marshall County. This union has been blessed by the birth of nine children, six of whom are living. Mr. Boyd is a Democrat and he and wife are members of the Cumberland Presbyterian Church. He has a good farm of 250 acres furnished with good buildings. He is a son of Joseph B. and Susan W. (Camden) Boyd. The father was born in North Carolina in 1810, and the mother in Virginia in 1809. They were married in 1831 and soon after settled in this county. At the end of six years they moved to Williamson County and engaged in merchandising. In 1846 he quit the mercantile business to engage in farming. Both parents were active members of the Cumberland Presbyterian Church, of which he has been an elder for about forty years. In 1885 his faithful companion was taken from his side by the hand of death. The father is living with his son Thomas.

THOMAS WESLEY BRENTS, D. D. and M. D. Thomas Brents, Sr., was born in the "Blue-grass State," and there married Jane McWhorter. They resided in the State until 1800, and then came to Marshall County, Tenn., and spent the remainder of their lives in agricultural pursuits. The father, although not an educated man, was a man of remarkable intellectual powers, superior to many of his associates in that particular. He and wife were not professed Christians, but they inclined to the Methodist Episcopal faith. He was an old-line Democrat and died at the age of sixty-two. The mother lived to be fifty-six years old. Thomas Wesley, our subject, was born in Marshall County, February 10, 1823. His early days were spent on a farm and in seeking an education in the old dirt-floor schoolhouse of early days, where the three "R's" were supposed to be sufficient for an education. Before attaining his twenty-first birthday he had never seen a grammar, but notwithstanding the many disadvantages under which he labored, he conceived the idea of gaining a better education, and began a course of private study, often burning the midnight oil in furtherance of his plans. He followed pedagoging about four years and became a disciple of Æsculapius and attended the Eclectic Medical College, of Memphis, Tenn., the Medical School of Nashville, and finally graduated, in 1855, from the Reform Medical College of Georgia, and was chosen demonstrator of anatomy, and later became professor of anatomy and surgery and held that position until the breaking out of the war. Owing to ill health he gave up his practice and moved to the country and devoted much of his time to the ministry, having started in that calling in 1850. He had acquired a thorough knowledge of Latin and his ministerial labors called for a knowledge of the Greek language, which he immediately began mastering. In 1841 he wedded Angeline Scott, who died in 1857, leaving five small children. Late in the same year he married Mrs. Elizabeth (Taylor) Brown, who bore him four children, two of whom are professional men: T. E., a physician, and John, a lawyer. Dr. Brents moved to Burritt in 1874 to educate his children in Burritt College, where three of them graduated. In 1882 he organized the present Bank of Lewisburg and acted as cashier for three years. In politics he is conservative, not having voted since 1856. For fifty-five years he has been a citizen of Marshall County, and whether as a physician, a professor or a minister of the gospel he has few equals and fewer superiors.

ALEXANDER BRYANT, of Marshall County, Tenn., is a son of John F. and Sarah (Amis) Bryant, and was born in Granville County, N. C., December 14, 1818. His parents were also born in North Carolina, and were married in that State, and became the parents of ten children. The father was a well-to-do farmer, and lived in his native State until 1837, and then moved to Tennessee, and located in Marshall County, and there died in 1857. He was a Democrat and for several years held the position of magistrate. The mother died in 1870. Alexander's early school advantages were very limited, never having attended school more than twelve months. After attaining manhood he began farming and has followed that calling through life. In 1842 he wedded Maria Wilkes, by whom he had eleven children. Both he and Mrs. Wilkes are members of the Cumberland Presbyterian Church. Mr. Bryant is a Democrat and as a farmer has met with well deserved success. He has been a resident of Marshall County for twenty-seven years, and has the confidence and respect of all who know him.

JOHN A. BRYANT, farmer, is a son of John F. and Sarah W. (Amis) Bryant, both natives of North Carolina; the father born in 1790 and the mother in 1794. After marriage, in 1837, they removed from their native State and came to Marshall County, where they spent the remainder of their days. This family consisted of ten children, six of whom are living. The father was an industrious tiller of the soil, owning nearly 800 acres of land. He was a Democrat and a man of fair education and good business qualities. His death occurred in 1857. After his death the mother lived a widow on the old homestead until 1870, when she, too, was called away. Our subject was born in North Carolina June 28, 1828, and his ancestors on both sides were of Irish extraction. He was reared on the farm, and owing to the demand for his services at home, received a very limited education. He worked for his father till twenty-one years of age, and then began his career as an independent farmer. In 1860 he wedded Sallie C. Fry, a native of Marshall County, born May 9, 1835, and to them were born four children. In 1862, Mr. Bryant enlisted in Company E, Eleventh Tennessee Confederate Cavalry and after twelve months' service was appointed brigade forage master, and a year later held a position in the ordnance department. During three years of faithful service he was never wounded nor taken prisoner. After peace had been declared he returned to the more peaceful pursuits of farming. He is a member of the Presbyterian Church, and for eight years held the position of magistrate He is a Democrat in politics. He owns over 500 acres of land, and for forty-nine years has been a resident of Marshall County.

JOHN R. BRYANT, farmer and stock raiser, was born February 17, 1849, in Marshall County. He was reared on the farm and received a common English education. At the age of seventeen he took charge of his father's farm and worked out the indebtedness of the estate. In 1870 he wedded Ada S. Pickens, a native of this county, born August 7, 1849. They are both active members of the Cumberland Presbyterian Church. In politics he is a Democrat. Mr. Bryant has a good farm of 173 acres, nearly all of which he has made by industry and close attention to business. Mr. Bryant has lived in Marshall County all his life, and is a good farmer and an honest, upright citizen. He is the son of William T. and Mary E. (Hill) Bryant. The father was born about 1822 in North Carolina, and about 1837 came with his parents to this county. The mother was born in Maury County in 1824, where they were married. They soon settled in this county and made it their permanent home. They have a family of four children—three boys and one girl. Two of the boys are farmers of the neighborhood, and the third is a cotton trader in Texas. The father is a Democrat in politics, and followed the calling of a farmer and stock raiser.

JOHN A. BURROW is a son of John and Catherine (Barron) Burrow, born, respectively, in Maury County and Giles County, in 1810 and 1811, and died in 1882 and 1881. They married and located in Alabama, residing there until 1879, when they returned to Tennessee and settled near the mother's birth-place, in Giles County. Both parents belonged to the Cumberland Presbyterian Church and the father was a Democrat. John A. was born in Lauderdale County, Ala., March 5, 1844. Owing to the breaking out of the war his educational advantages were retarded. He volunteered in Company E, Seventh Alabama Cavalry, and served two and a half years. He was in about twenty battles but did not receive a wound. After his return from the war he began tilling the soil and in 1872 he opened a store in Lawrence County, but at the end of one year was burned out, and soon after returned to the farm where he owns 641 acres of land. Three sons were born to his marriage with Ann E. Allen, whom he married in 1869. Mrs. Burrow died in 1876 and five years later he wedded Nannie Davis, who has borne him two children. He was one of the prime movers in building the Lynnville & Cornersville Turnpike and his efforts have been appreciated by those who know the advantage it has been to the county.

WILLIAM G. CLAYTON is a son of Stephen and Nancy (Hill) Clayton, who were natives of Tennessee and farmers by occupation. The former died in 1837 and the latter in 1826. William G. was born in Lincoln County, November 6, 1817, and received a common school education. In 1837 he wedded Jane S. Bachman, and to them were born eight children. William has followed in his father's footsteps and is a farmer. He started in life with little or no capital; but his hands and feet, step by step, climbed the ladder of success until he became one of the prosperous farmers of Marshall County, and commands the respect and esteem of all. His son, Dr. A. C. Clayton, was' born in Marshall County, February 26, 1842, and spent his juvenile days on his father's farm. He attended the common schools, and in 1862 enlisted in Company I, Fifth Tennessee Confederate Infantry. He was wounded so severely at the battle of Murfreesboro, that he was compelled to give up all ideas of further service. Toward the latter part of the war he spent some time in Texas, and after his return took a course of instruction in Richland Academy, and afterward taught school about seven terms. In 1876 he entered the medical department of Vanderbilt University, and graduated the following year. He has since practiced in Marshall County, and besides this has dealt in stock, lumber, and has been engaged in the milling business. He has a tan-yard in Lawrence County, a small farm in this county and a large one in Gibson County. In 1883 he wedded Mary E. Carter, who lived only about two years. The Doctor is a member of the Methodist Episcopal Church South and a Democrat. He has been a resident of the county about forty years, and has the respect and esteem of all.

DANIEL B. CLAYTON, farmer, of Marshall County, Tenn., is a son of William G. and Jane S. (Bachman) Clayton, and was born in the county where he now resides May 11, 1855. After attending the common schools he completed his education at Lewisburg, and then began the battle of life for himself. He taught one term of school and, in 1878, went to Texas and engaged in the mercantile business. After selling agricultural implements for a short time he opened a grocery store, which he managed two years with good results. He sold out and returned to Marshall County in 1881, and was united in marriage to Cora McCord, by whom he has one child, Mary Lucile. Both Mr. and Mrs. Clayton are active workers in the Methodist Episcopal Church South. They own 325 acres of land in the most fertile portion of Marshall County, it being considered one of the finest stock farms in the county. He takes great interest in raising fine stock, and is a stanch Democrat in his political views.

WILLIAM M. CLARK, son of Thomas and Betsey (Robinson) Clark, is a well-to-do farmer of Marshall County, Tenn., and was born in Giles County June 22, 1822. He was allowed to follow his own inclination in regard to schooling, consequently his education is very limited indeed. After working one year for wages he purchased seventy-five acres of land, largely on credit, and by the sweat of his brow has increased his farm to 375 acres. Two sons and one daughter are the results of his marriage with Mary Jones, which took place in 1849. After her death he married Betsey White, and two children have blessed their union. Mr. Clark and his first wife were members of the Methodist Episcopal Church South; his present wife is a member of the Cumberland Presbyterian Church. In former days our subject was a Whig, but is now a Democrat. His parents were North Carolinians by birth, and shortly after their marriage came to Giles County, Tenn., and followed farming for a livelihood. The father was twice married, his second wife being Nancy McCandless. Nine children were born to his first union and three to his last. The father was a Whig and died when about forty-five years old.

JOHN COWDEN, M. D., one of the leading physicians of Marshall County, is a son of William and Rhoda (Davis) Cowden, natives, respectively, of North Carolina and Tennessee. The father was born in 1806 and the mother in 1811. The father was a blacksmith and wagon-maker. They were married in 1828 and their family consisted of six children—three of whom died within two weeks of scarlet fever. Of the living, two are boys and one is a girl. One of the boys, William N., is a leading criminal lawyer of Lewisburg and the other appears at the head of this sketch. Both parents were united with the Christian Church and have ever lived in accordance with their profession. The father during his short life was an industrious, energetic worker, and was cut off in the bloom of manhood by the frosts of death. His death occurred in 1839. The mother was married again but after the death of her second husband has made her home with the Doctor. Dr. John Cowden was born October 6, 1834, in Marshall County, and received the rudiments of his education in the old-time subscription schools. At the age of sixteen he spent a year at an academy and then began the study of medicine with Dr. T. W. Brents. After studying about a year he took a course of lectures at Memphis and completed his medical education at Macon, Ga., graduating from that institution in 1854. He then began practicing and in 1856 he wedded Mary H. Leonard, a native of this county born January 23, 1837. To this union were born twelve children, ten of whom are living. The eldest son, Charles N., is a graduate of Vanderbilt University and is a practicing physician. Mr. and Mrs. Cowden are members of the Christian Church, and he is a Democrat in politics. He has the honor of being president of the Duck River Valley Railroad, besides being a director of the road since its completion. He has a farm of 200 acres and has followed his profession for thirty-one years.

THOMAS COLLINS, farmer, of Marshall County, Tenn., and son of Willis and Phœbe (Martin) Collins, is one of nine children and was born in the State of Georgia July 27, 1818. He was reared on a farm, and his early education was wholly and needlessly neglected. He was married at an early age, being only nineteen when he and Sarah Childs were united in marriage. Of the six children born to them only two are living: W. P. and Fannie. Since his marriage he has followed agricultural pursuits, and at one time was the owner of nearly 800 acres of land, the greater part of which he has given to his children. In 1884 his wife died, and, after living with his children a year, he was married to Mrs. Nancy E. (Clark) Judia. Previous to the war Mr. Collins was a Whig; since that time he has not cast a party vote. He has been a resident of Marshall County some thirty years, and has the confidence and respect of all who know him. Our subject's father and mother were born in North Carolina and Virginia, respectively, and were married in Georgia. The father was an overseer in the latter State, and came to Tennessee in 1826, where he became the possessor of nearly 1,000 acres of land. He was a soldier under Jackson, and in politics was an old-line Whig. He died in 1854. The mother lived to be about eighty-four years of age.

WILLIS P. COLLINS is the son of Thomas Collins (above written) and was raised on a farm in Giles County, Tenn., where he was born November 11, 1845. He received a common school education and like his father choose the free and independent life of a farmer. In 1866 he married Margaret Smith, who died in 1874, leaving four children. In 1875 he married Hannah G. Beard and to them were born five children. Mr. Collins and his wife are members of the Methodist Episcopal Church South. His first wife belonged to the Christian Church. After his first marriage Mr. Collins resided on a farm given him by his father until 1871 when he located on the farm of 257 acres where he now resides. He is considered one of the skillful farmers of the county and is a man who commands the respect of all.

DAVID COLLINS is a son of Jones Collins, who was born in 1791 in North Carolina. The mother, Sophia (Wright) Collins, was born in 1798, in Georgia. The father participated in the war of 1812, and in 1832 came to Marshall County, Tenn. He is a Jacksonian Democrat, and at the breaking out of the late war led some fourteen of his children and grandchildren to the front. He has always followed farming, and at one time was one of the most extensive land owners in the county. In 1875 the mother died. The father is now (1886) ninety-four years old and enjoys good health. The Collins family were among the earliest settlers of the county and are of Scotch-Irish descent. David Collins was born March 16, 1827, in Georgia. He had good educational advantages but did not improve them, which fact he has always regretted. At the age of seventeen he enlisted to serve in the Mexican war, and after a short service had his leg shattered by an ounce ball at Monterey, disabling him for further service. After he returned home he clerked, farmed, and at the age of twenty-two began operating the Allen Leper Mills. In 1853 he wedded Margaret Glenn, and to them were born five sons. Mr. Collins is a Democrat and the owner of 175 acres of land. His son, John C. Collins, was born September 15, 1858, in Marshall County. His rudimentary education was obtained in the common schools, and later he finished his education at Culleoka. After his return he kept several fine horses for about three years. In 1883 he came to Gill's Chapel and opened a grocery store in an old log house, his capital being $300. By good management he has built a new store-room, a nice frame residence and has increased his stock of goods many fold. He is a member of the Methodist Episcopal Church South and is a Republican in politics.

JAMES W. COLLINS is of Irish-Scotch descent and is a son of Elisha and Betsey (McGregor) Collins, who were born in North Carolina and Virginia in 1807. They came to Tennessee when young and here were married. Of their ten children seven are living. The father was a farmer and Democrat and died in 1872. The mother is yet living at the age of seventy-nine. February 15, 1832, is the date of our subject's birth which occurred in Marshall County. Being the eldest son he was obliged to assist his father on the farm, consequently his educational advantages were limited. At the age of twenty-one he began farming for himself and in 1861 volunteered in Company I, Second Mississippi Infantry. He was captured at Maryville, Tenn., but succeeded in making his escape. After the war he resumed farming and, in 1866, was united in marriage to Nancy McKnight, daughter of Ezekiel M. Mr. and Mrs. Collins have no children. They are members of the Methodist Episcopal Church South, and in politics Mr. Collins is a Democrat. He owns a farm of 185 acres, the fruits of his own labor.

HENRY L. COLLINS, one of the prosperous farmers of Marshall County, Tenn., was born September 28, 1845. His early education was wholly neglected, but he has overcome this deficiency by study during his leisure moments, and now has a fair general education. In 1863 he volunteered in Forrest's command Eleventh Tennessee Cavalry and after serving two years and receiving a slight wound he returned home and resumed farming. In 1866 he wedded Fannie Collins, by whom he had ten children, eight of whom are living. He is a Democrat and owns a 330-acre farm, one of the best in the county. He takes great pride in raising fine Holstien cattle, and some of his animals are the best in the county. His parents, Henry and Nancy E. (Cunningham) Collins, had both been married previous to their union. The father was married to Fannie Martin, by whom he had nine children, and the mother's first husband was O. P. Sheppard, by whom she had one child. Our subject, Henry Collins, is the only child born to their union. The father was a native of North Carolina, and moved from there to Georgia, thence to Tennessee in 1826. He was a Democrat and farmer and died in 1861, followed by his widow a year later.

SAMUEL A. CRUTCHER, farmer, is a son of Robert and Nancy L. (Childress) Crutcher, both parents born and reared in Virginia. The father was born in 1788 and the mother in 1800. They were united in marriage in 1815, and lived in Virginia till 1823, when they came to Tennessee and settled in Williamson County, where they passed the remainder of their days. They reared eleven children, nine of whom are living at the present time. The mother died in 1861 and the father in 1866. Our subject was born October 14, 1818, in Amherst County, Va., and when five years old came with his parents to Williamson County. He received a rather limited education, and at the age of twenty-one began the free life of a farmer. In 1843 he married Catherine P. Blackwell, a native of Kentucky, born February 22, 1822, and the fruits of this union were an interesting family of ten children, eight of whom are living. Having saved his earnings Mr. Crutcher bought a sixty-acre tract of land, which he afterward sold, and bought the farm of 282 acres where he now lives, going in debt for nearly all of it. By hard work and good management he paid for it in three years. Mr. Crutcher is a Democrat, and he and wife are church members, he of the Cumberland Presbyterian and she of the Methodist Protestant Church. For twenty-six years he has been a citizen of Marshall County, and enjoys the confidence and respect of all who know him.

ROBERT P. CRUTCHER, farmer and miller of Marshall County, Tenn., is a son of Robert and Nancy L. (Childress) Crutcher, and was born in Williamson County, Tenn., February 3, 1828. He made his home with his parents until twenty-seven years of age, and acquired a common school education, after which he began doing for himself. In 1855 he married Mary E. Thompson, who bore him three children: Hugh M., Mary A. and William B. (deceased). Hugh wedded Jennie Wallace, and is a farmer and miller; Mary is the wife of Whit Rone, also a farmer and miller. Mrs. Crutcher was born September 8, 1831, in Williamson County, and is a member of the Methodist Episcopal Church South. Soon after his marriage Mr. Crutcher located on the farm where he now lives. He also worked at the shoe-maker's trade, and had a good custom until 1859, when he opened a tan-yard where his mill now stands. Shortly after the close of the war he erected a small grist and saw-mill, which he ran with a ten-horse thresher engine, but soon tore this building down and erected a fine mill. He owned a farm of 400 acres, part of which he has given to his children, and now owns about 212 acres. He is a stirring business man, and upright in all his dealings with his fellow-men.

W. M. CRUTCHER, dentist, is a son of Robert and Nancy L. (Childress) Crutcher (for further particulars of parents see sketch of Samuel A. Crutcher), and was born November 16, 1833, in Williamson County. During his youth he had good advantages for receiving an education, but did not make the best use of them, a fact he has regretted all his life. In 1861 he enlisted in Company D, First Tennessee Infantry, Confederate Army, and during the four years of service was never taken prisoner. At the battle of Chickamauga he was struck by a minie-ball, inflicting an ugly flesh wound. Having returned and farmed a year he turned his attention to the profession of dentistry. In 1866 he married May L. Hays, who was born in Maury County, June 9, 1846. This union was blessed by the birth of nine children. Mr. Crutcher is a Democrat, and he and wife and three of the boys are members of the Missionary Baptist Church. Our subject has now practiced his profession in this country about nineteen years and has received a liberal patronage from the people.

WILLIAM A. DYSART, farmer, was born in Marshall County in 1831. He was reared on the farm, attended the district school in the winter seasons and received a good practical education. January 31, 1860, he married Elizabeth E. Bivins, and the union was blessed by three children: Clarence M., Anna L. and William E. Both parents are consistent members of the Presbyterian Church. November 8, 1862, Mr. Dysart volunteered in Company D, Fourth Tennessee Cavalry and was engaged in all the battles in which his company took part. His regiment was detailed through North Carolina as a body-guard for Jefferson Davis. Mr. Dysart remained with his command until it returned to Chattanooga, when his regiment was disbanded and he returned home. He is a Democrat and has voted that ticket since the Rebellion. He is one of Marshall County's most enterprising and energetic farmers, has a fine tract of land and his residence is beautifully located. Mrs. Dysart is a very intelligent and accomplished lady. Our subject's parents were Andrew and Jane (Ewing) Dysart. The father was born in North Carolina in about 1782, immigrated with his parents to Kentucky when quite young; then to Williamson County, and in about 1800 came to Marshall County. Here, in about 1815, he was married and became the father of thirteen children, eight of whom are living. He and wife are worthy members of the Old School Presbyterian Church. The mother died in 1867, and the father in 1868. Our subject's ancestors were of Scotch-Irish lineage. His grandfather was one of the brave men who fought in the Revolutionary war.

CHARLES A. DABNEY was born November 8, 1819, and received a common English education. At the age of eighteen he began to make his own way in the world. In 1865 the nuptials of his marriage with Miss Sallie Cox were celebrated. She is a daughter of Robert Cox, of North Carolina. In early life Mr. Dabney was a Whig in politics, but is now a strong supporter of Democratic principles. He is a wealthy farmer, and owns 741 acres of good land, the greater part of which he has made by his own industry. He has been a resident of Marshall County for over fifty years, and is one of the thrifty farmers and honest citizens of the county. His parents, John and Nancy (Cox) Dabney, were born, reared and married in North Carolina. They came to Tennessee in 1806, and located in what is now Marshall County when it was almost an unbroken canebrake. The father served as magistrate a number of years, and in politics was an old-line Whig. He died in 1857 and the mother in 1831.

ISAAC V. DARK, farmer, was born July 14, 1818, in Wilson County, Tenn., son of James and Martha (Gates) Dark, both natives of North Carolina. They were married in Wilson County, and afterward moved to this county, where the mother died. The father then married Sarah Fisher, went to Illinois, but finally settled in West Tennessee, where he died. He was a farmer and millwright by occupation. He was a soldier in the war of 1812, and participated in the battle of New Orleans. Our subject grew to manhood on the farm and received a common school education. In 1839 his marriage to Lydia C. Green was solemnized and the results of this union were the birth of eight children—three boys and five girls. Two of the boys, James and Harris, were soldiers in the late war. At Chickamauga the former received a wound in the foot from the effects of which he died. The second served until the close of the war. In 1876 our subject's first wife died and about five months later he married Martha Steward, by whom he had five children—three boys and two girls. Mr. Dark is a member of the Methodist Episcopal Church. For twelve years he served as magistrate, filling that office in an able and satisfactory manner. For about twenty-six years he worked at the shoe-making trade, being a first-class workman. At the present he is engaged in agricultural pursuits and has a good farm of 168 acres. He has been a resident of Marshall County for sixty-one years and is accounted a good farmer and an excellent citizen. He is a Democrat in politics.

GEORGE W. DAVIS, one of the leading liverymen of Lewisburg, was born on a farm in Marshall County, in 1855, and received a common school education. He is a son of Martin and Lizzie (Talley) Davis. The father was a farmer and a stanch Democrat. He died in 1866. The mother was a member of the Baptist Church, and died while she was yet comparatively young. At the age of nineteen the subject of this sketch, after tending bar some time, opened a saloon in Lewisburg, in 1877, and about five years later engaged in the livery business. He has been quite successful and is engaged in that business at the present time. In 1880 he was united in marriage to Mollie E. Richie, and to this union was born one child, Mabel C. In 1885 our subject's first stable was burned, and the same year he built the large brick that he now has. In politics Mr. Davis is, like his father, an ardent Democrat. For nine years he has been in business in Lewisburg and has succeeded well. He has a good stable well stocked.

WILLIAM M. DAVIS AND WILLIAM R. JAMES are members of the firm of Clayton, Davis & Co., millers, of Cornersville, Tenn. The former is a son of Nathan C. and Mary (Woods) Davis, who were born in the State and became the parents of seven children. The father was an agriculturist and a Democrat, and died in 1882. After his wife's death, in 1860, he married Mrs. Sallie Johnson, by whom he had five children. William M. was born August 23, 1851, and secured the rearing and education of the average farmer's boy. After attaining his majority he began farming for himself, and in 1876 married Ella M. McMahon, by whom he had two children: Minnie K. and Sallie J. In 1883 Mr. Davis engaged in his present business of grist and saw-milling, and is now making preparations to put in the patent rollers. Mr. Davis is a Democrat, and a man who attends closely to business, consequently he has prospered in his undertakings. William R. James, one of the above named firm, is a son of Pleasant L. and Emily (Freeland) James, who were born and passed their lives in Tennessee. Their family consisted of four children, our subject and one other son being the only living members. The father was a Democrat, and died in 1853. The mother's death occurred in 1862. William R. was born in Giles County, October 16, 1845, and was reared on a farm in Marshall County. In 1861 he volunteered in Company H, Third Tennessee Infantry, and was one of the defenders of Fort Donelson. He was captured and imprisoned at Chicago, and, after being exchanged at Vicksburg, returned to the army, but was soon discharged, being too young for the service. He then returned home and resumed farming. In 1869 he and Amanda K. Ferguson were united in marriage. She died in 1878, leaving four children. He then wedded Jennie McMahon, who died in 1884, having become the mother of two children. The following year Mr. James married Nannie McMahon, sister of his second wife. In 1884 he moved to Cornersville and in 1886 engaged in the milling business.

WILLIAM M. DOZIER, farmer, is a son of Zachariah and Cynthia A. (Johnson) Dozier, natives, respectively, of Missouri and Tennessee. The former was born in 1800 and the latter in 1809. The father moved, when young, to Kentucky, and finally to Rutherford County, where he was married. He was a farmer and a member of the Primitive Baptist Church, as was also his wife. He was a Democrat in politics. His death occurred in 1870. The mother died in 1885. William M. Dozier was born December 15, 1834, and, like the average country boy, received his education in the common schools. At the age of nineteen he went into the mercantile business as salesman, where he remained for eight years. In 1861 he enlisted in Capt. Webb's company of Eighteenth Tennessee Infantry as second lieutenant, and after nearly two years of faithful service he returned to his mercantile business. In 1868 he wedded Calidonia Talley, by whom he has two children: Ada M. and William Z. Mr. Dozier is a Democrat in politics, and he and wife are members of the Christian Church. For ten years he has successively and successfully held the office of constable. He has been a resident of Marshall County for over twenty-one years, and is considered one of the county's best citizens.

ALLAN L. EWING is a son of Lyle A. and Rebecca A. (Leeper) Ewing, born, respectively, in Georgia and Tennessee, in 1808. They became the parents of nine children, eight of whom lived to be grown. The father began life a poor boy and afterward opened a store in Farmington and became a wealthy man. He was magistrate of his district sixteen years and was an old-line Whig in politics. He died in 1853 and the mother in 1878. Our subject's ancestors on both sides were Scotch-Irish. He was born April 28, 1833, in Marshall County. His early school advantages were very good; besides this he attended Lewisburg Academy, Maryville College, and completed his education at Shelbyville University. After teaching about four years he turned his attention to farming, and in 1861 volunteered in Company H, Forty-first Tennessee Infantry. In 1863 he was captured at Farmington, Miss., and after an imprisonment of four months at Alton, Ill, he was exchanged at Vicksburg. After returning to service he was made sergeant. In 1864 he was again taken prisoner and would have been shot had it not been for a Union lad of seventeen. A drunken Federal soldier had leveled his gun to shoot him when the lad knocked aside the gun, the ball barely missing Mr. Ewing. He returned to farming after the surrender and in 1868 wedded Marian V. Palmer They are both church members, and in politics he is a conservative Democrat. He owns 353 acres of land besides a house and lot and grist-mill.

NEWTON B. EWING is a son of James Ewing, who was born in the "Keystone State" in 1782. After residing in Georgia for some time he came to Tennessee, and, soon after his marriage with Mary Neill, settled in Marshall County, where he reared a family of eight children. He was a Whig and acted as magistrate for many years. After the mother's death, in 1828, he wedded Mrs. Sarah How, and died in 1860. Our subject was born in Bedford County, Tenn., November 2, 1826, and inherits Scotch-Irish blood from his father. He received the education and rearing of the average farmer's boy, and at the age of nineteen began to battle his own way in the world by farming and trading. He owns 223 acres of land and is quite a successful farmer. In 1853 he married Florella J. Ewing, who was born May 2, 1835. They are members of the Presbyterian Church. During the war he served some time in Company H, Seventeenth Tennessee Infantry, although his health was very poor. Previous to the war he was a Whig, but is now a Democrat. He has lived within the limits of Marshall County all his life, and he and wife have passed thirty-three years of happy wedlock, and are surrounded by many warm friends and relatives.

DR. J.C. C. EWING, one of the good farmers of Marshall County, is a son of James V. and Elizabeth (Ewing) Ewing. The father was born in Wythe County, Va., in 1805 and was one of the most extensive farmers in this county. He was for many years magistrate, and held for several terms the position of chairman of the county court. He died in 1878. The mother was born near Athens, Ga., in 1813, and since the death of her husband has been living on the old homestead, and is now seventy-three years of age. Our subject was born November 12, 1839, in Marshall County, and his ancestors on both sides were of Scotch-Irish extraction. He was reared on the farm and had a fair opportunity for schooling, completing his education at Shelbyville. In 1860 he began the study of medicine under McClure & Johnson, of Lewisburg, and the same year took a course of lectures at the University of Nashville. The stirring events of the war cut short his medical pursuits. In 1861 he volunteered in Company H, Seventeenth Tennessee Infantry. During the four years of the war he never received a scratch nor was he ever taken prisoner. After returning home he practiced his profession four years at Lewisburg, and then completed his course at the Bellevue Medical College, and graduated from that institution in 1870. He then returned home and engaged in agricultural pursuits, and has continued that occupation up to the present time. Mr. Ewing has a farm of 500 acres, and is accounted a good farmer and an enterprising citizen. In politics he is conservative, voting for the man rather than the party.

GEORGE WYTHE EWING AND WILLIAM K. KERCHEVAL, editors and proprietors of *Marshall Gazette*, were born and reared in this county, and. while growing up, received their education in the common schools. The former (Mr. Ewing) took quite an extensive course under William Stoddert, D. D., embracing nearly the entire course of the University of Virginia. After completing his school days, he taught mathematics and language in Lewisburg Institute for two terms, and the same at Farmington Academy and some minor schools. Mr. Kercheval finished his education at Fayetteville, Tenn. In 1871 the *Marshall Gazette* was established, and, two years later, Mr. Ewing and two partners purchased the paper and office, and soon after Mr. Kercheval joined him; thus Mr. Ewing and he became sole proprietors, going in debt for the greater portion of it. Both were wholly unacquainted with the business, but notwithstanding they have made it a success and their crisp, newsy, eight-column paper has a circulation of about 1,100. George Wythe Ewing is a son of James S. Ewing, who was born July 5, 1824, in Maury County, and at the age of twenty began his career as a farmer, following that occupation for a period of fourteen years. In 1845 he wedded Eliza J. Rivens, by whom he had two children, only one of whom (our subject) is living. In 1859 the father came to Lewisburg and engaged in merchandising, following that business almost ever since. Both he and wife are worthy members of the Presbyterian Church, of which he has been an elder for about thirty-two years. For some time during the war he served as conscript officer in the Confederacy. He served as trustee of this county, and also as magistrate. He is a Democrat in politics, and the son of William D. and Rebecca (Ewing) Ewing, the former born in 1786, and died in 1872, and the latter born in 1791 and died in 1847.

J. BRITT EZELL, farmer, was born July 14, 1838, in Marshall County, and at the age of thirteen, with the consent of his parents, went to live with J. Britt Fulton, an uncle, who had no children of his own. While with him he received a good academic education. About the same time his uncle took a little girl, by the name of Sarah J. Reynolds, to raise. She and Britt grew up together, went to school together, and as time passed on childish affection gave place to the stronger affections of man and womanhood, and, in 1860, they were united in matrimony. To them seven children were born, five of whom are living. He is a Democrat in politics, and he and wife are members of the Methodist Episcopal Church. In 1861 Mr. Ezell volunteered in Company A, Fourth Tennessee Cavalry, Confederate Army. After about fifteen months' service as quartermaster and commissary, he was transferred to the purchasing commissary department, where he continued till the close of the war. During the whole time he was in the war he was neither wounded nor taken prisoner. Since that time he has been extensively engaged in farming and trading. When his uncle died he left a farm of 236 acres to our subject and wife, to which has been added sufficient to make it 670 acres. Our subject has lived in this county all his life, and is considered a good farmer and an enterprising citizen. He is a son of Joseph D. and Mary C. (Fulton) Ezell, both natives of Tennessee, the father born in 1810 and the mother in 1817. The father was a farmer, besides being engaged largely in trading and stock raising. For several years he held the position of magistrate, but was not a man who aspired to places of public trust. He died in 1880, leaving his widow and children well provided for. Since his death the mother has lived with her children.

REV. THOMAS B. FISHER was born February 5, 1844, in Marshall County, and was of German descent from his paternal ancestors and Irish from his maternal. He was reared on the farm and received a common school education. In 1862 he enlisted in Capt. Miller's Company, Eleventh Tennessee Cavalry, Confederate Army, where he remained till the close of the war. He and four brothers served in that contest; one of them received a wound, from the effects of which he died several years after the war. Having returned home, our subject attended school in his own county and took a course at Union University, graduating from the literary department in 1869. He then joined the Tennessee Conference, and has been engaged in preaching the word of God ever since. In 1872 he married Sallie H. Roberts, who was born in Marshall County, August 31, 1847. This union was blessed by the birth of four children: Wilson P., Fannie B. (deceased), John R. and Mary. Mrs. Fisher and her son Wilson are also members of the Methodist Episcopal Church South. In 1883 Mr. Fisher moved to the farm and has remained there ever since, but he still carries on his ministerial work. For seventeen years he has been actively engaged in the good cause, and his ability as a preacher is too well known to require comment. He is a son of John and Mildred (Stratton) Fisher. The father was born in North Carolina in 1806, and was the eldest of twenty-one children. The mother was born in November, 1810, in Maury County, and was the second wife of John Fisher. This union resulted in the birth of three children, all boys, two of whom are living. The father was a blacksmith and wagon-maker by trade until after he had passed the meridian of life, when he turned his attention exclusively to farming. He died in 1882 and his wife followed about three months later.

JOHN L. FITZPATRICK, a leading farmer of Marshall County, was born December 29, 1847, in Maury County. His youthful days were passed on the farm and in securing an education at the Mooresville school. At the age of twenty-five he left home and went to Texas on a grand buffalo hunt, and for five years was engaged in this pursuit. He killed some 3,000 buffalo and hundreds of deer, antelope and wolves. Having returned home he, in 1880, married Rebecca B. Grant, a native of West Virginia, born May 9, 1850. This union resulted in the birth of two children: Samuel W. (deceased), and John P. Mr. and Mrs. Fitzpatrick are members of the Methodist Episcopal Church. He is a Democrat in politics and owns 465 acres of the best land in his district. He is a son of Col. S. W. and Mary D. (Love) Fitzpatrick. The father was born in 1812 in Giles County and the mother in 1814 in Maury County, where they were married in 1832. They lived in this county until 1859 and then moved to Marshall County. In 1873 they returned to Maury County and there passed the remainder of their days. The father, three years previous to his death, joined the Methodist Episcopal Church. The mother was a member of the Primitive Baptist Church from girlhood. During the days of militia he held the position of colonel. He was a farmer by occupation, owning some 3,000 acres of land and 150 negroes, besides abundance of stock, but the war swept away many thousands for him. When Grandfather Fitzpatrick came to this county he brought his wife and household goods on a pony, himself walking, accompanied by six bear dogs and his rifle. At the age of thirty-six he determined to go to work, and as a result, when he died at seventy-two years of age he was worth $325,000. January, 1880, the mother died, and in December of the same year he too passed away.

ROBERT M. FOLLIS, a prosperous farmer of Marshall County, Tenn., was born in Giles County, Tenn, November 18, 1830. His early education was almost wholly neglected, and while growing up he learned the blacksmith's trade with his father. After becoming grown he attended school until he had learned the three "R's" and then resumed working at his trade. In 1851 he wedded Sarah Compton, by whom he had six children, all sons. She died in 1872, and the following year he married Mary Jones. To them were born three children. In 1862 he volunteered in Capt. Gordon's company, Eleventh Tennessee Cavalry, and served for nearly three years. He resumed his trade, and in 1882 abandoned work, owing to his right arm giving out. He has farmed since that time, and owns 326 acres of land, the most of which he has made by hard work. His parents, John and Elizabeth (Martin) Follis, were born in North Carolina and Kentucky, respectively. The father moved to Kentucky when young, and there married, and soon removed to Giles County, where he lived until his death. They were the parents of eleven children, and were members of the Primitive Baptist Church. He was an old-line Whig in politics, and died in 1845. After his death the mother moved to Illinois, and there died in 1882.

A. S. FOSTER, farmer, was born May 9, 1816, in Lincoln County. While growing he strongly desired an education, but the opportunities were not afforded. In 1836 he wedded Martha M. Cunningham, and nine children blessed this union. In 1883 his wife died, and the same year he wedded Fannie L. J. Foster. Our subject is a Democrat and a member of the Primitive Baptist Church. He has been magistrate and deputy sheriff, and is an example of what a young man of industry and determination can do, having started to keeping house with less than $100 worth of property, he arose by hard work and close attention to business to one of the heaviest tax payers of his community. For about thirty-two years he has lived in this county, and is accounted a good farmer and an enterprising citizen. He is a son of Frederick and Sallie (Broadaway) Foster. The father was born in 1793 in Kentucky, and the mother in 1797 in North Carolina. They were married in 1818, and located in Lincoln County, but soon moved to Illinois, where they remained seven years. They then returned to Lincoln County, where they spent the remainder of their lives tilling the soil. The father was a soldier in the Creek war, and a Democrat in politics. He died in 1838, and the mother followed in 1857.

JAMES E. FOWLER is a son of Alanthas L. and Tennessee A. (Fowler) Fowler. The father was born in Virginia in 1822, and the mother in Tennessee in 1831. Alanthas Fowler came to Tennessee in 1829, and married our subject's mother in 1848. To them were born four children, James E. being the only one living. The father served in the late war in Capt. McCure's company, Forty-first Tennessee Confederate Infantry, and was one of the defenders of Fort Donelson. After his capture and imprisonment at Camp Morton, some seven months, he was exchanged at Vicksburg, and served no more, owing to ill health. He has lived the quiet, independent life of a farmer, and casts his vote with the Democratic party. The mother died in 1860. He is now sixty-three years old, and has the confidence and respect of all who know him. James, his only child, was born August 25, 1851, in Marshall County. He was reared on a farm, and received a common school education. After taking a trip West for his health, he returned to the farm given to him, and in connection with his father is farming and raising stock. Anna M. Willis became his wife in 1882, and to them two children were born. Both husband and wife are members of the Christian Church, and James is a Democrat.

DR. F. FERGUSON, one of the leading practitioners of Marshall County, was born February 18, 1848, in that county, reared on the farm and had all the advantages that the common schools of those days afforded. He is a son of John F. and Amelia L. (Brittain) Ferguson. The father was a native of South Carolina and the mother of North Carolina. In early life they both came to what is now Marshall County, being among the early comers to that part of the State. For many years the father was a magistrate but his chosen profession was that of a farmer, being one of the most extensive in the community. After the death of the mother the father married Mary Brittain whose maiden name was Williams. In 1870 the father also passed away. In 1869 our subject began the study of medicine under Dr. J. B. Stephens of Nashville and late in the same year entered the medical department of the University of Nashville and graduated from that institution in 1871. He then opened an office in District No. 7, and has followed his profession there ever since. Besides what his practice brings him he has a good farm of 280 acres. In 1873 he wedded Sallie J. Robinson, who was born in this county August 21, 1855. To this union were born three children: John T., Maggie R. and James F. Mr. Ferguson is a Democrat in politics and he and wife are members of the Primitive Baptist Church. The patronage Mr. Ferguson has received and the financial advancement he has made render comments on his ability both as a farmer and a physician unnecessary.

GEORGE W. GARRETT. Levi Garrett, father of George W., was born in the "Palmetto State" in 1790, and when a small lad was taken to Virginia where he lived to be grown. He then came to Tennessee, having in his possession at the time of his arrival only a horse and 50 cents. He followed the occupation of farming and became the owner of 1,000 acres of land. He remained single until nearly fifty years of age, and then wedded Miss Davis, who was born in Tennessee in 1818, and to them were born eight children. The father was an 1812 soldier and in politics was an old-line Democrat. He died in 1867 and the mother nine years later. Jesse J. Garrett, son of Levi Garrett, was born in Marshall

County, October 1, 1846. His school days were limited and at the age of eighteen he enlisted in Company E, Eleventh Tennessee Cavalry, being an escort of Gen. Hood for a time and was with Forrest until the close of the war. He has been a farmer and owns 240 acres of excellent land. In 1868 he married Mary Ferguson, by whom he has had four daughters. She died in 1880 and since that time he and his children have kept house. Mr. Garrett is a Democrat. George W. Garrett, our immediate subject and son of Levi Garrett, was born October 27, 1852, in Marshall County. Like his brother he received a limited education and at the age of nineteen became an independent farmer on the place where he now lives. In 1873 he wedded S. L. Neren, daughter of Isaiah and Amanda (Hall) Neren, and to them were born five children. Mr. Garrett owns 196 acres of fertile land and is a stanch Democrat in his political views. He and Mrs. Garrett are members of the Cumberland Presbyterian Church.

THOMAS E. GARRETT, dealer in stoves and tinware, is a son of Jacob and Mary A. (Morris) Garrett, natives, respectively, of North Carolina and Maryland. The father died at the age of seventy-seven and the mother at the age of sixty-five. The father was a farmer, a Democrat, and he and wife were members of the Methodist Episcopal Church. Our subject was born September 23, 1842, in Sumner County, Tenn.; he passed his early days on the farm and attended the common schools. At the age of seventeen he began learning the tinner's trade with McClure, Buck & Co., of Nashville. After learning this trade, in 1877, he opened a store of his own in Lewisburg, and has been doing a good business since. In 1879 he wedded Elizabeth M. Brandon, and to this union were born two children. During the war he enlisted in Company F, Fifteenth Tennessee Cavalry, and served nearly two years. He then returned home and resumed his trade. Mr. Garrett is a Democrat, and he and wife are members of the Methodist Episcopal Church. Mr. Garrett has been a resident of Lewisburg for nine years, and is recognized as one of the wide-awake business men of the town.

ANDREW J. GRIFFIS, senior member of the firm of Griffis & Bro., of Robertson Fork, Tenn., is a son of T. M. and Nancy E. (Carner) Griffis, natives of Tennessee, where they grew to manhood and womanhood and were married. They spent the greater part of their lives in what is now Marshall County, and here raised their family of ten children. They were members of the Cumberland Presbyterian Church, and in politics the father was a Democrat. He served a short time during the late war and is now a prosperous farmer. The mother died in 1879. Andrew is of Irish-French descent and was born in Marshall County, July 22, 1847. He received a very limited education in his youth, but on reaching manhood he attended Cumberland University and afterward taught school a short time. He then began the mercantile business with A. D. Wallace. Since 1872 he and his brother have been in business together, and in connection with their store operate a large farm. Six children were born to his marriage with Bettie E. Tucker, which occurred in 1873. They are members of the Cumberland Presbyterian Church, and he is a Democrat politically.

SAMUEL T. HARDISON, M. D., one of the leading practitioners of Lewisburg, was born in Maury County, Tenn., February 13, 1841. He was reared on a farm and educated in country schools. At the age of nineteen he began the study of medicine under his father and in 1860 he entered the Reform Medical College, at Macon, Ga., where he took one course and then, in 1861, enlisted in Company G, Twenty-fourth Tennessee Infantry, Confederate States Army. Early in 1862 he was promoted to a position in the medical department of the army, serving in all four years. In 1865 Dr. Hardison began the practice of medicine at Lewisburg and has ever since continued in that profession, graduating in 1877 from the medical department of the University of Nashville. He has also been interested in the drug business, hardware trade, house building, livery business, planing-mill, and at present is a director of the Bank of Lewisburg. He has once been president of Marshall County Medical Society, having been a member of that society since its organization. He has also filled the office of vice-president of the Medical Association of Tennessee. Dr. Hardison was married in 1868 to Georgia Davidson, daughter of Dr. I. S.

Davidson, of Bedford County, Tenn., the fruits of this union being seven children. Both he and Mrs. Hardison are members of the Christian Church. Our subject is a relative of the American Gen. Howe, of Revolutionary fame. His parents, Dr. Joel and Jane (Long) Hardison, were natives of North Carolina; they were married in 1820, and eleven children, four of whom are living, blessed their union. The father was a Jacksonian Democrat; he died in 1873. The mother died in 1884.

HIRAM HARRIS, an old and prominent farmer, was born October 20, 1806, in North Carolina, and is a son of James and Nancy (Thompson) Harris, both natives of North Carolina. They were married in this State, and in 1808 came to Tennessee and located in Bedford County, where they spent the remainder of their days. The father followed agricultural pursuits, and during Indian troubles he was captain of a company under Jackson. In 1863 he died, and about seven years later his widow too passed away, both living to a ripe old age. Our subject was educated in the old-time schools, and at the age of twenty-one bought a farm of his own and began his career as a free and independent farmer. In 1837 he came to Marshall County, and has made this his home ever since. In 1828 he wedded Jane P. Johnson, who was born in Davidson County, Tenn., July 3, 1807, and to them were born eleven children. Mr. Harris is a Democrat, and he and wife are members of the Methodist Protestant Church. He has a fine farm of over 200 acres. He has been a resident of this county for nearly thirty years and is a highly respected citizen. He and wife are enjoying good health and fifty-eight years of wedded life.

ROBERT C. HARRIS, merchant at Silver Creek, was born September 24, 1856, in Marshall County, reared on a farm and educated in the common schools. At the age of seventeen he began working at the mechanic's trade and followed this exclusively for five years. In 1878 he opened a store of general merchandise at Silver Creek, where he has been successfully engaged ever since. In 1880 he was united in marriage to Mary A. Perry, a native of Marshall County, born December 20, 1857. The fruits of this union were two children: Lula M. and Homer T. For eight years Mr. Harris has held the position of postmaster at Silver Creek. He is a Democrat in politics. He is the son of James G. and Susan I. (Hill) Harris. The father was born in Wilson County in 1811, and the mother in Maury County in 1818. They were married in the latter county and after a short residence there moved to Marshall County to make this their permanent home. Their family consisted of seven children—five boys and two girls. Only the boys are living. Two are merchants, one is a teacher, and two are farmers. The father was twice married, before he wedded Miss Hill. He was a farmer, but worked at mercantile arts of nearly all kinds. He was a Democrat and for several years was a member of the County Court of Maury County. In 1882 he was called from the toils of earth. Since the death of her husband the mother has lived on the old homestead with her son.

VALENTINE O. HAYES, dry goods merchant, of Lewisburg, was one of seven children born to Hiram and Sallie (Webb) Hayes. The father was born in North Carolina and when young came to this State, and after marriage settled in this county. About 1856 he moved to Missouri, where the mother died. He was a blacksmith and a wood workman by trade. Our subject was born June 20, 1854, in Marshall County. After the death of his father, at the age of eight, he was bound out to a farmer, who gave him but little schooling though he furnished him abundance of work. On reaching manhood he worked for wages on the farm and spent the money in schooling himself. In 1877, he came to Lewisburg and entered the store of Montgomery Bro. as saleman, At the end of four years he opened a store of general mercandise. In 1874 he built the commodious brick building where he now conducts his business. For a short time he ran a hardware and a dry goods store, but having sold the former he made a specialty of the latter. In 1881 he wedded Zadie London, by whom he has two children. Mr. Hayes is a Republican in politics, and he and wife are members of the Cumberland Presbyterian Church. He is accounted one of Lewisburg's most enterprising citizens, and has erected three of the best buildings in the town. His building, where he is engaged in business, was the first business brick building erected in Lewisburg.

E. P. C. HAYWOOD, M. D., a resident of Marshall County, Tenn., is a son of George W. and Sarah B. (Dabney) Haywood, who were born in North Carolina and Tennessee in 1798 and 1809, respectively. The father was a physician and a highly educated man, having graduated from both a literary and a medical college. He was a skillful practitioner and in politics was a Whig. He died when about forty-nine years of age. His paternal ancestors were of English descent. The mother is of Scotch lineage and is yet living. Our subject was born in Marshall County September 5, 1845, and was reared on a farm and received an academic education preparatory to entering college, but the breaking out of the war changed his plans, and instead of attending school he, in 1864, enlisted in Gordon's Company, Eleventh Tennessee Cavalry, and served until the close of the war. He returned home and farmed until 1869, when he began studying medicine under Dr. Alfred White, and in 1870 entered the University of Nashville and graduated two years later. He practiced four years in Cornersville and then engaged in farming. Six children were born to his union with Isabelle Marsh, which took place in 1874. Both are members of the Methodist Episcopal Church South and in politics he is a Democrat. He owns a farm of 1,000 acres, and a one-half interest in a grist and flour mill.

WILLIAM L. HILL, farmer, is a son of William and Elizabeth (Arnold) Hill, natives of Virginia. After marriage they came to Tennessee and located in the Maury fraction of Marshall County, where they lived about thirty years. They then moved to West Tennessee, where they both died. The family consisted of nine children, six of whom lived to be grown. Our subject was born February 14, 1822, grew to manhood on the farm, and received a very limited education in the common schools of those early days. At the age of twenty-one he began farming, and has followed that occupation up to the present time. In 1851 he wedded Leanna Manire, and this union resulted in the birth of five children, three of whom are living: Amaca W., Lemuel R. and John R. The first is married to Catherine Wilson, by whom he has three children: Esther B., Eula R. and Maud. The other sons are living at home in single blessedness. Mr. Hill is a Democrat, and his wife, is a member of the Missionary Baptist Church. He has a fine farm of 248 acres, well stocked and furnished with abundance of running water. In fact there are few farms in the county superior to his. Mary A. R. Hill, deceased, was the wife of John F. Hill, by whom she had three children: Ida L., Rucker B. and Mary A. R., all living.

JOHN T. HILL, farmer, is a son of John R. and Elizabeth H. (Kennedy) Hill. The father was a native of Virginia, born in 1802, and when seventeen years old came with his parents to the Maury fraction of Marshall County. The mother was born in Kentucky in 1807, and when young also came to this county. They were married in 1829, and lived all their lives in what is now Marshall County. They were the parents of ten children. The father was a member of the Pleasant Hill Missionary Baptist Church, being named in honor of him. He is a Democrat in politics, and four years was deputy sheriff in Maury County and six years sheriff in Marshall County, being the first sheriff ever elected in that county. He was an energetic, industrious farmer, and was worth some $200,000 previous to the war. In 1878 the mother died and two years later the father passed away. Our subject's ancestors on his father's side were of English-French descent, and on his mother's of English. The father was a second cousin of Gen. D. H. Hill, of Virginia, and a cousin of Ben Hill, of Georgia. "Uncle Tom's Cabin" was based on the run-away of one of our subject's great-grandfather's (Kennedy) slaves. Our subject was born September 6, 1846, in this county, passed his early days on the farm and received a good English education. In 1884 he wedded Missie McLean, a native of Rutherford County, born June 3, 1851. Mrs. Hill is a member of the Methodist Episcopal Church. Mr. Hill is a Democrat and a thrifty farmer, owning 240 acres of good land. For forty years he has been a resident of Marshall County, and is considered one of the county's best citizens.

PERSIS D. HOUSTON, dentist, is a son of Benjamin F. and and Necie B. (Usery) Houston, both natives of North Carolina, the father born in 1805, and the mother in 1814. They were married in Marshall County in, 1834, and to them were born ten children, seven of whom are living. Both parents were active members in the Christian Church. Until forty-five years of age he was an infidel, but after his reformation he became zealous in the cause of Christianity. He had been a school-teacher in his early days, but of late years was a successful farmer. For many years he filled the office of magistrate, and during his entire life he was an industrious, energetic worker. In politics he was a Democrat. He died in 1861, and the mother in 1878. The father was a relative of Gov. Samuel Houston. The subject of this sketch was born January 8, 1843, in Marshall County, was reared on the farm and received an academic education. At the age of seventeen he began teaching in order to raise sufficient means for taking a course in college. But these plans were frustrated by the breaking out of the war. In 1861 he volunteered in Capt. R. C. Williams' company, and four years was engaged in the war's bloody struggles. After returning home he engaged in the mercantile business and later farmed for five years. Having studied and practiced the dental profession for a number of years he graduated from the dental department of Tennessee University in 1881. Previous to this, in 1868, he wedded Medora A. Pickens, by whom he had seven children, five of whom are living. Mr. Houston and wife are both members of the Christian Church. He has been alderman of Lewisburg for three terms. For twelve years Mr. Houston has successfully practiced his profession in his town.

JOHN W. HUTTON, a leading farmer of Marshall County, is a son of John and Susan (Watkins) Hutton, natives, respectively, of Kentucky and Virginia. The father was a Presbyterian and the mother a Methodist. In the bloody strife with the Indians in Kentucky the father took an active part. In 1809 they came to Tennessee when the woods were a mat of vines, and wild animals found their homes in the dense canebrake. The father died at the age of thirty, and in 1860 the mother followed him. Our subject was born August 6, 1809, in Franklin County, Ky., and spent the principal part of his time on the farm, and until eleven years of age had very good opportunities for schooling. At the age of eighteen he began to battle his own way in the world. After "overseeing" for four years, he purchased a tract of fifty acres in Rutherford County, and by hard work and good management is now one of the heaviest tax payers in the county. In 1833 he married Frances Moore, a native of Williamson County, born October 13, 1810. Fifty-three years of happy wedded life and ten children have blessed this worthy couple. Six of the children are living; all save one are married and pleasantly situated in life. Mr. Hutton had the honor of furnishing three brave boys for the war: Thomas, William and Polk. William sacrificed his life for home and State. Mr. Hutton is a stanch Democrat; and he and wife are members of the Cumberland Presbyterian Church. For thirty-six years he has held the office of magistrate. Mr. Hutton has lived in this county for thirty five years, and has gained a reputation beyond reproach.

THOMAS C. HUTTON, a leading farmer of Marshall County, and a son of J. W. and Frances (Moore) Hutton (for further particulars of parents see sketch of John W. Hutton), was born in Rutherford County November 19, 1835, on the field where the battle of Murfreesboro was fought. He received a good practical education, and when only fifteen years old superintended the moving from Rutherford County to this. At the age of twenty-one he began "overseeing" for his father, and this he continued until the breaking out of the war. In 1861 he volunteered in Company F, Seventeenth Tennessee Infantry, Confederate Army, and served for three years in that company. He then joined a company of cavalry, and continued with this until the close of the war. During four years of faithful service he was in eight hard-fought battles and many skirmishes. He had three horses shot from under him, and was never captured or wounded. The third day after his return home found him at work tilling the soil. In 1865 he wedded Margaret E. Robinson, by whom he had four children, only one of whom, Sallie, is living. In 1884 his wife died, and the following year he wedded Mary. C. Crowel, whose maiden name was Gordon. He is a Democrat in politics and a member of the Missionary Baptist Church. Mrs. Hutton is a member of the Primitive Baptist Church. Mr. Hutton has a fine, large farm, well stocked, and he is a man who takes an active part in all the enterprises of his community.

WILLIS M. HOPWOOD was born on the farm where he now resides February 1, 1813. His parents, Willis and Penelope (Moore) Hopwood, were born in the "Old Dominion," and in 1810 came to Tennessee, locating in Marshall County. The father was a minister of the gospel, and was among the first to accept the new doctrine that the Bible alone is the standard by which to measure Christian character. His labors were fully rewarded in this world by seeing many souls converted. He died in 1850, after a long and useful life. The mother died in 1868. Willis M. inherits Scotch-Irish blood from his ancestors. He received a good rudimentary education, and at the age of nineteen began earning his own living. He clerked in a store for two years, and for four years followed merchandising in Lewisburg, and has followed that and farming off and on ever since. He has filled the offices of constable, deputy sheriff and sheriff, serving in all about sixteen years, to the general satisfaction of the people. Julia A. Bills became his wife in 1846. Nine children were born to their union, seven of whom are living. Mr. Hopwood has been a Republican since the war; previous to that time he was a Whig. He is now seventy-three years old, and has never lived outside the county, nor more than seven miles from the place of his birth. Mrs. Hopwood is a member of the Cumberland Presbyterian Church.

JAMES N. HUNTER, a leading farmer of Marshall County, is a son of Ephraim and Mary (Elliott) Hunter. The father was a native of North Carolina, and when a boy came with his parents to Tennessee. About 1808 they removed to this county, and here Ephraim was married. His family consisted of eleven children, only one of whom is living. The father was a Democrat and served many years as magistrate. He followed farming and merchandising, besides running a carding machine and cotton spinner. The father died in 1857, and the mother in 1864. She was a member of the Cumberland Presbyterian Church. The subject of this sketch was born November 15, 1815, in Marshall County and while growing up worked in the factory and had very poor opportunities for schooling, attending the old subscription schools. At the age of twenty-two he began clerking in his father's store, where he remained for ten years. He then engaged in farming and this he has continued to the present time. In 1848 he wedded Cynthia Hays, by whom he had nine children. The eldest son, R. H., is a rising young physician of Texas. In politics Mr. Hunter is a Democrat and he and family are members of the Methodist Episcopal Church. In the days of militia, he held the position of colonel.

WILLIAM P. IRVINE, grocery and grain dealer, was born August 1, 1845, in Elkton, Giles County, where he grew up and received a common English education. His parents were Nathaniel and Narcissa (Davis) Irvine. The father was born in North Carolina, and the mother in Lincoln County, Tenn. After marriage they settled in Giles County, where they remained until 1852. They then moved to Georgia, where the father died. After his death the mother returned to Lincoln County, Tenn., and married H. N. Cowden. They located in this county, where they have lived ever since. The mother was a member of the Cumberland Presbyterian Church. In 1861 our subject volunteered in Company I, Thirty-second Tennessee Infantry, and remained in that company till 1864. He then joined Gen. Forrest's command, and served till the surrender at Gainesville, Ala., a period of over three and one-half years. He was imprisoned seven months at Camp Morton and Lafayette, Ind., and was exchanged at Vicksburg. He then returned and engaged in farming. In 1865 he wedded Eliza Garrett, and to them were born two children: Roy and Mamie. He is a stanch Democrat in politics, and is commissioner of this taxing district, and also one of the directors of the Bank of Lewisburg. In 1883 Mr. Irvine came to Lewisburg and opened the business in which he is now engaged. He is a good business man and has met with good success.

WILLOUGHBY A. JACKSON, a leading business man of Marshall County, was born October 7, 1834, in Wilson County, Tenn. He was a farmer boy and received a limited education, never having attended school more than nine months altogether. At the age of eighteen he left home, and after spending a year at Charleston, S. C., came to Marshall County and worked a short time in a livery stable. He then learned the saddler's trade and bought out the man for whom he worked, but at last he turned his attention to farming. In 1857 he married Margaret Phiper, by whom he had nine children, five of whom are living. He is a member of the Christian Church, and she of the Methodist Episcopal Church. In politics he votes for the man rather than the party, though he holds to Republican principles. At present he is the owner of 700 acres of land, three stores and two saw-mills, besides he is engaged in stock-trading. He is a resident of Marshall County, and is accounted one of the most stirring, energetic, successful business men of the county. He is a son of James and Martha (Evans) Jackson, both of whom were reared and married in North Carolina. In 1830 they came to Wilson County, and after living there fourteen years returned to North Carolina. In 1869 they returned to Tennessee, and after several moves they went to West Tennessee, where they passed the last years of their lives. They were both Baptists. The father served in the Seminole war and four years in the late war. In the first he held the position of orderly sergeant and captain, and in the last held the position of captain and colonel. The mother died in 1871, and two years later the father followed.

RICHARD T. JOHNSON. William Johnson, father of our subject, was born in Maury County, Tenn., in 1814, and was married to Eliza J. Mourton, who was born in Bedford County in 1819. They resided for a short time in Lawrence County, and then took up their abode in Giles County, where they spent the remainder of their lives. The father was an extensive farmer and stock raiser, and for many years filled the office of magistrate. He was married twice, and died in 1883. The mother's death occurred in 1867. Richard inherits English blood from both parents. He was born in Lawrence County, September 20, 1840, and his early schooling was limited to a few terms. In 1861 he enlisted in Company B, Second Tennessee Confederate Infantry. At the battle of Perryville, Ky., he received six wounds from one volley of the enemy, and although seriously wounded escaped with his life. He was in eighteen of the bloodiest battles of the war, and after serving two years was promoted to second lieutenant. In 1865 he wedded Laura A. Cochran, by whom he has had six children. Mr. and Mrs. Johnson are Methodists, and he, like his father, is a stanch Democrat. He owns a fine farm in Marshall County, and has been a resident of the county twenty-one years.

HON. A. JONES, M. D., one of the leading physicians of Cornersville, Tenn., and son of John R. and Martha A. (Lane) Jones, was born in Marshall County, May 15, 1839. His boyhood days were spent on a farm and in attending the common schools; later he attended the school of Pascal, at Nashville, and for some time studied medicine under Dr. Thomas Lipscomb. He graduated from the University of Tennessee in 1858, and later took a course of lectures at New Orleans, and another at Belleview Medical College at New York. In 1859 he opened an office in Cornersville, where he has since resided, with the exception of four years during the war. He served in Company H, Third Tennessee Infantry, as lieutenant, and after a short service was made surgeon of the Seventeenth Regiment. In 1862 he wedded Maxie Harris, by whom he had four children, three of whom are living. The Doctor is a member of the Methodist Episcopal Church South, and his wife is a Presbyterian. In 1871 he represented Marshall County in the State Legislature, and filled the position ably for one term. He is a Democrat, and owns and operates a farm of 235 acres. His parents were born in North Carolina, and were married in Tennessee. The father was a physician, but not liking that profession he took up farming, and eventually became one of the most successful farmers in the county. He was a Democrat, and died of the cholera in 1865. The mother died in 1885. She was of Welsh descent and the father of English.

JAMES F. KENNEDY, merchant of Cornersville, was born in Green County, Tenn., October 4, 1830, son of Daniel and Margaret (Kennedy) Kennedy, who were also born in Green County. They were the parents of seven children and were members of the Presbyterian Church. The father was a tanner and merchant, and quite an extensive farmer. He was magistrate a number of years and was a Whig in politics. He died in 1861 and the mother in 1877. Our subject assisted his father in the tan-yard, store and farm, and at the age of twenty-one began earning his own living. He worked for about ten years for wages, and in 1861 opened a store in his native county, but was compelled to abandon it, owing to the war. In 1866 he opened a store in Cornersville, Marshall County, Tenn., where he has carried on the business successfully ever since. His marriage with Hannah C. McGaughey was celebrated in 1852. They have had six children, five of whom are living. Mr. Kennedy owns a farm of 200 acres, and as a business man has met with good success. He is a stanch Democrat, and he and wife are members of the Presbyterian Church.

M. D. KELLEY, M. D., is a son of Cary T. and Nancy (Wilkins) Kelley, who were married in Giles County, and soon after settled on a farm, where they spent the remainder of their lives. They were Methodists and the father was a soldier in the war of 1812. He became a very prosperous farmer and was one of the first to introduce Berkshire hogs and Durham cattle into Marshall County. He was an old-line Whig and died in 1854. The mother lived until 1885. M. D. Kelley, our subject, was born September 6, 1832, in Giles County. At the age of seventeen he entered the Cumberland University and graduated in 1853. He then took a course in medicine at the University of Nashville and received the degree of M. D. in 1857. He spent some time in the State hospital and after three years' practice at Spring place in Marshall County, came to Cornersville in 1861, where he has since resided. In 1856 Margaret J. Gordon was united to him in marriage. To them were born three children—two sons and one daughter. The eldest son is a farmer and the other is studying for the ministry. The Doctor and his wife are members of the Methodist Episcopal Church South. He is conservative in politics, and is a successful physician of the county. He belongs to the Masonic, I. O. O. F., K. of H., K. of G. R., and Good Templar fraternities, and People's Mutual Life Insurance Company.

JOHN T. KERCHEVAL, a leading groceryman of Lewisburg, was born April 24, 1850, in Lewisburg, where he grew up and was educated. He is the son of Peter and Susan C. (Ewing) Kercheval, natives of Tennessee. They were married in this county and to them were born nine children. The father was a lawyer, being one of the ablest attorneys in his county. For many years he was clerk and master of the chancery court. He died in 1867 and the mother in 1883. The Kerchevals are of French descent. The name was formerly Cheval—a French word, meaning horse—and in some unknown way the Ker became prefixed. Dr. J. M. and Mayor Kercheval, of Nashville, are descendants of that name. Having prepared himself for Yale College, our subject had his plans frustrated by the death of his father. He then engaged in the dry goods business, as a salesman, where he remained for seven years. He then opened a grocery store in 1883, in which he has done a thriving business ever since. Having studied law under his father, he was admitted to the bar in 1871 and practiced three years. He was a promising young lawyer and had a good practice, but had not learned the art of economizing, consequently, at the end of three years, he found himself considerably in debt. He then began to retrieve his fallen fortunes and concluded to try merchandising. For ten years he has been engaged in that business at Lewisville, and has been quite successful.

WILLIAM M. KILLGORE is a son of Thomas Killgore, who was a native of Cocke County, Tenn., and there married Jane Cooper, who was born in the same place, and became the mother of five children. The father was a farmer until late in life, and then kept hotel for some time. About 1846 the mother died, and he afterward married Julia Smith, who bore him five children. Her death occurred in 1883. Previous to the war Mr. Killgore was a Whig. He is now a Republican, and is seventy-eight years of age. William M. Killgore was born in Cocke County, December 19, 1839, and was pursuing his studies at the breaking out of the war. In 1861 he volunteered in Company C, Thirty-first Tennessee Infantry, and during four years of service was in many hard-fought battles, but received only one slight wound. After the siege of Knoxville his regiment was mounted. In 1865 he came to Marshall County, where he has since resided and farmed. Penelope J. Blackburn became his wife in 1867 and died in 1874, leaving two sons. In 1877 he married Woodly Fain, and to them were born five children. Both Mr. and Mrs. Killgore are members of the Presbyterian Church, and in politics he is a Democrat.

ALFRED J LANE, farmer, was born February 8, 1848, on the farm where he now lives. While growing up he received a fair practical education in the common schools, and, like a dutiful son, remained with his parents until he was twenty-two years of age, when he went to Pulaski to clerk in a cotton factory. Two years later he returned to the farm, and in 1873 he was married to Mary A. Overton, a native of Texas, born February 19, 1853. Of this marriage three children was the result: John F., Mary D. and William J. Mr. Lane is a Democrat, and he and wife and eldest child are members of the Missionary Baptist Church. He has an excellent farm of 308 acres, well stocked. He has been a resident of this county for twenty-one years, and is accounted a good farmer and an enterprising citizen. He is a son of Joel and Susan H. (Carter) Lane, both natives of Tennessee. They were married in Maury County, and settled on the farm where Alfred now lives. Both parents were members of the Missionary Baptist Church. The father's chief occupation was farming, though he worked at blacksmithing, shoe-making, carpentering or whatever his inclinations suggested. Mechanical ingenuity runs through the Lane family. He died in 1854. The mother is still living, the wife of M. E. C. Overton, by whom she had ten children.

COL. JAMES HENRY LEWIS, attorney, of Lewisburg, was born September 17, 1837, in Maury County, Tenn. His grandfather, John C. Lewis, was a native of Virginia, and moved from that State to North Carolina, where he married a daughter of Nathan Forrest, near Orange Court House, at which place Fielding Lewis, father of the subject of this sketch, was born. Subsequently John C. Lewis, with his family, immigrated to Middle Tennessee. Fielding Lewis married Lydia Preston, in Sumner County, Tenn. Her father was a captain of Tennessee Volunteers, under Jackson, at New Orleans in 1815, and died soon after his return home from this campaign of disease contracted in the service. He was a member of the Preston family of Virginia and Kentucky. The grandmother, Lewis, was a member of the same family of which Gen. N. B. Forrest was a descendant, all at one time residents of Bedford and Marshall Counties. Lydia Lewis died in 1860, and Fielding Lewis in 1876. They were both members of the Cumberland Presbyterian Church. The husband was a farmer and mechanic, and was a relative of Gen. Meriwether Lewis, of the "Lewis and Clark Expedition" fame. Col. J. H. Lewis worked on a farm and in the shop until attaining his majority. His opportunities at school were limited, so that his education is almost entirely the result of his own efforts. At the age of twenty-one he began the study of law, and in October, 1859, was admitted to the bar. In 1861 he married Victoria J. Sims, who lost her father in the Mexican war. Her grandfather was John O. Cook, of Maury County, of whose family she was a member, being an orphan girl. Her other grandfather was Gen. Winn, of South Carolina. The result of this union is four children, three of whom are living. Both husband and wife are members of the Cumberland Presbyterian Church. Politically he is a firm Democrat. A short time before his marriage he enlisted in Company I, Second Battalion Tennessee Cavalry, Volunteers, as a private, and within a year was made captain of the company. After the consolidation of the Second and Eleventh Battalions the command was known as the First Regiment Tennessee Cavalry. He served as lieutenant-colonel of the regiment, and commanded the regiment for more than a year of the war. In the latter part of the war he commanded a brigade, including the command at the battles of Averysboro and Bentonville, N. C. After four years' service he returned home, located in Lewisburg and engaged in the practice of law, and served in the Legislature of the State—session 1871–72—as joint representative from Marshall, Giles and Lincoln Counties. Col. Lewis was largely instrumental in building the Duck River Valley Railroad, and served as president of the company two years prior to its lease to the Nashville, Chattanooga & St. Louis Railroad, having been a director before, and has been connected with the road ever since its building. He threw all of his energy and influence into the building of the road, and succeeded wherein most men would have failed. For twenty years he has practiced his profession, with ex-Gov. John C. Brown as his partner a portion of the time, and later with his brother, and now by himself. He is now the attorney for the Nashville & Chattanooga Railroad in Maury,

Marshall and Lincoln Counties. His ability as a lawyer is too well known to need comment, and he is a public-spirited citizen of the county, having done much for the schools, churches, and all other benevolent organizations of the county and State. The firm name, Lewis Bros., was dissolved in 1885, and Capt. Thomas F. Lewis, the junior member of the firm, is now a member of the bar at Jackson, Tenn.

BENTLEY A. LONDON, a prosperous young farmer of Marshall County, Tenn., is a son of N. B. and Cynthia A. (McConnell) London, both born in what is now Marshall County in 1825 and 1832. Soon after marriage they began farming, in which they were very prosperous. The father was a stanch Democrat, and died in 1869. The mother afterward married P. Fox and is still living. Bentley A. inherits English blood from his father and Irish blood from his mother. He was born October 4, 1855, in Marshall County. His early educational advantages being limited, when nineteen years of age he began his career as a farmer, and before reaching a legal age made several land trades. At the age of twenty he married Mattie A. Fox, by whom he has two children—Bettie M. and Bentley D. Mrs. London is a member of the Christian Church. Mr. London is a stanch Democrat, and is the owner of 140 acres of fertile land. In February, 1886, he and W. D. Fox purchased N. S. Hopwood's general merchandise store, and have been doing a good business ever since.

WILLIAM A. LONDON, a leading livery man of Lewisburg, Marshall Co., Tenn., is a son of Nathan B. and Cynthia A. (McConnell) London, who were born, reared and married in Marshall County. The father was a successful farmer, and served a short time in the late war, under Forrest. He was a Democrat, and died in 1869. His widow married Pervines Fox, Jr., by whom she has two children. Our subject was one of nine children, and was born November 23, 1857, in Marshall County. He was educated in the common schools, and at the age of nineteen began to do for himself. Since 1878 he has been engaged in the livery business in Lewisburg in partnership with different men, but since 1885 he and S. D. Davis have done business together, and are securing comfortable competencies. He also, in connection with McAdams & Sons, has done an extensive business in buying and selling horses and mules. In 1878 he wedded Mary E. Braly, by whom he has two daughters. Both Mr. and Mrs. London are members of the Christian Church. In politics our subject is a Democrat.

WILSON G. LOYD, clerk of the Circuit Court of Marshall County, is a son of Alexander M. and Louisa (Blackwell) Loyd. The father was a merchant, having sold goods in Bedford County for some time. In 1838 he removed to Texas for the purpose of surveying public lands. He was called from this world of toil at the early age of twenty-nine. Our subject was born April 26, 1838, in Lewisburg, but, his mother having died when he was but an infant, he was left to the care of an aunt at Shelbyville till nine years of age, after which he went to live with an uncle in Louisiana. At the age of seventeen he returned to this State and attended school three years, completing his education at Franklin College in 1859. He then went back to Louisiana and engaged as salesman in Alexandria till 1861, when he enlisted in Company B, Second Louisiana Infantry in the Army of Northern Virginia. At the battle of Gettysburg he received a slight wound, and it was the only one he received during the entire four years he was in service. In 1865 he wedded Victoria C. Meadows, and by this union became the father of eleven children, all living. Both Mr. and Mrs. Loyd are earnest workers in the Christian Church. In politics Mr. Loyd is a Democrat. In 1878 he was elected circuit court clerk, and has filled that position in a satisfactory manner. In 1885 he became book-keeper of the Bank of Lewisburg.

JOHN B. LUNA is a son of James G. and Rhoda C. (Stevens) Luna, native Tennesseeans. They were members of the Primitive Baptist Church. The father was a Democrat, and died in 1846, at the age of thirty-nine. The mother lived until 1880. John B.'s birth occurred in Marshall County August 29, 1844. At the age of fifteen he began earning his own living, receiving a common school education. For about eleven months he served in Company I, Eighth Tennessee Infantry, and then returned home and resumed farming. In 1864 he wedded Mattie Yowell, who died the following year. In 1870

Maggie Vaughn became his wife and seven children blessed their union. Both Mr. and Mrs. Luna are members of the Primitive Baptist Church, and, like his father, Mr. Luna is a Democrat. They possess 235 acres of land, and he is considered one of the best farmers of Marshall County. He gives much attention to raising fine stock and owns the two horses, Tom Hall and Chieftain, the latter of Black Satin stock. For forty-two years he has been a resident of Marshall County, and no man has been more intimately connected with the progress of the county than he.

SHELBY B. MARSH is a son of Simeon and Elizabeth (Shelby) Marsh, who were born in North and South Carolina, respectively. In 1812 they came to Tennessee and located in Marshall County, where the father became an extensive farmer and land speculator. The father was a Democrat, and died when about seventy years old. His ancestors were Revolutionary soldiers from the "Nutmeg State." The mother was related to Shelby, the second in command at the battle of New Orleans, and governor of Kentucky. Shelby B. Marsh was born in North Carolina. At the age of fifteen he began clerking in a store, and after following that occupation for a few years he began trading in negroes, making some $10,000 thereat. Seven children were born to his marriage with Elizabeth Jones, which took place in 1837. Two of the children died in infancy and Robert J. and Simeon were killed in the late war. Mr. Marsh is a stanch Democrat and has been remarkably successful in his business career. His wife is a member of the Missionary Baptist Church.

WILLIAM T. MARSH is a son of Shelby and Elizabeth J. (Jones) Marsh, and was born June 24, 1843, in Giles County, Tenn., and was reared by a father who, though very wealthy, was a believer in honest toil, and taught his sons to work. He acquired a good rudimentary education, and later attended Cumberland University. He then returned home, and has followed the free and independent life of a farmer up to the present time. He owns 930 acres of very fertile land, and is extensively engaged in stock raising. In 1871 Amelia Jackson became his wife. She is a daughter of Thomas R. and Elizabeth S. (Madry) Jackson, who were born in North Carolina and Missouri, respectively. They both came to Tennessee when young, and became the parents of ten children. The father was a Democrat, and died in 1883. His widow still lives, and has attained the age of seventy-two years. To Mr. and Mrs. Marsh were born three children—two sons and one daughter. Our subject and his wife are members of the Methodist Episcopal Church South, and he is a stanch Democrat.

JOHN L. MARSHALL, of the firm of Cowden & Marshall, of Lewisburg, is a son of James G. and Margaret J. (Bullock) Marshall, both natives of Tennessee. In early life the father was a teacher, but later engaged in the occupation of a farmer. Both parents were church members, the father being an elder for many years in the Presbyterian Church, and the mother an active member in the Methodist Episcopal Church. She died in 1863 and the father followed in 1871. He was a Democrat in politics. Our subject was born January 30, 1850, in Marshall County, and inherited Scotch-Irish blood from his father and English blood from his mother. He passed his youthful days on the farm and received an academic education. In 1869 he entered Cumberland University, where he completed his education. Having taught two terms he commenced the study of law and was admitted to the bar in 1875. He then became a partner of P. C. Smithson, and two years later dissolved partnership, practicing alone till 1883. He then became one of the firm to which he now belongs. In 1876 he wedded Mrs. M. L. (Swanson) Lyle, who died in 1881. Five years later he married Martha Steele. Mr. Marshall is an elder in the Presbyterian Church, and his wife belongs to the same church. He is a conservative Democrat, and is considered by all as an able and successful young lawyer.

JAMES M. MARTIN is a son of Henry and Maria (Tankersley) Martin. Henry Martin was born in North Carolina in 1802, and when young came to Tennessee and located in Bedford County, where he married Miss Tankersley, born in 1808. They were the parents of eighteen children, seven of whom are living. The mother was a member of the Christian Church, as was also the father until the last few years of his life, when he became a Universalist. He held the position of constable six years and that of deputy sheriff two years. During the late war he supported the Confederacy although too old to take an active part. The mother died in 1842 and two years later Mr. Martin married Mrs. Delilah Lamb, by whom he had six children. His death occurred in 1864. James M. was born September 6, 1822, in Williamson County, and secured a practical education. At the age of twenty he began working by the month and in 1845 married Nancy McGee, who was born February 21, 1826, in North Carolina, and died in 1856, having borne one child who died. In 1857 Mr. Martin took for his second wife Mary Stanfield, and seven children blessed their union. Husband and wife are members of the Methodist Episcopal Church South, and he is a stanch Democrat in politics and for some eight years has held the position of magistrate and has been constable nearly four years. He owns 260 acres of land and is known to be a thrifty farmer and an honest man.

HARDIN MAYBERRY is a son of Gabriel Mayberry, who was a Virginian by birth and married Rosanna Hardin, of South Carolina, by whom he had four children. They came to Tennessee when quite young and when Nashville was a small collection of cabins. The father was a Democrat and a prosperous farmer and lived to be seventy-five years of age. His widow outlived him but a few years. Grandfather Mayberry was a Revolutionary soldier at the age of seventeen, and was intimately associated with Gen. George Washington. Hardin, our subject, was born in Hickman County July 14, 1826, and was reared on a farm, receiving a common school education. Since attaining his twenty-first birthday he has farmed, and now owns a well stocked farm of 1,000 acres. In 1847 he married Cornelia E. Galloway, who died in 1856, leaving four children: Mary M., Harriet C. and two infants, deceased. Mr. Mayberry's second wife was Mrs. A. P. Blair, who bore him six children: Lawreston H., Emma P., Lula L., Harvey, Cora and Gabriella. Mr. Mayberry was a soldier in the late war, serving in Company A, Forty-eighth Tennessee Infantry, and was one of the defenders of Fort Donelson. After a two months' imprisonment at Camp Chase and five months' imprisonment at Johnson's Island he was exchanged at Vicksburg, and failing health caused him to be released. He served as first lieutenant about one year.

JOSEPH McBRIDE, clerk of the county court, was born December 27, 1827, in Lincoln (now Marshall) County, Tenn., and is of Scotch-Irish descent. He is a son of G. W. and Mary H. (Cook) McBride, natives, respectively, of North Carolina and Virginia. The father was a farmer, a Democrat in politics, and occupied the office of magistrate the greater part of his life. He died at the age of sixty-two and the mother at the age of sixty. Our subject grew to manhood on the farm and received a practical education in the common schools. In 1853 he wedded Mary A. V. Palmer, by whom he had ten children, seven of whom are living. Mr. McBride, like his father before him, is a stanch Democrat, and he and wife are members of the Cumberland Presbyterian Church. For nearly twelve years he has served as magistrate, and was also chairman of the county court a term. In 1882 he was elected to the position he is now occupying, and has filled that office in a highly satisfactory manner.

COL. W. L. McCLELLAND was born in North Carolina in 1815, and when a boy came with his parents to what is now Marshall County, Tenn. On reaching manhood he married Mary Chambliss, by whom he had three children. His wife died in 1854, and he wedded Sarah Chambliss, a sister of his first wife, by whom he had two children. He and both his wives were members of the Methodist Episcopal Church South. In early life he was a merchant, and later he took himself to farming, in which he was more than ordinarily successful. He twice represented his county in the State Legislature, and was chosen delegate to the Charleston and Baltimore Convention in 1860. During his life he was one of the most enterprising and energetic business men in his section. He died in 1883, leaving a widow and five children to mourn their loss. John R. is a lawyer of Nashville, Fernando, a farmer of Marshall County; Mattie, the wife of Capt. A. E. Read, of Louisiana; Ada lives at home, and Zana is the wife of W. W. Ogilvie, who has an interest in and charge of the old McClelland homestead. He was born in Maury County May 15, 1856, and attended Webb's school at Culleoka, and later the Tennessee University, completing the freshman year. He first opened a hardware store in Lewisburg, and in connection handled grain. His marriage with Miss McClelland was consummated in 1881. Mr. Ogilvie belongs to the Methodist Episcopal Church South, and in politics is a Democrat. In 1885 he moved to the farm, and is now extensively engaged in stock raising.

FERDINAND S. McCLELLAND may be mentioned as one of the prosperous farmers of Marshall County, Tenn. He is a son of Col. W. L. and Mary (Chambliss) McClelland, and was born February 7, 1841, in what is now Marshall County. His educational advantages were above the average, and he had reached his senior year in Cumberland University when the war broke out and he volunteered in Capt. Walker's company, Third Tennessee Infantry. He served four years and the last year and a half was lieutenant in the ordnance department. In 1866 he wedded Mary Y. Plattenburg, a native of Alabama, and to them were born seven children. At the close of the war he located in Alabama, where he was engaged in the culture of cotton four years. In 1870 he returned to Marshall County, Tenn., where he owns 150 acres of fine and well improved land. He is a conservative Democrat in politics and is a man of recognized ability. During the agitation of the State debt question he made many public addresses in favor of its payment in full. For thirty-seven years he has been a resident of Marshall County, and by his upright conduct and geniality has won the respect and esteem of all.

FREDERICK B. McCLURE, farmer of Marshall County and son of John and Sarah (Cooper) McClure. The father was born in North Carolina and there married Miss Jameson, who bore him five children. They came to Tennessee about 1811 and located in Rutherford County. His wife died and he then wedded Mrs. Cooper. To them were born four children. Both husband and wife were members of the Cumberland Presbyterian Church. The father was a tanner by trade and worked thereat in early life. Later he betook himself to farming. The mother died in 1845 and the father in 1848. Our subject was born in Rutherford County, August 15, 1827, but attended school very little in boyhood, owing to poor health. At the age of twenty he began farming and later purchased a farm in Marshall County. In 1862 he volunteered to serve in the commissary department, continuing until the close of the war. In 1866, after his return, he wedded a Miss McAfee, daughter of Green and Elizabeth (Scales) McAfee, and to their union were born five children, three now living. Mr. McClure is a stanch Democrat and is the owner of 163 acres of land in the garden spot of Marshall County.

HENRY G. McCORD was born August 12, 1847, in Williamson County, and is of Scotch-Irish descent. He received the rudiments of his education in the common schools and subsequently attended Cumberland University, and graduated from the literary department in 1873. He taught school for about three years, and then turned his attention to agricultural pursuits. In 1877 he married Lillie V. Ogilvie, who was born May 13, 1856. The fruits of this union were five children: Marks W., Harris O., Manella M., Joseph C. and Chamilla S. In 1864 Mr. McCord went out in Company C, Eleventh Tennessee Cavalry, Confederate Army, and served until the close of the war. He has a good farm of 269 acres, well watered and furnished with good buildings, and is considered a first-class farmer. He is a Democrat in politics, and he and wife are members of the Cumberland Presbyterian Church. He is a son of Cowden and Sallie A. (Williams) McCord. The father was born in Williamson County in 1809, and the mother was born on the farm where Henry now lives in 1826. They were married in Marshall County in 1844, and to them were born eight children, seven of whom lived to be grown, and six are living now. The father was a Democrat in politics, and for one term served as magistrate. He was also a farmer and an extensive one at that. The mother died in 1863, and in 1879 the father died also.

ROBERT A. McCORD, JR., member of the hardware firm of Woods & McCord, was born March 10, 1859, in Marshall County, son of Cowden and Sarah (Williams) McCord. (See sketch of Henry McCord for further particulars of parents.) Our subject was reared on the farm, and received a good common school education. At the age of twenty-two he began to battle his own way in life. In 1882 he came to Lewisburg, and in connection with Coffey & Woods engaged in the grain and agricultural business. In two years he transferred his line of business to hardware, in which he has succeeded remarkably well. In 1881 he was united in marriage to Bettie Whittsitt, and this union resulted in the birth of three children. In politics Mr. McCord is conservative, voting the Democratic ticket when good men are presented. He and wife are members of the Cumberland Presbyterian Church. He has, in the short space of four years, won a place among the first business men of the city.

HON. DILLISTON S. McCULLOUGH is a son of Richard and Nancy (Posey) McCullough, natives of Virginia and South Carolina, respectively. The father was born in 1803 and the mother in 1807. They were married in Rutherford County, Tenn., and were the parents of ten children, five of whom are now living. The father was a tiller of the soil and was quite successful in that occupation. In politics he was, respectively, a Whig, Know-nothing and Democrat. In 1878 the mother died and four years later the father died, too. Our subject was born May 11, 1838, in Rutherford County, and is of Scotch-Irish descent. He passed his youthful days on the farm and received his education in the district schools; later he took an academic course at Union Hill, and finished at Union University, where he graduated in 1860, with the degree of A. B. After teaching a term he volunteered, in 1861, to lead Company D, Eighth Battalion Tennessee Cavalry, which afterward became Starnes' regiment. Having served about twelve months he resigned his commission and joined the Eleventh Tennessee Cavalry. After the war he taught two terms, but not liking the nomadic life of a teacher, he turned his attention to agricultural pursuits, in which he is still engaged. In 1865 he married Martha J. Jordon, and to them were born three children: Ruben J., William R. and Dilliston. Mr. McCullough is a Democrat in politics and has not escaped public notice. In 1880 he was elected senator of the Thirteenth District, representing Marshall, Lincoln, Moore and Franklin Counties, and in 1883 he was elected to the same position by the Sixteenth Senatorial District, composed of Marshall and Williamson Counties. Mr. McCullough has been a resident of Marshall County for seventeen years, has a good farm of 180 acres, and is one of the county's best men.

COLEMAN R. McCULLOUGH, an enterprising farmer of Marshall County, and a son of Richard D. and Nancy (Posey) McCullough, was born February 25, 1842, in Rutherford County. He received a good practical education in the common schools, and in 1862 volunteered in Company C, Eleventh Tennessee Cavalry, Confederate Army. During nearly three years of faithful service he was engaged in eight hard-fought battles, but was never wounded or taken prisoner. After the war he engaged in farming, and in 1868 was united in marriage to Margaret R. McLean, a native of Marshall County, born October 21, 1844. This union was blessed by the birth of six children—two boys and four girls. Mr. McCullough is a Democrat in politics and a member of the Missionary Baptist Church. His wife is a member of the Cumberland Presbyterian Church. For four years our subject has filled the position of constable in a capable and satisfactory manner. He has a good farm of 300 acres, well stocked, and has been a resident of the county for twenty-eight years.

COL. CHRISTOPHER C. McKINNEY was born December 10, 1825 in Lincoln County, Tenn. He was reared on the farm and attended the old-time subscription schools. His parents were James and Temperance (Rowe) McKinney, natives, respectively, of Virginia and South Carolina. When young they came to this State, the father in 1808 and the mother two years later. After marriage they settled in Lincoln County where they passed the remainder of their days. The father was a member of the Methodist Church and the mother a member of the Primitive Baptist Church. Their family consisted of seven children, six of whom are living. The father was a farmer and carpenter and a soldier in the war of 1812. The father died in 1862 and the mother in 1880. Our subject after reaching twenty-one years of age began working for himself at $5 per month. After farming and milling for several years he opened a grocery store in

Petersburg in 1854. He then changed to the dry goods business and this he continued till the war. In 1849 he wedded Mary Luna, and this union resulted in the birth of seven children, six of whom are living. In 1861 Mr. McKinney enlisted in Company B, Eighth Tennessee Infantry, sharpshooters, as first lieutenant and from that arose to lieutenant-colonel of his regiment. At the end of four years' faithful service he returned and engaged in merchandising as salesman and book-keeper at Richmond, Tenn. In 1884 he opened a grocery store in this place where he has had a lucrative practice ever since. Mr. and Mrs. McKinney are active members of the Cumberland Presbyterian Church, of which he has been an elder for twenty-nine years. He is a Democrat, a good business man and a highly respected citizen.

G. A. McLANE, one of the firm of McLane & Co., proprietors of a saw and planing-mill, is a son of Jesse and Flora (Patterson) McLane, natives, respectively, of North Carolina and Virginia. They came to Tennessee at an early day, and were married in Marshall County, and there reared their family of seven children. Previous to this union the father had been married to Nancy Paton, by whom he had nine children. He was a Whig in politics. His ancestors were of Irish descent and his wife was of Scotch lineage. G. A. McLane was born August 14, 1836, in Marshall County. He only attended school about six months during his life, and when of age could scarcely write his own name, but by energy and ambition he overcame his deficiencies, and was a school-teacher for about three years, following farming at the same time. During the war he followed merchandising with Alfred McGahey at Shelbyville, but about three years later returned to the farm. In 1874 he engaged in his present business, and in 1885 moved to Lewisburg and became one of the above named firm. Eliza Whitsett became his wife in 1870. To them were born five children, only four of whom are living. Mr. McLane was a strong Union man during the war, and was strongly opposed to slavery. He was one of the men in his district to vote for the Union. In politics he is a stanch Republican. Mr. McLane has prospered in worldly goods, and owns a good farm, besides a saw and planing-mill.

JOSEPH A. McRADY, a native of Maury County, was born January 18, 1827, and is a son of Ephraim McRady. The father was born in Kentucky in 1800, and as his parents died while he was yet quite young, he was reared by an uncle. After reaching man's estate he wedded Sarah Wingfield, a native of Maury County, Tenn., born in 1806, and by this union became the father of two children: Joseph A., our subject, and Susan. Both parents were leading members of the Presbyterian Church. The father was a house carpenter by trade, but spent the latter part of his life in farming. In politics he was a stanch Democrat. In 1838 the mother died, and the father then married Margaret White, who was also a member of the Presbyterian Church. The father died in 1871. Our subject, during his youth, had the best of opportunities for an education. After finishing the common school course he entered Jackson College, Maury County, and graduated from that institution in 1846. After teaching a year he began to read law under Judge Dillahunty, and, in 1849, opened an office in partnership with Robert Payne, at Lewisburg. Here he continued five years. In 1852 he married Margaret E. Ewing, who was born February 14, 1833. This union resulted in the birth of nine children, seven of whom are living. The second son, Flarins S., is a rising young physician of Petersburg, Giles County. Our subject and wife are members of the Presbyterian Church, and he is a Democrat in politics. In 1861 he volunteered in Capt. Holden's company of the Fifty-third Tennessee Infantry, Confederate Army. He was soon appointed to the commissary department, and served in that capacity until the close of the war. He was captured at Fort Donelson and soon removed to Johnson's Island. Being sick when the roll for exchange of prisoners was called, a bushwhacker answered to Mr. McRady's name, and thus escaped. Our subject remained in prison twelve months. Since the war he has followed agricultural pursuits. He has a large farm of 430 acres, and has had reasonable success.

NEWTON McQUIDDY, farmer, born September 26, 1819, in Woodford County, Ky., was of Scotch-Irish descent on his father's side and English on his mother's. His parents were John and Achsah (Dale) McQuiddy, both natives of Kentucky. The father was born in 1790 and the mother in 1793. They had nine children, six of whom lived to be grown; three are living at the present time. The father was a farmer, though for several years, both in Kentucky and Tennessee, he ran a rope and bagging factory. He was a Whig, and a man who made the most of everything he undertook. At the time of his death, which occurred in 1863, he had over 1,500 acres of land. The mother died in 1881. Our subject grew up on the farm, and was educated in the schools of those early days. At the age of twelve he went to work in his father's factory, where he remained for about twelve years. In 1843 he married Nancy A. Shofner, a native of Lincoln County, born January 6, 1823. The fruits of this union were eleven children, nine of whom are living. Two of the boys, W. B. and J. C., are promising young ministers in the Christian Church. Mr. McQuiddy is a member of that church, and his wife a member of the Missionary Baptist Church. Mr. McQuiddy was a strong Union man during the war, and now votes with the Republican party. He has a farm of 1,200 acres, and is widely known and highly respected.

ROBERT MONTGOMERY, SR., usually called "Uncle Robin," a retired farmer of Marshall County, was born September 5, 1810, in South Carolina. He passed his youthful days on the farm in the summer months, and attended the common schools in the winter season. He was the son of Robert and Esther (Spence) Montgomery. The father was born in Ireland in 1784, and was of Scotch-Irish descent. He came to this country with his parents when but a lad and settled in South Carolina. After reaching the years of maturity he was married, and was living in South Carolina at the time of his death, which occurred in 1825. In 1830 the mother and her children came to Tennessee. Here the mother, after living a long and useful life, died in 1859. Our subject was married, June 5, 1855, to Margaret P. Ormand, of Alabama. The fruits of this union were three children: Mary E., now Mrs. Mount; John O. and Jane S., now Mrs. Wiggs, all living. Mr. Montgomery is a Republican in politics, and he and wife are members of the United Presbyterian Church. His son-in-law, I. T. Wiggs, was born October 21, 1846, in Marshall County, and received a fair education in the common schools. By his marriage to Jane L. Montgomery he became the father of one child, yet unnamed. He is a carpenter by trade, but has also followed the occupation of a farmer to some extent. Politically he is rather conservative, but inclines toward the Democratic party. He is the son of Needham B. and Elizabeth G. (Radford) Wiggs. The father was born in North Carolina in 1812 and the mother in Tennessee in 1815. The former died in 1876 and the latter in 1856.

JAMES J. MORGAN'S birth occurred in Maury County, Tenn., July 28, 1848, son of William B. and Martha L. (Huggins) Morgan, Tennesseeans by birth and residents of Maury County, after their marriage. Their children are James J., Lizzie C., David E. and Ella P. The father was a soldier in the late war in Capt. Holman's company, Fifty-third Tennesee Cavalry, and served nearly two years. He was captured at Fort Donelson and imprisoned at Camp Morton about seven months, but lived only a few weeks after being exchanged. After his death the mother lived with her children until 1877, when she, too, died. The father's people were Scotch-Irish, the mother's French Huguenots, who came to America at an early day. James J. Morgan's early education was limited, owing to the breaking out of the war. He resided with his mother and cared for her until her death. In 1879 he married Belle Davis, who was born in Marshall County, July 29, 1854, and four children have blessed their union: Mary E. (deceased), William C., Scott D. (deceased), and Alice. Mr. Morgan belongs to the Presbyterian Church and his wife to the Cumberland Presbyterian Church. He is a Democrat and owns a one-third interest in a well stocked farm of 260 acres.

ELISHA G. MORRIS, a leading miller and farmer of Marshall County, and a son of Allen and Margaret E. (Sawson) Morris, was born February 14, 1843, in Marshall County, and is of English descent. His parents were natives of North Carolina and South Carolina, respectively. The father was a farmer, and in connection with this ran a still-house.

Later he followed the trade of blacksmithing and milling. He died in 1862, and in 1886 the mother, too, passed away. Our subject received a good practical education in the common schools, and subsequently attended Chapel Hill Academy, but the breaking out of the war cut short all his plans. In 1861 he enlisted in the Fifty-fifth Tennessee Infantry, Confederate Army, and at the battle of Shiloh received a severe wound. At Petersburg he was captured, and after remaining in prison eight months was paroled and entered the service no more. In 1867 he wedded Chlora A. Hopkins, and this union was blessed by the birth of ten children, seven now living. The eldest son, William A., is a student at Goodman's Business College, the rest being at home Both Mr. and Mrs. Morris are members of the Methodist Episcopal Church. He is a Democrat in politics, and has made this county his home all his life.

JAMES J. MURRAY, one of the oldest attorneys of Lewisburg, Tenn., is a son of Henry and Matilda (Denney) Murray, born in North Carolina and Ireland, respectively. They both came to Williamson County, Tenn., when young, and were there married. This family consisted of eight children. The father was a farmer and Democrat, and died at the age of fifty years. The mother lived to the ripe old age of ninety-four. James' ancestors on his father's side were of English-Irish descent, and on his mother's Scotch-Irish. He was born in Williamson County June 20, 1830, and received a common English education. He was salesman in the mercantile business several years, and became a student of Blackstone under R. K. Kercheval. In 1857 he entered the Lebanon Law School and the same year was admitted to the bar and opened an office in Lewisburg, where he has since successfully practiced. In 1865 he wedded Mary A. Carothers, by whom he has five children. Mr. and Mrs. Murray are members of the Christian Church. In 1861 Mr. Murray enlisted in Company B, Fifty-third Tennessee Infantry, and rose to the rank of first lieutenant. He was slightly wounded at Atlanta and severely at Franklin. After his return he followed his profession and farmed on a limited scale. He made a specialty of raising fine jacks and also kept a fine horse of No. 1 pedigree. Mr. Murray is a talented lawyer and a Democrat in politics.

S. J. MURRELL is one of the twelve children of Richard and Sarah (Hale) Murrell, who were born in Sullivan and Washington Counties respectively. After their marriage they settled in Sullivan County, where they spent the remainder of their lives. The father held the office of magistrate for many years, and died at the age of forty-five. The mother lived to be about fifty-five years of age. Our subject was born and reared on a farm in Sullivan County. He was born March 9, 1820, and after attending the common schools completed his education in Holston College and Washington college, Tennessee. Caroline F. George became his wife in 1843, and to them were born six children, two of whom are dead. In 1862 he joined the Southern Army, serving in Trivet's company, and was out twenty-six months, twenty-two months of that time being spent as a prisoner at Johnson's Island. He served as second lieutenant. In 1865 he came to Marshall County, and is now one of the heaviest tax-payers of the county. He is a Democrat. Mrs. Murrell's death occurred in 1879. She was a second cousin of Lewis Cass, and also of Caleb Cushing. Since her death Mr. Murrell and his daughter Josephine have lived on the old home farm.

LAMBERT C. NEIL, horse trainer, of Marshall County, was born March 28, 1839, in this county. He was reared by his grandmother and received a limited education. At the age of fifteen he went to Texas and engaged as an overseer of a cotton plantation. In 1859 he went to California, and, after residing there three years, returned with a single companion on pack-horses. In 1862 he went out as an independent soldier in Capt. Carter's company, and later acted under Forrest. While transmitting an order from one fort to another he was captured and taken to Nashville, then to Louisville, and while being transported in a box car to Camp Chase, he cut out two planks and made his escape. In 1867 he married Letitia Talley, and to this union was born one child, Edgar. Mr. Neil is a Democrat and his wife is a member of the Christian Church. He has a good farm of 121 acres, and his principal business since the war has been training horses for the turf. He owns some well bred racers and trains for others on a fine half-mile track on his farm. He has trained of his own a pacing stallion, "Bay Tom" that makes his mile in 2:23; sold him for $1,500. Mr. Neil has also a trotting gelding "Blue Jay" that makes the distance in 2:29¼; sold for $1,450. "Sumicks," trial in 2:32, a bay gelding, "Fred. Neil" makes the mile in 2:29¼. Our subject has also trained for others a bay stallion, "Nettle Keyman," that makes the mile in 2:26¼, trial 2:21; sold for $1,500. Mr. Neil has a wide reputation as a horse trainer.

DAVID NIX is one of fourteen children born to the marriage of Robin and Fannie (Arnold) Nix. The father was born in Georgia, and was married to Miss Arnold in Marshall County. He was a Democrat and farmer, and after his wife's death he married Vicey Cheak. He died in 1880, lacking sixteen days of being one hundred years old. David inherits English blood from both parents. He was born in what is now Marshall County, April 20, 1818. He was allowed to have his own way in regard to attending school, and not knowing the value of an education he preferred working in the cotton fields to attending school, consequently, his education is none of the best. He began earning his own living at the age of eighteen, and after working as a farm laborer five years he purchased 100 acres of land largely on credit, which he paid for and increased to 500 acres. In 1843 he wedded Fannie Glenn, by whom he had ten children. Mr. and Mrs. Nix are members of the Christian Church, and in politics he is a Democrat.

HON. J. L. ORR is the son of John and Emily (Bagley) Orr, both natives of Marshall County (then called Bedford and Lincoln Counties); the former was born in 1811 and the latter in 1813. They were married in 1830 and were the parents of three children —two girls and one boy. The father followed the occupation of a farmer and served as colonel in the State militia. He was a Democrat in politics. His death occurred April, 1849. The mother died January, 1886. Our subject was born November 9, 1836, in Marshall County, and passed his early life in assisting on the farm and in attending the public school. He completed his education in Erskin College, graduating from that institution in August, 1860. January 29, 1874, he wedded Sally S. Williams, and this union resulted in the birth of four children: Julia, Daisy, Sallie and Robert Williams. In 1861 Mr. Orr enlisted in Company A, Fourth Tennessee Cavalry, commanded by Col. Baxter Smith, and was all through the war. He surrendered at Charlotte, N. C., May 4, 1865, and returned home. He held the rank of first lieutenant and was wounded slightly. He was in all the principal engagements of the southwestern army (except Shiloh). He served two terms in the State Legislature and is a Democrat in politics. He is a self-made man, and at one time taught in the common schools and worked for his father-in-law ten years. He is now doing business for himself as merchant and grain dealer, stock raiser, grain farmer, and is doing a successful business.

THOMAS A. ORR, farmer, was born February 9, 1827, in Williamson County, Tenn., and is a son of Robert and Mary A. (Cummins) Orr, natives of Williamson County, Tenn. In 1835 they moved to Giles County and five years later to Marshall, and here spent the remainder of their days. They were both members of the Cumberland Presbyterian Church. Our subject was reared on the farm and received a practical education in the common schools. Like a dutiful son he remained at home until he was twenty-two years of age. In 1848 he led to the hymeneal altar Minerva Vincent, a native of Marshall County, born July 17, 1830. The fruits of this union were twelve children, eight of whom are living. The eldest son, Joseph C. is a stock trader. The second, Robert A., is a rising young physician of Mooresville; William R., is a practicing physician at home. The rest of the boys are at home farming. Our subject has a fine farm of 500 acres and has been a resident of this county for a period of forty-seven years. Mr. Orr is a Democrat in politics and a member of the Cumberland Presbyterian Church.

ROBERT J. ORR is a son of Robert and Leah (Polk) Orr. The father was born in Maryland, May, 1765, was married in 1790 and immigrated to Williamson County, Tenn., 1800. In 1808 he moved to Marshall County, then known as Bedford County. The mother was of English descent and was born in 1768 and died in 1830. The father died January 5, 1855, and was of Irish lineage. The subject of this sketch was born February 11, 1813, at the old homestead. He worked on the farm until the death of his father, after which he worked for himself. He received a rather limited education in the district schools, and September 25, 1849, he was married to Sarah E. Laws. This union has been blessed by the birth of eight children: David L., Leah C., John M. (deceased), Martha M., Catherine O., Alfred D., Nellie M. and Robert J. Mr. Orr served as captain and colonel in the Tennessee militia until the Rebellion, but did not take an active part in the war. He held the office of magistrate for eighteen years to the entire satisfaction of the people. He is a Republican and a member of the Presbyterian Church and is a strong advocate of the cause of temperance. Mrs. Orr is a member of the Methodist Episcopal Church. Her father advocated the cause of the South, serving in the State Legislature before and after the war.

WILLIAM H. OGILVIE. Richard Ogilvie, father of William H., was born in North Carolina, and came to Tennessee about 1796, locating in Williamson County, where he farmed and eventually became the owner of 500 acres of land. He married Cynthia M. Wilson, a native of Georgia, and became the father of seven children. Williamson County was almost an unbroken canebrake at the time of his settlement, so that he had great difficulty in clearing his farm. He died in 1822 and the mother resided with her youngest son on the old homestead until her death. William H. Ogilvie was born in Williamson County December 17, 1818, and in his youth attended the old-time subscription schools, his studies extending to geography and grammar. At the age of twenty he married Elizabeth N. Demumbrane, born in Williamson County December 29, 1820. To them were born eight children, only two of whom are living. In 1853 Mrs. Ogilvie died, and the following year he was united in marriage to Mary R. Gentry, also a native of Williamson County, born December 16, 1825. They are the parents of three daughters. Mr. Ogilvie was a Whig until the war. Since that time has been a supporter of Democratic principles. He is a Royal Arch Mason and owns 700 acres of land.

MOSES PARK, an early settler of Marshall County, Tenn., is a son of Moses and Mary (Wier) Park, who were born in North Carolina, the father in 1780 and the mother in 1779. They came to Tennessee in 1804 and located in Williamson County first and Marshall County about 1812. They were the parents of eight children and members of the Cumberland Presbyterian Church. The father was an old-line Democrat and a hatter by trade, but the greater part of his time was spent in agricultural pursuits. The mother died in 1859 and he in 1864. Moses, our subject, inherits Irish blood from his mother; he was born in the county March 16, 1818, and his days have been passed as a tiller of the soil. He attended the common schools, and while in his "teens" learned the cabinet-maker's trade. He worked in Missouri for some time, and then returned and worked at his trade until his shop was consumed by fire, and then engaged in farming. Eight children were born to his marriage with Mary A. Davis, which occurred in 1842. His son, Jerome, died from exposure at Fort Donelson. Mr. Park is a Democrat, and by hard work and good management has become the owner of 800 acres of good farming land. He has also been quite extensively engaged in raising fine stock.

GEORGE M. PARK is one of six children and was born February 9, 1844, in Marshall County, Tenn. His parents, Hill and Nancy (Hayes) Park, were born in Tennessee and after marriage settled on a farm in Marshall County, where they are spending their declining years. Hill Park is a Democrat. George M. was educated in the common schools, and at the breaking out of the war between the North and South he enlisted with the Southern cause in Company H, Forty-first Tennessee Infantry. He was captured at the fall of Fort Donelson and was imprisoned at Camp Morton, Ind., and Chicago, and was exchanged at Vicksburg and immediately re-enlisted in the service, but was again taken prisoner, at Jonesboro, Ga., and held until the close of the war. During his four years' service he was only twice wounded, once at Chickamauga and once at Jonesboro. By his energy and good management he has become the owner of 150 acres of land, where he now lives. He was married, in 1867, to Mary J. Alexander, by whom he is the father of eight children—six sons and two daughters.

DR. THOMAS J. PATTERSON'S birth occurred June 13, 1828, in Marshall County, Tenn., on the farm where he now resides. He followed the plow in his youthful days, and received an academical education. He began the study of medicine under Dr. M. H. Scales after attaining his twenty-first birthday, and after reading about two years entered the medical department of the University of Louisville, from which he graduated in 1851. He entered upon his practice in Maury County, and after two years moved to Marshall County, where he has since lived. In 1856 he married Louisa H. Hardin, born December 29, 1832, in Maury County, and educated at Columbia, and eight children blessed their union. He acted as assistant surgeon for about eighteen months during the late war, and since that time has been a Democrat in politics. He is also a Mason, and the owner of 418 acres of land, well stocked. He devotes the most of his time to farming, but still practices among his old patrons. His parents, John and Sarah (Wilson) Patterson, were born in the "Palmetto State." The father moved to Kentucky when young, and finally to Marshall County, Tenn., in 1820, where he was married about five years later. The mother died in 1830, leaving two children, and the father wedded Sarah Lavender, who bore him four children, two daughters living. The father was an extensive farmer of his day, and is now in his eighty-fourth year. Our subject's wife is a daughter of Pleasant and Tabitha (Gentry) Hardin, born and married in North Carolina. They moved to Maury County, Tenn. at an early day, and became the parents of six children, all girls. The father died while in the prime of life, and after his death the mother and her daughters managed the farm. She died in 1873.

HON. JAMES M. PATTERSON, M. D., a leading physician of Marshall County, is a son of James and Mary (Reed) Patterson, born in South and North Carolina in 1794 and 1791, respectively. They were brought to this State when children, and after reaching years of maturity were married in 1818, and became the parents of nine children. They resided in Maury County until 1833, and then came to Marshall County, where the father carried on farming and stock raising on a rather extensive plan. The father was a Whig, and served as magistrate many years. He died in 1875, and his wife the year previous. James M. Patterson was born in Maury County, January 8, 1829, and secured a good early education. At the age of twenty-four he began the study of medicine under Dr. S. J. Rice, and about two years later entered the medical department of the University of Nashville, from which he graduated in 1858, among the first in his class. He began practicing in Maury County, and during the war was part of the time engaged as physician and surgeon. In 1860 he married Margaret S. Hardison, who was born November 10, 1836, and ten children were born to their union. Dr. Patterson is a member of the Methodist Episcopal Church South, and his wife of the Christian Church. He was a Whig previous to the war, but has since been a Democrat. In 1870 he represented Bedford and Marshall Counties in the State Senate, and filled that position very ably. He came to Marshall County in 1864, where he has followed his profession, and also farmed for twenty-two years.

DAVID B. PHILLIPS is a native of Lincoln County, Tenn., born February 11, 1842, and after having passed his youth on his father's farm, obtaining a common school education, he, in 1861, enlisted in Capt. Walker's company of Third Tennessee Infantry. During four years' service he was in over fifty battles and skirmishes, but was not wounded during his entire service. He was one of the defenders of Fort Donelson, and after being captured there was imprisoned at Chicago. Having bribed a guard with $5, he made his escape and rejoined his command at Granada, Miss. After the close of the war he engaged in farming, and in 1866 was united in marriage to Nancy V. Gordon, by whom he had two children, only Hallie now living. Mr. Phillips is a member of the Cumberland Presbyterian Church, and in politics is conservative, although on most occasions he supports the Democratic party. He owns ninety-four acres of land in the most fertile portion of Marshall County, Tenn., and is considered one of its prosperous farmers. His parents, John H. and Elizabeth H. (Parham) Phillips, were born in Montgomery County, Tenn., in 1804, and Virginia in 1806, respectively. They were married in Lincoln County in 1828, and there resided until 1852, when they came to Marshall County. They became the parents of three children and were members of the Cumberland Presbyterian Church. The father was a Whig, but later became a Democrat. He followed blacksmithing and farming and continued the latter occupation until his death in 1876. The mother has since resided with her children.

DAVID B. PICKENS, farmer, is a son of William H. and Hannah (Moore) Pickens. The father was born in South Carolina, in 1792, and when young came with his parents and settled on the farm where David now lives. The mother was a native of Kentucky, born in 1795. They were both members of the Cumberland Presbyterian Church, and he was a Democrat in politics. He died in 1872 and after his death the mother lived on the old homestead until 1882, when she too passed from life. She had been blind for nearly twenty years. Our subject was born August 9, 1816, on the farm where he now lives; while growing up he received a very limited education, and at the age of twenty-three he began working for himself. In 1842 he led to the altar Mary A. Meador, a native of Williamson County, born August 14, 1824, and nine children blessed this union; all with the exception of two are married and settled in visiting distance of home. Mrs. Pickens is a member of the Cumberland Presbyterian Church. Mr. Pickens is a Democrat and one of the most successful farmers of this county. For seventy years he has been a respected and honored resident of what is now, Marshall County.

THOMAS M. PORTER is a farmer and native of Marshall County, Tenn., born December 8, 1845. He attended school and assisted his parents on the farm, and in the latter part of the war, although only eighteen years of age, volunteered in Company A, Fourth Tennessee Cavalry, and although in many severe engagements, was not wounded or captured. Since the war he has made agriculture his chief business and is the owner of a well stocked farm of 225 acres. He is a son of Thomas N. and Mary F. (Hardin) Porter, who were born in Rutherford and Williamson Counties, Tenn., in 1820 and 1827, respectively. They were married in Maury County, but the greater part of their days were spent in what is now Marshall County. They became the parents of two sons—our subject and John N. The father was a Whig and died in the prime of life. His widow returned to Maury County and married E. H. McLean, by whom she had seven children. After his death she married William Reagen, who also died. She is a member of the Presbyterian Church and is fifty-nine years of age.

JOHN N. PORTER, the youngest son of Thomas N. and Mary F. (Hardin) Porter was born in what is now Marshall County, Tenn., September 24, 1847. While a youth, his opportunities for obtaining a schooling were exceedingly limited, owing to the breaking out of the war. At the age of sixteen he volunteered in Company C, Ninth Battalion of Cavalry, and was perhaps the youngest soldier that went out from Maury County. During eight months' service he was neither wounded nor captured. After the war he rented land about four years and then purchased a farm of his own, which now consists of 454 acres. Mary R. Rucker became his wife in 1868. She was born June 13, 1851, in Hickman County. Their children's names are as follows: M. Frances, Melville E., James R., Emma P., Lucy A., Thomas H., John A., Hardin Q. and Tabitha G. Both husband and wife are members of the Cumberland Presbyterian Church, and in politics Mr. Porter is a Democrat.

WILLIAM N. PYLAND, farmer, is a son of Hardin and Nancy (O'Neal) Pyland. The father was born in Rutherford County, Tenn., in 1813, and the mother in Marshall County, Tenn., about 1826. The father was a blacksmith by trade till the breaking out of the war, after which he engaged in agricultural pursuits. Both are members of the Missionary Baptist Church and both are still living. Our subject was born March 15, 1842, and received his education in the common schools. He inherited English blood from his father and Irish from his mother. At the age of nineteen he volunteered in Company D, Fourth Tennessee Cavalry, and remained in service nearly four years. He returned home and engaged in the free and independent life of a farmer. In 1867 he wedded Elizabeth Bills, a native of Marshall County, born August 29, 1848, and the fruits of this union were an interesting family of five children. Mr. Pyland is a stanch Democrat and he and wife are members of the Missionary Baptist Church. Mr. Pyland has been quite successful in agricultural pursuits, owning at the present time 233 acres of good land. For thirty-four years he has been a resident of this county and enjoys the respect and esteem of all who know him.

DR. THOMAS E. REED, a leading physician of Lewisburg, is a son of Andrew J. and Virginia E. (Nelson) Reed, both natives of Tennessee, where they grew to years of maturity and were married. Shortly after the latter event they moved to Giles County. The father was a farmer and in addition carried on merchandising for some time. He was a member of the Methodist Episcopal Church and the mother a member of the Presbyterian Church. The mother died in 1860 and afterward the father married Mary E. Scott, who became the mother of four children, two of whom are living. Our subject was born July 15, 1860, in Giles County, Tenn., and was reared on a farm. In boyhood he attended the country schools and afterward Giles College and Fayetteville Academy. In 1874 he took a course of lectures in the University of Virginia and in the spring of 1876 graduated from the medical department of Vanderbilt University. In the same year he commenced practicing his profession in Lewisburg. Dr. Reed married Virginia J. McRady and this union resulted in the birth of two children. For ten years Dr. Reed has practiced his profession in Lewisburg and the extensive patronage he has received says more for his ability and popularity as a physician than mere words can do. Dr. Reed, like his father, is a Democrat, and he and Mrs. Reed are members of the Presbyterian Church.

JOHN G. REYNOLDS was born July 21, 1858, in Marshall County, Tenn., and received a good common school education; son of John G. and Victoria (Liggette) Reynolds, both natives of Tennessee, he of Williamson County and she of Marshall County. After marriage they settled in Williamson County, where the father died. To them was born one child, our subject. The father was a Whig in politics, and his chief business was trading, being shrewd and successful at that. Besides he owned a good farm. In 1858 the mother removed to this county and wedded Capt. J. C. Cundiff, by whom she had seven children. At the age of twenty-one our subject began working on a farm of his own. In 1880 he was united in marriage to Ada W. Wilson, a native of Williamson County, born February 5, 1860. By this marriage two children were born: John T. and Clarence B. Mr. Reynolds is a Democrat in politics, and he and wife are worthy members of the Cumberland Presbyterian Church. He has a good farm of 125 acres, and as a farmer has met with very fair success. He is very fond of bird hunting, and is a sure shot.

JOHN D. ROBERTS (deceased) was born March 27, 1824, in North Carolina, and was the son of Bright and Mary (Silar) Roberts. When but an infant our subject was brought to Tennessee by his parents and grew up on the farm. He received his education in the common'district schools, and, his father dying when our subject was but three years old, he was left an orphan at thirteen by the death of his mother. He then went to learn the tailor's trade of his brother-in-law, William B. Holden. After working a short time he gave it up and turned his attention to the free and independent life of a farmer. In 1842 he wedded Susannah M. Wilson, who was born January 4, 1824, and who is a daughter of Aaron J. and Hannah (Martin) Wilson. To Mr. and Mrs. Roberts were born eleven children, seven of whom are living. The eldest son is a rising physician of Texas. During the late war our subject went out to serve his country, but failing health prevented his carrying a musket. He worked at his trade in the hospital when able. In 1860 he moved to Arkansas, where he owned nearly 1,000 acres, but in 1873 returned to this county. In 1884, after an active, useful life, he was summoned to lay down his burden and pass to that realm where toil, sorrow and death are not known. He was a Democrat in politics. Mrs. Roberts is a member of the Cumberland Presbyterian Church, and is living on her large farm of 450 acres, which is being conducted very successfully by her son, Sidney J., who is a stirring young business man, and promises to make one of the leading farmers of his community.

CAPT. W. M. ROBINSON, farmer, is a son of James and Maria (Mayfield) Robinson, who was born in Williamson County, Tenn., in 1805, and Bedford County, Tenn., in 1814, respectively. They were farmers and the parents of four children. The mother died in 1838, and the following year the father moved from Bedford County to Marshall County, and in 1844 married Mrs. Anna A. Wilhoite, whose maiden name was Warner. The father was a man of fine intellect and was a teacher for many years. He was a wide-awake and successful business man, and died when only forty-one years of age. Our subject is of Irish-English descent, and was born August 30, 1831. After receiving an academical education, he, at the age of eighteen, began to make his own way in the world by merchandising and lumbering, continuing almost continuously until the present time. Mary C. Orr became his wife August 26, 1841, and eight children were born to their union seven of whom are now living. In the late war he served in Company D, Fourth Tennessee Cavalry, and arose to the rank of first lieutenant, and was afterward commissioned captain of his company, being on staff duty the most of the time. He owns a fine farm of 550 acres, a saw-mill in Alabama, and an interest in a store at Farmington. He is a Democrat and a man who has made life a success financially.

C. J. SHEFFIELD, a leading farmer of Marshall County and a son of J. B. and Martha M. (Falwell) Sheffield, was born January 27, 1832, on the farm where he is now living. He attended the common schools, and afterward completed his education at Chapel Hill. At the age of eighteen he began farming, but soon turned his attention to school teaching, which he followed for several terms. In 1859 he began the mercantile business as salesman for King, Powell & Co. and before the close of the year had bought out Powell, and soon after he and Col. T. C. H. Miller purchased King's interest. In 1861 he volunteered in the Confederate Army, in Col. Haynes' company Fourth Tennessee Cavalry, and was wounded three times, but never captured during four years of service. About eighteen months after enlisting he was appointed sergeant, and soon after arose to second lieutenant, holding that position till the close of the war. He then returned home and engaged in farming, which occupation he has followed ever since. In 1874 he wedded Laura Dobson, a native of Williamson County, born November 23, 1850. This union resulted in the birth of three children: Samuel, Henry and Ephraim. Mr. Sheffield is a Democrat, and he and wife are members of the Cumberland Presbyterian Church. He has a good farm of 430 acres, the greater part of which he has made by stock raising and close attention to business.

NEWTON J. SMILEY, trustee of Marshall County, is a son of H. B. and Sarah (Lowry) Smiley, natives of Kentucky and South Carolina, respectively. The father's chief occupation was farming, though in early life he worked at the carpenter's trade. He was a soldier under Jackson in the war of 1812, and having lived to see the return of seventy-five winters was called from the trials and tribulations of earth. The mother was in her ninety-third year when she died. Our subject was born August 9, 1833, in the Bedford fraction of Marshall County, and was of Irish-Scotch descent. He was educated in the country schools, and having farmed until 1861, he volunteered in Company G, Thirty-second Tennessee Infantry as a private, and was one of the brave boys who defended Fort Donelson. After his capture and imprisonment at Indianapolis, Ind., he was exchanged at Vicksburg and re-entering the service was promoted to first lieutenant. After nearly four years of faithful service he returned home and soon after engaged in the mercantile business in which he was successful, though twice burned out. Previous to the war, in 1857, he wedded Catherine E. Hall, by whom he had seven children, all living. Both he and wife are members of the Cumberland Presbyterian Church. Like his father before him he is a warm Democrat. In 1884 he was elected to the responsible position that he is now occupying. In connection with his office he is engaged in tilling the soil.

THOMAS M. SMITH, farmer, is a son of Thomas S. and Lucinda (Blackwell) Smith, natives, respectively, of Virginia and Kentucky. They were married in Williamson County, Tenn., whither they immigrated when children. The father had been married previous to his union with Miss Blackwell, and by that union had one child, Merritt. By the second marriage he became the father of four children: Thomas M., Emeline F. (deceased), Susan A. and Sarah C. The father was a tiller of the soil, and quite a successful one at that. He died in 1843 and the mother followed in 1880. Our subject was born November 24, 1835, in Davidson County, Tenn., where his father had moved for a few years, to superintend a farm. His education was rather limited, but not enough to prevent him from having sufficient knowledge for all practical purposes. He farmed for his mother till 1879, when they bought the farm where he now lives. In 1861 he enlisted in Capt. Alexander's independent company, and after a year's service joined the Fourth Tennessee Cavalry, Confederate Army. He served all through the war without receiving a wound or being taken prisoner. Since that time he has been engaged in agricultural pursuits, and at the present has a farm of 235 acres. He is a Democrat in politics and has been a resident of this county for thirty-two years, and is considered an honest, upright citizen.

A. LAFAYETTE SMITH is a son of George W. Smith, who was born in 1822 in McNairy County, Tenn., and was married to Mrs. Martha (Fowler) Wilson (widow of Mark H. Wilson and the mother of five children). Mrs. Smith was born in 1818 and to her union with Mr. Smith were born five children. They were members of the Christian Church and the father was a well-to-do farmer and a Democrat. They came to Marshall County about 1853. After the mother's death Mr. Smith married Mrs. McDowery, to whom two children were born. The father died in 1884. Lafayette Smith was born December 25, 1846, and his educational advantages were such as could be obtained in the common schools. He began earning his own living at the age of nineteen, and in 1870 wedded Sarah T. Collins, and their union was blessed with seven children. His wife died in 1885 and the following year he married Margaret E. Goodrum. Mr. Smith is a Democrat and owns a fine tract of 350 acres of land.

PEYTON C. SMITHSON, one of the prominent attorneys of Lewisburg, is a son of John G. and Ann (Ladd) Smithson, both natives of Virginia, the former born in 1820 and the latter in 1818. They were married in Williamson County, this State, and became the parents of fifteen children, all of whom lived to be grown. Five of the boys are lawyers. Both parents are members of the Methodist Episcopal Church, the father being a local minister there, though his chief occupation is farming. He is a Republican in politics. Our subject was born in 1851, in Williamson County, and was of English descent on his father's side and Irish on his mother's. He assisted his father on the farm, and acquired sufficient education in the common schools to enable him to teach. After following this occupation for some time he entered Giles College and there completed his education. In 1874 he commenced reading law in his brother's office, and the following year was admitted to the bar. He subsequently opened an office in Lewisburg, where he has had a good practice ever since. In 1878 he wedded Ellen McClure, and to this union were born four children. Mrs. Smithson belongs to the Presbyterian Church. For two years Mr. Smithson held the office of mayor of Lewisburg. He is a Republican, though conservative in his views. For eleven years he has followed his profession in Lewisburg, and is one of that city's best attorneys.

JAMES C. SNELL, farmer, is a son of John A. and Mahala (Bills) Snell, who were natives of North Carolina. The father was born in 1809 and his wife in 1814. They were brought to Tennessee when young, and were married in Marshall County. Of their ten children eight are living. They were well-to-do farmers, and in former days raised cotton on the ground where the court house of Lewisburg stands. The father was constable four years, and was a Democrat in politics. He died in 1869, and his widow has since resided with her children. James C. was born July 22, 1833, in Marshall County, and received such education as could be obtained in his day. He began renting land at the age of twenty-one, but at the end of twelve years purchased 137 acres of land where he now lives. In 1857 he married Fannie Elliott, born in Marshall County in 1832, and died in 1877. In 1878 Mr. Snell was united in marriage to Melissa Ewing, who was born May 6, 1851, in Marshall County. Our subject has no children by either marriage.

JOHN STAMMER is a son of Thomas and Elizabeth (Wadley) Stammer. The father was born in Alabama in 1805, and the mother in Rutherford County, Tenn., where they were married by Squire Nash. Both parents were professors of religion. The father was a farmer and died in 1837, leaving a wife and four small children. The mother would go to the field with her children to hoe corn, pick cotton, or whatever else she could do toward making an honest living. While she succeeded in that she did vastly more—she sanctified honest toil with the sweat of a mother's brow, and taught her little ones the lesson of self-reliance. After three years she married J. R. Haskins, and is still living at the ripe age of seventy-seven. Our subject was born January 27, 1827, in Rutherford County, Tenn., and had very meager chances for schooling. At the age of eighteen he wedded Margaret A. Bigger, and to them were born three children, only one of whom is living. Three years later his wife died, and in 1851 he was married to Letitia Bigger, sister of his first wife, by whom she had seven children. In 1874 his second wife died, and in the same year he wedded Mrs. Lucinda Joyce, widow of D. F. Joyce, and this union resulted in the birth of four children. Mr. Stammer is a Democrat, and in 1862 enlisted in Company F, Twenty-third Tennessee Infantry, Confederate Army. He was captured and confined for nearly a year, but was at last released. He acted for some time as quartermaster-sergeant. Since the war he has farmed, and has 265 acres of good land. He is a Mason, and treasurer and superintendent of Eagleville & Chapel Hill Turnpike.

ALBERT B. STILLWELL, proprietor of the "Stillwell House," of Lewisburg, is a son of Osburn B. and Deborah L. (McCord) Stillwell, both natives of this State, where they grew up and were married. Their family consisted of three children, only one of whom, our subject, is living. One child died in infancy, and the other enlisted in the war and was captured at Fort Donelson. After lying in prison but a few days at Lafayette, Ind., he died from a relapse of the measels caused by exposure. The father was a tiller of the soil, and died while in the full strength of manhood. The mother then married John J. Elliott, by whom she had three children. She died in 1883. Our subject was born October 31, 1842, in Marshall County. His ancestors on his mother's side were Scotch-Irish, and on his father's probably Irish. He passed his boyhood days in assisting on the farm, and received a limited education. owing to the financial circumstances in which the family were left at the death of the father. In 1866 our subject began the mercantile business at Verona, and this he continued until 1878. Two years later he was elected trustee, and for four years filled that office in an able manner. In 1868 he wedded Mary K. Collins. Mr. Stillwell is a member of the Christian Church, and Mrs. Stillwell of the Methodist Church. In 1882 our subject purchased the hotel that he is now conducting.

CORNELIUS T. SWANSON, attorney, was born December 8, 1832, in Williamson County. His youthful days were passed in assisting on the farm and in attending the common schools. His education was completed in an academy. In 1858 he began reading law with John Marshall, of Franklin, and the following year was admitted to the bar. He then began the practice of his profession at Troy, Tenn. In 1861 he volunteered in Company H, Ninth Tennessee Infantry, as first lieutenant, and served a short time in the war when he was disabled by sickness for several months. After the reorganization of the army he joined the Fourth Tennessee Cavalry, and remained with that until the close of the war. After returning home he located in Franklin, and in 1868 wedded Emily C. Orr, and by her became the father of one child, Annie B. Two years after locating in Franklin he went to Mississippi to take charge of a cotton plantation, where he continued about six years. Finding that this was not a very lucrative business he returned to Tennessee and opened a law office in Lewisburg in 1877, where he has received his full share of patronage. In 1875 Mrs. Swanson died. Mr. Swanson is a Democrat in politics and has practiced his profession for nine years in Lewisburg. He is one of the first attorneys of Marshall County. He is a son of James and Anne M. S. (Zollicoffer) Swanson. The mother is a sister of Gen. Zollicoffer. Both parents are natives of this State. The father was born in 1802, and the mother in 1808. The father was a farmer and died in 1869, the mother died fourteen years previous to his death. The Swansons are of Scotch-Irish descent, and the Zollicoffers of Swiss.

WILLIAM P. THOMAS may be mentioned as one of the prosperous farmers of Marshall County, Tenn. His parents, T.W. and Lucy (Pierson) Thomas, were born in Virginia, and were there married, and soon after came to Tennessee and located in Rutherford County, where they lived until the death of the father, and then the mother and her five children located in Bedford County, and about 1850 came to Marshall County. The father was a stock trader and while on a tour in Alabama sickened and died William P. was born in Rutherford County, September 7, 1832, and as he was obliged to assist in supporting the family his school days were limited. He has acquired a practical business education, however, and is well to do in worldly goods, being the owner of 400 acres of land, which he has acquired by hard work. In 1861 he volunteered in Col. Haynes' company of cavalry and after a short service was discharged on account of rheumatic trouble. In politics he is a stanch Democrat, and is a Master Mason of Chapel Hill Lodge. He is a bachelor.

JOSEPH PERCIVAL THOMPSON is a son of John and Mary (Snell) Thompson, who were born in North Carolina. The father came to Tennessee with his parents when Nashville was a mere village. He spent the greater share of his life in Bedford County, where he farmed and practiced medicine. He served as surveyor and magistrate and represented his county one term in the State Legislature. He was a Democrat up to 1835 and then became a Whig. He died in 1857 and the mother in 1861. Joseph P. was born in Bedford County January 16, 1812. At the age of sixteen he began working as salesman, and in 1833 wedded Prudence Allison, by whom he had five children. She died in 1844 and the following year he married Myra Wallis. To them were born four children, two of whom lived to be grown. In 1850 his second wife died and two years later Margaret E. Fowler became his third wife. Since his first marriage Mr. Thompson has farmed. He is conservative in politics. Robert C. Thompson, his son, was born to his first marriage. He was born June 30, 1836, in Bedford County, and there lived until sixteen years of age and then came to Marshall County. He taught school for some time, although farming has been his chief calling through life. In 1858 he wedded Frances S. Wilson, by whom he had three children: Flora A., Thomas L. (who graduated with the class of 1886 from Vanderbilt University), and Minnie B. In 1861 Robert C. volunteered in Company H, Forty-first Tennessee Infantry. He was captured at Fort Donelson and imprisoned at Camp Morton, but re-entered service after being exchanged, but was so severely wounded at Atlanta that he was disabled from further service. He attained the rank of second lieutenant. Since the war he has farmed. He is a Democrat in politics, and is a man who takes deep interest in enterprises for the public weal.

JAMES A. WOODS, senior member of the firm of Woods & McCord, of Lewisburg, is a son of Francis B. and Margaret S. (Morrison) Woods, both natives of this State. After marriage they settled in this county, on the farm where they are still living. Their family consisted of eight children, six of whom are living. Both parents are members of the Presbyterian Church. For a number of years the father served as constable, though he was not an aspirant to places of public trust. He is now seventy-seven years old, and his wife is seventy-five. They have lived together fifty-four years. Our subject was born August 4, 1848, in Marshall County, and received his education in the country schools. Having prepared himself at Union Academy, of this county, in 1869 he entered Ann Arbor University and graduated in the classical course of the literary department in 1872. He then taught school one year, and began reading law under Walter S. Bearden, of Shelbyville, but failing health drove him from the profession of law, and after clerking for a short time he engaged in business at Lewisburg. In 1880 he wedded Nannie J. McCord, by whom he has two children: James W. and Bedford M. Mr. Woods is a Democrat, and he and wife are members of the Presbyterian Church. Mr. Woods has been alderman and commissioner of this taxing district for six years, besides he has been president of the Marshall County Temperance Alliance since its organization. He also holds a large interest in the firm of Coffey, Woods & Co.

WILLIAM H. WOOD, undertaker and dealer in furniture, is a son of William and

Amy (Smith) Wood. They were married in Massachusetts and came to Maury County, this State, between 1834 and 1840, to take charge of a large cotton factory. By trade the father was a machinist, being a first-class man in the business. For the last twenty-five years he has operated a chair factory. He has been magistrate for fourteen years, and since the war has been a Democrat. He is still living at the age of seventy-two. His wife is sixty-eight. Our subject was born September 20, 1841, in Maury County, was reared in town, and received a good practical education. While growing up he had learned the cabinet-maker's trade in his father's shop, and after reaching manhood he entered a book store as salesman, and two years later, in connection with R. D. Blum, opened a dry goods and clothing store in Columbia. Having bought out his partner, he sold the whole stock and engaged in the manufacture of chairs with his father and brother. He then sold out and worked in the cabinet shop of Lamb & Boyd, and later became superintendent of the water-works of Columbia. In 1866 he wedded Mary L. Bynum, and to this union were born six children—three of whom are living. Both Mr. and Mrs. Wood are active members of the Cumberland Presbyterian Church. Twice Mr. Wood has been elected alderman, and is now president of the corporation. In politics he is conservative, supporting the Democracy. For nine years he has been in business in Lewisburg, and the trade he has succeeded in getting speaks well for his ability as a business man.

JAMES M. WELBORN, farmer and stock raiser, is a son of Johnson and Elatia (Knight) Welborn. The father was born in Bedford County in 1814, and the mother in Rutherford County about 1822. After marriage they settled in Henderson County, and after a short residence came to this county in 1849. About twenty years later he moved to Texas, where they both died, the father in 1870 and the mother in 1880. The father was a Democrat, and a member of the Cumberland Presbyterian Church. He was a farmer and stock raiser and owned about 600 acres of land. Our subject, James M. Welborn, was born Feburary 12, 1841, in Henderson County, passed his youthful days in aiding his father on the farm and in attending the common schools, where he received a good English education. He was preparing for a course in the higher schools when the stirring events of the war broke into his plans. In 1861 he volunteered in the Confederate Army, Company F, Seventeenth Tennessee Infantry, and after eighteen months' service was transferred to Company A, Fourth Tennessee Cavalry. He received but one slight wound and was never captured during the four years he was in service. In 1865 he married Rosa L. Hutton, who was born August, 31, 1843, and five children blessed this union. Mr. Welborn is a Democrat in politics, and he and wife are zealous workers in the Missionary Baptist Church. He has a fine farm of 100 acres lying on the pike. In the line of fine stock, he keeps a fine horse of Traveler & Brooks stock, and two first class jacks.

JAMES W. WHITMAN, farmer, is a son of Rev. R. M. Whitman, a native of Boston, Mass., born in 1804. When a mere boy R. M. Whitman went with his parents to Virginia, where he lived quite a number of years. They then immigrated to Bedford County, and here he married Almedia Sanders (the subject's mother), and a native of Bedford County, born in 1815. To them were born nine children. After her death the father was married twice; first to Mrs. Jane Reed, who died in 1857, and then to Mrs. Ann Edwards, who still lives. The father died in Texas in 1873. He was an extensive farmer and stock trader, and in early life practiced medicine. He was also a preacher of the gospel. Our subject was born November 28, 1838, in the Moore fraction of Lincoln County. He was reared on the farm and received a poor education, owing to the demand for his labor at home. In 1861 he volunteered in Company K, Eighth Tennessee Infantry, Confederate Army, and went through four years of service without being wounded, and was only captured once, when he succeeded in making his escape in a few days. He served twelve months as captain of Company A, Twenty-eighth Tennessee Cavalry. After the war he went to Texas to engage in the mercantile business, where he remained ten years. In 1874 he returned to Tennessee and engaged in farming. In 1877 he married Ann E. Hutton, a native of Rutherford County, born August 14, 1841. In 1882 she died, and the following year he married Jennie P. Grigsby, of Giles County. This union resulted in the birth of one child, Robert G. Mr. Whitman is a staunch Democrat and a member of the Missionary Baptist Church. His present wife is a member of the Methodist Episcopal Church. He has a good farm of 497 acres, and as a farmer and stock raiser has been quite successful.

JOHN B. WILHOITE, farmer and stock dealer, is a son of William and Anna A. (Warner) Wilhoite, natives of North Carolina and Tennessee, respectively. The father was a miller, running successfully an old-style mill during his life. He was a Democrat, an attendant and his wife a member of the Missionary Baptist Church. He died at the age of thirty. In 1835 the mother came to this county, and soon afterward married James Robinson, father of Capt. Robinson. Her second husband died three years later. She died in 1876. Our subject was born December 23, 1830, in Bedford County, and did not have the best advantages for an education, but made the most of what he did have. After leaving the common schools he completed his education in Chapel Hill Academy. At the age of fifteen he took charge of the home farm, and a year later planned and superintended the construction of the grist and saw-mill at Fishing Ford, which he has run ever since. He is also the constructor of the dam furnishing water to the mills. In 1862 he volunteered in the Confederate Army in Capt. Miller's company of Eleventh Tennessee Cavalry, and after three years of faithful service returned home. In 1869 he wedded Lizzie T. Bullock, of Williamson County, born in 1846; the fruits of this union were three children, all living—Jacob, Mary and Addie. Mr. Wilhoite is a Democrat, a Royal Arch Mason and a member of the Missionary Baptist Church. Mrs. Wilhoite is a member of the Methodist Church. Our subject has considerable of this world's goods, and has lived in Marshall County for forty-six years.

WILLIAM E. WILKINSON, a prosperous young farmer of Marshall County, Tenn., is a son of Mack and Jane (Palmer) Wilkinson. The father was born in Giles County, Tenn., in 1816, and the mother in Virginia in 1819. To her marriage with Mr. Wilkinson were born six children. Mack Wilkinson was a soldier in the Seminole war, and for two terms filled the office of constable. He was a Democrat, and died in 1881. The mother is still alive and is sixty-seven years of age. Our subject is of Scotch-Irish and German descent, and was born in what is now Marshall County March 14, 1856. He was reared on a farm, and at the age of nineteen years began teaching in Arkansas, but failing health caused him to return to Tennessee. He was elected and served two terms as constable. In 1880 he wedded Mollie Cooper, by whom he had three children, all girls. Mrs. Wilkinson belongs to the Methodist Episcopal Church South. Since 1883 Mr. Wilkinson has resided on the farm where he now lives. He gives his support to the Democratic party, and is a prosperous farmer of the county.

HON. EWING A. WILSON was a prominent citizen and native of Marshall County, Tenn. He was born in 1818 and always resided in the county, and was prominently connected with its growth and prosperity. His early education was somewhat limited, but he acquired a good education through self-application and contact with business life. He held the positions of captain, major and brigadier-general of militia, and during the late war major of the Fourth Tennessee Cavalry, but failing health caused him to give up his army career. He represented his county three terms in the lower house of the State Legislature and was senator two terms. He was very public-spirited and assisted in every enterprise for the good of the county. He was president of the Marshall County Fair Association, and in the days of the Grange movement he was on the side of honest toil. As a financier he has been almost without a peer, and by good management became the owner of about 2,000 acres of land, which he distributed liberally among his sisters' children. For forty years he was a member of the Cumberland Presbyterian Church. He died in 1883, beloved and respected by all. As a Christian he was faithful, kind-hearted and true, wise as a legislator, and as a citizen had few equals. His parents were Aaron J. and Hannah (Martin) Wilson. The father was born in North Carolina and when young came to Rutherford County, where he married and became the father of seven children. The mother died in 1827 and he in 1831. They were members of the Cumberland Presbyterian Church.

JASPER A. YARBROUGH, register of Marshall County, is a son of George and Nancy E. (Gibbons) Yarbrough. The father was born in North Carolina and the mother in Tennessee. They were married in Tennessee, and their family consisted of ten children. Jasper's maternal grandparents had twenty-six children and his paternal had fourteen. Both our subject's parents were members of the Methodist Episcopal Church. The father was a well-to-do farmer and had the honor of furnishing three brave boys for the war, one of whom was killed. The father lived to be about seventy-six and the mother about seventy-four. Our subject, who was born November 7, 1839, in Marshall County, is a man three feet and nine and a half inches in height. He was reared on the farm and received a practical education in the common schools. Having picked up the shoe-maker's trade he worked at it for about eight years, besides teaching school. He was always a very handy workman and could make a suit of clothes, knit a pair of socks, or almost anything he turned his hand to. In 1874 he was elected register, and has held that position ever since with ability and to the satisfaction of the people. In 1881 he wedded Lizzie McKee. The fruits of this union were three children, two of whom are living. Mr. and Mrs. Yarbrough are members of the Methodist Episcopal Church. He has been a citizen of Marshall County for forty-six years. In politics he is a warm Democrat.

ABBOT, J.C.,0828
ABBOTT, C.R.,0827, Charles R.,
    1003, David,0815, Elizabeth,
    1058, Major,1058
ABBY, Harriet,0858
ABERNATHY, C.A.,0889, C.B.,
    0956, Hattie A.,0965, J.J.,
    0817, L.E.,0836, Tennessee,
    0988
ABRAHAMS, Hannah,1068
ABSTON, Fannie L.,0969, Mary,
    0969, Merry,0969
ACRES, Elizabeth,0963
ACUFF, J.W.,0879, William,
    0893
ADAMS & SIMMONS, (Mill),0863
ADAMS, Absalom,0809, Alex,
    0902, Alexr.D.,1190,
    Archibald,1126, Charmian,
    1077, Eldon,1077, Elizabeth,
    1190, Eveline W.,1190,
    Frances,1097, Harvey,1077,
    Henry,0822, J.,0807, J.N.,
    0843,0856, James N.,1077,
    James,0805, Jane E.,1190,
    Jane,1126
ADAMS, John Q.,0831, John W.,
    1126, John,0793,0801,0842,
    0888,0960, Joseph,1190,
    Ladie M.,1077, Mariah,1077,
    Mary H.,1126, Nathan,0892,
    R.L.,0890,0897, Rachel,
    1190, Robert L.,1190,
    Susannah,0761, T.Riggs,
    1190, William,0761, Wm.,0809
ADCOCK, Nancy,1083
ADKERSON, Clinton,1019, Ella,
    1019, George M.,1019, Ida,
    1019, James A.,1019,
    John H.,1019, John N.,1019,
    Katie N.,1019, Mabel,1019,
    Percilla,1019, Sallie M.,
    1019, Sallie,1019
ADKINS, J.P.,0764
ADKINSON, Anna,0941, J.,0764,
    Mary A.,0972, Oscar,0798,
    William,0764,0811
ADKISON, T.F.,0807
ADKISSON, Martha,0905
ADLE, Frank,0803
AFFLACK, John,0848
AGNEW, Addie C.,0904, Effie D.,
    0904, James F.,0904, John,
    0904, Rufus F.,0904, Sarah,
    0904, William,0904
AHRENS, Angelia,1093
AIGAN, ,0850
AIKINS, John,0956, Mary C.,
    0956
AKE, John,0871
AKIN, ,0776, A.N.,0759,0770,
    0773, Alfred N.,0904,
    Anderson,0909, Eliza C.,
    0904, J.C.,1126, J.H.,0787,
    J.K.,0753, James,0768,0939,
    Jas.T.,0753, John(Rev.),
    0776, John,0776, Mary L.,
    0918, Nathan B.,0752,
    Roxanna,0909, Samuel W.,
    0904, Samuel,0805
AKIN, Samuel,0808, Sarah D.,
    0920, Sarah,0904, Thomas,
    1126
AKINS, Caroline,0994, Williamson,
    0931
ALBERSON, Isaac,0796
ALDERSON, F.S.,0752, J.S.,
    0756, Tazwell S.,0752, W.S.,
    0782
ALDRIDGE, Alexander,0869,
    Jesse,0890
ALEXANDER, (Capt.),0896,1227,
    ,0776,0796, A.M.,0830,
    A.R.,0766, Abdon J.,0904,
    Abner,0842, Albert G.,1020,
    Andrew M.,1019, Andrew M.Sr.,
    1019, Annie E.,1020,
    Annie L.,0905, Annie,0911,
    Antoinette,0965, Archibald,
    0874, B.F.,1020, Benjamin,
    0857
ALEXANDER, Bessie W.,0905,
    Billy,0887, Blanch,0905,
    Capt.,0850, Caroline H.,
    0905, Catharine,1020,
    Charley R.,0905, D.W.,0895,
    Daniel,1020, Ebenezer C.,
    0965, Eleazer,0904, Eliza C.,
    0904, Eliza E.,0904,
    Eliza J.,1020, Elizabeth,
    0905
ALEXANDER, Elizabeth,1020,
    1178, Enola E.,0905,
    Ezekial,0863, George,0841,
    0844, J.H.,0799, J.M.,0902,
    J.N.,0764, J.W.,0775,0781,
    0782, Jesse W.,0965, Jesse,
    0838,0851, John C.,0904,
    John W.,0851, John,0815,
    0816,0893, Joseph B.,0905,
    Joseph W.,0905
ALEXANDER, Laura A.,0965,
    Laura L.,0905, Laura,0905,
    Lucy F.,0965, Madison H.,
    1020, Madison,1020, Marcus O.,
    0905, Mary C.,0905, Mary Cole,
    1143, Mary J.,1222, Nancy,
    1019, Nora L.,0965, Ophelia,
    1020,1046, Phoebe,0965,
    Randolph,0905, Rebecca,1020
ALEXANDER, Rev.,0839, Richd.,
    0796, Robert L.,1020, Ross,
    0905, Sallie B.,1073,
    Sarah R.,0905, Sarah,1020,
    Silas,0760, Thomas,0794,
    0822, Viola V.,0965,
    Volona L.,0965, W.H.,1047,
    Wm.,0776, Wm.A.,0758,
    Wm.C.,0965, Wm.E.,0965
ALFORD, A.J.,1126, Chirena I.,
    0916, D.M.,0877,1126,
    Margaret,1126, Nancy,1076
ALLAN, ,0863
ALLCORN & JOHNSON, ,0854
ALLCORN, John,0841,0845,0846,
    0847,0848,0853
ALLEN, ,0796,0886, Ann E.,
    1195, C.N.,0871, Capt.,0751,
    Charles,0797, David,0821,
    Eliza T.,0916, Elizabeth,
    1020,1127, Emmet C.,1021,
    Ewitt P.,1127, H.B.,0890,
    Hamblin,0916, Harris L.,
    1021, Isaac S.,1127, J.,
    0829, J.H.,0830,0832, J.S.,
    0819
ALLEN, J.W.,0764,0805,
    James E.,1127, James H.,
    1020, John H.,1127, John S.,
    0802, John,0779,0842,
    Lora V.,1127, Louisa,0906,
    M.G.,0764, N.J.G.,0855,
    Nathan,0764, Obadiah A.,
    1020, R.C.,0782, Rebecca C.,
    1192, Sanford,0808, Sarah E.,
    1021
ALLEN, Sarah,1127, Silvina,
    0916, Susan E.,1127,
    Thomas J.,1192, W.S.,0899,
    W.V.,0875, Walter,0841,
    William,0762,0853,1127
ALLEY, Martha,0969, Perna C.,
    0969, Walter,0969
ALLISON & COOK, ,1107
ALLISON & HALL, ,0874
ALLISON, ,0863, Andrew,1117,
    Dr.,0855, Elizabeth,1168,
    J.P.,0805, J.T.,0874,
    James,0794, Mary C.,0961,
    Mary W.,1045, Nancy,0997,
    Prudence,1229, R.P.,0854,
    Richard,0785, Robert,1168,
    Ruth C.,1168, Sallie,1074,
    T.C.,0875, T.J.P.,0759
ALLISON, Thomas,0800, W.M.,
    0889, William,0842,0870
ALLMAN, G.L.,0889, George T.,
    0903
ALMIRE, R.H.,0764
ALMONT, Hezekiah,0766
ALPIN, Joel,0848
ALSOP, G.M.(Dr.),1114
ALSTON, Jane D.,0986, Jane H.,
    0992, John,0992, Lucy A.,
    0992, Mary J.,0972, Sarah K.,
    1132
ALSUP, (Dr.),1101, A.H.(Rev.),
    1098, Carrie,1098, Gideon,
    0851, J.M.,0851, John,0842,
    S.T.,0844
AMBROSE, J.L.,0821
AMENT, Thos.W.,0753
AMIS, ,0778, Bruce E.,0905,
    Elizabeth,0911, John E.,
    0905, Jonas T.,0905,
    Mary J.,0947, Mary K.,0962,
    Rebecca T.(Mrs.),0905,
    Sarah W.,0910, Sarah,1194,
    Zurelda,0962
AMOS, Henry,0870
ANDERSON & GREEN, ,1176
ANDERSON, (Spring),0805, ,
    0863, Adaline,1021, Albert,
    0902, Andrew,0858, Berry G.,
    0965, Charles W.,1021,
    Clark C.,0906, D.B.,0852,
    Effie,0906, Eliza J.,0965,
    Elizabeth,0901,1109,
    Emily D.,1114, Emily M.,
    1021, Fannie,1077, Florence,
    1069
ANDERSON, Frank,0854,1114,
    Gen.,0962, George D.,1021,
    George W.,1021, George,
    0827, Harry I.,1021,
    Harry J.,1021, J.L.,0819,
    J.M.,0855, James C.,0809,
    0905, James L.,1021, James,
    0846,0853,0854, Joel,0809,
    John G.,0785, John H.,0874,
    John W.,0965
ANDERSON, John,0767, Joseph B.,
    1077, Joseph M.,1077,
    Joseph,0867,0895,0965,
    K.L.,0871, Kate Lee,1077,
    Lillie L.,1021, Lorenzo,
    0896, Lucinda,0905, Margaret,
    1141, Martha M.,1021,
    Martha M.,1021, Mary Dixon,
    1077, Mary W.,1000, Mary,
    1122
ANDERSON, Mattie C.,1021,
    Mattie,1021, Monroe,0851,
    Ora,0906, P.,0854, Patrick,
    0854,1077, Patten,0795,
    Paulden,0848, Pauldin,0854,
    Peter,0820, Prof.,0906,
    Robert B.,0965, S.,0965,
    S.C.,0857, S.M.,0855,
    Sallie T.,1021, Sallie,
    0965, Samuel,0827
ANDERSON, Samuel,0849,0870,
    1077, Sarah C.,0965,1149,
    1150, Sophia E.,0965, Susan,
    0936, T.,0854, T.C.,0858,
    Thomas W.,0965, Thomas,
    1109, Thompson,1077,
    Thos.(Rev.),0857, Thos.,
    0868, W.,0822, William,0809,
    0901,0905, Wm.,0766,0802,
    Wm.E.,0763
ANDERSON, Wm.P.,0965
ANDREAS, Capt.,0751
ANDREW, (& Co.),0804
ANDREWS & CO., ,0829
ANDREWS & MCGREGOR, ,0768
ANDREWS, Andrw. L.,0790, E.F.,
    0906, E.T.,0796, Eliz.H.,
    0987, Eliza,0965, Emily M.,
    0981, Ephraim,0906, Estella L.,
    1047, F.M.,0799, George,
    0965, J.H.,0770, J.L.,0799,
    James,0756,0780,0793,0966,
    Jane,0966, John T.,1047,
    John,0797,0966
ANDREWS, Jones,1190, Lucy J.,
    0966, Lucy,1190, M.L.,0796,
    0804,0839,0987, M.M.,0793,
    0797, Mark L.,0790,0797,
    0808, Mark Lydell,0965,
    Mary E.,0966, Mary K.,0962,
    Minerva,0966, Nannie R.,
    0966, R.E.,0771, Richard L.,
    0796, Sarah,0906, Tennessee,
    1190
ANDREWS, Thomas E.,0962, W.J.,
    0770,0771,0780, Wm.V.,1190
ANOLD, Ed,0818
ANTHONY, ,0863, Capt.,0851,

J.A.,0851, Jacob,0863,
John,0819, Lewis,0819,
Louis,0812, Thos.A.,0798,
William,0794
AOIDLETT, Rebecca A.,0952
APPLEBY, Jack,0896
ARMSTRONG BROS.,,0874
ARMSTRONG, ,0862,0897, Benj.,
0799, Benjamin F.,0966,
C.A.,0893,0898, Clinton A.,
1190, Elias J.,0750,
Elizabeth,1141, G.W.,0797,
0807, Gen.,0893, George,
1190, Hettie,1178, J.H.,
0854, J.L.(Dr.),0880, J.L.,
0820, J.W.,0856, James L.,
0872
ARMSTRONG, James,0749,0784,
0814, Jas.L.(Dr.),0880,
John,0762,0842, Maggie,
1191, Margaret E.,0919,
Margaret,1190, Mary,1177,
Nathaniel,0764, R.H.,0894,
Robert,0797,0823, W.H.,
0854, William,0966, Wm.,
0750,0805, Wm.W.,0966
ARNELL, D.R.,0750, Janie M.,
0917, Jas.M.,0782, S.M.,
0780, S.N.,0780, W.L.,0773
ARNOLD BROS.,,0874,0875,0878
ARNOLD, ,0863,0877, Belle,
1145, C.W.,0872, Chesley,
0872, D.D.,0871, Ed,1021,
Elizabeth,1207, Fannie B.,
1022, Fannie,1221, H.,0829,
Harriett,1021, Horace N.,
1021, Horace,1027, J.M.,
0764, John,0893, Josephine,
1061, Mary A.,1055, Nancy A.,
1145
ARNOLD, O.P.,0878, Thomas,
1145
ASBURY, Rev.,0860
ASHBRIDGE, Geo.W.,0779
ASHFORD, Thomas,0836
ASHTON, William,0793
ASHWORTH, Jaspar R.,0854,
Jasper R.,0854, Mary D.,
1112, Samuel,1112
ASKINS, Fred,0850
ASTON, Alex,0842, S.M.,0860
ATKINSON & MCCORD, ,0881
ATKINSON, ,0863, A.E.,1127,
Capt.,0792, Christina C.,
1127, Elizabeth C.,1127,
F.M.,1127, Frank,0870,
J.R.,1127, Jane,1127, John,
0865,0868,1008,1127, Juda,
1008, Mary A.,1127, Nancy,
1127, S.J.(Miss),1049, T.F.,
0789, W.E.,1127
ATKISSON, Emily,1191, L.P.,
0902, Mary A.F.,1169,
Mary O.,1191, P.A.,0902,
P.L.(Rev.),1191, P.L.,0897,
0902, Pleasant,1191,
Sophronia,1191, Squire,0886
ATWOOD, Bessie May,0966,
Jeneva V.,0966, John B.,
0966, John,0803,0966,
Maggie A.,0966, Mary,0966,
William F.,0966
AUBERY, Elizabeth,1167
AUGLIN, Capt.,0792
AUST, James,1078, Sarah,1078,
Thomas P.,1078, Thomas,1078
AUSTIN, Diana,1113, E.A.,0799
AUTRY & BRALEY, ,0897
AVENT & CARNEY, ,0828
AVENT & SMITH, ,0830,1022
AVENT, B.W.,0817,0835,
Bettie B.,1022, Frank,0818,
1022, J.M.,0823,0829,0830,
James M.,1022, James,0836,
0838,1022, Mary W.,1022,
Mary,1022, Sarah W.,1022
AVERY, Alln.,0854
AYDELOTTE, ,0775
AYDLOTTE, Thos.,0775
AYERS, ,0775, James,0842
BACCHUS, William,0842
BACHMAN, Jane S.,1195,1196
BADGETT, ,0750

BAGLEY, Elisha,0887, Emily,
1221, Frank,0869, Henry,
0887, Joab,0887
BAILEY, ,0776, A.M.,0781,
Albert H.,0967, C.A.,0977,
Catherine,0917, Elizabeth,
1121, George,0879, Henry M.,
0967, J.G.,0770,0771,0772,
John H.,0967, Leonora,0967,
Louise A.,0967, P.C.,0782,
Patrick R.,0967, Robert A.,
0967, Robert R.,0967
BAILEY, S.H.,0803, W.A.,0781,
0782, W.H.,0782, William T.,
0967, Wm.T.,0967
BAIN, Ann L.,1015
BAIRD & MARTIN, ,1022
BAIRD, Abigal,0838, Anna Y.,
0963, Edwin H.,0754,
Edwin M.,0755, Edwin,0755,
Frank,0848, J.B.,0843,
J.L.,0764, James S.,1022,
1023, James W.,0922, John,
0756,0863, Josiah M.,1023,
Martha,1120, Prucilla J.,
0922, Samuel,0849, Sarah J.,
0922
BAIRD, Sarah,1023, Seldon,
0842, Thomas,0764, W.E.,
0772,0898, Wm.D.,0838,
Zebulon,0842, Zenas,0898
BAKER & MEYERS, ,0856
BAKER, ,0775, Eliza,0999,
Elizabeth N.,1100, Elizabeth,
1078, German(Rev),0853,
Hardy,0849, Hartwell G.,
1191, Humphrey,1192,
John E.,1078, Lee,1078,
Mary E.,1078, Mary,1078,
Narcissa J.,1191, R.H.,
1078, Rev.,0835,0839,
Sallie,1192, Samuel,0836
BAKER, Wade,1078, William D.,
1078
BALCH, Alfred,0760,0761,0764,
0766,0794,0795,0820,0849,
0870, Amos,0863,0865,0867,
0869, D.L.,0804
BALDRIDGE, Susan,1075
BALDWIN, ,0810, Mattie,1173,
S.P.,0836
BALEMAN, Isaac,0793
BALEY, Benjamin,0818
BALL, Jerry,0870, Margaret,
0929
BALLANFANT, John,0759
BALLARD, George,1090, Octavia,
1089, William,0869
BALLE, Elizabeth,0821
BALLOW, R.S.,0790
BALT, Fredrick,0867
BALTES, George,0827
BALTS, Rebecca,1163
BANDY, Capt.,0850, Corrie E.,
1079, Edward F.,1079,
Epperson,1079, Harriet,
1079, Henry J.,1079,
Jonathan,1079, Lucinda,
1079, Maxie R.,1079,
Mildred C.,1079, Pierce J.,
1079, S.M.,1079, Sallie L.,
1079, Sudie S.,1079,
Virginia,1079, William P.,
1079
BANDY, William P.,1079, Wm.P.,
0852
BANGUSS, R.J.,0772
BANKS, Mary M.,0968, Mary,
0835, Nancy,0835, Thomas,
0800
BANTON, G.W.,0821,0837
BARBEE, Joseph,0843, W.J.,
0809
BARBER, J.L.,0819, John,0829,
Laura P.,1037
BARBOUR, P.P.,0757
BARBY, Brittain,0856, Ethelrid,
1103, Nancy,1103, Susanna,
1103
BARFIELD, Fred,0815,0820,0821,
Frederick,0814, Stephen,
0801, Tabitha H.,0996,
William,0830, Wm.,0826
BARHAM, Mary,0976

BARING, Amos,1023, Elizabeth,
1023, Ella,1023, Ethel,1023,
Josie J.,1023, Julia P.,
1023, Lizzie C.,1023, Lydia,
1023, Mammie L.,1023,
Mary E.,1023, Nancy,1023,
Sterling B.,1023, Tennie V.,
1023
BARKER, A.A.,0906, Alexander,
0906, Alfred H.,0907,
Alice B.,0906, Carrie H.,
0906, Emma,1147, Florence,
0907, George D.,0906,
George,0906, Hugh B.,0906,
Hugh,0906, John,0820, Kate,
0906, Margaret,0906,
Maria L.,0906, Myrtle J.,
0906, Nancy,0906
BARKER, Sarah E.,0934,
William A.,0906, Willie T.,
0907, Willis,0827
BARKESDAL, (Dr.),1142
BARKLEY, Alexander,0841
BARKSDALE, ,0838, James (Dr.),
0876, Jesse,0869, Wm.,0870
BARLAND, John,0919
BARLEY, S.H.,0798
BARLOW, ,0813
BARNARD, Alla D.,1135,
Elizabeth,1159
BARNES, Adaline,1018, Capt.,
0850, George,1018, Henry,
0841, J.M.,0901, Martha E.,
1165, Nancy,1018, Peter,
0881,1018, Pollie,1018,
Tabitha,1018
BARNETT, ,0813, Joseph,0808
BARNHILL, Maria,1188
BARNS, Mourning,1012, Tennie E.J.,
1012, Thomas,1012
BARR, Green,0842, Hugh,0779
BARRETT, (Rev.),0900, ,0863,
Amelia,0938, Callie,0938,
Capt.,0871, Charlie,1127,
Eugene A.,1127, James L.,
1127, Jane B.,1127, John A.,
1127, Leroy W.,1127,
Lucy B.,1127, Mary J.,0938,
Mary,1127, Sylvia,1069,
Wade,0938
BARRICK, J.R.,0967, Lou M.,
0967, Mattie A.,0967,
Thomas R.,0967
BARRON, Catharine,1195, James,
0841
BARROW, William,0843
BARRY, Redmond T.,0841
BARTER, John,0821
BARTLETT, Alma,1191, Andrew J.,
1191, Elizabeth,1191, John,
0874, Martha E.,1191,
William,0841
BARTON, D.J.,0848, Daniel J.,
1079, Eudora,1079, Gabriel,
1079, Jane,1079, Jerusha,
1189, Joseph,0820, Samuel,
0841,0843,1079, W.,0831,
William,1189
BARTOW, Col.,0999
BASHAW, Charlotte,1079,
Eulixis,1080, J.P.,1079,
1086, J.W.,1079, James B.,
1080, Kate E.,1080, Pierce,
1080, Salura,1080, Seluria,
1086
BASKETT, G.H.,0833
BASKETTE & STAMPS, ,0874
BASKETTE, J.H.,0877, W.T.,
0817
BASKETTE-JETT & CO., ,0874
BASS, Bettie,1112, Capt.,0850,
David,0849, Ezekiel,0847,
John,1112, Jordan,0843,
Malinda,1112, Nancy,1107,
Peter,0766, Sarah,0973,
Scott,0849, Solomon,0843,
Theophilus,0842
BASSHAM, W.T.,0782
BATE, (Col.),1062,1149, Capt.,
0792, Gov.,0962, W.B.,0785,
0796,0871, William B.,0824
BATEMAN, Dr.,0775, Harriet,
0970

BATEY, Benjamin,1023, Frances M.,
  1026, G.C.,1039, Martha,
  1046, Mary H.(Mrs.),1060,
  Tabitha,1023
BATTIN, M.,0821
BATTLE, Adaline,1023, Addie M.,
  1023, Alfred B.,1023,
  Bettie,1023, Frank P.,1023,
  Frank,1023, George S.,1023,
  James M.,1023, Joel A.,
  0797,0799,0825,1023, Joel,
  1023, Julia H.,1023, Paul,
  1023, W.S.,0799
BATY, America,1024, Fannie B.,
  1024, Granville C.,1024,
  Hal C.,1024, Lizzie G.,
  1024, Lucy L.,1024, Martha J.,
  1024, Rufus H.,1024,
  William G.W.,1024
BAUGHN, Daniel,0792, J.W.,
  0803, Jos.W.,0802
BAUGUSS, John T.,0906, John,
  0906, Louisa,0906, Robert J.,
  0906
BAUM, Moses,0822, Thomas,0822
BAVIREY, Capt.,0751
BAXTER(Black), James,0849
BAXTER, A.P.,1127, Capt.,0752,
  Dock,1127, E.,0796, Effie,
  1128, Eliza,0952, James M.,
  1128, James S.,0824,
  Joseph C.,1128, Judge,0796,
  Lucinda C.,1128, Mollie,
  1128, Nathaniel,0764,0892,
  Nathnl.,0796, Sarah R.,
  1128, William G.,1128
BAYLES, Charles,0805
BAYNE & SIMMONS, ,0898
BAYNE, Julia A.,0978
BEACHBOARD, Z.T.,0879
BEAGLE, William,0842
BEAL, Anna,0923
BEALE, ,0803, C.W.,0791
BEARD, ,0829,0861, A.E.,0857,
  Alexander,0843, Andrew,
  0851, Cynthia E.,1080,
  Cynthia,1024, Dr.,0858,
  0859, E.E.,0850,0855,0858,
  1080,1086, Hannah G.,1197,
  J.,0900, J.L.,0781,
  Margaret,1027, Marie L.,
  1024, R.,0829,0830, R.E.,
  0826, Richard,0832
BEARD, Richard,1024,1027,1080,
  Roena A.,1015, Sallie,1024,
  Sarah,1080, T.C.,0897,
  William E.,1024
BEARDEN, B.F.,1128, Isaac,
  0893, Maggie C.,1128,
  Susan M.,1128, Walter S.,
  1128,1229, Walter,0871
BEARS, S.H.,0829
BEASLEY, ,0838,0899, Archer,
  0899, Ephraim,0842, George,
  0830, Sol,0815
BEATIE, Susan J.,1095
BEAVERT, John,0797
BECK, ,0886, W.B.(Rev.),0783
BECKET, Geo.(Rev.),0783
BECKETT, Ann E.,0907, Geo.(Rev.),
  0780,0907, James,0898,
  Jane W.,0907, John Temple,
  0907, John W.,0907, Mary,
  0907, Rebecca,0907, Samuel,
  0907, Wm.P.,0907
BECKTON, Fannie,1063
BECKWITH, Alexr.W.,0907,
  Dolly C.,0907, Jonathan,
  0907, Mary,0907
BEDEL, Malissa,1103
BEDFORD, A.F.,0784, Elizabeth,
  1191, Henry,0822, J.B.,0797,
  Robert,0811,0821,0833,
  Sarah,1106, Thomas,0864
BEECH, (Farm),0893, ,0803,
  C.B.,0803, David,0969,
  Eugene L.,0967, Jane,1016,
  John J.,0967, John,0967,
  L.F.,0803, Martha C.,0967,
  Mary C.,0969, Robert A.,
  0967, Sallie,0983,0998,
  Sarah J.,0967, Sarah,0999,
  Sulula A.,1016, William,

1016
BEECHER, J.S.,0750, John S.,
  0780
BEEDY, Henry,0870
BEESLEY, Adelaide,1025,
  Alice G.,1025, Bettie O.,
  1025, Carrie E.,1025,
  Christopher E.,1025,
  Christopher,1024,1025,
  Emily M.,1021, Ethel L.,
  1025, Huston D.,1025, J.T.,
  1043, John R.,1025, John,
  1025, Martha A.,1025,1043,
  Mary O.,1025
BEESLEY, Mary S.,1025,
  Mattie T.,1025, Minnie P.,
  1025, Sarah G.,1025,
  Solomon,0821, Susan J.,
  1025, Susan W.,1025, Susan,
  1024, William A.,1025,
  William,1024,1025
BEGGER, John,0894
BEGLEY & SON, F.Y.,0856
BELCHER, Jerry,0849, John S.,
  0844, Sarah F.,1105
BELL & HUGGINS, ,0829
BELL & PHILLIP, ,0857
BELL, ,0776,0798, Byron,1081,
  C.H.,0859, E.,1147,
  Elizabeth J.,1192, Elizabeth,
  1192, Erastus P.,1080,
  Fielding,0867,1192, G.W.,
  1147, Geo.W.,0867, George F.,
  1081, James,1080, Jane E.,
  1190, Jane M.,1081, Jane,
  1073, John Jr.,0832, John,
  0766
BELL, John,0791,0795,0796,
  0802,0805,0814,0827,1058,
  1073,1104, Lizzie M.,1025,
  Lyda,1025, Martha A.,1192,
  Mary L.,0838, Mary,1080,
  Mattie,1147, Mollie E.,
  1031, Nellie,1025, Polly,
  1080, Robert F.,1025,
  Robert,1031,1080, Samuel S.,
  1081
BELL, Samuel,0814,0874,
  Sarah A.,1080, Thomas H.,
  1192, W.R.,0829, William R.,
  1025, Willie S.,1081
BELLAH, Moses,0821
BELMONT MILL CO., ,0830
BENGE, O.M.,0813
BENNET, T.J.,0818
BENNETT, ,0809, Drury,0834,
  H.S.,0990, Ida,1007, J.D.,
  1017, J.R.,0762, J.W.,0803,
  Jacob,0842, Jane W.,0990,
  Jas.R.,0763, John W.,0844,
  Joseph,0814, Lou M.,0990,
  Martha M.,0990, Mary A.,
  1157, Mary,1017, O.H.P.,
  0779, Rosanna,1029, Sallie A.,
  1063
BENNETT, W.H.,0855, William,
  1157
BENSHY, Elizabeth,1078
BENSON, Gabriel,0766, Mary,
  0973
BENTON, Mollie E.,0952,
  Thos.H.,0759,0761,0791,
  0794,0796,0797,0814,0820
BENZE, O.H.,0818
BERRY, C.R.,0890, E.E.,1122,
  James M.,1122, John M.,
  1103, John,1017, Mandy,1103,
  Mary,0956,0984, Penelope,
  0956, Sarah M.,1017, Thomas,
  0821,0984, Tom,0795,
  William,0766
BERRYHILL, Wm.,0768,0769,0778,
  Wm.M.,0760, Wm.W.,0767
BESTICK, R.W.H.,0791
BETHELL, P.C.,0770, W.D.,0770
BETTS & CO., T.O.,0968
BETTS, Clarissa,0967, Henry,
  0844, Margaret M.,0967,
  Thomas C.,0967, Thomas,0967
BEUMAN, James,0838
BICKETT, Samuel,0891
BICTON, F.E.,0837
BIDDINGTON, J.,0901

BIDDLE, Daniel M.,0907, Dr.,
  0908, Julia,0908, Mary,0907,
  William M.,0907
BIFFEL, Jacob(Col.),0937
BIFFLE, (Col.),0960, ,0776,
  A.B.,0787
BIGGER, Letitia,1228, Margaret A.,
  1228
BIGHAM, Elihu H.,1128,
  Granville H.,1128, J.J.,
  0968, James J.,0968,
  Mary J.,1128, Mary,1128,
  Robert B.,1128, Robert L.,
  1128, Roy B.,1128, Sallie A.,
  1128, Samuel B.,1128,
  Sue F.,1128, Susan,0968,
  William L.,1128
BILBRO, B.H.,0817
BILLINGS & RAGLAND, ,0855
BILLINGS, David,0842
BILLINGSLEY, John,0842
BILLINGTON, 0777,0886,
  Amanda F.,1192, James,1192,
  1193, Malissa,1192, Martha,
  1137, Matilda,1192, Reuben,
  1192, Sarah,1192, Thomas J.,
  1192, Wm.K.,1192
BILLS, (Dr.),0757, A.E.A.,
  1192, C.T.,1192, D.B.,0901,
  Daniel W.,1192, Elizabeth,
  1192, Elizaeth,1224, G.W.,
  1192, Isaac,0751,0760,0766,
  J.,0901, J.N.,0779,
  John A.,0890, John H.,0886,
  Jonathan,0890, Josie,1192,
  Julia A.,1209, Mahala,1227
BILLS, Mollie G.,1192, Rachel,
  1192, Rebecca C.,1192
BINFORD & WADE, ,1066
BINFORD, ,0897
BINGHAM, ,0775,0807, Alex,
  0893, Amelia,0968, Eliza,
  1001, J.J.,0764, James J.,
  0968, Jennie D.,0968,
  Laura Lee,0968, Luversa E.,
  0968, Sallie M.,0968,
  Thomas R.,0968, William F.,
  0968
BINKLEY, Margaret,1163
BIRD, ,0813
BIRMINGHAM, Jas.,0760
BISHOP, Capt.,0850, Henry,
  0891,0902, John,0822
BITTMANN, Katherine,1069
BIVENS, B.R.,0819, Josephine,
  1065, S.A.,0832
BIVINS, Elizabeth E.,1199
BIZZELL, Sarah,0906
BLACK, (Livery Stable),0767,
  Bessie,1036, Capt.,0752,
  Catharine W.,1025,1193,
  Claiborn W.,0892, Esq.,
  0774, Franke E.,1033, G.B.,
  0902, Gideon B.,0890,0892,
  Hilda,1095, James,0774,
  Josiah B.,0892, L.W.,0770,
  Mr.,0792, Samuel P.,0830
BLACK, Samuel P.,1025,1026,
  1033, Stokely,1095, T.C.,
  0817,0897,0902, Thomas C.,
  1025,1193
BLACKBORN, Anna R.,1061,
  Raven C.,1061
BLACKBURN, Elizabeth,1129,
  Gideon,0775,0782,0805,0807,
  J.N.,0807, John,0803,1129,
  Lucy J.,1129, Lucy,1129,
  Martha,1129, Mary M.,1129,
  Penelope J.,1211, Robert,
  1129, William,1128
BLACKINGTON, Mr.& Mrs.,0835
BLACKMAN, A.,0822, A.W.,0818,
  Ada L.,0908, Albert,0908,
  Ann,0908, Anna,0908,
  Bennett,0908, Charlie,0908,
  Edwin,0908, Eliza W.,0908,
  Gen.,0834, H.,0792,
  Henrietta,0999, John,0801,
  Louisa,0908, Mary,0908,
  R.C.,0830, Rufus K.,0908,
  Willie,0908
BLACKWELL, B.G.,0899, Catharine P.,
  1198, Charley D.,1129,

Delilia,1129, Elizabeth,
1192, J.D.,1162, James,1129,
John A.,1129, John N.,1129,
John,0862,0887,0901, Jos.,
0755, Josiah,0887, Louisa,
1213, Lucinda,1226, Martha,
1129, Mary A.,0975
BLACKWELL, Mary E.,1162, R.B.,
0871,0872, Robt.B.,0873,
S.B.,0864, Samantha A.,
1129, Samuel J.,1129,
Thomas J.,1129, William N.,
1129
BLAINE, Mr.,0865
BLAIR, ,0774,0813, A.P.(Mrs.),
1215, Ada V.,0908, Catherine C.,
0908, Ella,0908, G.H.,0779,
Geo.H.,0902, George D.,
0908, George H.,0901,
George,0775, Hazen,0862,
J.H.,0779, John H.,0908,
Julia H.,0908, Leonidas O.,
0908, McClary,0779
BLAIR, R.D.,0879, Sue Ella,
0908, Thomas W.,0908, Wm.,
0821
BLAKE, Elizabeth,0964, Ella,
1031, John M.,1193, John T.,
1193, John W.,1193, Joseph,
1031, Martha,1193, Mary A.,
1193, Prof.,0881,0882,
Susan M.,1128
BLAKELEY, James,0749
BLAKELY, James,0777, M.A.E.,
0920,0921
BLAKEMORE & CO., ,0864
BLAKEMORE, Cassie E.,1129,
Edward,0876, Eugene W.,
1130, Eugene,0863,1129,
Frank N.,1130, Frank,0876,
George F.,1129, J.(Dr.),
0880, John,0876, Ludie P.,
1130
BLALOCK, Capt.,0850
BLANKENSHIP, Benj.,0826,0839
BLANTON & BLANTON, ,0881
BLANTON & CO., ,0880
BLANTON & KELLER, ,0881
BLANTON, ,0813,0863, Annie,
1129, B.W.,0878, Benjamin W.,
1129, Benjamin,1129, Ella,
0908, F.E.(Mrs.),1129,
Family,0880, Lula,1129, M.,
0881, Martha,1129, Meredith,
0867,0880, N.C.,0829, Rob,
0829, Robert Lee,1129, W.C.,
0872, William,0827
BLAYLOCK, Charles,0841
BLCHEAIRS, N.,0758
BLECKER, Richard,0764
BLEDSOE, Arthur,0766
BLISS, J.G.,0803
BLOCKER, Elijah,0913, Martha,
0913
BLOODWORTH, Hardy,0891, Wm.,
0853
BLOUNT, Willie,0820
BLUM, R.D.,1230
BLYTHE, Andrew T.,0975,
Bettie J.,0975, Mary R.,
BOBO, ,0863, Casander,1146,
Elisha,0868,1146, Leslie,
0864, Lucy,1146
BOCK & WALTER, ,0829
BOCK, Adam,0829,0832,1026,
Estelle,1026, George I.,
1026, John A.,1026, John,
1026, Margaret J.,1026,
Margaretta,1026, Virginia C.,
1026
BOEHMS, J.H.,0829, W.G.D.,
0803
BOGLE, Robert,0891
BOLLES, Reuben,0827
BOLTON, Cordelia M.,0908,
Hattie J.,0908, Ida S.,
0908, John G.(Rev.),0908,
Pattie R.,0908, Samuel I.,
0908, Theresa,0909, Wm.T.,
0909
BOMAR, ,0863, Catharine,1163
BOMER, John,0869
BOND, ,0774,0775, Alice,1016,

Annie M.,0968, Benjamin F.,
0968, Bethenia D.,0968,
Bethenia,0968, Burke,0800,
0804, Charles A.,0968,
Elisha,0842, Eliza M.,0961,
Elizabeth,0968, Florence L.,
0968, George,0774, Henry M.,
0968, J.H.,0792, James D.,
0968
BOND, John D.,0968, John,0849,
0977, Laura E.,0968, Lett,
0838, Lizzie,1008, Lucy,
0968, Margaret,0968, Maria,
1011, Martha,0910, Mary L.,
0977, Mary M.,0968, Morris L.,
0968, Nancy D.,0968, Nancy,
0968, Nannie D.,0968, Page,
1016, Robert W.,0968
BOND, Sidney S.,0968, Susan V.,
0977, Thomas H.,0968, W.W.,
0807, William J.,0968,
William,0794,0968, Wm.M.,
0968
BONDWARD, Edward,0844,0846
BONE, Abner,0842, J.,0827,
Thomas,0842
BONNER, M.H.,0818
BOOKER, ,0751, Alice,1026,
George,0819, P.R.,0779,
Peter R.,0751,0754,0756,
0759,0760,0772,0794,
Ruth A.,0919, Stephen,0803
BOON, A.S.,0872
BOONE, Daniel,1051,1174,
Rhoda,1174, Sallie,1174,
William,1174
BORDERS, Susan H.,0951
BOREAN & BROS., ,0899
BOREN, J.W.,0899
BORING, Nancy,1076
BORUM, Rev.,0860
BOSKETT, (Dr.),0953
BOSS, Harriet,1079, James,
1079
BOSTANE, Andrew,0841
BOSTIC, Capt.,0851, Elizabeth,
1175
BOSTICH, John,0793
BOSTICK & ABSTON, ,0968
BOSTICK, ,0803, Bettie,1059,
Bithunia,1001, C.S.,0797,
Fannie L.,0969, Fannie M.,
0969, H.P.,0793,0802,
James A.,0968,0969,
James C.,0968, John C.,
0800, John,0794,0805,0851,
0968, Manoah H.,0968,
Martha E.,0968, Mary A.,
0969, Mary G.,0968
BOSTICK, Mary J.,0968,
Merry C.,0969, Nancy,0968,
R.W.H.,0796, Sallie P.,
0969, Sarah P.,0968,
Thomas H.,0851, Thomas K.,
0968, William,0968
BOSTWICK, E.R.,0893
BOSWORTH, Mary H.,1136
BOUNDS, Ann,1130, Bettie,1130,
1158, Fannie,1130, George W.,
1130, James C.,1130, John,
1130, June,1130, Mary A.,
1130
BOURKE, John,0870
BOWDEN, James M.,0902
BOWEN, ,0820, A.,0781,
John H.,0819,0820, R.M.,
0875, William,0815,0820
BOWERS & BROS., J.F.,0847
BOWERS, B.B.,0895, Rebecca,
0983, S.B.,0833, W.S.,0893
BOWLIN, Smith,0879,0880,1140
BOWLING, Albert M.,1130,
Edna Frank,1130, Elizabeth,
1130, F.M.,1130, Joseph,
1130, Mary Myrtle,1130,
Susan E.,1130
BOWLWARE, Judith,1146
BOWMAN, Dan,0821, Daniel,0820,
Dunklin C.,0969, Elizabeth M.,
0969, Elizabeth,1059,
George B.,0969, Inez B.,
0969, James G.,0969, James,
0812, Jennie B.,0969,

Joseph H.,0969, Maggie B.,
0969, Thomas B.,0969,
William H.,0969, William,
0969
BOXLEY, Harrison,0969, Hattie,
0969, James,0969, Mary,0969,
Nancy,0969, Philip,0969
BOYD, ,0777,0886, A.J.,0779,
A.T.,0759,0791, Aaron,0888,
Andrew T.,0909, B.F.,0896,
Capt.,0792, Elizabeth,0909,
J.B.,0752, J.G.,0799,
James,0801,0909, John Jr.,
0841, John,0841, Joseph B.,
1193, Mattie S.,1193,
Nannie,0945, Robert,0836
BOYD, Susan W.,1193, Thomas A.,
1193, V.C.(Corad),1092,
W.E.,0799, Wilmoth,1003
BOYER, ,0751, Joseph,0819
BOYLE, E.E.(Mrs.),1122
BOYLES, Charles,0794
BRACKEN, (Dr.),0757
BRADDOCK, Richard,0842
BRADEN, Alexander,0841, Belle,
1093, D.W.,1093, Isabella,
1115
BRADFORD, Benj.,0871, Benjamin,
0865, Edward,0820, Narciora,
1053, Narcissa,1043,
Theo.F.,0876
BRADLEY(Colored), Hugh,0849
BRADLEY, Anne E.,1018, E.,
0810, Eliza,1151, Elizabeth T.,
1005, Ella,1005, Gen.,0798,
John,0842,0843, Judith,
1108, Mr.,1050, R.H.,1018,
Robt.H.,0790, S.S.,0805,
Susan,0912, Thomas,0848
BRADLY, Thomas,0847
BRADSHAW, Amzi,0779,0902,
Elizabeth,0924,0942, Hugh,
0752, Wm.,0754,0758,0769,
0771,0778
BRADY, W.,0827, William,0828,
0831
BRAGG, (Gen.),0976, ,0787,
Capt.,1055, Gen.,0825,0834,
0873,1040
BRAHAN, John,0863
BRALEY, G.R.,0897, J.A.,0897,
J.D.,0902, W.A.,0897
BRALY, Mary E.,1213
BRAMBLET, L.M.,0822
BRAMBLETT, Ada B.,1131,
Elizabeth F.,1131, George D.,
1131, Idella,1131, James M.,
1131, Jennie,1131, John A.,
1131, John,1131, L.C.,1131,
Lunsford M.,0892, Mary J.,
1131, Newton A.,1131,
Walter T.,1131, William E.,
1131
BRAMBLITT, Lunsford M.,0892
BRAME, W.B.,0874
BRAMES, ,0863
BRAMLET, James,0795
BRAMLETT, Judge,0764, L.M.,
0761,0763,0819, Lunsford M.,
0850
BRANCH, Capt.,0850, Frances T.,
0909, James,0909, John T.,
0909, Joseph H.,0909,
Laura S.,0909, Malissa,
1103, Martha E.,0909,
Martha,0909, Mary S.,0909,
Nancy A.,0909, Nancy,1124,
Robert,0843, Ruth A.,0909,
Sarah E.,0909, William,0909
BRANCH, Willie T.,0909, Wm.M.,
0909
BRANDON, ,0897, Charles,0772,
Elizabeth M.,1205, George,
0820,0834, James,0863
BRANSON, William,0898
BRANTLEY, E.T.,0902
BRANTLY, Charlotte,1093
BRASHEAR, ,0812
BRASHEARS, Jesse,0874
BRASSFIELD, I.C.,0876
BRATTON, John,0848
BRAY, F.E.(Miss),1129
BRAYFORD, Ben,0874

BRAZEE, ,0876
BREATHITT, E.,0802, J.S.,0792
BRECKENRIDGE, George,0760
BRECKINRIDGE, (Gen.),0894,
  Gen.,0825
BRENNON & DEAN, ,0880
BRENNON, T.P.,0881
BRENT, Amanda,1109, Joe,1109,
  Solomon,0789, Sue,1109
BRENTS & MURRAY, ,0897
BRENTS, A.C.,0897, Angeline,
  1194, J.C.C.,0897, James,
  1194, John,1194, S.D.,0897,
  T.E.,1194, T.W.,0897,1196,
  Thomas Sr.,1194, Thomas W.,
  1194
BRETT, Alexander,1114,
  Bartholomew,0842, Hardy,
  1088, Jeffella,1114
BREVARD, Thomas,0858
BREWER, Elizabeth A.,1083,
  George,0841, James,0869,
  M.,1083, S.,1083, Thedford,
  0841
BREWINGTON, James,0857
BREWSTER, ,0774, Lyman D.,
  0776
BRIANTE, Nancy,0932
BRIDENTHALL, David,0836
BRIDGES, (Prof.),0900,
  Britton,0766, J.N.,0818,
  W.A.,0902
BRIEN, James M.,0849, James W.,
  0871, M.M.,0797
BRIGGS, Anna,0986, Dorithy M.,
  0986, I.W.,0792, Isaac W.,
  0986
BRIGHT, J.M.,0979, James,0863,
  John,0863, Martha R.,0979
BRINE, J.S.,0764, Judge,0765
BRITTAIN & ESCUE, ,0874
BRITTAIN & NEAL, ,0854
BRITTAIN, Amelia L.,1204,
  Columbus T.,1026, Frances M.,
  1026, Frankie D.,1026, J.F.,
  0890, James,0874, John W.,
  1026, John,1026, Joseph,
  0886, L.,1026, Margaret M.,
  1026, Martha M.,1026, Mary,
  1204
BRITTON, Abraham,0847, J.W.,
  1117, James H.,0850
BROADAWAY, Sallie,1204
BROADWAY, Lemuel,0867
BROCK & CODY, ,0803
BROCKAWAY, A.W.,0875
BROHAM, ,0803
BROOKER, Peter,0820
BROOKES, ,0775
BROOKS, ,0838, Alexr.N.B.,
  0969
BROOKS, Ann E.,1170, C.N.,
  0837, Capt.,0792, Christopher B.,
  0969, Christopher,0969,
  Eliza L.,0969, Emily T.,
  0994, Jas.W.,0779, John B.,
  0909, John(Rev.),0883,
  Kate B.,0969, Lizzie,0981,
  Martha A.,0969, Martha J.,
  0969, Martha,0969, Mary E.,
  0919
BROOKS, Mary E.,0969, Mary F.,
  0969, Mary,0909, Micajah,
  0761, Nancy,0994, Nannie B.,
  0994, Susan,0969, T.F.,0895,
  Thomas F.,0889, Thomas,
  0994, William W.,0969,
  William,0909,0969
BROTHERS, L.,1026
BROUGHTON, Mary,1030
BROWN & CO., John F.,0874
BROWN & DEASON, ,0881
BROWN & LITTLETON, ,0803
BROWN, (Gen.),1063, (Gov.),
  1023, ,0774,0801,0813,0853,
  A.F.,0753, A.H.(Dr.),0928,
  A.H.,0784,0963, A.S.,0878,
  1132, A.T.,0770, Aaron V.,
  0762, Abbie P.,1132, Ada,
  1026, Alexander,0869,
  Aley K.,1132, Alice E.,
  1132, Alice,1026, Allen,0764
BROWN, Annie L.,1131, Annie,
  1081, Armenia E.,1046,
  B.A.(Miss),0997, Benjamin,
  0967, C.,0773, Campbell,
  0770,0775,0781,0782,0785,
  0799, Candis,1081, Capt.,
  0752,0872, Catharine,1013,
  Cauras,1081, Charles E.,
  0963, Charlie B.,1081,
  Coleman,1013
BROWN, Comer N.,1132, Cora E.,
  1132, D.L.,0855, Daisy,1081,
  Daniel,0761,0774, David,
  0880, Dixon Lee,1081, Dr.,
  0758, Duncan(Rev.),0910,
  Duncan,0775,0776,0779,0782,
  Elizabeth,0909,0910,0963,
  1194, Enoch,1013, Ephraim,
  0791,0793,0801, Evaline,1026
BROWN, Fannie (Mrs.),0900,
  Fannie,1013,1081, Frank W.,
  1081, G.A.,1132, Gabe,0754,
  Garland,0848, H.A.,0782,
  H.H.,0783,0809, H.T.,0969,
  Harriet,1145, Harrison,
  0870, Hartwell H.,0783,
  Henry,0867,0870,1132,
  Horace,1026, Hugh,0775,0779
BROWN, Hugh,0910, Irene,1026,
  Isaac C.,0827, Isaac,1081,
  J.B.,1132, J.C.(Col.),0911,
  J.H.,0764, J.J.,1132, J.M.,
  0897,0902, J.N.,0750, J.R.,
  1131, J.T.,0819,0874,
  James B.,1132, James P.,
  1131, James W.,0910,1026,
  James,0752,0796,0875
BROWN, James,0887,0890,0891,
  Jane G.,1131, Jenette M.,
  0910, Jennie E.,0969,
  Jeremiah,0846, Jerre,0843,
  Jethro,0766, Jim,0758, Joe,
  0766,0778, John A.,0867,
  John C.,0785,0918,1003,
  1212, John S.,0910, John(Maj.),
  0783, John,0751,0754,0756
BROWN, John,0772,0779,0841,
  0843,0844,0869, Jordan H.,
  1081, Jos.(Col.),0784, Jos.,
  0752, Joseph E.,1131,
  Joseph,0759,0760,0761,0766,
  0769,0771,0778, Judge,0796,
  Kate,1131, L.S.,1132,
  Lillie,0910, Lucinda C.,
  1131, Lucy F.,1132, Lucy,
  1081
BROWN, Lula S.,1132, Lulecta,
  1081, Margaret S.,0969,
  Martha L.,1148, Mary A.(Mrs.),
  1131, Mary C.(Mrs.),0969,
  Mary F.,1013, Mary,0870,
  1026,1081,1082, Mattie A.,
  0967, Mattie L.,1036,
  Maud M.,1132, Mildred A.,
  0963,0964, Mr.,1013,
  Nancy J.,1131
BROWN, Nancy,0997, Nannie E.,
  1013, Nina,1026, Nora,0910,
  Paul M.,1131, R.C.,0768,
  R.S.,0819,0834, Rachel A.,
  1081, Rev.,0860, Robert S.,
  1026, Robert Saml.,1081,
  Robert,1026, S.L.,1132,
  Sallie,1161, Sally,1081,
  Samuel,1081, Sarah K.,1132
BROWN, Solomon,0909,1026,
  Sterling,0791,0839, Susan,
  1013, Susannah,1013, T.B.,
  1081, T.L.B.,0824, Thomas D.,
  1131, Thomas E.,1026,
  Thomas,0757,0779,0797,0969,
  0997, Virgia,0967, Virginia,
  1003,1013,1079, W.B.M.,0868,
  W.H.,0847,0854,0855
BROWN, W.H.,0963,1081,1102,
  W.Hugh,0910, W.L.,0762,
  William C.,1131, William,
  1131, Willie E.,0910, Wm.,
  0754, Wm.F.,0756, Wm.R.,
  0909, Wm.V.,0796
BROWNLOW, W.J.,0800,0895,
  Wm.Jr.,0894
BRUCE & MORGAN, ,0847
BRUCE, Elizabeth J.,1192,
James,0766, John,0827
BRUFF, James,0794
BRUTTON, Lucy,1107
BRYAN, Algernon,1082, Alice,
  1082, E.S.,1082, Elizabeth C.,
  1082, Ervin,1082, Hugh B.,
  1082, J.,0830, J.W.,1081,
  Margaret C.,1082, Mary,
  1082, Richard,0844,1082,
  Samuel H.,1082, Sarah A.,
  1082, Tennessee,1082,
  Thomas M.,1082, Unity,1082
BRYAN, Zula,1082
BRYANT & CO., W.M.,0875
BRYANT, Ada S.,1195, Alexander,
  1194, Andrew D.,0910,
  Andrew,0895, Arch S.,0907,
  Bessie M.,0911, Edward,
  0901,0911, Elizabeth,0911,
  1082, Emma J.,0911, Frank L.,
  0911, Hattie W.,0911,
  Ida R.,0910, Isaac H.,0910,
  J.L.,0893,0895, James H.,
  0911
BRYANT, James R.,0910, James,
  0851, Jane W.,0907, John A.,
  1194, John F.,0910,1194,
  John H.,1082, John R.,1195,
  John,0843,0880, Lizzie H.,
  0910, Maria,1194, Mary E.,
  1195, Mary,0910, Nancy,1157,
  Patrick H.,0910, Ralph G.,
  0907, Robertson,0764
BRYANT, Roland,0910, Sallie A.,
  0907, Sallie C.,1195,
  Sarah W.,0910, Sarah,1194,
  Sebastian C.,0907, Thomas H.,
  0910, Unity,1082, W.A.,0753,
  W.D.,0764, William T.,1195,
  William,0899,0910, Wm.T.,
  0910
BRYSON, Henry(Rev.),1140,
  Sarah,1140
BUCHANAN & WOODS, ,0874,1132
BUCHANAN, (Prof.),1095, A.H.,
  0757, Anna,0998, Beulah C.,
  0970, C.S.(Mrs.),1132,
  Capt.,0792, Claudius,0970,
  Dr.,0758, E.B.,0970,
  Elizabeth C.,0970, Esther,
  1140, George R.,0970,
  Gerald M.,0971, Hance H.,
  0970, Harriet,0970, Hattie,
  0970
BUCHANAN, Henry L.,0970,
  Henry S.,0970, J.K.,1115,
  James A.,0970, Jane T.,
  1037, Jimmie,0970, John A.,
  0969,0970, John B.,0970,
  0971, John M.,0970, John,
  0791,0970,0998,1037, Joseph,
  0970, Josephine E.,0971,
  Katherine L.,0970, Lillian M.,
  0971
BUCHANAN, M.Blanche,0971,
  Margaret,0970,1060, Martha,
  0970, Mary J.,0970, Mattie L.,
  0970, Mattie,0970, Moses R.,
  0970, Moses,0970, Nannie A.,
  0970, Nannie P.,0970,
  Nannie,0970, R.D.,0970,
  R.G.,0832, Robert S.,0970,
  Robert,0877, Sallie M.,0970
BUCHANAN, Samuel J.,0970,
  Sarah A.,0970, Sarah E.,
  1037, Sarah,0970,1037,1132,
  Scrap H.,0970, T.G.,1132,
  T.W.,1132, Tennessee L.,
  0970, Thomas W.,0874, Thos.,
  0805, Virginia L.,0970,
  W.C.,0897, William C.,0971,
  Willie E.,0970, Willie M.,
  0970
BUCKALOO, J.W.,0872
BUCKLEY, Thomas,0817
BUCKMAN, J.B.,0799
BUCKNER, ,0776, Alfred P.,
  0752, Mary,1092
BUDD, E.G.,0832
BUFORD, Capt.,0792, James,
  0789,0793, Mamie,0995,
  Priscilla,0923, S.,0801,
  Spencer,0793, Thomas S.,

BUGG, Albina G.,0964, Allen, 0807, Nancy,1006
BUIST, J.B.,0798
BULGETT, Thomas J.,0816
BULLARD, George H.,0854, Reuben,0847
BULLINGTON, G.(Miss),1152
BULLOCH, Ann L.,1015
BULLOCK, ,0777, Callie J., 1170, J.L.,0963, J.Lee,0759, J.R.,0764, J.S.,0764, John, 0777, Jonathan,0775, Lee, 1036, Lizzie T.,1231, Margaret J.,1214, T.Dick, 0804, W.P.,0890,0898
BUMPAS, Elizabeth,1032
BUMPASS, Capt.,0850, Wm.,0856
BUNCH, Isham,0774
BURCH, John,0849
BURDEN, Susan,0978
BURDETT & CO., ,0875
BURDETT, ,0862, Giles,0874, J.R.,0874
BURDETTE, Joel H.,0872
BURGESS & CO., ,0854
BURGESS & MATTLEY, ,0854
BURGESS, ,0834, Willis,0902
BURGH, Phillip,0808
BURGSDORF, L.,0829
BURK, G.W.,0817, John,0998, Lucy,0998, Margaret M., 0967, Mary,0961, Miles E., 0998, Sarah E.C.,0998
BURKE, Caldonia T.,1104, F.A., 0759, John,0816, Peggy,0998, Samuel,0998
BURKEEN, ,0875
BURKLEY, John,0795
BURKS, N.W.,0893, Sue F.,1128
BURNER, William,0805
BURNETT, Brooken,1006, Elizabeth,1173, Henrietta S., 1006, Henry,1016, Jane,1016, Joseph,0792, Margaret L., 1037, Sarah,1016
BURNEY, S.G.(Dr.),0859
BURNLEY, Sarah,0938
BURNS, (Dr.),0830, ,0767,0776, G.W.,0819, George,0849, Lucinda,0925
BURR, Aaron,0755, Mr.,1002, W.,0809
BURROUGHS, Sarah A.,1144
BURROW, Ann E.,1195, Banks, 0862, Callie,1153, Catharine, 1195, Freeman,0862, Harriet E., 1152, J.R.,1152, James,0871, John A.,1195, John,1195, Nannie,1195, Nimrod,0862, 0864, Philip,0862,0864,0871, Wilbourn,0862, Wm.,0862, 0871
BURRUS & WOODS, ,0830
BURRUS, F.R.,0829, Ophelia M., 1056, W.C.J.,0791
BURT, J.L.,0872, N.H.,0764, 0963, William,0819
BURTE, Laura,0957
BURTON, ,0823, E.F.,0826, Eliza,1030, Ervin,0830, F.N.W.,0832,0835, Hardy M., 1056, J.W.,0819,0829,1027, John W.,0826,1061, John, 0841,0871, Polly,1139
BURUS, Thomas,0803
BUSEY, J.,0857
BUSH, Fanny,1095, Theodica, 1110
BUSHROD, ,0895
BUSSY, Penelope,1160
BUTE, I.H.,0827, R.M.,0822
BUTLER & DRUMRIGHT, ,1027, 1031
BUTLER & DUMWRIGHT, ,0829
BUTLER, Fannie B.,1022, I.H., 1027, Isaac H.,1027, J.S., 0871, John A.,0824, John S., 1132,1133, Laura,1133, Mary A.,1133, Mary E.,1027, Mary,1133, Nancy E.,1132, Nancy J.,1133, Permelia, 1027, Rob,0827, Thomas G., 0824, Thomas O.,1027

BUTLER, Thos.,0755, W.R.,0819, 0831, William S.,1132, Wm.R.,0824
BUTNER, Buck,0880, John,0878
BUTT, Ada,0971, Arthur,0971, Clara,0971, Daniel,0799, Georgiana,0971, James,0971, Joanna,0971, Josiah,0971, Martha,0971, Mary,0971, Nathaniel,0971, Nettie, 0971, Olive,0971, Porterfield, 0971, Rebecca,0971, Theodore, 0971, Willie,0971
BUTTS, Elizabeth A.,1061
BYERS, ,0803, A.W.,0758, Anderson,0906, Kittie V.(Mrs.), 1038, M.A.,0851, Maria L., 0906, Sarah,0906, William, 0894, Wm.,0761
BYLES, Thomas,0843
BYNUM, Mary L.,1230, William, 0822
BYREN, Charles L.,0867
BYRES, Wm.,0807
BYRN, Annie,1108, Charley H., 1067, J.F.,0818, J.T.,0830, R.G.,1108, Sarah C.,1067, William B.,1067
BYRNE, Reason,0842
BYRUM, Elizabeth,0954
CABELL, Hugh,0827
CABLE, N.B.,0876, Philip,0868
CAFFE, Lety,0958
CAGE & CRUTCHER, ,0854
CAGE, Capt.,0850, John,0841
CAHAL, T.H.,0784, Terry H., 0764
CAHALL, Terry H.,0892
CAIN, G.J.,0831, George I., 0856
CALAHAN, J.W.,0890
CALDWELL & CO., T.M.,0874
CALDWELL, ,0862,0874,0877, Becky(Mrs.),1167, Cynthia, 0963, Dora M.,0911, Elizabeth, 0911, Ellen J.,0911, Emily O.,0911, Ernest,0871, Ernst,0877, J.C.,0874, John E.,0911, John S.,0911, Lennie M.,0963, Martha J., 1003, Mary E.,0911, Robert C., 0911
CALDWELL, Robina C.,0911, Sarah A.,0911,0958, Silas M.,0757, T.M.,0874, Thomas J.,0911, Thos.H., 0868,0871,0883, W.G.J.C., 0874, W.R.,0963, William H., 0911, Wm.A.,0763,0764
CALHOON & BROS, N.J.,0875
CALHOUN, Annie,1152, Corrie M., 1082, Elizabeth,1082,1152, Ewing G.,1082, John C., 1082, Lilla M.,1082, Mary, 1152, Mattie S.,1082, N.J., 1082, P.B.,1082, P.J.,1082, Samuel,0842, Thomas Wayne, 1082, Thomas,1082
CALLENDER, C.W.,0836
CALTON, Wm.,0890
CALVERT, Catharine,0950, Delia R.,0950, Joseph W., 0950, Saml J.,0779
CAMDEN, Susan W.,1193
CAMERON, Don,0804,0807, E., 0801, Ewen,0789,0801, W.D., 0772
CAMP, Sarah P.,1058, Sutherland M., 0793
CAMPBELL & HARMAN, ,0775
CAMPBELL, ,0778,0803,0809, 0863, A.J.,0786, Alexr., 0779,0809,0837,0850, Alfred, 1159, Andrew,0793,0804,0805, 0971,1008, Ann,0941, Arthur, 0868, Capt.,0751, David, 0765,0791,0796,0797,0892, Eliza E.,0904, Elvira,1027, G.W.,0796,0802, Geo.W.,0757
CAMPBELL, Geo.W.,0863, Gov., 0857, J.P.,0796,0837, J.S., 0779, James,0779,0971, Jane, 1149, Joe,0849, John A.,

1027, John,0759,0760,0761, 0971,0993, M.C.,0782, M.W., 0795, Margaret J.,0920, Margaret,0971, Nancy E., 1132, Nettie,1027, Patrick, 0797
CAMPBELL, Patrick,0971, Peter, 0827, Rebecca,0993, Robert, 0755,0774,0779, Robt.,0755, Robt.Jr.,0755, Sallie,1159, Sam,0821, Samuel,0819,1027, Sumpter,1027, Susan C., 1159, Victoria,1170, W.B., 0850,0893, W.C.,0781, William S.,0971, William, 0870
CAMPBELL, William,0971, Wm., 0801,0871, Wm.B.,0798
CAMPER, Ben,0849, Elizabeth, 1083, John,1083, Joseph, 1083, Mary J.,1083, S.E., 1083, Sallie,1083, Willie Lee, 1083
CANDLE, M.C.,0904
CANNADY, Elizabeth,1149
CANNON & SON, ,0830
CANNON, (Mill),0875, Alanson B., 1027, Alanson,1027, Annie W., 1027, Capt.,0792, Charles B., 1133, Charles L.,1133, Clement Sr.,1133, Clement, 0864,0865,0873,0874,0881, Cynthia G.,0972, E.C.,1048, 1058, Elizabeth E.,1027, Elizabeth,1027
CANNON, Franklin B.,1027, G., 1002, Gen.,0826, George M., 0916, Gov.,0784,1044, Henry, 0870,1133, J.C.,0829, J.L., 0823, JOhn,0874, James,0841, Jennie B.,0972, John B., 0972, John H.,1133, John T., 0871,1133,1164, Joseph L., 1027, Leah A.,0972
CANNON, Leah A.,1002, Letitia, 1163,1164, Lettie C.,1133, Lettie,1180, Lewis,0870, Lizzie H.,1133, Macon B., 1133, Margaret,1027, Maria L.,1133, Martha E., 0916, Martha M.,1179, Mary A.,1133, Mary R.,1133, Minnie,1027, Minos,1133, Nancy M.,0916
CANNON, Narcissa W.,1133, Narcissa,1133, Nellie L., 1027, Newton,0759,0779,0791, 0794,0803,0805,0971,0972, 1141,1164, Robert,0864,0869, 1133, Sallie C.M.,1133, Sally C.,1048, Sally C., 1122, Sally C.M.,1164, Samuel P.,0972, Sarah L., 1027
CANNON, Sarah,0869, Susan A., 0971,1141, Susan R.,1133, Susan,1133, T.A.,0821, Theophilus,0814, Thomas C., 1133, Thompson,0887, W.P., 1044, Walter S.,1133, William H.,1133, William P., 0971
CANTHERIN, ,0829
CANTHERON, James,0821
CANTRELL, (Judge),1115, Bailey,1083, Bettie,1083, Harriet P.,1083, Isaac, 1083, Kate,1083, Martha, 1083, Mary J.,1083, Mattie 1083, Minnie,1083, N.,0854, Nancy,1083, Robert,0849, 0850,0870,1083,1095,1137, William M.,1083
CAPERS, Bishop,1174
CAPERTON, ,0774
CAPLE, Branson,0896
CAPLINGER, Capt.,0850, John, 0843, Samuel,0843
CARD, Samuel,0862
CARDEN, A.G.,0824
CAREY, Letitia,1114
CARL, J.B.,0807, Jacob B., 0972, Jane B.,0972,1016,

Joseph,0972, Mary J.,0972,
Nannie Marion,1016
CARLIN, Joseph,0843
CARLISLE, William,0814
CARLTON, Blake,1028, Mary,
  1028, Thomas F.,1028
CARLYLE, Elizabeth,1176,
  James,1176, Virginia C.,
  1176
CARMACK, E.W.,0759,0770, S.W.,
  1036
CARMICHAEL, ,0826, A.,0805,
  0827, Alex,0815
CARNER, Nancy E.,1205
CARNEY & RANSOM, ,0829
CARNEY, E.W.,0874, L.H.,0826,
  0835,0839, Prof.,0835
CAROTHERS, James,1044, Jane,
  1044, Mary A.,1220, Robert,
  0805
CARPENTER, J.E.R.,0770,
  J.R.E.,0773, Samuel,1164
CARPENTER-MONTGOMERY, ,0898
CARR, Dabney,0854, Elizabeth,
  1082, Kate(Mrs.),1014
CARRIGAN, Jo.G.,0897
CARROL, Miss,0938
CARROLL, Deborah,0975, Prof.,
  0858
CARROTHERS, Sarah E.,1175
CARROUTH, James,0844, Walter,
  0841
CARSEY, Mary,1016, Thomas B.,
  1016, Thomas P.,1016
CARSON, ,0813, Alice,1083,
  Bell,1083, Capt.,0792,
  Cornelia,1083, Dora,1083,
  Farrer,0851, Ida,1083,
  J.W.,0793,0899, James W.,
  0793, James,0850,1083, Joe,
  0834, John D.,1083, Joseph,
  0842, Kit,1083, Laura,1083,
  Lucinda,1083, Nancy C.,1083
CARSON, Nancy,0965,0995,
  Walter,1083
CARTER & LESTER, ,1106
CARTER, (Capt.),1220, ,0801,
  A.C.C.,0802, Alma,0972,
  America,0972, Benj.,0779,
  Benjamin,0904, Callie,0972,
  Daniel F.,0774, Emma L.,
  0972, Estelle,1084, Fountain,
  0972, Frank F.,0972, H.H.T.,
  0819, Hugh,0972, Inez,1084,
  Isabella,1084, Jennie,1084
CARTER, John C.,0756, Lena,
  0972, Lucy,0972, M.B.,0799,
  0825,0893, Mary A.,0972,
  Mary E.,1196, Mattie A.,
  1062, Moscow B.,0972,
  Moscow,0802,0972, Moses B.,
  0799, Moses,0798, N.W.,0816,
  0896,1067, Pamelia,0972,
  Pollie H.,1157, S.A.,1105
CARTER, Sammie,1084, Samuel A.,
  1084, Susan H.,1212, Susan,
  1134, T.H.,0819, W.W.,0854,
  Walter,0972, William W.,
  1084, Willie W.,1084, Wm.,
  1105
CARTHEY, Lee,0894
CARTWELL, H.M.,0852, R.M.,
  0855
CARTWRIGHT, Dora,1122,
  Elizabeth,1122, Hezekiah,
  0815, John,0847, M.T.,0854,
  Mathew,0854, Nathan,0842,
  W.T.,0851,0854, Wilson T.,
  0857,1122
CARUTHERS, Abraham,0850,0858,
  James,0821, John,0766,
  Madison,0764, R.S.,0822,
  Robert L.,0858, Robert,
  0784,0789,0791,0794,
  Robt.L.,0849,0850, Sara H.,
  0945, Thos.,0799
CARVER, Elizabeth,1111, Isaac,
  1086, Jonas,1091, Martha,
  1091, Rachel A.,1086
CARWELL, Henry,0870
CASEY, J.L.,0805, J.M.,0803
CASKEY, Elmina,0996, Margaret M.,
  0935, Olivia C.,0941

CASON, (Chapel),0861
CASS, Lewis,1220
CASSITT, F.R.,0858
CASTEEL, John,0862,0871
CASTLEMAN, Artimenta,1084,
  Cynthia E.,1080, Cynthia,
  1024, Edward,1084, I.B.,
  0856, Jacob,1084, Jef L.,
  1084, John L.,1084, Joseph,
  0842, Lewis,0870, Robert,
  1084, Val,1084
CASTLEMEN, Boyd,0841
CATES, Caledonia C.,1134,
  Daniel E.,1134, Elizabeth,
  1134, Giles P.,1134,
  James P.,1134, Jestinie E.,
  1134, John R.,1134, John S.,
  1134, Joseph H.,1134,
  Levina,1134, Martha J.,
  1134, Mary A.,1134, Moses,
  0805, Phenettie F.,1134,
  Sadie R.,1134
CATES, William P.,1134
CATHEL, Capt.,0751
CATHEY, ,0776, Alexander,0761,
  Alexr.,0760, Capt.,0752,
  George,0863, Griffin,0759,
  Hugh,0901, John A.,0800,
  Mary M.,0994, Wm.,0754
CATHOM, James,0842
CATHRON, J.M.,0785
CATNER, Anna,1162, Hannah M.,
  1134, James,1134, John,1134,
  Lewis,1134, Margaret,1134,
  Martha,1134, Mary C.,1134,
  Peter,1134, Polly,1134,
  Sarah,1134, Susanna,1134,
  Thomas,1134, William,1134
CATOR, Moses,0807
CATTLES, America,0972
CAUGHRON, ,0775
CAUL, W.H.,0875
CAULESS, N.L.,0895
CAWTHON, Allie,1085, Emma Lee,
  1085, J.P.,1085, James Edw.,
  1085, Lunsford P.,1085,
  Mary A.,1085, Sue W.,1085,
  Susan,1085, Thomas F.,1085,
  Thomas P.,1085, William H.,
  1085
CAWTHORN, Alfred M.,1028,
  Anna M.,1028, James,1028,
  Mary A.,1028, Nancy,1028,
  Vienna,1028
CAYCE, ,0809, M.C.,0802,
  Sallie,0900, William,0802
CECIL, Anna M.,0954, James H.,
  0911, Julia,0911, Sarah,
  0934, W.J.,0764, Willie G.,
  0911
CHADWELL, Everett,0972,
  George,0972, James B.,0890,
  John,0972, Joseph T.,0972,
  Martha H.,0972, Mary,0972,
  Robert,0972, Sarah,0972,
  Thomas,0972
CHAFFIN & BROS., ,0768
CHAFFIN, Capt.,0752, E.H.,
  0768, Moses,0766, Nathan,
  0867
CHAMBERS, Bessie,1085, Bob,
  0870, Daisy,1085, Edna,1085,
  Eugene,1085, Evaline,1026,
  Fanny,1116, Gilbreth,1181,
  H.A.,1085, Henry,0854,
  Hortense,1085, J.D.,1085,
  J.S.,1111, John,1085,
  Lelia,1085, Lewis,0842,
  Louisa,1111, Marcia,1085,
  Margaret A.,1181
CHAMBERS, Martha A.,1006,
  Mattie,1176, Nancy,1006,
  Nellie,1101, Pauline,1085,
  Pearl,1085, Robert,0868,
  Sophia,1085, Thomas,1006,
  1026, W.R.,0850,1101, Woody,
  1085, Wylie,0870
CHAMBLISS, Mary,1215,1216,
  Sarah,1215, William,0894
CHAMP, John W.,0890
CHAMPION, Alexander,0973,
  Ann E.,0973, Elizabeth C.,
  0973, J.N.,0832, Joel,0973,

John R.,0973, Louisa J.,
  0973, Mary F.,0973, Mary,
  0973, Minnie J.,0973, Nancy,
  0973, Rebecca,0973, Susan I.,
  0973
CHANCE, Alexander,0841
CHANDLER, Caroline,0919,
  Fannie,1077, Henry,0842,
  Lucy,1081, W.D.,0855
CHANEY, David S.,0800
CHAPMAN, ,0774, A.S.,0800,
  E.N.,0893, Linsey,0851,
  Mary,1019, Saml.,0801
CHAPPELL, James,0841
CHARLTON, G.W.,0981, Margaret A.,
  0980,0981
CHATMAN, W.T.,0799
CHEAIRS, Annie,0911, Capt.,
  0752, J.W.,0775,0778,0781,
  0782, John M.,0911, John W.,
  0774,0911,0940,0959, John,
  0910, Laura B.,0910, M.T.,
  0774,0775, Martha,0910,
  Martin T.,0774,0910,
  Mary F.,0910, Mary L.,0959,
  N.F.,0785,0799, Nannie R.,
  0910
CHEAIRS, Nat.F.,0774, Nathaniel B.,
  0911, Nathaniel,0774,0910,
  Nathl.F.,0779, Sarah,0910,
  Susan T.,0911, W.M.,0782,
  Willie B.,0940
CHEAK, Vicey,1221
CHEATHAM, Ann,1009, James,
  0869, Joseph,0822, Maj.Gen.,
  0800, Peter,0766,0767,0769,
  Thomas,0834
CHEEK, Arthur B.,0912, Betsey,
  0925, C.L.,0912, Calvin B.,
  0912, Eliza J.,0912,
  Elizabeth,0912, Huston N.,
  0912, Ida L.,0912, James M.,
  0912, John L.,0912,0925,
  John T.,0912, John W.H.,
  0912, Joseph E.J.,0912,
  Lises E.,0912, Martha,0925
CHEEK, Nimrod P.,0912,
  Owen P.,0912, Susan E.,
  0912, Susan,0912, Van D.,
  0958, Wm.L.,0912
CHERRY, (Gen.),0922, Charlotte,
  1079, Daniel,0842, Jeremiah,
  0767,0769, Willie,0841
CHEVAL, ,1211
CHILDREN, James,0977, Jane P.,
  1010, Nancy,0977
CHILDRESS, A.,0840, Adrain D.,
  0912, Andrew,0827, Annette E.,
  0912, Capt.,0792,0823,
  Eloise,1064, Geo.,0772,
  George,0759,0770,0912,
  Henry,0793,0794, J.B.,0770,
  J.M.,0823, J.W.,0829,0830,
  0833, Joel,0790,0795,0815,
  0819,0826,0830, John W.,0822
CHILDRESS, John W.,1022,1027,
  John,0828, Mary W.,1022,
  Nancy B.,0912, Nancy L.,
  1198, Sarah,0946, Stephen,
  0789,0790,0794,0801,0805,
  W.G.,0803, W.S.,0792
CHILDS, Sarah,1197
CHINTON, Ann,0908
CHISHOLM, Isabel,0955, Jane,
  0955, Jennie R.,0955,
  Lewis C.,0955
CHISHOM, Capt.,0751
CHISM, Mary,1065
CHITWOOD, Stephen C.,0899
CHOCKLEY, J.C.,0878
CHRIESMAN, David V.,1009,
  George W.,0987, Jane,0987,
  Louella,1009, Lydia A.,
  1009, Martha E.,0987,
  Mary A.,0975
CHRISMAN, D.V.,0889
CHRISNHALL, Mr.& Mrs.,0838
CHRISTE, S.B.,0839
CHRISTOPHER, J.H.,0876
CHRISTY, Mr.,0828
CHURCH & JACK, ,0930,0931
CHURCH(Black), Andrew,0849
CHURCH, Abraham,0755,0777,

Allen B.,0912, Arthur,0913,
Bessie,0913, J.O.(Rev.),
0780, J.O.,0779, Jennette,
0913, Lucy,0912, Oatey,0913,
P.C.,0764, Robert C.,0912,
Stephen R.,0913, Tolitha,
0913
CHURCH/JACK & CO., ,0912
CHURCHHILL, Samuel,0841
CHURD, J.P.,0786
CINDER, ,0775
CISTHWAIT, G.D.,0829
CLADWELL Jr., John C.,0874
CLAGETT, Harriett,0916,0917
CLAIBORNE, (Gen.),0954, Mary,
1003
CLAIRY, W.F.,0879
CLAMPET, Ezekial,0842
CLAMPETT, Sarah,1014
CLAPTON, Walter,0842
CLARDY, Jerusha,1182, Peter E.,
0871
CLARK & COOK, ,0854
CLARK & MILLER, ,0879
CLARK, ,0837, Agnes A.,1113,
Betsey,1196, Christina C.,
1127, E.B.,0830, Ermine,
1170, Ida,0835, J.,0819,
J.N.,0837, James P.,0795,
L.J.,1113, Leslie,0848,
Margaret,1132, Martin,0840,
Mary J.,1067, Mary,1196,
Nancy E.,1197, Nancy,1174
CLARK, Nancy,1196, O.,0893,
Rachel A.,1188, Thomas,
1196, Vachel,0841, W.H.,
0877, W.M.,0799, William M.,
0880,1188, Wm.D.,0867
CLARKE, George,0843, Robert,
0867
CLARY & CO., ,0881
CLARY, Alla D.,1135, Ann,1135,
Benjamin,1135, Charley B.,
1135, Emma,1135, George,
1135, Irvin,1135, J.W.,1134,
James D.,1135, Mary A.,
1131, Mattie,1135, Nancy,
1131, W.F.,1160, William,
1131
CLAUD, Fannie,1013
CLAUDE, Nancy,0969
CLAXTON, Alice C.,1135,
Amanda I.,1135, Annie E.,
1135, Elizabeth A.,1135,
J.C.,1135, James J.,1135,
James,1135, Melvina J.,
1135, Minerva J.,1135,
Ophelia A.,1135, Philander P.,
1135, Temperance,1135,
Temperance,1135, William,
0849
CLAY, ,1133, Frances A.,1157,
Henry,1014,1034,1082,1116,
1165, John G.,0973, John Gillem,
0973, Nancy,0973, Sarah A.,
0973, Thomas J.,0973,
Thomas,0973
CLAYBROOK, Fred,0799, John S.,
0789
CLAYBROOKE, Annie W.,0974,
Eliz.T.,0973, Eliza M.,
0974, Elvira L.,0974,
Frederick,0974, James O.,
0973, Jane R.,0973, John P.,
0974, John S.,0973, Lucretia,
,0890, Laura A.,1210,
Levi,0889,0890,0898,0899,
0903, Maria R.,0913, W.P.,
0898, Wm.H.,0913
COCHRAN, Wm.J.,0913
COCKBURN, Capt.,0751, George,
0766
COCKE, ,0762
COCKRELL, ,0801, John,0887,
1120
COCKRILL, Capt.,0752
CODY, Will,0803
COE & MORRIS, ,0854
COE, Ella L.,1099, J.F.,0854,
0974, Mary E.,0973, Mary A.,0973,0974,
Mary E.,0974, Samuel P.,
0974, Sarah W.,0973, Sarah,
0973
CLAYBROOKE, Sarah,0974,
Susan F.,0974, Thomas W.,
0973, Virginia O.,0974,
William,0973
CLAYMASTER, Rebecca,0943
CLAYTON & DAVIS, ,0898
CLAYTON & OVERALL, ,0829,1028,
1030
CLAYTON DAVIS CO., ,1200
CLAYTON, ,0837,0838, A.C.,
0898,1195, Alexander A.,
1086, Ann E.,1085, B.,0816,
Benjamin,1028, C.C.,0830,

Cora,1196, D.D.,1085,
Daniel B.,1196, David,0773,
Emily H.,1028, H.H.,0817,
0818,0826,0829,0833,
Haddeassa,1029, Hattie A.,
1028
CLAYTON, Henry H.,1028, J.B.,
0833, J.C.,0826, James,1028,
Jane S.,1196, Jennie M.,
1028, John B.,1028, John,
1085, Joseph A.,0894,
Lockey,1028
CLAYTON, M.E.(Mrs.),0878,
Maria,1028, Mary E.,1196,
Mary Lucille,1196, Mary,
1028, Nancy,1195, Phoebe,
1196, Stephen,1195, William G.,
1196, William L.,1028,
Wm.G.,1195
CLAYWELL, A.F.,0855
CLEARLAND, H.P.,0868
CLEBURNE, Gen.,0750, P.R.,
0801,1069
CLEEK, ,0886, Joseph,0888
CLEMENT, ,0813, Beulah,1042
CLEMMONS, Elizabeth,1111,
Emma A.,1111, Thompson,
0842, William L.,1111
CLEMONS, Elizabeth,0930
CLEVELAND, Annie E.,1135,
Annie L.,1135, B.F.,0878,
1135, Benjamin,1135,
Caroline,1135, Carrie C.,
1135, Carrie,0870, E. (Mrs.),
0874, Eliza P.,1136,
Fannie L.,1135, G.A.,0875,
Georgia A.,1135, Harriet D.,
1135, Hattie D.,1135,
Jeremiah,1135
CLEVELAND, Jesse F.,1136,
Lizzie H.,1135, Lizzie,
1136, Mattie W.,1136, Mr.,
0865, R.M.,0878, R.M.Jr.,
1135, Robert M.,1135,
Robert,1135, Sallie E.,
1135, Sallie S.,1135,
Thomas S.,1135, Vannoy,
1135, William C.,1135,
William P.,1136
CLIFF, D.B.(Dr.),0799, D.B.,
0799,0825
CLIFFE, D.B.,0792,0804
CLIFTON, Capt.,0792
CLINE, Augusta,0915, Ella,
0915, John L.,0915
CLOIDE, Sallie Foster,1096
CLOPPER, John,0830
CLOUD, Joseph,0841,0890
CLOUSTER, W.G.,0803
CLOUSTON, Richard,0800
CLOYD, Ezekial,0842, Newton,
0856
CLUSKEY, M.W.,0824
CLUSKY, M.W.,0785
CLYMER, Samuel,0781, Thomas,
0848
COATES, P.H.,1166, Sarah B.,
1166
COBB, (Miss),0961, Ann L.,
0926, Jesse,0841, Robert L.,
0764, Susan,1001
COBBS, John W.,0871, Robt.L.,
0772
COBLER, Nicholas,0766
COCHRAN, ,0768,0899, Ascenith J.,
0913, David J.,0913, E.A.,
0827, H.B.,0772,0773, I.L.,
0772, J.T.L.,0764, James B.,
0913, James,0913, Jane,0913,

1099, Jesse F.,0847,
William,0820
COFFEE & WOODS, ,0897
COFFEE, Henry B.,0877, James,
0887, Jane C.,0928, John R.,
0877, John,0797,0820,0833,
0863, Nathan,0913, Rice,
0877, Wm.O.,0913
COFFEY & WOODS, ,1217
COFFEY BROS., ,0897
COFFEY, ,0863, A.N.,0898,
Allen,0902, Calvin,0895,
Hugh M.,0913, Hugh W.,0913,
J.A.,0753, J.H.,0764,
James,0901,0902, Jennie,
0913, John,0888, Joseph M.,
0913, Mary,0901, Ollie F.,
0913, Roy B.,0913, Sallie E.,
0913, Shirley E.,0913
COGGENS, Chaney(Miss),1170
COGGINS, John,0891
COHEA, Peter,0767
COHEE, Ann,0909
COKER, John M.,0913, Maggie J.,
0913, Sallie A.,0913
COLBERT, George,0796, James,
0796, Levi,0796
COLBURN, Mary,1086, Warren,
1087
COLDWELL, (Judge),1137,
Ballard,1136, Carrie,1136,
1137, Earnest,1136, Jane,
1136, John C.,1136, Mary H.,
1136, Mary J.,1136, Mary,
1137, Sarah E.,1136,
Thomas H.,1136
COLE, David B.,0848, Mary,
0974, W.T.,0842
COLEMAN, ,0777, B.,0821,
Blackman,0815,0818,0821,
0826, Edwin,1029, Ida,1029,
Mary E.,1029, Mary,0940,
Mattie J.,1148, N.A.,1148,
P.C.,0817, Robert A.,1029,
Tennie J.,1159, Thos.,0759,
W.B.,1029, W.W.,0779,
Walter,0764, Wm.J.,0851
COLES, W.T.,0854
COLLETT, W.J.,0799
COLLIER & EAGLETON, ,0829
COLLIER, Archie,0950, Don,
1137, Eliza F.,1137, G.W.,
0854, J.B.,0826, J.R.,0830,
Lockey,1137, Lulie J.,1064,
Martha,1137, Mary A.,1137,
Mary B.,1137, Mary,0950,
N.C.,0818,0826,0830,0832,
Nancy J.,1137,1161, Polly,
1161, Richard R.,1137
COLLIER, Sarah M.,0950,
William,0820,1137,1161
COLLINS & RANKIN, ,0875
COLLINS, ,0830, Betsey,1197,
Britton,0848, Capt.,0792,
Carrol,1029, David,1197,
E.T.,0790,0808, Edward E.,
1137, Edward H.,1029,
Elisha,1197, Ellen J.,1137,
Emmet C.,1137, Fannie,0974,
1197,1198, Franklin,0974,
Hannah G.,1197, Henry L.,
1198
COLLINS, Henry,1198, Ida J.,
1137, Isaac B.,0892, J.M.,
0897, James W.,1197, James,
0974, John B.,1137, John C.,
1197, John,0888, Jones,1197,
L.B.,0890, Lewis,0974,
Lizzie,1029, Lycurgus F.,
1137, M.,0974, Margaret,
1197, Mary K.,1228, Mary,
0974
COLLINS, Nancy E.,1198, Nancy,
1198, Phoebe,1197, Rosanna,
1029, Sally J.,0974, Sarah T.,1227, Sarah,1197,
Sophia,1197, Spencer D.,
1137, Squire,0848, Thomas,
1197, W.F.,0889,0895, W.J.,
1137, W.T.,1197, William,
0881,0974, Willis P.,1197
COLLINS, Willis,0893,1197,
Zibbie,0974

COLLINSWORTH, C.R.,0901, Geo.,
 0796
COLLIS, G.W.,0894
COLQUITT, W.L.,0764, William,
 0843
COMER, Ella,1138, J.J.(Rev.),
 1183, John B.,1138, John J.,
 1137,1138, John W.,0854,
 Martha P.,1138, Moltie P.,
 1138, Nannie J.,1138,1183,
 Reuben D.,1137, Samuel,
 1137, Sophronia A.,1138
COMPTON, ,0777, Cauras,1081,
 Howard,1081, Pattie,1081,
 Sarah,1203
COMSTACK, Clark M.,0882
COMSTOCK, S.G.,0768,0770,0772
CONAWAY, ,0863
CONGER, Thomas,0843
CONGERS, Thomas,0841
CONKEY, Zebina,0757
CONLY, Louisa,1061
CONNER, Addie B.,0914, Alfred,
 0914, India B.,0914, J.W.,
 0849, John W.,0855, Sidney,
 0914, Wm.R.,0913
CONROE, John,0841, Nicholas,
 0841
COOK & COOK, ,0856
COOK & OWEN, ,0854
COOK JR., D.,0854
COOK, (Mrs.),0979, ,0777,0803,
 0813, Alice,1087, Alvira,
 1086,1087, Ann Day,1160,
 Arch,0869, Bashie,1087,
 Betsy,0848, C.H.,0843,
 Charles H.,1086, Chloe N.,
 1086, Clark,1087, Cleopatra,
 1086, D.Lillian,1086, David,
 0832,1086,1087, E.C.,0796
COOK, E.C.,0800, E.K.,1086,
 1087, Ed C.,0799, Ed,0895,
 Eliza,1139, Elizabeth,0950,
 Ella,1086, Emily M.,1139,
 Emma,1086, Evalena,1086,
 Fanny,0974, G.W.,1138,
 Genevieve,0974, George,
 1087, Granville,0876,
 Green G.,1086, Green,1086,
 H.H.,0797
COOK, Harriet D.,0945, Harry,
 1087, Henry C.,1139,
 Henry Howe,0974, Henry,
 0794,0795,0797,0802, I.B.,
 0893, Isaac,0848, J.N.,0848,
 Jack,0844, James D.,0890,
 James E.,1086, James H.,
 1086, Jane(Mrs.),1044, Jane,
 1086, John O.,0777,1212,
 Joseph E.,0971
COOK, Joseph L.,1086, L.M.N.,
 1080, L.N.M.,1087, Lemuel N.M.,
 1086, Lewis,0974, Mamie,
 1087, Margaret Jane,0974,
 Martha L.,1086, Mary A.,
 1086, Mary E.,1139, Mary H.,
 1215, Mary J.,1086, Mary,
 1086,1087, Meddy,0931,
 Nancy,1139, Nora A.,1139
COOK, Oliver C.K.,1086, Peter,
 0814, Rachel A.,1086,
 Rebecca,0971,1174, Rosanna,
 1139, Salura,1080, Sambo,
 0892, Seleta Ann,1086,
 Seluria,1086, Susan,1087,
 Thomas,0797, W.A.,0763,
 W.C.,0829, W.J.,0892, W.W.,
 0795, William,0974,1086,1139
COOK, Wm.T.S.,1139, Zuella S.,
 1086
COOKE, Capt.,0792, John L.,
 0975, P.H.,0975, Sarah E.,
 0975
COONCE, Capt.,0850
COONRAD, Henry,0846, Michael,
 0846
COOPER & HILL, ,0768
COOPER, ,0750,0776,0863, A.G.,
 0893,0935, Albert C.,0914,
 Albert,0784, Alexander A.,
 1138, Algie B.,1138,
 Alice W.,1138, America L.,
 1138, Anna D.,0914, B.B.,

0759, Callie D.,0914,
 Callie T.,1138, Catharine,
 0914, Christopher,0845,
 Cicero W.,1138
COOPER, Constance,1138, Dr.,
 0757, Eddie A.,1138,
 Edmund Jr.,,0875, Edmund,
 0871,0875,0876, Edwin,0914,
 Ella L.,1138, George Lee,
 0914, George,1138, Gilley,
 1031, H.S.,0773, Henry V.,
 1138, Henry,0764,0769,0849,
 0858,0868,0870,0871,
 Horace L.,0771
COOPER, Horace S.,0759,0773,
 0914, J.B.,1138, J.C.,0894,
 James C.,0914, James H.,
 0914, Jane,1211, John L.,
 0867, John T.,0914, John,
 0870, Johnnie E.,1138, L.,
 0893, Lattie B.,1138,
 Lula S.,1138, M.,0784,
 M.D.,0772, Maggie M.,1138,
 Mary C.,1156
COOPER, Mary E.,1138, Mary,
 0914,1182, Mathew D.,0776,
 Matthew D.,0772,0914,
 Micajah T.,1138, Mollie,
 1231, R.T.,0785, Rebecca F.,
 1138, Rebecca J.,1138,
 Robert B.,0914, Robert M.,
 0752, Robert S.,1138,
 Robert,0914, Sallie,1138,
 Sarah A.,1138
COOPER, Sarah H.,0926, Sarah,
 1138,1216, W.C.,0879, W.F.,
 0764,0765, William E.,1138,
 Willis,0822, Wm.D.,0914
COOTS, Rebecca,1133
COPELAND, Arthur M.,0762,
 David,0760, Samuel,0842
CORE, Bettie J.,0975, Deborah,
 0975, J.D.,0975, Jesse G.,
 0975, John B.,0975, John D.,
 0975, Mary R.,0975, Richard E.,
 0975, Willie T.,0975
CORLETT, Annie P.,0975,
 David R.,0975, John C.,
 0975, Lucy J.,0975, Martha H.,
 0975, Marvin,0975, Mary A.,
 0975, Mary T.,0975, Sarah C.,
 0975
CORNEHAN, Elizabeth,1036
CORNEY & NEILEY, ,0874
CORTNER & CO., J.A.,0878
CORTNER, Albert E.,1134,
 Alexander F.,1134, Alexander,
 1134, Delilah,1134, George R.,
 1134, George,1134, Henry,
 1134, Letitia C.,1134,
 Mary E.,1134, Mary,1157,
 Roy E.,1134, Sarah E.,1134,
 Sarah,1181, Susan M.,1134,
 Victor H.,1134, William L.,
 1134
COSBEY, J.P.,0832
COSON, Margaret,1123
COTHRAN, J.N.,1048, J.P.,1139,
 Josephine,1048, Mary R.,
 1139, Polly,1139, Samuel,
 1139
COTTON, Alcenia G.,0976,
 Allen,0976, Amanda,0976,
 Lucila,0976, Lucinda J.,
 0976, Maggie,0976, Mary E.,
 0976, Mary,0976, Owen T.,
 0976, Park,0976, R.F.,0975,
 Robert A.,0976
COUCH, Catharine,1139,
 Emily G.,1140, James P.,
 0867, Jennie,1131, John R.,
 1139, Joseph,1139, Kittie,
 1139, Lester,1140, Lizzie,
 1140, Mary,1139, R.C.,0868,
 0872,1139, Reuben C.,1139,
 Robert W.,1139, Robert,1139
COUCH, Ruben C.,1140, T.P.,
 0799, William,1139
COURTNEY, ,0803
COVANTRY, (Mr.),0898
COVE, J.,0808
COVEY, Levi,0783

COVINGTON & LANDIS, ,0881
COVINGTON, Gen.Store,0881, J.,
 0881, James,0822
COWAN & CO., ,0874, O.,0875
COWAN & STRICKLER, ,0874
COWAN, Alexander,1140,
 Haddeassa,1029, Henry B.,
 1140, Jennie,1140, Mary A.,
 1161, O.,0874, Olive,1140,
 Oliver,0877,1140, Robert,
 1140, Sarah,1140, V.,0827,
 V.D.,0815, W.G.,0868,
 William B.,1140, William G.,
 1140, Wm.P.,0868
COWDEN & MARSHALL, ,1214
COWDEN & MOSS, ,0897
COWDEN & REED, ,0897
COWDEN, Brandon W.,0898,
 Charles N.,1196, H.N.,0890,
 1209, John,1196, Josie,1192,
 Mary H.,1196, Narcissa,
 1209, Rhoda,1196, W.M.,0897,
 W.N.,0890,0892,1191,
 William N.,1196, William,
 1196
COWEN, Addie,1102, Adeline,
 1087, Albert B.,1087,
 George W.,1087, J.N.,0843,
 James B.,1087, James,1087,
 John W.,1087, Julius E.,
 1087, Kate,1102, M.W.,1087,
 1102, Matthew W.,1087,
 Nancy,1087
COWER, O.,0768
COWLES, Alice,0976, Ann J.,
 0976, James B.,0976,
 John W.,0976, John,0976,
 Lucy,0976, Maggie R.,0976,
 Maggie,0976, Mary F.,0976,
 Mary,0976, Robert S.,0976,
 Sallie E.,0976, Samuel,
 0976, Susie,0976, William H.,
 0976
COX & GWINNETT, ,0857
COX, (Mr.),1030, ,1005,
 Andrew,1087, Beulah M.,
 1088, C.,0976, C.T.,0854,
 E.(Mrs.),0989, E.C.,0832,
 0833, Edgar E.,1088, Ella,
 0914, Emma,1029, Fannie O.,
 1088, Henry S.,0914, J.P.,
 0855,1087, J.T.,1010,
 Jackie Maud,1088, Jessie L.,
 1029
COX, John,0914, Louisa,1029,
 Maria,1087, Martha C.,0914,
 Martin S.,0914, Middleton,
 1029, Minos L.,1029, N.,
 0976, N.N.,0976, Nancy,1199,
 Pearsley,0887, Robert,1199,
 Sallie,1089,1199, Samuel,
 0988, Sarah A.,1087,
 Susan A.,0988, T.J.,1089
COX, Thomas W.,1029, W.Andrew,
 1088, William M.,1029
CRABTREE, William,0853
CRADDOCK, Charles E.,0830,
 Locky,1103, Nancy,1103,
 Richard,1103
CRAFT, H.,1035
CRAFTIN, Eliza A.,0950
CRAFTON, Mary,0933
CRAGNALL, Sarah,0979
CRAGWALL, Alabert O.,1088,
 Ellen B.,1088, James W.,
 1088, Sally,1088, Tepuple O.,
 1088, W.T.,1088, William J.,
 1088, Willie C.,1088
CRAIG & FLETCHER, ,0828
CRAIG, ,0776,0803,0809, A.,
 0809, B.B.,0782, Capt.,0752,
 Emmit P.,0915, Hattie,0915,
 James C.,0915, James F.,
 0915, James G.,0772, James,
 0760, John L.,0915, John W.S.,
 0915, John,0915,
 Joseph A.T.,0915, L.J.,
 0915, Lanella R.,0915
CRAIG, Lucinda,0915, Mary L.B.,
 0915, Mary M.,1015, Mary P.,
 0937, Mary,0915,0936,
 Nancy E.,0915, Nathaniel H.,
 0915, Rachel,0915, Robert J.,

0915, Robert R.,0915,
Robert,0915, Ruby,0915,
Sallie B.,0935, Sally,0948,
Saml.,0778, Samuel S.,0915
CRAIG, Samuel,0769, Stephen S.,
0914, Thompson S.,0915,
Virgie M.,0915, Wallace J.,
0915
CRAIGHEAD, David,0756,0795,
Jas.B.,0764
CRAIGMILES, Annie,1173,
Walter,1173
CRANE, John,0775
CRASS, F.H.,0833
CRAWFORD, ,0751,0774, A.T.,
0882, Alice,1093, Capt.,
0751,0752,0792, Dr.,0757,
Ellen P.,1033, Euphamie M.,
1171, J.C.,0854, John,0794,
1171, Jos.,0779, Nancy,1095,
W.P.,0879
CREIGHTON, James,0750
CRENSHAW, Daniel,0796, Mary,
1009
CRESON, Martha B.,1069
CRESSY, ,0768
CRICHLOW, (Mr.),1029, Emma,
1030, Helen M.,1030, J.H.,
0832, J.N.,0833, James H.,
1028,1030, James,0827,
Laila J.,1030, Newton C.,
1030, T.N.,0833, Thomas H.,
1030
CRISCOE, Joel,0869
CRISP, John H.,0947, John Henry,
0757
CRISTY, Thos.J.,0758
CRITTENDEN, (Gen.),0982, Gen.,
0991, John J.,0848, T.L.,
0825
CROCKER, E.B.,1178
CROCKET, G.S.,0819, J.A.,0829,
Louisa J.,1015, O.N.,0815
CROCKETT, America,1024,
Andrew,0995, Ann M.,1040,
Anthony,1071, Capt.,0792,
David,1071, Dr.,0803, G.S.,
0818,0828, R.P.,0824,
Samuel,0789,0801, Sarah Cath.,
1071, Sarah E.,0995
CROOKSHANKES, Anderson,1105,
Matilda,1105
CROSS, D.Jos.(Rev.),0785,
E.O.,0776, George,0870,
Joseph,0824
CROSSWAITE, Lt.,0825
CROSTHWAIT, Caroline,1030,
Eliza F.,1030, Eliza,1030,
Elizabeth,1030, G.D.,0817,
0819, George D.,1030,
George W.,1030, Lavina C.,
1030, S.,0833, S.D.,0818,
0838, S.N.,0818, Shelton,
1030
CROUCH, ,0863, Barton,0977,
Charles,0977, Eliza,0977,
John H.,0977, John,0977,
Lucy,0977, Mary,0977,
Molly,0977, Peter W.,0802,
Peter,0977, W.H.,0803,
William H.,0977, William,
0977
CROW, Bryant,0891, Matilda,
1107
CROWEL, Benjamin,1141, J.M.,
1141, Margaret,1141,
Mary C.,1208
CROWELL, ,0863, Edwin H.,1141,
Jennie L.,1141, Nancy A.,
1163, Susan A.,1141,
Thomas L.,1141
CRUDOUP, John J.,0856
CRUMP, Mattie D.,0905
CRUNK & FRIEND, ,0880
CRUNK, C.A.,0876, J.C.,0889,
James(Dr.),0880
CRUTCHER & MARSH, ,0898
CRUTCHER, ,0803, A.P.,1010,
Catharine P.,1198, David P.,
0977, Edmund,0853, Edward,
0848, Foster,0854, Henry L.,
0778, Hugh M.,1198, J.B.,
0799, James F.,0977,

James P.,0977, Jane E.,
0977, Jane P.,1010, Jennie,
1198, Magnes V.,0977,
Mary A.,1198
CRUTCHER, Mary E.,1198,
Mary T.,0977, May L.,1199,
Nancy L.,1198, Nancy,0977,
Robert P.,1198, Robert S.,
0977, Robert,0977,1198,
Samuel A.,1198,1199,
Sarah A.,1010, Sina V.,
0977, Susan C.,0977,
Susan V.,0977, Tennessee,
0977, W.M.,1198
CRUTCHER, William B.,1198,
William H.,0977, William,
0792,0862, Wm.,0880
CRUTCHFIELD, Dr.,0855
CULBERT, Capt.,0792
CULLEY, L.C.,1131
CULLOM, William,0834
CULLUM, Leslie,0771
CUMMING, ,0812
CUMMINGS, (Mill),0813, ,
0803, Charles,0842, Eleanor,
0901, Elizabeth,0901,
George,0842,0844, Henry G.,
0755, Hugh,0842, J.F.,0877,
James F.,1128,1165,1178,
John,0791,0901
CUMMINS & CROUCH, ,0977
CUMMINS, Lucy M.,1010,
Mary A.,1221, Mary,0979,
U.S.,0816,0818,0822,
William,1010
CUNDIFF, J.C.,0896,1225,
Victoria,1225
CUNNINGHAM, A.N.,0807, Aaron,
0759,0863, Alice,1045, C.W.,
0874, Clare G.,1141,
Cyrus W.,1141, Eliz.W.,
1141, Elizabeth,0935,1141,
Ewing B.,1141, Geo.,0876,
0888, Hattie S.,1141,
Horace L.,1141, J.A.,0878,
J.M.,1141, Jennie C.,1141,
Jeremiah,0874
CUNNINGHAM, Joseph A.,1141,
Kate T.,1141, L.,0890,
Lillie R.,1141, Lizzie T.,
1141, Martha M.,1204,
Mary J.,1141, Nancy E.,
1198, Rhoda,1139, S.A.,0877,
S.D.,1141, Susan A.,1141,
Vera C.,1141
CURD, Edgar,1088, Eliza,1088,
Elizabeth,1088, Ella,1088,
Elmer,1088, Emma,1088,
Gela,1088, J.N.,1088,
James A.,1088, John,1088,
May,1088, Sarah E.,1089,
Susan,1088, William E.,
1088, William,1088
CURL, Elvira,0926
CURRIN, J.,0827, R.P.,0789,
0794,0796,0802, Robert P.,
0802, Robt.P.,0790,0805
CURRY, John,0842, Rebecca,
1032
CURTHIRELL, L.(Miss),0909
CURTIS, Aaron,0796, Capt.,
0851, Henry,0849, James H.,
0868, Rebecca,0996
CURTISS, Alex,1141, B.M.,1141,
Fannie,1141, J.H.,1141,
James H.,1145, James R.,
1141, Mary,1145, Nola T.,
1141, Polk,1141, R.Dennie,
1141, Sallie E.,1141,
Teresa,1145, Teressa,1141,
Tint,1141
CUSHING, Caleb,1220
DABNER, W.W.,0920
DABNEY, Bethenia S.,0996,
Charles A.,1199, Cornelius,
0841, E.R.,0893, John,0841,
0850,0887,1199, M.J.(Miss),
1010, Margaret L.,0957,
Nancy,0968,1199, R.C.,0896,
Sallie,1199, Sarah B.,1207,
W.W.,0775
DADE, Maj.,0784,0797
DAILEY, P.H.,0795

DAKE, J.P.(Dr.),0908
DALBY, E.(Mrs.),0874
DALE & PHILLIPS, ,0896
DALE, Achsah,1219, E.W.,0766,
0771,0772,0782,0783, Edw.W.,
0783, Edward W.,0768, Lily,
0943, W.J.,0756,0768,
W.J.Jr.,0772, Wm.J.,0754
DALLIS, Willis,0870
DALLUM, ,0762
DALTON, Capt.,0792, Lucinda,
1083
DANCE, Russel,0828
DANCEY,Capt.,0792
DANDY, Howell,0865
DANIEL, Ann,1085, Harriet C.,
1145, John,0776,0870,
Mervin,0757, Susan,1085,
Travers,0769, William,0766,
Wm.,0759,0761
DANIELS, Wm.,0751
DARBY, W.J.,0859
DARDEN, B.G.,0785
DARK, Harris,1199, Isaac V.,
1199, James,1199, Lydia C.,
1199, Martha,1199,1200,
Sarah,1199
DARNALL, Delilia,1129
DARNELL, C.R.(Rev.),0899,
Emily M.,1139, William,1139
DARRACH, T.B.,0826,0829
DASHIALL, Alford,0882
DASHIELL, Lavinia J.,1048
DAUS, Joseph,0805
DAVENPORT, Sarah,1172
DAVID, Emily,1103, H.C.,1103,
Mary J.,1103, T.K.,1103
DAVIDSON & CALDWELL, ,0874
DAVIDSON & JETT, ,0874
DAVIDSON, ,0863, A.S.,0827,
Alice,1142, Anderson,0862,
Andrew D.,1142, Barkesdal,
1142, Capt.,0850, Cynthia,
0963, E.E.,0762, Elizabeth J.,
0916, Geo.W.,0916, George H.,
1142, George M.,0916,
George,0867,0874,0934,
Georgia,1205, H.L.,0870
DAVIDSON, Harriet E.,0934,
Hugh L.,0849,0870,0871,
0877, I.S.,1142,1206, J.,
0827, J.F.,0893, James W.,
0916, James,1181, John L.,
0867, John O.,0762, John R.,
1142, John,0760,0841,0961,
Judge,0882, Martha,0961,
Mary A.,1142, Mary Cath.,
1181
DAVIDSON, Mary E.,0934, Mau,
1142, Ophelia T.,0961, R.B.,
0871, R.V.,0878, Robt.B.,
0871, Sarah A.,1142, Sarah,
1142, W.H.,0764
DAVIS & CO., B.F.,0878, T.E.,
0854
DAVIS & LONDON, ,0897
DAVIS BROS., ,0856
DAVIS JR., Henry,0880
DAVIS, (Miss),1204, ,0751,
0778,0862, A.M.,0890, A.R.,
0854,1081, A.T.,1089,
Alabama V.,0977, Alfred,
0869, Alice R.,1089, Alice,
1089, Belle,1219, Benjamin,
0916, Bill,0849, C.W.,0789,
Charles E.,1142, Charles H.,
0977, Charles L.,1031
DAVIS, Cleopatra,1142,
Dora J.,0963, Eliza M.,
0916, Eliza T.,0916, Eliza,
0916, Elizabeth,1031,1081,
1102, Ella B.,1089, Ella M.,
1200, Ella,1031, Ellen,1101,
Elnathan G.,1142, Elnathan,
1142, Emma S.,1142, Ephraim,
0916, Eugene G.,1142
DAVIS, F.H.,0977, Felix Z.,
0916, Frank P.,1142, G.F.,
0875, G.W.,0790,0897,
Geo.W.,0897, George W.,
1200, Hay,0916, Henry,0819,
0820,0842,0862,0880,
Holland(Mrs.),0793, I.F.,

1089, Isham,0843,0844,0847,
J.C.,0894, J.K.,0897, J.W.,
0818
DAVIS, James H.,0842, James L.,
1089, James W.,1030,1031,
James,0847, Jane,0978,
Jeff,1087, Jefferson,1168,
Jeffie E.,1142, Jennie M.,
0916, John L.,0842, John R.,
0852, John W.,1142, John,
0789,1031, Joseph,0760,0848,
Judy A.,0949, L.,0820
DAVIS, L.,0821, Larkin,0843,
0847, Leah,0916, Lena Bell,
1142, Lizzie C.,1069,
Lizzie,1200, Lovey,1001,
Mabel C.,1200, Margt.Eliz.,
1089, Martha,0961,1001,
Martin,1200, Mary A.,0916,
0977,1222, Mary E.,1031,
1047,1142, Mary J.,1031,
Mary,0929
DAVIS, Mary,1030,1043,1200,
Mattie A.,1089, Mattie C.,
1081, Millie E.,1031,
Minnie K.,1200, Mollie E.,
1031,1200, Mollie J.,1142,
Molly L.,0929, Mr.,0756,
0758, N.J.,0799, Nannie,
1195, Narcissa,1209,
Nathan C.,1200, Nora E.,
1089, Omega H.,0916
DAVIS, Ovie W.,1089, Owen,
0929, Philander,0857, R.T.,
1089, Rachel J.,1089,
Rachel W.,1029, Rebecca,
1142, Rhoda,1196, Robert O.,
1031, Robert,0808,1081,
S.D.,1213, S.E.,1089, S.W.,
0824, Sallie J.,1200,
Sallie,1031,1200, Samuel B.,
1031
DAVIS, Samuel L.,1031, Samuel,
0888,0890,0893, Sarah A.,
0954, Sarah E.,1089,
Sarah M.,0950, Sarah,1076,
1132, Scott D.,0890, Sue H.,
1031, Susan,0968,1088, T.B.,
0878, Thomas,0842,0871,0874,
Thompson,0793, W.H.,0821,
W.P.(& Son),0892, W.P.,0890
DAVIS, W.P.,0893,1089,
William E.,0916, William G.,
1142, William H.,1030,
William L.,1031, William M.,
1200, William,0808, Willie J.,
1142, Wilson P.,0890,0897,
Wm.H.,0916
DAWS, Bros.,0802, Isaac,0892
DAWSON, Emma L.,1041, John,
0781,0915, Mann,0915,
Martha G.,0915, Martha G.H.,
0920
DE GRAFFENRIED, F.,0799
DE MUNBREUN, ,0788
DEACON, David,1173
DEADERICK, Thos.,0766
DEAN & KEITH, ,0880
DEAN, ,0863, Eliza,0965,
Henry,0868,0877, J.T.,0897,
John R.,0868,0871, John T.,
0870, Lucy,1146, Mary A.,
1181, Mary,1080, Thomas,
0862,0890
DEARENS, Capt.,0752
DEARING, W.L.S.,0850
DECKER, Jacob,0828
DEERING, (Maj.),1075
DEERY, ,0862, J.E.,0875,
James H.,0874, James,0874,
William,0874
DEGRAFFENRIED, John D.,0977,
M.F.,0977, M.M.,0977, May,
0978, Pattie,0978
DELK, Jacob B.,0932, Telitha,
0932
DEMMENT, C.,0819
DEMUMBRAN, Ann T.,0978,
Carrie D.,0978, Elizabeth,
0978, Francis E.,0978,
Hattie,0978, John F.,0978,
John W.B.,0978, Joseph T.,
0978, Mary A.,0978, Mary E.,

0978, Minnie M.,0978,
Sallie,0978, Wallace,0978,
William,0978
DEMUMBRANE, Charity E.,1005,
Eliz.N.,1222
DEMUMHANE, Capt.,0788, Wm.,
0788
DENHAM, A.W.,0764, Eleanor,
0929, Esther,0933, Mary M.,
0929, Nancy J.,0928, Peggie,
0928, Robert F.,0929,
Robert,0928
DENNEY, Matilda,1220
DENNING, William,1100
DENNIS, A.J.,0803
DENNISON, James,0872
DENNY, Alexander,0841
DENTON, E.A.,0782, Emma C.,
0947
DEPRIEST, Dr.,0767, H.,0766,
Horatio,0757,0759,0761,
0771,0778
DERRING, W.L.S.,0850
DERRYBERRY, ,0777, W.C.,0781
DESHA, Robert,0850
DESHEIL, A.H.,0807
DETH, Mary,1074
DEVAULT, Peter,0842
DEVER, Wm.,0750,0759
DEVEREUX, J.H.,0772
DEVORE, James,0817
DEW, Arthur,0842, Col.,0758,
J.H.,0764,0772, JOhn H.,
0764, John H.,0850, Mathew,
0854, Nathnl.,0854
DEWOLF, Jane,0835
DIBRELL, (Brigade),0800,
George,0849
DICKASON, Anna E.,0987, John,
0846
DICKENS, Andrew J.,1143,
Baxter B.,1031, Baxter M.,
1031, Charley G.,1031,
Clara A.,1143, Daniel,1142,
Edna F.,1031, Elizabeth C.,
1143, J.B.,1142,1143, James,
1031, Jasper F.,1031,
Jasper N.,1143, Jennie,
1143, John T.,1031, Malcolm A.,
1143
DICKENS, Martha E.,1031,
Mary J.,1031, Matilda F.,
1143, Matilda,1142, Nancy C.,
1031, Nancy J.,1143, Nancy,
1031, Nellie F.,1143,
Newton,1143, Quitnian,1031,
Rufus G.,1031, Sarah G.,
1143, Thomas P.,1031,
William C.,1143, William T.,
1031
DICKENSON, Eliza,1014
DICKERSON, C.J.,0773, Caleb J.,
0759, Henry C.,1143,
James W.,1143, John W.,
1143, Mary E.,1143, Nancy,
1143, W.G.,0772, W.H.,0869,
William J.,1143
DICKEY, John,0749,0759,
Squire,0749
DICKINSON, ,0762, Daniel,0815,
John,0794, W.G.,0784
DICKMAN, D.W.,0822, David,
0812
DICKSON, (Mr.),0810,0816,
0863, C.,0893, Capt.,0751,
D.W.,0836, David,0794,
Emily B.,0937, Ephraim,
0776, Isabel,0955, J.H.,
0817,0818, John,0815,0821,
Joseph,0820, Maria,0960,
Mary H.,1144, Priscilla,
0838, Thomas,0838
DIETRICH, Julius,0803
DILL, Gilley,1031, Isaac,1031,
J.M.,0818, James M.,1031,
Jestina,1031, Joseph W.,
1031, Mary,1031, Nettie F.,
1031, V.,0829
DILLAGE, George,0850
DILLAHAY, John W.,0938,
Louisa,0938, Nancy W.,0938
DILLAHUNTY, (Judge),1218,
Edmund,0763,0772,0779,0890,

0892,0945, Judge,0756,0763,
Jusge,0764
DILLARD & WILSON, ,0854
DILLARD, B.J.,1123, Capt.,
0850, J.L.W.,0871, J.O.,0854
DILLEHAY, Marcus G.,0946,
Mary,0946, Valderia A.,0946
DILLON, Coon,0851, Harriet,
1105, J.R.,0830, Martha,
1105, Thomas,1105
DINGES, D.W.,0855
DINWIDDIE, A.G.(Rev.),1143,
Emma,1144, Frank G.,1144,
Maggie L.,1144, Mary B.,
1144, Mary Cole,1143,
Rachael,1143, William,1143,
Willie H.,1144
DISMUKES, Elisha,0844, Z.T.,
0819
DITTO, William,0790
DIXON, Eunice,1172, Joseph,
0838, Margaret,0838, Martha,
0941, Mary,0838, Robert,
0870, Tilman,0863
DOAK, ,0813, A.A.,0750,
Danl.G.,0750, John,0841,
0845,0846, Robert,0783,
William R.,0824, William,
0785, Wm.R.,0824
DOBBIN, Jenette M.,0910
DOBBINS, A.N.(Mrs.),0919,
Alexr.,0749, Callie,0972,
J.G.,0764, Martha,0869,
William,0869
DOBSON, B.C.,0893, Benjamin,
0842, Laura,1000,1226,
Letitia,1000, Matthew,1000,
P.W.,0836
DODD, Alexander,0978, Jane,
0978, Luversa E.,0968,
Samuel,0978, Talbot F.,
0978,0979, William,0893,
Xernia,0978
DODGE, John,0783
DODSON & COPERTON, ,0768
DODSON & COX, ,1089
DODSON, Dorcus,1014, Eli,0986,
Elizabeth,0986, G.T.,1089,
Harry,1089, I.J.,1089,
Isaac J.,1089, Joseph,0934,
Kate,1090, Levina,1089,
Loretta,0916, Lucinda,0916,
Maggie A.,1090, Maggie,
1089, Manda,0920, Margaret,
0906, Maria R.,0913
DODSON, Mary S.,0986, Mary,
0909,0934, Mr.,0750,0770,
Octavia,1089, R.P.,0940,
Raleigh P.,0916, Sallie L.,
1089, Sallie,1089, Sarah J.,
1090, Stonewall J.,1090,
Tommie,1089, W.T.,0782,
W.W.,0920
DOE, John,0761
DOHERTY, George,0774,0863,
Mary,0774
DOLBY, Mary,1127
DONALD, Samuel,0782
DONALDSON, A.J.,0987, Andrew,
0832, Binkley,0795, D.W.,
0833, Robert,0834, Stokely,
0863
DONELSON, Andrew,0845, George,
0784
DONLEY, Mary,1073
DONNEL, George,1103, Nancy A.,
1103
DONNELL & YOUNG, ,0854
DONNELL, ,0841,0843, Adney,
0842, Cleopatra,1090,
David K.,0851, George,0837,
0860, John,0842, Mr.,0857,
Robert P.,1090, Robert,
0860, Samuel,0860, W.W.,
0850,0854, William W.,1090,
William,0841
DONNELLY, Peter,0874
DONNELSON, John,0844
DOOLEY, Capt.,0751,0792,
William,0759, Wm.,0778
DORAN, James,0833, Nancy,1019
DORIS, Thomas,0874
DORNAL, Calvin,1141

DORSET, Hallie B.,0917,
  Harriett,0917, Janie M.,
  0917, Marion,0917, Thomas J.,
  0917, Walter C.,0917
DORSETT, Harriett,0916,
  Laura R.,0916, Laura,0960,
  Lillie G.,0916, Mary E.,
  0916, Pauline,0916, T.J.,
  0960, Thomas J.,0916,
  Thomas,0916
DORTCH, D.R.,0764, Sarah,0906
DOSS, Alice I.,0979, Betty,
  0979, Edward L.,0979,
  Elizabeth,0979, John B.,
  0979, Maggie,0979, Martha,
  1102, Robert M.,0979,
  Robert R.,0979, Sawrie,
  0979, William W.,0979,
  William,0979
DOTSON, Elizabeth M.,0995
DOTY, ,0775
DOUD, ,0764
DOUGAL, W.R.,0857
DOUGHTY, Alma E.,1065, James,
  1115, Cynthia A.,1115, Mary C.,1115, W.N.,
  0830,0831, W.W.,1065
DOUGLAS, Bettie,0979, Bruce,
  0979, Byrd,0979, David,0841,
  Dr.,0775, Edwin H.,0979,
  Ellen,0979, Elmore,0845,
  George,0814, Harry L.,0850,
  0854, Hugh B.,0979, John W.,
  0824, Lee,0979, Margaret R.,
  0979, Martha R.,0979,
  Mary N.,0979, Richard,0979
DOUGLAS, Sarah,0979, T.L.,
  0808,0809
DOUGLASS, ,0793,0798
DOW, Lorenzo,0783
DOXIE, Daniel,0891
DOZIER, Ada M.,1201, Calidonia,
  1201, Cynthia A.,1200,
  William M.,1200, William Z.,
  1201, Zachariah,1200
DRAKE, B.L.,0808, Brittain,
  0842, Ephraim,0863, James,
  1097, Jane,1097, Margaret,
  1097, Richard,0842
DRAYTON & CO., John,0874
DRENNAN, John,1124, Mary,1124
DRENNON, Thomas,0842
DRIBRELL, G.G.,1107
DRIFOOS & CO., L.,0854
DRIFOOS, H.M.,0855, J.L.,0855,
  L.,0847,0854
DRIFOSS, Alice,1090, Annie Laura,
  1090, Carrie,1090, Eliza,
  1090, Frank,1090, G.L.,1090,
  Harry,1090, L.,1090, Laura,
  1090, Leopold,1090, Mary N.,
  1090
DRISKILL, A.F.,0809
DRIVER, W.T.,0824, William,
  0785
DROMGOOLE, G.C.,0819, J.E.,
  0816,0826,0829,0830,
  Marie L.,1024
DRUMMOND, Mr.,0779
DRUMRIGHT, Elizabeth,1032,
  Martha F.,1032, Richard,
  1031, W.B.,0832, William B.,
  1031
DRYDAW, Mary A.,1137, Morgan,
  1137
DRYDEN, ,0863, Annie,1144,
  Daniel D.,1144, David O.,
  1144, David,1144, Ella,1169,
  Hubert E.,1144, James N.,
  1144, John W.,1144, Lucinda E.M.,
  1144, Maggie H.,1144,
  Malinda,1144, Margaret,
  1186, Martha M.B.,1144,
  Mary H.,1144, Mary L.,1144
DRYDEN, Mattie M.,1165,
  Nancy C.,1144, Nathaniel L.,
  1144, Nathl.,0887, Nathl.L.Jr.,
  1144, Sarah J.,1144,
  Thomas F.,1144, Thomas,
  1144, William J.,1144
DUATT, Eliza,1069
DUDLEY, ,0979, B.W.,0960,
  Guilford,0794
DUFF, Hugh,0802

DUFFER, P.G.,0854
DUFFIE, Patrick,0825
DUGGAN & CLARK, ,0881
DUGGAN & HENDEN, ,0881
DUGGAN & SONS, ,0881
DUGGAN, ,0881, Algie A.,1144,
  B.F.,0881, Benjamin F.,
  1144, John,1144, Nancy A.,
  1144, S.S.,0881, Salome J.,
  1144, Salome,1147, Sarah A.,
  1144, Solon S.,1144
DUGGER, Catherine,0917,
  Corinna,0917, Daniel B.,
  0917, David,0917, Elizabeth L.,
  0917, Isolana,0917, Leroy S.,
  0917, Lorinda,0917, Samuel G.,
  0917, Shadrach S.,0917,
  Thomas J.,0917
DUKE, D.W.,0878, L.E.,1143
DUMONT, Gen.,0852
DUNAWAY, ,0863, Eliza,0985,
  J.M.,0871, M.E.W.,0871
DUNCAN, A.,0889, Andrew,0891,
  L.H.,0768, Lemuel,0754,
  Martha L.,0921, Saml.H.,
  0763
DUNLAP, ,0774, Lydia A.,1009,
  Marian,1095, Samuel,0775,
  W.C.,0902
DUNN, (Miss),1127, Capt.,0792,
  J.C.,0832
DUNNAGEE, Lutitia,0991
DUNNAWAY, Eliza,1017
DUNNIGAN, Sherwood,0888
DUNNINGTON, Bettie,0936, F.C.,
  0764
DURDIN, A.C.,0853
DURHAM, Thomas,0782
DUVALL, A.S.,0893
DWIGGINS, Ann,1144, B.F.,0874,
  Cassie C.,1145, Ethel E.,
  1145, H.C.,1144, Harry C.,
  1145, Mamie L.,1145, Mary,
  1145, R.S.,1144, Robbie E.,
  1145, Robert,0875
DYER, A.S.,0764, Annie H.,
  1145, Belle,1145, Capt.,
  0752, Charles,0870, Earnest G.,
  1145, Eliza,1145, Emily,
  1145, Grace B.,1145,
  Harriet,1145, Harry,1145,
  Henry C.,1145, James H.,
  1145, Joel,0815,0826,0827,
  Mary B.,1145, Mary J.,1140,
  1145
DYER, Roy,1145, Thomas,1145,
  William H.,1140,1145,
  William,1145
DYKE, ,0818
DYKES, Henry E.,1032, Henry,
  1032, Horace G.,1032,
  James M.,1032, John N.,
  1032, Rebecca,1032, Sallie,
  1032, Sidney B.,1032
DYSART, Alfred,0896, Andrew,
  1199, Anna L.,1199, Clarence M.,
  1199, Eli,0896, Elizabeth E.,
  1199, J.P.,0890, James P.,
  1164, Jane,1199, John,0886,
  0901, Leah,1164, Margaret,
  0901, Martha,0901, Sallie E.,
  1141, Susan,1164, William A.,
  1199
DYSART, William E.,1199
EAGLE & SHAFFNER, ,0875
EAGLETON & BYRN, ,0829
EAGLETON, Elvira,1027, Samuel,
  0832, W.C.,0831, William,
  0839
EAKIN & CO., ,0898
EAKIN & MOFFITT, ,0874
EAKIN, (Library),0874, ,
  0862, Alexander,0874,
  Brothers,0874, G.N.,0874,
  J.C.,0875, James,0870,
  Jas.(Colored),0869,
  John R.,0868,0877, John,
  0874, Spencer,0874, William S.,
EARHART, Jacob,0843
EARLEY, Sarah G.,0964
EARLY, (Bishop),1143, Bishop,
  0991, Martha R.,0991,
  Martha,1112

EARTHMAN, Anna,1033, Christine R.,
  1033, Elizabeth,1032,1033,
  Ella M.,1032, Fannie,1032,
  Hewett F.,1033, Ira O.,
  1032, Ira Overton,1033,
  James,1032, John B.,1033,
  Margaret,1032, Mattie T.,
  1033, V.K.S.,1032, W.B.,
  0830,0833,1032, W.W.,0832
EARTHMAN, Weber B.,1033,
  William W.,1033, Wm.B.,
  1032,1033, Wm.W.,1032
EASOM, Robert,0848
EASON, Amanda,0941, Reddick,
  0854
EASTES, J.B.,1100
EASTMAN, J.P.,0850,0855
EATHERLY, Andrew,1091,
  Ann Eliza,1091, Charles H.,
  1091, John W.,1091, John,
  1090, Lem R.,1091, Maggie A.,
  1090, Margaret J.,1091,
  Margaret,1091, Martha E.,
  1091, Mary F.,1091, Nancy C.,
  1091, Peggie,1090, T.Hugh,
  1091, Warren,1090, Wilson R.,
  1091
EATON, Dr.,0836, J.H.,0827,
  0836,0838, J.W.,0794,
  John H.,0794
ECHOLS, Capt.,0850, Joel,0842,
  Moses,0844
EDDE, James,0874
EDDINGS, Tempie,1124, William,
  0841
EDDINS, Martha,1119
EDDY, Emma,0803, James,0862
EDGAR, ,0751, Prof.,0858
EDGERTON, (Prof.),0806
EDMISTON, ,0775, Martha,0970
EDMONDSON, Barbara H.,0980,
  Barbara,0979, Bethenia H.,
  0979, Caroline,0980,
  Charles,0979, Const.P.C.,
  0979, David C.,0979,0980,
  Elizabeth B.,0980, Henry C.,
  0979,0980, Jane W.,0980,
  Jennie P.,0980, John A.,
  0980, John F.,0980, John,
  0979
EDMONDSON, John,0980, Margaret,
  0970, Martha,0980, Mary,
  0979,0980, Mira L.,0980,
  Priscilla,0980, Sarah,0979,
  Starnes W.J.,0980, Thomas,
  0979, William A.,0980,
  William H.,0979, Wm.,0789
EDMONSON, E.(Dr.),0982, John,
  0799,0825, William,0789
EDMUNDSON, Saml.,0793, Thos.,
  0801, Wm.,0793
EDMUNSON, Samuel,0791,
  William,0791
EDMUSTON, Capt.,0792
EDNEY, E.T.,0799, K.S.,0799
EDWARD, Arthur M.,1021,
  Elizabeth,1023, Sallie T.,
  1021
EDWARDS, ,0777,0813, Aaron,
  0842, Adongah,0751, Ann(Mrs.),
  1230, Capt.,0752, J.T.,0897,
  James,0843,1090, Jane,1127,
  Jarrett W.,0848, John,0815,
  0821,0842, Lavina S.,1043,
  Levina,1089, Margaret,0761,
  Owen,0814,0815,0821, Peter,
  0793,0801
EDWARDS, R.B.,0761, Robert,
  0842, Sarah J.,1090, Thomas,
  0848, Thos.,0760, W.,0821,
  W.T.,1043, William,0820,
  Wm.,0750
EELBECK, F.,0803, H.,0803,
  Henry,0808
EGGLESTON, Edmond W.,0980,
  Edward E.,0980, Hilu A.,
  0980, James F.,0980,
  Josiah C.,0980, Josiah,
  0980, Junius V.,0980,
  Robert W.,0980, Sarah J.,
  0980, Sarah M.,0980,
  Susan C.,0980, Susan,0980,
  Thomas B.,0980, William C.,

EGNEW, J.,0764, J.W.,0766
EICHBAUM, Catherine,0908,
  Eliza,0908, Wm.,0908
EICKHOFF, H.,0833
ELAM & EWING, ,0768,0918
ELAM, Annie,1033, Daniel,1033,
  David F.,1033, Ed,0827,
  Edward E.,1033, Edward,
  1033, Elizabeth,1033,
  Ellen P.,1033, Elnora,1185,
  Francis C.,1033, Franke E.,
  1033, Franklin,1033, J.J.,
  0772, James A.,1185, Mamie,
  1033,1053, Rebecca,1033
ELAM, Samuel B.,1033, T.J.,
  0818, Thomas J.,1033, W.R.,
  0770,0771, Wade H.,1033,
  Washington E.,1033
ELDER, Benjamin,0827
ELKIN, Alexander,0869
ELKINS, Angeline,1146,
  Asa W.(Rev.),1145, Charles,
  0870, Deletha,1145, Eli,
  1145, Evaline,1145, George T.,
  1146, James,1145, John W.,
  1146, Lafayette,1146,
  Lucinda,1146, Margaret A.,
  1146, Martha E.,1146,
  Mary A.,1146, Mary,1145,
  Nancy K.,1145
ELKINS, Nancy V.,1146, Nancy,
  1145, Richard,1145, Robert E.,
  1146, Sarah J.,1146, Sarah,
  1145, William S.,1145
ELKNS, William,0841
ELLET, James,0779
ELLETT, Anna L.,0917, Felix M.,
  0917, James K.,0917,
  John C.,0917, John H.,0917,
  Katharine,0917, Martha W.,
  0917, Ophelia,0917, Susan,
  0917, Thomas P.,0917,
  Wadkins B.,0917, William M.,
  0917
ELLINGTON BROS., ,0878
ELLINGTON, Addie(Mrs.),1093
ELLIOTT & CUNNINGHAM, ,0897
ELLIOTT, (Hotel),0803,
  0813, Addie L.,0980,
  Albert J.,1145, Alexr.,
  0980, Alice G.,1024,1025,
  Allen,0980, B.,1145,
  Charles E.,0980, Claude E.,
  0980, Deborah L.,1228,
  Deborah,1066, Excom A.,0980,
  Excom,0980, Fannie,1227,
  George,0980, Harriet C.,
ELLIOTT, Harriet L.,1145,
  Henry,0829, J.F.,1145,
  J.J.,0890, James L.,0980,
  James M.,1145, Jane,1066,
  Jeannette,0980, John J.,
  1228, John M.,0980, John,
  0888,0890, Josiah E.,0980,
  Josiah H.,0980, Josie,1145,
  Kittie,1163, Lillian H.,
  0980
ELLIOTT, Mary D.,0980,
  Mary J.,0980, Mary,1209,
  Mebane,0980, Minerva B.,
  0980, Nancy A.,1144, Nancy,
  0849,0901, R.,1145, Rebecca C.,
  1145, Robert,0901,0980,
  Samuel,0842,0890, Sarah K.,
  1145, Seth M.,0980, Seth,
  0980, Tennessee,1145, W.Y.,
  0791
ELLIOTT, William,0980
ELLISON, Charles,0869,
  Mary O.,1191
ELZEY, John J.,0891
ELZY, A.L.,0894
EMANUEL, J.,0854
EMERY & CO., ,0768
EMBRY, W.F.,0772, W.J.,0770,
  0773, W.M.,0770, Watt,0768
EMMERSON, J.C.,0893, Thos.,
  0762, W.W.,0893
EMMETT, W.C.,0827
ENGLAND, John,0901
ENGLISH, ,0777, Clara,0917,
  John W.,0918, John,0917,
  Martha,0959, Robert J.,

0918, Thomas Y.,0917,0918
ENLISS, ,0863
ENLOE, Asoph,0776
EPPERSON, Elizabeth,0917,
  Susan,0980
ERSKINE, Alexr.,0824, J.H.,
  0824
ERVIN, A.,0868, Robert,0877
ERWIN, ,0776, A.M.,0821,
  Alexander S.,0936, Andrew,
  0862, Bessie R.,0918, E.E.,
  0772,0773, Ephraim E.,0918,
  Harry,0878, Ida,0936,
  Jemima A.,0918, Joseph,
  0862, Josephus,0880,
  Mary C.,0936, Wm.E.,0759,
  Wm.H.,0918, Wm.J.,0936
ESKEN, Benjamin,0841
ESKEW, (Dr.),0757, Alice A.,
  1091, Andrew O.,1091,
  Andrew,1091, Benjamin,1091,
  J.C.,1091, James O.,1091,
  Lula B.,1091, Martha,1091,
  Matilda,1091, Viola G.,1091
ESSLEMAN, Ann,0941, Caroline K.,
  0941, James,0941
ESTES, Capt.,0792,0850, Dr.,
  0767, Ervin T.,0918, H.B.,
  0764, Hester J.,0918, L.B.,
  0756, Ludwell B.,0778, Mrs.,
  0775, Orvin T.,0918
ESTILL, Joseph,0882
ESTIN, Mr.,0773
ESTIS, L.B.,0769
ETHERLEY, Elizabeth J.,1116
ETHERLY, ,0843, Jonathan,0848,
  0852
EULES, Adam,1146, Allen F.,
  1146, Amelia,1152, Casander,
  1146, Della C.,1146,
  Dorothea,1146, Eli S.,1146,
  Elisha A.,1146, Ella J.,
  1146, Harriet E.,1146,
  John M.,1146, Lucy T.,1146,
  Lula B.,1146, Martin,1146,
  Mary E.,1146, Minnie A.,
  1146
EULISS, Martin,0877
EVANS & FITE, (Drs.),1167
EVANS & KEITH, ,0880
EVANS & SHEPARD, ,0874
EVANS, Cleo,0981, Daniel,0751,
  0759, David S.,1146, E.C.,
  0981, Eliza,1145, Elizabeth,
  0924,0995, Emily V.,1187,
  Emma S.,0981, Fannie D.,
  0939, G.W.,0981, Hampton,
  1187, Jackson Z.,0981, Jere,
  0849, John,0920, Judith,
  1146, Margaret E.,0981
EVANS, Martha C.,0914, Martha,
  1210, Mary B.,1163, Mary C.,
  1146, Mary F.,1146, Mary S.,
  0980, Mary,0993, N.P.,0875,
  Nancy H.,0981, Nancy,0932,
  Nathan,0864,1145, Philip,
  0939, Polk,0848, R.F.,0876,
  Robert F.,1146, S.W.,0981,
  Sally A.,0981
EVANS, Sammie E.,0920, Samuel,
  0869, Stella,1146, Thomas,
  0841, William G.,0980,
  William H.,0980
EVERETT, James,0842, John,
  0842,1088, Susan,1088
EVIN, Virginia F.,0933
EWBANKS, T.B.,0829
EWELL, ,0863, Richard S.,0775
EWIN, Henry C.,1002, John H.,
  0768, Theresa G.,1002
EWING & ADAMS, ,0897
EWING & BOREN, ,0897
EWING & BRO., ,0897
EWING & HOUSE, ,0989
EWING & RICHMOND, ,0854
EWING, ,0796,0863,0897, A.,
  0796, A.B.,0889, A.L.,0902,
  Allan L.,1201, Andrew,1033,
  1034, Capt.,0751,1009, Col.,
  0995, E.E.,0902, E.H.,0823,
  0829,1034,1058, Edwin H.,
  1033, Eliza J.,1202,
  Elizabeth,0918,1201, F.J.,

0772, Flavius J.,0918
EWING, Florella J.,1201,
  Florence,1058, Geo.Wythe,
  1202, J.C.C.,1201, J.L.,
  0898, J.S.,0902, J.W.,0833,
  0851, James L.,0888,
  James S.,0901,1202,
  James V.,0889,0890,0891,
  0918,1201, James,1103,1201,
  Jane,0902,1199, Josiah W.,
  1034, Lile A.,0898
EWING, Lile A.,0901, Lucinda C.,
  1103, Lyle A.,1201, Margaret E.,
  1218, Marian V.,1201,
  Mary L.,0918, Mary,1201,
  Nancy,1103, Nathan,1033,
  Newton B.,1201, Peyton,
  0854, R.C.,0771, R.M.,0796,
  Rebecca A.,1201, Rebecca,
  1202, Robert L.,0918
EWING, Robt.M.,0779, S.B.,
  0898, S.D.,1193, Sarah,1201,
  Susan C.,1211, W.E.,0791,
  William D.,1202, William,
  0800,0893, Z.W.,0894
EZELL, J.B.,0888, J.Britt,
  1202, Joseph D.,1202,
  Mary C.,1202, Sarah J.,1202
FAIN, D.N.,1023, Mamie L.,
  1023, R.W.(Dr.),0877,
  Woodly,1211
FAKES & CO., ,0855
FAKES & TAYLOR CO., ,1091
FAKES, Clarence,1091, Daisy,
  1091, Daniel R.,0854,
  Elizabeth,1091, Gertrude,
  1091, J.M.,1091, Mark,1091,
  Rosa A.,1091, Sally,1091,
  W.C.,1091
FALL, G.W.(Mrs.),1042
FALLS & CHRISTY, ,0827
FALWELL, Martha M.,1226
FANNING, Tolbert,0809
FARIS, ,0776, Ada,1034,
  Amanda R.,1147, Angre,1035,
  C.B.,1034, Cassie B.,1147,
  Charles R.,1035, Charley B.,
  1034, E.E.,1147, Eliza,1146,
  Elizabeth J.,1035, G.W.,
  1146, James R.,1034,
  John W.,1034, Julian L.,
  1147, Lee G.,1147, Lena M.,
  1034
FARIS, Lizzie,1034,1075
FARIS, Mary A.,1034, Mary J.,
  0960,1035, Mary,1034,
  Mattie,1035, Mr.& Mrs.,
  1035, R.W.,1035, S.I.,1147,
  Sallie,1034, Sue E.,1034,
  W.L.,1146, Walter R.,1035
FARISS, H.F.,0919, Hugh W.,
  0919, James,0919, Mary E.,
  0919
FARMER, B.W.,0826, Martha,
  1129, Samuel,0789,0790
FARNEY, Capt.,0751, John,0762
FARQUAHARSON, Robt.,0895
FARRAN, J.H.,0880
FARRER, John,0871
FARRIS, Alexr.,0754, Amanda M.,
  1192, C.J.,1192, James,0752
FATHERA, E.B.,0819
FAULKNER, Jesse,0761
FAUNTLEROY, ,0796
FAUSETT, Mary Jane,1171
FEATHERSTON, Gen.,0825, P.,
  0822, W.,0822
FEATHERSTONE, Abe,0869
FELLOWS, Mr.& Mrs., ,0835
FELTON, William,0819
FERGUSON, (Rev.),0809, ,
  0813, Amanda K.,1200,
  Amelia L.,1204, Col.,0873,
  Daniel,0814, David,0820,
  F.,0889,1204, Isaac,0797,
  James F.,1204, James,0896,
  John F.,1204, John T.,1204,
  Lucy,1129, M.,0781,
  Maggie R.,1204, Mary,1204,
  1205, Sallie J.,1204
FETCHER, John,0816
FIELD, ,0773,0828, John,0888
FIELDS, ,0774, David,0842,

L.P.,0864,0878, Martha J., 0983, Nelson,0805, Wm.,0805
FIELDS-MACKEY & CO., ,0878
FIGUERS, Bethenia H.,0943, Hardin P.,0942,0943, Lily, 0943, Louise A.,0967, T.N., 0770, Thomas N.,0943
FIGURES, ,0796,0897, David, 0801, H.P.,0770, J.N.,0770, Mathew,0842,0843,0845,0846
FINCH, ,0863, H.C.,0833, William,0862, Wm.P.,0862, 0871
FINDLEY, Samuel,0901
FINLEY, Almira,1092, Charles A., 1092, Charles,1093, Dr., 0836, Foster G.,1092, George,1092, Isaac,1093, J.J.,0850, J.R.,0835, James F.,0800, Jesse J., 1092, Jessie C.,1092, John B.,1092, Lucius,1092, Maggie,1092,1093, Mary Lewis, 1092
FINLEY, Mary,1092,1093, O.G., 1091,1092, Obadiah,1093, Samuel,1091, Sarah A.,1092, V.C.(Boyd),1092, Virgie Lee, 1092, William M.,1092, William,1093
FINNEY, H.E.,0879
FISH & REESE, ,0854
FISH, Monroe,0855
FISHER & EWING, ,0897
FISHER & ROBINSON, ,0899,1147
FISHER BROS, ,0854
FISHER, ,0863, Alice,1117, Amy,1179, Annie,1165, Ed, 0827, Edward,0826,0840, Elbert H.,1147, Elizabeth, 1147, Fannie B.,1203, George B.,1147, George W., 1147, Hugh C.,1147, J.,0808, J.C.,1147,1176, Jacob,0867, James D.,1147, Jane,0988
FISHER, John R.,1203, John, 0830,1203, Margaret,1168, Mary,1203, Mattie,1147, Michael,0874, Mildred,1203, Monroe,0896, Oscar B.,1147, Sallie H.,1203, Sarah,1199, Stella,1147, Thomas B., 1202, W.D.,0897, William D., 0902, Wilson P.,1203
FISHER, Wm.D.,0890
FITCH, H.D.,0769
FITE, C.C.,1146, E.C.,0852, J.L.,0855, Jennie M.,1146, Mary C.(Mrs.),1146
FITZGERALD, (Gr.Father),0931, ,0775, Caroline,0919, D., 1010, Elizabeth,0986, Francis M.,0919, Frank L., 0919, G.H.,0782, George V., 0919, John,0797, Lecey J., 0930, Lucy,0912, Margaret L., 0919, Margaret,0919, Maston, 0919, Willie L.,0919
FITZHUGH, John A.,0983
FITZPATRICK, ,0751, Capt., 0792, John L.,1203, John P., 1203, Mary D.,1203, Rebecca B., 1203, S.W.,1203, Samuel W., 1203
FLACK, James,0870
FLATH, Margaretta,1026
FLEISHMAN, ,0829
FLEMING, A.Brice,0981, Addie, 0981, Adelbert W.,0981, Albert,0981, Annie W.,0993, Bettie,0981, Blanche,0981, Capt.,0792, Charles,0981, David B.,0981, David R., 0981, Della,0981, E.L.,0981, Elizabeth,0981,0993, Ella E.,0920, Elmira,0981
FLEMING, Emily M.,0981, F.a., 0855, Fillmore,0981, George W.,0920, James,0981, Jane,0981, Joe,0981, John D.,0784, John O.,0920, John T.,0981, John,0981, Keziah,0981, Knox,0771,

L.G.,0920, Lee,0981, Lelia, 0981, Lizzie,0981, Malissa J., 0981
FLEMING, Malissa,0995, Malvina,0981, Manda,0920, Margaret E.,0919, Mary, 0981, Mattie,0920,0981, Mickey,0981, Mira,0981, Mixey,0981, Nathaniel,0920, 0981, Pauline,0981, Philip M., 0981, Q.C.,0893, Reams,0981, Robert,0981, Sallie,0981
FLEMING, Sam,0981, Sammie E., 0920, Samuel,0981, Sarah, 0981, T.J.,0772, Thomas F., 0919,0993, Thomas,0981, Virginia,0981, W.S.,0773, Watson,0981, William C., 0981, William O.,0920, William T.,0981, William, 0763,0841,0981,0993, Winnie, 0920
FLEMING, Wm.S.,0781,0919
FLEMING, Elizabeth H.,0980, Hilu A.,0980, J.J.,0753, J.S.,0782, Jane B.,0980, Josiah,0980, Sallie A., 0935, Samuel(Dr.),0967, T.A.,0750, W.S.,0764,0765, 0797,0892
FLEMMINGS, ,0749
FLETCHER, Elvira,1039, Florence,1058, Frank,0838, J.,0827, J.F.,0836,0838, John,0819,1035, Lucretia, 1035, M.L.,0818,0823,0830, Martha,1035,1044, Minos L., 1035, Montford,1044, R.F., 0878, Thomas,0870
FLOOD, Thomas,0842
FLOWERS, W.N.(Mrs.),1104
FLOYD, (Col.),0894, ,0812, 0863, Archibald C.,0920, 0927, David,0862, Delphia C., 1038, Gen.,0824, James E., 1038, John D.,0880, John W., 0920, Margaret J.,0920, Nannie,1180, W.W.,0894, Watson,0868
FLUTY, G.W.,0893, T.C.,0893
FLY, H.B.,0797, Ida,1029
FLYGS, Addie J.,0934, William, 0934
FOGELMAN, John,0870
FOGG, Francis B.,0764,1034, J.J.,0798
FOGLEMAN, ,0777, Geo.W.,0876
FOLLIS, Elizabeth,1203, John, 1203, Mary,1203, Robert M., 1203, Sarah,1203
FOMAN & SON, ,0875
FONDILL & BENNETT, ,1089
FONVILLE, A.R.,0854, Asa,0886 (Col.),1117, (Miss), 1117, John,0841
FORBS, John,0844
FORD, Dr.,0757, E.M.,0750, Mary,0891, Mr.,0853
FORGEY, (Dr.),0920, Addison H., 0920, Anna Lee,0920, Charles A.,0920, Hugh,0920, James H.,0920, L.B.,0775, Lunsford B.,0920, Salina, 0920, Sarah D.,0920, Thomas B.,0920, Walter E., 0920, William S.,0920
FORR, John C.,1080
FORREST, (Gen.),0976,1021, 1150,1168,1170,,0787, Gen., 0800,0872,0873,0999,1003, 1051, N.B.(Gen.),0886, N.B., 1009,1212, Nathan,1212
FORSYTH, Benjamin,1175
FOSS, John,0821
FOSSETT, Sarah,1154, W.T., 0893
FOSTER, (Mrs.),0808, A.S., 1203, A.W.,0848, Almira M., 1143, B.F.,0868,1147, Belle, 1093, Benjamin S.,1093, Caledonia T.,1143, Capt., 0752, Celia,1147, Charles R., 1147, E.N.H.,0787, Eliza J.,

1143, Elizabeth B.,0957, Elizabeth,0957, Elvira E., 0927
FOSTER, Ephraim W.,0779, Fannie L.J.,1204, Frances, 1147, Frederick,1204, G.W., 0802, Harriet M.,1147, Henry,1011, J.M.,0764, James J.,1147, James,0848, 0867,1147, Jennie,1143, John S.,1093, John,0841, 1093, Lela G.,1147, Malcolm A., 1143
FOSTER, Martha M.,1204, Mary A.,1143, Mary S.,1011, Nancy A.,1147, Prof.,0859, R.C.,0791,0795,0796,0802, R.G.,0792, R.V.,0859, Richard S.,0935, Richard, 0957, Robert C.,0764, Robert V.,1093, Robert, 0846,0847, Rufus H.,1093, S.D.,0792
FOSTER, Sallie A.,0935, Sallie B.,0935, Sallie, 1204, Sarah G.,1143, Sarah, 1093, Susan,1011, T.S.,0796
FOUNTAIN, Walter L.,0795
FOUNTAINE, (Family),1003
FOUST, Joseph,0843, Wm.E., 0848
FOUVILLE, F.F.,0871
FOWLER & DAVIS, ,0828
FOWLER, ,0813, Alanthas L., 1204, Anna M.,1204, H.,1035, Holman R.,0896, J.B.,0819, 0831, J.E.,0893, James E., 1204, John C.,1077, John R., 0898, Joseph C.,0957, Katie B.,1035, Ladie M., 1077, M.,0893, Margaret E., 1229, Martha,1227, Mary E., 0957
FOWLER, Mary R.,1077, R.,1035, Sallie,1035, Tennessee A., 1204, Thomas B.,1035, Walter W.,0957
FOX & SMITH, ,1035
FOX GILBERT & CO., ,1070
FOX, ,0813, Capt.,0792, Col., 0873, Cynthia A.,1213, Frances,0925, John,0900, 0925, Lizzie E.,1036, Lucy Catharine,1046, Martha,0925, Mattie A., 1213, P.,1213, Pervines Jr., 1213, Tennie,1035, W.D., 1213, W.R.,0830, William R., 1035,1036
FOX, William,1035,1070, Wm.R., 1036
FRALEY, R.A.,0897
FRAME, Bessie,1036, Irene H., 1036, John,1036, Lula T., 1036, Thomas,1036
FRANCIS, John M.,0753
FRANK & CO., J.,0829
FRANK, Willis,0892
FRANKLAND, ,0803, Joe,0803, Jos.,0803
FRANKLE & CO, A.,0874
FRANKLE & CO, H.,0874
FRANKLIN, A.,0761, Abner,0760, B.Andrew,0831, Benj.,0801, Joseph,1040, Mary L.,0924
FRAZIER, Amanda,1045, James, 0854,0855, T.N.,0823, Willis,0870
FRAZILL, T.F.,0879
FREELAND, Emily,1200, Jas.D., 0754
FREEMAN & WHITESCOWER, ,0855
FREEMAN, Emma,1147, Enid,1147, H.R.,0881,1147, Hartwell, 1147, J.M.,0879, James,0893, Josiah,1087, Maria,1087, Moses,0749, Nancy,1147, Pemelia,1124, R.,1145, S.T.,0875, Salome,1147, W.R.,0879, William,0817, 0818
FREEMAN-WHITESCARVER, ,0855
FREESE, Alice,1093, Angelia,

1093, Eva,1093, John H.,
1093, Katie,1093, Wessel,
1093
FRENCH, Chas.A.,0897
FRIER, Lucius,0770
FRIERSON & CO., ,0768
FRIERSON & FLEMING, ,0963
FRIERSON MAYES & CO., ,0940
FRIERSON, A.D.,0770,0771,0772,
Ada V.,0921, Albert,0875,
Anna E.,0920, Capt.,0752,
0784, D.P.,0771, Donna Maria,
0921, E.C.,0752,0753,0764,
E.J.,0867,0870, E.W.,0872,
Eli,0749,0751, Ella T.,
0920, Erwin J.,0892,
Eustatia,0921, G.P.,0764
FRIERSON, Gardner,0755,0768,
Goodloe M.,0921, Grace,
0921, H.R.,0881, Harriett A.,
0921, Horace,0771,0772,0773,
I.J.,0871, Ida J.,0921,
Ida,0921, Irene H.,0920,
Irwin J.,1136, J.B.,0750,
0759,0782, J.H.,0764, J.W.,
0782, J.W.S.(Dr.),0783
FRIERSON, J.W.S.,0750,0757,
0921, James A.,0750,
James M.,0920, James,0749,
Jane E.,0921, Jas.H.,0757,
John D.,0920, John S.,0776,
0921, John W.,0921, John,
0783,0921, L.D.,0892,
Lesey M.,0944, Lillie A.,
0920, Lucius,0770,0772,
Luther L.,0921
FRIERSON, M.A.E.,0920,0921,
M.G.,0772, M.L.,0772, M.S.,
0764, Martha G.,0920,
Martha G.H.,0920, Martha L.,
0921, Martha M.,0921,
Mary A.,0921, Mary J.,0921,
0929, Mary W.,0919, Milton B.,
0757, Moses G.,0760, Moses,
0749,0750,0759,0791
FRIERSON, Narcissa A.,0920,
Nettie,0920, R.M.,0964,
Robert L.,0921, Robert,
0749, S.,0759, S.D.,0764,
0765,0779, Sally R.,0920,
Saml.,0749, Saml.D.,0773,
0892, Saml.S.,0764, Samuel,
0917, Theodore,0750,0780,
0921, Thomas J.,0920,0921,
W.J.,0759
FRIERSON, W.J.,0779,0901,
Walter B.,0921, Willie T.,
0921, Willis R.,0921, Wm.,
0749,0754,0759,0760,0766,
0771, Wm.J.,0784
FRIZZELL, ,0803
FROST, Clarinda E.,1148, Dr.,
0880, Ebenezer,1148,
John E.,1148, John G.,1148,
John W.,1148, Joshua W.,
1148, Katie,1148, Martha L.,
1148, Mattie J.,1148,
Mattie L.,1036, Mattie T.,
1033, Nancy,1148, Nellie,
1025, S.B.,0808, W.A.,0874,
W.C.,0831
FROST, W.C.,1036, Walter C.,
1036,1148, William A.,1148,
William D.,1036,1148,
William W.,1148, Wm.A.,0877
FRY, O.N.,0753, Sallie C.,
1195
FUGETT, ,0863, Townsend,0871
FUGITT, A.D.,0878,0879,
Ada J.,1149, Alfred D.,
1149, Alfred T.,1149,
Annie N.,1149, Benjamin,
1149, Cassie M.,1149,
Glodolphus C.,1149,
Jane M.,1149, Jane,1149,
John N.,1149, Maggie N.,
1149, Mattie J.,1149,
Mollie B.,1149, Sallie E.,
FUGITT, Townsend,1149
FULLER, Chas.A.,0772, E.W.,
0875, John B.,0872
FULLERTON, W.D.,0791
FULTON, Charles,0981, J.B.,

0898, J.Britt,1202, J.S.,
1090, James,0870, Mary C.,
1202, P.,0749, Sarah M.J.,
0982, W.D.,0982
FUQUA, Elly,0856, Juda,1005,
Mary,1078
FURGASON, Sarah A.,1080
FURGUSON, Robert,0862, Robt.,
0871
FURR, (Mrs.),1192
FUSSELL, Eliza C.,0921,
Henry B.,0921, J.H.,0764,
0772,0773,0892, J.W.,0772,
Joe H.,0921,0922,0924,
John,0921, Margaret,0922
GADSDEN, Col.,0797
GADSEY, John E.,0802
GAIN, ,0861, Anthony,0850
GAINES, E.P.,0755, George S.,
1002
GAINS, John D.,0843, Mary,
1092
GALBRAITH, ,0863, Col.Bob,
0873, William,0867, Wm.,0868
GALBREATH, William,0865
GALE, Dr.,0757
GALLAGER, Mary,1151
GALLAHER, Tennie(Mrs.),1151
GALLAWAY, Charles R.,0922,
Elizabeth,0922, James A.,
0922, James E.,0922,
James L.,0922, Marion V.,
0922, Marion,0922, Mary,
0922, Prucilla J.,0922,
Robert,0922, Samuel,0850,
Sarah C.,0922, William R.,
0922, Wm.,0753
GALLOWAY, ,0777, Anna G.,0923,
Anna,0923, Cornelia E.,
1215, Enoch W.,0923, Enoch,
0923, George B.,0923,
Irvin T.,0923, J.B.,0787,
0923, James,0923, Jane,0923,
John B.,0923, John C.,0923,
Julia,0923, Margaret,0923,
Matthew J.,0922, Ola,0923
GALLOWAY, Pattison J.,0923,
Samuel W.,0923, Susan,0923,
W.,0779
GAMBELL, Ben,0874, Eliza Jane,
0867, Henry,0870
GAMBILL, ,0863, Aaron,1149,
Bradley,1149,1150, Charlotte,
1037, Elizabeth,1149,
James B.,1150, Jesse C.,
1150, Johsua C.,1150, Lucy,
1150, Marvin E.,1150,
Minerva,1150, Minnie E.,
1150, N.C.,1150, N.C.Jr.,
1150, Nancy L.,1150,
Nannie E.,1150
GAMBILL, Newton E.,1150,
Sallie J.,1150, Sarah C.,
1149,1150, Thomas J.,1150
GAMBLE, C.M.,0771, E.W.,0768,
0769,0770,0771,0772,0773,
0783, Jim,0870
GAMELIN, J.W.,0768
GAMMEL, William,0819
GAMON, Capt.,0752
GANAWAY & HENDEN, ,0881
GANAWAY, ,0813,0881, J.A.,
0881, Joshua(Dr.),0880,
R.P.,0877, Tom,0870
GANNAWAY, B.,0815,0836,0838,
Burrell,0826, Clarence E.,
1149, Cora L.,1149, Cornelius V.,
1149, Elija T.,1149,
Emma D.,1149, Horace B.C.,
1149, James W.,1149,
John A.,1149, John E.,1149,
John,1149, Josephus,1149,
M.R.,1149, Maggie E.,1149
GANNAWAY, Mary C.,1149,
Mary W.,1149, Nannie R.,
GANTT, Capt.,0792, George,
0759,0764,0787, Jacob,0801,
W.P.,0781
GARDNER, Mary,1162, W.,0827
GARLAND, F.,0828
GARNER, W.L.,0879
GARRET, Richard,0766
GARRETT, A.G.,0877, Capt.,

0792, Darington,1150,
Darlington J.,1150, Dolly,
0952, Eliza,1209, Elizabeth M.,
1205, Ella N.,1150, Eveline N.,
1190, Fane S.,1150, Fannie C.,
1150, Fannie,0939, George C.,
1048, George W.,1204,
Huldah G.,0952
GARRETT, Jacob,0794,1205,
Jesse J.,1204, John J.,
1150, Levi,1204, Lizzie L.,
1150, Lizzie,1029, Louis,
0809, Martha L.,1150,
Mary A.,1205, Mary B.,1137,
Mary,1205, N.G.,1070,
Nancy,1150, R.C.,1150,
Robecca G.,1150, Robert C.,
1150, S.L.,1205
GARRETT, Sallie,1048,1176,
T.P.,0897, Thomas,0794,
Thos.E.,1205, Tolitha,0984,
0985, W.B.,0829,0833, W.G.,
0829, William T.,1150,
William,0952
GARRISON, R.A.,0807, R.C.,
0779
GARRIT, Capt.,0752
GASLIN, William,0875
GASLING, William,0876
GASTON, John,0870
GATES, (Gen.),1128, Allen,
0891, Eliphas,1095, Elizabeth,
0891, James,0891, Lucy A.,
1094, Lucy,1095, Martha,1199
GATHIRE, Minerva Jane,1013
GAULT, Isaiah,1038, Mary,1038,
Mr.,0801
GAUNT, ,0863, Dan S.,1150,
James L.,1150, Joe U.,1150,
John T.,1150, L.T.,1150,
Lewis,1150, Margt.M.E.,
1150, Mary S.,1150, Mattie E.,
1150, Mollie E.,1150
GEARS & WILKERSON, ,0854
GEDDENS, Caroline A.,0923,
Carrie,0923, Eliza H.A.,
0923, James M.,0923, James,
0923, John W.,0923, Josephus T.,
0923, Matthew D.,0923,
Priscilla,0923, Tully,0923,
Wm.B.,0923
GEE, A.B.,0799, Elizabeth,
0932, John W.,0785
GENTRY, Celia,1147, Elizabeth,
1170, J.S.,0898, M.P.,0791,
0796, Martha A.,0982,
Mary R.,1222, Meredith P.,
0982, Nancy,1150, Rebecca B.,
0982, Reuben,0982, Tabitha,
1223, Theophilus L.,0982,
Watson M.,0982, Watson,0982
GEORGE, Caroline F.,1220,
Enoch,0808, Solomon,0842,
0844, W.H.,0851
GERMAN, Adalitia,0983, Alice,
0983, Daniel,0983, Eliza A.,
0953, Elizabeth,0983,
Graham,0983, Horace B.,
0983, M.,0791, Richard M.,
0983
GERMANY, N.C.,0863
GERMINY, Hal,0870
GHIST, Gen.,0750
GHOLSON, Capt.,0751
GIBBONS, Nancy E.,1232
GIBSON, Albert,0849, David,
0841, John,0842,0844,
Martha J.,1121, Thomas W.,
1121, Thomas,0770,0781,0862
GIDEON, James,0751,0795
GIFFORD, L.(Mrs.),0830
GILBERT, John,1070
GILBRAITH, ,0823
GILCHRIST, Danl.,0779, Malcom,
0863,0865, Wm.,0759,0871
GILES, Annie,0975, Martha A.,
1009, Mary E.L.,1161,
Wesley A.,0890
GILFINS, ,0813
GILHAM, Henry,0812
GILL, (Rev.),0807, ,0778,
Capt.,0752, J.J.,0877,
J.J.S.,0890, John J.,1151,

Loretta,0916, Martha C.,1151, Mary R.,1151, Sallie J.,1151, Sallie R.,1151, Sarah A.,1151, Susan S.,1151, Thomas,0762, Thos.,0759, W.W.,0877, Winston W.,1151
GILLEM, Charles,0842
GILLEN-WEBB & CO., ,0875
GILLESPIE & MABRY, ,0854
GILLESPIE, Alexander,0759, David,0754,0768, James,0821,0834, Jennie,0937, John,0782,0901, Z.R.,0753
GILLEY, Arthur T.,1036, Elizabeth,1036, Ephraim D.,1036, Jessie P.,1036, John A.,1036, John F.,1036, Mr.,1037, Nancy,1036, Peterson,1036
GILLIAM & PURDUE, ,0856
GILLIAM, Charles W.,0923, Cornelia C.,0912, Edward H.,0923, Estella,0923, Harrison O.,0912, Harrison,0814, Henry,0819, John H.,0923, Julia C.,0923, Martha,0923, Mary A.,0912, Robert,0923, Sarah P.,0923, Sarah,0923, Stephen M.,0923
GILLIAM, Thomas,0923, William,0827
GILLIAN, W.C.,0843
GILLIS, Eliza,1151, George D.,1151, Isabella,1151, J.S.,0874,1151, James,1151
GILMAN & MOORE, ,1019
GILMER, J.,0759
GILMORE, J.D.,0819
GIVENS, B.M.,0799, Helen,1157, Lina,1157
GLASS, John,0779, R.(Dr.),0803
GLEAVES, Annie T.,1094, Emma L.,1094, Eugene C.,1094, Guy T.,1094, James W.,1094, Jesse H.,1094, John,0842, Julia A.,1094, M.F.(Miss),1099, Rosa B.,1094, Thomas,0842
GLEN, Margaret,1197, W.B.,0898
GLENN, A.P.,0759, Daniel,0842, Fannie,1221, Giles H.,0848, Hugh K.,1126, John,0764, Lucretia E.,1126, Mary H.,1126
GODFREY, James,0842
GODOWIN, John B.,1037
GODUM, A.S.,0786
GODWIN, Saml.,0775
GOFF, A.C.,0784, Andrew,0789, 0793,0795,0806, Gracy(Mrs.),0793
GOFORTH, Josiah,0759
GOGE, Mr.,0863
GOLDEN, T.M.,0799
GOLDSTON, Eli,1119, Elizabeth,1119, John,0841, Sarah A.,1119
GOLDSTONE, ,0850
GOLING, Sarah E.,1136
GOLLADAY, Caroline M.,1117, E.I.,0852, Edward I.,0850, Samuel,1117
GOLLIDAY, Samuel,1116
GOMER, E.F.,0879
GONIGAL, Prof.,0881
GOOCH, Ada,0924, Alacy,0924, Benjamin E.,0924, Bertha,0924, E.,0989, J.S.,0819, John S.,0818,0825, Martha,0953, Mary C.,0924, Mattie,1063, N.,0989, Nancy E.,0924, P.H.,0924, Roland,0923, Rolena,0924, Sallie E.,0989, Thomas R.,0924
GOOCH, Thomas,0794, William,0849, Wm.S.,0924
GOOD, Hugh,0812
GOODALL, ,0850, D.L.,0785, 0824, David L.,0824, Park,0843

GOODBAR & MEANS, ,0854
GOODLOE, ,0812, Henry,0815, John M.,0766, Kate,1073, Mary A.,0921, Robert,0844, 0846
GOODLOW, Henry,0821
GOODNER, T.C.,0852
GOODRICH, Mary,0955, Mr.,0751, T.,0812, T.C.,0829,0831
GOODRUM, J.L.,0871, Jane G.,1131, Kate,1131, Margaret E.,1227
GOODWIN, ,0750, George M.,1037, George,1037, Henry M.,1037, Jane T.,1037, John Buchanan,1037, Joseph D.,1037, Ledocia,1037, Margaret L.,1037, Martha,0938, Mary A.,1110, Mary J.,1037, Nancy,1163, P.G.W.,0890, S.,0764, Sarah A.,1037
GOODWIN, Sarah E.,1037, Sarah,1037, Tennessee L.,1037, William H.,1037
GOOLITHAN, Hattie,1113, J.R.,1113
GORDON, (Capt.),0896,1203, , 0801, Adam E.,1152, Albert P.,1153, Amelia E.,1152, Amelia,1152, Amzi C.,1152, Anna B.,1153, B.,0755, Boling,0755, Callie,1153, Capt.,0792, Clawson R.,1153, Col.,0873, David,1152, Dosia,1153, Dr.,0880, Elizabeth,0924
GORDON, Euphus A.,1153, Family,0751, G.W.,0752, 0764, Geo.W.,0755,0778, George W.,0924,1152, Harriet E.,1152, J.E.,0753, James,0795, John A.,1152, John(Capt.),0784, John, 0754,0783, Louisa B.,1152, 1153, Margaret E.,1152, Margaret J.,1211
GORDON, Martin L.,1152, Mary C.,1152,1208, Mary L.,0924, Mary,1152, Mitchell S.,1152, Nancy V.,1223, Obediah,0854, Powhattan,0754,0755,0759,0777,0784, Richard D.,1152,1153, S.B.,0871, Samuel B.,1152, Samuel B.Jr.,1152, Thomas M.,0785
GORDON, W.B.,0764, W.C.,0773, W.O.,0753, William F.,1153, William J.,1152, Wm.B.,0924
GORE, Mary,1177
GORGEY, Hugh,0779
GORTH, Mattie T.,1014
GOSEY, James G.,0983, James,0983, Mary A.,0983, Mary T.,0983, Mattie L.,0983, Moses G.,0983, Rebecca,0983, Sarah E.,0983
GOSLING, Laura D.,1184, William,0868,1184
GOWAN, J.W.,0824, James,0871
GRACY, Elizabeth,0942, Joseph B.,0942, Sarah D.,0820
GRADY, E.,0820
GRAGG, Jennie,0913
GRAHAM, Capt.,0752, Cynthia,0983, Daniel,0761,0822, John,0793, Martha,1075, R.,0797, Saml.L.,0802, Sarah,1036
GRANBERRY, James M.,0921, Martha L.,0921
GRANBURY, ,0801, Gen.,0750
GRANDSTAFF & WATERS, ,0857
GRANDSTAFF, Arsula,1094, David W.,0848, David,1094, Frank,1094, Isaac,0843, J.B.,1094, Jane,1094, Margaret,1094, Martha,1094, Mary,1094, William D.,1094
GRANNIS, Hattie,1095, Henry,1095, Herbert W.,1095, John,1095, Lucy A.,1094, Marian,1095, William J.,1094

GRANT, ,0823, James F.,0800, James,0863, Jesse,1051, Rebecca B.,1203, Sarah R.,1128, Thomas U.,0918, U.S.,1051, Virginia T.,0918
GRANTSTAFF, (Dr.),1112
GRAVERLY, ,0803, J.M.,0803
GRAVES & GILLIS, ,0874
GRAVES, Bartlett,0841, Benjamin,0842, Dr.,0767, Easter C.,1116, Frances G.,1116, J.B.,0768, John,0842, Lorenzo J.,1116, Martin,0849, Mary,1054,1116
GRAY, (Miss),1065, ,0807, Alexr.,0754, Amos,0757, Andrew T.,0754, C.H.,0764, Charles M.,0810, E.H.,0893, J.B.,0790,0797, J.M.,0782, John B.,0755, Lillie G.,0916, Mary A.,0977, R.L.B.,0893, Samuel,0916, William,0842,0845,0846,0853
GRAYSON, W.J.,0824,0852
GREEN & FITZHUGH, ,0983
GREEN & MCGILL, ,0874
GREEN, ,0863, A.L.P.,0809, Annie M.,1038, B.,0983, B.F.,0867, Blount G.,1151, Canzada P.,1151, Charley B.,0983, Clifton H.,0984, Cora E.,0984, E.J.,0797, Elizabeth,0983, Ella M.,0983, Emily J.,1151, H.,0781, Harriet F.,1151, Henry,0983
GREEN, J.H.,0837, James B.,1151, James F.,1151, Jane,0983, Jessie B.,1151, John,0843,0900,0983, Jonathan,0841, Judge(Senr.),0858, Katie E.,0983, Lewis D.,1151, Lydia C.,1199, Madison G.,0983, Maggie,0983,1038, Martha J.,0983, Mary A.,0984
GREEN, Mary E.,1151, Mary J.,0983, N.,0858, Nance,0880, Nancy C.,1151, Nathan Jr.,0858, Nathan,0763,0854,0859, Nathaniel,0974, Norton,0814, Pollie,0983, R.,1117, R.E.,0822, Robert,0983, S.,0801, Salina F.,1151, Samuel E.,1151, Samuel,0822
GREEN, Sarah A.,0973,0983, 0984, Sarah M.,0983, Sarah,0973,1151, Susan C.E.,1151, Susan Patsie,0983, Tennessee A.,1151, Thomas B.,1151, Thomas,0844,0983, W.C.,0895, W.P.,0878, William B.,0973, William,1151, Willis K.,0983,0984, Zachariah,0796
GREENE, Gen,0762, Gen.,0784, General,0766, Nathaniel,0754,0909, Orville,0857
GREENFIELD, ,0777, Catharine,0924, Frances O.,0924, G.T.,0756, James T.S.,0924, Jane H.Y.,0917,0924, Jerard,0924, Thos.,0777, Zilpha,0924
GREENLEE, James,0863
GREER, ,0863, Caroline,1159, Jane H.,1187, Jesse,0795, Joseph,0863, Mary,1187, Rebecca,1097, Ruth,0863, Sherwood,0794
GREGG, ,0895
GREGOR, James,0870
GREGORY, Annie,1152, B.T.,1151,1152, Benj.C.,0875, Benjamin H.,1152, G.W.,0863, H.,0819, Joseph P.,1151,1152, Thomas,1152
GRESHAM, Jane W.,0907, Joseph,0894
GREVOR, Dr.,0757
GRIBBLE, Ann W.,1006, Cannon,1095, Clingman,1095, Gertrude,1095, Hilda,1095, J.S.,0850,1095, Nora,1095,

Power,1095, Robert E.,1095,
S.J.(Mrs.),1095, Vida,1095
GRIDER, Ananias A.,1152,
G.(Mrs.),1152, John H.,
1152, Sarah J.,1152
GRIFFIN, ,0775, Dr.,0859,
James O.,0773, William,0893
GRIFFIS, Andrew J.,1205,
Bettie E.,1205, Nancy E.,
1205, T.M.,1205
GRIFFITH, ,0776, J.O.,0779,
Jas.O.,0779, Spencer,0775,
Susan,0917
GRIGBY, (Farm),1084
GRIGG & SMITH, ,0856
GRIGGS, Adelaide,0984,
Daisy D.,0984, Dewitt C.,
0984, Edgar C.,0984,
Effie J.,0984, Elizabeth H.,
0984, Henry C.,0984,
James B.,0984, Jane,0984,
John A.,0984, John L.,0984,
John,0984, Lena,0984,
Lucy A.,0984, Lucy M.,0984,
Madison,0984
GRIGGS, Mary A.,0984, Mary E.,
0984, Mary,0984, Maude E.,
0984, Owen J.,0984, Ruby B.,
0984, St.Elmo,0984, Thomas J.,
0984, Virginia T.,0984,
William M.,0984, William,
0984
GRIGSBY, Amanda C.,1095,
Fannie,1095, Fanny,1095,
J.V.,1095, Jennie P.,1231,
John V.,1095, Lewis K.,
1095, Mary C.,1095, Mary W.,
1095, Thomas R.,1095
GRIM, W.T.,0877
GRIMES, ,0776, Alice M.,0924,
Archie,0925, Capt.,0752,
Elizabeth,0924, Fannie,
1117, Henry A.,0924, James,
1117, John A.,0924, John B.,
0925, Mary,1117, Minnie,
0925, Robert L.,0925,
Samuel H.,0925
GRIMMER, Jacob,0797
GRISWOLD, W.T.,0878
GRIZARD, Dr.,0880
GRIZZLE, Pomp,0849
GROSS, A.,0768, C.C.,0770
GROVE, Henson,0772
GROVES, J.B.,0771
GRUNDY, Felix,0760,0765,0794,
0795,0814,0820,0827,0839,
J.P.,0797, James P.,1034
GUEST, Addie E.,0927, James L.,
0927, Malinda,1144
GUGENHEIM, Rosa A.,1091
GUGGER, Charles,0827
GUILD, J.C.,0797,0823
GUILL, James,1124, Lucy,1124
GULLETT, James,0766,0783
GULLEY, C.C.,0892, Martha A.,
1177
GUM, John,0819
GUNTER, C.D.,0875
GURLEY, ,0751, Martin,0795
GUTHRIE, Capt.,0799, J.F.,
0799, Robert,0797
GUY, John,0834
GWYNN & HINDS, ,0855
GWYNN & PEYTON, ,0854
GWYNN, ,0750, Hugh,0842, John,
0750
HADDON, Anna G.,0923, S.W.,
0923
HADDOX, Amanda Ellen,0950,
Sarah,0981
HADLEY, Johnson,0841, Susan J.,
0997, Susan,0945, W.T.,0782,
Wm.,0796
HAGAN, James,0893
HAGER, B.D.,0843
HAGGARD BROS., ,0879
HAGGARD, A.L.,0879
HAGLE, Esther,1164, Magie L.,
1164, Peter,1164
HAILEY, Cora E.,0984, Elizabeth,
0984, Henry,0984, Joanna,
0984, Kittie,0984, Laura,
0984, Mary A.,0984, Mary,

0984, Richard T.,0984, W.F.,
0878, William N.,0984
HAINES, J.W.,0878, R.B.,0818,
William,0842
HALBACH, Blanch,1156
HALBERT, Mary Beatie,1095,
Nancy,1095, Pleasant,1095,
Susan J.,1095, Thomas Edwin,
1095, Wm.Hay,1095
HALE BROS., ,0880
HALE, ,0813, Branch P.,1037,
Charles V.,1037, Edgar P.,
1037, Elizabeth C.,1037,
Ellis H.,1037, J.P.,1102,
J.R.,0856, James D.,1037,
Joseph P.,1037, Laura P.,
1037, Lena,1102, Mary E.,
1037, Rufus O.,1037, Sarah,
1220, Thomas J.,1037, W.J.,
0824
HALE, William S.,1037
HALEY & SONS, R.S.,0855
HALEY, ,0813, Amelia,0968,
Anderson,1153, Annie B.,
0985, Beulah E.,0984,
Clarence B.,0984, E.T.,
1153, E.T.Jr.,1153, George,
1153, James,1153, John A.,
0985, John C.,0984, John,
0984,0985, Kate M.,0985,
Linus P.,0985, Lula H.,
0985, Martha,1153
HALEY, Mary B.,1153, Mary,
0984, Mattie E.,0985, N.W.,
1153, Nancy,1153, Nannie T.,
0985, Samuella,0985,
Susanna,1153, Tolitha,0984,
0985, William C.,0985,
William S.,1153, Willie D.,
0985, Young W.,0985
HALL & WARNOCK, ,0880
HALL, (Mill),0868, ,0823,0861,
0863, Albert S.,1038, Allen,
0880, Amanda,1205, B.I.,
0878, Bailey,0843, Capt.,
0792, Catharine E.,1226,
Catharine,0945, Charlotta,
1037, Charlotte,1037,
Delphia C.,1038, Dorcas,
1121, Edmund,0793,0794,
Eliz.Mason,1070
HALL, Eliza J.,1073, Ella F.,
1153, Emmett E.,1153,
Frances,0794, Francis,0793,
Frank,0895, H.,0879,
Harriet P.,1179, Hugh A.,
0902, J.W.(Rev.),0838, J.W.,
0819,0839, Jimmie S.,1037,
John B.,1038, John L.,1038,
John T.,1153, John V.,1153
HALL, John W.,1037, John,0779,
0793,0863,1037, Joseph E.,
1153, Joseph,0893, Joshua,
0867,1153, Julia A.,1038,
Larraphine,1037, Margaret,
1134,1153, Mary J.,1037,
Mary L.,1037, Rainy I.,
1038, Rev.,0860, Sammy B.,
1153, Samuel,1121, Sarah E.,
1037
HALL, Thomas J.,0901,1038,
Thos.J.(Rev.),0887,
Thos.J.,0779,0838, W.R.,
0799, William A.,1037,
William J.,1153, William,
0797,0854
HALLEY, J.B.,0854
HALLUM, Capt.,0850, George,
0848,0854, Robert,0848, W.,
1105
HAM, C.Davis,0925, Dolly,0952,
F.D.,0799, Henry,0925,
Lucinda,0925
HAMBLEN, Joseph F.,1096,
Martha,1096, Sallie Foster,
1096, W.F.,1096
HAMER, Fal.,0870
HAMILTON, ,0751,0803,0809,
Andrew J.,1097, Capt.,0778,
Celia L.,1121, David,0784,
Dr.,0776, E.,0807, E.H.,
0896, Eliza,0985, Emma J.,
0932, Fredonia,1097, George,

1097, H.,0821, Hans,0814,
0815,0820, J.B.,0772, J.P.,
0804,0882, J.T.,0807
HAMILTON, J.W.,1116, J.W.Jr.,
1096, James G.,0848,
James W.,1096,1097, James,
0820,0855,0985,1081,1096,
1117, Jas.W.,0832,0839,
John B.,0755,0756,0759,
0784, John C.,0846, John M.,
1096, Joseph,0842, Lizzie M.,
0985, Maggie,0985, Margaret,
1096
HAMILTON, Nannie,1096,1125,
Rebecca A.,1097, Rebecca,
1097, Robt.Hatton,1096,
Ruth Lee,1096, Samuel,1097,
Susan,0947, T.,1125,
William N.,0985, William,
0820,1096, Wm.,0869, Wm.E.,
0985, Wm.E.Jr.,0985
HAMLER, William,0849
HAMLET, Byrd,0789, Elizabeth,
0984
HAMLETT, Capt.,0752
HAMLIN, J.W.,0868, John W.,
0867
HAMMOND, ,0775, Abram,0773,
Isaiah,1157
HAMMONDS, Abram,0774
HAMMONS, W.N.,0899
HAMNER, A.M.,0757, Saml.A.,
0783
HAMPSON, Capt.,0792
HAMPTON, Ann,0985, Aubra A.,
0985, Daniel A.,0985, David,
0805,0985, Elizabeth,0985,
Emily C.,0985, Emily,0985,
Eva G.,0985, Hammeditha,
0985, Harris B.,0985,
James C.,0985, John H.,
0985, Joseph H.,0985,
Louella,0985, Louisa,0985,
Lulu B.,0985
HAMPTON, Mary E.,0985, Mary,
0985, Nancy E.,0985,
Richard C.,0985, Richard,
0985, Rufus S.,0985,
Thomas P.,0985
HANCOCK, Addie,1097, Ann J.,
1097, Benjamin,1097, C.C.,
1090, Carrie,1098, Dawson,
0842,0850,0854, Delta,1097,
E.D.,0829,0871, Ed,0830,
Ed.,0819, Etna,1097,
Frances,1097, Hallie,1097,
Hettie L.,1097, Homer,1098,
Howard,1098, J.B.,0858
HANCOCK, J.B.,0859,1098, J.E.,
1098, James H.,1097,
Julia J.,1098, Kate,1097,
Lewis,1097, Margaret,1097,
Martha,1098, Martin,0871,
1098, Myrtle,1097, Polly,
1097, R.A.,1097, Richard,
1097, Samuel L.,1097,
Sophia,1098, Walter,1097,
Wesley,1097
HANCOCK, William,1098
HAND, Mary J.,0957
HANDCOCK, Martha,1098
HANDY, ,0803
HANEY, Clarkey,1105, Elija,
1105, Othelda,1105
HANKINS, Arthur,0842, L.H.,
0772, Martha P.,1099,
Matthew C.,1099, S.E.(Miss),
1099, T.J.,0852
HANKS, ,0750, Capt.,0751,
Church,0750, Elijah,0750,
0751, Elisha,0932, Emily,
0932, H.,0790, Richard,0766,
Thomas,0750
HANNA, ,0776, Capt.,0751,
James P.,0798, Margaret,
0923, Samuel,0923
HANNAH, Amelia,1098,1099,
J.M.,1113, James,0842,
John M.,1098, John Matthew,
1099, Minnie,1113, William,
0855,1098
HANNER, J.P.,0804, James P.,
0985,0989, James P.Jr.,0986,

John W.,0985,0986, Lizzie McR.,
0986, Loulia A.,0986, Mary,
0986, Rachael E.,0985
HANNES, J.P.,0804
HANNIS, David,0840
HANNUM, W.L.,0761, Washington L.,
0761
HANSBROUGH, William,0812
HARALSON, Beulah,1099, Chorus,
1099, Etta G.,1099, J.S.,
1099, James,1099, Jara,1099,
Leonard,1099, M.F.,1099,
Margaret,1099, Mary,1099,
Samuel,1099, Sarah,1099,
Zara,1099
HARBIN, Dr.,0778, Elijah,0781
HARBISON, Capt.,0752
HARBOR, Christian,0893
HARDEE, (Gen.),0918, ,0825
HARDEMAN, ,0810, Almira,0943,
Constant,0833, Frank,0759,
0791,0808, John,0795,0805,
N.P.,0793, Thomas,0764,
0809, Thos.,0802,0803
HARDEN, Capt.,0792, Isaac,
0769, John,0901
HARDER, Margaret,0919
HARDGRAVE, James,0805
HARDIN, Alexander,0796,
Burgess,0890, Dr.,0779, H.,
0893, Isaac B.,0761, J.B.,
0761, J.O.,0775,0782,
Martin,0759, Mary F.,1224,
Pleasant,1223, Richard,
0761, Robert,0779,0901,0902,
Robt.(Rev.),0783, Rosanna,
1215, Tabitha,1223, Thomas,
0766
HARDIN, Thos.H.,0890
HARDING, Caroline,1030, Gen.,
0755, J.,0854
HARDISON & TATE, ,0897
HARDISON, ,0777,0897, Andrew J.,
0925, Eliza A.,0925,
Emily J.,0955, Georgia,
1205, Hampton E.,0925,
Hampton J.,0925, Hampton,
0925, Harriet,0925, Humphrey,
0925, Ira,0926, James H.,
0925, Jane,0925,1206,
Jesse P.,0925, Joel,0900,
0925,1206
HARDISON, John J.,0925,
John T.,0925, Joshua,0900,
Margaret S.,1223, Marshall E.,
0925, Mary F.,0925, Mary J.,
0925, Mary,0926, Melvin A.,
0925, Millie A.,0926, S.L.,
0900, S.T.,0889,0897,
Samuel T.,1205, Tallie,
0925, Texannah,0925,
Thomas C.,0925
HARDISON, Wm.W.,0925
HARDSION, S.T.,0889
HARDY, Drucilla,0935, Gen.,
0825, Lee,0849, Wash,0848
HARE, Mary,1052
HARGRAVE, Capt.,0792, R.K.,
0809
HARKREADER, Ella L.,1099,
John F.,1099, Judith,1099,
Mr.,1100, W.M.,0847, Wm.M.,
1099
HARLAN, D.B.,0772, Henry,0781
HARLING, D.,0782
HARMON, Ada,1155, C.,0819,
Robert,0801, Thomas,0801
HARNESS, John,0789,0793
HARNEY, C.A.,0802
HARPOLD, H.,0771
HARPOLE, ,0846, Adam,0842,
John,0845,0846,0850, S.,
0853
HARRALSON, Lee,0842
HARRINGTON, Elizabeth,1100,
H.,1100, Higdon,0844, L.,
1100, T.,0854
HARRIS, (Capt.),1023, (Gov.),
1091,1178, ,0813,0863, A.,
0813, Adlai O.,0768, Ann L.,
0926, Anna L.,0926, Annie M.,
1038, Arthur,0842, Baker W.,
1098, Burr,0854, C.A.,0796,

Edmond,0759, Edward,0841,
0863, Eliz.A.,1178, Eliz.J.,
0926, Eliza,0991
HARRIS, Elizabeth,1020,1178,
Ellen B.,1088, Etheldred P.,
0847, G.,0800, G.T.,0757,
Gov.,0851, H.H.,0814,
Hiram C.,0892, Hiram,1153,
1206, Homer T.,1206,
Isabell R.,1101, James G.,
1206, James L.,0980,
James P.,1038, James,1187,
1206, Jane P.,1038
HARRIS, Jane P.,1206, Janie R.,
1038, John C.,1038, John,
1153, Judith,0962, Julia J.,
1098, Kittie V.,1038,
Lucy A.,1153, Lula M.,1206,
Maggie,1038, Martha,0925,
Mary A.,1206, Maxie,1210,
Millard F.,0926, Mr.,1039,
1154, N.C.,0877, Nancy,1118
HARRIS, Nancy,1119,1147,1187,
1206, Newton C.,0867,
Plummer W.,0850, R.C.,0899,
R.J.,0856, Robert B.,1038,
Robert C.,1206, Robert G.,
1038, Robt.,0807, Sarah H.,
0926, Sarah M.,0980,
Sarah T.,1187, Sarah,1098,
1137, Simpson,0761,0822,
Susan I.,1206
HARRIS, Susie R.,1038,
Thomas A.,0926, Thomas F.,
0926, Thomas,0813,0821,
Virginia L.,0926, W.,0902,
W.D.,1101, William,0841,
0842,0842
HARRIS/FRIERSON & CO., ,0912
HARRISON, ,0863, Anna,0986,
Annie James,0986, Benjamin,
0764, Christiana,0986,
Covoda,0986, Edith,1000,
Gideon,0842, Goldie,0986,
H.H.,0765, H.P.,0799, J.A.,
0832, J.E.,0808, J.W.,0967,
0991, James W.,0986, Joe,
0849, Logan,0874, Louisa,
1049
HARRISON, Martha,0986,
Mary E.,1158, Mary J.,1000,
Mary,0907,0997, Modera,
0986, Nathaniel L.,0986,
R.P.,0874, Robt.P.,0871,
Stiff,0854, Thos.(Gen.),
0963, Turner L.,0986, W.C.,
0831, W.H.,1097, William,
0986, Wm.,0850, Wm.P.,1000
HARRN, Adlai O.,0779
HARSH, Eliza,1090, George,
0854
HART, A.,0859, Carrie B.,1154,
Catherine E.,1154, James H.,
1154, James,1154, John W.,
1154, John,0796,1154,
Joseph,0768, Lillian C.,
1154, Lucretia,1154,1155,
Mary A.,1154, Narcissa,
1154, Nathaniel B.,1154,
Rachel,1154, Sarah,1154,
Stephen,1154
HART, Susan,1154, Thomas,0878,
1154, Virginia,1154,
William G.,1154
HARTGROVE, James,0795
HARTIN, Henry,0764
HARTLEY, Ella,0965, Emeline M.,
0995, Laburn,0965,0995,
Nancy,0965, Sallie,0965
HARTMAN, A.,0829, Alex,0831,
Alexr.,0830
HARTPENCE, A.(Rev.),0783
HARTSFIELD, William,0850,1077,
Wm.,0854
HARTWELL, A.,0831, Mary,1071
HARWOOD, Mary E.,0929
HASEA, Fannie P.,0954, L.M.,
0954
HASKELL, J.,0795,0827, John,
0827, Joshua,0762,0826,0830
HASKINS, Elizabeth,1228, J.R.,
1228, Julia,1174
HASLETT, William,0862

HASSEL, Althea,1007
HASTING, ,0863, E.N.,0926
HASTINGS, Duncan,0926, Elvira,
0926, Henry,0862, John,0868,
0926, Joseph,0867, Mary,
0926, Robert,0862, Stephen,
0862
HATCHER & JOHNSON, ,0854
HATCHER, A.,0799, Abram W.,
0986, Charles W.,0987,
Elizabeth R.,0987, Ernest L.,
0986, George A.,0987,
James C.,0987, John E.,
0773, Lucy J.,0987, Lucy,
0986, Madeline,0987,
Mary S.,0986,0987, Robert A.,
0986, Sallie A.,0987,
William D.,0986
HATCHER, William,0986
HATCHETT & CALAHAN, ,0897
HATCHETT, John,0890,0891,0893,
0896
HATTON, (Gen.),1116, Robert,
0850,0851
HAWES, Isabella,1161
HAWKINS, ,1091, Alvin,1137,
Eleanor,0984, Elizabeth H.,
0984, Gov.,0871, J.M.,0895,
,0897, Lucas P.,0984, Marcus,
0849, Mariah J.,0984,
Mary A.,0984, Millie H.,
0984, Richard,0842, Rob,
0822, W.D.,0890, William,
0984
HAWKS, Annie T.,1094, Cassandra,
1094, Preston,1094
HAWTHORN, Adam,1036, Sarah,
1036
HAY ,0796, John,0893,
Richard,0796, W.A.,0799
HAYDEN & FISHER, ,0768
HAYES, ,0762, Andrew,0773,
Benjamin,0926, Capt.,0851,
Catharine,1048, Charles,
0926, Eliza B.,0927, Eliza,
0926, Fannie R.,0927,
Fannie,0927, George W.,
0920,0927, Hiram,1206,
James,0902,0926, Jane,1115,
John B.,0757, John D.,0927,
John,0850
HAYES, Margaret E.,0927,
Marica L.,0927, Marinie,
0926, Martha P.,0927,
Mary L.,0927, Nancy E.,
0927, Nancy,0927,1222,
Preston,0796, Sallie,1206,
Samuel D.,0926,0927,
Samuel,0926, Sarah W.,0927,
Thomas,1048, V.O.,0897,
Valentine O.,1206
HAYES, Whitman L.,0926,
William,0926, Wm.S.,0927
HAYNE, Robert Y.,0816
HAYNES & CO., J.A.,0854, W.R.,
0874
HAYNES HOLOWELL & CO., ,1039
HAYNES, (Col.),1192,1229, ,
0796,0803,0829, Anderson,
1100, Betty,0987, Ed,0803,
Elizabeth H.,0987, Elizabeth,
1100, Elvira,1039, Ivy J.C.,
1024,1039, J.A.,1100, J.B.,
0900,0902, J.H.,0897,
J.I.C.,0829,0831, J.M.,
0830,0897, J.R.,0894, J.W.,
0878
HAYNES, James,0886,0898,
John A.,0854,0855, John,
0887,1100, Kate S.,1154,
Lizzie,0987, Lucy L.,1024,
Margaret,1100, Martha,1100,
Mary B.,1154, Metta,0987,
Milton A.,0894, Minnie,
0987, Mollie E.,1154, N.J.,
0798,0804,0987, Narcissa J.,
1191
HAYNES, Narcissa,0987, Natus,
0987, P.C.,0896, R.R.,1154,
Sadie,1154, Sarah A.,1154,
Sophia M.,1039, T.E.,0791,
0804, Thos.Elliot,0987,
W.R.,1154, William R.,1039,

Wm.R.,1039, Wm.R.Jr.,1154
HAYS, Andrew,0795, Cynthia,
  1209, Dr.,0758, F.,1100,
  Fannie,1100, Harmon,0842,
  Hattie M.,1100, Henry,0781,
  James P.,1100, James T.,
  1100, John T.,0843, John,
  1186, Lee,1100, Lockie D.,
  1100, M.P.,1100, Marlinda,
  1100, Martha L.,1100,
  Mary E.,1100
HAYS, May L.,1199, Nancy E.,
  1186, Stokley,1100
HAYWOOD, E.P.C.,1207, G.W.,
  0899, George W.,0899,1207,
  Isabelle,1207, John,0762,
  0822,0841, Judge,0762,
  Sarah B.,1207
HAZELETT, ,0886
HAZELWOOD, John,0834, Rhoda,
  0834
HAZLETT, Spencer,0822, Wm.,
  0871
HEALAN, S.D.(Mrs.),0878
HEALEY, W.W.,0805
HEARN & HILL, ,0854
HEARN, ,0803, Alice F.,1049,
  Anna E.,0987, Cleopatra,
  1090, Drucilla,1120, E.M.,
  0852, E.Marcellus,0987,
  George,0843, John B.,0987,
  John,0848,0854, Louisa D.,
  0987, Mary Alice,0987,
  Milbry,1115, Mr.,0988,
  Nancy,1115, P.,0850, P.W.,
  0844
HEARN, Purnell,0841, T.R.,
  0844, W.R.,0812, Wash,0849,
  Whitson P.,0987
HEDGE, G.D.,0770, George,0768,
  J.M.,0770, James,0768,
  Most,0768, Saml.(Rev.),
  0782, W.R.,0779, Wm.R.,0768
HEGAN, Thomas,0831
HELEN, Maria,1028
HELM, (Lt.),0978, Elizabeth,
  1147, Fannie,1117, M.,0768,
  Meredeth,0766, Meredith,
  0755
HELMS, George,0854, John C.,
  1009, Thomas,0851, W.H.,0816
HELTON, Susanna,1134
HENDERSON & CO., ,0829,1112
HENDERSON & RUTLEDGE, ,0766
HENDERSON, (Rev.),0814,0821,
  ,0776, Agnes,1122, Amanda,
  1039, Andrew,0778, B.H.,
  0822, Bennett H.,0819,
  Capt.,0850, Clifford C.,
  1039, Col.,0823, Dorothea,
  1112, Elizabeth,0909,
  Estella,1039, Frances,0838,
  Frank,1039,1048, G.T.(Mrs.),
  0835
HENDERSON, G.T.,0824,0831,
  0835, H.M.,0821, Henrietta,
  1112, Henry,0838, Hortense,
  1039, Jack,0875, James F.,
  1039, James,0815,0982,
  John C.,0847, John H.,1002,
  John,0821,0838, L.,0808,
  Lizzie E.,1002, Logan,1039,
  Marcella,1106, Margaret E.,
  1039
HENDERSON, Mary,1106,1137,
  Medra,1039, Mr.,0768,
  Octavine,1039, Parson,0750,
  Preston,1112, R.K.,0831,
  Rob,0807, Robert,0782,0838,
  0839, S.,1122, Sallie M.,
  1009, Samuel,1009, Sarah M.J.,
  0982, Sophia D.,1048,
  Susana,0838, Temperance,
  0941
HENDERSON, Vansinderan,1039,
  Violet,1048, William,1106
HENDERSON, Wm.,0887
HENDLEY, (Mr.),0927, A.S.,
  0773, Elvira E.,0927,
  George S.H.,0927, H.L.,
  0772, Hiram L.,0927
HENDRICK, J.T.,0750, Joseph,
  0846

HENDRICKS & EDWARDS, ,0897
HENDRICKS, James,0888,0890,
  Jere,0842, Jeremiah,0841,
  Joseph,0843, W.W.,0902
HENLEIN, Moses,0829
HENRY, F.,0815,0826, M.M.,
  0819, Mary,1004,1061, T.B.,
  1061
HENSLEY, Rev.,0777
HENSON, Joseph,0820, T.C.,
  0879
HEPWORTH, Willis,0901
HERBERT, Dr.,0851
HERNDEN, Joseph,0751
HERNDON, ,0820, J.B.,0770,
  Jos.,0752, Joseph,0756,
  0760,0768,0783,0794,0818,
  0819
HEROD, John,0846
HERROD, John,0844,0846,0854,
  Lemuel,0846
HERRON, James H.,1011, M.M.,
  1011, Maria,1011
HESS, William R.,0849
HESSA, Margaret,1099
HEULETT, J.J.,0781
HEWETT, Caleb,0821
HEWGLEY, C.W.,1109, Josephine,
  1109
HIBBITTS, David C.,0848
HICKENBOTHAM, Joseph,0862
HICKERSON, Joseph,1162, Nancy,
  1162, Sallie,1162
HICKEY, A.C.,0892, John M.,
  0759
HICKLIN, A.M.,0762, Polly,
  0762
HICKMAN, Adaline,1021, Ewin,
  1002, Mary T.,1121, Snowdon,
  0841, William,0862, Wm.,0880
HICKS & JOHNSON, ,0854
HICKS BROS., ,0874
HICKS, ,0813, Alsie D.,1148,
  Bettie,1178, D.D.,1148,
  G.W.,1013, George,0777,
  James,0794,0795,0801,
  Malinda,1148, Patsy,0891,
  William,0822
HIGHT, Alice,1154, Eula R.,
  1154, Lucy J.,1154, Mary N.,
  1154, Mary,0950, Naomi E.,
  1154, Naomi,1154, Nola P.,
  1154, W.G.,1154, Wm.E.J.,
  1154
HIGHTOWER, Jennie,0974, R.R.,
  0803, Richard,0789,0793,0794
HILAND, Eliza,0952, Joseph D.,
  0952, Matilda J.,0952
HILDRETH, S.P.,0804
HILL, ,0775,0823,0827, A.P.,
  1108, A.W.,0764, Adeline,
  1087, Alexander,0927, Allen,
  0820, Amaca W.,1207,
  Annie B.,1039, B.,1087,
  Ben,1207, Betty,0987, C.A.,
  0819, Capt.,0792,0850,
  Catherine,1207, Charles H.,
  0988, Charley B.,1039, Col.,
  1158
HILL, D.H.(Gen.),1207, D.H.,
  1002, David,0807, Easter J.,
  0988, Eliza M.,1039,
  Elizabeth H.,1207, Elizabeth P.,
  0960, Elizabeth,0935,1207,
  Elmira,0928, Emma P.,0988,
  Esther B.,1207, Eula R.,
  1207, Florence S.,1039, H.,
  0796, H.R.W.,0774
HILL, H.R.W.,0808, Harry,0772,
  Herbert N.,1039, Hugh,0988,
  Ida L.,1207, Isaac,0910,
  J.C.,0889, J.Spencer,0928,
  J.W.,0800,0809, J.W.M.,
  0793, Jacob,1161, James B.,
  0927, James E.,0928,
  James N.,0988, James R.,
  0988, James W.,1039, James,
  0812
HILL, James,0819,0843,0927,
  0939, Jane,0927,0988, Jesse,
  0849, John F.,1207, John H.,
  0988, John M.,0854, John R.,
  0888,0889,0891,0988,1207,

John T.,1207, John W.,1039,
  John,0813,0814,0815,0819,
  0820,0821,0903, Joseph F.,
  0988, Leanna,1207
HILL, Lemuel R.,1207, M.F.,
  1087, Margaret C.,0988,
  Margaret F.,0928, Margaret,
  0910, Maria,0960, Martha,
  1096, Mary A.,0935, Mary A.R.,
  1207, Mary E.,1195, Mary J.,
  0939, Mary W.,0988, Mary,
  0928,1031, Matilda,0927,
  Mattie,0833, Maud,1207
HILL, Middleton,0935, Midleton,
  0927, Missie,1207, Nancy J.,
  0928, Nancy,0928,1195, Nona,
  0928, O.P.,0830, Olive,0927,
  Ophelia H.,0988, P.Y.,1113,
  Peggie,0928, R.F.,0796,
  Rachel,1045, Rebecca,1161,
  Richard,0793, Robert H.,
  0928, Robert,0754
HILL, Robert,0759,0760,0793,
  0988, Robt.,0807, Rucker B.,
  1207, Sadie C.,1039,
  Sallie A.,0988, Sarah E.,
  0928, Sarah M.,1039, Sarah,
  0910, Susan A.,0988,
  Susan E.,0988, Susan I.,
  1206, Susan J.,0988,
  Susie R.,1038, Talitia C.,
  0988, Thomas R.,0988
HILL, Thomas,0927, William C.,
  0960, William G.,1039,
  William L.,1207, William,
  1207, Wm.H.,0927, Wyatt,0891
HILLIARD, Isaac,0826
HILLIS, Samuel,0893
HILLS, I.H.,0895
HILLSMAN, John T.,1143, M.,
  0836
HILTON, Edward,0869
HIMES, Elizabeth,1134
HINDS & PETERS, ,0768
HINES, Sophia,1098
HINKLE, M.M.,0825
HINSE & HANNAH, ,0855
HIRSCH & CO., M.,1040
HIRSCH, H.,0833, Henry,1040,
  Minnie,1062, Moses,1040
HIRSH & CO., M.,0829
HIRST, Mathew,0821
HIST, Christopher,0827
HITE & TAYLOR, ,0875
HIX, ,0863, Ada,1155, Ailsey C.,
  1155, Asenith M.,1155,
  Benjamin F.,1155, Demarcus D.,
  1155, Emily,1132, Hulda,
  1155, J.H.,0875,1155, J.L.,
  0872,1155, James H.,1155,
  John A.,1155, John C.,0868,
  1132, John,1155, Joseph J.,
  1155, Lillie A.,1155
HIX, Louisa B.,1152,1153,
  Louisa F.,1155, Lucinda S.,
  1159, Malinda,1155, Martha A.,
  1155, Martha W.J.,1155,
  Mary E.,1155, Phineas,0880,
  Rebecca,1169, Sarah J.,
  1132, William S.,1155,
  William,0862, Wm.W.,1155
HOBBS, Bertha J.,0928,
  Clarence J.,0928, Cornelia B.,
  0928, Earnest W.,0928,
  Enna E.,0928, George W.,
  1171, James,0843, Jane A.,
  0928, Jane C.,0928, John C.,
  0928, Jordan,0928, Lizzie A.,
  0928, Maggie L.,0928,
  Martha O.,0928, Martha,0928
HOBBS, Sarah,1171, Susan E.,
  1127, Theodosia H.,1171,
  Thomas J.,0928, Thomas M.,
  0928
HOBSON, Alfred,0890, Drusilla,
  1103, Henry,1119, Lucy,1119,
  Polly,1113, Wm.T.,0851
HOCKS, Mrs.,0767
HODGE & SMITH, ,0829,1033,
  1040,1064
HODGE, A.A.,0771, Elisha,0842,
  Elizabeth,1049, Emma Sue,
  1040, Emma,1040, Florence,

1040, George C.,0844,
George W.,1040, John,0754,
0767,0768,0769, Lillian,
1040, Mary A.,1053, Mary J.,
1136, Molly,0977, Samuel H.,
0818,1039,1040, Sarah C.,
1039
HODGE, Wm.R.,0772
HOEHNLEIN, M.,0832
HOESLEY, Wm.(Rev.),0783
HOFFMAN, ,0828, J.,0835
HOGAN & MCMAHON, ,0802
HOGAN, J.(Jr.),0804, J.Jr.,
0802, William,0841
HOGE, Eliza A.,0928, George S.,
0928, Harvey,0988, Hervey,
0776, James H.,0988,
Lucy A.,0988, Moses,0928,
Thomas,0796,0804, Willie L.,
0928
HOGG, John,0846, Phoebe,1085,
Samuel,0850,0853, Thomas,
0855
HOLBERT, J.W.,0855
HOLCOMB, K.,0794
HOLDEMAN, C.V.,0803
HOLDEN, C.M.,0831, Catharine,
1004, G.W.,0818, W.B.,0889,
0895, William B.,1225
HOLDER, Gilbert E.,0869,
John W.,1154, Virginia,
1154, W.H.,0894, William,
HOLDING, R.,0768,0770,0773
HOLEMAN, Nancy M.,0916,
Robert M.,0848
HOLIWAY, Sarah A.,0983,0984
HOLLAND, ,0863, Asa,0888,
J.A.,0793, J.P.,0895,
James(Maj.),0784, Thos.,
0867, Thos.G.,0872
HOLLENELL & CO., ,0829
HOLLINGSWORTH, ,0797
HOLLINSWORTH, J.R.,0900
HOLLOWAY, Eunice,1115,
Ezekiel,1084, Levi,0841,
Maggie,1115, Richard,1115,
Sarah J.,1084
HOLLOWELL & CO., G.S.,1039
HOLLOWELL, Ann M.,1040,
Bessie,1040, Edwin C.,1040,
George S.,1039, Lena,1040,
Mary Ann,1040, Nancy P.,
1043, Nannie P.,1040, T.H.,
1043, Thomas R.,1039,1040,
Thomas,1040
HOLMAN & HOLMAN, ,1036
HOLMAN, (Capt.),1219, America,
1126, D.W.,0800, Isaac,1126,
Lee,0772, Marcia,1085,
Sophia A.,1085, W.F.,0875,
William S.,1085
HOLMES, D.Henry,0840, Henry,
0826,0827, J.,1108, James,
0816,0831, John,0816,0831,
0901, Lucinda R.,1108, Mary,
0901,1108, Sophronia,1191,
T.P.,0782, Virginia,1079
HOLT, ,0883, Albert A.,0929,
Berry D.,1155, Bettie,1155,
Blanch,1156, Cecil R.,1156,
Elizabeth,1155, Eva,0991,
H.F.,0868, H.H.,0871,
Henry,0867,1155, Herbert F.,
1156, Herrod F.,0867, Hulda,
1155, Isaac B.,0867, J.N.,
0902, James B.,1155
HOLT, James M.,0929, Jane B.,
1127, Jeremiah F.,0929,
Jeremiah,0929, Jerry,0929,
Jesse,0843, John H.,0991,
John W.,1155, John,0864,
0870, Joshua,0863, Josie,
0991, Lucretia,1155,
Mary E.(Mrs.),0991, Mary,
0929,1155, Mattie,1155,
Michael,0862
HOLT, Molly L.,0929, Nancy,
1031, Robert B.,0929,
Sullenger,0872, W.H.,0764,
William T.,1155, William,
0929, Willie,0991, Wm.L.,
0929
HOOD, (Gen.),0959,1205, Capt.,

0850, John B.,0824, John C.,
0800, Josephine,1045
HOOKER JR., Benj.,0856
HOOKER, B.F.,1130, Benjamin,
0842,1080, Capt.,0792, Cloe,
1111, J.,0837, Polly,1080
HOOPER, Elizabeth A.,1074,
P.(Mrs.),0830, W.J.,1074
HOOSER, Daniel,0871, Mary A.,
1133, Rebecca,1133, William,
1133
HOOTEN, John W.,0897
HOOVER, ,0813,0863, Albert A.,
1156, Alice D.,1156,
Anna M.,1156, Benjamin,
1156, Calladona J.,1156,
Charles M.,1156, Christopher,
1156, Clementine F.,1156,
Cleopatra,1156, E.R.,0901,
Edward C.,1156, Effie M.,
1156, Eliz.E.,1156, Elizabeth,
1156
HOOVER, Frances,1147, George C.,
1156, H.C.,1147, Harvey F.,
1156, Hugh L.,1156, James F.,
1156, James,0867,1156, John,
0815, M.J.,1156, Martha A.,
1156, Martha J.,1050,
Mary E.,1156, Mary J.,1128,
Nancy E.,1156, R.A.,0879,
Robt.W.,1156
HOOVER, Susan O.,1156, Susan,
1156, Thomas R.,1147,
Thomas,0821, W.,0818,
William,1128
HOOZIER, ,0863
HOPE & CO., ,0875
HOPE, Jane,1086
HOPEWOOD, Marshall,0892
HOPKINS, Carrie,1136, Chlora A.,
1220, James,0793, Lizzie,
1034, Margaret E.,1189, Mr.,
0775
HOPSON, George,1044, Mildred,
1044
HOPWOOD & MCGREGOR, ,0897
HOPWOOD DABNEY & CO., ,0896
HOPWOOD, Julia A.,1209, N.S.,
1213, Penelope,1209,
Willis M.,0896,1209,
Willis,1209
HORD, ,0863, Ada B.,1034
HORN, Abigail,1101, Bettie,
1100, Burrell,1101, Elizabeth N.,
1100, Etheldred P.,1100,
Fannie,1100, Isabell N.,
1101, J.M.,1101, James A.,
1100, James B.,1100,
Margaret A.,1100
HORNER & CO., ,0874
HORSELEY, ,0863
HORSLEY, A.S.,0773, Alf,0771,
Wm.,0753
HORTON & CARL, ,0803
HORTON, ,0793, H.C.,0808,
H.H.,0808
HOSKINS, C.H.,0988, Charles H.,
0988, Fannie E.,0988,
James T.,0988, John W.,
0988, Josie T.,0988,
Lulu T.,0988, Nannie E.,
0988, Robert J.,0988,
Robert T.,0988, Sterling F.,
0988, Tennessee,0988,
William B.,0988
HOUSE BROS., ,0803
HOUSE, Bettie,1023, Dudley P.T.,
0867, Evie,0989, J.& M.,
0803, John L.,0798, M.,1121,
Mansfield,0989, Mary,0958,
S.J.,0989, S.S.,0790,0797,
0798, Sallie J.,0989,
Samuel S.,0988,0989,
Sarah J.,0988, Susan E.,
1063, T.S.,0800, William,
0988
HOUSE, William,1014
HOUSTON & STILWELL, ,0899
HOUSTON, Abner,0886,0888,0890,
0896,0897, Benj.F.,1207,
C.P.,1156, C.P.Jr.,1156,
Caroline,0869, F.R.,0762,
J.D.,0878, Jane,1156,

Lilian,1156, Medora A.,
1208, Mrs. R.G.,0772,
Necie B.,1207, P.D.,0897,
P.Q.,0900, Persis B.,1207,
Russell,0764
HOUSTON, Sam,0850, Saml.,0795,
Samuel,0926,1208, Sidd,
0878, Syd,1156, W.A.,0890,
William(Jr.),0868
HOW, Sarah(Mrs.),1201
HOWARD, (Capt.),0786, Bradford,
0842, Emma J.,0911, Fana,
1167, Fannie,0929, J.D.,
0786, J.H.,0770, J.W.,0771,
0921, Jacob,0854, John A.J.,
0929, John K.,0850,0851,
John W.,0929, John,0929,
Margaret,0929,1174,
Mary J.,0921, Mary M.,0929
HOWARD, Mary R.,0929, Sallie,
1174, Thomas,0929, William,
0843, Wm.Jordan,0929
HOWE, (Gen.),1206, ,0974
HOWELL, Crawford,0836, Dandy,
0874, James,0813, John,0813,
0819, Moses,0849, R.B.,0838,
Thomas,0811, William,0814
HOWLAND BROS., ,0879
HOWLET, Martha,1035
HOWLETT, Adah B.,0930,
Addison B.,0930, Elizabeth,
0930, Isaac J.,0930, J.S.,
0889, Jennie L.,0930,
Kirby S.,0930, Lizzie D.,
0930, Mary I.,0930, Minnie M.,
0930, S.B.,0899,0930
HOWS, Ella,0992, Jack,0993
HOWSE, Adaline W.,1071,
Ambrose,1071, Martha L.,
1063, Mary E.,1053, Mary,
HOWSER, Alice E.,0939, F.O.,
0939
HOYL, J.D.,0872
HOYLE & CARPENTER, ,0898
HUBBARD, ,0823, J.L.,0843,
Nathan,0862, Thomas,0820
HUBBEL, ,0813
HUBBERT, J.M.,0859
HUDDLESTON, Alice,1101, J.W.,
0889,1101, Josie,1101,
Mary B.,1114, Mary,1101,
Nellie,1101, T.L.,0856,
Valeria,1114, W.W.,1101,
Winston,1114
HUDLESTON, Mary E.,1078, Mary,
1078, William W.,1078
HUDLOW, John,0872
HUDSON & CO., ,0880
HUDSON, A.B.,0760, C.Y.,0752,
Thomas,0862, William,0842
HUDSPETH, ,0750, James,0763,
Thomas,0761
HUEY, ,0777, James,0760,0766,
Susan,0912, Wm.G.,0912
HUFF, W.L.,0798
HUFFMAN, Alice,1157, Eliza,
1157, George C.,1156, John,
1157, Mary A.,1157, Mary,
1157, Martie J.,1157,
Sallie A.,1157, Thomas L.,
1157
HUFMAN, Angeline,1146
HUGGINS & SEAGRAVES, ,0855
HUGGINS, C.B.,0831, Camillus B.,
1040, Elizabeth W.,1040,
Jonathan,1040, Martha L.,
1219, Mr.,1041, Sallie,1012,
Sarah E.,1041, W.S.,0829,
0835
HUGH & DAVID, ,0843
HUGHES, A.M.,0772,0779,0892,
A.M.Jr.,1137, Alexr.R.,
0990, Amos,0764, Arch,0990,
B.R.,0989, E.(Mrs.),0989,
E.P.,0989, Elizabeth,0989,
Ennis,0990, Fannie,0989,
G.R.,0989, G.T.,0770,
George R.,0989, J.P.,0808,
James T.,0989, James,0988
HUGHES, L.B.,0990, Leander,
0990, Lee Sr.,0990, Leonard,
0990, Letitia,1000, Martha A.,
0990, Martha,0990, Mr.,0764,

0990, Nancy P.,0990, Nannie,
0989, Narcissie,0989,0990,
P.M.,0808, Richard,0989,
Susan E.,0988, Susan,0988,
Willie,0990
HUGHES, Wm.R.,0798, Wm.S.,
0989
HUGHLITT & HARRIS, ,0854
HUGLEY, Margaret,1096
HULEY, W.M.M.,0805
HULME, George,0794,0797,0801,
Permelia A.,0989, W.B.,
0797, William,0789, Wm.,0794
HUMBOLD, (Factory),1096
HUME, Alfred,1017, Anna M.,
1017, Mary,1017
HUMPHREYS, P.W.,0827, Parry W.,
0761,0794,0819,0820
HUMPHRIES, Fannie H.,0992
HUNGARFORD, Permelia A.,0989
HUNT, Alfred,0772, Betsy,0848,
David,0848, Father & Dau.,
0848, G.W.,0793, J.D.,0772,
J.S.,0757, Mary C.,1066,
Mary,0910, R.A.,0792,
Rosanna A.,1115, Samuel,
1116, Sarah C.,1067, Sion,
0789,0794, W.G.,0796,
William,0819
HUNTER & CO., ,0930
HUNTER, ,0775, Anna M.,0990,
Annie A.,0993, Aris M.,
0930, Bessie E.,0930, Capt.,
0850,0872, Charles P.,1156,
Cynthia,1209, Dr.,0776,
E.I.,0890, E.W.,1156,
Eliza J.,0935, Emily,1156,
Ephraim,0888,0890,1209,
Ethel,0930, Eugene D.,0930
HUNTER, Evan W.,0930, Frank W.,
1156, Fred,0930, George B.,
0990, Georgia,0930, Hendly B.,
0990, Henry,0990, Ida L.,
1156, Isaac,1119, J.B.,0894,
0896,1156, J.R.,0803,0875,
James B.,1156, James M.,
0930, James M.Jr.,0930,
James M.Sr.,0930
HUNTER, James N.,1209, James,
0842, Jane W.,0990, John H.,
0990, Lou M.,0990, Margaret B.,
1156, Margaret M.,1156,
Margaret,0929, Martha G.,
0915, Martha M.,0990,
Martha,1119, Mary A.,0930,
Mary C.,1156, Mary,0930,
1209, Mollie,0930, Mrs.,0997
HUNTER, R.H.,1209, R.P.,0894,
Rev.,0776, Robert P.,1156,
Roberta G.,0990, Sarah E.,
1156, Sarah M.,1156, Selina,
1119, Susanna,1156, Thomas H.M.,
1156, W.G.J.,0914,0930,
W.J.G.,0772, Wm.J.,0779
HURST, Bird,0820, James,0871,
Robert,0868, W.S.,1147
HURT, ,0777, Bird,0766, Capt.,
0751, Elisha,0902
HUSTON, C.P.,0874
HUTSON, J.L.,0871
HUTTON, Ann E.,1230, Frances,
1208, J.W.,1208, John D.,
0877, John P.,0868, John W.,
0889,1208, John,1208,
Margaret E.,1208, Margaret,
1063, Mary C.,1152,1208,
Polk,1208, Rosa L.,1230,
Sallie,1208, Susan,1208,
Thomas C.,1208, Thomas,1152
HUTTON, Thomas,1208, William,
1208
HYDE, Sallie,1192
HYERONEMUS, ,0803
ICEMEYER, Wm.R.,0827
IMPSON, John,0853
INDIAN, Big Foot,0784
INDIANS, Names,0796
INGLE, J.P.,0874
INGRAM, J.E.,0771, Julia,0911,
W.P.,0771,0773
IRELAND, Addie,1102, Benjamin W.,
1101, Benjamin,1117, David,
0842, Fannie,1101,1102,
Hanson,1102, Laura,1102,
Maggie,1101, R.M.,1101
IRVIN, Andrew,0995, B.B.,0789,
Eleanor,0997, Elizabeth,
0995, James P.,0998,
Marilda,0995, Robert I.,
0998, Robert,0998
IRVINE & BLACK, ,0897
IRVINE, Alex,0759, Eliza,
1209, Joe A.,0787, Mamie,
1209, Narcissa,1209,
Nathaniel,1209, Roy,1209,
W.P.,0897, William P.,1209,
Wm.,0759
IRWIN, Bertram M.;0930,
Dorcas,0941, Fannie,0930,
Horace O.,0930, J.D.,0821,
J.W.,0930, John,0853,
Knox H.,0930, Lelia I.,
0930, Mollie,0934, Wm.M.,
0930, Thomas G.,1041
ISACKS, Jacob C.,0795
ISOM, ,0776, James,0751, John,
1113, Mary C.,1113, Rebecca,
1113
IVES, Nathnl.,0772
IVEY, Charles S.,0871, F.B.,
0871, Thos.B.,0882
IVIE, C.D.,1184, Charles D.,
1041, Jennie,1184, Judith,
1041, Sallie,1041, T.B.,
1028, Thomas G.,1041
IVY, ,0813, A.W.,0799,
Frederick,0792, Isaac,0793
JACK, (Mr.),0913, Jack Wm.E.,
0931, John F.,0795, Lecey J.,
0930, Louisa,0931, Rosena S.G.,
0931, Samuel E.G.,0930,
William,0930
JACKSON, (Gen.),0977,1072,
Alex,0893, Amelia,1214,
Andrew,0827,0831,0863,1081,
Ann,0869, Calvin W.,0850,
Capt.,0792, Clara,1041,
Cora,1041, Elizabeth S.,
1214, Elizabeth Z.,1035,
Elizabeth,1084, Emma L.,
1041, Flora,1041, Gen.,0751,
0755
JACKSON, Gen.,0893,0998,1002,
1008,1033,1050, H.C.,0832,
Howell E.,0765,0962,
Indiana,1041, Isham,0848,
James,1210, Jennie,1084,
John A.W.,0891, John J.,
0971, John,1150, Margaret,
1210, Mark,0778,0784,
Martha L.,1150, Martha,
0971,1210
JACKSON, Nancy M.,1165,
Nathan R.,1041, President,
0765, Rebecca,1150, Ruth,
1041, Samuel,0974, Stonewall,
0798, Susan,1048, Thomas R.,
1084,1214, W.A.,0899,
Willoughby A.,1209, Wm.F.,
1041
JACOBS, Ann E.,0931, Edward G.,
0843, Elizabeth,1047,
Joseph R.,0931, Louisa,
0931, Neddie,0853, William,
0931, Wm.J.,0931
JAMERARY & TOMPKINS, ,1068
JAMERARY, Lizzie,1068
JAMES & COLLIER, ,0829
JAMES, A.S.,0772, Amanda K.,
1200, E.H.,0836, Emily,1200,
Emma C.,1072, G.N.,0810,
J.H.,0768, Jennie,1200,
Lazarus,0841, Louisa D.,
0987, Nannie,1200, Pleasant L.,
1200, Rev.,0860, William R.,
1200
JAMESON, (Miss),1216, Clarence H.,
0931, Elizabeth,0931,
Georgia,0930, H.D.,0816,
John W.T.,0931, John,0931,
Margaret R.,0931, Mary A.,
0930, Robert C.,0931,
Sarah A.,0911, Thomas E.,
0931, W.A.,0930, Wm.A.,0930
JAMISON & MILLER, ,0879
JAMISON, (Maj.),0786, A.,1110,
Atha T.,1042, Camilla T.,
1042, Ella,1042, Evis C.,
1042, Fannie,1110, Henry D.,
1041,1042, J.,1110, Maddie,
1042, Olivia M.,1046,
Robert D.,1041, Samuel P.,
1042, Sarah W.,1041, T.E.,
0786
JANUARY, J.A.,0826, R.W.(Mrs.),
0829, W.H.,0838
JARMAN, G.W.,0836
JARMON, Robert,0842
JARNETT, D.M.,0822
JARRATT, Mary F.,1076
JARRELL, A.J.,0874,1157,
Helen,1157, Martha,1157,
Wesley,1157
JARRETT, Bettie,1074, Claibourn R.,
0851, George,0844, J.A.,
0903, Rev.,0860
JARRIT, Capt.,0752
JASSEY, W.W.,0779
JEFFERSON, Pres.,0755, Thomas,
1020
JEFFRESS, Annie Lee,1157,
Frances A.,1157, James D.,
1157, Pollie H.,1157,
Sallie H.,1157, Thomas B.,
1157, Thos.Ewing,1157
JENKINS, (Col.),1192, Anna M.,
1042, Beulah,1042, Clement B.,
1042, Elizabeth,1192, G.A.,
0799, Henry,0805, Hiram H.,
1042, Hiram,1042, James F.,
1042, Kate B.,1042, Lizzie,
1042, Margaret C.,1185,
Mary A.,1042, Minnie S.,
1042, Nancy,1042
JENKINS, Nancy,1102, Ruby M.,
1042, Simon,1102, Thomas,
0854,1102, William,1185
JENNIER, Alf,0849
JENNING, Elizabeth,1174
JENNINGS & ATTWOOD, ,0857
JENNINGS, (Dr.),1082, A.L.,
0856,1102, Clement,0842,
Edmund,0843, Eliza J.,0942,
Eliza,0943, Elizabeth,1082,
Frank,0849, J.L.,1102,
J.M.,0856,1102, Jacob,0842,
Julia A.,1094, Lena,1102,
Mamie,1102, Martha,1102,
Narcissa,1154, Obediah,0779
JENNINGS, Peter(Negro),0828,
S.A.,1102, Sarah,1082,
W.S.,0785, William,0762,
0842
JERNIGAN, Amanda M.,1047
JEROME, C.W.,0882
JETT, James(Mrs.),0882, James,
0881, Prof.,0882, Wm. S.,
0874
JETTON & CLAYTON, ,0829
JETTON, (Col.),0811, J.L.,
0820, J.R.,0818, J.S.,0815,
0820,0821, John L.,0832,
Margaret,0838, Mr.,1068,
Nancy,1042,1076, R.B.,0839,
Rob,0827, Robert B.,1042,
Robert,0791,0815,0823,0827,
1042, Rufus,1028, S.,0820,
White,0819
JHNSON, Josiah,0834
JOB, Benjamin A.,1043,
Catharine,1042, Elihu C.,
1042, Elizabeth C.,1043,
James,1042, Lavina S.,1043,
Luke E.,1043, Martha A.,
1025,1043, Mary W.,1043,
Nancy P.,1043
JOBE, Nannie P.,1040
JOEY, David,0797
JOHN & CO., A.C.,0874
JOHN, John,0813
JOHNS, (Mr.),1103, Abe,0821,
Alfred,0822, Annie R.,1048,
C.L.,0854,1102, Catherine E.,
1052, Charles L.,1102,
Elizabeth,1056,1102, F.H.,
0822, H.G.,0847, John B.,
1048, John,0821, Joseph B.,
1056, Mildred C.,1056,
Nelson,0870, Wm.M.,0857
JOHNSON & HITE, ,0879

JOHNSON & VANCE, ,0855,1120,
1121
JOHNSON BROWN GIBSON, ,0991
JOHNSON, (Farm.),1050, (Mr.),
0932, (Mrs.),1082, ,0873,
0894,0895, A.W.,0903,
Addie L.,0991, Amos,0759
0760,0761,0791, Andrew H.,
0991, Andrew V.,0991,
Andrew,0797,0844,0931,0996,
1103,1136, Asbury,0849,
B.T.,0819, Benjamin,0832,
Berry,1117
JOHNSON, Bettie E.,1017, C.S.,
0799, Cassandy,1103,
Charles C.,1043, Columbus N.,
1043, Cordie G.,0932,
Cynthia A.,1200, Dolly,
1009, Duncan,0843, Edna,
1085, Eliza,1210, Elizabeth C.,
1067, Elizabeth,0962,1083,
Ella,0932, Emily,1103,
F.M.,0863
JOHNSON, Frank,0849,1134,
Gregory,0842, Harriet C.,
0990, Harriet L.,0991,
Horace E.,0932, Ida,1103,
J.B.,0763, J.C.,1103, J.D.,
0889, J.F.,0879, J.H.,1103,
J.M.,0871,0890, James E.,
0773, James P.,0990,0991,
James W.,0869,0991, James,
0761
JOHNSON, James,0815,0842,0843,
0847,0854,1103, Jane P.,
1206, Jane,1043,1079,
Jennie S.,0991, Jerry,0844,
Jesse S.,0991, Jesse,1009,
1092, John B.,0846, John C.,
0931, John Sr.,0789,0793,
John,0829,1043,1083,
Joseph M.,1103, Joseph,0853
JOHNSON, Joshua,1017, Julia,
0934, L.J.,0797, Laura A.,
1210, Lillian A.,0932,
Locky,1103, Louis,0990,
Lucy J.,1117, L.M.(Capt.),
0792, M.,0974, Margaret E.,
1039, Margaret K.,1009,
Martha,1116, Marvel,0934,
Marvin,0932, Mary C.,1134,
Mary E.,1071
JOHNSON, Mary J.,1103,
Mary L.,1092, Mary,1043,
1082,1092, Matthew,0789,
Meddy,0931, Minnie T.,1017,
Miranda,1117, Mr.,0828,
N.M.,0799, Nancy C.,1083,
Narcissie,0990, Pres.,0871,
Raymond R.,1043, Richard E.,
0991, Richard F.,1210,
Richard,1103
JOHNSON, Robert B.,1043,
Ruth A.,0919, Sallie(Mrs.),
1200, Sarah J.,0967, Sarah,
0808, Sillie G.,1043, Simon,
0767,0769, Tabitha J.,1043,
Tennie P.,0932, Thomas B.,
0990,0991,1071, Thomas,1082,
Tilman D.,1043, Virginia,
0931, W.A.,0766
JOHNSON, W.A.,0803,1121,
W.J.L.,0799, William A.,
0991, William,0808,0842,
1210, Wm.(Capt.),0792,
Wm.K.,0932, Xernia,0978
JOHNSTON, A.S.J.(Gen.),0873,
Benjamin,0815, Gen.,0825,
1069, Harriet,1113, I.,0794,
Joe E.,0764,0824, John,
0794, Joseph E.,0959,
Larkin,0821, Wm.,0790
JOICE, Capt.,0792, W.W.,0781
JOINER, Capt.,0850
JOLLY, Stephen,0872, Sue W.(Mrs.),
1060
JONES & BROS., ,1043
JONES, (Rev.),0809, ,0751,
0823, A.(Dr.),1210, A.,0818,
0889,0890,0898,0903, A.M.,
0819,1043, Aaron F.,0848,
Adeline,0958, Alacy,0924,
Albert B.,1158, Albert,

1043, Alfred,1103, Alverta,
0932, Ambrose,0841, Amelia A.,
1113, Amelia,0938,1098
JONES, Amzi,1043,1044,
Annie E.,1135, Betty,0979,
C.P.,0764, C.T.,0770,
Calvin,0800,0851,1103,
Capt.,0839,0850,0964,
Charles,1192, Charley,0786,
D.G.,0755, Edmond,0840,
Edmund,0830, Edwin,0936,
Elizabeth J.,1214, Elizabeth,
0932,1214
JONES, Elvira,1151,1152,
Emma J.,0932, Emma,1096,
Ernest,0932, Eulae E.,0932,
Fannie E.,1158, Fannie,
1158, G.W.,0785, George,
1043, Harriett,0932, J.,
0827, J.J.,0890, J.L.,0769,
0773, J.S.,0802, James B.,
0867, James C.,0816,0850,
James,0869
JONES, Jesse,0958, John F.T.,
0932, John L.,0932,1096,
John R.,0898,0982,1210,
John,0818,0826,0839,0840,
0841,0848,0870, Julia A.,
1087, Julia C.,0923,
Katie E.,1158, L.,0870,
L.E.,1157, Lawrence,0932,
Lemuel,0975, Lizzie H.(Mrs.),
1043
JONES, Lucy,1103, Malinda,
1104,1105, Malissa,1192,
Mandy,1104, Margaret B.,
1156, Martha A.,0982,1210,
Mary E.,1158, Mary M.,0952,
Mary Nancy Ann,0932, Mary,
0835,0936,1196,1203, Mary,
1210, Minnie,0932, Minos C.,
1158, Mrs.,0768,1044
JONES, Nancy A.,1103, Nancy E.,
0924, Nancy J.,1043, Nancy,
0932,0994,1157, Parthenia,
0952, Percilla,1019, S.H.,
0772, S.P.,0879, Sam,1035,
Saml.H.,0758, Samuel R.,
1158, Samuel,0847, Sarah E.,
0975, Sarah,0904,0958,
Susan S.,0995, Susanna,1103
JONES, T.J.,0875, T.M.,0759,
0892, Tallie,0932, Thomas J.,
1158, Thomas,0754,0851, W.,
0804, W.A.,0819, W.B.,0830,
W.C.,0770, W.E.,1043, W.T.,
0890, Walter,0932, William H.,
1158, William,0797,1103,
Willis,0932, Wm.J.,0932,
Wm.S.,1043
JORDAN & ELLIOTT, ,0830
JORDAN, Archer,1044, Clement J.,
1045, Clement,1044, Dr.,
0776, E.L.,0799,0805,0826,
0830, E.L.Jr.,0830, Edward L.,
1044, Elizabeth W.,1045,
Elizabeth,1044,1074, Emily,
0933, F.W.,0805, J.,0805,
James S.,1045, Jane,1051,
1075, John A.,1045
JORDAN, John,0791,0932,
Johnson,1045, Leah L.,1002,
Leland,1002,1044, Lulu B.,
1045, Maggie,1044, Martha J.,
1045,1217, Martha L.,1045,
Martha M.,0921, Martha,
0933,1044, Mary W.,1045,
Mary,0932,0933,1004,1044,
Minor C.,1045, Minor C.E.,
1045
JORDAN, Montford F.,1044,
Nancy B.,0958, Nannie,1004,
Newton,1004, Rachel,1045,
S.P.(Dr.),0778,0936, S.P.,
0921, Simon P.,0932,0933,
Sophia,0834, Thomas,0834,
Virginia C.,1026, W.,0805,
William,0834
JORDON, Louisa F.,1178
JOSEPH, J.,0773
JOSSEY, Sarah,0960
JOURDAN, E.L.,0830
JOURNEY, Cora L.,0933, E.T.,

0933, Frederic A.,0933,
Frederic V.,0933, John W.,
0933, Mahala C.,0933, Mary,
0933, Nathaniel T.,0933,
Virginia F.,0933, William,
0933, Wm.M.,0933
JOYCE, Anderson,1158, Bettie,
1130,1158, C.A.,1158, D.F.,
1228, Elizabeth,1158,
Emma E.,0934, Eula,0991,
J.H.,0764, Jackson,0991,
James,0891, Joseph,0991,
L.P.,1158, Lucinda,1228,
Lutitia,0991, Maggie,0991,
Mary E.,0991, S.A.,0991,
Samuel M.,0991
JOYCE, Thomas J.,1158, Thomas,
1130, W.W.(Dr.),0934
JOYNER, W.H.,0824
JUDIA, Nancy E.,1197
JUNKINS, B.W.,0779, Nimrod,
0813, P.H.,0779
JUSTICE & SON, H.A.,0880
JUSTICE, David,0794,0863,
R.L.,0879
Johnson, Amos,0759
KAIN, John,0841
KAINS, Ida,0870
KARR, ,0803, J.C.,0803,
James C.,0802
KAUFMAN, M.,0803
KAVANAUGH & BERRY, ,0766
KAVANAUGH, Charles,0841,0845,
0846
KEAL, Rushing Jas.,0834
KEARNEY, Capt.,0792
KEBBLE, H.P.,0829
KEE, George W.,0763
KEEBLE, E.A.,0815,0822,0826,
H.P.,0823,0830, Hattie A.,
1028, Richie H.,1050,
Walter,0833
KEEL, William,0837
KEELE, (Church),0883, Billy,
0883
KEELING, Elizabeth,1047
KEENAN, John,0766
KEESEE, Eliza,0964, T.W.,0771,
0964
KEITH & BAKER, ,0880
KEITH, Capt.,0872, George,
0799, Haywood,0891, Robert,
0849
KELLAMS, ,0886
KELLAR, A.M.,0757
KELLER, A.M.,0877, Francis H.,
0867
KELLEY, Cary T.,1211, D.C.,
0857, Daniel,0829, Dennis,
0842, John,0829, Joshua,
0842,0844, M.D.,0898,1211,
Margaret J.,1211, Nancy,
1211
KELLOM, William,0799
KELLY, Addie,1102, Annie,1102,
Capt.,0792, Edmund,0761,
Hanson,1102, Ritter,1125,
Sarah,1076, Thomas J.,0756
KELSEY, H.B.,0899, Robert,
0761
KELTON, Elizabeth,0838,
Jestina,1031
KENDALL, James,0842
KENDRICK, Jones,0762
KENNEDAY, Annie D.,0991, D.J.,
0991, David J.,0991, Eliza,
0991, Fannie H.,0992,
James W.,0991, Joseph S.,
0991, Martha R.,0991,
Richard,0991, Sallie H.,
0992, T.H.(Dr.),0991,
Theodore,0991
KENNEDY & ANST, ,0854
KENNEDY, ,0776,0803,0857,
A.A.,0787, B.,0827, Capt.,
0752, Chloe N.,1086, Daniel,
1210, Drusilla,1103,
Elizabeth H.,1207, G.A.,
0764, George,0841, Hannah C.,
1211, J.H.,0851,1103, J.N.,
0850, J.T.,1103, J.W.,1103,
James F.,0898,1210, James,
0841

KENNEDY, James,0891, John,
0827, Lucinda C.,1103, M.S.,
0901,0902, Margaret,1210,
Mary E.,1103, N.D.,1103,
S.A.,1103, Sidney,0914,
T.J.(Dr.),0785, T.J.,0824,
0889, Thos.J.,0750, W.C.,
0764, William B.,1103, Wm.,
0797, Wm.E.,0753,0763,0772
KENT, J.W.P.,0799
KERCHEVAL, ,0897, Emma,0900,
J.M.,1211, John T.,1211,
Maggie,1191, Mayor,1211,
Peter,1211, R.B.,0781,
R.K.,0890,0892,1220,
Susan C.,1211, W.R.,0899,
William K.,1202, Wm.F.,0781
KERCHEVALL, J.T.,0897
KERFORD, Capt.,0752
KERR, ,0778, A.M.,0933,
Andrew B.,0933, B.B.,0829,
C.(Moreen),0933, Capt.,
0752, Daisy E.,0934,
George D.,0934, H.H.,0826,
0829,1052, H.W.,0832, J.,
0829, Joseph B.,0933, Kate,
0933, Kint K.,0933, Louisa A.,
0934, Marshall B.,0933,
Marshall N.,0933
KERR, Mary E.,0933, Mary L.,
0933, Mary,0933, Mr.& Mrs.,
0934, Pearl W.,0934,
Rose M.,0934, Thomas,1027,
William A.,0934, William,
0762,0933, Wilson,0815
KERSEY, ,0777
KESLEY, T.A.,0809
KESTERSON, Rev.,0776
KETCHUM, Levi,0772
KETON, J.S.,1138, Moltie P.,
1138
KEYES, Ann M.,1112, George L.,
1045, Henry,1045, James H.,
1112, John W.,1045, Josephine,
1045, Martha,1045, Robert F.,
1045
KEYSER, Miss,0835
KIDDER, O.C.,0855
KIECHAM, J.B.,0893
KILBORN, Mrs.,0858, Myron,
0857
KILBRO, Samuel,0821
KILCREASE, Wm.,0759
KILEY, Capt.,0751
KILLGORE, Jane,1211, Julia,
1211, Thomas,1211, William M.,
1211, Woodly,1211
KILLOUGH, Alice,1045, James,
1045, Martin C.,1045,
Matilda,1045, William D.,
1045
KILPATRICK, Capt.,0751, Dr.,
0758, Saml.,0775, Thos.W.,
0775
KIMBRO, ,0863, Amanda,1045,
Argie L.,1159, Azariah,
1045, B.,0836, Charles H.,
1159, Clarence S.,1045,
Fitzie,1159, Frazier,1045,
Frederick D.,1159, Henry,
1159, Hoyt,1159, Ira,1159,
J.B.,0830, James,1159,
John B.,1045, John Bell,
1045
KIMBRO, John,0819, La Salle,
1045, Margaret,1159,
Martha A.,1159, Marvin L.,
1159, Minnie,1159, Riley J.,
1159, Riley,1159, Roy E.,
1159, Tennie J.,1159,
Walter,1159, William L.,
1159, Zannie,1159
KIMERY, Alice,1159, Bettie,
1159, Caroline,1159,
Edward L.,1159, Edwin,1159,
Frederick,1159, Harriet,
1159, Jackson G.,1159,
Joseph W.,1159, Leona,1159
KIMMONS, Evaline,1026
KINCADE, James,0876
KINCAID, Albert J.,1159, Alta,
1159, C.M.,1158, Cilena,
1159, Clingan,1158,1159,

Eliza C.,0921, Elizabeth,
1159, Erie,1159, Joseph,
0921, Louisa,1159, Sarah G.,
1159, Syrene,1159
KINCANNON, (Miss),1178
KINDEL, Ophelia,0917
KINDLE, Boyd W.,0934, Cecil,
0934, Felix M.,0934, Sadie,
0934, Sarah,0934, William R.,
0934
KING & POWELL, ,1226
KING, ,0863, Aohsah,1180,
Addie,0992, Albert E.,0993,
Alias,0992, Ann,1046,
Anna B.,1046, Anna M.,1046,
B.F.,0992, Benjamin,0992,
Berryhill,0766, Bessie L.,
0992, Bettie K.,1046, C.B.,
1180, Capt.,0752, Charles H.,
1046, Charles,0832
KING, D.G.,0799, D.W.,1122,
David,0880, Dorsey T.,1046,
E.J.,0831, Eliza,0992,
Elizabeth,0992, F.W.,0898,
Fannie G.,0992, George P.,
0992, George W.,1046, H.,
0799, Helen J.,1046,
Henry J.,1046, J.,0827,
0899, J.H.,0782
KING, James C.,0992, James M.,
1046, James Moore,1045,1046,
James R.,1046, James,0992,
Jeanette M.,1046, John A.,
0992, John B.,0992, John C.,
1046, John H.,1046, John M.,
0992, John W.,0992, Julia,
1046, L.,0781, Laura J.,
0992, Laura,1010
KING, Laura,1083, Leanna P.,
0992, Lucy E.,0992, Martha,
1046, Mary,1180, Mary E.,
0992, Mary F.,1046, Mary(Mrs.),
1122, Mary,0976,0992,
Morrison D.,1046, Nancy,
0968,0992, Needham,0880,
Nettie M.,1046, Olivia M.,
1046, Pattie B.,1046
KING, Rachel,0947, Ransom,
0842, Robert P.,1046,
Robert,0992, S.Moulton,
1046, Samuel,0841,0842,0860,
0902, Sarah J.,0992,
Sarah V.,0992, Sarah,0968,
Susan J.,0992, Susie N.,
0992, T.M.,0832, Thomas M.,
1046, Thomas S.,0992,
Thomas,0992
KING, W.E.,0799, Walter H.,
0992, William E.,0992,
William H.,1046, William,
0869,0968,0992,1083
KINMAN, G.C.,0805
KINNARD, A.,0792, Adella B.,
0993, Ann F.,0993, Claibourne H.,
0993, Claibourne Sr.,0993,
David O.,0790, Elizabeth,
0993, George,0993, Kate C.,
0993, Michael,0793, Mike,
0790,0792, Orlena C.,0993,
Rebecca M.,0993, Rebecca,
0993, Susan E.,0993
KINZER, Abraham M.,0934,
Addie J.,0934, Anna,0934,
Bamly,0934, Charles H.G.,
0963, E.C.,0963, Elizabeth,
0934, Ella M.,0963, Ella,
0939, Emarinthy C.,0914,
Emma E.,0934, Ethel G.,
0963, G.W.,0963, Geo.W.,
0781, Geo.Whitfield,0934,
George,0934
KINZER, Hannah,0940, Henry,
0934, James H.,0934, Jane,
0934, Jefferson D.,0934,
John W.,0934, Lennie M.,
0963, Lillie,0934, Marshall W.,
0934, Mary,0934,0955,
Mattie,0934, May F.,0934,
Mr.,0935, W.O.,0963,
Walter W.,0934, Wm.F.,0781,
Wm.J.,0963
KIOLON, Elizabeth,1100, F.,
1100, Thomas,1100

KIRBY, ,0850, E.,0764, Lewis,
0842, Malachi,0800
KIRCH, R.W.,0880
KIRK, Amanda R.,1147, Capt.,
0751, Edwin,1147, H.C.,0764
KIRKPATRICK, ,0751,0809,0830,
A.,1085, Anderson,1103,
Ann E.,1085, Curry B.,1104,
Donnell B.,1104, E.,1085,
Eliza,1103, Harry B.,1104,
J.D.,0853,0859, John D.,
1103,1104, Joseph,0842, Mr.,
0767, Susan,1104, T.E.,0807
KISER, Bettie,1159, Elizabeth,
0869, Louis,0870
KISSACK, A.M.,0781
KITCHEN, J.W.,0809
KITTRELL, Adaline,0993,
Anna L.,0993, Annie A.,
0993, Armesa,0993, Benjamin,
0993, Bettie,0993, Blanche,
0993, Cicily A.,0935,
Elizabeth H.,0935, Elizabeth,
0993, Eudora,0993, George M.,
0993, George W.,0935,
George,0935,0993, Hinton G.,
0935
KITTRELL, Jacob H.,0935,
Jacob,0993, James B.,0935,
James,0993, John,0993,
Josephine,0993, Joshua,
0935, Larissa K.,0935,
Larissa,0939, Laura R.,
0993, Loretta,0993, M.J.,
0993, Martha,0993, Phelix H.,
0935, Riddic(k),0993,
Robert H.,0993
KITTRELL, Rufus,0993, Ruth,
0935, Seth R.,0935, Sue,
0993, Thomas F.,0993,
Whitney F.,0993, William A.,
0935, William H.,0993,
William,0993, Zulika R.,
0935
KIZER, Riley,0869
KLINE, A.L.(Rev.),0783
KNAPP, Julia,0835
KNIGHT, ,0883, Absalom,0842,
Andrew J.,0935, Charles D.,
0935, Christiana,0935,
Dewitt C.,0935, Edward,
0849, Elatia,1230, Ellen,
0935, Horace,1103, J.W.,
0897, Jacob,0821, L.M.,0829,
L.W.,0897, Leathy L.,0935,
Lillie,0935, Luby,0935,
Lucy B.,1127
KNIGHT, Marlinda,1100,
Martha J.,0935, Mary,0935,
Minnie L.,0935, Minnie,
0935, N.D.,1103, Nancy M.,
0935, S.A.,1102, T.H.,1102,
Various L.,0935, W.M.,0935,
William,0821
KNOTT, Anderson B.,1158,
Annie,1158, Elizabeth,1158,
Iverson,1140, John,0867,
Julia B.,1158, L.B.,0868,
S.F.,0874, Sallie A.,1015,
Sallie J.,1140, Samuel F.,
1158, Thomas,0862, Willie,
1158
KNOX, ,0813, Armenia E.,1046,
Caroline,1059, John,0842,
Martha F.,1074, R.N.,0817,
0818, R.T.,1074, Robert N.,
1046, W.J.,0819, William F.,
1046, William,0842
KOHL, E.H.,0875
KOONCE, ,0860, John,0868,
Philip,0842
KUHN, Annette Estelle,0912,
E.,0780, Edward,0912
LACK, William,0874
LACRE, Ella,1138
LACY, E.M.,0872, Zachariah,
0872
LADD, ,0775, Ann,1227, Bamly,
0934, Nancy L.,1150, Robert,
0934
LAFAYETTE, Gen.,0802,0828
LAIRD, Alexr.,0768, Andrew,
0888, Capt.,0752, John H.,
0876, Margaret E.,1171,

Mary E.,0929, T.B.,0877
LAMB & BOYD, ,1230
LAMB, Abraham,0993,0994,
 Celia,0993, Charity,0993,
 Cora A.,0994, Davis,0993,
 Delilah,1215, Eliza J.,
 1048, Elizabeth,0993,
 George D.,0994, Gilbert H.,
 0993, Gilbert T.,0994,
 Hannah T.,0993, Henry,0870,
 Isham,0808, J.T.,0799,
 John,1048
LAMB, John,1082, Louis M.,
 0994, Luticia,0993, Martha
 0994, Mary F.,0994, Mary,
 0993,1082, Matilda A.,0993,
 Penina,0993, W.W.,0819,
 William H.,0994, William,
 0993
LAMPTON BROS., ,0854
LAMPTON, Gus,1093, Maggie,
 1093
LANCASTER, Adelia C.,0947,
 Ella R.,0935, Elmira,0928,
 Hope,0936, John,0845,
 Margaret M.,0935, Martha C.,
 0935,0936, Mary L.,0935,
 Mary,0946,1114, Michael,
 0936, Naomi,0935, Nathaniel,
 0936, Orison E.,0935,
 Samuel L.,0935, Susan,0936,
 Wm.H.,0935
LANCASTER, Wm.L.,0935, Wm.R.,
 0935,0936
LANDER, Bettie,0936, Frank D.,
 0936, L.B.,0769, Russell B.,
 0936
LANDERS, ,0863, Absalom,0867,
 Eliza J.,1182, Elizabeth,
 1182, Mary E.,1134, R.L.,
 0868, Rebecca F.,1138,
 Robert,1134, Susan,1134
LANDESS, Alfred G.,1159,
 George W.,1159, Grace C.,
 1159, Grace,1159, Henry D.,
 1159, Henry H.,1159, Henry,
 1159, Lucinda S.,1159,
 Mary F.,1159, Mittie M.,
 1159, Sarah M.,1159,
 Susan C.,1159, William G.,
LANDIS & BROS., ,0881
LANDIS & WINSETT, ,0881
LANDIS, ,0863, A.L.,0877,0894,
 Alice,1160, Bryant,1160,
 Florence,1160, G.L.,0881,
 George L.,1160, J.A.,1160,
 J.T.,0875, Margaret,1160,
 Robbie,1160, W.A.,0872
LANDRUM, John,0834
LANE & CRICHLOW, ,0829
LANE, (Widow),0849, Alfred J.,
 1212, America(Mrs.),1126,
 Bennett,1079, Emma,1030,
 G.W.,0802, Garret,0754,
 J.B.,0797,1030, J.F.,0848,
 J.T.,0850, Joel,1212,
 John F.,1212, John(Rev.),
 0839, John,0841,0865,
 Lucinda,1079, Martha A.,
 1210, Mary A.,1212
LANE, Mary D.,1212, Robert,
 1126, Sarah E.,1021,
 Susan H.,1212, William J.,
 1212
LANEARE, Elizabeth,0917,
 Howell,0917, Martha J.,0917
LANG, George,0792
LANGTRY, H.,0755, Henry,0768,
 Hillary,0779
LANIER, Lucy,1190
LANIUS, George W.,1079,
 Mildred C.,1079
LANNON, Coon,0843
LANOM, Caldonia T.,1104,
 Freddie,1104, Laura L.,
 1104, Lucy J.,1104, N.P.,
 1104, Nanny A.,1104, Nathan,
 1104, Sallie A.,1104,
 Sallie,1104, William J.,
 1104, William R.,1104
LARABEE, Benj.,0779
LARKIN, Jas.M.,0768
LARNE, John,0868

LARUE, Elizabeth,1190
LASH, John C.,0848
LASSITER, Alvira,1086,1087,
 Enos,1086
LATTA, John,0769,1010,
 Rebecca,1010, Sims,0758
LAUGHLIN, S.H.,0827, Saml.H.,
 0849
LAVANDER, A.,0900, Frances O.,
 0924
LAVENDER, Antoinette,0965,
 F.M.,0791,0825, Martha E.,
 1006, Nancy,1006, Nelson,
 0965,1006, Purmelia,0965,
 Sarah,1223, W.,0808
LAW, Dr.,0758, John S.(Dr.),
 0783, John S.,0757
LAWELL, Elizabeth,1160
LAWING, S.N.,0833, S.W.,0833
LAWRENCE, ,0892, Andrew S.,
 0867, Capt.,0792, Catharine,
 0950, Jane T.,0933, John,
 0843,0848, Mr.,0893
LAWS & SON, ,0897
LAWS, Daisy C.,0994, E.H.,
 0994, Hiram A.,0994,
 John W.,0898, John(Col.),
 0994, John,0889, Mary E.,
 0994, Mary F.,0994, Mary M.,
 0994, Sarah E.,1222
LEA, Abner,1137, Saml.P.,0776,
 Samuel,0800
LEACH, Gains,0843, James,0757,
 Wm.,0779
LEACOCK, H.T.,0810
LEATH, Ebenezer,0778, Mary J.,
 1070, Peter,0842, Sallie,
 1104
LEATHERMAN, J.M.,0819, M.F.,
 1058
LEATHERS, A.W.,0819, W.L.,
 0819
LEATON, William,0793
LEDBETTER, Capt.,0752,1034,
 John,0875, R.,0809,
 Richard,0818, Wilham,0818,
 William,0830, Wm.,0826,
 0832,0840
LEDFORD, ,0863
LEE, (House),0852, Amanda M.,
 1047, Anna E.,1047, Asa,
 1047, Elizabeth,1047,
 Elliott,1137, Gen.,0798,
 J.T.,0855, John J.,1047,
 Kate,1047, Lt.Gen.,0800,
 Mary M.,1047, Oder M.,1047,
 Polly,1097, Robert E.,0857,
 0948, Sarah E.,1047, Sarah,
 1074
LEE, Shelley J.,1047, Thomas E.,
 1047, William A.,1047,
 Zoror E.,1047
LEECH, Capt.,0850, William,
 0822
LEEPER, Rebecca A.,1201
LEFTWICH & CO., ,0874
LEFTWICH, Addison,0936,
 Albert,0936, Anna V.,0936,
 Arthur,0936, Charles W.,
 1160, Clayton W.,1160,
 Francis T.,0936, Jane,0936,
 Littleberry,1160, Maggie,
 1160, Mary,0936, Nina P.,
 1160, Sue M.,0936, Thomas E.,
 1160
LEFTWICK, A.,0758, J.W.,0758,
 James,0768
LEGGETT, Simpson,0764
LEGGON & BROS., ,0854
LEGRAND, Peter,0814,0815,0819,
 0820,0833
LEIGH, Benjamin,0966, Elizabeth,
 0966, Martha,0966
LEIPER & MENIFEE, ,0829
LEIPER, ,0777, Allen,0886,
 0901, Hugh,0777, J.A.,0829,
 James,0886,0901, John,0826,
 0832,0839,0901, Mary,0901,
 Phidellas,0901, Rebecca,
 0901, W.F.,0829,0832, W.T.,
 0831
LEMASTER, Joseph,0766
LEMON, J.P.H.,0820

LENT, ,0863
LENTZ, Babe,1160, Benjamin,
 1160, Eddie E.,1160,
 Elizabeth,1160, Ethan A.,
 1160, James M.,1160,
 John H.,1160, Mary L.A.,
 1160, Nancy,1139, Necy,1160,
 Penelope,1160, Robert M.,
 1160, Samuel J.,1160
LEONARD, John,0890, Mary H.,
 1196, T.B.,0889, W.J.,0890
LERNEAN, Daniel,0839
LESTER & CO., J.A.,0854
LESTER & SMITH, ,0854
LESTER & SON, H.D.,0854
LESTER, Albert D.,1106,
 Blanche,1106, Daniel R.,
 1105, Floyd H.,1106,
 Gertrude,1106, Henry D.,
 0848,1104,1105,1106, Isaiah,
 0822, J.A.,1084, J.D.,1105,
 J.R.,1105, Jennie,1105,
 Jessie F.,1106, Jimmie,
 1105, John A.,0854,1104,
 1105, John,1105
LESTER, Joseph A.,1106,
 Joshua,1118, Lucie,1118,
 Lucy A.,0988, Malinda,1104,
 1105, Marcella,1106, Marie,
 1105, Matilda E.,1105,
 Nellie,1105, Robert E.,
 1106, Sallie,1105, Wade H.,
 1106, William J.,1105,
 William,0842
LETHERMAN, ,0838
LEVEL, Sallie,1083
LEWIS, Estella L.,1047,
 (Family),1003, Andrew,0760,
 Elizabeth,1047, Fielding,
 1212, G.W.,0847,0854,
 George,0851, J.A.,0814,
 J.H.,0886,0889,0892,0896,
 1212, J.M.,0760, James Henry,
 1212, James M.,0751, James,
 0761,0863, Jas.M.,0760,
 John C.,1212
LEWIS, John W.,1047, Lydia,
 1212, Mahala,0946, Maj.,
 0767, Mary,1092, Meriwether,
 1212, Merriwether,0755,
 Nathaniel,1047, Seth,0794,
 Thomas F.,0892,1213,
 Victoria J.,1212, W.A.,
 0847, W.B.,0796, W.P.,0895,
 W.T.,0766, William,0851
LIDDON, A.,0827, Benj.,0821
LIDSEY, Jay,0816
LIGAN & BROS., ,0855
LIGAN BROS., ,0855
LIGGETT, Academy,0882, Robert,
 0891, Sampson,0781, W.C.,
 0781
LIGGETTE, Victoria,1225
LIGON, Richard L.,1121,
 Roseline,1121, Virginia,
LILLARD, ,0813,0837,0899,
 A.F.,0890, B.F.,0829,
 Flora,1058, Mary,1058,
 W.B.,0829, Wm.B.,0818
LILLIARD, B.F.,0830
LILLIE, Caroline,0994, Emma,
 0994, J.B.,0803, James,0994,
 Joshua B.,0994, Lucy A.,
 0994, Pryor,0994, Sallie M.,
 0994
LILLY, R.H.,0807
LINDER, William,0930
LINDSEY, James,0819, John,
 0751,0759,0760,0761,0766,
 Joseph,0819, Lewis,1089,
 M.,0809, Margt.Eliz.,1089,
 Moses,0797, N.Lawrence,0859
LINDSEY, (Dr.),0786, A.J.,
 0764, Adrain V.S.,1106,
 Eliza V.,1107, Eliza,1106,
 Frank,1106, Henry S.,1106,
 John B.,1106, Joseph W.,
 1106, Julia M.,1106,
 Kate S.,1106, Lucy,1107,
 N.Lawrence,1106, Nathaniel,
 1107, Philip,1106,1107,
 Phillip,0779
LINDSLY, Rev.,1092

LINEAU, David,0827
LINN, James M.,0779
LINSEY, Carter,0775
LIPSCOMB & CO., ,0874,0875
LIPSCOMB, ,0979, Ann Day,1160,
 Archibald A.,0936, Archibald,
 0936, Benj.B.,0936, Dorothea,
 0936, Emma,0936, George,
 0752,0784,0936, Ida,0936,
 Mary A.,1161, Mary C.,0936,
 Rebecca,1161, Theodocia E.,
 0936, Thomas,0876,0877,1160,
 1210, William,1160
LIPSCOMB, Wm.H.,0936
LISENBY, Mary,1128
LISTER, Alex,0797
LITTERER, William,1158
LITTLE, (Capt.),1170, ,0881,
 Montgomery,0872
LITTLEFIELD, E.B.,0766,
 Edw.B.,0754,0756,0759,
 John,0757
LITTON, Susan,1005
LIVELY, James,0848
LIVINGSTON, Sarah,1080
LLEWELLYN, Sarah J.,1144
LOCK, James,1141, Lizzie T.,
 1141, Susan,1133, William,
 0821
LOCKE, Carrie(Mrs.),1160,
 Henry,0842, Luira,0950,
 W.A.,0950
LOCKETT, Elizabeth C.,1008
LOCKHART, ,0775
LOGAN, Berry,0872, David,0793,
 J.W.,0750
LOGUE, C.,1107, Catharine B.,
 1107, Franklin L.,1107,
 J.C.,0843, James R.,1107,
 John,1091, Joshua C.,1107,
 Lucy A.,1107, Lucy,1120,
 M.,1107, Margaret E.,1107,
 Martha,1107, Mary E.,1107,
 Nancy,1107, Robert H.,1107,
 T.G.,1107, Tapley G.,1107
LOGUE, Tennessee,1107
LOIK, Robert,0832, Silas,0827
LONDON & KNUDSON, ,0897
LONDON, Bentley A.,1213,
 Bentley D.,1213, Bettie M.,
 1213, Cynthia A.,1213,
 Mary E.,1213, Mattie A.,
 1213, N.B.,1213, William A.,
 1213
LONG & MORGAN, ,0880
LONG & WATSON, ,0880
LONG, Archie,0937, Clarence B.,
 0937, David,0791,0925, Dr.,
 0776, Eliz.B.,0937, Emily B.,
 0937, Emily M.M.H.,0937,
 Eula,0937, Fannie B.,0937,
 Felix H.G.,0937, Frank,
 0937, Henry H.,0937, Henry,
 0936, Jane,0925,1206,
 Jennie,0937, Johnson,0785
LONG, Joseph S.,0937, Katie W.,
 0937, Lemuel,0776,0936,0937,
 Leon M.,0937, Leora,0928,
 Mary P.,0937, Mary R.,0949,
 Mary,0925,0936, Nicholas,
 0766, Rufus,0937, Sallie,
 1032, W.F.,0879, Washington,
 0937, William H.,0937
LONGLEY, Caleb,0768
LONGSTREET, ,0894
LOONEY & SONS, ,0768
LOONEY, A.M.,0759,0764,0798,
 A.N.,0922, Abraham,0763,
 R.F.,0764, W.J.,0897
LORDMORE, Thomas,0874
LORING, ,0786, Gen.,0798
LOSATER, Absalom,0842
LOTSPEECH, Elizabeth,1156
LOUDER, Nancy,1183
LOUIS, Capt.,0792
LOVE, (Capt.),0786,0787, ,
 0776, David,0759,0778,
 James,0759,0760,0761,
 Joseph,0766,0781, Mary D.,
 1203, Mattie,1021, Mr.,0792
LOVELACE, Henry,0870
LOVELL, Martha,1157
LOW, Ella G.,0998, Gabriel,
 0998, Mary,0869, Vina H.,
 0998
LOWDER, John,0767
LOWE, Calvin,1047, Effie S.,
 1047, Elizabeth P.,1047,
 Elizabeth,1047,1094, G.H.,
 0824, George K.,1047, Hudie,
 1029, James W.,1047, L.K.,
 1047, Leonard K.,1047,
 Leonard,1094, Lydia A.,
 0999, Margaret E.,1047,
 Mary D.,1047, Mary E.,1047,
 Neri,1047
LOWE, Rosa B.,1094, Rosy B.,
 1047, S.K.,1074, Sarah E.,
 1047, Sophia P.,1074,
 William T.,1047
LOWELL, James,0821
LOWERY, John,0821, Mr.,0828
LOWRY, James B.,0891, Sarah,
 1226, W.B.,0808
LOYD, Alexander M.,1213,
 James M.,1047, James,1047,
 Louisa,1213, Matilda,1047,
 Minnie,1161, Victoria C.,
 1213, W.G.,0890,0899, W.J.,
 0864, Wilson G.,1213
LUCK, Fannie,1125, Mary L.,
 1125, W.W.,1125
LUDWICK, Elizabeth,0951
LUKINS, J.,0828
LUMPKIN, Elizabeth,1088
LUMPKINS, John,0844
LUNA, B.F.,0893, Elisha,0893,
 J.B.,0893, James G.,1213,
 John B.,1213, Maggie,1214,
 Mary,1218, Mattie,1213,
 R.S.,0893, Rhoda C.,1213
LUNN, ,0899
LURK, Elias,0934, Elizabeth,
 0934, Margaret G.,0939,
 Mary J.,0934, Scott,0939
LURTON, Horace,0850
LUSK, ,0776, Samuel,0760
LUTTELOW, (Prof.),0900
LUTTERLOH, Mr.,0779
LYLE, M.L.(Mrs.),1214
LYNCH, Arthur B.,1048,
 Catharine,1048, Drucilla,
 1048, Ecasmur C.,1048,
 James S.,1048, Leonard,
 1048, M.S.,0819, Moses S.,
 1048, Oliver S.,1048,
 Robert H.,1048, Sallie,
 1048, Thos.,0779
LYNN, Andrew J.,1161, Isabella,
 1161, Jacob Sr.,1161, Jacob,
 1161, John A.,1161, Joseph T.,
 1161, Louise Jane,1161,
 Mary A.,1161, Mary E.L.,
 1161, Rebecca,1161, Sarah,
 1161
LYON, ,0751, Henry,0801, John,
 0766, Sarah,1049
LYPERT, Lawrence,1077,
 Mary Dixon,1077, Mary,1077
LYTHE, (Capt.),1046, Helen J.,
 1046
LYTLE, (Capt.),1145, Annie R.,
 1048, Archibald,0794,0815,
 0841, Catharine,1048, E.F.,
 0873, John,0832,0839,0840,
 1048, Julia(Mrs.),1048,
 Lavinia J.,1048, Lizzie S.,
 1048, Martha,1045, Mary E.,
 1048, N.H.,0829
LYTLE, Rebecca,1150, Robert,
 1048, Sallie E.,1048,
 Sophia D.,1048, Thomas B.,
 1048, Violet H.,1048,
 Violet,1048, W.F.,0835,
 W.H.,0818,1051, W.J.,0839,
 W.T.,0815, William H.,1048,
 William,0812,0813,0814,
 0815,0827,0835,0841,1048
MABRY, Benj.G.,0848
MACE, B.M.,0859,1086, Ella,
 1086
MACEY, Joe,0834
MACK, Dr.,0750,0779, E.G.,
 0938, Eliza,0939, J.B.(Rev.),
 0938, Judge,0762,0763,

Mollie,0938, Robert,0756,
 0762, S.B.(Mrs.),0781,
 William,0937, Wm.(Rev.),
 0783
MACKEY, John A.,0785
MACLIN, (Lt.),0786
MACON, H.H.,0819
MADDEN, Capt.,0792, Thomas,
 0809,0835, Thos.(Rev.),0783
MADDOX, Rev.,0860
MADISON, Dolly C.,0907, James,
 1161, L.,1137, Levi,1161,
 Minnie,1161, Nancy J.,1137,
 1161, Wm.D.W.,1161
MADRY, Elizabeth S.,1214
MAGATHEY, David,0841
MAGILL, James,0761
MAGNESS, David,0795, Jonathan,
 0795, Martha,1083, Mary,
 1083, Perry,1083
MAGRUDER, Mary,1071
MAHAFFY, Isaac,0848
MAHON, Abigail,0994, Brooks,
 0994, Dora P.,1016, George W.,
 0994, James,0994,1016, John,
 0994, Julie,0994, Martha M.,
 0994, Thomas E.,0994,
 Thomas E.Jr.,0994, Thomas Sr.,
 0994, William S.,0994
MAINRE, A.W.,0818
MAJOR, Fanny,1116, J.H.,1052,
 John,0897, Mattie,1116,
 Sallie,1035, Samuel,1116
MAJORS, Mary E.L.,1161,
 Noble L.,1161
MALLERY, Samuel,0821
MALLEY, John,0838
MALLORY, Andrew C.,0995,
 Clarence B.,0995, Clement W.,
 0995, D.B.,0819, Elizabeth,
 0981,0995, Harriet S.,0995,
 J.W.,0995, James H.,0995,
 John R.,0995, John W.,0995,
 John,0995, Josiah,0995,
 Lemuel P.,0995, Lucinda,
 0995, Malissa,0995, Mamie L.,
 0995
MALLORY, Mamie,0995, Martha J.,
 0995, Martha,0995, Mary A.,
 0995, Newton,0995, Philip,
 0995, Roger,0797, Sarah E.,
 0995, Susan S.,0995,
 William M.,0995
MALONE, ,0776
MALTHIS, W.G.,0819
MANCHESTER, W.,0827
MANEER, Silvina,0916
MANEY, ,0895, A.P.,0791,0795,
 Abram Jr.,0791, Abram,0791,
 Capt.,0792, Elizabeth M.,
 0969, Fanny,0838, George,
 0798, H.,0836, James H.,
 0795, James,0827,0828,0835,
 Jas.(Dr.),0836, R.R.,0893,
 T.H.,0838, Thomas,0796,
 0809, Thos.H.,0838, William,
 0969
MANGRUM, Edwin,0766, L.B.,
 0766
MANIER, T.H.,0878
MANIGAULT, ,0801
MANIRE, A.W.,0818,1048,
 Eliza J.,1048, Ella M.,
 1048, Florence E.,1048,
 J.A.,0901, John W.,1048,
 Josephine,1048, Julia A.,
 1048, Julia W.,1048, Leanna,
 1207, Lemuel,1048, Susan O.,
 1048, Susan,1048
MANKIN, Alice F.,1049,
 Benton P.,1049, Elizabeth,
 1049, J.E.(Miss),1049,
 Jessie J.,1049, John P.,
 1049, John,1049, Louisa,
 1049, Mardilla H.,1049,
 Mary L.,1049, S.J.(Mrs.),
 1049, Samuel W.,1049, Sarah
 1049, Welcom,1048,1049,
 William,0821
MANKINS, James,0867
MANLEY, J.E.(Mrs.),1049,
 Joseph,0807, W.R.,1049
MANN, Bettie,0981, Capt.,0850,

Edgar,0938, Henry W.,0938,
Joel,0847,0854, Josie I.,
0938, Lee,0938, Mary P.,
0938, William T.,0938,
William,0847,0854,0938
MANNING, William,0808
MANNS, G.W.L.,0794
MANNY, Ferdinand,0764, George,
1007
MANOR, Vienna,1028
MANSON VAUDY & CO., ,0874
MANSON, J.E.,0818, J.T.,0854,
Joseph T.,0850
MANY, Phillip,0801, Thomas,
0796
MARABLE, M.,0793
MARION, Gen.,0784
MARKS, A.S.,0819,0871,0894,
John,1125, L.,0773, Mary,
1125, Nancy,1125
MARR, Billy,0887, Jane,1129
MARRS, John A.,0874
MARSBY, Estella,0923
MARSH, Amelia,1214, Elizabeth J.,
1214, Elizabeth,1214,
Isabelle,1207, Robert J.,
1214, Shelby B.,1214,
Simeon,1214, William T.,
1214
MARSHAL, David,0854
MARSHALL, ,0863,0880, Daniel,
0820, David,0847,0853,
Elizabeth H.,1015, Fanny C.,
0974, G.,0790, Gilbert,0793,
Humphrey,0796, J.,0796,
J.H.,0836,0838, J.L.,0893,
0902, James G.,1214,
John L.,1214, John,0792,
0796,0799,0802,0806,0825,
0974
MARSHALL, John,1015,1228,
Lewis,0874, Lucien,0857,
M.L.,1214, M.M.,0807,
Margaret J.,1214, Martha,
1214, Mary,0956, Moses,0874,
0882, Solomon,0841, Wm.,
0791,0794
MARTIN, ,1133, A.B.,0832,
Abraham,0870,0871,0882,
Alice,1107, Amelia W.,0938,
Andrew B.,0858,1107,
Andrew,1107, Ann C.,0938,
Annie,1108, Barclay,0759,
0764,0765,0791,0871,
Barkley,0862, Bartlett,
0865, Benjamin F.,0986,
Bennett,1107
MARTIN, Bradley,0762, Burkley V.,
0939, Callie,0938, Capt.,
0752,0850, David,0767,0844,
Delilah,1215, E.W.,0775,
Elizabeth,0962,1049,1203,
Ella A.,0986, Ellen W.,
0939, Elsie M.,1108, Fannie,
1198, Fanny,1108,1120, G.M.,
0779, G.W.,0854
MARTIN, G.W.,0877, Geo.M.,
0761,0783, George E.,0938,
George M.,0759, George W.,
0938,0939,1108, George,0863,
1074, Hannah,1225,1231,
Helen,1107, Henry B.,0938,
Henry,0794,0938,0951,1214,
Ivy B.,0939, J.B.,1108,
J.R.,0827, Jacob T.,0800
MARTIN, Jacob,1049, James L.,
1108, James M.,0939,1214,
James T.,0938, James,0880,
Jane D.,0986, Jessie L.,
0938, John A.,1108, John D.,
0872, John H.D.,0938,
John J.,1049, John,0775,
1120, Josiah,0841, Judith,
1108, Julia C.,0923,
June F.,0938
MARTIN, Lillie G.,0939,
Lindsey C.,1108, Lizzie M.,
0939, Lucinda R.,1108, M.,
0821, Mahala T.,0951,
Marcus W.,1108, Maria,1214,
Martha,1107, Mary D.,1108,
Mary E.,0938, Mary J.,0938,
1108, Mary M.,0939, Mary O.,

1108, Mary,1049,1107,1108
MARTIN, Mary,1215, Mat,0862,
Matilda,1045,1107, Matt,
0871, Matthew,1107, Mattie H.,
0939, Nancy,1108, Narcissa,
0939, Ned(Negro),0856, Nora,
1095, North(Mrs.),1049,
Phoebe,1197, R.L.,0833,
Rachael,0867, Rachel P.,
1180, Rebecca,0914, Richard,
0863
MARTIN, Richard,0938, Rob,
0829, S.,0855, Sarah J.,
1074, Sarah T.,0939, Sarah,
0938, Seth Kittrell,0939,
Thomas G.,0939, Thomas T.,
0938, Thomas,0848, W.C.,
0817,0818, W.D.,1108, W.L.,
0836, W.P.,0765,0778,0792,
0892, William B.,0870,
William G.,0938
MARTIN, William L.,0850,
William M.,0938, William,
0791,0836,0841,0850,0922,
Willie T.,0939, Wm.,0803,
0819,0863, Wm.L.,0849,0870,
Wm.P.,0759,0764,0892
MASON, Daisy L.,1050, Dora C.,
1050, Elizabeth,1049,
Eulolia P.,1050, Frances J.,
1050, Isabella H.,1050,
John,0796, L.M.,0817, M.A.,
1050, Margaret J.,1056,
Martha J.,1050, Mary,0907,
Moss G.,1050, N.W.,0819,
P.P.,0830, Parthenia M.,
1050
MASON, Pleasant P.,1050, R.H.,
1050, Reynear H.,1049,
Richie H.,1050, Robert T.,
1050, Sanders,1050, W.N.,
0818, William N.,1050,
William,1049, Willie T.,
1057, Wm.A.,1050
MASS, Thomas,0841
MASSEY, Annie,0992, Ephraim,
0887,0898, Frances C.,0992,
Thomas J.,0992, W.G.,0890
MASTERSON, Mr.,0828
MATHER, ,0813
MATHERAL, John,0805
MATHERLY, Saml.H.,0854,
Samuel,0855
MATHEWS, "Old Davy",0749,
John,0761,0778, L.,0827,
Mary E.,1025, Mattie,1035,
Robert,0874, Stanley,0773,
0774, W.H.,0799
MATHIS & LOW, ,0875
MATHUS, Andrew,0871
MATLOCK, Gabriel,0797
MATTHEWS, ,0776,0777, Bedford L.,
0939, David,0784, Elenora,
0939, Eliza,0939, Fannie D.,
0939, Fannie,0939, Isham,
0966, J.B.,0824, Jerome,
0939, John,0760, Juba F.,
0939, Mary B.,0966, Mary D.,
0951, Minerva,0966, Newton,
0939, Robby,0939
MATTHEWS, Sallie E.,0939,
Samuel,0977, William,0939,
Wm.R.H.,0939
MATTLEY & CAMPBELL, ,0854
MATTLEY, Samuel T.,0854
MAULDEN, Harris,0893
MAUPIN, ,0863, Blan,1161,1162,
Gabriel,0868,1161,1162,
Joseph,1162, Marietta,1162,
Nancy R.,1162, R.P.,0878,
Sallie,1161,1162, Sarah Ann,
1162, Thomas H.,1162,
Thornton P.,1162
MAURY, A.P.,1003, Abram (Mrs.),
0808, Abram,0789,0793,0801,
0803,0805,1003, Caleb,0808,
F.C.(Mrs.),1003, Martha T.,
1002,1003, Mrs.,0969, Shaw,
0751, W.,0822
MAXEY, S.B.,0786
MAXFIELD, Thos.W.,0834
MAXWELL, David,0779, G.W.C.,
0764, James,0821, Jesse,

0863, Martha L.,1185, S.P.,
0766
MAY, ,0813, Capt.,0751,
Edmond,0761, Margaret J.,
0948, Sue,1065
MAYBERRY, A.P.,1215, Alice E.,
0939, Amercus C.,0995,
Columbus P.,0939, Cora,
1215, Cornelia E.,1215,
Elizabeth M.,0995, Elizabeth,
0934, Ella,0939, Emma P.,
1215, Fulton A.,0995,
Fulton,0995, G.W.,0807,
Gabriel,1215, Gabriella,
1215, George W.,0939
MAYBERRY, H.G.,0995, Hardin,
0781,1215, Harriet C.,1215,
Harvey,1215, Henry N.,0939,
Henry,0939, John H.,0995,
Lawreston H.,1215, Leonora,
0967, Lula L.,1215, Margaret G.,
0939, Margaret,0939,
Martha A.,0939, Mary J.,
0939, Mary M.,1215
MAYBERRY, Michael,0939,
Nannie,0995, Presley,0995,
Robert N.,0939, Rosanna,
1215, Virginia,0931,0939,
Wm.G.,0939
MAYES & FRIERSON, ,0768
MAYES WOOTEN & CO., ,0964
MAYES, ,0749,0751,0768, A.W.,
0750, Anna,1162, B.L.,0782,
Eliza J.,1162, Harriett F.,
1162, J.M.,0770,0772,0773,
J.M.S.,0750,0784, J.S.,
0749, James L.,1162,
James M.,0940, James,0841,
1162, John A.,1162, John M.S.,
0940, Maggie Lee,0940
MAYES, Martha A.,1162,
Mary E.,1162, Mr.,0770,
Pollie,1162, R.B.,0755,
Rebecca S.,0940, S.F.,0964,
Saml.,0756, Samuel,0750,
0784,0940, T.S.,1162,
Walter M.,0940, William W.,
1162, Willie B.,0940, Wm.,
MAYFIELD, A.J.(Dr.),0803,
Capt.,0792, Maria,1226,
Nancy,1175, S.S.(Dr.),0803,
S.S.,0792,1016, Thomas,
0812, W.S.,0898
MAYS, E.P.,0764, Eliz. P.,
0940, Fannie E.,0988, Kate,
1073, M.C.,0916, Miles C.,
0940, Miles H.,0940, Samuel,
1073
MCADAMS & SON, ,1213
MCADAMS, Irvin,0887, James,
0887, Josiah,0887
MCADOO, James,0842, Lockie,
1064, Mary,1064, Samuel,0842
MCAFEE, (Miss),1216, Elizabeth,
1216, Green,1216
MCALLISTER, Charles,0801,
J.S.,0799, John D.,0802,
Wm.,0796
MCALPIN, Lutitia A.,1016
MCAULEY, Mary,0941
MCBRAME, W.B.,0871
MCBRIDE & COMPTON, ,0899
MCBRIDE, Dora B.,0940, G.W.,
1215, Geo.(Negro),0887,
Geo.W.,0896, Hannah,0940,
Helena,0940, Hester J.,
0918, J.,0890, Jo,0902, Joe,
0899, John,0940, Joseph,
1215, Mary A.V.,1215,
Mary H.,1215, Mattie P.,
0940, Nancy A.,1147,
Robert L.,0940
MCBRIDE, Robert N.,0940,
Samuel,0813,0816,0818,0819,
0820, William D.,0940
MCBRIGHT, Alexr.,0814
MCCABE, Hugh,0808
MCCAIN, ,0776, John,0767,
Joseph,0767, Mrs.,0767,
Wm.T.,0782
MCCALEB, Rev.,0776
MCCALL, Andrew L.,0996,
Anna L.,0996, Dora M.,0996,

Emeline M.,0995, Lizzie E.,
0996, Louisa J.,0996,
Lucurgus,0995, Marilda,
0995, W.L.,0995, Wallace E.,
0996
MCCALLUM, ,0751, D.J.,0758
MCCANDLESS, Nancy,1196
MCCARDY, Capt.,0751
MCCARKIN, Capt.,0751
MCCARROLL, Israel,0774
MCCARTY, (Mr.),1087
MCCASLAND, James,0854
MCCAUL, R.F.,0800
MCCAULESS, N.L.,0895
MCCLAIM, Josiah S.,0844
MCCLAIN BROS., ,0855
MCCLAIN, (Bros.),1109,1115,
(Brothers),1089, (Mrs.),
0941, Alexander,1108,
Anson Brent,1109, Anson,
1109, Catharine,0940,
Elizabeth,0940, Hettie,
1108, J.T.,0854,1082,1089,
1109,1123, Jasper,1081,
Jennie,1108, John A.,1108,
John B.,1109
MCCLAIN, John,0940,0941,1109,
Josiah,0847, Jivonia,0940,
Lollie Bell,1109, Luther,
0940, Manerva,1108,1109,
Martha,0941, Mary,0940,
Minnie,1108, Newton,0941,
R.P.,0847,0850,1108,
Robert C.,0940, Rufus P.,
1109, Sue,1109, William T.,
0940
MCCLAIN, William,0841,0846,
0860
MCCLANAHAN, D.,0764, John B.,
1050, Mathew,0821, Matthew,
1050, Samuel,1050
MCCLANE, G.A.,0897
MCCLAREN, Nancy,1127
MCCLARION, Wm.,0799
MCCLARY, Samuel,0791,0801
MCCLEAN, ,0750, Chas.,0759,
W.W.,0900
MCCLEARY, David,0902
MCCLELLAN, George B.,1130
MCCLELLAND & HARRIS, ,0898
MCCLELLAND, (Miss),1216, Ada,
1215, Ferdinand,1216,
Fernando,1216, Hugh,0886,
0888,0890, John R.,1215,
Mary Y.,1216, Mary,1215,
1216, Mattie,1215, Sarah,
1215, W.L.,0889,1215,1216,
Zana,1215
MCCLISH, J.M.,0796, John,0755
MCCLORDEY, ,0863
MCCLORY, David,0789
MCCLURE & JOHNSON, ,1201
MCCLURE BUCK & CO., ,1205
MCCLURE, ,0886, Alexander,
0896, Augustus L.,1051,
Charlotte,1051, Curtiss H.,
1051, Elizabeth,1051, Ellen,
1227, Frank W.,1051,
Frederick B.,1216, James A.,
0874, James F.,1051,
John H.,1051, John,1051,
1216, Levi,1051, Margaret A.,
1051
MCCLURE, Mary J.,1051,
R.G.(Dr.),0889, R.G.,0890,
0895, Robert G.,0894,
Sarah E.,1051, Sarah,1216,
William G.,1051, William,
MCCLURE, Wm.,0886,0888,0890
MCCOLLOUGH, A.P.,0818, White,
0750
MCCOLLUM, E.A.,0895
MCCOMB, Rob,0820
MCCOMBS, Rob,0821, Robert,
0815
MCCOMICO & HAMNER, ,0802
MCCOMICO, G.,0805, James,0793,
M.L.,0796, W.L.,0791,0798
MCCONAN, J.W.,0808
MCCONICO, Rev.,0776
MCCONNELL, Cynthia A.,1213,
W.H.,0890, Wm.,0777
MCCONNICO, Lucinda,0932, Mary,

0930, Mr.,0789, Rhoda C.,
0955, Tennessee,0977, W.L.,
0962
MCCOOK, Gen.,0825
MCCORCLE, Elizabeth,1109
MCCORD & OGILVIE, ,0881
MCCORD, (Rev.),0900, Aaron C.,
0996, Allan,1135, Allen N.,
0793, Allen,1051, Ann,1135,
Anna V.,1051, Benjamin S.,
0996, Bettie,1217, Calvin,
0996, Chamilla S.,1216,
Cora,1196, Cowden,1216,
Deborah L.,1228, Elmina,
0996, Emmet A.,1051,
Fountain,0996
MCCORD, Harriet,0996, Harris O.,
1216, Henry G.,1216, J.,
0901, James A.,0996,
James C.,0996, James,0996,
Jane,1051, John H.,1051,
John Wesley,0996, John,
0996, Joseph C.,1216,
Joseph,0888,0890, Lillie V.,
1216, Macon S.,1074,
Manella M.,1216
MCCORD, Marks W.,1216,
Marshall P.,0996, Martha J.,
0996,1015, Mary,0996,
Milton A.,0996, Myra,0996,
Nannie J.,1229, Newton,
1015, R.A.,0902, Rebecca J.,
0996, Rebecca,0996, Robert A.Jr.,
1216, Russell F.,0996,
Russell,0996, Sallie A.,
1015
MCCORD, Sallie A.,1216,
Sarah J.,0996, Sarah,1051,
T.N.,0881, Thomas,1135,
W.H.,1074, William E.,1051,
William F.,0996, William H.,
1051
MCCORDY, R.C.,0889
MCCORKLE, Dr.,0855, William,
0850
MCCORMICK, Amanda,0941, Anna,
0941, Dorcas,0941, Dot,0941,
Lizzie D.,0941, Maury M.,
0941, Robert B.,0941,
William C.,0941
MCCORY, Capt.,0792
MCCOWEN, Alexr.,0802
MCCOY & CO., ,0803
MCCOY, ,0837, E.B.,0820,0821,
Ezekiel,0820, Henry,0813
MCCRACKEN, ,0775
MCCRARY, J.W.,0894, Jane,1165,
Nancy,1036, R.H.,0890,0893,
0894, Saml.,0793, Wade,0893
MCCREA, Richard,0902
MCCRERY, Thomas,0863, Wade,
0891
MCCRORY, Alva,1140, Annie,
1140, Eugene,1140, Hugh,
1186, Jame,1186, John,1140,
Sallie J.,1140, T.C.,0879,
Thomas C.,1140, Thomas F.,
1140
MCCUISTIAN, ,0863
MCCULLOCH, A.,0820, Alex,0819,
B.F.,0832, Benj.,0830
MCCULLOUGH, Benj.,0779,
Coleman R.,1217, D.J.,0890,
D.S.,0890,0896,1045,
Dilliston,1217, Frank,0848,
Margaret R.,1217, Martha J.,
1045,1217, Nancy,1217,
Nathan W.,0848, R.H.,0894,
Richard D.,1217, Ruben J.,
1217, William R.,1217
MCCURDY, David,0901, John,
0808
MCCURE, (Capt.),1204
MCCUTCHEN, Patrick,0791,0793,
Robert,0790, Saml.,0795,
Samuel,0791,0793
MCCUTCHIN, Capt.,0756
MCDANIEL, Collin,0794, J.J.,
0773
MCDERMOTT, J.,0827,0829, John,
0828,0833
MCDONALD & CO., ,0753
MCDONALD, Alexr.N.,0942,

Alexr.W.,0941, Allen,0941,
Angus,0941, Barnet A.,0942,
Caroline K.,0941, Donald G.,
0942, J.P.,0876, James B.,
0942, James E.,0941,
John O.,0942, John,0941,
Josephine,0993, Lizzie E.,
0942, Lura,0942, Luther B.,
0942
MCDONALD, Malcolm,0941, Mary,
0941, Olivia C.,0941,
Pinkney,0869, Sarah D.,
0942, Temperance,0941,
William E.,0942
MCDONALD-MCKINZIE, ,0855
MCDONNELL, B.W.,0858
MCDOUGAL, Mrs.,0829
MCDOWELL BROS., ,0875
MCDOWELL, D.N.S.,0757, E.C.,
0773, Edward C.,0942,
Horatio DePr.,0757, James,
0828, John L.,0942, Jos.C.,
0778, Joseph,0766, Nancy,
0942,1028, S.J.,0874, Saml.,
0771,0783, Samuel,0768
MCDOWERY, (Mrs.),1227
MCEWEN & DALE, ,0768,0942
MCEWEN, (Mr.),0893, ,0791,
Adalitia,0983, Alex,0815,
Capt.,0792, Christopher,
0803, Cynthia,0983, D.,0801,
David,0788,0789,0793,0794,
0996, J.B.,0788,0790,0796,
0797, J.L.,0796,0996, James,
0996, Jennie B.,0972,
John A.,0942, John B.,0789
MCEWEN, John B.,0972,0983,
0987, John L.,0793,0803,
1018, Margaret A.,0942,
Mary Alice,0987, S.D.F.,
0772, Samuel D.F.,0942,
Tabitha H.,0996, Thomas,
0794,0870, Wm.,0789
MCEWIN, Ebenezer,0779
MCFADDEN & SON, ,0829,1051
MCFADDEN, Anna E.,1051,
Edgar S.,1051,1052,
Elizabeth A.,1051, G.S.,
0829, Hollie,1051, J.S.,
0829, James S.,1051,
James T.,1051, Laura C.,
1051, S.G.,0833, Samuel,
1051, W.R.,0835,1051,
MCFALL, D.M.,0791, D.W.,0791,
Emma,0936, Wm.H.,0936
MCFALLS, W.H.,0787
MCFARLAND, (Miss),1169, Dicy,
1096, James,0842,0843,1096,
Jane,1096, Matilda,1091,
Van,0869, William,0843
MCFARLIN BROS., ,0879
MCFERRIN, J.A.,0808, J.B.,
0809, James,0809
MCGAFFERTY, Edward,0766
MCGAFFIN, Gen.Store,0881
MCGAHAH, James,0819
MCGAHEY, Alfred,1218, David,
0888,0890, Eliza,0933,
Geo.W.,0751
MCGAN, A.,0803
MCGARRAH, Margaret,1186
MCGAUGH, Wm.,0791
MCGAUGHEY, David,0899,
Hannah C.,1211
MCGAVACK, Randel,0805
MCGAVOCK, Bettie,0979, Carrie,
0996, Elizabeth,0996,
Frank Y.,1002, Hattie,0996,
J.R.,0979, James R.,0996,
John,0996, Mary,0996,
Randal,0996, Sarah,0996,
Theresa,1002, Winder,0996
MCGAW, J.P.,0768,0772,
Samuel P.,0759
MCGEE & KING, ,0766
MCGEE, ,0776, C.,0759,
William,0795,0860
MCGILL, ,0863, Elizabeth,1162,
Franklin,1162, Ida I.,1162,
James,1162, John A.,1162,
Kittie,1163, Lewis Cass,
1162, Lucy,1162, Mary E.,
1162, Mary,1162, Nancy,1162,

Priscilla,1162, Robert P.,
1162, Robert S.,1163,
Sallie,1162, Sarah J.,1162
MCGILL, Tennie,1151, Thomas B.,
1162, W.M.,1151, William,
0871,1162
MCGILVEY, W.,0796
MCGOWAN, E.H.,1163, Eddie,
1163, Florence,1163,
Henry C.,1163, Isabella,
1163, Margaret J.,1163,
Nancy A.,1163, Nancy F.,
1163, Rebecca W.,1163,
Rebecca,1163, Robert F.,
1163, Samuel G.,1163,
William C.,1163
MCGOWEN, E.(Rev.),1066, Lucy,
1066
MCGREGOR, ,0813, Albert,0849,
Andrew,0848, Betsey,1197,
W.A.,0770, W.C.,0890, W.F.,
0890,0896,0898
MCGREW, J.H.,0876, James H.,
1163, Joseph H.,1163,
Letitia,1163, Mary B.,1163,
Nancy,1163, Samuel J.,0876,
1163, William,0870,1163
MCGRUDY, Catharine,1071
MCGUIRE, Elizabeth,1155, J.P.,
0895, Jane,0966, Nancy B.,
0912, Patrick,0752,0754,
0766,0767,0768,0771,0772,
0779
MCHENRY, B.,0809
MCINTYRE, Capt.,0751, Charles,
0790
MCJIMSEY, Dr.,0767, John W.,
0757
MCKAIG, Mary,1181
MCKANNON, Daniel,0764
MCKAY & FIGUERS, ,0942,0943
MCKAY, (Mr.),0943, Alexander,
0943, Alexr.W.,0943,
Alice F.,0943, Anna E.,
0943, Ashley J.,0943,
Cameron H.,0943, Eliza J.,
0942, Eliza,0943, Elizabeth,
0944, John J.,0792, John P.,
0970, John,0791,0801,0807,
Margaret,0970, Mary,0928,
Mattie,0970
MCKAY, Phineas E.,0943, R.M.,
0770, Rebecca,0943, Richard A.,
0942,0943, Robert M.,0942,
0943, Robt.M.,0753,0770,
0772, Sallie R.,0943,
Thomas J.,0943, Thomas,
0789,0793, Thos.,0801, W.A.,
0797, William,0807
MCKEA, Duncan,0764
MCKEE, Capt.,0752, J.M.,0890,
Lizzie,1232, Louisa,0931,
Sarah A.,0953
MCKEITHEN, Dr.,0758
MCKENNON, Geo.N.,0781, W.R.,
0781
MCKENZIE, Alexander,1108,
Hettie,1108
MCKEY, William,0822
MCKINDRY, Rev.,0860
MCKINLEY & JACKSON, ,1064
MCKINLEY, Hiram,0848, J.J.,
0833, J.T.,0819,0832
MCKINNEY & CO., M.N.,0878
MCKINNEY, C.C.,0897, Christop.C.,
1217, David,0793, James,
1217, John,0791, Mary,1218,
Temperance,1217, Thos.,0801
MCKISSACK, ,0863, Alonzo,0943,
Archibald M.,0943, Daniel,
0865,0871, David,0874,
Ellina,0943, James,0868,
Orville W.,0943, S.(Dr.),
0774, William,0774
MCKNIGHT, ,0777,0813,0839,
A.B.,1108, A.D.,1052, A.M.,
0818, Alexr.,0813, Augustine,
0944, Cora,0944, D.M.,0819,
Ezekiel M.,1198, F.A.,0819,
J.J.,0832, James L.,1052,
James,0820,0821,0830,
Jas.T.C.,0824, Kate,0944,
Keziah,0944, Lelian,0944

MCKNIGHT, Lucy,1076, Luther,
0944, M.W.,0871, Mary,0944,
1052,1108, Mattie Lee,0944,
Moses,0849, Nancy,1198,
Samuel H.,0944, Samuel,
0944, Sarah,1023, Susie,
1052, Thomas,0889,0890,
W.J.,0829
MCKNOB, C.A.,0819
MCKSSACK, Alonzo,0775
MCLAIN, Eliza,1218
MCLANAHAN, Harriett,1021
MCLANE & BROS., ,0881
MCLANE, Flora,1218, G.A.,1218,
Jesse,1218, Sarah J.,0922
MCLAUGHLIN, Catharine,1052,
Ervin M.,1052, George W.,
1052, James M.,1052,
John R.,0818,0840, Joseph W.,
1052, Mary N.,1052, S.R.,
0822, Samuel,0840, Tennissee,
1052, William H.,1052
MCLAW, ,0894
MCLEAN, ,0775,0813, Capt.,
0751, E.B.,0819, E.H.,1224,
Edward,0902, Ephraim Jr.,
0759, Frank J.,0787, Jesse,
0887, Margaret R.,1217,
Mary T.,1075, Missie,1207,
R.O.,0895, Rachel,1190,
Sarah M.,1039, W.H.,0895,
W.S.,0889, W.W.,0900,
William,0896
MCLEAN, William,0899
MCLELLAN, Robt.,0795
MCLELLAND, N.L.,0903
MCLEMORE & BROS., ,0768
MCLEMORE, A.J.,0944,0996,
Albert S.,0997, Anna S.,
0997, Annie L.,0997,
Annie Lou,1060, Atkins P.,
0944, Bethenia S.,0996,
Bethenia,0997, Jamie,0944,
John D.,0944, Lemuel P.,
0944, Lesey M.,0944, Lesey,
0944, Lizzie M.,0997, M.M.,
0977
MCLEMORE, M.S.(Debrey),0944,
Mary M.,0944, Robert,0944,
Robina,0944, Sidney G.,
0944, W.S.,0796,0797,0800,
0804,0892,1060,1193,
Wickliffe F.,0944, William S.,
0996, William W.,0997,
Wm.S.,0765
MCMAHAN, Abraham,0870,0872,
Daniel,0789, J.H.,0802,
0804, Richard,0754, Samuel,
0867, William,0862, Wm.,0809
MCMAHON, D.,0797, Elizabeth C.,
0973, Ella M.,1200, Jennie,
1200, Nannie,1200
MCMAKIN, Capt.,0752
MCMANNIS, Capt.,0792
MCMAY, Capt.,0792
MCMEEN, Charles W.,0945,
Elizabeth,0944, Harriet D.,
0945, John A.,0944, John W.,
0945, Margaret R.,0931,
Thomas F.,0944, Thomas S.,
0945
MCMILLAN, Edward E.,1109,
Elizabeth,0940, Frank P.,
1109, Frank P.Jr.,1109,
Jane F.,1109, Josephine,
1109, Murray,1109, Robinson,
1109
MCMILLIN, R.,0859, Robinson,
0850
MCMINN, Gov.,0828, Hannah,
1054, Joseph,0795
MCMULLEN, Capt.,0792
MCMUNN, ,0767
MCMURRAY, Lt.,0799, S.T.,0757
MCMURRAY, Anna,1110, David,
1110, E.C.(Mrs.),1109,1110,
John M.(Rev.),1110, S.T.,
0959
MCNABB, William,0872
MCNAIRY, ,1120
MCNEIL, Dr.,0754,0767,
Gillespie,0757, Mary E.,
1055, Wm.,0757

MCNEILL, Capt.,0751, Wm.,0771
MCNEILLY, Thos.,0759
MCNIEL, William,0769,0771
MCNIELL, Wm.(Dr.),0783
MCNIGHT, Capt.,0850
MCNISH, Horatio,0793
MCNUTT, Capt.,0751, J.A.,0798,
John,0794
MCPEAK, Robert,0856
MCPHAIL & MCGILRAY, ,0766
MCPHAILT & ENGLISH, ,0803
MCPHERSON, (Gen.),1024,
Joseph,1018, Mahala H.,
1018, Mary,1018
MCQUIDDY, Achsah,1219, Geo.W.,
0772, H.C.,0899, J.C.,1219,
John,1219, Nancy A.,1219,
Newton,1218, W.V.,1219
MCQUIDLEY, Mr.,0767
MCRADY, Ephraim,1218, Flarins S.,
1218, J.E.,0897, Joseph A.,
1218, Margaret E.,1218,
Sarah,1218, Susan,1218,
Virginia J.,1225
MCRAY, William,0805
MCSPADDEN, William,0841
MCSPADDIN, William,0842
MCSWAIN, William,0847
MCTEE, Margaret,0951
MCWHIRTER, Geo.F.,0854,
George,0857, Jeremiah,0850
MCWHORTER, Jane,1194
MEACHAM, Matthew,0796
MEADE, (Bishop),0810
MEADOR, Mary A.,1224
MEADOW, Jos.,0797
MEADOWS, A.M.,0893, Joseph,
0823, Solomon,0889, Victoria C.,
1213
MEADWS, Jerry,0870
MEBANE, Alexander,0841,
Jeanette,0980, Martha E.,
1003, Mickie,1003, William,
1003
MEBANER, Capt.,0792
MEBLEY, ,0767
MEEK, Mr.,0803
MELCHAR, Kate R.,1054
MELDON BROS., ,0879
MELSON, Fannie,1158
MELTON, A.,0879
MENEES, George W.,0798, James,
0841,0845,0853
MENGEE, Joseph,0874
MENIFEE, Nimrod,0811,0820,
Willis,0897
MERCHANT, J.T.,0829
MERITT, Susan E.,1015, W.H.,
0799
MERRETT, Rebecca J.,1005,
Sally,0795
MERRILL, James,0803, S.S.,
0765
MERRITT, Alice,0999, James,
0795, John,0842,0978, Lewis,
0842, Nancy,0998, Sallie,
0978, Sarah A.,1154,
Stephen,0841, Susan,0978,
Thomas,0795, W.H.,0897
MESS, A.W.,0791
METCALF, Warner,0796
MEYERS, ,1021, John,0868,
William,0850
MIDDLETON, Capt.,0752
MILES & MCKINLEY, ,0829,1193
MILES, Alice E.,1066, Carolina,
1064, Catherine E.,1052,
Dicey,1052, Dr.,0855,
James H.,0867,0868, Nancy,
1052, Pattison,1052, Rachel,
0915, Thomas B.,1052,
Thomas,0795,0842,1052
MILIGAN, Jane,0913
MILLAM, W.W.,0835
MILLER, (Capt.),1202,1231, ,
0813,0880, A.,0821, A.G.,
0826, A.N.,0893, Adam,0888,
Alfred,0827,1053, Arthur,
1024, B.A.(Mrs.),0997,
Capt.,1041, Catharine,0945,
Dave,1033, E.M.,0890,0893,
Elizabeth,1047, Emily E.,
0961, G.H.,0879, Gertrude,

1095
MILLER, Harriett,0932,
  Henry A.,0776, I.D.,1052,
  I.M.,1053, Isaac,0880,
  J.E.,1095, J.L.,0759,
  James,0821, Jane,1043,
  Jemima S.,0945, Joe A.B.,
  0997, Joe E.(Miss),1073,
  John A.,0945,0997, John W.,
  0789,0797, John,0759,0760,
  0821,0870,0902
MILLER, John,0945,0997,1085,
  L.D.,0818, Maggie B.,0997,
  Mamie,1033,1053, Mary E.,
  1037, Mary M.,0997, Mary,
  1085, Melville J.,0945,
  Nannie,1096, Narciora,1053,
  Narcissa,1043, Nathaniel,
  1167, R.W.,0852, Rachel D.,
  1013, Rob,0816, Simon,0819
MILLER, Susan J.,0997, Susan,
  0945, T.C.H.,0890,0894,0896,
  1226, T.D.,0817, T.G.,0895,
  Temperance,1167, Thomas B.,
  0997, Thomas,0802,0872,
  W.G.,1096, W.W.,0897,0997,
  Washington W.,0945,
  William C.,0945, William W.,
  0997, Woody,1085
MILLFORD, J.,0821
MILLS, Capt.,0752, S.C.,0877
MILROY, Gen.,0873
MINOR, Henry,0820, I.P.,0754,
  Martha,0909
MIOT, Pamelia(Mrs.),0972
MISROON, Henry,1069
MITCHELL & SHEPARD, ,0874
MITCHELL & SPERRY, ,0874
MITCHELL, ,0775,0776,0833,
  0982, Addison,1053, Andrew,
  0775, Bates,1163, Benj.F.,
  0779, Bibbie B.,1163, Capt.,
  0751,0752,0823, Catharine,
  1163, Catherine,0904,
  David A.,0985, Edward,0842,
  0846,0850,0853,0854, Eliza,
  0985, Elizabeth,1163, Gen.,
  0829
MITCHELL, Gen.,0873, J.C.(Rev.),
  0783, J.C.,0779, James C.,
  0816,0849,0870, James W.,
  1163, James W.C.,1163, John,
  1163, Joseph,1163, Logan,
  1163, Margaret,1163, Mark,
  0814,0815,0819, Martha,1163,
  Martin,0814, Mary A.,1053,
  Mary E.,1053
MITCHELL, Mary,0985,1163, N.,
  0807, Nancy,1163, Oscar L.,
  1163, Robert H.,1163,
  Robert,0842, S.W.,0750,
  0773,0779, Saml.,0801,
  Samuel,0864, Sarah A.,1163,
  Sarah C.,1039, T.F.,1163,
  Thomas,0813,0819,0843,
  W.D.,0762,0764, William,
  0812,0818
MITCHELL, William,0819,0829,
  0831,1040,1053, Wm.,0832,
  Wm.C.,0844
MOBRY, Sarah,1037
MODRALL, N.P.,0902
MOFFET, Charlotte,1051
MOFFETT, James,0898
MOFFITT, O.D.,0792, Robert,
  0874
MOLDENHOLDER, J.,0855
MOLDER, Susan A.,1141
MONDAY, Col.,0852
MONROE, ,0767, A.,0809,
  N.Watson,0810
MONTAGUE, T.,0827, Thomas,
  0840
MONTFLORENCE, Jas.C.,0841
MONTGOMERY BROS.,,0897,1206
MONTGOMERY, Alice E.,1164,
  Denny,1164, Esther,1164,
  1219, Ethel,1164, Flora,
  1164, Gertrude I.,1164,
  Hoyle,1164,1164, Hugh,0815,
  J.O.,1164, Jane L.,1219,
  Jane S.,1219, Jimmie,1164,
  John O.,1219, John,0755,

L.P.,0794, Lillie,1164,
  Magie L.,1164
MONTGOMERY, Margaret P.,1219,
  Mary E.,1219, Mary,1164,
  R.S.,0897, Robert H.,1164,
  Robert Sr.,1219, Robert,
  1219, Robt.S.,1164, Susan,
  1164, Susie,1164, T.Clarence,
  1164, T.S.,1164, Thomas A.,
  1164, Thomas,1164
MOODY, C.J.,1133,1164,
  Charley E.,0997, Clement J.,
  1164, Ella B.,0997, G.W.,
  0876, George.W.,1164,
  Georgie,1164, Ida,0997,
  J.G.,0997, J.T.,0997,
  James A.,0997, John T.,
  0997, Letitia,1164, Mary Lou,
  0997, Mary O.,0997, Mary,
  0997, S.T.,0856
MOODY, Sallie C.M.,1133,
  Samuel S.,1164, Walter B.,
  0997, William P.,0997,
  William,0997, Winston G.,
  1164
MOON & BARNES, ,0881
MOON, Bertha Erie,1165,
  George,0879, J.M.,0881,
  James P.,1165, John R.,
  1165, Mary Ann,1165,
  Mary Myrtle,1165, Mattie M.,
  1165, Pleasant B.,1165,
  William U.,1165
MOONEY, Sarah J.,1152
MOORE & COX, ,0828
MOORE & PREWETT, ,0768
MOORE, (Gen.),1164, (Miss),
  1151, (Mrs.),0808, ,0813,
  0863, A.M.,1146, Alexander,
  0997, Ashley,0899, C.W.,
  1046, Capt.,0792,0850,
  D.B.(Rev.),1138, D.D.,0836,
  David B.,0848, Dicey,1052,
  Dora M.,0945, Eleanor,0997,
  Elijah,0842, Elizabeth,0979
MOORE, Frances,1208, G.W.,
  0890, George W.,0895,
  George,0822, H.O.,0808,
  Hannah,1224, Imogene,0945,
  J.,0803, J.A.,0785,0830,
  0893, J.C.,0827, J.L.,0781,
  1019, J.M.,0781, James A.,
  0818, James,0997, Jennie M.,
  1146, John A.,0864,0867,0872
MOORE, John C.,0826, John F.,
  0892, John T.,0754,0768,
  0783, John,0805,0808,0869,
  0927,0945,1008, Jonathan,
  0886, Julia R.,0945, Julia,
  1046, Laird B.,0945,
  Lillie B.,0945, Lucy,0945,
  Margaret,1174, Mary E.,
  1008, Mary J.,0945, Mary,
  0826
MOORE, Mary,1008, Mathew B.,
  0945, Matthew,0945, Mrs.,
  0802, N.I.,0781, Nancy,1112,
  Nannie,0945, Penelope,1209,
  R.N.,0787, R.W.,0893,
  Reuben,0945, Richard B.,
  0758, Robert S.,0945, S.,
  0801, S.B.,0759, Saml.B.,
  0755, Samuel,0807, Sarah,
  0945
MOORE, Sarah,0958, Susan,1156,
  Thomas,0795,0834,0868,
  Thos.D.,0888, W.F.,0764,
  0779, W.J.,0753, W.P.,0895,
  Walter,0945, Washington,
  0843, William F.,0945,
  William P.,0800, Wm.L.,
  0945, Ziza,0867
MOORHEAD, John,0751
MOREEN, C.,0933
MORELEY, ,0803
MORELY, Adaline,1023
MOREY, Ira,0807
MORGAN, (Gen.),1111, ,0838,
  0863,1091, Alice,1219,
  Allen,1069, Belle,1219,
  Benjamin,0833, Calvin,0770,
  David E.,1219, E.D.,0763,
  Elizabeth A.,1051, Ella P.,

1219, Gen.,0834,0968,
  George W.,1005, George,
  0869, Hattie E.,1069,
  Howard,0833
MORGAN, J.& A.,0768, J.A.,
  1068, J.H.,0817, Jack,0880,
  James A.,1069, James J.,
  1219, John H.,1032,1135,
  John,0852, Kate,1058,
  Lizzie C.,1219, Martha L.,
  1219, Martha,1170, Mary A.,
  1193, Mary E.,1219, Penelope,
  1167, Rachel,1170, Robert,
  0880
MORGAN, S.S.,0836, Sarah E.,
  1069, Scott D.,1219, Sylvia,
  1069, William B.,1219,
  William C.,1219, Wm.H.,0871
MORLEY, Bettie K.,1046,
  Thomas G.,1046
MORRING, Maggie,1160
MORRIS & CO., D.,0878
MORRIS, ,0813, A.D.,0859,
  Allen,1219,1220, Chlora A.,
  1220, Elisha G.,1219,
  George,0837, Henry,0891,
  Hugh,0841, J.L.,0808,
  Joel A.,0890, Leona,1119,
  Margaret E.,1219,1220,
  Mary A.,1205, Mary,0858,
  Matilda,1047, R.C.,1119,
  R.S.,0818
MORRIS, R.W.,0809, Rev.,0860,
  William A.,1220
MORRISON, Andrew,0901,
  Margaret S.,1229
MORSE, A.,0809, Adolphus,0809
MORTON & WILHOIT, ,0874
MORTON, ,0863, Ann F.,1175,
  Annie,1165, Bill,0870,
  C.E.(Miss),1182, Capt.,
  0792, Catharine W.,1025,
  1193, J.A.,0893, J.H.,0825,
  J.W.,0792,0898, Jacob,0874,
  1165, Jake,0799, James L.,
  1165, Jesse,0891, Joe,0820,
  John J.,1165, John W.,0990
MORTON, John W.,1016, John(Mrs.),
  0803, John,0869, M.L.,0875,
  Mark J.,1165, Martha E.,
  1165, Nancy M.,1165,
  Nannie R.,1165, Prof.,0775,
  0781, Q.E.,1165, Q.Emmet,
  1165, Rufus H.,1165, Samuel,
  0794, Sarah,1048, Tennissee L.,
  1052
MOSBEY, J.C.,1027
MOSBY & CO., ,0829
MOSBY, J.,0829
MOSELEY, Bessie,1165, Carrie Drue,
  1166, Edward A.,1165,
  Janie T.,1165, Jesse T.L.P.,
  1165, Maggie E.,1165,
  Mary S.,1165, Mary T.,1165,
  Mattie Louise,1165, Mattie,
  1165, Rebecca M.,1185,
  Rebecca,1186, Teressa,1141,
  Thomas G.,1165
MOSER, Elizabeth,1091
MOSES, Mary A.,1161
MOSIER, Henry,0842
MOSLEY, ,0863, Henry,0870,
  Peter,0846, Thos.B.,0880,
  Tom,0864
MOSS, A.W.,0798,0803, Alexander,
  0797, Alice M.,0924,
  Charles,0803, Eliza,1103,
  Elizabeth,1049, H.K.,0890,
  0893, J.D.,0785, Lou M.,0967
MOTHERAL, Emma T.,1005,
  Joseph,1005
MOTTLEY, Benjamin,0842,
  John D.,0850, Samuel T.,
MOUNT, Mary A.,1219
MOURTON, Eliza J.,1210
MOXLEY, George,1076, Joseph,
  0841
MOXLY, C.R.,0799
MUIRHEAD, John,0777,0854
MULINS, James,0871
MULLEN, James,0863
MULLIN, ,0863
MULLINS, (Mill),0875, Nancy,

1177, Olevia A.,0956,
William,0956
MUNBREUN, William,0793
MUNN, Capt.,0792
MUNOZ, Maria,1070
MUNTER, J.B.,0768
MURFREE, (Spring),0805, ,
0796,0823,0863, Ada J.,1054,
Esther L.,1042, Fannie D.,
1054, Hardy,0826,0841,1042,
Hordy,1054, J.B.,0817,0818,
0826,0829,0830,0832,0833,
James B.,1053,1054,
Jane R.,1054, Janie,0835,
Libbie M.,1054, M.B.,0817
MURFREE, M.B.,0832,0835,
Mary A.,1053, Mary R.,1054,
Mary,0830, Matthias B.,
1054, Talley,1054
MURFREESBORO MILL, ,0830
MURPHEY & BUCHANAN, ,0854,
0855
MURPHEY & CO., A.,0878
MURPHEY & STEPHENS, ,0878
MURPHEY, C.B.,0878, John,0871,
Louisa,0938, Mary E.,1027
MURPHY & WILSON, ,1123
MURPHY, ,0813, Anna,0959,
Hardy,0818, Henry,1048,
J.B.,0785, Margaret N.,
1182, Mary E.,1048
MURRAY, Cynthia,1057, G.H.,
0799, Henry,1220, J.J.,0895,
0898, James J.,0893,1220,
John T.,0897, L.L.,0889,
Mary A.,1220, Matilda,1220,
Mattie J.,0961, Shade,0961,
Thomas,0897, W.J.,0799
MURRELL, Caroline F.,1220,
James,0795, John A.,0795,
Josephine,1220, Richard,
1220, S.J.,1220, Sarah,1220,
William,0795
MURREY, Anna,0998, Ennis,0998,
John B.,0998, Maggie J.,
0998, Sallie E.,0998
MURRY, John M.,0878, Richard(Negro),
0856, Robert,0874
MUSE BROS., ,0899
MUSE, Geo.P.,0871, George P.,
1165, George,1166, Georgie A.,
1166, Henry K.W.,1166,
Isaac,0862, J.B.,0880,
James,1166, Jo C.,1166,
John T.,1166, Malinda M.,
1165, Mary A.,1166, Mary,
1180, Nancy,1102, Nannie,
1166, Orville,1165, Richard,
0862
MUSE, Sarah,1142, W.R.,0879,
Will J.,0868,1166
MYERS, Alexr.,0801, Bettie,
0942, G.W.,0826, Hampton,
0893, L.D.,0764, Leonard D.,
0942,0945, S.D.,0765,
Sara H.,0945, Shadrack,0792
MYRICK, Hillard,0757, John,
0759
NAFF, John,0836
NANCE, A.J.,0894, Betty M.,
1055, Carrie E.,1166,
Clement,1166, James E.,
1166, James W.,0888, James,
0939, Josiah C.,1055,
Julia E.,1166, L.J.,0898,
Martha A.,0939, Martha E.,
1166, Martha,0995, Mary,
1166, Reuben,1166, Sarah B.,
1166, Thomas H.,1166
NANCE, Thomas,1166, William G.,
1166, William T.,1166
NAPIER, ,1005, E.W.,0980,
Eliza A.,0928, John M.,
0761, M.C.,0755, Mary J.,
0980, Sarah M.,0761
NASH, Jerusha,1182, Squire,
1228, Thomas,0821, William,
0811,0812,0813,0814,0819,
0820,0821,0833
NATHAN & CO., M.,0829
NAYLOR, Arthur T.,1054,
Eugene B.,1054, Hannah,
1054, John M.,1054, Mr.& Mrs.,

1054, Wade H.,1054, William E.,
1054
NEAL & LIGAN, ,0855
NEAL & WARD, ,0853
NEAL, Alexr.,0851, Jake,0849,
James A.,1081, James,0834,
Jane M.,1081, Nancy,1125,
W.Z.,0853, William,0843
NEALEY, David,0870
NEASE, Katie,1172
NEELEY, ,0750,0775, A.E.,0764,
Capt.,0792, G.W.,0802,
George,0789,0793,0797,
Green T.,0867, J.N.,0863,
James,0789,0793, M.E.,0818,
S.M.,0782, W.W.,0782, Wm.,
0794,0805
NEELY, ,0803, Catherine C.,
0908, Elizabeth,0998,
Fannie,0998, George,0791,
Isaac L.,0998, Isaac,0998,
J.W.,0797,0798, John C.,
0998, Sarah E.C.,0998
NEGRO, Charles,0822, Jess,
0820, Sarah,0823
NEICE, Simpson,0864
NEIL & DARK, ,0897
NEIL & SHEARIN, ,0898
NEIL, (Mr.),1221, ,0863,
Alexander,0886, Andrew,
0886, C.C.,0889, E.J.,0896,
Edgar,1220, J.B.,0889,0897,
J.F.,0872, J.H.(Rev.),0839,
James H.,0871,0872,
James R.,0889, James,0886,
John L.,0871, John T.,0867,
0871, Lambert C.,1220,
Letitia,1220
NEIL, William,0869, Z.W.,0889
NEILL, Mary,1201
NEILSON, Patrick D.,1072,
Sarah H.,1071
NELSON & CANNON, ,0766
NELSON & IVY, ,0829
NELSON, ,0863, Agnes J.,1054,
Benjamin A.,1054, Capt.,
0792, J.,0829, J.H.,0828,
J.W.,0829,1041, James,1110,
John W.,0869, Joseph G.,
1054, Joseph W.,1054,
Kate R.,1054, Mary,1054,
Mathew,0830, Moses A.,1054,
Moses,1054, Pleasant,0759
NELSON, Pleasant,0772, R.M.,
0826, Theodica,1110, Thomas,
0811,0819, Virginia E.,1225
NEREN, Amanda,1205, Isaiah,
1205, S.L.,1205
NERING, John,0874
NERIS, Elena,1188
NETHERINGTON, ,0751
NEUGENT, David,0829,0833,
J.D.,0840, William,0821
NEULIN, J.,0766
NEVILS, Alice,0999, Annie C.,
0999, Augie V.,0998,
Edward M.,0999, Ella G.,
0998, Emmett,0999, J.W.L.,
0998, John L.,0998, John M.,
0999, Josiah W.,0998,
Josiah,0983,0998,0999,
Lydia A.,0999, Mary A.,
0983, Mr.,0999, Robert H.,
0999, Sallie M.,0998
NEVILS, Sallie,0983,0998,
Sarah,0999, Wm.W.,0998
NEVINS, J.G.,0799
NEW, William,0843
NEWBRY, James,0843
NEWBY, Foster,0849, Roland,
0843
NEWCOMB, N.,0799
NEWELL, S.C.,0779
NEWMAN, (Col.),1162, ,0813,
A.H.,0879, Mernira,1074,
T.W.,0894, Wm.H.,0824
NEWSOM, Ella V.,1005, James E.,
1005, Lucinda,0905, Sallie N.,
1005
NEWSON, Randolph,0868, Thomas,
0880, William,0874
NEWTON, Alexr.(Rev.),0881,
Fannie E.,1172, Geo.(Rev.),

0881, George,0779,0838, J.,
0876, James S.,1130, James,
0877, Ludie P.,1130
NICHOL, H.D.,1048, Lizzie S.,
1048, W.L.,0798
NICHOLLS, C.,0781
NICHOLS & NICHOLS, ,0768
NICHOLS, (Capt.),1061, C.G.R.,
0750, J.H.,0893, Joe,0819,
Willis,0764
NICHOLSON & GOODLOE, ,0766
NICHOLSON Sr., John,0764
NICHOLSON, ,0775,0796, A.O.P.,
0759,0762,0763,0764,0765,
0773,0774,0778,0922, Capt.,
0792, Hunter,0773,0787,
Martha,0928,1003, Mary A.,
1086
NILES, Charles,0826,0827
NILMS, James,0848
NIPPS, Bob,0849
NIX, David,1221, Fannie,1221,
Levina,1089, Robin,1221,
S.T.,1089, Vicey,1221
NIXON, ,0776, John,0776
NOAH, J.J.,0892
NOE, Peter,0813
NOELARD, Thomas,0821
NOLAN, Sarah,1014, Stephen,
1014
NOLEN, Benjamin,0801, Berry,
0794, Capt.,0792, David,
0766, J.S.,0898
NOLES, Nancy,0952
NOLIN, Bryant,0759
NORFLEST, P.F.,0836
NORMAN, ,0813, Amanda R.,1167,
Catharine J.,1167, Elizabeth A.,
1167, Elizabeth,1167, Henry,
1167, James L.,1167, P.W.,
1167, Sallie,1167, Sarah G.,
1167, T.E.(Mrs.),1167, T.H.,
0852, Thomas,0812, William,
0850
NORRIS, Capt.,0858
NORTH, ,0829, Alice,0999,
Ann W.,0999, Carrick H.,
0999, Eliza,0999, Elizabeth,
0999, Eloise,0999, H.B.,
0808,0976,0999, Henry B.,
0999,1014, Ida,0999,
James A.,0999, Jesse W.,
0999, Lucy,0999, Maggie,
0976, Margaret S.,0999,
Martha J.,0999
NORTH, Mary,0848,0933,0946,
1061, R.H.,0999, Robert J.,
0999, Sarah E.,1014,
Thomas B.,0999, William,
0822
NORTHCOTT, Benjamin,1136,
Jane,1136, R.S.,0831
NORTHEN, Saml.,0768
NORTON, E.A.,0898, H.W.,1142,
Jeffie E.,1142, Thomas,0768
NORVELL, A.S.,1142, Jane M.,
1149, John,1149, Mollie J.,
1142
NORVILLE, ,0863, John W.,0867,
John,0867, W.B.,0877,0879,
Wm.,0871,0878
NOTGRASS, Jerry C.,0782
NOWLIN, Bryan,0759, Callie M.,
0946, Fannie S.,0946, J.E.,
1130, J.O.,0889, J.S.(Dr.),
0889, J.S.,0889, Janway W.,
0946, Mattie Lee,0946,
Sarah H.,0946, Swanson,
0876, T.P.,0946
NOWLING, Swanson,0876
NUCKOLLS, G.S.,1044, Mary,
1044
NUMAN, Drucilla,1048
NUNN, John,0834, Malinda,1013,
William,0834
O'CONNER, Albert,0999, Anne,
0999, Annie,0999, Jerome J.,
0999, Laura,0999, Miles,
0999, William,0999
O'FLYNN, C.,0827, Charles,
0812
O'NEAL, ,0863, E.J.,1116,
J.H.,0868, John F.,0980,

John H.,0869, Martha A.,
1192, Matilda,0980, Nancy,
1224, Priscilla,0980,
William P.,0895
O'NEIL, Edmund,0785, John,
0867
O'REITLEY, J.C.,0750, James C.,
0751, James,0756
O'REILLY, Dr.,0767
OAKES, Jesse,0772, W.J.,0768
OAKLEY, ,0751, E.S.,0851,
Emily,0913, Levina,1134,
Martin W.,0888,0890,
Nathan,0848,0850,0851,
William,0842
OAKS, Capt.,0752
OATMAN, L.,0750
OBERALL, Eliza,1187
OCHILTREE, W.B.,1065
ODEN, Louisa,1029, T.H.,0808
ODER, T.H.,0797
ODIL, Rachael,1143
ODILL, W.A.,0775
ODUM & CO., J.F.,0855
ODUM, J.T.,1118
OFFICER, Berr,0849
OGDEN, S.,0840
OGILVIE, (Mr.),1216, Capt.,
0792, Cynthia M.,1222,
David,0778, Elizabeth N.,
1222, Lillie V.,1216,
Margaret,1160, Mary R.,
1222, Mattie,1135, R.,0792,
R.A.,0772,0899, Richard,
1222, Thos.J.,0868, W.W.,
1215, William H.,1222, Zana,
1215
OGLE, A.,0878
OGLEVIE & CRAWFORD, ,0879
OGLEVIE, T.J.,0879
OHRENNE, Ed,0833
OLD JOE, (Coachman),0758
OLDHAM, Capt.,0851, Judith,
1099, R.P.,0855
OLDS, Eliza A.,0925, James,
0925, Martha,0925, Thomas,
0808
OLIPHANT, ,0777, Capt.,0752,
James,0819, Saml.,0777
OLIVER, Althere E.,0947,
Carl L.,0946, Dalton A.,
0946, Edith,0946, Emma L.,
0946, Ethel,0946, G.Meldon,
0946, Hezekiah,0946,
Hillary G.,0946, Hilliary L.,
0946, Hubert L.,0946,
Mahala,0946, Milton L.,
0946, Valderia A.,0946
OLMSTEAD, C.G.,0802, C.S.,
0795
ORBORN, James,0899
ORDWAY, C.N.(Dr.),0779
ORGAIN & RAGLAND, ,1121
ORGAIN & WATKINS, ,0854
ORGAIN, J.F.,0847
ORGAN, W.M.,1122
ORMAN, Adam,0946, Anna L.,
0946, Capt.,0792, Henry,
0946, I.S.,0912, James S.,
0946, Jannie C.,0946, Julia,
0946, Maggie,0946, Martha,
0946, Mary,0946, Rhoda,0946,
Robert,0946, Sally B.,0946,
Sarah,0946, Wm.E.,0946,
Wm.L.,0946
ORMAND, Margaret P.,1219
ORR, A.F.,0852, Alfred D.,
1222, Catharine O.,1222,
D.F.,1167, Daisy,1221,
David F.,1167, David L.,
1222, David,0933, Emily C.,
1228, Emily,1221, F.M.,0894,
J.L.,0890,0896,0899,1221,
J.R.,0770, James,0893,
John Fain,1167, John M.,
1222
ORR, John,0887,1167,1221,
Joseph C.,1221, Julia,1221,
Leah C.,1222, Leah,1221,
Margaret,1190, Martha Ann,
1176, Martha M.,1222,
Mary A.,1167,1221, Mary C.,
1226, Minerva,1221, Minnie J.,
1167, Nellie M.,1222,
Penelope,1167, R.A.,0889
ORR, Robert A.,1221, Robert J.,
1221,1222, Robert,0902,1221,
Robin,0887, Robt.Williams,
1221, S.C.,0895, Sallie S.,
1221, Sallie,1221, Samuel,
0890, Sarah E.,1222, Sarah,
0933, Temperance,1167,
Thomas A.,1221, W.C.,1167,
William D.,0896
ORR, William M.,1167, William R.,
1221, Wm.D.,0868, Wm.M.,0891
OSBORN & BOCK, ,1026
OSBORN & CO., ,0880
OSBORN & JUSTICE, ,0880
OSBORN BOCK & CO., ,1070
OSBORN, ,0813,0863, Elizabeth,
1018, G.G.,0867,0877, H.,
0828,0829,0837, H.T.,0764,
Hannah,1018, J.,0829, J.C.,
0895, J.R.,0833, James,0888,
0891, Noble,1018, R.F.,0833,
W.C.,0833
OSBORNE, H.T.,0963,E.R.,0759
OSBURN, Capt.,0751
OSCEOLA, (Indian),0797
OSLIN, J.O.,0818,0833,
James O.,1055, James,1055,
Lucas,1055, Mary A.,1055
OTEY, (Rev.),0816, Bishop,
0750, J.H.(Rev.),0802, J.H.,
0803,0809, Jas.H.(Rev.),
0783, Jas.O.(Rev.),0779
OTT, W.A.,0881
OTTE, F.H.,0874
OTTENROSS, L.,0768
OTTS, J.M.P.(Rev.),0783
OVERALL, A.M.,0818,0831,
Asbury,1028,1029, Emma,
1029, Floyd,1029, G.W.,0818,
Gertrude,1029, Hudie,1029,
J.M.,0826,0829, James,1029,
John H.,1028, Lucretia H.,
1035, N.D.,0833, Rachel W.,
1029, Robert,0811
OVERTON, John,0973, Mary A.,
1212, Mec,1212, Sarah,0973,
Thomas,0822,0863
OWEN, Ambrose R.,1000,
Annie L.,1000, B.R.,1110,
Betsy,1000, Betty M.,1055,
Carrie L.,1000, Charity,
1000, Daniel,1123, Dr.,1096,
Elizabeth,1000, Eugenia S.,
1055, Fannie,1110, Floyd H.,
1000, G.H.,0894, Henrietta,
0999, Herbert H.,1000
OWEN, Hiram,1000, J.C.,0797,
Jabez,0790, Jennie,0974,
John C.,0949, John D.,0847,
1110, John F.,1000, John T.,
1000, John W.,1055, John,
0855,1110, Josiah W.,1055,
Judy A.,0949, Laura,1000,
Leila M.,1118, Letitia,
1000, Lillie V.,1055
OWEN, Madora,0949, Margaret J.,
0974, Martha L.,1055,
Mary A.,1055,1110, Mary E.,
0976,1055, Mary Y.,0976,
Mary,1000,1123, Nathan,
0974, Nathaniel,1055, O.C.,
0772,0773, Obadiah F.,1100,
Peter D.,1000, Peter,1000,
Polly P.,1000, Richard C.,
0999
OWEN, Richard C.,1000,
Richard G.,1000, Richard,
0976, S.C.(Miss),1123,
Sallie F.,1000, Sallie,
1055, Sally C.,1055,
Sarah G.,1000, Sidney,1118,
Stephen,0858, T.L.,0803,
Theo.,0803, Thomas E.,1055,
Thomas,1055, Urbane G.(Dr.),
0999, William B.,1055
OWEN, William T.,1000, Willie,
1000
OWENS, ,0775, Thomas,0791
OWENSBY, J.R.,0893
OXENDINE, Bill,0849
OZMENT & CO., J.H.,0854
OZMENT, Amanda,1111, Clara,
1111, Cleopatra,1086,
Emma A.,1111, Horace,1111,
J.Harrison,1111, James H.,
1086, John C.,1111, John,
0842, Jonathan,0842, Lenna,
1111, Martha,1086
PADGETT, D.C.,1000, H.G.,0808,
Henry G.,1000, L.P.,0955,
Mary W.,1000, Mr.,0963
PAGE, Almira,1001, Betty,1001,
Charity,1000, David D.,
1000,1001, Eudora M.,1001,
Frederick,1001, Harry H.,
1001, Harvey,1001, Hattie,
1113, Jacob S.,1000,
Jacob T.,1000, Jacob,1001,
Jason W.,1001, John D.,
1000, John J.,1001, John,
1001
PAGE, Katie,1001, Lewis,1145,
Lovey,1001, M.H.,0797,
Maggie,1001, Martha,1001,
Mary J.,1000, Mary L.,1000,
Mary Lou,0997, Nancy W.,
1145, Nancy,1001, Olivia E.,
1000, Rev.,0860, Robert W.,
1001, Sarah,1001, Thomas H.,
1000, W.G.,1113, Walter,1001
PAGE, Webb M.,1001, Wm.F.,
1000
PAINE, Guilford,0891, Mrs.,
0864, Rob,0809, Robert G.,
0892, Robert,0839
PAISLEY, William,0842
PALMER & PALMER, ,1056
PALMER, ,0830, Col.,1069,
Ella,1111, Gen.,0825, H.E.,
0826, Henry Clay,1111,
Henry,0849, Horace E.,1056,
1057, Horace,0831, J.B.,
0823,0824,0829,0830,0832,
Jane,1231, John,0855,1111,
Joseph B.,0826,1055,1056,
1057, Louisa,1111, Margaret A.,
1111
PALMER, Margaret J.,1056,
Marian V.,1201, Mary A.V.,
1215, Mary,1111, Mildred C.,
1056, Nancy,0834, Ophelia M.,
1056, Richard H.,1111,
Robert,0834, Sarah A.,1087,
Sarah,1111, William H.,
1056, William M.,1057,
William,0843,1111, Willie T.,
1057
PANKEY, Mr.,0803
PANNELL, M.J.(Miss),1179
PARHAM, Ann A.,0931, Eliza,
1001, Elizabeth H.,1223,
Florence,1001, George W.,
1001, John W.,1001, Nancy V.,
1001, Oscar,1001, Thomas J.,
0931
PARISH, Joel,0789
PARK, ,0902, A.,0803,0807,
Adelia C.,0947, Alexr.D.,
0750, Althere E.,0947,
Capt.,0792, Cash M.,0854,
Cordie D.,0947, Emma C.,
0947, Erastus J.,0947,
George M.,1222, George W.,
0947, Hill,1222, J.,0803,
J.J.A.,0947, James (Mrs.),
0808
PARK, James,0802,0808, Jerome,
1222, Katie L.,0947,
Martha E.,0947, Mary A.,
1222, Mary J.,1222, Mary L.,
0933, Mary,1222, Moses,0902,
1222, Nancy,1222, Rachael E.,
0985, Thomas H.,0947,
Thomas,0792,0802, W.,0803
PARKE, Joseph,0793, Reuben,
0793
PARKER, ,0863, A.F.,1167, B.,
1167, Charles G.,1167, Dora,
1167, Edward,1167, Fana,
1167, Frances,1057, Isaac,
0869, Isaiah,1167, Joseph,
1138, Lizzie,1167, Martha P.,
1167, Mary,1167, P.,0827,
Sallie,1162, Willie,1167

PARKES, J.L.,0803,0804,
  Thomas,0803
PARKHAM, Wm.,0774
PARKS, Dr.,1159, Harriet,1159,
  J.L.,0943, John M.,0893,
  John,0887, Mary(Mrs.),0972,
  R.,0795, Sallie J.,0989,
  Sarah J.,0988,0989
PARRISH, (Hotel),0803, ,
  0813, Emily E.,1070, Joel,
  0791, Louise T.,0964,
  Robert,0797, Samuel,0827
PARROTT, Sara R.,0948
PARSONS, ,0863, Anna L.,1168,
  Bunie C.,1168, Cynthia J.,
  1168, Elizabeth,1168, G.W.,
  1168, George A.,1168,
  George N.,1168, George W.,
  1168, John C.,1168, John W.,
  1168, Margaret,1168,
  Mary E.,1168, Mary F.,1168,
  Michael F.,1168, Newton H.,
  1168
PARSONS, Robert,1168, Ruth C.,
  1168, Safrone A.,1168,
  Sarah E.,1168, Sarah J.,
  1168, Strick,0863, Volney S.,
  1168, William J.,1168,
  Wm.C.,1168
PARTEE, ,0750, D.L.(Miss),
  0906
PARTLOW, Cloe,1111, Haywood R.,
  1111, James R.,1111,
  Margaret,1111, Martha E.,
  1111, May Ann,1111, Natlie M.,
  1111, Thomas A.,1111,
  Thomas,1111, William H.,
  1111
PASCHALL, Edwin,0804
PASSMORE, Richard,0775
PATRICK, Ephraim,0887,
  John N.,0898
PATTEN, James,0805, John,0763
PATTERSON, Alexr.,0821,
  Andrew,0886,0893,0903,
  Anna,0896, Burrell,0842,
  Camilla T.,1042, Clerky,
  1118, Cynthia,1057, Elijah,
  1118, Ella M.,1057, Flora,
  1218, Harriet C.,0990,0991,
  Hugh K.,1057, J.M.,0889,
  0890,0897, James M.,1223,
  James,0886
PATTERSON, James,0888,1223,
  John,0824,0843,1223,
  Margaret S.,1223, Mary J.,
  1057, Mary,1223, Naomi,1154,
  Prof.,0858, R.M.,0894,
  Robert,0886, S.J.(Mrs.),
  1057, Samuel,0822,0863,
  Sarah,1223, Thomas J.,1223,
  Thomas R.,1057, W.M.,0895,
  William K.,1057
PATTEY, J.W.,0879
PATTISON, Nancy,1052
PATTON & HARVEY, ,0843
PATTON & REEVES, ,0857
PATTON, ,0813, Agnes J.,1001,
  America,1122, Bithunia,
  1001, Capt.,0792, Catharine,
  1139, H.C.,1122, J.,0901,
  Jacob,0841, James H.,1124,
  James,0795,0808,0863,0886,
  1001,1140, Jason H.,1001,
  Jason,1001, John,0843,
  Joseph J.,1001, Margaret,
  1001
PATTON, Mary A.,0978, Mary B.,
  1001
PATTON, Rachel,1124, Robt.,
  0795, Sallie,1124, Samuel,
  0827, W.C.,0764, W.D.,0797
PATY & CO., B.F.,0829,1058,
  Burr F.,1058
PATY & LEATHERMAN, ,1058
PATY, Burr F.,1057, Frances,
  1057, John W.,1057, Mattie G.,
  1058, W.B.,0829
PAUL, Rebecca,0952
PAXTON, John,0899
PAYNE, Callie M.,0946,
  Elizabeth,1181, Fannie S.,
  0946, Henry,0842, J.D.,0877,

James,0849, M.,0872,0877,
  Mrs.,0867,0869, R.G.,0764,
  Robert,1218
PAYTON, John W.,0846,0848
PEA, George,0799
PEACE, William,0841
PEACH, Capt.,0792
PEACOCK, ,0863, James,0853,
  T.J.,0879, W.H.,0893
PEAK, J.W.,0821
PEARCE & ABBOTT, ,0829
PEARCE, John,0797, Robert,
  0760
PEARCY, R.B.,0856
PEARSHALL, James,0766
PEARSON, ,0863, Granville C.,
  1168, Hiram,1168, Kindred,
  0867, Matilda B.,1168,
  Stephen L.,0848, W.R.,0879,
  Wm.,0862
PEARSOn, Mitch,0870
PEAY, 0777, N.C.,0799
PECK, Catharine,1004, Jacob,
  0762
PEEBLES, Alice,0962, Catharine,
  1052, George,1074, Isham R.,
  1070, Martha C.,1074,
  Mary W.,1070, W.R.,0962
PEEL, Robert,0799
PEEPLE, ,0803
PEEPLES, Thomas,0792
PELLER, David W.,0964, Martha,
  0964
PEMBELTON, Dorothea,0936
PEMBERTON, A.R.,1125, J.D.,
  1125, William,0858
PENDELTON, Rev.,0836
PENDLETON, Lewis,0850,1112,
  Lizzie,1112, Mrs.,0843,
  Nancy,1112
PENEBAKER, Ed R.,0854
PENN, S.W.,0902
PENNINGTON, Martha,1137, W.W.,
  1137
PENUEL, A.G.,1118, Cornelia,
  1118, Hardy,0842, Minnie,
  1118, R.B.,1118
PEPER, Capt.,0792
PEPPER, Eliza,0870, Lizzie,
  1136, Westly W.,0869
PERCY, J.W.,0889
PERKIN & WHITE, ,0802
PERKINS, Bethenia H.,0943,
  Capt.,0792, Charles F.,
  1058, Daniel P.,1058,1059,
  Daniel,0789,0792,0793,0794,
  0805, Dr.,0803, Edwin M.,
  1002, Eliza M.,1002, Elvira,
  1002, Florence,1058, Hardin,
  1002, Henry C.,1002, J.W.,
  0796, Jennie,1058, Kate,1058
PERKINS, Laura,1002, Leah A.,
  1002, Leah L.,1002, Leah M.,
  1002, Leighla O.,1002,
  Letitia,1002, Lizzie E.,
  1002, Louisa,1002, M.T.(Mrs.),
  1003, Martha T.,1002,1003,
  Mary A.,0974, Mary M.,1058,
  Mary,1002,1003, Maud C.,
  1002, Morgan,1058
PERKINS, N.Edwin,1002, N.P.,
  0795,0802, N.T.,0791,0794,
  0821, Nancy,1002, Newton C.,
  1002, Nich.R.,0802,
  Nicholas T.,0805, Nicholas,
  0789,0794,0796,0803,0846,
  1002, P.,0803, P.G.S.,0791,
  0796, P.O.N.,0791, Peter,
  0801,1058, Rebecca W.,1058
PERKINS, Sally,0974, Samuel F.,
  1002, Samuel,0791,0794,0805,
  0974,1002, Sarah L.,1058,
  Sarah P.,1002,1058,
  Susan A.,0971, Susan,1002,
  T.F.,0791,0804, T.S.,0797,
  Theresa G.,1002, Theresa,
  1002, Thomas F.,1002,1044,
  Thomas F.Sr.,1001, Thos.F.,
  0800
PERKINS, Thos.F.Jr.,1002,
  Thos.H.,0789, W.T.,0790,
  William C.,1002, Wm.Ewin,
  1002, Wm.O'N.,0807

PERRY, (Com.),1086, ,0776,
  Alma A.T.,0947, Ann,0947,
  Annette,0947, Burkley,0939,
  Charles A.,0947, Elizabeth,
  0947, James S.,0947, Jerry,
  0952, John A.,0895, John S.,
  0947, Josiah A.,0947,
  Katy C.,0947, Lena,0947,
  Lulu J.,0947, Maggie A.,
  0947
PERRY, Mary A.,1206, Mary J.,
  0947, Mary M.,0952, Mattie H.,
  0939, Nancy E.,0947, Nathan,
  0947, Nathaniel,0848,
  Sarah M.,0952, Simpson,
  0947, Susan D.,0947, Susan,
  0947, W.L.,0836, W.N.,1023,
  Wiley T.,0758, William,
  0891,0947, Willie A.,0947
PERRYMAN, Sallie,1189
PETERS, James,0774, Jas.P.,
  0774, Wm.,0774
PETTNES, Sarah,0923
PETTUS, (Gen.),1029
PETTY, W.G.,0878
PETWAY, H.,0790, Hinchey,0801,
  0802
PEYTON, ,0776, A.D.,1081,
  Bailey,0844, Ephraim,0841,
  John W.,0842, Louis,1093,
  Lt.,0825, Mary,1093,
  Willie S.,1081
PHILIPS, Annie B.,0948,
  Eliza M.,0948, Hugh L.,
  0948, James M.,0948,
  Jesse H.,0948,0949,
  John O.,0949, Madora,0949,
  Margaret J.,0948, Mary W.,
  0948, Mary,0992, Mattie H.,
  0948, Robert L.,0949,
  Sarah V.,0992, Sarah Virginia,
  0948
PHILLIP, (Mill),0863, J.M.,
  0871
PHILLIPS & CLEMMONS, ,0857
PHILLIPS & HENDERSON, ,0857
PHILLIPS, Ada,1112, Benjamin,
  0842, Bessie,1112, Bettie,
  1112, Capt.,0852, David B.,
  1112,1223, David,1112,
  Eliza,1157, Elizabeth C.,
  1082, Elizabeth H.,1223,
  Elizabeth,1016, Eugene,
  1112, Garrett,0867,0871,
  1154, H.,0900, H.A.,1112,
  Hallie,1223
PHILLIPS, Hardin,1112,
  Harriet,0869, Hattie,1112,
  J.J.,0871, J.M.,0859, J.W.,
  0870, James B.,0869, Jesse,
  0869, John H.,1223, John M.,
  1112, John W.,0849,0873,
  John,0842, Joseph,0854,
  Josiah,1112, Julia L.,1172,
  Laura J.,1112, Lemuel H.,
  0759
PHILLIPS, Lizzie,1112,
  Malinda,1112, Margaret A.,
  0942, Margaret,1094,
  Maria E.,1074, Martha,1193,
  Mary D.,1112, Mary,1112,
  Mattie,1112, Miles,0868,
  Minerva,1150, Minnie,1112,
  Nancy V.,1223, Narcissa,
  1154, Richard,0868, Sallie,
  1112
PHILLIPS, Samuel,0868, Sarah,
  1151, T.W.,1112, Thomas,
  1111, W.S.,1113, William P.,
  1112, Wm.B.,0867
PHILPOTT, Charles N.,1169,
  Charles T.,1169, Demarcus,
  1169, Edward L.,1169,
  Elisha C.,1169, Ernest,
  1169, Jacob,1169, James,
  1169, John H.,1169, Joshua A.,
  1169, Minnie,1169, Nancy A.,
  1169, Rebecca E.,1169,
  Rebecca,1169, Sarah,1169,
  Thos.B.,1169
PHILPOTT, William,1169, Wm.,
  1169
PHIPER, Margaret,1210
PICK, J.,0983

PICKARD, ,0776, Alex S.,0947,
Capt.,0792, Hardy O.,0948,
Herbert B.,0948, Joseph L.,
0948, Josie C.,0948,
Katie G.,0948, Lewis C.,
0947, Mary D.,0948, Rachel,
0947, Sally F.,0948, Sally,
0948, T.S.,0784, William A.,
0948
PICKENS, Ada S.,1195, David B.,
1224, Hannah,1224, Mary A.,
1224, Medora A.,1208,
William H.,1224
PICKETT, Edward,0842, Emma,
1086, H.L.,1086
PICKLE, Andrew,1169, Annie C.,
1169, Catharine,1139,
Catherine,1169, Ella,1169,
George W.,1169, Henry J.,
1169, James M.,1169, M.A.,
1169, M.P.,1169, Major A.,
1169, Major,1139, Mary A.F.,
1169, Mary E.,1139, Minerva P.,
1169, Murry F.,1169
PICKLE, P.Murry,1169, Sarah E.,
1169, Wm.Franklin,1169
PIERCE, Annie,1059, Elizabeth,
1058, F.,1110, Franklin,
0765, Granville S.,1058,
Harriet,1079, Henry C.,
1058, Tennie,1059
PIERSON, Lucy,1229, Mary,0984,
William,0985
PIGG, ,0775
PILLOW, A.L.,0948, Abner,0766,
0948, Annie,0951, Anthony L.,
0948, E.T.,0759, Elizabeth T.,
0948, Ernest,0890, Eugene,
0770,0948, Evan Y.,0948,
Gideon J.,0750,0755,0763,
0785,0948, Gideon,0751,0784,
0841,0939,0948, Granville A.,
0753, James C.,0948
PILLOW, John,0948, L.C.,0898,
Mary F.,0948, Mary S.,0948,
Mordica,0948, Narcissa,
0939, Robert,0948, Robt.(Dr.),
0772, Sara R.,0948, W.H.,
0752, Way,0948, William H.,
0948, William,0762,0766,
0784, Wm.(Col.),0777
PINKSTON, E.T.,0799, Fannie,
0929, Lt.,0799, Mary A.,
0912, Vina H.,0998
PIPIN, Enos,0759
PIPPIN, Alabama R.,1060
PITMAN, Capt.,0850
PITT, Catharine,1042, F.E.,
0839, H.E.,0809
PITTS, John,1055, Mary A.,
1055, Susie,1052
PLACEBO, (Dr.),0757
PLATTENBURG, Mary Y.,1216
PLUMMER, J.R.(Rev.),1066,
J.R.,0836, James R.,0763,
0771,0783, Jas.R.,0752,0768
PODGETT, Elizabeth,1011
POGUE, Addie B.,0914, E.A.,
0914
POINDEXTER, ,0857
POINTER, (Capt.),0941 ,
0774, Capt.,0910, Elizabeth,
1003, Ellen,1003, H.P.,0782,
0785,0799, Harriet,1003,
Henry P.,1003, Henry Sr.,
1003, Henry Strange,1003,
Henry,0778,1003, Martha J.,
1003, Martha,1003, Mary,
1003, Sammie,1003, Susan T.,
0911
POINTER, Susan,1003, Thomas G.,
1003, Virginia,1003,
William,1003, Wilmoth,1003
POKE, B.,0799
POLK, (Gen.),0954, (Mrs.),
1042, ,0786, A.J.,0925,
Capt.,0752, Ezekial,0932,
Ezekiel,0761,0904,0931,
G.W.,0770, Gen.,0825,
George N.,0750, James K.,
0763,0765,0773,0892,0904,
0931,0933,0949,0950,0962,
0996,1100,1183, Jane M.,

0773, Jas.K.,0764
POLK, Jas.M.,0750, Leah,1221,
Leonidas(Rev.),0779,
Leonidas,0750,0782,
Lucius E.,0949, Lucius J.,
0750,0759,0772,0774,0779,
Lucius K.,0758, Mary R.,
0949, President,0758,
Rufus K.,0750,0949,
Sally M.,0949, Saml.,0754,
Samuel,0759,0760
POLK, Samuel,0766,0771,0773,
0774, Settlement,0750,
Thomas,0932, V.,0770, V.L.,
0770, W.A.,0799, W.H.,0762,
0764, Will,0770, William J.,
0949, William,0750,0751,
Wm. H.,0759, Wm.H.,0763,
0765,0963
POLLARD & SHATTUCK, ,1003
POLLARD, George W.,1003,
Isaac N.,1003, Joseph J.,
1004, Joseph,1003, Julia,
1004, Laura,1004, Malachi W.,
1003, Martha E.,1003,
Martha G.,1004, Martha,
1003, Mary J.,1003, Nancy D.,
1003, Newton N.,1003,
Robert L.,1003, Virginia A.,
1003
POLLARD, Wm.C.,1003, Wm.M.,
1004
POOL, ,0777, John,0871,
Seth P.,0844,0846,0847
POPE, Bettie O.,1025, Dolly(Etta),
0990, Harvey,0812, James K.,
0948, John,0805,0990, Lesey,
0944, Lucy,0990, Mary A.,
1130, T.A.,0804, W.L.,0764
PORCH, W.C.,0893
PORTER & DAVIS, ,0897
PORTER & HAFFEY, ,0802
PORTER & PARTEE, ,0768
PORTER & SPENCE, ,0827
PORTER, A.,1110, Alice A.,
1004, Amelia,1004, B.W.,
0752,0787, Bessie R.,0918,
Catharine,0949,1004,
Elizabeth T.,0948, Ellen A.,
1004, Emma P.,1224, Fannie P.,
0961, Florence E.,1004,
Hardin Q.,1224, Henry A.,
0949, Hugh V.,0949, Hugh,
0822
PORTER, Isabella,1004, J.B.,
0766,0801, James B.,0775,
0953, James H.,1004,
James R.,1224, John A.,
1224, John B.,0751, John N.,
0874,1224, Jos.B.,0754,
Joseph B.,0759, Joseph F.,
0949, Joseph,0791,0793, Lou,
1004, Lucy A.,1224, M.Frances,
1224
PORTER, Madison R.,0949,
Mary A.,0961, Mary F.,1224,
Mary J.,0953, Mary Jane,
0949, Mary R.,1224, Mary,
1004, Melville E.,1224,
Nimrod,0752,0756,0758,0773,
0961, Otey J.,0949, Reeves,
0841, Robert,1004, Saml.,
0757, Saml.S.(Dr.),0777,
Samuel S.,0755
PORTER, Samuel S.,0949,
Samuel,0949, Saunders,1004,
Stephen S.,1004, T.D.,0805,
T.J.,0759, T.L.,0787,
Tabathia G.,1224, Thomas H.,
1224, Thomas M.,1224,
Thomas N.,1224, Thomas S.,
0961, Thos.J.,0778, W.T.,
0759, Walter J.,0949,
Walter S.,1004
PORTER, William T.,0949,
William,0849
POSEY, Hollie,1051, Mr.& Mrs.,
0838, Nancy,1217
POTTER, Alice A.,1004,
Amanda Ellen,0950, Andre J.,
0950, Archibald,0803,
Austin W.,0949, Austin W.Jr.,
0950, Donaldson,0775,0950,

Ellen F.,0950, James O.,
0759, Jane,0950, Jas.O.,
0779, Mary A.,0950
POTTS, J.H.,0799, J.N.,0799
POWELL, ,0750,0838,0861,0892,
Capt.,0752, J.B.,0859,
Mary,0929,0984, Peter,0762,
R.J.,0817, Rev.,0859,
Ruth Lee,1096, Sallie,0984,
Sarah,1097, Thomas,0792,
0816,0984, William,1097
POWERS, Wm.,0851
PRATER, Caroline,1059, D.J.,
1059, Elizabeth,1068,
Fannie P.,1059, Lethie,
1059, Mary J.,1031, Mary L.,
1059, Monroe,1059, Sallie C.,
1059, William P.,1059
PRATT, Caroline,1011, Susanna,
1153
PRESGROVE, Wm.,0868
PRESTON, Alice,1112, Ann M.,
1112, Burdine,0849, Ella,
1112, James H.,1112,
John F.,1112, John,1112,
Laura,1112, Lydia,1212,
Martha,1112, Mattie,1112,
S.S.,0851,1112, S.S.Jr.,
PREWETT, Lemuel,0778
PREWITT, ,0813
PRICE & PATY, ,1123
PRICE, Jack,0849, John W.,
0854,1089, John,0878, M.A.,
0854
PRICHARD, J.D.,0799, W.C.,
0799
PRIDE, Mary,0907
PRIESTLY, Capt.,0850
PRIM, Nannie,0830
PRIMROSE, Mary,1176
PRINCE, Robert,0762,0764,
S.A.,0877
PRITT, Moses,0871
PROVIDENCE, J.,0853
PROVINE, Capt.,0850, Eleazer,
0841, J.C.,0837, John,0842
PRUETT, Lemuel,0759,0760
PRUIETT, Lethie,1059
PRUITT, ,0863, Willis,0877
PRYOR, Norton,0863
PUCKET, Eliz.(Mrs.),1121
PUCKETT, Frank,0842, Nancy,
1042, R.,0795,0801, Richard,
0791, Wm.P.,0869
PUETT, Thomas,0799
PUGH, A.J.,0787, John,0803,
Mary Jane,1006, T.P.,0803
PURCELL, James,0761, Mr.,0767
PURDAN, George,0891
PURDY, Robert,0826,0827
PURSLEY, Alice M.,1113, Ann,
1113, Brice B.,1113,
Edwin V.,1113, G.A.,1112,
Harriet,1113, Hattie,1113,
Lizzie A.,1113, Minnie,
1113, Philip H.,1113,
Sophia,1112, William B.,
PURYEAR, J.J.,0803, P.M.,0819
PUTNAM, ,0784, Matilda,1142,
W.S.,0879, William,0851
PUTWAY, William,0842
PYLAND, (Mr.),1225, Elizabeth,
1224, Hardin,1224, Nancy,
1224, William N.,1224
PYLE & HARTSFIELD, ,0855
PYLE & PORTER, & Co.,0854
PYLE, Caleb,0891
PYNER, Eliza,0998, Mason,0998
QUARLES, (Gen.),0786, ,0801,
A.J.,0857, Capt.,0850,
Elizabeth,1123, James,0842,
Lockey,1028, Roger,0842,
W.D.,0857
QUARTERMAN, W.A.,0772
QUESENBURY, Nicholas,0842,
William,0846
RABEY, Marcus L.,0864
RADFORD, Elizabeth G.,1219,
James,0849, Samuel,0891
RADLEY, W.C.,0782
RAGER, Anderson,0880, Saml.(Dr.),
0880
RAGLAND, Agnes A.,1113,

Amelia A.,1113, Amelia, 1099, Clark,1113, Hardin, 1099,1113, Hattie,1113, James H.,1113, Miss,1003, Pettis,1113
RAGSDALE, B.,0779, Baxter H., 0882, Benjamin,0797, Ed, 0793, James,0775, Jane P., 1038
RAIBOURN, W.K.,0878
RAINBOW, M.A.,0874, Martha (Mrs.), 0874
RAINES, Frances,1012, John, 1012
RAINEY, ,0896, Christiana, 1012, Elizabeth,1032, Jesse G.,1012, Martha,1175, W.S.,0764,0770
RAINS & SON, ,0768
RAINS, A.B.,0770,0771, J.B., 0770,0773, T.B.,0780,0964
RAINWATER, Wesley,0871
RAINY, Mary,1038
RALSTON, ,0777, Capt.,0792, Mrs.,1045, Sallie,0835
RAMBO, F.K.,0890
RAMSAY, Diana,1113, John H., 1113, William,1113
RAMSEY, ,0902, Dr.,0789, Ella Myrtle,1113, Jane, 1126, John I.,1113, John, 0887,0890,0898,0901, Joseph, 0837, Lucinda,1113, Mary C., 1113, R.,0822, R.L.,1126, Roxana,1113, Samuel,0886, 0887, Thos.K.,0850, W.,0819, William H.,1113
RANDALL, Kate,0906
RANDELLS, M.,1107
RANDLE, T.W.,0839
RANDOLPH, (Miss),1137, Annie, 1059, Beverly,1059, Catherine, 1059, Elizabeth C.,1059, Grief,0850, Henry S.,1059, John B.,1059, Lucy,1059, Peyton,0819, Sallie L., 1059, Walter A.,1059
RANEY, C.B.,1169, Catharine, 1169, Eunice,1170, John W., 1169, Margaret(Mrs.),1159, Victoria,1170, William,1170
RANKIN, A.F.,0902, Alexr.F., 1180, Alice F.,0943, Frances,1147, Maggie A., 1180, Mary,1180, R.D.,0879, Samuel,0834, Willis,0870, Wm.F.,0755, Wm.J.,0755
RANKINS, Sarah,1111
RANSOM & CO., ,0830
RANSOM & PERKINS, ,1059
RANSOM, (Mr.),1060, Bettie, 1060, Elizabeth,1059, G.W., 0833, Geo.W.,1059, George T., 1060, George,0819, J.A., 0830, J.B.,1058, John B., 1060, John,1059, Joseph, 0830,1074, Lillie,1164, M., 0817,0818,0829, Margaret A., 1178, Margaret,1060
RANSOM, Martha J.,1074, Mary M.,1058, Mary V.,1074, Mary,1034, Mr.,0767, R.M., 0832, R.N.,0829,0837, Richard,0818, S.H.,0798, Sue,1073, W.A.,0829,0830, W.C.,0889,0898,1164, Whit, 1074, Wm.A.,0829
RANSON, ,0830, Alfred,0867, R.P.,0809, Richard,0812
RAPP, W.A.,0829
RATCLIFF, F.G.,0797, Gideon, 0808
RATCLIFFE, Francis G.,1007, Martha,1007, Mary O.,1007
RATHER, J.T.,0833, James,0848, Martha F.,1032, William, 0812
RATLER, Temperance,1135
RAUNTREE, Elizabeth,0931
RAY, ,0863, Elizabeth,1127, Fletcher,0863, John,0855, 1077, Martha,1177, Peggy, 0848, Polly,1134, Sarah,

1134, Solomon,0848, Thomas, 0842, William,0841
RAYMOND, H.,0829, Jane,0835, Phoebe,0835
RAYSON, Robert,0867
RAZIER, Mary,1167
RAZIUS, Thomas,0797
REA, John C.,0950, John,0950, Luira,0950, Mary,0950, Nannie B.,0950, Thomas J., 0950
READ, A.E.,1215, Aldora,1170, Ann E.,1170, Callie J., 1170, Elizabeth,1170, George S.,1170, George W., 1170, J.C.,1170, James C., 1170, John B.,1170, Lou H., 1170, Martha W.,1170, Mary J.,1170, Mattie,1215, Richard L.,1170, Robert A., 1170
READ, Robert C.,1170, Robert, 1170, Sarah E.,1170, Wm.L., 1170
READING, Capt.,0751
READY, ,0813,0820, Alice,1107, Charles,0812,0813,0814, 0819,0820,0823,0826,0827, 0829,0834,1107, R.,0813
REAGEN, William,1224
REAGOR, James,0862
REAMS, Addie,0981, Henry,0981, Martha,0946,1007, Mattie, 0979, Robert,0808,0979
REASE, Joe T.,0974, Mary,0974
REAVES, ,0775, Alabama V., 0977, Benjamin,1170, Bettie F.,1170, Chaney, 1170, Dulcenia,1170, Emmet, 1170, Frances M.,1170, Iscm, 1170, Jane,1170, John,1170, Martha,1170, Mary J.,1170, Rachel,1170, Robert A., 1170, Robert,1170, William, 1170
RECORD, Geo.W.,0898, J.C., 0899, James C.,0888,0899, John W.,0888,0890, John, 0869, S.S.,0761
REDMAN, Ann T.,0978, Elizabeth, 0978, Julia,0978, Thomas J., 0978
REECE, Thomas B.,0843
REED & MCEWEN, ,0974
REED & TALLY, ,0829
REED, ,0796,0838, Andrew J., 1004,1225, Andrew,1004, Artimenta,1084, Henry,0841, J.,0837, J.H.,0831, J.L., 0890,0902, James,0828, Jane(Mrs.),1230, John N., 0820, John,0794,0868,0886, Mary E.,1225, Mary F.,1004, Mary,1223, Nancy,1004, Peter H.,1004
REED, R.D.,0826,0828,0837, R.W.,0818, Richard,0808, Sarah E.,1069, Silas,0819, T.E.,0889,0897, Thomas E., 1225, Thomas,0874, Virginia E., 1225, Virginia E.,1225, W.A.,0837, William F.,1004
REEDE, John W.,0855
REESE, ,0776, Elizabeth,0950, J.M.,0950, Jane,0950, M.J., 0950, Margaret,1111, Mary, 1111, R.H.,0950, Thomas B., 1111, W.B.,0763
REEVES, ,0863, A.T.,0818, Capt.,0792, Elijah,0754, Elizabeth W.,1185, Hooker, 0842, John,1114, Levi,0840, M.G.,0818, Moses,0851, Rhoda A.,1114, Sallie,1159, Sarah,1114, Sophia M.,1039, William,0851, Willis,0840
REGEN & BROS., ,0899
REID, ,0863, Dr.,0803, J.W., 1002, John,1002, Maud C., 1002, W.S.(Mrs.),1003
REIDENBERRY & TURNER, ,0875
REIDEOUT, ,0877
REISE, Thomas B.,0847

RENEAU, L.,0836
RENFRO, William,0784
RENFROE, Alice D.,0950, Delia R.,0950, Eliza A., 0950, Eliza C.,0950, J.L., 0764, James S.,0950, Joseph S.,0950, Mary A.E., 0953, Mary D.,0950, Narcissa E., 0950, Sarah M.,0950, William C.,0950, William, 0950
RENSHAW, J.,0827
RENT, J.A.,0847
REVIS, B.A.,0899, Lafayette, 0870
REYNEY, Honoroa,0956
REYNOLDS, ,0751,0803, Aaron, 0784, Ada W.,1225, Alice, 1089, Benj.,0759, Clarence B., 1225, E.P.,0989, Elizabeth, 0989, Gen.,0852, H.S.,0790, John G.,1225, John T.,1225, Mary,1152, Obadiah,1089, Sarah J.,1202, Victoria, 1225
REZER, Y.M.,0803
RHEA, Mathew,0779, W.H.,0824
RHODES, Kate,0849, Miss,0906, W.S.,0819
RICE & SANDUSKY, ,0874
RICE, Benjamin,0851, C.N., 0877, Clide Alexr.,1114, Fannie,1062, Fredonia,1097, Horace,0849, J.H.,1114, J.M.,1114, J.P.,0831, James,1097, Jeffella,1114, John P.,1062, John,0842, Mr.,0803, S.J.,1223, T.A., 1114, William,0842,0843
RICH & WRIGHT, ,0829
RICH, C.P.,1103, Charles,0842, S.A.,1103
RICHARDS, William,0842
RICHARDSON, ,0830, A.E.A., 1192, Alabama R.,1060, Annie Lou,1060, Augusta M., 1060, Augusta,1060, Bernice, 0849, C.R.,0803, J.D.,0823, 0829,0832, J.K.,0803, J.W., 0791,0817,0830, James D., 1060, James,1060, John E., 0818,1060, John W.,1060
RICHARDSON, John,0793, Mary, 1060, Nancy,1002, R.G.,0803, Sallie,1035, Samuel,0821, W.B.,0894, William M.,1060, Winnie,0920
RICHERSON, C.S.,0781, Sallie, 1015, T.H.,0781
RICHIE, Mollie E.,1200
RICHMOND, James,0842,0847
RICKETS, Robt.D.,0758
RICKETTS, Frank,0842
RICKMAN, Capt.,0872
RIDDLE, H.Y.,0850, Haywood Y., 0850
RIDLEY & RICHARDSON, ,1060, 1061
RIDLEY, ,0813,0830, Almira, 1061, Ann,0970, Annie,0951, B.L.,0819,0822,0829,0830, 0871,1022, B.L.Jr.,1061, Beulah C.,0970, Bromfield L., 0850, Bunk,1012, Capt.,0792, G.S.,0823,0829,1061, Hanley,1061, Henry,0834, Isabella,0970, J.W.S.,0770
RIDLEY, J.W.S.,0773,0951, James,0970,1061, Madge, 0951, Mary,1012, Minerva T., 0970, Moses,1057, Nannie P., 0970, S.J.(Miss),1057, Sarah E.,1041, Sarah,0970, Thomas,0795, Webb Jr.,0951, William,0825,0970, Willis, 0781, Wm.T.,1012
RIDOUBT, Susan J.,1025, Susan, 1024
RIDOUT, Elizabeth A.,1061, Jesse B.,1061, Mary,1061, Thomas,1061
RIED, John,0791
RIELLY, B.L.,0823

RIGGIN, Sarah,1078
RIGGINS, Nancy,1145
RIGGS, ,0886, A.S.,0809,
  Adam S.,1151, Catharine,
  1004, Earl,1004, Emmet,1004,
  Gideon W.,1004, Gideon,
  1004, Jordan,1004, Kate,
  1004, Lillie M.,1004,
  Oliver,1004, Polly,0991,
  Susan S.,1151
RINE, Betsey,0925
RING, Emma T.,1005, George,
  1004, Henry H.,1005,
  Hiram E.,1004, Leonidas R.,
  1005, Mr.,1005
RIPLEY, James,0869, T.B.,0836
RIPPY, Thomas,0870
RIVENS, Anna,1033, Eliza J.,
  1202
RIVERS, Henrietta,0999
RIVES, R.C.,0898
ROACH, ,0833, Jane,0950,
  John M.,0950, John,0842,
  Mr.,0858
ROAN & CABLE, ,0874
ROAN & MCGREW, ,0874
ROAN, Thomas,0874
ROANE, (Gov.),1084, Archibald,
  0761,1105, Harriet,1105,
  Hugh,0842, Isabella,1084,
  John S.,1105, John,1084,
  Judge,0795, Samuel C.,0850,
  1105, Samuel,1084, Wm.,0891
ROBB, H.W.,1111, Margaret A.,
  1111
ROBBINS, Ann,1085, Ruth,1085,
  Thomas,1085
ROBERSON, Nan,0870
ROBERTS & OSLIN, ,0830
ROBERTS, (Col.),0784, (Gen.),
  0759, Annie,0975, Benj.F.,
  1008, Benjamin,1005, Bishop,
  0965, Bright,1225, Charity E.,
  1005, Delilah,1005, Eliz.H.,
  1008, Ella,1005, Erskine P.,
  1061, Gen.,0758,0766, H.S.,
  0757, Isaac,0751,0759,0761,
  0766,0769
ROBERTS, Isaac,0778, James M.,
  1061, John B.,1225, John R.,
  0975, Josephine,1061, Juda,
  1005, Linsford M.,1061,
  Louisa,1061, Lucy J.,0975,
  Margaret L.,1123, Margaret,
  0922,1008, Mary A.,1053,
  Mary S.,1071, Mary,1225,
  Rebecca J.,1005, Robt.R.,
  0808
ROBERTS, Sallie H.,1203,
  Susannah M.,1225, W.T.,
  1005, William,1005,1071,
  Wm.,0764, Wm.R.,1005
ROBERTSON & RANSOM,,0793
ROBERTSON, (Gen.),0811,
  (Justice),0794, ,0813,
  Alice,1101, Capt.,0792,
  Elijah,0762, Ellen,1101,
  G.L.,0855, Hugh,1091,
  James,1101, Jane,0927,
  Jas.G.,0854, Lizzie E.,
  1036, Margaret,1159,
  Mary W.,1149, Mary,1123,
  Peggie,1090, Peyton,1101
ROBERTSON, Robt.D.,0780,0781,
  Tom,0849, V.,0821
ROBINS, J.,0900, May Ann,1111,
  R.P.,0895
ROBINSON & LIGGETT, ,0898
ROBINSON & PERRY, ,0854
ROBINSON, ,0899, A.B.,0898,
  Abram,0898, Anna A.,1226,
  1231, Baley P.,1005,
  Bellefield N.,1005, Betsey,
  1196, Catharine L.,1005,
  Catherine,1017, Churchwell,
  1114, Ella V.,1005, Emily D.,
  1114, G.L.,1114, George W.,
  1064, Hugh,0814,0815,0821
ROBINSON, Hugh,0826,0856,
  J.G.,0764, J.H.,0898,
  James C.,1005, James S.,
  0870, James T.,1005, James,
  1226,1231, Jane F.,1109,
  Jane,1168, Jessie,1054,
  Lavie M.,1054, Margaret E.,
  1208, Margaret F.,1177,
  Maria,1226, Mary C.,1095,
  1226, Mary,0916
ROBINSON, Mary,1114, R.W.,
  0793, S.B.,0793, Sallie J.,
  1204, Sallie M.,1005,
  Sallie N.,1005, Sarah A.,
  1087, Stephen,1114, Stewart,
  0916, Susan,1005, Susie N.,
  1005, T.L.,0802, Thomas H.,
  1095, W.A.,1087, W.D.,0824,
  0829,0832, W.M.,0896,1226
ROBINSON, Walter,1005,
  William,0813,0898, Wm.B.,
  0820, Wm.J.,1005
ROBISON, Fannie,1062, J.,0791,
  Mary,0951,1061,1124, R.W.,
  0790, S.B.,0817, Samuel B.,
  1061, W.D.,0818, William D.,
  1061
ROCKS, Manerva,1109
RODGERS, John A.,0803, Samuel,
  0795, W.A.,0790,0796
ROE, Richard,0761
ROGERS, A.G.,0857, Charlie E.,
  1062, Elisha,1062, Ellen T.,
  1173, J.W.,0810, James,0841,
  Julia,0908, L.A.,0819,1062,
  Maggie M.,1062, Martha,
  0990,1091, Mary,1062,
  Mattie A.,1062, Sallie M.W.,
  1062, Samuel,0820, Sarah,
  0996
ROLFFS, Anna Pugh,1006, J.H.,
  0804, John Henry,1006, John,
  1006, Kate,1006, Mary Jane,
  1006
ROLINSON, Catharine,1169
ROLL, Samuel,0795
ROLLAND, ,0774
ROLSTON, Alexander,1006,
  Margaret M.,1006
RONE, Mary,1198, Moxey,0893,
  Whit,1198
ROOKER, M.,0828
ROPER, Keziah,0944
ROSBOROUGH & KIDD, ,0773
ROSBOROUGH, J.H.,0764, Samuel,
  0846,0848
ROSCOE, Jas.W.,0824
ROSE, Robertson,0761
ROSECRANS, ,0825,0826, Gen.,
  0834
ROSENFELD, A.G.,0829, E.,0829,
  0833,1040,1062, Emanuel,
  1062, Gabriel,1062, I.,0829,
  M.,0829, Minnie,1062,
  Morris G.,1062, Ruby,1062,
  Sigmond,1062, Sylvia,1062
ROSENFIELD, E.,1052
ROSENTHAL & BRO., ,0829
ROSENTHAL & BROS., ,0768
ROSENTHAL, A.,0773
ROSENTHEL & BROS., ,0854
ROSER, W.T.,0902
ROSS, (Mr.),0877, F.A.,0902,
  Henry,0841,0845,0848,
  James,0890, Kate,0933,
  Malinda M.,1165, Manerva,
  1108, Robert,0892, S.M.,
  1079, Samuel,1079, Susan,
  1079, Thomas,0888,0891,0899,
  William,0842, Wm.T.,0892
ROSSER, W.L.,0807
ROSSON, William,0891
ROTHROCK, J.T.,0902
ROULET, W.,0833, William,0828,
  0829
ROUNDTREE, Maggie,1155, Mary,
  1155, William,1155
ROUNSAVILLE, Elizabeth,0983
ROUNTREE, Andrew,0951,0953,
  Charles W.,0951, Ellen,
  0955, Emily J.,0951, Ida R.,
  0951, Jane,0953, John J.,
  0951, John M.,0951, Johnnie E.,
  0951, Kansas L.,0951,
  Margaret J.,0951, Margaret,
  0951, Mary A.,0951, Mary,
  0951, Susan H.,0951,
  Thomas F.,0951
ROUNTREE, William A.,0951
ROWE, Temperance,1217
ROWLAND, ,0813, W.T.,0808
ROY, Eliza B.,0997, James,
  0880
ROYCE, A.S.,0810, M.S.,0803
ROYSTER, Sallie,1186
ROZELL, ,0803, Ashley B.,1006,
  Blackman L.,1006, Claybion W.,
  1006, Henrietta S.,1006,
  Henrietta,1006, Lizzie B.,
  1006, Lockie B.,1006,
  Logan D.,1006, Margaret M.,
  1006, Martha A.,1006,
  Martha C.,1006, Martha D.,
  1006, Mary T.,1006, Mary,
  1006
ROZELL, Rufard A.,1006,
  Ruford B.,1006, Solomon,
  1006, Wm.R.,1006, Yerbie P.,
  1006
RUCKEL, Kitty G.,1067
RUCKER, ,0820,0838, Benjamin,
  0840, J.,0820, J.F.,0818,
  J.J.,0818, James,0812,0813,
  Kitty G.,1067, Lucy,0986,
  Mary R.,1224, Ophelia,1046,
  Readyville,0814, S.R.,0826,
  0827, Thomas,0812,0813,0819,
  0820, Thos.Jr.,0837,
  Thos.Sr.,0837, W.M.,0819
RUCKER, W.R.,0827,0835,0840,
  William,0839, Wm.P.,0799,
  Wm.R.,0826,0828
RUDY, Catharine,0951, Charles,
  0951, Daniel,0951, Elizabeth,
  0951, Henry,0951, Herman,
  0951, Jacob L.,0951,
  Mary A.,0951, Mary,0951,
  Philip Z.,0951
RULE, Peter,0853
RUSH, Sarah,0910
RUSHING, Gen.Store,0881, M.R.,
  0824, W.A.,0819
RUSHTON, M.J.,0770, W.J.,0773
RUSS & CO., L.H.,0875
RUSS, A.J.,1171, Dr.,0880,
  Eunice,1171, Euphamie M.,
  1171, George H.,1171,
  Hannah,1171, Harry L.,1171,
  J.B.,0877, J.L.,0877,
  James Jr.,0877, James L.,
  1171, James,0877,1171, L.H.,
  1171, Lucy E.,1171, Margaret E.,
  1171, R.C.,0877,0897,
  Robert C.,1171
RUSS, Theodosia H.,1171,
  Thomas B.,1171, William,
  1171, Wm.L.B.,1171
RUSSEAU, Nancy,1162
RUSSEL, Abel,0820
RUSSELL & RANSOM, ,0831
RUSSELL, ,0775, Albert,0805,
  B.L.,1170, Col.,0773,
  Ermine,1170, H.H.,0799,
  J.H.,0764, James,0803,0808,
  M.M.,0949, Margaret,1126,
  Mary Jane,0949, Nannie,
  1166, Nona C.,0928, T.E.,
  0895, W.B.,0928, W.E.,0878,
  William,1126,1170, Wm.,0877
RUSSWURM, Almira,1061,
  John S.,1066, Mary L.,1066,
  Rebecca,1061
RUTH & SON, John W.,0874
RUTH, ,0863, Albert H.,1172,
  Anne C.,1172, Fannie E.,
  1172, George W.,1171,
  John W.,0874,1171, Weakley D.,
  1172
RUTHERFORD, (Gen.),0813, A.J.,
  0855, Bettie,0993, Eliz.H.,
  0935, Henry,0751,0789,0793,
  0794,0801, Sophia,1112
RUTLAND, Blake,0842, James B.,
  0850
RUTLEDGE & THOMPSON, ,0874,
  1172
RUTLEDGE, ,0823, Benjamin,
  0761, Eunice M.,1172, James,
  0751, John G.,1172, John H.,
  1172, John W.Jr.,1172,
  John W.Sr.,1172, John,1172,

Julia L.,1172, Katie,1172, Sarah,1172, Warner G.,1172
RUTLEGE, Matilda,1138, Sallie, 1138
RUTTLE & CO., W.A.,0768
RUTTLE, M.,0772, Mrs.,0768, W.A.,0771
RYALL & CO., T.C.,0875
RYALL, A.P.,1173, Albert P., 1172, Eliz.R.,1172, Elizabeth, 1172,1173, Ellie,1173, H.C., 0875, Henry C.,1172,1173, Johnston S.,1172,1173, Juliet S.,1172, Juliet, 1173, Mattie,1173, T.C., 0877, Thomas C.,1172, Thomas C.Jr.,1173, Thomas C.Sr., 1173
RYALL, Thomas,1172, Walter S., 1172, Walter,1173, William, 1172
SADDLER, Mary S.,0980
SAGELEY, W.W.,1068
SAILORS, "Salley",0862, "Sallie",0871
SAMPLE, John,0802
SANAWAY, B.,0826
SANDER, Frances J.,1066
SANDERS, (Chapel),0861, (Col.),1115, 0813, Alexander,1168, Almedia, 1230, Amelia E.,1152, Catharine,1168, David,0894, Elizabeth,0909,1031, Frances J.,1050, G.S.,1152, J.B.,0757, J.C.,0850, James,1114, Jane,1168, Jas.T.,0779, Jesse B.,1130
SANDERS, John C.,1114,1115, Ledocia,1037, Letitia,1114, Mary A.,1130, Nat,1114, Nora,1114, R.C.,0850,1114, Richard,0812, Russell,0848, Sarah,1099, Susan E.,1130, Tennessee L.,1037, Thomas, 1099, W.P.,0810, William, 0842
SANDFORD, ,0774, Catharine, 0924, George,0796, James T., 0756, Jas.T.,0779
SANDUSKY, (Dr.),1174, Annie, 1173, Cecil,1174, Dick R., 1173, Dick,1173, Elizabeth, 1173, Ellen T.,1173, Fannie, 1174, G.C.(Rev.),1173, G.C., 0876, Jacob,1173, John A., 1173, Nellie,1174
SANFORD, Col.,0774,0775, J., 0895, James,0760, Mary B., 0958
SANSOM, D.N.,0750, Dorrel N., 0771, Dr.,0767,0776
SANSON, Dowell N.,0772
SAPP, Mary,0932
SAPPINGTON, John,0801, R.B., 0794, Rebecca B.,0982, Thomas,0982
SATTERFIELD, Dr.,0758,0775
SAUNDERS, ,0813, Ralph S., 0877
SAVAGE, (Prof.),1074, Fannie F., 1074, G.M.,0834
SAVELL, T.M.,0781
SAWING, Sallie,1041
SAWSON, Margaret E.,1219
SAWYERS, H.,0799
SAY, Ann,0901, William,0901
SAYERS, Abner,1007, Ann M., 1012, Bettie E.,1007, James J.,1012, Jane,1007, Jimmie A.,1012, Mary E., 1012, Nancy,1012, Robert B., 1012, Robert,1012, Sarah J., 1012
SCABY, James,0843
SCALES, (Miss),1016, A.G., 0805,1006, Ab,0834, Allie A., 1006, Annie C.,1007, Bettie E.,1007, Charles E., 1006, Daniel,0834, Eliza L., 1006, Elizabeth,1216, Ella, 1007, Eva M.,1007, Fletcher A., 1006, Frances H.,1006,

Frances,1006, Frank B.,1006
SCALES, Frank E.,1007, James A.,1006, John,1007, Joseph D.,1006, Joseph G., 1006, Laura M.,1006, M.H., 1223, Melissa A.A.,1007, N., 0801, Nicholas,0775,0794, Peter S.,1006, Pleasant D., 1007, Risdon G.,1006, Sallie,1007, Samuel W.,1006
SCALES, Samuel,1007, Willis C., 1006, Wm.N.,1006
SCARCY, Bennet,0794
SCHOFIELD, Gen.,0800
SCHWARTS, W.A.,0878
SCOBEY, Anna B.,1079, Eudora, 1079, Robert C.,1079
SCOBY, Jane,1122
SCOTT, (Gen.),1175, ,0776, 0801,0863, Abner,0760, Andrew D.,0951, Andrew, 0951, Angeline,1194, Capt., 0751, Charles,0796, Elizabeth, 1174, Hattie,0915, Henry C., 0951, James F.,0951, James, 0791,0793,0849,0850,0871, John,0843, Joshua B.,0872
SCOTT, Leah,0951, Leroy,0947, Mahala T.,0951, Mary A., 0951, Mary D.,0951, Mary E., 1225, Miles E.,0951, Nancy E.,0947, Robert,0761, Samuel W.,0764, Samuel, 0915,0951, Sarah,0915, Thos.(Rev.),0783, William A., 0951, William J.,0951
SCRAPE, J.D.,0827
SCRIBNER, Alice O.,0952, Butler M.,0952, Butler N., 0952, George B.,0952, George W.,0952, James M., 0952, James N.,0952, James W.,0952, Jeremiah B., 0952, John A.T.,0952, John H.,0952, John,0952, Laura A.,0952, Lewis S., 0952, Malcia,0952
SCRIBNER, Margaret F.,0952, Marsus M.,0952, Mary E., 0952, Mary J.,0952, Matilda J., 0952, Mollie,0952, Nancy A., 0952, Nancy T.,0952, Nancy, 0952, Sarah B.,0952, Sarah C.,0952, Sue A.,0952, Susan R.,0952, Thomas C., 0952, Willie J.,0952
SCROGGIN, Maggie,1101
SCROGGS, (Dr.),1134
SCRUGGS, Allen M.,1007, Althea,1007, Angeline,0991, Drury,1007, Edward H.,1007, Edward Sr.,1007, Edward, 1007, F.P.,0809, Florence, 0991, Isabella,1008, J.E., 0862, John,1007, Joseph, 0991,1007, Lizzie,1008, Louie,1007, Mary(Mrs.),0862
SCRUGGS, Mattie T.,1007, Nancy,1007, Theo,1007, Thomas 1007, William,1007, Young,1007
SCUDDER, Elizabeth,1172,1173, James L.,0849,0870,0892, James,1873,0792, John,1173
SCURLOCK, Fannie B.,0937, James,0789,0792,0793
SEABRIGHT, George,0803
SEABURN, Kit,0850
SEAGRAVES, ,0775
SEAHORN & MCKINNEY, ,0874
SEAL, Bessie,0995, Nannie, 0995, W.H.,0995
SEALEY, James E.,0757
SEARCEY, ,0838
SEARCY, Bennett,0795,0841, John,0874, Julia,1048, Lucy,1059, Reuben,0842, Sarah,1048, Tabitha,1023, W.W.,0836, William,1048
SEARGROVE, Capt.,0752
SEARSEY, Sallie,1031, W.M., 0813, W.W.,0813,0821
SEAVY, Hial Paul,0952, Isaac,

0952, Rebecca,0952
SEAWELL, Benjamin,0846, William,0847
SEAY, (Chapel),0861, Daniel, 1105, Elizabeth,1105, George E.,0850, Marcus, 0849, Sarah F.,1105
SEBASTIAN, Dr.,0775
SEHORN, A.O.H.P.,0828,0832
SELLARS, Capt.,0751, James, 0760, Lard,0842
SELLERS, ,0750, E.J.Elvira, 0947, Hardy,0947, Jane,0923, Mary,0915, T.J.,0799
SENTER, Dewitt C.,1136
SERLEY, Jacob,0867
SETTLES, Joseph,0850
SEVIER, (Gov.),1184, John, 0759, T.F.,0798, Valentine, 1184
SEWELL & BILLS, ,0897
SEWELL, ,0768, Henry,0849, J.H.,0897
SHACKLEFORD, John,0850, R.D., 0766
SHACKLER, Philip,0841,0850
SHAFFER, Maggie Lee,0940
SHAFFNER, ,0863, John,0867, Marion,0870
SHAHL, Gen.,0750
SHANNER, ,0803
SHANNON & CO., ,0855
SHANNON, Alex,1115, Capt., 0792, Cornelia P.,1008, Dr., 0870, E.J.,1116, Elizabeth H., 1008, Elizabeth J.,1116, Elizabeth,1008, Ervin K., 1115, Eunice,1115, Finis E. 1116, Finis E.Sr.,1115, Finis Jr.,1108, Frusey, 1116, Henry,0841,1115
SHANNON, Isabella,1115, J.H., 1115, James R.,1115, James, 1108, Jane,1115, Maggie, 1115, Martha V.,1008, Mary C.,1115, Mary F.,1008, Mary J.,1108, Mary,1108, Nancy,1115, Nebar,1115, Norman P.,1115, Robert W., 1008, Robin,0842, Rosanna A., 1115
SHANNON, Samuel E.,1008, Samuel R.,1008, Sarah A., 1008, T.G.,0984, Tennessee E., 1008, Texannah,1116, Thomas G.,1008, Thos.,0751
SHAR, James,0863
SHARBER, Dr.,0774, E.Burk, 0953, Elizabeth,0905, Fannie P.,0953, J.W.,0775, James P.,0953, John E., 0785,0952, John P.,0953, John,0915, Joseph W.,0952, 0953, Lura,0953, Mary A., 0915, Mary E.,0953, Mary J., 0953, Nancy,0915, Parthenia, 0952
SHARBER, Walter S.,0953, William B.,0953
SHARON, ,0863
SHARP, A.,0821, Elizabeth, 1027, James,0815,0821, Jane B.,0980, John,0820, Joseph,0842,0844,0846, M.V.,0799, S.N.,0802
SHAW, Alexr.M.,1174, Ambrose D., 1174, Andrew J.,0953, Ann E.,1174, Barkley R., 0953, C.A.,1129, Christopher, 0862,0871, Edwd.Driskill, 1174, Elizabeth,0947,1174, Emily E.,0953, Hugh,0776, James P.,0953, James,0893, John Rufus,1174, John W., 1174
SHAW, John,0886,1174, Joseph B., 0953, Joseph J.,0953, Joseph,0953, Julia,1174, Mahala,1174, Margaret E., 0953, Martha H.,1174, Martha I.,0953, Martha, 0953, Mary A.E.,0953, Mary L.,1174, Mary O.,0953,

Mary,0929, Nancy,1174,
 Samantha A.,1129
SHAW, Susan O.,1174, Thomas B.,
 0953, William F.A.,0953,
 William S.,1174, Wm.M.(Rev.),
 1174, Wm.Marvin,1174
SHEAFE & SMITHSON, ,0830
SHEAFE, Charles A.,1062
SHEALEY, Lilian,1156
SHEAREN, Mary S.,1150
SHEARIN, Mollie F.,1177
SHEFFIELD, Ephraim,1226,
 Henry,1226, Jason B.,0888,
 Laura,1226, Martha M.,1226,
 Samuel,1226
SHEGOY, Robert,0755
SHEHAN, Chas.C.,0898
SHEHANE, G.H.,0893, J.F.,0893,
 Mirach,0893
SHELBY, Col.Isaac,0873,
 Elizabeth,1214, Henry,0850,
 0853
SHELTON, Bettie,0830, C.N.,
 0799, James R.,0772, James,
 0843, John B.,1063, John,
 0855,1063, Mary J.,1037,
 Monroe,0851, Sallie A.,
 1063, Susan E.,1063,
 William,0836
SHEPARD, (Store),0767, Agnes,
 1116, Alice,1116, Capt.,
 0792, Daniel G.,0851, Dr.,
 0880, E.,0875, Frances G.,
 1116, J.H.,0836, James,0834,
 John T.,0800, John,1116,
 Mattie,1116, S.G.(Rev.),
 1116, S.G.,0859, Samuel G.,
 1116, Samuel,1116
SHEPPARD, Clinton,0991,
 Mary E.,0991, Nancy E.,
 1198, O.P.,1198, Polly,0991
SHERMAN, Dr.,0779, Jos.(Rev.),
 0783, Wm.T.,0824
SHERRILL, Huldah,0844,
 William,0841
SHERROD, Capt.,0752
SHERWELL, L.S.,0810
SHIELD, Eliza,0959
SHIP, Daniel,0863
SHIPMAN, David,0863
SHIVER & CO., D.W.,0879
SHOAT, Joseph,0761
SHOFFNER, L.(Col.),1185,
 Sarah E.,1185
SHOFNER, Albert,1174, Austin,
 1174, Catharine,1174,
 Christop.H.,1174, Christopher,
 1174, Daniel W.,1174,
 Dorothea,1146, Elizabeth M.,
 1174, Elizabeth,1174,
 Frederick,1181, George F.,
 1174, Henderson,1174, Isom,
 1174, James B.,1174,
 Jeptha B.,1174
SHOFNER, John,1174, Martin,
 1174,1175, Mary A.,1181,
 Mary E.,1143, Mary,1181,
 Mitchell D.,1174, Monroe,
 1174, Nancy A.,1219, Nancy,
 1143, Newton M.,1174, P.W.,
 1143, Plummer W.,1174,
 Purline,1174, Rebecca,1174,
 Rhoda,1174, Sarah,1181,
 Wm.H.,1174
SHOPNER, Wm.J.,1174
SHORT, A.P.,0893, Andrew,1112,
 B.F.,1008, Capt.,0751,
 J.A.,1008, John B.,0892,
 Juda,1008, Judia,1228,
 S.S.,0790, Sally E.,1112,
 Thomas,0790, Wm.H.,1008
SHORTER, Easter C.,1116, J.R.,
 0855,1096,1116, James,1116,
 John,0848, Lorenza J.,1116,
 Martha P.,1116, Rebecca,
 1116, Salina,0920, Susie,
 1116
SHRIVER, ,0863, D.B.,0871,
 D.W.,0871
SHUMAN, Philip,0870
SHUTE, Abigail,0994
SHY, Maggie,0985, N.W.,0799
SIDBERRY, J.M.,0764

SIKE, W.H.,1069
SIKES, Bessie T.,1063, Bettie,
 1014,1063, Jesse,1063,
 Martha L.,1063, Mary L.,
 1063, Mary T.,1165, Mattie N.,
 1063, Mattie,1063, R.M.,
 0863, William H.,1063,
 William H.Jr.,1063
SILAR, Mary,1225
SIMMONS, ,0887, Alex,0843,
 Benjamin,0886, Capt.,0792,
 Charlie,0953, Edward,0953,
 Eliza A.,0953, Eva,0953,
 Harris H.,0850, James,0869,
 Mary A.,0953, Mary,1068,
 McKee,0953, Nannie,0989,
 Quinton,0953, Robert H.,
 0953, Sarah A.,0953,
 Thomas A.,0953
SIMMONS, Thomas D.,0953,
 Thomas G.,0953, Thomas,
 0794,0989, William C.,0953
SIMMS, James,0880,0899,
 Mary B.,0966, William,0851
SIMONS, Augusta,0915, Simpson,
 0840
SIMPSON, ,0875, Dr.,0761,
 George,0821,0833, Pins,
 0848, Robert,0858
SIMS, ,0863, A.C.,0782,
 Anderson,0870, Elizabeth,
 1063, John,0863, Leonard,
 0854, Mary A.,1133, Mathew,
 0842, R.H.,0877, Victoria J.,
 1212, Walter H.,0878
SINCLAIR, A.,0770, Maggie A.,
 0966
SINGLETON, Mary E.,1138,
 Robert L.,1138, Robert,
 0880, Robt.L.,0868
SITES, Capt.,0752
SIVLEY, Rebecca,1142
SKEEN, W.P.,0852
SKELLY, James,0795
SKERETT, Isadore,0841
SKIPWITH, G.S.,0779
SLAUGHTER, Reuben,0842
SLAVE, Bob,0867,0869, Clayton,
 0848, Joe,0848, John,0867,
 Martin,0892, Nelly,0794,
 Willis,0848
SLEDGE, Mr.,0788
SLOAN, John,0863
SLOCUM, John,0791
SMALL, Bennett,0815
SMALLING, Ann F.,1175,
 Benj.F.,1175, Benjamin,
 1175, Constantine,1175,
 Eliz.B.,1175, Elizabeth,
 1175, Forsyth,1175, James M.,
 1175, Mary C.,1175, Samuel,
 1175
SMEE, J.W.,0781
SMELL, Albert,0872, Jas.M.,
 0750
SMILEY & ARMSTRONG, ,0899
SMILEY, Catharine E.,1226,
 H.B.,1226, Jasper,0895,
 N.J.,0890, Newton J.,1226,
 Sarah,1226
SMITH & DAVIDSON, ,0768
SMITH & HODGE, ,0829
SMITH & LANHAM, ,0857
SMITH BROS.,,0878
SMITH, (Mill),0813, (Mrs.),
 0863, (Rector),0779, (Rev.),
 0809, ,0776,0777,0812,0813,
 0830,0863, A.H.,0819,
 A.Lafayette,1227, Agnes,
 1121, Alexander,0793,1040,
 Alice,1087, Amy,1230,
 Andrew J.,1175, Andrew,
 0902, Anna M.,0954,1176,
 Annie,1009
SMITH, Annie,1081,1087,
 Archibald,0795, B.B.(Bishop),
 0907, B.F.,0889, Baxter,
 0895, Benj.,0760, Bennet,
 0820,0821, Bennett,0815,
 0826, Bros.,0773, Bubie,
 1117, Capt.,0752,0850,0851,
 Carolina,1064, Carrie E.,
 0954, Charles G.,0850,

 Charles,0842
SMITH, Charles,0846, D.(Dr.),
 0797, D.A.,0779, Daniel D.,
 1064, Daniel,0843,1103,
 DeWitt H.,1064, Dr.,0753,
 E.Kirby(Gen.),0785,
 E.Kirby,0786,0824, E.S.,
 0850, Eddie W.,1117,
 Edgar P.,1050,1064,
 Effie M.,1009, Elizabeth C.,
 1008, Elizabeth W.,1040
SMITH, Elizabeth,0838,0954,
 1063, Eloise,1064, Emaline F.,
 1227, Emma,1040,1117,1175,
 Emmet,1175, Ephraim,1064,
 F.E.,0893, F.G.,0773, F.S.,
 0881, Fannie E.,1167,
 Fannie P.,0954, Fannie,
 0927,1063, Flora K.,0954,
 Francis S.,1008, Francis,
 0796
SMITH, Frank H.,0780,0954,
 Frank,0849, Franklin G.,
 0779,0780,0953,0954, G.W.,
 0819, Geo.L.,0842, George W.,
 1064,1227, George,0815,0842,
 1175, Green,0870, H.H.,0898,
 Henry,0854, Herbert,0868,
 Ida L.,1064, Isaac,0793,
 1081, J.,0821, J.L.,0752
SMITH, J.M.,0799, J.P.,0890,
 James B.,1117, James D.,
 1063, James G.(Dr.),0777,
 James G.,0757, James M.,
 1063, James,0760,0842,0898,
 1012,1116, Jane,0838,
 Jasper E.,1176, Jasper N.,
 1175, Jennie P.,1009,
 Jennie,1063, Jessie,1064,
 John A.,1175
SMITH, John E.,1175, John H.,
 1063, John M.,1175, John P.,
 1063, John,0813,0815,0819,
 0820,0826,0827,0830,0838,
 0863,0927,1009,1087,
 Joseph P.,1064, Joseph W.,
 1064, Josiah,0841, Julia E.,
 0954, Julia I.,0954, Julia,
 1211, Kirby(Gen.),1057
SMITH, Kirby,1065, L.,0764,
 Lafayette,1227, Laura,1090,
 Lelia,1117, Lockie,1064,
 Lorinda,0838, Louella,1009,
 Lucinda J.,0976, Lucinda,
 1226, Lucy A.,0994, Lucy J.,
 1117, Lulie J.,1064,
 Margaret A.,1009, Margaret E.,
 1227, Margaret I.,0954
SMITH, Margaret M.,1009,
 Margaret,1063,1134,1197,
 Martha A.,1009, Martha J.,
 1117, Martha M.,1026,
 Martha R.,1142, Martha,
 1012,1100,1116,1175,1227,
 Mary E.,1008,1103, Mary F.,
 1009,1117, Mary J.,1012,
 1066, Mary M.,1063, Mary W.,
 1043
SMITH, Mary,1064, Mattie G.,
 1175, Mattie,1176, McDaniel,
 0848, Merritt,1226, Miranda E.,
 1117, Morgan,1167, Moses,
 0751, Mrs.,0780,0802,0864,
 Mumford,0758, Munford,0764,
 0954, N.E.,0802, N.P.,0795,
 0796, Nancy A.,1175, Nancy,
 0927,0928,1175
SMITH, P.N.,0802, Parmelia,
 0848, Peter N.,0796,0809,
 Peyton,0837,0838, Polly,
 1134, R.& S.,0828, R.,0779,
 0827,0838, R.D.,0773,
 Reason,1142, Robert D.,
 0954, Robert E.,1175,
 Robert,0813,0819,0863,
 Robt.D.,0780, Robt.T.N.,
 0819, Ruth,1063
SMITH, Saline,1064, Sallie C.,
 1175, Sallie J.,1063,
 Sallie M.,0994, Sampson,
 0842, Samuel A.,1009,
 Samuel D.,1009, Samuel,
 0760,0761,1064

SMITH, Sarah A.,0954, Sarah C., 1227, Sarah E.,1175, Sarah M.,0980, Sarah T., 1227, Sarah,0945,1081,1142, Shadrack,0842, Sidney B., 1063, Simeon,0750, Susan A., 1227, Susan,0980,1185, T.B., 0799,0825, T.J.,0764, T.S., 0817, Theodore,0831
SMITH, Thomas M.,1226,1227, Thomas S.,1226, Thomas, 0794, Turner,0976, Virginia L., 0954, W.,0829, W.A.(Dr) 0780, W.A.,0954, W.Abe,0768, W.B.,0830, W.D.S.,0843, W.H.,0849,0855,1116, W.P., 0763, W.P.M.,0843, William C., 0954, William H.,1117
SMITH, William S.,1063, William,0789,0794,0805, 0813,0837,0842,0860,0896, Winfield,1117, Wm.,0794, 0801, Wm.A.,0780, Wm.H., 1008, Wm.M.,1009, Wm.N., 1009, Wm.N.M.,1009
SMITHSON & HODGE, ,0991
SMITHSON HODGE, ,1009
SMITHSON KENNEDY, ,1009
SMITHSON, (Mr.),1065, ,0803, Alma E.,1065, Ann,1009, 1227, Anne V.,1064, Chas.W., 1009, Dollie J.,0971, Dolly A.,1009, Dolly,1009, Elijah K.,1009, Ellen,1227, Fount,1064, George H.,1007, George W.,1009, James M., 1009, Janey,1010, Jesse W., 1009
SMITHSON, John G.,1064,1227, Joseph P.,1009, Louisa, 0971, Lydia O.,1009, Margaret K.,1009, Martha P., 1009, Mary E.,1009, Mary, 1009,1010, Nathaniel N., 1009, Noble,0892,1064, P.C., 0893,1214, P.G.,0799, Permelia,1009, Peyton C., 1227, Sallie M.,1009
SMITHSON, Sallie,1010, Sarah W.,1065, Sylvanus, 0971, Tandy S.,1009, Tandy, 1009, Wm.G.,1009
SMITHWICK, D.D.,0854
SMIZER, James,0755
SMOOT, Ann,0947, John M.,0768
SMOTHERMAN, Alice T.,1065, Eldridge,1065, Fred,1065, Joseph P.,1065, Joseph, 1065, Maggie,1032, Robert T., 1065, Sue L.,1065, Sue,1065
SNEED, ,0803, Abraham,1125, Ann J.,1097, Anna,1118, Annie,1097, Bethenia H., 0979, Constant P.C.,0979, Elizabeth,1125, Emily,1125, Fayette,0849, John,1097, 1118, Leathy A.,1118, May, 0978, Sallie,1019, Susan, 0979, W.H.,0791,0827
SNELL & CO., ,0827
SNELL, Elias,0893, Elizabeth, 1033, Fannie,1227, Harriett, 0929, J.C.,1176, James C., 1227, Jasper B.,1176, John A.,1227, Mahala,1227, Mary,1229, Sarah H.,1176, Thomas K.,1176, Virginia C., 1176, W.B.,1176
SNODDY, Robert,0862
SNOWDEN, R.B.,0798
SNYDER, ,0803, Susan Sevier, 1184
SOLOMON, Alice Cary,1176, Sallie C.,1176, Sue B., 1176, W.C.,1176, W.T.,1176, Wm.Tarver,1176
SOMERHALL, William,0828
SOPPINGTON, John,0794
SORRELL, Betsy,0891, Lucy, 0891
SOULE, Bishop,0835,0965
SOUTHALL, James,0793, P.H., 0782, Patrick H.,0954,

Patrick H.Jr.,0954
SOWELL, Albert B.,0955, Alice J.,0955, Barkley, 0955, Carrie E.,0955, Emily E.,0955, Emily J., 0955, Fannie P.,0955, Felix, 0955, James D.,0955, Jennie R.,0955, Nina,0955, Thomas W.,0955, Wallace T., 0955, William I.,0955, William J.,0955
SPAIGHT, Richd.Dobbs,0826
SPAIN & CO., ,0829
SPAIN, Lissie,0918, Sarah, 1093, Thomas,0829
SPAN, Martha A.,1159
SPARKMAN, Capt.,0752,0792, D., 1010, Dabney,1010, Ernest, 1010, James T.,1010, Latta, 1010, Laura,1010, Lena,1010, Lucy M.,1010, M.J.,1010, Mary P.,1010, Mary W.,0905, Nellie Ann,1010, Rebecca, 1010, Rosanna,1010, Seth C., 1010, Seth,1010
SPARKMAN, Tabitha C.,1010, Thomas W.,1010, William, 1010
SPARKS, Docie,1065, Fannie, 1065, Henry B.,1065, Ingraham T.,1065, J.W., 0830, James,1065, Jesse W., 1065, Josephine,1065, Massey C.,1065, Pollie,1162
SPEER, J.K.(Rev.),0901
SPENCE, Elizabeth,1066, Ellen S.,1066, Ellen,1066, Esther,1219, Florence,1066, Henry C.,1066, Henry,1066, J.C.,0828, Joe,0827, John C.,0828,1065,1066, John,0818,1065, Joseph, 0830, M.,0827, Marman,0826, 1066, Mary S.R.,1066, Mary, 1065
SPENCE, Thomas,0789, William J., 1066, William,0816,0829, 0830,0831,0835
SPENCER, ,0803, John,0758, 0759,0761,0769
SPENSER, B.F.,0766, John,0766, Zilman,0766
SPERRY, Lewis,0827
SPICER, Daniel,0842
SPILLARD, Mr.,0853
SPILLERS, R.T.,0853
SPINK, Capt.,0850
SPINKS(Colored), Burr,0849
SPINKS, John,0842
SPOTSWOOD, Nancy,1012
SPRADIM, Obediah,0846
SPRATT, Blythe,0808
SPRING, Abner,0842
SPRINGER, A.M.,0854
SPRINKLE, Dr.,0776, T.J.,0764
SPROTT, Absalom B.,1010, Blythe,1010,1011, Caroline G., 1011, Caroline,1011, Elizabeth,1011, Emma C., 1010, James F.P.,1010, James P.,1011, Jane,0987, Jimmie,1011, John A.,1010, John B.,1010, Joseph,1011, Mary S.,1011, Mary V.,1010, Minnie M.,1011
SPROTT, Nora P.,1010, Ophelia Z., 1010, Rachael J.,1011, Rachael,1010,1011, Sarah A., 1010, Sarah M.,1010, Thomas P.,1010, William H., 1011, Wm.H.,1011
SPRUCE, C.M.,1139, Mary E., 1139
ST.JOHN, H.J.,0824
STACEY, Capt.,0792, Joseph, 0842
STACKARD, George W.,0955, Sally,0955
STACY, Nancy,1108
STAFFORD, Lucinda,1146
STAGGS, Felix,0795
STALKER, Isabella,1151
STALLER, A.(Mrs.),0827, A.,

0827
STALLING, ,0863, E.,1139, Rosanna,1139
STALLINGS, Margt.M.E.,1150
STAMMER, Elizabeth,1227, John, 1227, Letitia,1228, Lucinda, 1228, Margaret A.,1228, Thomas,1227
STAMPS, Tom,0870
STANFIELD, Capt.,0792, Elizabeth,0911, Mary,1215
STANLEY, Austin C.,0955, Carrie I.,0955, Ellen,0955, Gen.,0800, Rhoda C.,0955, Thomas A.,0955, William W., 0955, William W.Jr.,0955, Wright,0955
STANTON, S.S.,1114
STARN, Col.,0873, J.W.,0977
STARNES, (Col.),1168,1175, , 0896, Augusta Mary,1060, James W.,0800
STATHAM, Mary,1062
STATLING, James,0867
STEED, Fanny,1108
STEELE, ,0863, A.A.,0890, A.H.,0890, Capt.,0752, J.P.,0819,0823, John P., 0850,0871,0892, Julia B., 1158, Lelia,0981, Margaret, 0910, Martha,1214, Mary, 0966, P.C.,0868, Robert, 0760, T.S.,0871,0877, William,0842
STEELEY, Eunice,1171, Lexy, 1171, William,1171
STEEN, Susan O.,1174
STEGALL, ,0893
STEINBRIDGE, John,0841
STEM, Elizabeth C.,1127, Jacob,1176, Mary,1176, Richard H.,0868,1176, Sallie,1176
STENSTON, Mary Ann,0869
STEPHENS, (Mr.),0956, Alexander H., 1034, Daniel,0877,0878, Dr., 0783, Etta,1177, Hardie, 1177, Henry H.,1177, Henry, 0868, Hiram,1177, Ida O., 0956, J.B.,1204, J.M.,0781, J.M.L.,1177, John,0877, 1177, Joseph,1177, Julia M., 1106, Kate,1177
STEPHENS, Leroy W.,0956, Lizzie,1177, Margaret F., 1177, Martha A.,1177, Martha,1177, Mary C.,0956, Mary,0914,0955,1177, Moses B.,1106, Moses,0779, Nancy,1177, Pearlie Lee, 1177, Ransom,1161,1177, Robert H.,1177, Sarah,1106, T.W.,0799
STEPHENS, Thomas M.,0955, Thomas N.,0956, Thomas, 1177, Tranquilla,1172, W.K., 0753, Walter S.,1177, William K.,0955,0956, Wm.H.,1177
STEPHENSON, (Gen.),1063, , 0750,0774,0863, Dr.,0750, Frances M.,0919, Grace, 0921, J.B.,0912, J.W.,0782, Jane E.,0921, Jas.N.,0749, Jas.W.,0776,0784, John, 0749, Lucinda C.,1128, Nancy C.,1144, Nathanl., 0749, Robt.,0874, Thomas, 0749, Thos.,0761
STEPHENSON, W.C.,0890
STERLE, Price C.,0867
STERLING, (Capt.),0987, Capt., 0852
STETWELL, A.B.,0897
STEUART, Margaret E.,0927
STEVENS, ,0813, Adaline,1011, Beulah,1011, Catherine, 0908, Edward,1011, Effie, 1011, Ernest,1011, Henry, 1011, James A.,1011, James W.,1011, Joseph,0793, Josephine,1011, Mary E., 1011, Nancy J.,1011, Nancy,

1011, Rhoda C.,1213, Robert L.,1011
STEVENS, Sarah,1011, Thomas, 1011, Walter D.,1011
STEVENSON, Gen.,0825, Moore, 0842, Rebecca,1161, Susan, 1011, V.K.,0816,1152
STEWARD, Martha,1200
STEWART, ,0786, A.P.,0858, George,0870, James,0848, 0870, Jane B.,0972, Lt.Gen., 0800, M.,0853, Margaret, 0971,1125, Mary,1008, May, 0838, Robert,0841, Salina F., 1151, Sallie,1055, Samuel, 0842, Thomas,0794,0849, William,0844,1008
STILES, Capt.,0850
STILL, Jeremiah,0841
STILLWELL, A.V.,0890, Albert B., 1228, Deborah L.,1228, Mary K.,1228, Osburn B., 1228
STINNETT, Benjamin,1161
STITT, Ferdinand,0789
STOCKARD, ,0776, A.W.,0773, Capt.,0751, Dr.,0776, Eliz.J.,0926, J.B.,0764, J.E.,0819, Jane,0934, Mary, 0955, Nathan,0955, Wm.,0754
STOCKELL, A.W.,0769,0770
STOCKETT, Stephen,0807, Thos.W.,0794
STOCKIRD, Alice E.,1066, Frances J.,1066, James E., 1066, James,1066, Jane,1066, John E.,1066, Mary C.,1066, Mary L.,1066, Nancy F., 1066, Rosalind D.,1066, Samuel R.,1066, Thomas A., 1066, Virginia L.,1066, William F.,1066, William, 1066
STOCKTON, L.D.,0902
STODDERT, William,1202
STOKES, ,0863, James F.,0849, 0871, T.J.,0893, William, 0821
STONE, ,0862, Birdie,0956, Capt.,0792, Charles,0854, Eliza,0977, Hendley,0794, I.,0893, Jessie,0956, John, 0847,0872,0956, Mary,0956, Sallie E.,1135, Samuel R., 0957, Samuel,0956, Susie D., 0957, Thomas,0814,0901, Uriah,0811, Walker J.,0956
STONE, William,0956
STRACHAUER, Louise G.,0952
STRAHL, ,0801,0895
STRAIGHT, (Gen.),1168
STRATTON, ,0777, Alice,1117, Caroline M.,1117, Caroline May, 1117, Fannie,1101,1117, Franceway C.,1117, Houston F., 1117, J.E.,0855,1117,1118, James G.,1117, James,1101, Leila M.,1118, Mary,1101, Mildred Owen,1118, Mildred, 1203, S.G.,0855
STRATTON, S.G.,1117, Samuel G., 0850, T.J.,0850,0854,0855, 1081, Thomas E.G.,1117, Thomas J.,1117
STRAYHONE, Daniel,0956, H.Eliz.B.,0956, Jennet E., 0956, John Alison,0956, Jos.Hart,0956, Mary C., 0956, Nellie C.,0956, Olevia A.,0956, Penelope, 0956, William D.,0956, Wm.Bascom,0956
STREET ANDREWS & CO., ,1066
STREET BURNS & CO., ,0829
STREET BYRN & CO., ,1066
STREET, ,0768,0829, Alexander, 1011, Ann P.,1012, Anthony G., 1011, Anthony,1011, Christiana, 1012, Claud P.,1012, David A.,1012, Elizabeth C., 1067, Eugene,0799,1012, Grief,1012, J.P.,0770,0772, 0773, James A.,1012,

James P.,1012, James,1011
STREET, Jennie,1012, John A., 1012, John M.,1012, John T., 0890, Lazinka U.,1012, Mary A.,1012, Mary J.,1012, 1066, Mary,1011,1012, Moffitt,1012, Nancy E., 1012, Park,0789,1011,1012, 1066, Parke,0752, Tennie E.J., 1012, W.M.,1066,1067, William M.,1066
STREET, Wm.D.,1012, Wm.M., 1012
STRIBBLING, Dr.,0775
STRICKLER, Benj.,0874
STRINGHAM, Capt.,0752, George, 0793, W.,0759
STRONG, Georgie,1164
STROUD, Angie,1118, Bernice, 1118, Cornelia,1118, Emma L.,1094, Garland,1118, L.D.,1118, Lucie,1118, Minnie,1118, Nettie,1118, O.B.,1118, Sarah,1161, Thomas,0851
STUART, J.A.M.E.,0802, Judge, 0763,0795, Kyle,0762, Thomas,0760,0762,0794,0796, 0820,0869,0870, Thos.,0760
STUDDART, John,0755
STUMP & JOHNSON, ,0766
SUBLETT, ,0813, A.C.,0831, 0832, G.A.,0826,0828,0831, 0840, W.A.,0813,0827
SUGGS, Acquilla,0842
SULLIVAN, (Mr.),1118, A.,1118, Daniel,0821, Emma,1074, Fletcher,0842, Flourence, 0956,0957, George,1125, Honora,0956,0957, J.N., 0897, James,0957, Jenkin, 0842, Jesse E.,1074, Jesse, 0842, John,0819,0957, Julia, 0957, Kate,0957, Margaret, 0957
SULLIVAN, Mary E.,1125, Mary J.,0957, Patrick S., 0957, Patrick,0956, S.,1118, Timothy,0957, W.M.,0782, Wm.M.,0758
SUMMERS, A.F.,0819, Bettie, 1178, Capt.,0751, Henry, 1177, Lewis,1177, Mary,1177, Mollie E.,1154, Odie P.R., 1178, Rachel,1192, Thomas, 1177, Walter W.,1177, Wattie R.M.,1178, William, 1178
SUMNER, Geo.B.,0880
SUMPTER, Nettie,1027
SUTTLE, Catharine,1020, Kate, 1178, Richard,1178
SUTTON, ,0863, Eliz.A.,1178, Elizabeth,1178, Ernest, 1178, Jane,1129, John L., 1178, John,1129,1178, Kate, 1178, Mary M.,1129, Narcissa, 1133, Stanford,0872, Walter F.,1178, William B., 1178, Wm.B.,0871
SWAIN, Charles,0847, Thomas, 0847
SWAN, Andrew,0842, John,0843, Rebecca,0907, Sallie,1048
SWANSON, Anne M.S.,1228, Annie B.,1228, C.T.,0893, Cornelius T.,1228, Emily C., 1228, J.,0802, J.S.,0946, James,1228, M.L.,1214, Richard,0808
SWEENEY, Annie L.,1013, Bonie L.,1013, Charles D., 1013, Edward L.,1013, John L.,1013, Lemuel F., 1013, Manerva J.,1013
SWEENY, Charles P.,1012, John, 0803, Josephus L.,1012, Sallie,1012
SWIFT, Catherine,1153, Flower, 1153, Margaret,1100,1153, Mary,1184
SWIM, James,0896, M.M.,0896
SWINDELL, W.G.,1116

SWINDLE & SHORTER, ,0854
SWINGLER, George,0841
SWINGLEY, Capt.,0850
SWISHER, Eliza,0985
SYKES, Jesse,0991, Sarah J., 0991, W.J.,0764
SYNNOTT, Anne,0999
SYPERT, Lawrence,0850,0854, Thomas,0841, William,0850
TACKETT, William,0849
TALBOT, Eli,0820
TALBOTT, Thomas,0795,0863, William,0846
TALIAFERRO, Ann M.,1012, Baldwin,1012, Nancy,1012
TALLEY, (Bros.),1103, Ada J., 1054, Calidonia,1201, D.H., 0830, Letitia,1201, Lizzie, 1200, Martin,0841, P.C., 1054, Spencer,0841, Thomas, 0799, W.W.,0850,0851
TALLY, D.H.,0829, J.P.,0894, Stephen,0890
TANKERSLEY, Maria,1214
TAPP, John S.,0850
TAPPAN, B.S.,0802,0809, E.S., 0802
TARLTON, James,0849
TARPLEY, Edward,1149, M.R., 1149, Pleasant,0851, Sterling,0842
TARPLY, John F.,0848
TARVER, A.Benjamin,1119, B.J., 0850,1118,1119, Benjamin, 0854,1118, George,1119, J.B.,1119, John E.,1119, Lucinda,1113, Lucy,1119, Mary,1101, Mattie E.,1119, Nancy,1118,1119, Nannie, 1119, Sallie C.,1176, Silas, 1118,1119, Walter A.,1119
TATE, Anderson,0842
TATUM, A.Frank,1119, Absalom, 0841, B.F.,0992, Edward L., 1119, Emily A.,1119, Ira J., 1119, Ira,1119, Martha E., 1119, Martha,1119, Mary E., 1119, Sarah A.,1119, Thomas E.,1119, William A., 1119, William B.,1119
TAYLOR & HESTER, ,0864
TAYLOR, Almira,1092, Annie R., 1178, Burt F.,0957, C.,0781, 0957, C.N.,1178, Caleb,0770, 0842, Callie D.,0957, Caroline,1119, Carrie Bell, 1013, Christina B.,1013, Clark,0957, Claybourne, 0957, Cornelia,0957, E.A., 1044, Earl F.,0957, Elbridge G., 1013
TAYLOR, Elizabeth B.,0957, Elizabeth,1194, Evaline, 1119, Floyd A.,0957, Frances N.,0957, G.D.,0809, Gen.,1055, Geo.C.,0759, George C.,0957, George, 1013, Georgie C.,0957, Hiram,1013, Isaac,1093, 1119, J.M.,0899, James H., 1119, James P.,1178
TAYLOR, James R.,0957, James, 0957,1013, Jasper,0957, John G.,0894, John M.,0759, 0760,0769,0820,1013, John N.,0857, John W.,1178, John,1013,1119, Joshua, 0843,0857, Kalabie M.,0957, L.,0770, Lashophine,1119, Laura C.,0957, Laura,0957
TAYLOR, Leona,1119, Lucy A., 0929, Lucy J.,1154, Maggie, 1044, Malinda,1013, Margaret A., 1178, Margaret,1013,1093, Martha,0957,1013,1045,1119, Mary E.,0957, Mary O.,1178, Mary,1013,1018, N.R.,0863, Nancy,1013, Perry,0842, Perrygan,1119
TAYLOR, Rachel D.,1013, Sallie,1013, Samuel,0766, Sarah J.,1015, Sarah P., 0957, Sarah,1119, Solomon,

1013, Stephen Allen,1013,
Stephen,1013, Susie D.,
0957, T.,0831, W.C.,0769,
0770, William C.,0957,
William,0834,0867,0957,
1013,1119, Wm.,0863
TAYLOR, Wm.,0864, Wm.A.,1013
TEAGUE, Dorothea,1112,
William,0842
TEAL, R.H.,0803
TELFORD, Hugh,0842, J.M.,0815,
John M.,0827
TEMPLE, Ann E.,0907, Burwell,
0794, H.B.,0797, Herbert R.,
1013, Mary F.,1013, Mary Y.,
0976, Roberta L.,1013,
Susan,1013, Wm.E.,1013
TEMPLER, Capt.,0792
TEMPLETON, Lucy,1150, Newton,
1150
TENNESON, A.,0834
TENNESSEE, Louisa,0931
TERRELL, (Dr.),0958, Alexr.C.,
0958, Anna,0958, Hezekiah,
0957, James,0958, Joel,0958,
Margaret S.,0957, Martha,
0986, Mary E.,0958, Mary,
0958, William J.,0958
TERRILL, John H.,0783
TERRY, Carena G.,0958, David,
0958, John M.,0958, John O.,
0958, Madison,0958, Mary E.,
1162, Nancy B.,0958,
Nannie S.,0958, Robert,
0867, Sarah A.,0958, Sarah,
0867, Zula,0958
THERENOT, Dr.,0776
THEVENOT, Dr.,0758, J.B.A.,
0757
THOMAS & CLAXTON, ,0879
THOMAS & TURLEY, ,0988
THOMAS, ,0764,0813,0863,
Altha G.,0803, Altha,0804,
Anthony,0867, Atha,0791,
0989,1013,1014, B.E.,0879,
Benj.,0759,0783, Bettie S.,
1186, Bettie,1014, C.O.,
0833, E.E.,1122, E.N.,0926,
E.R. (Mrs.),1044, Eliza,
1013, Elizabeth,1182, G.L.,
0771
THOMAS, Geo.H.,0825, Geo.L.,
0770, Isaac J.,0757, J.,
0838, J.E.,0758,0784,0935,
J.H.,0762,0764,0765,
James E.,0759, James H.,
0765,0890,0892,0948,0954,
0957, James,0842, Jane,1165,
1186, John,0763,0783,
Jonas E.,0926, Jonas(Col.),
0905
THOMAS, Joseph E.,1114, Lewis,
0870, Lucy,1229, Lula,0870,
Margaret I.,0954, Martha,
0905, Mary S.,0948, Mathew,
0891, Matt,0880, Mattie,
1165, Newton,0851, Rebecca T.,
0905, Robert,0844, S.J.,
0860, Sarah E.,1014,
Sarah W.,1041, Standards,
0872
THOMAS, T.W.,1229, William P.,
1229, William Sr.,1186,
William,0841,1013,1165,
1186, Wilson,0826, Woodlief,
1014
THOMASON, Caroline A.,0923,
J.R.,0764
THOMPSON & WARDLAW, ,0898
THOMPSON, (Miss),1133, (Mrs.),
1108, ,0753,0809,0820,0863,
A.P.,0854, Aaron,0896, Abe,
0815, Abraham,0826,0874,
Abram,0815, Absalom,0958,
Achsah,1180, Amy F.,1179,
Amy,1179,1184, Andrew,1125,
Annie E.,1180, Benjamin H.,
1180, Bettie,1063
THOMPSON, C.A.,0764, Capt.,
0950, Charles F.,1180,
Charles,0891,1179, David N.,
0959, David,0822, E.,0791,
0792, E.R.,0850, Elijah(Dr.),

0994, Eliz,0959, Elizabeth,
0947,1030, Ellen C.,1180,
Ellen F.,1180, Emma,1120,
Emmet,0870, Eunice M.,1172
THOMPSON, Eunice,1179, F.A.,
0902, Fannie E.,1120, Fanny,
1120, Flora,1229, Frances S.,
1229, G.W.,1184, Gen.,0784,
0797, George E.,1180,
George W.,1179, George,
0849,1120, Grace,1159, H.D.,
0822, Harriet P.,1179,
Harvey S.,0959, Hattie C.,
0959
THOMPSON, Hattie V.,1180,
Henry,0842, Hiram S.,1172,
Hugh,0975, Hulda B.,1179,
I.J.,0759, J.,0893, J.H.,
0877, J.M.,0823, J.R.,0832,
0836, J.T.,0782,0799,
J.T.S.,0781,0785, James B.,
1180, James M.,0959,
James T.S.,0958, James,
0842, Jane,0981
THOMPSON, Jason,1001, Jennie,
0963, John B.,1120, John C.,
0959, John F.,1179, John W.,
0868,0871,0874,1172,1178,
John,0790,0795,0814,0815,
0819,0820,0958,1229, Jos.H.,
0868, Jos.P.,0867, Jos.Percival,
1229, Joseph,0871, L.A.,
0893, Lawrence,0766
THOMPSON, Ledocia,1037,
Leo Duloney,0959, Letitia,
1179, Lettie,1180, Lillard,
0849,0850,0871, Lillord,
1120, Lucy,1120, Lydia,1179,
M.D.,0778, M.J.,1179,
Maggie A.,1180, Margaret E.,
1229, Martha M.,1179,
Martha,1120, Mary A.,0975,
1172
THOMPSON, Mary B.,0958,1180,
Mary E.,0957,0994,1120,
1198, Mary G.,1180, Mary L.,
1180, Mary P.,0959, Mary,
0972,1180,1229, Mattie,1120,
McNairy J.,0798, Minnie B.,
1229, Miranda,1125, Mixey,
0981, Mollie G.,1179, Moses,
1120, Myra R.,0959
THOMPSON, Myra,1229, Nancy,
1187,1206, Nannie,1120,1180,
Newcom,1179, Newcomb,1176,
Prudence,1229, Purdey,1179,
R.E.,1120, Richard,1179,
Ritter,1125, Robert C.,
1229, Robert E.,1180,
Robt.E.,1180, S.M.,0876,
Sam,0849,0852, Samuel,0868
THOMPSON, Samuel,1120,1161,
Sarah C.,0975, Sarah E.,
1180, Spurgen,1120, Sue B.,
1176, Susan,1001, Susie P.,
0959, T.A.,0771, Thomas C.,
1179, Thomas L.,1172,1229,
Thomas St.C.,0959, Thomas,
0819, Thos.,1172, Thos.J.,
0854, Thos.L.,0874
THOMPSON, Tranquilla,1172, W.,
1179, W.E.A.,1180, W.F.,
1179, W.V.,0764,0771,0787,
Warner,1179, William T.,
1120, William,0867, Wm.,
0795, Wm.W.,0759,0769,0778,
Zach,0864,0878,1180
THORNER, A.,0803
THORP, Mary,0936
THURMAN, ,0821
THURSTON, (Rev.),0882
THWEATT, ,0803, Nancy V.,1001,
W.H.,1001
TIDWELL, Rev.,0776
TILFERD, Mary R.,1133,
William H.,1133
TILFORD, ,0863, John M.,0812,
0815,0826, Nicholas,0826,
0830, Samuel,0812
TILLFORD, J.W.,0877,0878,
Lucy A.,1153
TILLMAN, Abraham,0882,
Abrahm M.,1181, Alice E.,

1164, Ambrose,0870, B.M.,
0870, Barclay M.,0849,
Daniel,0846, Edwin H.,1181,
Hattie A.,1181, Henry,0870,
J.D.,0890,0895, J.F.,1164,
James D.,1181, John,0862,
0864,0867,1180, Lewis Jr.,
0871
TILLMAN, Lewis Sr.,0871,
Lewis,0871,0872,0877,1133,
1180,1181, Mary Cath.,1181,
Rachel P.,1180, Sallie C.M.,
1133, Samuel E.,1181,
Samuel,0844
TIMBERVILLE, Capt.,0792
TINDALL, Mary J.,1003,
Noah B.,1003
TINDEL, Adeline,0958, Anderson,
0958, George W.,0958,
Jackson P.,0958, James M.,
0958, Lettie A.,0958, Lety,
0958, Lillie L.,0958,
Thomas J.,0958
TINDELL, R.W.,0781
TIPTON, James,0842
TITCOMB & FRIERSON, ,0767,
0768
TITCOMB & WILLIAMS, ,0964
TOBIAS & BROS., ,0829,1068,
A.,1040
TOBIAS, Abraham,1068, Amos,
1068, Daisy,1068, Emory Lee,
1068, Hannah,1068, Nettie,
1068, Solomon,1068, T.,0829,
Thomas,1068
TODD & BARKLEY, ,0828
TODD & CARNAHAN, ,0828
TODD & MORGAN, ,0829,1068
TODD, ,0813, Aaron,1068,
Andrew,1068, Catharine,
0949, Christopher,0755,
Eliza,1014, Elizabeth,1068,
George,1068, Herman A.,
1069, Hugh B.Jr.,1014,
Hugh Blair,1014, Ida F.,
1068, J.A.,1031, Jefferson,
1068, Josephine,1068, Kate,
1014, Martha B.,1069
TODD, Mary,1068, Mattie K.,
1068, Mattie T.,1014,
Nancy C.,1031, Palmer D.,
1069, Richard,1014, Thomas J.,
1068, William,1014
TOLLEY, W.P.,0890
TOLLIVER, J.P.,0854, Mary E.,
1120, Mary,1180, Zach,1120,
Zachariah,0850
TOLLMAN, Capt.,0752
TOLMIE, Alexr. McD.,1186,
Georgia M.,1186
TOMLINSON, (Capt.),0786,
(Mr.),0960, Anna,0959,
C.A.,0764, Irwin,0842,
John,0959, Martha,0959,
Mary S.,0959, William E.,
0959, William,0843
TOMPKINS & SINGLETON, ,1068
TOMPKINS, A.G.,0819, Albert G.,
1067, Albert S.,1068, J.M.,
0818,0823, James M.,1067,
James,0829, Kitty G.,1067,
Lizzie,1068, Margaret M.,
1068, Martha H.,1068,
Mary J.,1067, Rev.,0860,
Robert T.,1067,1068,
Roxana,1113, Speer T.,1068
TOMPKINS, Wade H.,1068
TOOMBS, Catherine,0960,
Edmund,0960, Elizabeth P.,
0960, John H.,0960, John,
0778,0960, Sabra,0960
TOON, ,0803, B.B.,1014,
Dorcus,1014, Fannie D.,
1014, Florence M.,1014,
James M.,1014, James,1014,
Michael M.,1014, Rufus C.,
1014, Sarah,1014, Vera P.,
1014, William B.,1014
TORN, Capt.,0751
TOWER, Benjamin,0846,0848
TOWLER, Catharine,0960, J.M.,
0772, Jos.,0773, Joseph M.,
0960, Joseph,0768,0769,0770,

0960
TRABUE, C.C.,0836,0838,
   Charles,0836
TRACEY, A.G.,0757
TRACY, Evans,0843
TRAIL, Emma R.,1184
TRATT, Benjamin,0822, Henry,
   0815
TRAVIS, R.E.,0809
TRAYLOR, ,0813
TRAYWICK, Abigail,1101
TREADAWAY, H.H.,0828
TREBBLING & SMITH, ,0855
TREWITT, Elijah,0841
TRIBBLE, Lewis,1103, Locky,
   1103
TRIGG, Alaman,0844, Alanson,
   0845, Daniel,0844, William,
   0843,0846,0853
TRIMBLE, Eliza,1106,1107
TROLINGER, A.J.,0875
TROLLINGER & TUNE, ,0874
TROTTER, John,0853
TROUSDALE, Gov.,0765, Wm.,
   0786,0797,0823
TROUT, Joseph,0842
TROXLER, Ambrose,1181,
   Anthony,1181, Daniel M.,
   1181, Delilah,1134, Edward,
   1181, Elizabeth,1181,
   George R.,1181, Isaac,1181,
   John A.,1181, John C.,1181,
   John,1181, Margaret A.,
   1181, Mary A.,1181, Micager,
   1181, Polly,1181, Sarah,1181
TROXLER, William T.,1181
TRUELOVE, Elizabeth,0910
TRUETT, A.,0804, Alice R.,
   1015, Alpheus,1014,1015,
   F.A.,0799, Henry M.,1014,
   1015, James M.,1015, Jennie,
   1015, John H.,1015, Lanie E.,
   1015, Richard E.,1015,
   Roena.,1015, Sallie A.,
   1015, Sarah J.,1015, Sarah,
   1014, Susan E.,1015,
   Susan J.,1015
TRUETT, William A.,1015
TUCKER, ,0861, Ada B.,0960,
   Appleton,0872, Bettie E.,
   1205, Carrie T.,1069,
   Collier B.,1069, Eliza,
   1146, Ellen M.,1069, Foster,
   0851, Frances M.,0957,
   Harriet,1139, J.F.,0773,
   J.H.,0799, J.P.,0773,
   Jesse P.,0960, Johnnie M.,
   1069, Joseph F.,0960
TUCKER, Lee S.,1069, Leonidas S.,
   1069, Lewis,1139, Lizzie C.,
   1069, Lucy,1139, Mary D.,
   0980, Mary J.,0960, Nannie May,
   0960, Oscar D.,1069, Silas,
   1069, Stephen,0808, T.M.,
   0785, Tennessee,1190,
   Thomas,0785,0799
TUDALE, Henry,0874
TULLOCH, John,0853
TULLOCK, John V.,0848
TULLOSS, J.E.,0797
TUNE & CO., ,0863
TUNE, ,0863, Bettie E.,1182,
   C.E.(Mrs.),1182, Charles W.,
   1182, Eliza F.,1182,
   Eliza J.,1182, Elizabeth,
   1158,1182, Emma S.,1182,
   Frances,1185, Horace G.,
   1182, J.C.,0875, James C.,
   1182, John C.,1182, John M.,
   1182, John,1182, Joseph E.,
   1182
TUNE, Kester L.,1182, Louis T.,
   1182, M.C.(Mrs.),1182,
   Mary A.,1182, Mary,1166,
   1182, Mattie J.,1182,
   Sallie,1182, Susan E.,1182,
   Thomas C.,1182, Thomas O.,
   1182, Thomas,1182, W.T.,
   0868, Will R.,1182, William R.,
   1182, William S.,1182
TUNE, William T.,1182,
   William,1166
TURLEY, ,0803, Judge,0989

TURNER, A.J.,0759,0764,
   Ann L.,1015, Anna T.,1015,
   Anthony I.,0760, Betsy,
   0891, C.R.,1015, Dick B.,
   1015, Dr.,0757, Elizabeth A.,
   1182, Elizabeth H.,1015,
   Elizabeth,1082, Henry,0846,
   James L.,1182, James R.,
   1015, James W.,1182, James,
   0797
TURNER, John N.,1015, John,
   1015, Joseph H.,1182,
   Joseph R.,1015, Lavinia,
   1182, Levi,0868, M.C.,0904,
   Maggie L.,1015, Manda P.,
   0904, Margaret C.,1082,
   Margaret F.,0952,1182,
   Margaret N.,1182, Martha E.,
   1191, Martha J.,1015, Mary,
   1182
TURNER, Nancy F.,1182,
   Nancy J.,0928, Sallie,1015,
   Sarah E.,1015, Sarah J.,
   1182, Tennessee M.,1182,
   Thomas,1082, William F.,
   1182, William H.,1015,
   William M.,1015, William,
   0904, Wm.K.,0823
TURNEY, Henry,0763, Peter,
   1137
TURRENTINE, ,0863, A.S.,1127,
   Alexr.,0872, Alice R.,1177,
   David A.,1176,1177,
   Eleanor F.,1176, Eleanor N.,
   1176, Ella F.,1153, Felix,
   1176,1177, James,1176,
   Lucy J.,1177, Martha Ann,
   1176, Mary A.,1127, Mollie F.,
   1177, Sallie A.,1177
TUTTON, John,0821
TYREE, Henry,0851
UNDERWOOD, Fines,0852,
   John C.,0832, Sue,0993
UNKNOWN, Eliza,1121, James,
   1121
UPSHAW, A.B.,0773
USERY, Matilda,0907, Mollie,
   0907, Necie B.,1207,
   William L.,0907
USSERY, Mary,0950
UZZELL, Ann,0909, Elisha,0766,
   0767,0783,0909, Mary Ann,
   0909
VAIL, R.A.,0768
VAN BUREN, ,0765, Martin,0996,
   1116
VAN CLEVE, H.P.,1063
VAN DORN, (Gen.),1065
VANCE, ,0863, Ann,1113,
   Drucilla,1120, Ed R.,1113,
   Ed.L.Jr.,1120, Edward R.,
   1120, Joseph T.,1121, Mary,
   1113, Nancy,0942
VANCLEAVE, J.M.,0895
VANDERFORD, Bertha E.,1069,
   Charles F.,1069, Charles R.,
   1069, Charles,1069, Eliza,
   1069, Eugene S.,1069,
   Florence,1069, Harry A.,
   1069, Mary F.,1069, Silas M.,
   1069
VANHOOK, B.J.,1121, Bettie V.,
   1121, Carrie,1121, Howard,
   1121, Huston,1121, Joel N.,
   1121, Mary T.,1121, Orrie,
   1121, Riley C.,1121,
   Virginia,1121
VANHOOSE, A.,0838
VANNATTA, C.C.,1183, Charity A.,
   1182, Christop.C.,1182,
   Delphia A.,1182, Eliza F.,
   1182, George W.,1182,
   Hibernah,1182, James,1182,
   1183, Jerusha,1182, John S.,
   1182, Joseph R.,1182, Katie,
   1183, Maria,1183, Martha,
   1182, Nancy,1183, Nannie D.,
   1183
VANNATTA, Samuel,1182
VANNOY, A.,0868,0871
VANTRASE, Jacob,0843
VARMORY, Bush,0869
VAUGH, ,0803, Drury,0837

VAUGHAN, Ada,1016, Andrew C.,
   1015, Dan E.,1016, Jessie E.,
   1016, Lulu E.,1016, Lutitia A.,
   1016, Margaret A.,1100,
   Mary M.,1015, Myrtle,1016,
   North(Miss),1049, Turner,
   0856, Williaim T.,1016,
   William,1015
VAUGHN, ,0803, A.C.,0803,
   Edmund,0842, Eliza G.,1124,
   Elizabeth C.,1037, Henry B.,
   1124, James,0827, Maggie,
   1214, S.,0802, Sallie,0960,
   Susan,1124, T.,0836
VAUGHT, Eli,1122, Josephine,
   1122, Mr.,0767, Nathan,0756,
   0783, Samuel,0819
VENABLE, ,0796, Joseph,0795,
   S.,0791,0796
VECORES, Amanda,1039
VERNATTI, George,0864
VERNER, W.H.,0902
VERNON, Ashlem,1012, Ellen,
   0993, G.,0805, Mary J.,1012,
   Matilda A.,0993, Nancy,
   1012, Obadiah,0993
VESA, John,0858
VESTAL, ,0750, John,0775
VICK & MILLER, ,0844
VICK, A.,1108, Allen W.,0848,
   Mary,1122
VICTOR, (Mill),0875
VINCENT, Minerva,1221, Sarah,
   1138, William,0819
VON BASTEL, Kate,1006
VOORHEES, W.N.,0786
VOORHIES, Catharine C.,0960,
   G.I.,0783, Peter I.,0767,
   Robt.I.,0761, William,0764,
   0767, Wm.,0762
VOSS, Jemima A.,0918, Taylor,
   0767
WADE, (Col.),0915, ,0774,0863,
   Allie,0835, Charles,0850,
   D.F.,0785, Elizabeth C.,
   1059, Elizabeth,1123,
   Ella M.,1123, H.P.,0782,
   Henry,0778, J.T.,0781,
   Leroy B.,1048, Levi,0854,
   M.B.,1123, Mary Anne,1071,
   Nannie,0835, Rebecca,1033,
   Violet H.,1048
WADE, W.T.,0800, Walter,1071
WADKINS, Ann,1144, Wm.,0891
WADLEY, Elizabeth,1227
WADLINGTON, Massey C.,1065
WADSWORTH, (Com.),1173
WAGGONER, Andrew,1016,
   Benjamin S.,1016, Emily K,
   1016, Flurida A.,1016,
   James I.,1016, Jane,1016,
   Joel S.,1016, John H.,1016,
   John,1016, L.M.,1016,
   Laurence,1016, Lee,1016,
   Mary F.,1016, Merry E.,
   1016, Neal S.,1016, Ophelia B.,
   1016
WAGGONER, Robert S.,1016,
   Sarah,1016, Sululia A.,1016,
   Thomas J.,1016, Vida P.,
   1016, William S.,1016
WAGSTER, James,0869
WAITE, Ada,1189, Ann B.,1189,
   George E.,1183, George,
   1183, James W.,1183,
   Nancy A.,1183, Nancy B.,
   1183, Rebecca A.,1189,
   Robert,1183, Rutha S.,1183,
   Warren S.,1183, Warren,1183
WALDEN, Robert,0799, S.J.Jr.,
   0875
WALDRON, Sallie H.,0992
WALKER, Addie,1121, Asberry,
   0960, C.,0807, Calvin H.,
   0757, Celia L.,1121,
   Cornelia L.,1121, Edna E.,
   1121, Edwin L.,1121,
   Elizabeth,1044, Henry,0791
   0793, J.A.,0759, J.K.,0764,
   J.N.,0787, J.S.,0768,
   James D.,1121, James S.,
   1003, James,0754
WALKER, James,0755,0756,0768,

0771,0773,0779, John B.,
0844, John C.,0764,0765,
0892, John,0796,0842,0887,
Joseph,0862,0863,0874,
Katie,1121, Laura,0916,
0960, Leth,0892, Lillia,
1121, Mary J.,0935, Mary,
0986,1028, Munroe V.,1121,
Nancy,1087
WALKER, Otey,0916,0960, R.A.,
0753, R.S.,0890, Richard S.,
1065, Richard,0886, Sally,
0955, Sarah E.,0960, Sarah,
0960,1192, Thomas,0795,0887,
W.C.,1121, W.W.,0893,
Wash.B.H.,1121, William C.,
1121, Wm.,0791
WALKINS, R.W.,0768
WALL, Byrd,0841, Clement,1183,
Edmond,0789, John B.,1183,
Martha E.,1183, Nannie J.,
1138,1183, Newton,0807,
S.V.,1138, Simeon V.,1183
WALLACE & BRO., J.W.,0874
WALLACE & CO., R.F.,0879
WALLACE, ,0886, A.D.,1205,
Alvin,1121, Catherine,1121,
Daisie,1121, Harvey W.,
1121, J.F.,1121, Jackson,
0868, James W.,1121, Jennie,
1198, Jesse,0797, John,0820,
Lillie,1121, Lizzie,1121,
Martha J.,1121, Mary,1049,
Matilda,1192, Mr.,0768
WALLACE, R.D.,0879, R.N.(Dr.),
0875, W.H.,1121, William,
0766,0894
WALLARD, Alligood,0841
WALLER, Elizabeth,1000, Joel,
1016, Nannie Marion,1016,
Obadiah,1016, Pierce,1000,
Sallie F.,1000
WALLIS, Myra,1229
WALLS, J.H.,0893
WALSH, John,0841, King,0849
WALTER & BENNER, ,0753
WALTER, Emily E.,1070, George,
0829,0832,1069, Kasper,1069,
Katherine,1069
WALTERS, Alice,1016, Dora P.,
1016, Eli A.,1016, J.E.,
1016, James,1016, Mary,1016,
Morris,1016, Nannie,1016,
Thomas,1016, Tommy,1016,
W.C.,1016
WALTHALL, (Gen.),0954,
Maj.Gen.,0825
WALTON, J.P.,1138, Sophronia A.,
1138
WAMACK, A.P.,1122, Agnes,1121,
1122, America,1122, California,
1122, Dorcas,1121, E.E.(Miss),
1122, Elizabeth,1121, J.S.,
1121, James R.,1122,
John K.,1122, Josephine,
1122, Jourdan,1122, Lucy,
1103, Mary,1122, Richard,
1121
WANNICK, Rob,0821
WANTLAND, Mahala C.,0933
WARD, Charles A.,1070, E.,
0821, Edward,0779, Elizabeth,
1073, H.,0772, Hillary,0764,
0892, Jackson J.,1070, John,
0842, Kate,1073, Mary J.,
1070, Pike,0849, William,
0871
WARDER, (Capt.),1184, India A.,
1184, James A.,0871,1183,
Laura D.,1184, Walter,1183
WARDLOW & THOMPSON, ,0874
WARDLOW, Hugh,0874
WARE, J.R.,0857, Permelia,
1027
WARFIELD, Mathias,0767
WARICK, Capt.,0850
WARMUTH, H.J.,0817,0818,
H.Joseph,1070, Joseph,1070,
Laura,1070, Maria,1070,
Mary W.,1070, Mitchell P.W.,
1070, Sallie A.,1070
WARNER, ,0863, Anna A.,1226,
1231, Emma R.,1184, Eunice M.,

1172, Eunice,1172, Frazer,
1184, H.B.,0902, Henry W.,
1184, Hugh,1184, John,0871,
1172, Mary,1184, R.Jr.,0897,
0898, Rev.,0886, Richard,
0890,0892,0893,0896,0899,
Saml.J.,0872, T.J.,0874
WARNER, T.J.,0875, Thomas W.,
1184, William D.,1184,
William F.,1184
WARNICK, William,0842
WARREN, Amy F.,1179, Amy,1184,
C.A.,0874, C.A.Jr.,1179,
C.A.Sr.,1179, Capt.,0792,
Charles A.,1184, Charles,
0842, David B.,0755, George,
1184, James,0870, John,0837,
Josephine,1184, Letitia,
1179, Martha H.,0975,
Mattie Lee,1184, Nancy B.,
1183
WARREN, S.(Miss),0827,
Stanley S.,1184, Susan Sevier,
1184, Theresa,0909, Thomas S.,
1184, William S.,1184,
William,0842
WARTMAN, Capt.,0792
WASHAM, Martha,0957
WASHINGTON, A.Isabella,1071,
Allen H.,1071, Beverly,
1071, Eliz.M.,1070, Francis W.,
1070,1071, Gen.,0871, Geo.,
1171, George,0909,0939,1070,
1116, James,1071, John Henry,
1071, John,1070,1071,
Sarah Cath.,1071, Thomas,
0849, Thos.,0795
WASHINGTON, W.H.,0823,1064,
Wm.,0823, Wm.Hunter,1071,
Wm.L.,0797
WASON, Mary E.,0934
WASSON, David,0842, Elizabeth J.,
0916, L.M.,0817, Margaret,
0838, Mariah,1077, Mrs.,
0839, Robert,0838
WASTON, James,0870
WATERHOUSE, Richd.,0785
WATERS & CO., ,0855
WATERS, Edgar,1106,1123, J.N.,
0890, James,0837, Kate S.,
1106, Mary,1112, Shelah,
0843, Thomas,0849, W.L.,0844
WATERSON, Henry,0774
WATKINS, A.,0831, Adaline W.,
1071, Archie W.,1122, Capt.,
0751, Catharine,1071,
Charles,0836, Dora,1122,
Elizabeth H.,0984, Emma Bell,
1122, Fannie,1117, J.M.,
0855,1122, Jane N.,0984,
Jane,1122, Joel,0796,
Joseph,0835, Lena May,1122
WATKINS, Louise S.,1071, M.J.,
0854, Mary Anne,1071,
Mary S.,1071, Mary,1071,
1122, Moses,0984,1122,
Saml.B.,1071, Samuel S.,
1071, Susan,1208, T.C.,0826,
T.H.,0770, Thomas S.,1071,
Thomas,1071, W.,1071,
Wilson L.,1071, Wm.,0797,
Wm.P.,0818
WATSON, (Dr.),1048, ,0828,
Dr.,0837,0838, John,0801,
0805,0844, Kate,1017, Laura,
1112, Martha,1182, Rufus L.,
0848, Sallie,1017, Thomas J.,
1017, Thomas,0842, William T.,
1112
WATTERSON, H.M.,0876
WATTS, Eleanor,0929
WEAKLEY, H.,0832, Mary J.,
1031, Robert,0766,0791,0811,
0812,0814,0833, Robt.,0759,
Sallie,0960, Samuel,0814
WEATHERBY, James M.,1100,
M.P.(Miss),1100, Nancy,1100
WEATHERLY, Lockie W.,1064
WEATHIER, Jesse,0791
WEAVER, Wm.,0867
WEBB, (Capt.),1200, (Prof.),
0955, ,0813, A.M.,0882,
B.F.,0824, B.W.,1095,

Benjamin,0871,1185, Bob,
0870, Capt.,0792, Elizabeth W.,
1185, Elnora,1185, Fannie E.(Mrs.),
1167, Frances,1006, G.S.,
0818, Isaac,1167, Isham,
0844, J.M.,0882, J.S.,0819
WEBB, James,0897, Madison H.,
1185, Messrs.,0781, Nancy,
0973, Ross,0851, S.J.,1095,
Sallie,1206, T.E.(Miss),
1167, W.R.,0772,0773,0781,
0882, W.S.,0790,0805,
William,0760, Wm.S.,0793
WEBBER, Margaret,1032
WEBSTER, Ada B.,0960, Fannie P.,
0961, Frank W.,0961,
Hyleman A.,0961, J.C.,0781,
James H.,0961, James J.,
0961, Jonathan,0874,0961,
Kate W.,0961, Lizzie D.,
0961, Mary A.,0961, Mary C.,
0961, Mattie J.,0961,
Robt.P.,0755, Robt.T.,0755
WEBSTER, Roenia C.,0961,
Sarah J.,0960, Virginia M.,
0961, W.J.,0770, William J.,
0961, William J.Sr.,0961
WEIR, David,0778, Joseph,0842,
Prof.,0859
WEISSINGER, Anna M.,0961,
Charles M.,0961, Eliza M.,
0961, Emily E.,0961,
George J.,0961, Henry Y.,
0961, Leonard A.,0961,
Leonard,0961, Mary L.,0961,
William M.,0961
WELBORN, Elatia,1230, James M.,
1230, Johnson,1230, Rosa L.,
1230
WELDON, Robert,0796
WELHAMS, Nathl.W.,0795
WELKISEN, Elizabeth J.,1088,
Isaac J.,1088, Sally,1088
WELLS, ,0774, Capt.,0792,
Catherine,1017, Coleman,
1016, E.T.,0804, Edgar J.,
1185, Edward T.,1017,
Elizabeth,1016, Ethel,1185,
Frances,1185, Giles,1017,
Hebert,1185, J.H.,0897,
James C.,1017, John C.,
1016, John H.,0874, John W.,
1017
WELLS, John W.,1185, M.C.(Miss),
1182, Margaret C.,1185,
Miss,0773, Posthenia E.,
1017, Richard P.,1017,
Richard,1017, Robert, Sarah E.,
1185, Sarah F.,1017,
Susan M.,1185, Susan,1185,
Thomas E.,1185, Thomas P.,
1185, Virginia H.,1017
WELSH, James,0759, Mitchell,
1114, T.A.,1114
WELTON, ,0813, Joseph,0821
WEMS, Catherine,0960
WENDEL, (Dr.),0830,1048,
Christopher,1072, D.D.,
0818,0819,0831,0835,0839,
David,0819,0826,0827,1071,
1072, Emma C.,1072, J.E.,
0829,1033, James E.,1071,
1072, R.S.,0818,0829,0833,
1033, Robert S.,1072,
Sarah H.,1071, William,0829
WEST, J.D.,0836, John,0880,
M.C.,0890,0897,0902,
Moses C.,0890
WESTALL, Eliza M.,1039
WESTBROOK, Betsy,1011, Nancy,
1011, Thornton,1011, W.C.,
0819
WESTERVELT, Ann W.,1006,
Eliza L.,1006, Peter A.,
1006
WESTFIEL, ,0803
WETON, George,0821
WHARTEN, Jessee,0794
WHARTON, (Rev.),0809, Anna S.,
0997, B.F.,0818, Jesse,0846,
Joseph,0854, W.H.(Dr.),
0997, W.H.,0802, William,
0843

WHEATON, Jesse,0822
WHEELER, (Gen.),1107, ,0800,
 Col.,,0993, E.D.,0817,
 Edward,0855, Etta Valonie,
 1185, Gen.,0800,0873,
 James T.,0984, John W.,
 1185, Malissa A.,1185,
 Martha L.,1185, Mary Ann,
 1185, Nathaniel M.,0868,
 Thos.,0867, W.W.,1185,
 William D.,1185
WHILTHORN, W.J.,0871
WHITAKER, Bettie S.,1186,
 Katie,1148, Mattie M.,1186,
 Philander,1185, Rebecca M.,
 1185, Roberson A.,1185,
 Sarah A.,1151, William T.,
 1186
WHITBY, Martha,0966
WHITE & PRICE, ,0854
WHITE, (Capt.),1028, (Mrs.),
 1185, ,0803,0830,0863,
 Alexander,0807, Alfred,
 1207, Anna,1186, Ary A.,
 1186, Ary,1186, Azile,1073,
 B.M.,0818, B.R.,0803,
 Bartley N.,1073, Benj.,
 0801, Berry,0762, Betsey,
 1196, Bettie,1074, Burrell G.,
 1073
WHITE, C.S.(Miss),1132,
 Carter,0844, Chapman,0789,
 0791,0792,0793, Coral,1123,
 David,0791, Dr.,1123, E.A.,
 0854, E.M.,0961, Edward,
 0854, Eliza J.,1073,
 Elizabeth,1073,1074,1168,
 1186, Ella M.,1123, Ethel,
 1123, Frank,0819,1073,
 Frankie,1073
WHITE, George A.,1074,
 George M.,0961, George,
 0834, Grover C.,0961, H.L.,
 0770,0790, Henry H.,1073,
 Henry,1073, Holland,0792,
 Hugh L.,1074, Isaac H.,
 1186, Isabella,1008, J.B.,
 0752,0764,0829, J.H.,0818,
 0819, J.L.,0854, J.T.,0799,
 James D.,1119
WHITE, James E.,0961, James L.,
 0961,1073,1186, James R.,
 1186, James,0772,0961, Jane,
 1073, Joe E.(Mrs.),1073,
 John H.,0817,1074, John M.,
 1073, John V.,1074, John W.,
 0850,0854,0876,0961,1122,
 John,0766,0779,0790,0805,
 0843,1186, Joseph,0791
WHITE, Joseph,1186, Julia W.,
 1048, Julia,1186, Kate,1073,
 Kenneth,1123, L.W.,0855,
 Levi B.,1073, Levi,1073,
 Lewis,0962, Lucy,0766,
 Lula,1186, Mabel,1123,
 Margaret E.,0961, Margaret,
 1186, Martha F.,1074,
 Mary A.,1074, Mary L.,1073,
 Mary,1017
WHITE, Mary,1073,1186, Mrs.,
 0783, Nancy,0962,1186,
 Nellie Ann,1010, Opal,1123,
 Pattie,0961, Peyton H.,
 1074, Purmelia,0965, R.C.,
 0874, R.L.C.,0853,1122,
 Richard,0874, Robert,0834,
 0863,1186, S.N.,0824,1035,
 Sallie B.,1073, Sallie(Mrs.),
 1167
WHITE, Sallie,1017, Sally C.,
 1122, Sally W.,1073,
 Sarah A.,1074, Sarah J.,
 1074, Sarah,1074, Stephen,
 1073, Sue,1073, Susan,1119,
 1186, T.P.,0772, Thomas A.,
 1186, Thomas C.,1186,
 Thomas Sr.,1186, Thomas V.,
 1074, Thomas,0783,1186,
 Thos.B.,0802
WHITE, Thos.D.,0824, W.J.,
 0800, W.W.,0799, Walter C.,
 1186, Walter M.,1073,
 Wharton,0757, William B.,

1073, William D.,1186,
 William R.,1073, William T.,
 1074, William,0793,0842,
 1017, Willie E.,0961
WHITEFIELD, Abraham,0769
WHITEHEAD, ,0863
WHITELOCK, Abraham,0766
WHITESETT, Elder,0838
WHITESIDE, ,0762,0776, H.C.,
 0822, India B.,0914, James,
 0761,0821, Maggie C.,1128,
 T.C.,1128, Thomas S.,0914,
 Thomas,0760,0868, Thos.,
 0759, Thos.C.,0849,0870,
 Wm.H.,0871
WHITESIDES, Thos.C.,0871
WHITFIELD, Anna E.,1017,
 Capt.,0792, Clifton B.,
 1017, Harrison,1019,
 Jimmie D.,1017, John H.,
 1017, Julia W.,1017, Mary,
 1019, Mattie H.,1017,
 Nancy A.,1018,1019,
 Sarah M.,1017, Thomas W.,
 1017, William B.,1017
WHITING, Mr.,0767
WHITMAN, Almedia,1230, Ann E.,
 1230, Ann,1230, James W.,
 1230, Jane,1230, Jennie P.,
 1231, R.H.,0874, R.M.(Rev.),
 1230, Robert G.,1231
WHITNEY, ,0863, Grant,0876,
 Madge,0951, Wm.O.,0874
WHITON, W.H.,0772
WHITSEN, William,0818
WHITSETT, Eliza,1218, James,
 0819,0820
WHITSITT, May F.,0900
WHITSON, Capt.,0751, David,
 0877, George D.,1074,
 George,1074, H.K.,0878,
 Hygene,1074, Lurenza D.,
 1074, Maria E.,1074, Mary,
 1074, Mernira,1074, S.K.,
 0880, W.,0829, William W.,
 1074, William,1074
WHITTAKER, Col.,0758, J.J.,
 0836
WHITTEMORE, Maggie T.,1186,
 Nancy,1186, Wm.B.,1186,
 Wm.H.,1186
WHITTHORNE, B.B.,0875,
 Brom R.,1173, Juliet,1173,
 W.C.,0759,0764,0765,0973,
 W.J.,0759, Wash.Curran,
 0962, Wm.J.,0898
WHITTINGTON, Clarissa,0967
WHITTSITT, Bettie,1217
WHYTE, Robert,0762
WICK, Alex W.,0832
WIER, David,0779, Mary,1222
WIGG, J.M.,0833, J.W.,0832
WIGGINS, A.F.,1187, Benjamin F.,
 1187, Bessie F.,1187, David,
 1187, Edward H.,1187,
 Emily V.,1187, Fannie E.,
 1187, Hampton E.,1187,
 Harbert,1187, Harrel,1186,
 Henry,0863, Hundley,1187,
 J.Greer,1187, Jane H.,1187,
 John S.,1187, John W.,1186
WIGGINS, John W.,1187,
 Mary J.,1187, Mary,1187,
 Sallie,1186, Sarah E.,1187,
 Thomas H.,1187, William J.,
 1187
WIGGS, Elizabeth G.,1219,
 I.T.,1219, Jane L.,1219,
 Jane S.,1219, Needham B.,
 1219
WIGHT, ,0812, Fannie L.,1135
WILBOURN, Daniel,0841
WILBURN, Henry M.,0958
WILEY, (Miss),1151, Moses A.,
 0754
WILFORD, Wm.L.,0779
WILHOIT & BROS., ,0874
WILHOIT, (Mill),0863, Joseph,
 0863, W.W.,0874
WILHOITE, Addie,1231, Anna A.,
 1226,1231, Anna M.,1017,
 Annie E.,1017, Bettie E.,
 1017, Eliza,1017, Hulda B.,

1179, Jacob,1231, James T.,
 1017, Jimmy Y.,1018,
 John B.,1231, Lettie C.,
 1133, Lizzie T.,1231
WILHOITE, Mary,1231, Minnie P.,
 1018, Phillip,1133, William,
 1231, Willie,1018, Young,
 1017
WILHORTE, Narcissa,0896
WILKES, Alice,0962, Anna Y.,
 0963, B.L.,0956, Capt.,0751,
 Dora I.,0963, Elizabeth,
 0962, Geo.W.,0771, George,
 0768, Ida O.,0956, Izora,
 0962, J.H.,0772, James H.,
 0963, Jennie,0963, John B.,
 0888,0889, John,0891,
 Joseph T.,0963, Judith,0962
WILKES, Lennie M.(Mrs.),0963,
 Maria,1194, Mary K.,0962,
 Mr.,0963, N.R.,0764,0773,
 0963, Nathl.Robards,0962,
 R.A.,0759,0781, R.A.L.,
 0759, Richard A.L.,0962,
 Richard,0962, Sallie A.,
 0913, W.H.,0781,0895, Wm.,
 0888,0891, Wm.H.,0962,
 Zurelda,0962
WILKINS, James,0768, Nancy,
 1211
WILKINSON, Gen.,0797, George H.,
 1071, Hubbard P.,1071, Jane,
 1231, Mack,1231, Mary E.,
 1071, Mollie,1231, William A.,
 1071, William E.,1231
WILLBURRY, John,0850
WILLEFORD, Clara,0917
WILLIAMS & COVINGTON, ,0855
WILLIAMS & GLENN, ,0898
WILLIAMS & LANDIS, ,0881
WILLIAMS & MOON, ,0881
WILLIAMS, (Mrs.),0985, ,
 0750,0776,0850,0863, A.,
 0764, Ada,1018, Adaline,
 1018, Alex,0776,1123,
 Almeda,1187, Archibald D.,
 0964, Ary A.,1186, Benj.,
 0899, Benjamin,0890, Berry,
 1018, Bettie,1123, C.Foster,
 0750,0772, Capt.,0792,0850,
 Charles,0834
WILLIAMS, Charlie,1018,
 Chesley,1074, Clem W.,1018,
 Cornelia,1083, D.C.,0853,
 1122, Daniel,0819, David,
 1137,1187, Dixon C.,1105,
 Dr.,0776,0880, E.F.,0890,
 E.T.,0898, Earnest,1118,
 Edward,0777,1075, Elijah,
 1117, Eliz.W.,1141, Elizabeth,
 0834
WILLIAMS, Elizabeth,1018,1074,
 Ellen C.,1180, Elvira,1187,
 Emma,1074, Fannie F.,1074,
 Fannie P.,1018, Freeman,
 1018, Grace,0838, Granville,
 1075, H.,0773, H.H.,0830,
 1044, Harrison,0870,
 Hattie J.,0908, Helena,
 0940, Herbert,1118, Horace,
 1075
WILLIAMS, Ida J.,1137,
 Isaac H.,0888,0890, Isaac,
 0869, J.,0815, J.C.,0834,
 J.H.,1123, J.J.,0764, J.W.,
 0808, James C.,1074,1075,
 James H.,1187, James,0842,
 0848,1074, Jasper,0849,
 Joel,0793, John P.,1044,
 John W.,1018, John,0766,
 0821
WILLIAMS, John,0841,0898,
 Joseph,0842,0870,1018,1187,
 Joshua I.,0759, Joshua L,
 0963, Joshua,0759,0765,1018,
 Jourdan,1018, Lafayette,
 1187, Levi,1018, Lottie G.,
 0964, Lou,1187, Luke,1018,
 Macon S.,1074, Mahala C.,
 1123, Margaret I.,1123
WILLIAMS, Margaret,0939,1123,
 Martha C.,1018, Martha J.,
 1074, Martha,0941,1018,1105,

Mary F.,1117, Mary H.,1018,
Mary T.,1075, Mary V.,1074,
Mary,1204, Mattie M.,1123,
Mildred(Mrs.),1044, Minnie,
1075, Miss,1032, Mollie J.,
1187, N.S.,0854
WILLIAMS, Nancy,1018, Nathnl.,
0760, Nathnl.W.,0795, Noble,
1018, Oliver,0863, Peter,
0812,0888, Phoebe,0965,
Polly,1117, R.B.,1123,
R.C.,0893,0894,1208, R.E.,
0834, R.M.,1083, Rachel,
1018, Robert E.,1074,
Robert,0803,0899,1018,
Robt.L.,0854
WILLIAMS, Rosanna,1010, S.,
0782, S.C.(Mrs.),1123, S.R.,
0855, Sallie A.,1216,
Sallie S.,1221, Sallie,
1074, Saml.H.,0758,0760,
0775, Samuel H.,0762,
Samuel K.,1187, Samuel L.,
1018, Samuel W.,0964,
Samuel,0821,1075, Sarah G.,
0964, Sarah H.,0946
WILLIAMS, Sarah T.,1187,
Sarah,1051,1137, Selden R.,
0854,1081, Seldon R.,1105,
Seth,0849, Sophia P.,1047,
1074, Susan,1018, T.C.,0799,
Thomas L.,1018, Thomas S.,
1075, Thomas,0841, W.D.,
0940, William H.,1123,
William,0853,0887,0888,0899
WILLIAMS, William,1018, Wm.,
0793, Wm.D.(Gen.),0964
WILLIAMS-KIRKPATRICK, ,0843
WILLIAMSON & BEARD, ,1080
WILLIAMSON, Abbie L.,1075,
Albina G.,0964, Alfred F.,
1075, Bob,0849, C.S.,0962,
Capt.,0792,0850, Charles S.,
0963, Charles T.,1075,
Cuthbert,0963, Eula D.,1075,
Gen.,0789, Geo.C.,0963,
George C.,0964, Horace S.,
1075, Izora,0962, J.T.,0759
WILLIAMSON, J.W.,0843,
James G.,0963, Jane,1075,
John A.,1075, John J.,0772,
John T.,0773,0785,0963,
0964, John,0842, Judith,
0963, Lizzie,1075, Maggie E.,
1075, Margaret,1111,
Mildred A.,0964, Mr.,0773,
P.K.,0850, Porter,0849,
Richard W.,1075
WILLIAMSON, Sallie,1105,
Samuel,0963, Sue M.,1075,
Susan,0923, Thomas,0789,
1075,1111, W.H.,0850,0851,
0870,1107, William,1105,
Wm.H.,0849
WILLIE, Jedediah,0848
WILLIFORD, Prof.,0778, Wm.L.,
0775
WILLIS, Anna M.,1204, Rev.,
0860
WILLSON & JENNINGS, ,0776
WILLY, W.A.,0851
WILSON & WATERS, ,0855,1123
WILSON, (Col.),0974, ,0803,
0863, Aaron J.,1225,1231,
Ada W.,1225, Adaline,0998,
Andrew,0842, Annie,1140,
Capt.,0792,0850, Catherine,
1207, Cynthia M.,1222,
David,0845, E.A.,0889,0890,
E.D.,0771, Eaton G.,1123,
Ewing A.,1231, Frances S.,
1229
WILSON, H.,0901, Hannah,1225,
1231, J.B.,0805, J.D.,0818,
J.H.,0792, J.T.,0800,0819,
J.T.B.,0830, J.W.,0819,
James,0795, John A.,0800,
John R.,1091, John,0789,
0794,0795,0842,0869,0900,
1018,1075, Joseph C.,0848,
Joseph T.B.,1075, Lizzie,
1042
WILSON, Mahala,1174, Margaret A.,

1001, Margaret J.,1091,
Margaret L.,1123, Margaret,
0838,1001, Mark H.,1227,
Martha E.,1183, Martha,
0938,1001,1075,1227,
Mary E.,1142, Mary P.,0938,
Matilda B.,1168, Matthew,
1007, Mattie S.,1193,
Melissa A.A.,1007
WILSON, Nancy,1042, P.,0821,
Robert,0834, S.E.,0902,
Samuel,0811,0815,0819,0821,
0822,0841,1001, Sarah A.,
1074, Sarah,1119,1223,
Susanna,1156, Susannah M.,
1225, Thomas,0794,0821,0844,
0888,0938,0998, Thos.,0795,
W.B.,0759, W.V.,0770
WILSON, W.W.,1123, William,
0842,0843,0847,0848, Wm. B.,
0759
WILT, G.W.,0836
WILTS, John,0874
WINCHESTER & CAGE, ,0854
WINDEL, B.S.,0817, J.E.,0817,
R.S.,0817
WINDER, Carrie,0996
WINEFORD, Benjamin,0841
WINFORD, Bern,0851, James C.,
0843, Jerome,1071, Louise S.,
1071
WING, C.P.(Rev.),0783, Gomar,
0758
WINGFIELD, A.M.,0759, Mary M.,
0939, Sarah,1218
WINN, (Gen.),1212, Alex,0799,
0825, M.J.(Miss),1156, Mary,
1182, Richard(Gen.),0784
WINNETT, Mrs.,0879
WINRO, Henry,0874
WINSEPP, Eliz.(Mrs.),1049
WINSETT & COVINGTON, ,0881
WINSETT & ELKTON, ,0881
WINSETT & MCLANE, ,0881
WINSETT, Jason,0793,0867,
John,0842
WINSLOW, (Col.),1014
WINSTEAD, Anne E.,1018,
Elizabeth,1019, Harrison W.,
1019, Ida,1019, James M.,
1019, John M.,0790,0793,
0798,1018,1019, John,1019,
Katie Niel,1019, Lucy T.,
1019, Maggie A.,1019,
Mary E.,1019, Mary,1019,
Meredith P.G.,1019,
Nancy A.,1018
WINSTEAD, Robert O.,1019,
Thomas E.,1019, Walker W.,
1019, William E.,1018,1019,
William,1019, Winfield S.,
1019
WINSTON, C.K.,0836, Cassie E.,
1129, Isaac,0842, Joseph,
0891, T.F.,0893,0895
WINTER, A.J.,1088, Ella,1088,
Rachel J.,1189, Wilburn R.,
0848
WINTERS, ,0775, Maj.,0774
WISDOM, W.H.,0868
WISE, David,0807
WISEMAN, John,0852, Rev.,0860
WISENER, W.H.,0888,0890,0892,
Wm.H.,0871,0876, Wm.H.Jr.,
0871
WITHERINGTON, Jos.,0797
WITHERSPOON, C.W.,0770, Isaac,
0842, John,0794, Lucinda,
0916, Rebecca S.,0940, S.E.,
0782, Saml.,0749,0760,0778,
Thomas H.,0759, W.,0801,
W.O.,0758
WITHOITE, Anna E.,0985, Eliza,
0985, Liza,0985, Young,0985
WITT, Ira C.,0771
WOLDRIDGE, F.S.,0758, J.,0773,
N.,0796, W.P.,0768,0948,
Walter P.,0771
WOLLAND, J.T.,1192, Mollie G.,
1192
WOMACK, (DR.),0898, Michael,
0862,0871, Mr.,0853
WOOD, ,0863, A.J.,1149, Amy,

1230, Ann,1046, David,0760,
E.,0822,2129, Elena,1188,
Eliza T.,1187, Eliza,1187,
Gen.,0873, George B.,0874,
George,0869, Horace O.,
1187, Hughes,1076, J.P.,
1188, James G.,1187, James,
1187, John A.,1187, John E.,
0880
WOOD, Johnson W.,1178,
Joseph O.,1188, Judith,
1041, Lizzie,1076, Louisa E.,
1015, Louisa F.,1178, Lucy,
1076, Martha C.,1188,
Martha H.,1187, Martha J.,
1015, Martha,1129,1134,
Mary L.,1188,1230, Mary O.,
1178, Melissa J.,1187,
Nancy P.,1187
WOOD, Nora W.,1188, O.C.(Miss),
0989, Rachel A.,1081, S.H.,
0817, Samuel,1134, Sarah A.,
1187, Sarah,1076, Thomas H.,
1076, Thomas W.,1187,
Thomas,0824, W.G.,0878,
W.H.,0897, W.M.,1129,
William H.,1229, William J.,
1187, William T.,1015
WOOD, William W.,1188,
William,0868,1188,1229,
Winnie L.,1188, Wm.,0763,
0766,0767
WOODARD, Cal(Mrs.),0855,
Eliza J.,1162, J.A.,1162,
James,0870, Martha A.,1162,
W.R.,1162
WOODFIN, (Mrs.),0979, Alice,
1188, Emma L.,1188, Ida,
1188, James M.P.,1188,
Judith,0963, Maggie L.,
1188, Maria,1188, Mollie E.,
1188, Moses,1188, Nicholas,
1188, Rachel A.,1188,
Samuel N.,1188, Samuel,
1188, William J.,1188
WOODKINS, William,0851
WOODRUFF, John,0766
WOODRUM, Jacob,0842, Wood,
0856
WOODS & MCCORD, ,0897,1216,
1229
WOODS, (Maj.),1076, B.G.,0824,
Bedford M.,1229, Bedford,
0902, Capt.,0752, D.T.J.,
0799, Emily,1191, F.H.,0901,
Francis B.,1229, Francis H.,
0887,0901, Frank,0902,
George B.,1132, J.A.,0902,
1132, James A.,0899,1229,
James W.,1229, John,0818
WOODS, John,0819,1075, Joseph,
0874, Josiah,0842, Margaret S.,
1229, Margaret,1132,
Mary F.,1076, Mary,1200,
Nancy,1076, Nannie J.,1229,
Peyton,0856, S.O.,0902,
Susan,1075, T.H.,0832,
Thomas,1075, William,0865,
Wm.,0871,0872
WOODWARD, Martha C.,1188
WOOLARD & BROS., J.A.,0855
WOOLARD, Harriet,0925, J.M.,
0854
WOOLDRIDGE, Eliza,0964, F.S.,
0803, Ferdinand,0964,
Louise D.,0964, Louise T.,
0964, Walter P.,0964
WOOLEN, J.Matt,0855, John,
0842
WOOTEN, Elizabeth,0964, Emma,
0965, Hattie A.,0965, J.C.,
0772, James C.,0964,
John T.,0965, Shedrick O.,
0964, Wm.B.,0965
WOOTON, T.F.,0864
WORD, C.B.,0873, C.C.,0872,
Charles,1124, Cuthbert,
0862, Elizabeth,1123,1124,
James,0880, John,1123,
Martha A.,1155, Pemelia,
1124, R.Q.,1123, Thomas,
0842, Thos.S.,0862
WORKE, Jane,1156

WORMLEY, Hugh W.,0763,
  John C.,0778, John,0766,
  W.B.,0764
WORTHAM, ,0863, James,0867,
  0871,0873, John,0871,
  N.W.B.,0757, Robt.C.,0872,
  Thos.,0752, W.H.,0854,
  William,0842
WORTHMAN, Capt.,0752
WRATHER, James,0841,0842,
  Mary E.,1029
WRAY, Archbd.,0754, F.,0799,
  Martha E.,1111, William,
  1111
WREN, ,0751,0775, Howell,0842,
  Thomas,0784
WRIGHT & VAUGHAN, ,0856
WRIGHT, Alex M.,0815, Alice B.,
  1124, Amanda,1111, Annie E.,
  1135, Annie,1124, Cora,1124,
  Eliza G.,1124, Elizabeth,
  1111, Emma C.,0947, G.W.,
  0843, George W.,1124,
  Graham C.,1124, Hollis,
  1111, J.K.,1124, J.M.Sr.,
  0819, Jackie Maud,1088
WRIGHT, Jacob,0815, James K.,
  1124, James,1088, Jane,0950,
  John M.,1100, John V.,0892,
  1036, John,0841,0853,1124,
  Lee,1124, Lena,1124, Lewis,
  1124, Lucy,1124, Maggie S.,
  1124, Marcus J.,0904,
  Margaret J.,1124, Mary J.,
  1166, Mary,1124, Matilda,
  0907
WRIGHT, Monroe A.,1124,
  Moses R.,1135, Nancy,1131,
  1148, Nathan,0779, Rebecca,
  1020, Sophia,1197, Tempie E.,
  1124, Tempie,1124, Thomas,
  1137, W.M.,0796, Whitfield,
  1166, William H.,1124,
  William,1124
WYATT, Edward,0848, J.B.,0893
WYLAND, R.C.,0870
WYNN, Albert,0854, Bolin,0844,
  George K.,0846, George,
  0841, J.B.,0854, John K.,
  0841, John,0844,0846,0850,
  L.A.,0854
WYOONE, Martha P.,1116
YANCEY, ,0774, Phillip A.,
  0802
YANDELL, Dr.,0837, L.P.,0827
YARBROUGH, George,1232, J.A.,
  0890,0898, Jasper A.,1232,
  Lizzie,1232, Nancy E.,1232,
  Vina H.,0998
YARDLEY, Thomas,0813
YARNELL, Lewis,0848
YATES, Joseph,0793
YEARGAN, H.,0818
YEARGIN, B.W.,0799
YELL, A.D.,1189, Abner W.,
  1189, Ada,1189, Adah,1189,
  Ann B.,1189, Annie,1189,
  Archibald,0871, Benjamin B.,
  1189, Benjamin,1189,
  Bettie A.,1189, Bettie,
  1189, Charley,1189, Edith N.,
  1189, Frances M.,1189,
  Francis M.,1188, G.E.,1189,
  George C.,1189
YELL, Gordentia W.,1189,
  James A.,1189, James C.,
  1188, James,1189, Jerome,
  1189, Jerusha,1189, Joshua,
  1189, Judia,1188, Nancy B.,
  1189, Rutha S.,1183,
  Warren S.,1189
YERGER & GOLLADAY, ,0854
YERGER, G.S.,0796, Samuel,
  0849,0850
YOAKUM, Capt.,0823, H.,0826,
  0839
YOES, John S.,1189, Joseph W.,
  1189, Margaret E.,1189,
  Marzie S.,1189, Rebecca A.,
  1189, Sallie,1189, Thomas,
  1189, William T.,1189
YORK, T.J.,0799
YOUNG, ,0863, A.R.,1125, A.T.,
  0856,1125, Arsula,1094,
  Capt.,0751, D.,0988,1125,
  David,1125, Earnest,1076,
  Effie L.,1125, Effie,1125,
  Elbert W.,1125, Emily,1125,
  Etna,1097, Evan,0768,0779,
  Foster,1125, Frank,0842,
  G.D.,1125, George,1125
YOUNG, H.,1125, Henry,0776,
  Hiram,0836, Holly,1125,
  J.M.,1125, J.W.,1125,
  Jacob,1097, James W.,1125,
  James,0848,1124,1125, Jane,
  1094, Joseph D.,1125,
  Joseph,0821,1076,1125,
  Laura,1125, Margaret E.,
  1125, Margaret,1125,
  Marshall,1090
YOUNG, Martha,1087, Mary E.,
  1125, Mary F.,0948, Mary L.,
  1125, Mary,1125, Miranda,
  1125, Nancy,1076,1124,1125,
  1143, Nannie,1125, Omar A.,
  1125, Palace,1125, Pallas,
  1125, Robert H.,1076,
  Robert,1124,1125, Samuel,
  1087, Sarah E.,1125, Sarah,
  1076
YOUNG, Sarah,1125, Stacy,1094,
  Susan,1087, William B.,
  1125, William F.,1125,
  William,1125
YOURIE, ,0813, W.E.,0817,0818
YOWELL, J.A.,0890, J.M.,0890,
  Joel,0888, Mattie,1213
ZEIGER, Mary,0951
ZILLNER, A.,0752, Arnold,0769
ZOLLICOFFER, (Gen.),1228, ,
  0894, Anne M.S.,1228,
  Felix K.,0773,0776,
  Frederick,0776, John J.,
  0760,0776, John,0761

www.ingramcontent.com/pod-product-compliance
Lightning Source LLC
Chambersburg PA
CBHW020633300426
44112CB00007B/97